Butterworths
Commercial Law in New Zealand

Butterworths
Commercial Law in New Zealand
Second Edition

General Editors:

John H Farrar LLM PhD
Barrister of the High Courts of Australia and
New Zealand, Professor of Law at Victoria
University of Wellington

Andrew Borrowdale BA (Hons) LLM PhD
Barrister and Solicitor of the High Court, Senior
Lecturer in Law at the University of Canterbury

Specialist Authors:

Andrew Borrowdale BA (Hons) LLM PhD
Senior Lecturer in Law at the University of
Canterbury

John F Burrows LLM PhD
Barrister and Solicitor of the High Court,
Professor of Law at the University of Canterbury

John H Farrar LLM PhD
Professor of Law at Victoria University of
Wellington

Jeremy N Finn MA LLB (Hons)
Barrister and Solicitor of the High Court, Senior
Lecturer in Law at the University of Canterbury

Lindsay F Hampton BA LLM
Barrister and Solicitor of the High Court, Senior
Lecturer in Commercial Law at the University
of Canterbury

Richard J Scragg LLB (Hons) LLM
Barrister and Solicitor of the High Court, Senior
Instructor in the Institute of Professional Legal
Studies, Canterbury

Stephen M D Todd LLM
Barrister (Inner Temple), Associate Professor
of Law at the University of Canterbury

Wellington
Butterworths
1992

The Butterworth Group

New Zealand	Butterworths of New Zealand Ltd 203-207 Victoria St, CPO Box 472, WELLINGTON and NML Plaza, 41 Shortland St, PO Box 2399, AUCKLAND
Australia	Butterworths Pty Ltd, SYDNEY, MELBOURNE, BRISBANE, ADELAIDE, PERTH, CANBERRA and HOBART
Canada	Butterworths Canada Ltd, TORONTO and VANCOUVER
Ireland	Butterworth (Ireland) Ltd, DUBLIN
Malaysia	Malayan Law Journal Sdn Bhd, KUALA LUMPUR
Puerto Rico	Equity de Puerto Rico, Inc, HATO REY
Singapore	Malayan Law Journal Pte Ltd, SINGAPORE
United Kingdom	Butterworth & Co (Publishers) Ltd, LONDON and EDINBURGH
USA	Butterworth Legal Publishers, AUSTIN, Texas; BOSTON, Massachusetts; CLEARWATER, Florida (D & S Publishers); ORFORD, New Hampshire (Equity Publishing) and ST. PAUL, Minnesota.

National Library of New Zealand
Cataloguing-in-Publication data

Butterworths commercial law in New Zealand / general editors, John
    H. Farrar, Andrew Borrowdale ; specialist authors, Andrew
    Borrowdale ... [et al.]. 2nd ed. Wellington, N.Z. :
Butterworths, 1992
    1 v.
    First ed. published 1985.
    Includes index.
"Successor to Leys and Northey Commercial law in New Zealand
    (7 ed.) "--Pref.
    ISBN 0-409-78964-X (hbk.)
    ISBN 0-409-78900-3 (pbk.)
    1. Commercial law--New Zealand. I. Leys, W. C. S. (William
Clifton Selwyn), 1902- .Leys and Northey Commercial law in
New Zealand. II. Farrar, John H. (John Hynes), 1941-
III. Borrowdale, Andrew. IV. Farrar, John H. (John Hynes),
1941- . Butterworths commercial law in New Zealand. V. Title.
VI. Title: Commercial law in New Zealand.
    346.9307

© Butterworths of New Zealand Ltd 1992

Preface

This edition of *Butterworths Commercial Law in New Zealand* is significantly longer than its predecessor. A comparison of the case tables for this and the previous edition discloses the rapid growth in the number of New Zealand decisions in commercial law now reported in specialist reports and consequently reflected in the text of this book. Statutory developments account for new chapters on Fair Trading by Jeremy Finn and the Motor Vehicle Securities Act by Richard Scragg. In anticipation of its implementation John Farrar has contributed a short chapter on the proposed personal property regime. Other chapters, especially Competition and Hire Purchase, have been wholly or substantially rewritten.

We are grateful to Julie Bremner of Butterworths for her part in cajoling this edition into print. The law is stated as at 30 September 1991.

John Farrar
Faculty of Law
Victoria University
Wellington
December 1991

Andrew Borrowdale
Law School
University of Canterbury
Christchurch
December 1991

Preface to the first edition

This work is a successor to Leys and Northey "Commercial Law in New Zealand" (7 ed). I was asked at short notice to edit a new edition and was given licence to produce a new work. The present book which represents a team effort of some past and present members of the Canterbury Law Faculty is the beginning of a new work. The shortness of time meant that we could not re-write the whole book and we have used parts of Leys and Northey. The result is as follows:

Part 1:   Is entirely new.
Part 2:   General principles of Contract and Quasi-Contract is entirely new.
Part 3:   Sale of Goods is almost entirely new work. Bailment and Carriage of Goods is entirely new. Credit Contracts Act is almost entirely new work. Cheques, Suretyship and Guarantees, Agency and Partnership have been substantially rewritten. Insurance is entirely new.
Part 4:   Chattels, Securities and Hire Purchase are revised and in places rewritten. The Floating Charge is new.
Part 5:   Competition Law is new.
Part 6:   Insolvency is revised and in places rewritten.
Part 7:   The Resolution of Commercial and Consumer Disputes is new except that some parts of the old chapter on Arbitration have been used.

It is our intention to rewrite Parts 4 and 6 in future editions and the new Fair Trading and Commerce Bills will necessitate further changes in due course. A brief note on the Fair Trading Bill follows this preface and the Commerce Bill is referred to in Part 5. It is also likely that the newly established Law Commission will turn its attention to the reform of Sale of Goods and Chattel Security. Another development likely to occur in the future will be the preparation of new Insolvency Rules to conform as far as possible with the new High Court Rules. In the meantime the Insolvency Rules 1970 SR 1970/245 as amended remain in force. We have attempted to accommodate changes in the text occasioned by the new rules in other areas.

The Law is stated as at 1 January 1986.

The division of labours is indicated generally in the Table of Contents. Responsibility for Part 2, General Principles of Contract and Quasi-Contract, was divided between three authors. John Burrows wrote chapter 2, Part 2 of chapter 3, Part 1 of chapter 4, Parts 1, 2, 3 and 4 of chapter 7, Part 1 of chapter 8 and chapter 9. Jeremy Finn prepared Parts 1, 3 and 4 of chapter 3, Parts 3 and 4 of chapter 4 and Parts 3 and 4 of chapter 5. Stephen Todd took responsibility for Part 2 of chapter 4, Parts 1 and 2 of chapter 5, chapter 6, Parts 5, 6 and 7 of chapter 7 and Parts 2 and 3 of chapter 8.

John H Farrar
Faculty of Law
University of Canterbury
Christchurch

Table of contents

Contents

Table of cases

A

Table of Cases

Table of Cases

Table of Cases

Table of Cases

C

Table of Cases

Table of Cases

D

E

F

G

H

Table of Cases

I

J

K

L

Table of Cases

M

Table of Cases

Table of Cases

Table of Cases

Q

R

Table of Cases

S

Table of Cases

Table of Cases

Table of Cases

T

Table of Cases

U

Table of Cases

Table of Cases

Z

Table of statutes, statutory regulations and related matters

Table of Statutes

Table of Statutes

Table of Statutes

Table of Statutes

Table of Statutes

Part I

INTRODUCTION

Chapter 1

THE NATURE, SCOPE AND HISTORICAL DEVELOPMENT OF COMMERCIAL LAW

SUMMARY

1.1 THE NATURE AND SCOPE OF COMMERCIAL LAW

The term "Commercial Law" is an illustration of how many words tend to have a core of certainty and penumbra of uncertainty in their meaning: H L A Hart, *The Concept of Law*, (1961) ch VII. Professor R M Goode, a distinguished English Professor of Commercial Law, defines Commercial Law as that branch of law which is concerned with rights and duties arising from the supply of goods and services in the way of trade: *Commercial Law* (1982), 35. He recognises that it is usual to treat Commercial Law as confined to *personal* property and the provision of services but he argues that at certain points it is entwined with Land Law on such matters as fixtures and security for advances. His book is extremely persuasive but it should be remembered that Professor Goode is interested in Land Law as well as more conventional Commercial Law. Commercial Law has a core of certainty in topics like sale of goods, hire purchase, chattel security, negotiable instruments and guarantees. Beyond that there is a penumbra of topics such as insurance, arbitration and insolvency which may be considered. Pure Land Law as opposed to questions of legal and equitable priority is probably better taught elsewhere.

3

In New Zealand law as in English law there is no distinct body of law called "Commercial Law", we do not have a commercial code and generally there is no special status afforded to merchants or traders as is the case in Continental European countries. Commercial Law is part of the general civil law but this has not always been so in English law as we shall see. Even today there are areas of law such as the core topics we have mentioned which have a more distinctly mercantile character than others and these we shall concentrate on in this book. A lot of Commercial Law can be viewed as applications of general contract principles to specific areas and hence a learned work such as *Chitty on Contracts* has two volumes: Vol 1 General Principles and Vol 2 Specific Contracts. Some subjects such as insolvency do not, however, fit easily into this neat system. Indeed Insolvency Law, like Commercial Law, represents a sort of legal crossroads where numerous areas of law meet.

Commercial Law also interrelates with another body of law which is emerging and is gradually acquiring a distinctive character. This is the law of Consumer Protection. The legislature is increasingly producing legislation to protect consumers in commercial transactions. Much of this relates to the provision of goods on credit. Consumer Protection Law is mainly statute law.

The resolution of commercial and consumer disputes can also be regarded as a proper part of a Commercial Law course as these areas arguably call for special attention by the legal system. They tend to be the areas where the system is prepared to innovate. Thus in ch 51 in addition to conventional litigation, which we deal with briefly, we also deal with private negotiation, arbitration, small claims, mediation and conciliation.

Underlying the law is a number of interests. The term "consumer" is ambiguous. It can refer to a buyer of goods or a borrower of money or someone who combines both attributes. In a sense we are all consumers but conventionally the law excludes the business purchaser/borrower from much of the protection of consumer protection legislation. On the other side of the transaction are the manufacturers and retailers/wholesalers and the financial institutions. Further and beyond these there is the rather more abstract concept of the public interest. In Commercial Law this is primarily concerned with maintaining the efficiency and integrity of markets. There is, however, no general requirement of good faith such as one finds in German law and the Uniform Commercial Code of the USA. There is a proposal to introduce such a requirement into Sale of Goods statutes in the Canadian provinces and this may eventually influence reform here.

1.2 THE SOURCES OF COMMERCIAL LAW

Modern Commercial Law is contained in statute, statutory regulation and case law precedents augmented by custom and usage. Historically the general order of development was as follows:

usage → custom → precedents → code

This is oversimple in that it suggests that precedent was always reduced to statute form which is not the case. Only some case law has been codified.

Modern Commercial Law grew out of the customs and usages of merchants which were known as the Law Merchant. Some were written down and became a code of international commercial customs. Eventually the Law Merchant was absorbed into the Common Law. The Common Law on Bills of Exchange, Partnership, Sale of Goods and Marine Insurance was codified at the end of the nineteenth century and early this century. Commercial custom and usage continue to be of some importance although it has been argued by Lord Devlin that it has been killed by the written contract and especially standard forms of trade associations and international bodies: (1951)14 MLR 249. While of some force this overstates the case. Nevertheless where custom and usage is in issue today it tends to be argued in contract as an express or implied term.

Even when the law is codified precedent is still important as the Courts are called upon to interpret the statutory provisions.

1.3 THE LAW MERCHANT AND THE COMMON LAW

There were three key periods in the history of the Law Merchant. The first was the period up to 1606 which is characterised by the Law Merchant as a special law administered by special Courts for a special class of people: TE Scrutton, "General Survey of the History of the Law Merchant" in *Select Essays in Anglo-American Legal History*, (1907-9) Vol 3, 7, 8. Gerard Malynes, writing in 1622, regarded the Law Merchant as customary law approved by the authority of all Kingdoms and not a law established by the sovereignty of any prince: *Consuetudo vel Lex Mercatoria* (1662). Lord Mansfield, Lord Chief Justice of England in the eighteenth century, described it as the "Law of all nations": *Luke v Lyde* (1759) 97 ER 614. The special Courts were the Courts of merchants at markets and fairs which became known as Pie Powder Courts from the French for dusty feet. The Courts were generally informal affairs presided over by merchants and handling merchants' disputes. There were similar Courts at ports. Some of these Courts were the subject of express legislation.

The second period is the period from 1606 until 1756 which is when Lord Mansfield became Chief Justice of England. This is characterised by the decline of the special Courts and the handling of Law Merchant in the Common Law Courts as custom, not as law. At first the custom only applied if the plaintiff or defendant was a merchant. The content of the Law Merchant was treated as a jury matter and this impeded the development of Commercial Law.

Fortunately this changed in the third period which dates from 1756 until the end of the nineteenth century. Lord Mansfield and his successors built up the Law Merchant as an integral part of the Common Law relying on the writing of foreign jurists for international custom and special juries of merchants for current trade customs and findings of fact.

The final stage of development is when the common law including the Law Merchant is codified.

1.4 THE CODIFICATION OF COMMERCIAL LAW

As a result of the Utilitarian movement in the nineteenth century there was a trend towards codification of the common law in the second half of the nineteenth century. The trend was most successful in relation to Commercial Law. There is a tendency to regard this as explicable by reference to a single set of reasons concerning commercial pressure for legal rationality. However, apart from the fact that a small number of reformers was interested in all this legislation, the influences differed from statute to statute. The UK Bills of Exchange Act 1882 was the result of a lawyer's initiative which was taken up by the banking community. The Partnership Act 1890 was the result of a larger exercise promoted by the Chambers of Commerce. The Sale of Goods Act 1893 was primarily the result of lawyers' initiative which received some but not extensive commercial support. The Marine Insurance Act 1906 had some support from the shipping industry, especially local support in Liverpool: see R B Ferguson (1977) 4 BJLS 518.

The lawyers such as Lord Herschell and Sir Mackenzie Chalmers who promoted codification believed that it would produce greater certainty, make legal reasoning more logical and ultimately make the task of reform easier. The immediate aim was not, however, reform of the substance of the law: M Chalmers (1886) 2 LQR 126; (1903) 19 LQR 11.

1.5 CONSUMER PROTECTION

In early law the church and state sometimes intervened in the market place to proscribe usury, regulate prices and unfair market practices. However, by the nineteenth century most restrictions had disappeared and the dominant philosophies were laissez-faire and caveat emptor – in other words a free market in which the buyer must beware. This is not to say that there was no state intervention in the nineteenth century but legislation such as the Sale of Goods Act was drafted on the basis of freedom of contract.

A growing awareness of the imperfections in the market place in the real world in an age of increasing mass manufacturing of goods has led to the growth of the consumer protection movement at home and overseas: see A A Tarr (1983) 5 Otago L R 397. This has assumed a non party political force which has acted as a permanent interest group lobbying the legislature. In New Zealand consumer protection was institutionalised by legislation in the form of the Consumer Institute and Consumer Council. In the spirit of "Erewhon" we have recently seen a countertrend promoted by the Treasury and the Ministry of Consumer Affairs.

The earliest consumer protection legislation was passed against the adulteration of food and drink and to regulate weights and measures. In the nineteenth century regulation of carriage of goods and persons was introduced. In this century we have had, inter alia, price controls and legislation on hire purchase, door to door sales, layby sales, unsolicited goods and credit contracts. We deal with most of the modern statutes later. The aims of modern consumerism are:

    (a) to promote competition;
    (b) to improve consumer information and to educate the public;
    (c) to improve the quality and safety of goods;
    (d) to redress inequality of bargaining power; and
    (e) to facilitate consumer redress.

Much of modern reform of Commercial Law has been consumer protection legislation. Some overseas commentators argue that the time has come to take stock: P S Atiyah, *The Rise and Fall of Freedom of Contract*, (1979) ch 22. New Zealand has not gone as far as many other Western countries but a balancing act needs to be done to weigh up costs and benefits of state regulation: Tarr, op cit 416.

1.6 CREDIT, SECURITY AND THE LAW

1.6.1 The present approach

Today most individuals and companies seek credit. Credit means either the deferment of payment for goods delivered or services rendered or the straight lending of money. New Zealand law, true to its Common Law inheritance, has treated these as separate things with resulting confusion. In reality they are two aspects of the same thing—the transfer of purchasing power from one set of persons to another set of persons, against a promise to repay the principal with interest: Report of the Committee on Consumer Credit, Vol 1, 1 (Cmnd 4596, 1971) (UK).

A creditor will often have imperfect knowledge of the debtor. He or she will of course take steps to check the creditworthiness of the debtor and his or her ability to service the debt. To protect himself or herself further the creditor will often seek security to avoid the cost of regular surveillance of the debtor's activities.

1.6.2 The role of security

The economic role of security is to ensure the debtor's performance by creating a set of rights against his property or that of a third party. This confers two advantages on the credit providers – the right of preference and the right of pursuit. The first is a right to be paid out of the particular assets in preference to and in priority to unsecured creditors and secured creditors ranking subsequent to him or her. The second enables the creditor to follow the assets into the hands of certain third parties. Examples of the different types of security are shown in the diagrams on the following pages. In the case of a floating charge a major inroad is made into the secured rights by the company's power to dispose of assets in the ordinary course of business free of the charge until crystallisation. In addition to securities which create a right against property there are personal guarantees and indemnities which are sometimes loosely described as collateral security. These simply confer personal rights against the guarantor but not against his or her property unless a mortgage or some other form of security is given or judgment is obtained and enforced against him or her.

Apart from the Credit Contracts Act 1981, which regulates disclosure and the financial side of credit, the law relating to credit transactions at present lacks any functional basis. Its approach is based on legal abstractions such as title, property or possession rather than commercial reality. Hire purchase, for instance, has been treated as more akin to sale than security although the objectives are usually the same as a chattel security. The law fails to distinguish clearly between consumer and commercial transactions although there are arguably different policy objectives between the two. There are crucial differences between corporate and non corporate credit transactions. There are separate systems of registration under the Chattels Transfer Act 1924, the Companies Act 1955 and the Motor Vehicle Securities Act 1989 which differ in certain respects. There is no rational policy in relation to third party rights especially as they are affected by notice. The law employs a bewildering variety of forms – conditional sale, true hire purchase in the sense of bailment with an option to purchase, chattel security, chattel leasing, Land Transfer mortgages, the floating charge and so on. The results often vary considerably with the form used. The result is that the law is excessively technical and frequently fails to provide just solutions to common problems. It is unsuited to modern commercial requirements and fails to deal with everyday problems in a realistic fashion.

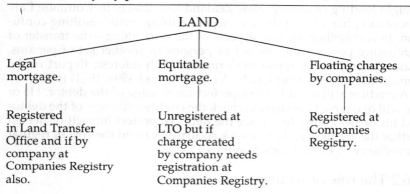

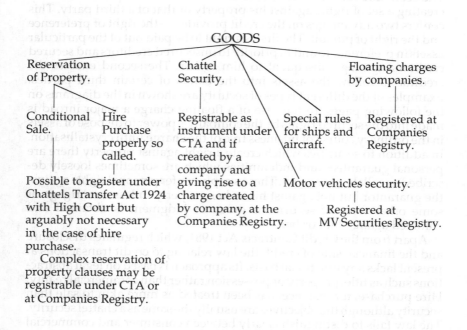

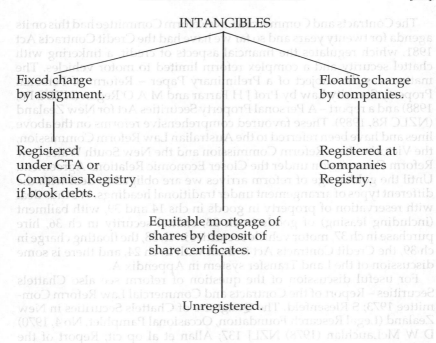

INTANGIBLES

Fixed charge
by assignment.

Floating charge
by companies.

Registered
under CTA or
Companies Registry
if book debts.

Registered at
Companies
Registry.

Equitable mortgage of
shares by deposit of
share certificates.

Unregistered.

To some extent the problem lies in the nature of personal as opposed to real property. Goods are of comparatively less value than land; they are usually depreciating and destructible; they are usually indistinguishable from other items of the same genus; and they are mobile and can usually be sold easily and without formality. Intangible property suffers from the inherent abstraction of the property and the limited methods which the law has developed for creating security over it. For these reasons security over goods and intangible property lags behind the simplicity and precision of the Land Transfer System.

1.6.3 The need for reform

A good system of commercial and consumer securities requires simple and cheap formalities for creation of the security; a comprehensive system of registration of securities with priorities dependent on time of perfection; and non discrimination of tax and other laws between different types of security: D E Allan et al, *Credit and Security in Australia* (1977), ch 1.

In New Zealand, therefore, there is a need for reform:

1 to introduce centralised registration of all credit transactions which involve security in the widest sense. This should be the subject of a computer link up between the main centres.

2 to assimilate all forms under a common system based on a functional approach such as is done under art 9 of the US Uniform Commercial Code and the Ontario Personal Property Security Act.

3 to assimilate corporate and non corporate transactions.

4 to provide for a common regime for third party rights.

The Contracts and Commercial Law Reform Committee had this on its agenda for twenty years and so far we have had the Credit Contracts Act 1981, which regulates the financial aspects of credit, a tinkering with chattel security and a complex reform limited to motor vehicles. The matter was the subject of a Preliminary Paper – Reform of Personal Property Security Law by Prof J H Farrar and M A O'Regan (NZLC P6, 1988) and a report – A Personal Property Securities Act for New Zealand (NZLC R8, 1989). These favoured comprehensive reforms on the above lines and have been referred to the Australian Law Reform Commission, the Victorian Law Reform Commission and the New South Wales Law Reform Commission under the Closer Economic Relations Agreement. Until the golden age of reform arrives we are obliged to deal with the different types of arrangement under traditional headings. We thus deal with reservation of property in goods in chs 14 and 39, with bailment (including leasing) of goods in ch 23, chattel security in ch 36, hire purchase in ch 37, motor vehicle securities in ch 38, the floating charge in ch 39, the Credit Contracts Act is dealt with in ch 24, and there is some discussion of the Land Transfer system in Appendix A.

For useful discussion of the question of reform see also Chattels Securities – Report of the Contracts and Commercial Law Reform Committee 1973; S Riesenfeld, The Quagmire of Chattels Securities in New Zealand (Legal Research Foundation, Occasional Pamphlet, No 4, 1970) D W McLauchlan (1978) NZLJ 137; Allan et al op cit; Report of the Committee on Consumer Credit op cit; R M Goode (1984) 100 LQR 234.

1.7 INTERNATIONAL INFLUENCES

1.7.1. The Commonwealth influence

New Zealand as a colony of the United Kingdom inherited the English Law as it stood on 14 January 1840, so far as applicable to the circumstances of New Zealand: English Laws Act 1908, s 2.

The principal modern significance of this is that New Zealand inherited the English common law and equity. The nineteenth century codes did not extend to New Zealand but were used as the model for New Zealand legislation. In most cases the New Zealand Acts are almost verbatim copies. The English influence has continued as the dominant influence until the last decade. Although that decade corresponds with the United Kingdom's membership of the EEC the change has been coincidental and cultural rather than immediately derived from that fact.

The major characteristics of the last decade have been: (1) the failure by New Zealand to reform the Sale of Goods Act 1908 except in certain minor respects; and (2) the attempt by New Zealand to codify areas of the general law of Contract.

The former omission is almost inexplicable but the latter represents an ambitious attempt by a part time committee to carry out a project originally conceived then suspended by the English and Scottish Law Commissions. The resulting statutes, the Minors Contracts Act 1969, the Illegal Contracts Act 1970, the Contractual Mistakes Act 1977, the Contractual Remedies Act 1979 and the Contracts (Privity) Act 1982 are partly reform, partly codification. They opt for general principle and judicial discretion but seem to work well in practice. The major difficulty seems to be the complicated relationship of the Contractual Remedies Act 1979 to the Sale of Goods Act 1908.

United Kingdom, Australian and Canadian law reform ideas still influence New Zealand but New Zealand is now prepared to strike out on its own.

1.7.2 CER

New Zealand and Australia share a number of common characteristics: they are geographically isolated outposts of European settlement in the Southern Hemisphere and adjacent to each other; they are former British colonies; in the early history of colonisation, New Zealand's closest economic ties were with Australia in terms of labour, trade and banking; they have distinctive cultural similarities; they share the inheritance of a common law but are struggling towards a sense of national identity; each has an indigenous population which is becoming more conscious of its rights; both were prejudiced by the United Kingdom joining the EEC.

All this makes it inevitable that there will be close contact between the two countries. There has long been a free movement of labour between them. The Courts of both countries refer to the precedents of the other system, as well as English precedents. Australia has abolished appeal to the Judicial Committee of the Privy Council and New Zealand may do so in the near future. The appellate Courts of both countries reveal a greater willingness to depart from English authority which they consider unsound, as well as on the traditional ground of differing local circumstances. Both countries have at times borrowed from the other's legislation although this has perhaps been less frequent than one would have expected. The reasons for this are the common trait of looking to London in the past coupled with the complexities of Australian federalism in practice.

CER is the name given to the Australia/New Zealand Closer Economic Relations Trade Agreement which was a treaty entered into between the governments of the two countries on 13 April 1982. The Treaty is principally concerned with the establishment of a free trade area. This objective must be seen in the context of the concept of economic integration.

Economists distinguish between five forms of economic integration – restricted free trade areas, free trade areas, customs unions, common markets and economic unions. The lowest level of integration is a restricted free trade area in which some but not all trade restrictions are abolished. A free trade area involves the abolition of all trade restrictions with each country retaining its own restrictions against imports from non-member countries. A customs union involves the abolition of trade restrictions between the member states and the adoption of a common external tariff system. A common market involves the removal not only of trade restrictions but restrictions on the movement of labour, capital and enterprise. An economic union is a common market with a harmonisation of national economic policies. The ultimate stage is total economic union in which all monetary and fiscal policies are unified. An economic union of this kind while falling short of political union requires establishment of a supranational authority whose decisions are binding on member states. Under CER, Australia and New Zealand have moved from a restricted free trade area towards a free trade area. There is talk of further union and some of the moves taken recently foreshadow closer economic integration, if not ultimate political integration. The CER Agreement itself is rather vague but the matter has been the subject of a Memorandum of Understanding between the Government of Australia and the Government of New Zealand on harmonisation of business law. This was signed in Christchurch on 1 July 1988. A wide range of topics was included under the heading of Further Development of Business Harmonisation. These included consumer protection, sale of goods and services, competition law, insolvency and commercial arbitration. Obligations of each government under the Memorandum of Understanding are to keep the other government informed of proposed reforms in the business law area and, where feasible and appropriate, to consult in the harmonisation of the laws in question.

For detailed discussion see J H Farrar "Harmonisation of Business Law Between Australia and New Zealand" (1989) 19 VUWLR 435 and the materials there cited.

1.7.3 International legal activity

In the twentieth century there has been a number of international organisations such as UNIDROIT and UNCITRAL involved in the harmonisation of International Trade Law. New Zealand has mainly been affected by work on international bills of exchange, bankers' commercial credits (another method of international payment of export trade transactions) and carriage of goods by sea. Reference should also be made to the 1980 United Nations Convention on Uniform Sales. Added to these is the important contribution of private international bodies such as the International Chamber of Commerce which is active in particular in codifying price-delivery terms (INCOTERMS) and international arbitration. It is perhaps in this blend of public and private international legal organisation activity that we see the resurgence of the Law Merchant: see Leon E Trakman (1980) 12 *Journal of Maritime Law and Commerce* 1; and R M Goode, *Commercial Law* 988-989.

Common law Judges at the highest level are prepared to consult the new legal materials as a source of international commercial custom and law: see Lord Diplock in *United City Merchants (Investments) Ltd v Royal Bank of Canada* [1982] 2 All ER 720 noted by JH Farrar in [1982] *All England Law Reports Annual Review* 19.

Part II

GENERAL PRINCIPLES OF CONTRACT AND QUASI-CONTRACT

Chapter 2

INTRODUCTION: THE NATURE OF CONTRACT

SUMMARY

2.1	DEFINITION
2.2	FREEDOM OF CONTRACT
2.3	STATUTORY INTERVENTION
2.4	SIMPLE CONTRACT AND DEED
2.5	CONTRACTS AND OTHER TRANSACTIONS

2.1 DEFINITION

A contract may be defined as an agreement between two or more persons which is intended to be enforceable at law. The most common sort of contract is one whereby the parties make reciprocal promises to each other – for instance A promises to sell B a house in return for $150,000 promised by B; C promises to work for D in return for a weekly wage of $600 promised by D. The possible subject matter of contracts is infinite.

The essential elements of a simple contract may be listed as follows:

(a) There must be agreement between the parties as to the terms of their bargain. This agreement is normally arrived at by a process of offer and acceptance, whereby one party makes the other an offer containing the terms on which he is prepared to do business, and the other accepts that offer. It used commonly to be said that a contract involved a "consensus ad idem" or meeting of the minds. Although such a statement has its uses, it must surely be treated with caution. Evidence of agreement must be gleaned objectively, ie by looking at what a person has said and done rather than at what he or she thinks in his or her innermost mind; what is relevant is what a reasonable person would understand that person to have agreed to rather than what he or she secretly *thought* he or she was agreeing to. (See however the discussion of Mistake, in 5.3).

(b) The parties must have intended to create legal relations. There are some arrangements of a purely social or domestic kind (for instance an invitation to dinner), and certain "gentlemen's agreements" where it would be unrealistic to suppose either party intended that the matter should be enforceable in the Courts.

15

(c) There must be consideration. This is an expression of the essential bargain nature of contract. Each party gives the other something and each party gets something in return. Thus in the example of the sale of the house given above, the consideration for A's promise to transfer the house to B is B's promise to pay $150,000, and vice versa. A promise for which there is no consideration is not enforceable – for instance a promise to give $1,000 to a friend as a wedding present.

(d) Both parties must have the capacity to contract. As we shall see later in this book, minors (persons under 20) have limited capacity, as do persons who are mentally ill, and persons who are bankrupt.

2.2 FREEDOM OF CONTRACT

In contract, traditional theory has it that it is the parties who formulate their own obligations, the law's main function being to determine whether a contract has been made, to interpret it, and to enforce it.

Of course it has never been true that the law will enforce *any* contract: for instance if a contract is illegal (an extreme example being a contract to commit a crime), or if it has been induced by misrepresentation or duress, or, in some cases, if the parties have entered their arrangement under some fundamental mistake, a Court may refuse to enforce the resulting "contract". But in the nineteenth century the common law for the most part held very strongly to the tenet that the parties were the sole arbiters of their contract. Within the very generous limits outlined above they could contract about anything they wished, and agree on any terms they liked. A Court could not refuse to enforce a contract just because it was unreasonable; nor could the law impose obligations on parties which they had not agreed on themselves.

However, in the twentieth century certain inroads have been made into these old principles. Most of them are due to the realisation that in many contract situations one party is in a better bargaining position than the other: that is true of most cases where a citizen, perhaps not very businesslike, is contracting with a large corporation. Such citizens' interests require the protection of the law to make sure that the contracts they enter into do not cause them injustice. The problem has been exacerbated by what are known as "standard form contracts". Many commercial organisations have a standard form of contract containing many terms in what one Judge has described as "regrettably small print". Customers know that if they do not agree to these terms and sign them, without alteration, they will not get the purchase or service they desire. To speak of freedom of contract, or freedom of negotiation, in such a situation, is unrealistic; rather one party is forcing an arrangement on the other. The old theories of contract are not really adequate to deal with such a situation.

To meet such problems of the market place, the law of contract has developed in several ways. One technique which has evolved is for the Courts to interpret consumer contracts, as far as they can, in favour of the consumer. Thus, if a clause in such a contract is to some extent vague or ambiguous, it will be given the construction most favourable to the consumer. This is often called the "contra proferentem" rule. Likewise if it can be shown that a contract is "unconscionable" in that one party has taken improper advantage of some weakness in the other, the Court may set the contract aside: see 5.2.3. But there are limits as to how far the Courts can go, and most of the major changes in recent years have been by statute.

Thus there are statutes which impose on the parties to certain types of contract mandatory obligations which they cannot contract out of: examples are the conditions and guarantees of quality in the Hire Purchase Act 1971 and the Motor Vehicle Dealers Act 1975, and the obligations imposed on landlords and tenants by the Residential Tenancies Act 1986. Other statutes give parties a "cooling off" period during which they may think better of a contract they have entered and withdraw from it without penalty: examples are to be found in the Credit Contracts Act 1981 and the Door to Door Sales Act 1967. The Credit Contracts Act 1981 also gives the Court power to "re-open" a credit contract which it finds to be harsh and oppressive and the Employment Contracts Act 1991 (which in some respects increases freedom of bargaining in respect of employment contracts) nevertheless empowers a Court to refuse to enforce clauses in such contracts which are harsh and oppressive. These examples of state intervention in contract are a far cry from the old "freedom of contract". Indeed, the New Zealand Law Commission is currently considering whether there should be a general statutory provision empowering the Courts to give relief in respect of all unfair contracts. See their discussion paper "Unfair Contracts", 1990.

2.3 STATUTORY INTERVENTION

Quite apart from these instances of consumer protection, there are other modern statutes in New Zealand which substantially change certain aspects of the law of contract. The most important of these statutes are the Minors Contracts Act 1969, the Illegal Contracts Act 1970, the Contractual Mistakes Act 1977, the Contractual Remedies Act 1979 and the Contracts (Privity) Act 1982. In each case the common law had been unsatisfactory in that it was either too complicated or too harsh. For instance in the areas of illegal contracts and mistake the common law took an "all or nothing" approach: the contract was either valid and enforceable, in which case the parties must perform it whatever the injustice, or else it was totally void and unenforceable. The pattern of the new statutes is to give the Court more flexibility. For instance in our two examples of illegality and mistake the Courts are given a discretion to validate the contract, or to enforce part of it, or even in some instances to vary it. This is a substantial departure from the certainty of the old common law.

These statutes give the New Zealand law of contract a flavour of its own. They are discussed more fully later in this chapter. They make it dangerous to use English text-books in the law of contract.

2.4 SIMPLE CONTRACT AND DEED

A contract may be entered into in a special form known as a deed (sometimes called a specialty contract). In New Zealand, by virtue of s 4 of the Property Law Act 1952, a deed must be signed by the party to be bound, and must be attested by at least one witness who adds his place of abode and calling or description. Except where the party is a corporation, sealing is not necessary. There used to be many differences in consequence between a contract by deed and a simple contract, but today many of them have disappeared. However two very important differences remain. The first is that in a deed consideration is not necessary; it is enough that one party has entered into a promise in the solemn form of a deed. The second, which is related to this, is that a party to a deed can be bound even though the person who is to benefit has not signed the deed or assented to it. In other words a deed imposes an obligation because it is made in a particular form, not because of any element of bargain, nor because of contractual assent. In fact one can have a deed with only one party.

2.5 CONTRACTS AND OTHER TRANSACTIONS

(a) A contract can be distinguished from a transfer. A contract creates an obligation to do, or forbear from doing, something in future, whereas a transfer is an actual conveyance of an interest in property from one person to another which has the effect of presently vesting ownership in that other. However the distinction is not always simple. Sometimes a contract itself has the effect of passing ownership of property to a buyer: for instance under s 20 r 1 of the Sale of Goods Act 1908, where there is an unconditional contract for the sale of specific goods the property in the goods passes to the buyer when the contract is made. Moreover quite often a document which transfers property contains also promises or covenants which will continue to bind one or more of the parties even after the transfer is complete: a fencing covenant in a transfer of land for example.

(b) A contract must also be distinguished from a trust. In a trust, one person (the trustee) holds property on behalf of another (the beneficiary) and is bound to deal with it for the benefit of that other. While the trustee is the legal owner of the property, the beneficiary is said to have beneficial, or equitable, ownership of it.

(c) Contract is to be distinguished from tort. A tort is the breach of a non-contractual obligation which one citizen owes to another: examples of torts are assault, defamation, and negligence. Winfield said that the main differences between contract and tort are: (i) that duties in tort are defined by the law while in contract they are defined by the parties; and (ii) that in tort the duty is towards persons in general while in contract it is towards a specific person or persons. However in recent times the tort of negligence has been expanding to the point where if a person by careless words or conduct causes foreseeable harm to another he or she may well be liable to that other in tort. At times tort can invade what some regard as the province of contract. Thus if a person commits a careless act in the course of performance of a contract he or she may in some situations be liable in both tort and contract. (However in New Zealand, because of a case called *McLaren Maycroft & Co v Fletcher Development Co Ltd* [1973] 2 NZLR 100, the situations in which concurrent liability can exist are limited). It is possible that a party's liability in tort may extend even to persons who are not parties to the contract: thus a solicitor who, allegedly negligently, failed to carry out his client's instructions to draft a will was held to owe a duty in tort to a potential beneficiary under the will when his client died: *Gartside v Sheffield Young and Ellis* [1983] NZLR 37.

Moreover if one makes a careless statement, or even a careless promise, to another person which that other relies on to his detriment, it may well be that an action in negligence will lie, even though there would be no action in contract because of a lack of consideration or lack of intention to contract: see for instance *Meates v Attorney-General* [1983] NZLR 308 (although there is some doubt about the effect of that decision, cf *Shing v Ashcroft* [1987] 2 NZLR 154). Some believe that we are approaching a day when much of the law of contract will be swallowed up in the law of tort, but it is difficult to believe that this is so. As long as parties are able to regulate their obligations by their own agreement there will have to remain a "law of contract".

(d) There has also been substantial development in recent years in what is known as promissory estoppel or equitable estoppel. This development is leading to a position that if party A induces a belief or expectation in party B, and party B relies on it to his or her detriment, the Courts may hold party A to his or her word if it would be unconscionable not to do so. At times, this doctrine can have the effect of enforcing a promise made by party A simply because it has been relied on, even though there may be no consideration for it. It is still unclear how far this new development will go, but it could emerge as a method of enforcing promises outside the normal confines of contract. This type of estoppel will be more fully discussed below in 3.2.11.

Chapter 3

FORMATION OF A CONTRACT

SUMMARY

3.1   AGREEMENT
3.2   CONSIDERATION
3.3   FORM
3.4   INTENTION TO CREATE LEGAL RELATIONS

3.1 AGREEMENT

As has been outlined above in 2.1, for there to be a contract, there must be apparent agreement between the parties. The Courts look to see if the dealings between the parties have reached a stage where a reasonable bystander with knowledge of the parties' actions and the terms of any communications between them would see them as having reached a mutual understanding as to the terms of their agreement and as having shown a willingness to be bound by those terms.

There are two important corollaries to the objective view of agreement. The first is that the Courts look to the legal effect of communications rather than to the descriptions given to them by the parties. Thus what is described by a person as "an offer" may not, in law, be an offer.

It is important to note that where one person is simultaneously involved in transactions with several other persons, a statement or action by him may have legal effects in relation to more than one transaction, and may even have different legal effects in the different contexts. Examples can be seen in the auction sales cases cited in 3.1.3 infra.

Secondly, the parties' respective states of mind are assessed by inference from their conduct. There may be cases where a person's actions are influenced by mistake, misrepresentation, duress or incapacity and thus the inferences to be drawn from his or her conduct do not accurately represent his or her real state of mind. This will not prevent there being an agreement, on the objective view, but the agreement may not be binding as a contract. Elements which may prevent an agreement being binding as a contract are discussed in ch 5, infra.

3.1.1 Offer and acceptance

The normal approach to ascertaining whether there is a contract is to look at the dealings between the parties to see if at some point one party has expressed a clear willingness to be contractually bound to the other on sufficiently definite terms. This will be the offer. If the other party indicates a willingness to be bound on those same terms there is an acceptance and an agreement comes into existence.

It is only safe to say that this is the normal approach, because there are some cases where contractual liability has been held to exist where no such clear statements can be found. Thus in *Clarke v Dunraven* [1897] AC 59, an entrant in a race organised by a yacht club was held to be contractually bound to other entrants in the race by virtue of their respective entries. On the agreement approach each entry would have to be regarded as having been an offer to any other competitor to abide by the yacht club rules (which differed from the general law regarding liability for damages) and at the same time be an acceptance of the offers made by the other entrants. In *NZ Shipping Co Ltd v A M Satterthwaite and Co Ltd* [1975] AC 154, [1974] 1 NZLR 505, the acceptance by a cargo-owner of terms offered by a shipping firm was held by a majority of the Privy Council to create an offer to a third party, the stevedores, who unloaded the cargo. These cases do not fit easily with the normal approach, but as Lord Wilberforce said in *Satterthwaite's* case [1975] AC 154, 157; [1974] 1 NZLR 505, 510:

> English Law, having committed itself to a rather technical and schematic doctrine, in application takes a practical approach, often at the cost of forcing the facts to fit uneasily into the marked slots of offer, acceptance and consideration.

However in the vast majority of contractual transactions, it is possible to identify an offer and an acceptance.

3.1.2 Bilateral and unilateral contracts

The distinction between bilateral and unilateral contracts may be of importance as in some cases different rules may apply. The essential distinction between them is on the basis of *promises* made. In a bilateral contract, the agreement is an exchange of promises – A promises to hand over A's car to B and B promises to pay to A the agreed price. There is thus a promise on both sides of the contract.

In a unilateral contract, only one side makes a promise and in exchange for the promise receives not a promise but an act. Thus, in a common form of unilateral contract, A offers (promises) a reward to anyone returning a lost item. B makes the contract by performing in reliance on A's offer. B also performs B's obligations under the contract at the same time. At no time does B make any promise to A.

3.1.3. The offer

(a) OFFERS AND INVITATIONS TO TREAT

An offer signifies a person's willingness to enter into a legally binding arrangement. There must therefore be both an indication of the terms which would govern such an arrangement and an indication of willingness to be bound by those terms. It is the presence of this latter element that distinguishes an offer from an invitation to treat. An invitation to treat is a statement which indicates that its maker may be prepared at some future stage to enter into a contract as to the matters mentioned in the invitation to treat. It is a statement of a person's willingness to enter into negotiations which may ultimately lead to a contract: it is not of itself intended to give rise to any contractual nexus. The question of certainty as to terms is discussed below, at 3.1.7.

Thus in *Harvey v Facey* [1893] AC 552, an inquiry "Will you sell us Bumper Hall Pen? Telegraph lowest cash price?" was answered in these terms "Lowest price for Bumper Hall Pen £900", and the Court held there was no offer to sell to the would-be buyer. The owner had not indicated a willingness to sell, but had merely supplied information which could be used to formulate an offer. It was the inability of the would-be purchaser to establish the vendor's willingness to be bound which was fatal to his case in *Boulder Consolidated Ltd v Tangaere* [1980] 1 NZLR 560, which is now perhaps the leading New Zealand case on this area of the law.

(b) OFFERS AND INVITATIONS TO TREAT IN SOME SPECIAL CASES
There are a number of special instances which have involved the classification of statements as offers or invitations to treat, and it must be stressed that although the following generally represents the legal position, changes in terminology used or exceptional circumstances may alter the position in individual cases.

(1) Shops: A display in a shop window is normally only an invitation to treat: *Fisher v Bell* [1961] 1 QB 394; [1960] 3 All ER 731. In effect, since shop sales will normally be bilateral contracts, the shop window display is treated under the principle governing advertisements.

The same rule will usually apply to displays of goods within a shop. These are normally an invitation to treat by the shopkeeper. The contractual offer is made by the customer who approaches the cash desk intimating a willingness to buy the thing in question and the shopkeeper may accept or refuse this offer: *Pharmaceutical Society of Great Britain v Boots Cash Chemists (Southern) Ltd* [1953] 1 QB 401; 1 All ER 482.

(2) Tenders: A call for tenders is an invitation to treat, indicating an interest in forming a contract, but clearly without wishing to be bound to a contract with any particular tenderer. The tenders received will, therefore, be the offers and may be accepted or rejected at will. (The customary rubric in calls for tenders that the highest or any tender will not necessarily be accepted is not necessary and is presumably only included because of an excess of caution or habit.)

(3) Advertisements: An advertisement will not normally be an offer but an invitation to treat if the contemplated contract is a bilateral one though it will often be an offer if the contract would be a unilateral one. The difference is essentially that, as explained above (3.1.2), in a unilateral contract one party lays down all the essential terms and these are then accepted by performance by the other party. In most unilateral contracts

it is the other party's performance of the stipulated action, not his identity, which is vital. The Courts are therefore readier to assume that a statement which requires performance by the other party is intended to give rise to a contract than they are to hold a statement seeking some other person's expressed agreement and promise is a contractual offer. If one is to rely solely on another's promise, one would wish to have the opportunity to verify the worth of the promise.

In some cases the wording of a tender or an advertisement may explicitly or impliedly make promises as to the procedure that will be followed in determining how an offeree will proceed in handling offers that result from the advertisement or request for tenders. In such cases the same statement can have more than one effect in law. For instance, it is clear law that an auctioneer's advertisement that an auction would take place on a certain date and place is merely an invitation to treat as regards the holding of the sale, and, a fortiori, in regard to the sale of any items advertised: *Harris v Nickerson* (1873) LR 8 QB 286. However, in *Warlow v Harrison* (1859) 1 E & E 309 the Court considered that an advertisement that an auction would be held "without reserve" (ie that the highest bidder would get the item put up for sale) was a contractual offer, addressed to any person who bid in reliance on it, that there would be no reserve price on the item. The making of a bid is the doing of an act in reliance on that offer, and thus is the acceptance of the offer. There is then a contract that the sale will be without reserve. It should be noted that the bid has two separate legal effects – as an offer to purchase and, as noted, as an acceptance of the offer as to the procedure of the sale. (Auction sales are governed by the Sale of Goods Act 1908, s 59(2) and see Property Law Act 1952 s 51.) Similar decisions have been reached in cases involving advertisements and tenders. In *Markholm Construction Ltd v Wellington City Council* [1985] 2 NZLR 520, it was held that the defendant, by advertising sections for sale at stipulated prices and stating that a ballot would be held if there was more than one applicant for each section, had made an offer, accepted by the supply of a application for a section, that the advertised ballot would take place, with the section then to be sold to the winner of the ballot. A similar contract was found in *Blackpool and Fylde Aero Club Ltd v Blackpool Borough Council* [1990] 3 All ER 25, where it was held that the Council, by inviting tenders for a concession to operate pleasure flights from its airfield, were contractually obliged to consider each tender submitted in accordance with the terms of the invitation to tender.

3.1.4 Offer and acceptance

The contract is made when the party to whom it is addressed (the offeree) accepts the offer; ie signifies a willingness to be bound by the terms the offeror has proposed. This simple statement however involves several corollaries which must be discussed further. Attention must be given to whether the offeree is entitled to accept the offer, whether the offer is still in existence and what constitutes a valid acceptance.

(a) WHO MAY ACCEPT AN OFFER?
An offer may be made to an individual, or to a class of persons or to the world at large. If it is made to a specific person, he or she alone may

accept. An offer can validly be made to the whole world, in the expectation of a contract being made by those members of the public who respond to it: *Carlill v Carbolic Smoke Ball Co* [1893] 1 QB 256. That was a case of unilateral contract where the defendant advertised that it would pay £100 to any person who contracted influenza after using one of its smoke balls. The plaintiff on fulfilling those conditions was held entitled to recover £100. It is unlikely that, unless very specific terms are used, the Courts would hold that a statement to the whole world which would or could result in a multitude of bilateral contracts was more than an invitation to treat.

If the offer is to a class of persons, anyone not included in that class cannot validly accept: *McMahon v Gilberd* [1955] NZLR 1206. In that case, a bottle dealer could not take advantage of higher refunds offered to customers for the return of the manufacturer's bottles.

(b) DURATION OF THE OFFER
An offer exists and may be accepted until it has lapsed, has been withdrawn or has been rejected.

(1) Lapse: An offer will lapse either at the end of any time limit specified in it or on the passing of a reasonable time. What is a "reasonable time" will, naturally, vary according to the circumstances and nature of the transaction. In *Ramsgate Victoria Hotel v Montefiore* (1866) LR I Ex 109 an offer to take up shares in a company was held to have lapsed when no acceptance had taken place in a period of nearly six months. In other circumstances a shorter time period might be sufficient. There is a useful discussion of this area in *Manchester Diocesan Council for Education v Commercial and General Investments Ltd* [1970]1 WLR 241; [1969] 3 All ER 1593.

An offer will also lapse, if not previously accepted, on the death of the offeree: *Re Irvine* [1928] 3 DLR 268. There is no clear authority as to the position of an offer where the offeror dies prior to a purported acceptance. It is possible that if the contract is one that can be carried out by the deceased's personal representative the offer does not lapse; but an offer of personal services would clearly lapse on the death of the offeror.

(2) Withdrawal or revocation: An offer may be revoked at any time prior to its acceptance unless there is a separate contractual undertaking to keep it open for a specified period. This is so even if the offer was originally stated to remain open for a fixed period: *Routledge v Grant* (1828) 4 Bing 653.

The exception to the general rule that the offer is freely revocable is the case of an option agreement supported by consideration. Options may be regarded either as a conditional contract for the main subject matter (the condition being the exercise of the option) or as a contractual arrangement to keep an offer of the substantial contract open. The latter seems the preferred view in New Zealand, see *Alexander v Tse* [1988] 1 NZLR 318, 324-5. The distinction may be relevant in terms of remedies for breach, but makes no difference to the rule here that an offer contained in an option is not revocable at will. There is a masterly summary of the law relating to options in the judgment of Gibbs J in *Laybutt v Amoco Australia Pty Ltd* (1974) 48 ALJR 492.

Revocation of an offer is only effective when it is communicated to the offeree. Until such time as the revocation comes to his or her notice, the offeree is still free to accept the offer: *Byrne and Co v Van Tienhoven and Co* (1880) 5 CPD 344 and *Stevenson and Co v McLean* (1880) 5 QBD 346.

Notice of revocation need not come directly from the offeror. It is sufficient if the offeree has information which would inform a reasonable person that the offeror no longer intended to be bound by the offer to the offeree: *Dickinson v Dodds* (1876) 2 ChD 463; *King v Homer* (1913) 33 NZLR 222.

Offers of unilateral contracts pose two problems in relation to revocation which do not occur in bilateral contracts. The first is that by its nature, an offer of a unilateral contract is often made to persons not known to the offeror. The offeror, therefore, cannot communicate directly with each offeree to revoke the offer. Although there is no direct Commonwealth authority, it seems likely that the American rule in *Shuey v US* (1875) 92 US 73 would be adopted. According to that rule, an offeror who has made an offer through public media may validly revoke the offer by similar publicity in similar channels, even though the revocation does not actually reach all persons who come to know of the original offer.

The second problem is whether an offer of a unilateral contract may be revoked while the offeree is in the course of performing the acts required for acceptance. Strict adherence to the general rules of offer and acceptance would suggest that revocation may occur at any time before acceptance is complete, and this is the view taken in some American cases (see eg *Petterson v Pattberg* (1928) 248 NY 86). However, in *Errington v Errington* [1952] 1 KB 290, the English Court of Appeal appeared to hold that an offeror cannot revoke an offer when he or she knows the offeree intends to accept and has done acts towards acceptance in reliance on the offer. This view is supported obiter, by Goff LJ in *Daulia Ltd v Four Millbank Nominees* [1978] 2 WLR 621; 2 All ER 557. The position in New Zealand is thus uncertain.

(3) Rejection and counter-offers: An offer is terminated if it is rejected. Rejection includes outright refusal, but in this context also includes any variation of the terms of the original offer. If the offeree indicates a willingness to be bound but on terms that are different from those proposed by the offeror the offeree is making a counter-offer. This extinguishes the original offer, and, of course, does not of itself result in a contract: *Jones v Daniel* [1894] 2 Ch 332; *Cross v Davidson* (1899) 17 NZLR 576.

It must be stressed that a counter-offer's rejection of the original offer turns on the indication by the offeree that he insists on new or different terms. Thus the making of remarks about the offer, not intending to insist on their tenor as terms of the agreement is not a counter-offer: *Simpson* v *Hughes* (1897) 76 LT 237. The critical question is whether a reasonable person in the shoes of the offeror would consider that the offeree had insisted on terms different from those proposed by the offeror (thus a counter-offer) or had merely been exploring the possibility that other terms might be available. The two may be hard to distinguish, but it is the question of intention which is vital, rather than any particular form of words or conduct: *Powierza v Daley* [1985] 1 NZLR 558. If additional words are used which introduce an apparent conflict, but the additional words are inherently meaningless, the Court may disregard them, and hold there is no counter-offer (*Nicolene Ltd v Simmonds* [1953]1 QB 543).

It is also possible to have replies to an offer which do not amount either to a rejection or an acceptance. These will include both requests for further information as to the true meaning of the offer, as in *Stevenson v Maclean* (1880) 5 QBD 346, and conditional acceptances as in *Frampton v McCully* [1976]1 NZLR 270. As to the latter, see 4.3.1 infra.

Once the counter-offer is made, the original offeror is free to accept it or reject it. If it is rejected, the original offeree cannot seek to accept the original offer unless the original offeror has expressly or impliedly renewed it: *Hyde v Wrench* (1840) 3 Beav, 334; 49 ER 132. Renewal will be implied if the offeror indicates a preparedness to stand by the original terms: *Livingstone v Evans* (1925) 4 DLR 762.

(c) STANDING OFFERS

It should be noted that there is one kind of offer which can continue despite acceptance. This is what is called a "standing offer". A standing offer is an indication of willingness to perform certain obligations (eg to supply goods at a certain price) as and when requested. Even if the offer is accepted on one occasion it continues and can be accepted on other occasions. Revocation of a standing offer is possible, but will only be effective from the time it is communicated and acceptances made before revocation is effective are legally binding: *Great Northern Railway v Witham* (1873) LR 9 CP 16.

3.1.5 Acceptance

The rules regarding the acceptance of a contractual offer are, in general, simpler to apply than those which have been discussed above as to offers. The importance of the rules regarding acceptance is that the acceptance of an offer, which thus brings about the contract defines the time of the contract's coming into existence, its terms and the location of the contract. This last may be important for determining matters of jurisdiction. The rules regarding acceptance can be summarised thus:

(a) ACCEPTANCE MUST BE IN RELIANCE ON THE OFFER

This requires that the offeree know of and intend to accept, the offer: *R v Clarke* (1927) 40 CLR 227; *McMahon v Gilberd* [1955] NZLR 1206. It should not matter that other motives are present as well as reliance on the offer. The view expressed here is generally now preferred, though in some English cases reliance is hard to establish (eg *Williams v Carwardine* (1833) 5 C&P 566; *Upton-on-Severn RDC v Powell* [1942]1 All ER 220).

(b) CROSS-OFFERS ARE NOT OFFER AND ACCEPTANCE

This may originally have started as a different rule from the reliance rule, but its rationale is similar. Offers, even if identical in the terms proposed, from both parties are not offer and acceptance: *Tinn v Hoffman and Co* (1873) 29 LT 271.

(c) THERE MUST BE AN OVERT ACT OF ACCEPTANCE

It is not sufficient for acceptance that the offeree decide to accept the offer. There must be some manifestation of acceptance: *Brogden v Metropolitan*

Railway Co (1877) 2 App Cas 666. In that case the offeree's writing of "approved" on a draft contract (which act was not made known to any other person) was not acceptance – but his conduct in abiding by the terms of the draft contract for a considerable period was a sufficient act of acceptance. Conduct or words or both may sufficiently indicate acceptance.

(d) ACCEPTANCE MUST BE SUFFICIENTLY COMMUNICATED TO THE OFFEROR
In general, the offeree must convey to the offeror the information that he or she has accepted the offer: *Brogden's case* (supra); *Kennedy v Thomassen* [1929] Ch 426. However, what is necessary to convey acceptance may vary considerably according to the circumstances.

It is possible for the offeror expressly or impliedly to waive the offeree's obligation to communicate acceptance: *Carlill v Carbolic Smoke Ball Co* [1893] 1 QB 256. Implied waiver in a bilateral contract may be difficult to establish: *Latec Finance Co v Knight* [1969] 2 NSWR 79, but in unilateral contracts such as in *Carlill's* case it will be the norm.

The law itself allows a major exception to the requirement of communication of acceptance. This occurs where what are known as the posting rules apply.

(1) The posting rules: These rules provide that where a letter is used as the method of conveying acceptance, acceptance is complete on the posting of the letter: *Adams v Lindsell* (1818)1 B & Ald 681;106 ER 250. This will be so even if the letter is delayed in the post *(Dunlop v Higgins* (1848)1 HLC 381), or is lost and never arrives *(Household Fire and Carriage Accident Insurance Co v Grant* (1879) 4 ExD 216).

The same rule applies to telegrams: *Cowan v O'Connor* (1888) 20 QBD 640. If the telegram is garbled in transmission, it is the form in which it is handed in for transmission that is legally effective: *Henkel v Pape* (1870) LR 6 Ex 7.

Where a person seeks to establish acceptance by the posting rules, it is for that person to establish that the letter or telegram was properly despatched: *Re London and Northern Bank, ex p Jones* [1900] 1 Ch 220.

The posting rules will be applicable to acceptances where it is reasonably appropriate to use the post or a telegram: *Henthorn v Fraser* [1892] 2 Ch 27. Even in such circumstances, they may be ousted by a stipulation, express or implied, in the offer requiring acceptance to be communicated or requiring acceptance to be communicated in a particular way. The posting rules will not apply if the offeror has indicated a wish to receive the acceptance before it will be effective. In *Holwell Securities Ltd v Hughes* [1974]1 WLR 155;1 All ER 161 an option had to be exercised "by notice in writing" and mere posting of a letter of acceptance was ineffective. There may be exceptional cases where the whole circumstances are such that neither party can have intended to risk being bound by communications which might be delayed or never arrive: *Tallerman and Co Pty Ltd v Nathan's Merchandise (Victoria) Pty Ltd* (1957) 98 CLR 93.

If the offeror has stipulated a particular mode of reply to the offer, the offeree must accept by that mode or one no less advantageous to the offeror: *Eliason v Henshaw* (1819) 4 Wheaton 225; *Tinn v Hoffman* (1873) 29 LT 271 and *Manchester Diocesan Council for Education v Commercial and General Investments Ltd* [1970] 1 WLR 241; [1969] 3 All ER 1593.

One matter which is not yet clearly settled is whether a posted letter of acceptance can be revoked prior to receipt by some faster method of communication. If the letter would not be effective until receipt, it appears it can be: *A to Z Bazaars v Minister of Agriculture* 1974 (4) SA 392. However, if the letter is effective as an acceptance on posting, such New Zealand authority as there is would suggest the acceptance is not revocable: *Wenkheim v Arndt* (1874) 1 NZ Jur 73; *Sommerville v Rice* (1911) 31 NZLR 370. There is an old Scottish case, *Dunmore (Countess) v Alexander* (1830) 9 Sh (Ct of Sess) 190 which would suggest the contrary, and the point cannot be regarded as conclusively decided.

(2) Instantaneous communications: Such methods of communication as the telephone, telexes and radio are not governed by the posting rules. Communications by these means are treated as if "inter praesentes" – as if the parties were present in the same place. The onus there is on the offeree to make certain the acceptance is received by the offeror: *Entores Ltd v Miles Far East Corporation* [1955] 2 QB 327; 2 All ER 493, and *Brinkibon Ltd v Stahag Stahl GmbH* [1982] 1 All ER 293. The House of Lords in the latter case indicated that where communication between the parties by telex or other means will not in fact be instantaneous, as where the message is sent out of office hours, the rule outlined may not apply and reference may have to be made to the intention of the parties, sound business practice and consideration of where the risk of non-communication should lie to determine when acceptance takes place.

(e) THE OFFEROR CANNOT STIPULATE FOR SILENCE TO BE CONSENT
The offeror cannot validly state that the onus is on the offeree to refuse the offer: *Felthouse v Bindley* (1862) 11 CB (NS) 869; *Fairline Shipping Corporation v Adamson* [1974] 2 WLR 824; 2 All ER 967.

3.1.6 Ascertaining the full meaning of the offer

It must be stressed that in many cases the full terms of the contract will not be contained within the words of the offer. Other terms may be implied into the contract (as to which see ch 4.4 infra) or terms may be incorporated into the contract though not expressly included in the offer. The classic instances of these are conditions limiting or excluding certain types of contractual liability. These may be taken as terms of the contract provided reasonable notice of them is given to the offeree prior to his acceptance. This point is further discussed in relation to exclusion clauses etc in ch 4.2. infra.

3.1.7 Certainty and agreement

Even though the parties have purportedly gone through the procedures of offer and acceptance, it does not mean that there is automatically a binding contract. The agreement resulting from offer and acceptance must be sufficiently clear and unambiguous that the Courts can determine the nature and extent of the obligations created by the agreement. If this cannot be done, there is no contract. Whether or not the agreement is sufficiently certain will depend on the terms used and the nature and provisions of any agreement. If the Courts can find a way of making the contract sufficiently certain, they will usually do so. Questions of lack of certainty may arise in different situations. The most common cases arise where the alleged agreement has not been fully delineated by the parties in that the agreement lacks one or more terms of importance or has apparently left that term to be determined in the future. In such cases, much depends on whether there is some external mechanism available to fill in the blank left by the parties and thus make the agreement sufficiently clear and certain, or whether certainty could only be achieved by the further negotiations of the parties themselves. In the former case there is a contract, in the latter there is not. There may also be cases where there is an appearance of a complete agreement which is vitiated because the wording used does not reveal any single clear meaning.

(a) INCOMPLETE AND FUTURE AGREEMENTS
The common law does not recognise a contract to make a contract: *Von Hatzfeldt-Wildenburg v Alexander* [1912] 1 Ch 284. Nor will it recognise an agreement to negotiate: *Courtney and Fairbairn v Tolaini Bros* [1975] WLR 297. The decisions in these cases are premised, at least in part, on the futility of any remedy the Court could give in the circumstances. The Courts cannot compel the parties to come to an agreement at a later date. However a contract which requires one party to give the other an opportunity to be heard at some future date before some action is taken is different and may well be enforceable: *Rothmans of Pall Mall (NZ) Ltd v Attorney-General* [1991] 2 NZLR 323.

If the parties to an agreement have expressly left something to be determined in the future by the parties themselves, then there is no contract: *May and Butcher v The King* [1934] 2 KB 17; *Willets v Ryan* [1968] NZLR 863. In such cases, there has been no indication of willingness to undertake certain and binding obligations. This has prevented there being a true offer and acceptance. However, an agreement will not be void for lack of certainty if the matters not yet agreed can be resolved by reference to some external factor or by the use of some machinery which can produce a result if there is no agreement between the parties. If the matter left unsettled can, in terms of the agreement, be resolved in only one way, there is no uncertainty: *Havenbar Ltd v Butterfield* (1974) 48 ALJR 225.

Nor is there insufficient certainty if one party, or one party's agent, is to determine finally the terms of the agreement by using terms which are common or usual in an area or trade or profession: see *Coachman Properties Ltd v Panmure Video Club Ltd* [1984] 2 NZLR 200 and *Robertson Enterprises Ltd v Cope* [1989] 3 NZLR 391.

Equally, there is sufficient certainty if the Courts can fill in the matters left incomplete by using some external standard which the parties have indicated shall be used for that purpose. This kind of case is exemplified by *Hillas v Arcos Ltd* (1932) 147 LT 503, where the price of timber to be delivered could be ascertained by reference to an official price list mentioned in the apparently vague agreement. Other terms of the bargain could be determined by the use of implied terms or by reference to the parties' earlier dealings.

(b) USE OF MACHINERY PROVISIONS
Frequently the parties to an agreement wish to leave some matter to be

determined in the future. To avoid the difficulties of future agreements, there is a provision that, if the parties do not agree as to some future matter, the point in question shall be determined by the application of an agreed procedure – as, for instance, the sale and purchase of something at a price to be fixed by a valuer. Such terms are usually referred to as "machinery provisions". A common example is the use of an arbitration clause to resolve a matter left for future decision. Where a contract has been partly executed and difficulties arise as to matters which were apparently reserved for future agreement, the Courts may hold that an arbitration clause can be used to bring sufficient certainty. This requires that the clause be drafted widely enough to cover failure to agree on the matter left for future decision, and that there be sufficient guide-lines by which the arbitrator can approach the issue. For examples of the use of arbitration clauses, see *Foley v Classique Coaches Ltd* [1934] 2 KB 1, and *Attorney-General v Barker Bros* [1976] 2 NZLR 495. Arbitration clauses can, of course, only apply if there is some contractual force in the document giving rise to the obligation to accept arbitration.

If the machinery provided to resolve a matter left undetermined itself turns out to be defective, as where property is to be bought "at valuation", but there is no provision for what is to happen if the parties do not agree on a valuer, the Courts can either remedy the deficiency or substitute some other form of machinery to determine the matter: *Sudbrook Trading Estates Ltd v Eggleton* [1983] 1 AC 444. The reasoning in *Sudbrook* is that if the parties have intended their respective obligations to be determined *objectively*, as with a sale at "market price", remedying the deficiency is in fact giving effect to the parties' intentions. That reasoning has been extended in *Money v Ven-Lu-Ree Ltd* [1988] 1 NZLR 685 (HC); [1988] 2 NZLR 414 (CA); [1989] 3 NZLR 129 (PC) to cover cases where the parties have shown an intention to have their principal obligations fixed objectively, but have provided machinery which never fully provided a means for this to be done.

Because the parties must have intended that any matter left undetermined be settled on an objective standard, the *Sudbrook* and *Ven-Lu-Ree* principle cannot apply where the parties have either reserved a matter for them to decide later on a subjective basis (as in *Willetts v Ryan* [1968] NZLR 863 – the payment of money "by mutual arrangement") or have stipulated for a particular machinery provision which need not operate on an objective basis (as with the use of a price-fixing committee in *Nelson v Cooks McWilliams Wines Ltd* [1986] 2 NZLR 215). Neither of course, can the principle be used where there is an existing, workable machinery provision, even if some other machinery might be more effective or convenient: *Northern Regional Health Authority v Derek Crouch Construction Co Ltd* [1984] 1 QB 644, [1984] 2 All ER 175.

There are other approaches to future agreements which may be applicable in some cases. The Courts may be able to imply a term to fill in a gap, as was done in regard to price and delivery in *Hillas v Arcos Ltd*, supra. However the Courts may not imply a term which essentially creates a bargain the parties themselves have refused to make: *Aotearoa International Ltd v Scancarriers A/S* [1985] 1 NZLR 513. The Courts can clarify and give effect to the substantive obligations imposed by the bargain the parties have made; the Courts cannot imply new substantive obligations to rewrite such a bargain.

A further possibility is to read the agreement as creating a right of pre-emption. This latter class is illustrated by cases such as *Smith v Morgan* [1971] 2 All ER 1500. The owner of land gave an option over a piece of land but without specifying the price. The Court held that this created a right in the grantee of the option to have first opportunity to purchase the land, if and when the owner wished to sell, and the price the vendor could ask was to be no more than the vendor would ask of any other purchaser. This way of getting around the problems of future agreements can be used in other contexts, for example, in *Adaras Developments v Marcona Corporation* [1975] 1 NZLR 324 a right of pre-emption over any development of mineral resources was upheld.

(c) MEANINGLESS TERMS

If the parties have used some ambiguous or meaningless term in their agreement the contract may be void for uncertainty. In *Scammell v Ouston* [1941] AC 251; 1 All ER 14, a vehicle was to be purchased "on hire-purchase terms" but there was no indication of which form of hire-purchase was intended. Since there were a number of possibilities with different legal consequences, there was insufficient certainty for there to be a contract. If the meaningless words are not in any way vital to the agreement, they can be ignored by the Court: *Nicolene Ltd v Simmonds* [1953] 1 QB 543. (In that case the words "We trust the usual conditions of acceptance apply" were excised as there were no such conditions.) This will not usually be the case.

3.2 CONSIDERATION

A simple contract is a bargain, and consideration is an essential element of it. A promise is not binding if it is purely gratuitous; it is only binding if the other party has supplied something in return for it. That which is supplied in return is called the consideration for the promise. Thus, in a contract to sell a motor car for $5,000 the consideration for the promise to transfer the car is the promise to pay $5,000; likewise the consideration for the promise to pay $5,000 is the promise to transfer the car. Consideration is variously defined. In *Currie v Misa* (1875) LR 10 Ex 153, at 162, Lush J said:

> A valuable consideration . . . may consist either in some right, interest, profit or benefit accruing to one party, or some forbearance, detriment, loss or responsibility given, suffered or undertaken by the other.

This "benefit – detriment" definition is one of the best known, and is helpful provided it is recalled that the terms "benefit" and "detriment" are sometimes used in a somewhat artificial sense. *Pollock on Contracts* (13th ed, 1950) 133 defined consideration as follows:

> An act or forbearance of the one party, or the promise thereof, is the price for which the promise of the other is bought, and the promise thus given for value is enforceable.

This definition is perhaps the best, emphasising as it does, by its reference to price, the necessary element of *return* which binds the consideration and the promise together.

3.2.1 Executory, executed and past consideration

The distinction between executory and executed consideration is best drawn by illustration. Where A promises B that A will pay B $3,000 if B will promise to paint A's house, the consideration is executory ie one promise is given in return for another, and both parties have obligations in future under the contract. If, however, C promises D to pay D $100 if D will supply C with information, the consideration is executed: it is the *act* of supplying the information. Thus, the consideration in a bilateral contract is executory; in a unilateral contract it is executed. However past consideration is no consideration at all. If E has done an act and F later promises to pay E $50, E has not furnished consideration. The element of bargain is missing: the act was not done in return for the promise because the act was completed when the promise was made.

Thus in *Re McArdle* [1951] Ch 669; [1951] 1 All ER 905, a woman made various improvements to a house forming part of the estate of McArdle. The following year the beneficiaries signed a document stating: "in consideration of your carrying out certain alterations and improvements ... we the beneficiaries ... hereby agree that the executors shall repay to you . . . the sum of £ 488 in settlement of the amount spent on such improvements." It was held that there was no contract, the promise to pay having been given for past consideration.

However if the act done in the past was done *at the request* of the party who later promises to pay, the result may be different. In that case, it may be possible at the outset to *imply* a promise by the party requesting the act to pay for it. If that is so, the later promise may be treated as fixing the amount of the payment.

In *Re Casey's Patents, Stewart v Casey* [1892]1 Ch 104, A and B, who owned certain patent rights, wrote to C that: "in consideration of your services as the practical manager in working our patents, we hereby agree to give you one-third share in the patents." C had already performed these services when the promise was made, and it was thus argued that the consideration for the promise, being past, was ineffective. It was held however that when the services were initially performed there was an implication that they would be paid for, and the subsequent promise could thus be treated, in Bowen LJ's words:

> either as an admission which evidences or as a positive bargain which fixes the amount of the reasonable remuneration on the faith of which the service was originally rendered.

That case was applied in *Casey v Commissioner of Inland Revenue* [1959] NZLR 1052. Loans were made by a wife to her husband. Many years later the loans were repaid with interest. The Revenue alleged that the amount in excess of the loans was a gift, but the Court held it was indeed interest, the payment of which was in the contemplation of the parties when the loans were made.

There are certain statutory exceptions to the rule that past consideration is no consideration. For example the Bills of Exchange Act 1908, s 27, provides that any antecedent debt or liability is sufficient consideration to support a bill of exchange; and under the Law Reform (Testamentary Promises) Act 1949, s 3(2)(a) the promise to make testamentary provision is binding although the services may have been rendered prior to the making of the promise.

3.2.2 Consideration must be given by the promisee

At common law if A and B made a contract under which A promised, for consideration supplied by B, to confer a benefit on C, C could not enforce the promise because C was not a party and had supplied no consideration. However in respect of contracts made after 1 April 1983, the Contracts (Privity) Act 1982 provides that in such circumstances C can enforce the promise despite the fact that C has supplied no consideration. (See ch 5). However unless the contract between A and B is by deed, A must receive consideration from B, the other party, before A's promise is thus enforceable by C.

3.2.3 Adequacy of consideration

The Courts generally do not inquire into adequacy of consideration. That is to say, they are not concerned to see that the consideration for a party's promise is equal in value to the value of the promise. The parties themselves are the sole judge of value. Thus, if I agree to sell my late model Jaguar motor car for $500 this will be an enforceable bargain. Thus, for example, in *Re Murphy* [1933] NZLR s 83 an agreement to transfer land to a Council was held enforceable even though the only consideration was that the transferor be permitted to use cottages on the land for ten years rent free, that the Council pay the costs of transfer, and that the land be called "Murphy Park". And in *Chappell and Co Ltd v Nestle Co Ltd* [1960] AC 87, Nestles, as an advertising scheme, promised to give a record to anyone who sent in one and sixpence and three wrappers from Nestles chocolate bars. It was held that, quite apart from the money, the three wrappers were valuable consideration, even though they themselves were of no money value and were thrown away by Nestles on receipt.

Parties sometimes take advantage of this rule to render binding a promise which would otherwise be gratuitous: for instance an option to purchase land may be rendered enforceable by a consideration of 10 cents and an agreement to lease land by a promise to pay a peppercorn rental.

Adequacy of consideration is sometimes relevant, however. If it can be shown that a person has improperly taken advantage of some special weakness in another (for example, senility) and has thus obtained a bargain which is grossly unfair to the weaker party, the contract may be set aside as being unconscionable. Inadequacy of the consideration supplied to the weaker party is one thing that will be taken into account in such a situation: see 5.2.3.

3.2.4 Forbearance as consideration

Consideration may consist in forbearing, or promising to forbear, from doing something you were otherwise at liberty to do. Thus in the famous American case of *Hamer v Sidway* (1891)124 NY 538 an uncle was held bound by a promise to pay his nephew $5,000 if he did not smoke, drink, swear or gamble until he was 21.

Forbearance as consideration is seen most often in the cases on forbearance to sue and compromise of suit. Forbearance to sue arises where A owes B a debt, and in consideration of B's refraining from suing A for a time, promises to grant B a benefit such as a security over his or her property. The period of forbearance need not be for any particular time, provided there is some degree of forbearance; and there need not be an express promise to forbear provided it can be inferred that the forbearance which in fact results was the direct consequence of an arrangement between the parties: *Alliance Bank* v *Broom* (1864) 2 Dr & Sm 289. A compromise of suit arises when two parties settle a disputed claim by one against the other for an agreed payment. This is very common. Actions for negligence, or defamation, for example, are often "settled out of Court" in this way. In this case the consideration, much as in the case of forbearance to sue, is the abandonment by one party of a right to sue the other on the original claim.

Although slightly different, the two categories of case raise very similar problems. In particular, what happens if the original claim was of doubtful validity in law, and might have failed had it been brought to trial? Can it be said that by abandoning it, or forbearing to sue on it, the party is giving up anything of any value at all? The law takes the pragmatic view that provided the party honestly believes he or she had a chance of success if the claim ever came to trial, the forbearance or compromise is good consideration: the party is giving up what he or she considers a *chance* of success. Thus in *Couch* v *Branch Investments Ltd* [1980] 2 NZLR 314, Mr and Mrs C promised, in consideration of B Ltd forbearing for one month to take action against them on a hire purchase agreement, to give a mortgage over their two houses. This promise was held binding even though the validity of the hire purchase agreement was suspect. As Cooke J said in *Moyes and Groves Ltd v Radiation (NZ) Ltd* [1982]1 NZLR 368, 371, "The Courts are very slow to reject a compromise of a bona fide claim as consideration on the mere ground that on subsequent analysis it may be seen to have had small prospects of success."

3.2.5 Performance of an existing duty

There is no consideration if the promisor under the agreement secures nothing more than that to which he or she is already entitled. However this proposition is not quite as uncomplicated as it at first appears.

3.2.6 Performance of a public or statutory duty

If all that the plaintiff has done is to promise to do what he or she is already legally bound to do, he or she cannot enforce performance of the defendant's promise; there is no consideration for that promise. In *Collins v Godefroy* (1831)1 B & Ad 950, C sought to recover a payment promised by G for giving evidence in a Court case. As C, who had been subpoenaed to appear as a witness, was obliged by law to give evidence he could not recover the payment from G.

However if the plaintiff supplies or promises to supply *more* than the law obliges him or her to do, he or she does give good consideration: the plaintiff is then doing something he or she need not otherwise have done.

Thus in *Glasbrook Bros v Glamorgan County Council* [1925] AC 270 a colliery owner wanted a permanent garrison of police stationed on its premises during a strike, but the police superintendent thought a mobile force was enough. He finally acceded to the owner's wishes in return for a promise to pay £ 2,200. It was held that although the police were bound by law to provide protection the superintendent had a discretion as to the type of protection, and providing more than he deemed necessary constituted good consideration for the promise to pay. Again, in *Black White and Grey Cabs Ltd v Reid* [1980]1 NZLR 40 the provision by a taxi company to its drivers of a more extensive radio telephone communication service than the Transport Act required it to provide was held to be good consideration for a return promise by the drivers.

Statements have occasionally been made (eg by Denning LJ in *Ward v Byham* [1956] 1 WLR 496) that even if the promisee is doing no more than he or she was obliged to do he or she ought (at least in some cases) to be deemed to be supplying consideration, simply because the other party is getting what he or she wanted. However this view cannot be said to represent the law at the moment.

3.2.7 Performance of an existing contract with a third person

If C promises A some benefit if A performs (or promises to perform) a contract which A has made with B, it may appear at first sight that there is no consideration for C's promise, simply because A is already bound by contract with B to do the same thing. A would thus not appear to be providing anything additional to C. However it now appears to be established law that there is consideration in such a case.

In *Shadwell v Shadwell* (1860) 9 CB (NS) 159 it was held that a promise by C to pay his nephew an annuity if he married B, to whom the nephew was already engaged, could be enforced. The majority of the Court was able to find a detriment to the nephew in acting on the promise and incurring liabilities, and a benefit to C, who was interested in the marriage. There was a similar holding in a commercial case, *Scotson v Pegg* (1861) 6 H & N 295. These cases were followed in *New Zealand Shipping Co Ltd v AM Satterthwaite Ltd* [1974] 1 NZLR 505 where the Privy Council held that by unloading a vessel under contract with B, A (a stevedoring company) was supplying consideration for another promise by C, even though A was doing no more than its contract with B obliged it to do.

These cases are perhaps not easy to reconcile with principle, unless it be on the basis that in response to C's promise A forgoes a privilege he or she would otherwise have had to join with B in cancelling their contract.

3.2.8 Performance of an existing contract with the promisor

If B promises A an additional benefit if A performs, or promises to perform, an existing contractual obligation which A owes to B, it is well established that A supplies no consideration for B's new promise. A is doing no more than he or she was already bound to do. A variation of one party's contractual obligation requires a corresponding variation on the other side. Thus in *Stilk v Myrick* (1809) 2 Camp 317, two seamen deserted during a voyage and the captain promised the remainder of the crew that if they would perform the extra duties the wages of the two deserters would be divided amongst them. It was held that the promise was not binding, because they had in their original agreement undertaken to do all they could under the emergencies of the voyage. Likewise in *Cook Islands Shipping Co Ltd* v *Colson Builders Ltd* [1975] 1 NZLR 422 a shipping company contracted to carry goods at a set freight. On encountering difficulties, it indicated it would only be prepared to proceed if the other party paid an additional sum over and above the freight. The other party agreed. It was held that this promise was not binding because the shipping company was doing no more than it was already obliged to do under the original contract.

Of course if, in return for B's promise, A promises something over and above his or her existing obligation there is good consideration. In accordance with principle this extra performance need not be large. In *Moyes and Groves Ltd v Radiation (NZ) Ltd* [1982] 1 NZLR 368 a buyer ordered goods from a seller for the price of $400. The goods had to be imported from India, and contrary to expectations they did not arrive for nearly three years. Not only had the parties actually forgotten about the contract in the interim: the cost of the goods was now $2,700. The buyer eventually agreed to pay $2,700. It was held that this promise to increase the price was enforceable: the seller had an arguable claim that because of the long delay the original contract had been abandoned, and his giving up this claim was consideration for the buyer's new promise.

In recent years there have been indications that the Courts are prepared to take a relaxed attitude to the requirement of additional consideration in this situation. The most significant case is *Williams v Roffey Bros & Nicholls (Contractors) Ltd* [1991] 1 QB 1. A contractor, employed to refurbish a block of flats, subcontracted the carpentry work to the plaintiff at a price of £20,000. When it became clear in the course of doing the work that the plaintiff would not be able to finish at this price, the parties mutually agreed to raise it by another £10,500, payable in instalments on the completion of each flat. It was held by the Court of Appeal that the new arrangement was enforceable, and that the Judge's finding that there was consideration for raising the price should not be disturbed. The new arrangement benefited both sides: in particular, the head contractor, having ensured that the plaintiff could now complete the subcontract, would avoid having to pay penalties for late completion, and would not have to expend time and trouble searching for a replacement subcontractor. These practical benefits were sufficient to constitute consideration for the rise in payment. As Glidewell LJ put it, the head contractor had obtained, in practice, a benefit, or obviated a "disbenefit". It is difficult to avoid the conclusion that the Court here was anxious to uphold an arrangement because it was commercially sensible and reasonable. However, he did point out that if the plaintiff had extracted the promise of extra payment by economic duress, the promise would have been unenforceable. If the Courts are to take an increasingly flexible approach to consideration in this situation some such qualification is essential.

3.2.9 Payment of part of a debt

A promise by a creditor to accept less than the amount of a debt from a debtor is not binding, because it is not supported by consideration. The debtor, who is actually paying *less* than he or she is obliged to do, supplies no consideration in return for the creditor's promise to relieve him or her from a portion of the debt. This rule, originally laid down in *Pinnel's case* (1602) 5 Co Rep 117a, was affirmed by the House of Lords in *Foakes v Beer* (1884) 9 App Cas 605. The rule still stands, but it has not been popular, and a large number of qualifications and exceptions have grown up. Thus:

(a) If a part payment, expressed to be in full satisfaction, is made by a third person and not the debtor him- or herself, it discharges the whole debt: *Hirachand Punamchand v Temple* [1911] 2 KB 330. This is based on the notion that it would be a fraud on the third person for the creditor to sue the debtor for the balance.

(b) A composition with a number of creditors whereby each creditor agrees to accept part of his debt in full satisfaction binds all creditors: *Cook v Lister* [1863]13 CB (NS) 543. Again, fraud lies at the basis of this exception.

(c) An important statutory exception exists in New Zealand. Section 92 of the Judicature Act 1908 provides that an acknowledgment *in writing* by a creditor or any person authorised by the creditor in writing of the receipt of part of the debt in satisfaction of the whole debt operates as a discharge of the whole debt. The acknowledgment must be *in writing,* and part payment must have been *received.*

(d) If the debtor pays part of the debt in a different way (eg in kind), or at an earlier time, from that in which he or she was obliged by the contract to pay, he or she will be discharged, for the new element amounts to consideration for the discharge. It was at one time believed that a part payment by negotiable instrument discharged the whole debt because this was payment in a different manner, but this view is now largely discredited. As Lord Denning said in *D and C Builders Ltd v Rees* [1966] 2 QB 617, 623:

> No sensible distinction can be taken between payment of a lesser sum by cash and payment of it by cheque. The cheque, when given, is conditional payment. When honoured, it is actual payment. It is then just the same as cash. If a creditor is not bound when he received payment by cash, he should not be bound when he receives payment by cheque.

(e) It has been held in New Zealand that the rule in *Foakes v Beer* only applies to liquidated debts. If the amount of the debt is unliquidated, or in dispute, an acceptance of a payment "in full settlement" serves as an accord and satisfaction, or compromise, which extinguishes the debt. This was held in *Homeguard Products (NZ) Ltd v Kiwi Packaging Ltd* [1981] 2 NZLR 322. The other holding in the *Homeguard* case – that the act of banking a cheque tendered in full settlement amounts to acceptance of that condition – has been modified in subsequent cases. This topic is more fully dealt with at 8.2.1, below.

3.2.10 The *High Trees* principle: promissory estoppel

In *Central London Property Trust Ltd v High Trees House Ltd* [1947] KB 130
Denning J established a principle which is capable of relieving people
from their obligations, despite a lack of consideration for the release. In
that case, the plaintiff had leased to the defendant a block of flats at a
rental of £ 2,500 per annum. When it became difficult for the lessee to let
the flats profitably during the war, the lessor wrote to the lessee agreeing
to accept a reduced rent of £ 1,250 per annum. The reduced rent was paid,
and accepted, until the beginning of 1945, at which time the flats were all
let again. An action was brought to recover £ 625, being the difference
between the rental stated in the lease and the reduced rental for the
quarters ending in September and December 1945. Denning J held that
the full rental was payable for the period covered by the action, but said
that despite the lack of consideration for the landlord's concession the
full rental would not have been recoverable during the war when the flats
were not full. He expressed the doctrine on which he relied as follows:

> . . . a promise intended to be binding, intended to be acted on and in fact acted
> on, is binding as far as its terms properly apply.

Denning J derived this principle from earlier cases in equity. Among
them was *Hughes v Metropolitan Railway Co* (1877) 2 App Cas 439 in which
Lord Cairns had said:

> . . . if parties . . . enter upon a course of negotiation which has the effect of
> leading one of the parties to suppose that the strict rights arising under the
> contract will not be enforced, . . . the person who otherwise might have
> enforced those rights will not be allowed to enforce them where it would be
> inequitable having regard to the dealings which have thus taken place
> between the parties.

In other words, the *High Trees* doctrine can operate to release a person
from performing his or her obligations, even though there is no consideration for that release. The doctrine is often called "promissory estoppel".

However, the Courts were initially very cautious about the *High Trees*
doctrine, perhaps because of the fear that it might subvert the doctrine of
consideration, the very basis of the law of contract. There are signs that
the Courts are today prepared to be bolder in this regard. It may be
helpful to outline, first, the conditions originally imposed by the Courts
on the doctrine; and to proceed (in 3.2.11) to indicate the more recent
developments.

The conditions originally imposed were as follows:

(a) The doctrine was said only to apply where the parties are in a
contractual relationship and one releases the other from part of his or her
contractual obligation. It was said not to apply to undertakings given
before the contract is entered into: *McCathie v McCathie* [1971] NZLR 58.

(b) The doctrine was said not to found a cause of action in itself. In
other words a party cannot sue to enforce an undertaking of the kind
made in the *High Trees* case; it operates only as a defence or, at most, as
a support for an independent cause of action. The doctrine is "a shield not
a sword": *Combe v Combe* [1951] 2 KB 215.

(c) The promise not to insist on strict performance of the contractual obligations must be clear and unequivocal: *The Scaptrade* [1983] 1 All ER 301, affd [1983] 2 All ER 763.

(d) Since the *High Trees* doctrine had its origins in equity, a party can only plead it if he or she has acted equitably. Thus in *Re Goile, ex parte Steelbuild Agencies Ltd* [1963] NZLR 666 a debtor was told that if he paid part of his debt by an immediate downpayment and monthly instalments, he would be excused the balance of it. It was held that even if the *High Trees* doctrine could ever be applicable in such a situation it could not be pleaded here because the debtor had failed to pay any of the instalments under the new arrangement and thus could not be heard to take advantage of an equitable doctrine.

(e) The opinion was expressed that the *High Trees* doctrine can only apply where a creditor releases an obligation in advance of its falling due, and not where he or she attempts to release a debt which has already fallen due and where the debtor is thus in breach. In other words it can apply in a case like *High Trees* itself where the landlord released the tenant from its obligation to pay *future* instalments of rent in full, but not in a case like *Foakes v Beer* where the debt has already fallen due and owing: *Homeguard Products Ltd v Kiwi Packaging Ltd* [1981] 2 NZLR 322, 331, per Mahon J.

(f) The view was taken in New Zealand that the *High Trees* doctrine cannot be successfully pleaded unless the person to whom the promise of release was made has altered his or her position in reliance on it. It is sometimes said that he or she must have relied on it to his or her detriment, although the difference between these two ways of putting the matter is slight (see *Connor v Pukerau Store Ltd* [1981] 1 NZLR 384 at 388 per Cooke J). The essential point is that if the promisee has done nothing to change his or her position, it will normally not be *inequitable* for the promisor to resile from his or her promise. Thus in *Commissioner of Inland Revenue v Morris* [1958] NZLR 1126 a mother transferred to her son a debenture worth £10,000. He was to pay £125 every six months. As each payment fell due she "waived" it. It was held, on the mother's death, that these sums had not been effectively released, and that the whole debt was still owing. The plea on the basis of the *High Trees* doctrine failed because, in the words of Gresson P and Cleary J at 1131:

> The essence of the doctrine is that a person is not permitted to enforce strict legal rights when it would be unjust that he should be allowed to do so, having regard to the dealings which have taken place between the parties. But those dealings must amount to one party having been led by the attitude of the other to alter his own position . . . (I)n this case there is no evidence that the debtor did anything, or in any way altered his position, in reliance upon the waiver.

However in P v P [1957] NZLR 857 the Public Trustee as the administrator of Mrs P (an inmate of a mental hospital) wrote to P advising him that on payment of arrears of maintenance he would be under no further liability under a separation agreement. Later, the Public Trustee sued for further payments. The *High Trees* doctrine was pleaded in defence, and succeeded. McGregor J said, 859-60:

> In the belief induced by this letter that such payment would be a final settlement under the deed, the appellant . . . refrained from any proceedings

under the Divorce and Matrimonial Causes Act 1928 to set aside or vary the postnuptial settlement effected by the provisions of the deed. It seems to me it would be inequitable now to allow the respondent to enforce the rights which the appellant had been led to believe would not be enforced.

(g) It has also been said that the *High Trees* doctrine is mainly suspensory in operation. What this means is that a promise to release someone from an obligation may be withdrawn, and the original obligation reinstated, provided this can be done without causing inequity (or, as some would say, detriment) to the promisee. This feature of the doctrine (about which there has also been some disagreement) was thus expressed by the Privy Council in *Ajayi v R T Briscoe* [1964] 1 WLR 1326:

> The principle . . . is that when one party to a contract in the absence of fresh consideration agrees not to enforce his rights an equity will be raised in favour of the other party. This equity is, however, subject to the qualifications (1) that the other party has altered his position, (2) that the promisor can resile from his promise on giving reasonable notice, which need not be a formal notice, giving the promisee reasonable opportunity of resuming his position, (3) the promise only becomes final and irrevocable if the promisee cannot resume his position.

In *P v P* for instance, it seems that the Judge must have held it inequitable for the Public Trustee to revert back to the original contractual rights. However in *Tool Metal Manufacturing Co Ltd v Tungsten Electric Co Ltd* [1955] 1 WLR 761 a different result was reached. An agreement made between the appellants and respondents provided for the use by the respondents of inventions belonging to the appellants and for "compensation" for that use. Compensation payments were made until the outbreak of war in 1939. In 1942 the appellants agreed to suspend enforcement of payments until a new contract was made; negotiations for that new contract were unsuccessful. In 1945 the respondents sued for breach of contract and the appellants counterclaimed for compensation. The House of Lords awarded compensation to the appellants from 1947, on the basis that reasonable notice had been given by the appellants of the resumption of their contractual rights. There was no suggestion that the appellants would at any stage have been entitled to claim retrospectively for payments back to 1942.

Despite these cautious limitations, it cannot be said that everyone was agreed on the exact scope of the *High Trees* or "promissory estoppel" doctrine. As late as 1972, it was said in the House of Lords that the *High Trees* line of cases "may need to be reviewed and reduced to a coherent body of doctrine by the Courts." (*Woodhouse AC Israel Cocoa Ltd v Nigerian Produce Marketing Co Ltd* [1972] AC 741, 757 per Lord Hailsham LC).

However, in very recent times there are strong indications that the doctrine is capable of considerable expansion, and that the Courts may be prepared to throw off at least some of the conditions we have just outlined. To these developments we now turn.

3.2.11 The future of promissory estoppel

For many years, in addition to "promissory estoppel", there has been another doctrine of equity known as "proprietary estoppel". Its origins are of considerable antiquity. In essence, the doctrine provides that if an owner of land leads another to believe that that other may have an interest in that land, and on the faith of that understanding the other expends money on the land, the owner of the land may be prevented from denying that that interest exists. To take a simple example, if A leads B to believe B may have a right-of-way over A's land, and in reliance on that B expends money constructing a garage or laying a concrete drive, a Court in its equitable jurisdiction may well require A to allow B to exercise the right of way; or at least to compensate B in some way for B's disappointed reliance. The doctrine is thus used as a cause of action.

What is very apparent is that there are close affinities between this proprietary estoppel and promissory estoppel: both depend on persons suffering detriment through reliance on another's word. This common principle has recently been pointed out by the Courts. For instance, Cooke P has said (in *Gillies v Keogh* [1989] 2 NZLR 327, 331):

> The tide is setting or has set, I think, against the view . . . that proprietary estoppel and promissory estoppel are entirely separate and take their origins from different sources . . . [A broader approach] identifies a general principle asserting the unfairness or unjustice of resiling from underlying assumptions that have been acted upon.

If this common principle is accepted, it means that some of the limitations initially placed on promissory estoppel have been too restrictive.

In Australia there has been a recent dramatic liberalisation. The most important case is *Waltons Stores (Interstate) Ltd v Maher* (1988) 164 CLR 387. In that case, it was agreed that M, the owner of land, would demolish an old building on it, erect a new building designed especially for Waltons, and lease it to Waltons. Although the contract documents were never signed, Waltons intimated that they were content with the draft, and that Maher could assume all was well if he did not hear to the contrary by the following day. Nothing having been heard, Maher commenced the demolition and rebuilding. After a substantial time (Waltons being aware of these operations) Waltons told him they were no longer interested. It was held by the High Court of Australia that, although no contract had ever been properly entered into, Waltons had led Maher to believe that a contract was going to be signed. Since he had relied, to his obvious detriment, on that understanding, it would be unconscionable for Waltons to go back on it. Maher must have a remedy, and in the circumstances of the case it should be damages in lieu of specific performance. The basis of the decision is estoppel: Waltons were estopped from going back on the understanding they had induced in Maher. Some members of the Court referred to it as "promissory" estoppel, other as "equitable" estoppel.

It will be seen immediately that the first two limitations on promissory estoppel outlined in 3.2.10 above were abandoned in this case. This was not a promise made between persons in a contractual relationship. There was in fact no contract between the parties at all. Moreover, it looks very much as though "estoppel" was here being used as a cause of action: the detriment incurred through reliance on Waltons' word was the essence of the plaintiff's claim.

How far this expansion of estoppel will be taken remains to be seen. But in New Zealand there have been indications that our Courts may be prepared to adopt a similarly liberal approach to the once rigid qualifications on promissory estoppel.

(a) Promissory estoppel has recently been applied in a case where there was no contractual relationship between the parties: *Burbery Mortgage Finance & Savings Ltd v Hindsbank Holdings Ltd* [1989] 1 NZLR 356. (This was a case where one secured creditor of a debtor was held bound by an understanding it had induced in another creditor, that the goods the subject of the security would not be sold.) *McCathie v McCathie* (supra at 3.2.10) was not mentioned. Likewise, in *Harris v Harris* (1989) 1 NZ ConvC 190, 406 the plaintiff was held to an understanding communicated *before* a contract was entered into that an obligation to pay money under it would not be enforced.

(b) In the *Burbery* case McMullin J said that Burbery "might be said to have been using the doctrine of estoppel as a sword and not a shield. However, it is unnecessary to discuss the implications of that issue".

In this country estoppel has recently been used as the basis of a number of decisions, and while some of these could readily have been based on traditional doctrine, the judgments are marked by general references to the unconscionability of resiling from understandings which have induced people to act to their detriment. Thus:

• Parents were held unable to claim a debt due under a contract with their son and daughter-in-law because they had intimated before the contract that it need not be paid: *Harris v Harris* (1989) 1 NZ ConvC 190, 406.

• A landlord had to allow tenants a renewal of a lease when they had, with the landlord's acquiescence, renovated the premises on the understanding they would get it: *Andrews v Colonial Mutual Life Assurance Society Ltd* [1982] 2 NZLR 556.

• Racehorse owners were held able to run their horses in a certain race because their entry fee had been accepted some time before: *Mortensen v New Zealand Harness Racing Conference* (High Court, Auckland, CP 1812A/90, 11 December 1990).

• A mortgagor was held unable to treat interest rises as invalid because he had for some time paid the increased amounts without objection: *Westland Savings Bank v Hancock* [1987] 2 NZLR 21.

• It has been said that the rights of a de facto spouse in property owned by the other spouse may be resolved by this doctrine: *Gillies v Keogh* [1989] 2 NZLR 327.

However, it should not be assumed that all members of the judiciary are equally committed to this new liberalism. Nor is it clear how far these developments will go. It is likely that the Courts will soon attempt more clearly to chart the boundaries of the doctrine. It has already been emphasised that estoppel still requires a clear and unequivocal statement or promise: *Travel Agents Association of New Zealand Inc v NCR (NZ) Ltd* (High Court, Wellington, CP 1069/90, 27 March 1991) per Eichelbaum J.

It has also been said by Cooke P that today it is perhaps "fashionable or easy" for lawyers to become "preoccupied" with promissory estoppel: *Minister of Education v De Luxe Motor Services* [1990] 1 NZLR 27, 33.

3.3 FORM

Although most contracts can be made wholly or partly orally, there are some cases where a written document is required for validity or enforceability. Although it may, in some cases, be difficult to distinguish between invalidity and unenforceability, it is a useful analytical device. The distinction is sufficiently discussed infra.

3.3.1 Contracts where writing is required for validity

These transactions are ones where writing, and in some cases a particular form of writing, is required before there is, in law, a contract.

They include transactions in the nature of a contract (such as recognisances and judgments) and deeds. A deed is a document in which a person undertakes to do some act. It is enforceable even in the absence of consideration of the act to be undertaken. The formal requirements for a deed are set out in the Property Law Act 1952, ss 4 and 5.

More truly contractual arrangements in this class include bills of exchange and promissory notes (Bills of Exchange Act 1908, ss 3 and 84), assignments or mortgages of life insurance policies (Life Insurance Act 1908, ss 43 and 44), transfers of company shares or debentures (Companies Act 1955, s 84), assignments of copyright (Copyright Act 1962, s 56) and matrimonial property agreements (Matrimonial Property Act 1976, s 21). The first two of these are treated in more detail elsewhere in this book. In all these cases the transaction is invalid, and cannot be relied on by either party in the absence of writing in the due form. The statutory requirements however do not extend to invalidation of transactions of a different legal character regarding such subject matters. Thus the sale of a copyright may be made orally and the purchaser may rely on the contractually-acquired proprietorial rights, even though he or she cannot rely on an oral assignment of the rights.

3.3.2 Contracts where writing is required for enforceability

Here a contract which is not in writing (or in some cases evidenced in writing) is unenforceable by one or both parties. The fact that it is unenforceable by one party does not make the contract void, and it may be used as a defence in some cases or may be a cause of action for the party against whom it is unenforceable.

There are a number of statutory provisions which as a form of consumer protection make certain kinds of oral contract unenforceable against the consumer. These include hire purchase agreements (Hire Purchase Act 1971, s 5) credit contracts (Credit Contracts Act 1981, s 48) (as to both of which see chs 37 and 24) and real estate agency commission contracts (Real Estate Agents Act 1976, s 62) although oral collateral contracts between parties to a contract required to be in writing may still be valid and enforceable: *Industrial Steel and Plant Ltd v Smith* [1980] 1 NZLR 545.

A similar policy underlies acknowledgements of part-payments in full satisfaction of a debt (Judicature Act 1908, s 92) and of statute-barred debts (Limitation Act 1950, s 26). In both of these cases an oral promise is unenforceable.

A slightly different situation arises with the Contracts Enforcement Act 1956. Here the statute requires evidence in writing, by way of a contract or memorandum or note of such a contract, before the contract is enforceable (s 2). The Act applies to contracts of guarantee (as to which see ch 27) and contracts for the sale or disposition, mortgage or charging of land. It does not apply to sales of land by order of the High Court or through the Registrar of that Court, to certain dispositions of Maori land or to actions under the Law Reform (Testamentary Promises) Act 1949 (as to which see *Public Trustee v Bick* [1973] 1 NZLR 301). The Act does not affect the law relating to part-performance, which, as one major way of avoiding the Act, is discussed infra.

It should be noted that although contracts coming under the Contracts Enforcement Act may not be enforceable against one party, that party must specifically plead the Act if he or she wishes to rely on the statutory unenforceability: *Boviard v Brown* [1975] 2 NZLR 694; High Court Rules, R 133. The oral agreement may also be used as a defence in a related action — eg for the return of a deposit.

The requirement that the contract be evidenced in writing can be satisfied by a document executed after the oral contract was made, or by the joinder of documents which together constitute a sufficient written record. Parol evidence may be used to link documents together: *Pearce v Gardner* [1897] 1 QB 688, but it must be clear that the full terms of the contract appear on the linked documents. For example a written offer may be linked to a receipt for a deposit paid to the vendor as in *Saunderson v Purchase* [1958] NZLR 588; but a written offer coupled with a receipt naming another party as the payer is not sufficient, even though parol evidence could prove the actual payer to be acting as the purchaser's agent: *Timmins v Moreland Street Property Ltd* [1958] Ch 110; 1957] 3 All ER 265.

The document or documents must contain the names or identification of the parties, the subject matter of the contract and the consideration for it (except in contracts of guarantee) and all material terms other than those which would be implied by law. If there is a term omitted which is solely for the plaintiff's benefit, he or she may waive it (*North v Loomes* [1919] 1 Ch 378) and a plaintiff may concede a term solely for the defendant's benefit which has been omitted and enforce the contract as evidenced in writing with that omitted term added to it: *Scott v Bradley* [1971] Ch 850; 1 All ER 583. Most importantly, the documents must indicate the existence of a binding agreement. A "subject to contract" agreement, even though evidenced in writing is not sufficient; *Tiverton Estates Ltd v Wearwell Ltd* [1974] Ch 112; [1973] 2 All ER 437.

The documents relied on must also contain the signature of the person against whom the contract is to be enforced. The signature may, in appropriate cases, be that of a person authorised by the party to be charged to sign the document, or even of a person to whom the signing was sub-delegated, as long as the sub-delegate's signature can be seen as a purely ministerial or administrative step: *Parkin v Williams* [1986] 1 NZLR 294. The Courts have also held sufficient what is known as the "fiction of the authenticated signature" – a written or printed name of the party inserted by the party or an authorised agent in such a way as to be intended to authenticate the party's involvement. The criteria for the use of this fiction are discussed in a number of cases where somewhat different expositions of the tests to be applied have been given: see *Short v Graeme Marsh Ltd* [1974] 1 NZLR 723; *Sturt v McInnes* [1974] 1 NZLR 729 and *Van der Veeken v Watson's Farm (Pukepoto) Ltd* [1974] 2 NZLR 146.

3.3.3 Part performance

In certain circumstances evidence of acts done in reliance and toward performance of the contract may allow an oral contract not evidenced in writing to be enforced. The doctrine of part-performance originated in equity to mitigate the harshness of rules which required evidence in writing. If one party to an unenforceable contract stands back and allows the other party to incur expense or otherwise incur some detriment, the Courts will not allow the inactive party to profit by inaction or use the statute as a cloak for fraud. Since the decision of the House of Lords in *Steadman v Steadman* [1976] AC 536; [1974] 2 All ER 977, the law has been somewhat unsettled. It is, however, suggested that the proof of acts done which can only be explicable by there being a contract between the parties is sufficient to invoke the doctrine of part-performance, and thus to avoid the requirements of the Contracts Enforcement Act. In exceptional circumstances, the payment of money may be a sufficient act of part-performance *(Steadman's* case, supra), but usually something more is needed. In *Boviard v Brown* [1975] 2 NZLR 694, the securing of mortgage finance and insurance cover for the property allegedly to be purchased and the instruction of a solicitor to prepare a contractual document were held to be sufficient to invoke the part-performance doctrine. These acts were not explicable without there being a contract for sale and purchase of the property, and the former two were acts toward performance. It must be stressed that acts done in reliance on an unenforceable contract which are not directed at some aspect of performance are insufficient to invoke the doctrine: *Boutique Balmoral Ltd v Retail Holdings Ltd* [1976] 2 NZLR 222.

3.3.4 Contracts by non-natural person

There are legal entities, such as companies and incorporated societies, which have legal personality but whose acts must be performed through its servants. There is therefore a need for special rules relating to execution of contracts by such bodies. Most of these artificial persons are bound by rules akin to those found for companies in s 42 of the Companies Act 1955. Where the contract, if made by natural persons, would have to be in a deed, the company must contract in writing under the seal of the company. If the contract is one which, if made between natural persons, would require to be in writing, and signed by the parties, it is sufficient if it is made in writing signed by a person acting under the authority of the company. If the contract could be made orally by natural persons, it can be made orally by any agent or servant of the company acting under its authority.

3.4 INTENTION TO CREATE LEGAL RELATIONS

As we have seen there must be an agreement and consideration before there can be a contract. However, these alone do not make a contract. The

Courts insist that the parties must be taken to have intended to give their agreement binding legal effect. As Atkin LJ put it in *Rose and Frank Co v J R Crompton and Bros Ltd* [1923] 2 KB 261, 293; [1924] All ER Rep 245, 252:

> To create a contract there must be a common intention of the parties to enter into legal obligations, mutually communicated expressly or impliedly. Such an intention ordinarily will be inferred when the parties enter into an agreement which in other respects conforms to the rules as to the formation of contracts. It may be negatived impliedly by the nature of the agreed promise or promises as in the case of offer and acceptance of hospitality or of some agreements made in the course of family life between members of a family. . . .

Thus in agreements on purely social matters or between close relatives there is a presumption that no new legal relationship has to be created. In business agreements the reverse is true, and the person seeking to show that no legal effect was intended requires clear proof *(Edwards v Skyways Ltd* [1964] 1 WLR 349; 1 All ER 494). Examination of the cases indicates the scope of these classes and the ways in which the presumption may be rebutted.

3.4.1 "Domestic" arrangements

Both social and familial agreements are normally not enforceable because the parties are presumed not to have intended to allow legal redress to be taken for any breach. This is most clearly seen in agreements between husband and wife *(Balfour v Balfour* [1919] 2 KB 571, where an agreement as to an allowance during the subsistence of the marriage was not enforceable) and parents and children *(Jones v Padavatton* [1969] 1 WLR 328; 2 All ER 616 where an allowance during study was held not to be legally enforceable) .

The presumption against legal effect is rebutted by evidence that the parties clearly had legal effects in mind (as with joint entries into contests where division of expenses and any prizes is agreed: *Welch v Jess* [1976] 2 NZ Rec Law (NS) 185, *Simpkins v Pays* [1955] 1 WLR 975; 3 All ER 10); or where the subject matter of the contract is such that enforceable rights must have been contemplated *(Parker v Clark* [1960] 1 WLR 286; 1 All ER 93 – devising a house by will) or where existing legal relations are to be altered by the agreement (as with separation agreements or contracts altering the statutory division of matrimonial property (as to which see s 21 of the Matrimonial Property Act 1976)).

3.4.2 "Business" arrangements

The presumption in favour of legal relations is hard to rebut. A clear statement that the agreement is not binding in law but in honour only suffices *(Rose and Frank Co v J R Crompton and Bros Ltd* (supra)). The Courts look to the reality of the transaction rather than the words used, so that phrases such as "ex gratia", which normally deny a legal duty, may not be enough to prevent an obligation being enforceable *(Edwards v Skyways Ltd* supra). In most circumstances the words "subject to contract" will indicate a postponement of any legal effect of the document (see the discussion of conditional contracts, ch 4.3, infra and the cases therein cited).

There will be exceptional occasions where although an agreement can be spelled out of discussions between organisations who would normally come within the business relationships class, no contract is formed. Three particular cases require mention – agreements between a Government and a subject; agreements between unions and employers, and "letters of comfort" used in some financial transactions.

Where a Governmental agency makes an agreement with a subject, the purpose of the transaction must be examined. If the transaction is essentially a commercial one, the normal rule applies and there is a presumption that legal relations were intended: see *Rothmans of Pall Mall (NZ) Ltd v Attorney-General* [1991] 2 NZLR 323, 326. However, if the agreement relates to issues of policy and governmental discretion, there is a presumption that the agreement was not intended to give rise to enforceable contractual rights or obligations: *Meates v Attorney-General* [1979] 1 NZLR 415, apparently accepted on this point on appeal to the Court of Appeal [1983] NZLR 308; *Australian Woollen Mills Ltd v Commonwealth of Australia* [1956] 1 WLR 11; [1955] 3 All ER 711.

Agreements between an employer and unions representing the employees of the employer have generally been regarded as being presumed not to be intended to give rise to legal relations, unless the agreement forms part of a system of registered awards or agreements: see *Ford Motor Co v AUEFW* [1969] 2 All ER 481 and *Re Andrew M Paterson Ltd* [1981] 2 NZLR 289. However these cases may well require review by the Courts in due course. The reasoning in the *Paterson* case was in part founded on the then inability of individual employees to enforce any rights that such a union/employer agreement might create. That rule has now been abrogated by the Contracts (Privity) Act 1982: see 6.3.5.

The Employment Contracts Act 1991 creates a regime where employee/employer relations are to be based on particular contracts rather than the old system of awards and agreements, and unions can represent employees but not be a party to any contracts made by the employees. In such a regime, agreements between unions and employers may well be regarded as being primarily business documents, and therefore presumably intended to be binding.

"Letters of comfort" have become a not uncommon tactic in certain financing transactions, whereby the owners or directors of a company give an assurance, falling short of a guarantee, that they will attempt to ensure that the company will make payment of moneys borrowed or otherwise owing. This assurance is known as a "letter of comfort". The question is usually whether the maker of the assurance is contractually liable on it should the debtor become insolvent or otherwise default on its obligations. While particular words might in some cases be held to create such a liability, the Courts have generally held that such assurances are not binding – in part at least because there was no apparent intention to undertake a legally binding obligation: see *Kleinwort Benson Ltd v Malaysia Mining Corporation Berhad* [1989] 1 All ER 785; 1 WLR 379 and *Bank of New Zealand v Ginivan* [1991] 1 NZLR 178.

Chapter 4

THE TERMS OF THE CONTRACT

SUMMARY

4.1 EXPRESS TERMS
4.2 EXCLUSION CLAUSES
4.3 CONDITIONAL CONTRACTS
4.4 IMPLIED TERMS

4.1 EXPRESS TERMS

The most common express terms in a contract are promises: that is say, terms by which one party expressly promises that he or she will do certain acts for, or pay money to, the other. But not all contractual terms are promises in the strict sense. Some are in the nature of guarantees about present facts – for instance a guarantee that the subject-matter of the contract is in a certain state. Breach of such a term is remediable by damages, or cancellation of the contract, just as much as breach of a promise. A contract may also incorporate terms which contain no element of undertaking at all: for instance there may be *conditions* which make the obligations of one or both the parties conditional on a certain event occurring; and *exclusion clauses* which exclude or limit the liability of one of the parties for breach (4.2 infra).

The Contractual Remedies Act 1979 uses the word "stipulation" rather than the word "term", but it appears to mean the same thing. The Act recognises a category of "essential" stipulation, that is to say a stipulation the performance of which is so essential to a party that any breach of it permits cancellation of the contract by that party. Other stipulations are not in this "essential" category, but breach of them may still justify cancellation of the contract if it substantially affects the contract as far as the innocent party is concerned. (See infra 7.3.)

4.1.1 Contracts oral and written

Except where a statute provides that all the terms of a particular type of contract must be in writing, one can have a contract which is partly oral and partly in writing. An old rule of the common law, the "parol evidence rule", used to state that parol evidence cannot be adduced to add to a written contract, but that rule has weakened substantially over the years. Courts are now quite prepared to find that parties intended that a written document should be only part of their bargain, and that their total agreement should include oral terms as well. Thus in *AM Bisley and Co Ltd v Thompson* [1982] 2 NZLR 696 it was held that a written contract to supply a harvesting machine "ASAP" (as soon as possible) was supplemented by an oral term that the machine was to be installed before the next harvest season. When this was not done damages were awarded. And in *Mendelssohn v Normand Ltd* [1970] 1 QB 177 it was held that an oral promise by a car park attendant that a car would be kept locked was part of the contract, and that an exclusion clause in the written contract must be construed subject to it.

An oral term will not be held to be incorporated in the contract if it directly contradicts a written term. In *Wakelin v Jackson* (1984) 2 NZCPR 195 for instance Henry J stated that it was not permissible to adduce evidence of an oral representation that the turnover of a business, warranted in the written contract to be $6,000 per week, was in fact $7,000 per week. However even here there is now more latitude than would previously have been thought acceptable. In the *Bisley* case the Court of Appeal, citing an earlier unreported judgment of its own, thought there might be a distinction between an oral term which conflicts with a main provision, or the main object, of a written contract, and an inconsistency with an ancillary provision of the contract (p 701-702). They even thought it "seriously arguable" that a promise not to exercise the strict legal rights arising from a written contract ought not to be regarded as "contradictory" to the written contract. There are, for instance, English cases where an oral undertaking has been held to override a statement in a written contract that no warranties were given by the vendor: eg *Couchman v Hill* [1947] KB 554.

4.1.2 Collateral contracts

Sometimes an oral statement or promise will be held not to be a term of a single contract which also contains written terms, but to form a separate contract by itself which stands alongside the written contract. The correct analysis of such a "collateral contract" is that the statement or promise is given in consideration of the entry into the written contract. In *Heilbut Symons and Co v Buckleton* [1913] AC 30, Lord Moulton said at 47:

> It is evident . . . that there may be a contract the consideration for which is the making of some other contract. "If you will make such and such a contract I will give you one hundred pounds" is in every sense of the word a complete legal contract. It is collateral to the main contract, but each has an independent existence . . . .

It is a difficult question when a Court will decide that the oral term is a collateral contract and when part of the main contract. It is no secret that policy considerations have often guided that determination. (See Cooke J in *Industrial Steel and Plant Ltd v Smith* [1980] 1 NZLR 545, 557). Thus a collateral contract has been found to exist where the main contract was of a kind which by law was required to have all its terms in writing

(Industrial Steel v Smith, supra); where the main contract was illegal and thus unenforceable *(Strongman (1945) Ltd v Sincock* [1955] 2 QB 525), and where the oral statement was made by a person who was not party to the main contract and thus was by virtue of the doctrine of privity unable to be sued on it *(Shanklin Pier Ltd v Detel Products Ltd* [1951] 2 KB 854). In the light of New Zealand statutory developments, such as s 6 of the Contractual Remedies Act 1979 and the Illegal Contracts Act 1970, and also the relaxation of the parol evidence rule, it is felt that the device of the collateral contract (for "device" is all it really is) will need to be used less now than used to be the case. However, a good example did arise recently. In *Kenneth Williams & Co Ltd v Thomas* (1990) 1 NZ ConvC 190, 583 a prospective purchaser of a section was told there would be "no state rentals" in the subdivision. It was held that this oral promise, which did not contradict the written contract, could be enforced as a collateral contract.

As in the previous paragraph, a collateral contract will not be found where it would contradict the provisions of the main contract. (See for instance *Donovan v Northlea Farms Ltd* [1976] 1 NZLR 180). But there is currently a liberalisation of views on what amounts to "contradiction" for this purpose (see 4.1.1 supra).

4.1.3 Construction of express terms

Questions often arise as to what one of the terms of a written contract means. Many parts of the law of contract are now heavily dependent on the "construction" or "interpretation" of particular terms: whether an exception clause on its true construction covers a particular breach; whether a deposit clause allows flexibility as to time of payment; the effect of a condition requiring "solicitor's approval". Extrinsic evidence is admissible to construe terms. The approach which has been adopted is that expounded by Lord Wilberforce in *Reardon-Smith Line v Yngvuar Hansen-Tangen* [1976]1 WLR 989. One is entitled to put oneself in the shoes of the parties at the time they signed their contract by studying the background to the contract, and the circumstances surrounding its formation (the "factual matrix"). One is then better able to appreciate their purposes in contracting, and the meaning they would be likely to give the words and phrases in the contract. The "surrounding circumstances" include "the genesis of the transaction, the background, the context, the market in which the parties are operating" (ibid 995). On occasion, the pre-contractual "communings" of the parties have been looked to as part of the background: *Eastmond v Bowis* [1962] NZLR 954. However ultimately the test is an objective one: the actual intentions of one or both of the parties are irrelevant, and direct evidence of these intentions is not admissible: *Quainoo v New Zealand Breweries Ltd* [1991] 1 NZLR 161. This is because, as McMullin J has said, in the absence of such a rule there would be no end to an exchange of views as to what each party had in mind: *Driffill v Frank Driffill Ltd* (Court of Appeal, CA 218/87, 10 February 1989).

It is unclear whether subsequent conduct of the parties is admissible to prove their intention at the time of the contract: *James Wallace Pty Ltd v William Cable Ltd* [1980] 2 NZLR 187, 195 per Richardson J.

4.2 EXCLUSION CLAUSES

The parties to a contract are free, subject to certain limited statutory restrictions, to exclude or limit their liability for breach of contract. A party who seeks to rely on an exclusion clause must, however, be able to show (i) that the clause is part of the contract; and (ii) that it does in fact cover the events which have happened.

4.2.1. Contractual documents

The document relied on as containing notice of the excluding or limiting term must have been intended to have contractual force. In *Holmes v Burgess* [1975] 2 NZLR 311, for example, it was held that an exclusion clause in an auctioneer's catalogue did not apply to a private agreement for the sale of a colt which the parties had negotiated after the colt had failed to sell by auction, even though the purchaser had signed a purchase note acknowledging his familiarity with the conditions of sale in the catalogue. The Judge considered that the parties did not intend that the document should form part of their contract. The vendor simply wanted a written record of the sale and the purchaser thought he was facilitating the registration of the transfer of the colt.

4.2.2 Incorporation of signed documents

If a contractual document containing an exclusion clause is signed by a party, then the orthodox view, laid down in *L'Estrange v Graucob* [1934] 2 KB 394, is that in the absence of fraud or misrepresentation that party is bound even if he or she did not read the document. Recently, however, in *Crocker v Sundance Northwest Resorts Ltd* (1989) 51 DLR (4th) 321 the Supreme Court of Canada took a different view. The plaintiff, when in an intoxicated condition, entered a competition at the defendants' ski resort involving racing on inflated rubber tyres. He signed an application form containing a clause purporting to release the defendants from any liability to the competitors. In the course of the race the plaintiff was thrown off his tyre and seriously injured. He sued the defendants, alleging negligence in organising an inherently dangerous competition and allowing an intoxicated person to participate. It was held that the claim succeeded and that the contractual waiver was not binding, it not having been read by him or known to him or drawn to his attention. On this view the question whether an exclusion clause is part of a contract turns on the rules about notice set out below, irrespective of whether the contract has been signed.

4.2.3 Incorporation by notice

An exclusion clause may be incorporated into a contract by giving reasonable notice of its existence to the party adversely affected by it. This may be done orally (subject to the parol evidence rule, supra para 4.1.1) but normally it will be by giving a ticket or putting up a sign stating liability is excluded. In determining the effect of the notice the following factors must be taken into account.

(a) TIME OF NOTICE
Sufficient notice of the clause be given before or at the time of making the
contract. A belated notice is of no effect. Thus in *Olley v Marlborough Court
Ltd* [1949]1 KB 532 a notice on the wall of a hotel bedroom was not part
of a contract previously made at the reception desk of the hotel. Similarly,
in *Thornton v Shoe Lane Parking Ltd* [1971] 2 QB 163 a clause on the back
of a parking ticket issued by an automatic machine at the entrance to a
carpark came too late to affect the terms upon which a customer entered
the park.

The position may be different where a customer in a shop makes a
purchase and is given a document containing limiting terms. It may well
be that the acceptance of the money and handing over the document is
a counter offer by the shopkeeper to sell the goods on the proffered terms,
which the purchaser is free to accept or reject. The customer in *Thornton's*
case had no such opportunity. However it must, of course, be clear,
unlike in *Chapelton's* case, that the document is intended to be contractually binding.

(b) DEGREE OF NOTICE
It is a question of fact whether the steps taken to bring the notice to the
attention of the other party are reasonably sufficient in all the circumstances. *Harvey v Ascot Dry Cleaning Co Ltd* [1953] NZLR 549 will be taken
as an example. The plaintiff left a suit with the defendants for cleaning.
He was handed a docket which was folded in two and which he placed
in his pocket unread. The docket had printed on it a clause in large letters
limiting the liability of the defendants to ten times the charge for the work
done. The suit was damaged and the plaintiff claimed its full value. The
Court held that the folding of the docket was immaterial, that the
defendants had done what was reasonably sufficient to give notice of the
condition and that the plaintiff was, therefore, bound by it.

An exclusion clause may be incorporated by reference to another
document. In *Thompson v LM and S Railway* [1930] 1 KB 41 the plaintiff
bought a railway ticket which stated on the back that it was issued subject
to the conditions set out in the railway company's timetables, which
could be bought for 6d. These conditions included (on p 552) an exclusion
clause. It was held that the defendants had given reasonable notice of the
clause and that the plaintiff was bound. The finding of fact made here
was, perhaps, a harsh one but, the principle involved is unexceptional.

The plaintiff in *Thompson's* case was in fact illiterate and could not have
read the clause even had she known about it. The Court regarded this as
immaterial. If, however, the defendant knows at the time of the contract
of the plaintiff's illiteracy or other disability he or she may have to take
extra steps to give adequate notice of the conditions upon which the
contract is made.

If an exclusion clause is unusual, unexpected or of especially far
reaching effect, a higher degree of notice is required. In J *Spurling Ltd v
Bradshaw* [1956]1 WLR 461 Denning LJ said of some clauses he had seen
that they "would need to be printed in red ink on the face of the document
with a red hand pointing to it before the notice could be held to be
sufficient". The *Spurling* principle was applied in *Interfoto Picture Library
Ltd v Stiletto Visual Programmes Ltd* [1989] QB 433, although the case does
not involve an exclusion clause. (It really seems to be about penalty

clauses: see infra para 7.5.4.) The plaintiffs hired photographic transparencies to the defendants. One of the conditions of the hiring, contained in a delivery note which the defendants did not read, was that very high "holding fees" be paid if the transparencies were not returned within 14 days. The plaintiffs' claim for these fees failed. The Court said that a party to a contract seeking to enforce particularly onerous or unusual conditions had to show that the conditions had been fairly and reasonably brought to the attention of the other. The plaintiffs had, however, done nothing in this respect.

(c) PREVIOUS COURSE OF DEALING

Notice of an exclusion clause may be inferred from a previous consistent course of dealing between the parties. In *Kendall and Sons v William Lillico and Sons Ltd* [1969] 2 AC 31 the sellers sold goods to the buyers under an oral contract and the next day sent them a "sold note" containing an exemption clause. As this "sold note" came after the contract had been made, it was too late in itself to be of any effect. However, there had been a consistent course of dealing between the parties over the previous three years during which the sellers had, after each oral contract, sent the buyers a "sold note" containing the same clause. The House of Lords held that the previous dealing sufficed to give reasonable notice of the exemption clause to the buyers.

A term may also be implied into a contract pursuant to a general course of dealing amounting to a trade custom even though the parties have not dealt with each other before: *British Crane Hire Corp Ltd v Ipswich Plant Hire Ltd* [1975] QB 303: and see infra, para 4.4.2.

4.2.4 Construction of the contract

An exclusion clause which has successfully been incorporated into a contract still requires to be interpreted. The general rule adopted by the Courts here is one of strict construction. A party who wishes to exclude or limit liability for the consequences of his or her own breach of contract must use very clear words. Indeed, the Courts have sometimes searched for strained and artificial meanings to be given to these clauses in order to limit or reduce their efficacy. This kind of approach has recently been under attack and is certainly not appropriate for all cases, as the House of Lords has been at pains to make clear. The latest UK cases should, however, be treated with a measure of caution because legislative intervention in the form of the UK Unfair Contract Terms Act 1977 has alleviated the harsher consequences which can flow from the enforcement of wide-ranging exclusion clauses and this in turn has influenced judicial thinking as regards the need for a strict interpretation of these clauses.

(a) CONSTRUCTION CONTRA PROFERENTEM

The strict canon of construction which the Courts have commonly adopted is known as the contra proferentem rule. It requires that an exclusion clause be strictly construed against the interest of the party who seeks to rely on it. Any ambiguity or other doubt will be resolved in a way least favourable to that party. One example from many is *Beck and Co Ltd v Szymanowski and Co Ltd* [1924] AC 43. A contract for the sale of cotton provided "the goods delivered shall be deemed in all respects in accordance with the contract". The seller delivered a short quantity. The House of Lords held that the clause did not apply because it related to goods delivered and the damages claimed were for goods *not* delivered.

An important aspect of the contra proferentem rule is that clear words must be used before a party will be held to be exempt from liability in negligence: see generally *AM Bisley and Co Ltd v Thompson* [1982] 2 NZLR 696. For example, where a clause in a contract for processing meat at a freezing works stated that "the wool, meat and skins are uninsured and are held at the owner's risk" it was held that these words simply gave notice to the owner that the meat was held at his risk in respect of accidental loss or damage and did not prevent the owner suing the processor in negligence: *Producer Meats Ltd v Thomas Borthwick and Sons Ltd* [1964] NZLR 700; and see *Securitas (NZ) Ltd v Cadbury Schweppes Hudson Ltd* [1988] 1 NZLR 340. Furthermore even if a party's only liability is in negligence the wording must make it clear that negligence is excluded. Thus a clause to the effect that the defendants were "not responsible for damage caused by fire to customer's cars on the premises" was held to operate only as a warning as to the legal position in the absence of negligence: *Hollier v Rambler Motors Ltd* [1972] 2 WLR 401. The word "negligence" need not, however, be mentioned expressly for the defendant may make it clear that the exemption is from any conceivable liability. In *George Mitchell Ltd v Finney Lock Seeds Ltd* [1983] 2 AC 803 a clause in contract for the supply of Dutch winter cabbage seed excluded "all liability for any loss or damage arising from the use of any seeds or plants supplied by us and for any consequential loss or damage arising out of such use . . . or for any other loss or damage whatsoever". It was held by the House of Lords, reversing the Court of Appeal on this point, that this condition unambiguously limited the supplier's liability and that being the case there was no principle of construction that could properly be applied to confine the effect of the limitation to breaches of contract arising without negligence on the part of the suppliers. This approach has also been taken in New Zealand. In *Kaniere Gold Dredging Ltd v Dunedin Engineering and Steel Co Ltd* (1985) 1 NZBLC, 102,223, where the relevant clause referred to "no liability of any kind whatsoever", Holland J said that it could not be inferred that these words meant "no liability of any kind whatsoever other than a claim in negligence".

In *Ailsa Craig Fishing Co Ltd v Malvern Fishing Co Ltd* [1983] 1 All ER 101 Lord Wilberforce thought that a clause *limiting* rather than *excluding* liability should be clearly and unambiguously expressed and construed contra proferentem but was not to be construed as rigidly and strictly as an exclusion clause, since a limitation clause was more likely to accord with the true intention of the parties. This view was accepted by Cooke P in *SGS (NZ) Ltd v Quirke Export Ltd* [1988] 1 NZLR 52, his Honour observing that a Court should be especially slow to interpret a clause as in effect totally negating contractual liability. His Honour was, however, also attracted by the contrary view of the High Court of Australia in *Darlington Futures Ltd v Delco Australia Pty Ltd* (1986) 161 CLR 500 to the extent that a clause ostensibly of limitation but in effect of virtual exclusion should be approached for what it really is.

(b) DEVIATION CASES

There are a number of decisions to the effect that a shipowner who deviates from the agreed or usual route thereby loses the benefit of an exemption clause in the contract of carriage: see eg *Joseph Thorley Ltd v Orchis SS Co Ltd* [1907] 1 KB 660. A bailee who stores goods in a place other than agreed or who without authority parts with possession of the goods similarly is unable to rely on such a clause: *Lilley v Doubleday* (1881) 7 QBD 510. The shipowner or bailee is regarded as having performed something fundamentally different from that which was agreed, and as having thereby "stepped out of the contract", so that clauses designed to apply to the contracted voyage or bailment are held on their true construction to have no application to the deviating voyage or bailment.

(c) FUNDAMENTAL BREACH OF CONTRACT

In the years up to the decision of the House of Lords in *Suisse Atlantique* [1967] 1 AC 361 the Courts in some cases did more than construe exemption clauses strictly, but actually held them to be ineffective as a matter of *law* where the breach of the party seeking to rely on such a clause was so serious as to be termed "fundamental": see, for example, *Karsales Ltd v Wallis* [1956] 1 WLR 936. By treating the doctrine of fundamental breach as a rule of law the Courts were able to disregard an inconvenient exclusion clause completely, irrespective of the intention of the parties. In *Suisse Atlantique,* however, the Lords laid down that there was no blanket rule that an exclusion clause would not apply in the case of a fundamental breach of contract. It was simply a matter of construction of the contract and an appropriately worded clause could cover such a breach. Lord Wilberforce did, however, recognise that the more serious the breach, the clearer the language that would be needed to cover it.

Subsequent Court of Appeal decisions in England paid lip service to *Suisse Atlantique* but in reality ignored it. When the matter came before the House of Lords again in *Photo Production Ltd v Securicor Transport Ltd* [1980] AC 827 these decisions were overruled and the doctrine of fundamental breach rejected once more. The House also took the opportunity to discuss the policy issues underlying their decision.

The facts of this case certainly disclosed a serious breach of contract. The plaintiff factory owner employed the defendant security company to conduct security patrols of their premises at night and during weekends. One night the patrolling officer lit a small fire inside the factory. The fire got out of control and the factory and its stock, worth £615,000, were destroyed. The plaintiffs sued the defendants, who relied on an exemption clause in the contract which provided: "Under no circumstances shall [Securicor] be responsible for any injurious act or default by any employee of [Securicor] unless such act or default could have been foreseen and avoided by the exercise of due diligence on the part of [Securicor] as his employer". The plaintiffs did not allege that the defendants were negligent in employing the officer concerned. The Court of Appeal held the exclusion clause could not apply by reason of Securicor's fundamental breach of contract but this decision was reversed by the House of Lords. Their Lordships affirmed that the question whether an exemption clause applied to a fundamental breach was one of construction of the whole contract, including the exemption clause. The wording here was seen as clear and unambiguous and perfectly adequate to cover the defendants' position. This result was, moreover, thought to be fair and reasonable as well as technically correct. Lord Wilberforce observed that Securicor agreed to provide a service for a very modest charge, provided no equipment and had no knowledge of the value of the factory or of the efficacy of any fire precautions. In these circumstances nobody could consider it unreasonable that the risk assumed by Securicor should be a modest one and that Photo Productions should carry the substantial risk of damage or destruction. In similar vein Lord Salmon thought that any businessman entering the contract could have had no doubt as to the real meaning of the clause and would have made his insurance arrangements accordingly.

The House of Lords returned to this matter once again in *George Mitchell Ltd v Finney Lock Seeds Ltd*, discussed supra. Their Lordships were at pains to deprecate the strained interpretation put on the clause in question by the majority in the Court of Appeal to the effect that the wording did not cover negligence. As Lord Bridge put it, some of the judgments below had come dangerously near to reintroducing by the back door the doctrine of fundamental breach which had been so forcibly evicted by the front door in *Photo Productions*.

(d) APPRAISAL

We are now in a position to consider where these developments overseas leave the New Zealand Courts.

(i) The doctrine of fundamental breach clearly no longer exists as a separate rule of law (although the seriousness of a breach will be relevant in construing an exclusion clause in any particular case). In *Kaniere Gold Dredging Ltd v Dunedin Engineering and Steel Co Ltd*, supra, Holland J doubted whether the doctrine had in fact ever become part of New Zealand law. He also observed that in the absence of any statutory reform injustice might sometimes be produced if exclusion clauses were left to operate, but was satisfied that it would be irresponsible for a Judge sitting at first instance in New Zealand in 1985 to attempt to revive the doctrine.

(ii) Construction contra proferentem certainly remains appropriate for "consumer" cases, there being as yet no New Zealand equivalent of the UK Unfair Contract Terms Act. The Courts may take a slightly more lenient approach in "commercial" cases for the reasons expounded in *Photo Productions*.

(iii) The rule of construction is subject to certain rather ill-defined limits. A difficult problem arises where performance is totally different than that bargained for. Suppose, for example, a contract is to sell beans, and peas are delivered and the contract contains an exclusion clause so widely drafted as to cover even such gross misperformance. The issue was raised but not resolved in *George Mitchell Ltd* where Lord Bridge merely observed that the instant case was not of the "peas and beans" variety. In *Suisse Atlantique* Lord Reid suggested that a Court might refuse to give effect to a clause if it would "lead to an absurdity" or "defeat the main object of the contract". Lord Wilberforce thought likewise if it would "deprive one party's stipulation of all contractual force" and "reduce the contract to a mere declaration of intent". His Lordship also referred to the rationale behind the "deviation" cases with seeming approval. In *Photo Productions* Lord Diplock confirmed that the agreement must "retain the legal characteristics of a contract", which arguably this type of case might not. Perhaps the Courts might justify rejection of the clause in such cases so as to give effect to the construction of the contract as a whole. Again, it might also be argued that there has been a total failure of consideration, giving the party who has not received the agreed performance the right to restitution in respect of his or her own performance.

4.2.5 Common law restrictions

(a) FRAUD AND MISREPRESENTATION

In *L'Estrange v Graucob* supra, Scrutton LJ mentioned fraud and misrepresentation as exceptions to the principle that a person is bound by a document he or she signs. His Lordship's observations in this respect were applied in *Curtis v Chemical Cleaning Co Ltd* [1951]1 KB 805. Here a statement by a shop assistant that an exclusion clause in an agreement for cleaning a wedding dress covered only damage to beads and sequins whereas it did in fact exempt from liability for all damage, had the result that the cleaners could not then rely on the clause.

(b) COLLATERAL CONTRACT

An exclusion clause in a document by reference to which the parties contracted may be overridden by an express inconsistent undertaking given before the contract. Thus in *Mendelssohn v Normand Ltd* [1970]1 QB 177 an oral promise by a carpark attendant that he would lock the plaintiff's car took priority over an exclusion clause in a ticket subsequently given to the plaintiff.

4.2.6 Statutory intervention

There has been some limited and piecemeal statutory intervention which may restrict or negate the efficacy of exclusion clauses in particular cases. Some important examples will be given.

(a) HIRE PURCHASE CONTRACTS

By the Hire Purchase Act 1971, s 51 a term in a hire purchase agreement purporting to contract out of the provisions of the Act is ineffective.

(b) SMALL DISPUTES

By the Disputes Tribunals Act 1988 s 18(6) a Disputes Tribunal is required to determine a dispute according to the substantial merits and justice of the case and in doing so must have regard to the law but is not bound to give effect to strict legal rights or obligations. By s 18(7) a Tribunal may disregard any provision in an agreement or document bearing upon a dispute that excludes or limits (a) conditions, warranties or undertakings, or (b) any right, duty, liability or remedy that would arise or accrue in the circumstances of the dispute if there were no such exclusion or limitation.

(c) MINORS' CONTRACTS

Contracts with minors under 18 are prima facie unenforceable and contracts with minors under 20 which are unconscionable or which contain harsh or oppressive terms may be cancelled in the discretion of the Court: Minors' Contracts Act 1969, ss 5, 6: see infra para 5.1.1. Exclusion clauses could be caught by these general provisions.

(d) PRE-CONTRACT NEGOTIATIONS

It is not uncommon to find clauses in contracts which attempt to exclude liability for misrepresentation. A common form of such clause is to the effect that the purchaser "acknowledges that he is purchasing in reliance on his own judgment, and not in reliance on any statements made by the vendor". Section 4(1) of the Contractual Remedies Act 1979 limits the effectiveness of such clauses. It provides:

(1) If a contract, or any other document, contains a provision purporting to preclude a Court from inquiring into or determining the question –
(a) Whether a statement, promise, or undertaking was made or given, either in words or by conduct, in connection with or in the course of negotiations leading to the making of the contract; or
(b) Whether, if it was so made or given, it constituted a representation or a term of the contract; or
(c) Whether, if it was a representation, it was relied on –
the Court shall not, in any proceedings in relation to the contract, be precluded by that provision from inquiring into and determining any such question unless the Court considers that it is fair and reasonable that the provision should be conclusive between the parties, having regard to all the circumstances of the case, including the subject-matter and value of the transaction, the respective bargaining strengths of the parties, and the question whether any party was represented or advised by a solicitor at the time of the negotiations or at any other relevant time.

Section 4(2), to similar effect, provides that the Court may also go behind a clause which purports to preclude a Court from inquiring into or determining whether a person had actual or ostensible authority to make a statement, promise or undertaking.

It has been pointed out (McLauchlan (1988) 18 VUWLR 311) that interpreted literally the section seems to mean that the Court cannot inquire into whether a statement or promise has been made until it has first determined that it is not fair and reasonable to treat the clause as conclusive. As predicted, the Courts have not in fact tended to approach the section in this way: rather, they have investigated the making of the statement or promise *before* deciding whether the clause should be conclusive. Recently, however, in *Ellmers v Brown* (1990) 1 NZ ConvC 190, 216 Somers J said that there was an argument that the circumstances to which the Court could have regard would exclude any details of the circumstances in which it is alleged the promise was made, the relative weight of the promise and probably even the alleged nature of the promise. It would be unfortunate if this dictum were to herald a more restrictive approach towards s 4 in the future. So far it seems to have worked quite satisfactorily.

Two cases, one going one way and one the other, will be taken as examples. In *M E Torbett Ltd v Keirlor Motels Ltd* (1984) 1 NZBLC 102,079 a contract for the sale of a coffee lounge contained an exclusion clause in terms caught by the section. During negotiations for the purchase the defendant had misrepresented the amount of the weekly wages bill. In applying s 4 Casey J took into account the importance of the subject-matter of the representation, the large amount of money involved and the fact the misrepresentation was deliberate. This was "precisely the kind of case the Contractual Remedies Act was intended to cover" and in the circumstances his Honour was satisfied it would be unjust to allow the defendant to rely on the clause. On the other hand in *Herbison v Papakura Video Ltd* [1987] 2 NZLR 527 a disclaimer in respect of representations made prior to the sale of a video business was held to be conclusive between the parties. Henry J relied, inter alia, on the following factors: (1) the transaction involved the sale of a business at a substantial figure; (2) there was no disparity between the bargaining strengths of the parties; (3) the parties were in receipt of competent legal and accounting advice; (4) the precise wording of various special terms, included in which was the disclaimer, was the subject of detailed negotiation; and (5) the schedule which comprised the misrepresentation was originally included as a warranted document and was deliberately replaced by another, specially drafted, clause.

In *Torbett's* case it was held, adopting the common law rule (*S Pearson & Son v Dublin Corporation* [1907] AC 351) that an exclusion clause could never apply in the case of fraud. On the other hand in *Shotover Mining Ltd v Brownlie* (High Court, Invercargill, CP 96/86, 30 September 1987) and *Bird v Bicknell* [1987] 2 NZLR 542 fraud was treated simply as a factor in determining what was "fair and reasonable" in the circumstances.

(e) FAIR TRADING ACT 1986
Sections 9-14 of the Fair Trading Act prohibit conduct in trade which is misleading or deceptive and certain false representations in connection with the supply of goods or services or in relation to land: see infra Chapter 10. Persons who suffer loss or damage caused by conduct in breach of the Act may institute civil proceedings for the amount of the loss or damage. The words of the Act are mandatory and it seems, therefore, that any term in a contract purporting to contract out of the provisions of the Act can be of no effect. There is Australian authority on similar legislation in support of this view: see *Petera Pty Ltd v E A J Ltd* (1985) ATPR 40-605; *Clark Equipment Australia Ltd v Covcat Pty Ltd* (1987) ATPR 40-768. Possibly, however, a tradesman's disclaimer could be formulated in such a way as to remove from his statement any potential it might otherwise have to mislead or deceive, so there is no breach of the Act in the first place. For example, a dealer advertising an appliance described as four years old might add that he or she had no personal knowledge of the history of the goods and thus could not guarantee its age.

4.2.7 Reform

The Law Commission has recently issued a discussion paper (Preliminary Paper No 11 (1990)) making a broad review of "unfair" contracts or terms of contracts, and as part of this putting forward suggestions for the reform of the law relating to exclusion clauses. The main features to the scheme, including its possible treatment of exclusion clauses, are set out infra, para 5.2.5.

4.3 CONDITIONAL CONTRACTS

Here we are concerned with transactions where the parties contemplate the occurrence or non-occurrence of some event affecting the dealings between them. The occurrence or non-occurrence of the event is a condition and normally is apparent in the agreement by words such as "subject to" or "on condition that". Many of the older textbooks and cases use the terminology of a "condition precedent" or a "condition subsequent" – the failure of the former preventing contractual liability, the failure of the latter discharging a contract. The use of this style of terminology can be misleading and has been the subject of some judicial criticism: see *Hunt v Wilson* [1978] 2 NZLR 261, 267 and *Robertson Enterprises Ltd v Cope* [1989] 3 NZLR 391.

It is preferable to look at the practical effect of conditions and at some of the more common types of conditions used.

4.3.1 Conditions affecting the formation of any agreement

If an offer is made subject to a condition, there can be no valid acceptance until the condition is fulfilled and there is a complete offer. Thus in *Buhrer v Tweedie* [1973] 1 NZLR 517, the vendor altered some terms of the original offer, thus making a counter offer. He also stipulated that his "acceptance" (ie counter-offer in law) was subject to his solicitor's approval. It was held that until that approval was given, there was no offer capable of being accepted.

Where a condition is put on an acceptance, the position will generally be different. A conditional acceptance will normally be a counter-offer and therefore not act as an acceptance at all: *Reporoa Stores Ltd v Treloar* [1958] NZLR 177; *Frampton v McCully* [1976]1 NZLR 270. It is suggested in the latter case that if the condition is as to some trivial matter or as to something which the law would regulate by an implied term, then the conditional acceptance might be effective. The scope of any such exception to the general rule must be limited.

4 3.2 Conditions delaying the enforceability of a concluded agreement

Here the parties have concluded their agreement, but the agreement does not have contractual force until the condition is fulfilled.

The commonest form of such a condition is "subject to contract", in its usual sense. Normally where the parties have reached an agreement but have employed the phrase "subject to contract" or words to that effect there is a presumption that the parties have intended to postpone any contractual obligation until the formal contract is prepared and executed: *Carruthers v Whitaker* [1975] 2 NZLR 667; *Concorde Enterprises Ltd v Anthony Motors Ltd* [1981] 2 NZLR 385 and *Holmes v Australasian Holdings Ltd* [1988] 2 NZLR 303.

This presumption can be rebutted by evidence that the parties intended the arrangement to have immediate contractual effect, as in *Newton-King v Wilkinson* [1976] 2 NZLR 321 and *France v Hight* [1990] 1 NZLR 345. If performance of some of the terms of the contract has to occur before a formal contractual document can be prepared, the Courts will usually hold that the first arrangement was intended to be contractually binding until subsumed into the formal contract. Thus in *Branca v Cobarro* [1947] KB 854 and *Reid Motors v Wood* [1978] 1 NZLR 319 the implementation of financial arrangements had to take place before a contractual document could have been completed, and so documents expressed to be "provisional" and "subject to formal contract" were held to be fully enforceable. A similar result was reached in *Walmsley v Christchurch City Council* [1990] 1 NZLR 199.

There will also be exceptional "subject to contract" cases where final details of the agreement are to be settled by the parties themselves in the contract document. Such an agreement is not enforceable because there is as yet no complete offer and acceptance: *Winn v Bull* (1877) 7 ChD 29. Note, however, that if the parties leave an adviser to draft the final version of the contractual document in accordance with the local custom and practice for such documents, the contract is likely to be binding: *Coachman Properties Ltd v Panmure Video Club Ltd* [1984] 2 NZLR 200 and *Robertson Enterprises Ltd v Cope* [1989] 3 NZLR 391.

If the normal rule applies that the parties have postponed contractual liability until the formal execution of a contractual document, it follows that either party is free to withdraw from the arrangement at any time until the document is executed. This may be the position even if the arrangement reached does not include the words "subject to contract" if the parties have had abortive earlier negotiations as to the same subject matter which were subject to contract; see *Cohen v Nessdale Ltd* [1982] 2 All ER 103.

4.3.3 Conditions suspending some elements of performance of a binding contract

If an agreement contains a term of this nature, the parties are contractually bound to each other and are not free to withdraw until and unless the condition fails of fulfilment. Equally, substantial performance of the contract is not required until the condition is fulfilled. Depending on the nature and terms of the condition, there will usually be an obligation on one or both parties to attempt to ensure the condition is fulfilled.

The commonest conditions of this type, which also serve as illustrations of the principle, are "subject to solicitor's approval", "subject to finance" and conditions as to approval required by statute, eg planning permission. In all of these cases the parties are contractually bound but cannot insist on performance of the major elements of the contract (eg the payment of the price and the transfer of the title) until the condition is fulfilled.

"Subject to solicitor's approval" will be taken to mean "subject to the solicitor's approval as to matters within his or her sphere of expertise". The solicitor must give approval if the conveyancing aspects of the transaction are reasonable – he or she may not purport to refuse approval on the substance of the bargain: *Provost Developments Ltd v Collingwood Towers Ltd* [1980] 2 NZLR 205. The same principle would apply to any other professional person who might give advice on a specialist point.

If the circumstances are such that the approval does relate to the substance of the bargain there is no binding agreement but only a conditional offer or acceptance: *Frampton v McCully* (supra).

"Subject to finance" clauses are now clearly recognised as not preventing the formation of a contract: *Connor v Pukerau Stores Ltd* [1981] 1 NZLR 384. Unless specific rates of interest etc are mentioned in the condition it will be interpreted as referring to finance at reasonable rates. Where the condition refers to the obtaining of some permission or approval required by statute, the contract is binding until the approval is clearly unobtainable: *Neylon v Dickens* [1977] 1 NZLR 595 (CA), [1978] 2 NZLR 35 (PC).

A common feature of all these types of conditions is that the Court can use the objective standard of reasonableness to determine whether a condition can be taken as fulfilled.

4.3.4 Conditions terminating contractual liability

These are the simplest form of condition in theory. The contract subsists and must be fully performed but comes to an end on the happening of the specified event. If a contract calls for payments to A "while A is studying law", the contract terminates if A ceases to study law.

4.3.5 Fulfilment of conditions

In general, a condition is fulfilled when the specified event occurs, rather than at the time when the other party receives notice of the event: *Meehan v Jones* (1982) 56 ALJR 813; *Mekol Pty Ltd v Brown* (1966) 40 ALJR 327 and *Dunsford v Tate* (1971) 1 NZCPR 600. The position may be different where only one party does or can know whether the stipulated event has occurred. Notice may be required in such a case.

The normal rule is that a party on whom the burden of obtaining fulfilment of the condition falls must make all reasonable efforts to perform the condition. Thus the purchaser who has to seek suitable finance may be obliged to seek finance from the vendor or to use other property as security: *Connor v Pukerau Stores Ltd* (supra). There is no obligation, however, to take all possible steps if these are not reasonably likely to succeed: *North Shore Demolition Ltd v McKay* [1978] 1 NZLR 454. If, however, the contract uses a term requiring the party to make more than reasonable efforts, the burden imposed may be stringent: see *Innes v Mars* [1982] 2 NZLR 68 and *Innes v Ewing* [1989] 1 NZLR 598.

If a party to a contract fails to take reasonable steps to perform the condition, this will amount to a breach of an implied term, entitling the recovery of damages. Perhaps more pertinent, if these steps to fulfill the condition have not been taken, that party will not be able to rely on the failure of the condition and the contract will become in effect unconditional on that point: *Provost Developments v Collingwood Towers Ltd* (supra) and *Connor v Pukerau Stores Ltd* (supra). If no time limit is provided for fulfilment, a term will be implied that the condition must be fulfilled within a reasonable time.

If the other party makes fulfilment of the condition impossible, the condition will be treated as fulfilled: *Mahoney v Lindsay* (1981) 33 ALR 601.

4.3.6 Waiver

Any condition which can be classed as for the benefit of one party alone can be waived. Waiver operates to render the contract unconditional on that point. The party seeking to waive must make it clear to the other party that he or she does not regard occurrence of the condition as essential. No particular form of words is required to convey waiver: *Williams v Kirk* [1988] 1 NZLR 452. Indeed waiver may be made by conduct: see, for example, the waiver of time limits by acquiescence in the other party's delay in *Neylon v Dickens*, supra. There are some conditions which cannot be waived, as for instance where a statute requires consent to be given by some authority. The commonest example of this in the reported cases is the requirement of consent under the Land Settlement Promotion and Land Acquisition Act 1952.

The most difficult issue in waiver is in determining whether a condition may be unilaterally waived. The long-standing rule is that a condition may only be waived unilaterally if it is solely for the benefit of the party waiving seeking to waive it. For instance, a "subject to finance" condition is normally one that is solely for the benefit of the purchaser: *Connor v Pukerau Stores Ltd* (supra), but this is not so if the condition affects the date at which possession is to change: *Daubney v Kerr* [1962] NZLR 319; or the vendor is also a mortgagee and the finance condition thus affects the security for the money owing: *Karangahape Road Village International Ltd v Holloway* [1989] 1 NZLR 83, 110. There are also some cases where the contractual provision for termination affect the right to waive a condition. In *Moreton & Craig v Montrose Ltd (in liquidation)* [1986] 2 NZLR 496 the Court held that a provision that the contract would be "null and void" on the failure of a condition provided benefits for both parties, in that the legal position was more certain and that each had a possibility that the contract would cease to be binding. This meant that the condition was not solely for the benefit of either party to the contract and could therefore not be waived. This kind of implied benefit to both parties cannot, of course, take priority over any stipulation in the agreement as to the status of a condition: *Hawker v Vickers* [1991] 1 NZLR 399.

4.4 IMPLIED TERMS

Implied terms are those terms which are included in a contract even though they do not appear on the face of the agreement between the parties. In most cases terms are implied to give efficacy to a contract and to resolve a difficulty for which the parties have not provided. Implied terms may be implied by law or implied by custom or implied in fact.

4.4.1 Terms implied by law

These may be laid down by statute or laid down by the common law. Those by statute may be either mandatory or supplementary terms. Mandatory terms are those which apply to a contract and override any contrary term expressed in the agreement. Examples of this kind of term may be found in the Hire Purchase Act 1971 in regard to such matters as the right to pay the balance due, repossession and assignment. These are discussed in detail, infra ch 37.

Supplementary terms are those which a statute provides will apply only if the parties have not made express provision as to that matter. The clearest examples are in the Sale of Goods Act 1908 in regard to such matters as quality of the merchandise and delivery. These are discussed in detail in ch 15, infra.

The third kind of term implied in law is the term implied by the common law. These are of rather less importance now than in earlier years because many of the terms implied by the common law are now embodied in statutes (eg the Sale of Goods Act 1908). A term implied by the common law is one which is implied into a contract because such a term is needed to give efficacy to that class of contracts. Thus in *Liverpool City Council v Irwin* [1976] AC 239; 2 All ER 39, the House of Lords held that a term should be implied into agreements between the owner and tenants of a multi-storey building that the owner keep the lifts and stairs in reasonable condition. Such an obligation is necessary to make such agreements generally effective. Similarly, a term may be implied into a contract of employment that the employee take reasonable care to prevent injuring fellow-employees: *Lister v Romford Ice and Cold Storage Co* [1957] AC 555.

Before such a term will be implied into any particular contract of this class it must be clear it does not contradict the express terms of the particular contract.

4.4.2 Terms implied by custom

These are terms implied from the background of trade usages against which the contract has been formed. If a particular custom in some trade or locality is so well-known that anyone dealing in the area would or should have known of it, it may be implied into an agreement. The threshold of "notoriety" is high; *Woods v NJ Ellingham* [1977] 1 NZLR 218. Even if the custom is universal, it cannot be implied into a contract if it is contrary to an express term; *Les Affreteurs Reunis SA v L Walford Ltd* [1919] AC 801 or is inconsistent with the tenor of the whole contract: *London Export Corporation Ltd v Jubilee Coffee Roasting Co* [1958] 1 WLR 661; 2 All ER 411.

4.4.3 Terms implied in fact

These differ from terms implied by the common law in that the Courts are concerned with the circumstances of the individual contract, and not with considerations of what is reasonable and necessary in a class of contracts: *Shell UK Ltd v Lostock Garage Ltd* [1977] 1 All ER 481.

The tests for implying a term in fact have been authoritatively stated by the Privy Council in *BP Refinery (Westernport) Ltd v Shire of Hastings* (1977) 52 ALJR 20 as:

(a) It must be reasonable and equitable – the Courts will not imply an term that is unfairly advantageous to one or the other party. Thus in *Aotearoa International Ltd v Scancarriers A/S* [1985] 1 NZLR 513, the Privy Council refused to imply into a contract for shipping goods a term requiring the shipper to guarantee that space was available. Such a term would have radically altered the bargain made by the parties, as well as being inequitable in the circumstances. This still leaves a considerable discretion in the hands of the Court. It must be noted that the fact a term, if implied, would be reasonable is not, of itself, enough to imply it: *Trollope and Colls Ltd v NW Hospital Board* [1973] 1 WLR 601.

(b) It must be necessary to give business efficacy to the contract. If the contract cannot work without a term being implied as to some matter, then this test is met. If it can work without the implied term, although perhaps less fairly, the term is not to be implied. A good example of a term needed for business efficacy can be found in *Inca Ltd v Autoscript (NZ) Ltd* [1979] 2 NZLR 700. The defendant manufacturer agreed to sell goods to the plaintiff at the same rates of discount it gave other wholesalers. It was held a term should be implied that the manufacturer would inform the plaintiff of what that discount was, from time to time, as otherwise the plaintiff could not ensure the contract was being observed.

(c) The term must be "obvious". This requires the Court to be certain of what the parties would have provided had the matter been drawn to their attention at the time of the formation of the contract: *Shirlaw v Southern Foundries Ltd* [1939] 2 KB 206, 227. If it is clear that some provision would have been made, but it is not clear which of a number of possibilities would have been adopted, there can be no term implied: *Trollope and Colls v NW Hospital Board*, supra.

(d) The term must be capable of clear expression.

(e) The implied term must not contradict any express term of the contract.

The five probanda in *BP Refinery (Westernport) Ltd v Shire of Hastings* have been treated as defining the law in this country: see *Devonport Borough Council v Robbins* [1979] 1 NZLR 1; *Prudential Assurance Co Ltd v Rodrigues* [1982] 2 NZLR 54 and *Aotearoa International Ltd v Scancarriers A/S* [1985] 1 NZLR 513. Some recent Australian cases have indicated that where a contract has been partially executed, the Courts need not adhere rigidly to the five probanda discussed above: see the views of Deane J in *Hawkins v Clayton* (1988) 78 ALR 69 at 91-93; *Hospital Products Ltd v United States Surgical Corporation* (1984) 156 CLR 41; 55 ALR 417 and *Codelfa Construction Pty Ltd v State Rail Authority of New South Wales* (1982) 149 CLR 337. The point appears open in New Zealand.

Chapter 5

VITIATING ELEMENTS

SUMMARY

5.1   INCAPACITY
5.2   DURESS, UNDUE INFLUENCE AND UNCONSCIONABILITY
5.3   MISTAKE
5.4   ILLEGALITY

5.1 INCAPACITY

An essential element in a binding contract is that the parties to it should possess full legal capacity. Certain persons lack such capacity and are incapable, wholly or in part, of binding themselves by a promise or, sometimes, of enforcing a promise. These persons are minors, persons of unsound mind, and bankrupts. The position as regards corporations also deserves special mention.

5.1.1 Minors

By the Age of Majority Act 1970 s 4 a minor is a person who has not attained the age of 20.

The contractual capacity of minors is governed by the Minors' Contracts Act 1969. The provisions of the Act are a code replacing the rules of common law and equity on this matter: s 15(1). The Act is subject to any other enactment making a contract binding on a minor: s 15(3). It applies to contracts made, compromises and settlements agreed to and discharges and receipts given after 1 January 1970: ss 1(2), 15(2).

The broad scheme of the Act is to divide minors' contracts into separate categories according to the marital status or age of the minor and, to a limited extent, the nature of the contract in question.

(a) MARRIED MINORS

Minors who are or have been married have full contractual capacity: s 4. However, nothing in the Act entitles a trustee to pay money to a minor or deliver property to him or her otherwise than in accordance with the terms of the trust, nor does the Act entitle such a person to enter into an agreement whereby a trust is extinguished or its terms varied: s 16.

(b) CONTRACTS APPROVED BY A DISTRICT COURT
An application may be made by or on behalf of a minor for approval of a contract which is to be entered into by a minor. If it is approved the contract has effect as if the minor were of full age: s 9.

(c) CONTRACTS OF MINORS OVER 18 AND CERTAIN OTHER CONTRACTS
Contracts made by minors who have attained the age of 18, those made by any minor pursuant to s 75 of the Life Insurance Act 1908 and contracts of service entered into by any minor have effect as if the minor were of full age: s 5(1). If, however, the Court is satisfied that, at the time the contract was entered into, the consideration for the minor's promise or act was so inadequate to be unconscionable or that any provision imposing an obligation on the minor was harsh or oppressive, it may cancel the contract or decline to enforce it against the minor or declare that the contract is unenforceable against the minor in whole or in part and may also make an order as to compensation or restitution of property: s 5(2). Some special types of contract are excepted from this power of intervention, in particular contracts of apprenticeship: see s 5(4).

It is clear that s 5 has only a relatively narrow field of operation and that the wording quite deliberately is different from that in s 6, dealing with those under 18. The focus in s 5 is solely on the inadequacy of the consideration for the minor's promise or the harshness of the terms. The section cannot, it seems, be extended so as to allow any other consideration to be brought into account, such as the fact that an 18- or 19-year-old may have bought something he or she does not need or cannot afford. See *Morrow & Benjamin Ltd v Whittington* [1989] 3 NZLR 122 at 126, discussed infra.

(d) CONTRACTS OF MINORS UNDER 18
Contracts made by minors who have not attained the age of 18 (other than contracts of life insurance and of service) are unenforceable against the minor but otherwise have effect as if the minor were of full age: s 6(1). A Court may, however, inquire into the fairness and reasonableness of such a contract at the time it was entered into and if satisfied it was fair and reasonable may enforce it against the minor, declare it to be binding on him or her in whole or in part, make an order entitling the other parties to cancel the contract and make an order as to compensation or restitution of property: s 6(2)(a). If the Court finds that the contract was not fair and reasonable it may cancel the contract, make an order entitling the minor on such conditions as the Court thinks just, to cancel the contract and, again, make a compensation or restitution order: s 6(2)(b). The Court has a wide discretion in exercising these powers and may take into account all relevant considerations including the circumstances surrounding the making of the contract, the subject matter of the contract and the age of the minor: see s 6(3).

The only reported case in which s 6 has been applied is *Morrow & Benjamin Ltd v Whittington* [1989] 3 NZLR 122. The plaintiff stockbrokers started to buy shares for the defendant when he was a 15-year-old minor. The defendant originally paid for the shares in cash but over the next two and a half years the plaintiffs allowed him to purchase on credit to ever increasing amounts. On 20 October 1987, when the share market collapsed, his total debt was over $35,000. The shares realised about $5000 and the plaintiffs, seeking to recover the balance, applied for an order under s 6 that the contracts be declared enforceable. Thorp J noted the different phraseology of s 5 and s 6 and thought that it must follow that the s 6 test of "fairness and reasonableness" is not satisfied by establishing that there was consideration and the contract was not harsh or oppressive. Fairness and reasonableness was not to be assessed as between consenting and informed adults, excluding consideration of the age of the minor, for that would disregard the essential purpose of the legislation. His Honour thus was satisfied that the circumstances in which the contracts were made had to be brought into account, and on this basis decided that they were fair but were not reasonable. The plaintiffs were aware of the defendant's minority, the contracts were for the purchase on credit of highly speculative investments, the plaintiffs knew the minor's means were inadequate and that he was relying on resale to pay for the shares and they regarded him as unreliable yet failed to implement their normal credit controls.

(e) ORDERS FOR COMPENSATION OR RESTITUTION

The nature and extent of the power of the Court in ss 5(2) and 6(2) to order compensation or restitution of property is set out in s 7. Any party, a guarantor or indemnifier (see below) or anybody claiming through these persons may seek such relief in the discretion of the Court: s 7(1). An order made pursuant to this power may vest the whole or part of the property concerned in any party to the proceedings or may direct a party to transfer or assign the property to any other party: s 7(2).

(f) GUARANTEES AND INDEMNITIES

While a minor's contractual capacity is limited as described, persons of full capacity may enter into binding contracts of guarantee or indemnity in respect of a minor's obligations: see s 10.

(g) MISCELLANEOUS PROVISIONS

The 1970 Act contains miscellaneous other provisions covering the settlement of claims by minors (s 12), the jurisdiction of District Courts (s 14) and of Disputes Tribunals (s 14A) and life insurance by minors and dealings by minors with insurance policies (s 17).

5.1.2 Persons of unsound mind

When a person lacks, wholly or partly, the competence to manage his or her affairs in relation to his or her property, the Court may appoint a suitable person to act as manager of the property, pursuant to Part III of the Protection of Personal and Property Rights Act 1988. A person subject to such a "property order" is incapable of exercising personally any of the powers thus vested in the manager: s 53(1). Any disposition of property and every contract involving property (except for necessaries, as to which see below) which is entered into by that person is, unless it is entered into with the leave of the Court, avoidable by that person or by his or her manager: s 53(2). If any transaction is so avoided, the Court may make such order as it thinks just for adjusting the rights of the parties and of any other person who has received any property or money comprised in the transaction, not being a person who has received the property or money from a person in good faith and for valuable consideration or who claims through such a person: s 53(6). If the person from whom relief is sought received the property or money in good faith and has altered his or her position in reliance on having received an indefeasible interest in it then the Court may deny relief wholly or in part if in its opinion it is inequitable to grant relief: s 53(8).

A person who is not subject to a property order may nonetheless be incapable because of senility or other incapacitating circumstances of handling his or her own affairs and in particular may lack any, or any adequate, understanding of the nature and effect of contractual relations with others. The validity of a contract made by such a person was considered by the Privy Council in *O'Connor v Hart* [1985]1 NZLR 159; (1986) 12 NZULR 87, where the following principles were laid down: (i) a contract entered into by a person of unsound mind is voidable at that person's option if it is proved that the other party knew of the unsound-ness of mind when the contract was made; (ii) where, however, a contract is entered into by a lunatic who is ostensibly sane in circumstances where the other contracting party does not know of the lunatic's lack of capacity, its validity is to be judged by the same standards as apply to a contract made by a person of sound mind; (iii) the contract is not, therefore, voidable for "unfairness" unless such unfairness creates an independent ground for relief in equity, as where undue influence has been exercised or the bargain is "unconscionable" (as to which see infra, paras 5.2.2, 5.2.3). Applying these principles, it was held, reversing the decision of the Court of Appeal ([1983] NZLR 280) that a disposition of farmland, apparently at an under-value, made by a senile man of 84 could not be rescinded for want of capacity and unfairness because the purchaser did not know of the senility and had conducted himself in relation to the sale in a way that was above reproach.

The test for determining whether a person is of unsound mind was considered by the Court of Appeal in *Scott v Wise* [1986] 2 NZLR 484, [1986] NZLJ 331, where it was held that the capacity required is related to the transaction. The question is whether the contracting party can understand the general nature, as opposed to the details, of the transac-tion in which he or she is engaging when it is explained to him or her. As for the other party's knowledge, the Court pointed out that there is a distinction between concluding a contract and making a gift. In order to avoid a contract the incapacitated party must show that the other knew of the incapacity, but to avoid a voluntary transaction the donor need only establish that he or she in fact lacked capacity, subject to some equitable defence like laches.

These principles were applied recently in *Dark v Boock* [1991] 1 NZLR 496. The plaintiff, aged 87 and suffering from senile dementia, signed a document purporting to grant to the defendant the right to live in the plaintiff's property for the rest of the defendant's life. This was expressed to be in consideration for the defendant's "looking after (the plaintiff and her) affairs heretofore". The Public Trustee as manager of her affairs applied to have the arrangement set aside. Heron J held: (i) that the plaintiff lacked capacity properly to understand the document: and (ii) that the nature of the document was essentially one of gift and that it was voidable as such. His Honour thought that the result would be the same even if the document was seen as contractual, for the defendant's solicitor, when visiting the plaintiff at her nursing home, acquired constructive knowledge of her lack of capacity. Here, then, the knowledge of the principal was imputed from the knowledge of her agent.

There does not seem to be any good reason why the rules governing contracts made by insane persons should not also apply to contracts made by drunken persons. In *Peeters v Schimanski* [1975] 2 NZLR 328, however, Cooke J accepted that there was a distinction between extreme intoxication which deprived a person of his or her reason and rendered his or her consent void and drunkenness which deprived a person merely of his or her business sense and which rendered the contract voidable at his or her suit on equitable grounds. This decision may have to be reconsidered in the light of *O'Connor v Hart* for no similar distinction was drawn in that case, the lunatic's contract being treated as at most voidable, whatever his or her state of mind.

An insane or drunken person to whom necessaries are sold and delivered must pay a reasonable price for them: Sale of Goods Act 1908, s 4. Necessaries are articles or services which a person needs and which are suitable to his or her "condition in life": see *Chapple v Cooper* (1844) 3 M & W 252.

5.1.3 Corporations

A corporation is in law a legal person distinct from the persons who conduct its affairs. A corporation may be a corporation sole or a corporation aggregate. The former consists of a single person occupying a particular office eg the Public Trustee. The latter is a body of persons united together into one entity which may be maintained by a constant succession of members.

The contractual powers of a corporation aggregate depend upon how it was created. There are three methods.

(a) ROYAL CHARTER
The corporation has all the powers possessed by an individual, subject to any special limitations contained in the charter. A contract made beyond the powers given in the charter is not void but the charter becomes liable to forfeiture.

(b) SPECIAL ACT OF PARLIAMENT
The corporation has only such special powers as are expressly or impliedly given to it by its Act of incorporation. Contracts made outside these powers are void.

(c) REGISTRATION UNDER THE PROVISIONS OF AN ACT OF PARLIAMENT
Formerly a company incorporated under the provisions of the Companies Act 1955 had only the powers conferred by the objects clause of the memorandum of association. Contracts made beyond those powers

were ultra vires and void: *Ashbury Railway Carriage Co v Riche* (1875) LR 7 HL 653. However the law was reformed by Companies Amendment Acts in 1983 and 1985, which inserted a number of new sections into the 1955 Act. The position now may be summarised as follows:

(i)   A company registered after 1 January 1984 has the "rights, powers and privileges" of a natural person whereas a company registered before that date may alter its memorandum and resolve that it shall have such powers: s 15A.

(ii) Any registered company, even where objects are stated, has full capacity to make any conveyance or transfer any real or personal property: s 18A(1).

(iii) Shareholders or debenture holders may seek to stop an ultra vires act by applying to the Court for an injunction, in which case the party dealing with the company is entitled to relief in respect of losses (other than the loss of anticipated or future profits) resulting from the company's failure to perform: s 18A(2)-(4).

(iv) An agent who makes a contract which is outside the powers of a company is acting outside the scope of his or her authority. The company nonetheless is bound, unless the other party knew or by reason of his or her position with or relationship to the company ought to have known of the lack of capacity or lack of authority: s 18C.

Broadly, then, innocent third parties may make contracts with companies without risk of their being set aside but members of the company can still seek internal redress.

The Companies Bill 1990 continues this scheme. The constitution of a company, if it has one, may, but is not required to, state the objects of the company: cl 9(1); a company has the capacity, rights, powers, and privileges of a natural person: cl 9(2); an act of a company is not invalid merely because the company did not have the capacity, the right or the power to do it: cl 10(1), and the fact that an act is not, or would not be, in the best interests of the company does not affect the legal capacity of the company to do the act: cl 10(2). Internal redress, again, may be available: certain interested persons may apply for an injunction to restrain conduct that would contravene the constitution of the company: cl 138; shareholders or directors may bring derivative actions: cl 139; and shareholders may bring personal actions against directors: cls 143, 144. As for transactions by agents, a company is bound by the acts of its directors, employees and agents in its dealings with outsiders unless the outsider knows about any non-compliance with the constitution or lack of the customary authority to exercise a power: cls 11, 155, 156.

5.1.4 Bankrupts

When a person is adjudicated bankrupt, all his or her property vests in the Assignee by virtue of the Insolvency Act 1967, s 42. Generally speaking the bankrupt's power to make a valid disposition of his or her property ends on the commencement of bankruptcy.

5.2 DURESS, UNDUE INFLUENCE AND UNCONSCIONABILITY

The consent of one of the parties to a contract may have been obtained by illegitimate pressure or influence or the circumstances of the making of the contract may have been unconscionable. A measure of relief from the consequences of unfair bargains of this kind is provided both at common law and in equity and also by special statutory provision.

5.2.1 Duress

A contract which has been obtained by improper pressure is voidable at common law on the ground of duress. Early cases required that the pressure be by way of actual or threatened violence to the person or to property. It is clear now, however, that duress can take other forms, and in particular that economic pressure alone may suffice.

In deciding whether duress is made out the first question is as to the nature of the pressure or threat. In *Universe Tankships Inc of Monrovia v International Transport Workers Federation* [1983] 1 AC 366 the House of Lords held that the victim's apparent consent must be induced by pressure which the law does not regard as legitimate. Pressure is illegitimate if it amounts to a legal wrong, as where the threat is of unlawful conduct, or if the threat itself is unlawful, as where it amounts to blackmail. It follows that a plea of economic duress will not succeed where at the time the pressure is exerted there are no existing contractual relations between the parties and one does no more than strike a hard bargain, or where there is an existing contract and one induces a new agreement simply by threatening to enforce it, for in neither case can the pressure be seen as illegitimate. (Whether relief might be available in equity in these circumstances is discussed infra, paras 5.2.2, 5.2.3.) Economic duress usually will only be available in relation to a variation of an existing contract brought about by an unlawful threat not to perform it.

Whether an illegitimate threat actually constitutes duress must be determined by reference to its coercive effect in the particular case. In *Pao On v Lau Yiu Long* [1980] AC 614 (PC) Lord Scarman put the question as being whether there has been "a coercion of the will so as to vitiate consent", but it seems that this should not be taken to suggest that the victim's will must be totally overborne. Probably his Lordship meant only that the illegitimate pressure must be a reason for entering the contract, for he went on to say that in deciding the question of coercion it is material to enquire whether the person alleged to have been coerced protested, whether he or she had an alternative course open to him or her such as an adequate legal remedy, whether he or she was independently advised and whether after entering the contract he or she took steps to avoid it.

Pao On's case itself illustrates that an unlawful threat does not necessarily constitute duress. The threat was to break a contract with a company unless the defendants, who were shareholders in the company, gave a guarantee against loss resulting from performance of the contract. It was held that there had been commercial pressure to give the guarantee but no coercion: the defendants considered the matter thoroughly and formed the opinion that the risk in giving the guarantee was more apparent than real. On the other hand in *Atlas Express Ltd v Kafco Ltd* [1989] 1 All ER 641 a claim by carriers who refused to carry out a contract to deliver the defendants' goods until the defendants promised to pay more than the agreed contract rate was unsuccessful. The defendants were heavily dependent on the plaintiffs performing the contract and the second agreement thus was vitiated by economic duress. Alternatively there was no consideration for the defendants' promise (supra, para 3.2.8).

It is difficult to establish duress where the parties to a contract genuinely dispute their rights and liabilities and then agree to a compromise. It will be recalled that in *Moyes and Groves Ltd v Radiation NZ Ltd* [1982] 1 NZLR 368 (supra, para 3.2.8) a buyer of goods from India agreed to pay the cost, rather than the contract, price for the goods when they arrived two years late and where the seller otherwise proposed to return them to their Indian suppliers. The Court was satisfied both that the seller bona fide had considerable grounds for believing that the original contract had been abandoned and that the new arrangement was a prudent and sensible compromise between the parties. The Court specifically warned that a finding of economic duress should not be made too lightly.

The same kind of issue can arise where a party to a contract performs unsatisfactorily, agrees under some pressure to do further work and then repents of the agreement. In *Walmsley v Christchurch City Council* [1990] 1 NZLR 199 it was held that a printer who had done work of unacceptable quality, entitling his customer to reject it, had not been coerced by the customer into making a new contract under which he would pay the reprinting costs. The contract had been concluded under conditions of some urgency but the printer was given time to take advice and decide what to do and his consent was a genuine recognition of the situation.

5.2.2 Undue influence

The doctrine of undue influence may be invoked where the parties to a contract or gift enjoy a special relationship of trust or confidence and the transaction subsequently is challenged by the weaker party. Equity will presume that the stronger party procured the transaction by exercising undue or improper influence over the will of the other. The onus is on the stronger to rebut the presumption, even where that party obtained no personal benefit from the transaction, and unless he or she can do this it will be set aside.

Relationships where the presumption applies as a matter of course include those between parent and child, solicitor and client, doctor and patient, trustee and beneficiary, religious advisor and disciple and, in certain circumstances, fiancé and fiancée. The doctrine is not, however, confined to these relationships. Rather, "the principle applies to every case where influence is acquired and abused, where confidence is reposed and betrayed": *Smith v Kay* (1859) 7 HLC 750 per Lord Kingsdowne. Once the requisite relationship is proved, the presumption comes into play. For example, in *Goldsworthy v Brickell* [1987] Ch 378 the presumption was held to apply to the grant of the tenancy of a farm with an option to purchase given by an old man of 85 to a neighbouring farmer whom the old man relied on for help round the farm and trusted implicitly.

Similarly in *O'Sullivan v Management Agency and Music Ltd* [1985] QB 428 it applied to an exclusive management agreement made between a young and inexperienced musician and his internationally recognised business manager. On the other hand in *Re Brocklehurst* [1978] Ch 14 the grant by an old man to a local garage proprietor with whom he was friendly of a 99 year lease of valuable shooting rights on his estate was held not to give rise to the presumption. The Court was satisfied on the evidence that it was the old man who had in fact tended to dominate the garage proprietor during their friendship rather than vice versa.

A relationship of dominance by one party over the other is not sufficient of itself to allow a transaction to be set aside for undue influence. In *National Westminster Bank v Morgan* [1985] AC 686 the House of Lords held that it must also be shown that the impugned transaction was wrongful in that it constituted a manifest and unfair disadvantage to the person seeking to avoid it. In this case a wife had, at the instigation of her bank manager, executed in favour of the bank a legal charge over her home as security for a bridging loan granted by the bank, this to refinance an existing building society loan secured by way of mortgage on the house. The husband failed to repay the loan and the bank brought proceedings for possession. The wife's defence that the manager had exercised undue influence over her failed because: (i) the relationship between the wife and the bank had never gone beyond the normal business relationship of banker and customer; and (ii) the transaction had not been disadvantageous to the wife, it having been the only way to save her home from repossession by the mortgagee.

The presumption of undue influence is rebutted if the party benefiting can show that the transaction was the result of the free exercise of independent will: *Inche Noriah v Shaik Allie Bin Omar* [1929] AC 127 per Lord Hailsham LC. An obvious way of doing this is to show that the other party received independent legal advice which was both competent and based on knowledge of all the material facts. There is, however, no invariable rule that independent advice must be taken. In *Re Brocklehurst* the Court also held that even if the circumstances had given rise to the presumption, it was rebutted by evidence showing that the gift was the spontaneous and independent act of the donor.

Sometimes a contract is made as a result of undue influence exerted by a third party. Suppose, for example, that a wife is improperly induced by her husband to guarantee advances to the husband from his bank. The guarantee can only be set aside if (i) the husband was acting as agent for the bank, or (ii) the bank had actual or constructive notice that the guarantee had been procured by the exercise of undue influence: *Bank of Credit and Commerce International SA v Aboody* [1990] 1 QB 925.

The right to rescind a contract or revoke a gift is lost if the victim affirms the transaction after the influence has ceased or if third parties have acquired an interest in the subject matter in good faith and for value.

5.2.3 Unconscionable bargains

Equity may also intervene in respect of unconscionable bargains when unfair advantage is taken of persons who are poor and ignorant or who for some other reason are in need of special protection. The doctrine of the unconscionable bargain clearly has much in common with undue influence but is not reliant on any element of personal influence.

The doctrine has been applied in New Zealand in a number of cases at first instance and on appeal. *Moffatt v Moffatt* [1984] 1 NZLR 600 is a recent example. After 18 years of marriage the parties had instructed a solicitor to prepare a separation agreement. The wife, who was under stress and anxious to have the separation finalised, ceded in the agreement her entire interest in the matrimonial home and the furniture and furnishings. Before signing she acknowledged in writing that she had been advised by the solicitor to seek independent advice but had chosen not to do so. The Court considered this was a marginal case but was nonetheless satisfied that the strain on the wife, her ignorance of the value of the home and her lack of any independent advice in combination created a situation of serious disadvantage. The husband knew of her condition and had taken unconscientious advantage of it. The agreement thus was regarded as unfair and unconscionable and was set aside accordingly.

It is not essential that actual knowledge by one of the other's position of disadvantage should always be proved. It is sufficient that the stronger party ought to have known. In *O'Connor v Hart* [1985] 1 NZLR 159, discussed supra, para 5.1.2, the purchaser did not know of the vendor's senility or have cause to suspect it. The agreement was upheld for, as Lord Brightman put it, there was no equitable fraud, no victimisation, no taking advantage, no overreaching or other description of unconscionable doings which might have justified the intervention of equity to restrain an action by the purchaser at law. In the opinion of the Court the respondents had failed to make out any case for denying to the purchaser the benefit of a bargain which was struck with complete propriety on his side. On the other hand in *Nichols v Jessup (No 1)* [1986] 1 NZLR 226, *(No 2)* [1986] 1 NZLR 237 an owner of land was relieved of her contractual obligation to grant a right of way over it to her neighbour. The owner was "ignorant about property matters", "unintelligent and muddle headed" and her business judgment "was likely to be swayed by wholly irrelevant considerations". The agreement was of little or no benefit to her yet of very great benefit to the neighbour. The "glaring" imbalance in the arrangement should have alerted him to the owner's inability to appreciate the consequences of the bargain. Again, in *Dark v Boock* [1991] 1 NZLR 496, the facts of which have been given supra para 5.1.2, the Court thought that it would be unconscionable to allow the arrangement between the plaintiff and the defendant to stand. The defendant's solicitor ought to have known of the plaintiff's incapacity yet he went ahead and obtained the plaintiff's signature to a document which was highly advantageous to the defendant and only of marginal benefit to the plaintiff. The reasoning here perhaps is open to question. The Judge equated unconscionable conduct by the defendant's agent with unconscionable conduct by the defendant personally. He seemed to think that the defendant acted innocently, for he remarked that she had been occupying the house "in complete good faith".

5.2.4 Oppressive credit contracts

By ss 9-14 of the Credit Contracts Act 1981 a Court has power to re-open a credit contract which is oppressive, harsh, unjustly burdensome, unconscionable or in contravention of reasonable standards of commercial practice. If it does this it may make such orders as it thinks necessary to remedy the matters which caused it to intervene. See infra, ch 24.

5.2.5 Reform

In the spring of 1990 the Law Commission issued its Preliminary Paper No 11, entitled "Unfair Contracts". The Commission invited submissions on a detailed statutory scheme for reform, stressing that it was not committed to the scheme nor to any form of legislative intervention in this area. The main features to the suggested scheme are as follows:

(i) There is a test of unfairness which restates and clarifies the common law of unconscionability. Broadly, for a contract to be unfair there should be a serious imbalance of power, one party taking undue advantage of that imbalance and a substantial disparity of result.

(ii) A term of a contract is also unfair if it is harsh or oppressive. This extends to other contracts the law which deals with oppressive terms in credit contracts.

(iii) Certain types of term, such as penalty clauses or exclusion clauses, are mentioned as possibly justifying proscription either altogether or in "consumer" transactions, or as being made subject to a "fair and reasonable" test.

(iv) The Courts may review the exercise of contractual powers in an oppressive manner. Once again this extends to contracts generally the law applicable to credit contracts.

(v) The Courts have enlarged and more flexible powers to grant relief where a contract or contractual terms are unfair, or contractual powers are used oppressively.

(vi) Within its scope of application the scheme is meant to replace the common law governing the reopening of "unfair" contracts under the heads of unconscionability, undue influence and duress. It is not intended merely to add a new statutory remedy to those now available.

5.3 MISTAKE

All cases of mistake in contracts – those where the true facts were not appreciated by, or known to, one or both parties – are now governed by the Contractual Mistakes Act 1977. The common law rules relating to mistaken contracts were often difficult to apply, and frequently produced apparently unfair results. The Contractual Mistakes Act was intended to make clearer and more simple provisions for the Courts to grant relief from the effects of mistake in appropriate cases and to provide more flexible and just remedies. It may not entirely have succeeded, at least as yet, in that aim. As the Act has been considered in more cases, most of its provisions have become clear, but there remain some areas of uncertainty and difficulty.

5.3.1 The grounds for relief

A person seeking relief for mistake must satisfy the provisions of s 6 as to a qualifying mistake. If the mistake does not come within s 6, he or she cannot get any relief under the Act. Before considering s 6, it must be noted that the term "mistake" is not fully defined in the Act.

(a) WHAT IS A "MISTAKE"?
Section 2 provides:

> (1) "Mistake" means a mistake, whether of law or of fact.
> (2) For the purposes of this Act, and without limiting the meaning of the term "mistake of law", but subject to section 6(2)(a) of this Act, a mistake in the interpretation of a document is a mistake of law.
> (3) There is a contract for the purposes of this Act where a contract would have come into existence but for circumstances of the kind described in section 6(1)(a) of this Act.

This definition is more than somewhat lacking in clarity, and, so far, the case law has done little to give any greater certainty to the law. Generally the Courts have taken the view that anything which was a mistake at common law is to be regarded as a mistake for the purposes of the Act: see *Slater Wilmshurst Ltd v Crown Group Custodian Ltd* [1991] 1 NZLR 344, 357. There are some matters which are clear. Any mistake for which relief under the Act is sought must be a mistake made prior to or at the point of entering into the contract. A mistake, made after the contract has been formed, as to the operation of agreed and understood terms cannot be relied on. So in *N B Hunt & Sons Ltd v Maori Trustee* [1986] 2 NZLR 641 a mistaken application of an agreed rent review clause was held to be a matter for which relief under the Act could not be given.

The Act will apply to mistaken beliefs. These are taken as mistakes of fact, at least as long as the belief relates to present or past fact: *Shivas v Bank of New Zealand* [1990] 2 NZLR 327, 356. A mistaken belief, for the purposes of the Act, can exist where the party claiming mistake did at one time know the true facts, but has since forgotten them, as in *Slater Wilmshurst Ltd v Crown Group Custodian Ltd*, supra. In that case the defendants contracted to sell a building to the plaintiffs, each forgetful of the fact that the tenant of the building had a right of pre-emption over the building. In such cases, the mistake alleged can, albeit with some difficulty, be described as involving a turning of the mind to the relevant issue. It is probable that there is no "mistake" where the mind never turns to the relevant issue at all. A party who gives no thought to whether a particular matter exists or not is ignorant of it, rather than mistaken as to it.

This definition does go further than the common law in one respect – the inclusion of mistake of law. Such mistakes could not be relied on for relief at common law, although equity did recognise them in some, limited circumstances. While generally any mistake in the interpretation of a document is a mistake of law, the importance of the inclusion of mistakes of law is limited by s 6(2)(a) of the Act, which disentitles reliance on a mistake as to the interpretation of the contract itself. This is exemplified by *Shotter v Westpac Banking Corporation* [1988] 2 NZLR 316. There the applicant sought relief for a mistake as to the extent of a guarantee that he had signed. This mistake was one going to the meaning of the contractual document. Relief under the Act was barred by s 2(2).

Section 2(3) makes it clear that the Act applies to cases where contracts would never have come into existence at common law because of a mistake by one or both parties. The provision appears to endorse the objective view of contract formation: see 3.1 above. If a reasonable bystander would think that there was a contract, then there will be one for the purposes of the Act, even in fact if there was no true agreement on the facts actually existing: *Mechenex Pacific Services Ltd v TCA Airconditioning (New Zealand) Ltd* [1991] 2 NZLR 393, 397.

(b) MISTAKES WHICH MAY GIVE RISE TO RELIEF

Assuming there is an identifiable mistake, the applicant for relief must then satisfy each of the criteria for relief in s 6. Section 6 enables relief to be granted where mistake by one party is known to the opposite party or is common or mutual. It provides that:

(1) A Court may in the course of any proceedings or on application made for the purpose grant relief under section 7 of this Act to any party to a contract—
(a) If in entering into that contract—
(i) That party was influenced in his decision to enter into the contract by a mistake that was material to him, and the existence of the mistake was known to the other party or one or more of the other parties to the contract (not being a party or parties having substantially the same interest under the contract as the party seeking relief); or
(ii) All the parties to the contract were influenced in their respective decisions to enter into the contract by the same mistake; or
(iii) That party and at least one other party (not being a party having substantially the same interest under the contract as the party seeking relief) were each influenced in their respective decisions to enter into the contract by a different mistake about the same matter of fact or of law; and
(b) The mistake or mistakes, as the case may be, resulted at the time of the contract—
(i) In a substantially unequal exchange of values; or
(ii) In the conferment of a benefit, or in the imposition or inclusion of an obligation, which was, in all the circumstances, a benefit or obligation substantially disproportionate to the consideration therefor; and
(c) Where the contract expressly or by implication makes provisions for the risk of mistakes, the party seeking relief or the party through or under whom relief is sought, as the case may require, is not obliged by a term of the contract to assume the risk that his belief about the matter in question might be mistaken.

The Act thus requires that an applicant for relief establish three distinct and different matters before relief is available. These are

(i)   a mistake of the kind set out in s 6(1)(a);
(ii)   an unequal exchange of value arising from the mistake;
(iii)   that the contract did not impose on the applicant for relief the onus of bearing any risk of mistake.

It should be noted that in all instances, the person seeking relief need only have been *"influenced"* in the decision to enter the contract by the mistake. The Courts have placed little emphasis on this element, but it reflects a lower threshold than the "fundamental" mistake needed at common law.

(c) A MISTAKE QUALIFYING FOR RELIEF UNDER s 6(1)(A)

The simplest form of qualifying mistake is that of unilateral mistake known to the other party, as provided for in s 6(1)(a)(i). This head of mistake has not been the subject of any extensive judicial discussion since the Act came into force. The section was designed primarily to cover the common law "rogue" cases, where a fraudulent purchaser passed himself or herself off as a person of substance. The subsection provision will cover these cases (though the application of the Act to them may be limited by s 8: see 5.3.2, infra) but will also have effect where one party seeks to take advantage of an erroneous belief formed independently by the other party.

More common have been cases arising under s 6(1)(a)(ii), where both parties have been influenced in deciding to enter the contract by a shared misapprehension as to the true state of affairs. This cases are usually referred to as "common mistake" cases. The operation of the subsection can be seen in *Ware v Johnson* [1984] 2 NZLR 518 where the parties to a contract for the sale and purchase of a kiwifruit orchard both believed that the orchard would be producing commercial quantities of fruit by a certain date. The orchard did not do so because of the long-term effects of herbicide sprays used. Prichard J accepted that was a common mistake as to the likely date of commercial production. As *Ware v Johnson* itself shows, common mistake cases may well overlap with cases of innocent or negligent misrepresentation under the Contractual Remedies Act 1979.

Section 6(1)(a)(iii) presents rather more of a conceptual problem. On its wording, the section ought to apply in cases where the parties were both mistaken, but in different ways, about the same matter. Suppose A contracts to buy a car from B, thinking the car to be only two years old; B thinks it is five years old and it is in fact three years old. A and B have made different mistakes as to the same matter – the age of the car. Cases where there are genuine different errors as to the same matter of fact will be rare.

A major source of difficulty with subs (iii), indeed with the whole Act as a result, is that the subsection was apparently also intended to allow relief in the circumstances known at common law as "mutual mistake". As illustrated in the classic case of *Raffles v Wichelhaus* (1864) 2 H & C 906; 159 ER 375, this comprised cases where the parties had reached an apparent agreement but the terms used were not being used in the same sense. The latent ambiguity meant that there was no real agreement. However "mutual mistake" is itself a misleading term; in reality such cases do not involve mistakes by both parties. One party is right, the other wrong, about the true meaning of the contract or agreement. The stumbling-block is that the Court cannot determine which party is right and which is wrong.

The first case under the Act to reach the Court of Appeal was *Conlon v Ozolins* [1984] 1 NZLR 489. In that case a majority of the Court held that relief was available in just such a "cross-purposes" case. The contract concerned the sale of land owned by the appellant to the respondent. The contract provided for the sale of four lots of land, one of which was contiguous to the appellant's home and was used by her as part of her garden. It was separated from the other three lots by a fence. The purchaser believed the area to be sold to be four lots. Woodhouse P and McMullin J took the view that the appellant's mistake (that the contract did not provide for the sale of the lot used as part of her garden) and the respondent's "mistake" (that the vendor intended to sell all four lots) were different mistakes about the same matter of fact (the boundaries of the land to be sold). Somers J dissented, holding that there were not different mistakes about the same matter of fact. Somers J took the view that s 6(1)(a)(iii) was not applicable to "either-or" situations of this kind. One party must have been correct in his or her view of the true facts, and therefore it could not be said that the parties were both mistaken.

The Court of Appeal reconsidered the issue in *Paulger v Butland Industries Ltd* [1989] 3 NZLR 549. In that case Paulger sent to the creditors of a company, of which he was the managing director, a letter in which he urged them to maintain supplies to the company, and finished with the words, "The writer personally guarantees that all due payments will be made". Later the respondent sued on the alleged guarantee in the letter. Paulger sought relief under the Contractual Mistakes Act, arguing, inter alia, that subs (iii) applied. The allegation was that each party had made different mistakes as to the same matter, the source of the funds to pay any creditors, Paulger thinking it would come from a sale of assets by the company, the creditor thinking that the money would come from Paulger personally. In essence, this posed the same legal issue as did *Conlon v Ozolins:* whether there was a qualifying mistake where two parties had formed different views about the effect of a document, where one of the parties was in fact right and the other wrong. The Court of Appeal in *Paulger* held that relief was not available under the Act. It held that *Conlon v Ozolins* was a decision on its own particular facts, thereby losing any authority it had, but did not specifically overrule it. However, it now seems clear that there is no mistake under s 6(1)(a)(iii) where one party thinks his or her plain words mean something other than they do when objectively examined. Thus if A says something which means X, and B thinks it means X, the fact that A thinks it means Y is no ground for relief. It should also be noted that the actual decision in *Paulger*'s case was supported on the basis that the alleged mistake would also have been a mistake as to the interpretation of the contractual document, and therefore relief was prevented by the combined effect of ss 2(3) and 6(2)(a). The prominence given to those sections may well indicate that the Court will be less willing to construe a mistake as going to a matter outside the contractual document.

(d) SECTION 6(1)(b) – INEQUALITY OF EXCHANGE
Even though there may have been a mistake qualifying under s 6(1)(a), no relief can be granted unless a substantially unequal exchange of value has resulted. Thus if a party to a mistaken contract gets a thing different from that which was intended, but the thing received is of comparable value to that which was intended, there is no relief under the Act. The Courts have given little detailed consideration to the interpretation of the phrases "substantially unequal" and "substantially disproportionate". At most, it emerges as a matter of degree, and perhaps of impression on the particular facts. In *Conlon v Ozolins* [1984] 1 NZLR 489, one of the few cases where disparity of value has been seriously in issue, the majority of the Court of Appeal held, differing from the trial Judge, that s 6(1)(b) was satisfied. The evidence as to valuation left the value of the land unresolved. The disparity in price was perhaps 25 per cent on the vendor's valuation, less than 10 per cent on the evidence called by the purchaser. The higher differential might well be thought to be "substantial"; the

lower is less clearly so. By way of contrast, in *Wijeyeratne v Medical Assurance Society of NZ Ltd* [1991] 2 NZLR 332, the payment of a substantial insurance premium when no insurance cover was obtained was treated as being a manifest case of inequality of exchange.

(e) SECTION 6(1)(c) – PROVISION FOR RISK OF MISTAKE
This subsection simply means that if the parties have in some way contemplated that one or other or both may make assumptions as to the circumstances which are wrong, the person who is to carry the risk of error cannot seek relief if it turns out that there was indeed a mistake. Express provision for risk of mistake is not common; ascertainment of boundaries in real estate transactions being perhaps the most usual. Implied risk of mistake may be more common. The class of case where s 6(1)(c) can apply is illustrated by *Dennis Friedman (Earthmovers) Ltd v Rodney County Council* [1988] 1 NZLR 184, 192. The plaintiff had carried out works for the Council and now sought extra payment for costs incurred because the physical conditions under which the work had to be performed had made the work slower and more expensive than had been envisaged. However, the terms of the contract had required the plaintiff to satisfy himself as to the conditions in which the work would be performed. Relief was refused on the basis that the contractor was required to assume the risk of the conditions not being as he expected, or could reasonably have foreseen, them to be. As the difficulties were reasonably foreseeable, s 6(1)(c) prevented relief.

5.3.2 Relief for mistake

Section 7 of this Act gives the Court very wide powers to achieve what it thinks is a fair result to an applicant who seeks relief. The Court may enforce the contract, in whole or in part, or cancel it, or vary it. It may order the payment of restitution or compensation or order the vesting of property in particular persons. These powers can be exercised with or without conditions being attached.

It should be noted that this relief may be sought by a party to the mistaken contract or by someone to whom it is material to know whether relief would be granted, and relief may be given to a party to the contract or to someone claiming through or under that party.

This very wide discretion to grant relief or withhold it is subject to certain limits however. The Court is to have regard to who caused the mistake in determining whether to give relief (s 7(2)). It cannot give relief to a person who has affirmed the contract after discovering his or her mistake (s 6(2)(b)) and it is not to exercise its powers to grant relief in such a way as to prejudice the security of contractual relationships generally (s 4(2)).

More importantly, the powers of the Courts are limited where property which was the subject matter of the contract has passed into the hands of a third party. Dispositions by a party to the mistaken contract to a third party who acts without notice of the mistaken contract and furnishes good consideration cannot be invalidated by any order of the Court under the Act (s 8). This provision causes considerable difficulty in the "rogue" cases. The central problem is that there are two different transactions by the rogue, either or both of which may be mistaken contracts for the purposes of the Contractual Mistakes Act. On one view, the rogue is a party to a mistaken contract between himself or herself and the vendor of property, and therefore the subsequent purchaser from the rogue is then protected by s 8. On another view, the critical contract is the one between the rogue and the subsequent purchaser. The Courts can then adjust matters as between the purchaser and the vendor without falling foul of s 8. The issue is discussed in detail by McLauchlan (1983) 10 NZULR 199 and (1986) 12 NZULR 123 and also in *Cheshire Fifoot and Furmston's Law of Contract* (7th NZ edition) pp 253-54. Until the issue is resolved by the Courts, the effect of s 8 must remain obscure.

In determining how to use its powers to grant relief, the Courts must have regard to the statutory guide-lines provided by s 7(2), which requires the Courts to take into account the extent to which the applicant for relief, or the person through whom such an application is made, "caused" the mistake, and s 4(2) which enjoins the Courts to ensure the preservation of contractual certainty generally. Although neither provision has received any detailed consideration by the Courts, it is clear that the approach of the Courts is now in general harmony with them. If one party, or that party's agent, has deliberately or carelessly induced a mistaken belief on the part of the other party, relief under the Act will generally not be available: *Australian Guarantee Corporation (NZ) Ltd v Wyness* [1987] 2 NZLR 326. It is also clear that the Courts will generally be reluctant to allow a party to gain relief under the Act from which that party would be disentitled under the general law; see *Slater Wilmshurst Ltd v Crown Group Custodian Ltd* [1991] 1 NZLR 344, 358.

5.3.3 The relationship of the Act to other areas of law

The Contractual Mistakes Act is a code (s 5) and as such completely replaces the old law of mistake, including evidential rules which might have prevented one party proving his or her mistake (*Conlon v Ozolins*, supra, overruling *McCullough v McGrath's Stock and Poultry Ltd* [1981] 2 NZLR 428).

There are a number of areas which may impinge on mistaken contract cases which are preserved (s 5(2)) including rectification, non est factum, undue influence, fraud, misrepresentation, breach of fiduciary duty, illegality, frustration, recovery of money paid under a mistake of fact (ss 94A and 94B of the Judicature Act 1908) and the discretion to refuse a decree of specific performance. It is important to note that nothing in this section prevents an applicant for relief for mistake seeking alternative remedies under a heading not affected by the Contractual Mistakes Act. Thus relief under the statute can be sought along with a plea of non est factum *(Conlon v Ozolins)*, or mistake and misrepresentation may be coupled together: see, for example, *Ware v Johnson* [1984] 2 NZLR 518. Indeed cases of misrepresentation generally involve mistakes, either by the person innocently or negligently representing the true facts or in the mind of a person to whom a deliberate misrepresentation is made. In such cases relief is available under the Contractual Remedies Act 1979. However, damages for misrepresentation under the Contractual Remedies Act are available as of right; relief under the Contractual Mistakes Act is discretionary. It is therefore not surprising that litigants have generally preferred to rely on misrepresentation rather than mistake. A similar procedure would be possible in most of the other preserved areas;

there is no reason why a claim for relief in mistake could not be made as an alternative to, say, one for relief for a contract procured by undue influence.

5.3.4 Rectification

This equitable doctrine allows the Court to amend the terms of a written document in some circumstances. The document may be a contractual document or an instrument creating an interest in land such as a lease: *Wellington City Council v New Zealand Law Society* [1988] 2 NZLR 614, affirmed [1990] 2 NZLR 22; or a mortgage: *Barber v Barber* [1987] 1 NZLR 426; *Westland Savings Bank Ltd v Hancock* [1987] 2 NZLR 21.

The most common ground for rectification is that the document fails to record accurately the parties' common intention. In these cases it is not essential that a prior oral contract has been made which was later reduced to writing; it suffices if the written document which concludes the formation of the contract wrongly expresses a common contractual intention of the parties: *Joscelyne v Nissen* [1970] 2 QB 86; 1 All ER 1213.

A very good example of the operation of the doctrine in this kind of case is provided by *Dundee Farms v Bambury Holdings* [1976] 2 NZLR 747, affirmed by the Court of Appeal [1978] 1 NZLR 647. Here the parties entered into an agreement for the sale and purchase of a farm. The farmland was held in three titles, but in the formal agreement for sale and purchase a fourth piece of land was also listed. This land, though also owned by the vendor, was several miles from the farm. The Courts held that the clear intention of the parties was the sale of the farm only and thus the document should be rectified by removing from it the reference to the separate piece of land.

Relief by way of rectification is not available where the parties were affected by some mistake in their decision to enter the agreement actually reached, but the mistaken agreement has been correctly recorded. In *Frederick E Rose London Ltd v William H Pim Jnr and Co* [1953] 2 QB 450; 2 All ER 739, a written contract for horsebeans was not rectified. The parties had conducted their negotiations on the mistaken assumption that horsebeans could be supplied to consumers as "feveroles" when, in fact, they could not. The Court held the parties had in contemplation the supply of horsebeans and that was what the contract provided.

Any person seeking rectification undertakes a severe evidential burden. There will need to be clear evidence of a common intention which was not reflected in the contractual document. The party seeking rectification must establish, on the balance of probabilities, not merely that the contractual document is incorrect, but that there existed an agreement in different terms. If there was an earlier contractual agreement in the same terms as the one now sought to be rectified, there is a particularly heavy onus to show that the common intention of the parties had altered since the earlier document: *Barber v Barber*, supra. When the Court is determining whether the document correctly recorded the parties' intentions, it may look at the parties' actions to see whether or not their actions indicate agreement with the document. In *Westland Savings Bank Ltd v Hancock* supra, the plaintiff bank sought rectification of a mortgage document to include a provision for regular review of the interest rate, a provision which was usual in its mortgages. Evidence that the parties had previously acted as if the clause had been included (the bank by altering the rates charged, and the defendant by acquiescing in such changes) was admissible to show the common intention of the parties.

Rectification may also be available where only the applicant for relief was mistaken as to the contents of the contractual document, provided that the Court is satisfied that it is inequitable for the document to apply in its extant form. This may be because one party realises, prior to the completion of the document, that an error has been made and keeps silent in order to obtain a benefit under the document which would not otherwise have been received. The issue is whether enforcement of the document in its terms would be inequitable: *Westland Savings Bank Ltd v Hancock*, supra. This does not require proof of sharp practice or fraud by a party, it can be enough that the party seeking rectification is now in a disadvantaged position: see *Bates v Wyndhams* [1981] 1 All ER 1087 and *Roberts and Co v Leicestershire CC* [1961] Ch 555; 2 All ER 545.

Rectification is a discretionary remedy. It may be refused, even if the normal grounds for it are made out, if there has been excessive delay in seeking the remedy or if it would be otherwise unfair to the other party to the agreement. What will be excessive delay, or unfairness, will depend on the particular facts of each case: see *Barber v Barber* and *Wellington City Council v New Zealand Law Society*, supra.

5.3.5 Non est factum

This plea in answer to an action based on a document is literally "This is not my deed". Its origins lie in the medieval common law applied to persons who were unable to verify the contents of documents which they had executed – the blind and the illiterate. In later centuries it has widened to allow the plea to be used by persons able to check the document but who have not done so.

The law relating to non est factum is largely that laid down by the House of Lords in *Gallie v Lee* [1971] AC 1004; sub nom *Saunders v Anglia Building Society* [1970] 3 All ER 961. In that case an elderly woman attempted to use the doctrine to invalidate the transfer of the lease of her house. She had intended to transfer it to her nephew to allow him to raise money on the security the lease offered. The document she executed, without verifying the contents – her spectacles were broken – in fact was a transfer by sale to Lee, a confederate of her nephew, and did not include her intended reservation of a life tenancy of the property. Lee raised a mortgage on the property and decamped with the proceeds.

The House of Lords held the plea was not available. Two prime requisites for it to apply are that the document signed is one that is of a "radically" or "fundamentally" or "basically" different nature from what it is believed to be, and that there has been no negligence or lack of care by the signatory. Both of these points were decided against the appellant – the transfer to Lee was not sufficiently different from a transfer to her nephew and she had not taken adequate care in signing the document.

As *Gallie v Lee* and subsequent cases show, the factual and legal basis for non est factum is hard to establish. The plea requires very clear evidence of the signatory's mistake. Perhaps more importantly, the plea is rarely going to be available to a person of full age and intelligence. In *IFC Securities v Sewell* [1990] 1 NZLR 177 the defendants, who were sharebrokers, were held liable on personal guarantees they had given for the indebtedness of loans to a company in which they held shares. The Judge held that even if the defendants had been mistaken as to the documents they signed, they were of full age and competence, and could not be allowed to claim they did not appreciate the nature of the documents they had signed. *IFC Securities v Sewell* can be contrasted with the successful raising of the plea in *Chiswick Investments v Pevats* [1990] 1 NZLR 169. In that case the defendant had signed a loan document as a witness, but had expressly indicated he was not signing as a guarantor of the loan, a matter provided for in the same document. It was held that the signature as a witness amounted, in law, to a signature to the guarantee as well. However, the defendant was not liable on the guarantee as his plea of non est factum was successful. The document clearly had a radically different effect from that which he expected, or which any ordinary person would have expected. In effect he had made a reasonable mistake as to the effects of his signature, and could therefore not be said to have been negligent or careless as to the content of the document.

The restrictive approach to the availability of non est factum is firmly based in policy considerations; where the plea succeeds, it can jeopardise third parties who may have relied on the validity of the document now impugned. The importance of this policy consideration was accepted in *Conlon v Ozolins* [1984] 1 NZLR 489. Where no third party is or has been involved, the plea may be more readily available. It is clear that where one party has signed a document under a mistake which was induced or caused by the party now seeking to rely on the document, the Courts will allow the plea more readily: *Petelin v Cullen* (1975) 6 ALR 129, 49 ALJR 239; *Landzeal Group Ltd v Kyne* [1990] 3 NZLR 574, 580-81. However, this relaxation only applies, even in the absence of third parties, if the party seeking to enforce the document was at fault in causing the mistake: *Conlon v Ozolins*, supra.

5.4 ILLEGALITY

5.4.1 General

At common law illegal contracts posed great conceptual and practical difficulties to the Courts. The law was eventually greatly modified in New Zealand by the enactment of the Illegal Contracts Act 1970. The common law regarding illegality is therefore not always of relevance, and some aspects are not discussed in great detail here. The common law rules developed from the Courts holding various kinds of contracts to be illegal and therefore unenforceable, because the contracts in some way involved some matter which was seen as damaging to society. The harm had, however, to be perceived as serious enough to justify the imposition of the sometimes harsh and unfair consequences of holding the contract to be illegal. Public policy is therefore at the root of all the common law rules, and is still of great importance under the Act.

5.4.2 What is an "illegal contract"?

The Illegal Contracts Act does not define what is or may be an illegal contract, although s 3 provides:

Subject to s 5 of this Act, for the purposes of this Act the term "illegal contract" means any contract that is illegal at law or in equity, whether the illegality arises from the creation or performance of the contract, and includes a contract which contains an illegal provision, whether that provision is severable or not.

Thus the common law rules defining an illegal contract are still operative although, as discussed infra, several of them are modified by the provisions of the Act. The final part of s 3 referring to severability concerns the common law doctrine of severance. Under that doctrine the Courts could sometimes enforce the legal parts of a contract which contained some illegal provisions by severing from the contract these illegal provisions. This could only be done where the substance of the whole agreement was not radically affected by the severance: *Goldsoll v Goldman* [1915] 1 Ch 292; *Attwood* v *Lamont* [1920] 3 KB 571. The doctrine of severance now survives only in regard to restraint of trade cases and there only in the statutory form set out in s 8 of the Illegal Contracts Act. This area is discussed infra, para 5.4.6.

(a) CONTRACTS WHICH ARE VOID BUT NOT ILLEGAL
The common law rules relating to contracts contrary to public policy distinguished between contracts which were void and those which were illegal. There were three recognised categories of cases where the contract might be void but not illegal – contracts ousting the Court's jurisdiction, contracts in restraint of trade and contracts prejudicing the freedom and security of marriage. Contracts in restraint of trade are considered infra para 5.4.5. The others merit brief discussion.

(1) *Contracts ousting the Court's jurisdiction:* The common law position as to these is specifically preserved by s 11 of the Act and so the Courts can continue to hold the view that any provision which purports to deprive one or both parties to a contract of the right to seek legal redress is illegal: *Lee v Showmen's Guild of Great Britain* [1952] 2 QB 329. A provision in a contract which requires the right to seek legal redress to be exercised in a particular way, for example, only after attempting to resolve a dispute by going to arbitration, is not illegal: *Scott v Avery* (1865) 5 HL Cas 811.

(2) *Contracts affecting the freedom and security of marriage:* Contracts which attempt to prevent a person from marrying at all, or very heavily restrict their marital opportunities were invalid at common law: see *Lowe v Peers* (1768) 4 Burr 2225, as was any contract which had a likelihood of imperilling an existing secure marriage: see *Fender v St John Mildway* [1938] AC 1. In view of changes in social policy, it may be doubted whether the rule continues in its full breadth, or indeed at all.

(b) ILLEGALITY AT COMMON LAW
The categories of common law illegality are now closed: *Fender v St John Mildway* [1938] AC 1. Thus only the recognised heads of illegality exist. These can be summarised as being:

(1) *Contracts in breach of a statute:* see p 89.

(2) *Contracts to commit a crime, a tort or a fraud on a third party:* As to commission of a tort, see *Mallalieu v Hodgson* (1851) 16 QBD 689. The

common law regarded any contract where the parties had agreed to the commission of a crime as illegal: eg *Bigos v Boustead* [1951] 1 All ER 92, whether or not the parties were aware that their acts would be criminal: *Belvoir Finance Co v Stapleton* [1971] 1 QB 210. This element of the rule is affected by the Illegal Contracts Act 1970, in that not all acts in breach of a statute are illegal (see below), and the good faith of the parties is of considerable importance in determining whether to grant relief: see 5.4.4.

(3) *Contracts directly or indirectly interfering with the course of justice:* This line of cases is exemplified by contracts to pay money to stifle a prosecution or to reimburse a person who has paid money for such a purpose: *Slater v Mall Finance and Investment Ltd* [1976] NZLR 1, affirmed [1976] 2 NZLR 685; *Barsdell v Kerr* [1979] 2 NZLR 731. If a term of a contract has the effect of hindering investigation of an offence, it may be illegal under this head; thus in *A v Hayden* (1985) 56 ALR 82 a contractual term of confidentiality which would have prevented an employer from divulging the names of employees to the police was struck down. The common law rule also prohibited contracts for maintenance (the stirring up of civil litigation by supporting a person to bring an action without due cause) and champerty (assistance with litigation in which one has no personal interest in return for a share of any eventual reward).

(4) *Contracts to defraud the revenue:* Any contract which seeks to defraud local or national governments of taxation properly due is illegal: *Napier v National Business Agency Ltd* [1951] 2 All ER 264; *Alexander v Rayson* [1936] 1 KB 169. However the rule requires that the aim of the contract is such an evasion; it is not enough that some contractual provision might enable one party to evade taxation: *Herbison v Papakura Video Ltd (No 2)* [1987] 2 NZLR 720.

(5) *Contracts which injure the State in its relations with other states:* This will include trading with the enemy in time of war as well as contracts which involve or contemplate performance by acts which are illegal in the country in which they will be committed: *Foster v Driscoll* [1929] 1 KB 470; *Regazzoni v KC Sethia (1944) Ltd* [1958] AC 301. The rule appears now to include contracts which require acts which are contrary to the public policy of both the foreign state and the country where legal proceedings are brought, even if the acts are not illegal in either country: *Lemenda Trading Co Ltd v African Middle East Petroleum Ltd* [1988] QB 448.

(6) *Contracts injuring the public service:* These will include contracts not to serve in the armed forces as well as contracts to use improper influence to affect the award of honours: *Parkinson v College of Ambulance Ltd* [1925] 2 KB 1, or to affect the decision of a governmental official: *Lemenda Trading Co Ltd v African Middle East Petroleum Ltd*, supra.

(7) *Contracts which promote sexual immorality:* This rule is not now applied as broadly as in some earlier cases. In the older cases, any contract in which performance was related to, or tainted by, sexual intercourse outside marriage, would be considered illegal. That attitude has now largely passed away: compare *Pearce v Brooks* (1866) LR 1 Ex 213 with *Somma v Hazlehurst* [1979] 1 WLR 1014.

(c) ILLEGALITY BY BREACH OF A STATUTE

At common law, there was great difficulty in determining whether a contract was or was not void for breach of a statute. It is common in modern statutes for the Act itself to stipulate what the position is to be if a contract would breach its provisions. This may be to make any such contract invalid because of the breach, but to exclude relief under the Illegal Contracts Act 1970 (as with the Credit Contracts Act 1981, the Commerce Act 1986 and certain types of wagering and gaming contracts under the Gaming and Lotteries Act 1977). The statute may even provide that a breach of the Act does not make the contract illegal at all: for example, the Employment Contracts Act 1991, s 25. Most, though not all, of the remaining difficulties are resolved by s 5 of Illegal Contracts Act which provides:

> A contract lawfully entered into shall not become illegal or unenforceable by any party by reason of the fact that its performance is in breach of any enactment unless the enactment expressly so provides or its object clearly so requires.

It is possible to analyse contracts in breach of a statute as coming within one of three categories. These are:

(1) *Contracts which are not illegal but are void or unenforceable:* There are many rules of law which prescribe certain formalities which must be observed in any contract (eg see ch 2.3) and provide that such contracts are void and unenforceable if the requirements as to form or procedure are not met. If a statutory rule as to form or procedure is not complied with, the contract is void or unenforceable, but it is not illegal.

(2) *Contracts which are void and illegal at their inception:* Here we are concerned with cases where certain types of contract, at least in some circumstances, are made unlawful by a statute. Examples may be found in such statutes as the Land Settlement Promotion and Land Acquisition Act 1952, s 25(4) (aggregation of farm land); the Companies Act 1955, s 62 (provision of funds by a public company for purchase of its own shares) and the Race Relations Act ss 3-7 (discrimination in regard to services, accommodation etc). In most cases the illegal nature of the contract will be explicit, but in some cases it may be established by inference: as to which see *Lower Hutt City Council v Martin* [1987] 1 NZLR 321.

(3) *Illegality because of the mode of performance:* Here the contract will be one which could be performed entirely within the law, but one or both parties breach the law in performing their respective contractual obligations. If, for instance, the completion of a contract requires a licence or approval of some kind, the contract can be lawfully performed by obtaining the licence or approval. If no licence is obtained the contract will be illegal: *Carey v Hastie* [1968] NZLR 276. (If the parties originally contemplated performance without the requisite licence, the contract would be illegal at inception: *Bigos v Bousted* [1951] 1 All ER 92).

The common law position in regard to this third category has been modified by s 5 of the Act. The Courts now have to look to whether the statute regulating conduct involved in performance of a contract expressly or impliedly makes the contract illegal if the statute is contravened. It may be difficult to establish an implied intention of Parliament to make a contract illegal merely because some part of the performance of the contract breaches some element of a statute. The point is well illustrated by *Automobile Centre (Auckland) Ltd v Facer* [1974] 2 NZLR 767 where Cooke J held that a breach of the requirement (imposed by reg 86 of the Traffic Regulations 1976) that every car being sold have a current warrant of fitness did not make the contract for the sale of the car illegal. The object of the regulation was road safety, not consumer protection, and thus the purpose of the regulations was not being frustrated.

5.4.3 The consequences of illegality

These are provided by s 6 of the Illegal Contracts Act which provides, in s 6(1):

> Notwithstanding any rule of law or equity to the contrary, but subject to the provisions of this Act and of any other enactment, every illegal contract shall be of no effect and no person shall become entitled to any property under a disposition made by or pursuant to any such contract.

Thus the whole contract is illegal and has no effect. No interest in any property which is the subject matter of, or the consideration for, the contract passes, and thus the owner of such property can reclaim it. There is a savings provision in s 6(2) which preserves the position of any third party dealing, in good faith and without knowledge of the illegality, with one of the parties to the illegal contracts. In effect, the Act secures for such a third party the rights he would have acquired to any property had the original contract been valid and capable of passing interests in the property to the person with whom he dealt.

5.4.4 Relief in illegal contract cases

The most important effect of the Illegal Contracts Act was to give the Courts a discretionary power to alleviate the effects of illegality in proper cases. This power is granted and delimited by s 7 of the Act which provides that relief by way of restitution, compensation, variation or validation (in whole or part) of the contract or otherwise may be granted to any party to an illegal contract or someone claiming through or under such a party "Notwithstanding the provisions of s 6 of this Act, but subject to the express provisions of any other enactment". (s 7(1)).

The main issue raised by s 7(1) has been the determination of the meaning of "subject to the provisions of any other enactment". After some uncertainty in the early discussions of the statute, it is now clear that a mere statement that a contract is unlawful and of no effect does not oust the jurisdiction of the Courts to grant relief under s 7: *Harding v Coburn* [1976] 2 NZLR 577; *Ross v Henderson* [1976] 2 NZLR 589, affirmed by the Privy Council [1977] 2 NZLR 458. The reasoning of the Court of Appeal in these cases was that if a statute declared a contract to be unlawful and of no effect, it was establishing the state of affairs in which the Illegal Contracts Act was intended to operate – such invalidity is a prerequisite for relief. There may be a few instances where the statute breached provides for a particular result in all cases. Such a provision may be seen as so inconsistent with discretionary relief under the Illegal Contracts Act as to show a legislative intention to oust any jurisdiction under the Act to grant relief: see *Harding v Coburn* [1976] 2 NZLR 577, 585ff. However, such a result will be uncommon. The Courts have generally been reluctant to find that the jurisdiction to grant relief has been excluded. In *National Westminster Finance New Zealand Ltd v South Pacific Rent-a-car Ltd* [1985] 1 NZLR 646 it was held that a statute which provided for a particular result to apply on breach did not oust jurisdiction under the Illegal Contracts Act. The Court of Appeal held that the statutory remedy was contingent on the contract remaining illegal; if the illegal contract was validated, it was not to be considered as illegal and in breach of the statute, and therefore the specific remedy provided ceased to apply. Discretionary relief under the Illegal Contracts Act was therefore not inconsistent with the statute's own fixed remedy. Later decisions have gone even further than *National Westminster Finance New Zealand Ltd v South Pacific Rent-a-car Ltd* in interpreting the statutes so as to preserve the capacity to grant relief. In *Re AIC Merchant Finance Ltd* [1990] 2 NZLR 385, the Court of Appeal was dealing with an application for relief by persons who had deposited moneys with a finance house, where there was at the relevant time no valid prospectus to enable them to rank as secured creditors. The Securities Act 1978 provided that its provisions were to have effect notwithstanding anything to the contrary in any other enactment. The Court of Appeal held that the statutory priority of the Securities Act provision meant that validation of the contracts was not possible. However other forms of relief could be granted, if appropriate. In the result, the receiver was ordered to treat the unsecured creditors as if there had been a valid security; an order which had an effect indistinguishable from validation.

The power to grant relief, although very wide, is subject to certain limitations. The Court is to have regard to the conduct of the parties (s 7(3)(a)), any knowledge they may have had of the facts or law giving rise to the illegality (s 7(4)) and, in breach of statute cases, the object of the statute and the penalty, if any, provided for a breach of it (s 7(3)(b)). The Court may have regard to other matters (s 7(3)(c)) but is subject to an overriding factor that relief shall not be given if it is not in the public interest to do so.

The extent of the discretion given by the section makes it impossible to give more than a general indication of the way in which the Courts use the powers conferred by the Act. The primary question will be whether the policy underlying the statute or common law rule which created the illegality would be frustrated by the granting of relief in the particular circumstances before the Court. A good example is the line of cases concerned with breaches of the Land Settlement Promotion and Land Acquisition Act 1952, the aim of which is to prevent individuals attaining an undue aggregation of land. The Courts have been willing to validate such contracts where no real issue of aggregation could arise, as in *Harding v Coburn* [1976] 2 NZLR 577 and *Hurrell v Townend* [1982] 1 NZLR 536, but where a real issue as to aggregation arose, the contract has been varied to make it conditional on the necessary official consents under the Act being obtained, as in *McLachlan v Taylor* [1985] 2 NZLR 277 and *France v Hight* [1987] 2 NZLR 38, affirmed [1990] 1 NZLR 345. The same pragmatic approach has been adopted in many other contexts. That same public interest requirement will prevent validation or relief in cases of serious criminal conduct or interference with justice: *Barsdell v Kerr* [1979] 2 NZLR 731; *Slater v Mall Finance and Investment Co Ltd* [1976] 2 NZLR 1; [1976] 2 NZLR 685.

If relief is to be available, its form is essentially to be considered on the basis of fairness as between the parties. The Courts take the view that s 7 is not to be used to increase the penalties applicable to a party who breaches a statute: *Broadlands Rentals v RD Bull Ltd* [1976] 2 NZLR 595. Equally, relief will not be granted if it would result in an unfair windfall profit to one party: *House v Jones* [1985] 2 NZLR 288. The extent to which the party seeking relief was aware of the illegality is highly relevant: *Hurrell v Townend* supra, and *Leith v Gould* [1986] 1 NZLR 760. Other aspects of the conduct of the parties may be relevant, delay in seeking a remedy may operate to prevent relief: *House v Jones* supra. The interests of any third parties affected must also be considered, and, where appropriate, their positions safeguarded: see as examples *National Westminster Finance New Zealand Ltd v South Pacific Rent-a-car Ltd* supra, and *Re AIC Merchant Finance* supra.

5.4.5 Contracts in restraint of trade

The common law regarded contracts which acted in restraint of trade – ie limited the freedom of one or both parties to carry on as they saw fit their trade, profession or employment – as prima facie void as being contrary to public policy. However, if the restraint could be shown to be reasonable, the restrictive covenant (the operative part of a restraint of trade contract) would be held valid. The onus of proving validity is on the person seeking to enforce the covenant: *Blackler v NZRFL* [1968] NZLR 547 and the cases discussed therein.

The Courts have recognised that to establish the validity of a restraint of trade agreement, it must be shown that:

(a) There is a valid interest to be protected: *Vancouver Malt and Sake Brewing Co v Vancouver Breweries Ltd* [1934] AC 1. A bare promise not to compete at all, in any business, would be void, since no one interest is shown to be protected: *Townsend v Jarman* [1900] 2 Ch 698.

(b) That the restraint of trade is reasonable in the circumstances. Reasonableness here comprehends both reasonableness inter partes and reasonableness in terms of public interest. It is also clear that the tests of reasonableness will vary according to the type of interest which is sought to be protected by the restrictive covenant.

The Courts have been quite content to uphold restrictive covenants which are part of a contract for the sale and purchase of a business. The protection of the goodwill of a business purchased is seen as a reasonable and acceptable business practice: *Nordenfeldt v Maxim Nordenfeldt Guns and Ammunition Co* [1894] AC 535; *Brown v Brown* [1980] 1 NZLR 484. The same fairly generous line is taken toward other forms of trade or business regulation, whether this takes the form of market regulation by "solus" agreements (*Esso Petroleum Co Ltd v Harpers Garage (Stourport) Ltd* [1968] AC 269; [1967] 1 All ER 699) or of a trade, profession or calling (*English Hop Growers Ltd v Dering* [1928] 2 KB 174; *Dickson v Pharmaceutical Society of Great Britain* [1967] Ch 708; 2 All ER 558).

These "business" cases can be contrasted with contracts involving a restrictive covenant on future employment or competition between an employer and employee. The trade secrets or consumer goodwill that an employee may acquire from his or her employment are interests of the employer such as can be protected (*Herbert Morris Ltd v Saxelby* [1916]1 AC 688; *H and R Block Ltd v Sanott* [1976]1 NZLR 213), but the Courts do tend to impose a harsher test of reasonableness in such cases: *Mason v Provident Clothing and Supply Co Ltd* [1913] AC 724; *Sanott's* case, supra.

Reasonableness will also depend on the extent and duration of the restriction imposed on the party or parties. If the covenant is unduly long, it is invalid. In the *Esso* case (supra) the covenant for 21 years was invalid, another for four years was valid. In *Brown v Brown*, supra, a 20-year restriction was too long—though in an exceptional case a life ban was upheld: *Connor Bros Ltd v Connors* [1940] 4 All ER 179. Similarly, an overly-wide geographical limitation may be invalid (*Brown v Brown*, supra) although, again, in exceptional circumstances a world-wide covenant was upheld as to that element against an armaments manufacturer (*Nordenfeldt's* case, supra). Where the interest to be protected is not substantial, only restrictions which are very limited in space and time are likely to be valid: *Landzeal Group Ltd v Kyne* [1990] 3 NZLR 574. The wider the covenant, the harder it will be to justify it, especially if one party has the power to abuse the covenant: *McEllistrim v Ballymacelligott Co-op Society* [1919] AC 548 and *Kemp v NZRFL* [1989] 3 NZLR 463.

Reasonableness inter partes will also be affected by the respective bargaining strengths of the parties. If the parties have reached a genuine arm's length agreement, it will be relatively rare for the Courts to review the parties' views of reasonableness, but where there is no such true "bargain" a restraint of trade clause is much more closely scrutinised: *Brown's* case (supra); *A Schroeder Music Publishing Co Ltd v Macauley* [1974] 1 WLR 1308. Indeed, this is the rationale for the Court's less generous approach to employer-employee restrictive covenants.

The public interest is also relevant to reasonableness and a restrictive covenant may be invalid if it is unreasonable in the public interest even though it is reasonable inter partes: *Kores Manufacturing Co Ltd v Kolak Manufacturing Co Ltd* [1959] 1 Ch 108; [1958] 2 All ER 65. Regard must also be had in any restrictive trade practice contract to the Commerce Act 1986, as to which see ch 41 infra.

5.4.6 Restraint of trade contracts and the Illegal Contracts Act

Nothing in the Act affects the doctrine of restraint of trade: s 11(a), but s 8 does give the Courts considerable power to modify unreasonable, and thus invalid, contracts in restraint of trade. There may be some jurisdictional difficulties with restraints of trade provisions in contracts of employment. Disputes as to such contracts will, under the Employment Contracts Act 1991, come before Employment Tribunals, but that Tribunal's jurisdiction does not include the exercise of powers under the Illegal Contracts Act. If the case can be brought before the ordinary Courts or the Employment Court, relief under the Illegal Contracts Act is possible. It is to be hoped that this anomaly will be rectified.

If the contract is valid at common law, it can be enforced by ordinary action in the Courts. In practice, the bulk of cases under the Act arise where the person bound by a restrictive covenant seeks relief under the Act, in the hope that the restraint of trade provision will be declared invalid or will be modified in such a way as to prevent liability arising under it. If the restrictive contract is void only because of unreasonableness, the Courts may sever the unreasonable element and enforce the rest of the contract, or modify the covenant so as to make it reasonable as at the time the contract was entered into, or may decline to enforce it at all. This power is much wider than that given by the common law doctrine of severance (as to which see 5.4.2 supra) and has been exercised in a number of cases such as *H and R Block Ltd v Sanott* [1976] 1 NZLR 213, *Brown v Brown* [1980] 1 NZLR 484 and *Landzeal Group Ltd v Kyne* [1990] 3 NZLR 574. The Courts have shown themselves willing to rewrite restrictive covenants in regard to both duration and geographical scope.

Chapter 6

PRIVITY AND ASSIGNMENT

SUMMARY

6.1   GENERAL
6.2   THE IMPOSITION OF CONTRACTUAL LIABILITIES UPON
        THIRD PARTIES
6.3   THE ACQUISITION OF CONTRACTUAL RIGHTS BY THIRD
        PARTIES
6.4   THE ASSIGNMENT OF CONTRACTUAL RIGHTS

6. 1 GENERAL

There are two limbs to the common law doctrine of privity of contract, one to the effect that a contract cannot impose liabilities on a stranger to it and the other to the effect that a contract cannot confer enforceable rights on a stranger. Legislative intervention in the form of the Contracts (Privity) Act 1982 has left the burden aspect of the doctrine untouched but has largely abrogated the benefit aspect as regards contracts made on or after 1 April 1983, when the Act came into force.

In addition, the benefit of a contract may be transferred to another by way of assignment. This constitutes a well established exception to the privity rule.

6.2 THE IMPOSITION OF CONTRACTUAL LIABILITIES UPON THIRD PARTIES

The general rule is that two persons cannot, by any contract into which they enter, impose liabilities on a third person not a party to the contract. The reason for the rule is simply that a person should not be subjected to contractual obligations without his or her consent. The rule is nonetheless capable of causing injustice or inconvenience in practice and is subject to certain exceptions. When examining these it is helpful to distinguish between contracts concerning land and contracts concerning chattels. Furthermore, the possibility that a person who acquires property in disregard of contractual provisions binding others may be liable to one of the contracting parties in tort should also be taken into account.

6.2.1 Contracts concerning land

At common law the burden of a covenant did not run with the land, except in the case of covenants made between landlord and tenant. In equity, however, the vendor of freehold land could attach to the land restrictive covenants as to its use which would bind future purchasers in certain circumstances. The leading case is *Tulk v Moxhay* (1848) 2 Ph 774. Tulk owned land in Leicester Square and sold the garden in the centre to one Elms, who agreed not to build upon it but to preserve it in its existing condition. The garden was resold several times and finally it was purchased by Moxhay, who was aware of the covenant as to its use. He stated that he intended to build on the land in breach of the covenant and Tulk sought an injunction to restrain him from doing so. The injunction was granted, the Court holding that Moxhay could not in good conscience disregard a contractual obligation affecting the land of which he had notice at the time of purchase.

Originally the rule in *Tulk v Moxhay* was thought to apply whenever a defendant bought land with notice, actual or constructive, that it was subject to a restrictive covenant. It was, however, later confined to cases where the person seeking to enforce the covenant retained in the vicinity land capable of being benefited by its protection: *London County Council v Allen* [1914] 3 KB 642.

The position at common law and in equity has been supplemented by statute (Property Law Act 1952, ss 63, 64), the combined effect of all three being to make the benefit and burden of restrictive covenants relating to land enforceable by and against successors in title of the original parties to the covenant unless a contrary intention is expressed in the instrument containing the covenant. Successors in title include the owners and occupiers for the time being of the land affected by the covenant.

For further discussion of this matter see Hinde, McMorland and Sim *Land Law*, ch 11.

6.2.2 Contracts concerning chattels

Shortly after *Tulk v Moxhay* was decided it was sought to apply the principle there laid down to a contract concerning a chattel, namely a ship under charterparty. In *De Mattos v Gibson* (1858) 4 De G & J 276 the charterer of a ship sought an interlocutory injunction to restrain the mortgagee of the ship from selling it in disregard of the charter. The defendant knew of the charter at the time of the mortgage. In granting the injunction Knight Bruce LJ observed:

> Reason and justice seem to prescribe that, at least as a general rule, where a man by gift or purchase acquires property from another, with knowledge of a previous contract lawfully and for valuable consideration made by him with a third person to use and employ the property for a particular purpose in a specified manner, the acquirer shall not, to the material damage of the third person, in opposition to the contract and inconsistently with it, use and employ the property in a manner not allowable to the giver or seller.

This reasoning did not form part of the concurring judgment of Turner LJ and when the case came for trial before Lord Chelmsford LC ((1859) 4 De G & J 288) a final injunction was refused on the basis of a finding that the defendant had not in fact interfered with the performance of the charterparty.

The far-reaching principle asserted by Knight Bruce LJ thereafter received little overt support until the Judicial Committee of the Privy Council reached its decision in *Lord Strathcona SS Co v Dominion Coal Co* [1926] AC 108. The respondents had a long term charterparty of a ship. The ship was later purchased by the appellants who agreed to honour the terms of the charter. The appellants later went back on their undertaking and contended that they were not bound by the charterparty as they were not in privity with the respondents. The Judicial Committee approved Knight Bruce LJ's dictum and granted an injunction restraining the appellants from using the vessel contrary to the charterparty. The Court regarded the case as falling within the *Tulk v Moxhay* doctrine and thought that whether the subject matter was land or a chattel the principle to be applied was the same.

This reasoning has been criticised on the basis that in the case of land, as has already been seen, the plaintiff should retain adjacent land for the benefit of which the covenant was taken. It is hardly possible to apply this "adjacency" principle to movable chattels. Thus in *Port Line v Ben Line Steamers Ltd* [1958] 2 QB 146 Diplock J observed that the charterer under a time charter had no proprietary or possessory rights in the ship to constitute an "interest" in the ship to which the covenant in the charterparty related. His Honour was, indeed, firmly of the view that *Strathcona* had been wrongly decided. Alternatively, he was prepared to distinguish it, observing that the purchaser in that case had express notice of the terms of the charter and had covenanted with the vendor to perform it, whereas in the case before him the purchaser was aware only of the existence but not of the terms of the charter.

Notwithstanding the doubts of Diplock J it is clear that the *Strathcona* case represents the law in New Zealand. Even in England both *De Mattos v Gibson* and *Strathcona's* case were accepted as correct by Browne-Wilkinson J in *Swiss Bank Corporation v Lloyd's Bank Ltd* [1979] Ch 584. (The judgment was varied on appeal but without further discussion of the present issue: see [1982] AC 584). Unfortunately the scope of the principle remains uncertain. Arguably it applies only to the very special case of a ship under charterparty: *Clore v Theatrical Properties Ltd* [1936] 3 All ER 463 per Lord Wright. Actual as opposed to constructive notice of the charterer's rights must be shown: and, at least according to Diplock J in the *Port Line* case, damages cannot be awarded and the only remedy is by way of injunction.

The difficulties in principle in giving a remedy to a time charterer of a ship stem, as has been seen, primarily from his or her lack of any proprietary or possessory interest in the vessel. He or she merely has a contractual right to control its use. Where actual possession of a chattel is transferred to another, for example by way of a contract for hire, it seems that this does give a "proprietary" interest in the chattel to the hirer which can be protected against the claims of a third party who subsequently buys the chattel. There do not appear to be any clear decisions on the point but it has been argued that there is no good reason why the owner of goods should be able to convert the hirer's right to possession into a right to damages by selling the goods over his head: see *Cheshire, Fifoot & Furmston's Law of Contract* (7th NZ edn, 1988) (Burrows, Finn and Todd) p 400.

Thus far we have considered the rights of the charterer or hirer of a chattel in circumstances where the original owner has sold or mortgaged the chattel regardless of his or her interests. Where, however, the owner sells property to another and attempts to impose conditions on its use as regards all future purchasers, the privity rule clearly prevents the owner from enforcing those conditions. For example, the vendor of goods cannot impose minimum resale price restrictions upon a third person who subsequently acquires the goods, whether or not that person had notice of the conditions: *McGruther v Pitcher* [1904] 2 Ch 306. (Note that resale price maintenance of goods is now prohibited by statute: Commerce Act 1986, ss 37, 38; ch 41.)

6.2.3 Inducing breach of contract

A person who acquires a chattel with knowledge of an existing covenant affecting its use may be liable in tort for wrongfully interfering with the contractual rights of the covenantee. *British Motor Trade Association v Salvadori* [1949] Ch 556 is an example. The purchasers of cars from the plaintiffs covenanted with the plaintiffs that they would not re-sell the cars except as provided in their covenants. The defendants induced the purchasers to resell cars to them in breach of the covenants and were held liable to the plaintiffs for inducing breach of their contract with the purchasers. It was made clear that the fact that the contracting party was willing to be induced was no defence if inducement had taken place. The defendant must, however, have *caused* the breach and if the contractor has already decided not to perform, the inducement should not give rise to liability.

6.3 THE ACQUISITION OF CONTRACTUAL RIGHTS BY THIRD PARTIES

The common law principle that no-one except a party to a contract can acquire rights under it received its most authoritative exposition in the judgment of Viscount Haldane in the House of Lords in *Dunlop Pneumatic Tyre Co Ltd v Selfridge and Co Ltd* [1915] AC 847. His Lordship said:

> My Lords, in the Law of England certain principles are fundamental. One is that only a person who is a party to a contract can sue on it. Our law knows nothing of a jus quaesitum tertio arising by way of contract. Such a right may be conferred by way of property, as, for example, under a trust but it cannot be conferred on a stranger to a contract as a right to enforce the contract in personam.

The inability of a third party to enforce a contract made for his or her benefit may have startling consequences. It means, for example, that a simple contract to pay money to a third person is unenforceable by the third person: *Tweddle v Atkinson* (1861)1 B & S 393; a widow may be unable to enforce a contract between her husband and his employer for the payment of an annuity to her after the husband's death: *Re Schebsman* [1944] Ch 83; family and friends may be unable to sue on a contract for a holiday tour made by one person on their behalf. Such examples could be multiplied. Indeed in recent years the rule came to be widely criticised both in the Courts and elsewhere on the grounds that it was unjust and out of step with common experience. In England Lord Scarman in *Woodar Investment Development Co Ltd v Wimpey Construction (UK) Ltd* [1980] 1 WLR 270 called for a reconsideration of the doctrine and Lord Diplock in *Swain v Law Society* [1983] 1 AC 598 described it as "an anachronistic shortcoming that has for many years been regarded as a reproach to English private law". In Australia in *Trident General Insurance Co Ltd v McNiece Bros Pty Ltd* (1988) 165 CLR 107 three members of the Full Court of the High Court of Australia held that in certain circumstances a third party could sue on a contract of liability insurance, and contemplated also that as regards contracts generally when an appropriate case arose the Court might reconsider and abrogate the traditional rules. Further developments in these countries are awaited. For New Zealand, at least, reform has been achieved by the Contracts (Privity) Act 1982. The provisions of this Act will be discussed below, but first there are some preliminary matters to consider. The privity rule has never been absolute. The promisee has rights which may be asserted for the benefit of the third party in certain circumstances. The principle itself is subject to qualifications and exceptions quite apart from the 1982 Act. All this will remain important for third party beneficiaries to contracts made before 1 April 1983, to which the Act does not apply (s 15) and in some respect to contracts made after that date, as will be explained below.

6.3.1 Remedies of the promisee

A third party may in fact receive the promised benefit if the promisee takes action to enforce the contract. There are several possible remedies which may be available for the promisee.

(a) SPECIFIC PERFORMANCE
If the promisee can require the promisor specifically to perform the contract, the third party will then receive the promised benefit. A well known example is the decision of the House of Lords in *Beswick v Beswick* [1968] AC 58. A coal merchant transferred the business to his nephew who promised that he would, after the uncle's death, pay £ 5 a week to his uncle's widow. After the uncle died the nephew failed to pay as promised. The widow thereupon sued him both in her own right and as administratrix of her husband's estate. The claim in her private capacity failed by reason of the privity doctrine but she succeeded in her action on behalf of the estate and obtained an order for specific performance of the contract.

When specific performance is obtained it will provide the third party with a complete remedy. It is, however, only available in the discretion of the Court: see infra para 7.6.1.

(b) DECLARATION
Where a promisor expressly or by implication promises he or she will not sue a third party, that party cannot rely on the promise as a defence to any action brought by the promisor. The promisee may nonetheless obtain a

declaration that the promise is binding on the promisor, effectively
preventing the promisor from suing the third party: *Snelling v John
Snelling Ltd* [1973] QB 87.

(c) DAMAGES
The promisee may recover substantial damages for a breach of contract
by the promisor if the promisee can show that he or she personally has
suffered loss notwithstanding that performance was to be rendered to a
third party. For example, a promisor who fails in breach of contract to pay
debts owed by the promisee to a third party is liable in damages to the
promisee, for the debts remain undischarged: *Price v Easton* (1833) 4 B &
Ad 433. Similarly, damages are recoverable if the promisee comes under
a legal obligation to pay damages to the third party if the promisor does
not fulfil his or her promise. It may also be sufficient if the promisee
comes under a *moral* obligation to compensate the third party. This may
be inferred from *Beswick's* case where Lord Upjohn explained that
damages in that case would be nominal because the promisee had no
other assets. Seemingly they could have been substantial if the estate
would otherwise have been in a position to make alternative provision
for the widow, even without any legal obligation to do so.

In *Jackson v Horizon Holidays Ltd* [1975] 1 WLR 1468 Lord Denning MR
took the view that the promisee was entitled to damages even where loss
was suffered only by the third party. The plaintiff made a contract with
the defendants for a holiday in Sri Lanka for himself, his wife and two
children. The holiday turned out to be a disaster and the plaintiff sued for
breach of contract. The Court of Appeal held that the plaintiff could
recover damages not only for his own discomfort and disappointment
but also for that suffered by his wife and children. This result may be
justified on the majority view that the plaintiff was recovering for his
own disappointment that a family holiday had been spoilt. Lord Denning,
however, relied on a dictum of Lush LJ in *Lloyd's v Harper* (1880) 16 ChD
290, 321 to the effect that where a contract is made with A for the benefit
of B, A can sue on the contract for the benefit of B and recover all that B
could have recovered if the contract had been made with B himself. Lord
Denning thought that the plaintiff here could recover specifically for the
others' loss and also said that the damages, when received, would be
money had and received to the use of the third parties.

Jackson's case was considered by the House of Lords in *Woodar Investment Development Ltd* v *Wimpey Construction Ltd* [1980] 1 WLR 277 where
Lord Wilberforce said it was probably right on the facts, either as a broad
decision on the measure of damages or possibly as an example of a type
of contract – examples of which were persons contracting for family
holidays, ordering meals in a restaurant for a party, hiring a taxi for a
group – calling for special treatment. His Lordship disagreed, however,
with the basis on which Lord Denning put his decision, regarded *Lloyd's
v Harper* as a case turning on the rules of agency and affirmed the general
principle that a plaintiff promisee must show actual loss in seeking to
recover damages.

A clear disadvantage of these three remedies from the point of view of
the third party is that they all depend on the promisee actually deciding
to sue. The third party cannot compel an unwilling promisee to institute
proceedings. In *Beswick's* case, for example, if the nephew had been
appointed administrator of the estate, obviously the widow would never
have received the promised annuity.

A promisee who wishes to sue may still do so regardless of the Contracts (Privity) Act, but, as will be seen, a more certain remedy is now available for the third party himself or herself.

6.3.2 Trusts of contractual rights

A trust is an equitable obligation to hold property on behalf of another. A person may be a trustee not only of money or a tangible thing but also of a chose in action (a right that may be enforced by legal action) such as a debt. Thus a promisee under a contract may constitute a trust of the right to which he or she is entitled in favour of a third party. The property which is the subject matter of the trust is here the contractual right and the beneficiary can enforce the trust just as can a beneficiary under a trust of tangible property.

Unfettered use of the trust concept could effectively outflank the privity doctrine but the Courts have kept its potential in this respect firmly in check. In particular, there must be clear evidence that the promisee intended to create a trust. In *Swain v Law Society* [1983] 1 AC 598, for example, the House of Lords held that the UK Law Society was not the trustee of the benefit of insurance contracts entered into by it on behalf of all practising solicitors. Only rarely has the requisite intention been established to the Court's satisfaction, perhaps because the creation of a property right in the beneficiary prevents the parties from rescinding or varying the contract so as to deprive the beneficiary of that right. Furthermore, the enactment of the Contracts (Privity) Act means that there is little need to seek a remedy for the beneficiary via the law of trusts. Where, however, it is clear that a trust *has* been created, it is not limited or affected by the Act: s 14(1)(e). In particular this means that the arrangement cannot be varied without the consent of the beneficiary. How far variation is permitted where the 1982 Act applies is discussed infra, para 6.3.5, sub-para (c).

By s 75A of the Life Insurance Act 1908 a life insurance policy expressed to be for the benefit of the spouse or children of the policy holder creates a trust in favour of the named beneficiaries.

6.3.3 Exclusion clauses and third parties

A person may acquire rights or become subject to liabilities as a principal where his or her agent makes a contract with another on his or her behalf. The general rules of agency are examined infra, ch 28. Only one aspect of these rules will be considered here. This concerns the position where an exemption clause in a contract between two parties purports to affect a third.

There are a number of cases in which stevedores who have negligently damaged goods have sought to take the benefit of an exclusion clause in a contract between the consignor and consignee of the goods. The leading authority is *Scruttons Ltd v Midland Silicones Ltd* [1962] AC 446. A drum of chemicals was shipped from New York to London under a bill of lading which included a clause limiting the liability of the carrier to the sum of $500. Stevedores employed by the carrier damaged the drum and claimed the benefit of the limitation clause. The House of Lords held that they were not parties to the contract of carriage and hence could not rely on the clause. However, the question whether the stevedores could have been protected if the carriers had contracted as agents on their behalf was left open. Lord Reid said on this matter:

> I can see a possibility of success of the agency argument if (first) the bill of lading makes it clear that the stevedore is intended to be protected by the provisions in it which limit liability, (secondly) the bill of lading makes it clear that the carrier, in addition to contracting for these provisions on his own behalf, is also contracting as agent for the stevedore that these provisions should apply to the stevedore, (thirdly) the carrier has authority from the stevedore to do that, or perhaps later ratification by the stevedore would suffice, and (fourthly) that any difficulties about consideration moving from the stevedore were overcome.

In *New Zealand Shipping Co Ltd v AM Satterthwaite and Co Ltd* [1974] 1 NZLR 505 the Privy Council held that the clause in the bill of lading at issue satisfied these four conditions. It provided that no servant or agent (including independent contractor) of the carrier was to be liable for any act or default in the course of his employment; that every limitation applicable to the carrier should be available to such persons; that for the purpose of the clause the carrier should be deemed as acting as agent for such persons; and that they should to this extent be or be deemed to be parties to the contract. Lord Wilberforce regarded the bill of lading as having brought into existence a bargain, initially unilateral but capable of becoming mutual, between the shipper and the stevedores made through the carrier as the stevedores' agent. This became a full contract when the stevedores performed the services by discharging the goods. Their work provided the consideration for the promise notwithstanding that they were already bound by contract with the carriers to do it: see supra, para 3.2.7.

Satterthwaite's case was distinguished in *Herrick v Leonard and Dingley Ltd* [1975] 2 NZLR 566 where McMullin J held that three of Lord Reid's four propositions were not met. The clause in question referred only to agents and servants and did not make it clear independent contractors were also protected; there was no clear indication that the carrier was contracting as agent for the stevedores; and there had been no prior authority for or later ratification of the terms of the carrier's contract.

This matter came before the Privy Council once more on appeal from Australia in *Salmond and Spraggon (Australia) Pty Ltd v Port Jackson Stevedoring Pty Ltd* [1981] 1 WLR 138. Here the stevedores had safely unloaded the goods and deposited them in their warehouse but then had negligently allowed them to be stolen. The stevedores relied on a clause in the bill of lading identical in material respects to that in *Satterthwaite's* case. The High Court of Australia gave judgment for the consignees, two members of the Court rejecting *Satterthwaite* and two distinguishing it on the basis that the stevedores' immunity ended once the goods reached the warehouse and that thereafter they acted on their own behalf. The Privy Council allowed the stevedores' appeal, affirmed *Satterthwaite's* case and held that the stevedores were still acting for the carriers when the goods were in the warehouse.

Nothing in the 1982 Act limits or affects, inter alia, the law of agency: s 14 (1)(d). If Lord Reid's four conditions are met the beneficiary of an exclusion clause can still rely upon it as a principal to a contract made by an agent on his or her behalf. If, however, the intention is to contract not as *agent* for another *but for the benefit of* another, without making the other a contracting party, the Privity Act may then come into play: see infra, para 6.3.5, sub-para (b).

Even where the *Scruttons* agency argument might apply, a simpler approach taken in some recent cases tends to indicate that it has become redundant. Instead of asking whether the defendant has excluded his or her negligence liability in a contract with the plaintiff, one asks whether the defendant has excluded liability by a non-contractual notice. Such a notice can bind an entrant coming on to land provided it is sufficiently brought to his or her attention: *Ashdown v Samuel Williams* [1957] 1 QB 409. Again, the maker of a statement is at liberty to make it clear in the statement that he or she assumes no responsibility for the words or that he or she is not in any event liable for them: *Hedley Byrne & Co v Heller & Partners Ltd* [1964] AC 465. It now seems clear that the same principle can apply where the excluding notice happens to be in a contract or arrangement made between the plaintiff and another. In *Smith v Eric S Bush* [1990] 1 AC 831 the purchaser of a house applied for a mortgage to a building society which instructed a valuer to carry out a mortgage valuation. The mortgage application form contained a disclaimer of liability for the accuracy of the report covering both the building society and the valuer. The House of Lords held that the exclusion notice provided the valuer with a defence at common law to an action for negligence by the purchaser. (Their Lordships went on to hold that the notice was rendered ineffective by special statutory provision, which has no counterpart in New Zealand). Again in *Norwich City Council v Harvey* [1989] 1 All ER 1180 it was held not to be just and reasonable to exclude a sub-contractor from the protection of a provision in a contract between an owner and a contractor which put the risk of damage to the building on the owner, presumably because the owner had notice of it.

6.3.4 Property Law Act 1952, s 7

Section 7 of the Property Law Act 1952 provides a clear statutory exception to the privity rule in the case of benefits conferred by *deed* made before 1 April 1983, the date of commencement of the Contracts (Privity) Act. It provides that any person may take an immediate benefit under a deed, although not named as a party thereto. By ss 13 and 14(2) of the 1982 Act, s 7 is repealed so far as deeds made after that date are concerned but otherwise continues to apply. For discussion see *Cheshire, Fifoot & Furmston's Law of Contract* (7th NZ edn, 1988) (Burrows, Finn & Todd) pp 387-388.

6.3.5 The Contracts (Privity) Act 1982

In May 1981 the Contracts and Commercial Law Reform Committee presented to the Minister of Justice a Report on Privity of Contract. The Committee observed that there are means of avoiding the rigours of the privity doctrine and in proper cases the Courts have usually been able to give effect to the intentions of the contracting parties. The reported cases in which those intentions have been frustrated by the doctrine were seen as relatively few. However, the Committee looked in vain for a solid basis of policy justifying the frustration of contractual intentions. Thus it proposed quite fundamental changes to the doctrine and incorporated in its report a draft Bill designed to give effect to its recommendations. That Bill, with minor amendments, became the Contracts (Privity) Act 1982.

The purpose of the Act, broadly, is to allow an intended beneficiary of a contract between others to enforce the benefit conferred by the contract, yet not to interfere too much with the autonomy of the contracting parties. The Act lays down rules concerning who can sue under it, protects the beneficiary by setting limits on the normal right of contracting parties to vary or discharge the contract and provides for the defences available to the promisor in an action by the beneficiary.

(a) MEANING OF "BENEFIT"
The Act applies where a deed or contract confers a benefit on a third party. Section 2 defines "benefit" as including:

(a) Any advantage; and
(b) Any immunity; and
(c) Any limitation or other qualification of –
　　(i)　　An obligation to which a person (other than a party to the deed or contract) is or may be subject; or
　　(ii)　　A right to which a person (other than a party to the deed or contract) is or may be entitled; and
(d) Any extension or other improvement of a right or rights to which a person (other than a party to the deed or contract) is or may be entitled.

An inquiry as to whether a third party has obtained a benefit in these terms should normally be straightforward. The specific inclusion in the definition of any "immunity" or "limitation or qualification of a right" clearly contemplates the conferring on a third party of a benefit by way of an exclusion clause. This possibly creates difficulty, for s 4, as will be seen, refers to the right of the third party beneficiary to "enforce" the promise conferring the benefit, seemingly presupposing that it is the beneficiary who is bringing the action. The section is not very aptly worded in the case of a benefit asserted by way of defence. Presumably the third party can be treated as enforcing a promise conferring an immunity, by pleading it in his or her defence to a claim by the promisor.

(b) THIRD PARTY BENEFICIARIES
Section 4 is the key provision of the 1982 Act. It states:

> **4. Deeds or contracts for the benefit of third parties** – Where a promise contained in a deed or contract confers, or purports to confer, a benefit on a person, designated by name, description or reference to a class, who is not a party to the deed or contract (whether or not the person is in existence at the time when the deed or contract is made) the promisor shall be under an obligation, enforceable at the suit of that person, to perform that promise:
> Provided that this section shall not apply to a promise which, on the proper construction of the deed or contract, is not intended to create, in respect of the benefit, an obligation enforceable at the suit of that person.

The onus is on the third party to show that he or she has been "designated" in terms of s 4. The proviso allows the contracting parties to establish that, even so, the beneficiary was not intended to have an action.

The requirement of designation clearly is crucial. Persons who happen to benefit from the performance of a contract but who are not sufficiently designated by it cannot sue. Most judicial discussion of the requirement so far has been concerned with the position of nominees. Where there is a contract with X "or nominee", the question is whether the nominee can enforce as a third party beneficiary of the contract under s 4.

In *Coldicutt v Webb and Keeys* (unreported, High Court, Whangarei, A50/84, 1 June 1983) it was held that the nominee could sue, because (i) he had been designated by description, and (ii) the only purpose of the words "or nominee" was to give the nominee the right to complete the contract. Subsequent cases have held the contrary. In particular in *Field v Fitton* [1988] 1 NZLR 482, a decision of the Court of Appeal, Bisson J said that whether a nominee who is not a party might have the benefit of the Act will depend on the nominee being defined with sufficient particularity to come within the designation prescribed in s 4. His Honour said that it is difficult to treat a bare nominee not designated by name as a person identified by description or as being within a designated class of persons. The nominee could be anyone at all. If the nominee is not named the word nominee in the contract should be qualified by the addition of a descriptive phrase or the addition of the particular class within which the nominee falls so as to specify or identify the nominee in the manner required by s 4.

In *Karangahape Road International Village Ltd v Holloway* [1989] 1 NZLR 83 Chilwell J thought that even a designated nominee could not sue. His Honour maintained that until the nomination is made no person is identified. Identification requires the further act of nomination. The benefit referred to in s 4 is one conferred by the promise contained in the contract, not one conferred by a party with a right to nominate. *McElwee v Beer* (unreported, High Court, Auckland, A 445/1262-85, 19 February 1987) and *Brown v Healy* (unreported, High Court, Auckland, A 147/84, 25 July 1988) are to the same effect.

The distinction between a benefit under the contract and a benefit by act of one of the parties may yet be rejected in the Court of Appeal: certainly it was not mentioned in *Field*'s case. The logic of the distinction does not seem to be compelling, for it can equally well be argued that the benefit is still conferred by the contract notwithstanding that the precise identity of the particular beneficiary is left to be ascertained. As a matter of commercial convenience, moreover, it would seem sensible to let at least a designated nominee have an action, if not to return to the view taken originally in *Coldicutt*'s case.

Some obiter remarks in the earlier decision of the Court of Appeal in *Gartside v Sheffield, Young & Ellis* [1983] NZLR 37 possibly could be regarded as consistent with the approach taken in *Karangahape*. Richardson J here denied that a legatee whose hopes of receiving a benefit under a will had been dashed by the untimely death of the testatrix could sue as a third party beneficiary of an implied term in the contract between the testatrix and her solicitor, that the solicitor would draw up and present the will to the testatrix for execution with all due diligence. His Honour explained that the contract of retainer between solicitor and client did not include any provision for the benefit of a third party; that benefit arose only when the contract was properly carried out and was not conferred by the contract itself. By contrast, however, on one view at least the benefit to a nominee can be seen as flowing from the contract, which in its very terms gives a party a power to nominate another to take a benefit under that contract.

Where the beneficiary is designated, and assuming that his or her benefit is conferred by the contract, either of the contracting parties may still seek to show that it was not intended that the promise should create an obligation enforceable at the suit of the beneficiary. An express agreement about enforceability is conclusive of the matter. Otherwise, on the requisite intention being denied, the Courts will look for some clear evidence suggesting that enforcement by the beneficiary was in fact contemplated. In *Field v Fitton*, supra, the mere addition of the words "or nominee" without more was not sufficient to impute an intention to the parties to create an obligation on the vendors enforceable at the suit of the nominee.

It is apparent from the words in parenthesis in s 4 that an otherwise qualifying beneficiary does not actually have to be in existence at the time the deed or contract is made. In principle, then, it would seem that the section can apply in the case of a contract purportedly made for a company before the company has been incorporated; and this was confirmed early on in *Palmer v Bellaney* (1983) ANZ Conv R 467 and more recently in *Speedy v Nylex New Zealand Ltd* (unreported, High Court, Auckland, CL 29/87, 3 February 1989). However, a word of caution is needed here. Section 4 applies where a contract is made *for the benefit of* a company yet to be formed, not where it is made *on behalf of* the proposed company. There is a distinction between A and B intending to bind themselves by contract, some benefit under which is to go to C (a company to be formed), and A contracting with B as agent for C, it being intended that the contract should be with C on C being incorporated. In the latter case C can enforce only if it ratifies the contract after its incorporation pursuant to s 42A of the Companies Act 1955. The requirements of s 42A are discussed infra, para 28.3.2.

(c) VARIATION OR DISCHARGE OF THE CONTRACT

Conferment of a right of action on a third party beneficiary raises questions as to the ability of the contracting parties to vary or cancel the contract. Sections 5, 6 and 7 seek to balance their respective interests.

Section 5 sets out the circumstances which, subject to ss 6 and 7, preclude the variation or discharge of the contract without the consent of the beneficiary. These are, in brief, that the position of the beneficiary has been materially altered by his or her own or another's reliance on the promise, that the beneficiary has obtained judgment upon the promise and that the beneficiary has obtained the award of an arbitrator upon a submission relating to the promise. As regards the first of these, material alteration in the position of the beneficiary, it could be helpful to draw comparisons with cases concerning the circumstances in which a promisor may be estopped from reneging on his or her promise: supra, para 3.2.10.

Section 6 makes it possible to contract out of this regime. The section allows the contracting parties to vary or discharge the contract (a) by agreement between the parties and the beneficiary, or (b) pursuant to express provision in the contract which is known to the beneficiary and the beneficiary had not materially altered his or her position in reliance on the promise before the provision had become known to him or her.

Even where the beneficiary has acted in reliance on the promise, and a right to vary has not been reserved by the contract, the contracting parties' hands are not completely tied. Section 7 allows either party to apply to a Court to authorise variation or discharge upon such terms or conditions as it thinks fit. In particular, the Court can require that the promisor pay to the beneficiary such sum by way of compensation as the Court thinks just. Compensation normally will be confined to the reliance loss of the beneficiary since, ex hypothesi, the rights of the beneficiary no longer stem from the contractual will of the parties: Coote (1984) NZ Recent Law 107, 114. In an appropriate case, however, such as where restitution is not possible, the Court may order payment of the plaintiff's full expectation loss.

(d) ENFORCEMENT BY THE BENEFICIARY
Section 8 should be read together with s 4. It confirms that the obligation imposed on the promisor by s 4 can be enforced at the suit of the beneficiary as if he or she were a party to the deed or contract and takes away the defences of the beneficiary not being a party and not having provided consideration. The beneficiary can obtain full contract damages and also equitable relief.

(e) DEFENCES
It is a natural corollary of the principle that the beneficiary's rights stem from the contract that the promisor may assert any contractual defences he or she may have in answer to a claim by the beneficiary. Thus s 9(2) provides in substance that, in a claim by a beneficiary against a promisor, the promisor may rely on any defence, counterclaim, set-off or otherwise which would have been available to him or her if the beneficiary had been a party or if the beneficiary were the promisee. By s 9(3) the defences of set-off or counterclaim can only be utilised if the subject matter of the set-off or counterclaim arises out of or in connection with the deed or contract in which the promise is contained. Finally, by s 9(4) the beneficiary is liable on a counterclaim only if he or she elects with full knowledge of the counterclaim to proceed with his or her claim against the promisor and his or her liability is limited to the value of the benefit conferred on him or her by the promise.

(f) THIRD PARTY CLAIMS IN NEGLIGENCE
The Contracts (Privity) Act is not concerned with claims by third parties in the tort of negligence. The mere fact that the negligence may have been committed in the course of the performance of a contract is immaterial. A engages B to build a wall, B does so negligently and the wall later collapses onto C's car. C sues B in negligence, not on the contract between A and B. *Donoghue v Stevenson* [1932] AC 562 holds that B's liability is based upon his failure to take care to avoid acts or omissions which he can reasonably foresee would be likely to injure his "neighbour", meaning someone who is so closely and directly affected by his act that he ought reasonably to have him in contemplation as being so affected when directing his mind to the act or omission called in question. (See Todd *The Law of Torts in New Zealand* (1991) Ch 4). Deciding this question has nothing to do with contract or privity.

Tort compensates for damage to or loss of something the plaintiff already owned or possessed, such as bodily health (subject to the accident compensation scheme), property, financial wellbeing, reputation. It does not generally compensate for the loss of a financial expectancy, which is left to the law of contract. In the example given above C had a sound car before it was damaged by B's negligence, and so ordinary tort principles can apply. Suppose, however, that C is a subsequent owner of the wall and he sues B, not for separate damage done to other property but *for the cost of rebuilding the wall*. C's complaint now is not that he had a good wall which has been damaged but that he has bought an already defective wall. His claim thus is for his unfulfilled expectation that he was buying a good wall.

Certain leading cases in England, notably *Anns v London Borough of Merton* [1978] AC 728, for a time allowed this kind of loss to be recoverable in a negligence action, but recently they have all been discarded. In *D & F Estates Ltd v Church Commissioners for England* [1989] AC 177 the House of Lords held that building owners who were allegedly negligent in failing properly to supervise plastering contractors doing work in a flat owed no duty of care to the lessees of the flat in respect of the cost of replacing the defective plaster. The claim by the lessees was seen as essentially an action for breach of a warranty of quality, for the loss of a bargain, which could lie only in contract. Likewise, and for the same reasons, in *Murphy v Brentwood DC* [1991] 1 AC 398 it was held that a claim in tort against a local authority for negligently inspecting a defective building could not be maintained. In New Zealand, on the other hand, the Court of Appeal has adhered to the position formerly held in England, confirming in a number of cases that a builder or inspector may be liable in negligence to a subsequent purchaser in respect of the cost of putting right defects in the construction of a house: see *Bowen v Paramount Builders (Hamilton) Ltd* [1977] 1 NZLR 394; *Mount Albert BC v Johnson* [1979] 2 NZLR 234; *Stieller v Porirua CC* [1986] 1 NZLR 84.

It seems quite clear that a subsequent purchaser of defective property cannot maintain an action under the Privity Act, not being designated or intended to have an action. Whether the tort action will survive the developments in England remains to be seen. It might in fact be possible to give a remedy which does not amount to the impermissible enforcement of a building contract at the suit of a non-party. Sir Robin Cooke has suggested extra-judicially ("An Impossible Distinction" (1991) 107 LQR 46) that a warranty need not necessarily be contractual and, drawing on American cases, that the Courts could recognise a warranty on the part of a builder, actionable at the suit of subsequent purchasers not in contractual privity, that care has been taken to build a reasonably sound and habitable dwelling. The warranty would operate quite independently of the terms of the original building contract and thus would not be affected by any limitations or exclusions of liability contained in the contract. It seems likely that the Courts here will in fact wish to continue to afford a remedy to the building owner, whether in negligence or by way of a warranty of habitability. The attitude of the Privy Council is, however, another matter.

6.4 THE ASSIGNMENT OF CONTRACTUAL RIGHTS

Personal rights to property which can only be claimed or enforced by action (in the sense of litigation) and not by taking physical possession are known as choses or things in action. A chose in action may be legal or equitable. A *legal* chose is one which is enforceable at common law and this includes, in particular, a debt or other right under a contract. Further examples of legal choses are company shares, bills of exchange, patents and copyright. An *equitable* chose is one which originally was enforceable only in equity, examples being a share in a trust fund or a legacy.

Both legal and equitable choses may be assigned to another person on meeting certain qualifying conditions. Assignment involves the transfer of the benefit of the chose in action by the party entitled to that benefit (called the creditor or assignor) to a third party (called the assignee) as a result of which the assignee becomes entitled to sue the person liable under the contract (called the debtor). Our discussion will be concerned primarily with the assignment of contractual rights, which are, as noted above, legal choses, but for the sake of completeness any special rules governing the assignment of equitable choses will also be mentioned.

6 4.1 No assignment at law

Contractual rights are not generally assignable at common law, although an exception has always been made in the case of assignments to or by the Crown. In addition, negotiable instruments are freely transferable by the custom of merchants or by statute: see infra, para 25.2.

6.4.2 Assignment by statute

Section 130(1) of the Property Law Act 1952 sets out a statutory method of assignment. It provides in substance that any absolute assignment in writing of any debt or other legal or equitable thing in action, of which express notice in writing has been given to the debtor, is effectual in law (subject to all equities) to pass to the assignee the legal or equitable right to the debt or thing in action as from the date of the notice.

It may be seen that there are three conditions which must be satisfied to make a valid assignment under the statute:

1   It must be absolute. An assignment is not absolute if: (i) it is subject to a condition; or (ii) is by way of charge whereby the assignee becomes entitled to payment out of a particular fund but not to the fund itself; or (iii) is of part of a debt.
2   It must be written.
3   Written notice must be given to the debtor. No special form of words is required so long as the meaning is clear: see *Van Lynn Developments Ltd v Pelias Construction Co Ltd* [1966]1 QB 607.

The meaning of the "subject to equities" proviso will be considered infra, para 6.4.4.

Consideration is not necessary to the validity of a statutory assignment. An assignment which satisfies the requirements of s 130 transfers the chose in action by virtue of the section itself and consideration is irrelevant.

6.4.3 Assignment in equity

Section 130(1) does not forbid or impair the efficacy of equitable assignments and these may be made with a minimum of formality and restriction. Thus an assignment which fails to meet the conditions laid down by the statute may nonetheless be good in equity.

1   A non-absolute assignment may take effect in equity provided that it is "complete" (the meaning of which will be considered below).
2   Equity does not require an assignment to be in any particular form and insists only that the assignor should have made clear his or her intention to make the assignment: *Peacocke Land Co Ltd v Hamilton Milk Producers Co Ltd* [1963] NZLR 576 (CA). By statute, however, the disposition of an equitable interest must be in writing signed by the person disposing of the same or his agent: Property Law Act 1952 s 49A(3). An oral assignment of an equitable chose is, therefore, void. An equitable assignment of a legal chose may be made orally.
3   As between assignor and assignee notice to the debtor is unnecessary to complete the title of the assignee. Notice is nonetheless advisable for at least two reasons. In the first place, if the debtor pays the assignor before receiving notice of the assignment he or she cannot be compelled to make a second payment to the assignee. Secondly, an assignee who first gives notice to the debtor of the assignment has priority over other assignees provided he or she was unaware of any prior assignments when the assignment was made: *Dearle v Hall* (1828) 3 Russ 1.

The equitable assignment of a chose in action, if completed, need not be supported by consideration. The gift is both valid and irrevocable in the same way as is the gift of a pound note by delivery of possession: *Re McArdle* [1951] Ch 669 per Sir Raymond Evershed MR. If, however, the assignment is incomplete the assignor can change his or her mind and revoke it. The assignee cannot enlist the aid of equity in such a case for it is well settled that equity will not assist a volunteer (ie a person who has not given consideration). Whether a gift has been "completed" hinges on whether any act remains to be done by the assignor in order to perfect the assignment and this in turn depends on the requirements, if any, for the transfer of the particular chose at law. For example, the voluntary assignment of a debt may be achieved simply on the creditor clearly expressing an intention to make the assignment there and then, for nothing else needs to be done on his or her part. On the other hand, if a creditor only promises to assign *in the future* an existing debt, he or she has not done everything necessary to transfer the chose to the assignee and the promise can only operate as a contract to assign, which requires consideration like any other contract: see *Pulley v Public Trustee* [1956] NZLR 771. A purported assignment of a right which does not yet exist, such as a future debt, must likewise be supported by consideration.

The effect of an absolute equitable assignment of an equitable chose in action is to pass the assignor's entire interest in the chose to the assignee. The assignee may sue in his or her own name to recover the chose and need not join the assignor, who has no interest in the proceedings. Where, however, an assignment of an equitable chose is not absolute the assignor retains an interest in the subject matter of the assignment and here the assignee must join the assignor as a party. If the assignor will not join as co-plaintiff he or she must be joined as co-defendant along with the debtor. The dispute may then be resolved by the Court with all interested parties before it. Similarly, where the chose assigned is a legal chose, the legal interest is retained by the assignor who must, therefore, be joined as a party, whether the assignment is absolute or non-absolute.

6.4.4 "Subject to equities"

An assignee under both a statutory and an equitable assignment is said to take "subject to equities". What this means is that the debtor can plead against the assignee any defences that he or she could have pleaded against the assignor. The assignee cannot take more than the assignor had to give. Any defects in the title of the assignor, as may arise, for example, by reason of mistake, illegality, misrepresentation or non-performance by the assignor, may all be pleaded by the debtor in answer to a claim by the assignee. The debtor can also set off a claim for unliquidated damages for breach of the contract by the assignor, whether the breach occurred before or after notice of the assignment had been given.

Where the Contractual Remedies Act 1979 applies the debtor may cancel for misrepresentation or breach or set off any claim for damages and if the debtor has already paid the assignee before discovering any of these matters he or she arguably may even be able to recover damages from the assignee: see the 1979 Act s 11, infra, para 6.4.6.

An example of an assignee taking subject to equities is *Field v Fitton* [1988] 1 NZLR 482. The Court of Appeal held here that the assignees of the equitable interest of the purchasers of land "must accept the burdens of the contract along with its benefits". The assignees had failed to fulfil or secure the fulfilment of all the assignor's liabilities under the contract, entitling the vendors to cancel and putting an end to the equitable interest of the assignor and his assignees in the land.

Where the debtor has a claim arising out of a transaction other than the contract assigned, it can only be set off against the assignee if the claim accrued before the debtor had notice of the assignment: *Business Computers Ltd v Anglo African Leasing Ltd* [1977] 1 WLR 578.

6.4.5 Contractual rights which are not assignable

The parties to a contract are free to make it a term of their own contract that the rights under it shall not be assignable. There are, furthermore, certain contractual or other rights which cannot be assigned in any event, either under s 130 or in equity:

1   There are many statutory restrictions on assignment based on considerations of public policy. For example, pensions, social security benefits and maintenance payments ordered in matrimonial proceedings cannot be assigned.
2   The right to claim unliquidated damages for breach of contract cannot usually be assigned after the contract has been broken. This

is because a bare right to litigate smacks of the tort of "maintenance", which is the improper stirring up of legal proceedings by a stranger not directly concerned in them. However, the assignment of a right to sue may validly be made where the assignee has a "genuine commercial interest" in the subject matter of the action, as where the assignee is a creditor of the assignor: *Trendtex Trading Co Ltd v Credit Suisse* [1982] AC 679 (HL); *Brownton Ltd v Edward Moore Inbucon Ltd* [1985] 3 All ER 499; and see *First City Corporation v Downsview Nominees Ltd* [1989] 3 NZLR 710 (on appeal [1990] 3 NZLR 265).

3   The benefit of a contract of a "personal" nature cannot be assigned. Contracts where one party relies on the particular skills and qualifications of the other or which otherwise involve a relation of special confidence fall into this category. Thus a contract of employment cannot be assigned by the employer so as to oblige the employee to work for another: *Nokes v Doncaster Amalgamated Collieries Ltd* [1940] AC 1014. Normally contracts for the sale of land are capable of assignment because personal considerations are not important: *HEB Contractors Ltd v Verrissimo* [1990] 3 NZLR 754. Where, however, the parties to a contract are defined as including their respective assigns, the contract is assignable by one without the consent of the other save in exceptional circumstances: *Peacocke Land Co Ltd v Hamilton Milk Producers Co Ltd* [1963] NZLR 576.

6.4.6 The transfer of contractual liabilities

The discussion here will proceed initially without regard for the provisions of s 11 of the Contractual Remedies Act 1979. The effect of that section on the position at common law will be examined thereafter.

Assignment is the transfer of a *right* to a third person. The only way in which contractual *liabilities* may be transferred is by novation. Where novation takes place a new contract between debtor, creditor and third party under which the debt owed by the debtor is henceforth owed to the third party replaces the former contract between debtor and creditor. The essential point about novation is that it requires the agreement of all the parties: see *Karangahape Road International Village Ltd v Holloway* [1989] 1 NZLR 83.

Rights as well as duties may be transferred by novation but it is a simpler matter for a creditor who wishes to transfer a contractual right to proceed by way of assignment as he or she need not then seek the consent of the debtor.

To say that a contracting party cannot, save by novation, transfer his or her liabilities to another does not mean that that party cannot engage another to perform the contract on his or her behalf. A creditor cannot object to vicarious performance unless the contract forbids it or unless the contract is 'personal' in the sense that one party has contracted for the particular skill and expertise of the other: *Robson and Sharpe v Drummond* (1831) 2 B & Ad 303. Vicarious performance is, however, quite different from assignment or novation, for one debtor is not thereby *substituted* for another. The original debtor remains liable to the other contracting party for the due performance of the contract and the third party is not liable to that contracting party for non performance or defective performance, although he or she may, of course, be liable on a separate contract with the debtor.

Section 11 of the Contractual Remedies Act 1979 might be thought to cast doubt upon the principle that contractual liabilities are not assignable. The first three subsections are in these terms:

(1) Subject to this section, if a contract, or the benefit or burden of a contract, is assigned, the remedies of damages and cancellation shall, except to the extent that it is otherwise provided in the assigned contract, be enforceable by or against the assignee.

(2) Except to the extent that it is otherwise agreed by the assignee or provided in the assigned contract, the assignee shall not be liable in damages, whether by way of set-off, counter-claim or otherwise, in a sum exceeding the value of the performance of the assigned contract to which he is entitled by virtue of the assignment.

(3) Unless it is otherwise agreed between the assignor and the assignee, the assignee shall be entitled to be indemnified by the assignor against any loss suffered by the assignee and arising out of—
(a) Any term of the assigned contract that was not disclosed to him before or at the time of the assignment; or
(b) Any misrepresentation that was not so disclosed.

These provisions appear to be drafted on the erroneous assumption that the burden of a contract is freely assignable. In view of the wording of subs (1) – "If, … the burden of a contract is assigned…" – it is apparent that the section does not create any power to assign liabilities but operates only when an assignment of the burden has been made. As this cannot be achieved at common law the section is in this respect without effect.

To the extent that s 11 is concerned with the assignment of the benefit of a contract it confirms that the assignee may invoke the remedies provided in the 1979 Act. It appears, moreover, that the assignee may be liable for any breach of contract by the assignor. Subsection (1) states, inter alia, that if the benefit of a contract is assigned, the remedies of damages and cancellation are enforceable *against* the assignee. Thus where an assignment is made of an executory contract under which the assignor purports to transfer both the benefit and the burden of the contract, it seems that: (i) non-performance or mis-performance by the assignee cannot amount to a breach of contract as between the assignee and the other contracting party, since the burden of the contract cannot be assigned; and (ii) the other party can nonetheless enforce against the assignee his or her remedy of damages for what is strictly a breach of contract by the assignor. The same result must follow even where the assignee has undertaken no responsibility for performance of the contract. This argument assumes that the reference in subs (1) to enforcement against the assignee is not to be read as referable only to the assignment of the burden of the contract.

If the assignee becomes liable for the assignor's breach in this way, his obligations are limited by subs (2) to "the value of the performance of the assigned contract to which he is entitled by virtue of the agreement" unless "it is otherwise agreed by the assignee or provided in the assigned contract". Probably the "value" of the contract in this context is to be determined by the Court on an objective basis. Any excess would have to be recovered from the assignor who, as has already been seen, remains fully liable on the assigned contract.

There are two specific statutory exceptions to the rule of non-assign-ability of contractual liabilities: (i) A purchaser of land subject to a mortgage becomes personally liable to the mortgagee on the mortgage: Property Law Act 1952, s 104, confirmed in the 1979 Act, s 11(4)(a); (ii) An assignee from a vendor (owner) under a hire purchase agreement may be liable in damages to the purchaser (hirer): Hire Purchase Act 1971, s 18 (infra, ch 37), confirmed in the 1979 Act, s 11(4)(b).

6.4.7 Assignment by operation of law

The automatic transfer of contractual rights and liabilities may occur upon the death or bankruptcy of one of the contracting parties.

(a) DEATH
On the death of a contracting party, all causes of action subsisting against or vested in him survive against or for the benefit of the estate: Law Reform Act 1936, s 3. The personal representatives may thus sue or be sued on the deceased's contracts, although in the latter case their liability is limited to the value of the assets in their hands. The general rule does not apply to contracts of a personal nature, where the death of either party brings the contract to an end.

(b) BANKRUPTCY
The effect of an adjudication in bankruptcy is discussed infra, ch 43.

Chapter 7

MISREPRESENTATION AND BREACH

SUMMARY

7.1	MISREPRESENTATION
7.2	TYPES OF BREACH
7.3	CANCELLATION FOR BREACH AND MISREPRESENTATION
7.4	ENTIRE CONTRACTS AND SUBSTANTIAL PERFORMANCE
7.5	DAMAGES
7.6	EQUITABLE REMEDIES
7.7	LIMITATION OF ACTIONS

7.1 MISREPRESENTATION

Before a contract is finally entered into there is often an exchange between the parties, oral or written, in which one party makes statements to the other about the subject matter of the contract. These statements sometimes contribute to the decision of the other party to enter the contract. If it later turns out that one or more of the statements were false, (ie if they were misrepresentations), the original party may have two remedies:

(i) he or she may be able to claim damages; and
(ii) he or she may, if the misrepresentation was of a serious kind, be able to cancel the contract.

The present section will deal with the remedy in damages. The remedy of cancellation will be discussed in para 7.3 infra.

7.1.1 Damages for misrepresentation

The main provision in New Zealand dealing with damages for misrepresentation is s 6 of the Contractual Remedies Act 1979. This section applies to all contracts, including contracts for the sale of goods, entered into after 31 March 1980. It makes very substantial changes to the pre-existing law which was an unfortunately complicated amalgam of common law and equity. For the old law, which still applies to contracts entered into before 1 April 1980, reference should be made to earlier editions of this book. Section 6(1) of the Act provides:

(1) If a party to a contract has been induced to enter into it by a misrepresentation, whether innocent or fraudulent, made to him by or on behalf of another party to that contract —

(a) He shall be entitled to damages from that other party in the same manner and to the same extent as if the representation were a term of the contract that has been broken, and

(b) He shall not, in the case of a fraudulent misrepresentation, or of an innocent misrepresentation made negligently, be entitled to damages from that other party for deceit or negligence in respect of that misrepresentation.

7.1.2 The meaning of misrepresentation

The Act does not define "misrepresentation", so one must assume it bears the meaning it had at common law. A misrepresentation is a representation which is false.

(a) A representation is a statement which relates to a matter of present or past fact, not one which relates to the future. Thus a statement that something will happen in future, or that the maker of the statement intends to do something in the future, is not actionable as a representation. It will only be actionable at all if it is a promise which forms part of a contract.

However this dichotomy between present or past on the one hand and future on the other is not always straightforward. In the first place, if the maker of the statement does not have the intention which he or she says he or she has, he or she will be taken to have misstated a fact, for as Bowen LJ said in *Edgington v Fitzmaurice* (1885) 29 ChD 459, 483:

The state of a man's mind is as much a fact as the state of his digestion. It is true that it is very difficult to prove what the state of a man's mind at a particular time is, but if it can be substantiated, it is as much a fact as anything else.

In that case a company issued a prospectus inviting subscriptions for debentures and stating that the funds were to be used to complete alterations to buildings and the purchase of equipment. In fact the directors intended to use the money to pay off liabilities. It was held that the prospectus was a misrepresentation of fact for it stated that the directors had an intention which they simply did not have.

Secondly, many statements expressed as projections of the future have been held by the Courts to imply statements of present fact. For instance a projection that the throughput of a garage business would be 200,000 gallons within three years was held to contain an implied assurance that the forecast was based on careful and adequate research *(Esso Petroleum Ltd v Mardon* [1976] 1 QB 801); a statement by the seller of a kiwifruit orchard that the orchard would produce in 1982 was held to imply an assurance that the vines were presently of such quality that they would produce at the time stated *(Ware v Johnson* [1984] 2 NZLR 518); and a "budget forecast" for a company was held to imply that the present state of the company was such as to justify the forecast: *New Zealand Motor Bodies Ltd v Emslie* [1985] 2 NZLR 569.

(b) A statement of *opinion* which turns out to be erroneous is not actionable as a misrepresentation. Thus, in *Bisset v Wilkinson* [1927] AC 177 the vendor of land which had not previously been used as a sheep farm told a buyer that the land had a carrying capacity of 2,000 sheep. It was held that in the circumstances this amounted to no more than a statement of the vendor's opinion and was thus not actionable. However, as with the last criterion the matter is not always so simple. If the maker of the statement does not hold the opinion he or she proclaims he or she is misstating a fact; and particularly where the facts are not equally well known to both sides, an apparent statement of opinion by the one who has the greater knowledge may be held to incorporate a statement that he or she knows facts which justify the opinion. On this latter ground also the statements in *Esso Petroleum Ltd v Mardon* and the *Emslie* case could be treated as ones of fact.

(c) "Mere puff", or exaggerated sales talk, is not treated by the law as misrepresentation; to hold that it was would put a stop to age-old advertising practice. Thus, to describe land as "uncommonly rich water meadow" is not misrepresentation. But where the assertion goes beyond generalities and refers to verifiable particulars, it may become a representation.

(d) A representation must be of fact, not of law, to be actionable. However the distinction between fact and law is often notoriously difficult to draw, and it has been said that the Judges have failed to propound a workable differentiation. However, in some cases a statement may contain elements of both fact and law; often such statements will be classified as statements of fact and held to be actionable.

(e) Generally speaking, silence is not a misrepresentation. A seller who stands by, saying nothing, and allows a purchaser to deceive him- or herself about the qualities of what is for sale does not commit an actionable misrepresentation. However, in certain circumstances silence may be actionable. First, silence may distort a positive representation: to tell only half the story, and leave out material qualifications, may result in a representation which is not really the truth. Thus a statement, accurate as far as it went, that a property was let, was held to be a misrepresentation because it omitted to state that the tenants had been given notice to quit (*Dimmock v Hallett* (1866) 2 Ch App 21); and a statement that the nearest competition to a food bar was 1 mile away was held to be a misrepresentation because it omitted to state that a licence had just been granted for one to open around the corner: *Wakelin v Jackson* (1984) 2 NZCPR 195. Secondly, a statement which is true when it is made becomes a misrepresentation if the facts later change in a material way before the contract is finally made; in such a case the maker of the statement is under an obligation to inform the other party of the change. It should also be noted that at common law there are a few types of contract, known as contracts *uberrima fides*, where one party is obliged to disclose facts to the other; the best known of such types of contract is the contract of insurance. However the remedy for non-disclosure in such cases has always been rescission only, and it could not seriously be argued that such non-disclosure is a "misrepresentation" for the purposes of claiming damages under s 6 of the Contractual Remedies Act; that view is supported by *Banque Keyser Ullmann SA v Skandia (UK) Insurance Co Ltd* [1990] 1 QB 665 affd [1990] 3 WLR 364.

7.1.3 The making of the misrepresentation

To be actionable, the misrepresentation must be made *by or on behalf of another party to the contract*. Thus, a contracting party may be liable for a misrepresentation made by his or her agent; in some cases the agent may also be personally liable in tort. (See below, 7.1.6).

A misrepresentation may be express or implied, and may be inferred from acts or conduct as much as from words.

7.1.4 Inducement

A party may only recover damages if the misrepresentation *induced* him or her to enter the contract. *Jolly v Palmer* [1985] NZLR 658 provides an example of a case where inducement was held to exist. An agent for the sale of a house falsely stated to prospective purchasers that its government valuation was $21,000 whereas in fact it was only $15,500. The purchasers, in reliance on this statement, paid more for the property than they otherwise would. It was held that they had been induced by the representation: they would not have bought at the figure they did had they known the true position. (However the misrepresentation was held not sufficiently substantial to allow cancellation: infra 7.3.2).

The following would be examples of situations where the misrepresentation could not be said to have induced the contract: where the matter misrepresented is not material to the plaintiff – for instance a case where a prospectus wrongly named X as a director of the company, but the plaintiff had never heard of X: *Smith v Chadwick* (1882) 20 ChD 27, affd (1882) 9 App Cas 187; where the plaintiff never knew of the existence of the misrepresentation or learned of it only after the contract was made; where the plaintiff knew of its falsity; where the plaintiff did not allow the misrepresentation to affect his or her judgment. An illustration of this last point is *Attwood v Small* (1838) 6 Cl & Fin 232, in which a vendor of a mine made incorrect statements about its earning capacities. The buyers, far from accepting the vendor's word, required the appointment of experts to investigate the claims; they confirmed the vendor's statements. It was held that the buyers had not relied on the vendor's statements but rather on their own investigations.

There is no requirement in s 6 that the misrepresentation be the sole inducement to contract – it is enough if it forms one of the inducements. Thus, in *New Zealand Motor Bodies v Emslie* (supra) the plaintiff recovered damages although the budget forecast was only one of the things that induced it to buy: the desire to rationalise the industry was another.

Despite the fact that the section on its face indicates no such requirement, it has been said in the Court of Appeal that in addition to the misrepresentation inducing the contract, either the person making the misrepresentation must have intended to induce it, or the representation must have been such as would induce a normal person to contract: *Savill v NZI Finance Ltd* [1990] 3 NZLR 135. These were requirements at common law, and have been read into the section. They are likely to have the effect that a plaintiff will be unable to rely on trivial misstatements, or misstatements which at the time they were made were unrelated to any impending contract.

7.1.5 Damages

The successful plaintiff in a case of misrepresentation is entitled to damages as if the representation were a term of the contract. Thus, the action is equivalent to one for breach of contract, and the damages awarded will be the contract measure: *Walsh v Kerr* [1989] 1 NZLR 490. In this sort of case, that will normally be the sum required to put the plaintiff in the position he or she would have been in had the representation been true. Thus, damages will normally be the difference between the value of the subject matter had the representation been true, and its value as it in fact is.

It should be noted, however, that s 6 equates misrepresentation to breach of a term only for the purpose of recovering damages. For other purposes they remain distinct. For example, an exclusion clause excluding liability for one may not extend to the other: *Wilsons (NZ) Portland Cement Ltd v Gatx-Fuller Australasia Pty Ltd (No 2)* [1988] 2 NZLR 33, 37 per Prichard J.

7.1.6 Actions in tort

Section 6(1)(b) provides that in the case of a fraudulent or negligent misrepresentation the innocent party will not be entitled to damages against the other party in tort for deceit or negligence. Although in some cases a deceit action might have resulted in higher damages, the legislature has opted for simplicity, and has provided that the action against the other party is to be in contract alone. However the prohibition on suing in tort is confined to actions against the other party or parties to the contract. If the misrepresentation was made by an agent who is not himor herself a party, a tort action will probably lie against that agent: see *Wakelin v Jackson* (1984) 2 NZCPR 195 and *Shing v Ashcroft* [1987] 2 NZLR 154, 158 per Cooke P.

7.1.7 Exclusion clauses

It is not uncommon to find clauses in contracts which attempt to exclude liability for misrepresentation. A common form of such clause is to the effect that the purchaser "acknowledges that he is purchasing in reliance on his own judgment, and not in reliance on any statements made by the vendor." Section 4(1) of the Contractual Remedies Act 1979 limits the effectiveness of such clauses. It provides:

(1) If a contract, or any other document, contains a provision purporting to preclude a Court from inquiring into or determining the question—
(a) Whether a statement, promise, or undertaking was made or given, either in words or by conduct, in connection with or in the course of negotiations leading to the making of the contract; or
(b) Whether, if it was so made or given, it constituted a representation or a term of the contract; or

(c) Whether, if it was a representation, it was relied on —
the Court shall not, in any proceedings in relation to the contract be precluded by that provision from inquiring into and determining any such question unless the Court considers that it is fair and reasonable that the provision should be conclusive between the parties, having regard to all the circumstances of the case, including the subject-matter and value of the transaction, the respective bargaining strengths of the parties, and the question whether any party was represented or advised by a solicitor at the time of the negotiations or at any other relevant time.

This effectively means that despite the existence of such a clause the Court can go behind it, and look to the truth of the matter. If it finds that a false representation was in fact made, and that it did in fact induce the buyer, it may award damages. In a number of cases this has happened. For example, in *Bird v Bicknell* [1987] 2 NZLR 542 the buyers of a franchise were told (falsely) that the chemical process involved was a secret known only to them and the inventor. It was held that the purchaser could claim damages despite clauses in the contract to the effect that the buyers acknowledged the vendor gave no warranty, and that the buyers purchased solely in reliance on their own judgment. In all the circumstances, particularly the fact that the vendor had been fraudulent, it was not fair and reasonable "that the disclaimer clauses should be conclusive". However a different conclusion was reached in *Herbison v Papakura Video Ltd* [1987] 2 NZLR 527 when the Court found it was "fair and reasonable" to allow reliance on a similar disclaimer clause. Factors favouring the conclusiveness of the clause were the substantial price, the equivalence in bargaining strengths of the parties, the fact that both were competently legally advised, the precise wording of the contract and the business experience of the purchasers, and the fact that the disclaimer was not part of the standard form but was contained in a special clause drafted with particular reference to the facts of the case.

Section 4(2), similar in effect to s 4(1), provides that the Court may also go behind a clause which purports to preclude a Court from inquiring into or determining whether a person had actual or ostensible authority to make a statement, promise or undertaking.

7.1.8 The Fair Trading Act 1986

The Fair Trading Act 1986, based closely on the Australian Trade Practices Act 1974, will often provide another means of obtaining redress for misrepresentation. Section 9 provides:

No person shall, in trade, engage in conduct that is misleading or deceptive or is likely to mislead or deceive.

Sections 10-14 more specifically prohibit the making of various types of false statement and misleading conduct in relation to goods, services, land and employment. Section 43 gives the Court a discretion to grant various types of relief and remedy where those sections have been infringed. There is, for instance, power to order payment of the amount of any loss or damage suffered, power to direct that goods be repaired, power to vary any contract, and power to avoid any contract.

It is quite clear that, although the Act as a whole, particularly s 9, extends well beyond contract, it does cover misrepresentations *made in trade* which induce contracts. In many cases, then, it will provide an alternative cause of action to that in s 6 of the Contractual Remedies Act 1979. In some ways the Fair Trading Act is wider: "misleading conduct", while it certainly covers misrepresentation, may go wider and cover conduct which is not strictly a misrepresentation; there is a greater range of remedies available under it; damages are not confined to the contract measure; and (most importantly) it enables an action against anyone engaging in misleading conduct in trade *whether a party to the contract or not*. In other ways, however, it is narrower than s 6 of the Contractual Remedies Act: it only applies to conduct "in trade" and thus does not affect private sellers; and damages is a discretionary remedy only, and does not follow as of right as it does under the Contractual Remedies Act. In a number of cases the Fair Trading Act and the Contractual Remedies Act have been pleaded as alternatives: see for instance *Savill v NZI Finance* [1990] 3 NZLR 135.

A plea under the Fair Trading Act failed in *Mills v United Building Society* [1988] 2 NZLR 392 where the purchasers of a lease found it was a "Friedlander" worth far less than they thought. They alleged that the vendor's conduct in not clearly indicating its value to them was misleading. It was held, however, that it was not. The purchasers had been given a copy of the lease, and told to see a solicitor. The Court emphasised that the principle of caveat emptor had not been abrogated by the Fair Trading Act. Whether conduct is "misleading" is a question of fact.

7.2 TYPES OF BREACH

A breach of contract consists simply of a failure by one party to perform his or her promises under the contract. Thus if a party agrees to transfer property on a particular date and fails to do so, he or she is in breach; so is the builder who promises to build according to specification but departs from the specification; so is the shipowner who undertakes in a contract of charter to provide a seaworthy vessel, and provides one which is not seaworthy.

It should be recalled that many contracts contain implied as well as express terms. A failure to perform an implied promise is just as much a breach as if the promise were express.

There may also be what is described as an "anticipatory breach". This is perhaps, strictly speaking, not a breach at all, but rather an advance threat that a breach will take place at a future time. Thus, if I agree to transfer land to you on 1 November, but on 15 October repudiate the contract by unequivocally stating my intention not to perform on 1 November, this is a threat of breach. However, mainly for reasons of convenience, the law allows the innocent party to treat this repudiation as a breach in itself, and immediately to cancel the contract and sue for damages. Thus, in *Hochster v de la Tour* (1853) 2 E & B 678, D was engaged by H as a courier, his employment to begin on June 1. Prior to that date H said he would not employ D after all. D accepted this, put an end to the contract, and sued for damages. Despite certain doctrinal difficulties, it was held that D was entitled to do so. The fact that H might have again changed his decision prior to June 1 did not prevent D from recovering damages. On the other hand, the innocent party in such a case is not obliged to accept the repudiation and cancel the contract: he or she may if he or she wishes keep the contract on foot and attempt to persuade the other to perform when the time arises. If the innocent party follows this line of action, he or she is not in fact treating the repudiation as a breach at all. This law is preserved by the Contractual Remedies Act 1979, and will be dealt with more fully in that context later. (See 7.3.3).

The Contractual Remedies Act 1979 also recognises another type of anticipatory breach. In s 7(3)(c) it permits cancellation of the contract, in serious cases, where "it is clear that a stipulation in the contract will be broken by another party to that contract." This would seem to go beyond repudiation and encompass cases where, despite the fact that a party professes willingness to perform, it is quite clear that he or she will be unable to do so. An innocent party who attempts to cancel the contract in such circumstances may take a risk: there may be room for difference of opinion in a particular case whether it is *clear* that the stipulation in question is going to be broken.

7.3 CANCELLATION FOR BREACH AND MISREPRESENTATION

In the case of more serious breaches of contract and misrepresentations, the innocent party, in addition to the right to claim damages, has the option of cancelling – ie putting an end to – the contract. Sections 7 to 9 of the Contractual Remedies Act 1979 (which apply to all contracts made after 31 March 1980) define the types of breach and misrepresentation for which cancellation will lie, and describe the effects of cancellation. It should be noted at this point that the innocent party is never *obliged* to cancel; he or she merely has a *right* to do so.

7.3.1. Repudiation

Section 7(2) of the Act codifies what was formerly the common law on this subject. It provides that the innocent party may cancel the contract if the other party *repudiates* it by making it clear that he or she does not intend to perform the obligations under it, or to complete such performance. Repudiation, in other words, is a refusal to perform the contract. It may happen at the time when performance is due, or before that date, in which case it is described as an anticipatory repudiation. *Hochster v de la Tour* (supra 7.2) is an example of an anticipatory repudiation. A repudiation may be made in words or by conduct. An example of repudiation by conduct is *Forslind v Bechly-Crundall* 1922 SC 173 where a seller of timber was held to have repudiated when he delayed for a long time in performing, provided a galaxy of weak excuses, and indulged in what the Court described as "shilly-shallying". In all the circumstances the only conclusion a reasonable person could draw was that he did not intend to perform at all.

However, whether it is in words or by conduct the evidence of repudiation must be clear, and a Court will not find it lightly. Thus in *Schmidt v Holland* [1982] 2 NZLR 406 the purchasers of a house who went to the vendor and asked if she would "let them out of" the contract were held not to be repudiating. They were simply asking her if she would agree to a release, and were not unequivocally stating that they were not going to perform. However their later conduct did amount to a repudiation: they did not settle on due date, and bought another house. This, obviously, was clear evidence that they did not intend to proceed with this first purchase. The vendor was entitled to cancel.

It can also be repudiation for a party to express an intention to perform the contract in a way which departs substantially from the true contractual obligations. As Lord Wright said in *Ross T Smyth & Co Ltd v T D Bailey Son and Co* [1940] 3 All ER 60, 72:

> I do not say that it is necessary to show that the party alleged to have repudiated should have an actual intention not to fulfil the contract. He may intend in fact to fulfil it, but may be determined to do so only in a manner substantially inconsistent with his obligations, and not in any other way.

This was the position at common law, and is almost certainly still so under the statute. However, once again it must be clear that the party is *refusing* to perform the contract according to its true construction. In *Starlight Enterprises Ltd v Lapco Enterprises Ltd* [1979] 2 NZLR 744 L agreed to manufacture 4000 bags for S at a price of $3. After making 571 bags, L purported to raise the price for the remainder of the contract to $4.10 per bag. S treated this as a repudiation and tried to cancel the contract. It was held that L had not repudiated. It had been mistaken in believing it could raise the price; there was no evidence that when that error was pointed out to it it would still refuse to supply at the original price.

The stance of the Courts in requiring strong evidence of repudiation (and there are English cases to similar effect) means that it is dangerous for the innocent party to jump to the conclusion that the other party is repudiating. This has the effect of promoting communication with the other party to determine just how firm is that party's determination not to proceed.

7.3.2 Serious breaches and misrepresentations

In addition to being able to cancel for a repudiation, the innocent party can also cancel, by virtue of s 7(3), if one of the following has occurred:

(a) He [the innocent party] has been induced to enter into it [the contract] by a misrepresentation, whether innocent or fraudulent, made by or on behalf of another party to that contract; or

(b) A stipulation in the contract is broken by another party to that contract: or

(c) It is clear that a stipulation in the contract will be broken by another party to that contract.

However in each of these cases cancellation is only possible if the breach or misrepresentation is serious enough. Section 7(4) defines the degree of seriousness required. Its provisions are as follows:

(a) BREACH OF ESSENTIAL TERM

Firstly, the innocent party can cancel (by virtue of s 7(4)(a) of the Act) if:

(a) The parties have expressly or impliedly agreed that the truth of the representation, or as the case may require, the performance of the stipulation is essential to him.

This perpetuates something rather like what was described at common law as the "condition": a term of the contract which is so important that the parties intend that any breach of it should justify cancellation. Sometimes the parties make this clear by providing expressly in the contract that a certain term is "of the essence". In *New Zealand Tenancy Bonds Ltd v Mooney* [1986] 1 NZLR 280, for instance, the contract provided that the time specified for payment of the deposit was strictly of the essence of the contract. It was held that timeous payment was an essential term entitling cancellation if it was not complied with. Another example is provided by the old case of *Bannerman v White* (1861) 10 CB (NS) 844. B sued W for the price of hops delivered to W. Before purchasing W had asked if sulphur had been used in their cultivation and made it clear that if it had he was not interested in buying: he "would not even ask the price." B assured him sulphur had not been used. When it was found that sulphur had in fact been used, it was held that W was entitled to cancel. It is likely that the Courts will reach a similar conclusion where one party makes it clear that he or she will not enter a contract unless he or she receives a certain promise or assurance: see *Young v Hunt* [1984] 2 NZLR 80, 86. More difficult are the cases where it has to be determined whether the parties have *impliedly* agreed that a stipulation is essential. A line of English cases holds that certain time stipulations in shipping contracts are essential – eg a term that a buyer will give a seller 15 days notice of the readiness of a vessel for loading (*Bunge Corporation v Tradax Export SA* [1981] 1 WLR 711); it is likely that these cases would be followed in New Zealand, for such is the importance of certainty in mercantile contracts of this kind that the parties would probably be held to have "impliedly agreed" on the essentiality of such stipulations here also.

It should be noted, however, that it is not enough that one party alone privately treats a certain term as essential: *both* parties must "expressly or impliedly" have agreed that it is.

(b) ESSENTIAL BREACH (OR MISREPRESENTATION)

There are many terms in most contracts which are not essential in the sense just outlined. Nevertheless, some breaches of these inessential terms may have such far-reaching effects that they justify the innocent party in cancelling.

It should be noted that this applies not just to breaches of a stipulation, but also to misrepresentations and cases where it is clear that a breach is going to take place: see para. 7.3.2 above.

The tests the Act lays down are to be found in s 7(4)(b) as follows. The innocent party may cancel if:

(b) The effect of the misrepresentation or breach is, or, in the case of an anticipated breach, will be –
 (i) Substantially to reduce the benefit of the contract to the cancelling party; or
 (ii) Substantially to increase the burden of the cancelling party under the contract; or
 (iii) In relation to the cancelling party, to make the benefit or burden of the contract substantially different from that represented or contracted for.

In such a case it would not be reasonable to require the innocent party to continue with the contract. Just when a breach has effects which are "substantial" is of course a question of degree to be determined in each case. One common law case would be likely to be decided in the same way under the Act. In *Aerial Advertising Co v Batchelors Peas Ltd (Manchester)* [1938] 2 All ER 788, the plaintiffs entered into a contract with the defendants to fly over various towns trailing a streamer advertising the defendants' peas. The pilot was to telephone the defendants each day for instructions. He failed to telephone on two days, November 10 and 11. On November 11, Armistice Day, he flew over Salford's main square during the two minutes' silence trailing a streamer reading "Eat Batchelor's Peas." There was outrage among the citizens, and Batchelor's Peas received many letters and phone calls telling them their product would be boycotted. This breach of contract by Aerial Advertising Ltd was held sufficiently serious to justify Batchelor's Peas in cancelling the contract; the pilot's conduct, said Atkinson J, made it wholly unreasonable for the defendants to carry out the contract.

Likewise, it has been held in New Zealand in a case under the Act that a purchaser of a house could cancel when, contrary to his vendor's undertaking in the contract itself, the vendor was aware of two unsatisfied council requisitions on the property. These requisitions required the owner of the house to re-site a washing machine which currently operated on the back porch, and to rebuild a decking around the house and a swimming pool. The expense involved would be substantial in proportion to the price the purchaser had paid: the Court held that the benefit of the contract was thus substantially reduced, and its burden increased, as far as the purchaser was concerned: *Gallagher v Young* [1981] 1 NZLR 734.

On the other hand it was held insufficient to entitle cancellation when the turnover of a business was represented to be $600 a week when in fact it was $563 a week (*Young v Hunt* [1984] 2 NZLR 80); and when a misrepresentation as to the Government valuation of a house led to the purchaser paying 11 per cent too much for it (*Jolly v Palmer* [1985] 1 NZLR 658). It has been said that "substantiality" in s 7(4)(b)(iii) involves an assessment taking into account both subjective and objective factors: *Sharplin v Henderson* [1990] 2 NZLR 134, 137 per Cooke P.

It would seem that the Act does not differ very much from what used to be the common law on cancellation, or "discharge", for breach. In essence the question is one of degree, and once again it is important for an innocent party not to be too ready to cancel. If he or she makes an incorrect judgment that a breach is substantial enough to justify cancellation the innocent party may him- or herself be held in breach.

7.3.3 Option to cancel

The innocent party is not *obliged* to cancel in respect of a serious breach; this is simply an option he or she has. This was so at common law, and is the case also under the Act. The guilty party cannot unilaterally terminate a contract, which he or she is bound to perform, by breaking it. This position is graphically illustrated by *White and Carter (Councils) Ltd v McGregor* [1962] AC 413. An advertising contract for three years was made between the parties. The advertiser repudiated the contract almost immediately, but the repudiation was not accepted by the contractor, who continued to display advertisements for the period of the contract.

It was held that the contractor was entitled to recover the full contract price and was not obliged to cancel and sue for damages. This case has been the subject of criticism on the ground that it does not seem consistent with the rule that an innocent party should mitigate the loss; but it is consistent with the principle that the innocent party has a right to performance of the contract. The New Zealand Contracts and Commercial Law Reform Committee has studied the case, and has recommended that no action be taken by the legislature to reverse it.

If the innocent party elects not to cancel in respect of an *anticipatory repudiation*, he or she is in fact treating that repudiation as not being a breach at all. He or she cannot sue for damages on the basis of it without cancelling. As Asquith LJ said in *Howard v Pickford Tool Co Ltd* [1951] 1 KB 417, 421, "An unaccepted repudiation is a thing writ in water and of no value to anybody: it confers no legal rights of any sort or kind." In *Avery v Bowden* (1855) 5 E & B 714, B agreed to load A's ship at Odessa with wheat within a specified period. B's agent informed the master of the ship that no cargo would be loaded, but the master insisted on waiting for the cargo. Before the period fixed by the contract had expired, war broke out and the contract could not be performed. As the contract had been frustrated (see 8.1) before A had cancelled it, A could not successfully sue B. Likewise, in *Ferco-metal SARL v Mediterranean Shipping Co SA* [1989] 1 AC 788 a charterer was held entitled to exercise a contractual right to cancel even though the charterer had previously repudiated: the shipowner had elected to affirm the contract, which thus remained on foot in all respects. Lord Ackner stated at 801:

> The anticipatory breaches by the charterers not having been accepted by the owners as terminating the contract, the charterparty survived intact with the right of cancellation unaffected.

However while the innocent party always has in law merely an option and not an obligation to cancel, there may be some situations when the practicalities are such as to virtually force cancellation. One would be the situation in *Harbutt's Plasticine Ltd v Wayne Pump and Tank Co Ltd* [1970] 1 QB 447 where a breach by a manufacturer in installing machinery led to a fire which in turn led to a complete destruction of the factory in which the machine was being installed. Another may well be the case of an employee who is wrongfully dismissed: refusal to accept this dismissal and cancel the contract can lead to a practical impasse.

7.3.4 Affirmation

Under s 7(5) of the Act:

> (5) A party shall not be entitled to cancel the contract if, with full knowledge of the repudiation or misrepresentation or breach, he has affirmed the contract.

Thus, if one party clearly elects to keep the contract on foot after a serious breach by the other party, he or she will not be allowed later to cancel in respect of *that* breach. Thus in *Gray v Thomson* [1922] NZLR 465 it was held that a purchaser of land could not cancel in respect of a deficiency in area when, knowing of the deficiency, he remained in possession, continued to pay instalments of the purchase price, and requested compensation in respect of the deficiency.

It has been held in England that to be held to have affirmed a contract the innocent party must not only have known of the existence of the breach, but must also have known of the right to cancel: *Peyman v Lanjani* [1984] 3 All ER 703. However, in New Zealand this question has been left open, it being said that the question is always whether there has been a real and genuine affirmation: *Hughes v Huppert* [1991] 1 NZLR 475.

What conduct will be sufficient to amount to affirmation will depend on the facts of the case. For example will the issuing of a writ of specific performance inevitably be held to amount to affirmation? It is not uncommon practice for a vendor whose purchaser has repudiated to "keep his options open" by both issuing a writ of specific performance and putting the property on the market: presumably in such a case the evidence of affirmation could not be said to be sufficiently unequivocal: see *Stine v Maiden* (unreported, High Court, Auckland, 8 November 1984, M 269/84, Thorp J). In a number of cases the Courts have preferred to find that, rather than affirming, the party is simply keeping his or her options open. Thus in *New Zealand Tenancy Bonds Ltd v Mooney* [1986] 1 NZLR 280 even a long delay after the purchaser's breach did not amount, in the circumstances, to an affirmation.

However if a contract is affirmed after a breach, the innocent party may of course cancel in respect of a further breach after the date of affirmation, provided it is sufficiently serious. Thus in *Jolly v Palmer* (supra 7.3.2) a vendor affirmed after his purchaser's repudiation, but the conduct of his purchaser after the affirmation evinced a continuation of the repudiation. The vendor was held to be entitled to cancel on the basis of that later conduct.

7.3.5 Notice of cancellation

Section 8(1) and (2) provide as follows:

(1) The cancellation of a contract by a party shall not take effect—
(a) Before the time at which the cancellation is made known to the other party: or
(b) Where it is not reasonably practicable to communicate with the other party, before the time at which the party cancelling the contract evinces, by some overt means reasonable in the circumstances, his intention to cancel the contract.
(2) The cancellation may be made known by words, or by conduct evincing an intention to cancel, or both. It shall not be necessary to use any particular form of words, so long as the intention to cancel is made known.

The rule that cancellation does not take effect till made known to the other party is extremely important. In *Schmidt v Holland* [1982] 2 NZLR 406 a seller, after a purchaser's repudiation, resold the house to someone else. It was held that cancellation of the first contract had not been effected because the first purchaser had not been notified and the vendor had thus not laid the basis for a claim for damages for the loss of the contract. It will be seen that this could have very serious consequences, particularly if the original purchaser changed his or her mind and revoked his or her repudiation before being notified of the cancellation. In cases subsequent to *Schmidt v Holland* the Courts have tried to mitigate the harshness of the decision. In *Innes v Ewing* [1989] 1 NZLR 598

Eichelbaum J thought that a repudiating purchaser might be said to waive the need for communication of cancellation. In *Chatfield v Jones* [1990] 3 NZLR 285 the Court of Appeal preferred to leave this waiver solution open, but did say that if a vendor resells (as in the *Schmidt* case) even a much later notification that the resale has taken place can render the cancellation effective against the first purchaser: in that case it was held that even the documents in the vendor's ensuing action for damages amounted to a sufficient communication of the fact that the contract had been cancelled. There is clearly a logical difficulty here, and it may be that reform of the words of s 8(1) is required to bring it into line with the solution the Courts seem determined to reach.

The cancellation may be made known by words or conduct, and no particular form of words is necessary. In *Auckland Waterbed Co v Progressive Finance Ltd* (unreported, High Court, Christchurch, 24 May 1984, A 31/84, Chilwell J) a clear statement by one party in response to the other's breach that he was stopping his cheque was held to be a sufficient notification of cancellation.

It remains to be seen what conduct will be regarded as "overt means reasonable in the circumstances" for the purpose of s 8(1)(b). In *Car and Universal Finance Co Ltd v Caldwell* [1965] 1 QB 525 the purchaser of a car, whose cheque bounced, disappeared. The vendor told the AA and the police to attempt to recover the car. It was held that this was a sufficient rescission of the contract. No doubt a similar holding would be made under the Act.

7.3.6 The effect of cancellation

Cancellation, whether for breach or misrepresentation, is not rescission ab initio; it is cancellation for the future only. Section 8(3) and (4) provide:

> (3) Subject to this Act, when a contract is cancelled the following provisions shall apply:
> (a) So far as the contract remains unperformed at the time of the cancellation, no party shall be obliged or entitled to perform it further;
> (b) So far as the contract has been performed at the time of the cancellation no party shall, by reason only of the cancellation, be divested of any property transferred or money paid pursuant to the contract.
> (4) Nothing in subsection (3) of this section shall affect the right of a party to recover damages in respect of a misrepresentation or the repudiation or breach of the contract by another party.

Section 8(3)(a) provides that all unperformed obligations under the contract come to an end at the moment of cancellation. This proposition is normally simple of application, but is perhaps misleading in the case of certain secondary obligations. If the contract contains, for example, an arbitration clause or a liquidated damages clause, a too literal reading of the section might suggest that these "obligations" cease to bind the parties on cancellation. But this is an unlikely result. Since the right to damages continues after cancellation (s 8 (4)) it seems likely that provisions governing that right, and its enforcement, survive cancellation also. Lord Diplock's analysis in *Photo Production Ltd v Securicor Transport Ltd* [1980] AC 827 of termination for breach at common law may well be apposite under the statute too. He said that cancellation terminates only the primary contractual obligations (eg the obligations to provide the services and pay the price), but not the secondary obligations such as the duty to pay damages; indeed those secondary obligations actually replace the primary ones on cancellation.

In *Brown v Langwoods Photo Stores Ltd* [1991] 1 NZLR 173 Cooke P said he was not satisfied that cases of this type need give rise to difficulty. (Compare the doubts of Wylie J in *NZI Life Ltd v Partington Consultants Ltd* (High Court, Auckland, M 1842/90, 13 December 1990).) However, more difficulty might arise in other cases. Take the case where an employment contract contains a covenant by the employee not to compete with the employer after leaving the job. If the contract is cancelled because of the employee's breach, does the restraining covenant continue to bind him or her? In *Broadcasting Corporation of New Zealand v Nielsen* (1988) 2 NZELC 96040 it was held that such a clause did continue to bind, despite s 8(3)(a), because it was *expressed* to apply after termination of the contract, and under s 5 of the Act express contractual provisions take precedence over the Act.

However, a difficulty of far greater practical importance has arisen, and indicates that the apparently simple wording of s 8(3)(a) is by no means as straightforward as it looks. In *Pendergrast v Chapman* [1988] 2 NZLR 177 the vendor quite legitimately cancelled a contract to sell land because the purchaser had not paid the deposit on time as the contract required. It was held, despite s 8(3)(a), that the vendor could, after cancellation, sue to recover the unpaid deposit as a debt due and owing. This was not to require the party to "perform" the contract further; it was merely to claim a debt which had accrued due before cancellation and continued afterwards. The principle of that case applies not just to deposits, but to any debt which fell due under the contract before it was cancelled. That was affirmed in *Brown v Langwoods Photo Stores Ltd* [1991] 1 NZLR 173 where periodic payments under a franchise agreement, unpaid before cancellation, could be claimed afterwards as a debt due and owing. This is another situation, then, when it is easy to be misled by a first reading of the words of the section.

Section 8(3)(b) provides that cancellation alone does not undo what has been done under the contract before it was cancelled: money which has been paid is not divested, nor is property which has been transferred. Imagine, for instance, a case where the purchaser of land on a long term agreement for sale and purchase has paid over half the purchase price but then repudiates, whereupon the vendor cancels the contract. The cancellation alone does not divest the vendor of the proportion of the purchase money which he or she has received: he or she remains entitled to it. Likewise, if a person who has bought a business cancels the contract, property (for instance stock-in-trade) which has vested in that person remains that person's property; the original vendor does not automatically become re-entitled to it.

7.3.7 The discretion

However a situation such as that just described could lead to manifest injustice. The Act therefore confers on the Court a discretion to make orders granting relief in such circumstances. Section 9(1)-(4) provide as follows:

(1) When a contract is cancelled by any party, the Court, in any proceedings or on application made for the purpose, may from time to time if it is just and practicable to do so, make an order or orders granting relief under this section.

(2) An order under this section may:

(a) Vest in any party to the proceedings, or direct any such party to transfer or assign to any other such party or to deliver to him the possession of, the whole or any part of any real or personal property that was the subject of the contract or was the whole or part of the consideration for it:

(b) Subject to section 6 of this Act, direct any party to the proceedings to pay to any other such party such sum as the Court thinks just:

(c) Direct any party to the proceedings to do or refrain from doing in relation to any other party any act or thing as the Court thinks just.

(3) Any such order, or any provision of it, may be made upon and subject to such terms and conditions as the Court thinks fit, not being in any case a term or condition that would have the effect of preventing a claim for damages by any party.

(4) In considering whether to make an order under this section, and in considering the terms of any order it proposes to make, the Court shall have regard to:

(a) The terms of the contract; and

(b) The extent to which any party to the contract was or would have been able to perform it in whole or in part; and

(c) Any expenditure incurred by a party in or for the purpose of the performance of the contract; and

(d) The value, in its opinion, of any work or services performed by a party in or for the purpose of the performance of the contract; and

(e) Any benefit or advantage obtained by a party by reason of anything done by another party in or for the purpose of the performance of the contract; and

(f) Such other matters as it thinks proper.

Such an order for relief, and the terms on which it is made, are thus entirely in the Court's discretion, and are not the subject of firm rules. An application for relief may be made by the party, a person claiming through or under a party, or any other person if it is material for him or her to know if relief will be granted.

In *Worsdale v Polglase* [1981] 1 NZLR 722 P agreed to buy a house from V for $60,000. $6,000 was paid as deposit. P then repudiated, whereupon V cancelled and resold the house for exactly the same price. P then sued to recover back his deposit, less land agent's commission. The Court, exercising its discretion, refused this claim, holding that a deposit is an earnest for the performance of a bargain, and thus the defaulting purchaser should not recover it back unless it is excessive in amount or it is otherwise unconscionable for the vendor to retain it. In *Gallagher v Young* (supra 7.3.2) an order was made that the purchasers recover the whole of their purchase price after cancellation. And in *Young v Hunt* [1984] 2 NZLR 80, when a purchaser repudiated after going into possession of a coffee bar and after paying the vendor $11,300, the Court in its discretion revested the plant and fittings in the vendor, and allowed the purchaser to recover the sum of $5,000 from the vendor, being the $11,300 plus a small allowance for a misrepresentation which had misled the purchaser, *less* the amount which the vendor had lost as a result of the purchaser's cancellation.

No order may be made which deprives a person, not being a party to the contract, of any property acquired by him or her in good faith and for valuable consideration (s 9(5)). Nor may an order be made in respect of any property if a party to the contract has so altered his or her position in relation to it that it would be inequitable to make such an order (s 9(6)).

Section 9, in empowering the Court to order the payment of such sum as it thinks just, is in extremely wide terms. Although its primary purpose was to allow the Court to order the restitution of money paid (for instance, the refund of part payments etc), the section is perhaps widely enough framed to allow an award in the nature of compensation. In *Burch v Willoughby* (1990) 3 NZELC 97,582 for instance, an employee who had been wrongfully dismissed was awarded under s 9 compensation for hurt feelings. The correctness of this decision may be questioned.

7.3.8 Damages

A party to a contract is not precluded by the cancellation of the contract or by the granting of relief under s 9 from recovering damages in respect of a misrepresentation, repudiation or breach. But the value of any relief granted under s 9 is to be taken into account in assessing such damages, (s 10(1)).

7.3.9 Exclusions and savings

Section 5 of the Act provides:

> 5. **Remedy provided in contract** — If a contract expressly provides for a remedy in respect of misrepresentation or repudiation or breach of contract or makes express provision for any of the other matters to which sections 6 to 10 of this Act relate, those sections shall have effect subject to that provision.

It is thus open to the parties expressly to provide in the contract for their own remedies for breach, or their own variations of remedies such as cancellation. If they do so, their express contractual provisions will prevail over the Contractual Remedies Act insofar as they are inconsistent with it. Thus, the form of agreement for sale and purchase drawn up by the Law Society in conjunction with the Real Estate Institute lays down a special procedure (the serving of a settlement notice and consequent cancellation) if a purchaser of land does not settle on due date; a party may rely on this to the exclusion of the Contractual Remedies Act, if he or she wishes, in the event of such a failure to settle. But this clause is limited in scope. It does not, for instance, cover matters such as repudiation, misrepresentation or indeed any type of breach other than a failure to settle on due date; to those things the general law, ie the Act, applies. The clause also specifically provides that the remedies it lays down are "without prejudice to any other remedy" the party may have, eg remedies under the Act. In some situations, therefore, an innocent party may be able to elect whether to proceed under the Act, or under the express contractual provisions.

Section 15 of the Act provides that:

> Except as provided in sections 4(3), 6(2), and 14 of this Act, nothing in this Act shall affect—
> (a) The law relating to specific performance or injunction;
> (b) The law relating to mistake, duress, or undue influence;
> (c) The doctrine of *non est factum*;

(d) The Sale of Goods Act 1908;
(e) The Frustrated Contracts Act 1944;
(f) Thc Limitation Act 1950;
(g) Sections 117 to 119 of the Property Law Act 1952 (which relate to relief against forfeiture under leases);
(h) Any other enactment so far as it prescribes or governs terms of contracts or remedies available in respect of contracts, or governs the enforcement of contracts.

The most important of these savings is para (d). The Sale of Goods Act 1908, and not the Contractual Remedies Act, governs the "cancellation" of contracts for the sale of goods. Basically, in such a contract, if there is breach of a "condition", as opposed to a "warranty", the party may "treat the contract as repudiated" and reject the goods. Hardie Boys J said in *Finch Motors Ltd v Quin (No 2)* [1980] 2 NZLR 519 that apart from the important changes introduced by ss 4 and 6 of the Contractual Remedies Act 1979, there may be little scope for the application of the new Act to contracts for the sale of goods. This is a matter of great significance. It means that what is probably the most common type of contract is treated differently with regard to cancellation for breach. Law reformers may have to consider whether there would be advantages in bringing sale of goods into line with other sorts of contract.

7.3.10 The Fair Trading Act 1986

It will be recalled (7.1.8) that, if there has been misleading conduct in trade, one of the orders a Court can make is that a contract be declared void. Such an order – which is discretionary in the Court – might in some cases of misrepresentation be an alternative to cancellation under the Contractual Remedies Act 1979.

7.4 ENTIRE CONTRACTS AND SUBSTANTIAL PERFORMANCE

The common law knows a category of contracts called "entire contracts". An entire contract is one in which the parties have agreed, impliedly or expressly, that complete performance by one party is a condition precedent to the liability of the other. The most common example is the lump-sum contract, where A agrees to pay B a single sum of money when a piece of work, for instance a building, is completed by B. The rule at common law in such a case was that until B's work was completed, B was entitled to no payment at all. The agreed price is not due under the terms of the contract, and in the face of those express terms one cannot imply a term that B is entitled to a smaller amount in proportion to what has been done. There are a number of common law decisions where such a ruling caused considerable hardship: most of them involve builders who had partly completed a house or other structure and then abandoned the work. Likewise in *Vigers v Cook* [1919] 2 KB 475 an undertaker was entitled to nothing when, through the use of an inappropriate coffin which broke open, the funeral service had to take place in church without the coffin present; this was so despite the fact that the service, and the eventual burial, took place. And in *Bolton v Mahadeva* [1972] 1 WLR 1009 the plaintiff was held entitled to recover nothing in respect of the installation of a central heating and hot water system because the system emitted harmful fumes and heated inefficiently; the contract was treated as an entire contract in which payment was due on *completion* only.

To alleviate such hardship the common law developed a doctrine known as "substantial performance". If the performance of the contractor, although not literally complete, could be said to be substantially so, the Court would award him or her the contract price subject to a counterclaim for damages in respect of the uncompleted work. Thus in *Hoenig v Isaacs* [1952] 2 All ER 176 an interior decorator agreed to decorate a room, and provide it with furniture, for £ 750. This was held to be an entire contract. The work was done, but not entirely to the client's satisfaction: the door of a wardrobe needed replacing and a bookshelf which was too short required to be remade. It was held that the plaintiff was bound to pay the price, less the cost of putting right the defects.

The current law in New Zealand on entire contracts is not clear. If such a contract is frustrated before completion the Frustrated Contracts Act 1944 (infra 8.1.6) will apply and enable the Court to award reasonable compensation. But if one party is in breach in failing to complete an entire contract the question arises as to the impact of the Contractual Remedies Act 1979. A Court might conceivably say that since the condition of payment (ie completion) has not taken place, payment has never fallen due, and the matter is outside the Act. However since the Act is a remedial one the Courts are likely to give it a more liberal interpretation than this. They are likely to regard the question as being whether the failure to complete is a repudiation under s 7(2), a breach of an essential term under s 7(4)(a), or a breach which has in the circumstances substantially reduced the benefit of the contract to the contracting party under s 7(4)(b). If the answer is affirmative to any of these questions the other party could cancel, and the Court would then have a discretion under s 9 to make a just order granting relief. In a case such as *Bolton v Mahadeva* such an order could well consist in a requirement that the contractor be paid something for his or her services. Difficult questions would still remain, however, if the innocent party in this situation refused to cancel, but kept the contract open and insisted on completion. There would then be no scope for the operation of s 9.

7.5 DAMAGES

An action for damages is always available on any breach of contract. If the plaintiff has in fact suffered no loss he or she will recover merely nominal damages. Normally, however, the plaintiff will claim substantial damages. We shall consider four questions: (1) the general principles governing the quantification of damage in contract; (2) the remoteness rules limiting the kind of loss which may be recovered; (3) the requirement that the plaintiff should take reasonable steps to mitigate his or her loss; and (4) the validity of clauses which fix in advance the damages to be payable by a defaulting party.

7.5.1 Quantification of damages

(a) GENERAL PRINCIPLES
The victim of a breach of contract may suffer various different types of
losses for which damages may be recovered.

(1) Loss of bargain: The plaintiff's primary entitlement is to be compensated for loss of his or her bargain and thus get the benefit of what was
promised. An award of damages on this basis thus puts the plaintiff in the
position he or she would have enjoyed if the contract had been performed: *Stirling v Poulgrain* [1980] 2 NZLR 402, 419. For example, in
Williams v Kirk [1988] 1 NZLR 452 a vendor seeking damages for repudiation by the purchaser of a contract for the sale of land could recover the
difference between the contract price and the lower price obtained by
him on subsequently reselling the land. Again, in *Ryan v Hallam* [1990]
3 NZLR 184, one of the many cases arising out of the stock market crash
of October 1987, a vendor of shares at a pre-determined price was entitled
to receive from the defaulting purchaser the difference between the price
and the (much lower) value of the shares at the date fixed for settlement.
Recovery of damages based on difference in value in contracts for the sale
of goods is discussed in chapter 20.
    In some cases, such as where building work done under a contract is
defective, there are two possible bases of assessment: the difference in
value between what was promised and what was supplied, and the cost
of rectifying the breach. The Courts take a pragmatic attitude and adopt
whichever seems appropriate: see *Bevan Investments Ltd v Blackhall and
Struthers (No 2)* [1978] 2 NZLR 97 (CA).

(2) Reliance loss: The plaintiff may claim for expenses incurred in reliance
on the contract and here he or she is put in the position as if the contract
had never been made. Thus in *McRae v Commonwealth Disposals Commission* (1951) 84 CLR 377 the plaintiffs contracted to buy from the defendants an oil tanker said to be wrecked on a reef north of Samarai. It turned
out that no such tanker existed. The Court held that the plaintiffs could
recover as damages for breach of contract the agreed purchase price and
the costs incurred in fitting out a salvage expedition, being expenditure
wasted in reliance on the promise that there was a tanker at the locality
given.

(3) Restitution: A plaintiff who has paid money or given other benefits
under the contract may claim that they be restored to him. Such a claim
is not strictly one for "damages"; and where cancellation is sought under
the Contractual Remedies Act 1979 the prima facie position is that
property already transferred under the contract remains transferred (s
8(3)(b)), but the Court has a discretion to order restitution under s 9:
supra, paras 7.3.6, 7.3.7.

    The plaintiff in any particular case may not, of course, suffer more than
one of these types of loss or a claim under one head or another may not
be maintainable for some reason. Thus if the plaintiff claims for loss of
bargain he or she must be able to prove the value of his or her expectations; some other basis for assessment must be chosen if the inquiry as to

anticipated profits becomes too speculative: *McRae v Commonwealth Disposals Commission* supra. Restitution of money paid under a contract can, in general, only be awarded if there has been a total failure of consideration: *Fibrosa* case [1943] AC 32. Where more than one type of claim is, however, available, the plaintiff may elect which he or she wishes to pursue: see *CCC Films (London) Ltd v Impact Quadrant Films Ltd* [1985] QB 16. Indeed there is no objection to combining the various types of claim but not so as to recover more than once for the same loss: *Herbison v Papakura Video Ltd (No 2)* [1987] 2 NZLR 720. It might, for example, be necessary to expend money in reliance on a contract in order to earn the anticipated profits; both losses cannot then be recovered.

A breach of contract may in addition involve the innocent party in extra expenses or cause further harm such as damage to property and these losses also are recoverable. An example is *Parsons Ltd v Uttley Ingham Ltd* [1978] QB 791 where the plaintiff pig farmer recovered damages for loss of his pigs from the supplier of a hopper which in breach of contract had not been properly ventilated, causing the pignuts stored in it to go mouldy and the pigs which ate the nuts to die.

(b) DATE OF QUANTIFICATION

The date by reference to which damages for breach of contract will be assessed may assume considerable importance in times of high inflation and rising costs. The date of breach is usually taken as the starting point. Thus on a refusal to accept or deliver goods, the damages are prima facie measured by the difference between the contract and the market price at the time when the goods ought to have been accepted or delivered: Sale of Goods Act 1908 ss 51(3), 52(3), infra, paras 20.1, 20.2. The general rule may, however, yield to the Court's power in the interests of justice to fix such other date as may be appropriate in all the circumstances: *Stirling v Poulgrain* [1980] 2 NZLR 402, 420. If the innocent party acting reasonably only discovers the breach some time after it has been committed and then acts with reasonable promptitude, for example by doing necessary repairs to a defective building, he or she may be compensated for the actual costs incurred: *Bevan Investments* case, supra. Furthermore, the innocent party may know of a breach but be unable to act on it, for example by making a substitute contract or putting right a defect, because he or she lacks the means to do so or because it would not make sense, from a commercial point of view, to incur further expense while issues of both liability and quantum remain in dispute. Damages may then be assessed as at the date of trial: *Wroth v Tyler* [1974] Ch 30: *Bevan Investments* case, supra.

While damages may be assessed at a date later than breach or at trial in order to compensate an innocent party, they may not be so assessed to the benefit of the defaulting party. Thus on a breach of contract to buy land, a rise in the value of the land after the date of the breach is disregarded: *Turner v Superannuation & Mutual Savings Ltd* [1978] 1 NZLR 218.

(c) DAMAGES AND TAX LIABILITY

In *British Transport Commission v Gourley* [1956] AC 185 the House of Lords held that where an award of damages includes compensation for loss of income that would have been assessable to tax, the damages must be calculated by reference to the net loss of income after deducting the tax that would otherwise have been paid. The rule presupposes that the damages award itself would not be subject to income tax when paid. *Gourley's* case concerned a claim for damages in tort for loss of earnings and was followed in New Zealand in respect of a similar claim in *Smith v Wellington Woollen Manufacturing Co Ltd* [1956] NZLR 491 (CA). The principle involved could be equally applicable to contractual claims for loss of earnings or profits but in *North Island Wholesale Groceries Ltd v Hewin* [1982] 2 NZLR 176 the Court of Appeal declined so to extend it and held that in claims for compensation for loss of office any potential income tax liability should not be taken into account when calculating the damages awarded. The approach taken in *Hewin's* case was affirmed in *Horsburgh v New Zealand Meat Processors Industrial Union of Workers* [1988] 1 NZLR 698. *Smith's* case has not been formally overruled but with the advent of the accident compensation scheme the problem can no longer arise in the context of a tort action.

7.5.2 Remoteness of damage

(a) GENERAL PRINCIPLES

A defendant is not liable for damage caused by his or her breach of contract but which nonetheless is too remote a consequence of it. The test of remoteness to be applied here was laid down by Alderson B in the leading case of *Hadley v Baxendale* (1854) 9 Exch 341, 354:

> Where two parties have made a contract which one of them has broken, the damages which the other party ought to receive in respect of such breach of contract should be such as may fairly and reasonably be considered either arising naturally, ie according to the usual course of things, from such breach of contract itself, or such as may reasonably be supposed to have been in the contemplation of both parties, at the time they made the contract, as the probable result of the breach of it.

There are thus two limbs to the principle, the first dealing with normal and the second with abnormal loss. Normal loss is presumed to be in the contemplation of the parties. For abnormal loss to be recoverable it must be shown that such loss was or should have been in the contemplation of both parties when the contract was made. The defendant need not have expressly agreed to compensate the plaintiff for the loss. It is sufficient if he or she ought to have seen that the loss was likely to be caused by the breach.

It is instructive to see how these principles were applied to the facts of *Hadley v Baxendale*. The plaintiffs, who were mill owners in Gloucestershire, engaged the defendant carriers to take a broken mill shaft to Greenwich as a pattern for a new one. The defendants promised to deliver the shaft at Greenwich the following day but due to their neglect it was delayed in transit so that there was a stoppage of several days at the mill. The plaintiffs' claim for damages for loss of profit caused by the delay failed. The stoppage was not the "natural" consequence of the delay: it could not have been foreseen by the carrier that delay would keep the mill idle. The plaintiffs might have had a spare shaft or been able to get one. Nor could the stoppage have been contemplated by *both* parties as the probable result of the breach, for the defendants were not told that any delay would keep the mill idle.

The rule in *Hadley v Baxendale* has been considered and applied on many occasions since 1854. An important case where it received careful examination is *Victoria Laundry (Windsor) Ltd v Newman Industries Ltd* [1949] 2 KB 528 where Asquith LJ reformulated the test in terms of whether the loss was "reasonably foreseeable as liable to result from the breach". This gave rise to the view that the same test governed remoteness of damage in both contract and tort but when the matter came before the House of Lords in *The Heron II* [1969] 1 AC 350 it was made clear that liability in tort was wider than in contract, and for good reason. Lord Upjohn said why. A tortfeasor is liable for any damage which he can reasonably foresee may happen as a result of a breach of duty, however unlikely it may be, unless it can be brushed aside as far-fetched: The *Wagon Mound* cases *(No 1)* [1961] AC 388: *(No 2)* [1967] 1 AC 617. A tortfeasor usually is a stranger to the innocent party but he or she is a neighbour for the purposes of the law and is bound to act with due regard for his or her neighbour's rights whoever he or she may be. If he or she fails in such a duty the law has rightly laid down a stringent test for the assessment of damages. In contract, however, the parties have only to consider the consequences of the breach to the other: it is fair that the assessment of damages should depend on their assumed common knowledge and contemplation and not on a foreseeable but most unlikely consequence.

Various expressions were used by their Lordships to describe the higher degree of probability required to satisfy the test of remoteness in contract. Lord Reid thought that the party in breach was liable for losses "not unlikely" or "quite likely" to result. Lord Morris referred to losses that were "contemplated" by the parties. Lord Hodson preferred "liable to result" from the breach as the test. Lord Pearce rejected the phrase "on the cards" used at one point by Asquith LJ in favour of loss "within the contemplation of the parties". Lord Upjohn adopted the phrases "a real danger" or "a serious possibility". It cannot thus be said that the House of Lords has laid down a single test for determining which losses resulting from the breach will be covered by an award of damages. Indeed, it may be that the test to be applied is incapable of any more precise formulation than as laid down by Alderson B in *Hadley v Baxendale* itself. In the words of Sellers LJ when *The Heron II* was before the English Court of Appeal, "the phrases and words of *Hadley v Baxendale* have been hallowed by long user and gain little advantage from paraphrases or substitutes".

The decision of the Court of Appeal in *Isaac Naylor and Sons Ltd v New Zealand Co-operative Wool Marketing Association Ltd* [1981] 1 NZLR 261 illustrates the principles of remoteness of damage in operation. The plaintiff sued for losses caused by delays on the part of the defendant in taking delivery of and paying for wool which the defendant had contracted to purchase from the plaintiff. The contract provided for payment in the United Kingdom in sterling and the value of this currency fell during the period of delay. The Court held that exchange losses were recoverable if the criteria ordinarily applied in damages cases in contract were satisfied. On the facts the loss was not too remote because: (1) the risk of loss from fluctuating exchange rates was fairly and reasonably within the contemplation of the parties as international wool traders, bringing the case within the first limb of *Hadley v Baxendale;* and (2) (per

Richardson J) the defendant knew that the plaintiff would be remitting the purchase money to New Zealand and would be detrimentally affected by adverse movements in the exchange rate during the period of delay and so the circumstances fell within the second limb of the rule as well.

(b) UPSET AND DISTRESS

Whether ordinary remoteness principles can apply to the claim by the victim of a breach of contract for compensation in respect of vexation, annoyance and distress caused by the breach for long has been a matter of controversy, but recently the question has been resolved so far as the law in New Zealand is concerned.

The source of the difficulty is the decision of the House of Lords in *Addis v Gramophone Co Ltd* [1909] AC 488, where it was held that a manager who had been wrongfully dismissed by his employer in a harsh and humiliating way could recover damages for loss of salary and commission but not for injured feelings. The *Addis* rule seemed to be that damages for non-pecuniary loss could not be recovered in a contract action, but this proposition soon came to be seen as too sweeping. In *Wilson v United Counties Bank Ltd* [1920] AC 102 the House of Lords held that a trader who had contracted with a bank to manage his business could recover damage to his credit and reputation after the bank's mismanagement led him into bankruptcy. It has also been recognised in a number of cases that the rule does not apply in the case of contracts to provide enjoyment or prevent distress. Thus damages for loss of enjoyment of the amenities of a social club may be awarded on the plaintiff being expelled in breach of contract from the club: *Byrne v Auckland Irish Society* [1979] 1 NZLR 351. A package tour operator who provided the plaintiff with sub-standard accommodation on a skiing holiday was liable for the plaintiff's disappointment and loss of a pleasurable holiday: *Jarvis v Swan's Tours Ltd* [1973] 2 QB 233. Solicitors who failed in breach of contract to obtain a non-molestation order to protect the plaintiff from the unwelcome attentions of a rejected suitor were held liable for the plaintiff's mental distress and suffering when the molestation continued: *Heywood v Wellers* [1976] QB 446.

The Courts in England so far have not been prepared to go any further. In *Hayes v James and Charles Dodd* [1990] 2 All ER 815 the Court of Appeal affirmed that damages for mental distress caused by a breach of contract cannot be recovered simply on the basis that the distress was reasonably foreseeable or should reasonably have been within the contemplation of the parties. Staughton LJ said that such damages should not be awarded in any case where the object of the contract was not comfort or pleasure, or the relief of discomfort, but simply carrying on a commercial activity with a view to profit. It is not clear that all contracts can easily be fitted into one or other category, and at all events in New Zealand an approach more in accordance with general principle has now emerged. The ground was laid in *Horsburgh v New Zealand Meat Processors Industrial Union of Workers* [1988] 1 NZLR 698 and *Hetherington v Faudet* [1989] 2 NZLR 224, where the Court of Appeal expressed reservations about *Addis'* case and said its application in present day New Zealand calls for consideration. Then in *Whelan v Waitaki Meats Ltd* [1991] 2 NZLR 74 Gallen J undertook an exhaustive review of the question. His Honour observed that the view that the law does not permit general damages to be awarded for breach of contract is inconsistent with much authority decided after *Addis*, whereas to treat the decision as laying down a specific rule applying to breaches of contracts relating to employment is difficult to justify in law and in logic. He thus preferred the view taken in Canada, that *Addis* is no more than an illustration of a principle that in commercial contracts such damages are inappropriate as not being foreseeable. In the result his Honour was prepared to award substantial damages for distress to an employee wrongfully dismissed in an abrupt and high-handed way after 29 years' service with the employer.

If any uncertainty about the matter remained even after *Whelan*, it has effectively been put to rest by the legislature. A Tribunal or Court settling a claim by an employee under the personal grievance procedure in the Employment Contracts Act 1991, which procedure applies to all employment contracts, is empowered by s 40(1)(c)(i) to provide for payment to the employee of compensation for "humiliation, loss of dignity and injury to the feelings of the employee". In *Air New Zealand Ltd v Johnston* (Court of Appeal, 91/90, 26 June 1991), Cooke P, after referring to *Whelan* with approval, said that the 1991 Act had now put the point beyond all doubt. Certainly, then, in the unlikely event of a dismissed employee bringing an action for wrongful dismissal rather than using the 1991 Act procedures, the Courts are not going to continue to apply *Addis*. Indeed in any common law action it is clear that *Hadley v Baxendale* principles will apply and the question will be simply whether upset and distress were within the reasonable contemplation of the parties.

For further discussion see Dawson "General Damages in Contract for Non-Pecuniary Loss" (1983) 10 NZULR 232.

7.5.3 Mitigation

A plaintiff should take reasonable steps to mitigate or reduce the loss caused by a breach of contract. The burden is on the defendant to prove that there has been a failure to mitigate, but if the defendant succeeds in showing this the plaintiff cannot recover compensation for loss flowing from that failure. Thus an employee who has been dismissed in breach of contract must seek other employment and so reduce the loss caused by the breach: *Brace v Calder* [1895] 2 QB 253. Where a buyer refuses to accept the contract goods the seller must use his or her best efforts to sell to other purchasers: *Pacific Overseas Corporation Ltd v Watkins, Browne and Co (NZ) Ltd* [1954] NZLR 459. Exactly what steps are reasonably required of the plaintiff is a question of fact in each particular case. In *Payzu Ltd v Saunders* [1919] 2 KB 851, for example, a seller of goods agreed to give credit and then refused to deliver except for cash. It was held that the buyer was bound to mitigate by accepting such delivery instead of buying elsewhere on a rising market. On the other hand in *Pilkington v Wood* [1953] Ch 770 the purchaser of a house was not obliged to embark upon complicated litigation against the vendor for having conveyed a defective title, in mitigation of a claim against his solicitor for negligently investigating the title. *Treloar v Henderson* [1968] NZLR 1085 is a similar case. On a breach of a contract to buy land the vendor is not obliged to resell (*Pendergrast v Chapman* [1988] 2 NZLR 177), but if in fact the vendor does seek to resell he or she should offer the land at a proper price having regard to the state of the market, take adequate steps to advertise and promote the sale and keep the property in reasonable order and condition: *Sullivan v Darkin* [1986] 1 NZLR 214.

It was made clear in *James Finlay and Co v NV Twik Hoo Tong HM* [1929] 1 KB 400 that a plaintiff is under no obligation to risk injury to himself or herself, his or her character, business or property in order to reduce the damages payable by the other party. A buyer of goods thus was not required to enforce against sub-buyers the strict terms of a sub-contract in mitigation of a claim against the sellers where such a course would ruin his commercial reputation.

Loss may also be said to be mitigated if some benefit in fact accrues to the plaintiff as a result of the breach. In *British Westinghouse Co v Underground Electric Rys Co of London* [1912] AC 673 it was held by the House of Lords that if a plaintiff has taken reasonable and prudent steps to protect himself or herself from the consequences of a breach of contract, then in order to assess the damages for the breach any loss sustained by the plaintiff must be balanced against any gain to him or her incidentally derived from his or her steps in mitigation. The gain should, however, arise directly out of the conduct aimed at lessening the consequences of the breach. This principle was applied by the Court of Appeal in *I T Walker Holdings Ltd v Tuf Shoes Ltd* [1981] 2 NZLR 391. The plaintiff agreed to purchase from the defendant a factory in the course of construction but the building was not completed by the contract date. The plaintiff moved into another factory and claimed damages including, inter alia, the cost of the other factory's lease and of outfitting the premises. It was held that the plaintiff's loss was the expense caused by its being deprived of the premises at the agreed time (ie the cost of the lease and the outfitting) less the resale value of the remainder of the lease.

7.5.4 Damages fixed by the contract

The parties to a contract may, at the time of entering into it, provide that in case of breach the party in default should pay to the other a sum certain specified in the contract. Such provision may reflect good business sense and be advantageous to both parties. It enables them to envisage the financial consequences of a breach; and if litigation proves inevitable it avoids the difficulty and the legal costs, often heavy, of proving what loss has in fact been suffered by the innocent party: *Robophone Facilities Ltd v Blank* [1966] 1 WLR 1428 per Diplock LJ. It cannot, however, be used in effect as a means of forcing the offending party to perform the contract. The distinction which must be drawn here is between a genuine pre-estimate of damage on the one hand and a penalty on the other. The first is a form of liquidated damages and is perfectly valid even though the stipulated sum may not be exactly the amount of the loss. The second operates *in terrorem* and will not be enforced by the Courts.

Whether a clause genuinely pre-estimates the damage or operates as a penalty is a question of construction. The description given to it by the parties is relevant but not decisive. In *Dunlop Pneumatic Tyre Co Ltd v New Garage and Motor Co Ltd* [1915] AC 79 Lord Dunedin summarised the rules for distinguishing between them. They are as follows:

(i) It is a penalty if the sum stipulated for is extravagant or uncon-
    scionable in amount in comparison with the greatest loss that
    could possibly follow from the breach.

(ii) It is a penalty if the breach consists only in not paying a sum of
    money, and the sum stipulated is greater than the sum due to be
    paid.

(iii) There is a presumption (but no more) that it is a penalty when a
    single lump sum is made payable on the occurrence of one or more
    of several events, some of which may occasion serious and others
    only trifling damage.

(iv) It is no obstacle to the sum stipulated being a genuine pre-estimate
    of damage that the consequences of breach are such as to make
    precise pre-estimation impossible. On the contrary that is just the
    situation when pre-estimated damages was the true bargain be-
    tween the parties.

In this case the defendants bought tyres from the plaintiffs and agreed
that they would not: (1) tamper with the manufacturer's mark; (2) sell
below the list price; (3) sell to any person "suspended" by the plaintiff;
(4) exhibit or export tyres without the plaintiff's written consent. They
agreed to pay to the plaintiffs £ 5 per tyre sold or offered in breach of the
agreement. It was held that the provision for payment of £ 5 was not
penal. The presumption that a sum payable on several events was penal
was rebutted by the fact that the damage caused by each of those events
was of such an uncertain nature it could not be accurately ascertained.

The distinction between liquidated damages and a penalty has been
considered in a number of recent cases. For example, in *General Finance
Acceptance Ltd v Melrose* [1988] 1 NZLR 465 an agreement to lease a
computer contained a formula for calculating damages which, if it were
applied, would mean that the owner would recover significantly more as
a result of the hirer's default than it would have recovered had the
agreement run its course. The clause was, therefore, penal and unenforceable. In *Turner v Superannuation & Mutual Savings Ltd* [1987] 1 NZLR
218 the forfeiture of a deposit of 5.5 per cent of the purchase price of
property was held to be a penalty where the contract provided for the
recovery of full damages in addition to retention of the deposit. In *Jobson
v Johnson* [1989] 1 WLR 1026 a clause providing for the repurchase of
shares if the purchaser defaulted on certain instalment payments was
penal, because the repurchase was at a fixed price irrespective of the
gravity and consequences of the breach.

The rules as to penalties normally only apply in the case of a *breach* of
contract. A clause under which a sum is payable only on some other event
is, therefore, not a penalty: *Export Credits Guarantee Dept v Universal Oil
Products Co Ltd* [1983] 1 WLR 399 (HL). However, where a clause
provides for payment on several events, one of which is a breach while
the others are not, the position is uncertain. At least if the contract is in fact
determined by breach the law as to penalties will apply. The problem
arose in *Bridge v Campbell Discount Co Ltd* [1962] AC 600. The hirer of a car
under a hire purchase agreement paid a deposit and the first instalment
by way of repayment of the price and then notified the owner that due to
unforeseen personal circumstances he would not be able to pay any more
and asked when and where he would have to return the car. Shortly
afterwards he did in fact return it. The owner then sued for two-thirds of

the hire purchase price under a clause in the agreement providing that if the agreement were terminated, the hirer should deliver up the vehicle and pay arrears and interest plus "by way of agreed compensation such further sum as may be necessary to make the rental paid and payable equal to two thirds of the hire purchase price". The majority of their Lordships thought that the hirer had reluctantly felt compelled to break the agreement and had never had the slightest intention of exercising his option to terminate. They went on to decide that the clause was penal and hence invalid. The sum payable was said to be compensation for depreciation yet it *decreased* with each payment made by the hirer whereas the depreciation obviously increased the longer the hirer kept the goods. In the words of Lord Radcliffe it was "a sliding scale of compensation but a scale that slides in the wrong direction".

Whether the clause would have been enforceable if the hirer had lawfully terminated the contract was left undecided. Authority prior to *Bridge's* case (eg *Associated Distributors Ltd v Hall* [1938] 2 KB 83 (CA)) holds that no question of penalty then arises. There is, however, much to be said for the contrary view for otherwise, as Lord Denning observed in *Bridge's* case, it means that equity commits itself to an absurd paradox: it will grant relief to a person who breaks his or her contract but will penalise the person who keeps it.

For special statutory provision concerning minimum payment clauses in hire purchase agreements, see infra, para 37.3.3.

Where the sum stipulated is held to be a penalty the plaintiff can still recover damages in the ordinary way, but must, of course, establish his or her actual loss in accordance with the principles governing quantification of damage discussed in para 7.5.1.

7.6 EQUITABLE REMEDIES

7.6.1 Specific performance

A decree of specific performance is an equitable remedy whereby the Court may order that the contract be performed as promised. The orthodox view at least is that it is available only when the ordinary remedy for breach of contract, damages, would not be an adequate remedy: *Loan Investment Corporation of Australasia v Bonner* [1970] NZLR 724 (PC). Thus it will usually be ordered at the suit of a buyer of land or a house because the particular subject matter is unique and so damages for refusal to perform the contract can be seen to be inadequate. On the other hand it will rarely be granted in the case of a contract for the sale of goods, for normally the buyer can easily be compensated in damages: see infra, para 20.2.2. Again, a breach of a contract to lend or borrow money is seen as readily compensatable in damages.

It may be that the Courts have taken, or have appeared to have taken, too rigid an approach to the grant of this remedy. The action for breach of contract exists to protect a person's expectation that a contract will be performed and arguably that expectation is best met by recognising specific performance as a primary, routine remedy. Indeed it has been argued that recent New Zealand cases have moved away from treating the remedy as a secondary alternative to damages, and that they demonstrate that the discretion is exercised as one to refuse the remedy should it be inappropriate rather than to grant it if damages are inappropriate: see Beck "Specific Performance in the New Zealand Courts from 1970" (1987) 6 OLR 420.

On any view specific performance, unlike damages, is not available as of right. As for the factors to be taken into account in the exercise of the discretion, arguably a distinction should be drawn between those which go to the question of the *validity* of the agreement and those which go to the appropriateness of the remedy in the particular circumstances. Some cases have denied the remedy where the plaintiff has acted unconscionably or unfairly (for example *K v K* [1976] 2 NZLR 31) or where the defendant has made a mistake as to the subject matter of the contract (for example *Wallace v McGirr* [1936] NZLR 483), but such cases should, it seems, be determined in accordance with ordinary principles of unconscionability (supra, para 5.2.3) or mistake (supra, para 5.3). It is not clear that there is room for a half-way house where, say, an agreement is not so unconscionable as to be unenforceable but is sufficiently unconscionable as to confine the plaintiff to his or her remedy in damages.

Putting aside questions such as these, the Courts bring into account a number of other factors which bear upon the appropriateness of granting specific performance in all the circumstances of the case.

(i) Specific performance may be refused on the ground of severe hardship to the defendant, such as where the cost of performance to the defendant is out of all proportion to the benefit which performance will confer on the plaintiff: *Tito v Waddell (No 2)* [1977] Ch 106. In contrast is the case where performance simply will put the defendant in financial difficulty. In *Brett Wotton Properties Ltd v Cameron* (High Court, Rotorua, A 3/83, 29 July 1986) a mere change in tax laws rendering a contract uneconomic was seen as an irrelevant consideration.

(ii) It is generally seen as undesirable and unworkable to attempt to force upon an unwilling party the performance of a contract for personal services: see *Rigby v Connol* (1880) 14 Ch D 482. Specific performance may, however, be awarded if the evidence shows that it is unlikely to lead to serious practical difficulties: see *Thomas Borthwick & Sons (Australasia) Ltd v South Otago Freezing Co Ltd* [1978] 1 NZLR 538, discussed infra, para 7.6.2.

(iii) The plaintiff may be confined to his or her remedy in damages in cases where the proper performance of the contract is likely to require constant supervision by the Courts: *Ryan v Mutual Tontine Association* [1893] 1 Ch 116.

(iv) It is relevant to ask whether the plaintiff has delayed in seeking to enforce the contract: *Hickey v Bruhns* [1977] 2 NZLR 71.

(v) Sometimes a Court may adhere to a principle of mutuality and thus refuse specific performance at the suit of one party where it would not be available at the suit of the other. For example, an infant may be denied the remedy if it would not be ordered against the infant. For discussion of the principle see *Price v Strange* [1978] Ch 337.

7.6.2 Injunction

A party may in some circumstances be restrained by injunction from committing a breach of contract and thus in effect be compelled to perform the contract. An injunction may be prohibitory or mandatory. A prohibitory injunction may be granted in the case of a negative promise requiring the defendant to refrain from doing what he or she has promised not to do. The Court is not concerned here with the balance of convenience or inconvenience and will not deny the remedy merely because any advantage to the plaintiff might be seen as outweighed by the detriment to the defendant. As was observed by Lord Cairns LC in *Doherty v Allman* (1878) 3 App Cas 709, 720, the injunction does nothing more than give the sanction of the process of the Court to that which already is the contract between the parties. The Court retains a residual discretion, however, and the nature of the covenant and the surrounding circumstances must be taken into account: *McBean and Pope Ltd v Coley* [1965] NZLR 966. A mandatory injunction is restorative and orders an existing breach of contract to be undone. In this case disproportionate hardship to the defendant, as with a claim for specific performance, is clearly relevant: *Charrington v Simons* [1970] 2 All ER 257.

It was noted above that the Courts generally decline to order specific performance in the case of contracts for personal services. So also an injunction will not be issued if its effect is to oblige the defendant to perform a contract which is not otherwise specifically enforceable. In *Lumley v Wagner* (1852)1 De GM & G 604 Mlle Wagner was engaged to sing exclusively at Mr Lumley's theatre. During the currency of the contract she agreed to sing for a competitor and refused to sing for Mr Lumley. The Court granted an injunction restraining Mlle Wagner from singing elsewhere during the term of her contract with Mr Lumley. This operated as an inducement to carry out her contract but did not compel it for she could have taken other employment which did not involve singing. An injunction ordering the defendant not to take employment in any capacity with a person other than the plaintiff would, however, have been tantamount to specific performance of a contract for personal services. *Lumley's* case was applied in *McBean and Pope Ltd v Coley*, supra, where McGregor J refused an injunction where the effect would have been either to render the defendant idle and without employment or to force him to return to the employment of the plaintiff.

Whether an injunction would "effectively compel " performance of a contract for personal services was considered recently by the English Court of Appeal in *Warren v Mendy* [1989] 1 WLR 853. The plaintiff had entered into a contract to manage the affairs of B, a talented boxer, and sought an injunction restraining the defendant from acting as manager of B in his place. The Court rejected the argument that an injunction would not be compulsive because of the possibility that B could be managed by someone else: the plaintiff might seek relief against any other manager as well and in any event B took the view that he needed the services of the defendant.

In these "personal services" cases the Courts are exercising a discretion, not applying a rule. In *Thomas Borthwick & Sons (Australasia) Ltd v South Otago Freezing Co Ltd* [1978] 1 NZLR 538 the appellant freezing company and the respondent exporter had entered a contract whereby

(i) the appellant would buy stock at prices notified by the respondent, process it and sell it to the respondent, and (ii) the appellant would not handle stock on behalf of anyone else. Wild CJ in the Supreme Court granted an injunction restraining breach of this latter promise and in the Court of Appeal this decision was affirmed. Cooke J put the question as being whether the relations which an injunction seems likely to compel the parties to maintain are such as to make the remedy undesirable in principle. His Honour recognised that co-operation and mutual confidence were needed if the contract was to operate with maximum efficiency, yet the machinery for its enforcement involved routine matters, it was unlikely that the personnel involved in the day to day carrying out of the contract would be influenced by the litigation, and all the troubles between the parties only emerged after the appellants were taken over by another company.

It is not essential that the negative stipulation the breach of which a party seeks to restrain be spelt out in express terms. The Courts may be prepared to imply a negative covenant from an express positive covenant so long as it is clear precisely what it is the defendant has undertaken not to do. For example in *Hill and Plummer Ltd v Pinchin Johnson and Co (NZ) Ltd* [1957] NZLR 758 a positive covenant on the part of the defendant manufacturer to promote the sale of the plaintiff's goods in a certain area by and through the plaintiff company was held to carry with it an implied negative covenant not actively to seek the direct sale of the goods in that area. An injunction was issued restraining any breach of that implied covenant.

It is possible that negative stipulations of the kind under consideration may be attacked as operating in restraint of trade. Under s 8 of the Illegal Contracts Act 1970 the Court can modify unreasonable restraints and enforce what is left: supra, paras 5.4.5, 5.4.6.

7.7 LIMITATION OF ACTIONS

By s 4(1) of the Limitation Act 1950 an action founded on simple contract or tort shall not be brought after the expiration of six years from the date on which the cause of action accrued. In the case of contracts under seal the period is twelve years: s 4(3). A cause of action accrues in contract not when the damage is suffered, which is the relevant date in the tort of negligence, but on the date when the breach takes place.

If on that date the person to whom the right of action accrues is under a disability, the action may be brought within six years from the date when the person ceases to be under the disability or dies: s 24. "Disability" means infancy or unsoundness of mind: s 2(2).

When an action is based on the fraud of the defendant, or the right of action has been concealed by fraud, or when an action is for relief from the consequences of a mistake, the period does not begin to run until the plaintiff has discovered the fraud or mistake or could with reasonable diligence have discovered it: s 28. In *Inca Ltd v Autoscript (NZ) Ltd* [1979] 2 NZLR 700 Mahon J thought that concealment of a right of action by "fraud" means wilful concealment in breach of either a fiduciary duty or a special duty of disclosure inherent in the contract made by the parties or in some other legal relationship to which they had become committed. In this case a supplier agreed to sell goods to a purchaser at current wholesale prices less "the usual trade discount" and the supplier failed to keep the purchaser informed of its discount rates. It was held that the purchaser's action for breach of contract had been "concealed by fraud" in the relevant sense.

In the case of a claim to a debt or other liquidated sum an acknowledgement of liability or a part payment by the debtor starts time running afresh, even if given or made after the period of limitation has expired: s 25(4). The acknowledgement must be in writing and be signed by the person making it: s 26(1). An acknowledgement of a debt or other liquidated claim binds only the person making the acknowledgement and his or her successors whereas a part payment binds co-debtors as well, unless it is made after the expiration of the limitation period when it binds the payer alone: s 27(5),(6).

The periods of limitation prescribed in the Act do not apply to claims for purely equitable relief (s 4(9)) but such claims are subject to the equitable doctrine of laches, whereby equitable remedies such as claims for rectification, specific performance or injunction are barred by reason of undue delay in asserting them. In *Lindsay Petroleum Co v Hurd* (1874) LR 5 PC 221 Lord Selborne said that the doctrine applies where it would be "practically unjust" to give a remedy . In *Neylon v Dickens* [1987] 1 NZLR 402 the Court of Appeal noted that the length of the delay and the parties' actions during the interval were important factors in deciding whether it would be inequitable to allow a claim to proceed.

In 1988 the Law Commission issued Report No 6 "Limitation Defences in Civil Proceedings" proposing that the law of limitation of actions be reformed in a number of respects.

(1) The Limitation Act 1950 should be repealed and replaced by a new statute, called the Limitation Defences Act.
(2) There should be a common limitation period which would apply to all civil proceedings, the period commencing on the date of the act or omission by the defendant of which the plaintiff complained.
(3) The standard period should be three years.
(4) The standard period would not start if the plaintiff lacked knowledge, actual or constructive, of any of the following facts:
    (a) the occurrence of the act or omission:
    (b) the identity of the person responsible;
    (c) that the act or omission has caused harm; and
    (d) that the harm is significant.
(5) The period should also be extended in the case of infancy, incapacity and prior agreement between the parties.
(6) Subject to certain exceptions, such as concealment of the right of action by fraud, there should be an overall long stop period of 15 years.

So far Parliament has not acted on the Law Commission's recommendations.

Chapter 8

DISCHARGE OF CONTRACT

SUMMARY

8.1   FRUSTRATION OF CONTRACT
8.2   DISCHARGE BY AGREEMENT
8.3   DISCHARGE BY OPERATION OF LAW

8.1 FRUSTRATION OF CONTRACT

Sometimes, before the parties have been able to complete performance of their contract, a disastrous event occurs, beyond the control of either of them, which renders further performance impossible or substantially impossible. In such cases the contract is said to be frustrated, and both parties are completely discharged from their obligations.

The doctrine of frustration is a relative newcomer to the common law, not being thoroughly established till the case of *Taylor v Caldwell* (1863) 3 B & S 826. Before that time contractual promises had normally been thought of as absolute: if a person made a contract and was prevented from performing it he or she had to pay damages even though the failure was due to no fault of his or her own.

8.1.1 Some examples

Frustration of contract occurs only in extreme cases. The following are examples only: the list should not be treated as exhaustive.

(a) THE SUBJECT MATTER OF THE CONTRACT CEASES TO EXIST

Taylor v Caldwell (1863) 3 B & S 826, the seminal case on frustration, provides a good example. T agreed to hire a hall to C for a series of concerts. Before the scheduled time for the concerts the hall was accidentally burnt down. It was held that the contract was discharged and that neither party had any further obligation under it.

147

(b) A PARTY TO A CONTRACT FOR PERSONAL SERVICES DIES OR BECOMES PHYSICALLY INCAPABLE OF PERFORMING

Thus, a contract by a pianist to give a concert on a certain day was held to be discharged when the pianist became too ill to perform: *Robinson v Davison* (1871) LR 6 Ex 269. Likewise, a contract of employment was frustrated when the employee was sent to borstal: *F C Shepherd & Co Ltd v Jerrom* [1987] QB 301.

(c) THE PURPOSE OF THE CONTRACT BECOMES IMPOSSIBLE OF ATTAINMENT

In *Krell v Henry* [1903] 2 KB 740 the defendant agreed to rent a flat from the plaintiff on June 26 and 27 1902. The purpose of the letting, as both parties knew, was so that the defendant could view the coronation procession of Edward VII. The procession and indeed the coronation, did not take place on the appointed day because of the King's illness. It was held that the contract of letting was discharged by frustration. The case was an interesting one, because literal performance of the contract as it was written – a lease for two days – was possible. But as Vaughan Williams LJ said at 749:

> You have first to ascertain, not necessarily from the terms of the contract, but if required from necessary inferences, drawn from surrounding circumstances recognised by both contracting parties, what is the substance of the contract and then to ask the question whether that substantial contract needs for its foundation the assumption of a particular state of things. . .

The decision might have been different if it could have been shown that viewing the procession was not the sole purpose of the letting, and that the tenant would still obtain some substantial benefit from it even though the procession were cancelled: cf *Herne Bay Steam Boat Co v Hutton* [1903] 2 KB 683.

(d) THE SPECIFIED MODE OF PERFORMANCE HAS BECOME IMPOSSIBLE

A contract will be held frustrated if it was to be performed in one way only, and that mode of performance has become impossible. An example would be a contract to carry goods on a named ship which is then wrecked: *Nickoll and Knight v Ashton Edridge and Co* [1901] 2 KB 126. However the doctrine will not apply if there are a number of possible modes of performance only one of which is rendered impossible, even if that is the one which one party expected to use. Thus, a contract by a timber merchant to supply "Finland birch timber" was held not frustrated when the merchant was unable to import the timber from Finland as a result of the presence of warships in the Baltic. As far as the buyer knew there might have been several sources of supply. "The sellers agreed to deliver timber at Hull, and it was no concern of the buyers as to how the sellers intended to get the timber there": *Blackburn Bobbin Co Ltd v Allen* [1918] 2 KB 467, 469 per Pickford LJ. It has been said, for this reason, that a contract for the sale of unascertained goods will almost never be frustrated.

(e) PERFORMANCE IS RENDERED ILLEGAL BY LEGISLATION

If, after the contract is entered into, legislation renders its performance illegal, the contract is discharged and the promisor excused from performance. In *Rayneon (NZ) Ltd v Fraser* [1940] NZLR 825 a contract of hire of a neon sign for a dentist was held to be discharged by legislation passed two years later which made this form of advertising illegal.

(f) DELAY AND OBSTRUCTION

If performance of a contract is delayed, or otherwise hindered, by external events it may be held frustrated – but only if the delay is so long, or the obstruction so extreme, that continued performance of the contract would be performance of a totally different kind from what the parties had initially contemplated. In *Bank Line Ltd v Capel and Co* [1919] AC 435 the defendants let a steamer to the plaintiff for trading purposes for 12 months from April. As a result of a government wartime requisition it was not available until September. The contract was held to be frustrated. An April to April charter was a very different thing from a September to September charter; the seasons being different the available produce would be different also. According to Lord Sumner the identity of the chartered service had been destroyed, and the charter as a matter of business had become quite different. On the other hand in *FA Tamplin Steamship Co Ltd v Anglo-Mexican Petroleum Products Co Ltd* [1916] 2 AC 397 a five-year charter of a tanker was held not to be frustrated by a government requisition when the charter still had nearly three years to run, despite the fact that the requisition was to be of uncertain duration and had actually run for 15 months when the case was heard. The majority of the House of Lords took the view that the interruption was not of such a kind as to destroy the identity of *this* charter. The charter had no particular purpose which could be frustrated, nor was the length of the delay in proportion to the total length of the charter sufficient to change its nature. This case, however, was a marginal one, and was decided by a bare majority of three to two in the House of Lords.

These delay cases raise the question of the point of time at which the contract can be said to be frustrated: in other words, does one have to wait until the delay has lasted so long that the nature of the adventure has changed, or does one make a decision at an early stage that the delay is likely to last so long that the contract should be regarded as discharged immediately? With an eye no doubt to commercial convenience, authority has established that the second of these possibilities is the correct one. As Lord Sumner said in *Bank Line Ltd v Capel and Co* [1919] AC 435, 454:

> The probabilities as to the length of the deprivation and not the certainty arrived at after the event are material. The question must be considered at the trial as it had to be considered by the parties when they came to know of the cause and the probabilities of the delay and had to decide what to do. . . . The contract binds or it does not bind, and the law ought to be that the parties can gather their fate then and there. . . .

Whether or not the delay is such as to bring about frustration must be determined on the evidence of what has occurred and what is likely to occur; sometimes it will be necessary to wait upon events for a time before one can answer that question confidently: *Pioneer Shipping Ltd v BTP Tioxide Ltd* [1982] AC 724, 752 per Lord Roskill.

8.1.2 The test of frustration

It is difficult to formulate a test which covers all kinds of frustration of contract. The most commonly accepted test is one which was formulated in the delay and obstruction context, and is particularly appropriate to that. In *Davis Contractors Ltd v Fareham Urban District Council* [1956] AC 696, 728-9 Lord Radcliffe said:

> ... Frustration occurs whenever the law recognises that without default of either party a contractual obligation has become incapable of being performed because the circumstances in which performance is called for would render it a thing radically different from that which was undertaken by the contract. *Non haec in foedera veni.* It was not this that I promised to do.

This test has been quoted many times since, and it has been said that in a case where frustration is pleaded the circumstances of the case should always be tested against it: *Pioneer Shipping Ltd* v *BTP Tioxide Ltd* [1982] AC 724, 752 per Lord Roskill. The test is not easy to satisfy. It is never enough just that obstructions have made performance more onerous, more expensive, or slower. There must have been a real change in the nature of the obligation.

Thus the following obstructions to contractual performance, severe though some of them be, have been held insufficient to frustrate the contract:

1   Shortages of labour and materials meant that performance of a contract to build 78 houses in eight months for £ 94,000 took 22 months and cost the builder £ 115,000 (*Davis Contractors Ltd v Fareham Urban District Council* [1956] AC 696);

2   The closure of the Suez Canal meant that goods had to be carried via the Cape of Good Hope which would cost more and take four weeks longer (*Tsakiroglou and Co Ltd v Noblee and Thorl GmbH* [1962] AC 93);

3   After a contract to purchase a property had been concluded the property was designated by the Department of the Interior as a place of special architectural and historic interest which reduced its value from the £ 1,700,000 it would have been worth as a site for redevelopment to £ 200,000 (*Amalgamated Investment and Property Co Ltd v Walker* [1977] 1 WLR 164);

4   A 10-year lease of a warehouse became less beneficial to the lessee when the access road was blocked off for a period of over a year (*National Carriers Ltd v Panalpina (Northern) Ltd* [1981] AC 675).

No doubt some of these decisions were influenced not just by the gravity of the interruption but also by the fact that contracting parties have traditionally been expected to bear the risk in contracts of certain kinds. Thus a purchaser of land has always been understood to bear the risk of fluctuations in the value of the property after the contract is made, just as a builder in giving a quote is expected to take the risk that the building operation will prove more difficult and perhaps more costly than expected.

8.1.3 The theory of frustration

In some of the older cases the doctrine of frustration was said to be based on an implied term in the contract. This theory held that when the Court determined a contract to be frustrated, all it was doing was to give effect to what must have been the intention of the parties in the situation that had arisen. (See for instance *Taylor v Caldwell* (1863) 3 B & S 826.) This was really only paying lip service to the nineteenth century view that contractual obligations were defined solely by the parties themselves. Nowadays a rather more realistic view is taken, namely that it is the law itself which imposes a just solution on the parties. However, as in any matter of contract, the intentions of the parties are never entirely irrelevant. For one thing, in applying Lord Radcliff's test of frustration it is essential to know the true nature of what was undertaken by the contract; this is a matter of construction. For another, it remains true, as we shall see, that parties can expressly provide in their contract that even the most disastrous event will *not* discharge it.

8.1.4 Self-induced frustration does not discharge the contract

A disruptive event only discharges the contract if it occurs independently of the fault or default of the parties. If either of them can be said to have caused the event the contract is not frustrated. Rather the guilty party is in breach of the contract, whereupon the other party will have the option to cancel and may sue for damages. As Lord Sumner said, "reliance cannot be placed on a self-induced frustration": the *Capel* case supra, 452.

In *Maritime National Fish Ltd v Ocean Trawlers Ltd* [1935] AC 524 M operated five trawlers fitted with otter trawling gear. One of these was chartered from O. Legislation made it illegal to use an otter trawl without a government licence. Only three licences were issued to M. M allocated the licences to three vessels owned by itself, and then said the contract of charter with O was frustrated. The Court held that M could not rely on its own act in allocating licences to other vessels as frustrating the contract.

Sometimes the question of whether a frustrating event was "self-induced" can raise very difficult questions of causation. For instance in one case (*Constantine Line Ltd v Imperial Smelting Corporation Ltd* [1942] AC 154) a ship which had been chartered to go to Australia was wrecked by an explosion in her boiler room while still in harbour. The cause of the explosion was unknown. It was held that since performance was impossible the contract was frustrated; in such a case the party who was alleging that the doctrine of frustration did not apply had the onus of proving that the other party's fault had caused the disaster. In this case, in the absence of any evidence of the cause, that onus was not discharged.

There is then the question of what precisely is meant by "fault" or "default" of a party. For instance, what if in the *Constantine* case it could be shown that the explosion had been caused by non-deliberate but nevertheless careless conduct by the ship's engineers? In such a case what degree of carelessness would be necessary? That question has not been answered satisfactorily, but in the *Constantine* case Lord Russell said at 179:

The possible varieties [of negligence] are infinite, and can range from the criminality of the scuttler who opens the sea cocks and sinks his ship to the thoughtlessness of the prima donna who sits in a draught and loses her voice. I wish to guard against the supposition that every destruction of corpus for which a contractor can be said to some extent to be responsible, necessarily involves that the resulting frustration is self-induced.

(See also *Paal Wilson and Co A/S v Partenreederei Hannah Blumenthal* [1983] 1 AC 854, 910 per Lord Brandon.)

An interesting variant is the case of *F C Shepherd & Co Ltd v Jerrom* [1987] QB 301 where a contract of employment was held to have been frustrated when the employee was sent to borstal for committing a crime. Although it might be said that this frustration was self-induced, it was held that the imposition of the sentence was the act of the Judge rather than the employee; and in any event the employee (who did not wish the contract to be held frustrated) could not rely on his own default to achieve this end.

8.1.5 Foreseeability

Sometimes at the time of their contract the parties foresee the disruptive event which later occurs. Sometimes they actually provide for it in their contract. For instance leases sometimes provide what is to happen in the event of destruction of the premises by earthquake and contracts of charterparty sometimes provide what is to happen in the event of government requisition of the ship. In such cases the express contract must govern, and if the parties have said their contract is to remain alive despite this event, there will be no room for the doctrine of frustration. However the Courts have traditionally given such clauses a narrow interpretation. In several cases they have said that the clause before them was not clearly enough expressed to cover the devastating event which in fact happened (eg *Jackson v Marine Insurance Co Ltd* (1874) LR 10 CP 125), so that the contract was frustrated despite the clause.

More problematic are cases where the parties at the time of the contract foresee the destructive event which later happens, but say nothing about it in their contract. Sometimes the true construction of their conduct will be that they are prepared to take the risk of the event happening, and to continue with their contract regardless; in such a case the event when it happens will not frustrate the contract (eg *Hawkes Bay Electric Power Co v Borthwick* [1933] NZLR 873). But it may be that in other cases the mere fact that the event was foreseen, or foreseeable, by them will lead to no such conclusion: they may well simply have hoped that it would not happen, but have been prepared to "leave it to the lawyers to sort it out" if it did. This was the view of Lord Denning in *The Eugenia* [1964] 2 QB 226, 234. However the law on this is not entirely clear, and in one of the latest statements of the doctrine in the House of Lords, Lord Brandon said it was an essential feature of frustration that there must be an outside event "not foreseen or provided for by the parties": *Paal Wilson and Co A/S v Partenreederei Hannah Blumenthal* [1983] 1 AC 854, 909.

8.1.6 The consequences of frustration

Frustration "brings the contract to an end forthwith, without more and automatically": *Hirji Mulji v Cheong Yue SS Co* [1926] AC 497, 505 per Lord Sumner. It does not render the contract void ab initio, but terminates it for the future only, so that the parties are not obliged to perform it any further.

The common law applied this concept entirely logically, but often created injustice in so doing. A party whose contractual obligations had fallen due before the frustrating event had to perform them, but was excused from performing any which fell due afterwards. Thus one could have a case where one party had received a substantial benefit from the other before the date of frustration, but was excused from paying anything for it because the contractual date for payment was after the frustrating event. Likewise one party who had received an advance payment from the other at the commencement of the contract might be entitled to retain it even though he or she had performed very little of the return obligation before the frustrating event intervened: see for instance *Chandler v Webster* [1904] 1 KB 493 and the *Fibrosa* case [1943] AC 32.

It was left to statute to provide the remedy. The current New Zealand statutory provision is the Frustrated Contracts Act 1944 which is almost an exact copy of the 1943 English Act of the same name. The Act does not in any way alter the common law on the definition of frustration, or on the circumstances in which it occurs. It regulates only the *consequences* of frustration. It contains two major provisions.

First, s 3(2) governs the case where money has been paid, or has fallen due for payment, by one party before the frustrating event. It provides that in such a case money actually paid can be recovered, and that moneys payable cease to be payable:

> All sums paid or payable to any party in pursuance of the contract before the time when the parties were so discharged (in this Act referred to as the time of discharge) shall, in the case of sums so paid, be recoverable from him as money received by him for the use of the party by whom the sums were paid and, in the case of sums so payable, cease to be so payable.

However if the party to whom these moneys were paid or payable has incurred expenses in performing his or her part of the contract before frustration, the Court may allow him or her to offset a sum in respect of those expenses. The proviso to s 3(2) provides:

> Provided that, if the party to whom the sums were so paid or payable incurred expenses before the time of discharge in, or for the purpose of, the performance of the contract, the Court may, if it considers it just to do so having regard to all the circumstances of the case, allow him to retain or, as the case may be, recover the whole or any part of the sums so paid or payable, not being an amount in excess of the expenses so incurred.

By way of example, if a builder has partly constructed a house, and has received $80,000 in progress payments before frustration occurs, the owner will be entitled to recover the $80,000 less such sum as the Court allows the builder to reimburse him or her for the expenses he or she has incurred; these no doubt will be very substantial. In estimating the expenses, the Court may include a reasonable sum for overheads and in respect of work or services performed personally: s 3(4).

The limitations on this subsection 3(2) should be noted:

(i) It applies only when money has been paid, or fallen due for payment, *before the time of discharge*. It is only out of such money that the other party can claim his or her expenses.

(ii) It applies only to expenses incurred *before* the time of discharge, and not to expenses incurred *after* such time. (It is possible to imagine cases where a party incurs expense in ignorance that a frustrating event has occurred.)

(iii) A party falling within the subsection who incurs expenses before the time of discharge will not necessarily be entitled to all of them; he or she is entitled only to such sum as the Court allows him or her.

Secondly, s 3(3) allows a party whose part performance has conferred a benefit on the other party before the contract is discharged to recover some compensation from that other:

> Where any party to the contract has, by reason of anything done by any other party thereto in, or for the purpose of, the performance of the contract, obtained a valuable benefit (other than a payment of money to which the last preceding subsection applies) before the time of discharge, there shall be recoverable from him by the said other party such sum (if any), not exceeding the value of the said benefit to the party obtaining it, as the Court considers just. . . .

In assessing the "just sum" (which need not be the full value of the benefit, although it cannot be more) the Court must have regard to any expenses that the party benefiting has incurred in performing his or her part, and also to whether the value of the benefit has been affected by the frustrating event. In *BP Exploration Ltd v Hunt* [1979] 1 WLR 783 affirmed [1981] 1 WLR 232 and [1983] 2 AC 352 the Court awarded a "just sum" of 35 million dollars to BP when land on which they had been developing an oil field under contract with Hunt was expropriated by the Libyan government; the Court of Appeal could find no reason to upset this exercise of the Judge's discretion.

It will be seen that, while the statute provides for the relief of the parties in a far more satisfactory manner than did the common law, it still does not ensure complete justice. It is doubtful, for example, whether its provisions would cover facts like those in *Appleby v Myers* (1867) LR 2 CP 651. In that case, the plaintiffs contracted to erect machinery on the defendant's premises in return for a price of £459 payable on completion. When the machine was nearly complete a fire destroyed it, together with the building in which it was housed. It was held at common law that the plaintiff could recover no part of his price. It is doubtful whether he would be any better off under the Act. Since no money was paid, or payable, before the frustrating event, s 3(2) would not operate to allow the plaintiff reimbursement of his expenses; and since the fire took place before any valuable benefit was conferred on the defendant, it is difficult to see that s 3(3) would assist him either, unless a most artificial interpretation were to be placed on the concept of "benefit".

One other provision of the Act should be noted. Where it appears to the Court that a part of any contract to which the Act applies can properly be severed from the remainder of the contract, being a part wholly per-formed before the time of discharge, or so performed except for the payment in respect of that part of the contract of sums which are or can be ascertained under the contract, the Court must treat that part of the contract as if it were a separate contract and had not been frustrated: s 4(4).

It should be noted, finally, that by virtue of s 4(5) certain types of contract are excluded entirely from the operation of the Frustrated Contracts Act 1944. They are:

(i) a contract for the carriage of goods by sea or a charterparty (except a time charterparty or a charterparty by way of demise);

(ii) a contract of insurance;

(iii) a contract to which s 9 of the Sale of Goods Act 1908 applies, or any other contract for the sale of specific goods where the contract is frustrated by reason of the fact that the goods have perished.

8.2 DISCHARGE BY AGREEMENT

A contract is created by agreement and may be discharged by agreement. In accordance with ordinary principle the discharge must be supported by consideration provided by each party. In the case of a contract which is still executory no difficulty arises. Each party promises to release his or her rights in consideration of a similar release by the others and the agreement thus generates its own consideration. Where, however, a contract has been wholly executed by one party, a promise to discharge the other from further performance must either be under seal or be supported by separate consideration to be contractually binding.

8.2.1 Accord and satisfaction

Discharge in return for some new consideration is called "accord and satisfaction". This was defined by Scrutton LJ in *British Russian Gazette Ltd v Associated Newspapers Ltd* [1933] 2 KB 616 in these terms:

Accord and satisfaction is the purchase of a release from an obligation whether arising under contract or tort, by means of any valuable consideration not being the performance of the actual obligation itself. The accord is the agreement by which the obligation is discharged. The satisfaction is the consideration which makes the agreement operative.

As has already been seen, a promise to accept payment of a smaller sum in satisfaction of a larger is not a good discharge of the debt: *Pinnel's* case (1602) 5 Co Rep 117a, supra, para 3.2.9. A promise by the debtor to confer a benefit not otherwise contractually due to the creditor may, however, constitute consideration for the acceptance of the smaller sum. Thus receipt by the creditor of some satisfaction different in kind, or receipt of a lesser sum at an earlier date or in a different place discharges the debt. Moreover the rule in *Pinnel's* case does not apply to a claim for an unliquidated sum. The value of the claim is uncertain and thus it may validly be compromised: *James Wallace Pty Ltd v William Cable* [1980] 2 NZLR 187. Similarly where the claim is for a liquidated sum but the amount of the claim is genuinely disputed, acceptance of a lesser sum than that claimed may bind the creditor.

Whether or in what circumstances there is an accord and satisfaction in cases where a creditor has banked a cheque tendered in full satisfaction of a disputed debt has been a matter of some controversy. In *Homeguard Products (NZ) Ltd v Kiwi Packaging Ltd* [1981] 2 NZLR 322 Mahon J held that as a matter of law the mere act of banking the cheque effects a binding accord. In *HBF Dalgety Ltd v Morton* [1987] 1 NZLR 411 Hillyer J declined to follow *Homeguard*, holding instead that the question is one of fact. The plaintiff, a real estate agent, sold a farm for the defendants, who thereby became liable to pay agency charges calculated according to the scale of the New Zealand Real Estate Institute. The defendants sent a cheque for a lesser sum, being their "estimate of costs on a 'work done' basis". The plaintiff banked the cheque and at the same time sent a letter stating that the cheque was not regarded as satisfying their claim. The defence of accord and satisfaction failed because (i) the debt was not genuinely disputed and hence there was no consideration for any accord, (ii) it was not clear that the cheque was being offered in full and final settlement, and (iii) there was no accord because the plaintiff had made it clear that the cheque was not accepted as full settlement. Subsequent cases, for example, *Dunrae Manufacturing Ltd v CL North & Co Ltd* [1988] 2 NZLR 602, *James Cook Hotel Ltd v Canx Corporate Services Ltd* [1989] 3 NZLR 213, *Haines Haulage Co Ltd v Gamble* [1989] 3 NZLR 221 and *Budget Rent A Car Ltd v Goodman* [1991] 2 NZLR 715, have endorsed the *Dalgety* approach.

Clearly an important consideration in these cases is how quickly the creditor notifies the debtor that there is no accord. Any substantial delay in this respect may lead the debtor reasonably to believe that his or her offer of settlement has been accepted. The question is always whether the creditor actually agreed to accept the offer in full satisfaction or led the debtor reasonably to believe that he or she had so agreed.

An influential article on this topic by Professor D McLauchlan deserves careful study: see "Cheques in Full Satisfaction" (1987) 12 NZULR 259, updated in (1989) NZ Recent L Rev 399.

There are two important statutory exceptions to the rule that a unilateral discharge requires consideration. First, a written acknowledgement by the creditor of the receipt of part of a debt in satisfaction of the whole debt discharges the debt: Judicature Act 1908, s 92, supra para 3.3.2. Secondly, no satisfaction is required for the discharge of a bill of exchange or promissory note provided that the discharge is in writing or the bill delivered up to the person liable: Bills of Exchange Act 1908, ss 62, 90.

8.2.2 Variation

In the case of contracts required to be in writing by the Contracts Enforcement Act 1956 (supra, para 3.3.2) it is important to distinguish between discharge by such an alteration of terms as substitutes a new contract for the old, and a variation whereby the original contract continues as varied. This is because the discharge of any contract, including one governed by the Contracts Enforcement Act, may be by oral agreement. The variation of a contract required to be in writing must, however also be in writing, for the statutory requirements apply to the whole contract, not merely part of it. An example will show the consequences of the distinction. An oral agreement for the discharge of a contract for the sale of land is effective. If the parties have at the same time sought to create a new contract concerning the same subject matter, this will be unenforceable for want of writing. Conversely, oral variation of the written contract is without effect and leaves the contract intact.

Whether there has been a mere variation of terms or a discharge depends upon the intention of the parties in each particular case. In *Morris v Bacon and Co* [1918] AC 1, Lord Haldane said that for a contract to have been discharged, "there should have been made manifest the intention in any event of a complete extinction of the first contract and not merely the desire of an alteration, however sweeping, in terms which leave it still subsisting".

8.2.3 Waiver

Where an oral variation of a contract is made at the request of one party for his or her sole benefit, problems of both form and consideration may arise. If the contract is required by statute to be in writing, a strict insistence that the variation also be in writing could allow the statute to be used as an instrument of fraud. For example, a buyer of land might ask that the date for completion be postponed yet later seek to avoid his or her obligations under the contract by alleging that the seller did not complete on the due date and that the purported variation of the contract was ineffective for lack of writing. Furthermore, in any case where one party to a contract has granted a concession as to its performance to the other, the validity of the concession might be attacked on the ground that it was granted without consideration. In order to meet these difficulties the Courts developed a supposed distinction between a variation on the one hand and a waiver or forbearance on the other. While a variation takes effect as a contractually binding arrangement, a waiver has rather more limited legal effects: (i) the party for whose benefit the waiver was granted cannot refuse to accept the varied performance: see, for example, *Levey and Co v Goldberg* [1922] 1 KB 688; (ii) if the varied performance is actually carried out, neither party can claim damages on the ground the performance was in breach of the original contract; and (iii) the waiver binds the party who grants it only while it continues. His or her forbearance lacks any contractual effect and thus he or she may revoke it but first must give to the other party reasonable notice of his or her intention to do so: *Charles Rickards Ltd v Oppenheim* [1950] 1 KB 616.

The nature of the distinction between variation and waiver has been described as "tenuous" (Treitel) and "visionary" (Cheshire and Fifoot). It provides an uncertain and unsatisfactory foundation for the Courts' endeavours to give effect to the intention of the parties. Equity provided a better solution to the problem with the development of the doctrine of promissory estoppel, as first propounded by the House of Lords in *Hughes v Metropolitan Railway* (1877) 2 App Cas 439. This doctrine looks not to an elusive analytical distinction incapable of precise formulation but to the effects of the waiver or forbearance on the position of the parties. Its scope has been discussed supra, para 3.2.10. There is, perhaps, a good deal to be said for the view which regards waiver merely as a species of estoppel: see *Oppenheim's* case, supra, per Denning LJ; *Brikom*

Investments Ltd v Carr [1979] QB 467. In one respect, however, it may be that promissory estoppel is more limited than waiver. For an estoppel to operate the promisee has to alter his or her position in reliance on the promise, arguably to his or her detriment. This requirement has never been regarded as necessary for waiver.

8.2.4 Provisions for discharge in the contract itself

The parties may agree at the outset that the contract shall be discharged in certain events and make provision in the contract accordingly.

A continuing contract may contain a provision making it determinable at the option of one or both parties upon notice. For example, a contract of employment will usually specify a fixed period of notice for its determination. In the absence of such a provision the Courts may sometimes be prepared to imply a term that the contract be terminated by reasonable notice by either party.

A contract may also be discharged for failure of, or on the occurrence of, a condition contained within it: supra, para 4.3.

8.3 DISCHARGE BY OPERATION OF LAW

8.3.1 Merger

Where a party to a contract takes from the other party a security for performance of a higher nature than that which the party already possesses, his or her remedies on the minor security or cause of action are merged in and extinguished by the higher security. Thus where the parties to a simple contract embody its contents in a deed, the simple contract is discharged. Before merger takes place it must always be shown that the two securities secure the same obligation and are made between the same parties.

A judgment in favour of a plaintiff operates by way of merger, his or her cause of action being merged in the judgment.

8.3.2 Alteration of a written instrument

Any material alteration of a written instrument deliberately made by the promisee or his or her agent without the consent of the promisor discharges the contract except as against the party making or assenting to the alteration. A "material" alteration is one which alters the legal effect of the instrument, usually by imposing a greater liability on the promisor. The reason for the rule is that "no man shall be permitted to take the chance of committing a fraud, without running any risk of losing by the event, when it is detected": *Master v Miller* (1791) 4 Term Rep 320 per Lord Kenyon CJ.

Special statutory provision has been made regarding bills of exchange. A bill shall not be avoided as against a holder in due course, though it has been materially altered, if the alteration is not apparent and the holder may enforce payment of it according to its original terms: Bills of Exchange Act 1908, s 64.

8.3.3 Bankruptcy

The effect of an adjudication in bankruptcy is to vest in the Assignee all such property (with certain exceptions) as belongs to or is vested in the bankrupt at the commencement of his or her bankruptcy or is acquired by or devolves on the bankrupt before his or her discharge: Insolvency Act 1967, s 42. A contract is not, however, necessarily determined by the bankruptcy of one of the parties. Ordinarily the benefit of any contract made by the debtor passes to the Assignee subject to the Assignee's power to terminate the contract: Insolvency Act 1967, s 76.

Chapter 9

QUASI-CONTRACT

SUMMARY

9.1   THE TYPES OF QUASI-CONTRACTUAL RELIEF
9.2   UNJUST ENRICHMENT

9.1 THE TYPES OF QUASI-CONTRACTUAL RELIEF

"Quasi-contract" covers a range of situations where the law requires one person to pay a sum of money to another. It is really separate from contract, and is dealt with under the heading of "contract" for convenience only.

Sir Percy Winfield QC in *The Laws of Quasi-Contracts* (1952), defined quasi-contractual liability as:

> Liability, not exclusively referable to any other head of the law, imposed upon a particular person to pay money to another particular person on the ground that non-payment of it would confer on the former an unjust benefit.

Formerly, it was suggested that the plaintiff could succeed in quasi-contract if a contract could be implied by law in his or her favour. The fiction of the implied contract has been severely criticised and has effectively been abandoned. Lord Atkin in *United Australia Ltd v Barclays Bank Ltd* [1941] AC 1, was particularly outspoken. He stated at 27-29:

> . . . to find a basis for the actions in any actual contract whether express or to be implied from the conduct of the parties was in many of the instances given obviously impossible. The cheat or the blackmailer does not promise to repay to the person he has wronged the money which he has unlawfully taken: nor does the thief promise to repay the owner of the goods stolen the money which he has gained from selling the goods. . . . These fantastic resemblances of contracts invented in order to meet requirements of the law as to forms of action which have now disappeared should not in these days be allowed to affect actual rights. When these ghosts of the past stand in the path of justice clanking their mediaeval chains the proper course for the Judge is to pass through them undeterred.

Illustrations of quasi-contract include:

(a) Actions for the recovery of money where there has been a total failure of consideration. Since the enactment of the Contractual Remedies Act 1979 there will probably be less scope than in the past for the quasi-contractual action in this situation. If one party is in breach in failing to supply the consideration, the other party may cancel and claim repayment in the Court's discretion under s 9.

(b) Actions on a quantum meruit. Quantum meruit is available in a number of situations. First, it is available where work has been done or goods supplied on the understanding that a reasonable price would be paid. Secondly, in cases where there is an inference that a party has agreed to accept part performance and pay for it, a quantum meruit can be secured. A third instance is where the plaintiff has done work under a void contract. For instance in *Craven-Ellis v Canons Ltd* [1936] 2 KB 403; [1936] 3 All ER 1066, a person who had acted as managing director of a company without a valid appointment was held to be entitled on the basis of quantum meruit to reasonable remuneration for his or her work. Another instance of the quasi-contractual remedy at common law was where the innocent party to a contract which had been broken by the other party could claim in respect of work he or she had done before the breach. Such cases would now be dealt with under the Contractual Remedies Act 1979.

(c) Actions to recover money paid under constraint. A party who has been compelled to pay money for which another is liable may recover the amount thus paid from the other. But to succeed he or she must show both that he or she was coerced to pay the money, and that it is money which the other was legally liable to pay. No action will lie at the suit of a person who voluntarily pays money on behalf of another.

(d) Actions for money had and received to the use of another. For example, if an agent has made an unauthorised profit, the principal can recover that profit, including any bribe that the agent may have received; and if a person has received, even innocently, stolen money without giving full consideration, it can be recovered: *Lipkin Gorman v Karpnale Ltd* [1991] 3 WLR 10.

(e) Actions for money paid at the request of another. If A pays money to B with an instruction to pay it to C, C (when C is notified that B will pay him) has an action against B for "money had and received" to C's use.

(f) Money paid under a mistake. At common law an action would lie to enable X to recover money he or she had paid to Y by mistake, but only if the mistake was one of fact. However by an amendment to the Judicature Act in New Zealand this relief was extended also to a case where the mistake was one of law.

Section 94A(1) of the Judicature Act 1908 (added in 1958) provides that, subject to the provisions of subs (2), where relief in respect of any payment that has been made under mistake is sought in any Court, whether in an action or by way of defence, set off, counterclaim, or otherwise, and that relief could be granted if the mistake was wholly one of fact, that relief shall not be denied by reason only that the mistake is one of law, whether or not it is in any degree also one of fact. Subsection (2) makes it clear that the section does not enable relief to be given in respect of any payment made at a time when the law requires or allows, or is commonly understood to require or allow, the payment to be made or enforced, by reason only that the law is subsequently changed or shown not to have been as it was commonly understood to be at the time of the payment. The section is concerned with the case where an individual makes a mistake as to the law, not with the case where a Court decision shows that there has previously been a common misunderstanding of the law.

Section 94B provides that relief, whether under s 94A or in equity or otherwise, in respect of any payment whatsoever that is made under mistake, whether of law or of fact, shall be denied wholly or in part if the payee received the payment in good faith and has so altered his or her position in reliance on its validity that the Court, having regard to all possible implications in respect of other persons, considers it inequitable to grant relief. The section does more than limit the operation of the new s 94A. It also provides a defence in cases of payments made under mistake in certain other cases (eg tracing proceedings in equity as in *Ministry of Health v Simpson* [1951] AC 251; [1950] 2 All ER 1137). The purpose and effect of ss 94A and 94B are discussed in an essay written by RJ Sutton which appears in *The A G Davis Essays in Law* (Butterworths, 1965) ch 9 and in (1969) 3 NZULR 232.

In a case on s 94B, North P in *Thomas v Houston Corbett and Co* [1969] NZLR 151, 164 said of that provision:

This is an entirely new provision introducing a doctrine of alteration of position hitherto unknown to English law. Previously in order to resist an action by a plaintiff to recover money paid under a mistake of fact in these circumstances the defendant was required to prove a true estoppel: see *R E Jones Ltd v Waring and Gillow Ltd* [1926] AC 670; [1926] All ER Rep 36. That is no longer the position in New Zealand. Now the Court is entitled to look at the equities from the point of view of both sides. It is now possible for a defendant who brings himself within the provisions of this section to resist recovery of the money paid to him under a mistake of fact or law.

In that case, a legal firm paid £ 840 into a client's trust account on the faith of a fraudulent representation by a clerk of the firm. In view of the reliance of the payee on the payment the Court, "balancing the equities", held the client entitled to retain £ 560. However the relief provisions of s 94B are not available unless the party has altered his or her position in reliance on the validity of the payment in such a way as to make it inequitable that he or she should have to repay all the money: *KJ Davies (1976) Ltd v Bank of New South Wales* [1981] 1 NZLR 262. Sections 94A and 94B are not affected by the Contractual Mistakes Act 1979: see s 15(2)(d) of that Act.

9.2 UNJUST ENRICHMENT

The above are the well-established categories of quasi-contract. Underlying them all may be said to be a principle that one person should not be unjustly enriched at the expense of another. Arguably that same principle underlies certain equitable doctrines—for example the remedy of tracing (under which a beneficiary may follow trust property into the hands of a person who has taken with knowledge of the trust: eg *Ministry of Health v Simpson* [1951] AC 251) and the device of constructive trust (a trust arising by operation of law where a person holds property which in equity should belong to another).

From time to time it has been argued that it is time that "unjust enrichment" emerged as a principle in its own right. But when such a claim has been made in a case which falls outside one of the *established* categories of quasi-contract or equitable doctrine the common response in the past has been that such general principle does not (yet) exist, and that it is necessary to bring one's case under one of the established categories. Thus in *Carly v Farrelly* [1975] 1 NZLR 356 a purchaser was held unable to recover insurance moneys paid to the vendor when the house he had agreed to buy was destroyed by fire. Mahon J said in response to an argument based on unjust enrichment (p 367):

> ... I think I am being asked to apply a supposed rule of equity which is not only vague in its outline but which must disqualify itself from acceptance as a valid principle of jurisprudence by its total uncertainty of application and result. . . . No stable system of jurisprudence could permit a litigant's claim to justice to be consigned to the formless void of individual moral opinion.

The Judge concluded that he could only base his judgment on settled principles. (See also Mahon J in *Avondale Printers and Stationers Ltd v Haggie* [1979] 2 NZLR 124, 144-155).

However times may be changing. In 1983 the New Zealand Court of Appeal indicated that the door may not be completely closed to such an argument. *Hayward v Giordani* [1983] NZLR 140 was a case involving the possible property rights of a de facto husband who had contributed money to his de facto wife and had done a "tremendous amount" of work renovating and upgrading a house belonging to her. It was held that a common intention could be proved that the property should be equally shared. But Cooke J, referring to an argument based on constructive trust, said:

> The scope of [the doctrine of unjust enrichment] in New Zealand is unsettled. Safely if tritely one can say that it may be evolving. The law of unjust enrichment ... cannot have ceased growing at some climactic date in England, any more than tort law stopped before *Donoghue v Stevenson*.

In other cases on the property rights of de facto spouses Cooke P has gone further, saying that there is no significant difference between the notion of imputed common intention used in the English cases, and the unjust enrichment concept used by the Supreme Court of Canada. "Normally it makes no practical difference in the result whether one talks of constructive trust, unjust enrichment, imputed common intention or estoppel": *Gillies v Keogh* [1989] 2 NZLR 327, 370. (See also *Pasi v Kamana* [1986] 1 NZLR 603 and *Oliver v Bradley* [1987] 1 NZLR 586.) Further impetus has been given to a doctrine of unjust enrichment by the House of Lords cases *Lipkin Gorman v Karpnale Ltd* [1991] 3 WLR 10 which held that an innocent recipient of stolen money who had not given full consideration for it must pay an equivalent sum to the true owner. Lord Goff of Chieveley said such an action for money had and received is founded simply on the fact that "as we say nowadays, for the third party to retain the money would result in his unjust enrichment at the expense of the owner of the money" (at 27). (See also *Powell v Thompson* [1991] 1 NZLR 597 at 607 per Thomas J.)

The growth of Restitution as a separate subject of study in universities and academic writings seeking to rationalise the underlying basis of restitutionary remedies, is also beginning to have effect on the acceptance of "unjust enrichment" as a doctrine. This is a subject of growing importance and interest. However, it is clear that if unjust enrichment is to become increasingly an articulate basis of decision it will have to be subject to principled development. Richardson J has pointed to the unsatisfactory nature of "treating fairness in the round as the ultimate test": *Gillies v Keogh* [1989] 2 NZLR 327, 344.

PART III

FAIR TRADING

Chapter 10

FAIR TRADING ACT 1986

SUMMARY

10.1 GENERAL
10.2 MISLEADING AND DECEPTIVE CONDUCT IN TRADE
10.3 SPECIAL INSTANCES OF MISLEADING OR DECEPTIVE CONDUCT
10.4 RELATIONSHIP OF FAIR TRADING ACT AND OTHER AREAS OF LAW
10.5 REMEDIES AND PROCEDURAL MATTERS
10.6 CONSUMER INFORMATION AND PROTECTION PROVISIONS

10.1 GENERAL

The Fair Trading Act 1986 is primarily a consumer-protection statute, but one which may be of relevance in a wide range of circumstances, including some cases which do not appear at first sight to be concerned with consumer issues. The statute was largely derived from Part V of the Trade Practices Act 1974 of the Commonwealth of Australia, as amended in 1977. The Australian Act is, for constitutional reasons, confined to corporations but there is now legislation in most states which applies to both corporations and individuals. The New Zealand Courts have repeatedly stressed the assistance to be gained from Australian decisions, and also indicated that in general the Courts should aim, so far as is reasonably practicable, at consistency with those decisions: for example, *Taylor Bros Ltd v Taylors Group Ltd* [1988] 2 NZLR 1, 26, 39. However, the Courts have also stressed that the primary consideration is the wording of the statute, rather than any particular judicial interpretation of it. In all cases the essential issue will be whether or not the words of the statute apply to the particular facts established: see *Taylor Bros Ltd v Taylors Group Ltd,* supra, and *Trust Bank Auckland Ltd v ASB Bank Ltd* [1989] 3 NZLR 385, 388.

The Act makes unlawful a number of specific kinds of business or trade malpractice, as well as laying down broad general prohibitions on conduct which is, or may be, misleading or deceptive. Most of the prohibitions provide for both civil and criminal liability; however the most general and frequently litigated section, s 9, only creates civil liability for any contravenor. There are also special provisions dealing with product safety standards and the recall by manufacturers or distributors of faulty or unsafe items: see 10.6.

Unlike most earlier consumer protection legislation, the Act is designed to allow enforcement of its provisions by actions brought against alleged infringers by rival traders, as well as by a regulatory agency, the Commerce Commission, or by persons who have suffered loss as a result of conduct in breach of the Act. While criminal prosecutions will normally be launched by the regulatory agency, civil remedies are open to it as well as to any other applicant for relief under the Act: as to remedies, see 10.5. The Courts have recognised the public policy implicit in allowing enforcement of the Act by rival traders: see, for example *Taylor Bros Ltd v Taylors Group Ltd* [1991] 1 NZLR 91, 93. Manifestly, the bringing of proceedings by individuals minimises the costs to the state, and may well result in more appropriate results than if enforcement were left to persons directly suffering losses from misleading or deceptive conduct. The consumer who has suffered loss is primarily concerned with restitution or compensation; the rival trader with ensuring the termination of unfair procedures by a competitor in the market place. The Fair Trading Act therefore allows the ethical trader to protect his or her position by having the Court terminate unethical practices indulged in by a rival, whether or not there has been actual loss by way of loss of trade or goodwill. [The next para is 10.1.2.]

10.1.2 Criminal and civil components

The Act is designed so that most of its provisions may be enforced by criminal or civil proceedings. Criminal proceedings will involve a number of significant differences from civil proceedings. First, and most significantly, the standard of proof will be higher; the prosecution will have to prove the infringement beyond reasonable doubt, rather than on the balance of probabilities standard which suffices for civil proceedings. If a penalty is exacted for breach of the statute, it will normally be directed at punishing the offender for his or her conduct, rather than at compensating a victim of that conduct for any losses incurred, although the Court may, even in a criminal prosecution, order compensation or restitution: see s 43. Other differences are that a prosecution will normally be brought by an agency of the state rather than a disgruntled individual; the proceedings will be different in form; there will be differences in the rules as to what evidence is admissible. These differences may not always be of great moment, but they will on occasion be important.

10.1.3 Liability for the conduct of others

One matter which may be of great significance is the extent to which an individual or corporation may be liable for the acts of servants or employees or agents. Here the applicable rules come from the special provisions of s 45 of the Fair Trading Act. These are to a significant extent different from the rules that would be applicable at common law. They may be summarised as follows:

(i) In all proceedings under the Act a corporation will be liable for the acts of any director, agent or employee acting within the scope of his or her actual or apparent authority: as to the meaning of these terms, see 28.4. For example, if a real estate agent misleads prospective tenants, the landlords are answerable: *Brown v Jam Factory Pty Ltd* (1981) 53 FLR 340; *Mr Figgins Pty Ltd v Centrepoint Freehold Pty Ltd* (1981) 36 ALR 23. The corporation will also be liable for the acts of any other person done on the instructions of, or with the consent or authority of, any director, agent or employee who has actual or apparent authority to so instruct or consent: s 45(2). Proof of the actual authority will be essential where it is alleged that a person or corporation is answerable for the acts of a person who is not formally an agent or employee: see *Adelaide Petroleum NL v Poseidon Ltd* (1990) 98 ALR 431. Any person other than a corporation is liable for the acts of an agent or servant acting within the scope of his or her apparent or actual authority: see s 45(4).

(ii) If a mental element is required to be shown, then it will always be sufficient to show that an employee or agent acting within the scope of his or her actual or apparent authority had the relevant state of mind. In the case of a corporation, the state of mind of a director will also be sufficient: see s 45 (1), (3).

(iii) In many cases the agent or employee may be liable jointly with the principal or employer for misleading conduct: see, for example, *J F & B E Palmer Pty Ltd v Blowers & Lowe Pty Ltd* (1987) 75 ALR 509, another real estate agent case.

(iv) The personal liability of the employee or servant, or in the case of a company, a director, in relation to offences committed by the company will be governed by the normal rules of the criminal and civil law. Such a person will only be liable in the criminal law if he or she comes within s 66 of the Crimes Act 1961. This will require at the least knowledge of the essential elements of the offence committed by the company or employer, as well as an act of encouragement or assistance by the defendant: see *Cardin Laurant Ltd v Commerce Commission* [1990] 3 NZLR 563.

One question that may well be critical is whether disobedience to instructions is sufficient to take an employee or servant outside the scope of authority conferred. The normal position in the criminal law is that it does not. In the law of agency, disobedience by the agent may take the agent outside the scope of his or her actual authority, but not necessarily outside any apparent authority. The issue has not yet arisen in New Zealand, but there is Australian authority which indicates that there are limits on an employer's liability for the acts of agents or servants. The principle appears to be that if the employee does acts unconnected with the employer's business, the employer is not liable for them. A good example of this is provided by *Cooper v Snyman* (1989) 91 ALR 209, affirmed (1990) 97 ALR 364. In that case the first defendants had been employed by a company which sought advertisers for, and arranged the printing and distribution of, the "Yellow Pages" part of the Brisbane telephone book. While in that employment, the defendants had arranged for the insertion of misleading and deceptive descriptions of a business with which they were connected. It was held that the employer company was not liable for those actions, since the employees in arranging the advertisements were not acting in furtherance of the employer's activities but for their own purposes.

10.2 MISLEADING AND DECEPTIVE CONDUCT IN TRADE

10.2.1 "In trade"

The Fair Trading Act only applies to conduct or statements which are "in trade". The word "trade" is defined thus in s 2(1):

> "Trade" means any trade, business, industry, profession, occupation, activity of commerce, or undertaking relating to the supply or acquisition of goods or services or to the disposition or acquisition of any interest in land.

The word "business" is itself further defined as:

> "Business" means any undertaking –
> (a) That is carried on whether for gain or reward or not; or
> (b) In the course of which –
>   (i) Goods or services are acquired or supplied; or
>   (ii) Any interest in land is acquired or disposed of whether free of charge or not.

These definitions have not, as yet, been the subject of any substantial judicial comment in the New Zealand Courts, but it is probable that the term "trade" will be interpreted in much the same way as the cognate phrase "in trade or commerce" used in the Australian Trade Practices Act. The Australian cases indicate that the following principles will apply when determining whether or not conduct takes place in "trade":

(a) Conduct by a private individual outside the normal scope of his or her occupation or business is not normally conduct "in trade". Thus a sale of land which was not used as farm land by a farmer was not something done "in trade": see *O'Brien v Smolonogov* (1983) 53 ALR 107. Note that any person providing services as a part of a business activity involved in the promotion or implementation of the transaction will be acting "in trade". Thus the vendor of a private dwellinghouse may not be acting in trade, but a real estate agent or auctioneer acting for the vendor will be: for example, see *Latella v L J Hooker Ltd* (1985) 5 FCR 146.

(b) Where a member or employee or agent of a corporation or other composite entity indulges in misleading or deceptive conduct toward another employee, agent or member, there is no relevant conduct "in trade". The statute is aimed at the protection of consumers, not the regulation of the internal affairs of commercial entities. Thus in *Concrete Constructions (NSW) Pty Ltd v Nelson* (1990) 92 ALR 193 the High Court of Australia held that there could be no action under the Trade Practices Act for an alleged misleading statement made by one of the appellant's employees toward the respondent, another employee.

(c) Almost any conduct by a commercial enterprise which is directed at the public or members of it will be conduct "in trade". This will include advertising conducted by that enterprise: *Larmer v Power Machinery Pty Ltd* (1978) 29 FLR 490.

(d) The sale of the assets of a business or of the business itself to another for use in trade is itself conduct "in trade": *Bevanere Pty Ltd v Lubidineuse* (1985) 59 ALR 334.

(e) Things said or done in an attempt to preserve activities of a trade or business, or indeed the existence of the business or trade, will be conduct "in trade". This can be illustrated by the unusual case of *Hay v Chalmers* (1991) 3 NZBLC 102,000. Here the plaintiff was an accountant and ran a business as a provider of financial services. The defendant, who ran his own mechanic's business, was in financial difficulties and sought to delay the payments of moneys owing by alleging to his own creditors that the plaintiff had embezzled money belonging to the defendant and was under investigation for it. The plaintiff's business, predictably, largely collapsed as a result of the circulation of these statements. Fraser J held that as the statements had been made as a part of defendant's seeking extension of time to satisfy debts due by him, they were made "in trade". Similarly, an organisation may be acting in trade when the relevant conduct is designed to protect or enhance the commercial interests of the organisation of its members. In *Australian Federation of Consumer Organisations Inc v Tobacco Institute of Australia* (1991) 98 ALR 670, the Tobacco Institute had, as a part of a campaign against legislative restrictions on the advertising of tobacco products, issued advertisements which questioned, inaccurately in some instances, claims about the harm done by passive smoking. The Court held that taking part in a campaign to influence public opinion frequently would not be conduct "in trade"; however in these circumstances it was. The critical element was that the campaign was designed to safeguard the commercial interests of advertisers and distributors in being able to advertise tobacco products.

(f) Organisations or individuals who have as their primary occupation or pursuit something which is not a "trade" or "business" may still be held to be acting "in trade" if activities undertaken which are incidental to the primary purpose are properly to be characterised as having a trading or business character. An obvious example is provided by entities such as sports clubs, which may have a non-trading principal aim, but act "in trade" in activities undertaken to raise funds for the club: see as examples *R v Judges of Federal Court; ex p Western Australian National Football League (Inc)* (1979) 143 CLR 190; 23 ALR 439 and *Hughes v Western Australian Cricket Association (Inc)* (1986) 69 ALR 660 at 671. There must however be a real and substantial element of conduct of a trading nature; it is not enough that the relevant activities are small in extent and purely incidental to a primary non-trading purpose: *Attorney-General (ex rel Elisha) v Holy Apostolic and Catholic Church of the East (Assyrian) Australia NSW Parish Association* (1989) 98 ALR 327. A trade or professional association may have a primary non-trading purpose of regulating the conduct of members or providing advocacy and representation for such members, conduct which would not normally be "in trade". However, if the association engages in activities of the nature of trade to raise funds for its primary purposes it will be classed as acting in trade: see *Conference & Exhibition Organisers Pty Ltd v Australian Beauty Trade Suppliers Ltd* (1990) 96 ALR 439, affirmed (1991) 99 ALR 473 where the defendants, who were a company operating as a trade association, were held to be involved in trade in arranging an annual show, the organiser of which paid a substantial fee to the company.

Even where an organisation which has a primary non-trading aim or purpose is considered to engage in trade because of its fund-raising or other financial transactions, liability will only attach to conduct which is a part of the trading rather than the non-trading activities. Thus in *E v Australian Red Cross Society* (1991) 99 ALR 601 it was held that the Red Cross Society could be classed as a trading corporation because a substantial part of its activities were in the nature of trade, even though done to provide funds for non-trading and charitable purposes. However, the conduct on which the plaintiff brought his action, the supply of blood and blood plasma to hospitals, was done gratuitously as part of the charitable activities. Liability did not attach to it.

10.2.2 News media exception

The Act makes specific provision for the position of news media who may publish material which is alleged to be misleading or deceptive. Under s 15, the media are exempt from liability under the Act in relation to the publication of any matter which is not an advertisement for, or related to, business activities. The specified kinds of business activity are the supply, possible supply, or promotion of the supply, of goods or services or the sale or connection with the sale or grant of an interest in land. The precise limits of this exemption are not entirely clear because of the difficulties inherent in defining what are or are not business activities and therefore outside the protection of s 15. In *Sun Earth Homes Pty Ltd v Australian Broadcasting Corporation* (1990) 98 ALR 101, the Court refused to strike out a claim for misleading conduct alleged to have occurred in radio broadcasts of advertisements of a TV programme involving investigation by ABC staff of consumer complaints. The Court held that such advertisements might well not be protected by the Australian equivalent of s 15, since they could well be held to be advertising by ABC of a service provided by the ABC itself to consumers, a conclusion rendered more probable in that the ABC used material from the television programme in books on consumer affairs that it co-produced and offered for sale.

There is a further protection in s 44(4) of the Act for the media and for others whose business is the publication, or arranging for the publication, of advertisements. Such persons are protected from civil or criminal liability under the Act if they prove that the advertisement, or material on which it was based, was received in the ordinary course of business and the defendant did not know and had no reason to suspect that the publication of the advertisement, or the information contained in it, would be a contravention of the Act.

10.2.3 Conduct

The Act requires that there be some relevant conduct by the defendant. However, s 2(2) makes it clear that conduct for the purposes of the Act includes not only the doing of an act but also refusing or omitting to do an act. Conduct also includes making it known that an act will or, as the case may be, will not be done. The scope of "conduct" is therefore very wide. The range of matters which may be relied upon to constitute "conduct" may perhaps be illustrated by consideration of some particular instances.

(1) *Misrepresentations:* In general, anything that would be a misrepresentation for the purposes of the law of contract (as to which see 7.1.2), will be misleading or deceptive conduct for the purposes of the Fair Trading Act.

However, it must be remembered that the test of whether a statement is a misrepresentation or is misleading conduct requires the Court to look not only at the meaning which the maker of the statement intended it to convey but also at the meaning that an ordinary person would take from the statement. Often a statement will convey to the hearer further implications which the hearer would assume to be consequent upon what has actually been said. The point is well illustrated by *P C Brixton Autos Ltd v Commerce Commission* [1990] NZAR 203. In that case the appellant had offered a motor vehicle for sale, stating the odometer readings of the vehicle. The actual mileage done by the vehicle was considerably greater than that shown, the odometer readings having been falsified at some time before the vehicle came into the appellant's hands. It was nevertheless held that the appellant had correctly been convicted of a breach of the Act. As Holland J (at 208) put it:

> A statement by a motor vehicle dealer that a vehicle he is proposing to sell has x kilometres on the odometer is, in the absence of qualification or explanation and in ordinary circumstances, a representation that the vehicle, since new, has travelled approximately the stated number of kilometres.

However, note that if the statement made is accurate, and would not be misinterpreted by an ordinary person, it does not become a misrepresentation, or misleading conduct, merely because the person hearing it interprets it in some unusual and unintended way: see *Savill v NZI Finance Ltd* [1990] 3 NZLR 135. It will be possible to sue on the basis of a representation made to an agent of the plaintiff, if the plaintiff was intended to be influenced by the representation: *Netaf Pty Ltd v Bikane Pty Ltd* (1990) 92 ALR 490.

(2) *Promissory statements:* A promissory statement is unlikely to be a misrepresentation at common law, but it can be relevant conduct for the purposes of the Act. In *Adelaide Petroleum NL v Poseidon Ltd* (1990) 98 ALR 431 it was held there was misleading conduct where the defendant entered into a bargain to provide financial assistance to the plaintiff because the defendant had an undisclosed intention not to honour the agreement unless certain events occurred.

(3) *Silence where there is a duty to speak:* The case of *Mills v United Building Society* [1988] 2 NZLR 392 is the leading New Zealand authority on when silence might amount to misleading conduct. In that case the defendant had advertised for sale, as a mortgagee's sale, a leasehold interest in a block of flats. The plaintiff made enquiries of the defendant's agent, and was told that UBS were trying to recover about $210,000 plus GST. The agent declined to give any estimate of the value of the building. The agent

further informed the plaintiff that the land was held under a "Friedlander" lease, and supplied a copy of the lease document. The plaintiff purchased the property at the mortgagee's sale but later discovered further facts, which led to the bringing of the action. The plaintiff found that UBS had initially only advanced $100,000; the remainder of the sum sought at the sale was arrears of interests and other costs. He also found out that the "Friedlander" lease denied him, as lessee, any compensation for improvements to the land when the lease terminated. The property was therefore worth much less than he had thought, or paid. The High Court and Court of Appeal held that there was, on the facts, no misleading or deceptive conduct by UBS or its agents. The Courts held that a failure to give information could only be misleading or deceptive conduct where there was a duty to give full information. The Courts held that the relationship between vendor and purchaser in a contract of sale is not one which would normally create such a duty.

However there are, as *Mills v UBS* recognises, certain cases where one party may be under a duty to disclose to the other any relevant information in his or her possession, either as to the whole transaction or as to a part of it. These generally follow the common law as to contract, but may go some little distance beyond it. From *Mills* and the Australian law, the leading Australian cases being *Rhone-Poulenc Agrochimie SA v UIM Chemical Services Pty Ltd* (1986) 68 ALR 77 and *Collins Marrickville Pty Ltd v Henjo Investments Pty Ltd* (1987) 72 ALR 601, it can be said that there will be a duty of disclosure, and that silence may amount to misleading or deceptive conduct, in the following circumstances:

(i)   Where there is a fiduciary element in the relationship between the parties. The fiduciary element may arise from the nature of the contract: as with contracts of insurance or contracts of guarantee, see, for example, *Kennard v A G C (Advances) Ltd* (1986) ATPR 48,127. It may also arise because of the relationship of the parties; solicitors and clients, parents and children, trustee and beneficiary are all recognised fiduciary relationships. Or it may arise on the particular facts of the transaction; see the cases discussed in 5.2.2. It may be that the Courts will apply a somewhat lower threshold of reliance and confidence in cases under the Fair Trading Act. In *Sutton v A J Thompson Pty Ltd (in liquidation)* (1987) 73 ALR 233 it was held that a vendor of a business who was on friendly terms with the purchaser, and knew that the purchaser would be affected in his decisions by that friendship owed a duty to make full disclosure of all the facts relevant to the transaction. The facts of the case would not appear to have been enough to give rise to a fiduciary duty at common law.

(ii) Where a statement is made which is literally true, but which omits mention of other matters which make what was said inaccurate. Failure to mention the related matters is in effect deceiving by telling only a part of the truth. A very good example is furnished by *Collins Marrickville Pty Ltd v Henjo Investments Pty Ltd* (1987) 72 ALR 601. In that case the plaintiffs had purchased a restaurant from the defendants. The defendants had accurately stated the restaurant's turnover figures, but had failed to disclose that the turnover was achieved by operating in breach of the restaurant's licence. That omission was misleading conduct. For other examples of the same principle, see *P C Brixton Autos Ltd v Commerce Commission* [1990] NZAR 203, and *Collier Constructions Pty Ltd v Foskett Pty Ltd* (1990) 97 ALR 460.

(iii) Where one party makes a statement which is then true, but subsequently fails to disclose the occurrence of a material change in the circumstances. In *Bevanere Pty Ltd v Lubidineuse* (1985) 59 ALR 334, it was held that a failure to disclose that employees of a hair dressing establishment, on whom the purchaser was known to be intending to rely, had determined to leave and set up a rival business was misleading and deceptive.

However, the general rule remains that in the absence of any such duty to disclose, silence is not misleading conduct. In the context of commercial transactions, it seems the Courts will not easily be moved to find such a duty. An instructive recent decision is that in *David Securities Pty Ltd v Commonwealth Bank of Australia* (1990) 93 ALR 271. The plaintiffs had arranged to borrow substantial sums in foreign currency, the loans being arranged through the defendants. When the value of the Australian dollar fell heavily against the loan currency movements, the plaintiffs lost heavily. The principal allegation was that the bank had been guilty of misleading conduct by failing to advise as to techniques available to safeguard the borrower against such losses. It was accepted that the bank had indicated there were risks attached to such a loan, and had directed the borrower to an accountant with some expertise in the field. The Federal Court of Appeal held that there was at most in the circumstances a duty to warn that risks were attached to the transaction. This had been done; there was no further duty to advise as to possible alternative courses of conduct.

The reasoning of the judgments in *David Securities Pty Ltd* and *Mills v United Building Society* may foreshadow the development of a rule to deal with commercial transactions which present unusual features. In such cases there might well be a duty on a party who is aware of the unusual feature, and aware that the other does not know of it, to put the less-informed party on notice of the existence of the unusual feature. The duty would not extend to describing the exact nature of the unusual feature, or its possible effects or ways to avoid it. The creation or recognition of such a duty has not as yet been explicitly considered by any Court. However, the adoption of such a rule would, it is suggested, explain and reconcile most of the cases in the area, as well as providing what appears to be a workable test for commercial purposes.

10.2.4 Mere puffery

The common law excluded from the law of misrepresentation any statement which was classed as "mere puffery", that is, statements of commendation or deprecation which did not convey any real element of fact. To state that something is "a great bargain" or even that it is "a wonderful product" is therefore normally a matter of mere puffery. However, a statement which conveys a definite element of fact is not mere puffery, and may therefore have effect as a representation. A similar rule would appear to apply under the Fair Trading Act. It may be illustrated by *Given v Pryor* (1979) 39 FLR 437. In that case the Court held there was misleading conduct in advertising for sale certain land which was described as "a wonderful place to live". The land was not zoned residential, and special permission for building was required. It was held that the advertisement carried an implied, and misleading, representation that the land could be used for residential purposes. The distinction was emphasised again in *Schindler Lifts Australia Pty Ltd v Debelak* (1989) 89 ALR 275. The plaintiff company was engaged in the supply and maintenance of lifts. The defendants had worked for the plaintiffs, prior to its purchase by overseas interests. The defendants then left the plaintiff's employment and set up in opposition. The plaintiff brought an action alleging false or misleading conduct by the defendants by way of comments made to prospective customers about the ability of the plaintiff to offer adequate levels of service. Pincus J held that the comments were generally no more than "mere puffery", statements of disparagement which would be discounted because of their nature and source by those persons who heard them. It may perhaps have been different if it had been shown that the defendants had spoken in similar terms to a person who was unaware of the history of the parties, and therefore in a position to be discriminating as to the validity of the comments. A similar line has been taken in cases involving advertisements: see *Colgate Palmolive Pty Ltd v Rexona Pty Ltd* (1981) 58 FLR 391 and *Dewhirst & Kay Rent-A-Car Pty Ltd v Budget Rent-A-Car System Pty Ltd* (1986) 8 FCR 1.

10.2.5. Labelling

It is clear that a statement made on a label attached to goods will be treated as a representation concerning the goods, for which the retailer will normally be liable: see, for example, *Cardin Laurant Ltd v Commerce Commission* [1990] 3 NZLR 563. Although the display of goods with a marked price falls short, on general principle, of a contractual offer, the display is to be taken for the purposes of the Fair Trading Act as being made "in connection with the supply of goods". Any misleading or deceptive elements of the label may therefore involve a breach of the Act. It seems that unless there is a timeous and suitable counter to the misleading label, liability under the Act will be incurred. A correction made too late may be ineffective in preventing liability. In *Foodtown Supermarkets Ltd v Commerce Commission* [1991] 1 NZLR 466, the appellant displayed, in its supermarket, food items with displays and labels indicating a lower price than was actually charged by the computerised central check-out system. The only evidence before the Court came from customers who had realised the difference and disputed the issue. These customers were supplied with the goods at the price displayed. It was held that there was a breach of s 13 (g), despite the later charging of the price displayed.

The relative positions of the retailer and manufacturer of goods which are wrongly labelled were considered in *Allied Liquor Merchants Ltd v Independent Liquor (NZ) Ltd* (1989) 3 TCLR 328. In that case the defendants had produced and marketed a range of products described as gin, rum, vodka or whisky. Each actually contained a lower percentage of alcohol than such spirits normally contained. The products were labelled prominently with the name of the product and a figure representing the amount of proof spirit, for example "Gin 62". The labelling also carried, less prominently, the actual composition of the liquid. It was held that the labelling amounted to a breach of s 9, because the prominence of the name of the spirit was such as to swamp all the other descriptions. It therefore conveyed a false representation as to the quality of the goods. The manufacturer was therefore guilty of a breach of the Act by affixing the label chosen. The manufacturer sought to evade liability by arguing that it should not be answerable for the conduct of the retailer, which may have contributed to any misleading of the public. Gault J held that any person who supplied goods labelled in such a way as to prevent any other realistic manner of description must be answerable for the offer and sale of those goods under the name and description given by the supplier. Any failure by the retailer to clarify the position cannot be seen as excusing the manufacturer or supplier from liability. On that basis, both the manufacturer and the retailer may be liable under the Act for any defective or misleading labelling.

10.2.6 "Misleading or deceptive or likely to mislead or deceive"

The most important concept in the Fair Trading Act is the requirement that conduct be actionable if it is misleading or deceptive or likely to mislead or deceive. Unfortunately, the concept is also one of the most difficult concepts to define. The Courts have generally been loath to place glosses on the wording of the statute and have insisted that essentially the issue will be one of applying the words of the statute to the particular facts of any case. The variety of circumstances in which the words may fall to be applied is so wide as to make any precise definition impossible, but there are certain broad general principles which are useful starting points in considering the statute.

One helpful, and frequently cited, discussion of the issues is that of Wilcox J in *Chase Manhattan Overseas Corporation v Chase Corporation* (1985) 63 ALR 345, 354-55. That case was one where it was alleged that the misleading or deceptive conduct lay in the adoption of a name sufficiently similar as to cause confusion in the market. However, the principles are, mutatis mutandis, applicable to all forms of misleading or deceptive conduct.

> The legal principles relevant to the determination of the question whether the use by a corporation of a particular name amounts to conduct which is actually or potentially misleading or deceptive may, I think, be summarised as follows:
> (a) Conduct cannot, for the purposes of sec 52, be categorised as misleading, or deceptive, or likely to be misleading or deceptive, unless it contains or conveys a misrepresentation: *Taco Company of Australia Inc v Taco Bell Pty Limited* (1982) ATPR para 40-303 at p 43,751; (1982) 42 ALR 177 at p 202.
> (b) A statement which is literally true may nevertheless be misleading or deceptive: see *Hornsby Building Information Centre Pty Limited* (1978) ATPR para 40-067 at p 17,690; (1978) 140 CLR 216 at p 227. This will occur, for example, where the statement also conveys a second meaning which is untrue: *World Series Cricket Pty Limited v Parish* (1977) ATPR para 40-040 at p 17,436; (1977) 16 ALR 181 at p 201.
> (c) Conduct is likely to mislead or deceive if this is a 'real or not remote chance or possibility regardless of whether it is less or more than 50 per cent' *Global Sportsman Pty Limited v Mirror Newspapers Limited* (1984) ATPR para 40-463 at p 45,343; (1984) 55 ALR 25 at p 30. [This aspect may now need qualification in relation to ss 10-14, see 10.3.1 below.]

(d) The question whether conduct is, or is likely to be, misleading or deceptive is an objective one, to be determined by the Court for itself, in relation to one or more identified sections of the public, the Court considering all who fall within an identified section of the public 'including the astute and the gullible, the intelligent and the not so intelligent, the well educated as well as the poorly educated, men and women of various ages pursuing a variety of vocations': *Taco Company* at ATPR p 43,752; ALR p 202. Evidence of the formation in fact of an erroneous conclusion is admissible but not conclusive: *Global Sportsman* at ATPR p 45,343, ALR p 30.

(e) Ordinarily, mere proof of confusion or uncertainty will not suffice to prove misleading or deceptive conduct: *Parkdale Custom Built Furniture Pty Limited v Puxu Pty Limited* (1982) ATPR para 40-307; (1982)149 CLR 191. However, where confusion is proved, the Court should investigate the cause; so that it may determine whether this is because of misleading or deceptive conduct on the part of the respondent: *Taco* at ATPR p 43,752; ALR p 203.

It is obvious that the principles are interrelated, rather than distinct, approaches to the issue before the Court in any particular case. Whether a statement is a misrepresentation will depend on the audience to which it is addressed, as well as whether it is in itself untrue. If true, it may still carry with it a secondary, false meaning. Most of Wilcox J's statements are clear and require little discussion.

One vital distinction is between conduct which is merely confusing and conduct which is misleading or deceptive. Something is not misleading or deceptive merely because members of the public may be caused to wonder whether two products come from the same source or are otherwise linked. The causing of uncertainty in the mind of the public, or of the relevant section of it, is not of itself enough to show that there has been misleading or deceptive conduct. It is evidence from which the Court may infer that members of the public were deceived; it is not of itself decisive of the issue. Evidence of widespread confusion makes the drawing of an inference of misrepresentation or deception easier: see for example *Taylor Bros Ltd v Taylors Group Ltd* [1988] 2 NZLR 1 and *Trust Bank Auckland Ltd v ASB Bank Ltd* [1989] 3 NZLR 385. Even where there is evidence of confusion it must be shown that the confusion proceeds from the acts of the defendant: *Hornsby Building Information Centre v Sydney Building Information Centre* (1978) 18 ALR 639; 140 CLR 216. The plaintiff need not prove that all of the public took the same meaning from the defendant's conduct or statements; it is sufficient if a significant proportion of the target audience form a particular erroneous belief: *Siddons Pty Ltd v Stanley Works Pty Ltd* (1991) 99 ALR 497.

It must be borne in mind that there is no requirement that the conduct be intended to mislead or deceive. Indeed, evidence that a person was aware that his or her conduct might cause confusion in the marketplace does not, of itself, establish that there was any misleading or deceptive conduct: see *Murray Goulburn Co-operative Co Ltd v New South Wales Dairy Corporation* (1990) 92 ALR 239. However, if there is evidence of any intentional element in the conduct which rendered it deceptive in the sense of conduct designed to cheat or ensnare or mislead customers, the position is different. If a person deliberately sets out to cause confusion among prospective customers as to the nature or sources of a product or service because he or she sees that this will be to his or her commercial benefit, the Court may infer that the person believed that their actions would mislead or deceive, and thus render more probable the finding that the public were in fact deceived. This is illustrated by *Telmak Teleproducts (Australia) Ply Ltd v Coles Myer Ltd* (1989) 89 ALR 48. The defendant had imported and sold a dry-frying convection pan of a kind similar to that produced and marketed by the plaintiff. The defendant had deliberately used packaging which was very similar to that of the plaintiff's product in an attempt to gain a benefit from the plaintiff's television advertising of its product. The Court determined that the defendant had believed that the sales of their products would be advanced by these tactics. This was evidence from which it could be inferred firstly that the defendant expected to sell its products to persons who wrongly thought they were buying the advertised product, and further, that that expectation was evidence from which it could be inferred that the packaging was misleading or deceptive.

10.3 SPECIAL INSTANCES OF MISLEADING OR DECEPTIVE CONDUCT

The Act contains a number of prohibitions on misleading or deceptive conduct in specific activities, as in connection with offers of employment: s 12 and, in even more specialised cases s 22; as to the nature or quality or other attributes of goods: s 10, or services: s 11. There is also a prohibition on the use of false representations in relation to goods or services: s 13, and in relation to land: s 14. Some aspects of these particular provisions are more specifically discussed below, but it is necessary first to consider the relationship of these provisions with the general provision in s 9 and also the inter-relationship of the specific provisions.

10.3.1 Relationship of ss 9-12 and s 13

The first matter is the relationship of s 13 with the more general provisions of ss 9 - 12. Section 13 defines a "false representation" in very broad terms. Almost any false statement as to nature, condition, origins, history, or quality of goods or services will involve a breach of the section. It is clear that the same conduct may be relied on to establish both a breach of s 9 and of one of the more specific sections; indeed in civil proceedings it is normal for the case to be considered almost solely on the s 9 ground. However, criminal liability may attach to breaches of ss 10 - 14, other than in relation to s 14(2), whereas it does not attach to a breach of s 9. This allows enforcement of the Act by criminal rather than civil sanctions. Further, misleading or deceptive conduct in relation to transactions affecting an interest in land or the supply of goods or services is only unlawful if the conduct occurs "in trade", whether under s 9 or a more specific provision. In relation to employment, there is no requirement that the prohibited conduct occur "in trade".

The provisions of ss 9 -12, prohibiting misleading or deceptive conduct, are aimed at different kinds of behaviour from those in ss 13 and 14 dealing with false representations. The relationship between the provisions was discussed in *Sound Plus Ltd v Commerce Commission* (1991) 3 NZBLC 101,989. Anderson J stated that ss 10 and 11 are primarily concerned with conduct or statements which, accurate in themselves, are true, but which become misleading because they could be construed as something which would be untrue. By contrast, s 13 is primarily concerned with false representations which may be taken as true. Anderson J also expressed the view that s 10 is concerned primarily with public dealings, s 13 with "more restricted" or individual transactions.

It may also be that the standard of proof required as to the deceptive character of the conduct is higher for ss 10-13 than it is for s 9. In *TPC v J & R Enterprises Pty Ltd* (1991) ALR 325 it was held that the word "likely" in the Australian equivalent of s 9 was different in meaning from "liable" in the equivalent of s 11. The latter required proof of a probability, apparently a more than 50 per cent chance, that the public would be misled or deceived; the former required something less than this.

10.3.2 Misleading conduct in relation to employment

The general provision in s 12 which prohibits, in relation to the offer or potential offer, of employment to any person, any conduct which is misleading or deceptive, or is likely to mislead or deceive the offeree as to the availability, nature, terms or conditions, or any other matter relating to that employment.

There is only one reported New Zealand case on the section, *Sinclair v Webb & McCormack Ltd* (1990) 3 NZELC 97,405. In that case Sinclair was offered employment by the defendants if he migrated to New Zealand. The major point in dispute related to a promise to pay the plaintiff's moving costs, a promise which was not fulfilled. The Court held that there was no liability under s 12; what was alleged was essentially a breach of a contractual term. Failure to adhere to a contractual promise was not of itself proof of misleading or deceptive conduct at the time the promise was made. The Court expressed the view that cases involving a dispute which was essentially only as to an alleged breach of the contract of employment should be dealt with as a matter of contract, rather than under the umbrella provisions of the Fair Trading Act.

The special provisions of s 22 may also be of relevance to employment cases. That section prohibits the making of false or misleading representations as to profitability or risk or other material aspects of a business activity which are represented as being one that can wholly or substantially be carried out from the representee's place of residence or in which the representee is invited to participate by the performance of work, with or without investment of moneys.

10.3.3 Misleading conduct in relation to goods and services

The general provisions in relation to goods and services are ss 10 and 11. These sections proscribe any person acting in trade from engaging in any conduct that is liable to mislead the public as to the nature, characteristics, suitability for a particular purpose, or quantity of any goods or services, as well, in relation to goods alone, of any misleading conduct as to the manufacturing process of the goods.

Both goods and services are very extensively defined in the Act. It is noteworthy that the definition of goods may well be wider than that provided in the Sale of Goods Act 1908: see 12.2. For the purposes of the Fair Trading Act "goods" includes ships, aircraft, vehicles, animals, fish, minerals, trees, and crops, whether on, under, or attached to land or not, as well as gas or electricity. Although the statutory definition is not exhaustive, forms of personal property which are not "goods" will presumably not be included. Thus it is probable that money in the form of coins and notes, cheques and intangible property are not included. However, perhaps surprisingly, it has been held that shares are "goods" for the purposes of the Fair Trading Act: see *CPB Industries Ltd v Bowker Holdings No 16 Ltd* (1987) 3 NZCLC 100,035 and *Miln v Stratford Fisheries Ltd* (1988) 4 NZCLC 64,428.

The definition of services is even more extensive. It includes any rights, benefits, privileges, or facilities arising from any contract for the performance of work (ie a contract for services) for insurance, for the provision of credit, as well as any contract between a customer of a bank and the bank . The Act also includes in the definition any contract for the provision, or use or enjoyment, of facilities for accommodation, amusement, the care of persons or animals or things, entertainment, instruction, parking, or recreation, as well as any contract under which there is a conferral of rights, benefits, or privileges in return for remuneration by way of royalties, levies and the like. However, the definition of services explicitly excludes rights or benefits in the form of the supply of goods or the performance of work under a contract of service.

The terms of s 11 are generally quite clear and therefore leave relatively little doubt as to what constitute "services". However, there are some matters worthy of note. One important matter is that action to enforce rights created by a contract for the supply of services is not necessarily to be taken as being connected with the supply of services. For example, the statutory definition includes all contracts relating to the lending of money or the extension of credit, thereby including all mortgages. However, a mortgagee exercising its powers of possession and sale of properties which were the security for the mortgage is not supplying "services" to the mortgagor: *National Australia Bank Ltd v Sproule* (1989) 98 ALR 570.

10.3.4 Misleading conduct in relation to land

Section 14 of the Act prohibits false representations or other misleading conduct in relation to any interest in land. "Interest" is defined in the section to include both legal and equitable interest, as well as a right of occupancy of the land, or of a building or part of a building on the land including rights from shareholding in a company owning the land or building. The section prohibits the making of false representations concerning the nature of any interest in the land to be acquired, or the price payable for the land, the location of the land, the characteristics of the land, the use to which the land is capable of being put or may lawfully be put, or the existence or availability of facilities associated with the land.

The provisions of s 14 are largely self-explanatory. Perhaps the most significant phrase is "the use to which the land is capable of being put or may lawfully be put". This wording will obviously have effect in relation to town-planning or other controls on the uses which may be made of the land: cf *Given v Pryor* (1979) 39 FLR 437. However, it appears that the section does not remove the general principle of the "caveat emptor" from contracts for the sale of land. It appears clear that the Fair Trading Act has not altered the common law principle that there is no implied warranty of fitness of purpose in a contract for the sale of land. In *Bradford House Pty Ltd & Ors v Leroy Fashion Group Ltd* (1982) 46 ALR 305, the plaintiff had leased a commercial building from the defendant. The plaintiff intended to use it to store commercial printing materials, including large and heavy rolls of paper, which would be moved by forklift. The defendant's agent was aware of this intended purpose and failed to warn the plaintiff that the structure of the building might not withstand the loads intended to be placed on it, as indeed it did not. It was held that there was no duty to warn that the building might not be suitable. Thus, unless some other matter creates a duty to warn (as to which see 10.2.3), s 14 will only attach liability to express statements as to the suitability of land for a particular purpose.

10.4 RELATIONSHIP OF FAIR TRADING ACT AND OTHER AREAS OF LAW

The rules and causes of action provided by the Fair Trading Act overlap to a considerable extent with other rules of law which affect liability for commercial practice and behaviour. In appropriate cases, actions may be brought in reliance on both the Act and an alternative proceeding at common law. This has, perhaps, been a more marked phenomenon in Australia than in New Zealand. In contractual cases, this may reflect the alterations to the common law rules relating to misrepresentation made by the Contractual Remedies Act 1979. Certainly these changes have eased the task of the plaintiff in some circumstances. In non-contractual cases, particularly those involving an allegation of passing off, the coupling of the common law action with one under the Fair Trading Act is the norm.

While a full description of the relevant rules governing the various causes of action would be out of place in this work, the following summary represents the most significant elements of the relationship between the Fair Trading Act and other relevant rules of law.

(1) *In cases where the parties entered a contractual relationship:* The plaintiff may rely on misrepresentation under the Contractual Remedies Act 1979: see 7.1, or the Fair Trading Act. Under the Contractual Remedies Act the plaintiff must establish a misrepresentation; under the Fair Trading Act, both conduct which does mislead and conduct which is deceptive are actionable. In contract it is irrelevant whether the misrepresentation was innocent, negligent or deliberate; under the Fair Trading Act the defendant may escape liability by showing a reasonable belief that any representation made was true: see 10.5.6. Reliance on the representation by the representee, ie that the misrepresentation induced the contract, must be shown in a contractual action to establish liability. Such reliance is not essential under the Fair Trading Act, but damages will be likely to be small unless reliance is established. The measure of damages may well be different. Loss of potential profit is usually recoverable in contract; it will be rare in fair trading cases. One vital difference is that a contractual provision excluding or limiting liability may well prevent a successful action in contract; it will not have this effect under the Fair Trading Act.

(2) *Tortious liability for misrepresentation or deceit:* At common law an action may be brought for negligent misrepresentation or for deceit. Negligent misrepresentation requires proof that the maker of a statement owed the recipient a duty of care, that there was a representation made and that the statement was made without reasonable care being taken to ensure its accuracy. The standard of care needed will vary according to the circumstances of the case. Once these elements are shown, and it is shown that the plaintiff relied on the misrepresentation and suffered loss as a result, there will be liability at common law, absent, of course, is any relevant contractual exclusion of liability. Deceit requires a deliberate misrepresentation, rather than a merely negligent one, but also requires reliance leading to a loss. By contrast, the Fair Trading Act does not require an actual misrepresentation. Again without proof of a representation, and reliance on it, damages may well be small.

(3) *Defamation:* There may also be cases where an action under the Act can be coupled with an action for defamation. This is particularly likely to be the case where the conduct complained of is not directed to the plaintiff, but to others. A good example is furnished by *Hay v Chalmers* (1991) 3 NZBLC 102,000, the facts of which are given at 10.2.1 supra. Defamation is essentially the making of statements which have a tendency to lower the subject of the statement in the eyes of those members of the public who become aware of the statements. Truth is not always a perfect defence; there are other special rules relating to privilege and fair comment which may provide defences. Both in defamation and fair trading it is no defence that the statement was believed to be true, though under the Fair Trading Act a honest belief based on reasonable grounds may be a defence.

(4) *Intellectual property and passing off actions:* Lastly, but far from least important, is the overlap with actions relating to intellectual property. There are a number of statutes which provide protection for designers, authors and inventors, for example, Designs Act 1953, Trademarks Act 1953, Copyright Act 1962 and Patents Act 1953. Falsely claiming to be the author, inventor etc of a product may involve liability under both the Fair Trading Act and the more specialised statute. Indeed, falsely claiming that a product or service is protected by one of the statutes would be a misleading representation in relation to the quality of the goods or the service: see, for example, *Rhone-Poulenc Agrochimie SA v UIM Chemical Services Pty Ltd* (1986) 68 ALR 77. In addition, the Fair Trading Act specifically outlaws the forgery or unauthorised use of a trademark: s 16, and the importation of goods to which a false trademark has been applied: s 26.

The most common action involving elements of intellectual property which is likely to coincide with a Fair Trading Act action is a claim in tort for passing off. The essential requirements for a passing off action have been stated many times in slightly different ways. The following summary is largely drawn from the speeches of Lord Diplock and Lord Fraser in *Erven Warnink BV v J Townend and Sons (Hull) Ltd* [1979] AC 731, 742 and 755-6 respectively. The plaintiff must show firstly that his or her business consists of, or includes, selling in a particular geographical location a class of goods, or providing a particular kind of services, to which the particular trade name applies. Secondly, it must be shown that the class of goods, or services, is clearly defined, and that in the minds of the public, or a section of the public, the trade name distinguishes that class from other similar goods or services. Thirdly, it must be shown that the goods or services have acquired a goodwill in the market because of the reputation they carry. Fourthly, the plaintiff must show that he or she has a real or substantial interest in the goodwill attaching to the goods or services. Lastly, it must be shown that the plaintiff has suffered, or is likely to suffer, substantial damage to his or her property in the goodwill by reason of the defendant selling goods which are falsely described by the trade name to which the goodwill is attached. This last element requires proof of infringement, ie that the defendant, while acting in the course of his or her trade, has misrepresented the origins or characteristics of the goods or services to prospective customers or ultimate consumers of the those goods or service, and proof of loss to the plaintiff. If the defendant's conduct produces harm to the plaintiff's interests, and the harm was reasonably foreseeable, liability for passing off is established.

As can be seen from this analysis, there are very great similarities between an action for passing off and the requirements for an action under the Fair Trading Act. However, the two proceedings are not identical. The statutory proceedings are open to a wider class of persons in that there is no requirement that the plaintiff be the owner of any goodwill in the services or goods. Nor need there have been actual damage to the plaintiff's goodwill. The most significant element is, however, that in the tort of passing off the plaintiff must show that the defendant has caused actual confusion in the market place as to the provenance of the goods or services. Under the Fair Trading Act it is sufficient if there is a serious risk of such a confusion. It must be borne in mind that slightly different rules may apply where an action is brought to restrain a person from commencing acts which might amount to passing off from those that apply where the conduct has already occurred.

(5) *Limitation periods:* One significant difference between any of the common law actions and one under the Fair Trading Act is the difference in the limitation period. In most cases a claim at common law can be brought within six years of the cause of action occurring. Under the Fair Trading Act the claim must be brought within three years from the time when the matter giving rise to the application arose: s 43(5). This would appear to be three years from the date of the relevant misleading or deceptive conduct.

10.5 REMEDIES AND PROCEDURAL MATTERS

The Act provides a number of different remedies. These are contained in ss 41, 42 and 43.

10.5.1 Disclosure orders

The most specialised of the remedies is the power under s 42 to order a defendant to make disclosure of information, to the public generally or to sections of it, or to publish statements so as to counteract earlier misleading conduct. Such orders can only be made on an application by the Commerce Commission.

10.5.2 Injunctions

Under s 41, the High Court may grant an injunction to restrain the occurrence or continuance of misleading or deceptive conduct by any person, or to enjoin the activities of any person assisting such conduct, or being "knowingly concerned" in the conduct: s 41(e). A person will only be considered to be "knowingly concerned in" a contravention by another if he or she has actual knowledge of the essential matters which go to make up the contravention: *Yorke v Lucas* (1985) 158 CLR 661, 61 ALR 307; *Crocodile Marketing Ltd v Griffith Vintners Pty Ltd* (1989) 91 ALR 273. In the latter case Cole J refused to extend liability to cases of constructive knowledge.

The normal rules relating to injunctions are significantly relaxed by s 41(3) and (4). The first of these subsections provides that it is not necessary that the Court be satisfied that without the injunction the defendant would continue or repeat the infringing conduct; the second that the Court be satisfied that there is a risk of substantial damage to any person if the injunction is not granted. In practice injunctions will usually be sought by the Commission or by rival traders, who are more concerned with preventing unfair business practices and competition, rather than by individual consumers whose primary objective is likely to be compensation for losses already suffered.

10.5.3 Orders for cancellation or variation of the contract

Other forms of relief are available under s 43. That section gives to the Courts very wide powers to make orders of various kinds. The most important are orders to cancel or vary the contract: s 42 (1) (a) and (b), to restore money or other property: s 43 (1)(c), or to order compensation for loss or damage. This last power differs from the common law or the Contractual Remedies Act 1979 in that the award of damages is discretionary. The case law has also shown that the principles on which damages are to be assessed are generally those applicable in tort, rather than in contract. The issue of damages is discussed further at 10.5.4.

While the normal approach of the Courts has been to award damages where there is clear loss flowing from misleading or deceptive conduct, there have been cases where the Court has, as a matter of discretion, held that no relief should be granted. In *Parkdale Custom Built Furniture Pty Ltd v Puxu Pty Ltd* (1982) 149 CLR 191,199 it was said that the Courts should withhold relief from a party who had failed to take reasonable care of his or her own interests. Such a restriction may be rare, but there may be cases where it is important particularly if there was something in the circumstances to make the applicant for relief aware of the need to verify information given by the defendant: see *Sutton v A J Thompson Pty Ltd (in liq)* (1987) 73 ALR 233.

10.5.4 Damages

The question of the correct approach to the award of damages has not yet arisen for substantial discussion in New Zealand. The Australian Courts have repeatedly indicated that the normal approach of the Courts, once the decision is made to order the payment of damages or compensation, is to use the tort measure to determine the quantum of damages: see *Gates v City Mutual Life Assurance Society Ltd* (1986) 160 CLR 1. Therefore the approach is to award such a sum as will put the plaintiff in the position in which he or she would have been but for the misleading conduct. The applicant for relief must, of course, establish that any loss arose from the particular misleading or deceptive conduct alleged and proved: see *Pappas v Soulac* (1983) 50 ALR 231.

This may lead to difficulties in some cases. Two which have received particular attention are those where the misleading conduct has been directed at the public generally, but the plaintiff alleges a loss as a result; the other is where the misleading conduct has enticed the plaintiff into entering a bad bargain, or a losing contract. In the first of these, the Court may have great difficulty in determining to what extent any misleading conduct was causative of particular losses. A very good example is provided by *Cooper v Snyman* (1990) 97 ALR 364. In that case the misleading conduct alleged was in listing a florist's business in a telephone directory in such a way as to make it appear that it was located in a particular area, which it was not, and in terms which made could cause confusion between it and the florist's business operated by the plaintiff. The plaintiff proved a substantial decline in her turnover after the misleading advertisements appeared, but could not establish that this was substantially due to the unfair competition, rather than to a general decline in consumer spending which had affected the revenues of all florists in the area at the relevant time. The plaintiff therefore recovered only relatively small damages.

Difficulties may also arise in calculating the appropriate level of damages where the misleading or deceptive conduct has influenced the plaintiff into entering a contract which entails a continuing loss, as with the purchase of a business which runs at a loss. If the circumstances are such that avoiding the contract is not appropriate, the Court has a difficult task in assessing the appropriate damages. The Australian Courts have taken the view that generally, but not invariably, the purchaser should be awarded damages for all the loss flowing directly from the misleading or deceptive conduct, including trading losses incurred: see *Gould v Vaggelas* (1984) 157 CLR 215; 56 ALR 31; *Netaf Pty Ltd v Bikane Pty Ltd* (1990) 92 ALR 490 and *Henjo Investments Pty Ltd v Collins Marrickville Pty Ltd* (1989) 89 ALR 539. However, damages are not normally available for consequential losses, such as trading losses, if these were attributable to external factors, such as competition from other parties or general economic circumstances.

In other, exceptional, cases, the appropriate test for damages may be the loss of the value of a bargain, and thus be more akin to the contractual measure of damages. In *Adelaide Petroleum NL v Poseidon Ltd* (1990) 98 ALR 431, the plaintiffs had sought assistance from other companies in the reconstruction and refinancing of the plaintiff's activities. The defendant had diverted the plaintiff from negotiations with a third party by promises which, it was held, were not intended to be kept: see 10.2.3. When those dealings broke down, the plaintiff negotiated again with the third party, and obtained assistance, on less favourable terms than it would earlier have received. It was held that the appropriate measure of damages was to award a sum equivalent to the benefits of the bargain promised by the defendant, less the value of the benefits received from the eventual contract with the third party.

Exemplary damages are probably not available under the Fair Trading Act. The point does not appear to have been decided in New Zealand, but there is Australian authority that only compensatory damages are available: *Cooper v Snyman* (1989) 91 ALR 209, 235 and *Musca v Astle Corporation Pty Ltd* (1988) 80 ALR 251, 262. The damages may include compensation for distress and inconvenience: *Sinclair v Webb & McCormack Ltd* [1990] 3 NZELC 97,405.

10.5.5 Effect of exclusion and disclaimer clauses

It is common in consumer transactions for a contract to make provision limiting in some way the liability of one of the parties to the contract. There may be a number of different techniques used. Limitation clauses generally provide for a monetary limit on any liability arising under the contract; exclusion clauses deny liability arising from certain events or from certain kinds of legal obligation. This may be done directly or by clauses which provide that one party acknowledges that he or she relied on his or her own judgment in entering the contract and that there was therefore no reliance on any conduct or representations by the other party or his or her agents. For the contractual position, see 4.2 and 7.1.7 supra.

There is as yet no New Zealand authority as to the effect of such a provision on a claim under the Fair Trading Act, but it is unlikely the Courts would give great effect to them. The Australian case law indicates that any contractual provision which purports to exclude liability for pre-contractual representations will not prevent liability arising under the statute: *Petera Pty Ltd v E A J Pty Ltd* (1985) ATPR 40-605. The position will be different if the clause does not deny liability generally, but expressly indicates that the particular representations are based on information supplied by a third party and that the contracting party takes no responsibility for its accuracy: see *Yorke v Ross Lucas Pty Ltd* (1985) 158 CLR 661.

The position of disclaimer clauses, whereby one party acknowledges that he or she has not relied on any representations made by the other party, is less clear. In most cases, it has been held that such a clause has no effect at all: see, for example *Dorotea Pty Ltd v Christos Doufos Nominees Pty Ltd* [1986] 2 Qd R 91 and *Collins Marrickville Pty Ltd v Henjo Investments Pty Ltd* (1987) 72 ALR 601. However the more recent case of *Netaf Pty Ltd v Bikane Pty Ltd* (1990),92 ALR 490 indicates that the issue is not as clear cut as the earlier cases would indicate. In *Netaf v Bikane* it was held that although such a clause does not of itself prevent a claim being brought under the Act, the clause can still be of evidential significance in determining whether any alleged representation was made, or if made was relied on. If that approach is adopted in this country, an acknowledgement in the contract that no representation was made, or if one was made it was not relied on, may place a evidential obstacle before any person seeking relief under the Fair Trading Act. Any plaintiff who has made such an acknowledgement would have to satisfy the Court that the earlier acknowledgement should be disregarded in the light of the particular facts of the case. Such a flexible approach would appear to be desirable in New Zealand as it will allow the use of such clauses as a protective device in appropriate cases without jeopardising the policy aims of the statute. Such a rule would also maintain a degree of harmony with the provisions of the Contractual Remedies Act 1979 in relation to disclaimer clauses: see 7.1.7.

10.5.6 Statutory defences

In s 44 the Act provides, for a restricted number of defences to criminal charges under the Act. It will be a defence if the defendant proves any one of the three defences under s 44 (1):

   (a) That the contravention was due to a reasonable mistake;
   (b) That it arose from reasonable reliance on information from a third party;
   (c) That the cause of the contravention was the act or default of a third party or accident or other cause beyond the defendant's control and that the defendant had taken reasonable precautions and exercised due diligence to avoid the contravention.

The defences have not received significant judicial analysis. The wording is clear and relatively little exegesis is necessary. The Courts have stressed that the requirement of reasonable grounds in the defence of reliance on information from others is important. In *Cardin Laurant Ltd v Commerce Commission* [1990] 3 NZLR 563, it was held that a defendant who had received information from an unknown person within the relevant government Ministry had not reasonably relied on it as the information indicated, to the defendant's knowledge, the reversal of a long-standing Ministry policy. In those circumstances reliance was only reasonable where the defendant had taken steps to verify the accuracy of the advice and the identity of its provider. A recent Australian decision, *TPC v J & R Enterprises Pty Ltd* (1991) ALR 325, is also informative as to aspects of the possible defences. In that case it was held that a defendant may lose a defence of reasonable mistake or reasonable reliance where the circumstances alter so that the reasonable grounds for the belief or the reliance no longer exist.

10.6 CONSUMER INFORMATION AND PROTECTION PROVISIONS

10.6.1 Unfair trade practices

The Fair Trading Act has, in ss 17-25, a number of specific provisions dealing with specific unfair trade practices.

(1) *Improper advertising or promotion:* The first group of practices prohibited are those directed at the improper promotion or advertising of goods or services. It is unlawful to use "bait" advertising: s 19. This is defined as the advertising of goods or services at specific prices, where either there is no intention to provide them at that price, or the advertiser cannot supply the goods or services for a reasonable period and in reasonable quantity. "Reasonable" here is to be judged in the light of the nature of the advertisement and the market in which the advertiser operates. The statute provides a defence for advertisers who remedy the unavailability of goods or services they have advertised by arranging for supply by a third party at the same price. The Act also prohibits the offer of gifts or prizes where the offeror has no intention of supplying the gift or prize as offered: s 17.

(2) *Improper practices:* The Act makes it unlawful to use physical force or harassment or coercion in connection with the supply or possible supply of goods or services, or in connection with payment therefor: see s 23. Such behaviour might well also be unlawful under other statutes. The same can be said of s 21, which makes it unlawful for any person to demand or accept payment for goods or services where that person does not intend to supply the services, or intends to supply materially different goods or services, or does not have reasonable grounds for believing that the goods or services will be supplied within any specified time, or within a reasonable period, if no time was specified. There are also restrictions on referral selling: s 20, and prohibitions on trading stamp schemes: s 18, and pyramid selling schemes: s 24.

10.6.2 Product safety standards and recall orders

The Act makes provision, in s 32, for the Minister of Consumer Affairs to make a range of orders where he or she is satisfied that this is the appropriate way to deal with goods which do not meet a product safety standard or are otherwise to be classed as unsafe but which have reached the hands of the public. The Minister may order the public disclosure of information relating to the goods, or order that the product be recalled, or order that the supplier repair or replace the goods or refund to the customer the price paid or such lesser sum as is appropriate in the light of any use the customer may have had of the goods. The operation of the section has been extensively discussed in *Isaac v Minister of Consumer Affairs* [1990] 2 NZLR 606. In that case Tipping J held that the section requires that if the Minister is contemplating the issue of any order under s 32, he or she must first give notice to the supplier of the essential elements relied on as justifying the making of the order and afford the supplier a reasonable opportunity to answer the case made. The Judge also indicated that the Minister would normally be required as a matter of substantive fairness to treat different suppliers of the same goods in essentially the same way.

Part IV

SPECIFIC CONTRACTS

Chapter 11

SALE OF GOODS – INTRODUCTION

SUMMARY

11.1 SALE IS A SPECIES OF CONTRACT

Although historically sale developed as a species of contract, particular rules have developed in relation to the sales of different types of property. There are, for instance, important differences between the sale of goods and sale of land. These difficulties are now accentuated by the fact that contracts other than sale of goods are subject to the whole of the provisions of the Contractual Remedies Act 1979. Except for the significant changes introduced by ss 4 and 6, the Contractual Remedies Act does not apply to matters covered by the Sale of Goods Act. One consequence of this is that the old common law division of contractual terms into conditions and warranties still survives in relation to contracts for the sale of goods: Contractual Remedies Act 1979, s 15 and *Finch Motors Ltd v Quin (No 2)* [1980] 2 NZLR 519.

11.2 THE SALE OF GOODS ACT 1908 IS A CODE

Before the end of the nineteenth century the law relating to sale of goods consisted of case law principles developed at common law, the law merchant and in equity supplemented to some extent by statute. In 1893 the UK Parliament passed the Sale of Goods Act 1893 which was used as a model by countries in the Commonwealth. New Zealand adopted the Act in 1895 and the present legislation is the Sale of Goods Act 1908. The original Act was stated to be "an Act for codifying the Law relating to the Sale of Goods". The draftsman of the statute, Sir Mackenzie Chalmers, said that as originally drawn the Bill endeavoured to reproduce as exactly as possible the existing law, leaving any amendments that might seem desirable to be introduced in committee. Amendments were introduced so that the Act is not in fact a pure code. Nevertheless, it is treated as a code for the purpose of interpretation of statutes. The correct method of interpreting such a code was stated by Lord Herschell in *Bank of England* v *Vagliano Bros* [1891] AC 107, 144-5 where he said that the proper course is in the first instance to examine the language of the statute and to ask what is its natural meaning, uninfluenced by any considerations derived from the previous state of the law. However, if provisions in the code are doubtful, technical or unusual it is legitimate to look at the earlier authorities. There needs, however, to be a special ground of this kind. *Bank of England v Vagliano Bros* was in fact a case on the Bills of Exchange Act 1882 but it has been followed in cases relating to the Sale of Goods Act.

11.3 THE VITALITY OF THE COMMON LAW

Section 60(2) of the Sale of Goods Act provides that the rules of the common law, including the law merchant, save insofar as they are inconsistent with the provisions of the Act continue to apply to contracts for the sale of goods. In particular, the subsection refers to the rules relating to the law of agency and the effect of fraud, misrepresentation, duress or coercion, mistake, or other invalidating cause. Although, as we have seen, the matters covered by the Sale of Goods Act are not subject to the whole of the Contractual Remedies Act 1979, s 4 which relates to statements during negotiations and s 6 which relates to fraud and misrepresentation extend to sale of goods and the Contractual Mistakes Act 1977 and the Illegal Contracts Act 1970 both apply in place of the common law. However, because of s 60(2) the rest of the rules of the common law continue to apply save insofar as they are inconsistent with the express provisions of the Act. This has resulted in a tension between the dynamism of the common law and the rigours of the code. In *Ashington Piggeries Ltd v Christopher Hill Ltd* [1972] AC 441, 501, Lord Diplock said:

> unless the Sale of Goods Act . . . is to be allowed to fossilise the law and to restrict the freedom of choice of parties to contracts for the sale of goods to make agreements which take account of advances in technology and changes in the way in which business is carried on today, the provisions set out in the various sections and subsections of the code ought not to be construed so narrowly as to force on parties to contracts for the sale of goods promises and consequences different from what they must reasonably have intended.

One particular area which has been affected is the classification of contractual terms. The Act applies a simple dichotomy of contractual terms into conditions and warranties. At common law there has been increasing recognition in recent years of the innominate term. Such terms cannot be classified from the beginning but have to be assessed by reference to the effect of breach. The Courts have recognised that such terms can co-exist with the Sale of Goods Act classification.

11.4 THE EFFECT OF THE CODE ON EQUITY

Section 60(2) does not expressly refer to equity. The question arises as to
whether the term "common law" used in the subsection is used in a
narrow or broad sense. In a broad sense it would include equity. In
Riddiford v Warren (1901) 20 NZLR 572, the Court of Appeal said obiter
that what is now s 60(2) did not include equity. Williams J said that s 60(2)
amounts to a legislative statement that in contracts for the sale of goods
the fusion of law and equity has not interfered with the rules of the
common law and the law merchant. The case was concerned with
rescission on the ground of innocent misrepresentation which would
have been the subject of equitable redress. The Court held that on the
facts there was no misrepresentation but also said that at the time no
equitable relief had ever been granted in respect of the contract of sale of
goods and that to grant it would be inconsistent with the statutory
scheme. The case has now been effectively overruled on this point by
s 6 of the Contractual Remedies Act 1979 and on the general point some
doubts must now arise in the light of the later Court of Appeal decision
in *Thomas Borthwick and Sons (Australasia) Ltd v South Otago Freezing Co
Ltd* [1978] 1 NZLR 538. That case was concerned with an application for
an injunction. Cooke J delivering the judgment of the Court said that
s 60(2) was intended, at least primarily, to preserve rules of substantive
law on matters not covered by the express provisions of the statutory
code. The Court found nothing in s 60(2) or elsewhere in the Act or in the
ratio decidendi of *Riddiford v Warren* to exclude the discretionary jurisdiction to grant the equitable remedy of injunction. The Court thought that
insofar as *Riddiford v Warren* contained statements suggesting that the
rules of equity had no application at all to contracts for the sale of goods
they were clearly obiter. *Riddiford v Warren* was followed by the Full
Court of the Supreme Court of Victoria in *Watt v Westhoven* [1933] VLR
458 but both cases were not followed by the Full Supreme Court of South
Australia in the recent case of *Graham v Freer* [1985] 35 SASR 424. The
Borthwick case does not appear to have been cited but *Graham v Freer* is
consistent with it.

11.5 REFORM

Apart from piecemeal consumer protection legislation which is dealt
with in ch 15 below, New Zealand has not attempted any major reforms
of the Sale of Goods Act 1908. In 1977 the Contracts and Commercial Law
Reform Committee produced a Working Paper on Warranties in Sales of
Consumer Goods. This anticipated some of the reforms which were later
contained in the Contractual Remedies Act 1979 and dealt with implied
terms, remedies and manufacturers' liability. Although the Working
Paper was referred to the legislative draftsmen it has not been implemented. The matter was the subject of the Vernon Report to the Department of Justice – D H Vernon *An Outline for Post-Sale Consumer Legislation
in New Zealand* – which was criticised for not having paid enough
attention to Australian Law: see D Harland (1988) 3 Cant LR 410. The
Ministries of Commerce and Consumer Affairs are now promoting
revised reform proposals in respect of the supply of goods and services
and the Law Commission, proposals in respect of "Unfair Contracts".

Meanwhile piecemeal reforms have taken place in the UK, Australia and Canada. The Ontario Law Reform Commission, whose earlier proposals influenced the 1977 Working Paper, has since produced a more comprehensive report on the Act as a whole which has been approved by the Uniform Law Conference for Canada with minor amendments. Although the USA had legislation on the Sale of Goods Act model it replaced it by more modern law in art 2 of the Uniform Commercial Code. This has influenced many of the Ontario proposals. Lastly, the law relating to international sale of goods was the subject of a United Nations Convention on a Uniform Law for International Sales in 1980. This too has had some influence on the Canadian proposals. The time is now ripe for a comprehensive review of the Sale of Goods Act 1908 in the light of these developments. Whether New Zealand will stay within the main stream or opt for an application to sale of goods of the Contractual Remedies Act 1979 remains to be seen.

Chapter 12

DEFINITIONS

SUMMARY

12.1 SALE AND AGREEMENT TO SELL
12.2 GOODS
12.3 MONEY CONSIDERATION CALLED "THE PRICE"
12.4 SALE DISTINGUISHED FROM OTHER CONTRACTS

12.1 SALE AND AGREEMENT TO SELL

Section 3(1) of the Sale of Goods Act 1908 provides that "a contract of sale of goods is a contract whereby the seller transfers or agrees to transfer the property in goods to the buyer for a money consideration, called the price". A distinction is drawn in s 3(4) between a sale and an agreement to sell. Where under a contract of sale the property in the goods is to be transferred from the seller to the buyer the contract is a sale. Where the transfer of the property in the goods is to take place at a future time or subject to a condition the contract is an agreement to sell. "Property" is defined in s 2(1) as meaning the general property in goods and not merely a special property. The Act later equivocates between property and title but the reference to general property excludes the situation of persons having a limited proprietorial interest in the goods. An agreement to sell becomes a sale when the time elapses or the conditions are fulfilled subject to which the property in the goods is to be transferred: s 3(5).

The significance of the distinction is as follows:-
(1) Apart from export contracts, a sale is a contract coupled with an immediate transfer of property to the buyer; an agreement to sell is merely a contract. The property is to pass at a future time.
(2) A sale is executed; an agreement to sell is executory;
(3) A sale gives the buyer a right *in rem*, ie a right to claim the thing itself; an agreement to sell confers no right to demand possession, but merely a right *in personam*, ie a right to damages if the seller refuses to deliver the thing to the purchaser.

(4) If the buyer defaults after a sale is made, the seller can maintain an action for the contract price. If default is made under an agreement to sell, the seller cannot sue for the contract price; he or she can sue only for damages to compensate him or her for having to sell the goods to someone else on the available market, if there is one.

(5) Risk passes with the property in the goods. If there has been a sale of goods and they have been destroyed, the buyer suffers the loss whether they are in the physical possession of the seller or the buyer. If the goods are subject to an agreement to sell, property remains with the seller and he or she suffers the loss.

12.2 GOODS

Goods are defined in s 2(1) as including all chattels personal other than money or things in action. Thus, dollar notes and coins are not goods unless they are sold as antiques or rare or beautiful objects. In *Moss v Hancock* [1899] 2 QB 111 a Golden Jubilee £5 piece sold as a curiosity was held to be within the definition of goods. Stocks and shares and cheques are not goods. The statutory definition also provides that the term "goods" includes emblements, growing crops and things attached to or forming part of the land which are agreed to be severed before sale or under the contract of sale. The term "emblements" was defined by Adams J in *Scully v South* [1931] NZLR 1187 as *"fructus industriales*, the growing crops of the soil which are annually produced by the labour of the cultivator". A distinction was drawn in Roman law which has subsequently been adopted in English and New Zealand law between *fructus industriales* and *fructus naturales. Fructus industriales* are crops intended to be harvested within one year which are produced by the labour of man. *Fructus naturales* are items such as grass and trees where the labour employed in the planting is so small in relation to the natural growth that they are regarded as the natural produce of the soil. *Fructus industriales* are clearly goods when harvested whereas the position of *fructus naturales* is less certain. Difficult classification questions arise as to whether a particular contract for the sale of timber, for example, is a sale of goods or a contract for the sale of an interest in the land. To a certain extent this is dealt with by the latter part of the statutory definition of goods. Where the goods are already severed or there is an obligation to sever the contract is usually held to be a sale of goods. Where, however, the grantee has a right to enter on the land without an obligation to sever the contract is likely to be regarded as an agreement relating to an interest in the land: *Egmont Box Co Ltd v Registrar-General of Lands* [1920] NZLR 741. The sale of a house to be moved on a trailer has been held in Australia to be sale of goods: *Symes v Laurie* [1985] 2 Qd R 547. It has been held in Australia that a sale of a computer system, including both hardware and software is a sale of goods: *Toby Constructions Products Pty Ltd v Computa Bar (Sales) Pty Ltd* [1983] 2 NSWLR 48.

12.2.1 Species of goods

Goods are classified in two different ways in the Act. Section 7 distinguishes between existing and future goods. Existing goods are goods which are owned or possessed by the seller at the time of the contract.

Future goods are goods to be manufactured or acquired by the seller after the making of the contract. Where under a contract of sale the seller purports to make a present sale of future goods, the contract operates as an agreement to sell the goods: s 7(3). A further distinction is drawn between specific and unascertained goods. Specific goods are defined in s 2(1) as goods identified and agreed on at the time a contract of sale is made. Unascertained goods are not defined but are goods not so identified and agreed upon. There is in fact an intermediate category which is not referred to in the Act but which can be referred to as "quasi specific" goods. This is the situation where goods are part of a larger body of specific goods. Until the contract goods are separated from the bulk there is no passing of property in the goods: *Re Wait* [1927] 1 Ch 606.

12.3 MONEY CONSIDERATION CALLED "THE PRICE"

The Act stipulates that there must be a money consideration. This simply means that the consideration must be measured in money. It can in fact be satisfied in whole or in part by the delivery of goods of equivalent value: *Aldridge v Johnson* (1857) 7 E & B 885; *Davey v Paine Bros Ltd* [1954] NZLR 1122. Where there is no money consideration expressed the contract is not sale of goods but barter or exchange. We discuss this below in 12.4.1. Section 10 provides for ascertainment of the price. Section 10(1) provides

> The price in a contract of sale may be fixed by the contract, or may be left to be fixed in a manner thereby agreed, or may be determined by the course of dealing between the parties.

Section 10(2) provides "Where the price is not determined in accordance with the foregoing provisions the buyer must pay a reasonable price". What is a reasonable price is a question of fact depending on the circumstances of each particular case: s 10(3). Section 10 seems to be more flexible than the general law of contract but still predicates the need for some machinery. In the absence of such machinery the Courts may say that there is no contract: *May and Butcher Ltd v The King* [1934] 2 KB 17; *Coupe v Rangitikei Produce Distributors Ltd* (unreported, High Court, Wellington, M65/81, 8 August 1983, Ongley J); [1983] BCL 718; [1984] RL 3. Section 11 contains provisions dealing with a price which is to be fixed by the valuation of a third party. Where the third party cannot or does not make such a valuation the agreement is avoided. However, if the goods or part of the goods have been delivered and appropriated by the buyer he or she must pay a reasonable price for them: s 11(1). Where the third party is prevented from making the valuation by the fault of the seller or buyer, the innocent party may maintain an action for damages against the party at fault: s 11(2): see *Van Straalen v Rupert* (unreported, High Court, Hamilton 28 May 1974, M92/83, Tompkins J; Cap L 7/23/5).

12.4 SALE DISTINGUISHED FROM OTHER CONTRACTS

Contracts of sale of goods are governed by the Sale of Goods Act 1908. Other contracts are governed by the common law, equity and the contract legislation. Some but not all of the latter applies to contracts governed by the Sale of Goods Act. It is, therefore, necessary to distinguish between sale and other contracts.

12.4.1 Exchange

We have seen that s 3(1) provides that a contract of sale of goods is a contract whereby goods are to be sold for a money consideration. Where the consideration consists of other goods or some other valuable consideration not money or no monetary consideration is expressed the transaction is one of exchange or barter. Where the goods are to be paid for partly in money and partly in other goods at a fixed value the contract may be treated as one of sale for the total sum: *Aldridge v Johnson* (supra). In such circumstances the Courts have sometimes been prepared to regard the contract as one of sale of goods even where no fixed value has been put on the goods: *Routledge v Mackay* [1954]1 All ER 855. The law relating to exchange or barter is undeveloped and the Courts seem to be inclined to treat such contracts as analogous to contracts of sale, although they do not come within the Sale of Goods Act 1908: *Halsbury's Laws of England*, Vol 41, para 601.

12.4.2 Labour and materials

A distinction is drawn between a contract for sale of goods and a contract for labour and materials. A contract of sale of goods is a contract the substance of which is the transfer of property in and the delivery of possession of goods to the buyer: *Lee v Griffin* (1861) 1 B & S 272; *Samuels v Davis* [1943] 1 KB 526. Where the main object is not the transfer of goods but the skill and labour in the production and the materials are purely ancillary the contract will be regarded as one of labour and materials: *Robinson v Graves* [1935] 1 KB 579. The Courts seem to prefer the substance test although at times they have paid attention to the ownership of the materials, the value of the skill and labour and the result. The better view seems to be that the latter are simply factors which have to be weighed in assessing what is the substance of the contract. The distinctions drawn in the cases are sometimes rather fine. Thus in *Robinson v Graves* (supra) the defendant agreed orally to commission the plaintiff artist to paint a lady for 250 guineas but repudiated the contract before it was completed. In an action for the price it was held by the English Court of Appeal that it was a contract for labour and materials not sale of goods as the substance of the contract was the skill of the artist. The distinction between the two types of contract at that time was important. Contracts for the sale of goods of the value of more than £10 had to be in writing. Contracts for materials and labour did not. Where the contract involves both the supply of materials and the provision of services it will often be difficult to classify it. In *Young and Marten Ltd v McManus Childs Ltd* [1969] 1 AC 454 the House of Lords were faced with such a contract. In that case a builder had subcontracted the job of putting a roof on a house. The subcontractor had to supply tiles corresponding to certain specifications. The House of Lords held that the main object of the contract was the provision of materials and labour or services not sale of goods. They nevertheless stressed the undesirability of drawing unnecessary distinctions between the two types of contract. For a recent case on the distinctions see, however, *Printcorp Services Ltd v Northern City Publications Ltd* [1990] BCL 1604, the subject of a useful case note by C Hawes [1991] NZLJ 3.

12.4.3 Mortgage

Section 60(3) provides that the provisions of the Act do not apply to any transaction in the form of a contract of sale which is intended to operate by way of mortgage, pledge, charge, or other security. Thus it is a question of substance, not form, whether a particular transaction is a mortgage or sale of goods. The essence of a mortgage of goods is the transfer of the property in the goods to secure a debt: *Re Hardwicke, ex parte Hubbard* (1886)17 QBD 690, 698. Simple reservation of property by an unpaid seller is conventionally regarded as a sale whereas more complex clauses tend to be construed as charges: *Clough Mill Ltd v Martin* [1984] 3 All ER 982 (CA). See ch 39 post.

12.4.4 Hire purchase

Whereas a contract of sale involves a transfer of the property in the goods in a hire purchase contract possession is given but the property in the goods remains with the vendor until all the instalments have been paid. A hire purchase agreement may take one of two forms. It may consist of a contract of hire, coupled with an option to purchase. Thus in *Helby v Matthews* [1895] AC 471 the owner of a piano agreed to let a customer hire the piano for 36 months at a rental of 10/- per month. The piano was to remain the property of the owner until all the instalments had been paid. The hirer could terminate the hire by returning the piano. The House of Lords held that this was not a contract of sale.

An alternative form is that of conditional sale. In such an agreement there is no right to terminate and the conditional purchase constitutes an agreement to sell within the Sale of Goods Act 1908: *Lee v Butler* [1893]1 ER Rep 1200. However, the distinction between the two forms of hire purchase is now obscured by the fact that consumer protection legislation equates them for many purposes. See ch 37 post.

12.4.5 Gift

Whereas a contract of sale of goods involves transfer of the property in goods for a money consideration a gift involves a transfer of the goods without consideration. The law will not generally perfect an imperfect gift: *Re Rose* [1949] Ch 78; [1952] Ch 499. In the context of goods this would usually mean a handing over of the goods. A complete gift of goods, where possession remains with the donor, must be effected by an instrument registered under the Chattels Transfer Act 1924. See ch 36 post.

Chapter 13

FORMALITIES AND CONTRACTUAL EFFECT

SUMMARY

13.1   FLEXIBILITY
13.2   THE BATTLE OF THE FORMS
13.3   AUCTION SALES — SPECIAL RULES
13.4   CONTRACTUAL TERMS

13.1 FLEXIBILITY

A contract of sale of goods can be made in a wide variety of ways. The Act is very flexible. Section 5 provides that it may be made in writing (either with or without a seal), by word of mouth, or partly in writing and partly by word of mouth and may even be implied from the conduct of the parties. Where a contract is by word of mouth or is to be inferred from conduct there may be problems of evidence if litigation ensues.

Formerly there was in s 6 a requirement of writing for contracts of the value of £10 or upwards but s 6 was repealed by s 4(1) of the Contracts Enforcement Act 1956 for contracts made after the passing of that Act. There also used to be additional requirements for contracts by corporations but most trading corporations are now governed by s 42 of the Companies Act 1955 which allows similar flexibility.

13. 2 THE BATTLE OF THE FORMS

A practical problem which sometimes arises is the so called "Battle of the Forms" where there is no single contract document but an exchange of printed forms containing different terms. The Courts, in seeking to ascertain offer and acceptance, tend to adopt "the last shot" rule that there is a contract on the basis of the last of the printed forms sent and received without objection. However, this is not an inflexible rule of law but simply a matter of construction of the documents as a whole: *Cleave v King* (1879) NZLR 3 CA 277; *Butler Machine Tool Co Ltd v Ex-Cell-O Corp (England) Ltd* [1979]1 All ER 965. The Courts attempt to give business contracts efficacy by reasonable implication even if the conflicting terms were irreconcilable: see Lord Denning MR in *Butler Machine Tool Co Ltd v Ex-Cell-O Corp* supra at 969a.

13.3 AUCTION SALES—SPECIAL RULES

Section 59 sets out special rules which apply to auction sales. These are:

1 Where goods are put up for sale by auction in lots, each lot is prima facie deemed to be the subject of a separate contract of sale.

2 A sale by auction is complete when the auctioneer announces its completion by the fall of the hammer, or in other customary manner: until such announcement is made any bidder may retract his bid.

3 Where a sale by auction is not notified to be subject to a right to bid on behalf of the seller, the seller shall not bid himself or employ any person to bid at such sale, nor shall the auctioneer knowingly take any bid from the seller or any such person. Any sale contravening this rule may be treated as fraudulent by the buyer.

4 A sale by auction may be notified to be subject to a reserved or upset price, and a right to bid may also be reserved expressly by or on behalf of the seller.

5 Where a right to bid is expressly reserved, but not otherwise, the seller, or any one person on his behalf, may bid at the auction.

In New Zealand most sales by auction in the agricultural sector take place on the New Zealand Stock and Station Agents' Association Conditions of Sale, a copy of which is set out in Appendix E to this book. It is to be noted that under these conditions although risk passes on the fall of the hammer, property does not pass until the price is paid.

13.4 CONTRACTUAL TERMS

13.4.1 Former significance of distinction between terms and misrepresentations

Before the Contractual Remedies Act 1979 the position regarding misstatements inducing a contract was complicated and unsatisfactory. First it had to be ascertained whether the misstatement was a representation or contractual term and this depended on the presumed intention of the parties. If it was a representation damages would not lie unless it was fraudulent or, in certain circumstances, negligent. In other cases even where the representation was relatively minor the only remedy was rescission and this was easily lost. If, on the other hand, the misstatement was regarded as a contractual term a claim for damages could always be made. If the term was regarded as a condition the contract could be discharged. The distinction then between being a term or not a term of the contract was crucial and the cases revealed oversubtle technicalities: see JF Burrows [1980] 1 Canta LR, 82, 84-5.

13.4.2 The new law

The Contractual Remedies Act has accomplished a desirable reform by providing in s 6 that if a party is induced to enter a contract by any misrepresentation, innocent or fraudulent, then he or she will be entitled to damages as if the representation were a contractual term and he or she will not be entitled to damages for deceit or negligence. Section 6 applies to contracts of sale of goods falling within the Sale of Goods Act 1908.

13.4.3 Express and implied terms

In most contracts the parties will expressly provide for the most important matters. The language which they use will not necessarily be conclusive of the legal classification of the terms by the Courts. The matter is ultimately one of construction of the contract as a whole. The Sale of Goods Act 1908 contains a number of implied terms which apply unless they are excluded by the contract: s 56. The principal implied terms are set out in ss 14-17. Section 14 deals with the implied undertaking as to title etc; Section 15 with sale by description; Section 16 with implied conditions as to fitness or quality and s 17 with sale by sample. In addition certain other parts of the Act such as s 20 set out rules for ascertaining the parties' intention. Section 20 deals with the parties' intention as to the time at which the property in the goods is to pass to the buyer.

13.4.4 Conditions, warranties and innominate terms

The wording of the Sale of Goods Act 1908 seems to envisage a dichotomy of contractual terms into conditions and warranties. Warranty is defined by s 2(1) as meaning "an agreement with reference to goods which are the subject of a contract of sale, but collateral to the main purpose of such contract, the breach of which gives rise to a claim or damages, but not to a right to reject the goods and treat the contract as repudiated". There is no statutory definition of condition but it can reasonably be inferred from the definition of warranty and the wording of s 13 of the Act that a condition is a term, the breach of which gives rise to a right to treat the contract as repudiated. A useful discussion of the distinction between condition and warranty appears in the judgment of Jordan CJ in the NSW case of *Tramways Advertising Pty Ltd v Luna Park (NSW) Ltd* (1938) 38 SR (NSW) 632, 641-642 where he said:

> The question whether a term in a contract is a condition or a warranty, ie an essential or a non-essential promise, depends upon the intention of the parties as appearing in or from the contract. The test of essentiality is whether it appears from the general nature of the contract considered as a whole, or from some particular term or terms, that the promise is of such importance to the promisee that he would not have entered into the contract unless he had been assured of a strict or a substantial performance of the promise, as the case may be, and that this ought to have been apparent to the promisor.... If the innocent party would not have entered into the contract unless assured of a strict and literal performance of the promise, he may in general treat himself as discharged upon any breach of the promise, however slight. If he contracted in reliance upon a substantial performance of the promise, any substantial breach will ordinarily justify a discharge. In some cases it is expressly provided that a particular promise is essential to the contract, eg by a stipulation that it is the basis or of the essence of the contract . . . but in the absence of express provision the question is one of construction for the Court, when once the terms of contract have been ascertained.

In recent years there has been the emergence, or some would say the re-emergence, of a third type of contractual term – the innominate term. This can in fact be traced back to the eighteenth century. The essence of the innominate term is that its effect depends upon the breach. The approach is first look and see what the event is that constitutes the breach then to ask oneself what did the parties when they entered into the contract intend their rights should be if that particular breach occurred. The Court presumes that fairminded persons intended that monetary compensation should be recoverable for loss caused by the breach if the contract were broken in such a way as to deprive a party of substantially the whole benefit it would have received from its due performance. The modern case law on the innominate term dates from *Hong Kong Fir Shipping Co Ltd v Kawasaki Kisen Kaisha Ltd* [1962] 2 QB 26; a decision of the English Court of Appeal has been followed in later cases in the English Court of Appeal and House of Lords: *Cehave NV v Bremer Handelsgesellschaft MBH* [1975] 3 All ER 739 and *Reardon Smith Lines Ltd* v *Hansen Tangen* [1976] 2 Lloyd's Rep 621. It has been accepted in New Zealand in *Holmes v Burgess* [1975] 2 NZLR 311. At first sight it is a little difficult to accommodate the innominate term within the framework of the Sale of Goods Act 1908. However, for once the orthodox view is that expressed by Lord Denning MR in *Cehave NV v Bremer Handelsgesellschaft* ibid 746 g-h and 747a where he said that the division into conditions and warranties was not exhaustive:

> It left out of account the vast majority of stipulations which were neither 'conditions' nor 'warranties', strictly so called, but were intermediate stipulations, the effect of which depended on the breach. The cases about these stipulations were legion. They stretched continuously from *Boone v Eyre* (1779) 1 Hy Bl 273n in 1779 to *Mersey Steel v Naylor* [1881-5] All ER Rep 365. I cannot believe that Parliament in 1893 intended to give the go-by to all these cases, or to say that they did not apply to the sale of goods. Those cases expressed the rules of the common law. They were preserved by [s 60(2) of the 1908 Act]....

13.4.5 Treating conditions as warranties

Section 13 of the Sale of Goods Act 1908 deals with the circumstances in which a condition can be treated as a warranty. Section 13(1) provides that whether a contract is subject to any condition to be fulfilled by the seller the buyer may waive the condition or may elect to treat the breach of such condition as a breach of warranty and not as a ground for treating the contract as repudiated. Section 13(2) contains a general provision that whether a stipulation is a condition or a warranty depends in each case on the construction of the contract. A stipulation may be a condition though described as a warranty in the contract. Section 13(3) deals with the case of a contract of sale which is not severable where the buyer has accepted the goods or part thereof. In such a case the breach of any condition can only be treated as a breach of warranty and not as a breach of condition unless there is a term of the contract, express or implied, to that effect. The effect of s 13(3) was described by Lord Loreburn LC in *Wallis, Son and Wells v Pratt and Haynes* [1911] AC 394, 395 when he said:

> That does not mean that it was really a breach of warranty or that what was a condition in reality had come to be degraded or converted into a warranty.

It does not become degraded into a warranty ab initio, but the injured party may treat it as if it had become so, and he comes entitled to the remedies which attach to a breach of warranty.

13.4.6 Stipulations as to time

Section 12(1) of the Sale of Goods Act 1908 provides that unless a different intention appears from the terms of the contract, stipulations as to *time of payment* are not deemed to be of the essence of a contract of sale. Section 12(2) provides that whether any other stipulation as to time is of the essence of the contract or not depends on the terms of the contract. As McCardie J pointed out in *Hartley v Hymans* [1920] 3 KB 475, 483 this is different from both the common law and law merchant which did not make the question depend on the terms of the contract unless of course there was an express term on the point. The approach was rather to look at the nature of the contract and the goods in question. In practice in commercial contracts stipulations as to time of delivery are considered to be of the essence even in the absence of an express term: see *Bowes v Shand* (1877) 2 App Cas 455, 463 and the other cases cited in Benjamin's *Sale of Goods* (3 ed) by AG Guest and others para 588, fn 94. In the shipping law case of *Bunge Corpn v Tradax SA* [1981] 2 All ER 513 the House of Lords held that stipulations as to time in commercial contracts were generally to be treated as conditions and not innominate terms because the reason for such a clause was to enable each party to organise his or her affairs to meet obligations arising in the future under the contract and not merely to determine, with the benefit of hindsight, the appropriate remedy after a breach had occurred. This was particularly the case where there was a string of contracts.

Chapter 14

PASSING OF PROPERTY

SUMMARY

14.1   SIGNIFICANCE OF PASSING OF PROPERTY
14.2   INTENTION PARAMOUNT
14.3   THE STATUTORY PRESUMPTIONS

14.1 SIGNIFICANCE OF PASSING OF PROPERTY

There are a number of reasons why it is important to determine when the property in the goods passes from the seller to the buyer. The first reason is allocation of risk. If the goods are damaged then the risk, prima facie, falls on the person with the property. Section 22(1) provides that unless otherwise agreed the goods remain at the seller's risk until the property is transferred to the buyer. When property is transferred to the buyer the goods are at the buyer's risk, whether or not delivery has been made. These two general rules are affected by delay due to the fault of either party. We discuss the question of risk in more detail in 18.1. The second reason why it is important to determine when property passes is insolvency. If the seller remains in possession but the property has passed the goods are not subject to the seller's bankruptcy. Where, however, it is the buyer who is made bankrupt the goods in such a case form part of his or her assets. The third reason is that under ss 19 and 21 it is possible to insert a provision in the contract providing that property, or a right of disposal, remains in the seller until the price has been paid. A simple reservation of property or right of disposal is regarded as a matter of sale, although its effect is to achieve a measure of security: see *Len Vidgen Ski & Leisure Ltd v Timaru Marine Supplies (1982) Ltd* [1986] 1 NZLR 349; *Multiwall Packaging Ltd v Packaging House Ltd* (unreported, High Court, Auckland, CP 277/90, 5 March 1990). Where the terms of the contract make a buyer in possession the bailee or agent of the seller with regard to subsales it has been held that there may be an equitable right of tracing available to the seller: *Aluminium Industrie Vaassen BV v Romalpa Aluminium Ltd* [1976] 3 All ER 522. However, this equitable right does not prevent a good title being acquired by a *bona fide* purchaser for value without notice under s 27(2): *Dayton Moneyweight Scale Co Ltd v Mather* (1923)18 MCD 86; *Re Interview Ltd* (1975) IR 382; *Four Point Garage Ltd v Carter* [1985] 3 All ER 12. Where the contract contains a more complex reservation of property clause which purports to extend to the manufacture of new goods using the goods supplied it may be construed by the Courts as a charge which will be void for non-registration either under the Chattels Transfer Act 1924 if granted by an individual or under s 102 of the Companies Act 1955 if granted by a company. The topic of reservation of property is discussed in more detail at 39.6 post. The fourth reason why the passing of property is important is that generally the seller can only sue for the price if the property has passed: s 50. Where the property has not passed the seller has a remedy in damages for non-acceptance: s 51. The principal significance of this is that if the market falls the seller, in the case of a contract where property has passed, can still sue for the full contract price. He or she is also not under a duty to mitigate his or her loss. One thing which may seem surprising about the concept of property in the Sale of Goods Act is that it is possible for a third party to acquire title to goods dealing with a person who did not have the property in them. The circumstances in which this can take place are known as the exceptions to the rule *Nemo dat quod non habet* and are dealt with in ch 16 post.

There is an increasing feeling that the use of the abstract concept of property as a determining factor in deciding the rights and liabilities of the parties leads to unnecessary complications and technicalities. The US Uniform Commercial Code has abandoned the concept of property for these purposes and adopted a more pragmatic approach. The comment to art 2-101 states: "The purpose is to avoid making practical issues between practical men turn upon the location of an intangible something the passing of which no man can prove by evidence, and to substitute for such abstractions words and actions of a tangible character". These ideas have influenced the recent Canadian proposals and will no doubt be considered when the Sale of Goods Act 1908 is eventually reformed.

14.2 INTENTION PARAMOUNT

The general rule is set out in s 19(1) which states that where there is a contract for the sale of specific or ascertained goods, the property in them is transferred to the buyer at such time as the parties to the contract intend it to be transferred. For the purpose of ascertaining the intention of the parties regard is to be had to the terms of the contract, the conduct of the parties and the circumstances of the case. However, s 18 provides that in the case of a sale of unascertained goods no property in them is to be transferred to the buyer unless and until the goods are ascertained. Thus if goods are part of a larger bulk no property under the Sale of Goods Act is transferred until there is severance from the bulk and there is no equitable property which continues to exist outside the Act: *Re Wait* [1927] 1 Ch 606.

14.3 THE STATUTORY PRESUMPTIONS

Section 20 sets out a number of so-called "rules," which are presumptions for ascertaining the intention of the parties and which apply unless a different intention appears.

14.3.1 Specific goods – rules 1, 2 and 3

Rule 1 provides that where there is an unconditional contract for the sale of specific goods in a deliverable state the property in the goods passes to the buyer when the contract is made and it is immaterial whether the time of payment or delivery, or both, is postponed. Formerly, the Courts were obliged to adopt a non-technical interpretation of "unconditional" because of the wording of s 13(3). Section 13(3) formerly provided that where a contract of sale was not severable and the buyer had accepted the goods or part thereof or where the contract was for specific goods the property in which had passed to the buyer, the breach of a condition to be fulfilled by the seller could be treated as a breach of warranty. The joint effect of r 1 and the old wording of s 13(3) was that a buyer could be deprived of his or her right to reject the goods when property passed which, in this case, was when the contract was made. The Courts, therefore, ought to argue that "unconditional" meant not subject to a condition and the Courts bent over backwards to find that there was a condition. Now, however, in the light of the amendment to s 13(3) by the Contractual Remedies Act 1979 which has removed the offending words "or where the contract is for specific goods the property in which has passed to the buyer", "unconditional" can now be given its natural meaning as not being subject to a condition precedent or subsequent.

The term "deliverable state" is defined in s 2(4) as being in such a state that the buyer would, under the contract, be bound to take delivery of the goods. In *Underwood v Burgh Castle Brick and Cement Syndicate* [1922] 1 KB 343 the plaintiff sold a condensing engine to the defendant. At the time of the contract it was cemented to the floor. It was held that it was not in a deliverable state so no property had passed. These words were also considered in *Philip Head v Showfronts Ltd* [1970] 1 Lloyds Rep 140, where the plaintiff had sold carpets to the defendant which the plaintiff was required to lay. The carpet was delivered to the defendant's premises but was stolen before it could be laid. An issue before the Court was whether the property had passed prior to the time of the theft. Mocatta J held that one was entitled to apply everyday common sense to this question. A householder purchasing carpet under a contract providing that it should be delivered and laid would be surprised to find that carpeting in bales which he or she could hardly move deposited in their garage was then in a deliverable state and their property. The crucial facts here seem to have been that the carpet was in a heavy bundle which was difficult to move and the seller was under an obligation to lay it.

Rule 2 provides that where there is a contract for the sale of specific goods, and the seller is bound to do something to the goods for the purpose of putting them into a deliverable state the property does not pass until such a thing is done and the buyer has notice of it. In the *Underwood* case the engine was broken while being lowered on to a railway truck. The English Court of Appeal held that the property had not passed under r 2. Where goods are to be altered for a buyer they will not be in a deliverable state until the alterations have been carried out. Property in the goods, therefore, will not pass until this has taken place and the buyer has notice.

Rule 3 provides that where there is a contract for the sale of goods in a deliverable state, but the seller is bound to weigh, measure, test or do some other act or thing with reference to the goods for the purpose of ascertaining the price, the property does not pass until such act or thing is done and the buyer has notice of it. Thus in *Farm Products Co-operative v Belkirk Poultry Farm Ltd* [1965] NZLR 1012 a contract for the sale of poultry provided that the price was to be fixed by valuation. It was held that property in the poultry did not pass until the valuation had taken place. However, it is important to note that r 3 only applies where the acts are to be done by the seller. In *Nanka Bruce v Commonwealth Trust Ltd* [1926] AC 77 A sold cocoa to B at an agreed price per lb. It was agreed that B should weigh the cocoa to ascertain the extent of his debt to A. It was held that since the weighing was not to be carried out by the seller the necessity of weighing the goods did not prevent the property passing to B before the price was ascertained.

14.3.2 Unascertained goods – s 18 and s 20, r 5

As we saw in 14.2 in the case of unascertained goods no property is transferred unless and until the goods are ascertained. This rule is implicit in the logic of property as understood by the Sale of Goods Act. Once the goods have been ascertained then the goods are subject to the general rule contained in s 19(1), property passes when the parties intend it to pass. In the absence of evidence of such an intention r 5(1) applies. Rule 5(1) provides that where there is a contract for unascertained or future goods by description and goods of that description and in a deliverable state are unconditionally appropriated to the contract either by the seller with the assent of the buyer or by the buyer with the assent of the seller, the property in the goods thereupon passes to the buyer. Such assent may be express or implied and may be given before or after the time when the appropriation is made. The central concept is that of unconditional appropriation. This was considered by Pearson J in *Carlos Federspiel v Charles Twigg and Co* [1957] 1 Lloyds Rep 240. In that case an English company agreed to sell 85 bicycles to a Costa Rican company. The bicycles were packed in cases and the cases marked with the buyer's name and address on them. Arrangements were made to ship the bicycles, but before they could be shipped the seller became insolvent. It was held that the property had not passed to the buyer. Pearson J summed up the matter as follows:

1   The element of common intention is always to be borne in mind. A mere setting aside or selection by the seller of the goods he expects to use in performance of the contract is not enough because he can always change his mind. To constitute appropriation the parties must have had or be reasonably supposed to have had an intention irrevocably to attach the contract to those goods so that those goods and no others are the subject of the sale.
2   The appropriation takes place by agreement, although in some cases the buyer's assent is conferred in advance by the contract or otherwise.
3   An appropriation by the seller with the assent of the buyer always involves an actual or constructive delivery of the goods. There is a distinction between delivery and appropriation. Delivery is the transfer of possession, whereas appropriation is the transfer of ownership. Where there is a constructive delivery the seller becomes bailee for the buyer.
4   Where, under the contract, the goods are at all material times still at the seller's risk that is prima facie an indication that the property has not passed to the buyer.

5   Usually, but not necessarily, the appropriating act is the last act to be
     performed by the seller. If there is a further act, an important and decisive
     act to be done by the seller, then there is prima facie evidence that
     probably the property does not pass until the final act is done.

In *Donaghy's Rope and Twine Co v Wright Stephenson and Co* (1906) 25
NZLR 641 the defendants in December 1903 ordered 26 tons of binder
twine from the plaintiffs, delivery to be made in 1905. In April 1905 the
defendants, having requested 13 tons, wrote to the plaintiff asking it to
store the balance on their behalf until the next season. The plaintiff agreed
to do this and in its reply stated "you will, of course, attend to the
insurance at your end". Later in the month the store and twine were
destroyed by fire. The plaintiff sued for the price. Cooper J held that there
had been unconditional appropriation of the twine and the property had
passed to the defendants. The defendants, therefore, bore the risk of loss
and were liable for the price. The decisive point was when the plaintiff
communicated that it would hold the goods in store for the defendants.
A problem with this case is that no one other than the seller could tell
which goods were meant for a particular buyer. It is arguable that there
should be some objective evidence such as an entry in the seller's books
and records, otherwise it is difficult to reconcile this with the first
proposition of Pearson J in *Carlos Fiederspiel v Charles Twigg and Co* supra.
     Rule 5(2) deals with a particular instance of unconditional appropria-
tion. It provides that where, in pursuance of the contract, the seller
delivers the goods to the buyer or to a carrier or other bailee (whether
named by the buyer or not) for the purpose of transmission to the buyer,
and does not reserve the right of disposal, he or she is deemed to have
unconditionally appropriated the goods to the contract.

14.3.3 Sale or return contracts – s 20, r 4

Rule 4 deals with a special situation which really does not fall within the
same subject matter as r 1-3 and r 5. It deals with the specific topic of sale
or return contracts. It provides that where goods are delivered to the
buyer on approval or "on sale or return" or other similar terms the
property passes to the buyer: (a) when he or she signifies their approval
or acceptance to the seller or does any other act adopting the transaction;
and (b) if they do not signify their approval or acceptance but retain the
goods without giving notice of rejection then if the time fixed for return
arrives or if no time has been fixed, on the expiration of a reasonable time.
What is a reasonable time is a question of fact. An illustration of r 4(b) is
Poole v Smiths Car Sales (Balham) Ltd [1962] 2 All ER 482. In that case a car
dealer who supplied two secondhand cars to another on sale or return in
August. A sale of one of the cars was made in September. In October
numerous requests were made for the return of the other car and a letter
dated 7 November said that unless it was not returned by 10 November
it would be considered as sold. It was returned two weeks after this date.
The English Court of Appeal held that having regard to all the circumstances of the case, the fact that the vehicles were handed over when the
dealer who supplied them was on holiday, the quick sale of the first car,
the decline in the secondhand car market and the second dealer's
acknowledgment that there was no prospect of a sale by October and the

repeated requests for the return, the proper inference was that a reasonable time had passed and with it the property. The plaintiff was, therefore, entitled to sue for the sale price.

Chapter 15

IMPLIED TERMS IN FAVOUR OF BUYER

SUMMARY

15.1 TITLE

Section 14 of the Sale of Goods Act sets out three obligations with regard to title which must be fulfilled by the seller unless the circumstances of the contract show a different intention. First, s 14(a) provides that there is an implied *condition* on the part of the seller that in the case of a sale he or she has a right to sell the goods and that in the case of an agreement to sell he or she will have a right to sell the goods at the time when the property is to pass. The term "a right to sell" is not defined and probably does not mean right in the strict sense but power. In other words, the seller must be the owner or have the authority of the owner to sell. In *Niblett Ltd v Confectioners' Material Company Ltd* [1921] 3 KB 387 the seller agreed to sell a quantity of tins of condensed milk at a price to include insurance and freight from New York to London. The buyer paid the price on receipt of the shipping documents. When the tins arrived it was found that they bore labels with the brand name "Nissly". The Nestle Company claimed that the word infringed their trade mark. The goods were detained by the Customs and the buyer was obliged to remove the name or brand in order to get possession of the goods and could only sell them at a loss without any distinctive marks. The English Court of Appeal held that the defendant had broken the implied condition in s 14(a). As Scrutton LJ said, at 398 "If a vendor can be stopped by process of law from selling he has not the right to sell".

Secondly, s 14(b) provides that there shall be an implied *warranty* that the buyer shall have and enjoy quiet possession of the goods and thirdly s 14(c) provides that there shall be an implied *warranty* that the goods are free from any charge or encumbrance in favour of any third party, not declared or known to the buyer before or at the time when the contract is made. It is possible for the implied terms under (a), (b) and (c) to overlap but this will not always be the case. In *Microbeads AG v Vinhurst Road Markings Ltd* [1975]1 All ER 529, the defendant English company bought some special machinery for making road markings from the plaintiff, a Swiss company. A couple of years later another English company claimed that these machines infringed their patent. Under patent law a person only acquired rights and privileges after publication of the complete specification. In this case the publication was almost a year after the date of the sale. It was held that there was no breach of s 14(a) because at the time of the sale the Swiss company had the right to sell but there was a breach of s 14(b) as the buyer was not able to enjoy quiet possession.

Where there is a breach of s 14(a) the buyer may (1) sue for damages by electing under s 13(1) to treat the breach of condition as a breach of warranty (see *Blake v Melrose* [1950] NZLR 781); or (2) rescind the contract and recover the price on the grounds that there has been a total failure of consideration. This is not the normal contractual remedy, but is preserved by s 55 of the Act. It is possible that by exercising his or her right to claim that there has been a total failure of consideration the purchaser may get a benefit which goes beyond reasonable compensation. In *Rowland v Divall* [1923] 2 KB 500 the plaintiff bought a car from the defendant and used it for four months. He then discovered that the car did not belong to the defendant who had bought it in good faith from someone without title. It was held by the English Court of Appeal that the buyer could recover the whole purchase price and that the seller was not entitled to any set-off in respect of the four months use of the car. A similar result occurred in *Butterworth v Kingsway Motors Ltd* [1954] 2 All ER 698 where the seller misunderstood her rights under a hire purchase agreement, sold the car and then paid off the hire purchase debt. Before she had paid off the debt the plaintiff, who had had the use of the car for nearly a year, received a notification from the finance company claiming the car. He, therefore, claimed rescission for a total failure of consideration and it was held that he was entitled to do so. As the market value of the car had dropped from £ 1,275 to £ 800 this enabled the plaintiff effectively to receive a windfall of £ 475. It is possible to argue that these decisions basically rest on a fallacy which springs from the word "property". Property in English law does not mean ownership in the sense of absolute dominion but relative title. The seller in *Rowland v Divall* did transfer a title which was good against all the world, except the person with a better title. It would be fairer if the matter was treated as a question of damages for breach of warranty and the plaintiff limited to recovering his actual loss. The Contracts and Commercial Law Reform Committee in its Working Paper of 1977 recommended such a solution. In the case of a sale by a registered motor vehicle dealer these problems are now remedied by the Motor Vehicle Dealers Act which is discussed in 21.4. The cases, however, still apply to a private sale.

A residual question is whether it is possible for the seller to "feed" his or her title and bar a claim by the buyer. Pearson J indicated obiter in *Butterworth* that to hold otherwise would be extraordinary. In the Northern Irish case of *West (HW) Ltd v McBlain* [1950] NI 144 Sheil J rejected the idea since "you can never revivify that which never had life". The matter should be clarified by statute to allow the possibility. See generally Ellinger (1969) 4 VUWLR 168.

15.2 COMPLIANCE WITH DESCRIPTION

Section 15 of the Sale of Goods Act provides that where there is a contract for the sale of goods by description there is an implied *condition* that the goods shall correspond with the description. If the sale is by sample as well as by description it is not sufficient that the bulk of the goods correspond with the sample if they do not also correspond with the description. The two essential ingredients in the first part of s 15 are: (1) that the goods have been sold by description; and (2) that they in fact correspond with the description.

15.2.1 Sale by description

The question of what is a sale by description is surprisingly not easy to answer. In *Taylor v Combined Buyers Ltd* [1924] NZLR 627, Salmond J said that all sales of unascertained goods are necessarily sales by description in as much as, in the absence of any description, there will be nothing to determine the subject matter of the contract and the obligations of the vendor. In the case of specific goods, however, it is possible to sell them without reference to any description. The goods might conceivably be identified merely by their presence. Nevertheless even in the latter case they are usually sold by description in some sense. They are sold as being of some specified and disclosed nature. An animal is sold as a horse, or a cow, a precious stone is sold as a diamond or a ruby. In the Judicial Committee of the Privy Council in *Grant v Australian Knitting Mills* [1936] AC 85, Lord Wright elaborated on this latter idea. He said that there could be a sale by description even though the buyer was buying something displayed before him or her on the counter

> ... a thing is sold by description, even if it is specific, so long as it is sold not merely as the specific thing, but as a thing corresponding to the description eg woollen undergarments, a hot water bottle, a second-hand reaping machine, to select a few obvious illustrations.

Thus the unfortunate Dr Grant who purchased a pair of combinations from the counter which were later found to contain sulphites from which he contracted dermatitis was held to have bought the goods by description. Similarly, in *Godley v Perry* [1960] 1 WLR 9 the plaintiff, a six-year-old child, bought a plastic catapult from the defendant shopkeeper. Due to defective manufacture it broke when the plaintiff used it and he suffered an injury. Edmund Davies J held that where a child asked for a catapult and one is sold to him over the counter that is no less a sale by description than one where an order is placed on the strength of a catalogue. A most bizarre case is that of *Beale v Taylor* [1967] 3 All ER 253 where the defendant seller sold a car which he believed to be a 1961 Herald Convertible with a 1200 cc engine. He advertised the car as "Herald Convertible, white, 1961 £190". The plaintiff read the advertisement, contacted the seller and had a test run in the car. As he was not insured he did not drive. He bought the car and found defects in the steering. He took the car to a garage which informed him that instead of being a 1961 Herald 1200 cc car it was in fact an amalgam of two different cars. Only the back portion was of that description. The front portion which contained the engine was an older 948 cc model. The car was in fact unsafe on the road. The English Court of Appeal held that there had been a sale by description. This seems to have been largely because the buyer had relied in part on the newspaper advertisement.

15.2.2 Description relates to the identity of the goods

As the law stands there is a conflict between *Taylor v Combined Buyers Ltd* supra and a House of Lords' decision in England. In *Taylor v Combined Buyers Ltd*, Salmond J took a wide view of what constitutes description in the case of unascertained goods based on the fact that in such case the description is not a statement but a promise. He thought that "every description and every part of the description is material, whether it relates to kind or quality, essential or unessential attributes". On the other hand in the case of specific goods he thought that description meant a statement of the "kind, class or species to which the article belongs". In the House of Lords case of *Ashington Piggeries Ltd v Christopher Hill Ltd* [1972] AC 441 all five members of the House of Lords applied a distinction between identity and quality, not distinguishing between specific and unascertained goods. If the statement referred to the identity of the goods it constituted description. If it related to other matters, then it related to the quality of the goods which was covered by s 16. In *Ashington Piggeries* U had developed a formula for a special mink food called "King Size". He approached Christopher Hill who agreed to make it up. One of the ingredients was herring meal which Christopher Hill obtained from N, a Norwegian firm. The mink food proved noxious to thousands of mink due to a preservative in the herring meal called DMNA. Ashington Piggeries refused to pay for the food and Christopher Hill brought an action for the price. Ashington Piggeries counterclaimed for breach of implied conditions under the Sale of Goods Act. It was conceded by the parties that the sale was by description, so the only relevant issue in this context was whether it corresponded with the contract description. Applying the identity-quality distinction four of the five Law Lords held that the presence of the DMNA did not prevent the herring meal from being herring meal. It was simply a matter of quality. There was no loss of identity. There was, therefore, no breach of s 15. It should be noted, however, that in *Reardon Smith Lines Ltd v Hansen Tangen* [1976] 2 Lloyds Rep 621, 626 Lord Wilberforce seemed to acknowledge that there is a distinction between specific and unascertained goods. See also *Burlington Canning Co v Campbell* (1908) 7 WLR 544, 549 (Manitoba). However, at the moment it cannot be regarded as settled that there is a distinction between the two as Salmond J suggested. It is unfortunate that *Taylor v Combined Buyers Ltd* does not appear to have been cited in the House of Lords in *Ashington Piggeries* or subsequent cases. It has been argued that to limit description to identity is to take a test devised to shelter buyers from the effect of exception clauses and use it to diminish the rights given to buyers by the Sale of Goods Act: see B Coote [1976] 50 ALJ 17, 24.

15.2.3 Description and reliance

It has been held by the majority of the English Court of Appeal in *Harlingdon & Leinster Enterprises Ltd v Christopher Hull Fine Art Ltd* [1990] 1 All ER 739 noted by Brown (1990) 106 LQR 561 that the description must have a sufficient influence on the sale to become an essential term of the contract and the correlative of influence is reliance. Nourse LJ said that ". . . reliance by the buyer is the natural index of a sale by description . . . for all practical purposes". Slade LJ was less dogmatic as to whether reliance was essential but thought it relevant to the question whether it was a term of the contract. Stuart-Smith LJ dissented, having difficulty understanding the relevance of reliance. Stuart-Smith LJ's reasoning is preferred by Cynthia Hawes "Sales of Goods" in *Essays in Commercial Law* (Borrowdale and Rowe (eds)) 169 at 173. In that case an art dealer sold another art dealer a painting described by the seller as a Münter for £6,000. The seller acknowledged he was not an expert. The painting was a forgery, only worth £50-100. The Court of Appeal held that there was no breach of the English equivalent of s 15.

15.2.4 Degree of correspondence with description

The old approach of the Courts was to treat this matter strictly. The rationale of the strict approach was that contracts of sale of goods were often commercial contracts for goods which would be the subject of one or more sub-sales, and a degree of precision was, therefore, desirable. This approach can be illustrated by the House of Lords' decision in *Arcos Ltd v Ronaasen and Son* [1933] AC 470. In that case the seller agreed to supply a quantity of timber in staves one-half inch thick. On arrival in London it was discovered that 85% were larger than this but only by 1/16th of an inch. It was, nevertheless, held by the House of Lords that the buyer was entitled to reject. Lord Atkin said that if a written contract specifies conditions of weight, measurement and the like they must be complied with. A ton does not mean about a ton or a yard about a yard. There might be microscopic deviation which businessmen and their lawyers would ignore but apart from this the conditions of a contract must be performed. However, in a number of more recent cases the strict approach has been criticised and distinguished by the Courts. Thus in the *Reardon Smith* case Lord Wilberforce, supra, said at 626 that he was not prepared to accept that the authorities on description should be extended. Some of them were excessively technical and due for fresh examination in the House of Lords.

Sometimes the Courts have been prepared to recognise that a description is not to be taken literally. If goods are known in the trade as being of a certain type they may correspond to their description even when on a literal interpretation of the description they fail to comply. Thus in *Grenfell v Meyrowitz Ltd* [1936] 2 All ER 133, the plaintiff purchased a pair of flying goggles described as being made with "safety glass". During a flying accident the glass splintered and injured his eye. The English

Court of Appeal held that there was no breach of s 15 because it had been established that in the trade safety glass meant glass manufactured in a particular way and the glass in question had been manufactured in that way.

15.3 FITNESS FOR PURPOSE

The basic rule as regards quality of goods at common law was *caveat emptor*. This rule is still preserved by the Sale of Goods Act 1908. The opening words of s 16 provide that "subject to the provisions of" the Act "and of any statute in that behalf, there is no implied warranty or condition as to the quality or fitness for any particular purpose of goods supplied under a contract of sale...". This general rule is, however, subject to s 16(a) and (b). Section 16(a) deals with the fitness of goods for their purpose and s 16(b) deals with a requirement of merchantable quality. Although logically merchantable quality is a more general requirement as to quality, the statutory wording limits merchantable quality to sales by description. This is the reason, therefore, why the subsections are in this particular order. The draftsman of the Act thought that these two subsections probably went further than the cases and narrowed down the rule of caveat emptor. The history of interpretation of s 16 has been somewhat surprising: Benjamin's *Sale of Goods* (2 ed) para 791. Early doubts as to whether a sale was by description and the precise meaning of merchantable quality caused many litigants to argue that their case fell under fitness for purpose. The result was that fitness for purpose was widely interpreted to cover almost all sales: Benjamin op cit. This was at the expense of the development of merchantable quality.

Section 16(a) provides:

Where the buyer, expressly or by implication, makes known to the seller the particular purpose for which the goods are required, so as to show that the buyer relies on the seller's skill or judgment, and the goods are of a description which it is in the course of the seller's business to supply (whether he is the manufacturer or not), there is an implied condition that the goods shall be reasonably fit for such purpose:

Provided that in the case of a contract for the sale of a specified article under its patent or other trade name, there is no implied condition as to its fitness for any particular purpose.

15.3.1 Sale in the course of a business

The goods must be of a description which it is in the course of the seller's business to supply whether he is the manufacturer or not. This excludes private sales. The meaning of this phrase was considered by Lord Wilberforce in *Ashington Piggeries Ltd v Christopher Hill Ltd* [1972] AC 441, 476 where he said ". . . what the Act had in mind was something quite simple and rational; to limit the implied conditions of fitness or quality to persons in the way of business, as distinct from private persons . . .". He later went on to say that he had "no difficulty in holding that a seller deals in goods of that description if he accepts orders to supply them in the way of business". With regard to the description element in s 16(a) Lord Wilberforce made it clear that this meant goods of that kind.

In New Zealand it seems that there must be a degree of regularity of similar sales for a sale to be "in the course of business": *Colmar & Brunton Research Ltd v Tomes Statistical Research Ltd* (Unreported, High Court, Auckland, A 721/82, 22 May 1990).

15.3.2 Making the purpose known

Section 16(a) requires that the buyer expressly or by implication makes known to the seller the particular purpose for which the goods are required. Where purpose is communicated expressly there will usually be no problem. Where, however, it is left as a matter for implication there may be. Goods may have two types of purpose – a general or normal purpose and a special purpose. Thus I may purchase a new Mazda car for routine driving or I may purchase it for use in rally driving. In *Taylor v Combined Buyers* [1924] NZLR 627, 629, Salmond J said, however, that the expression "particular purpose" in s 16(a) was not limited to special purpose but was capable of including the general purpose itself. Thus there is no magic in the word "particular". A communicated purpose, if stated with reasonable precision, will be a particular purpose within s 16(a). In the *Ashington Piggeries* case supra Lord Wilberforce stated, at 877, "the word 'particular' means little more than 'stated' or 'defined'." In the case of most consumer sales the purpose is very easily implied. In *Frost v Aylesbury Dairy Co* [1905] 1 KB 608 the plaintiff purchased milk which was infected by typhoid and his wife died as a result of consuming some of the milk. It was held that it was unfit for the purpose which was human consumption. Similarly, in *Priest v Last* [1903] 2 KB 148, a man purchased a hot water bottle for his wife which burst and scalded her. It was held that this was not fit for the purpose. In this case the purpose was simply the general purpose and this could quite easily be implied from the facts. Where, however, the buyer wants the goods for a special purpose there must either be express communication of that purpose or some other evidence from which it can be implied. In *Griffiths v Peter Conway Ltd* [1939] 1 All ER 685 a woman who had an abnormally sensitive skin purchased a Harris Tweed coat which gave her dermatitis. It was found that it would not have affected an ordinary person. In this case, in view of her sensitivity, she failed to communicate that what she needed was a coat for a person with abnormally sensitive skin. Since she had done nothing to communicate this to the seller this was not a breach of s 16(a).

A problem arises where goods may have more than one purpose. Is it sufficient that it should simply be fit for one particular purpose? The matter was considered by the House of Lords in *Henry Kendall and Sons v William Lillico and Sons Ltd* [1969] 2 AC 31 and *Ashington Piggeries Ltd v Christopher Hill Ltd* [1972] AC 441. In *Kendall v Lillico* groundnuts were sold "for compounding into food for cattle and poultry". It was held by the House of Lords that this was sufficient to communicate to the seller that food would be used as an ingredient in the diet of pheasants. In a way this was rather strange since pheasants are not poultry. The House of Lords held that poultry food had several normal uses and feeding pheasants was an ordinary and normal use of the goods. In *Ashington Piggeries Ltd v Christopher Hill Ltd* supra, the House of Lords held that the requirement was satisfied provided that the seller was aware that the buyer might use goods for a particular purpose. Thus, in that case, the Norwegian supplier of the herring meal knew generally that it was fed to mink and so, therefore, it was in breach of s 16(a) in supplying poisoned herring meal. In the case of goods which have a wide variety of uses this view of the law imposes on the seller a potentially wide responsibility. Hence one particular writer has referred to a "general particular purpose": Franzi [1977] 51 ALJ 298. In *Aswan Engineering Establishment Co v Lupdine Ltd* [1987] 1 All ER 135 the English Court of Appeal held that goods were of merchantable quality if they were suitable for one or more purposes which they might, without abatement of price, reasonably be expected to be used but they were not required to be suitable for every purpose within such a range of purposes for which such goods were normally bought.

15.3.3 Reliance on the seller's skill and judgment

Not only must the buyer communicate his or her particular purpose but this must be "so as to show that the buyer relies on the seller's skill and judgment". In the case of consumer sales the Courts have been very ready to hold that there has been reliance. Thus in *Grant v Australian Knitting Mills Ltd* [1936] AC 85, the case of the unfortunate Dr Grant and his impregnated combinations, Lord Wright said at 99

> the reliance will seldom be express, it will usually arise by implication or the circumstance; thus to take a case like that in question, of a purchase from a retailer the reliance, in general, will be inferred from the fact that the buyer goes to the shop in the confidence that the tradesman has selected his stock with skill and judgment.

In *Kaata v Swiss Built Ltd and Anor* [1990] DCR 265 it was held that a customer who buys a car from an apparently reputable licensed motor vehicle dealer would normally rely on the seller's skill and judgment unless the buyer and seller are equally knowledgeable about the subject matter.

Where, however, the matter is not a consumer sale, it becomes more complicated. In many commercial sales the seller and buyer will be equally knowledgeable about the quality of goods. In *Kendall v Lillico* supra both the importer and wholesaler were members of the same trade association. It was argued, therefore, that this ousted any question of reliance. However, the House of Lords held that this was not so. There was no presumption of reliance either way. That being the case the Court looked at the evidence available to decide whether in fact there was reliance and found that there had been reliance since the seller thought that the buyer had always dealt "in a nice line of ground nut extraction". In *Ashington Piggeries Ltd v Christopher Hill Ltd* Lord Guest said that the question in each case was whether in all the circumstances the inference can be drawn that a reasonable man in the shoes of the seller would realise that he was being relied upon. If the inference can be drawn then the Court will hold that there has been reliance unless the seller can produce rebutting evidence. If the inference cannot be drawn the Courts will hold that there has been no reliance unless the buyer can produce affirmative evidence of reliance. In *Feast Contractors v Ray Vincent Ltd* [1974]1 NZLR 212 the appellant cartage contractor bought a secondhand engine from the respondent garage owner. The appellant's employee, who was experienced in engines, inspected the engines and told the seller the purpose for which his employer wanted one. The employee selected an engine but did not inspect any part of the interior. After two days of running the engine broke down. Mahon J held that the inference would not necessarily be drawn from mere disclosure of purpose in a case where the contract of sale was being completed between buyer and seller who were equally knowledgeable in relation to the subject matter of the sale. It had not been established that the appellant was relying on the respondent's skill and judgment. Note, however, that the reliance need only be partial; it need not be total and exclusive reliance. However, initial reliance may be superseded by the buyer's acts. In *Zip Holdings Ltd v Ados Chemical Co Ltd* (Unreported, High Court, Wellington, CP 88/83, 23 November 1988) the defendant supplied glue for bonding sheets of cloth in the manufacture of electric blankets which proved ineffective. Ellis J held that initial reliance by the plaintiff on the defendant's advice had been superseded by its own tests. The claim under s 16 therefore failed. Compare *Hunter Engineering Co Inc v Syncrude Canada Ltd* (1989) 57 DLR (4th) 321 (S Ct of Canada) (design fault seller's responsibility).

15.3.4 Fitness for purpose

The meaning of fitness for purpose can sometimes be difficult to answer. In *Ashington Piggeries Ltd v Christopher Hill* it was conceded that toxic herring meal was unfit for the purpose. Similarly, in *Kendall v Lillico*, poisonous nuts were accepted as being unfit for feeding pheasants. However, in the latter case Lord Pearce said "in deciding the question of fact the rarity of the unsuitability would be weighed against the gravity of its consequences". Thus, if food was merely unpalatable on rare occasions it might be reasonably fit for the purpose but it would not be reasonably fit for the purpose if on such rare occasions it killed the consumer.

15.3.5 Nature of liability

Once liability is established under s 16(a) the seller's liability is absolute. In *Taylor v Combined Buyers Limited* [1924] NZLR 627, 629 Salmond J said "the liability of the seller is not limited to defects which might have been avoided by the due use of his skill and judgment, but is an absolute liability for all defects which in fact make the goods unfit for the buyer's purpose, even though such defects were latent and undiscoverable". Thus in *Frost v Aylesbury Dairy*, supra, where the plaintiff's wife died from typhoid contracted from contaminated milk, the defendant dairy was held liable notwithstanding the elaborate precautions which it had taken.

15.3.6 The proviso to s 16(a)

The proviso states that in the case of a contract for the sale of a specified article under its patent or other trade name there is no implied condition as to its fitness for any particular purpose. Thus in *Wilson v Rickett Cockerell and Co Ltd* [1954] 1 QB 598, the plaintiff purchased a consignment of Coalite from the defendant which, unknown to either party contained an explosive. The explosive blew up in the plaintiff's fireplace causing damage. It was held that although the Coalite was unfit for the purpose there was no liability under s 16(a) because it had been purchased under a trade name. The theory behind the proviso is that if the purchaser purchases something under a trade name he or she is assumed to be relying on his or her knowledge and the manufacturer's reputation rather than the seller's skill and judgment. In the case of consumer sales this is manifestly unreasonable. In a number of cases the Courts have insisted that the trade name must be a real trade name acquired by established usage and not merely the name which the seller gives to the goods. In *Bristol Tramways Co v Fiat Motors Ltd* [1910] 2 KB 831 the buyer purchased a Fiat omnibus which, to the knowledge of the seller, was to be used for heavy passenger traffic in a hilly location. The bus was unfit for the purpose but the seller pleaded the proviso. The English Court of Appeal rejected the seller's defence. The use of a trade name did not bring the proviso into operation. Even a sale under an established trade name will not necessarily bring the proviso into operation. In *Baldry v Marshall* [1925] 1 KB 260 a buyer asked for a car suitable for touring and was recommended a Bugatti 8 cylinder. He then ordered the car on a printed order form which referred to "one 8 cylinder Bugatti car". Although the English Court of Appeal accepted that this was a sale under a trade name the circumstances of the sale excluded the operation of the proviso. It was only where the goods had been specified under their trade name in such a way as to indicate that the buyer is satisfied that it will answer his purpose that the proviso applies. In *Taylor v Combined Buyers Ltd*, supra at 631, Salmond J went so far as to say that the proviso only applies where the defect is common to all goods sold under that trade name. If this test had been applied the decision on s 16(a) in *Wilson v Rickett Cockerell and Co* would have been different. Needless to say *Taylor v Combined Buyers Ltd* was not cited in that case.

15.3.7 Time and durability

It is not clear from the wording of the section at which time the goods must be reasonably fit for their purpose. Obviously they should be fit for the purpose at the time of sale and arguably when the property passes if this is later. If goods are unfit for the purpose soon after the purchase then this may be evidence that they were not fit for the purpose at the time of sale: see *Priest v Last* (supra) where the hot water bottle burst after five days' use and there was held to be liability under s 16(a). In some jurisdictions there is an express provision that the goods should be fit for the purpose for a reasonable time after delivery and the 1977 Working Paper contains such a provision in its proposed warranty of acceptability: Working Paper on Warranties in Sales of Consumer Goods, July 1977, 14. The latest proposals of the Ministry of Consumer Affairs favour such a reform.

15.4 MERCHANTABLE QUALITY

Section 16(b) provides:

> Where goods are bought by description from a seller who deals in goods of
> that description (whether he is the manufacturer or not), there is an implied
> condition that the goods shall be of merchantable quality:
>   Provided that if the buyer has examined the goods, there shall be no
> implied condition as regards defects which such examination ought to have
> revealed.

This requires: (1) that the goods must be bought by description; (2) that
the seller must deal in goods of that description whether he is the
manufacturer or not. We have discussed both these requirements above
in 15.3; and (3) the goods must be of merchantable quality.

15.4.1 Merchantable quality

The meaning of merchantable quality has proved difficult in the cases. It
is arguable that it is a concept which is applicable to commodity sales
amongst merchants and not consumer sales. However, the Act requires
that it be applied to all types of sale. The case law has alternated between
three different approaches to merchantable quality. These are: (a) saleability; (b) acceptability; and (c) usability. Merchantable was defined by
Lord Ellenborough in *Gardiner v Gray* (1815) 4 Camp 144, 145 as "saleable
in the market under the denomination mentioned in the contract". In
Taylor v Combined Buyers Ltd [1924] NZLR 627, the plaintiff sued the
defendant, inter alia, for a breach of s 16(b), arguing that the new
Calthorpe car which he had purchased from the defendant had numerous defects. Salmond J at 646 said that

> The question whether goods are of merchantable quality or not can in no case
> be determined in *abstracto* by reference merely to the goods themselves. The
> question must always be asked and answered with reference to the particular
> description under which the goods are sold. . . . This means, as I understand
> the matter, are the goods of such a quality and in such a state and condition as
> to be saleable in the market, as being goods of that description, to buyers who
> are fully aware of their quality, state, and condition, and who are buying them
> for the ordinary purpose for which goods so described are bought in the
> market?

Salmond J applied this test and held that the description under which the
car was bought was that of a "new Calthorpe car". As the car had a
number of defects it was unsaleable to a purchaser who wished to acquire
a "new Calthorpe car" and was aware of the condition of the particular
car. The acceptability approach was adopted by Farwell LJ in *Bristol
Tramways v Fiat Motors* [1910] 2 KB 831, 841 where he said that merchantable
quality meant "that the article is of such quality and such condition that
a reasonable man, acting reasonably, would after a full examination
accept it under the circumstances of the case in performance of his offer
to buy that article whether he buys it for his own use or to sell again". This
is not an entirely satisfactory test as Lord Reid pointed out in *Henry
Kendall and Sons v William Lillico and Sons Ltd* [1969] 2 AC 31. Lord Reid

thought that what was meant was that a reasonable man in the shoes of the actual buyer would accept the goods as fulfilling the contract which was in fact made. The usability approach was adopted by Lord Wright in *Cammell Laird and Co Ltd v Manganese Bronze and Brass Co Ltd* [1934] AC 402 and Lord Reid in *Kendall v Lillico* supra. Lord Reid in the latter case slightly modified Lord Wright's definition to read as follows:

> [Merchantable quality means] that the goods in the form in which they were tendered were of no use for any purpose for which goods which complied with the description under which these goods were sold would normally be used and hence were not saleable under that description. This is an objective test, "were of no use for any purpose" must mean "would not have been used by a reasonable man for any purpose . . .".

In *Kendall v Lillico* K, a wholesale dealer and member of the London Cattle Food Association, imported some "Brazilian groundnut extractions". He sold some of these to L who in turn subsold them to S. S made the groundnuts into a meal which was sold to H who fed them to the birds. Unknown to all concerned the groundnut extraction contained a poison which killed a large number of the birds. While the groundnuts were poisonous to poultry they could be fed to cattle. The majority of the House of Lords held that they were of merchantable quality under s 16(b) in spite of being contaminated by poison. Lord Reid held, applying the above definition of merchantable quality that as cattle food producers were prepared to buy them at the full price notwithstanding the contamination the goods were merchantable under their general description of "groundnut extractions". The question of merchantable quality could not be divorced from the contract description. If a buyer wants goods for one of several purposes for which the goods delivered do not happen to be suitable though they are suitable for other purposes for which goods for that description are normally bought then he cannot complain. He should indicate the particular purpose for which he required the goods. The test ultimately is objective.

Lord Reid's test was applied in the later House of Lords case of *BS Brown and Son Ltd v Craiks Ltd* [1970] 1 All ER 823. In that case B was a textile merchant who ordered cloth from the seller cloth manufacturers. The purchaser wanted the cloth for dresses but did not tell the seller. The seller manufactured material which conformed with the contract description but was unsuitable for dressmaking because of irregularities in the weaving. It was, however, suitable for industrial use. The buyer paid 36p per yard for the material and there was evidence that there was a market at 30p per yard. It was held that the cloth was of merchantable quality as it could be used for industrial purposes. Lord Reid's test was also affirmed in the later House of Lords case of *Ashington Piggeries v Christopher Hill Ltd* [1972] AC 441 where it was conceded that the goods were not of merchantable quality.

The three House of Lords cases were considered by Mahon J in *Feast Contractors Ltd v Ray Vincent Ltd* [1974]1 NZLR 212. This was the case of the cartage contractor who purchased a secondhand engine from a garage proprietor. We have already considered it under fitness for purpose. Mahon J, after considering the House of Lords cases, said that, while recognising the modern reappraisal which had been necessary from the creation of so many new types of commercial contracts involving features not in existence at the time of the enactment of the original legislation, in the ordinary uncomplicated contract for the sale of goods there was little difference between Salmond J's definition in *Taylor v Combined Buyers Ltd* and that of Lord Reid in *Kendall v Lillico*. It is worth noting in this respect a statement made by Lord Reid in *Brown and Son v Craiks Ltd* supra where he said

> ... Judicial observations can never be regarded as complete definitions; they must be read in the light of the factors and the issues raised in the particular case. I do not think it possible to frame except in the vaguest terms, a definition of merchantable quality which can apply to several kinds of cases.

15.4.2 Relevance of price

Merchantability cannot be entirely divorced from the contract price. In *Grant v Australian Knitting Mills* [1936] AC 85 the Privy Council held that goods must be commercially saleable under the contract description without abatement of the price. In *Brown v Craiks Ltd* supra it was thought that this was too widely stated and that goods are unmerchantable when they are only saleable at a substantially lower price. Lord Guest said that the price should not be "a throw-away price". In *Finch Motors Ltd v Quin (No 2)* [1980] 2 NZLR 519, 525 Hardie Boys J said: "In many cases, the difference between the price paid pursuant to the contract and the price payable for the goods as they in fact were may be a factor in determining their saleability under the contract description".

15.4.3 A congeries of minor defects

A congeries of minor defects can result in goods not being of merchantable quality. In *Spencer v Rye* (1972, The Guardian, December 19, noted by M Whincup (1975) 38 MLR 66C) the radiator on a new car boiled over every 100 miles. Croom Johnson J held that the car was not fit for the purpose but he also said that various other "very irritating" defects which included a broken throttle cable, a door needing to be re-hung, roof leaks, excessive use of oil, defective boot catch and paint runs would not in themselves have justified rejection since they only caused inconvenience and all were eventually cured. More recent cases, however, indicate a change of attitude by the Courts. A congeries of defects might, in certain circumstances, amount to a breach of s 16(b), where the goods sold are new goods which are advertised as high quality items and the defects cannot be easily cured. Thus in *Rogers v Parish (Scarborough) Ltd* [1987] QB 933 (CA), a new Range Rover had defects in the engine, gear box, body work and oil seals but was roadworthy. After repeated attempts by the seller to repair it the buyer rejected it. The English Court of Appeal held that it was not of merchantable quality. In *Bernstein v Pamson Motors (Golders Green) Ltd* [1987] 2 All ER 220, Rougier J held that in determining whether any particular defect or feature rendered a new car unmerchantable, the Court had to consider (a) whether the car was capable of being driven in safety, (b) the ease or otherwise with which the defect could be remedied, (c) whether the defect was of such a kind that it was capable of being satisfactorily repaired so as to produce a result as good as new, taking into account not only the part or parts at the site of the defect but also any other potential damage, (d) whether there was a succession of minor defects to be taken into consideration, and (e) in appropriate cases, any cosmetic factors. The case involved a new Nissan Laurel car which broke down not long after it had been bought. The plaintiff had driven it for 140 miles and had it for three weeks. It was held that he could no longer reject it and his total damages were limited to £232.90 in respect of getting home after the breakdown, loss of a full tank of petrol, a sum to compensate him for a spoilt day and five days' loss of use of the car. For a recent New Zealand decision in the District Court see *Kaata v Swiss Built Ltd and Anor* [1990] DCR 265 when a secondhand car could not be driven without consuming a large quantity of oil and was held to be unmerchantable. It was also unfit for the purpose. In spite of keeping the car for five weeks there was held not to have been acceptance. See too *Shine v General Guarantee Corp Ltd* [1988] 1 All ER 911 (CA – sale of "enthusiast's car"). For sales by motor vehicle dealers see 21.4 post.

15.4.4 Significance of cost of alterations

Goods may nevertheless be held to be not of merchantable quality in spite of the fact that the cost of altering or repairing them is small. Thus, in *Winsley Ross v Woodfield Importing Co* [1929] NZLR 480, a broken shield and set-square on a thicknessing machine could be put right at a maximum cost of £1, but Smith J held that the de minimis rule did not apply and that there was a breach of s 16(b). To hold otherwise would, he thought, in fact oblige the buyer to pay £91 for a new machine which he had agreed to buy for £90. Similarly, in *Jackson v Rotax Motor and Cycle Co* [1910] 2 KB 937 a consignment of motor horns were sold of which a considerable portion were found to be dented and badly polished. Although these defects could be put right at low cost the English Court of Appeal was unanimous in holding that there had been a breach of s 16(b). There seems to be some contradiction between the approach of the Courts in cases such as *Spencer v Rye* (supra) and these two cases.

15.4.5 Secondhand goods

A purchaser of secondhand goods can obviously not expect the same quality as a purchaser of new goods. In *Bartlett v Sidney Marcus* [1965] 2 All ER 753 there was a sale of a secondhand Jaguar car. The purchaser knew that there was something wrong when he bought it but the defect turned out to be much worse than he expected. The English Court of Appeal held that the car was of merchantable quality. A buyer must realise when he or she buys a secondhand car that defects may appear sooner or later. Nevertheless recent cases suggest perhaps greater sympathy for the poor buyer of a "rogue car". In *Shine v General Guarantee Corp* [1988] 1 All ER 911, 915 f Bush J said: "A car is not just a means of transport: it is a form of investment (though a deteriorating one) . . .". See too *Kaata v Swiss Built Ltd* (supra 15.4.3). In New Zealand in the case of a sale by a licensed motor vehicle dealer there will be a statutory warranty. This is discussed in 21.4.

15.4.6 Time and durability

As with fitness of purpose, the Act is not very clear on the time when the goods must be of merchantable quality. Similar principles apply. The goods must obviously be of merchantable quality at the time of sale and possibly also when the property is to pass if this is later. If goods are shown to be not of merchantable quality within a short period after delivery this may be evidence that they were not of merchantable quality at the time of the sale. Also there is nothing in the Sale of Goods Act about spares which can be very important to the question of durability. In some other jurisdictions the legislation has been amended to provide expressly for spares and the Working Paper on Warranties in Sales of Consumer Goods recognises that in the case of new goods, spare parts and repair facilities should be available for a reasonable time after the sale from commercial trade sources, at or within short distance from the seller's place of business unless the buyer knew, or ought to have known, before the sale of the risk of the unavailability of parts or repair facilities: Working Paper on Warranties in Sales of Consumer Goods, July 1977, 14. This is favoured by the latest proposals of the Ministry of Consumer Affairs.

15.4.7 Proviso

The proviso to s 16(b) states that "if the buyer has examined the goods there shall be no implied condition as regards defects which such examination ought to have revealed". The proviso only applies where the buyer has examined the goods. He or she is under no duty to examine the goods. Also the proviso does not apply to latent defects which could not have been discovered by reasonable examination. Nevertheless, there are occasional problems which arise with the operation of the proviso. In *Thornett and Fehr v Beers and Son* [1919] 1 KB 486 the defendant purchased some barrels of glue from the plaintiff. The plaintiff offered the defendant the opportunity to inspect but since he was in a hurry the defendant merely looked at the outside of the barrels. The glue was defective. It was held that the defect would have been noticeable if the defendant had opened the barrels and so s 16(b) did not apply. The case seems to be wrong in principle in that the proviso refers to "such examination" and this would seem to refer to an examination which actually took place: PS Atiyah's *Sale of Goods* (8 ed), 150.

15.5 TRADE USAGE AND EXPRESS TERMS

Section 16(c) provides that an implied warranty or condition as to quality or fitness for a particular purpose may be annexed by trade usage. A question of trade usage is one of fact in a particular case. Section 16(d) provides that an express warranty or condition does not negative a warranty or condition implied by the Sale of Goods Act unless inconsistent with it. The relationship between an express term and s 16(a) and (b) is ultimately a matter of construction of the contract.

15.6 CORRESPONDENCE WITH SAMPLE

A contract of sale is a contract for sale by sample where there is a term in the contract, express or implied, to that effect: s 17(1). Where there is an express provision there will usually be no problem. Where, however there is no express provision the matter is more problematic. In *Drummond v Van Ingen* (1887) 12 App Cas 284, 297 Lord Macnaghten said that the contract will be a sale by sample if the object of the sample is to "present to the eye the real meaning and intention of the parties with regard to the subject matter of the contract which owing to imperfections of language, it may be impossible to express in words". The fact that a sample is produced during negotiations is not, therefore, sufficient to make the contract a sale by sample. Most sales by sample in practice are commercial sales of commodities rather than sales of consumer goods. Assuming that there is a sale by sample s 17(2) provides that there is an implied condition:

(a) that the bulk shall correspond with the sample in quality;
(b) that the buyer shall have a reasonable opportunity of comparing the bulk with the sample; and
(c) that the goods shall be free from any defect, rendering them unmerchantable, which would not be apparent on reasonable examination of the sample.

The requirement in (a) that the bulk shall correspond with the sample in quality is essentially a factual question. In *E and S Ruben Ltd v Faire Bros and Co* [1949] 1 KB 254 rubber was sold by sample. When the rubber was delivered it was found to be crinkly and folded, unlike the sample. Although this was a defect which could easily be put right by warming and pressing out the crinkles and folds it was held to be a breach of s 17(2)(a). Section 17(2)(b) is self explanatory. As regards s 17(2)(c) a buyer is not expected to carry out every test that might be practicable. As Edmund Davies J said in *Godley v Perry* [1960] 1 WLR 9, "not extreme ingenuity, but reasonableness, is the statutory yardstick".

15.7 CONTRACTING OUT

The basic rule is set out in s 56 of the Sale of Goods Act 1908. It is in essence freedom of contract. Section 56 provides:

> Where any right, duty, or liability would arise under a contract of sale by implication of law, it may be negatived or varied by express agreement or by the course of dealing between the parties, or by usage, if the usage is such as to bind both parties to the contract.

Thus the statutory implied terms can be varied by either an express term or an implied term arising from the course of dealing or usage. Unlike the United Kingdom and Australia, New Zealand has not excluded this rule in the case of consumer sales except under the specific legislation discussed in ch 21, although there were general proposals to do so in the 1977 Working Paper which we discuss in 15.9. At the moment the only statutory protection (apart from this specialist consumer legislation, and the provisions relating to minors and small claims: see ch 3 ante and 51 post) that a buyer has against an exclusion clause is under s 4 of the Contractual Remedies Act 1979. Section 4(1) of the Contractual Remedies Act 1979 provides that if a statement as to quality or fitness is made by the seller during negotiations for a contract, any provision in the contract purporting to preclude a Court from determining the question (a) whether the statement was made or given, (b) whether if it was made or given, it constituted a representation or term of the contract or (c) whether, if it was a representation, it was relied on, does not preclude the Court from determining any such question unless the Court considers it fair and reasonable that the provision should be conclusive between the parties, having regard to all the circumstances. See ch 7 ante.

In addition the Courts have applied certain principles which are as follows:

1   The Courts may hold that in the circumstances the exclusion clause was not part of the contract: *Thornton v Shoe Lane Parking* [1971] 2 QB 163.

2   Such clauses are strictly construed: *Hawkes Bay and East Coast Aero Club Inc v McLeod* [1972] NZLR 289 (CA). Thus a clause excluding liability for breach of warranty will not cover breach of condition even though for remedial purposes it is treated as a breach of warranty under s 13: *Wallis, Son and Wells v Pratt and Haynes* [1911] AC 394. Exclusion of implied terms will not exclude an express term: *Andrews Bros Ltd v Singer and Co Ltd* [1934] 1 KB 17.

3   Where there is an ambiguity it will be construed *contra proferentem* ie against the person who inserted the clause. Thus in *Webster v Higgin* [1948] 2 All ER 127 an exclusion clause was held not wide enough to cover a collateral warranty by the owner's agent. The Courts seem willing to search for ambiguities in such clauses in worthy cases. However since the Unfair Contracts Terms 1977 the English Courts have said that although that view still applied the relevant words are, if possible, to be given their natural, plain meaning. A limitation clause is not to be construed as strictly as an exclusion clause since an agreed limitation of liability is more likely to accord with the true intention of the parties: *Ailsa Craig Fishing Co Ltd v Malvern Fishing Co Ltd* [1983] 1 All ER 101 (HL). The 1977 Act allows exclusion clauses which are reasonable. There is no such provision in force in New Zealand, but see generally *Kaniere Gold Dredging Ltd v The Dunedin Engineering and Steel Co Ltd* (1985) 1 NZBLC 99-024.

4   The Court may hold that the clause is repugnant to the main purpose of the contract. In *Sze Hai Tong Bank Ltd v Rambler Cycle Co* [1959] AC 576 the seller agreed to sell a consignment of cycles to a buyer in Singapore. Under the bill of lading for the carriage by sea of the cycles to Singapore a clause provided that the responsibility of the carrier ceased after the goods were discharged from the ship. After arrival in Singapore the goods were wrongly delivered to the buyer without production of the bill of lading before it had paid. The buyer defaulted and the carrier was held liable. The Judicial Committee of the Privy Council thought that the extreme width of the exclusion clause would run counter to the

main object and intent of the contract. The clause had, therefore, to be limited to enable effect to be given to that object and intent.

5   The Courts have held that unless negligence is the only liability to which the words could apply, general words of exclusion do not extend to negligence: *Alderslade v Hendon Laundry Ltd* [1945] KB 189; *Producer Meats (North Island) Ltd v Thomas Borthwick and Sons (Australia) Ltd* [1964] NZLR 700 (CA); *Hawkes Bay etc Aero Club Inc v McLeod* (supra) (CA). See the useful discussion in D Yates, *Exclusion Clauses in Contracts* (2 ed) 141 et seq.

6   The Courts may hold that there has been a misrepresentation as to the effect of the clause: *Curtis v Chemical Cleaning Co* [1951] 1 KB 805; *Holmes v Burgess* [1975] 2 NZLR 311.

7   The Courts may hold that a collateral warranty overrides the operation of the clause: *Couchman v Hill* [1947] KB 554.

8   In the past the Courts have made use of the doctrine of fundamental breach of contract but today the effect of such a breach on the contract is one of construction although the more radical the breach the clearer must be the language used if it is to be covered. However there is no single formula. One must look at the nature of the contract, the character of the breach and its effect on future performance and make an estimate of the final result: *Photo Production Ltd v Securicor Transport Ltd* [1980] AC 827 (HL); *SGS (NZ) Ltd v Quirke Export Ltd* [1988] 1 NZLR 52 (CA).

The position is, therefore, fragmented and unsatisfactory. There is a need for further legislative reform which will probably now have to await a review of the Sale of Goods Act as a whole. For general discussion of exclusion clauses see B Coote, *Exception Clauses* (1964) and D Yates, *Exclusion Clauses in Contracts* (2 ed), Chin Nyuk-Yin, *Excluding Liability in Contracts* (1985) and 4.2 ante.

15.8 PRODUCTS LIABILITY

The Sale of Goods Act 1908 is simply concerned with the relationship between seller and buyer. It does not deal with the relationship between manufacturer and the ultimate consumer. There is no privity of contract between the manufacturer and the consumer where the sale is from an independent retailer. This does not, however, mean that the buyer is without a remedy. He or she has in fact the following possible courses of action:

1   He or she can sue the retailer who can in turn sue the distributor who can sue the manufacturer, assuming in each case that the statutory implied terms have not been excluded.

2   He or she may possibly have rights under the contract between the retailer and the distributor by virtue of s 4 of the Contracts (Privity) Act 1982 if there is a promise which confers a benefit and a reference to him or her as a person or a class benefitted but a reference to consumers generally may not be a sufficiently precise designation. See, however, B Coote [1984]10 *Recent Law* 107, 115-6: see 6.3.5 ante.

3   He or she may be able to sue the manufacturer on a collateral warranty on the basis that the manufacturer's "guarantee" was the

consideration for him or her entering into the contract with the retailer: *Shanklin Pier Ltd v Detel Products Ltd* [1951] 2 KB 854; *Murray v Sperry Rand Corporation* (1979) 96 DLR (3d) 113.

The manufacturer's guarantee might be negotiated as part of the overall contract of sale with the retailer acting as the manufacturer's agent for that particular purpose.

4   The buyer can sue the manufacturer for the tort of negligence under the principle in *Donoghue v Stevenson* [1932] AC 562 laid down by Lord Atkin at 599. This covers physical damage. In the past, the cost of putting right a defect in the goods could only by recovered in contract but in certain circumstances it may now be claimed in tort: *Junior Books Ltd v Veitchi Co Ltd* [1983] AC 520. See also *Lambert v Lewis* [1981] 1 All ER 1185, 1192, per Lord Diplock.

5   He or she may be able to sue the manufacturer for breach of statutory duty where there is legislation governing the sale of the particular class of goods.

A recent case which illustrates 1 and 4 is *Milne Construction Ltd v Expandite* [1984] 2 NZLR 163 where glue was used by Milne for constructing a garage floor, for the Auckland Electricity Board, which glue was held to be unfit for the purpose of bonding concrete, partly on the ground of the inadequacy of the manufacturer's instructions. It was, however, of merchantable quality. The Board as second plaintiff sued the manufacturer for negligence and recovered damages. Moller J held that the instructions, recommendations and warnings as to the use of the glue were negligently inadequate.

Products liability is governed in Australia by federal legislation under Part V the Trade Practices Act 1974-78 and is the subject of proposals in the 1977 Working Paper which we discuss in 15.9.

15.9 REFORM PROPOSALS

In July 1977 the Contracts and Commercial Law Reform Committee of the Department of Justice produced a Working Paper on Warranties in Sales of Consumer Goods. After some consultation the matter was referred to the law draftsman but so far no legislation has been introduced. Although there does not seem to be a clear programme to revive the 1977 Working Paper as such it is nevertheless useful to examine some of its main proposals as they provide some indication of what may eventually appear in the proposed reform bill. First, the Committee gave a fairly wide ambit to the concept of consumer. By "consumer sale" was meant a sale of goods to an "end user" (other than a sale by auction or by competitive tender) by a seller in the course of a business where goods: (a) are of a type ordinarily bought for private use or consumption; or (b) are sold to a person who does not buy or hold himself out as buying them in the course of a business. The term "end user" meant a person who bought goods other than for the purpose of resale. The main recommendations of the Working Party were:

1   A statement of the minimum liabilities of the seller of goods in a consumer sale;
2   Provisions governing recourse by the seller against the manufacturer and importer of goods, the subject of a consumer sale.

15.9.1 Proposed minimum liabilities of seller

As in the case of the Contractual Remedies Act 1979 the Working Party proposed an abolition of the condition-warranty distinction. All representations relating to goods would be treated as contractual if their natural tendency was to induce the buyer to purchase and the buyer was so induced. Representations for this purpose would cover labelling and advertisements. A new single concept of warranty was proposed with a new set of remedies which are discussed below. Section 14 of the Sale of Goods Act 1908 would be amended to make allowance for the use of goods sold without title before the defect in title was discovered and to provide that the ordinary consequences of acceptance would not apply to a defect in title. Section 15 would be abolished in the light of the proposals regarding representations. Instead of s 16(a) and (b) there would be a new warranty of acceptability which would have two aspects – ordinary acceptability and special acceptability. Ordinary acceptability roughly corresponds with fitness for purpose and special acceptability to a special purpose but in certain circumstances special acceptability could cover a normal purpose made known by the buyer. The warranty of acceptability would require goods to be durable for a reasonable time after delivery and in the case of new goods (other than disposable goods) the availability of spares and repair facilities for a reasonable time unless the buyer knew or ought to have known before the sale of the risk of these not being available. The Working Paper divided breaches into two categories – those which are and those which are not of fundamental character. In the case of a less important breach the seller would have a reasonable opportunity to repair the breach if it is repairable. If he or she failed to do so the buyer would have the right to have the repairs done elsewhere at the seller's expense. He or she would also have a right to damages to the extent that they could be proved. Basically the use of exemption clauses to exclude, restrict or diminish express or implied warranty rights or remedies would be prohibited in a consumer sale. This would even extend to sales of second hand goods and goods sold with disclosed defects, although the standard required under the warranty of acceptability would be lower. Any exclusion clause would be void and the use of such clauses would constitute a criminal offence. An express right would be conferred on the seller of recourse against his or her supplier and so on back to the manufacturer or importer. In relation to these commercial sales contracting out would be permitted, provided that it was fair and reasonable.

15.9.2 The manufacturer's liability

The Working Paper recommended that the lack of consideration or privity would be no bar to an action by the buyer against the manufacturer who should be liable in all respects as if he or she had made a consumer sale to the buyer on the statutory terms. This would resemble the law in force in Australia. Having said this the Committee then expressed doubts as to whether these provisions were desirable or necessary for reasons that are not entirely convincing. First they thought that the proposed rights of the seller to have recourse to distributors and manufacturers might well achieve most of what was intended. It is questionable whether this is so since it seems to go little further than the existing law as a matter of practice. Secondly, the Torts and General Law Reform Committee had already advised there was no need to reform the law as to manufacturer's liability in tort. In view of the rather moribund character of that Committee this is hardly a convincing reason. Thirdly, it was said that there were exceptional difficulties in implying a contract between parties who had never had any relations. This is a mystifying comment since the implication of such a contract is not logically necessary in the case of a statutory reform of this kind and there is ample proximity between the parties for the purpose of the law of tort. Where a consumer completes a manufacturer's '"guarantee" there is either a contractual nexus or something approximating thereto. While the Working Paper did not propose to force manufacturers to give "guarantees" it did propose to regulate the use and content of such guarantees when they were offered. Many of the requirements relate to form but some relate to substance. Thus it was proposed a manufacturer should undertake at least to repair or replace any defective part free of charge to the consumer whether for the part or for repair or make him a fair allowance for the defective goods on the purchase of new goods. The guarantee should cover all the major components and state clearly the duration of the "guarantee". The duration should be extended by any period during which the goods are out of use pending repair. The "guarantee" should not exclude or limit the express or implied warranties or remedies. The new Act should empower the making of regulations to complete the legislative scheme and adjust it to the circumstances and needs of particular industries.

The Committee was not convinced that a separate agency should be established for the enforcement of consumer rights in New Zealand. In 1984 the Labour Government set up a Ministry of Consumer Affairs. This has continued under the National Government but is in effect a branch of the Ministry of Commerce. It has not been very effective in promoting reform, other than the Fair Trading Act 1986 which is the subject of Chapter 10 above. With regard to reform of the Sale of Goods Act 1908 in general it is submitted that there are two basic alternatives. The first is to revise the Act in the light of the Contractual Remedies Act 1979. The second is to recognise that the Sale of Goods Act inter alia relates to export trade and that it would be undesirable for the New Zealand Sale of Goods Act to be too far out of line with other Commonwealth countries, particularly Australia. In the light of CER it would be sensible for a Joint Committee to be set up between the states of Australia and New Zealand to harmonise and reform the Sale of Goods Act and consumer protection legislation. Such a reform initially would not only be desirable in the interests of trade but it would also act as a model for smaller countries in South East Asia and the South Pacific.

Chapter 16

SALES WITHOUT TITLE

SUMMARY

16.1 NEMO DAT QUOD NON HABET

We have seen in ch 14 the rules which relate to the passing of property. Where property has not passed to a buyer, subject to certain exceptions, he or she cannot confer a good title on a sub-buyer. This is part of a more general rule which is often expressed in Latin – *nemo dat quod non habet*, no one can give a better title than he or she possesses. This general rule is the subject of s 23(1) of the Sale of Goods Act 1908 which provides that subject to the provisions of the Act "Where goods are sold by a person who is not the owner thereof . . . the buyer confers no better title to the goods than the seller had . . .". However, the rule is subject to certain exceptions which are necessary in the interests of justice. In *Bishopsgate Motor Finance Corp v Transport Brakes Ltd* [1949] 1 KB 332, 336-7 Denning LJ said

> In the development of our law, two principles have striven for mastery. The first is the protection of property. No one can give a better title than he himself possesses. The second is the protection of commercial transactions. The person who takes in good faith and for value without notice should get a good title. The first principle has held sway for a long time, but it has been modified by common law itself and by statute so as to meet the needs of our times.

In essence the law is faced with a conflict between two proprietary interests – the interest of the true owner and the interest of a bona fide buyer without notice. The exceptions to the general rule are contained in the wording of ss 23(1) and (2), 25, 26, 27, and 28. The wording of s 23(1) protects a person who buys from someone selling goods with the authority or consent of the owner and also deals with the situation where the owner is, by his or her conduct, estopped from denying the seller's authority to sell. Section 23(2)(a) provides that nothing in the Act shall affect the provisions of the Mercantile Law Act 1908 which deals with the authority of a mercantile agent to dispose of goods and s 23(2)(b) deals with the validity of a sale under a special common law or statutory power of sale or under the order of a Court of competent jurisdiction. Section 23(2)(c) excludes sales of motor vehicles protected by the Motor Vehicle Securities Act 1989. Section 24 provides that the law relating to market overt does not apply in New Zealand. Only certain sales fell under this heading. Section 25 deals with a sale under voidable title. Section 26 deals with the revesting of property in stolen goods on the conviction of an offender and s 27 deals with a sale by a seller or buyer in possession after a sale. Section 28 deals with the effect of writs of execution. We will now deal with the more important exceptions in detail.

16.2 ESTOPPEL

The basis of this exception is the wording in s 23(1) "Unless the owner of the goods is by his conduct precluded from denying the seller's authority to sell". There are two species of estoppel for this purpose – estoppel by representation and estoppel by negligence. Estoppel by representation can be divided into estoppel by conduct and estoppel by express words.

16.2.1 Estoppel by conduct

In order to constitute an estoppel by conduct it must be proved: (1) that there was a representation of fact; (2) that it was not ambiguous; and (3) that the injured party relied on it. In *Mercantile Bank of India Ltd v Central Bank of India Ltd* [1938] AC 287 a merchant pledged some railway receipts with the Central Bank of India in return for a cash advance. Railway receipts were documents which enabled the holder to obtain delivery of goods which had been despatched to him on the railway. In accordance with its usual practice the bank returned the receipts to the merchant to enable him to get clearance of the goods. The merchant fraudulently pledged them to the Mercantile Bank of India. The merchant was subsequently declared insolvent and an action was brought by the Central Bank for conversion. The Mercantile Bank argued that the Central Bank was estopped by its conduct from denying that the merchant had the right to pledge the goods. The Judicial Committee of the Privy Council said that this was not so. A railway receipt, though a document of title, was simply an authority to take delivery of the goods and possession of such a document did not amount to any representation that the holder had implied authority or right to dispose of the goods. The possession of the railway receipts no more inferred a representation than the actual possession of the goods. In *New Zealand Securities and Finance Ltd v Wrightcars Ltd* [1976] 1 NZLR 77, W agreed to buy a car from Wrightcars from $3,100 and it was agreed that no property should pass until the price had been paid in full. W gave Wrightcars a cheque but asked them not to present it until he had made arrangements with a finance company to finance the purchase. The finance company intended to send its cheque direct to Wrightcars but W asked the cheque to be sent direct to him, saying he had already given Wrightcars a cheque. The finance company checked with Wrightcars to confirm this and thereupon sent a cheque to W. W's cheque to Wrightcars was dishonoured and he fell into arrears with payment under his agreement with the finance company. Wrightcars repossessed the car and sold it for $2,800. The finance company sought to recover this amount from Wrightcars. O'Regan J held that Wrightcars was precluded by its conduct from denying W's authority to sell the car to the finance company, having told the company that W had paid for the car. In *Eastern Distributors Ltd v Goldring* [1957] 2 All ER 525 estoppel was again successfully pleaded. In this case M wished to raise a loan on the security of his car and he got together with a dealer to deceive a finance company. Hire purchase forms were drawn up as if the car belonged to the dealer and M to acquire it on hire purchase. M did not pay his instalments and later sold the van to Goldring, an innocent buyer. The Court upheld the finance company's claim that M was estopped from denying the finance company's title. He had misrepresented to the finance company that the van belonged to the dealer.

In *Henderson v Williams* [1895]1 QB 52, A was induced by the fraud of B to sell goods in a warehouse of which the defendant was warehouseman. Because of the fraud the contract between A and B was void for mistake. On the instructions of A the defendant transferred the goods in his books to the order of B. B then sold to the plaintiff who was rather suspicious of B and made inquiries of the defendant. The defendant supplied a written statement that he held the goods to the order of B and later on endorsed this to the effect that he held the goods to the order of the plaintiff. There was a dispute between the parties as to the ownership of the goods. It was held that A and the defendant were estopped from denying the plaintiff's title. In the case of the defendant this was because he had represented in writing that the goods were held to the plaintiff's order.

16.2.2 Estoppel by negligence

In order to constitute estoppel by negligence there must be shown to have been a breach of a duty of care. Normally there is no duty of care on an owner of property to see that it does not get lost or stolen. In *Mercantile Credit Ltd v Hamblin* [1964] 3 All ER 592 the defendant wished to borrow money on the security of her car and approached a dealer whom she knew personally. He gave her some hire purchase forms to sign in blank. Thinking that these were mortgage documents she signed them but retained possession of the car. The dealer in fact completed the forms so as to represent an offer by himself to sell the car to the plaintiff finance company and an offer by the defendant to have the car on hire purchase from the finance company. The English Court of Appeal held that the defendant was not bound by the hire purchase agreement. Although in the circumstances she owed a duty of care there had been no breach as it was not unreasonable for her to trust the dealer. In *Moorgate Mercantile Co Ltd v Twitchings* [1976] 2 All ER 641 the question of estoppel by negligence was considered by the House of Lords in a case which involved special arrangements made by English finance companies to record and supply information concerning hire purchase agreements. Since there is no such scheme in New Zealand we will not concern ourselves with the details but with the discussion of principle by Lord Wilberforce. He said at 645-646 that the law has taken the robust line that a person who owns property is not under a general duty to safeguard it.

> He is not estopped from asserting his title by mere inaction or silence because inaction or silence, by contrast with positive conduct or statement, is colourless; it cannot influence a person to act to his detriment unless it acquires positive content such that that person is entitled to rely on it.

Although he recognised that the authorities applied the test of a duty of care in negligence he thought that there was some danger of bringing with that test some of the accretions which it had gained – proximity, propinquity, foreseeability which might be useful in other contexts but not here. He said that what we are looking at here is an answer to the question whether, having regard to the situation in which the relevant transaction occurred, as known to both parties, a reasonable man, in the position of the "acquirer" of the property would expect the "owner" acting honestly and responsibly if he claimed any title in the property, to take steps to make that claim known to, and discoverable by, the "acquirer" and whether, in the face of an omission to do so, the "acquirer" could reasonably assume that no such title was claimed. So instead of the relatively simple concept of the duty of care we now have a more complicated concept of an honest and responsible owner and a "reasonable" acquirer. It is submitted, with respect, that this does not greatly improve matters. In such a case in any event a black and white solution in terms of property rights is never satisfactory. It is better for the law to opt for a system of apportionment such as has been suggested by the Ontario Law Reform Commission in its Report on Sale of Goods in 1979, vol 2, 318.

16.3 SALE BY MERCANTILE AGENT

Section 23(2)(a) provides that nothing in the Act shall affect "the provision, of the Mercantile Law Act 1908, or any other enactments enabling the apparent owner of goods to dispose of them as if he were the true owner thereof . . .". Section 3(1) of the Mercantile Law Act 1908 provides that "Where a mercantile agent is, with the consent of the owner, in possession of goods . . ., any sale, pledge or other disposition of the goods made by him, when acting in the ordinary course of business of a mercantile agent shall . . . be as valid as if he were expressly authorised by the owner of the goods to make the same; provided that the person taking under the disposition acts in good faith, and has not at the time of the disposition notice that the person making the disposition has no authority to make the same". In order for s 3(1) to apply, therefore, the following must be satisfied.

First, the disposition must be by a mercantile agent. Section 2 of the Mercantile Law Act defines this as "an agent, having in the ordinary course of business as such agent, authority either to sell goods, or to consign goods for the purpose of sale, or to buy goods, or to raise money on the security of goods". In *Davey v Paine (Motors) Ltd* [1954] NZLR 1122, 1128 North J said that although at one time the tendency was to give the term a restricted meaning a more liberal attitude now prevailed and he held that a person "in a fairly substantial way of business as a secondhand car dealer . . . accustomed to sell cars on behalf of principals" was a mercantile agent. In *Nicholson v Bank of New Zealand* (1894) 12 NZLR 427, it was held that a carrier did not become a mercantile agent on being entrusted with the sale of goods on a single occasion. On the other hand, in the New South Wales case of *Mortgage Loan and Finance Co of Australia v Richards* (1932) 32 SR (NSW) 50, 58, it was held that an isolated transaction might be sufficient since the business of mercantile agents, like any other, must have a beginning.

Secondly, the mercantile agent must be in possession of the goods with the consent of the owner. Under s 3(4) of the Mercantile Law Act there is a presumption that the owner's consent has been given. The older cases held that where consent was obtained by a trick this negatived consent. However, this is no longer valid. In *Paris v Goodwin* [1954] NZLR 823, it was held by Turner J that even though a person had obtained possession of a car registration book in circumstances amounting to larceny by a trick this did not prevent it being obtained by consent.

Thirdly, the disposition must be in the ordinary course of business of a mercantile agent. This was described by Buckley LJ in *Oppenheimer v Attenborough* [1908] 1 KB 221, 230 as "within business hours, at a proper place of business, and in other respects in the ordinary way in which a mercantile agent would act, so there is nothing to lead a third party to suppose that anything wrong is being done, or to give him notice that the disposition is one which the mercantile agent had no authority to make". See *Frost v Johnson* (Unreported, High Court, Auckland, CP 632/86, 6 August 1986) (transactions with hire purchase agreements so common as to be in the ordinary course of business of a mercantile agent).

Fourthly, the third party must take in good faith and without notice of the lack of authority.

Let us now examine how these principles have been applied in some of the cases. In *Paris v Goodwin*, supra, the plaintiff bought a Vauxhall Velox from Porter Motors, but was dissatisfied with it and saw a man called Flanagan with a view to selling it. Flanagan was in business under the name Eden Car Sales and advertised his business extensively in the newspapers and on the radio, indicating that he sold cars on commission. Flanagan suggested that the car should be put in for repairs and the plaintiff handed over the car. Later Flanagan said a buyer wanted to see the registration papers. The plaintiff handed over the certificate of registration to Flanagan. The car was sold to intermediate parties and eventually came into possession of the defendant who was an innocent buyer. The question was whether the defendant had good title. Turner J held that Flanagan was a mercantile agent since in the customary course of his business he had been shown to have authority to sell the cars of his principals. Even though the circumstances in which he gained posses-sion of the car and the certificate constituted larceny by a trick this did not negative consent for the purpose of s 3. The defendant, therefore, succeeded.

In *Davey v Paine Bros (Motors) Ltd* supra the plaintiff advertised his Austin A40 car for sale. S replied to this advertisement saying that he was not a buyer himself but that he would sell the car on the plaintiff's behalf.

An agreement was signed to this effect. The plaintiff handed over the car to S and later handed over the registration papers. The car was sold to the defendant. North J held that S was a mercantile agent because there was a body of evidence showing that he was in a fairly substantial way of business as a secondhand car dealer. He was in possession of the car with the consent of the plaintiff and the method of sale of the defendant which involved a trade-in of used cars was in the ordinary course of business. The defendant had acquired the car in good faith and without notice. There was no evidence before the Court to justify the conclusion that the defendant dealt with S differently from its other customers.

In *Stadium Finance Ltd v Robbins* [1962] 2 All ER 633, the English Court of Appeal held that where the owner retained the ignition keys the sale of the car without the keys was still a sale of goods but if the registration book and the ignition key were missing it was not a sale in the ordinary course of business. In *Astley Industrial Trust Ltd v Miller* [1968] 2 All ER 36 a car was consigned to L because D had requested a car of that kind. D ran a self-drive hire car business and merely handled secondhand cars as a sideline. D was held not to be in possession in a capacity as mercantile agent but simply as the operator of a car hire business.

16.4 SALE UNDER A VOIDABLE TITLE

Section 25 of the Sale of Goods Act 1908 provides that where the seller of goods has a voidable title thereto, but his title has not been avoided at the time of the sale, the buyer acquires a good title to the goods, provided he buys them in good faith and without notice of the seller's defect of title. The classic problem falling within this section is whether a contract is void or voidable for mistake. Some cases of mistake of identity turn on subtle distinctions. It seems that the contract between the owner and the original buyer will be void if: (1) the buyer's identity was a vital factor for the owner in deciding to enter into the contract; and (2) the owner was intending to deal with someone other than the actual buyer. In *Lewis v Averay* [1972] 1 QB 198 L advertised his car for sale and a rogue answered the advertisement claiming to be Richard Green, a well known film actor. The rogue showed L a pass for Pinewood Studios as proof of identity and L accepted his cheque. The cheque was dishonoured. The rogue then posed as L and sold to A, an innocent buyer. The English Court of Appeal held that there was a contract between L and the rogue and A had acquired a good title. Lord Denning MR said that where a person was dealing with someone who was present before him a presumption in law was that there was a contract even though there was a fraudulent impersonation by the rogue of another. The contract could be avoided for fraud but it was still a good contract until then.

On the other hand in *Ingram v Little* [1961] 1 QB 31 a rogue falsely claiming to be H went to the home of the plaintiffs and negotiated to buy their car. They were unwilling to accept payment by cheque until the rogue told them that he was H who had substantial business interests and lived in a large house nearby. One of the plaintiffs consulted a telephone directory and confirmed the name and address. They then sold the car to the rogue who sold it to the defendant who acquired it in good faith. The majority of the English Court of Appeal held that the offer was made solely to H and, therefore, the rogue was incapable of accepting it. The distinction between the two types of case is very technical and it is unsatisfactory for the law to be based on such fine distinctions. It is arguable that cases such as *Ingram v Little* now fall under the Contractual Mistakes Act 1977 because of s 2(3), which provides for a deemed contract. Section 8 of that Act gives priority to the rights of a bona fide third party without notice and arguably achieves the same result as *Lewis v Averay* when read with s 2(3). This changes the common law but suffers from the same basic rigidity. This is paradoxical since the Act was introduced to give greater flexibility. However, see DW McLauchlan (1983) 10 NZULR 199 for an alternative view and a valuable discussion of the issues. See also (1991) 14 NZULR 229. What is needed is some provision for apportionment of the loss such as Devlin LJ recommended in *Ingram v Little* supra at 73-74 when he said:

> The true spirit of the common law is to override theoretical distinctions when they stand in the way of doing practical justice. For the doing of justice, the relevant question in this sort of case is not whether the contract was void or voidable, but which of two innocent parties shall suffer for the fraud of a third. The plain answer is that the loss should be divided between them in such proportion as is just in all the circumstances. If it be pure misfortune, the loss should be borne equally; if the fault or imprudence of either party has caused or contributed to the loss, it should be borne by that party in the whole or in the greater part.

His proposal was rejected by the English Law Reform Committee in its Twelfth Report on Transfer of Title to Chattels (1966 Cmnd 2958). The Committee recommended a solution similar to that now adopted in New Zealand. See the criticisms by PS Atiyah (1966) 29 MLR 541.

The seller's title must not have been avoided at the time of sale. In *Car and Universal Finance Co Ltd v Caldwell* [1965] 1 QB 525 there was a sale of a car to a rogue who gave a cheque that was subsequently dishonoured. The owner on discovering this immediately informed the police and the Automobile Association. The English Court of Appeal held that the owner could rescind by taking all steps open to him where he was unable to communicate with the rogue. Section 27(2) of the Sale of Goods Act which protects a buyer in good faith from a buyer in possession does not appear to have been cited. This might have had the effect of conferring a good title on the innocent buyer from the rogue. See 16.6 below. Apart from this the result in the *Caldwell* case is similar to that adopted by s 8(1) of the Contractual Remedies Act 1979. See ch 7 ante.

16.5 SALE BY SELLER IN POSSESSION

Section 27(1) of the Sale of Goods Act provides that:

> Where a person, having sold goods continues or is in possession of the goods, or of the documents of title to the goods, the delivery or transfer by that person, or by a mercantile agent acting for him, of the goods or documents of title under any sale, pledge, or other disposition thereof, or under any agreement for sale, pledge, or other disposition thereof, to any person receiving the same in good faith and without notice of the previous sale, shall have the same effect as if the person making the delivery or transfer were expressly authorised by the owner of the goods to make the same.

The effect of this subsection is that a buyer to whom property has passed may nevertheless be divested of his or her title. The result is the same as if the seller had the authority of the buyer to sell to the third party. Formerly, it was held that the seller had to be in possession of the goods as seller and not in some other capacity such as bailee. In *Pacific Motor Auctions Pty Ltd v Motor Credits (Hire Purchase) Ltd* [1965] AC 867 the Privy Council departed from these earlier authorities. In that case a motor dealer had entered into a display agreement with the plaintiff finance company which enabled him to sell his cars to the plaintiff but retain possession of them and sell them on the plaintiff's behalf. The dealer got into financial difficulties and the plaintiff revoked his authority to sell. Later the same day the dealer sold a number of cars on display to the defendant. The High Court of Australia held that the defendant received no title.

Section 27(1) did not apply because the dealer was in possession as bailee, not as seller. However, the Privy Council reversed this decision and held that the defendant had received a good title under the subsection. The words in s 27(1) "continues in possession" were intended to refer to the continuity of physical possession regardless of any private transactions between the seller and the buyer, which might alter legal title. Section 27(1) refers to "sale, pledge or other disposition". In *Worcester Works Finance Ltd v Cooden Engineering Co Ltd* [1972] 1 QB 210 the English Court of Appeal held that the word "disposition" was very wide but did not cover a mere transfer of possession. To fall within the subsection there had to be a transfer of some interest in the goods. The fact, of that case were that Cooden sold a car to Griffiths who posed as a dealer and sold it to Worcester. He then resold it to Griffith's customer, Millerick who never took delivery and never paid any deposit or any instalment under his hire purchase agreement with Worcester. The car remained in Griffiths' possession. Cooden sought to rely on the equivalent of s 27(1), arguing that Griffiths was a person who, having sold goods to Worcester, continued in possession of them. The Court held, following the *Pacific Motor Auctions* case, that it did not matter what private arrangement had been made by the seller with the buyer if there was continuity of physical possession. Griffiths was, therefore, a person who continued in possession until the car was retaken by Cooden. The next question was whether the retaking of possession by Cooden was a disposition by Griffiths. The Court held that disposition was a very wide word that extended to all acts by which a new interest in property was created. When Cooden retook the car because Griffiths' cheque had not been met there was a transfer back to them of property in the car. By retaining the goods they impliedly gave up their remedy on the cheque. The Court also held that Cooden acted in good faith without notice of the sale to Worcester.

16.6 SALE BY BUYER IN POSSESSION

Section 27(2) of the Sale of Goods Act provides that:

> Where a person having bought or agreed to buy goods, obtains, with the consent of the seller, possession of the goods or the documents of title to the goods, the delivery or transfer by that person, or by a mercantile agent acting

for him, of the goods or documents of title, under any sale, pledge, or other disposition thereof, or under any agreement for sale, pledge, or other disposition thereof, to any person receiving the same in good faith and without notice of any lien or other right of the original seller in respect of the goods, shall have the same effect as if the person making the delivery or transfer were a mercantile agent in possession of the goods or documents of title with the consent of the owner.

Provided that if the lien or other right of the original seller is expressed in an instrument duly registered under [the Chattels Transfer Act 1924], and if the person selling, pledging, or disposing of the goods or agreeing so to do is the mortgagor or bailee named in such instrument, then the person receiving the goods shall be deemed to have had notice of the contents of such instrument.

Provided further that, in the case of a motor vehicle, if the lien or other right of the original seller is created or evidenced by, or arises under, a security interest registered under the Motor Vehicle Securities Act 1989, then the person receiving the motor vehicle shall be deemed to have notice of the existence of that security interest and the registered particulars in respect of it.

Whereas s 27(1) deals with a sale by a seller in possession s 27(2) deals with the converse situation, that of a buyer in possession. This means that even though the seller retains property in the goods, if he delivers possession of the goods the buyer may divest him of his title by selling the goods to a third party. There are three important elements in s 27(2). First the subsection refers to a person "having bought or agreed to buy goods". Where a person has actually bought the goods then normally property will pass to him and if this is so then he can confer a good title without the need of the subsection. It is arguable, therefore, that the word "bought" is unnecessary: PS Atiyah, *The Sale of Goods* (8 ed), 376.

Secondly, the wording "shall have the same effect as if the person making the delivery or transfer were a mercantile agent..." has given rise to difficulties in the cases. As the subsection is worded, it would appear to create a statutory analogy and indeed this is what it was held to do in *Jeffcot v Andrews Motors Ltd* [1960] NZLR 721. In that case it was argued that the subsection could not apply unless the buyer in reselling the goods was acting as a mercantile agent. It was held that this was not so. The section operated to validate the sale as if the buyer in possession were a mercantile agent. It did not require that he should act as though he were a mercantile agent. On the other hand, in the later English case of *Newtons of Wembley Ltd v Williams* [1965] 1 QB 560 a different interpretation was given. In that case a rogue purchased a car and persuaded the seller to accept a cheque. The seller insisted that the property should not pass until the cheque was cleared but allowed the rogue to drive it away. Needless to say the cheque was dishonoured and the seller took steps to trace the car by informing the police and the other agencies. Before the car was found the rogue sold it and it was subsequently resold to the defendant. The main issue was whether the sale by the rogue was within the equivalent to s 27(2). The English Court of Appeal held that the rogue was a person who had agreed to buy and the defendant had purchased it in good faith. However, for the rogue to pass a good title under the subsection he had to be treated as if he were a mercantile agent. Since he was not in fact a mercantile agent he could only fall within the subsection if he was acting in a way in which a mercantile agent would normally act.

Such an interpretation narrows down the scope of the protection of the subsection and it is submitted that the earlier New Zealand case is preferable.

Thirdly, the subsection refers to the person being in possession of the goods or documents of title "with the consent of the *owner*". This reference to the owner contrasts with the wording at the opening of the subsection which refers to the obtaining of possession "with the consent of the *seller*". Since the subsection refers to two different people a literal interpretation would suggest that even if the original seller had no title a sub-purchaser from the buyer in possession could obtain a good title because he would be deemed to have taken with the consent of the *owner*. However, in *Elwin v O'Regan and Maxwell* [1971] NZLR 1124, Beattie J equated seller and owner. In that case the plaintiff purchased a car from Maxwell who had obtained the car from Broadlands Finance Co which in its turn had acquired it from Nevin who had had the car on a hire purchase agreement of the classic *Helby v Matthews* type in Australia. O'Regan was an agent of the Australian hire purchase company which was seeking repossession of the car. Elwin claimed damages in conversion and detinue. Beattie J held that Nevin, having acquired the car under a hire purchase agreement, was not a person who had bought or agreed to buy within s 27(2) but Maxwell was. However, he held that a strict interpretation of s 27(2) would produce a startling conclusion. He, therefore, interpreted "owner" as "seller", thus limiting the scope of the section. He could not accept that stolen goods finding a haven with a third or fourth purchaser should give title. The principle of *nemo dat quod non habet* should apply. A similar view was taken in *National Employer's Mutual General Insurance Association Ltd v Jones* [1990] 1 AC 24 (HL).

The proviso to s 27(2) is a cross reference to the Chattels Transfer Act 1924 and Motor Vehicle Securities Act 1989. Registration under those Acts constitutes notice of the registered instrument. This has particular significance in the case of the conditional sale type of hire purchase.

16.7 SPECIAL POWERS OF SALE

Section 23(2)(b) provides that nothing in the Sale of Goods Act affects the validity of any sale under special common law or statutory power of sale or the order of a Court of competent jurisdiction. An example of a common law power is the right of the sheriff after seizing goods in execution to sell them. Reference should also be made to s 28 which deals with the effect of writs of execution. These bind the goods as from the time of execution but without prejudice to the title of a bona fide purchaser for value without notice from the *debtor*. An example of a statutory power of sale is the power of a mortgagee under para 7 of the Fourth Schedule to the Chattels Transfer Act 1924 and ss 94 and 99 of the Property Law Act 1952 to realise the mortgaged property in the event of default by the mortgagor.

16.8 MOTOR VEHICLE SECURITIES ACT 1989

See ch 38.

Chapter 17

PERFORMANCE AND NON-PERFORMANCE

SUMMARY

17.1 DUTIES OF SELLER AND BUYER
17.2 DELIVERY
17.3 THE BUYER'S RIGHT OF EXAMINATION
17.4 ACCEPTANCE
17.5 REJECTION

17.1 DUTIES OF SELLER AND BUYER

The seller's duty is to deliver the goods and the buyer's duty is to accept and pay for them in accordance with the terms of the contract: s 29. Delivery is the voluntary transfer of possession from one person to another: s 2. Delivery does not necessarily mean despatch of goods to the buyer. If there is no provision relating to delivery in the contract of sale, it generally rests on the buyer to go and get his or her goods from the seller. Delivery may be actual or constructive. Delivery is constructive when the means of obtaining possession of the goods is transferred, eg, by delivering the key of a warehouse where the goods are stored. It may be made by the transfer of a document of title, eg shipping documents, or by attornment – the acknowledgement by a person holding the goods that he or she will act on a delivery order.

Delivery and payment are concurrent conditions unless otherwise agreed. The seller is entitled to withhold delivery until the buyer is prepared to pay the price in exchange for the possession of the goods: s 30.

If payment is to be in cash the tender of a cheque or credit card will not be sufficient unless the seller agrees: *Green & Ryall v SJ Ramsay Ltd* (Unreported, High Court, Rotorua, 103/79, 18 April 1986).

17.2 DELIVERY

17.2.1 Basic rules

These are laid down by s 31 of the Sale of Goods Act 1908. Whether it is for the buyer to take possession of the goods or for the seller to send them to the buyer is a question depending in each case on the contract between the parties: s 31(1). Unless otherwise agreed, the following rules apply:

(a) The place of delivery is the seller's place of business, if he or she has one or, if not, his or her residence. If specific goods are somewhere else at the time of the contract with the knowledge of the parties, then that place is the place of delivery (s 31(2));

(b) If the seller is to send the goods and no time is fixed, he or she is bound to send them within a reasonable time (s 31(3));

(c) If the goods at the time of sale are in the possession of a third party there is no delivery until the third party acknowledges to the buyer that he or she holds the goods on the buyer's behalf but this does not affect the rights of a third party who has received a document of title issued by the seller (s 31(4));

(d) Demand or tender of delivery must be made at a reasonable hour which is a question of fact (s 31(5));

(e) Unless otherwise agreed the expenses of making the goods deliverable are to be borne by the seller (s 31(6)).

17.2.2 Delivery of wrong quantity

Section 32(1) provides that if the seller delivers less than the quantity contracted for, the buyer may reject the goods delivered or he or she may accept and pay for them at the contract rate. If the seller delivers more than the quantity contracted for, the buyer may:

(a) reject the whole delivery; or
(b) retain the quantity contracted for and reject the rest, or
(c) accept the whole delivery and pay for it at the contract rate: s 32(2).

It should be noted that delivery of the wrong quantity entitles a buyer to reject the goods tendered, whereas defective quality must be held to be a breach of condition before there is a right of rejection.

Where the seller delivers goods of a different description together with some of the goods contracted for (described in the Act as "mixed goods"), the buyer may reject all the goods or retain only those in accordance with the contract; s 32(3). The term "mixed" in the Act means simply "accompanied by". Thus, if a buyer ordered five dozen fine China teasets and received three dozen fine China teasets and two dozen of Delft he or she would be entitled to reject the five dozen sets or retain the three dozen China sets and pay for them at the contract rate.

In *London Plywood and Timber Co Ltd v Nasic Oak Extract Factory and Steam Sawmills Co Ltd* [1939] 2 KB 343 L sent its representative to Yugoslavia to inspect timber it was purchasing. The representative branded all timber he approved with a distinctive hammer mark. L paid the full price and freight amounting to £ 4,894 due on the shipment of the timber to London. More than half the timber making up the quantity was unbranded when it arrived in London. The dispute was referred to an arbitrator who referred his award in the form of a special case to the Court. The Court confirmed his award that "mixed" goods had been delivered and that L could reject the whole consignment and recover the full price, freight, interest, damages and costs.

Where part only of a larger quantity contracted for has been delivered, the buyer is not bound to pay for the part delivered before the time fixed for the delivery of the whole and if the seller fails to complete his or her contract the buyer may reject the part delivered: *Shipton v Casson* (1826) 5 B & C 378.

The provisions of s 32 are subject to any usage of trade, special agreement or course of dealing between the parties: s 32(4). Where words of approximation such as "about" or "more or less" are used, a reasonable variation must be allowed, depending on the nature of the goods and the circumstances of the case: *Carson v Union Steamship Co of NZ Ltd* [1922] NZLR 778.

17.2.3 Delivery by instalments

Where delivery by instalments has been agreed the question arises what happens if some instalments prove defective. The basic rule is contained in s 33(2). This provides:

> Where there is a contract for the sale of goods to be delivered by stated instalments, which are to be separately paid for, and the seller makes defective deliveries in respect of one or more instalments, or the buyer neglects or refuses to take delivery of or pay for one or more instalments, it is a question in each case depending on the terms of the contract and the circumstances of the case, whether the breach of contract is a repudiation of the whole contract or whether it is a severable breach, giving rise to a claim for compensation but not to a right to treat the whole contract as repudiated.

The subsection was discussed in *Bignell and Holmes v Partridge Co Ltd* [1923] GLR 657 (CA) where the buyer ordered 50 tyres but only 39 were delivered. It was held that the seller was not entitled to deliver the goods by instalments and the buyer was entitled to reject the goods. On the other hand in *Maple Flock Co Ltd v Universal Furniture Products (Wembley) Ltd* [1934] 1 KB 148 in the English Court of Appeal Lord Hewart CJ said where there is a sale by instalments that: "The matters to be considered are first, the ratio quantitatively which the breach bears to the contract as a whole and secondly, the degree of probability or improbability that such a breach will be repeated". In that case there was a sale of 100 tons of rag flock to be delivered by instalments every three weeks of 1-1/2 tons each. The first 15 instalments were satisfactory but the 16th was not. The next four were. The Court held that the buyer was not entitled to reject. Only one instalment was defective and there was only a remote prospect of a further breach.

17.2.4 Delivery to carriers

Where the seller has to send goods to the buyer, delivery to a carrier is prima facie delivery to the buyer. The seller must make a reasonable contract with the carrier and if he or she neglects to do so and loss or damage occurs in transfer, the buyer may decline to accept delivery and hold the seller responsible in damages: s 34(1),(2).

Where carriage involves sea transit, eg in a fob contract, the seller must give sufficient notice to the buyer to enable him to insure. Otherwise, the goods will be at the seller's risk. It is likewise incumbent on an exporter using air transport to notify the consignee in time for him or her to insure or else to take out insurance cover, not only while the aircraft is in flight but also from "warehouse to warehouse", as is usual in marine insurance. Where the seller agrees to deliver goods at his or her own risk at the place other than where they are sold the buyer must, unless otherwise agreed, take any risk of deterioration in the goods necessarily incident in the course of transit: ss 34 and 35.

17.3 THE BUYER'S RIGHT OF EXAMINATION

Where there is a delivery to the buyer of goods which he or she has not previously examined, he or she is not deemed to have accepted them unless and until he or she has had a reasonable opportunity of examining them for the purpose of ascertaining whether they are in conformity with the contract: s 36. The opportunity must allow an adequate examination, not merely a cursory one but the buyer is obliged to make his or her examination within a time which is reasonable in the circumstances.

Unless otherwise agreed, the buyer is entitled to ask for a reasonable opportunity to examine the goods, and prima facie the time and place for this will be the time and place of the delivery of the goods, but this presumption is subject to the terms of the contract: *Perkins v Bell* [1893] 1 QB 193. If the place of delivery is not a reasonable one for the examination of the goods, the purchaser's premises may be held to be a reasonable place for examination: *Molling and Co v Dean and Son Ltd* (1901) 18 TLR 217.

Again if the place of delivery is unsuitable for an adequate examination, it appears that examination may be postponed until arrival of the goods at a place with proper facilities. This applies particularly in export sales, where goods may be packed and constructively delivered in one country and the place of examination will be the port or town in the country to which they are being despatched.

In *The Canterbury Seed Company v The JG Ward Farmers Association* (1894) 13 NZLR 96, 108, the Court of Appeal held that where an inspection is to take place must depend upon the terms and circumstances of the contract. Where a merchant orders by correspondence goods from another at a distance, the purchaser has a right to inspect the goods at the place which will be reasonably supposed to be the destination of the goods, and that, in the absence of special circumstances or incidents in the contract, must be taken to be the place where the purchaser carries on business.

All that the Act provides is that the buyer be given a reasonable opportunity to examine the goods. Acceptance does not depend on whether he or she examines them or not. If he or she does not take advantage of his or her opportunity and does some act in relation to the goods inconsistent with the seller's ownership, he or she will be deemed to have accepted them. A buyer who accepts goods with an obvious defect may well find that not only has he or she lost his or her right to rejection but he or she may also be debarred from recovering damages for breach of warranty.

It appears that when the Act was drafted in England in 1893, it was envisaged that specific goods would have been examined and accepted by the buyer in terms of s 37 before the contract was made. However, numerous cases have established that specific goods may be sold by description and that the buyer is entitled to demand an examination on delivery after the contract has been made, although his or her only remedy may be the recovery of damages through the operation of s 13(3).

Many goods sold today may require lengthy examination to determine, for example, whether specific goods sold by description by a dealer in such goods are reasonably fit for the purpose for which they were bought or, alternatively, are of merchantable quality. Salmond J in *Taylor v Combined Buyers Ltd* [1924] NZLR 627 stated, p 651:

> What amounts to reasonable examination, and to reasonable delay for the purpose of examination, is a question of fact which depends on the nature of the article sold and the nature of the defects alleged. There are cases in which these defects are discoverable at once or on a mere cursory inspection. There are other cases in which the defects are so far latent that some form of investigation, or even user, and some consequent delay, may be essential for their discovery, but if such user or such delay exceeds what is reasonably necessary for this purpose it amounts to an acceptance which destroys the right of rejection and relegates the purchaser to his right to damages as for a breach of warranty. . . . The purchaser has done more than merely try the car for the purpose of ascertaining its defects. He has used the car for his own purposes to a substantial extent and for a substantial period and has thereby obtained for himself the benefit of part of the consideration for which he paid the purchase money to the vendor.

The learned Judge added at 651-52:

> He [the buyer] cannot, however, enlarge his rights against the vendor by reason of his own want of knowledge in this respect. If he was personally unable to inspect the car at once, so as to ascertain its true condition without undue user and undue delay, it was his duty to entrust that examination to some expert on his own behalf. If this had been done many of the defects would doubtless have been ascertained at once. Even, however, if the defects were so far latent as to be undiscoverable except by the process of extended use. I am not prepared to say that this circumstance would have saved the buyer's right of rejection. There may be articles whose failure to conform to the contract may be undiscoverable until they have been so far used that the purchaser has obtained a substantial part of the benefit of his purchase. I am not prepared to say that in such a case the purchaser can still reject and recover the purchase-money on the plea that he did no more than was necessary for the effective inspection of the goods. In such cases it may be that the purchaser is necessarily limited to a claim for damages, inasmuch as he cannot avoid the operation of s 37 in taking away his right of rejection.

The learned Judge after demonstrating that the buyer, through the use of the Calthorpe car for some months, had received a substantial part of the consideration for which he had contracted, was not prepared to let the buyer reject the goods and recover the price for breach of the condition of merchantable quality. Having accepted the goods (s 37), he was entitled only to damages as for a breach of warranty.

17.4 ACCEPTANCE

Prior to 1979 it was thought that s 36 was subordinate to s 37 in that if a buyer did an act inconsistent with the rights of the seller, notwithstanding the fact that the buyer had not had any opportunity to examine the goods, he or she was deemed to have accepted them.

The most common example of an act inconsistent with the seller's rights is a sub-sale by the purchaser.

In *Hardy and Co Ltd v Hillerns and Fowler* [1923] 2 KB 490 a cargo of wheat was sold and delivered to a sub-purchaser on the day of its arrival. The original buyer examined the wheat two days after arrival and found that it was not in conformity with the contract, but the English Court of Appeal held that the resale was an act inconsistent with the ownership of the seller by a buyer after goods had been delivered to him and that as this, in accordance with s 37 of the Act, was an acceptance of part of the goods, the original buyer could not reject the goods.

In the United Kingdom, s 4(2) of the Misrepresentation Act 1967 ended the effect of *Hardy and Co Ltd v Hillerns and Fowler*. In New Zealand the Contractual Remedies Act 1979, s 14(1)(b) has resolved this problem by amending s 37 to make that section expressly subject to a reasonable opportunity of inspection under s 36.

Section 37 as amended now provides that a buyer is deemed to have accepted the goods:

(a) When he intimates to the seller that he has accepted them; or
(b) Except where s 36 otherwise provides, when goods have been delivered to him, and he does any act in relation to them inconsistent with the ownership of the seller; or
(c) When, after the lapse of a reasonable time, he retains the goods without intimating to the seller that he has rejected them.

As regards (b), acts inconsistent with the ownership of the seller giving rise to the presumption of acceptance by the buyer may arise in a number of ways.

If a buyer requests the seller to despatch the goods directly to a sub-purchaser he or she may expressly or impliedly waive his or her right of examination. Thus in *Ruben Ltd v Faire Bros and Co Ltd* [1949] 1 KB 254 the seller agreed to sell a buyer rolls of rubber material. The buyer asked the seller to despatch half the material to a sub-purchaser, to whom the buyer had resold it. The sub-purchaser rejected the rubber on the ground that it did not correspond with the sample, which he was entitled to do. The seller sued the original buyer for the price and succeeded. The contract between them was held not severable and consequently the buyer's action in dealing with part of the goods amounted to acceptance and deprived him of his right of rejection.

Crucial factors in determining whether a sub-sale is inconsistent with the right of the seller are who has the duty of delivery, and where is to be the place of examination. If examination is to be at the buyer's factory, then delivery on a sub-sale will be an act inconsistent with the right of the seller. However, this will not be the case if the contract of supply requires the seller to deliver to the buyer's order. In such a case the place of examination will most likely be found to be at the point of delivery. In such a case a sub-sale and a direction to the seller to deliver directly to the sub-purchaser will not be inconsistent with the seller's right to get the goods back from the place of delivery in the condition originally despatched. (Compare *Ruben Ltd v Faire* with *Hammer and Barrow v Coca Cola* (infra).)

In cif contracts, conditional property passes with the receipt of the documents, but dealing with the documents does not deprive a buyer of his or her right to reject goods on arrival unless he or she forwards them on to another destination and thus destroys the seller's reversionary right to be able to recover legally rejected goods at their contract destination. In *Kwei Tek Chao v British Traders and Shippers Ltd* [1954] 2 QB 459 which involved a claim by the buyer against the seller on a forged bill of lading, Devlin J made the following points:

1   In a cif contract the buyer has two rights of rejection; he or she can reject the documents if they are not in order, or he or she can reject the goods on arrival if they are not in accordance with the documents.

2   The documents confer only conditional property on the seller. No dealing with the documents amounts to a final acceptance of the goods. The buyer still has his or her rights of examination and objection on the arrival of the goods.

Assignment of the plaintiff's interest in a motor vehicle to a finance company under a hire purchase agreement under an arrangement made by the dealer was held not to be an act inconsistent with the dealer's ownership: *Kaata v Swiss Built Ltd and Anor* [1990] DCR 265.

The question of what is a reasonable time for the purposes of (c) is a question of fact: s 57. In *Kaata v Swiss Built Ltd* five weeks was held not to be the lapse of a reasonable time. Cf *Bernstein v Pamson Motors (Golders Green) Ltd* [1987] 2 All ER 220 (three weeks held to constitute acceptance). Normally five weeks would be the lapse of a reasonable time. In *Kaata v Swiss Built Ltd* the facts were extreme. The plaintiff had been falsely imprisoned until she purchased the vehicle. The Court was prepared to declare the contract void ab initio for breach of s 23 of the Fair Trading Act 1986.

17.5 REJECTION

The draftsman of the Sale of Goods Act aimed at stability and certainty in sales of goods. Such an objective was reasonable and desirable in an age when the quality and efficiency of goods could normally be determined by visual inspection or by simple trial. If a buyer has seen and agreed to take specific goods, or if goods had been delivered to him or her and he or she had commenced to use them, it seemed reasonable that if the buyer later found the goods to be defective he or she should be satisfied with damages and the seller should not have to take back goods, which are now secondhand.

Section 13(3) of the Act provides that where a contract of sale is not severable, and the buyer has accepted the goods or part thereof, the breach of any condition to be fulfilled by the seller can only be treated as a breach of warranty, and not as a ground for rejecting the goods and treating the contract as repudiated, unless there is a term of the contract, express or implied to that effect.

This section, which prevents rejection of goods not corresponding with the description or seriously defective in quality, or unfit for the buyer's purpose, because he or she has accepted them by doing some act inconsistent with the seller's rights, can have harsh consequences for the buyer.

Richmond J's judgment in *Hammer and Barrow v Coca Cola* [1962] NZLR 723 illustrates the difficulty of applying the law of performance and non performance in practice. For this reason we shall examine it in some detail.

Coca Cola arranged for the manufacture and distribution of its produce through various distributors in New Zealand. Its Auckland distributor was the Northern Bottling Co Ltd. Coca Cola organised an advertising campaign in which retailers were to be supplied with ("champion not beginners") yo-yos artistically finished with an advertising slogan on them. Coca Cola ordered 200,000 yo-yos for resale to its distributors from the plaintiff in Christchurch. The plaintiff was to arrange for the carriage of 85,000 yo-yos to be sent by the plaintiff to the Northern Bottling Co Ltd in Auckland. The yo-yos were roughly finished and many of them did not work. 85,000 of the yo-yos were sent by the plaintiff to the Northern Bottling Co on the following dates:

| 2-9 September | 51 cartons |
| 19 September-7 October | 97 cartons |

The Northern Bottling Co sold 22 cartons of yo-yos to retailers and had 14 cartons returned to them with a flood of complaints as the yo-yos were not playable. In the meantime the Northern Bottling Co had been inspecting and sorting the yo-yos, sandpapering and otherwise trying to improve them. In all, the Northern Bottling Co had either sold or otherwise dealt with 28 cartons.

Richmond J held that the "playability" of the yo-yos was fundamental to the contract and on the evidence found that 80% of the yo-yos were defective. Accordingly as the quantitative ratio of defective yo-yos was so substantial and as the plaintiff, despite complaints and requests for replacement stock, had done nothing, this breach was likely to continue and Coca Cola was entitled to rescind the contract for further deliveries.

His Honour found that the factory door was the place of delivery. Although the place of delivery is generally the place for examination it may be clear that examination cannot conveniently be carried out at the place of delivery, or the place of delivery may be unsuitable through the nature of the goods, or the type of examination required, particularly where goods might have to be unpacked and then repacked. His Honour held that the plaintiff was contractually bound to arrange the carriage of the yo-yos to the premises of the Northern Bottling Co and that these premises were the place for examination and, if justified, rejection of the goods. In this respect His Honour's view, although unorthodox at the time, is strengthened by the amendment to s 37 discussed above.

His Honour also decided that when they were despatched to Auckland the yo-yos were not in accordance with the contract description and that the property in these yo-yos would not pass to Coca Cola until they had been accepted by it. The transport of these goods in accordance with the terms of the contract could not be regarded as an act inconsistent with the ownership of the seller. The sub-sale to Northern Bottling Company Ltd, therefore, was not an acceptance of the goods.

His Honour found that 28 cartons of yo-yos had either been sold to retailers or worked on to improve their playability and that being bound as he was to take the view most favourable to the defendant he also found that these 28 cartons came from the first consignments of 51 cartons. The contract was severable, and it was not unreasonable to deal with the first 51 cartons, the second 97 cartons and the remaining yo-yos separately.

As 51 cartons had been accepted and the property in them had passed to Coca Cola, the defendant was liable for the price: s 50(1). However, there was nevertheless a breach of the condition of merchantability which had now to be treated as a breach of warranty: s 13(3). Following s 54(3), the measure of damages was, prima facie, the difference between the value at the time of delivery to the buyer and the value they would have had, if they had complied with the warranty. Richmond J found that the defective yo-yos, embellished with advertising slogans, were unsaleable, that no replacement stock was available, and accordingly allowed Coca Cola's counterclaim for damages, which equalled the total amount of the price claimed by the plaintiff.

As we have seen s 37 is now made expressly subject to s 36 so that the buyer has a right of examination unless he or she waives it.

The consequences of a wrongful rejection of the goods by the buyer can be serious. It constitutes a repudiation which the seller is entitled to accept as a discharge of the contract. If, however, the seller decides not to treat the rejection as repudiation the wrongful rejection will be ineffective. If the property has passed the seller will be able to sue for the price. If he or she elects or is obliged because property has not passed, to sue for damages then he or she must take reasonable steps to mitigate his or her loss: see RM Goode, *Commercial Law* 359 and ch 20 post.

Chapter 18

RISK, PERISHING AND FRUSTRATION

SUMMARY

18.1   RISK
18.2   PERISHING BEFORE CONTRACT
18.3   PERISHING AFTER CONTRACT

18.1 RISK

Risk is not defined in the Sale of Goods Act 1908 and it has been said that the meaning of risk is not constant but depends on whether the party in question is the seller or the buyer: RM Goode, *Commercial Law*, 194. Indeed, Dr LS Sealy has written, "The truth is that risk is a derivative, and essentially negative, concept – an elliptical way of saying that either or both of the primary obligations of one party shall be enforceable, and that those of the other party shall be deemed to have been discharged, even though the normally prerequisite conditions have not been satisfied": [1972] CLJ 225, 226. The Sale of Goods Act links risk with the passing of property. Section 22(1) of the Act provides that "Unless otherwise agreed, the goods remain at the seller's risk until the property therein is transferred to the buyer; but when the property therein is transferred to the buyer the goods are at the buyer's risk, whether delivery has been made or not". Where, however, the delivery has been delayed through the fault of either buyer or seller the goods are at the risk of the defaulting party as regards any loss which might not have occurred but for his or her default. Thus although the Act links risk with property this is only a prima facie rule as the marginal note to the section indicates. In other words it does not apply if there is a contrary agreement between the parties. Secondly, where one party is at fault the risk may shift to him or her even though the property does not vest in him or her. Thirdly, the rule does not affect the responsibilities of either party as a bailee of the goods: s 22(2). Fourthly, there are further rules in the Act which apply to goods in transit: see s 34(2) and (3) and s 35 which we have already discussed in ch 17 supra.

18.2 PERISHING BEFORE CONTRACT

Section 8 of the Sale of Goods Act 1908 provides that where there is a contract for the sale of specific goods and the goods without the knowledge of the seller have perished at the time when the contract is made the contract is void. This rule has been said to be based on the ground of common mistake (*Bell v Lever Bros Ltd* [1923] AC 161, 217) or on the ground of impossibility of performance or an implied condition precedent that the goods exist (*Bell v Lever Bros Ltd*, supra 224 and *Solle v Butcher* [1950]1 KB 671, 681). In so far as it is based on common mistake the Contractual Mistakes Act 1977 may be relevant. However, s 5 of that Act provides that it is intended to displace the rules of common law and equity and, therefore, it is arguable that it does not affect this express provision of the Sale of Goods Act. Nevertheless, the point is not free from doubt since the Sale of Goods Act is a code of the common law and it is likely that the draftsman of the Act had in mind the House of Lords decision in *Couturier v Hastie* (1853) 5 HL Cas 673 when he drafted the section. However the issue in that case was whether there was a total failure of consideration and not whether the contract was void so it is arguable that the section does not precisely codify the common law. If that is the case then clearly the Contractual Mistakes Act will not apply.

The section only applies to specific goods. Generic goods, ie goods defined by description only, come within the maxim *genus num quam perit* – the class never perishes; *Re Thornett and Fehr v Yuills* [1921] 1 KB 219.

The meaning of perish in the section is not free from doubt. Obviously if goods have been physically destroyed they have perished but it is possible to argue that perish also covers cases where the goods are no longer commercially saleable under their contract description: PS Atiyah, *The Sale of Goods*, (8 ed) 81. In *Rendell v Turnbull* (1908) 27 NZLR 1067 table potatoes were sold which, unknown to either party, were unfit for human consumption because of second growth. It was held that the contract was void under s 8 since second growth destroyed the nature of the potatoes as table potatoes. On the other hand in a later English case *Horn v Minister of Food* [1948] 2 All ER 1036 it was held that rotten potatoes which could not be used were still potatoes as long as they were in a form which permitted of their being called potatoes. It is submitted that *Rendell v Turnbull* is preferable. In *Asfar v Blundell* [1896] 1 QB 23 dates which had been submerged under water for two days and had become impregnated with sewage were argued to have perished for insurance purposes. The insurers, however, argued that there had been no total loss. Lord Esher MR, with characteristic common sense, said that while the insurers' argument might commend itself to a body of chemists, it would not do so to businessmen. The test was whether as a matter of business the thing had altered. That test would seem applicable in the context of s 8. A more problematic question is whether goods which have been stolen have perished. Where this is the case the goods may be later recovered in which case they have obviously not perished. However, where they have not been recovered within a reasonable time it is arguable that they have perished: cf PS Atiyah, *The Sale of Goods*, (8 ed) 83. Another difficult question is what happens where only part of the goods have perished. In *Barrow Lane and Ballard Ltd v Phillips and Co Ltd* [1929] 1 KB 574, a consignment of nuts was held to be an indivisible whole and, therefore, to fall within s 8. In that case the plaintiff contracted to sell to the defendant 700 bags of ground nuts, which were believed to be in certain warehouses. In fact 109 of the bags had disappeared, presumably stolen, at the time when the contract was made. The seller delivered the remaining bags and the buyer paid the price at the contract rate for them. The seller then claimed the price for the missing bags and the buyer quite reasonably refused to pay. Wright J held that the contract was for a parcel of 700 bags and this was different from a contract for 591 bags. The parties were contracting about something which, at the time of the contract, did not exist. Although the decision was fair in the circumstances of the case the principle laid down by Wright J seems rather odd and a different approach was adopted in the later case of *Sainsbury Ltd v Street* [1972] 1 WLR 834 in which s 8 was not argued. In that case the defendant agreed to sell a crop of about 275 tons of barley to be grown on his farm. Due to a crop failure only 140 tons were produced which the defendant sold to a third party at a higher price. McKenna J held that, while the contract was frustrated as to the part of the crop which had failed this did not exonerate the defendant from supplying them under the terms of his contract with the plaintiff. *Sainsbury v Street* seems a fairer and more sensible solution.

Lastly, it may be held in certain circumstances that the seller expressly warranted the existence of the goods in which case he or she will be liable in spite of the fact that they did not exist at the time of the contract: *Macrae v Commonwealth Disposals Commission* (1951) 84 CLR 377.

18.3 PERISHING AFTER CONTRACT

Section 9 of the Sale of Goods Act 1908 provides that where there is an agreement to sell specific goods, and subsequently the goods, without any fault on the part of the seller or buyer, perish before the risk passes to the buyer, the agreement is thereby avoided. This section appears to be a partial codification of the common law of frustration. Unlike the general law of frustration s 9 only applies where goods have perished before the risk passes to the buyer. In practice it will be of limited scope since, unless otherwise agreed, s 20 rule (1) will result in property in specific goods passing at the time when the contract is made and under s 22 prima facie risk passes with property. Where, however, s 9 does apply it is expressly provided in s 4(5)(c) of the Frustrated Contracts Act 1944 that the provisions of that Act do not apply. The result of this is that where a case falls under s 9 of the Sale of Goods Act the common law rules on frustration of contracts apply. Instead of the discretionary relief under the 1944 Act the parties are immediately discharged from all obligations under the contract and any money paid over can be reclaimed as if there had been a total failure of consideration. However, there can be no recovery where the failure of the consideration is only partial. Where the buyer can recover the price the seller is not allowed to set-off any sum for the cost which he or she has incurred. Where there has been part performance no claim can be made for the benefit of that part performance: see further RG Lawson, *Law of Sale and Hire Purchase in New Zealand*, 78. The position is highly unsatisfactory and the matter was under review by the Contracts and Commercial Law Reform Committee, prior to its demise.

Chapter 19

BREACH OF CONTRACT – SELLER'S REAL REMEDIES

SUMMARY

19.1   REMEDIES IN GENERAL
19.2   WITHHOLDING DELIVERY
19.3   LIEN
19.4   STOPPAGE IN TRANSIT
19.5   SELLER'S RIGHT OF RESALE

19.1 REMEDIES IN GENERAL

Remedies in Sale of Goods can be divided into two categories – real and personal. Real remedies are rights over the goods themselves. Personal remedies are monetary claims against the parties or controlling their conduct.

Where property in the goods has not passed and the seller still retains possession he or she may withhold delivery and resell in the event of continued default by the buyer. Where property in the goods has passed an unpaid seller has the following real remedies:

1   a lien on the goods in his or her possession;
2   a right of stoppage in transit where goods are in the hands of a carrier; and
3   a limited right of resale.

Personal remedies of the seller are an action for the price or damages for non-acceptance. The buyer's remedy is to claim damages for non-delivery or for breach of warranty.

Where the seller is in default the buyer may have a right to bring a claim for specific performance but this being an equitable remedy is discretionary.

263

19.1.1 Unpaid seller defined

Section 40(1) of the Sale of Goods Act 1908 provides that the seller is deemed to be an unpaid seller when:

(a) The whole of the price has not been paid or tendered; or
(b) A negotiable instrument has been received as conditional payment and it has been dishonoured.

"Seller" includes any person in the position of a seller, as for instance an agent of the seller to whom the bill of lading has been indorsed: s 40(2).

Thus, a New Zealand importer could arrange for a confirming house in London to buy goods on his or her behalf. The confirming house would have to pay the English exporter but if it had not been paid by the importer it would have all the remedies of the unpaid seller against him or her.

On the other hand, a buyer of goods, who has rejected them but had previously paid the price, cannot claim to be in the position of an unpaid seller in order that he or she may retain possession of the goods until he or she recovers the purchase price: *Lyons v May* [1923] 1 KB 685.

19.2 WITHHOLDING DELIVERY

If the property in the goods has not passed to the buyer, the unpaid seller has a right to withhold delivery or stop his or her goods in transit, co-extensive with the right of lien and stoppage in transit where the property has passed to the buyer, he or she can, in the exercise of his or her common law rights, rescind the contract and deal with the goods as he or she thinks fit. Accordingly, if a buyer either expressly, or by his or her conduct impliedly, repudiates a contract, the seller can accept his or her repudiation and resell the goods which were the subject matter of the contract and also recover any loss arising from the expense of reselling and any difference between the contract price and the resale price.

Section 41(2) provides for what might be regarded as a quasi-lien, in so far as it states that the unpaid seller has a right of withholding delivery co-extensive with his or her or her right of lien and stoppage in transit where the property has passed to the buyer. The statutory provision appears to add little to the common law although it clarifies the legal position in regard to instalment contracts. Thus, in *Ex parte Chalmers* (1873) 8 Ch 289 where goods were to be delivered to the buyer in monthly instalments, payment to be made within a fortnight of each delivery, and the buyer became insolvent during the course of the contract, the seller, being unpaid for one instalment, was held to be entitled to refuse to deliver the next instalment until payment for both instalments had been made.

19.3 LIEN

Where the property has passed to the buyer, the seller may exercise a lien on the goods, or a right to retain them for the price, while he or she is in possession of them: s 41(a).

The unpaid seller's lien is set out in s 42, and is a right to retain possession of the goods until payment if:

(a) The goods have been sold without any stipulation as to credit; or
(b) The term of credit has expired; or
(c) The buyer has become insolvent.

Insolvency is defined in s 2(3) as ceasing to pay debts in the ordinary course of business or an inability to pay one's debts as they fall due and does not necessarily involve bankruptcy or winding-up.

The lien is exercisable although the seller is in possession as an agent or bailee for the buyer: s 42(2).

The seller does not need to have sole possession of the goods to exercise his or her right of lien – he or she can exercise it even if he or she has been allowing the buyer access to the goods: *Wrightson v McArthur and Hutchisons* [1921] 2 KB 807. If the seller has deposited goods with a bailee, he or she can still exercise his or her lien, but not if the goods have been so mixed with other goods that they have lost their separate entity, eg where gold bars were stored with other gold bars: *Dollfus Meig and Cie v Bank of England* [1950] Ch 333.

The lien is lost if credit is subsequently allowed, for example by the acceptance of a bill of exchange payable at a future date. In such a case, the property will be vested in the buyer who will have the right to demand possession of the goods at any time before the bill matures. The buyer will not have this right if the seller can show that in fact he or she is insolvent. The amount that the seller can demand before release of the lien is limited to the price; he or she cannot claim anything extra for storage arising out of the lien, nor can he or she demand the payment of any damages before selling the goods. If the seller is demanding more than the price and will not release the goods, the buyer may bring an action for damages for non delivery: *Albemarle Supply Co Ltd v Hind and Co* [1928] 1 KB 307, 318.

To free the goods from the lien, anyone can pay the purchase price. A sub-purchaser can demand delivery on tender of the purchase price.

The right to exercise the lien only arises when the seller is "unpaid" when he or she should have been paid.

In *Mount Ltd v Jay and Jay Ltd* [1959] 3 WLR 537 it was held that where a seller, knowing that he or she was going to be paid out of the proceeds of a resale by the buyer, assents to a sale, then the seller loses his or her right of lien. In such a case there is a clear inference that the first buyer will not be paid and consequently will not be able to pay until he or she has given a delivery order or some similar document to the sub-purchaser.

Generally, delivery of goods to a common carrier for transport to the buyer puts an end to the seller's lien, but if the circumstances show that the carrier is the seller's agent, not the buyer's, the lien is not lost. Where, for example, the seller has undertaken responsibility for delivering the goods at the buyer's premises, or where the seller has reserved the right of disposal and thereby retained both the right to the property and possession of the goods, the seller is not deemed to have lost possession.

A seller, who, on delivery to a carrier, receives a receipt that the carrier holds the goods on account of the seller retains his or her lien until delivery to the buyer.

The seller may give a buyer constructive possession by an unconditional delivery to him or her of a document of title, such as a bill of lading.
The indorsement to the buyer and delivery to him or her of a bill of lading
is legal delivery and transfers conditional property in the goods to him.
It gives him or her legal control over goods which are still being shipped.

Where documents, other than documents of title, entitling the buyer
to take delivery are issued the unpaid seller can still refuse delivery and
repudiate the contract. This is not a case of claiming a lien as property has
not passed to the buyer. Delivery orders and warrants issued by dock
owners or warehousemen do not usually pass the property in the goods
to the buyer, but they nevertheless confer on him or her an insurable
interest as the risk in regard to destruction or deterioration passes to the
buyer. A seller can also retain legal possession of goods under an fob
contract by demanding a receipt for them in his or her own name when
he or she delivers the goods free on board. A seller holding such a receipt
can claim the bill of lading from the shipping company: *Ruck v Hatfield*
(1882) 5 B & Ald 632.

A mere appropriation of the goods by setting them aside, or putting
the buyer's address on them, or even packing them under the buyer's
orders in receptacles provided by him, does not divest the seller of his or
her lien: *Goodall v Skelton* (1794) 2 HB 316. However, once the seller loses
possession of the goods the mere fact that he or she recovers possession
does not revive his or her lien: *Jacobs v Latour* (1828) 5 Bing 130. In *United
Plastics Ltd (in Liq) v Reliance Electric (NZ) Ltd* [1977] 2 NZLR 125 it was
held that an unpaid vendor's lien requires uninterrupted possession,
and cannot be revived by the return of the goods to the vendor for repair.

Where a part delivery has been made, the lien may still attach to the
remainder of the goods unless the circumstances show an agreement to
waive it: s 43. If the unpaid seller has contracted to deliver goods by
instalments, he or she cannot withhold delivery of future instalments
because the previous instalment has not been paid for, unless the buyer
is insolvent or the circumstances show that he or she intends to repudiate
the contract: *Steinberger v Atkinson* (1914) 31 TLR 110.

Under s 44 the unpaid seller loses his or her lien:

(a) When the goods have been delivered to a carrier or other bailee for
    transmission to the buyer without reserving the right of disposal;
    or
(b) When the buyer or his or her agent lawfully obtains possession of
    the goods; or
(c) By waiver of the lien: *Mount Ltd v Jay and Jay Ltd*, supra.

The term "lawfully" in s 44(1)(b) above does not seem to mean anything
more than "with the consent of the buyer". If this is so, even if the seller
consented to possession through larceny by a trick, he or she would have
lost his or her lien.

In *Jeffcott v Andrew Motors Ltd* [1960] NZLR 721 F persuaded J to hand
over a car and registration papers to him in return for a worthless cheque.
F, the following day, sold the car to A in another town. A did not suspect
any irregularity. J at first claimed that no property in the car had passed
to F and that A could acquire no title from him. This submission was later
abandoned but J then contended that before F could confer a good title

on A under s 27(2) he must have had the car with the consent of J and be acting as a mercantile agent. The Court of Appeal held that although F gained possession by the subterfuge of a worthless cheque, nevertheless as F's possession arose through voluntary delivery it was with consent. The section validated the sub-sale "as if the buyer in possession were a mercantile agent"; it did not require F to act as a mercantile agent. The final submission on behalf of J was that he was entitled to an unpaid seller's lien (s 42) and that the lien had not been lost because s 44 provides that an unpaid seller loses his or her lien: "when the buyer or his or her agent lawfully obtains possession of the goods", and that F had obtained possession unlawfully. Hutchison J, at 731 held that the unpaid seller's lien was a possessory lien only and that the lien here was dependent on F's right of retention. The only sound inference then was that as F had obtained possession with J's consent, but through an unlawful act by F the unpaid seller's lien was not finally lost, but could revive again if J again obtained possession of the car. Gresson P and Cleary J did not consider that they were called upon to decide the point.

Thus J's action for possession of the car or alternatively damages failed.

The lien may be waived expressly or by implication. It is waived by implication where the seller agrees to take a term bill (eg a bill of exchange payable 30 days after sight) or takes a security for the price the conditions of which are inconsistent with the existence of the lien implied by law or where he or she dispenses with payment or tender of the price by repudiating the contract or refusing to deliver the goods. He or she does not, however, lose his or her lien by reason only that he or she has obtained judgment for the price of the goods.

19.4 STOPPAGE IN TRANSIT

This right of the unpaid seller applies only where the buyer becomes insolvent: s 41(b). The moment a seller loses possession, his or her common law right of lien is replaced by the right of stoppage in transit if the goods have not come into the possession of the buyer. This is a right to stop goods in the course of transit to the buyer, and to retake possession of them if the buyer has become insolvent. As in the case of lien, the seller may retain possession of the goods until the buyer pays or tenders the price: s 45. This right exists even though the period of credit has not expired and lasts until the goods reach the buyer or his or her agent. As in the case of lien, the seller, by exercising this right, does not rescind the contract nor does the property in the goods revest in him. The exercise of these rights does not put an end to the contract with the buyer. In short, the exercise of the right of lien or stoppage in transit does not carry by itself an automatic right of resale of the goods.

In distinguishing between the seller's right of lien and his or her right of stoppage in transit, it is necessary to notice that the seller's lien attaches when the buyer is in default, whether he or she is solvent or insolvent, whereas the seller can stop the goods in transit only when the buyer is insolvent. For stoppage in transit to be available the seller must have lost both the possession and the property in the goods.

19.4.1 Duration of transit

Goods are deemed to be in transit from the time they have left the seller's possession until they come into the possession of the buyer or of a carrier or other intermediary who has agreed to hold them for the buyer. It is immaterial how many people handle the goods before they reach their destination and there is no implication that the goods must be in motion. They may be stationary in the hands of a forwarding agent awaiting suitable transport. At any time when they still remain between the buyer and the seller, whether in a storage shed or in the course of transport, the seller retains the right to prevent their being diverted to an insolvent buyer. Transit does not end until the goods have come into the hands of some one who holds them for the buyer and for some purpose other than that of merely carrying them to the destination fixed by the contract or in accordance with the directions given by the buyer to the vendor.

Section 46 deals with the duration of transit; transit is ended if the buyer or his or her agent obtains delivery before the goods arrive at their destination or, if on arrival of the goods at the destination, the carrier acknowledges to the buyer that he or she holds the goods on the buyer's behalf, even though the buyer requests that the goods be carried to a further destination.

If the transit has been stopped by the buyer and the movement of the goods will not be resumed without further orders from him or her, then transit is at an end and the unpaid seller's right to stop and claim the goods is lost: *Reddall v Union Castle Mail Steamship Co* (1914) 84 LJKB 360.

If the carrier wrongfully refuses to deliver the goods to the buyer, transit is at an end. If the seller wrongfully stops delivery of the buyer's goods he or she may be liable for detinue or conversion.

If the goods are rejected by the buyer and the carrier or bailee retains possession of them, transit is not at an end even if the seller refuses to take them back.

There can be no valid exercise of the right of stoppage in transit while goods are in the post: *Postmaster-General v Jones and Co Ltd* [1957] NZLR 829.

When part of the goods have been delivered, the remainder may be stopped in transit unless the circumstances of the delivery of the part show an implied agreement to give up the whole of the goods. If the goods have been delivered to a ship chartered by the buyer it depends on the circumstances whether the master holds them as a carrier or as the buyer's agent.

19.4.2 How stoppage in transit is effected

This can be exercised either by taking actual possession of the goods or by giving notice to the carrier or to his or her agent or principals in time to stop delivery. When notice of stoppage in transit has been given to the carrier, he or she must re-deliver the goods according to the directions of the seller and at the seller's expense: s 47. He or she must comply with the notice or he or she will be liable to the seller for conversion of his or her goods. The carrier has a lien for unpaid freight which has priority over the unpaid seller's right to get back his or her goods: *Booth SS Co v Cargo Fleet Iron Co* [1916] 2 KB 570.

Where goods have been forwarded *by air*, the consignor, subject to the common law consequences of breach of contract, can, whether he or she is an unpaid seller or not, direct the goods to another consignee, stop them at any landing in the course of the journey or direct them to be returned to him or her provided that transit has not ended. Transit ends when the goods are tendered to the consignee at the airport of destination. This right is exercisable whether the consignee is insolvent or not; Warsaw Convention First Sched, art 72. The Carriage by Air Act 1967 gives effect to the Warsaw Convention for the unification of certain rules relating to international carriage by air (1929) as amended by The Hague Protocol (1955) and the Guadalajara Convention (1961).

19.4.3 Resale by the buyer

Subject to the provisions of the Act, the unpaid seller's statutory right of lien or stoppage in transit is not affected by any sale or other disposition of the goods by the buyer unless the seller has assented thereto. If documents of title have been lawfully transferred to the buyer and he or she has transferred them to a third party who has taken them in good faith and for value, the seller's right of lien or stoppage in transit is defeated. If the transfer is by way of pledge or other disposition for value, the unpaid seller's right of lien or stoppage in transit can only be exercised subject to the rights of the transferee: s 48.

19.5 SELLER'S RIGHT OF RESALE

The contract of sale between the seller and the original buyer is generally not rescinded by the seller's exercise of his or her statutory right of lien or stoppage in transit, but where a seller, having exercised this right of lien or stoppage in transit, resells, the second buyer acquires a good title against the original buyer. Under s 49(3) and (4) an unpaid seller is entitled to resell the goods:

    (a) Where the goods are perishable, or
    (b) Where the unpaid seller gives notice to the buyer of his or her
        intention to resell and the buyer does not, within a reasonable
        time, pay or tender the price; or
    (c) Where the right of resale has been expressly reserved in the
        contract.

An unpaid seller in possession who resells under (a), (b) or (c) above is deemed to have rescinded the original contract of sale.

Mere failure to pay the price is not necessarily repudiation of the contract by the buyer, but if the seller gives him or her notice to pay by a certain date, time is made of the essence and the seller can, if the buyer still fails to pay, accept the repudiation and resell the goods.

19.5.1 Resale at a loss

The seller can claim as damages for non acceptance any loss suffered through the resale price being less than the contract price and the expense of resale.

19.5.2 Resale at a profit

The statutory power of resale is conferred by s 49(3) of the Act which empowers an unpaid seller, where the goods are of a perishable nature or where the seller gives notice of his or her intention to resell, and the buyer does not within a reasonable time pay or tender the price, to resell the goods and recover from the buyer damages for any loss occasioned by the latter's breach of contract. It was held by the English Court of Appeal in *Ward v Bignall* [1967] 1 QB 534 that the exercise of the power of resale rescinds the contract, so that the unpaid seller's action to recover any loss must be for damages for non-acceptance and not for the balance of the purchase price. The true measure of damages then falls to be decided pursuant to s 51(3). The earlier New Zealand case of *Commission Car Sales (Hastings) Ltd v Saul* [1957] NZLR 144, which followed the case of *Gallagher v Shilcock* [1949] 2 KB 765 in holding that no rescission occurred and that the unpaid seller resold the goods as an agent of the buyer with the result that the unpaid seller had to account to the buyer for any surplus received, must be treated as no longer good law, *Gallagher v Shilcock* being overruled by *Ward v Bignall*. The question of why s 49(3) does not expressly provide that the contract in question is rescinded when a power of resale is exercised although such a provision is found in s 49(4) was also explained in *Ward v Bignall*. There it was said that the latter subsection covers the case where the contract itself provides for resale and that the unpaid seller would, by the act of reselling in such a case, be complying with the terms of the contract and the contract would therefore continue in existence.

It would appear to be immaterial whether property in the goods in question has passed or not at the time of resale in considering the effects of exercising the power to resell, for property in the goods must either have remained with the unpaid seller or revests in him or her by virtue of the seller's act of reselling. The reasoning of the Court in *Ward v Bignall* suggests that the result in that case would have been the same whether property had passed to the buyer or not, and that it was unnecessary to decide the point.

It was also held in *Commission Car Sales (Hastings) Ltd v Saul* that the right of resale under s 49(3) is exercisable only if the unpaid seller has never lost physical possession of the goods in question. However, there was no mention of this point in *Ward v Bignall*, and, in view of the rejection by the Court in that case of the reasoning underlying *Commission Car Sales*, the authority is perhaps doubtful.

Ward v Bignall was followed in New Zealand in the case of *Reid Motors Ltd v Wood* [1978] 1 NZLR 319 in which the question of calculating the damages due to an unpaid seller arose. The buyer in the case had paid a deposit by way of a trade-in of a car on the purchase of two others. It was held that the facts in the case indicated that the parties intended that the deposit should be a part payment of the purchase price, and not merely an earnest, or security, to bind the bargain, and that the unpaid seller was obliged to give credit to the buyer in calculating the actual loss which the seller had suffered.

Chapter 20

BREACH OF CONTRACT – PERSONAL REMEDIES

SUMMARY

20.1   REMEDIES OF SELLER
20.2   REMEDIES OF BUYER
20.3   INTEREST, SPECIAL DAMAGES AND RECOVERY OF MONEY PAID

20.1 REMEDIES OF SELLER

20.1.1 Action for price

Section 50(1) provides that where property in the goods under a contract of sale has passed to the buyer and the buyer wrongfully neglects or refuses to pay for them according to the terms of the contract the seller may bring an action for the price against him or her.

An action for the price can also be brought where the price is payable on a particular date, irrespective of delivery and the buyer wrongfully neglects or refuses to pay. This is so even though the property has not passed and even though goods have not been appropriated to the contract: s 50(2). The reason for this latter, rather exceptional, rule is that the buyer's promise amounts to an independent and unqualified obligation to pay: CM Schmitthoff, *The Sale of Goods* (2 ed), 172.

It should be noted, however, that under s 12(1), unless otherwise agreed, stipulations as to time of payment are not of the essence of a contract of sale. Although non payment may give rise to an action for the price under s 50(1) it will not constitute repudiation of the contract. Delivery and payment are concurrent conditions unless otherwise agreed: s 30. Where payment is made by cheque this is only conditional payment. The seller's right to sue for the price is suspended but revives if the cheque is dishonoured and there is also an action on the cheque itself.

The value of an action for the price is that this is a liquidated claim and there is no duty on the seller to mitigate his or her loss. It is increasingly common practice for sellers to purport to impose an interest charge on the expiration of a period of credit. See, for example, *McHaffie v Pyne*

Gould Guiness Ltd (1990) 3 NZBLC 101, 846 (interest at 25 per cent on unpaid price for stock bought at auction).

20.1.2 Damages for non-acceptance

Where the property in the goods has passed to the buyer the seller can either sue for the price or for damages for non acceptance under s 51. Where property has not passed the seller's only remedy is to sue for damages for non acceptance.

Section 51(2) deals with measure of damages and provides that this is the estimated loss directly and naturally resulting, in the ordinary course of events, from the buyer's breach of contract. This is a statutory restatement of the first limb of the rule in *Hadley v Baxendale* (1854) 9 Exch 341 (see 7.5.2 ante for a discussion in the context of the general law of contract).

Unlike the action for the price a claim for damages for non acceptance obliges the seller to take steps to mitigate his or her loss. However his or her duty is simply to act reasonably, not to nurse the interests of the buyer: *Harlow and Jones Ltd v Panex (International) Ltd* [1967] 2 Lloyd's Rep 509. Thus he or she need not accept the buyer's offer to take the goods at a reduced price.

Section 51(3) then provides that where there is an available market for the goods the measure (for the purposes of s 51(2)) is prima facie the difference between the contract price and the market price at the time when the goods ought to have been accepted or if no time was fixed for acceptance, when there was refusal to accept. The Courts have equivocated over the meaning of available market. In *Dunkirk Colliery Co v Lever* (1878) 9 ChD 20, 24, 25 James LJ thought of it in terms of a fixed place when he said:

> What I understand by a market in such a case as this is, that when the defendant refused to take the 300 tons the first week or the first month, the plaintiffs might have sent it in waggons somewhere else, where they could sell it, just as they sell corn on the Exchange, or cotton at Liverpool: that is to say, that there was a fair market where they could have found a purchaser either by themselves or through some agent at some particular place.

In *W L Thompson Ltd v Robinson (Gunmakers) Ltd* [1955] 1 Ch 177, 187, however, Upjohn J thought that it referred to the situation in a particular trade. He said:

> Had the matter been res integra I think that I should have found that an "available market" merely means that the situation in the particular trade in the particular area was such that the particular goods could freely be sold, and that there was a demand sufficient to absorb readily all the goods that were thrust on it, so that if a purchaser defaulted, the goods in question could readily be disposed of.

A third and more sophisticated approach was adopted by Jenkins LJ in *Charter v Sullivan* [1957] 2 QB 117, 128 when he said:

> I doubt if there can be an available market for particular goods in any sense relevant to [s 51(3) of the Sale of Goods Act 1908], unless those goods are

available for sale in the market at the market or current price in the sense of the price, whatever it may be, fixed by reference to supply and demand as the price at which a purchaser for the goods in question can be found, be it greater or less than or equal to the contract price.

For useful discussion of the concept of available market see RM Goode, *Commercial Law*, 360 and the earlier article by R Lawson (1969) 43 ALJ 52. The problems which arise in the operation of s 51 can be illustrated by the latter two cases. In *WL Thompson Ltd v Robinson (Gunmakers) Ltd* [1955] 1 Ch 177 there was an agreement to sell a new Vanguard car. The day after the contract the buyer told the seller that it would not take delivery. At the time the local demand was insufficient to absorb the supply of new Vanguards. It was held that there was no available market and, therefore, s 51(3) did not apply. The seller could recover the loss of profit on the sale. On the other hand in *Charter v Sullivan* [1957] 2 QB 117 on similar facts involving a Hillman Minx car the seller was able to sell the car to another buyer a week later. The local demand was sufficient to absorb supply. It was held by the English Court of Appeal that the seller could recover only nominal damages. Section 51(2) was applied instead of s 51(3). In most cases, however, s 51(3) will provide a workable rule.

Where special damages could be claimed under the second limb of *Hadley v Baxendale* (see 20.3 below) then they can be claimed by the seller by virtue of s 55 of the Sale of Goods Act 1908. The seller must take reasonable steps to mitigate the loss. Where the goods cannot be immediately resold it may be reasonable to resell in the future market to insulate the seller against future changes in the market value: *Gebruder Metelmann GmbH & Co KG v NBR (London) Ltd* [1984] 1 Lloyd's Rep 614.

20.2 REMEDIES OF BUYER

20.2.1 Action for non-delivery

Under s 52(1) where the seller wrongfully neglects or refuses to deliver the goods to the buyer, the buyer may maintain an action against the seller for damages for non-delivery. In other words the rule is the first limb of *Hadley v Baxendale*. Section 52(3) likewise applies the concept of the available market as a prima facie rule for the purposes of s 52(2). Section 52(3) provides that where there is an available market for the goods in question the measure of damages is prima facie to be ascertained by the difference between the contract price and the market or current price of the goods at the time or times when they ought to have been delivered, or if no time was fixed, then at the time of the refusal to deliver. Similar principles apply mutatis mutandis as apply under 20.1.2.

Of particular relevance here is whether a buyer can recover for loss of profit and damages on a subsale where goods cannot be obtained on the market. It seems that something more than mere knowledge of the fact or likelihood of a subsale is necessary for the case to fall under the second limb of *Hadley v Baxendale* and s 55 of the Sale of Goods Act 1908. Knowledge of special circumstances such as an unusually large profit on the subsale is necessary: *The Arpad* [1934] P 189. In *Kwei Tek Chao v British Traders and Shippers Ltd* [1954] 2 QB 459 Devlin J said that there were cases where the normal rule did not operate because something different was contemplated as where goods were of special manufacture known to be bought for resale and it was known that they could not be bought on the market. In such a case loss of profit was the appropriate measure. Likewise in "chain" contracts where the seller knew not only that the goods were bought for resale but that the buyer could only honour his or her contract in the "chain" by selling those very goods.

20.2.2 Specific performance and injunctions

Section 53(1) of the Sale of Goods Act 1908 provides that in an action for breach of contract to deliver specific or ascertained goods the Court may, if it thinks fit, on the application of the plaintiff, by its judgment direct that the contract shall be performed specifically, without giving the defendant the option of retaining the goods on payment of damages.

It will be rare that such an order will be made since normally damages will be an adequate remedy. However it has been granted in the case of a ship which had unique qualities as far as the buyer was concerned (*Behnke v Bede Shipping Co Ltd* [1927] 1 KB 649) and a mandatory injunction of equivalent effect was granted in respect of a contract to supply oil at the time of the first oil embargo: *Sky Petroleum Ltd v VIP Petroleum Ltd* [1974] 1 All ER 954. The Court of Appeal has made it clear in *Thomas Borthwick and Sons (Australasia) Ltd v South Otago Freezing Co Ltd* [1978] 1 NZLR 538 that the equitable jurisdiction to grant injunctions is preserved.

20.2.3 Damages for breach of warranty

Section 54(1) of the Sale of Goods Act 1908 deals with a breach of warranty by the seller or the situation where the buyer elects or is compelled under s 13(3) to treat a breach of condition as a breach of warranty. The remedies open to the buyer are: (a) to seek an abatement of the price; or (b) to maintain an action for damages.

Section 54(2) applies the first limb of *Hadley v Baxendale* as the measure of damages and s 54(3) lays down a rule in the case of a breach of warranty of quality. Here the loss is prima facie the difference between the value of the goods at the time of delivery and the value they would have had if they had answered to the warranty.

Again special damages may be recoverable under s 55. A buyer has a duty to mitigate his or her loss but he or she is not expected to spend money to render defective goods merchantable in a speculative attempt to sell them: *Hammer and Barrow Ltd v Coca Cola* [1962] NZLR 723, 735. This case involved a sale of 200,000 "champion" yo-yos. A consignment of 85,248 were delivered of which 80% were defective. "Champion" yo-yos were not common in New Zealand. In the absence of a special advertising campaign to arouse "a craze" for yo-yos of this kind the Judge thought that the market would be extremely limited and repair work and alterations to the yo-yos would be spending money on a highly speculative venture.

20.3 INTEREST, SPECIAL DAMAGES AND RECOVERY OF MONEY PAID

Section 55 of the Sale of Goods Act 1908 provides that nothing in the Act shall affect the right of the buyer or the seller to recover interest or special damages in any case where by law interest or special damages may be recoverable, or to recover money paid where the consideration for the payment of it has failed.

Whether a seller or buyer is entitled to interest under a contract of sale depends on the contract. Normally this will only concern the seller who may reserve a right of interest on the unpaid price. At common law and under the Act interest is not payable but in equity interest at a reasonable rate could be charged on a purchaser who obtained possession without paying the purchase price: *Tom the Cheap (WA) Pty Ltd v Allied Leasing Corpn Pty Ltd* [1980] WAR 47. Where judgment is obtained the Court may award interest on the judgment debt: Judicature Act 1908, s 87 (as amended).

We have already discussed special damages above. In essence s 55 preserves the second limb of the rule in *Hadley v Baxendale*.

The latter part of the wording preserves the common law remedy of recovery of money paid when the consideration has failed. This is most relevant in a claim for breach of s 14(a): see *Rowland v Divall* [1923] 2 KB 500. The rule in *Hadley v Baxendale* has no application to such a claim which is a species of quasi contractual claim rather than a claim in contract.

Chapter 21

SPECIAL CONSUMER SALES

SUMMARY

21.1	DOOR TO DOOR SALES
21.2	UNSOLICITED GOODS
21.3	LAYBY SALES
21.4	SALE OF MOTOR VEHICLES

21.1 DOOR TO DOOR SALES

The Door to Door Sales Act 1967 (as amended) regulates agreements for the sale of goods and the provision of services on credit if the agreements are made other than at the appropriate trade premises.

The purpose of the Door to Door Sales Act 1967 was to protect persons who decide to buy goods or services under pressure by salesmen visiting their homes or interviewing them at places where the seller does not normally carry on business. Sales for cash are not affected by the Act. The transactions affected are credit-sale agreements, ie arrangements to pay for services by instalments, hire purchase agreements and hiring agreements which entitle the hirer to apply the rental payments as payment of the purchase price and retain goods as his or her own. Sales of books and ancillary services, eg annotation of law books on credit terms, are also subject to the Act. Door-to-door salesmen found that the provisions of the Act could be circumvented if they offered services at the same time as they persuaded people to buy their goods. However, the Door to Door Sales Amendment Act 1973, s 3, makes credit arrangements and credit sale agreements for the performance of any work or services, whether in addition to the supply of goods or not subject to the provisions of the Act.

The definition of the type of "credit agreement" with which the Act is concerned is found in s 2 of the principal Act, which must be read with the amendments contained in the Schedule to the Door to Door Sales Amendment Act 1973. The Act does not apply if the transaction takes place at the appropriate trade premises, which are now defined in the Schedule to 1973 Amendment Act. The Act does not apply if the salesman called at the buyer's premises on the invitation of the buyer. It does not

277

apply to sales to companies, or to business and other people who are
using the goods for their business or profession. For example, a salesman
selling a tractor on credit terms to a farmer at his or her farm is not subject
to the Act. Sales of perishable goods are not included: s 2. Credit sales of
books or printed matter or any hire purchase agreement or hiring
agreement of any goods where the total price does not exceed $20 and
any other credit sale where the total purchase price does not exceed $40
are excluded from the Act: s 2 (as amended).

The Court is not precluded by any provision in the agreement from
determining whether any statement, representation or warranty, oral or
written, is a term of the agreement unless it considers that it is fair and
reasonable that the provision should be conclusive between the parties:
s 11A. This overlaps with s 4(1) of the Contractual Remedies Act 1979. In
addition there is a general provision against contracting out in s 12. Any
transaction entered into in evasion of the Act is unenforceable except that
any money paid can be recovered: s 12(2).

When the seller or any other person guarantees the goods, the guarantee must be put into writing and a copy of it must be given to the buyer
at the time the agreement is made: ss 4, 5, Door to Door Sales Amendment
Act 1973.

The Act provides a "cooling off" period for the buyer or hirer, in that
the buyer or hirer has seven days clear after the day on which the
transaction took place to cancel the agreement or, if the seller neglects to
comply with the provisions of the Act, then the period for cancellation is
extended to one month: s 7.

To comply with the provisions of the Act the seller must see that the
agreement is in writing signed by all parties and that a copy is given to
the buyer. The agreement shall show the full name and address of each
seller, the amount of the "total cost of credit", the "finance rate" and the
"cash price" as defined in the Credit Contracts Act 1981. The agreement
shall also state the amount of each payment, the number and frequency
of each payment and the dates and places the payments are due. The
agreement and copy must include a notice to the customer setting out his
or her rights if he or she wishes to cancel the agreement, and also a notice
of cancellation: s 6. If the seller fails to comply with the statutory
requirements, he or she cannot enforce the agreement nor any supporting guarantee or security: s 5.

A buyer wishing to terminate the transaction must give written notice
to the seller within the period mentioned above: s 7. He or she need not
take the goods back to the seller's premises, but must, however, make the
goods available for collection at his or her own premises: s 10.

21.2 UNSOLICITED GOODS

A contract of sale of goods requires offer and acceptance. Where goods
are sent unsolicited or invoices are sent in respect of unordered goods it
might be possible for a fraudulent or unscrupulous seller to claim that
there is acceptance by the recipient's failure to act. The Unsolicited Goods
and Services Act 1975 was passed to protect the public from such
activities.

"Unsolicited" for the purposes of s 2(1) of that Act means in relation
to goods sent to any person that they are sent without any prior request
made by him or her or on his or her behalf.

The Act broadly protects the recipient by:

(a) giving him or her or her certain rights (ss 3, 6) and
(b) making certain conduct on the part of the sender a criminal offence (ss 4, 5, 7 and 8).

The rights conferred by s 3 are to treat the goods as an unsolicited gift if:

1   the recipient neither agreed to acquire or return them;
2   the sender does not take possession within three months of the recipient receiving them and the recipient does not unreasonably refuse to permit the sender to do so;
3   the sender does not respond to a notice sent to him or her less than 30 days before the end of the three month period.

The rights conferred by s 6 are in effect immunities. The recipient is not liable to pay for the goods unless he or she has agreed to acquire them or does any act inconsistent with the ownership of the sender. He or she is only liable for loss or injury to the goods due to wilful and unlawful actions during the three month period.

The offences are:

1   to make demands for payment: s 4;
2   to make threats: s 5;
3   to order goods without authority: s 7;
4   to send invoices for unordered goods or services: s 8.

There is a defence to ss 4, 5 and 8 if the accused has reasonable cause to believe he or she has a right to payment, otherwise liability is absolute *Harding v Police* [1981] 2 NZLR 462.

For a useful commentary on the Act see IH Williams (1976) 7 NZULR 190. The Act has still not been brought into force.

21.3 LAYBY SALES

The Layby Sales Act 1971 contains provisions protecting buyers of goods on layby. For the purposes of the Act layby sales are sales of goods at retail where the goods are not to be delivered to the buyer until the buyer has paid the whole or a part of the purchase price, and the whole or part of the purchase price is to be paid by instalments over a fixed or ascertainable period; alternatively the whole or part of the purchase price may be payable during or at the end of a certain period of time. Sales of goods to be delivered by instalments where the whole of the purchase price of each instalment is payable at the time of delivery of the instalment is not a layby sale: s 3(1).

Sales of goods where the price exceeds $1,000 and motor vehicles sold by licensed motor dealers are not subject to the Layby Sales Act 1971: s 4.

Before the Act many layby sale contracts provided that cancellation of the contract by the buyer entailed the loss of deposit and all instalments paid. This type of provision could be grossly unfair where the buyer could not complete his or her contract through loss of employment or illness and the goods were of a type which could be resold without appreciable loss. On the other hand, if the goods were fashion goods which might at the time of default have gone out of fashion, the seller's loss might be substantial. The Layby Sales Act 1971 provides protection for the seller against loss but prevents him or her from getting a windfall at the buyer's expense.

Notwithstanding s 22 of the Sale of Goods Act 1908, the risk in goods sold on layby does not pass from seller to buyer until the property is transferred to the buyer and the goods are delivered to him or her: s 6.

A buyer of goods to the value of more than $10 is entitled on tender of 25 cents to the seller to a statement of his or her position with regard to the goods, setting out the purchase price, the amount paid, the seller's estimate of the value of the goods at the time of notice of cancellation of the sale, and the amount estimated to be due to the seller or buyer, as the case may be: s 7(1) and (5).

Before the Layby Sales Act 1971 came into force, a seller normally retained both the possession and property in goods bought by this method. But if the contract provided for property passing to the buyer before delivery, he or she also had to carry the risk in goods over which he or she had no control. A particular risk the buyer had to carry could well arise where the seller, being a company, was wound up or, being an individual, was adjudicated bankrupt. As the goods sold on layby were the property of the insolvent seller they passed to the liquidator or the Official Assignee, as the case might be. This meant that the layby buyer's only right was to prove as an unsecured creditor, with the probable result that he or she would receive only a small percentage of what he or she had paid, having lost the right to pay off and receive the goods he or she thought he or she had bought. Had the property in the goods passed to the buyer as in an ordinary instalment sale he or she would, as an owner of the goods, have had precedence over the interests of both secured and unsecured creditors.

Under the Act except where the price is $5 or less the buyer may at any time before the full purchase price is paid and irrespective of the seller being adjudicated bankrupt or going into receivership cancel the sale by giving written or oral notice to that effect: s 8. Section 9 of the Act sets out the rights of the seller and buyer on cancellation. Where there has been a cancellation the retail value of generic goods sold on layby shall be deemed to be the same as when they were purchased; if the goods were specific the retail value remains unchanged if cancellation occurs within one month – no account is taken of possible deterioration.

Under s 10 if the seller is adjudicated bankrupt or goes into receivership or liquidation a buyer on layby is entitled, whether the goods have been appropriated to the sale or not, to pay the balance owing and get delivery of the goods. If there are insufficient goods available to fulfil the contracts with the buyers, the earlier buyers shall have priority over the later buyers.

A buyer who has failed to make any payment to the seller in the three months preceding the filing of the petition in bankruptcy, the commencement of winding up or the appointment of a receiver, shall not be entitled to complete his or her purchase as set out above. The same restriction applies to officers or employees of the seller and to their spouses.

Layby buyers who, being unable to complete their purchases owing to a shortage of goods on the bankruptcy, receivership or liquidation of the seller are entitled to a refund from the seller, are treated as preferential creditors over all other secured creditors and over creditors secured by a floating charge: s 11.

No provision in the agreement itself can nullify the buyer's rights under the Act: s 13.

For a useful note on the Act see RG Lawson (1972) 5 NZULR 181.

21.4 SALE OF MOTOR VEHICLES

Contracts of sale of motor vehicles by a motor vehicle dealer fall within the Motor Vehicle Dealers Act 1975 as amended. This Act was passed to promote and protect the interests of consumers. It extends not only to sale of goods but also contracts of exchange, leases for sale arrangements and hire purchase agreements.

The legislation provides for the licensing of motor vehicle dealers and setting up of the Motor Vehicle Dealers Licensing Board and Institute. Dealers are required to be licensed by the Board and to be members of the Institute. A fidelity guarantee fund is set up by s 30 to which dealers must contribute. Claims by a buyer can be made against the fund in the event of default by a dealer.

An elaborate system of duties, registration of salesmen and regulation of dealings is prescribed by Parts IV, V, VI and VII. Part VII is most relevant for our purposes. Section 89(1)(a) implies a condition that the seller of a new or secondhand vehicle is the true owner or is duly authorised by power of attorney from him or her to sell, exchange or lease the motor vehicle. This is a stronger obligation than s 14(a) of the Sale of Goods Act 1908. Section 89(1)(b) provides that the vehicle will be free from any charge or encumbrance in favour of a third party unless it has been disclosed. Section 90 specifies the particulars which must be displayed in the case of the sale of secondhand vehicles and s 91 with odometer readings. Section 92 then divides second hand vehicles into four categories A, B, C and D based on age and odometer readings and s 93 specifies the obligations of quality which apply to non trade transactions. Different obligations apply to the different categories of vehicles.

Complaints against a licensed dealer can be made via the Institute to the Motor Vehicles' Disputes Tribunal which in the event of default by the dealer can pay compensation out of the fidelity fund or rescind the contract: s 100. However under s 98(1) the Disputes Tribunal is limited to a total sum in dispute not exceeding $3,000 or to a larger sum when both parties to the dispute consent in writing. See also ss 100(1A) and 101A(2).

Section 107(1) provides that the provisions of Part VII shall have effect notwithstanding any provision to the contrary in any contract, sale or other agreement. Section 107(2) provides that ss 14 and 56 of the Sale of Goods Act 1908 and s 11(a) of the Hire Purchase Act 1971 are to be read subject to the provisions of Part VII of this Act. Section 108 expressly provides that disputes involving ss 14-16 of the Sale of Goods Act 1908 or ss 11-13 of the Hire Purchase Act 1971 may be referred to the Disputes Tribunal by both parties by agreement in writing. Appeals lie from the Disputes Tribunal to the District Court on the grounds set out in s 133(1). The decision of a District Court Judge is then final: s 133(2).

Where matters have been decided by the Disputes Tribunal then, subject to the right of appeal, this gives rise to res judicata: *Gray v Phillips Mills Ltd* (1983) 2 DCR 105.

Sale of motor vehicles is now subject to the consumer protection provisions of the Motor Vehicle Securities Act 1989. This is described in Chapter 38, post.

Chapter 22

EXPORT TRADE CONTRACTS

SUMMARY

22.1   EXPORT SALES
22.2   THE APPLICABLE LAW
22.3   TYPES OF EXPORT TRADE SALE CONTRACTS
22.4   INTERNATIONAL CONVENTIONS ON UNIFORM LAWS

22.1 EXPORT SALES

For the most part the Sale of Goods Act 1908 deals with sales of goods to be performed in New Zealand. However the Act is capable of applying to export and import sales. In such cases the provisions of the Act will often be negatived or varied by usage and the express terms of standard form documents. Some of the usages and practices have developed because of the length of time of sea voyages and the interest of both seller and buyer in dealing with the commercial documents as if they were the goods themselves prior to arrival at the destination. The principal document for this purpose has traditionally been the bill of lading which acts as a receipt by the carrier, proof of the contract of affreightment and a document of title in respect of the goods.

22.2 THE APPLICABLE LAW

It is important for both exporter and importer of goods to know by what system of law the contract is governed. Any complicated issue will, of course, need to be submitted for professional opinion. However, the basic rule in relation to contracts is that the *proper law* of the contract is paramount in determining the creation, validity and effect of a contractual obligation. The term "proper law" of the contract means the system of law by which the parties intend the contract to be governed, or, where their intention is neither expressed nor to be inferred from the circumstances, the system of law with which the transaction has its closest and most real connection: *Mount Albert Borough Council v Australasian Temperance and General Mutual Life Assurance Society Ltd* [1938] AC 224 (PC).

Where the parties expressly select the law by which their contract is to be governed, and this selection is bona fide and legal and not contrary to public policy, the Court will determine the parties' rights and obligations in accordance with this proper law: *Vita Food Products Inc v Unus Shipping Co Ltd* [1939] AC 277 (PC), *Golden Acres Ltd v Queensland Estates Pty Ltd* [1969] Qd R 378.

Where there is no express choice of the proper law the Court is faced with the task of ascertaining by what law the parties' rights and obligations are to be determined. The Court may decide that there is an implied or inferred choice of law in the parties' contract; for example, in accordance with the principle *qui elegit judicem elegit jus*, the selection of a particular Court or arbitration centre as the only forum to which disputes arising out of the contract may be submitted, gives rise to a very strong inference that the law administered by that Court or arbitrator is intended to be applied to the contract: *Compagnie d'Armement Maritime SA v Compagnie Tunisienne de Navigation SA* [1971] AC 572.

When the intention of the parties to a contract with regard to the law applicable to it is not expressed and cannot be inferred from the circumstances, the contract is governed by the system of law with which the transaction has its closest and most real connection: *Monterosso Shipping Corp v International Transport Workers Federation* [1982] 3 All ER 841. In determining the proper law in this situation all the relevant facts such as the place where the contract was made, the nationalities of the parties, where performance was to take place, the currency stipulated for payment under the contract and the form of the contract must be weighed in the balance: *Amin Rasheed Shipping Corp v Kuwait Insurarce Co; The Al Wahab* [1984] AC 50; [1983] 1 All ER 873.

22.3 TYPES OF EXPORT TRADE SALE CONTRACTS

In international sale of goods specialist terms of trade and usage have developed which in the past often differed from place to place. Also contracts necessarily vary according to the wishes of the parties to them. To standardise usage and promote uniformity of law the International Chamber of Commerce has published "Incoterms", International Rules for the Interpretation of Trade Terms. These only apply if the parties incorporate them into their contract but in practice they are often adopted. The following is a list of special trade terms:

ex works (the seller's works, factory or warehouse, where the goods are
    situate);
for/fot (free on rail/free on truck; named departure point);
fas (free alongside; named port of shipment);
fob (free on board; named port of shipment);
c & f (cost and freight; named port of destination);
cif (cost, insurance and freight; named port of destination);
ex ship (named port of destination);
ex quay (duty paid by the seller or duty on buyer's account, according to the
    agreement of the parties);
delivered at frontier (named place of delivery at frontier; this clause can only
    be used in terrestrial sales and the two countries separated by the frontier
    should be indicated);
delivered duty paid (named place of destination in the country of importation);

fob airport (named airport of departure);
free carrier (named point);
freight carriage paid to (named point of destination)
freight carriage and insurance paid to (named point of destination).

The last three are to be used for container transport. "Free carrier" equates with fob, "freight/carriage paid to" to c & f, and "freight/carriage and insurance paid to" to cif. See generally *Schmitthoff's Export Trade* (9 ed) ch 2. Of these terms the most important are cif, fob and ex ship.

22.3.1 Cif contracts

Cif stands for cost, insurance and freight. A cif contract is a contract of sale of goods performed by the seller by delivery of the *shipping documents* to the buyer. That does not mean, however, that it is a sale of documents, not goods. "It contemplates the transfer of actual goods in the normal course, but if the goods are lost, the insurance policy and the bill of lading contract – that is the rights under them – are to be taken to be, in a business sense, the equivalent of the goods": per Lord Wright in *Ross T Smyth and Co Ltd v T D Bailey Son & Co* [1940] 3 All ER 60, 70. The normal shipping documents are:

(a) the bill of lading, or way-bill, evidencing the contract of carriage by sea;

(b) the insurance policy or certificate, evidencing the contract of marine insurance; and

(c) the invoice, evidencing the contract of sale: *Johnson v Taylor Bros & Co Ltd* [1920] AC 144, 155. See also *Cardale & Scott v Clarke & Co* [1922] NZLR 83, 86 per Salmond J.

Thus in *Smyth's* case at 67-8 Lord Wright described the cif contract in these terms:

The contract in question here is of a type familiar in commerce, and is described as a cif contract. The initials indicate that the price is to include cost insurance and freight. It is a type of contract which is more widely and more frequently in use than any other contract used for purposes of sea-borne commerce. An enormous number of transactions, in value amounting to untold sums, are carried out every year under cif contracts. The essential characteristics of this contract have often been described. The seller has to ship or acquire after that shipment the contract goods, as to which, if unascertained, he is generally required to give a notice of appropriation. On or after shipment, he has to obtain proper bills of lading and proper policies of insurance. He fulfils his contracts by transferring the bills of lading and the policies to the buyer. As a general rule, he does so only against payment of the price, less the freight which the buyer has to pay. In the invoice which accompanies the tender of the documents on the "prompt" – that is, the date fixed for payment – the freight is deducted, for this reason. In this course of business, the general property remains in the seller until he transfers the bill of lading. . . .

In *Bignell & Holmes v Partridge & Co (NZ) Ltd* [1924] NZLR 769 Hosking J said in the Court of Appeal that it was not essential in order to produce the effects of a cif contract that it should be so headed or described or that "those fateful initial letters" should be used if it was clear that the parties intended that some or all of the incidents corresponding to those where the contract was strictly cif were employed.

The cif price includes the freight charges and the insurance premium. The cost of unloading the goods on arrival and the import duties have to be borne by the buyer. Under a cif contract, it is not material whether the goods arrive safely at the port of destination. If they are lost or damaged in transit, the marine insurance policy should cover the loss or damage and, by virtue of the transfer of the bill of lading and the insurance policy to the buyer, the buyer has direct contractual claims against the shipowner or the insurer.

The duties of a seller under a cif contract are, therefore:

1   To ship at the port of shipment goods of the contract description or buy goods already shipped within the agreed time.
2   To procure a contract of carriage by sea, under which the goods will be delivered to the destination contemplated by the contract on usual terms.
3   To arrange for an insurance upon the terms current in the trade which will be available for the benefit of the buyer.
4   To make out an invoice for the goods debiting the buyer with the agreed price.
5   To tender the bill of lading, the policy or certificate of insurance and the invoice to the buyer within a reasonable time after shipment so that the buyer may obtain delivery of the goods, if they arrive, or recover for their loss, if they are lost on the voyage: see Hamilton J in *Biddell Bros v E Clemens Horst Co* [1911] 1 KB 214, 220 and Lord Atkinson in *Johnson v Taylor Bros & Co Ltd* [1920] AC 144, 155.

The bill of lading must be a "clean" bill ie free from any indorsement qualifying the statement "shipped in good order and condition".

The bill of lading tendered must correctly state the date of shipment, otherwise the buyer can reject the goods: *Finlay v Kwik Hoo Tong* [1929] 1 KB 400. This is because where a time of shipment is specified it is usually construed as a condition and not merely a warranty: *Boyes v Shand* (1877) 2 App Cas 455 (HL).

Where no time is stated the goods must be shipped within a reasonable time: *Thomas Borthwick (Glasgow) Ltd v Bunge and Co Ltd* [1969] 1 Lloyd's Rep 17. The goods must be shipped by the usual route unless otherwise agreed: *Postlethwaite v Freeland* (1880) 5 App Cas 599, 616 (HL).

Under a cif contract the buyer has a right to reject the documents and also a right to reject the goods. These two rights are quite separate. This was very clearly stated by Devlin J in the leading case of *Kwei Tek Chao v British Traders and Shippers Ltd* [1954] 2 QB 459. In that case BTS sold bleaching chemicals to K, shipment to be made not later than October 31. The goods arrived at the quay on October 31 but were in fact shipped on November 3. The date of shipment shown on the bill of lading was forged to show a shipment in October, but BTS was ignorant of and not a party to the forgery. In ignorance of the forgery K paid the price and received the documents, but before the goods arrived K discovered it. K took delivery, but as the market had fallen was unable to sell the goods.

Devlin J held that the bill of lading was not a nullity as the forgery did not go to the heart of the contract but merely a limb; but K, although he had not rejected the documents, still had a separate right to reject the goods and could recover the difference between the contract price and the market price. Cf *International Ore & Fertilizer Corporation v East Coast Fertiliser Co Ltd* [1987] 1 NZLR 9 (CA).

If the buyer accepts documents which disclose that the goods were not shipped in conformity with the contract he or she is estopped from later trying to reject them but he or she can still reject the goods if they fail to comply with the contract. In *Panchaud Freres SA v Etablissements General Grain Co* [1970] 1 Lloyd's Rep 53 P sold some Brazilian maize to E. The contract was cif Antwerp and provided that shipment was to take place "during the period of June/July 1965" and that the bill of lading was to be considered "proof of date of shipment in the absence of evidence to the contrary". The goods were, in fact, shipped on August 1 to 12, 1965, but the bill of lading was backdated and gave as the date of shipment July 31, 1965. However, a certificate of quantity issued by a superintendent company which supervised the loading in Brazil stated that they had drawn samples on August 10 to 12, 1965, and this certificate was tendered together with the bill of lading. The English Court of Appeal held that by accepting the documents and paying for them the buyer was aware that the goods were shipped later than provided in the contract and was precluded afterwards from complaining of the late shipment or the defect in the bill of lading.

Normally only a bill of lading evidencing the contract of shipment must be handed over and a delivery order or mate's receipt will not suffice: *Re Denbigh, Cowan and Co and R Atcherley and Co* (1921) 90 LJKB 836 (CA). It is, however, common in trans-Tasman trade to issue an ocean way-bill rather than a bill of lading. The buyer has less rights under an ocean way-bill which merely has contractual force and is not a document of title. It is non negotiable. For a useful article comparing bills of lading and ocean way-bills see W Tetley QC (1983) 14 *Journal of Maritime Law and Commerce* 465.

The duties of the buyer are:

(a) to pay the price, less any freight charges, on delivery of the documents. The buyer cannot defer payment until after he or she has inspected the goods (*Clemens Horst Co v Biddell Bros* [1912] AC 18);

(b) to pay the cost of unloading at the port of destination according to the bill of lading; and

(c) to pay all import duties and wharfage charges, if any.

Property in the goods normally passes with the transfer of the bill of lading but risk passes with shipment. Section 22 of the Sale of Goods Act 1908 does not apply to cif contracts. During the voyage, therefore, the goods are at the risk of the buyer. This risk will usually be covered by the insurance, but if the goods are lost from a peril not covered by the ordinary policy of insurance current in trade, the buyer must nevertheless pay the full price on delivery of the documents: *C Groom Ltd v Barber* [1915] 1 KB 316. As Salmond J said in *Cardale & Scott v Clarke & Co* [1922] NZLR 83 at 86, whether the goods arrived at their destination or go to the bottom of the sea is a matter with which the seller is in no way concerned.

In *Manbre Co v Corn Products Co* [1919] 1 KB 198 it was held that even if the seller knows that the goods have been lost at the time the shipping documents are tendered, the seller can still compel the buyer to take and pay for them.

The property passes when the documents are accepted by the buyer, but "what the buyer obtains, when the title under the documents is given to him, is the property in the goods, subject to the conditions that they revest if upon examination he finds them to be not in accordance with the contract": per Devlin J obiter in *Kwei Tek Chao v British Traders and Shippers Ltd* [1954] 2 QB 459, 487. If, however, the goods are not ascertained at the time the documents are taken up no property in the goods will pass until the goods become ascertained. Ascertainment can take place by exhaustion. Thus where goods sold formed part of a bulk cargo and the remainder of the bulk cargo was unloaded in Rotterdam and Hamburg ascertainment by exhaustion took place in Hamburg and property then passed to the buyer: *The Elafi* [1982] 1 All ER 208.

Where risk but not property has passed to the buyer at the time of the damage, he or she cannot maintain an action for the tort of negligence against a third party: *Leigh and Sillivan Ltd v Aliakmon Shipping Co Ltd* [1986] AC 785 (HL).

In a c & f contract the seller is obliged to arrange for the carriage of the goods to the place of destination and to pay the freight, but he need not insure the goods.

22.3.2 Fob contracts

Under an fob contract it is the duty of the seller to deliver the goods over the ship's rail at the port of shipment on board the ship named by the buyer. The cost of sea freight and marine insurance has to be borne by the buyer.

There are two types of fob contracts, the strict or classic type and fob contract providing for additional services. Under the strict fob contract the arrangements for shipment and insurance are made by the buyer direct. The buyer is a party to the contracts of carriage by sea and marine insurance. Under this type of contract the buyer has to name to the seller an effective ship and the port of shipment, ie a ship ready, willing and able to carry the goods away from the port of shipment within the stipulated shipping time. This is the condition precedent to the seller's duty to bring the goods or make them available for loading at the port of shipment: *Sutherland v Allhusen* (1886) 11 LT 666. If the buyer fails to nominate an effective ship, the seller cannot make such nomination. In this case the seller's remedy is an action for damages for non-acceptance of the goods but not an action for the price: *Colley v Overseas Exporters* [1921] 3 KB 302.

In an fob contract with additional services the parties have agreed that the arrangements for the carriage by sea and insurance shall be made by the seller, but for and on behalf of the buyer and for his or her account: see *Schmitthoff's Export Trade* (9 ed) 16 et seq, on which this is based. In such a case the seller is entitled to a commission for the additional services unless otherwise agreed. In this kind of case the buyer need not name an effective ship.

In both types of fob contract the cost of putting the goods on board ship has to be borne by the seller. Delivery is complete when the goods are put on board ship. The risk under s 22(1) of the Sale of Goods Act 1908 passes to the buyer when the seller has placed the goods safely on board ship whether they are specific or unascertained and even though property has not yet passed. The seller should give notice of the shipment to the buyer so as to enable the buyer to insure. If the seller fails to do this, the goods will be at his or her risk: *Wimble Sons and Co v Rosenberg and Sons* [1931] 3 KB 743. In that case it was held by a majority of the English Court of Appeal that s 34(3) of the Sale of Goods Act 1908 applied to an fob contract. See also *May v Newman* [1923] NZLR 1328,1332. It should be noted that the section does not apply to a cif contract.

Unless otherwise agreed, the property passes to the buyer when the goods are placed on board ship: *Meredith v Winstone Ltd* (1914) 33 NZLR 232.

In *Carlos Federspiel and Co SA v Charles Twigg and Co Ltd* [1957] 1 Lloyd's Rep 240 a Costa Rican buyer bought from an English company a number of bicycles "fob UK port" and paid the purchase price in advance. The bicycles were packed into cases, which were marked with the buyer's name and port of destination and registered for shipment in a named ship that was to load them at Liverpool. The cases containing the bicycles had not been sent to the port when a receiver and manager was appointed for the sellers. It was held that property in the goods had not passed to the buyer.

It is settled law that even under an fob contract there is a right of rejection upon delivery if proper grounds for rejection exist and there is no general law that the place of shipment is the place of inspection: *Pacific Produce Co Ltd v Franklin Co-operative Growers Ltd (in liq)* [1968] NZLR 521.

There is no general rule that in the case of an fob contract for sale of goods in respect of which export restrictions exist that there is an obligation on the buyer to obtain an export licence which will be implied into the contract in the absence of express stipulation between the parties. Each case depends on the contract and the surrounding circumstances of the case: *AV Pound and Co Ltd v MW Hardy and Co Inc* [1956] AC 588.

22.3.3 Ex ship contracts

Under an ex ship or arrival contract the seller must procure that the goods themselves arrive at the place of destination and the contract is not performed with the shipping documents. In deciding whether a particular contract is a cif contract or an ex ship contract, regard must be had to the intention of the parties, as evidenced in their agreement and the description of the contract used by the parties is not decisive.

Thus in *Comptoir d'Achat etc v Luis de Ridder Ltd* [1949] AC 293 a Belgian company bought 500 tons of rye from an Argentine company on April 24 1940. The terms were cif Antwerp. The goods were part of a larger consignment, and the documents tendered to the buyer included a delivery order addressed to the seller's agents in Antwerp and instructing them to release 500 tons to the buyer. The buyer paid against the documents, but the ship carrying the goods was diverted to Lisbon because Antwerp had fallen into German hands. At Lisbon the goods were sold for a price less than the buyer had paid. It was held by the House of Lords that the contract which was not expressed in readily intelligible terms was not in fact a cif contract although described as such but was a contract to deliver at Antwerp. Since there was a frustration of the adventure the consideration had totally failed and the buyer could recover the money paid.

The duties of the seller under an ex ship contract are:

(a) to deliver the goods to the buyer from a ship which has arrived at the port of delivery;
(b) to pay the freight or otherwise discharge the shipowner's lien, and
(c) to furnish the buyer with a delivery order, or some other effectual direction to the ship to deliver.

In this case the documents do not take the place of the goods. The property in the goods and the risk do not pass until the goods are over the ship's rail at the port of delivery. There is no obligation on the seller to effect an insurance on the buyer's behalf: *Yangtsze Insurance Association v Lukmanjee* [1918] AC 585. Thus s 34 of the Sale of Goods Act 1908 has no application.

22.4 INTERNATIONAL CONVENTIONS ON UNIFORM LAWS

It is clearly desirable that the laws which different states apply to the international sale of goods should be uniform as far as is possible. An early attempt at uniformity was the approval by a diplomatic conference at the Hague in 1964 of two conventions, on the International Sale of Goods and the formation of Contracts for the International Sale of Goods. In 1980 at Vienna the United Nations adopted a convention on Contracts for the International Sale of Goods. This is intended to supersede the Hague Conventions and is more comprehensive in scope. The Vienna Convention came into force in 1988 after ten states (including the United States and Australia) had either acceded to it or ratified it. As of 1991 New Zealand had neither implemented the Hague Conventions nor bound itself to the Vienna Convention.

Chapter 23

BAILMENT AND CARRIAGE OF GOODS

SUMMARY

23.1   DEFINITION
23.2   POSSESSION
23.3   BAILEE'S DUTY
23.4   BAILOR'S DUTY
23.5   SUB-BAILMENTS
23.6   CARRIAGE OF GOODS

23.1 DEFINITION

> Bailment eludes precise definition because the term covers a host of legal relationships which have as a common denominator only that one is in possession of another's chattel. Possession is the salient feature, but the forms and incidents of bailment are miscellaneous.
>
> *Crossley Vaines' Personal Property* (5 ed, 1973) 70.

A bailment, therefore, arises whenever one person (the bailee) knowingly and willingly comes into possession of goods belonging to another person (the bailor). The ownership of the chattels bailed stays with the bailor, but the bailee has possession: see *Motor Mart Ltd v Webb* [1958] NZLR 773, 780-785. Bailments are a very common everyday occurrence. For example, if a person consigns goods to some destination by way of New Zealand Rail, or lends a watch to a friend, or leaves his or her car at a garage for repairs, such a person has bailed his or her goods, watch, or car, as bailor. Alternatively if a person borrows a library book or hires skis or purchases a car pursuant to a hire purchase agreement such a person is a bailee of the book, skis, or car, as the case may be.

In *Coggs v Bernard* (1703) 2 Ld Raym 909; 92 ER 107, Sir John Holt CJ identified six categories of bailment from Roman law, namely, gratuitous loans, gratuitous safekeeping, gratuitous bailment of chattels for something to be done to them, bailment of chattels for reward for something to be done to them, pledge of chattels as security for moneys advanced, and hire. However, it is doubtful whether any value is derived from such classification today and as Turner J pointed out in *Motor Mart Ltd v Webb* [1958] NZLR 773, 784, the transaction of bailment is by no means a closed set and the learned Judge declined to assume that "under the pressures and stresses of modern legal necessity, some new mutation may not have burst into flower, of a quality to startle the author of the Institutes were he or she privileged to behold it".

A bailment arises either by virtue of a relationship of possession or by virtue of contract between the parties. Where bailment arises by contract, the rights and remedies that arise at common law may be qualified and/or excluded by the terms of the contract and the contract of bailment may be subject to certain statutory controls; for example, the Hire Purchase Act 1971. However, not all bailments are based on contracts. Diplock LJ observed in *Morris v C W Martin and Sons Ltd* [1966] 1 QB 716, 731 that:

> The legal relationship of bailor and bailee of a chattel can exist independently of any contract, for the legal concept of bailment as creating a relationship which gives rise to duties owed by a bailee to a bailor is derived from Roman law and is older in our common law than the legal concept of parol contract as giving rise to legal duties owed by one party to the other party thereto.

So in *Walker v Watson* [1974] 2 NZLR 175 a gratuitous loan of a motorcar, where there was no element of contract present nor consideration moving from the bailee to the bailor, was held to be a bailment. The bailee assumed a duty to exercise reasonable care of the chattel entrusted to her custody. See also *Gilchrist Watt and Sanderson Pty Ltd v York Products Pty Ltd* [1970] 1 WLR 1262 (PC). Therefore there does not have to be a contractual relationship between the parties for one to become the bailee of the other and it is perhaps best to regard bailment as a transaction *sui generis*.

23.2 POSSESSION

23.2.1 Bailment vs licences

An essential element of bailment is the transfer of possession. Possession is an extremely difficult term to define but it is clear that something more than mere custody is required before a person can be said to be in possession of goods for purposes of a bailment. Whether the relationship between parties is that of bailor and bailee or only that of licensor and licensee depends upon the intention of the parties as ascertained from all the circumstances. Consider the following cases.

In *Ashby v Tolhurst* [1937] 2 KB 242 the plaintiff had parked his car on land owned by the defendant, paid one shilling to an attendant and was issued with a ticket. When the plaintiff returned, the attendant told him that he had just given the car to the plaintiff's "friend". The car was never recovered. The ticket was headed "Car Park ticket" and stated "The proprietors do not take any responsibility for the safe custody of any cars or articles there, nor for any damage to the cars or articles however caused, nor for any injuries to any persons, all cars being left in all respects entirely at their owner's risk". It was held by the Court of Appeal that the relationship between the parties was that of licensee and licensor and not that of bailee and bailor because there was no transfer of possession from the plaintiff. Sir Wilfrid Greene MR emphasised that the car park ticket itself was of crucial importance as this document revealed that a right to park the car had been given but that the owner of the car is not thereby to have claims against the proprietors of the car park. Moreover, Romer LJ said at p 255:

> It is true that, if the car had been left there for any particular purpose that required that the defendants should have possession of the car, a delivery would rightly be inferred. If, for instance, the car had been left at the car park for the purpose . . . of being driven to some other place or indeed for the purposes of safe custody, delivery of the car, although not actually made, would readily be inferred. But it is perfectly plain in this case that the car was not delivered to the defendant for safe custody.

Another useful example is *Tinsley v Dudley* [1951] 2 KB 18. In this case the owner drove his motorcycle into a covered yard of a public house. There was no attendant to look after vehicles in the yard and no charge was paid. The motorcycle was stolen. It was held that there was no bailment as the motorcycle had not been delivered into the possession of the defendant who was unaware that it had been brought onto his or her premises. No transfer of possession, actual or symbolical had occurred.

Conversely in *Shorters Parking Station Ltd v Johnson* [1963] NZLR 135, an arrangement between a garage proprietor and vehicle owner was held to constitute a bailment. The respondent had an arrangement with the appellant whereby the respondent's car, used by an employee, was garaged during business hours on the appellant's premises. This arrangement had subsisted for about five years and £ 5 per month was charged. When the car was brought into the building the driver either parked it in a position indicated by an attendant employed by the appellant or left it for the attendant to park, in each case the key being left in the car so that it could be moved if necessary. The car was stolen from the appellant's premises as a result of negligence on the part of the appellant's employees in allowing an unauthorised person to remove it. Hardie Boys J held, at p 138:

> Here delivery over of possession was much more than symbolical; it was actual, it was for safe custody; it was a bailment for reward. The intention of both parties to the contract is available from a long course of conduct to show that those were the elements of their bargain and that it was not a matter of mere license to occupy space.

See also *Ulltzen v Nicols* [1894] 1 QB 92; *Wellington Racing Club v Symons* [1923] NZLR 1; *Sydney City Council v West* (1965) 114 CLR 481.

Therefore it is a question of fact whether in all the circumstances the parties intended a bailment. The intention of the parties may be quite plain from the documents, if any, that evidence their transaction, or may be deduced from the surrounding circumstances. Factors which may be of significance in inferring the parties' intention are as follows:

1   Whether the means of access or control over the chattel has passed; the delivery of keys to a vehicle may amount to a symbolical delivery of possession.

2   The procedures in question may be significant; for example, in *Sydney City Council v West* (1965) 114 CLR 481, 486, a card had to

be presented to an attendant "to obtain release" of a vehicle and had to be presented to an attendant "for time stamping and payment" before taking delivery of the vehicle.

3   The physical geography of the premises may be significant as a delivery over of possession for safe custody will more readily be inferred where the layout is conducive to security: see *Wellington Racing Club v Symons* [1923] NZLR 1, 2; *Ashby v Tolhurst* [1937] 2 KB 242, 249.

These are only three of the many factors that may have an impact in the decision as whether a bailment or licence was created. The intention of the parties must be ascertained from all the circumstances of the particular case. Generally, see Palmer *Bailment* (1979), pp 195-213.

23.2.2 Common intention that possession shall pass

The most common method whereby possession passes is delivery. For possession to pass by delivery, however, there must be a receipt and acceptance and a common intention that possession shall pass, as a person does not become a bailee against his or her will: *Crossley Vaines' Personal Property* (5 ed 1973), p 83. For example, in *Neuwith v Over Darwen Industrial Co-operative Society* (1894) 63 LJQB 290 a committee hired the defendant's concert hall for an evening performance. No mention was made of rehearsals but the orchestra rehearsed in the hall on the same afternoon without objection. After the rehearsal, Neuwith, one of the players, left his musical instrument in a small room off the hall. The caretaker, who had no notice of this, was obliged to move the instrument in order to light the gas and in so doing damaged it. It was held that there was no bailment and no liability. But in *Southland Hospital Board v Perkins Estate* [1986] 1 NZLR 373 it was held that the hospital board, having accepted a patient with his or her possessions into a hospital, had a responsibility as bailee to take due care of those possessions in the event of the patient's death, even though the hospital board may have had no actual intention to act as bailee.

The proposition that a person cannot become a bailee against his or her will means that where goods are sent without request or arrangement, by one person to another, who does not hold himself or herself out to receive them, the person to whom they are sent is under no liability to the sender for their safe custody or protection. Of course, the recipient must refrain from causing intentional damage to the goods and must not prevent the sender from recovering the goods. The Unsolicited Goods and Services Act 1975 provides that the recipient of unsolicited goods is not liable to make any payment for such goods unless the recipient agrees to acquire them or does any act in relation to them which is inconsistent with the ownership of the seller, or liable for any loss or injury to the goods other than loss or injury arising from his or her wilful and unlawful disposal, destruction or damage: s 6. The recipient of unsolicited goods may deal with those goods as if they were an unconditional gift once the time periods for the recovery of such goods by the sender have expired: s 3. Generally, see Williams (1976) 7 NZULR 192.

In the case of a casual finding of a lost chattel in a public place there is no obligation on the finder to take charge of it at all. If, however, the finder actually takes it into his or her custody, and is somehow negligent and causes loss or damage to the goods, the finder may be liable for the damage caused. Thus in *Helson v McKenzies (Cuba Street) Ltd* [1950] NZLR 878 the Court of Appeal held that the finder of a handbag, having voluntarily assumed possession or custody of it, thereby incurred responsibility to deliver it to its true owner. The finder had failed adequately to discharge this responsibility in that the handbag had been delivered to a person who claimed it, but who was not the true owner, after a perfunctory investigation unattended by any attempt to investigate the claimant's right by referring to the handbag's contents. Again, the finder was under no obligation to assume custody of the handbag in question, but having voluntarily done so, a duty to take reasonable care arose. Generally, see *Parker v British Airways Board* [1982] 2 WLR 503 (CA).

23.2.3 Redelivery of identical goods

If the transaction is such that the identical goods delivered are to be returned to the bailor or are to be delivered to his or her nominee, the contract is one of bailment, but if the goods are delivered on a contract for a money consideration or for some other consideration and the identical goods are not to be returned either in original or in altered form the transaction is a sale: *Chapman Bros v Verco Bros and Co Ltd* (1933) 49 CLR 306, 316; cf *Harding v Commissioner of Inland Revenue* [1977] 1 NZLR 337. Provided the identical subject matter is to be redelivered, either as it stood or in altered form, the transaction is one of bailment. In the *Chapman* case farmers delivered unmarked bags of wheat to a wheat merchant. The terms of the transaction required the merchant to buy and pay for wheat on request by the farmer, or failing such a request, on a specified date, or to return an equal quantity of wheat of the same type; but there was no obligation to return the identical bags. Although the contract referred to the wheat merchant as "storers" it was held by the High Court of Australia that the transaction was necessarily one of sale as the property in the wheat passed to the merchant on delivery. It would have been a bailment if the identical wheat had to be returned even if it had been ground into flour; that is, identical subject matter in altered form, as is the case with a motorcar returned by a garage after repairs.

23.3 BAILEE'S DUTY

23.3.1 The duty is to take reasonable care in the circumstances

The most common question that arises is the liability of the bailee. What standard of care must the bailee exercise in relation to the bailed chattels? In *Coggs v Bernard* (1703) 1 Ld Raym 909; 92 ER 107, Sir John Holt CJ assessed the degree of care required with reference to the kinds of bailment which he or she derived from the Roman law. For example, where a bailment is for the benefit of both parties, such as hire, the bailee is liable for ordinary negligence; where the bailment is for the benefit of the bailor alone, such as deposit without reward, the bailee is liable only for gross negligence; and, where it is for the benefit of the bailee alone, such as the gratuitous loan of goods, the bailee is liable even for slight negligence. The application of these varying standards of care occasioned much difficulty, and today the terms "ordinary", "gross" and "slight" have been abandoned in favour of the broader proposition that the bailee is bound to take reasonable care of the bailor's goods according to all the circumstances or the situation. As Ormerod LJ stated in *Houghland v R R Low (Luxury Coaches) Ltd* [1962] 1 QB 694, 698:

> For my part, I have always found some difficulty in understanding just what was "gross negligence", because it appears to me that the standard of care required in a case of bailment, or any other type of case, is the standard demanded by the circumstances of that particular case. It seems to me that to try and put a bailment, for instance, into a watertight compartment – such as gratuitous bailment on the one hand, and bailment for reward on the other – is to overlook the fact that there might well be an infinite variety of cases, which might come into one or the other category. The question that we have to consider in a case of this kind, if it is necessary to consider negligence, is whether in the circumstances of this particular case a sufficient standard of care has been observed by the defendants or their servants.

So now the duty of care required of the bailee depends upon the circumstances of the case.

While recognising that factual situations are as innumerable as they are diverse the following two examples illustrate the scope of the standard of care expected of a bailee.

In *Nairn Aviation Ltd v Johnston* (unreported, High Court, Greymouth, A 19/81, 26 June 1981) the facts were as follows. A Cessna aircraft, flown by the defendant as a student pilot undergoing instruction from the plaintiff company as owner of the plane, crashed and was a total "write-off". The defendant was practising a forced simulated landing exercise when the plane's wing clipped a tree causing the plane to crash. The defendant was a bailee of the aircraft and was obliged, therefore, to exercise reasonable care in all the circumstances of the case. Casey J found that the defendant's conduct did not fall short of the reasonable standard of care and skill expected of him. While he endeavoured to perform this exercise too close to the ground, the learned Judge found that he was not told nor aware of the minimum safe height for a forced simulated landing exercise and his endeavours to extricate himself from his predicament when he discovered he was too close to the ground were all that could have been expected from a pilot of his limited experience in this situation, especially having regard to the shortcomings in his instruction and supervision.

In *Petersen v Papakura Motor Sales Ltd* [1957] NZLR 495 a motorcar, bailed to the defendants for sale on behalf of the plaintiff, was stolen from the defendants' showroom and wrecked. The evidence showed that the thief or thieves had broken into the unlighted building by breaking the staple on an outside padlock fitment on a side door, and, once inside, had opened the front door from within and had driven the plaintiff's car away through the front doorway. The car had been left unlocked with the ignition key in the dashboard but it was not contended that this was negligent. However, Turner J held that in all the circumstances of this case the locking device used on the side door fell below the required standard of what a reasonably careful man would use in like circumstances and he gave judgment for the plaintiff. Turner J also found that the defendants had failed to take adequate precautions so to secure the front door to prevent any thief who gained entry from driving the car out through this door, and, while the failure to maintain an interior light did not in itself amount to negligence, it was a circumstance which affected the defendants' duty adequately to secure the front door from within, for in dark premises a burglar could work more easily and securely. See too *Conway v Cockram Motors (Christchurch) Ltd* [1986] 1 NZLR 381.

The Court will take into consideration the subject matter of the bailment, the nature of the bailment, and the skill professed by the bailee. If the goods are unusually fragile or perishable, or even if their great value or portability make them unusually attractive objects of theft, then presumably the bailee must take these factors into consideration. Reward or lack of reward may also be a relevant consideration; for example, a bailee who is paid to hold something in safekeeping may be expected to take greater precautions than someone who performs a similar function as a favour for a friend. Where the bailee is a professional carrying out the bailment in the course of a business, or holds himself or herself out as having a certain expertise, the bailee is bound to use such skill as his or her situation or profession implies: *Wilson v Brett* (1843) 11 M & W 113. Finally, it should be noted, that if an uncommon or unexpected danger arises, the bailee must use efforts in proportion to the danger to ward it off: *Brabant v King* [1895] AC 632; cf *Britain and Overseas Trading (Bristles) Ltd v Brooks Wharf and Bull Wharf Ltd* [1967] 2 Lloyd's Rep 51.

23.3.2 Onus of proof

The loss of, or damage to, a chattel while it is in the possession of a bailee raises a prima facie inference of negligence against him or her. The bailee, in order to escape liability for such loss or damage, must prove that the loss or damage was sustained notwithstanding the exercise of reasonable care in the circumstances: *Petersen v Papakura Motor Sales Ltd* [1957] NZLR 495, 498-499; *EMI (New Zealand) Ltd v Holyman and Sons Pty Ltd* [1976] 2 NZLR 566, 575. The position is the same whether the bailment is for reward or is gratuitous: *Southland Hospital Board v Perkins Estate* [1986] 1 NZLR 373.

The bailee is not obliged to show that the loss happened in some way which he or she could account for, and that in relation to that particular matter and that particular moment of time proper care was taken. As Sir Gorrel Barnes stated in *Bullen v Swan Electric Engraving Co* (1906) 22 TLR 275; affirmed (1907) 23 TLR 258, this would enhance the burden upon a bailee to an absurd extent if the bailee had to prove not only that he or she had taken every reasonable care but also that he or she knew how the loss happened. Consequently in *EMI (New Zealand) Ltd v Holyman and Sons Pty Ltd* [1976] 2 NZLR 566, Beattie J held that the bailee had discharged the onus of disproving the inference of negligence which arose following the disappearance of radios and recorders by demonstrating that it had exercised all reasonable precautions to guard against the danger of theft – notwithstanding that the defendant could not put its finger on the actual point of time when the goods were pillaged. See also *Port Swettenham Authority v T W Wu and Co Ltd* [1979] AC 580.

The onus upon the bailee may, in exceptional circumstances, be otherwise. For example, in *Mitchell v London Borough of Ealing* [1978] 2

WLR 999 the plaintiff squatter was evicted by Court order from a flat owned by the defendant council. The plaintiff accepted an offer by the Council to store her furniture in a lock-up garage until she could collect it and take it away. A request was made for the return of the goods and an appointment to effect the delivery of the goods made. However, the Council representative failed to keep the appointment and it was almost a month later pursuant to a fresh arrangement that the parties finally met at the garage. They discovered that the furniture had been stolen and the plaintiff sued the Council. O'Connor J held that although the Council had exercised reasonable care, its negligent failure to return the goods at the time requested converted the Council from a gratuitous bailee (under a duty to take reasonable care) to a bailee strictly responsible, and thereafter the Council held the furniture at its peril and became insurers of the furniture. O'Connor J placed an interesting gloss upon the ordinary rule as to onus of proof; namely, whenever it is uncertain whether a loss has occurred during the period of a bailee's responsibility as a bailee or during the later period of his or her liability as insurer, the onus is upon the bailee to identify the time of the loss. However, the local authority was unable to discharge this onus.

The general rule as to onus of proof also may be qualified where the bailee disappears with the chattel and dies. In *National Trust Co Ltd v Wong Aviation Ltd* (1969) 3 DLR (3 ed) 55 an aircraft rented from Wong Aviation Ltd disappeared and no trace of it or the pilot was ever found. The pilot was quite experienced, the aircraft was in satisfactory flying condition and had sufficient fuel for the purpose of the projected flight. Wong Aviation contended that there was a bailment and therefore the onus lay on the bailee's executors to disprove the inference of negligence that arose. The Supreme Court of Canada held that in these circumstances it was sufficient for the executors to adduce a reasonable explanation of what occurred, without having to go further and prove affirmatively that the bailee had exercised reasonable care. It would be unrealistic to impose the normal rule as to onus of proof upon parties who had no knowledge of the circumstances. The Court held that there was no liability to make good the loss as the executors had produced an explanation of the loss (bad weather conditions) which, on the scarcity of the evidence available, was as consistent with the facts as was the bailor's allegation of negligence.

Generally, though, the bailor must prove that a bailment existed and that the chattel bailed was lost or damaged during the bailment; the onus is then on the bailee to show that the loss did not happen in consequence of his or her neglect to use such care and diligence as was reasonable in the circumstances of the case.

23.4 BAILOR'S DUTY

If a chattel is hired for a special purpose, the duty of the bailor is to supply a chattel as fit for the purpose for which it was hired. For example, in *Smith v Stockdill* [1960] NZLR 53, the Linen Flax Corporation provided a pulling machine with which the defendant was required to harvest on his farm a linen flax crop. The plaintiff, who was a servant of the defendant, was injured when his leg came into contact with moving parts of the pulling machine that were insufficiently guarded. Henry J held that, in the circumstances, there was an implied warranty that the machine was reasonably fit for the purpose for which the parties intended it to be used, and that this warranty had been breached for the machine in operation was dangerous to the operator and could be operated only in breach of the Machinery Act 1950. Therefore, the amount in damages which the defendant was responsible to pay the plaintiff was recoverable in full from the Corporation. See also *Francis v Cockerill* (1870) LR 5 QB 501; *Southland Harbour Board v Vella* [1974] 1 NZLR 526 (CA). Of course bailments regulated by statute such as hire purchase agreements have terms as to fitness and merchantable quality implied into the contract by virtue of the statute: Hire Purchase Act 1971, ss 12, 13. In the case of gratuitous bailments it was held in *Coughlin v Gillison* [1899]1 QB 145 that the bailor is under a duty to disclose to the bailee any defect in the goods rendering them unsuitable for the purpose for which they are to be used.

23.5 SUB-BAILMENTS

If a person (the principal bailor) delivers goods to a second person (the bailee) for transporting, repairing, storing, or the like, and if that second person consigns the goods to a third person (the sub-bailee), the third person assumes the obligations of a bailee towards the principal bailor. The nature of these obligations will, as in the case of an ordinary bailment, vary according to the circumstances of the particular situation. The sub-bailee owes concurrently the same duties to the original bailee, whose obligations to the bailor are not extinguished by the sub-bailment: *Morris v C W Martin and Sons Ltd* [1966]1 QB 716; *Mason v Attorney-General* (unreported, High Court, Hamilton, A 15/78, 10 June 1983; Bisson J).

The bailor has a right of action against the sub-bailee for any breach of his or her duties either if the bailor has the right to immediate possession of the chattels or if they are permanently injured or lost. The relationship between the bailor and the sub-bailee exists independently of any contract between them or of any attornment and the obligation to take care arises out of the delivery and voluntary assumption of possession of the bailor's goods: *Gilchrist Watt and Sanderson Pty Ltd v York Products Pty Ltd* [1970] 1 WLR 1262 (PC); *Balsamo v Medici* [1984] 1 WLR 951, 959.

23.6 CARRIAGE OF GOODS

23.6.1 Introduction

A special type of bailment is that of carriage of goods. Given the vital role of transportation in the commercial arena, this topic of carriage of goods has been isolated for particular attention as against the background of the law pertaining to bailments in general.

The international carriage of goods by sea from any port in New Zealand to any port outside New Zealand is governed by the Sea Carriage of Goods Act 1940 and the Rules contained in the Schedule to this Act. These Rules, known as The Hague Rules having first been formulated at a meeting of the International Law Association at The Hague in 1921, may be modified or enlarged by express agreement. In addition to the provisions of the Sea Carriage of Goods Act 1940, international sea carriage is regulated by statutes such as the Shipping and Seamen Act 1952 and the Mercantile Law Act 1908. In the case of international carriage of goods by air, the liability of carriers is largely regulated by international agreements, particularly the Warsaw Convention of 1929 as amended and supplemented by a subsequent Protocol and Convention. These have been adopted in New Zealand by the Carriage by Air Act 1967.

Contracts for the carriage of goods within New Zealand are governed by the Carriage of Goods Act 1979. This Act applies to every carriage of goods, not being international carriage, whether the carriage is by land, water or air, or by more than one of those modes: s 5(1). Every contract of domestic carriage is covered by this Act whether or not it is incidental to the carriage of passengers and whether or not the carrier is at the same time also engaged in international carriage: s 5(2), (3).

Constraints of space dictate that the balance of this chapter is devoted to a consideration of domestic carriage of goods as regulated by the Carriage of Goods Act 1979, and readers are referred to standard texts on international carriage for a comprehensive treatment of this latter subject. See, for example, M Davies and A Dickey, *Shipping Law* (1990); *Payne and Ivamy's Carriage of Goods by Sea* (13 ed 1989).

23.6.2 Definitions

The Carriage of Goods Act 1979 (hereinafter referred to as "the Act") defines a carrier as meaning a person who, in the ordinary course of his or her business, carries goods owned by any other person: s 2. A distinction is drawn between a "contracting carrier", who as principal or agent of any other carrier enters into the contract of carriage with the contracting party, and the "actual carrier", who is the carrier in possession of the goods at the material time. The term "goods" receives a wide definition and means goods, baggage and chattels of any description and includes animals, plants, money, documents and all other things of value.

The law is modernised so as to take account of current methods of transport where goods are often aggregated, transported in containers or on pallets. Limitations are imposed upon the amounts for which carriers may be held liable and these limits are stipulated by reference to the "units of goods" lost or damaged: s 15. Section 3 defines this term as follows. With bulk cargo, this is the unit of bulk, weight or measurement upon which the freight for that type of cargo is customarily computed or adjusted. With containerised cargo, palleted, packaged or unitised goods, the unit is the container, pallet, package or unit. In relation to baggage the unit refers to each item of baggage and, as far as other goods are concerned, the unit is each item of the goods. For the purpose of determining the limit of liability of any carrier under s 15 of the Act in respect of each unit of goods the relevant time for assessment is when the goods are accepted for carriage by the actual carrier or, where the carriage is undertaken by more than one carrier, by the first actual carrier. It is irrelevant that the goods may be repacked, aggregated or separated from other goods at any stage of the carriage: s 3(2).

In *W D & H O Wills (New Zealand) Ltd v Wolters Cartage Ltd* [1991] 3 NZLR 119 a consignment of cigarettes was stolen while in the possession of the carrier. The bulk of the cigarettes were loaded on pallets holding 24 cartons each and each pallet was then stretch-wrapped. Each pallet load was held to constitute a unit of goods. However 146 cartons had been loose stacked on top of the stretch-wrapped pallets, as there was insufficient space to carry them in the vehicle in pallets. It was held that each carton, having been accepted by the carrier as an individual item, was also a unit of goods.

23.6.3 Liability of the carrier

The *common law* distinguishes between common carriers and private carriers. The common carrier holds himself or herself out to carry passengers or goods for anyone choosing to employ him or her; he or she must carry on business as a carrier and cannot reserve the right to accept or reject the transport of goods, save in certain limited circumstances – for example, the common carrier could refuse to carry goods when his or her conveyance was full or where the goods were improperly or insufficiently packed: see *New Zealand Express Co Ltd v Minahan* [1916] NZLR 816; *Luddit v Ginger Coote Airways Ltd* [1947] AC 233 (PC); *Geering v Stewart Transport Ltd* [1967] NZLR 802 (CA). If the common carrier wrongfully refuses to carry any goods he or she may be sued for damages in tort: *Crouch v London and North Western Railway* (1854) 9 Ex 556. The common carrier is the virtual insurer of the safety of the goods that he or she carries and is liable for any damage to, or loss of, those goods unless the loss arose from an act of God, or the acts of the Queen's enemies or an inherent vice in the thing carried: see *Redhead v Midland Railway Co* (1869) LR 4 QB 379, 382. Conversely, private carriers reserve the right to reject the transport of goods and are not necessarily liable if goods are lost or damaged; the private carrier of goods must demonstrate that the loss or damage was not caused by his or her neglect but will escape liability if he or she rebuts the inference of negligence that arises: *Hobbs v Petersham Transport Co Pty Ltd* (1971) 124 CLR 220.

However, the Act abolishes the genus of common carrier. Section 28(1) of the Act provides that:

> . . . subject to the provisions of any enactment and of any contract entered into by the carrier, no carrier is under any duty or obligation to accept or carry goods that are offered to him for carriage.

Moreover, it is provided that no carrier is liable for loss of or damage to any goods carried by him or her *except in terms of his or her contract of carriage and the provisions of the Act or, where he or she intentionally causes the loss or damage:* s 6. The parties to a contract of carriage are free to make their own terms in respect of any matters covered by ss 10, and 18 to 27 of the Act; that is, the liability of the actual carrier and rights of action as against the carrier, and where they do so, the relevant section or sections shall, in relation to that matter, have effect subject to those express terms.

For the purpose of determining upon whom liability for loss of or damage to any goods falls, every contract of carriage is deemed to be one of four kinds:

(a) A contract for carriage *at owner's risk* under which the carrier is liable only for loss or damage caused intentionally by him: s 8(1)(a). No contract of this kind is effective unless it is in writing, expressed to be at owner's risk and signed by the parties or their agents; or, before or at the time the goods are accepted the contracting party or his or her agent signs the following statement:

> These goods are to be carried at "owner's risk". This means that the carrier will pay no compensation if the goods are lost or damaged, unless he or she intentionally loses or damages them.

This statement must be conspicuous and must be separately signed by the contracting party or his or her agent: s 8(5); compare the Hire Purchase Act 1971, s 12(1)(d). Moreover, no contract of carriage "at owner's risk" shall have effect as such unless the freight is fair and reasonable having regard to the risk that the carrier undertook: s 8(9). If the freight is not fair and reasonable then the contract of carriage shall have effect as a contract for carriage "at limited carrier's risk".

(b) A contract for carriage *at limited carrier's risk*, is a contract whereby the carrier is liable for loss of or damage to the goods in accordance with ss 9, 14 and 15 of the Act: s 8(1)(b).

(c) A contract for carriage *at declared value risk*, is one under which the carrier shall be liable for the loss of or damage to any goods up to an amount specified in the contract and otherwise in accordance with ss 9, 14 and 15 of the Act: s 8(1)(c). Such a contract will only be effective as such if it is in writing and the freight is fair and reasonable in the light of this risk undertaken by the carrier – otherwise the contract will be treated as a contract for carriage "at limited carrier's risk": ss 8(6), 9.

(d) A contract for carriage *on declared terms* is a contract under which the carrier shall be liable for the loss of or damage to the goods in accordance with the specific terms of the contract: s 8(1)(d). This kind of contract is to be treated as a contract for carriage "at limited owner's risk" *unless* the contract is freely negotiated between the parties, it is reduced to writing, and is signed by the parties or their agents: s 8(7). In determining whether the agreement was freely negotiated a Court must have regard to the respective bargaining strengths of the parties, any course of dealing between them, the value of the transaction, any extraordinary features about the goods or the route over which they are to be carried, and any other matters that the Court considers relevant: s 8(8).

Identifying the category into which a particular contract for carriage falls is facilitated by various presumptions in s 8. If one of the four terms – "at owner's risk", "at limited carrier's risk", "at declared value risk", "on declared terms" – is used in the contract of carriage then the contract is deemed to fall into that category: s 8(2). Subject to this, the kind of contract of carriage to be entered into in a particular course is a matter for agreement between the parties: s 8(3). Where the contract does not purport to be of a particular kind it is deemed to be a contract for carriage "at limited owner's risk": s 8(4).

Section 9 of the Act deals with the liability of the *contracting carrier*. This carrier is, subject to the other provisions of the Act, liable to the contracting party for the loss of or damage to goods while he or she is responsible for the goods, whether or not the loss or damage is caused wholly or partly by him or her or by any actual carrier: s 9(1). The responsibility of the contracting carrier for goods commences when he or she accepts the goods for carriage in accordance with the contract and ends upon delivery to or collection by the consignee: s 9(2), (3). This responsibility may end before delivery or collection upon non-payment of freight which is due on or before delivery, or where the goods are to be collected by the consignee and that person does not after five days' notice effect collection: s 9(3). The liability of the contracting carrier under s 9 of the Act is subject to the other provisions of the Act; therefore where the contracting carrier enters into a contract for carriage "at owner's risk" pursuant to the provisions of s 8 he or she does not assume any liability for the loss of or damage to any goods. With a contract for carriage "on declared terms" the liability of the contracting carrier is to be assessed in accordance with express provisions of the contract between the parties and s 9(1) does not apply. However, the contracting carrier who enters into a contract for carriage "at limited carrier's risk" or "at declared value" risk may be held liable pursuant to s 9.

The prima facie position of *actual carriers* is dealt with in s 10 of the Act – prima facie because, again, the provisions of this section are expressed to be subject to the other provisions of the Act. Where one actual carrier is involved he or she is, subject to the terms of his or her contract with the contracting carrier, liable to the contracting carrier for loss of or damage to the goods whether he or she has caused or contributed to it, from the time he or she accepts the goods until such time as the contracting carrier's responsibility ends in accordance with s 9(3) and (4): s 10(2). Where two or more actual carriers are involved they are, subject to the terms of their respective contracts, jointly and severally liable to the contracting carrier for the loss of or damage to the goods: s 10(3). The liability of each is assessed in accordance with the proportion of freight payable to him: s 10(7).

Where the contracting carrier is liable to the contracting party for the loss of or damage to any goods but the contracting carrier is insolvent or cannot with reasonable diligence be found, the contracting party is entitled to the same rights against each actual carrier as the contracting carrier has under s 10(3)(b); that is, each actual carrier is liable to the contracting party for loss of or damage to the goods while they are his or her separate responsibility: s 11(1). However, the actual carrier(s) has the same rights against the contracting party as he or she would have had under the contract if the proceeding had been brought against him or her by the contracting carrier – including the right of set-off: s 11(3).

As far as baggage is concerned, the Act provides that a carrier is not liable with respect to baggage pending his or her acceptance of it for carriage, or pending its collection from him or her after the completion of the carriage: s 12(1). Particular limitations are imposed on the liability of a carrier for hand baggage: s 12(2). Contracts of successive carriage by air also receive special attention in s 13, and ss 8 to 12 of the Act do not apply in respect of such contracts: s 13(2).

23.6.4 Limitation or exclusion of liability of the carrier

The carrier may by the terms of the contract for carriage exclude all liability for the loss of or damage to the goods. Such exclusion of liability must be in accordance with the provisions of the Act for it to be effective, for example, by the incorporation of a conspicuous statement explaining the effect of a contract for carriage "at owner's risk" which is separately signed by the contracting party or his or her agent: s 8(5)(b).

However, notwithstanding any of the other provisions of the Act, s 14 provides that:

> ... a carrier is not liable as such for the loss of or damage to goods occurring while he or she is responsible for them under a contract of carriage to the extent that he or she proves that the loss or damage resulted directly and without fault on his or her part from –
> (a) inherent vice; or
> (b) any breach of either of the terms implied in the contract by section 17 of this Act; or
> (c) seizure under legal process; or
> (d) saving or attempting to save life or property in peril.

Inherent vice means some default or latent defect in the things carried themselves which tends to cause damage or destruction to those goods; for example, in *Jahn v Turnbull Scott Shipping Co Ltd; The Flowergate* [1967] 1 Lloyd's Rep 1, cocoa beans were damaged by moisture emanating from the beans themselves, and this was held to be an inherent vice in the beans. As far as s 17 is concerned, s 17(1) provides that in every contract of carriage there is implied on the part of the contracting party a term: (a) that the goods tendered are fit to be carried and stored in accordance with the contract; and (b) that the provisions of any other legislation relating to the consignment have been complied with; for example, the Radiation Protection Act 1965, and the Dangerous Goods Act 1974. These implied terms may be subject to variation where the contracting party discloses to the carrier prior to acceptance of the goods for carriage any material particular that would otherwise constitute a breach of either of the terms: s 17(2). Similarly, at common law, a carrier was relieved of liability for damage caused by faulty packing by the consignor: *Gould v South Eastern and Chatham Railway Co* [1920] 2 KB 186. And, at common law, the consignor was taken to warrant that the roads were safe and fit for carriage and was obliged to give reasonable warning of any danger: *Great Northern Railway v LEP Transport Co* [1922] 2 KB 742. The third circumstance enumerated in s 14 as excusing a carrier from liability is where the loss or damage to the goods is caused, without fault on his or her part, by seizure under legal process. Clearly, the carrier cannot be held liable for something totally outside his or her control. Finally, no liability is incurred where the carrier proves that the loss or damage resulted directly and without fault on his or her part from "saving or attempting to save life or property in peril". This has long been recognised as a circumstance excusing a carrier from liability; for example, in a 1908 case a ferryman was held not to be liable for goods thrown overboard from his barge to lighten the load on the occasion of a sudden storm where this jettison was necessary to save the lives of those on board: *Mouse's* case (1608) 77 ER 1341.

For purposes of the Act, where a carrier is liable for the loss of or damage to goods, his or her liability is limited in amount in each case to the sum of $1,500 for each "unit of goods" lost or damaged or, in the case of a contract "at declared value risk", the amount specified in the contract: s 15(1). These limits do not apply where the loss of or damage to the goods is intentionally caused by the carrier, or where the liability for damages arises out of the terms of the contract for some reason other than the loss of or damage to the goods, or where damages consequential upon the loss of or damage to the goods are sought: s 15(2).

Carriers' employees are liable to the owner of goods only if they intentionally cause loss of or damage to any goods being carried by the carrier: s 16.

23.6.5 Actions against carriers

Generally speaking, no action may be brought against a contracting carrier for damage or partial loss of goods unless written notice giving reasonable particulars of the alleged damage is given within 30 days after the date on which the carrier's responsibility for the goods ceased: s 18(1). Moreover, the contracting carrier may not take action against an actual carrier unless he or she notifies the actual carrier of a claim within 10 days of receiving it: s 18(2). These time limits do not apply where there is fraud, and no notice is required if it is apparent from all the circumstances of the case that the carrier is or ought to be aware of the damage or partial loss: s 18(3). A carrier may consent to an action being brought against him or her notwithstanding that notice of the claim was not properly given, and a Court may grant leave for an action to be brought where the failure to give notice was due to mistake or other reasonable cause and no material prejudice to the intended defendant has resulted from this failure: s 18(5), (6), (7).

Except where there is fraud by the carrier, an action against a carrier must be brought within 12 months from the date on which the carriage should have been completed in accordance with the contract (in the case of lost goods) and within 12 months from the date when notice was served (in the case of damaged goods): s 19(1), (2). Again the carrier may consent to an action being brought against him or her out of time, and, in the absence of such consent, the Court may grant leave to bring the action within the six year limitation period governing actions in contract: s 19(3), (4). The delay in bringing the action must not materially prejudice the carrier and must have been occasioned by mistake or other reasonable cause: s 19(6).

Finally, as far as actions against a carrier are concerned, an action against a contracting carrier may be brought by a consignee, who is not the contracting party, provided the property in the goods has passed to the consignee: s 20(1). The contracting carrier is entitled to raise the same defences as against the consignee as he or she would have been entitled to raise as against the contracting party: s 20(2).

23.6.6 Rights of carriers

A carrier may sue for the recovery of *freight* payable under a contract of carriage when he or she ceases to be responsible for the goods in accordance with the provisions of the Act: s 21(1). This does not affect the right of a carrier to insist upon payment in advance for any carriage: s 21(2). Any action for the recovery of freight may be brought against the consignee, to whom the property in goods has passed, but who is not the contracting party: s 22(1). The consignee has the same liability as the contracting party for the payment of freight, but may raise the same defences and counterclaims: s 22(2).

The carrier is given a *lien* over the goods by s 23 of the Act. The carrier must give notice of his or her intention to exercise this right of retention of the goods to the owner of the goods – in this context, the contracting party or consignee if property in goods has passed to that person and he or she is not the contracting party – and must specify the amount and particulars of the claim and require the owner to pay or secure to the carrier the amount of the freight claimed and all recoverable expenses: s 23(3). Recoverable expenses refer to all expenses and charges reasonably incurred in removing, preserving and storing the goods, and in arranging and conducting their sale: s 23(1), (6). In exercising the lien a carrier may remove and store the goods in premises reasonably convenient for collection, and must take all reasonable steps to preserve the goods: s 23(4). If, within 2 months after the date on which the carrier serves notice of the claim on the owner, payment in full of all the freight owing and recoverable expenses so far incurred has not been tendered to the carrier, the carrier is entitled to sell the goods by public auction: s 23(5). Then follows the balancing of accounts that is, where the proceeds of the sale exceed the amount owing the carrier must refund the excess to the owner, but in the case of deficit, the deficiency constitutes a debt owing to the carrier by the owner: s 23(6), (7). Finally, it is provided in s 23(8) that nothing in s 23 shall limit or affect the right to have and enforce a general lien over any goods to which a carrier may be entitled by virtue of any contract of carriage. Thus, the parties may agree by an express provision in the contract of carriage that the carrier may exercise a lien over goods in respect of sums owing to him or her for freight on the carriage of other goods of the same owner, or in respect of any other debt due from that owner to the carrier – such a lien is known as a general lien. The lien conferred by the Act is an "active and particular lien over the goods"; that is, it extends over the goods in question for the sum owing for the freight for the carriage of those goods on the carriage in question, and is "active" in the sense that the carrier is afforded a right to sell the goods to raise the money owing to him.

The Act confers rights of *disposal* upon the carrier in respect of certain other categories of goods. Where goods are unclaimed or rejected by the consignee, the carrier may remove the goods at that person's expense to suitable premises for storage: s 24(1). The carrier has an active and particular lien over those goods and may exercise this lien in the manner and extent outlined in s 23, save for one departure; that is, the carrier must before selling the goods offer to carry them to the consignor if the consignor agrees to pay all charges owing: s 24(2), (3). If, at any time while perishable goods are subject to a contract of carriage or a carrier's lien, the goods appear to be deteriorating and are likely to become offensive the carrier may sell them to best advantage, or, if sale is not reasonably practicable, destroy or dispose of them: s 25(1). Again there must be a balancing of accounts between the parties and if the goods are destroyed or otherwise disposed of the carrier may recover all reasonable expenses incurred from the contracting party: s 25(2), (3). If a carrier believes, on reasonable grounds, that any goods are dangerous or about to become dangerous and that it is necessary to destroy them in order to avoid threat to life and limb, the carrier may do so and recover his or her reasonable expenses from the contracting party: s 26.

Finally, a carrier is under no liability under the Act or otherwise for the sale, destruction or disposal of goods in accordance with ss 23-26 of the Act. This, however, does not affect any liability for any loss or damage that had already occurred in respect of the goods before the sale, destruction or other disposition: s 27.

23.6.7 Miscellaneous

Proceedings under the Act can be brought against a New Zealand agent of an overseas contracting carrier if the contract is to be performed wholly or partly in New Zealand and the agent plays some part in relation to the contract: s 29.

Other statutes relating to goods of a particular nature and class, such as the Dangerous Goods Act 1974, are not limited or affected by the provisions of the Carriage of Goods Act 1979 and in the event of inconsistency arising the other statute prevails: s 30.

The Act applies to goods carried by the Railways Corporation: New Zealand Railways Corporation Act 1981, s 18.

Chapter 24

CREDIT CONTRACTS ACT 1981

SUMMARY

24.1   INTRODUCTION
24.2   RE-OPENING OF OPPRESSIVE CREDIT CONTRACTS
24.3   DISCLOSURE
24.4   CREDIT ADVERTISEMENTS
24.5   PROHIBITION OF CERTAIN FINANCIERS AND TERMS
24.6   MISCELLANEOUS

24.1 INTRODUCTION

Credit may be provided in an infinite variety of ways but credit transactions fall basically into two categories; namely deferred payment sales and loans.

There are two major types of deferred payment sales in New Zealand; that is, credit sales and hire purchase agreements. In everyday use the term "hire purchase" is used interchangeably with terms such as "time payment", "instalment plan" and other fanciful terms, all of which are commonly used to refer to any method of purchasing goods by instalments. However as mentioned earlier the feature that distinguishes hire purchase agreements from other instalments sale and credit sale agreements is that, while possession of goods subject to a hire purchase agreement is given to the purchaser at the time of sale or delivery, property in the goods remains with the vendor until all the instalments have been paid.

Conversely in a credit sale arrangement property in the goods is transferred to the purchaser at the time of sale or delivery of the goods and the passing of property is not contingent upon the payment of the full purchase price. Retailers provide directly to consumers an enormous amount of credit for the purchase of goods and services. There is the familiar buying "on account" where retailers allow credit to certain responsible customers. Alternatively many retail outlets operate a type of evolving credit – often termed a budget account. This is a system whereby the customer agrees to pay so much a month and at the same time can have goods on credit up to a certain value. As the customer's repayments reduce his or her outstanding debt, he or she can then buy more goods or "top up" his or her debt to the arranged maximum amount.

As a further alternative most retailers accept payment by a credit card. There are two main types of credit card in New Zealand namely, (i) three party cards; and (ii) two party cards. With respect to the former variety the first party is the cardholder, the second party is the outlet that accepts the card, and the third party is the bank or credit card company that issues the card. In this case the credit is not provided by the retailer but by the bank or credit card company operating the scheme. As regards two party cards, again the cardholder is the first party and the retailer the second party. There is no third party though because the retailer issues its own card. These two party credit cards are often called "in house" cards and are offered on store charge accounts by most of the big business houses in New Zealand.

Although the terms of deferred payment sales in New Zealand vary, for example, as between credit sales, conditional sales and true hire purchase agreements, the common denominator is that the buyer of goods and services is permitted to pay the price of the goods or part of it at a later date and is, or may be, subject to term charges or interest charges for this privilege.

The second major category of credit transactions are loans. The primary sources of loan moneys in New Zealand are the banks and the finance houses who provide credit to consumers to facilitate the purchase of realty, goods and services. Banks provide credit through loans or the extension of overdraft facilities, the former usually being a loan of a fixed sum at a fixed rate of interest to be paid off by fixed regular instalments, while the latter is an arrangement whereby a customer may borrow on his or her current account.

Loans and deferred payment sales serve a similar objective in the usual case, namely to enable a consumer to purchase certain goods and services. Furthermore if a person has insufficient cash to acquire a particular chattel, for example, he or she may enter into a hire purchase agreement or raise a loan from a finance company or bank. Such a lending institution may require the borrower to execute an instrument by way of security over the particular chattel, which has the effect of transferring the property in the chattel to the lender. In effect, therefore the position of the secured lender is the same as that of the seller under a hire purchase agreement; that is, property in the goods is retained until such time as the amount owing, including interest charges, is paid. Another obvious similarity between deferred payment sales and loans is that the purchaser and borrower respectively, pay a charge for the privilege that is afforded them.

The rapid expansion of the credit industry in recent times has brought significant and obvious advantages. In addition to advancing the business of those in industry, commerce and finance, the growth of credit enables consumers to purchase realty, goods and services as opportunity or desire arises with less reference to the immediate cash position. However, as Ison, *Credit Marketing and Consumer Protection* (1979), p 14, comments:

[The growth of credit marketing] has also provided the opportunities and incentives for predatory practices, deceit and other abuses. Complaints have been voluminous about, for example, misleading advertising, fraud, the concealment of credit terms, high pressure tactics, defective goods, dubious accounting methods and oppressive collection tactics. These problems were not created by the expansion of new forms of consumer credit, but they may have been aggravated. For example, it is often thought to be easier for a high-pressure salesman to induce a signature on an instalment contract than to induce a signature on a cheque for the same amount.

Furthermore, it is clear that there is a substantial difference between the simplicity evidenced by the "buy now, pay later", "easy terms" type of exhortation and the complicated credit contract that the consumer actually signs. It is probably fair comment to assert that the average person who, for example, buys goods on credit is usually only interested in the practical aspects of the transaction and is seldom aware of the precise nature of his or her legal rights and obligations. The complexity of documentation and apathy of the buying public are contributing factors.

Concern over the dramatic increase in the availability and use of credit led the Minister of Justice in 1968 to instruct the now defunct Contracts and Commercial Law Reform Committee (referred to as "the Committee" in what follows) to study the law relating to moneylending transactions and to other agreements involving the extension of credit with a view to recommending necessary reform. The result of the Committee's deliberations and consultations was the lengthy *Report on Credit Contracts* presented in July 1977. Many of the recommendations in this Report received statutory recognition in the Credit Contracts Act 1981.

This Act, which came into force on 1 June 1982, has four basic objectives, namely:

(i) to prevent oppressive credit contracts and conduct;
(ii) to ensure that all terms of credit contracts are disclosed to debtors before they become irrevocably committed to them;
(iii) to ensure that the cost of credit is disclosed on a uniform basis in order to prevent deception and encourage competition; and,
(iv) to prevent misleading credit advertisements.

In order to attain the objectives the legislature has provided for the re-opening of oppressive credit contracts, the disclosure of information, the regulation of credit advertisements, and for the prohibition of certain financiers and terms. The Credit Contracts Act repealed the Moneylenders Act 1908 and amended the Hire Purchase Act 1971 to maintain uniformity and consistency in the regulation of credit contracts. Section 52A of the Hire Purchase Act states that the provisions of the Credit Contracts Act that apply to hire purchase agreements shall apply thereto in addition to the provision of the Hire Purchase Act, and neither Act shall limit the provisions of the other.

24.2 RE-OPENING OF OPPRESSIVE CREDIT CONTRACTS

24.2.1 General

The Courts of Equity have long asserted a limited jurisdiction to set aside harsh and unconscionable bargains. Such jurisdiction exists whenever one party to a transaction is at a special disadvantage in dealing with the other party because illness, ignorance, inexperience, impaired faculties, financial need, or other circumstances affect his or her ability to protect his or her own interests, and the other party takes unconscionable advantage of the opportunity thus placed in his or her hands: *Blomley v Ryan* (1956) 99 CLR 362, 415; supra 5.2.3.

Under the Moneylenders Act and the Hire Purchase Act the Court had a limited power to a contract, and the Committee favoured the retention and expansion of this power for two reasons: namely, (i) without purporting to control the terms of lending agreements and without fixing rate ceilings, it enables the Courts to grant a remedy to a debtor against a harsh and unconscionable financier; and (ii) while the doctrine does not interfere with ordinary transactions it is a useful weapon against those financiers who employ sharp practices and drive hard bargains: *Credit Contracts Report*, para 7.06. The Committee therefore recommended: (i) that wide application be given to the doctrine that entitles the Courts to re-open harsh and unconscionable transactions; (ii) that guidelines should be provided concerning the Court's exercise of its discretion; and (iii) that the jurisdiction of the Court should not be confined to an examination of the terms of the agreement but should extend to a review of the subsequent exercise of the powers under the agreement: *Credit Contracts Report*, paras 7.66-7.67. These recommendations were accepted and Part I of the Credit Contracts Act makes extensive provision for the re-opening of credit contracts.

24.2.2 What is a credit contract?

Section 3 of the Credit Contracts Act 1981 defines a credit contract to mean a contract under which a person provides or agrees to provide money or money's worth in consideration of a promise by another person to pay a sum or sums of money exceeding in aggregate the amount of the first mentioned money or money's worth or a contract under which a person agrees to forbear from requiring payment of money owing in consideration of a promise by another to pay a sum of money exceeding in aggregate the original amount owing. Section 3 extends the operation of the above definition to any contract where the credit arises by virtue of one person lending the other person the money; or one person selling or agreeing to sell property or provide services to the other in consideration of a promise by the other person to pay in the future for that property or those services; or any contract of bailment (whether or not with an option to purchase) where the bailee agrees in the future to pay sums of money. Any or all of these contracts will be credit contracts if the sum or sums of money contracted to be paid exceed in aggregate the amount of the loan, or the cash price of the property or services provided, or the cash price of the bailed goods. The section also includes as a "credit contract" any contract whereby a person assigns his or her right to receive money in the future in consideration of the assignee promising to pay a lesser sum of money than the debt assigned: s 3(1)(f). Excluded from the definition are leases of real property and contracts for the sale of property or the provision of services where the agreed price of the property or services is the total amount payable for the property or services and is to be paid within two months from the date the contract is made.

It is an essential element of a credit contract under s 3(1)(a) that the borrower undertakes to repay a greater sum than the money or money's worth originally provided. For the purpose of determining whether a contract is a credit contract, s 3(3)(b) lists certain amounts which are not included as part of the sum or sums of money promised to be paid in the future. Such amounts include any reasonable amount payable for incidental services to the borrower: s 3(3)(b)(i). This is relevant in determining whether a contract between a credit card holder and the credit card operator is a credit contract for the purposes of the Act. If the contract has a money transfer function only, the card holder does not promise to pay a greater sum than originally provided, unless any joining fee and annual fee charged by the card operator is not payable for incidental services. In *South Pacific Credit Card Ltd v Kay* [1986] 2 NZLR 578 it was held that holders of American Express cards received substantial literature and other membership benefits which constituted incidental services; the contract between the card operator and card holder in that case was therefore not a credit contract.

Section 3(3)(b)(ii) refers to any reasonable amount payable as a result of a default under the contract by the promisor. In *McHaffie v Pyne Gould Guiness Ltd* (1990) 3 NZBLC 101,846 M took delivery of stock which he had purchased at an auction from PGC but did not pay for it until almost two years had elapsed. It was a condition of the sale that interest would be charged at the rate of 25 per cent if payment was not made within 14 days of the sale. It was held that the interest claimed by PGC fell within s 3(3)(b)(ii). The only evidence was that interest rates of between 25 and 29 per cent capitalised annually were being charged and paid for unpaid amounts on stock purchases by farmers generally. Accordingly it could not be said that the interest claimed by PGC was other than reasonable; cf *Wrightson NMA Ltd v Mead* (1984) 1 NZBLC 102, 093.

A collateral contract may be deemed to form part of the credit contract by virtue of s 4(1). Section 4(1)(b) provides that where it is a term of a credit contract that another contract or deed be entered into for the purpose of giving security for the credit provided under the credit contract, then that other contract or deed shall be deemed to form part of the credit contract for the purposes of the Act. Thus a guarantee or mortgage required by the credit contract is deemed to form part of it. Whether a guarantee or mortgage as such constitutes a credit contract in its own right is doubtful. In *UDC Finance Ltd v Lloyd* (unreported, High Court, Auckland, CP 297/86, 16 September 1986, Wylie J) it was held that a guarantee is not a credit contract. In *Elia v Commercial & Mortgage Nominees Ltd* (1988) 2 NZBLC 103,296 a mortgage was held to constitute a credit contract because the mortgagor undertook liability as a principal debtor, a factor distinguishing that case from *UDC Finance*. However subsequent cases have not followed this reasoning: see, for example, *Stewart v Westpac Banking Corporation* (unreported, High Court, Auckland, CP 1883/90, 24 August 1991, Thorp J); cf *Baggott v Samuel* (1990) 3 NZBLC 101,534. Generally see S D Walker "Guarantees and the Credit Contracts Act" [1989] NZLJ 290.

The definition of credit contract is extremely broad and is designed to embrace all contracts whatever their form, the function or one of the functions of which is the provision of credit. Submissions were made to the Committee that commercial loans should not be subjected to the unconscionability doctrine, but the Committee considered that not only would it be difficult to draw a clear line of demarcation between the "categories" of consumer and commercial transactions, but that it would be contrary to their intention to enable the Courts to prevent or redress the unconscionable assertion of economic or legal power whenever it may arise: *Credit Contracts Report,* para 7.15. For similar reasons, the Committee recommended that transactions between financiers and companies should not be exempted and that the Courts should have the power to re-open transactions irrespective of the amount lent: *Credit Contracts Report*, paras 7.17-7.18. The definition of credit contract in s 3 of the Act is framed in accordance with the recommendations of the Committee and relief, therefore, may be given against almost every type of unconscionable bargain and conduct of a party to a credit contract. Generally, see Dugdale, *The Credit Contracts Act 1981* (1981), pp 16-22.

24.2.3 Re-opening provisions

Section 10(1) of the Act provides that the Court may re-open any credit contract where the Court considers that:

(a) The credit contract, or any term thereof is oppressive; or
(b) A party under a credit contract has exercised, or intends to exercise, a right or power conferred by the contract in an oppressive manner; or
(c) A party under a credit contract has induced another party to enter into the contract by oppressive means.

A party is deemed to be exercising a right or power under the contract where the party refuses to agree to the early termination of the contract, or to vary or waive any term of the contract, or imposes conditions on such agreement: s 10(2).

As to when a term or the exercise of a power is "oppressive", s 9 defines oppressive to mean oppressive, harsh, unjustly burdensome, unconscionable or in contravention of reasonable standards of commercial practice. These words mean something much more than unfairness: *Shotter v Westpac Banking Corporation* [1988] 2 NZLR 316, 342. In *Didsbury v Zion Farms Ltd* (1989) 1 NZ ConvC 190,229 at 190,238 it was said that the intention of s 9 is to give the Courts a power to intervene in any case when there is a sufficiently serious element of unfairness. There a number of factors to be considered in testing oppressiveness were identified: the relative status of the parties; the nature and extent of the default; the way in which the default arose; the implications for the borrower; the attitude of the lender; the existence of a collateral purpose; and the general appearance of the contract throughout.

Section 11 of the Act provides guidelines to assist the Court in deciding whether to re-open a credit contract. This section provides:

(1) No credit contract or term of a credit contract, or act performed pursuant to or in relation to a credit contract, shall be considered to be oppressive in the contract, term, or act would not have been considered oppressive at the time at which, and in the circumstances in which, it was made or performed.

(2) In deciding whether paragraphs (a) to (c) of section 10(1) of this Act apply in respect of a credit contract and whether to re-open the contract under that section, the Court shall have regard to –

(a)   All the circumstances relating to the making of the contract, the exercise of the right or power conferred by the contract, or the inducement to enter the contract, as the case may be; and

(b)   Such of the following matters as are applicable (if any):

(i) Whether the finance rate for the contract, or any amount payable by the debtor under the contract (whether or not on default by the debtor), is oppressive:

(ii) Where a debtor is in default under the contract, whether the time given to the debtor by or pursuant to the contract to remedy the default is oppressive having regard to the likelihood of loss to the creditor:

(iii) Where the creditor has required, as a condition of early repayment of the credit outstanding under the contract, that the debtor pay interest for a period subsequent to the date of repayment, whether the amount of interest is oppressive having regard to the expenses of the creditor and the likelihood that the amount repaid can be reinvested on similar terms:

(iv) Where the creditor has refused to release part of any security relating to the contract or has agreed to such a release subject to conditions whether the refusal is, or the conditions are, oppressive having regard to the amount of the credit and the extent of the security that would remain after the release; and

(c)   Such other matters as the Court thinks fit.

(a) OPPRESSIVE CREDIT CONTRACT OR TERM THEREOF

The Courts have been slow to find that a particular term of a contract is per se oppressive. This is particularly so where the contract is a standard contract in general use in the business community, or has been approved by the borrower being an experienced businessperson: see *Shotter v Westpac Banking Corporation (No 2)* (1990) 3 NZBLC 101, 902, at 101,912; *Cambridge Clothing Co Ltd v Simpson* [1988] 2 NZLR 340, 344. However by s 11(2)(a) the Court may have regard to all the circumstances relating to the making of the contract, and it may be easier to show that in context the credit contract was oppressive, especially where the bargaining strength of the parties is unequal and the lender has brought pressure to bear upon the debtor. In *Elia v Commercial & Mortgage Nominees Ltd* (1988) 2 NZBLC 103, 296 the plaintiff E had secured borrowings by a company from the defendant lenders by mortgages over his home. E was unable to read English and did not understand the implications of the transactions into which he was entering. It was held that although the transactions were themselves standard the lenders had taken advantage of E. Their unconscionable dealing constituted oppressiveness for the purposes of the Credit Contracts Act. On the other hand oppressiveness is unlikely to be found where the person seeking to reopen the credit contract is intelligent, well able to understand the nature of the transaction and is not subjected to undue pressure to enter into it: see, for example, *Jenkins v NZI Finance Ltd* (1990) ANZ ConvR 422 (CA); *Bank of New Zealand v McLellan* (1989) 2 NZBLC 103, 710.

(b) EXERCISE OF POWER OR RIGHT IN OPPRESSIVE MANNER

Although the terms of the contract may not be oppressive, the lender's exercise of rights and powers under the contract may well be oppressive.

In *Manion v Marac Finance Ltd* [1986] 2 NZLR 586 M reluctantly gave a mortgage over his property to secure borrowings by a company to establish a stud farm. It was the understanding of all the parties that M's security was no more than an interim measure and that the stud farm once acquired would be substituted as security. This the lender refused to do. It was held that the exercise by the lender of its powers under the mortgage was oppressive.

In *Didsbury v Zion Farms Ltd* supra the borrower through an oversight paid interest due for one quarter some three weeks late. The lender invoked a penalty clause claiming penalty interest for that quarter, and when the borrower reluctantly paid penalty interest after the date specified for payment, the lender claimed penalty interest for succeeding quarters as well. Wallace J considered that the power to claim penalty interest was exercised in an oppressive manner. First, the borrower's default was inadvertent. Secondly, the lender had by acting in an uncooperative manner contributed to confusion as to the meaning of the penalty interest clause. Thirdly, there was an inference that the lender may have been acting for a collateral purpose by seeking to recover by penalty interest the shortfall in the purchase price it had hoped to obtain on the related sale transaction. Fourthly, the claim to penalty interest if upheld would produce a manifestly unfair result and quite disproportionate to the borrower's default. On the other hand, the mere exercise of the power of sale when the defaults have been remedied and payments are up to date is not of itself oppressive, unless there is some other factor present: *Grose v Development Finance Corporation of New Zealand* (1987) 1 NZBLC 102,646. In that case the defaults relied upon by the lender were not isolated instances arising through mistake. In other cases, however, the Courts have indicated that it may well be oppressive to insist upon the exercise of a power of sale where the arrears have been paid and the lender can give no good reason for so insisting: see, for example, *Hart v Haydon* (1982) 2 NZCPR 115; *Robinson v United Building Society* (unreported, High Court, Dunedin, CP 35/87, 7 May 1987, Tompkins J). This is especially so where it is suspected that the lender's motive in proceeding is to recover the proceeds of the sale in order to reinvest them at a higher rate of interest.

(c) INDUCED TO ENTER CONTRACT BY OPPRESSIVE MEANS

A good example is *Gibson v Dealer Discounting (Canty) Ltd* (unreported, High Court, Christchurch, A 140/82, 3 April 1984, White J) where G gave a security in order to prevent the prosecution of her husband for fraud and the lender knew and intended that the threat of prosecution would induce her to enter into the contract.

Each case must, of course, depend largely on its own circumstances and it is unlikely that the Courts will be prepared to lay down general guide-lines.

It is not permissible to use hindsight in deciding whether a credit contract or term thereof, or act to be performed to or in relation to the credit contract, is oppressive: s 11(1). Save for this restriction, it is clear that the Act gives the Court a very wide discretion. For example in *Italia*

Holdings (Properties) Ltd v Lonsdale Holdings (Auckland) Ltd [1984] 2 NZLR 1 it was alleged that a condition of a mortgage loan was oppressive in terms of s 10(1)(a) of the Act. The applicant, a property dealer, obtained from the defendant a mortgage loan which he needed to complete a land purchase. A condition of the loan was that the applicant purchase other land from the defendant at what was alleged to be a gross over-value and give back a mortgage to the defendant. Vautier J held that the condition as to the purchase of the other land did not of itself make the contract oppressive. The applicant was an experienced land dealer, independently advised, and was not obliged to accept the loan on this condition. The defendant, like other lenders in high risk areas, was entitled to impose what would in other circumstances appear to be harsh terms to bolster its security. The over-value at which the other land had been sold to the applicant could not of itself in the circumstances import oppressiveness or a contravention of reasonable standards of commercial practice. The present case was not one in which one party was relatively naive and inexperienced; both were business entities which had had dealings in the field for some years. Moreover the particular transaction complained of had not been entered into by the applicant in great haste as negotiations had extended over a substantial time. Therefore, Vautier J declined to exercise his discretion to re-open the transaction under the Credit Contracts Act 1981.

Where the Court considers that there is a credit contract, and that any term or the exercise of any power or any act thereunder is oppressive, then providing proceedings seeking the re-opening are instituted not later than six months after the date on which the last obligation to be performed under the contract is performed, the Court may re-open the contract: s 12. Upon re-opening, the Court may make such order as it thinks necessary to remedy the matters that caused the Court to re-open the contract and without limiting the Court's power, s 14 provides that the Court may order an account to be taken, or vest in any party to the contract the whole or any part of any property that is the subject of the contract, direct any party to the contract to pay to the other party such sum as the Court thinks fit, order that any obligations outstanding under the contract may be extinguished, altered or performed, set aside any contract or terms thereof, or any security given under the contract, or direct any party to the contract to do, or to refrain from doing any act or thing. Note that only a party to the credit contract may seek to re-open it: *Titcombe v Twin Valley Developments Ltd* (1991) 1 NZ ConvC 191,015.

24.3 DISCLOSURE

24.3.1 Transactions to which the disclosure provisions apply

The Act endeavours to ensure that debtors are appraised of information relating to the credit transaction they have entered. The preamble to the Act recites that the Act is designed, inter alia, to ensure that all the terms of credit contracts are disclosed to debtors before they become irrevocably committed to them. However, the identification of transactions that should be subject to the rules as to disclosure is a controversial and difficult issue. While the term "credit contract" must be defined widely with a view to subjecting most credit contracts to the unconscionability doctrine, such a wide definition would be unsuitable in respect of the disclosure requirements. For example, the small investor in a company or the depositor of money with a bank should not be obliged to inform the company and the bank, respectively, of the terms of the transaction: *Credit Contracts Report*, para 8.23. Consequently, the Credit Contracts Act 1981 restricts the requirements as to disclosure to a narrower class of credit contracts than that embraced by the general definition. The disclosure provisions apply in the main to "controlled credit contracts" and categorisation of this limited class of credit contracts has been done by reference to the following considerations: (a) Status of the Creditor; (b) Status of the Debtor; (c) Nature of the Transaction.

(a) STATUS OF THE CREDITOR

A controlled credit contract is defined in s 15(1) as meaning:

> ... a credit contract – (a) where the creditor, or one of the creditors, for the time being is a financier acting in the course of his or her business; or (b) which results from an introduction of one of the parties to the contract to another such party by a paid adviser; or (c) that has been prepared by a paid adviser.

Clearly the intention of the legislature is to exclude from the ambit of the disclosure provisions transactions where the credit is extended by private persons. As the Committee remarked, at para 8.24 of their Report:

> Simple loans or other credit transactions between members of a family or between neighbours and friends, should not, we think, be subjected to the legal formalities appropriate to transactions at arms length of a more formal nature.

Furthermore, while a person who is in the business of extending credit can be expected to acquaint himself or herslef with the statutory rules and to comply with them the same cannot be said of the private creditor, such as a private individual making a casual loan to a friend, or disposing of his or her car on instalment terms. In any event, if any term of such a private credit transaction is oppressive, or is oppressively exercised, the Court may reopen the contract.

The basic definition of controlled credit contracts refers therefore, to credit transactions where the person extending the credit is a financier, or where the credit contract is made through, or prepared by, a paid adviser.

The term "financier" embraces those persons who carry on the business of providing credit, or who make a practice of providing credit in the course of a business, or who make a practice of entering into credit contracts in their own names as creditors on behalf of other persons: s 21(1). The question as to whether a person is a financier, or not, may be answered more easily by reference to the regularity of transactions, than by reference to the difficult concept of carrying on business as a financier.

The Credit Contracts Act 1981 demands disclosure, not only in credit contracts where the credit is extended by financiers, but also in those credit contracts where paid advisers are involved: s 15(1)(b),(c). The term "paid adviser" encompasses any person who acts for reward as an adviser to, or as a trustee, nominee, or agent of one or more of the parties to a credit contract: s 2(1). Clearly the legislature's intention is that the activities of professional intermediaries such as solicitors, mortgage brokers and trustees should be regulated. Therefore the disclosure provisions apply to credit contracts made through the instrumentality of these intermediaries and to credit contracts prepared by such persons notwithstanding the fact that both creditor and debtor may be private persons. However, such transactions negotiated through or prepared by, paid advisers are clearly distinguishable from the private transaction in the strict sense where both parties will usually be in a position of equal bargaining power.

(b) STATUS OF THE DEBTOR

Exempted from categorisation as "controlled credit contracts" are those credit contracts where the debtor can be presumed to be capable of looking after himself or itself. For example, the disclosure provisions do not apply where the debtor himself or herself is a financier and consequently must himself or herself know and comply with laws which oblige him or her to make disclosure to others: s 15(1)(d). Similarly where the debtor is the Crown, a local authority or a Government agency, or a large company, or where the total amount of credit outstanding between the same creditor and debtor is not less than $250,000, then the disclosure provisions do not apply: s 15 (1)(d), (f).

The Credit Contracts Act 1981 also ensures that members of the public who subscribe for debentures or securities issued by companies are not covered by the disclosure provisions as it would be absurd if the investor had to make statutory disclosure of terms better known to the debtor: s 15(1)(g). Similarly, no sound basis for disclosure exists where every party to a credit contract is a body corporate related to every other such party to the contract: s 15(1)(e).

The Committee considered whether the reasoning, that no disclosure be required where the debtor can be presumed to look after his or her own interests, would justify the exclusion from the ambit of the disclosure provisions transactions in which the debtor is a businessperson: *Credit Contracts Report*, para 8.27. However, the Committee concluded that ordinary businesspersons could not be treated in the same way as financiers in that they did not possess the same financial expertise. This is undoubtedly the case with many unincorporated traders, small partnerships and even small companies that are ill-equipped to bargain on equal terms with creditors and so it is appropriate that they should enjoy the full benefit of disclosure.

(c) NATURE OF THE TRANSACTION

The nature of certain transactions renders them for various reasons unsuitable for the imposition of general or even limited disclosure requirements. Consequently, some transactions are for sound reasons of business efficacy exempt from the disclosure provisions. For example, where banks' customers, without obtaining the prior consent of their respective banks, "go into overdraft" or exceed the agreed limit of overdraft facilities extended to them, an intolerable burden would be placed upon banks if they were obliged to make statutory disclosure whenever such an overdraft was created or extended: s 15(2). Similarly contracts that facilitate and form part of import/export transactions, and contracts entered into pursuant to a registered superannuation scheme are exempt transactions: s 15(1)(j),(k).

Other contracts such as those entered into pursuant to revolving credit contracts and those for the modification of controlled credit contracts are exempted from the general disclosure provisions in that special provision is made for these contracts: ss 15(1)(h), (i); 17, 18. For the same reason credit agreements made otherwise than at appropriate trade premises are subject to the rules specified in the Door To Door Sales Act 1967 and are exempt transactions for purposes of the disclosure provisions of the Credit Contracts Act 1981: s 15(1)(l).

24.3.2 What must be disclosed?

The Committee observed, at para 8.04 of their Report, that the simple answer is to require disclosure of all the terms of the contract. However full disclosure of all the terms was regarded as being unsatisfactory for the following reasons: (i) debtors are seeking understanding as much as they are seeking information and consequently disclosure must be in a form that renders it intelligible to the average person. To provide too much information is self defeating as a debtor can absorb only so many items of information at one time and beyond this he or she loses interest or does not have the inclination to digest the multitude of facts, and the law of diminishing returns comes into play; (ii) many contract terms are incorporated by reference to other documents and various terms are implied by statute into contracts. If the debtor is to be appraised of *all* the terms then he or she would need copies of all statutory instruments that impinge upon the transaction that he or she is entering and he or she would also need copies of any other documents or terms that are incorporated by reference; (iii) if on the occasion of each and every credit transaction there was a meticulous and exhaustive perusal of all the express *and* implied terms, business efficacy would be severely impaired.

These considerations led to the irresistible conclusion that a balance had to be struck. There is an optimum level of information that the debtor needs if he or she is to make a relatively informed decision about the merits of a credit transaction and is to compare its costs with that of alternative sources and methods of finance. Clearly financial particulars are of the essence in credit transactions and disclosure of financial particulars performs both a descriptive and shopping function in that this form of disclosure enables the debtor to determine whether the utility of the loan or instalment sale justifies the price, and disclosure of these financial matters provides the means whereby debtors may shop effectively for credit by comparing prices from different sources. Not surprisingly, therefore the Committee emphasised the disclosure of financial particulars and recommended as well the disclosure of the *express* terms of the credit transaction.

(a) FINANCIAL PARTICULARS
It is desirable that financial particulars be given in meaningful, uniform manner that would be readily intelligible to the average consumer. This task is complicated at the outset by the number and variety of credit

transactions in existence with the resultant difficulty of stipulating a method of disclosure applicable to credit transactions in general.

In order to enable the proverbial person-in-the-street to compare terms offered to him or her by different financiers the Committee recommended that two vitally important financial details, namely, the total cost of credit and the finance rate be quoted in a uniform manner by the various sources: *Credit Contracts Report* para 9.08. Lack of uniformity in the methods adopted in indicating the price that a debtor has to pay for the credit extended to him or her makes comparison between the credit charges of different suppliers of credit and the relative merits of borrowing as between one type of financial institution and another difficult, if not impossible, to determine. For example, the financier may express the credit charge rate as a flat rate, simple rate, reducible rate, compound rate, add-on rate, nominal rate or effective rate; moreover, the rate may be expressed on an annual basis, monthly or other periodic basis. In these circumstances a meaningful comparison of credit costs is unlikely and the full play of market forces is not able to operate with the consequence that the consumer may pay more for his or her credit than he or she needs.

The key elements of financial disclosure in the Credit Contracts Act 1981 are the "total cost of credit" and the "finance rate". The finance rate, as defined in s 6, being the rate that expresses the total cost of credit as a percentage per annum of the amount of credit is perhaps the item of information that will have the greatest impact upon consumers seeking and comparing credit sources. However, the most vexed question in the field of financial disclosure is: What items ought to be treated by law as comprising the total cost of credit? The resolution of this question is vital for the following reasons:

1   The division of the debtor's total indebtedness as between the amount of the credit and total cost of credit may determine whether a transaction is outside the upper financial limit of the legislation, the characterisation of the transaction as oppressive, and so on. For example, the implied term as to merchantable quality is not implied into hire purchase agreements where the cash price of goods disposed of exceeds $15,000: Hire Purchase Act 1971, s 12(1)(c), and the Hire Purchase (Specified Sums) Order 1980.

2   The computation of the finance rate is totally dependent upon the calculation of the total cost of credit. It is not possible to determine the rate of the credit charge imposed in a particular transaction unless it is known what comprises the charge itself.

3   The inclusion of certain items in the total cost of credit may be supported for the purpose of rate disclosure but inappropriate for the calculation of rebates and if the total cost of credit is to remain constant in any legislation this may require some compensating adjustment where rebates are in issue.

The Committee recommended that certain disbursements should not form part of the total cost of credit, and this is implemented in the Credit Contracts Act 1981. Total cost of credit is defined as the total of all money or money's worth payable by the debtor by virtue of the credit contract, less the amount of the credit provided pursuant to the contract *and* certain specified fees and charges: s 5. For example, amounts payable in respect of incidental services to the debtor, or for legal services relating to the credit contract, or the reasonable costs of surveys, inspections or valuations or property, do not form part of the total cost of credit inasmuch as they are reasonable: s 3(3). Some of the disbursements that are excluded from constituting part of the total cost of credit are very liberal dispensations in light of the strong case that can be made for regarding the total cost of credit as being represented by the excess of *all* the debtor's repayment obligations over the amount of credit provided to him or her. What is vitally important is that the true cost to the debtor, and not the net return to the creditor, should be reflected. Moreover, it is open to speculation as to the number and quantum of charges that will gain exemption under the head "reasonable amount payable for incidental services", s 3(3)(b)(i).

The position is clarified to a certain extent that "incidental services" are defined as meaning benefits (not being benefits that consist in the provision of credit) such as the provision by the lender of insurance or services for the protection, maintenance or preservation of the property: s 2(1). What benefits outside the scope of those mentioned in the amending legislation will qualify as an open question. The more exemptions granted the less accurate and useful a disclosure will be, as it will not reflect the total cost of borrowing.

Turning now to the finance rate, this is defined as the rate that expresses the total cost of credit as a percentage per annum of the amount of credit *and* that is either: (i) calculated by the financier himself by reference to the formula given in the First Schedule to the Act; or (ii) correctly derived or calculated from tables, or in accordance with a formula, prepared and published by the Government Actuary: s 6.

Disclosure of financial particulars is not always a straightforward task. Where the amount of credit and the total cost of credit are agreed upon and stipulated in the contract there is no difficulty in effecting disclosure of these particulars and the finance rate which is dependent upon them. However consider the following examples:

(a) A financier may agree to advance 80 per cent of the cost of an engineering contract subject to a specified limit and here the amount of credit will not be determined at the time the contract is made; or, a contract may be made whereby the interest payable is held to the prevailing bank rate from time to time. How is disclosure to be effected in these circumstances? Where the amount advanced is uncertain the legislature's solution is that if the credit is not to exceed a known maximum amount then the amount of credit shall be decreed to be that maximum amount or, if there is no such maximum amount, the amount of credit shall be that amount which in the creditor's opinion will be advanced: s 5(2)(a). In relation to transactions with a varying interest rate a similar solution is adopted; that is, if the interest rate or other component of the total cost of credit is subject to variation calculations shall be on the basis of the terms prevailing at the time the contract is made or, where such rate or other component is not known at the time of contracting, the rate or amount will be that figure that the creditor deems to be likely: s 5(2)(c).

(b) In open-end credit transactions, the creditor allows the debtor to draw at his or her discretion for amounts needed by the debtor from time to time up to an agreed ceiling; for example, bank overdraft arrangements and credit cards enable the debtor to charge his or her purchases to a financier if and when needed up to a specified limit. With these transactions not only is the amount of credit indeterminable in advance, but the total cost of credit is dependent upon the debtor's debiting and repayment patterns. The solution adopted in the Act is that while the financier must disclose the maximum amount of the credit and the basis of the calculation of the credit charge, there is no requirement that the finance rate be disclosed in such cases: Second Schedule, Part I, cl 2, 4, 6. Furthermore at the end of each billing period the financier must disclose the details outlined in Part III of the Second Schedule to the Act; that is, the opening balance, details of the credit provided, amounts paid by the debtor during the billing period, the amount and description of each charge payable under the contract that does not form part of the total cost of credit and that has been charged during the billing period, the cost of credit and the interest rate. Obviously with these transactions, known as "revolving credit contracts", it is not possible to give the actual finance rate in advance, but if the debtor knows the rate to be applied to any amount owing at the end of any billing cycle, this may be of more significance to him or her.

(b) OTHER PARTICULARS
It is obviously important that the debtor should be able to identify and locate the financier to whom he or she is indebted and the Credit Contracts Act 1981 provides that the name and address of the financier must be provided: Second Schedule, Part I, cl 1. Furthermore, all terms of the contract, other than terms implied by law, must be disclosed: Second Schedule, Part I, cl 6.

Save for certain penalty and termination clauses, no restraint is placed on the nature of terms that may be agreed upon, but in light of the extensive re-opening provisions such restraints are strictly unnecessary. With deferred payment dispositions of goods a statement of rights must be incorporated in the disclosure document outlining the debtors' legal rights under the Act: Second Schedule, Part I, cl 8. This topic will be dealt with below, but the underlying premise is that if a debtor is ignorant of these rights then obviously he or she cannot even begin to exercise these rights – disclosure in a prominent fashion goes a long way towards rectifying this ignorance.

24.3.3 When should a disclosure be made?

This question can only properly be answered by reference to the objectives of disclosure. Succinctly stated these objectives are:

(a) To facilitate comparison shopping; that is, to ensure that before commitment to a particular credit transaction the consumer has the information before him or her to compare the various sources of credit available.

(b) To facilitate rational choice as between credit and cash. If the consumer has adequate information about the cost of credit more intelligent decisions about the use of credit compared with buying for cash may be made.

(c) To ensure that persons who enter into credit contracts are aware of their rights and obligations under that contract.

(d) To ensure that during the term of a credit contract the debtor can ascertain his or her position under that contract.

If all these objectives are to be met there has to be provision for disclosure of information before a debtor is committed to a particular contract, and provision must also be made for post-contract disclosure.

(a) PRE-COMMITMENT DISCLOSURE

It is well recognised that disclosure at or immediately before the conclusion of a particular credit transaction is inadequate in itself, for by then the debtor usually will be psychologically committed to the transaction and disclosure will have only a limited effect, if at all. Credit contracts are notoriously complicated documents and it would be totally unrealistic to expect a prospective debtor to even read, let alone understand, such a document when at the point of signature. Very few persons would insist on a time for consideration, especially when goods are to be acquired pursuant to the credit contract. How then is disclosure to be effected so as to facilitate comparison shopping for credit, the rational use of credit compared with buying for cash, and to ensure prior familiarity with the terms of credit transactions?

The solution adopted by the Credit Contracts Act 1981 is to afford the debtor a right to cancel the credit contract within three working days of the required disclosure being made to him: s 22. The Act provides that every creditor who enters into a "controlled credit contract" must ensure that initial disclosure of the contract is effected before the contract is made or will be made not later than the end of the fifteenth working day after the contract was made: s 16. Initial disclosure is to be given in one or more legible documents and must encompass all the information, statements and other matters specified in the Second Schedule: ss 20, 21. After such disclosure is made the debtor has three working days to consider his or her position. The joint objective of these provisions is to ensure that the debtor has sufficient information at his or her disposal to assess the merits and demerits of a particular transaction and the three "days of grace" enable the debtor to determine not only whether he or she wishes to be finally bound, but also to ascertain whether more attractive terms are available elsewhere.

Cancellation has the effect of extinguishing the debtor's liability and entitles him or her to recover payments made and goods tendered in part exchange or for any other purpose: s 23(1). Furthermore, the creditor must ensure that all security given by the debtor pursuant to the credit contract is released and, subject to certain exceptions, the debtor is not liable to pay any part of the cost of credit or other charges: s 23(1)(b), (c). It is vitally important to note that the purchaser who has received goods cannot cancel completely; he or she can only cancel "the credit part" of the contract: s 22(2). Generally, therefore, where a debtor has entered into a credit sale or hire purchase agreement for the purchase of goods he or she may cancel the credit provisions of the contract by giving written notice of cancellation to the creditor or dealer and by paying the cash price not later than 15 working days after giving notice. Dugdale, *The Credit Contracts Act 1981* (1981), p 52, comments:

It was designed to avoid a situation where for example someone could take delivery of a car under a hire purchase agreement on a Friday, use it until the following Wednesday and then with some thousands more miles on the clock, return it and demand his deposit back.

Moreover, cancellation is precluded altogether in the case where the credit is provided for a specified period not exceeding two months and no part of the credit is used, with the knowledge of the creditor, to pay amounts owing to the creditor under another credit contract: s 22(4). This provision is designed to prevent the debtor from taking advantage of a series of "cooling-off" periods to his or her own benefit in short term transactions, but is also framed in such a way to avoid the potential abuse of a creditor evading the cancellation provisions by a series of short term contracts of the "roll over" variety with a particular debtor.

How effective then are these measures when assessed against the Committee's primary objective to enable the public to shop for credit? Consider the purchase of goods and services on credit terms. Very rarely will advertisements do more than indicate the availability of credit and the desirability of, say, buying now rather than later. If a prospective debtor wishes to be appraised of financial particulars in sufficient detail to make an informed choice, he or she will have to visit or contact each alternative credit outlet. Needless to say this will be a time consuming exercise and it may well be that the prospective debtor will settle for the first loan or credit transaction that "sounds" reasonable, rather than acquaint himself or herself with the terms available from a large number of creditors before making a selection. True "shopping for credit" would entail the latter course of action. In the usual case the debtor will first consider the question of credit at the time when he or she sees goods that are to his or her liking; if the debtor elects to buy those goods pursuant to a credit sale agreement or hire purchase agreement initial disclosure will usually be effected at or immediately before the conclusion of the particular transaction. Such a debtor is not entitled to return such goods in terms of the cancellation provisions and so if he or she elects to cancel the credit provisions of the contract he or she must "front up" with the cash within 15 days of giving written notice of such cancellation. If the debtor does not have funds to meet the cash price he or she must frantically scour the credit market in the three day "grace" period after the initial disclosure in an endeavour to find an alternative, and cheaper, avenue of finance. It is suggested that this would not be an attractive, and hence likely, proposition for the average debtor who has the desired goods in hand. Consequently, it is suggested that significant practical barriers could stand in the way of the Act, achieving one of its primary objectives; namely, the shopping for credit. A prominent statement of the rights under the cancellation provisions must accompany the disclosure documentation in the case of deferred payment dispositions of goods: Second Schedule, Part I, cl 8.

The great advantage of reconsideration is that it ensures a reasonable period of time for detached evaluation of the financial and other data, as well as an opportunity to compare alternative credit arrangements, for the debtor who avails himself or herself of the opportunity. Furthermore, the existence of the cancellation provisions may have a beneficial impact in making creditors more reticent and cautious in the construction of their contracts and imposition of charges for credit – the same could be said for re-opening provisions.

(b) POST-CONTRACT DISCLOSURE

One objective of the disclosure provisions is to ensure that during the term of a credit contract the debtor can ascertain his or her position under the contract. Post-contract disclosure under the Credit Contracts Act 1981 may be briefly canvassed under the following heads:

(a) Request disclosure. A debtor or guarantor under a controlled credit contract may request in writing that the creditor disclose to him or her all or part of the information specified in Part IV of the Second Schedule of the Act; for example, outstanding payments required: ss 19, 21(1)(b). Upon receipt of a specified fee the creditor must ensure that disclosure of the information or documents requested shall be made not later than the end of the fifteenth working day after the day the fee is received. In order to avoid vexatious inquiries and the disruption of normal business, a creditor is relieved of compliance with a request if disclosure of the information or documents requested has been made during the three months preceding the receipt of a request: s 19.

(b) Modification disclosure. The Act also makes provision for the situation where the terms of a controlled credit contract are modified or varied and such a contract is known as a modification contract: s 17. Where a creditor enters into a modification contract he or she must ensure that disclosure of the information specified in Part II of the Second Schedule is made; for example, disclosure of all the terms of the modification contract, other than those implied by law, must be made: ss 17, 21(1)(a). Such a modification contract is subject to the cancellation provisions: ss 22(1), 23(1)(d).

(c) Continuing disclosure. Where revolving credit contracts are involved the legislature has recognised that a different disclosure provision is needed by virtue of the distinct nature of this credit. A creditor under a revolving credit contract must ensure that not later than the end of a specified period after the end of each billing period during which credit has been provided under the contract or the whole or part of the cost of credit has become due, that the creditor discloses all the information specified in Part III of the Second Schedule to the Act; that is, disclosure of the opening and closing dates of the billing period, the opening and closing balances, as well as details of the amounts paid, credit provided, charges and cost of credit, is required: see ss 18, 21(1)(a).

This comprehensive set of provisions ensures that a debtor may ascertain his or her position during the currency of a credit contract. Disclosure of financial particulars, such as the amount outstanding under a credit contract, is of vital importance to a debtor, eg a purchaser under a hire purchase agreement may complete the purchase of goods by paying the unpaid balance at any time during the continuance of the agreement and if the purchaser does so he or she is entitled to certain statutory rebates. However, it is not only the financial particulars that are of concern to debtors, but other terms as well. The Act ensures that a debtor has, or may obtain, a copy of the agreement encompassing all the terms of the credit contract other than those implied by law, and where any variation of those terms occurs, the terms of the contract effecting that variation must be disclosed.

24.3.4 Method of disclosure

Disclosure must be made by providing to each person to whom disclosure must be made disclosure documents which comply with s 21. This may be done either by delivering the disclosure documents to each such person or by sending them by post to the last place of residence or business of that person known to the creditor or to an address specified by that person for the purpose of receiving the disclosure documents: s 20(1); see *IFC Securities Ltd v Sewell* [1990] 1 NZLR 177.

Note that where a debtor has conferred a power of attorney with unqualified power to borrow and the attorney subsequently borrows on behalf of the debtor, disclosure may be made to the attorney and need not be made to the debtor personally: *National Australia Finance Ltd v Fahey* [1990] 2 NZLR 482.

24.3.5 Sanctions for non-compliance

The Credit Contracts Act 1981 provides for basic sanctions for non-compliance with the disclosure provisions.

First, no person other than the debtor may enforce a controlled credit contract, or any right to recover property to which the contract relates, or enforce any security given pursuant to the contract, until the requisite disclosure is made: s 24; subject, however to ss 31-33.

Secondly, failure to make disclosure results in a loss to the creditor of part or all of the total cost of credit payable under the contract: ss 25-28. The exact computation of the amount forfeited is dependent upon the nature of the disclosure provision that is breached and the time when disclosure is made. For example, if initial disclosure is not made in accordance with the Act the debtor's liability to pay a specified amount is extinguished: s 25. This specified amount is the smaller of: (a) An amount equal to three times the part of the total cost of credit that relates to the period from the day the contract is made until the earlier of the following days: (i) The day on which initial disclosure is made; (ii) the day that is eight months after the day the contract is made; (b) the total cost of credit payable under the contract: s 25(2). Accordingly for any medium or long term contract it is highly unlikely that a creditor will forfeit the total cost of credit, but will forfeit a lesser amount.

Notwithstanding non-compliance with the disclosure provisions outlined in the Act relief may be accorded the creditor who shows that:

(a) the failure was due to inadvertence or to events outside the control of the creditor; and

(b) disclosure was made as soon as reasonably practicable after the failure was discovered by the creditor or brought to his or her notice; and

(c) where disclosure documents relating to the contract state as the finance rate of the contract a rate that is less than the correct finance rate, the creditor has reduced the finance rate of the contract to the rate disclosed in those documents; and,

(d) the creditor has compensated or offered to compensate the debtor under the contract for any prejudice caused the debtor by the failure: s 31.

In these circumstances the penalties for non-compliance do not apply. Even where the creditor cannot satisfy these criteria the creditor may apply to Court for an order directing that the penalties not apply or that a lesser penalty be imposed: s 32. In exercising its discretion the Court must have regard to whether the creditor is a financier, the extent and reasons for non-disclosure, whether the debtor has been prejudiced by the non-disclosure and any other circumstances as the Court thinks fit: s 32(2). Finally the penalties for non-disclosure may be waived by a debtor provided he or she has received written notice of the failure and his or her rights that arise from the failure: s 33.

In considering whether relief should be granted under s 32 the Court will take into account whether the breach of disclosure was deliberate, whether the borrower was misled and whether the penalty is disproportionate: see, for example, *Anderson v Burbery Finance Ltd* [1988] 2 NZLR 196 (CA). In *United Fisheries Ltd v Patrikios Holdings Ltd* [1989] 3 NZLR 56 (CA) the appellant, a fish wholesaler, had supplied fish to the respondent on the basis that payment was to be made weekly. The respondent never kept to these terms and the appellant then charged interest at the rate of 0.4 per cent per week on overdue accounts. At trial it was held that the transactions were controlled credit contracts. Since it was common ground that the appellant had failed to disclose the finance rate as required by the Act the penal provisions of s 25 became operative. Without relief the effect would have been to extinguish the liability of the respondent to pay interest for two years, but the trial Judge allowed a reduction of one-third, thereby expunging interest for 16 months. On appeal this order was varied, the Court of Appeal considering that a reduction of approximately one-tenth was more appropriate. The failure to disclose was not a deliberate evasion of the Act and was of no consequence to the respondent, which never accepted that it was liable to pay interest at all.

24.4 CREDIT ADVERTISEMENTS

A very broad definition of "credit advertisement" is given in the Act in that any information, sound, image or other matter that is communicated to the public by whatever means and that notifies or implies the availability of credit, falls within the scope of the definition: s 34. The theory that a credit purchaser becomes hypnotised by a product to the extent that he or she is less concerned with financial details than a cash purchaser carried sufficient weight with the Committee for them to recommend that specific provision be made for misleading credit advertisements: *Credit Contracts Report*, para 10.06. Such advertisements must not contain any information, sound, image or other matter that is likely to deceive or mislead a reasonable person with regard to any particular that is material to the provision of credit: s 35.

The phrase "likely to deceive or misled" is not defined but is certain to be interpreted on similar lines to the construction of s 9 of the Fair Trading Act 1986 which provides that no person shall, in trade, engage in conduct that is misleading or deceptive or is likely to mislead or deceive: see 10.2.6 supra.

Logically any inquiry into whether a particular credit advertisement is likely to mislead or deceive must have as its focal point the intended audience of that communication. A strict view as to composition of that audience is adopted in Australia and the United States. As Murphy J observed in *Parkdale Custom Built Furniture Pty Ltd v Puxu Pty Ltd* [1982] 42 ALR 1, 19:

> The prudent buyer may be misled, but not all buyers are prudent. The [Trade Practices] Act aims to protect the imprudent as well as the prudent. In applying a similar provision of the Consumer Protection Act 1969 (NSW) the Industrial Commission said that an advertiser's responsibility extended to readers both shrewd and ingenuous ... educated and uneducated and ... inexperienced in commercial transactions ... an advertisement may be misleading even though it fails to deceive more wary readers (see *CRW Pty Ltd v Sneddon* [1972] 72 AR (NSW) 17, 28).

Similarly, in *Florence Manufacturing v J C Dowd and Co* 178 F 73 (1910) it was held that the advertisement must be looked at from the perspective of potential impact on the ignorant, the unthinking and the credulous who in making purchases do not stop to analyse but are governed by appearance and general impressions. However the New Zealand legislature has taken a much more lenient view in that the question as to whether a credit advertisement is "likely to deceive or mislead" must be assessed as against the standard of the reasonable person. Therefore it would not be enough that an advertisement had the potentiality to effect an individual whose comprehension and sophistication fell beneath this hypothetical level of understanding embraced by a reasonable person. Moreover, such a credit advertisement must be likely to deceive or mislead a reasonable person with regard to a particular that is material to the provision of credit.

While the Credit Contracts Act 1981 proscribes misleading advertising it does not set out to achieve full and comprehensive disclosure of information in credit advertisements. Mandatory disclosure of financial particulars in *all* credit advertisements would not only promote "shopping for credit" but would have a highly beneficial competitive effect. However, notwithstanding these obvious advantages, and statutory requirement of disclosure of certain particulars in credit advertisements is fraught with complications. For one thing, mandatory rate disclosure in credit advertisements would place an unduly heavy burden upon financiers in that it would enjoin flexibility. Financiers must be able to vary their interest rates and other charges according to the circumstances of each transaction, eg the estimated risk, the size of the loan required, whether it is to be secured or unsecured, the period, the category of goods for which finance is to be provided and so on. For this reason mandatory rate disclosure in credit advertisements is inappropriate given that it would be likely to deceive or mislead prospective debtors if the advertised rate were not the rate at which transactions were actually consummated. Flexibility could be introduced by permitting financiers, whose rates vary according to the factors outlined above, to advertise a range of rates. However the danger with this approach is that considerable scope for abuse is introduced in that the prospective debtor could be lured by the quotation of a relatively low rate at the lower end of the scale and then subjected to pressure to consummate a transaction at the upper end of the scale.

Considerations such as these led to the adoption of a compromise between the extremes of mandatory disclosure of certain particulars such as the interest rate, other charges and the cash price of property or services, on the one hand, and the absolute prohibition against the disclosure of these particulars, on the other. Therefore, where an advertisement contains no indication of the interest rate or other charges at which credit may be provided, there is no obligation upon the financier to disclose the finance rate in that advertisement; but, where such an indication is given in a credit advertisement then the finance rate must be identified and displayed with equal prominence: s 36. Similarly any advertisement that gives the deposit payable in respect of a deferred payment disposition of property or services must also stipulate the cash price of the property or services, and describe it as such: s 37. Given that there are varying degrees of specificity in financial advertising the approach adopted in the Credit Contracts Act 1981 appears to offer the best possible solution. While many loans, for example, are subject to widely fluctuating interest rates and other charges dependent upon the prospective debtor's particular financial circumstances, loans by banks are normally available at a known rate to all customers – there is no question of varying the rate according to the degree of risk as, either, the customer is considered credit-worthy enough to qualify for a loan at the going rate, or, he or she is refused the loan altogether. There is no sound reason to preclude such a lender from advertising its rate or rates, but at the same time it is not equitable, nor indeed practicable, to require similar disclosure by other lenders whose rates are variable.

As far as enforcement is concerned, s 38 provides:

> If a credit advertisement contravenes any of sections 35 to 37 of this Act, every person whom the advertisement states or implies is a person from or through whom credit can be obtained commits an offence, and is liable on summary conviction to a fine not exceeding $5,000:
>   Provided that a person shall not be convicted under this section in respect of any such contravention if he or she proves –
> (a) That neither he, nor any person acting on his or her behalf, had any knowledge of the advertisement before it was made; or
> (b) That he or she took all steps reasonably possible on his part to stop the communication of the advertisement to the public.

In *The Credit Contracts Act 1981* (1981), p 66, Dugdale comments that:

> the effect of this section is that the prosecution need do no more than identify the defendant as the creditor referred to in the contravening advertisement. The onus then passes to the defendant to establish that neither he or she nor his or her agent had any knowledge of the advertisement prior to its communication to the public, or else that if he or she did . . . he or she did all he or she could to stop the publication.

24.5 PROHIBITION OF CERTAIN FINANCIERS AND TERMS

The Credit Contracts Act 1981 does not contain any registration requirement for persons who provide finance, but does provide that the District Court may prohibit or restrict certain persons from acting as financiers: s 39. For example, a person who has been convicted of an offence against the Act or of a crime involving dishonesty may be prohibited from providing credit. Any person may apply to the District Court for an order under this section: s 39(2).

As mentioned earlier, the basic approach of the legislature is that the parties should as far as possible have a free hand in the negotiation and determination of the terms of their credit contracts. This is, in the light of the re-opening provisions, unlikely to lead to abuses as the presence of extensive re-opening provisions is a significant deterrent and means of rectifying oppressive terms. However, there are two types of clause that are specifically dealt with by the Act:

(a) PENALTY CLAUSES

Section 40(1) provides that no credit contract shall contain a term to the effect that, if a debtor fails to comply with a term of the contract, an amount payable by the debtor under the contract will be increased, or will not be reduced, to another amount. This provision incorporates in the Act the common law rule against penalties, and catches the backdoor device of providing for interest at a higher rate reducible for prompt payment: see *Wallingford v Mutual Society* [1880] 5 App Cas 685, 702. Note, that it is permissible to provide for an increase in the finance rate or interest rate payable under a credit contract in the limited circumstances outlined in s 40(2).

(b) TERMINATION CLAUSES

Section 41(1) provides that no credit contract shall contain a term to the effect that all or part of the credit under the contract will become immediately payable to the creditor under the contract or that the finance rate will be increased (or will not be reduced) to another rate if an application is made to re-open the contract, or to seek an order to prohibit or restrict the activities of a financier, or if any of the disclosure sanctions are invoked. In the absence of such a provision a creditor could endeavour to prevent or deter a debtor from seeking relief, say, under the re-opening provisions, in that immediate repayment of the principal sum could loom ominously in the debtor's mind.

24.6 MISCELLANEOUS

The provisions of the Credit Contracts Act 1981 shall have effect notwithstanding any provision to the contrary in any contract or agreement: s 43. Moreover the Act applies to contracts whether made before or after the commencement of the Act, save for certain limited exceptions: s 53; see also *Sharplin v Broadlands Finance Ltd* [1982] 2 NZLR 1, 8. Finally, the fact that a contract has been entered into in contravention of any of the provisions of this Act or that an act which contravenes the provisions of the Act has been committed in the course of performance of any contract shall not make that contract illegal, or, except as expressly provided in the Act, make that contract or any provision of that contract unenforceable or of no effect: s 44.

Chapter 25

CHEQUES

SUMMARY

25.1 GENERAL

This chapter is concerned with the legal principles governing the use of cheques. Cheques form the most common class of bills of exchange. In turn, bills of exchange are a species of negotiable instrument.

The law governing bills of exchange is contained in the Bills of Exchange Act 1908. In addition, the Cheques Act 1960, which forms part of the 1908 Act, deals exclusively with cheques, and confers certain protections and immunities upon paying and collecting banks. As well as this set of statutory rules, recourse must be made to case law where the statutes are silent on a particular point. Section 98(1) of the 1908 Act provides as follows:

> The rules of common law, including the law merchant, save in so far as they are inconsistent with the express provisions of this Act, shall continue to apply to bills of exchange, promissory notes, and cheques.

In *International Ore & Fertilizer Corporation v East Coast Fertiliser Co Ltd* [1987] 1 NZLR 9 the Court of Appeal affirmed the importance of adhering to fundamental principles of English law about bills of exchange.

25.2 NEGOTIABILITY

An instrument can be given the status of a negotiable instrument either by statute (eg the Bills of Exchange Act 1908), or by long-standing and universally accepted custom: *Goodson v Hawera Lawn Tennis and Croquet Club Inc* [1931] NZLR 1096, 1101.

The following are the essential characteristics of a negotiable instrument:

(1) Title to the instrument passes by delivery (in the case of instruments payable to bearer) or by delivery and indorsement (in the case of instruments payable to order). In the case of bills of exchange, this rule is contained in s 31 of the 1908 Act. A bill is payable to bearer if it is expressed to be so payable, or if the last indorsement on it is in blank (ie the simple signature of payee or indorser). A bill is payable to order if it is expressed to be so payable, or if expressed to be payable to a particular person (including a "special" indorsement, that is, one which indorses the cheque not in blank, but payable to a specific person): s 8.

(2) A holder for value of a negotiable instrument can sue on it in his or her own name, that is, without having to join any prior holders in any action. A "holder" of a bill of exchange is defined in the 1908 Act as "the payee or indorsee of a bill who is in possession of it, or the bearer thereof": s 2.

(3) A bona fide transferee for value of a negotiable instrument takes the instrument free from any defects of title of prior parties. In the context of bills of exchange such a transferee is known as a "holder in due course". Section 29 of the 1908 Act defines a holder in due course as a holder who has taken a bill, complete and regular on the face of it, before the bill became overdue, without notice of any previous dishonour of the bill, in good faith and for value, and without notice of any defect of title of the transferor. Every holder of a bill is presumed to be a holder in due course: s 30. Thus a bona fide transferee for value of a negotiable instrument can acquire a good title even through a thief. A holder in due course enjoys a privileged status under the law in that he or she has an absolute title to the instrument and its proceeds. There is, however, one exception to this principle, for the holder's claim may be defeated where there has been a prior forgery on the instrument. Although the general rule is that no person can acquire title through a forgery, it will be seen that various exceptions and estoppels against the person whose signature is forged are raised by the Bills of Exchange Act. For example, by s 24 a person whose signature has been forged is generally not liable on the bill unless that person is by his or her conduct estopped from setting up the forgery or want of authority for his or her signature.

Certain cheques and other bills of exchange are not negotiable, and clearly no person can acquire a good title to such an instrument from a person having no title or a defective title even if he or she takes in good faith and for value. It is only where the instrument is truly *negotiable* in the sense already described that such a transferee can enjoy the special position of a holder in due course.

The characteristic of negotiability should be contrasted with that of transferability. Transferability relates to the process of passing title to an instrument, whereas negotiability is a concept which describes the quality of the title that is passed.

In the case of assignment, notice to a debtor or other person liable under the instrument is required whereas no such notice is required in the case of negotiable instruments. By virtue of negotiation, the holder of a cheque can sue in his or her own name upon it: s 38. An assignee does not necessarily have this right. Furthermore, an assignment, whether legal or equitable, is always *subject to equities;* that is, the assignee takes subject to any rights which the party liable or third parties may have against the assignor, and the assignee can only acquire the same title as was possessed by the assignor. But a person who takes a negotiable instrument for value and in good faith takes it *free from equities,* that is, free from the rights of third parties and free from any defects in title of a prior holder. Finally, whereas consideration is presumed to have been given in the case of a negotiable instrument (s 30), it must be proved to have been given in the case of some assignments.

Nowadays many drawers of cheques are concerned to protect themselves and their funds by nullifying or restricting the negotiability of cheques, so that they retain little of their traditional negotiability. The methods by which such restrictions are sought to be achieved are dealt with below.

25.3 DEFINITION OF "CHEQUE"

25.3.1 General

A cheque is a bill of exchange drawn on a banker payable on demand: s 73(1), Bills of Exchange Act 1908.

As cheques are bills of exchange, s 73(2) of the Act provides that the provisions of the Act applicable to a bill of exchange payable on demand also apply to a cheque, except as otherwise provided in Part II of the Act.

There is no statutory definition of the word "bank", although s 2 of the Act defines a "banker" as including "a body of persons, whether incorporated or not, who carry on the business of banking" (see also Banking Act 1982, s 2). For the purposes of the law relating to cheques, it will be sufficient to state that a bank must be a concern which, at the very least, conducts current accounts on behalf of its customers. This includes the payment of cheques drawn on such accounts and the collection of cheques for customers: *United Dominions Trust Ltd v Kirkwood* [1966] 1 QB 783; cf *Re Roe's Legal Charge* [1982] 2 Lloyd's Rep 370. If these elements are absent, then the Bills of Exchange Act 1908 and the Cheques Act 1960 will not come into play.

By amalgamating the statutory definitions of "bill of exchange" (1908 Act, s 3) and cheque (s 73), we arrive at the following composite definition of a cheque:

A cheque is an unconditional order in writing, addressed by a customer to his or her bank, requiring the bank to pay on demand a sum certain in money to or to the order of a specified person, or to bearer.

25.3.2 Elements of the definition

(a) UNCONDITIONAL ORDER
A cheque must be an *unconditional order.* It must be an *order* of an imperative nature and not merely a request. Accordingly, an instrument in the terms "Please let the bearer have £100, and place it to my credit, and

you will oblige me" is not a cheque. On the other hand, the addition of the word "please" to an unconditional order does not in itself deprive the instrument of the character of a cheque.

The order must also be *unconditional*. The drawer cannot impose any conditions upon the drawee banker, as for example, by requiring a particular form of receipt to be completed as a condition of payment. Such an instrument would not be a cheque: *Bavins Jnr and Sims v London and South Western Bank* [1900] 1 QB 270. Such a request may, however, be made of the payee or holder to acknowledge receipt of the sum represented by the cheque, and the completion of such a receipt by the holder or payee does not amount to a condition of payment as between the drawer and the bank: *Thairlwall v Great Northern Railway Co* [1910] 2 KB 509. Thus the drawer may insist on the completion of such a form on the cheque before *presentment* for payment, and it is only the *order* to pay as between the drawer and the banker which must be free of conditions. The distinction between these two directives is indeed a vague one. If the direction is contained in the body of the instrument and runs in terms such as "Pay T Smith provided the receipt below is duly signed" - these words are taken as a direction to the payee only and do not render the instrument conditional.

On this point, s 3(3) states that a bill is rendered conditional by an order to pay out of a particular fund, but an unqualified order to pay, coupled with: (a) an indication of a particular fund out of which the drawee is to reimburse himself or herself or a particular account to be debited with the amount; or (b) a statement of a transaction giving rise to the bill, is unconditional. In other words, if it is an order free from conditions or instructions, it is not vitiated by an indication of a particular fund from which the drawee may reimburse himself or herself. For example, in *Peacocke and Co v Williams* (1909) 28 NZLR 354, a "bill" was addressed to the drawee requesting the payment to P of £ 150 and stating "deduct same from moneys coming to me on account of contract . . .". It was held that the instrument was a bill of exchange. The actual order to pay was unconditional and unequivocal and the words quoted above were merely an indication of a particular fund for reimbursement.

(b) IN WRITING

Although writing is essential, the 1908 Act does not specify that cheques have to be written on paper. However, it could be argued that it is an implied term of the banker-customer relationship that only the bank's printed forms should be used. The following is an example of a typical form of cheque issued by a bank and filled in by the drawer.

(c) ADDRESSED BY CUSTOMER TO BANK

Section 6(1) of the 1908 Act requires that the drawee (the person to whom the order is given) must be named or otherwise indicated on a bill with reasonable certainty.

This part of the definition contemplates that the person giving the order (the drawer) and the person receiving it (the drawee) shall be two distinct legal persons. It will be realised that "bank cheques" do not conform to this requirement, since such instruments are basically orders to pay addressed by a bank to itself. However, s 5(2) of the Act provides that where drawer and drawee are the same person, the holder of the instrument may treat it, at the holder's option, either as a bill of exchange or as a promissory note. The same applies where the drawee is a fictitious person or a person not having capacity to contract.

(d) SIGNED BY THE DRAWER

The drawer's signature is essential for a cheque to be enforceable. A forged and unauthorised signature is of no effect unless the party against whom it is sought to enforce the cheque is precluded from pleading the forgery or lack of authority: 1908 Act, s 24(1). One instance of where a person is estopped from claiming that a signature is a forgery is where a person becomes a party (ie indorses the cheque) subsequent to the forgery. As against a holder in due course, such a person is estopped from setting up the forgery: s 55(2)(d). A person can sign a cheque as agent for another (s 92(1)), but must clearly indicate that he or she is signing in a representative capacity, so as to exclude personal liability on the cheque: s 26.

Section 25 provides that a signature by procuration operates as notice that the agent has but a limited authority to sign, and the principal is bound by such signature only if the agent so signing was acting within the actual limits of his or her authority. Thus it is a warning to a transferee to ascertain that the agent is acting within the scope of his or her authority. By s 23, no person is liable upon a bill as drawer, indorser, or acceptor unless he or she has signed it as such, but a person who signs a bill in a trade or assumed name is treated as liable thereon as if he or she had signed his or her own name. Similarly, the signature of the name of a firm is treated as equivalent to the signature of the names of all persons liable as partners: s 23.

The position regarding the signing of cheques by rubber stamp facsimile remains unclear. Nowhere does the Act define "signature". In *Goodman v J Eban Ltd* [1954] 1 QB 550; [1954] 1 All ER 763, concerning the signature, by means of a facsimile rubber stamp, to a solicitor's bill of costs, Denning LJ (as he then was), in a dissenting judgment appeared to doubt whether a bill of exchange or a cheque could be signed by means of a rubber stamp. Sir Raymond Evershed MR and Romer LJ did not address themselves to the case of bills of exchange. They held that as the plaintiff solicitor had been shown to have placed the stamp on the letter himself, the letter had to be taken to have been duly "signed" by him within the meaning of the Solicitors Act 1932 (UK).

It remains an open question whether this decision is applicable to cheques by analogy, although it would clearly be unreasonable to require bankers to act on anything but the handwritten signature of the drawer. If signing by rubber stamp was allowed in the case of bills of exchange a bank would have no way of knowing which signatures were genuine and which were unauthorised. Customer and banker could, of course, enter into a contract entitling the bank to pay (and debit) cheques "signed" in this way.

(e) PAYABLE ON DEMAND

A bill is payable on demand: (a) if it is expressed to be payable on demand, or at sight, or on presentation; or (b) if no time for payment is expressed therein: s 10(1).

The date on a cheque is not essential to its validity as a legally enforceable instrument, for by s 3(4)(a) a bill is not invalid merely because the date is omitted. In practice, however, banks do not pay cheques which do not bear a date, and return undated cheques for completion, despite the fact that, by virtue of s 20, any holder has prima facie authority to fill up any omission of any material particular on a bill as he or she thinks fit. Such a completion of an inchoate instrument must be done within a reasonable time to render the instrument enforceable against persons who become parties thereto prior to completion. However, if such an instrument is negotiated to a holder in due course after completion it shall be valid and effectual for all purposes in his or her hands: s 20(2). By s 13(1) there is a presumption that a date of drawing, acceptance, or indorsement on a bill of exchange is the true date unless the contrary is proved.

(1) Post-dated cheques: Section 13(2) of the 1908 Act provides that bills of exchange are not invalid merely by reason of being either antedated or postdated.

In drawing a postdated cheque, the drawer's clear intention is that it should not be payable until that date arrives. If the bank does pay a postdated cheque prematurely, and subsequently dishonours other cheques because payment of the first cheque has exhausted the funds in the customer's account, it will be liable to pay to the customer damages for wrongful dishonour: *Pollock v BNZ* (1902) 20 NZLR 173.

Therefore, if it pays the cheque too soon, the bank cannot debit the account. It may be able to debit the account when the postdate arrives, but could take the risk of something occurring to the account to frustrate the act of debiting as against a credit balance.

A postdated cheque can be transferred prior to the due date: *Royal Bank of Scotland v Tottenham* [1894] 2 QB 715. Presumably, therefore, a person can become a holder in due course of such a cheque prior to the due date.

In *Brien v Dwyer* (1978) 141 CLR 378 the High Court of Australia indicated that a post-dated cheque is not a cheque proper for the purposes of the Bills of Exchange Act. In that case a contract for the sale of land required the purchaser to pay a specified sum by deposit, and permitted payment by cheque. The issue was whether tender by the purchaser of a post-dated cheque constituted compliance with the contract. It was held that it did not. But the High Court went further. Barwick CJ said at p 387

> The cheque spoken of in [the contract] is a cheque proper, i e an order on a bank for immediate payment. A post-dated cheque is a bill of exchange of a different order.

However in *Hodgson & Lee Pty Ltd v Mardonius Pty Ltd* (1986) 5 NSWLR 496 the New South Wales Court of Appeal took a different view. There two post-dated cheques had been given to the plaintiff by the third defendant in respect of some plumbing work which the plaintiff had performed. The cheques were duly presented, for payment, to the bank on which they were drawn, but were dishonoured. The plaintiff then sued the drawer, among others, for the amount due on the cheques. The defence was that the cheques were not strictly speaking cheques at all, but merely bills of exchange payable at some future time, and that the plaintiff had failed to prove, as he was bound to do in order to succeed, that the cheques had each been presented for payment on the date on which each fell due. The Court of Appeal refused to apply the dicta in *Brien's* case, citing earlier authority tending to show that a post-dated cheque is a cheque proper, and invoking also s 13 of the Bills of Exchange Act, which says that a bill is not invalid by reason only that it is antedated or post-dated.

(2) Stale cheques: Section 45 (2) (b) appears to require that a cheque, being a bill payable on demand, be presented within a reasonable time after its issue in order to render the drawer liable upon it, and within a reasonable time after its indorsement in order to render the indorser liable.

However s 74 of the Act makes s 45 inapplicable to cheques. Section 74 is generally regarded as the ruling enactment as to cheques, impliedly excluding the drawer from the operation of or any right under s 45 arising from the holder's failure to present within a reasonable time. As s 74 clearly contemplates only the special, if remote, circumstance of the failure of a banker having funds of the drawer in hand after a reasonable time for presentment of the cheque has elapsed, its general effect is therefore taken to render the drawer of a cheque continuously liable to a holder for the normal six-year limitation period applicable to contractual rights. In other words, unless a drawer suffers actual damage through a delay in presentment, as specifically defined and provided for in s 74, the drawer is not discharged by reason of the fact that the cheque had not been presented within a reasonable time, but remains liable to a holder on the cheque for six years from the date of its issue: see *Cox and Walsh v Burton* [1933] NZLR 249, and the cases cited therein at pp 254-255, per Ostler J. Quaere whether, if the rights of a *drawer* of a cheque under s 45 are abrogated by s 74, the rights of an *indorser* of a cheque remain intact under the earlier section?

It is the practice of banks in New Zealand to return for the drawer's confirmation any cheque which appears to have been outstanding for more than six months, although this practice has never received judicial sanction. Such a cheque is regarded as "stale" and the holder is usually instructed to "refer to drawer" for this confirmation. The banks consider that their authority to pay the cheque has lapsed after this period, but this does not, of course, mean that the cheque is then unenforceable by the holder, who may still sue upon it during the limitation period should the drawer refuse to confirm it as an order that the drawee bank will honour.

Although a cheque remains a valid order in law for the limitation period, the banking practice of refusing to honour "stale" cheques has become so well established that perhaps it must be taken to have become an implied term of the contract between banker and customer, so that no action for the wrongful dishonour of such a cheque would now be entertained by the Courts.

(f) SUM CERTAIN IN MONEY

Section 9 of the Act provides that the sum payable by a bill is a sum certain within the meaning of the Act although it may require payment (a) with interest; (b) by stated instalments; (c) according to an indicated rate of exchange, or according to an indicated rate of exchange to be ascertained as directed by the bill.

As a rule, the amount of a cheque is stated both in words and in figures, but it sometimes happens that the words specifying the amount payable differ from the figures. To allow for this contingency, s 9 (2) provides that where the sum payable is expressed in words and also in figures, and there is a discrepancy between the two, the sum denoted by *the words* is the amount payable. The practice of bankers, however, is to pay the smaller amount or to offer to do so. This is done as a safeguard for the drawer but, although there is no decided authority on the point, it is probable that the drawer who created the difficulty in the first place would have no ground for complaint if a higher sum expressed in words was paid. The statute is explicit that it is this sum that is the amount payable.

It is also banking practice to refuse to honour cheques where no sum payable is expressed in words at all, and to return such instruments marked "Amount required in words". Moreover, in the above case of a discrepancy between the amounts expressed in words and figures, some banks will decline to rely on s 9 (2) and return the cheque marked "words and figures differ" for clarification by the drawer. Either course of action by the banker appears sanctioned by established practice so that bankers may not be strictly obliged to comply with the direction of s 9 (2).

Where the amount payable is stated in error, and yet the intention of the drawer is plain on the face of the instrument, a bank as a general rule should not refuse payment on this account. Thus, if a cheque is drawn "Pay one hundred to . . . or bearer", then a banker would be justified in paying if the amount in figures is given as "$100". Nevertheless, it is probably sound practice always to return such cheques to the drawer for clarification.

(g) PAYABLE TO OR TO ORDER OF SPECIFIED PERSON, OR TO BEARER

A bill is payable to order if expressed to be so payable, or if expressed payable to a particular person, and does not contain words prohibiting transfer or indicating an intention that is non-transferable: 1908 Act, s 8(4).

A bill is payable to bearer if expressed to be so payable, or if the only or last indorsement thereon is in blank: s 8(3); as to "indorsement in blank": s 34(1). The example shown in (b) above is a cheque payable to bearer whereas the following is an example of a cheque payable to order.

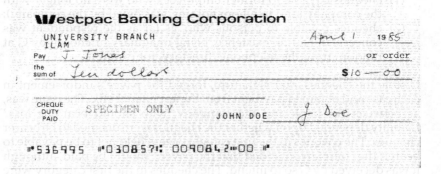

Where a bill is not payable to bearer, the payee must be named or otherwise indicated on the cheque with sufficient certainty: s 7(1). Therefore, instruments payable to "Cash or Order" are not cheques at all (*Orbit Mining and Trading Co Ltd v Westminster Bank Ltd* [1962] 3 All ER 565), but nevertheless are instruments to which the protective provisions of the Cheques Act 1960 apply.

Where the payee is a fictitious or non-existing person the bill may be treated as payable to bearer: s 7 (3). From this, it follows that the forgery of the indorsement of such a payee will not affect the title of subsequent holders because, as the bill can be treated as a "bearer" bill, no indorsement is required for its negotiation. Any such indorsement would therefore be superfluous. Although the name of the payee may be that of an existing person, it may be "fictitious" for legal purposes if the bill is not intended to be payable to that person. In *Bank of England v Vagliano Bros* [1891] AC 107, a trusted clerk of the defendant had on a series of bills forged both the names of real drawers and payees. Clearly the named payees had not and were never intended to have any right upon or arising out of the bills. The employee obtained the name of the defendant as acceptor on the bills by fraud, and had then proceeded further to forge the indorsement of the named payees and obtained cash for himself on the bills at the bank. When the fraud was discovered, the question arose whether those bills were rightly charged to the defendant's account. The majority of the House of Lords held that the bank was entitled to debit the account with the amounts on the ground that the named payee was a fictitious or non-existing person within the meaning of the Act, and the documents might therefore be treated as bills payable to bearer, there being no intention on the part of the drawer to benefit the named payee under the bills.

Therefore, if the mind of the drawer is directed towards a specific existing person, whom the drawer intends to receive the money, then such a payee is not a fictitious or non-existing person, even though by reason of fraud on the part of a third party in obtaining the cheque, such person could never have acquired any rights on it.

In *Royal Bank of Canada v Concrete Column Clamps (1961) Ltd* (1976) 74 DLR (3d) 26 G, an employee of the respondent company engaged in the fraudulent practice of "payroll padding". In preparing pay cheques for the signature of the authorized signing officer over a period of a year and a half, G included more than 1000 cheques which should not have been paid. These fell into two categories:

(1) cheques payable to former employees who were no longer with the company (and to whom nothing was owed by the company);
(2) cheques payable to persons who, as far as the respondent was concerned, had no existence, being imaginary or chosen by G at random from the telephone directory, for example.

G stole the cheques after signature, forged the payee's indorsement in each case and obtained payment from the appellant bank. The issue was, as between the bank and the company, who should bear the loss? Liability depended upon whether the cheques were deemed to be bearer cheques. The cheques in the first category were held not to be payable to bearer: the company intended that the payees should be paid, although it was deceived by G so to intend. The cheques in the first category were bearer cheques, payable either to non-existing persons or persons to whom it was not intended that anything be paid. Cf *Fok Cheong Shing Investments Ltd v Bank of Nova Scotia* (1981) 123 DLR (3d) 416.

25.4 PARTIES TO A CHEQUE

25.4.1 General

At the inception of a cheque there are three parties to it. The person who gives the order to pay is termed the *drawer*. The person to whom the order is given is the *drawee* (in the case of a cheque referred to as the "paying" bank). The person in whose favour the bill is drawn is the payee

When the bill is "delivered" to the payee, he or she becomes the first holder of it. "Delivery" is simply the transfer of possession, actual or constructive from one person to another. A party to a bill cannot be held liable on it until delivery: s 21. Accordingly, the drawer incurs no liability to the payee before delivery to the latter.

A "holder" is defined as the payee or indorsee of a bill who is in possession of it, or as the bearer of the bill: s 2.

The holder may now transfer the cheque to another party. In terms of the Act, a cheque is "negotiated" when it is transferred from one person to another in such a manner as to constitute the transferee the holder of it: s 31(1). A cheque payable to bearer is negotiated by delivery, whilst a cheque payable to order is negotiated by indorsement completed by delivery: s 31.

Negotiation, therefore, involves the giving of a direction by the payee to the drawee to pay a third party. This direction is an "indorsement". The payee becomes the first "indorser" and the transferee is the first "indorsee".

There are several possible forms of indorsement. If the indorser merely signs his or her name on the back of the cheque then this is an "indorsement in blank", which has the effect of rendering the cheque payable to bearer: s 34. However, if the indorser signs and also names a particular indorsee, then the cheque retains its character as an order cheque, since the drawee must pay either that person or his or her subsequent indorsee: s 34(2). Furthermore, the holder of a cheque may direct payment to a named indorsee only, with no further right of negotiation. This is a "restrictive indorsement": ss 35, 36(1).

In fact, the Act contemplates cheques which prohibit transfer from even the original payee: s 8(1).

25.4.2 Transferor and transferee by delivery

Where the holder of a cheque payable to bearer negotiates it by delivery without indorsing it, he or she is called a "transferor by delivery", and he or she is not liable on the instrument. However, by s 58 (3) a transferor by delivery warrants to any immediate transferee for value that the cheque is what it purports to be, that the transferor has a right to transfer it, and that at the time of the transfer the transferor is not aware of any fact which renders it valueless.

25.4.3 Holder

We have seen that the "holder" is the payee or indorsee of a cheque who is in possession of it, or the bearer: s 2. Where a bill is in the actual possession of an agent, the principal may nonetheless qualify as a holder of the bill by virtue of constructive possession of the bill: *Silk Bros Interstate Traders Pty Ltd v Security Pacific National Bank* (1989) 16 NSWLR 446.

The bearer is the person who is in possession of a cheque payable to bearer.

Since possession is all that is required with a bearer cheque, then a drawee would be justified in paying the cheque to any bearer, even if that person had no true entitlement to it, as long as the drawee had no knowledge of such a defect in title: s 59. A crossed bearer cheque must, however, be paid either to the true owner or a bank: s 79 (2).

A holder may negotiate an order cheque, or present it for payment. The holder may sue on the cheque in his or her own name (s 39(a)) and give a discharge to a drawee whose payment is in due course: s 38 (c). The holder has a prima facie authority to fill in blanks on a cheque (s 20(1)) and to insert the date of issue, if such is omitted: s 12. He or she may convert an order cheque into a bearer cheque by indorsement in blank, and reconvert it back into an order cheque: s 34. However, a cheque which starts life as a bearer cheque cannot be converted into an order cheque: *Miller Associates (Aust) Pty Ltd v Bennington Pty Ltd* [1975] 2 NSWLR 506.

However, if a holder of a cheque is not a holder for valuable consideration, then the holder's claim on it will fail.

Section 27(1) provides that valuable consideration for a cheque may be constituted by: (a) any consideration sufficient to support a simple contract; or (b) any antecedent debt or liability.

Every party whose signature appears on a cheque is prima facie deemed to have become a party to the cheque for value: s 30 (1). Furthermore, where value has at any time been given for a cheque, then the holder is deemed to be a holder for value as regards all parties to the cheque who became parties prior to that time: s 27 (2).

In other words, the holder does not himself or herself have to give value. It is enough if value was given by some party in the chain between the holder and the intended defendant.

For instance, A gives a cheque payable to B in payment of a debt. B indorses it to C for value. C then gives the cheque to D as a gift. D is therefore, a holder for value as regards A and B, since they became parties before value was last given. However, D is not a holder for value as against C.

25.4.4 Holder in due course

A holder of a cheque is constituted, pursuant to s 29, as a holder in due course, if he or she takes the cheque under the following conditions:

1　the cheque must have been complete and regular on its face;
2　he or she must have become the holder before the cheque was overdue, and without notice that it had been previously dishonoured, if such was the case;
3　he or she must have taken the cheque in good faith and for value, without notice of any defect of title of the transferor. As to what are "defects of title" for this purpose, see s 29(2).

The holder in due course is one who enjoys the fullest possible rights over a negotiable instrument. He or she can acquire a title to a cheque free from equities and defects in the title of the transferor: s 38. Thus, the holder in due course could acquire title from a thief, or from someone who has acquired a cheque for a consideration which has wholly failed, such as where the original holder took the cheque as payment for defective goods.

He or she must, however, be a "holder", as defined in s 2. If therefore, the holder takes the cheque under a forged indorsement, then he or she cannot be a "holder", since a forgery is of no effect: s 24. Even to this, however, there is an exception: s 55(2) of the Act provides that an indorser is precluded from denying to a holder in due course the genuineness and regularity of the signatures of the drawer and all prior indorsers. Thus, in the above example, the holder would not technically be a holder in due course, but he or she would have the rights of one as against any indorser who became a party to the cheque subsequent to the forgery.

It is also mandatory that the cheque should be complete and regular on its face at the time the person claiming to be a holder in due course took it. This means that one who takes an inchoate instrument cannot be a holder in due course of it, even though the Act gives that person authority to complete it. It also means that there must be nothing apparent on the face of the cheque which gives rise to suspicions. This would include unauthenticated erasures or alterations, or differences between the payee's name and the indorsement on a bill: eg *Arab Bank Ltd v Ross* [1952] 2 QB 216. Cf *Heller Factors Pty Ltd v Toy Corporation Pty Ltd* [1984] 1 NSWLR 121.

The cheque must not be overdue (see s 36(3)) or have been previously dishonoured. Either of these facts, if present, should give rise to suspicions on the holder's part that all is not well.

The cheque must be taken for value. We have already examined the question of value. A transferee need not give full value for a cheque in order to qualify as a holder in due course, but absence of full consideration may indicate bad faith on his or her part.

The payee of a cheque cannot be a holder in due course. In other words, the cheque must be negotiated: *RE Jones Ltd v Waring and Gillow Ltd* [1926] AC 670. There must be no notice of any defect in title. There is no comprehensive definition of "defect in title" in the Act, but s 25(2) provides that the term includes the title of a person who obtains a cheque:

... by fraud, duress, or force and fear, or other unlawful means, or for an illegal consideration. ...

or negotiates a cheque "in breach of faith, or under such circumstances as amount to a fraud".

A holder (whether for value or not) who derives title to a cheque through a holder in due course, and who is not a party to any fraud or illegality affecting it, has all the rights of that holder in due course as regards all parties to the cheque prior to that holder: s 29(2). Thus, a holder claiming through a holder in due course is not deprived of the rights of the latter even where he or she has knowledge of the fraud or illegality, as long as he or she is not a party thereto.

This rule indirectly protects the holder in due course, since he or she does not, in order to dispose of the cheque, have to find a transferee who knows nothing of the irregularity.

Every holder of a cheque is prima facie deemed to be a holder in due course; but if in an action on the cheque it is admitted or proved:

(a) that the issue, or subsequent negotiation of the cheque is affected with fraud, duress, or force and fear, or illegality; or

(b) that the cheque was drawn as part of, or pursuant to a credit contract, as defined in the Credit Contracts Act 1981, and that one or more of the provisions of that Act have not been complied with, or that any of paras (a) to (c) of s 10(1) of that Act apply, in respect of the contract –

the burden of proof is shifted, unless and until the holder proves that:

(c) in any case to which para (a) above applies, subsequent to the alleged fraud or illegality value has in good faith been given for the cheque; and

(d) in any case to which para (b) above applies, value has been given for the cheque in good faith and without knowledge of the non-compliance or any oppressiveness: s 30(2) and see *Begley Industries Ltd v Cramp* [1977] 2 NZLR 207.

As noted above, the holder in due course holds the cheque free from any defect of title of prior parties, as well as from mere personal defences available to prior parties among themselves, and may enforce payment against all parties liable on the cheque: s 38(b). "Personal defences" is not defined in the Act, but will include contractual defences available as between the original parties to the bill.

25.5 RIGHTS AND LIABILITIES OF PARTIES

25.5.1 General

No-one is liable on a cheque, whether as drawer or indorser, unless they have signed it as such: s 23. It is not necessary that the drawer or indorser sign the cheque with his or her own hand for liability to follow; it is sufficient if the drawer's or indorser's signature is written on the cheque by some other person with the drawer's or indorser's authority: s 92. In *R J Bowling Motors Ltd v Kerr* (1988) 2 NZBLC 103, 341 Mr and Mrs Kerr operated a joint cheque account; their cheques bore the preprinted names "R L & M F Kerr", and the drawee bank had a mandate to pay their cheques drawn over the single signature of either Mr or Mrs Kerr. Unbeknown to his wife Mr Kerr drew a cheque in favour of the plaintiff which was dishonoured. Mr Kerr having left for Australia, the plaintiff sued Mrs Kerr on the cheque itself. For the plaintiff it was necessary to establish that Mrs Kerr had signed the cheque. It was argued that the combination of her preprinted name and the written signature of Mr Kerr constituted the "writing" of Mrs Kerr's signature by her agent. McGechan J held that a person is not liable on cheques unless his or her signature actually is written on the instrument, either directly by the person sought to be held liable or by someone with authority. In any event, Mr Kerr had no actual or apparent authority to sign.

In the case of a partnership, the signature of the name of the firm is equivalent to the signature by the person so signing of the names of all persons liable as partners in that firm: s 23(b). Where the name of the firm is preprinted on the cheque, it is not necessary to link the manuscript signature with printed name, by words such as "on behalf of", for example: *Ringham v Hackett* (1977-1986) 10 LDAB 206.

The holder of a bearer cheque who negotiates it does not incur liability on the cheque itself (s 58) since it is negotiated by delivery alone, without indorsement. But the transferor does warrant to the immediate transferee, if the latter is a holder for value, that the transferor has a right to transfer it, and that at the time of transfer the transferor is not aware of any fact which renders it valueless: s 58(3).

A signatory to a cheque incurs to subsequent parties the liability for its payment and is precluded from denying to a holder in due course the genuineness of the signature of prior parties: ss 54-55.

It should be observed that some parties to a cheque are only liable on it because of an estoppel resulting from their signature on it. For example, title to a cheque cannot be derived through a forged signature (s 24) but, as against a holder in due course, an indorser is precluded from denying that the signature of the drawer and any prior indorser is genuine: s 55(2).

The estoppels only operate, however, in respect of the signatures of prior parties. Therefore, a holder in due course could not sue an indorser where the signature of a subsequent indorser is forged.

Before looking at the liability of each party to a cheque it can be seen that the chain of rights runs back from the holder through prior indorsers to the drawer. Each party in the chain can claim against prior parties. Therefore, any party sued by the holder can recover in turn against his or her predecessors.

25.5.2 The drawer

The drawer is the person primarily liable on a cheque. By virtue of s 55(1), the drawer of a cheque, by drawing it:

(a) Engages that on due presentation it shall be accepted and paid according to its tenor, and that if it is dishonoured the drawer will compensate the holder or any indorser who is compelled to pay it, provided that the requisite proceedings on dishonour are duly taken;

(b) Is precluded from denying to a holder in due course the existence of the payee and the payee's then capacity to indorse.

It should again be noted that the general undertaking of the drawer may be limited in accordance with s 16(1). Although it is unlikely to be invoked, a drawer could qualify his or her signature by adding the words "sans recours", or "without recourse to me", in which case the drawer does not undertake to pay the holder in the event of dishonour. Apart from this unlikely limitation, the drawer guarantees payment of the cheque by the drawee to a holder, and also reimbursement of an indorser who has been compelled to pay it on dishonour.

25.5.3 The drawee

Section 53 of the Act provides that a bill does not of itself operate as an assignment of the drawer's funds in the hands of the bank. If a cheque is dishonoured, a holder has no claim against the bank and must therefore look to the drawer or indorsers, if any.

25.5.4 The payee (or indorsee)

A payee or an indorsee can incur no liability to the holder unless he or she has actually signed the cheque: s 23.

25.5.5 The indorser

The liability of an indorser of a cheque is similar to that of the drawer in that the indorser also engages that on due presentation it shall be paid according to its tenor, and that if it is dishonoured the indorser will compensate the holder or a subsequent indorser who is compelled to pay it, provided that the requisite proceedings on dishonour are duly taken: s 55(2)(c). Moreover, the indorser is precluded from denying (i) to a holder in due course the genuineness and regularity in all respects of the drawer's signature and all previous indorsements, and (ii) to his or her immediate or a subsequent indorsee that the cheque was at the time of his or her indorsement a valid and subsisting cheque and that the indorser had a good title thereto.

It will be recalled, first, that a person signing a cheque otherwise than as a drawer or indorser, ie a stranger to a cheque, will incur the liability of an indorser to a holder in due course (s 56), and secondly, that it is always open to such a stranger or a genuine indorser to negative or limit liability under s 16.

It also appears that, under s 45, an indorser (but not a drawer) is discharged from liability unless the cheque is presented for payment within a reasonable time of its indorsement: see the discussion supra.

25.5.6 Agents

Where an agent signs a cheque as drawer or indorser, and adds words to his or her signature indicating that he or she signs for or on behalf of a principal, or in a representative character, the agent is not personally liable thereon; but the mere addition to the signature of words describing him or her as an agent, or as filling a representative character, does not exempt the agent from personal liability: s 26(1).

The agent must, therefore, state on the face of the cheque that he or she signs for another person, otherwise the agent will be personally liable on it. However, if the director of a company signed a cheque "John Smith, Director, H Smith Ltd", then he or she would be personally liable, since the words after his or her name are descriptive only, and do not sufficiently indicate that Smith is signing as agent. Signature for and on behalf of the company is necessary here: see *Elliott v Bax-Ironside* [1925] 2 KB 301; *Jones and Son v Sears* (1915) 17 GLR 392. On the other hand, express qualification of a company signature is not necessary where the form of the cheque shows that the company alone is intended to be bound. In *Bondina Ltd v Rollaway Shower Blinds Ltd* [1986] 1 All ER 564, B Ltd had supplied goods to the defendant company and in payment was issued with two post-dated cheques which were dishonoured on presentation. The cheques were drawn on preprinted cheque forms on which the name of the company was printed below the space for the drawer's signature. The personal unqualified signatures, in ink, of two directors of the company appeared below the company's name. At the bottom of the cheque forms there was printed a line of figures designating the number of the cheque, the branch of the drawee bank at which the account was held, and the number of the account itself, which was the account of the company. In an action on the cheques B Ltd joined the two directors on the basis that by signing the cheques without qualification they were personally liable. The English Court of Appeal held that the directors were not personally liable. By signing the directors had adopted all the printing and writing on the cheques, and in particular the printing of the company's name and the numbers which designated the company's account. The effect was to show that the cheque was drawn on the company's account and not on any other account. Thus it could not be a case of joint liability of several persons, of which the company was only one. Since preprinted cheque forms are now invariably used, the decision in *Bondina* means that it is only in rare cases that an unqualified personal signature on a company cheque will entail personal liability.

25.6 ENFORCEMENT OF LIABILITIES ON CHEQUES

25.6.1 General

With a bill that is payable on demand (eg a cheque), the bill matures immediately, and the holder, therefore, simply presents it to the drawee for payment.

Section 47 of the 1908 Act refers to dishonour by non-payment. It provides that a bill is dishonoured by non-payment: (a) where it is duly presented for payment and payment is refused, or cannot be obtained; or (b) where presentment is excused (see s 46) and the bill is overdue and unpaid. Where a bill is dishonoured by non-payment an immediate right of recourse against the drawers or indorsers accrues to the holder: s 47(2). Unless presentment for payment is excused, a bill must be duly presented for payment. If it is not so presented, the drawer and indorsers are discharged from liability to the extent by which they are prejudiced by the omission: s 45(1).

Presentation for payment is not, however, necessary in order to render the drawer liable on a cheque where the drawee is not bound, as between the drawee and the drawer, to pay the cheque, and the drawer has no reason to believe that the cheque would be paid if presented: s 45(2)(c). An example would be where the drawer has insufficient funds in his or her account to cover the cheque, and has no pre-arranged overdraft facility with the bank.

25.6.2 Notice of dishonour

Where a cheque is dishonoured by non payment, notice of dishonour must be given to the drawer and each indorser (unless notice is excused), and any such party to whom notice is not given is discharged to the extent that he or she is prejudiced by the omission: s 48.

The notice must be given by or on behalf of the holder, or indorser: s 49(a). It cannot be given, therefore, by other persons so as to affect those liable on the bill. Notice need not, however, be in any particular form: s 49(e).

Notice must be given within a reasonable time after dishonour: s 49(m).

Once the holder gives notice, it enures for the benefit of all subsequent holders and all prior indorsers having a right of recourse against the party to whom it is given: s 49(c). Notice of dishonour is not required in various cases:

1 When, after the exercise of reasonable diligence, notice as required by the Act cannot be given or does not reach the drawer or indorser sought to be charged;
2 By waiver, express or implied, either before the time of giving notice of dishonour has arrived, or after the omission to give due notice;
3 As regards the drawer –
   (i) where drawer and drawee are the same person;
   (ii) where the drawee is as between the drawee and the drawer under no obligation to pay the cheque, as in the case of a cheque dishonoured by the drawee bank for lack of funds;
   (iii) where the drawer has countermanded the cheque: s 50(2).

In addition to these cases, delay in giving notice is also excused where it is beyond the control of the party giving it: s 50(1).

25.6.3 Suing on the cheque

Where a cheque is dishonoured, the holder may sue all parties liable on it. Where a cheque is tendered as the means of payment under a contract, but is dishonoured, then the holder has the option of also suing on the contract, since dishonour restores the contractual duty to pay should the cheque not be honoured.

However, a claim on a cheque is more expeditiously realised, and usually without regard having to be paid to defences arising from the underlying contract, in respect of which the cheque was given.

The measure of damages on a dishonoured cheque includes, of course, the amount of the cheque. As well, interest can be claimed from the time of presentment for payment: s 57.

The primary right of action on the cheque lies with the holder, but an indorser who has been compelled to pay may recover from the drawer, or a prior indorser: s 57. In other words, a party can recover from prior parties, but only once he or she has made payment. In order to ensure recovery from someone, the holder should usually sue all parties liable on the cheque in one action.

25.6.4 Defences to claims on cheques

As a general rule a bill of exchange is treated as if it were cash. Accordingly only very limited defences arising from the underlying contract in respect of which the bill was given can be raised. The drawer of a cheque, who is sued by the payee on the cheque itself, can rely only upon the defences of failure of consideration (total or partial), illegality or fraud: *International Ore & Fertilizer Corporation v East Coast Fertiliser Co Ltd* [1987] 1 NZLR 8. A claim for unliquidated damages under the underlying contract is no defence to an action on a cheque: *Nova (Jersey) Knit Ltd v Kammgarn Spinnerei GmbH* [1977] 1 WLR 713.

(a) ABSENCE OR FAILURE OF CONSIDERATION

As we have seen, valuable consideration must have been given for a cheque before it can be enforced. The Bills of Exchange Act 1908 codifies, in relation to bills of exchange, the common law rules relating to valuable consideration, but with some modifications.

Thus, valuable consideration for a bill may be constituted by:

(a) any consideration sufficient to support a simple contract; or
(b) an antecedent debt or liability: s 27(1).

Every party who signs a cheque is prima facie deemed to have given value for the cheque: s 30(1). This presumption may, however, be rebutted on the facts of any particular case.

The Act further provides that where value has at any time been given for a cheque, the holder is deemed to be a holder for value as regards all parties to the cheque who became parties prior to the time when the value is given: s 27(2).

The entire failure of consideration has the same effect as its original absence. For instance, if A gives B a cheque in payment for some goods, and B fails to deliver the goods, then B cannot sue A on the cheque.

Even a partial failure of consideration, as, for instance, where B delivers some only of the goods, is a defence where the failure is in an ascertained and liquidated amount: *Thoni GmbH and Co KG v R T P Equipment Ltd* [1979] Lloyd's Rep 282.

The total unsuitability of a motor vehicle for the purpose for which it was bought, where that purpose was known to the seller at the time of sale, constitutes a defence of total failure of consideration to an action brought by the seller on the cheque given in payment for the vehicle: *Finch Motors Ltd v Quin* [1980] 2 NZLR 513, *Finch Motors Ltd v Quin (No 2)* [1980] 2 NZLR 519. In *Spencer v Crowther* (1986) 1 NZBLC 102 488,

C agreed to purchase a house from S but refused to complete after the agreement became unconditional. Subsequently a cheque given by C to S for the deposit on the purchase was dishonoured. Although S could not have sued for the deposit after electing to cancel the agreement, the contract arising from the cheque was distinct from the underlying transaction. As there was no suggestion of fraud or illegality, C was liable to pay on the cheque unless he could show failure of consideration. Prichard J held that S had given consideration by agreeing to accept the cheque in place of legal tender.

(b) FAILURE TO PRESENT BILL IN TIME

As far as indorsers are concerned, a cheque must be presented within a reasonable time after its indorsement in order to render the indorser liable: s 45(2)(b).

As regards the drawer, a cheque must be presented within a reasonable time after its issue in order to render the drawer liable. In the case of cheques, however, the drawer is only discharged from liability to the extent to which he or she has suffered actual damage through the delay: s 74(a). Mere delay, then, is not enough to discharge the drawer in the case of cheques.

(c) NO NOTICE OF DISHONOUR

As with the previous defence, availability of this defence depends on whether the defendant is the drawer or the indorser.

Any indorser to whom notice of dishonour is not given is discharged to the extent that he or she is prejudiced by the omission: s 48. Notice may be given as soon as the bill is dishonoured, and must be given within a reasonable time thereafter: s 49(m).

If a bill is dishonoured when in the hands of an agent (eg in the hands of a customer's bank for collection), then the agent may either himself or herself give notice of dishonour to the parties liable on the cheque or give notice to his or her principal, who must then give those parties notice: s 49(o). Obviously, a bank collecting a cheque for its customer is more likely to give notice of dishonour immediately to the customer.

As regards the drawer, the same provisions apply: s 48. Regard should be paid here to the circumstances in which notice of dishonour is not necessary. These were examined earlier. In particular, in the case of a cheque notice of dishonour need not be given to the drawer where the drawee bank is under no obligation to pay the cheque, eg where there are insufficient funds in the account. The same applies where the drawer of a cheque has countermanded payment.

(d) CONTRACTUAL INCAPACITY

Capacity to incur liability as a party to a cheque is co-extensive with capacity to contract: s 22(1).

Therefore, a person who does not possess full contractual capacity, and who signs a cheque, can plead that lack of capacity, in an action brought against him.

For instance, the contractual capacity of minors has already been examined (see ante).

A cheque drawn or indorsed by a minor can still be enforced in the normal way against the other parties to it: s 22(2).

351

The statutory estoppels, referred to earlier, are of relevance here. The drawer is precluded from denying to a holder in due course the payee's capacity to indorse at the time of the drawing of the bill: s 55(1).

(e) CHEQUE INCOMPLETE WHEN SIGNED
If a blank cheque is signed, but not delivered for the purpose of completion, the signatory is not liable on it even to a holder in due course: s 20(1).

(f) CONDITIONAL DELIVERY
The delivery of a cheque may be conditional, or for a special purpose only, and not for the purpose of transferring the property in the cheque: s 21(2)(b). If the condition is not fulfilled, the drawer can plead the non-fulfilment as a defence. However, this defence cannot be pleaded as against a holder in due course, since a valid delivery of the cheque by all parties prior to the holder in due course so as to make them liable to him or her is conclusively presumed: s 21(3).

The issue of conditional delivery has arisen in the context of accord and satisfaction. Is accord and satisfaction established where a debtor sends his or her creditor a cheque, for a lesser amount than is claimed by the creditor, in full and final settlement and the creditor banks the cheque? (This topic is discussed fully above, para 8.2.1.) In *Homeguard Products (NZ) Ltd v Kiwi Packaging Ltd* [1981] 2 NZLR 322 Mahon J held that a cheque given in full and final settlement is delivered on conditional terms, ie that it is accepted in full and final settlement, and property in the cheque does not pass to the recipient until that condition is complied with. Having banked such a cheque, the recipient cannot then disclaim the condition, for it would otherwise have committed the tort of conversion.

This reasoning has not been adopted in subsequent cases. In *Equitable Securities Ltd v Neil* [1987] 1 NZLR 411 it was said that s 21(2)(b) of the Bills of Exchange Act merely allows an exception to the parol evidence rule. It does not mean that the recipient of the cheque is bound by any condition should he or she bank it; rather it is still necessary to show that the recipient understood the condition and its precise terms. In *James Cook Hotel Ltd v Canx Corporate Services Ltd* [1989] 3 NZLR 213, s 21(2)(b) was interpreted to refer to conditions which wholly suspend the operation of a cheque, whereas the condition that a cheque is paid in full and final settlement does not prevent the operation of the cheque as a whole. Non-suspensory conditions fall foul of the parol evidence rule and accordingly evidence of such conditions is not admissible.

(g) FORGED OR UNAUTHORISED SIGNATURE
Where a signature on a cheque is forged or unauthorised then generally speaking it is wholly inoperative, and no right to retain the cheque or to give a discharge therefor or to enforce payment against any party thereto can be acquired through or under that signature, unless the party against whom it is sought to retain or enforce payment of the cheque is precluded from setting up the forgery or want of authority: ss 24(1), 54(2)(a), 55.

Banks are given special protection in relation to cheques, in that payment by a bank of a cheque with a forged indorsement, in good faith and in the ordinary course of business, is deemed to be payment in due course: s 60(1).

As to want of authority, s 25 provides that a signature by procuration operates as notice that an agent has but a limited authority to sign, and the principal is bound by such signature only if the agent in so signing was acting within the actual limits of his or her authority. The abbreviation "pp" is usually employed to denote signature by procuration, with the name of the principal placed before the abbreviation.

(h) MATERIAL ALTERATION
Where a cheque is materially altered (s 64(2)) without the assent of all parties liable on the cheque, it is avoided except as against a party who has himself or herself made, authorised, or assented to the alteration, and subsequent indorsers, provided that, where a cheque has been materially altered, but the alteration is not apparent, and the cheque is in the hands of a holder in due course, such holder may avail himself or herself of the cheque as if it had not been altered, and may enforce payment of it, according to its original tenor: s 64(1).

Therefore, as against holders not in due course, assenting parties are liable to the extent of the cheque as altered, whereas non-assenting parties are not even liable on the cheque according to its original tenor.

(i) FRAUD
It is clear that if the plaintiff himself or herself obtained a cheque by fraud, this is a defence to any action by that person. The position is less clear as regards the rights of a present holder, where a prior holder had obtained a cheque by fraud.

If the fraud renders the contract void, as for instance where a person is fraudulently induced to sign a document on the representation that it is not a bill of exchange at all, then the signatory can escape all liability, as long as he or she signed without negligence: *Foster v MacKinnon* (1869) LR 4 CP 704.

In most cases, however, fraud only renders a cheque voidable. Therefore, it would afford no defence to a claim by a holder in due course: s 38(b).

(j) DURESS AND UNDUE INFLUENCE
The same principle applies here as under (i), namely, that bills obtained by duress or undue influence will only be enforceable in the hands of a holder in due course.

(k) ILLEGAL CONSIDERATION
If the consideration for a cheque is illegal, then it cannot be recovered on except by a holder in due course: note s 30(2).

A consideration may be illegal either at common law (eg contracts against public policy) or by statute (eg Gaming Act 1908).

For instance, a bill or promissory note given to stifle a criminal prosecution is unenforceable by illegality, as being contrary to public policy: *Barsdell v Kerr* [1979] 2 NZLR 731. So also with "negotiable" instruments given in relation to gaming, or wagering contracts (*Ladup Ltd v Shaikh* [1982] 2 WLR 172), and instruments connected with transactions which contravene hire purchase regulations: *Stenning v Radio and Domestic Finance Ltd* [1961] NZLR 7.

The Illegal Contracts Act 1970 may provide relief by way of validation and respect of bills given on illegal consideration.

(l) CHEQUE OVERDUE
Where an overdue cheque (see s 36(3)) is negotiated, it can be negotiated only subject to any defect of title affecting it at its maturity, and thenceforward no person who takes it can acquire or give a better title than that which the person from whom he or she took it had: s 36(2).

(m) CHEQUE PREVIOUSLY DISHONOURED
Where a cheque that is not overdue has been previously dishonoured, any person who takes it with notice of the dishonour takes it subject to any defect of title affecting it at its dishonour: s 36(5). This, however, does not affect the title of a holder in due course, who in any case is required to have taken a bill without notice of any previous dishonour: s 29(1)(a).

In relation to both (k) and (l), it should be remembered that the term "defect of title" is partly defined by s 29(2). It should also be remembered that a holder in due course takes free from both prior defects in title and from mere "personal defences" available to prior parties as amongst themselves: s 39(b). The term "personal defences" is not defined by the Act, but presumably includes claims arising from matters which are collateral to the cheque itself, such as rights of set-off. It seems also that an original absence of consideration, and also a total failure of consideration, is regarded as a personal defence: *Sturtevant v Ford* (1842) 4 M & G 101.

25.7 DISCHARGE OF A CHEQUE

A cheque is treated as discharged when all rights of action in it are extinguished, that is, where no party remains who can sue or be sued on it.

The first means by which a cheque can be discharged is by payment of it in due course by or on behalf of the drawee: s 59(1).

"Payment in due course" is defined as being payment made at or after the maturity of the cheque to the holder thereof in good faith and without notice that his or her title to the bill is defective: s 59(1). Thus, payment to a person claiming under a forged indorsement will not discharge a cheque but a bank payment a cheque in such circumstances may have a defence against the true owner of the cheque, if it has acted in good faith and in the ordinary course of business: s 60.

A cheque which is paid by a drawer or indorser remains in being for the purpose of the taking of recourse against prior parties. The cheque is not discharged in such cases, but only remains in being for these limited purposes: s 59(3).

Secondly, a cheque is discharged where the holder absolutely and unconditionally renounces his or her rights against any party to the cheque. However, a holder in due course who takes without notice of the renunciation retains the right to sue any party: s 62.

Thirdly, where a cheque is intentionally cancelled by the holder or the holder's agent, and the cancellation is apparent on the cheque, it is discharged: s 63(1). In fact, any party to a cheque can be discharged from liability by the holder or the holder's agent intentionally cancelling that party's signature. In such a case an indorser who would have had a right of recourse against the party whose signature has been cancelled (ie subsequent indorsers) is also discharged: s 63(2). In other words all parties prior to the party whose signature is cancelled remain liable on the cheque.

Fourthly, where a cheque is materially altered, it is generally avoided as against prior parties who did not assent to the alteration, but is enforceable by a holder in due course where the alteration is not apparent, and remains enforceable against the person who made the alteration and subsequent indorsers: s 64.

Chapter 26

BANKING

SUMMARY

26.1 GENERAL

26.1.1 Relationship between bank and customer

The relationship between a bank and its customer is well settled as being that of debtor and creditor, and founded on the ordinary law of contract. The bank is ordinarily the debtor of the customer, holding the customer's funds for him or her, and undertaking to repay them on the customer's demand. If the customer's account is overdrawn, then the normal relationship is reversed; the bank becomes the creditor of the customer. Some of the rules governing the relationship were spelled out by Atkin LJ in *Joachimson v Swiss Bank Corporation* [1921] 3 KB 110, 127:

> The bank undertakes to receive money and to collect bills for its customer's account. The proceeds so received are not to be held in trust for the customer, but the bank borrows the proceeds and undertakes to repay them. The promise to repay is to repay at the branch of the bank where the account is kept, and during banking hours. It includes a promise to repay any part of the amount due against the written order of the customer addressed to the bank at the branch, and as such written orders may be outstanding in the ordinary course of business for two or three days, it is a term of the contract that the bank will not cease to do business with the customer except upon reasonable notice. The customer on his part undertakes to exercise reasonable care in executing his written orders so as not to mislead the bank or to facilitate forgery. I think it is necessarily a term of such contract that the bank is not liable to pay the customer the full amount of his balance until he demands payment from the bank at the branch at which the current account is kept.

See too *Re Loteka Pty Ltd* (1989) 15 ACLR 620.

The bank becomes a debtor of its customer upon deposit of money. In *Balmoral Supermarket Ltd v Bank of New Zealand* [1974] 2 NZLR 155 an employee of the plaintiff had handed over a sum or money for deposit to the defendant's teller. While the teller was in the process of counting the money, robbers entered the bank and stole the uncounted cash. It was held that until money to be deposited has been checked and the bank has accepted it for deposit, the money has not been deposited and the bank has not become the debtor of the customer in respect of that money.

As to who is a customer, the Judicial Committee in *Commissioners of Taxation v English, Scottish and Australian Bank Ltd* [1920] AC 683, held that the *duration* of the relationship with the bank was not of the essence. It was sufficient that a person's money had been accepted by the bank on a footing that they undertook to honour cheques up to the amount of his or her credit to constitute him or her a "customer" for these purposes, irrespective of the duration of this connection.

The actual terms of the contract between bank and customer will vary according to the circumstances of each case, and also according to the particular function that a bank is performing for a customer at the time. In the collection and payment of cheques, banks perform two distinct functions: (a) that of "paying bank", and (b) that of "collecting bank".

26.1.2 Liability to third parties

While the general rule is that a bank is a creditor of its customer for the amount deposited in an account, and that the customer has only a contractual right to repayment of the funds, which belong to the bank, the bank may nonetheless be affected by the rights of third parties in respect of those funds. First, the funds may be the subject of a so-called Quistclose trust. In *Barclays Bank Ltd v Quistclose Trust Ltd* [1970] AC 567 it was held that the bank could not set off debts owed it by its customer against funds to the credit of the customer's account when it knew that those funds had been deposited by a third party for a specific purpose. When that purpose failed, there arose a resulting trust in favour of that third party.

Secondly, a bank is vulnerable to liability as a constructive trustee where it has received funds in breach of trust, or has assisted a breach of trust. In each case the bank must account for such funds if it has knowledge of the breach of trust. In the first category, knowing receipt, constructive knowledge suffices to fix the bank with liability, whereas the bank is liable in the second category only if it either has actual knowledge of the trustee's fraudulent or dishonest design or shuts its eyes to the obvious: *Lipkin Gorman v Karpnale Ltd* [1989] 1 WLR 1340 (CA), 1355.

In *Westpac Banking Corporation v Savin* [1985] 2 NZLR 41 (CA) A Co sold boats on behalf of clients and paid the proceeds into its account with the appellant bank which was overdrawn. The bank received those funds to the extent that the overdraft was diminished. A Co had no right to the proceeds of sale and by treating the funds as if they were its own property, A Co was in breach of its fiduciary duty to its clients. The bank had constructive knowledge of that breach and was therefore liable to account to the clients of A Co for the funds received.

26.2 THE PAYING BANK

The obligation of a bank to honour cheques drawn upon it by its customers is the most important of its duties. The various aspects and elements of this obligation are listed below.

26.2.1 The bank must obey its mandate

This is the first, and most basic, aspect of the paying bank's duties. The bank will only be entitled to debit its customer's account if it has paid his or her cheque strictly in accordance with the customer's instructions. This is qualified, however, by the customer's obligation to give clear instructions to the bank, as will be seen below.

The bank has no mandate to pay a cheque where the signature of the drawer is forged. Accordingly a paying bank can never debit a customer's account where it has paid a cheque over the forged signature of the drawer. Furthermore, where the account is operated on the basis that an agent of the customer may sign its cheques, the bank must ensure that the person signing as agent of the drawer has the authority to do so.

The obedience by a bank to its customer's mandate may result in loss to the customer. For instance, if the customer draws a cheque payable to bearer, to send to one of his or her creditors, but the cheque is lost before it reaches the creditor, then the bank will be quite justified in paying that cheque to anyone who presents it, since such person will be the "bearer" of the cheque. It does not matter that that person has no title to the cheque, since the customer is taken, by having drawn the cheque payable to bearer, to have authorised the bank to pay it to anyone who presents it. As we shall see later, banks do have certain statutory protections conferred on them when paying order cheques to persons not entitled to them.

Although the bank's duty is, above all, one to obey its customer's mandate, there are nevertheless circumstances in which the bank will be under a duty to refuse to pay its customer's cheques, on the ground that the funds in the account are being employed for some illegal purpose. If the circumstances were such that the bank was put on inquiry as to the existence of such illegality, it will be no defence that it has acted in accordance with its customer's mandate.

26.2.2 The bank is only under an obligation to pay cheques that are properly presented and in proper form

Crossed cheques must be presented for payment through the medium of a bank account. For crossed cheques see 26.7.2 infra.

The bank has the right to an unambiguous mandate. The cheque drawn by the customer, therefore, should be clear in its directions to the bank. Should the mandate be ambiguous, the bank will be justified in paying the cheque pursuant to a reasonable interpretation which it places on the cheque, and the customer cannot dispute the debiting of the account as a result: *Joint Stock Bank Ltd v MacMillan* [1918] AC 777.

If the date on a cheque is omitted, the bank will usually return the cheque, although it does have power under the Act to insert the date itself: s 20(1).

If a cheque is presented after a certain period has elapsed from its ostensible date of issue (usually six months in practice), the bank will usually return it unpaid.

Banks are much less concerned with indorsements on cheques today than they used to be. This is largely because s 2 of the Cheques Act 1960 provides that where a bank in good faith and in the ordinary course of business pays a cheque drawn on it which is not indorsed or is irregularly indorsed it shall not in so paying, incur any liability by reason only of the absence of, or irregularity in indorsement, and is deemed to have paid the cheque in due course (see also Bills of Exchange Act 1908, ss 60, 80). However, as a matter of practice banks still require indorsements where cheques payable to order are presented for cash, and also in the case of instruments not covered by the provisions of the Cheques Act 1960.

26.2.3 There must be funds available

The bank is only required to pay a cheque if the customer has sufficient funds to his or her credit or the cheque is within the limit of an agreed overdraft: *Joachimson v Swiss Bank Corp* [1921] 3 KB 110, 127; *Rouse v Bradford Banking Co Ltd* [1894] AC 586.

In ascertaining the amount which stands to a customer's credit, the bank has the right to combine all accounts which the customer maintains in the same right, unless by agreement this right is excluded.

However, the customer has no similar right to combine his or her accounts, although the drawing of a cheque on an account the balance of which is not enough to meet it (or which is overdrawn up to the agreed limit) may be taken as authority to the bank to combine with another account sufficiently in credit in order that the cheque may be paid.

The bank must honour a cheque only if the funds in the account are sufficient to honour the whole of the amount of the cheque. The bank need not pay only part of the cheque, since the cheque is not an assignment of funds in the bank's hands: s 53.

Cheques must be honoured by the bank in the order in which they are presented. If two or more cheques are presented simultaneously for payment, but the balance is insufficient to pay all of them the bank should pay so far as is possible. It is thought that the bank should pay the smallest of the cheques first, since dishonour of a small cheque has a more adverse effect on a customer's credit than dishonour of a larger one.

Money is not available to the drawer as soon as it is paid in, since the bank is to be allowed time to make the necessary entries. However, the interval is likely to be negligible today, except in the case of cheques paid in for collection. In such a case, it is usually a term of the banker-customer contract that the customer has no right to draw against uncleared effects. The mere crediting of a customer's account with the amount of a cheque does not confer on the customer a right to draw on those proceeds, until the cheque is actually cleared: *A L Underwood Ltd v Bank of Liverpool* [1924] 1 KB 755.

26.2.4 The decision to pay or dishonour

The bank must usually, when a cheque is sent to it by another bank for payment, pay the cheque or dishonour it by the end of the next business day. If the cheque is simply presented to it over the counter, it must decide there and then whether or not to pay. The bank cannot postpone its decision, and a request to represent the cheque amounts to dishonour: *Bank of England v Vagliano Bros* [1891] AC 107, 141.

26.2.5 Bank's duty of care

In paying a customer's cheque or transferring money out of the account of a customer, the bank is acting as the customer's agent. It is an implied term of the contract between the bank and the customer that the bank will observe reasonable care and skill in executing the customer's instructions: *Barclays Bank plc v Quincecare Ltd* [1988] 1 FTLR 507. In that case the chief executive of the defendant company had defrauded the company by obtaining the transfer of its funds by the bank to his solicitors and ultimately to the United States. It was argued that the bank was liable for the loss of the money because in acting on the fraudster's instructions it had failed to exercise proper care and skill. The test of liability was stated to be as follows: a banker must refrain from executing an order if and for as long as the banker is put on inquiry in the sense that he or she has reasonable grounds for believing that the order is an attempt to misappropriate the funds of the company. See too *Lipkin Gorman v Karpnale Ltd* [1989] 1 WLR 1340 (CA), 1356. Even where the bank is found to have acted without proper care and skill, it may raise the defence of contributory negligence on the part of the customer: *Lipkin Gorman* supra 1360. But this does not apply where the bank has paid a cheque on which the customer's signature as drawer has been forged.

26.2.6 Wrongful dishonour of cheques

A customer whose cheque has been wrongfully dishonoured (but not the payee) is entitled to claim damages from the bank.

First, the customer may base his or her action against the bank on breach of contract. The normal rule in contract is that only actual damages proved to have resulted from the breach are recoverable. However, if the customer is a trader, he or she can recover substantial damages without having to show actual damage. The damages are for injury to the trader's commercial credit: *Baker v ANZ Bank Ltd* [1958] NZLR 907, 909. The question, then, is when is a customer a "trader"? The answer must be that the customer's activities must be shown to have a mercantile character, in the widely-accepted sense of the term.

In *Hill v National Bank of New Zealand Ltd* [1985] 1 NZLR 736 the plaintiff was a member of a partnership carrying on the business of management consultants. The partnership bank account was held with the defendant bank which reduced the partnership's overdraft limit without reasonable notice. Following the reduction in the overdraft limit the bank dishonoured a cheque drawn for $500 in favour of the partnership's accountant and returned it to the payee marked "R/D". The Court awarded damages of $500 for breach of contract, without actual damage being proved. However the modesty of the award was suggested by the facts that the dishonour was known only to the bank officials and the payee of the cheque, and damage to the partnership's reputation could have been minimised by a phone call to the payee.

Non-traders must allege and prove actual, special damage: *Gibbons v Westminster Bank Ltd* [1939] 2 KB 882.

Secondly, the customer may have an action against the bank for defamation. Defamation is, basically, constituted by writing or printing or oral statements which are untrue, and which disparage a person's reputation to a third party. When a cheque is dishonoured, the paying bank will usually put a note on it indicating the reasons for its dishonour. It is this writing which may give rise to an action in defamation, where a cheque is wrongfully dishonoured. Under this head, a non-trader is not restricted to recovering only nominal damage. In other words, proof of actual damage is unnecessary here.

The liability of the bank for defamation depends on the form of the words which it uses on the cheque, and whether those words import the intimation that the drawer of the cheque has failed to provide the bank with sufficient funds to meet the cheque. Words which convey such a meaning tend to lower a person in the estimation of right-thinking members of society.

The words "refer to drawer" have been held to be defamatory (*Jayson v Midland Bank Ltd* [1968] 1 Lloyd's Rep 409, *Hill v National Bank* supra), as have "Present Again" (*Baker v ANZ Bank Ltd* supra) and "Not Sufficient" (*Davidson v Barclays Bank Ltd* [1940]1 All ER 316). It should always be remembered that there is no defamation if the words complained of are true. The paying bank, therefore would be well advised to make the answer on a dishonoured cheque as neutral, and as specific as possible, since the more precise the answer, the easier it will be to substantiate.

If the bank is unable to justify an answer that is prima facie defamatory, then the damages which will be awarded against it will depend on

> ... the position and standing of the plaintiff, the nature of the libel, the mode and extent of the publication, the absence of any retraction or apology, and the whole conduct of the defendant from the time when the libel was published, down to the very moment of verdict: *Baker v ANZ Bank Ltd* [1958] NZLR 907, 911.

In *Davidson v Barclays Bank Ltd,* it was argued for the bank that a defamatory answer on a cheque was protected by the defence of qualified privilege, so that no action lay.

At common law, the defence of qualified privilege lies where:

> the person who makes [the] communication has an interest or a duty, legal, social, or moral, to make it to the person to whom it is made, and the person to whom it is so made has a corresponding interest or duty to receive it: *Adam v Ward* [1917] AC 309.

Where this requirement is fulfilled, the plaintiff must show that there is "malice" in order to succeed in an action for defamation. "Malice" here means that the communication is made for some motive other than that for which the occasion is privileged: *Clark v Molyneaux* (1877) 3 QBD 237.

In *Davidson's* case, it was argued that the bank was under a duty to make a communication to the payee or that the communication was made on a matter of interest common to both parties. Hilbury J held that a privileged occasion must exist prior to the making of a communication, and that the bank could not "by making a mistake, create the occasion for making the communication". The defence was, therefore, held not to lie: [1940] 1 All ER 316, 322.

26.3 LIABILITY OF THE PAYING BANK

26.3.1 Payment in due course

Having paid the cheque of a customer which has been drawn on it, the paying bank may debit the account of the customer for the amount of the cheque so paid provided the bank has adhered to the customer's mandate to pay and has made payment in due course.

Under s 59(1) of the Bills of Exchange Act 1908 a cheque is discharged by payment in due course by or on behalf of the paying bank. "Payment in due course" means payment to the holder of the cheque in good faith and without notice that the holder's title is defective: s 59(2). A person who takes a cheque bearing a forged signature, whether of the drawer or indorser, cannot be the holder of the cheque, since s 2 of the Act defines "holder" as meaning the payee or indorsee of a cheque who is in possession of it or the bearer. A forged signature is a nullity and precludes any person who takes for qualifying as the holder. By contrast, a person taking a bearer cheque which bears a forged indorsement will still be the bearer, and therefore the holder, since the indorsement was not necessary to pass title to him or her. Payment to that person constitutes payment in due course if the bank acts in good faith and without notice, and the bank is accordingly entitled to debit the drawer's account.

26.3.2 Absence of mandate

(a) FORGED OR UNAUTHORISED SIGNATURE

The paying bank clearly has no mandate to pay a cheque on which the signature of the drawer is forged or made without authority, and may not debit the account of the customer for the amount of the cheque. Where the signature of an indorser is forged, the bank is protected by s 60: for which see infra 26.3.4.

(b) MATERIAL ALTERATION

The mandate given by the drawer of the cheque is for payment of the sum for which the cheque is drawn. If subsequently that sum is fraudulently altered for a greater amount, the paying bank is liable for payment exceeding the original amount.

(c) COUNTERMAND

By s 75 of the Act, the duty and authority of a bank to pay a cheque on it by a customer are determined by:

(a) countermand of payment, and,
(b) notice of the customer's death.

However, a bank may pay cheques drawn on it, notwithstanding that it has notice of the drawer's death, if the cheque is presented not more than ten days after the date of death, unless: (a) the cheque is dated after that date; or (b) the bank receives a notice of countermand by a person who claims to be entitled to a grant of administration in respect of or to be a beneficiary of the drawer's estate: s 75(2).

As to the authority of a bank upon the bankruptcy of its customer, see Insolvency Act 1967, s 49.

A countermand is an instruction to the bank that the order contained in a particular instrument is revoked. In relation to cheques, the issue of a countermand is often referred to as "stopping payment" on the cheque. When notice of such an order is given to a bank, the effect is that the banker may not debit the amount of the cheque to its customer's account if it pays the cheque, nor can it recover the payment from the person who received the money unless the recipient acted without good faith or had no title. A countermand need not be in writing, but this form is preferable. Some banks will prefer that their own printed forms be completed by the drawer by way of confirmation and record of the countermand. This will serve to avoid later misunderstandings, and possible actions for wrongful dishonour etc.

The drawer's right to stop payment of a cheque exists up to the last moment when payment may be made or refused by the banker. In *Capital Associates Ltd v Royal Bank of Canada* (1970)15 DLR (3d) 234, the customer and another depositor had accounts at the same branch of the defendant bank. The plaintiff depositor lodged the customer's cheque for credit in its own account, and the cheque was received for deposit and marked "paid" by the bank. However, payment of the cheque was countermanded by the drawer before the transaction was recorded by the bank's central computerised posting process, which was done overnight. The question for the Quebec Supreme Court was whether the bank acted properly as regards its depositor customer in re-marking the cheque "payment stopped". It was held that the countermand was still given in time to require the bank, in its role as drawee, to refuse payment, and to justify it, in its role as collecting bank, in removing the proceeds, from the payee's account. The payee had not presented the cheque for payment, but rather for deposit, and the less formal procedures appropriate to that transaction had been followed in the case. The bank, it was held, did not give any new promise to pay or to do any other act which might preclude it from debiting its customer's account with the amount of the dishonoured item in accordance with the terms of the banking contract between them.

This decision was cited in *HH Dimond (Rotorua 1966) Ltd v Australia and New Zealand Banking Group Ltd* [1979] 2 NZLR 739, where the bank received countermand of authority to pay between 11.20 and 11.30am. The cheque had been received from a computerised data processing centre at 9am but it would not have been processed until 2.30pm. The Bank's instructions about dishonour included this sentence:

> Instruments which are presented to the branch through the computer centre output without a request for a special answer, may be dishonoured up until 3pm on the business day following the date on which they were debited in the branch books.

The Bank dishonoured the cheque pursuant to that instruction and reversed the entries at the computer centre. It was held that payment was stopped before the cheque was "paid" by the banker.

Drawers who wish to countermand payment of their cheques should express themselves in clear and unambiguous terms, and must accurately describe the date, payee, and amount of the cheque, or the bank will not be obliged to stop payment: *Giordano v Royal Bank of Canada* (1972) 29 DLR (3d) 38. A customer must provide sufficient details to enable the banker to identify which cheque is being countermanded, and the details given must be exact. It has been held that where cheques are misdescribed by the customer by using the wrong date of the cheque, or the wrong number of it, the bank will not be held responsible to the customer for paying such a cheque: *Hilton v Westminster Bank Ltd* (1926) 43 TLR 124; *Shapera v Toronto-Dominion Bank* (1970) 17 DLR (3d) 122.

A telephone call or an unauthenticated telegram may reasonably be acted upon by a bank, at least to the extent of postponing payment of the cheque pending confirmation by the drawer. A banker should in any case of countermand be as certain as circumstances permit that the instructions emanate from the drawer of the cheque or the drawer's known agent. In an Irish case, *Reade v Royal Bank of Ireland* [1922] 2 Ir R 22, a telegram was held to be an effective countermand. However, in *Curtice v London City and Midland Bank Ltd* [1908]1 KB 293, the delivery of a telegram in the circumstances of that case was held not to constitute sufficient notice to the bank of a countermand. The plaintiff drew a cheque on October 31, 1906, and on the same day, but after business hours, he telegraphed to countermand payment. The telegram was delivered to the bank's letter box that evening but due to an oversight on the part of the bank staff was not brought to the notice of the manager until 2 November. The cheque had been presented and paid the day before. The notice of the countermand must therefore be brought to the actual notice of the management of the bank for it to be an effective countermand. It could be that in this case the oversight of the bank staff amounted to negligence, in which case it seems reasonable that an action against the bank for negligent disregard of a countermand order (breach of contract) would lie.

In *Royal Bank of Canada v Wildman (Boyce, Third Party)* (1966) 57 DLR (2d) 683, a cheque was drawn on a bank in a specified city, but with no indication as to which of two branches in that city was the drawee. Payment was countermanded by the drawer at the branch where his or her account was held, but the cheque was presented and paid at the other branch. The question for the Court was whether the notice to the bank was an effective countermand. It was held that the drawer had done all that he or she was required to do for an effective countermand, and he or she was under no obligation to any other branch to give notice of his or her stop payment order. The bank's claim as holder in due course also failed, because the bank paid the cheque as drawee, notwithstanding that it had been paid by a branch other than the one where the drawer had an account.

It has been shown that while a countermand will effectively terminate the authority of a bank to pay a cheque, it will not deprive a holder of an action against the drawer upon it.

26.3.3 Bank's defences

(a) CUSTOMER'S NEGLIGENCE

The defence of the paying bank which has paid a forged cheque that the loss was caused by the negligence of the customer is limited by the rule that it is only negligence of the customer in or immediately connected with the drawing of the cheque itself which relieves the bank from liability: *London Joint Stock Bank Ltd v Macmillan* [1918] AC 777 (HL); *National Bank of New Zealand Ltd v Walpole* [1975] 2 NZLR 7 (CA). This rule was reaffirmed by the Privy Council in *Tai Hing Cotton Mill Ltd v Liu Chong Hing Bank Ltd* [1986] AC 80. In that case an employee of the appellant company had forged a large number of cheques which had been paid by the respondent banks. It was found that the company's internal structures and controls for preventing such fraud were inadequate, if they existed at all. The banks argued that the company owed them a duty to take reasonable precautions in the management of its business with the banks to prevent forged cheques being presented to them for payment. This argument failed, and the company was entitled to recover from the banks the amount debited from its accounts on payment of the forged cheques. Much the same approach was taken by the Supreme Court of Canada in *Canadian Pacific Hotels Ltd v Bank of Montreal* (1988) 40 DLR (4th) 385 on similar facts. There the bank argued that a distinction should be drawn between sophisticated and non-sophisticated customers, and that in the case of the former, the customer owed the bank a duty to maintain an adequate system of internal accounting controls for the prevention and minimisation of loss through forgery.

However the bank will not be liable where the customer is negligent in the drawing of the cheque itself. Put differently, the customer is under an obligation to draw the cheque in such a way as not to facilitate its fraudulent alteration. Usually this means the alteration of the amount for which the cheque is drawn: see, for example, *Varker v Commercial Banking Co of Sydney* [1972] 2 NSWLR 967. But a customer must take care also in describing the payee. In *Commonwealth Trading Bank of Australia v Sydneywide Stores Pty Ltd* (1981) 55 ALJR 574 the drawer of a cheque was held to be in breach of its duty to the paying bank to take reasonable precautions to prevent fraudulent alteration. The cheque was drawn payable to "CAS or order" ("CAS" being an acronym for "Computer Accounting Services") and this was fraudulently altered by an employee to "CASH or order".

(b) BREACH OF DUTY TO WARN

A customer is under a duty to warn the paying bank if the customer knows of or has reason to suspect that his or her cheques have been forged. By failing to warn, the customer is estopped from asserting the forgeries against the bank or is deemed to have adopted them. In *Brown v Westminster Bank Ltd* [1964] 2 Lloyd's Rep 187 the customer, an elderly woman, was estopped from asserting that the bank had paid over 300 forged cheques drawn on her account. Her bank manager had periodically inquired as to the regularity and on each occasion she had either confirmed that her statements of account were correct or had made no comment. From the sheer number of cheques involved it was inferred that she must have realised that her signature was being forged, and should have advised the bank accordingly.

(c) VERIFICATION CLAUSE
A customer is under no obligation to check his or her bank statement to ensure that no forged or unauthorised cheque has been paid: *Kepitagalla Rubber Estates Ltd v National Bank of India Ltd* [1909] 2 KB 1010. But banks frequently rely upon a verification clause in terms of which a customer's statement of account is deemed to be correct unless the bank is advised otherwise within a specified period. An effective verification clause means that the customer is precluded from subsequently asserting that the statement is inaccurate by virtue of the payment of forged or unauthorised cheques. However the Courts are reluctant to uphold a verification clause except where it is expressed in the clearest terms. In *Tai Hing* supra one such clause provided that the balance shown in the monthly statement would be deemed to be correct if the bank was not notified of any error within 10 days of receipt. This was held not to be conclusive. Such a clause was not sufficiently explicit in bringing home to the customer the seriousness of the obligation to check statements and the seriousness of the failure to do so.

(d) RATIFICATION
Since the paying bank acts as the customer's agent in paying his or her cheques, the customer can ratify the act of a bank which pays a cheque which it is not authorised to honour. For instance, a director of a company ought to be authorised to draw on the company's account jointly with another director. If he or she draws a cheque without obtaining that other person's signature, the board of directors might still adopt the director's act, with full knowledge that the cheque had been improperly drawn. The company could not then complain of the payment of the cheque: *London Intercontinental Trust Ltd v Barclays Bank Ltd* [1980] 1 Lloyd's Rep 241.

26.3.4 Statutory protection of the paying bank

(a) BILLS OF EXCHANGE ACT 1908, s 60
We have seen that if a bank pays an order cheque bearing a forged indorsement to the "indorsee", it does not pay the cheque in due course. However, the bank may not be in a position to know whether an indorsement is forged or not.

Section 60 of the 1908 Act is designed to afford the paying bank some protection here. It provides:

> Where a bill payable to order on demand is drawn on a banker, and the banker on whom it is drawn pays the bill in good faith and in the ordinary course of business, it is not incumbent on the banker to show that the indorsement of the payee or any subsequent indorsement was made by or under the authority of the person whose indorsement it purports to be and the banker is deemed to have paid the bill in due course, although such indorsement has been forged or made without authority.

Payment of the cheque must, first, be in good faith. Section 91 of the Act provides that something can be done in good faith for the purposes of the Act even though it is done negligently.

Secondly, the cheque must be paid in the ordinary course of business. What is in the usual course of business is of course, largely a matter for the banks, and the Court will be guided by their evidence on such a question. It must be the universally adopted, recognised, or customary form of business for banks in general. Therefore, if a crossed cheque is paid over the counter, for example, this could hardly be payment in the ordinary course of business. Neither would payment of a cheque bearing an irregular indorsement. This latter proposition, however, is subject to the provisions of the Cheques Act 1960, examined below.

It is not certain whether a banker who acts negligently can nevertheless be considered to be acting in the ordinary course of business. In *Carpenter's Co v British Mutual Banking Co* [1938] 1 KB 511, the Court of Appeal was divided on the issue. It would seem reasonable to assume that the ordinary course of business includes acting with due care, and that, in any event, the bank's duty to take care has not been expressly abrogated by statute.

(b) BILLS OF EXCHANGE ACT 1908, s 80

Section 80 of the Act provides as follows:

> Where the banker on whom a crossed cheque is drawn pays it in good faith and without negligence, if crossed generally, to a banker, and if crossed specially, to the banker to whom it is crossed, or to his agent for collection being a banker, the banker paying the cheque, and, if the cheque has come into the hands of the payee, the drawer shall respectively be entitled to the same rights and be placed in the same position as if payment of the cheque had been made to the true owner thereof.

Unlike s 60, s 80 is not specifically confined to cheques bearing forged indorsements of the payee. However, it is confined to crossed cheques, whereas s 60 is not. On the other hand, s 80 extends to certain instruments other than cheques whilst s 60 does not.

Given that s 60 provides protection in respect of forged indorsements, s 80 will not need to be relied upon in many cases. Although s 80 requires that payment be made "without negligence", whereas s 60 requires that payment be made "in the ordinary course of business", it has already been observed above that the two tests lead to similar results, since the better view is that negligent payment is not payment in the ordinary course of business.

(c) CHEQUES ACT 1960, s 2

Section 2 of the Cheques Act provides as follows:

> Where a banker in good faith and in the ordinary course of business pays a cheque drawn on him which is not indorsed or is irregularly indorsed, he shall not, in doing so, incur any liability by reason only of the absence of or irregularity in, indorsement, and he shall be deemed to have paid it in due course.

On its face s 2 goes much further than s 60 (which it may have been intended to replace, although this did not come about) or s 80 of the Bills of Exchange Act. The purpose of the provision is to relieve banks from the necessity of checking to see whether all cheques presented to it for payment have been indorsed at all or properly indorsed. The paying bank may rely upon the collecting bank to ensure that the cheque is properly indorsed: *Hill Construction Ltd v Housley* (unreported, High Court, Auckland, CP 923/86, 8 December 1986, Smellie J). Cf *Bank of New South Wales v Derham* (1979) 29 ACTR 3.

26.3.5 Actions by true owner

The true owner of a cheque may have an action in conversion against the paying bank. The term "true owner" is not defined by statute, but it will, of course, include a holder in due course of a cheque. Thus, if a cheque payable to bearer is stolen and negotiated to a holder in due course, the latter, and not the person from whom the cheque was stolen, is the true owner: *Smith v Union Bank of London* (1875) 1 QBD 31.

If, however, an order cheque is stolen, and an indorsement forged thereon, the payee remains the true owner. The true owner, therefore, is the person who, under the provisions of the Bills of Exchange Act, is regarded as the person having property in the instrument. He or she is, in other words, the last person to whom the cheque is validly transferred.

Defences as against the true owner are as follows:

(a) Payment in due course (see above);
(b) Bills of Exchange Act 1908, s 60 (see above);
(c) Bills of Exchange Act 1908, s 80 (see above);
(d) Cheques Act 1960, s 2 (see above);

26.4 RECOVERY OF MONEY PAID BY MISTAKE

The more usual circumstances in which a bank may seek to recover money it has mistakenly paid away are as follows:

1   where payment is made on a cheque, contrary to the drawer's countermand;
2   where payment of a cheque has been made, but the drawer has insufficient funds in the account to meet it;
3   where a cheque on which the drawer's signature has been forged is paid;
4   where payment is made contrary to the customer's mandate, and none of the defences previously discussed are available to the bank as against the customer.

In all of these cases, it can be seen that the bank may be anxious to recover the money from the person to whom it was paid and may be able to do so on the ground that it paid the money under a mistake, that is, in the belief that the person was entitled to be paid.

A mistaken payment may be recovered directly from the payee, or it may in equity be traced and recovered from the payee's bank account: *Chase Manhattan Bank v Israel-British Bank (London) Ltd* [1981] 1 Ch 105.

It has not always been easy to describe the circumstances in which money is recoverable on the ground of mistake of fact or law, but the following basic principles can be enumerated:

(a) The mere fact that the paying bank honours its customer's cheque is no representation to the payee that it is a genuine cheque. Therefore, the bank is not estopped, on this ground alone, from recovering the money from the payee: *National Westminster Bank Ltd v Barclays Bank International Ltd* [1975] QB 654.

(b) The mistake must be fundamental, in the sense that it caused the bank to pay the cheque. Furthermore, it has been held that the mistake must be as to a fact which, if true, would make the person paying liable to pay the money. In other words, a mere voluntary payment will not support recovery. However, more recent cases have taken the view that money is recoverable as long as the mistake was fundamental to the payment, even though the payor would not have been liable to pay if the supposed fact had existed. Alternatively, it could be asked whether the payor would still have paid, whether or not there was a mistake: *Commercial Bank of Australia Ltd v Younis* [1979] 1 NSWLR 444.

(c) In *Barclays Bank Ltd v W J Simms, Son and Cooke (Southern) Ltd* [1979] 3 All ER 522, Robert Goff J, after a thorough review of the authorities, concluded that if the payment discharged an existing debt owed to the payee (or to a principal on whose behalf the payee is authorised to receive the payment) it is irrecoverable. Briefly, the facts of the case were that the bank mistakenly paid a cheque after it had received a countermand. It was held that since the payment was made without the customer's mandate, it was not effective to discharge the debt which the customer owed to the payee. The money was, therefore, recoverable from the payee.

(d) In some cases it has been said that the mistake, in order to ground recovery, must be a mistake as to some matter between the party paying and the party receiving. In *Barclays Bank Ltd v W J Simms, Son and Cooke (Southern) Ltd,* Robert Goff J expressly rejected the sub-rule. Indeed, if such a rule were to be applied it would exclude the case where a bank in error pays a stopped cheque. The mistake here is one between the bank and the drawer, not between the bank and the payee.

(e) The claim of the bank may fail if the payee has in the meantime "changed his position". In New Zealand this defence appears in statutory form, as s 94B of the Judicature Act 1908, which provides that relief may be denied wholly or in part:

> ... if the person from whom relief is sought received the payment in good faith and has so altered his position in reliance on the validity of the payment that in the opinion of the Court, having regard to all possible implications in respect of other persons, it is inequitable to grant relief, or to grant relief in full, as the case may be.

The statutory wording does not change the criteria for establishing the change of position defence from those which operate at common law in other jurisdictions. Obviously, each case depends on its own facts, to a very large extent. The recipient of the moneys must obviously not have known of the bank's mistake when he or she took the money, otherwise he or she cannot be said to have acted in good faith.

The mere fact that the payee has spent the money is not enough to establish a change of position. It depends very much on what the money has been spent on. If the money is spent on ordinary living or business expenses, then a "change of position" is unlikely to be established (see

KJ Davies (1976) Ltd v Bank of NSW [1981] 1 NZLR 262; cf *Skyring v Greenwood* (1825) 4 B & C 281). If, on the other hand, money has been invested in a company which has gone into liquidation, then it may be unjust to require a bona fide recipient of moneys to repay them: see *Holt v Markham* [1923] 1 KB 504. Again, on the other hand, expenditure which would have been incurred even if the mistaken payment had not been received is not sufficient as a change of position: *United Overseas Bank v Jiwani* [1977] 1 All ER 733.

(f) Money paid by mistake to a person may be deposited in his or her own bank account. It seems clear that the money can be recovered by suing the payee's bank, at least if that bank has not in the meantime paid the money out of the account. In other words, the mere crediting of the money to the payee's account will not constitute such a change of position as will found a defence for the bank against action by the payor. Neither could the payee's bank seek to assert a lien or right of set-off against such money in the account, unless it had changed its position by making advances to the payee, by way of overdraft, on the strength of the money paid in.

(g) At common law, with regard to negotiable instruments, there is a principle to the effect that where money is paid on such an instrument to a person innocent of any knowledge of mistake it cannot be recovered if the payee's position might, not necessarily would, be affected if he or she had to refund. Thus stated, the rule means that the payee need not show an actual change of position.

The rule is thought to be justified by the commercial importance of preserving the security of negotiable instruments which have been negotiated to an innocent holder for value. The payee of a cheque should have the right to spend the proceeds without fear of a legal liability to repay them. The leading case is *Cocks v Masterman* (1829) 9 B & C 902, in which the plaintiff bankers paid a bill of exchange, but discovered a day later that the acceptance of their customer on the bill had been forged. It was held that the plaintiffs could not recover the money from the holder's bankers. The ground for decision was that the holder of a bill is entitled to know, on the day when it becomes due, whether it is an honoured or dishonoured bill. Therefore, if he or she receives the money and is suffered to retain it for a day, as the holder in the instant case was, then if the payor sues him or her to recover the money on the ground of mistake, he or she can argue that the money is irrecoverable because the payor's delay might have caused him or her harm, by affecting his or her right to give notice of dishonour to prior parties. In other words, the holder is deemed to have changed his or her position.

Such a defence cannot, therefore, arise where the holder is under no obligation to give notice of dishonour, as would be the case where an instrument is forged, and, therefore, not a negotiable instrument at all. Another example is where the drawer has countermanded payment, see *Imperial Bank of Canada v Bank of Hamilton* [1903] AC 49, 58 and Bills of Exchange Act 1908, s 50(2).

In any event, s 50(1) of the Bills of Exchange Act 1908 provides that:

> Delay in giving notice of dishonour is excused where the delay is caused by circumstances beyond the control of the party giving notice, and not imputable to his default, misconduct, or negligence. When the cause of delay ceases to operate notice must be given with reasonable diligence.

It seems, therefore, more rational, in the light of this provision, to allow money to be recovered from someone who has been paid on a negotiable instrument, as long as delay in giving notice of dishonour is excused. Furthermore, the Privy Council indicated in one case that it regarded the rule as being a stringent one, which should not be extended to cases where notice of the mistake is given in reasonable time, and no loss has been occasioned by the delay in giving it: *Imperial Bank of Canada v Bank of Hamilton* [1903] AC 49, 58.

26.5 THE COLLECTING BANK

26.5.1 General

As a major part of its undertaking to its customers, a bank is obliged to collect cheques and other instruments which the customers lodge for their credit.

The bank will, in most cases, act merely as an agent or conduit pipe to receive payment from the bank on whom the cheques are drawn and to hold the proceeds at the disposal of its customer.

In other, more rare, cases, the bank will become more than a mere agent. If it receives the cheques in its own right, as a purchaser for value, it will be collecting them on its own behalf. It can, therefore, qualify as a holder in due course of the cheques; it can sue on the cheque in its own name if the cheque is dishonoured. If it becomes a holder in due course, then it can incur no liabilities to the "true owner" of the cheque, since it will itself then be constituted as the true owner.

To become a holder in due course, the bank must, of course, satisfy all the requirements of s 29 of the Bills of Exchange Act 1908. If, for instance, the bank purchases a cheque whilst at the same time knowing that it is not the property of its customer, then it will not have satisfied all of those requirements. Furthermore, it should be remembered that if a cheque received for collection is crossed "not negotiable", and the customer's title to it is defective, then by virtue of s 81 of the Bills of Exchange Act 1908 the bank will be unable to obtain a better title to it than the customer possessed.

As will be seen, the Cheques Act 1960 removes the need for a collecting bank to examine indorsements on cheques. To qualify as a holder in due course, the bank would normally have to have, however, an indorsement so as to constitute it as a "holder", unless the cheque is payable to bearer. Section 3 of the Act deals with this apparent inconsistency by providing that a bank which gives value for, or has a lien on, a cheque payable to order which the holder delivers to it for collection without indorsing it shall have such rights (if any) as it would have had if, upon delivery, the holder had indorsed it in blank.

In any case, by virtue of s 5(1)(b) of the Cheques Act 1960, a bank which having credited a customer's account with the amount of a cheque, receives payment for itself, is protected against liability to the true owner, if it has acted in good faith and without negligence. A bank which collected a cheque merely as agent for its customer is prima facie liable in conversion to the true owner, but this liability is also subject to the protection of the Cheques Act 1960, considered below.

The question, then, is when does the collecting bank give value for a cheque, so as to constitute itself as a holder for value, or in due course? First, the bank may give value by allowing the customer to draw against the cheque before it is cleared: *National Bank Ltd v Silke* [1891] 1 QB 435. However, the mere crediting of a customer's account with the amount of a cheque does not constitute the giving of value by the bank: *AL Underwood Ltd v Barclays Bank Ltd* [1924] 1 KB 775; *National Australia Bank Ltd v KDS Construction Services Pty Ltd* (1987) 163 CLR 668.

This is merely an accounting procedure, which is always liable to be reversed if the cheque is dishonoured on presentation. In order for the bank to have given value, it must be shown either that there was, in addition, a prior arrangement that the customer should be able to draw against uncleared cheques, or, the honouring of an uncleared cheque, without any prior arrangement: *Capital and Counties Bank v Gordon* [1903] AC 240; *Westminster Bank Ltd v Zang* [1966] AC 182, 210.

There can certainly be no implied agreement that a customer may draw against uncleared cheques if, as is usually the case, there are printed words on the customer's paying in slips which expressly negative such a right.

There must be a nexus between the cheque and its drawing. It must be shown that the bank intended to collect the cheque on its own behalf as the price of the drawing, ie that (whether by prior arrangement or otherwise) it allowed a further drawing, on the strength of the cheque and would or might have refused such drawing if the cheque had not been given.

What if the cheque is credited to an account which is already overdrawn, and thus operates to reduce the overdraft? Section 27(3) of the Bills of Exchange Act 1908 provides that where the holder of a bill has a lien on it arising either from contract or by implication of law, he or she is deemed to be a holder for value to the extent of the sum for which he or she has a lien. A bank clearly has a lien on any cheques delivered into its possession by a customer, provided that the customer is indebted to the bank. The bank is, therefore, a holder for value of the cheque, at least to the extent of the amount of the overdraft: *Re Keever* [1957] Ch 182.

This will be so even though the bank is the customer's agent for collection: *Barclays Bank Ltd v Astley Industrial Trust Ltd* [1970] 2 QB 527. The bank will, however, lose its lien if it returns the cheque to its customer: *Westminster Bank Ltd v Zang* [1966] AC 182, 205.

26.5.2 Duties of collecting bank

(a) The collecting bank has a duty to collect promptly and diligently cheques which the customer has deposited for collection. The bank will be liable to the customer for any damage caused as a result of the delay. For example, the indorser of a cheque will be discharged by the omission to present the cheque within a reasonable time after its indorsement, as long as he or she has been prejudiced by the omission: s 45. The drawer is discharged to the extent of any actual damage he or she has suffered through the delay: s 74(c).

The time within which a bank must present a cheque for payment is not specifically set out by statute, but regard will be paid to the current usages of banks (ie the system of clearing cheques through Databank) and the facts of the particular case: ss 45(2), 74(b).

(b) If the cheque is dishonoured upon presentation, then the collecting bank itself will give notice of dishonour to the parties liable on the cheque, in the manner required by the Act, but only if it itself is intending to enforce the cheque as a holder for value. In most cases, in fact, the bank will simply give notice of dishonour to parties liable on the cheque: s 49. However, the question of notice of dishonour will not arise in most cases, since non-payment of a cheque will usually be due either to countermand by the drawer, or lack of funds to meet the cheque, and each of these factors excuses notice of dishonour: s 50.

(c) The collecting bank always runs the risk that it will collect a cheque for someone whose title to it is in some way defective. If it does so, then it will be liable to the true owner, in damages, for the value of the cheque.

The bank may be liable for the tort of conversion, or alternatively, in quasi-contract, for money had and received. The measure of damages under either head of claim is identical.

Alternatively, the collecting bank may be liable in equity as a constructive trustee, if it collects a cheque in circumstances where an intelligent person would see that a breach of trust would thereby be committed, or would be likely to be committed: *Coleman v Bucks and Oxon Union Bank* [1897] 2 Ch 243.

26.5.3 Protection of collecting bank

The true owner of a cheque has an action for conversion against the collecting bank which collects the cheque on behalf of a person who has no title, or a defective, title to the cheque. At common law liability for conversion is absolute. Section 5 of the Cheques Act 1960 cuts down the liability of a collecting bank by imposing a qualified duty to take reasonable care to refrain from taking any step which the bank foresees is, or ought reasonably to have foreseen was, likely to cause loss or damage to the true owners: *Marfani & Co Ltd v Midland Bank Ltd* [1968] 1 WLR 956, 972.

(1) Where a banker in good faith and without negligence
(a) Receives payment for a customer of an instrument to which this section applies; or
(b) Having credited a customer's account with the amount of any such instrument receives payment for himself,
and the customer has no title, or a defective title, to the instrument, the banker shall not incur any liability to the true owner of the instrument by reason only of having received payment thereof.

The crucial question in most cases concerning s 5 is whether the collecting bank has acted "without negligence". The bank must prove its lack of negligence.

The Act does not define negligence, but this is hardly surprising given the wide variety of circumstances which come before the Courts. Indeed, the Courts have also refused to lay down rules or statements which will determine what is negligence and what is not. Each case must be determined on its own circumstances.

At the same time, however, one cannot ignore some statements of apparently general application, which the Courts have made whilst at the same time deciding cases very much on their individual facts. Thus, it is said that the conduct of a collecting bank should be judged according to the "ordinary practice of bankers," although such practice may not always be a conclusive guide: *Commissioners of Taxation v English, Scottish and Australian Bank Ltd* [1920] AC 683, 689. The recognition of the ordinary practice of bankers shows that the Courts acknowledge that there must be some limits to the obligation of a collecting bank. A bank is not expected to be abnormally suspicious, since the honest majority of its customers will resent being subjected to a cross-examination which gives the impression that the bank doubts their honesty. However, the Courts will expect banks to make investigations, for example, when a doubt is raised as to a person's true entitlement to a cheque. The extent of the investigation to be undertaken will depend on "what, in the circumstances, a fair-minded banker, paying due regard to the reasonable exigencies of banking business . . . would consider it prudent to do in order to protect the interests of the true owner": *London Bank of Australia Ltd v Kendall* (1920) 28 CLR 401, 417. Clearly then, a bank will not be held liable merely because it has not subjected an account to a microscopic examination. It is not expected that bank officials should also be amateur detectives.

On the other hand, it will not usually be valid for a bank to plead that the exigencies of banking business operate as a defence to a charge of negligence. In other words merely because bank officials are very busy is no answer, if they have in fact shown a lack of care.

The situations in which a collecting bank is regarded as not having acted "without negligence" can be divided into cases where the bank is careless in opening the account and cases in which the carelessness is directly related to the cheque received for collection.

26.5.4 Negligence in opening the account

In several cases, collecting banks have been held to be negligent in not making due inquiries about a customer, when an account is opened. Information should usually be obtained not only as to the customer's respectability but also as to all matters relating to him or her which are obviously relevant to the possibility of his or her using his or her account to obtain payment of cheques which the customer has fraudulently converted to his or her own purposes.

Thus, it has been held that a bank is negligent if it fails to "take up references": *Ladbroke v Todd* (1914) 30 TLR 433. Also, the bank may be held to have been negligent if it fails to ascertain the occupation of the prospective customer and the name of his or her employer: *Lloyds Bank Ltd v EB Savory and Co* [1933] AC 201. This reason is that revelation of the customer's occupation may reveal that he or she has the opportunity of misappropriating his or her employer's cheques.

If the bank were not then to ascertain the name of the employer, then it could not guard against the danger, which was fully known to it, of the customer paying in cheques stolen from his or her employers. In a more recent case, however it was thought that this was a "hard doctrine" as far as the bank was concerned, and that "it cannot at any rate be the duty of the bank continually to keep itself up to date as to the identity of a customer's employer." *Orbit Mining and Trading Ltd v Westminster Bank Ltd* [1962] 3 All ER 565, 579. In any event, less reliance is placed upon references in modern banking practice and cases such as *Ladbroke v Todd* may no longer be reliable authorities.

As a limitation on the bank's duty to make inquiries, it has been judicially stated that:

It does not constitute any lack of reasonable care to refrain from making inquiries which it is improbable will lead to detection of the potential customer's dishonest purpose if he is dishonest, and which are calculated to offend him and may be drive away his custom if he is honest: *Marfani Co Ltd v Midland Bank Ltd* [1968] 1 WLR 956, 977.

On the other hand, if bank officials fail to make inquiries which they should have made, there is, at the very least, a heavy burden on them to show that such inquiries could not have led to any action which could have protected the interests of the true owner.

26.5.5 Negligence when cheque presented for collection

The collecting bank may be considered negligent in connection with specific cheques received for collection in several types of case.

First, a cheque may be payable to the customer who is paying it in, but he or she may not have a good title to the cheque, and the circumstances may be such as to put the bank on inquiry as to this fact. For example, a bank might be considered negligent if, without making due inquiry, it credits to the private account of an agent a cheque payable to him or her in his or her representative capacity: *Marquess of Bute v Barclays Bank Ltd* [1955] 1 QB 202.

Then again, an agent might forge cheques of his or her employer and make them payable to himself or herself. The bank should make some inquiry here, in order to satisfy itself as to the agent's title.

If the agent pays a bearer cheque into his or her own account then the circumstances might justify inquiry, despite the form of the cheque. For instance, in *Commercial Bank of Australia Ltd v Flannagan* (1932) 47 CLR 461, F drew a cheque "Pay State Tax or bearer". F's agent to pay his tax paid the cheque into his own account. The bank officer asked the agent why he was paying the money into his private account. The agent replied to the effect that money was owed to him by the principal. It was held that the bank had not, in the circumstances, made sufficient inquiries. The form of the cheque required further proof that the agent was entitled to it.

Secondly, a bank is sometimes considered negligent if, without making due inquiry, it collects for one person's account cheques which are payable to a third party. These cases are as follows:

1   Cheques which are payable to the customer's employer: *Hanna's Lake View (Central) Ltd v Armstrong and Co* (1900) 16 TLR 236; *Francis and Taylor Ltd v Commercial Bank of Australia Ltd* [1932] NZLR 1028.
2   Cheques drawn by an employer in favour of a third party: see eg *Orbit Mining and Trading Co Ltd v Westminster Bank Ltd* [1963] 1 QB 794.
3   Cheques payable to public office holders: see eg *Ross London County Westminster and Parrs Bank* [1919] 1 KB 678.

4   Cheques crossed "Account Payee Only": *Importers Co v Westminster Bank Ltd* (1927) 96 LJKB 919: infra 26.7.4.

26.5.6 Mitigation of bank's negligence

Contributory negligence is available as a defence to an action in conversion: *Helson v McKenzies (Cuba St) Ltd* [1959] NZLR 878. Therefore, if the true owner of a converted cheque has in some way contributed to the conversion by his or her negligence, then his or her damages may be reduced. In *Australian Guarantee Corporation (NZ) Ltd v National Bank of New Zealand Ltd* (unreported, High Court, Wellington, CP 18/88, 4 August 1988, McGechan J) AGC gave one T three cheques payable to named payees (supposedly the sellers of vehicles to T, which sales AGC was financing) with the intention that T would deliver the cheques to those persons. The cheques were crossed and marked "not negotiable – credit bank a/c payee only". T deposited them in an account held with the National Bank in the name of his panelbeating business. The bank questioned T as to his title to the cheques, and accepted his explanation that the sales had fallen through but that AGC was content to lend him the money in any event. AGC successfully sued the bank for conversion; the bank was negligent in failing to contact AGC to satisfy itself as to T's title. But AGC was itself negligent as to 20 per cent in giving T the cheques in the first place, and damages were liable to be reduced by that proportion. The Australian Courts have refused to allow contributory negligence as a defence to conversion: see, for example, *Australian Guarantee Corporation Ltd v Commissioners of the State Bank of Victoria* [1989] VR 617.

Similarly, "the defence" of estoppel is theoretically open to the collecting bank, if it can show that the true owner had said or done something which led it to believe on reasonable grounds that it would be in order for the bank to collect the cheques on behalf of its customer. However, it has been held that the mere fact that an employer does not inform the collecting bank when he or she discovers that an employee has been misappropriating his or her cheques cannot be taken as condonation of the wrongs, so as to operate as an estoppel: *Lloyds Bank Ltd v Chartered Bank of India, Australia and China* [1929] 1 KB 40. In other words, the bank cannot argue that it was "lulled to sleep" by the employer's actions in respect of past frauds, so as to be able to assume that the transactions were valid. To the contrary, each repetition of a fraudulent transaction should aggravate rather than allay suspicion.

Further, the true owner may be held to have ratified the actions of a customer who has converted a cheque belonging to him or her. To constitute ratification there must be full knowledge of what has happened, and unequivocal adoption of it after the knowledge has been gained. If such knowledge does not exist, then mere repetition of misappropriation of cheques does not, by itself, amount to ratification: *Bank of Montreal v Dominion Gresham Guarantee and Casualty Co Ltd* [1930] AC 659, 666. The adoption of the acts in question can be implied.

The measure of damages for conversion by a collecting bank is the face value of the cheque, plus damages for consequential loss which was reasonably foreseeable: *Harrisons Group Holdings Ltd v Westpac Banking Corporation* (1989) 51 SASR 36. However, the damages are reduced by any amount which the true owner of the cheque receives out of the proceeds of conversion, but the onus is upon the bank to prove any such recovery: *Hunter BNZ Finance Ltd v ANZ Banking Group Ltd* [1990] VR 41.

The weight of authority suggests that it is no defence that any inquiry which the bank might have made would not have revealed its customer's lack of good title to a cheque deposited for collection: *Hunter BNZ Finance Ltd v C G Maloney Pty Ltd* (1988) 18 NSWLR 420.

26.5.7 Bank's right to indemnity

If the collecting bank has no defence to an action in conversion by the true owner, it has a right to be indemnified by its customer in respect of the sum claimed: *Bavins Jnr & Sims v London and SW Bank Ltd* [1900] 1 QB 270. This right to indemnity may, however, be removed if the liability of the bank is due to its own default or breach of duty. For example, a fraudulent shop manager steals cheques from some third person. The cheques are not payable to his employer. He forges the payee's indorsements, cashes the cheques through the shop till, and pays the cheques into his employer's account. The bank makes no inquiry concerning the third-party cheques. When the frauds come to light, the bank is sued by the true owner of the cheques. The bank's defence under the Cheques Act 1960 fails since it is not found to have acted "without negligence". The Court might deny the bank an indemnity from its customer, because it failed to draw his attention to the fact that a number of third-party cheques, apparently unconnected with the customer's business, were being passed through the customer's account by the manager of one of his shops.

26.6 PROTECTION OF THE DRAWER

Nowadays, it is seldom that a cheque is drawn with anything like its traditional negotiability in mind. They are drawn primarily for the purpose of settling debts and the drawer is therefore concerned that it should be paid to the named payee. Thus, the original purpose of drawing a cheque, namely to create a negotiable instrument, has become of secondary importance.

Since the majority of cheques are not now intended to be negotiable or even transferable, it is clear that any mandate or authority for payment addressed to the bank by the customer would serve the same purpose. It is an historical accident that these mandates in modern usage are based upon and take the form of bills of exchange.

An indorsee too may be concerned to restrict the negotiability of a cheque to ensure that it is paid only to his or her order. He or she may achieve this result by means of a restrictive indorsement: s 35. By s 36 (1) a bill which is negotiable in its origin continues to be negotiable until it has either been restrictively indorsed, or discharged by payment or otherwise. Various methods by which the drawers and indorsees of cheques may cancel or limit the transferability and negotiability of cheques will now be discussed.

26.6.1 Words prohibiting transfer

To ensure that a cheque reaches a named payee and is paid only to that person a drawer may use adequate words prohibiting transfer under s 8(1) as already described. However, the more usual course to restrict the transfer of cheques in practical effect is by the use of various "crossings".

26.6.2 Crossings

A crossing is a direction to the paying bank to pay the cheque only to another bank. The forms of crossings are set out in s 76 of the Bills of Exchange Act, which provides:

(1) Where a cheque bears across its face an addition of –
(a) The words "and Company", or "bank", or any abbreviation thereof, between two parallel transverse lines, either with or without the words "Not negotiable", –
(b) Two parallel transverse lines simply, either with or without the words "Not negotiable", – that addition constitutes a crossing, and the cheque is crossed generally.
(2) Where a cheque bears across its face an addition of the name of a banker, either with or without the words "Not negotiable", that addition constitutes a crossing, and the cheque is crossed specially and to that banker.

Two kinds of crossing are recognised in this section; special crossings, and general crossings.
The following are examples of general crossings:

NOT NEGOTIABLE | AND COMPANY | BANK | ACCOUNT PAYEE ONLY

A crossing must be on the face of the cheque and should be across the middle, though in practice it is found in a variety of positions.

The following are examples of special crossings:

BANK OF NEW ZEALAND	WESTPAC BANKING CORPORATION CENTREVILLE	LLOYDS BANK NOT NEGOTIABLE	WESTPAC BANKING CORPORATION M MCLEOD & CO.

The words "bank" or "and company" are based on earlier mercantile practices and are no longer in common use. Two parallel transverse lines simply will suffice: s 76(1)(b). These lines are essential to a general crossing but not to a special crossing, for which the simple addition of the name of the banker on the face of the cheque is sufficient: s 76(2).

In *Hunter BNZ Finance Ltd v C G Maloney Pty Ltd* (1988) 18 NSWLR 420 it was argued that the cheque was not crossed because the parallel transverse lines extended only a quarter or so across the face of the cheque and were therefore not "across its face" within the terms of s 76. This argument was rejected; the test is whether the transverse parallel lines sufficiently reveal their status, and in the present case they could perform no other function than to act as a crossing.

It should be noted that the words "not negotiable" are not required for the crossing as such. The effect of these words upon a crossed cheque is covered by s 81. Further, nothing in s 81 requires that the words be placed between the two parallel transverse lines of the crossing.

THE EFFECT OF CROSSINGS

A general or special crossing on a cheque without the words "not negotiable" in no way affects the r transferability of that cheque. It merely ensures that the cheque will not be paid otherwise than through a bank, and if a bank pays it in disregard of the crossing instructions, it will incur liability to the true owner of the cheque for any loss he or she may sustain owing to the cheque having been so paid. The crossing itself, without the words "not negotiable", means only that the holder cannot cash the cheque over the counter, but must lodge it with a bank if it is crossed generally, and with the named bank if it is crossed specifically. Section 79 of the Act provides:

(a) Where a cheque is crossed specially to more than one banker, except when crossed to an agent for collection being a banker, the banker on whom it is drawn shall refuse payment thereof.

(b) Where the banker on whom a cheque so crossed is drawn nevertheless pays the same, or pays a cheque crossed generally otherwise than to a banker, or if crossed specially otherwise than to the banker to whom it is crossed, or his agent for collection being a banker, he is liable to the true owner of the cheque for any loss he may sustain owing to the cheque having been so paid.

(c) Where a cheque presented for payment does not at the time of presentment appear to be crossed, or to have had a crossing which has been obliterated, or to have been added to or altered otherwise than as authorised by this Act, the banker paying the cheque in good faith and without negligence shall not be responsible or incur any liability, nor shall the payment be questioned by reason of the cheque having been crossed, or of the crossing having been obliterated or having been added to or altered otherwise than as authorised by this Act and of payment having been made otherwise than to a banker, or to the banker to whom the cheque is or was crossed, or to his agent for collection being a banker, as the case may be.

The inadequacy of crossing simpliciter as a means of reducing the risks involved in the drawing of cheques became apparent when the Courts began to hold that such crossings left the negotiability of cheques unaffected. In *Smith v Union Bank of London* (1875) LR 1 QBD 31, a crossed cheque was stolen and negotiated to a bona fide holder for value who had it collected by his bank. The cheque had been drawn to the order of the payee who had indorsed it in blank before the theft, thereby making it payable to bearer. By the general principle of negotiability the title to the cheque had passed from the payee, and he could no longer maintain an action for conversion whether the paying bank had acted wrongly or not. The payee sought to allege that the negotiability of the instrument was restricted because of the crossing. The Court of Appeal held that the original payee had ceased to be the true owner of the cheque, and that the form of crossing did not restrict its negotiability.

26.6.3 Effect of the words "not negotiable"

It was because of the need for some further protection that the "not negotiable" crossing was introduced by the legislature to negate effectively the negotiable character of cheques while leaving their transferability unimpaired. Section 81 provides:

Where a person takes a crossed cheque bearing on it the words "Not negotiable", he shall not have and shall not be capable of giving a better title to the cheque than that which the person from whom he took it had.

Although the cheque may be passed from hand to hand, such a crossing has been described as constituting a warning to prospective transferees that they take it at their own risk as subject to any prior defects in title: *Great Western Rly Co Ltd v London and County Banking Co Ltd* [1901] AC 414. In that case, Lord Brampton stated:

The object of s 81 is obvious. It is to afford to the drawer or the holder (s 77) of a cheque who is desirous of transmitting it to another person as much protection as can reasonably be afforded to it against dishonesty or accidental miscarriage in the course of its transit, if he will only take the precaution to cross it, with the addition of the words "not negotiable", so as to make it difficult to get such cheque so crossed cashed until it reaches its destination (422).

The case of *Wilson and Meeson v Pickering* [1946] KB 422 shows that s 81 applies even where the person taking the cheque is the named payee thereof. A blank crossed cheque drawn by the appellants and marked "not negotiable" was handed to the appellant's secretary (Mrs Paice), who was instructed to fill it in for £ 2 and insert the Commissioners of Inland Revenue as payees. She filled in the cheque for £ 54 4s 0d and inserted the name of the respondent (to whom she was indebted) as payee. The respondent, who acted bona fide, paid in the cheque to her bank and secured payment. She was held liable to repay the moneys to the appellants.

It is clear, then, that the drawer can afford himself or herself a fair measure of protection by the use of this crossing. The drawer will be under no obligation to pay the cheque if it falls into the wrong hands through dishonesty or accidental miscarriage, even though the person claiming took it in good faith and for value. The drawer may countermand payment of the cheque, and, even if it has already been paid to an innocent holder subsequent to a defect in title, the proceeds may be traced and recovered by the true owner of the cheque. The law intends innocent takers of cheques crossed "not negotiable" to understand that they take at the risk of acquiring no title at all to it if there is a prior infirmity in the title.

26.6.4 Effect of words "account payee", or "account payee only"

Such a crossing does not cancel the transferability of the cheque: *National Bank v Silke* [1891] 1 QB 435. In that case the cheque was crossed specially to the National Bank and was marked "account of J F Moriarty". The question for determination was whether the payee could transfer it by indorsement to the bank. It was held that the words amounted to nothing more than a direction to the bank to carry the amount to the credit of Moriarty's account when they received it, but did not prevent its renegotiation or transfer.

Commercial and judicial attitudes to cheques crossed in this manner began to change in the early portion of the twentieth century, and it became the practice of banks to make inquiries whenever a customer paid such a cheque in for collection and was not himself or herself the payee, and in *Ladbroke v Todd* (1914) 30 TLR 433, it was held to be negligent not to do so.

It now seems firmly established that a bank has a duty to inquire as to the circumstances of cheques crossed "Account payee" or "Account payee only" deposited for credit to an account other than that of the payee.

In *Importers Co Ltd v Westminster Bank Ltd* [1927] 2 KB 297, I sent crossed cheques marked "Account payee only" to S for delivery to the payee. S forged indorsements by the payees, added his name below and paid them into his own account with the H Bank. The H bank indorsed them to the order of W. The cheques were cleared and the proceeds were credited to the H Bank. It was held that the H Bank was a "customer" within the meaning of s 82, and that the respondents were protected by that section, having discharged the onus of negativing negligence on their part. There was nothing on the cheques to put the respondents as a collecting bank upon inquiry as to the regularity of the indorsement. Bankes LJ stated at 302:

> The principal point of the appellants' argument is that the cheques being all crossed and marked, "Account payee only", that marking amounted to a direction to any one handling the cheques that they were only to deal with them in such a way that the proceeds must pass into the account of the payee, and that anybody who disregarded that direction acted contrary to the express direction on the face of the cheque, and must be taken to be acting negligently, and, if a bank, to be without the protection of s 82. As I understand it, the respondents' answer to that contention is that while that form of marking is a direction to the banker of the person in whose favour the cheque is drawn, it has no application to those who are merely clearing bankers, seeing that it is not in their power to comply with the direction, because the cheque comes to, and is passed on by, them in pursuance of a mandate and in such circumstances that they cannot control the ultimate destination of the money. To that Mr Pritt, for the appellants, says that such a contention does not avail the respondents who, when a cheque comes to them as collecting bankers in this form, must do one of two things: either refuse to deal with it at all, because they cannot comply with the direction on it, or, if they deal with it, they do so knowing that they are doing something which is irregular in disregarding the direction, and therefore, as wise people, they ought only to undertake the business where, knowing it is irregular, the person for whom they are acting is of sufficient standing to indemnify them if any trouble arises.
>
> If I have put the case on the one side and on the other correctly, that last contention, it seems to me, renders this class of business altogether impossible.

And Atkin LJ said at 309:

> . . . one knows very well that cheques are occasionally drawn marked "Account payee" and sent to a person who has no banking account. I do not agree that those cheques are of no value to that person. I see no reason why such a person should not request someone who has a banking account to present and get the cheque cleared for him. I agree that there is a duty upon the bank which takes a cheque in those circumstances to see that, in fact, they are collecting the money for the account of the payee, and that the proceeds, when received, will go to the payee.

The question was again discussed by the Judicial Committee in *Universal Guarantee Pty Ltd v National Bank of Australasia Ltd* [1965]1 WLR 691, where it was stated:

> The addition of the words "a/c payee" or "a/c payee only" refer to the payee named in the cheque and not the holder at the time of presentation: *House Property Co of London v London County and Westminster Bank* (1915) 84 LJKB 1846; 31 TLR 479, but they do not prevent, at law, the further negotiability of the cheque. The words merely operate as a warning to the collecting bank that if it pays the proceeds of the cheque to some other account it is put on inquiry and it may be in difficulty in relying on any defence under section 88 of the Act in an action against it for conversion of the cheque: per Scrutton LJ in *A L Underwood Ltd v Bank of Liverpool and Martins* [1924] 1 KB 775, 793; 40 TLR 302 (CA). These words do not cast on the paying bank, paying the cheque to a banker, any additional obligation to satisfy itself that the collecting bank is collecting it on behalf of the named payee. That is entirely the responsibility of the collecting bank (697).

The marking "account payee only" constitutes a warning to the collecting bank that it should not collect a cheque for a person other than the named payee without satisfying itself as to the title of its customer. If it fails to make inquiry it acts negligently and cannot rely upon the protection afforded by s 5 of the Cheques Act 1960. This is so even if the cheque appears to be properly indorsed: *Hunter BNZ Finance Ltd v C G Maloney Pty Ltd* (1988) 18 NSWLR 420.

In *New Zealand Law Society v ANZ Banking Group Ltd* [1985] 1 NZLR 280 Broadlands Finance agreed to lend $50,000 to a company T Ltd for the purchase of two trucks. The application for the loan was made by a solicitor C who was also a director of T Ltd. Broadlands advanced the funds by way of two cheques payable to T Ltd, crossed and marked "not negotiable account payee only". The cheques were delivered to C who deposited them in his trust account held with the ANZ. The bank made no inquiry as to his title to the cheques. The funds never reached T Ltd because C misappropriated them. T Ltd as the true owner of the cheques claimed against the Law Society Fidelity Fund, which compromised the claim and took an assignment from Broadlands of the latter's rights against the bank. In deciding the question of negligence Davison CJ adopted the test established in *Commissioners of Taxation v English, Scottish and Australian Bank* [1920] AC 683, viz whether the transaction of paying in any given cheque coupled with the circumstances antecedent and present was so out of the ordinary course that it might have aroused doubts in the banker's minds and caused them to make inquiry. Davison CJ found that the bank had not acted negligently. Factors of importance were that:

(a) it was established banking practice in New Zealand to credit solicitors' trust accounts with cheques payable to a third party, for it is in the nature of such accounts that they hold funds for third parties;

(b) the manager of the branch concerned knew C and had no reason to suspect his integrity, particularly since there had been no untoward dealings with the account; and

(c) C was a director of the payee.

This is possibly an unusual case; generally the mere failure to make inquiry is itself evidence of negligence. Cf *National Commercial Banking Co of Australia Ltd v Robert Bushby Ltd* [1984] 1 NSWLR 559, 574. See too *Commercial Securities & Finance Ltd v ANZ Banking Group Ltd* [1985] 1 NZLR 728; *Thackwell v Barclays Bank plc* [1986] 1 All ER 676.

Section 77 provides that a cheque may be crossed generally or specifically by the drawer, or by any holder of an uncrossed cheque. Where a cheque is crossed generally, then the holder may cross it specially, and may also add the words "not negotiable" to a crossing, whether special or general. Where a cheque is crossed specially to a banker, that banker may again cross it specially to another banker for collection. A banker with whom an uncrossed or generally crossed cheque is lodged for collection may cross it specially to itself. By s 78 a crossing authorised by the Act is a material part of the cheque, and no person may obliterate or add to or alter the crossing except as authorised by the Act.

Section 4 of the Cheques Act 1960 offers some protection to the drawer by providing that an unindorsed cheque which appears to have been paid by a banker on whom it is drawn shall, in the absence of proof to the contrary, be sufficient evidence of the receipt by the payee of the sum payable by the cheque. A presumption that the payee has received his or her money on which the drawer can rely is therefore raised. It is therefore incumbent on the payee to adduce sufficient evidence to the contrary.

Chapter 27

SURETYSHIP AND GUARANTEES

SUMMARY

27.1 INTRODUCTION

27.1.1 General

A guarantee is a promise by one person (the guarantor) to answer for the debt of another person (the principal debtor). This promise is made to the creditor of the principal debtor. The promise involves the undertaking by the guarantor of a secondary liability, that is, one which arises upon the debtor's defaulting on his or her primary obligation to the creditor.

A guarantee is a very common form of security utilised by lenders. For instance, the directors or principal shareholders of a small private company which borrows money from a bank will usually be required by the bank to guarantee personally repayment of the loan. These guarantees thus act as collateral security to securities given over the company's assets. Commercial guarantees of this sort are long, complex documents, which are drafted by the banks with a view to restricting the freedom of action of the guarantor as much as possible, whilst at the same time conferring a considerable degree of latitude in favour of the bank. Reference to some common terms in such documents will be made below.

A guarantee may be contrasted with an indemnity. The distinction between a guarantee and an indemnity was clearly shown in *Birkmyr v Darnell* (1704) 1 Salk 27, where the Court stated:

> If two come to a shop and one buys, and the other, to gain him credit, promises the seller "If he does not pay you, I will", this is a collateral undertaking (a

387

guarantee). . . . But if he says "Let him have the goods, I will be your paymaster, or I will see you paid", this is an undertaking as for himself (an indemnity) and he shall be intended to be the very buyer and the other to act but as his servant.

Therefore, a guarantee is a secondary or "back-up" undertaking, whereas an indemnity gives rise to a primary or "first-line" liability. Whether the transaction is an indemnity or a guarantee depends upon the intention of the parties.

27.1.2 Form

Section 2 of the Contracts Enforcement Act 1956 requires that a contract of guarantee be in writing. No such requirement applies to contracts of indemnity. It should be noted that if the guarantee is not the sole or predominant object of the parties, but is incidental to a larger transaction, then s 2 may not apply to the guarantee element: *Sutton and Co v Grey* [1894] 1 QB 285.

The Contracts Enforcement Act 1956, s 3 provides that the consideration for a guarantee need not appear in writing. However, consideration must still in fact exist for the guarantee, unless it is given under seal, ie by deed.

A promise to pay a debt incurred by a third party prior to the giving of the promise is past consideration and cannot support the guarantee. Some other consideration requires to be proven in such a case. The usual form in respect of past debts is for consideration to be constituted by the creditor forbearing to sue the principal debtor, in return for the guarantee. This forbearance need not be expressly stated, but is usually implied from the very taking of the guarantee: *Clegg v Bromley* [1912] 3 KB 474, 491. The forbearance to sue must, to constitute good consideration, be given at the request of the guarantor: *Combe v Combe* [1951] 2 KB 215.

An agent may sign on behalf of a guarantor, even if the agent is himself or herself a co-guarantor, but an agency signature by the other contracting party, ie the person in favour of whom the guarantee is given, is not effective: *Bank of New Zealand v Mulholland* (1991) NZBLC 101,970.

27.1.3 Capacity

Under s 15A of the Companies Act 1955 a company registered after 1 January 1984 has the rights, powers and privileges of a natural person. Prima facie, therefore, such a company has unrestricted capacity to give a guarantee. However there are two practical limitations as far as the enforcement of corporate guarantees are concerned. Where a company gives a guarantee without any benefit accruing to the company (for example, a guarantee securing the personal debt of a director), the directors in procuring the guarantee possibly do not act bona fide in the best interests of the company and for a proper purpose. Accordingly they have no authority to procure the guarantee which may be unenforceable at the instance of a third party with notice of lack of authority: see *Rolled Steel Products (Holdings) Ltd v British Steel Corporation* [1985] 3 All ER 52 (CA).

Secondly, procurement by a parent company of a guarantee given by a subsidiary in favour of a third party may amount to abuse of a corporate power: *ANZ Executors & Trustee Co Ltd v Quintex Australia Ltd* (1990) 8 ACLC 980.

27.1.4 Lender liability

A guarantor may be able to avoid liability under a guarantee on account of the conduct of the creditor before, or at the time of, the giving of the guarantee. Generally the complaint of the guarantor is that the creditor has failed to make proper disclosure, or that the guarantor was subject to undue influence, or that the contract of guarantee is unconscionable. "Lender liability" refers to the responsibility of the lender for conduct of this kind.

(a) NON-DISCLOSURE

A creditor who takes a guarantee must disclose to the guarantor anything that might not naturally be expected to take place between the debtor and the creditor: *Hamilton v Watson* (1845) 12 Cl & Fin 109; *National Mortgage and Agency Co of New Zealand Ltd v Stalker* [1933] NZLR 1182. However, this duty of disclosure has always been restrictively interpreted by the Courts. The very fact that a creditor seeks a guarantee is sufficient to put the guarantor upon notice that the creditor mistrusts the debtor's creditworthiness. Accordingly the creditor need not disclose that the debtor's credit is dubious or that previous dealings with the debtor have been unsatisfactory. In *Goodwin v National Bank of Australasia Ltd* (1968) 117 CLR 173 G gave the bank a mortgage securing the indebtedness of his son and daughter-in-law to the bank. Unbeknown to G, his son had guaranteed the liability of a third person to the bank a week previously. The son's liability under this guarantee came within the security which G had given the bank, and when the bank sought to enforce the security, G argued that the bank should have disclosed to him the existence of the guarantee. It was held that the bank was under no duty of disclosure, since the existence of the guarantee was not an unexpected circumstance. On the other hand, in *Westpac Banking Corporation v McDougall* (1988) 2 NZBLC 103,218 it was held that disclosure should have been made to a guarantor where the loan guaranteed was far greater than that normally permitted by the bank's lending policy, and there was an unusually close relationship between the manager of the bank and the person at whose instigation the guarantee was signed.

Following the decision in *Shotter v Westpac Banking Corporation* [1988] 2 NZLR 316 it appeared that the limitations of the rule in *Hamilton v Watson* might be avoided, at least in the case of a bank taking a guarantee from its own customer. In that case S gave an "all moneys" mortgage to the bank with a limit of $100,000 securing the liability of a company which had borrowed that amount as bridging finance for a development scheme. S was not aware, and was not told, that the company already owed the bank some $500,000. The loan of bridging finance was largely recovered and S did not dispute his liability to the bank for the balance. The bank, however, sought payment of the full amount of the guarantee on the basis that the company's other liabilities to the bank exceeded that amount. Wylie J accepted that the bank was under no duty to disclose under the rule in *Hamilton v Watson*. But Wylie J held that a bank owes its customer a duty of explanation, warning or recommendation of separate advice when it should reasonably suspect that:

(1) the customer may not fully understand the meaning of the guar-
     antee and the extent of liability thereunder; or
(2) there is some special circumstance known to the bank which it
     should reasonably suspect might not be known to the prospective
     guarantor and which might be likely to affect that person's deci-
     sion to enter into the guarantee.

Accordingly, in *Shotter's* case, it was held that the bank should have
disclosed the existence of the company's other debts to the bank.

Subsequent cases have not followed *Shotter*: see *Westpac Banking
Corporation v McCreanor* [1990] 1 NZLR 580; *Shivas v Bank of New Zealand*
[1990] 2 NZLR 327. A major difficulty is distinguishing a duty of care in
tort, as held to exist in *Shotter*, from the duty of disclosure under the rule
in *Hamilton v Watson*. Furthermore, in *Shivas* it was said that a guarantor
is already adequately protected under the rule in *Hamilton v Watson*.

(b) UNDUE INFLUENCE

Undue influence and unconscionable bargain are discussed above paras
5.2.2, 5.2.3. While the doctrines of undue influence and unconscionable
bargain are closely related, they are nonetheless quite distinct. A finding
of undue influence negates sufficiency of consent on the part of the
defendant. Generally it is only infrequently that actual undue influence
on the part of an institutional lender itself will be shown. In the case of a
bank and its customer, for example, the relationship is not ordinarily one
which gives rise to a presumption of undue influence: *National Westminster Bank plc v Morgan* [1985] AC 686 (HL). In *Shotter's* case supra Wylie
J considered that the bank was not in a position to dominate or influence
the guarantor. He had considerable commercial experience, had given a
guarantee twice before, and was in contact with solicitors from whom he
could have sought advice if necessary.

On the other hand, an institutional lender may be vulnerable to a
finding that it is tainted by the undue influence exercised by some other
party (usually the debtor) in order to obtain the giving of a guarantee. In
Contractors Bonding Ltd v Snee (unreported, Court of Appeal, CA 35/91,
6 November 1991) the Court of Appeal reviewed the numerous English
authorities and McKay LJ summarised the position as follows:

> The mere fact that a person has entered into a contract with a creditor or lender
> as a result of undue influence will not of itself entitle that person to have the
> contract set aside. Some further element is necessary which affects the
> conscience of the creditor or lender. If the undue influence has been exercised
> by the agent of the creditor or lender, that is sufficient. Where the creditor
> entrusted the third party with the task of obtaining execution of the document,
> that may be sufficient to make that person the agent of the creditor, but that
> is a question of fact. In cases not amounting to agency, the question is whether
> the circumstances are such that the creditor is to be regarded as having notice
> of the exercise of undue influence, or of circumstances which would give rise
> to a presumption of undue influence. Where the procurement of execution of
> the document is entrusted to someone such as the debtor who has a motive for
> ensuring its execution, this will be a relevant factor to take into account, but
> ... the mere fact that the document is sent to the debtor for execution by himself
> and his guarantor is not of itself sufficient.

(c) UNCONSCIONABLE BARGAIN

A guarantee will be set aside if the guarantor is in a vulnerable position and the party taking the guarantee has as a result gained an unfair advantage through the unconscientious use of its greater power. In *Commercial Bank of Australia Ltd v Amadio* (1983) 151 CLR 447 Mrs and Mrs A executed a mortgage and guarantee securing the indebtedness to the bank of a company controlled by their son. The bank gave them no advice as to the nature of the documents or the extent of their liability. In fact the son had misrepresented the terms of the documents to his parents, who were elderly, unfamiliar with written English and patently did not understand the implications of their executing the documents. It was held that Mr and Mrs A were under a special disadvantage, and that it was unconscientious for the bank to enforce the security with knowledge of their position. See too *Elia v Commercial & Mortgage Nominees Ltd* (1988) 2 NZBLC 103,296.

However, the Courts are wary of finding that a person is under a special disadvantage merely because he or she is inexpert in commercial matters. In a succession of cases wives who have secured their husbands' business borrowings have failed to show unconscionability: see, for example, *Alexander v Westpac Banking Corporation* (unreported, Court of Appeal, CA 90/90, 14 August 1990); *Jenkins v NZI Finance Ltd* (1990) ANZ ConvR 422 (CA).

27.2 LIABILITY OF GUARANTOR

The nature of a guarantor's obligation and the manner in which it arises is revealed in a passage from the speech of Lord Diplock in the House of Lords in *Moschi v Lep Air Services Ltd* [1972] 2 All ER 393, 401:

> It is because the obligation of the guarantor is to see to it that the debtor performs his own obligations to the creditor that the guarantor is not entitled to notice from the creditor of the debtor's failure to perform an obligation which is the subject of the guarantee, and that the creditor's cause of action against the guarantor arises at the moment of the debtor's default and the limitation period then starts to run. It is also why, where the contract of guarantee was entered into by the guarantor at the debtor's request, the guarantor has a right in equity to compel the debtor to perform his own obligation to the creditor if it is of a kind in which a Court of equity is able to compel performance. (See also *Fahey v MSD Spiers Ltd* [1975] 1 NZLR 240 PC).

Apart, however, from this general principle, the guarantor's obligations are determined as to nature and extent by the terms of the guarantee.

The extent and nature of the guarantor's liability depends upon the contract of guarantee. The contract will define the amount for which the guarantor is liable and the circumstances in which his or her liability arises. The guarantor's liability may arise on non-payment by the debtor or on the happening of an event provided for in the contract, on which the guarantor becomes liable to pay. It must be emphasised that the contract of guarantee is made between the creditor and the guarantor. Hence, in the absence of agreement between the creditor and the guarantor, decisions or admissions made by the principal debtor to the creditor are not binding on the guarantor. The creditor need not sue the principal debtor when default is made; the creditor need not attempt to realise on securities held by him, or even demand payment from the debtor before suing the guarantor (see *DFC Financial Services Ltd v Coffey* [1991] 2 NZLR 513 (PC)), unless the guarantee requires that this be done. The more common types of guarantee are:

(a) *A specific guarantee.* This is a promise so worded as to refer to one particular transaction and it is discharged immediately the obligation arising under that transaction has been satisfied, whether by the principal debtor or the guarantor, eg "Lend X $50 and I will repay you if he does not". This guarantee will not extend to any further loans to X.

(b) *A continuing guarantee.* This extends to a series of transactions and is not affected by payments by the principal debtor from time to time. The liability of the guarantor is to pay the final balance owing by the debtor. For example, if the X Co has a current account with a bank (the overdraft being guaranteed by A, one of the directors of the X Co), A's liability is the amount of the overdraft at the time the company fails to pay when demand is made by the bank.

(c) *A guarantee up to a certain fixed amount.* If the guarantor undertakes to guarantee payment for goods to the value of $200 supplied to X, this may mean that once X has bought $200 worth of goods, the guarantee will not cover any further purchases. On the other hand, it may mean that X may purchase goods from time to time and that the guarantee will cover a final liability not exceeding $200. Each case must be determined by the language used and the intention of the parties.

(d) *A guarantee by several guarantors.* The amount recoverable from each of several guarantors, liable under the same guarantee for a fixed sum, depends on whether each of them has made himself or herself liable for that sum or whether the prescribed sum represents their aggregate liability. In the former case, the full amount would be recoverable from each guarantor in the latter case, payment of the prescribed sum by one cannot discharge the others from liability under the guarantee. There may be a joint guarantee in which case all guarantors have the right to insist on being sued together. Where judgment is recovered against one of them even though it is unsatisfied, it is a bar to any action against the others: *Kendal v Hamilton* (1879) 4 App Cas 504.

A common form of guarantee required by lenders or people supplying goods is known as a "joint and several" guarantee which is usually worded in such a way that any one of the guarantors can be called on to pay the full amount or all the guarantors can be called on to pay their individual proportion of the amount guaranteed.

27.3 RIGHTS OF THE GUARANTOR

27.3.1 General

A guarantor has certain rights as against the principal debtor, the creditor, and against any co-guarantors if necessary. As will be seen, these rights may in part be limited or removed by the express terms of the guarantee contract.

27.3.2 As against creditor

As against the creditor the guarantor has a right not to have his or her liability under the guarantee brought about by the creditor's own fault. If the creditor releases a security without the consent of the guarantor, the latter's liability under the guarantee is discharged not absolutely but pro tanto: *National Bank of New Zealand Ltd v Murland* [1991] 3 NZLR 86.

The extent to which a guarantor is liable will frequently depend upon the success with which assets of the debtor are disposed of in order to defray the principal debt. It is accepted that a receiver in getting in and selling the assets subject to a security owes a duty of care to a guarantor: *Davy v Nathan Securities Ltd* (1989) 4 NZCLC 65,321, and the position is the same for a mortgagee conducting a mortgage sale: *Clark v UDC Finance Ltd* [1985] 2 NZLR 636. But the Courts have refused to find that the creditor owes a duty of care to the guarantor. In *China & South Sea Bank Ltd v Tan* [1990] 1 AC 536 (PC) T guaranteed a debt which was secured by the mortgage of shares. The security was ultimately nugatory because the shares became worthless. The guarantor argued that the creditor owed him a duty of care in terms of which the creditor should have realised its security before the value of the shares evaporated. The Privy Council held that the creditor owed no such duty. Lord Templeman said:

> The surety contracts to pay if the debtor does not pay and the surety is bound by his contract. If the surety . . . is worried that the mortgaged securities may decline in value then the surety may request the creditor to sell and if the creditor remains idle then the surety may bustle about, pay off the debt, take over the benefit of the securities and sell them. No creditor could carry on the business of lending if he could become liable to a mortgagor and to a surety or to either of them for a decline in value of mortgaged property, unless the creditor was personally responsible for the decline (545).

See too *Davis v Bank of New Zealand* [1991] 1 NZLR 745. While prejudicial conduct by the creditor during the subsistence of the guarantee may discharge the guarantor (for example, where the creditor connives at the default by the debtor), the Courts have confined such conduct to narrow categories: see *Bank of India v Trans Continental Commodity Merchants Ltd* [1983] 2 Lloyd's Rep 298, 301-302; *Westpac Securities Ltd v Dickie* [1991] 1 NZLR 656 (CA); *Coffey v DFC Financial Services Ltd* (1991) 5 NZCLC 67,403 (CA).

A guarantor who has paid the debt of the principal debtor is subrogated to all rights possessed by the creditor in respect of the debt: Judicature Act 1908, s 85. Furthermore, a guarantor who has paid the principal debt is entitled to all securities held by the creditor (Judicature Act 1908, s 54). He or she is entitled to receive such securities in the same condition as they were received by the creditor, and if the creditor has lost any of the securities, the guarantee is discharged to that extent: *Taylor v Bank of New South Wales* (1886) 11 App Cas 596; *National Bank of New Zealand v Chapman* [1975] 1 NZLR 480.

However, the guarantor has no right to compel the creditor to sue the principal debtor before suing him or her on the guarantee, unless he or she undertakes to indemnify the creditor for the risk, delay and expense he or she thereby incurs.

Finally, on being sued by the creditor under the guarantee, the guarantor may avail himself or herself of any set-off or counterclaim which the debtor possesses as against the creditor: *Bechervaise v Lewis* (1872) LR 7 CP 372.

27.3.3 As against principal debtor

As against the principal debtor, the guarantor has the right to compel him or her to perform his or her obligation to the creditor, even before the debtor has been called upon to pay under the terms of the guarantee: *Moschi v Lep Air Services*, supra; *Ascherson v Tredegar Dry Dock and Wharf Co Ltd* [1909] 2 Ch 401.

Once the guarantor has paid the creditor, he or she may require repayment to him or her of such sums by the principal debtor, by suing in quasi-contract. In addition, as noted above, the guarantor is entitled to stand in the shoes of the creditor, and to use all the remedies and securities available to that creditor.

Where the guarantor, who has guaranteed the principal debtor's account at a bank is compelled by the bank to pay, the guarantor, notwithstanding that the principal debtor's debt to the bank is statute-barred, can recover against the principal debtor the payments made by him or her: *Fuller v Perano* [1941] NZLR 44.

27.3.4 As against co-guarantors

A guarantor who has paid more than his or her share of the common liability is entitled to compel contribution from his or her co-guarantors whether they are bound jointly and severally or severally. This right will exist notwithstanding that the co-guarantors are bound by different instruments, or became guarantors without being aware of the existence of any co-guarantors: Judicature Act 1908, ss 85–86.

The right to contribution is not founded on contract but is the result of general equity arising at the inception of the contract of guarantee on the ground of equality of burden and benefit: see *Trotter v Franklin* [1991] 2 NZLR 92. There is no right of contribution when guarantors are bound by different instruments for portions of a debt due from the same debtor, the guarantee of each being a separate and distinct transaction, or where it is expressly arranged by contract that each shall be individually answerable only for a given portion of one sum of money due from the principal debtor.

The guarantor can, before payment, by action against his or her co-guarantors, compel them to contribute towards the liquidation of the common liability. If one of the guarantors is sued, he or she will normally cite the other co-guarantors as co-defendants. The individual liability of each guarantor will then be determined at the same time as their collective liability under the guarantee.

The right to contribution after payment does not arise until the guarantor has paid more than his or her proportion or share of the common liability, ie more than he or she was legally bound to pay.

For example, if there is a joint and several guarantee by A, B and C of an overdraft up to $900 and payment of $270 is demanded from A, he or she will have no right of contribution against B and C if the overdraft is to continue to be supported by the guarantee. If, however, A is entitled to have the guarantee discharged on making such a payment, the total liability under the guarantee is $270 towards which he or she can claim contribution of $90 from each of his or her co-guarantors.

In *Stirling v Burdett* [1911] 2 Ch 418 some guarantors had paid more than their share of interest on a mortgage debt and premiums on a life policy. It was held that their right to contribution had not arisen as the principal, interest and premiums together constituted one debt, and they had not yet paid their due proportion of that debt.

The amount recoverable from each co-guarantor is always regulated by the number of solvent guarantors. For example, if A, B and C jointly guaranteed the payment of $300 and A become insolvent, B (who had paid the full amount) could recover $150 from C. Where each guarantor is liable for an equal amount, all contribute equally towards the common debt and if not equally liable, then proportionately to the amount for which each is liable.

If a co-guarantor is adjudicated bankrupt and the other guarantor has paid off the whole debt, the latter can prove in the bankruptcy for the whole debt for which the bankrupt is severally liable. But he or she cannot receive from the bankrupt estate more than the excess over and above the amount of his or her own proportionate contribution. For example, if A, B and C jointly and severally guaranteed a debt of $900, and upon B becoming bankrupt, the whole sum of $900 was claimed from A, A could prove in B's bankruptcy for the aggregate liability of $900. If B's estate paid 25 cents in the dollar, A would be entitled to receive the sum of $225 as a contribution towards the liability under the guarantee. In such a case, A would be entitled to claim contribution from C, the remaining solvent guarantor, of $337.50, being half of the balance of the liability owing. On the other hand, if B's estate paid 50 cents in the dollar, the maximum amount payable by way of dividend in respect of proof for $900 would be $300, being B's original proportionate liability.

Co-guarantors are entitled to the benefit of all securities which have been obtained by one of their number whether they knew of the existence of such securities or not.

27.4 DETERMINATION OF GUARANTEE

The guarantee will be determined in the following cases (subject to express terms to the contrary in the contract of guarantee):

27.4.1 Where the debtor pays the debt

Payment of the debt determines the guarantee unless the guarantee is a continuing one, that is, one which covers whatever debts may be incurred by the debtor from time to time, during the currency of the guarantee. However, if the debt is paid to the creditor so that the guarantor is discharged, nevertheless the payment may be attacked as a voidable (or fraudulent) preference: see Insolvency Act 1967, s 56; Companies Act 1955, s 309; and see also *Re M Kushler Ltd* [1943] Ch 248.

In such a case, the creditor will have to refund the money to the Official Assignee or liquidator, and can then proceed against the guarantor on the guarantee, as before. Alternatively, the guarantor who has been preferred by the payment can be joined as a party to an application by a liquidator for recovery of the money paid and recovery can be made directly from him or her: see Companies Act 1955, s 310(3). This is useful to the creditor where the guarantor has had his or her securities returned to him or her on payment having been made, since he or she is probably then under no duty to return the securities to the bank, in the event of the payment being adjudged a voidable preference: *Re Conley* [1938] 2 All ER 127.

27.4.2 Where the guarantor volunteers payment of the principal debt

In such a case, where the debt is paid off prematurely, the guarantor cannot seek his or her indemnity from the debtor until the time when the debt would have fallen due has passed.

27.4.3 Where the guarantor gives notice of termination

Thus, in the case of a continuing guarantee over a bank overdraft, the guarantor can determine the guarantee as to future advances at any time by notice, and by paying what has accrued due up to that time, up to the limit of the guarantee: *Beckett v Addyman* [1882] 9 QBD 783.

This right to determine the guarantee by notice is thought even to exist in the case of a guarantee for a specified period of time, but only if the bank was not bound to make further advances to the principal debtor: *Re Grace* [1902] 1 Ch 733.

27.4.4 Where the guarantor dies

In fact, the mere death of the guarantor does not put an end to a guarantee. Termination only takes place when notice of death reaches the creditor, unless the guarantee provided for a period of notice to be given by the deceased's personal representatives: *Bradbury v Morgan* (1862) 1 H & C 249; *Re Sherry* (1884) 25 ChD 692.

27.4.5 Notice of guarantor's mental incapacity

When the bank receives notice of the mental incapacity of the guarantor the guarantee is determined: *Bradford Old Bank Ltd v Sutcliffe* (1918) 23 Com Cas 299.

27.4.6 Joint and several guarantees

Where the guarantee is joint and several, neither the death nor the mental disorder of one of the guarantors ends the liability of his or her co-guarantors: *Beckett v Addyman* supra; *Bradford Old Bank Ltd v Sutcliffe*, supra.

Similarly notice by one co-guarantor will not determine his or her liability is not effective to determine the liability of any of the co-guarantors, unless the guarantee actually makes provision for termination by one only of them: *Egbert v National Crown* Bank [1918] AC 903.

27.4.7 Bankruptcy of guarantor

The bankruptcy of a guarantor does not of itself determine the guarantee, but for practical purposes the creditor will find that the security is terminated, and that the creditor is limited to proving in the bankrupt's estate in respect of his or her liability under the guarantee: *Boyd v Robins* (1859) SCB (NS) 597.

27.4.8 Change of parties

In the absence of a contrary provision a guarantee is revoked by a change in the constitution of any of the parties thereto. For instance, a continuing guarantee for a partnership's debts is revoked by a change in the constitution of the firm: see Partnership Act 1908, s 21, *Prescott etc and Co Ltd v Bank of England* [1894] 1 QB 351.

27.4.9 Material variation

Any material variation of the terms of the contract between the creditor and the principal debtor will discharge the guarantor, unless the guarantor consents to it. This is so even if the guarantor is not prejudiced by the variation: see *Ward v National Bank of New Zealand* (1883) 8 App Cas 755; *National Bank of Nigeria Ltd v Awolesi* [1964] 1 WLR 1311; *Royal Bank of Canada v Gorgulis* (1980) 98 DLR (3d) 335.

27.4.10 Release and giving time

The release of the principal debtor discharges the guarantor, as does the existence of a binding agreement between the creditor and the debtor to give the latter extra time to pay, as long as the extra time is given without the guarantor's consent. Again, no prejudice to the guarantor need be shown: *Brown v Aimers* [1934] NZLR 414.

27.4.11 Non-disclosure

As noted above, mere non-disclosure by the creditor to the guarantor of matters which may be material to his or her liability will not necessarily discharge the guarantee, but a failure to answer honestly questions actually put by the guarantor regarding matters which he or she reasonably regards as material and which he or she could reasonably assume to be within the knowledge of the creditor will have such an effect.

As a general rule, whenever a guarantor is induced by a material misrepresentation of the creditor to undertake his or her obligation he or she will be entitled under the Contractual Remedies Act 1979 to seek cancellation of the contract. The silence of the creditor may be held to amount to a positive misrepresentation of the nature of the liability being assumed, in appropriate cases. The creditor should ensure that the guarantor is under no misapprehension as to the nature of his or her liability.

397

27.4.12 Interference with right to security

Any act of the creditor which interferes with the right of the guarantor to receive securities held by the creditor, upon making payment under the guarantee, will discharge the guarantor from liability to the extent of such interference. Thus, where there is a mortgage security given in respect of a guaranteed debt, the creditor must hold it for the benefit of the guarantor so that the latter may, upon paying such debt, obtain a transfer of the mortgage in its original unimpaired condition. If the creditor does not fulfil his or her duty in this respect the guarantor is discharged.

The same principle applies where the creditor, without the guarantor's consent, substitutes one security from the debtor for another, or merges one security in another, or relinquishes any security: *National Bank NZ Ltd v Chapman* [1975] 1 NZLR 480.

27.4.13 Release of debtor

The guarantor is discharged from liability where the principal debtor is expressly or impliedly released from liability. In like vein, the guarantor will be released if the principal debt is void. For instance, in *Coutts and Co v Browne-Lecky* [1947] 1 KB 104, an infant was granted an overdraft by the bank guaranteed by two guarantors. It was held that as the contract by the infant was void under the Infants Act, the guarantors were not liable. There was no "debt" the payment of which they had guaranteed. See also *Robinson's Motor Vehicles Ltd v Graham* [1956] NZLR 545.

27.4.14 Release of co-guarantors

A release of one of several or joint and several guarantors without the consent of the others will discharge those others. Even where guarantors are only severally bound, the release of one will release the others to the extent that they have by the release of the one lost their right to seek contribution from him or her: *Carter v White* (1883) 25 ChD 666.

27.4.15 Irrelevance of principal debtor's bankruptcy

Neither the discharge in bankruptcy of the principal debtor nor the acceptance by creditors of a composition discharges the guarantor: Insolvency Act 1967, s 116: see *Quainoo v New Zealand Breweries Ltd* [1991] 1 NZLR 161 (CA).

27.5 GUARANTEES IN PRACTICE

Many of the principles discussed above are allowed limited or no effect in many standard form commercial guarantees, such as those employed by banks. Express clauses often operate in this way. The effect of most such clauses is to give the creditor the utmost freedom of action, whilst restricting or removing completely rights which the guarantor would have enjoyed either at common law or in equity. Some of the more important of such clauses are as follows:

27.5.1 Consideration clause

As we have seen, the Contracts Enforcement Act 1956 provides that the consideration for a guarantee need not appear on the face of the document. In practice, however, it invariably does appear.

Guarantees are often expressed to extend to both existing and future advances to the principal debtor, by the creditor and are not limited to the lending of any specific sum.

Although the mere existence of an antecedent debt is not good consideration of itself for the guarantee, the consideration is actually constituted by the creditor's forbearing to sue the debtor, in return for the guarantee. This forbearance to sue need not be expressly stated, since it is implied from the very taking of the guarantee (see above).

27.5.2 Guarantor's liability

Without repeating the voluminous clauses in standard-form guarantees word for word, it can be said in summary that the guarantor usually accepts responsibility for every possible amount which the principal debtor may owe to the bank, at the time when a demand is made on him or her by the creditor. The requirement for the making of a demand removes any doubts which might exist as to when the guarantor's liability accrues, thus also making clear the point from which time begins to run for limitation purposes.

Although the guarantor's liability is expressed to be for all amounts owing by the principal debtor, in practice his or her liability is also stated to be limited to a stated amount. There are several reasons why the guarantor's liability is expressed in this apparently contradictory manner. First, the guarantor's liability is expressed to be for all sums owing since, if liability was stated in terms of a specific sum lent, the creditor would run the risk of inadvertently releasing the guarantor should it lend either more or less than the stated sum. Secondly, if the guarantor guaranteed only a stated proportion of the principal debt, and paid it, then he or she would be entitled to a proportionate share in any security held by the creditor for the whole debt. This would obviously prejudice the creditor. Therefore, if the guarantee is for all amounts owing, but limited to a specific sum, then payment of that specific sum does not entitle the guarantor to a proportionate share in the securities.

Thirdly, if the debtor is made bankrupt, a guarantor can usually prove in his or her estate for amounts paid under the guarantee. If, however, the guarantor's liability is expressed in the way described above, he or she has no such right: *Re Sass* [1896] 2 QB 12; *Re Houlder* [1929] 1 Ch 205. In fact, the guarantor is usually expressly debarred, in any event, from proving in the principal debtor's bankruptcy or liquidation.

27.5.3 Bank's power to vary contract with debtor

As we have seen, the guarantor may be discharged from his or her obligations if the creditor varies its contract with the principal debtor, or grants him or her time, at least without the guarantor's consent. Standard guarantee forms always remove the risk of this occurring by giving the creditor power to make such variations or to grant time to the principal

debtor: *Perry v National Provincial Bank of England* [1910] 1 Ch 464;
Compare *Barnes v Trade Credits Ltd* [1981] 2 All ER 122; *Pogoni v R & W H
Symington & Co (NZ) Ltd* [1991] 1 NZLR 82 (CA).

27.5.4 Guarantor cannot take security

It is obviously of benefit to the creditor to ensure that it has no competition from the guarantor in the event of the liquidation or bankruptcy of
the principal debtor. If part of the amount advanced by the creditor was
unsecured, the assets of the debtor which might have been available to
the creditor could be depleted by charges created in favour of the
guarantor. This is prevented by a prohibition on the taking of securities
from the debtor by the guarantor.

27.5.5 Determination of guarantee

The guarantee usually provides that the death or notice of the death, of
the guarantor does not of itself determine the guarantee, but that notice
of discontinuance of liability must be given to the creditor by the
deceased's executors or administrators.

In other cases, the guarantor can usually determine the guarantee by
giving notice to the creditor. His or her liability, however, is only
determined in respect of advances not yet made to the principal debtor.
In respect of advances already made, his or her liability remains, and it
is usually expressly provided in bank guarantees that, notwithstanding
valid notice of determination having been made, either by the guarantor
or his or her personal representatives, the guarantor's liability for advances made remains intact notwithstanding subsequent payments into
or out of the debtor's account. If this provision was not made, then
subsequent payments into the account would wipe out the guarantor's
liability, under the rule in *Clayton's Case* (1816) 1 Mer 572 whilst payment
out would constitute advances for which the guarantor was not liable:
see *Westminster Bank Ltd v Cond* (1940) 46 Com Cas 60. Alternatively, the
bank can protect its position by stopping the account upon determination.

27.5.6 "A continuing security"

The guarantee is usually expressed to be a "continuing" guarantee,
which is not discharged in whole or in part by the mere fact that the
debtor's account with the creditor may appear at any particular time to
be in credit. Again, this clause operates to exclude the rule in *Clayton's
Case*. If the Rule was not excluded, each sum paid into the account of the
debtor after the execution of the guarantee would reduce pro-tanto the
guarantor's liability.

27.5.7 Power of creditor to take additional securities

If the creditor took other securities for the same debt, the guarantor might
argue that the guarantee was intended to be replaced by these and that
he or she is therefore discharged. The creditor is therefore usually given
power to take additional securities. Furthermore, the guarantee usually

provides that the creditor's right to enforce the guarantee is not to be affected by any misconduct of the creditor in enforcing these other securities. This provision is probably suspect today, and the guarantor of a debt may be able to argue successfully that his or her liability only arose because of negligence of the creditor in realising its other securities over the debtor's property, and that he or she should have a counterclaim against the creditor in respect of that negligence. Against this, however, is the fact that the guarantee is usually expressed to be a "principal obligation". Could the creditor therefore argue that its right to proceed against the guarantor is unaffected by its choice to proceed against its other securities first? This argument could be bolstered by another provision which usually appears, to the effect that the creditor is under no obligation to marshall in favour of the guarantor any other securities held by it from the debtor.

27.5.8 Bankruptcy or liquidation of principal debtor

The creditor may have released the guarantee upon the receipt of another security from the principal debtor or upon a payment by him or her to it. Such securities or payments may, however, be invalidated in the debtor's bankruptcy or liquidation. The creditor might, therefore, have to give up its security or return the payment. In such a case, the guarantee will provide that the guarantor's liability is to revive.

27.5.9 Evidence as to amount owing by debtor

Admissions made by the principal debtor as to the amount owing by him or her are not evidence as against the guarantor: Ex *parte Young* (1881) 17 ChD 668, 671.

The creditor might, therefore, have difficulty in adducing the evidence necessary to obtain judgment against the guarantor. This problem is met by a clause which provides that a certificate signed by the creditor as to the amounts owing shall be conclusive evidence as against the guarantor: *Dobbs v National Bank of Australasia Ltd* (1935) 53 CLR 643.

27.5.10 Changes in constitution of parties

We have seen that a guarantee is revoked by a change in the constitution of the principal debtor, eg where the debtor is a partnership. An express clause usually provides to the contrary, but it is often also provided that the guarantee can be determined by the guarantor giving notice to the creditor.

27.5.11 Guarantor as principal debtor

If the principal debtor was labouring under some contractual incapacity which makes it impossible for the creditor to enforce the debt which he or she owes, then the guarantor would usually be discharged also. An express clause will therefore provide that the guarantor is not to be discharged in such circumstances, and that he or she is deemed for that purpose to be a principal debtor of the creditor.

27.5.12 Disclosure

We saw that the creditor has, at the outset, certain obligations of disclosure vis a vis the intending guarantor. Creditors attempt to minimise their liability in this regard by inserting a clause into the guarantee which declares that the guarantor has not signed the guarantee in reliance on any information given to him or her by the creditor (whether voluntarily or at his or her request), and that the creditor was under no duty to disclose details of the debtor's account to the guarantor.

27.5.13 Joint and several guarantors

If several persons agree to act as guarantors, but not all of them sign the document, then those who have signed will not be bound, as we have seen. The guarantee will usually meet this rule by providing for those who signed the guarantee to be liable on it.

Chapter 28

AGENCY

SUMMARY

28.1 GENERAL

An agent is a person who is engaged for the purpose of bringing his or her principal into contractual relations with third persons. The agent may have general authority or his or her authority may be restricted to acts of a certain kind. Thus the power of an agent to bind his or her principal to legal obligations depends largely upon the circumstances of the case and the intentions of the parties, or, more particularly, the intentions of the principal with regard to the width of the authority that is to be conferred on the agent.

28.2 TYPES OF AGENTS

Agency may be universal, general or special. A universal agent has unrestricted authority to contract on behalf of his or her principal. A general agent has only the power to represent his or her principal in the usual course of a particular business, trade or profession. A special agent is appointed for a specific purpose not falling within the usual business of the agent.

Examples of particular types of agent are as follows.

403

28.2.1. Attorneys

An agent may act with the authority of a power of attorney, which is "a formal instrument by which one person empowers another to represent him or act in his stead for certain purposes" (*Bowstead on Agency*, p 47). Powers of attorney are strictly construed and are interpreted as giving only such authority as they confer expressly or by necessary implication: *Bryant, Powis and Bryant Ltd v La Banque du Peuple* [1893] AC 170, 177.

28.2.2 Mercantile agents

The Mercantile Law Act 1908 defines a mercantile agent as "an agent having in the customary course of his business as such agent authority either to sell goods, or to consign goods for the purpose of sale, or to buy goods, or to raise money on the security of goods" (s 2).

This definition reflects and enshrines earlier decisions of the Courts on the definition of the term "factor" which preceded the present term "mercantile agent": see *Stevens v Biller* (1883) 25 ChD 31, 37 per Cotton LJ; *Dexter Motors Ltd v Mitcalfe* [1938] NZLR 804.

Despite the use of the words "in the customary course of his business" in the Act, to be a "mercantile agent" it is not necessary to carry on business normally as such. What is necessary is that authority is given to deal with goods in the manner described in the above provision: *Hayman v Flewker* (1863) 13 CBNS 519.

28.2.3 Brokers

A broker is a person employed to make bargains and contracts between persons in matters of trade and commerce. He or she is a negotiator between other parties. Unlike mercantile agents a broker takes no possession of goods, nor does he or she determine their destination: *Fowler v Hollins* (1872) LR 7 QB 616, 623 per Brett LJ; see also *Stafford v Conti Commodity Services Ltd* [1981] 1 All ER 691.

Examples of brokers include stockbrokers and insurance brokers. The former deal with the sale of stock and shares, while the latter arrange policies of insurance. Some types of brokers are regulated in their activities by their own special sets of rules. For example, the Sharebrokers Act 1908 provides for the issue of licences to sharebrokers before they are to be entitled to practise as such (s 3).

28.2.4 Del credere agents

Del credere agents, in return for an extra commission, promise that they will indemnify the principal, if the third party with whom they contract in respect of goods fails to pay what is due under the contract. The del credere agent is only secondarily liable to the principal, that is, as a surety for the person with whom he or she dealt: *Morris v Cleasby* (1816) 4 M & S 566. However, a contract of del credere agency is one of indemnity, not of guarantee, and therefore does not need to be in writing: *Couturier v Hastie* (1852) 8 Exch 40.

The del credere agent will only be liable to the principal for the other party's failure to pay what is due under the contract, and for no other breach of contract on that party's part: *Thomas Gabriel and Sons v Churchill and Sim* [1914] 3 KB 1272.

28.2.5 Auctioneers

Auctioneers are agents whose ordinary course of business is to sell by public auction. If given possession of the goods to be sold, they will be "mercantile agents" within the Mercantile Law Act.

Auctioneers occupy an unusual position, in that they are agents for both parties to the sale which they negotiate (*Hine v Whitehouse and Calan* (1806) 7 East 558), and may personally sue for the price of goods sold by them as auctioneer, even if their commission has been paid: *Chelmsford Auctions Ltd v Poole* [1973] 1 All ER 810.

An auctioneer who sells goods to which the vendor had no title will be liable in conversion to the true owner, even though he or she has acted innocently, and merely as an agent: *Barker v Furlong* [1891] 2 Ch 172; *RH Willis and Son v British Car Auctions Ltd* [1978] 1 WLR 438.

The Auctioneers Act 1928 provides for the licensing of auctioneers, creates various offences arising out of non-compliance with the Act and states that nothing in the Act limits any civil remedy in respect of any matter constituted an offence under the Act.

28.2.6 Barristers and solicitors

Barristers and solicitors will frequently involve their clients in legal responsibility for the agreements made on their behalf both in and out of Court. For instance, they have implied authority to compromise a suit without reference to the client for instructions: *Waugh v HB Clifford and Sons Ltd* [1982] 1 All ER 1095. On the other hand, a solicitor has no implied authority to receive a notice on behalf of his or her client: *Singer v Trustee of the Property of Munro* [1981] 3 All ER 215.

28.2.7 Estate agents

The Real Estate Agents Act 1976 defines "real estate agents" as persons who act, or hold themselves out to the public as ready to act, for reward as an agent in respect of the sale or other disposal of land or of businesses, or the purchase of the same, or in respect of letting or leasing of land (s 3). Real estate agents must be appointed in writing, otherwise they cannot recover commission for any work done (s 62); *Markham v Dalgety* [1974]] NZLR 192; *McKillop v Borthwick* [1976] 2 NZLR 482; *Previews Inc v UEB Industries Ltd* (1986) 1 NZBLC 102, 287. The agent must be able to point to a writing which appoints that agent in respect of the particular work or service for which he or she is claiming commission: *Walsh v Beasley, Packard & Chamberlain Ltd* (1988) 2 NZBLC 103, 075. The Act also contains provisions relating to the treatment by real estate agents of money received by them during the course of their business (ss 55-60), and preventing them from taking personal benefits or interests from commissions to sell or purchase, except in certain circumstances (s 63).

A real estate agent is not generally held out as having general authority to sell on any terms or at any price (*Shortal v Buchanan* [1920] NZLR 103n). The agent's authority, as held out, is merely to sell on the terms specified by his or her principal.

28.3 FORMATION OF AGENCY

The relationship of principal and agent may be created in one of the following ways.

28.3.1 Express or implied contract

In general, an agent may be appointed orally or in writing, even where the agent is to make a contract required to be evidenced in writing under s 2 of the Contracts Enforcement Act 1956. However, other statutes do require written evidence of an agent's appointment, for certain purposes. For instance, s 15(1) of the Companies Act 1955 requires that an agent have written authority to sign a company's memorandum of association on behalf of his or her principal.

As with other contracts the agency relationship may be impliedly created by the conduct of the parties, without any express agreement. The circumstances must raise the implication that one person has given another authority to act on his or her behalf.

28.3.2 Ratification

Ratification occurs where a person has performed certain acts, purportedly on behalf of another, but in fact without that person's authority. If the "principal" adopts the unauthorised act of the "agent", then the effect is the same as if there had been a prior authorisation by the principal to do exactly what the agent has done. The ratification is ante-dated to take effect from the time of the agent's act.

Whether the principal has in fact ratified or adopted what the agent has done is a question of fact. In *Centrepac Partnership v Foreign Currency Consultants Ltd* (1989) 2 NZBLC 103, 641 it was held that a principal had not ratified an agent's unauthorised entering into certain contracts merely by instructing the agent shortly afterwards to enter into similar contracts (and then revoking the authority).

The requirements for a valid ratification are as follows:

1   The agent whose act is sought to be ratified must have purported to act for the principal: *Keighley, Maxsted & Co v Durant* [1901] AC 240. Furthermore, the principal must be ascertained or at least be "capable of being ascertained" at the time of the contract: *Watson v Swann* (1862) 11 CBNS 736. Thus the principal cannot ratify where the person contracting does not indicate that he or she is acting as agent or where the principal is not identified or identifiable. It is not easy to reconcile these principles with the position where an agent acts *with the authority of* an undisclosed principal. Here the general rule is that the contract is enforceable by that principal even though the existence of the agency was not disclosed to the other contracting party: infra, para 28.7.2. Obviously enough, the only person who can ratify an agent's act is the person on whose behalf it was expressed to be done: *Barclays Bank Ltd v Roberts* [1954] 3 All ER 107.
2   At the time the act was done the agent must have had a competent principal, ie one who himself or herself was qualified to act in law

as the agent did. The requirement is not satisfied if, say, the agent purported to act for a principal who was an infant or was insane. Formerly the rule was important in the case of pre-incorporation contracts. At common law a company not in existence at the time of the contract could not as a principal be bound by or take a benefit under a contract, nor could it ratify the contract: *Kelner v Baxter* (1866) LR 2 CP 174. However, s 42A of the Companies Act 1955, introduced in 1983, provides that a company may ratify a contract made in its name or on its behalf within such period as may be specified in the contract, or if no time is specified, within a reasonable time after incorporation. Clauses 157 to 160 of the Companies Bill 1990 are intended substantially to re-enact s 42A. Clause 157(5) makes it clear that the new regime operates to the exclusion of the Contracts (Privity) Act 1982. The company must, therefore, ratify under the Companies Act if it wants to be able to enforce the contract. Where, however, a contract is made not in the name of or on behalf of, but simply *for the benefit of*, a company to be formed, the Privity Act can still apply and the company can enforce the contract without being bound by it: supra, para 6.3.5.

3 Before ratification can validly take place the principal must be aware of all the material facts. For example X on Y's behalf enters into a mortgage agreement, which in fact is invalid. Afterwards Y acts in such a way as to indicate that he or she is ratifying X's actions. His or her ratification, however, will be of no effect if he or she did not know that the transaction was invalid: *Savery v King* (1856) 5 HLC 627. On the other hand, the principal may be liable for unauthorised acts of the agent, even in the absence of complete knowledge, if the circumstances warrant the clear inference that the principal was adopting the acts of the supposed agent whatever their nature or culpability: *Marsh v Joseph* [1897] 1 Ch 213.

4 It has been said that there can be no ratification of a legal nullity, such as a forgery. For example, it has been held that a principal cannot purport to ratify the forgery of his or her name to a promissory note by his or her agent: *Brook v Hook* (1871) LR 6 Exch 89. A principal could, however, be bound by a forged signature by the operation of an estoppel: *Greenwood v Martins Bank Ltd* [1933] AC 51. Acts which are not void ab initio, but are merely voidable, may be ratified prior to avoidance.

5 The principal must possess the capacity to ratify, at the time of ratification. Another way of stating this principle is to say that ratification cannot operate to displace or upset proprietary or contractual rights which have arisen prior to ratification. For instance, an agent for the vendor of goods may send an unauthorised notice of stoppage in transitu to the assignee in bankruptcy of the buyer. The principal may subsequently purport to ratify the notice of stoppage but will be prevented from doing so in order to displace the accrued right of the buyer's assignee in bankruptcy to obtain possession of the goods: *Bird v Brown* (1850) 4 Exch 786.

6 Ratification must be effected within a reasonable time after the contract is made: *Re Portuguese Consolidated Copper Mines Ltd* (1895) 45 Ch D 16.

7 Ratification must be complete. The principal cannot adopt the favourable parts of a transaction and disaffirm the rest: *Union Bank of Australia v McClintock* [1922] 1 AC 240.

28.3.3 Agency of necessity

Agency of necessity occurs where an unforeseen situation has arisen which carries with it sudden danger to the property, or similar interests of the person on whose behalf acts are performed. For instance, if a ship or its cargo is in danger, the master may sell or otherwise deal with the cargo, or the ship itself, and the acts of the master, although not expressly authorised, will bind the ship's owners. There must, however, be some urgent necessity arising from accident: *The Bonita* (1861) 1 Lush 252. In considering what is necessary, any material circumstances must be taken into account eg danger, distance, accommodation, time and expense: *James Phelps and Co v Hill* [1891] 1 QB 605, 610 per Lindley LJ.

Furthermore, it must be impossible for the ship's master to communicate with the owners of the ship or the cargo and ask for instructions: *The Australia* (1859) 13 Moo PCC 419. This rule severely limits the operation of agency of necessity, in the light of modern communications. The master must also act bona fide and for the benefit of either the shipowners or cargo owners: *Tronson v Dent* (1853) 8 Moo PCC 419.

The doctrine of agency by necessity has been stated in general terms by Lord Simon of Glaisdale in *China Pacific SA v Food Corp of India, The Winson* [1981] 3 All ER 688, 697 h-j as follows:

> One of the ways in which an agency of necessity can arise is where A is in possession of goods the property of B, and an emergency arises which places those goods in imminent jeopardy. If A cannot obtain instructions from B as to how he or she should act in such circumstances, A is bound to take without authority such action in relation to the goods as B, a prudent owner, would himself have taken in the circumstances.

It is more uncertain, however, as to whether the doctrine of agency of necessity applies where someone has acted, in an emergency, to safeguard the life or health of another, lacking authority to do so. Cases where the doctrine has so extended could be explained as the application of restitutionary principles, based on the notion of unjust enrichment.

The Matrimonial Property Act 1976, s 49, abolished the special position of a married woman living apart from her husband having power to bind him by contracts for necessaries. Section 49 also abolished a married woman's power to pledge her husband's credit for household expenses, including clothing.

28.4 AUTHORITY OF AGENTS

The nature of the agent's authority to bind his or her principal is the central feature of the agency relationship. Upon it depend not only the legal relations of the principal and his or her agent, but also the relations between principal and agent and third parties.

As a general rule the principal is only bound by acts of the agent that are within the latter's authority. Furthermore, an agent acting beyond his or her authority may be liable to his or her principal for breach of contract, or to the third party for breach of the implied warranty of authority.

28.4.1. Actual authority

As the term implies, actual authority is that which has actually been conferred on the agent in terms of his or her contract with the principal: see *Freeman and Lockyer v Buckhurst Park Properties (Mangal) Ltd* [1964] 1 All ER 630, 644 per Diplock LJ.

Actual authority may be expressly conferred, as in the case of a resolution of a board of directors which authorises two of their number to sign cheques. Secondly, actual authority may be implied from the nature of the business which the agent is employed to transact. Thirdly, actual authority may include the agents' usual, or customary, authority. This is the authority which an agent in that particular trade, business, or profession would normally or usually possess, in the absence of any limitation imposed by the principal. It is the authority which knowledge-able persons, dealing with the agent, would expect to go with that particular trade, etc. For example, appointment by a board of directors of one of their number as managing director will carry with it all such authority as is usually associated with that office: *Hely-Hutchinson v Brayhead Ltd* [1976] 3 All ER 98, 102 per Lord Denning MR.

The extent of an agent's implied or usual authority will of course vary considerably with the nature of the business in which he or she is employed, and with the customs or usages which normally govern and define the performance of his or her everyday employment.

For instance, mercantile agents may sell goods entrusted to them for sale in their own name (*Boring v Corrie* (1818) 2 B & Ald 137), and may receive payment of the purchase price: *Drinkwater v Goodwin* (1775) Cowp 251. They may sell in any way they think best, including on credit terms: *Houghton v Matthews* (1803) 3 Bos and P 485. While at common law a mercantile agent has no authority to pledge goods, the agent may yet by so doing affect or extinguish his or her principal's title, in view of s 3 of the Mercantile Law Act 1908.

Brokers may act in accordance with the usages and rules of the market in which they normally deal, although not if such usage or rule is illegal or unreasonable: *Robinson v Mollett* (1875) LR 7 HL 802.

Auctioneers have implied authority to sign a contract on behalf of both vendor and purchaser: *Rosenbaum v Belson* [1900] 2 Ch 267. They may only receive payment in cash, and cannot give credit: *Williams v Evans* (1866) LR 1 QB 52. They cannot warrant the goods which they sell: *Payne v Leconfield* (1882) 51 LJQB 642.

If a reserve price is advertised, the auctioneer has no authority to sell at below the reserve.

Estate agents have authority to sign contracts for sale and purchase on behalf of their principals, if they are employed actually to sell the property: *Keen v Mear* [1920] 2 Ch 574. The agent does not have implied authority to ask for and receive a deposit on behalf of the vendor: *Sorrell v Finch* [1976] 2 All ER 371.

A servant has not, merely from the act of service, authority to pledge his or her employer's credit: *Bary and Co v Bryant* (1907) 26 NZLR 232.

Solicitors have implied authority to receive payment for debts they are instructed to sue for: *Yates v Freckleton* (1781) 2 Doug KB 623. They may bind their clients to the compromise or abandonment of an action (*Re Newen* [1903] 1 Ch 812), but may not compromise an action not yet begun: *Macaulay v Polley* [1897] 2 QB 122.

28.4.2 Apparent authority

A person who by words or conduct has allowed another to appear to the outside world as his or her agent, with the result that third parties deal with him or her as agent, cannot afterwards repudiate this apparent agency if to do so would injure third parties: *Pole v Leask* (1863) 8 LT 645, 648 per Lord Cranworth. As it is sometimes expressed, a person's apparent or ostensible authority creates an agency by estoppel.

There may be an agency of this kind where the agent has no actual authority at all, but the more usual situation is for there to be an agency relationship, but the authority of the agent is limited by agreement between the parties. In this latter case the doctrine of estoppel operates so that the apparent authority of the agent supplements his or her actual authority, and broadens the scope of the principal/agent relationship so as to make the former liable for the latter's unauthorised acts. The requirements for agency by estoppel can be summarised as follows:

(a) there must be a representation, express or implied, by the principal that the agent has his authority to enter into the particular transaction: *Broadlands Finance Ltd v Gisborne Aero Club* [1975] 2 NZLR 496 (CA). The matter is judged from the viewpoint of a reasonable person dealing with the alleged agent: *Credit Services Investments Ltd v Evans* [1974] 2 NZLR 683 (CA);

(b) the third party must rely on such representation, that is, must contract believing that the principal will be bound;

(c) the third party must alter his or her position as a result of such reliance: *Freeman and Lockyer v Buckhurst Park Properties (Mangal) Ltd* [1964] 2 QB 480, 503 per Diplock LJ.

The representation referred to above must be clear and unequivocal, made either by words or conduct. An implied representation of authority can be made by the entrusting to an agent of certain duties in the normal course of his or her work, the representation being that he or she has the authority to do those things: *Lloyd v Grace, Smith and Co* [1912] AC 716.

The agent must appear to be acting in a way in which a person in his or her position would normally act, otherwise it cannot be argued that he or she reasonably appeared to have the necessary authority. In *United Bank of Kuwait v Hammoud* [1988] 3 All ER 418 it would have appeared to a bank that a solicitor's undertaking given as security for a loan was within the ordinary business of the solicitor where it was given in the context of an underlying transaction of a solicitorial nature. The solicitor thus had ostensible authority to bind his partners and his principal and the undertaking could be enforced against them.

The representation must be made to the person who relies upon it: *Farquharson Bros v King and Co* [1902] AC 325, 341 per Lord Lindley. It must be made intentionally or negligently. It must be the proximate cause of leading the party mistakenly to believe that the principal had actually conferred the requisite authority upon the agent. In other words, if the third party knew, or ought in the circumstances to have known, that the agent's authority was limited, he or she cannot plead such proximity as to found an estoppel. If, for example, the agent acts for his or her own benefit and the third party is aware of this, such will operate as notice of a lack of authority. Similarly, estoppel will be rebutted where the transaction is of such an unusual nature that any reasonable person in the position of the third party would be put on inquiry.

The agent cannot himself or herself enlarge the scope of his or her apparent authority. It is the principal's representation that creates the authority, not the agent's assertion that he or she has that authority: *Armagas Ltd v Mundogas SA* [1986] AC 717; *Savill v Chase Holdings (Wellington) Ltd* [1989] 1 NZLR 257. Thus a real estate agent with authority to accept payment of a deposit could not exceed the limits laid down by the express terms of the contract by asserting to the purchaser that he was entitled to accept late payment: *New Zealand Tenancy Bonds Ltd v Mooney* [1986]   1 NZLR 280. Again, a husband had no apparent authority to sell a jointly owned car on behalf of his wife simply because he said he had authority or because he was in possession of the registration papers: *RJ Bowling Motors Ltd v Kerr* (1988) 2 NZBLC 103, 341.

28.5 DUTIES OF THE AGENT

(1) Where the agency is contractual, the agent must perform what he or she has undertaken to perform. The agent has no obligation, however, to perform an undertaking that is either illegal or null and void: eg *Cohen v Kittell* (1889) 22 QBD 680, a gaming contract.

Where an agency is non-contractual, ie gratuitous, the agent is not liable for non-performance, but is liable for negligent performance of the undertaking.

(2) The agent must act in accordance with the authority which is conferred. That is, he or she must act within his or her express and implied authority, or within the bounds of prevailing trade customs or usages: *Cunliffe-Owen v Teather and Greenwood* [1967] 3 All ER 561.

(3) The agent must perform his or her undertaking with due care and skill, whether the agency be contractual or gratuitous. However, the standard of care required may vary, depending on whether the agency is gratuitous or for reward.

In the case of contractual agency, the agent must exhibit such skill and care as an agent in his or her position would normally possess and exercise. Regard is thus had to the nature of the agent's business. In *Stafford v Conti Commodity Services Ltd* [1981] 1 All ER 691, commodity futures brokers invested money on a client's behalf, but at a loss. Mocatta J rejected allegations of negligence on the brokers' part, holding that they had acted in accordance with normal practice in the commodity futures market. The client had accepted the risk of loss in such a volatile and uncertain market. On the other hand in *Hooker v Stewart* [1989] 3 NZLR 543 (CA) a real estate agent was in breach of his duty when he assured his principals, without any or any adequate foundation, that a prospective purchaser of their property was a man of substance and dissuaded them from consulting their solicitor before signing an agreement for sale. In *Cee Bee Marine Ltd v Lombard Insurance Co Ltd* [1990] 2 NZLR 1 (CA) an insurance broker was liable for failing to arrange appropriate cover for the principal's building. The broker's duty was to assess the risk to be insured, to obtain the best possible cover at the most economical rates and, if his or her efforts fail, to report this to the principal and seek further instructions.

As to gratuitous agents, they must exercise the care that a reasonable person would exercise in respect of his or her own affairs, or, if the agent has held himself or herself out as possessing the skill necessary for a particular undertaking, the care which is reasonably necessary for that undertaking: *Moffatt v Bateman* (1869) LR 3 PC 115. In *Chaudry v Prabhakar* [1989] 1 WLR 29 a gratuitous agent was liable for giving negligent advice to a friend about the condition of a second hand car.

(4) Generally speaking, an agent may not delegate his or her functions to another. The agent's obligation is to act personally — delegatus non potest delegare: *Allam and Co Ltd v Europe Poster Services Ltd* [1968] 1 All ER 826, 832 per Buckley J.

However, there are exceptions to this general rule. Obviously, the agent may delegate if permitted to by law or by contract. Secondly, if the function delegated is purely ministerial, and not involving confidence or the exercise of discretion, this is permissible. In *Parkin v Williams* [1986] 1 NZLR 294 attorneys acting for the elderly owners of a house decided that the property should be sold by auction. The property was passed in but subsequently the auctioneer, with the authority of the attorneys, sold it to one of the bidders. The power of attorney did not contain express power for the attorneys to delegate the signing of a contract of sale, but as the attorneys had agreed to all the terms the signing was only a mechanical act and was within the implied authority conferred under the power of attorney. On the other hand, there can be no such delegation if the agency is an employment to which personal skill is essential: *John McCann and Co v Pow* [1975] 1 All ER 129, 132 per Lord Denning MR.

The principal may consent to the delegation, or may ratify it subsequently. Consent to delegation may be implied where it is obvious that the performance of the agent's undertaking requires that he or she employ subordinates, for example, where the agent is a company. Consent may also be implied where delegation is within the usual authority of the agent.

Where delegation is allowed, the agent is liable to the principal for the sub-agent's breaches of duty: *Swire v Francis* (1877) 3 App Cas 106. Generally, delegation creates no privity of contract between principal and sub-agent, although tortious duties may be created: see, eg *Moukatoff v British Overseas Airways Corp* [1967] 1 Lloyd's Rep 396.

(5) The agent cannot deny the title of the principal to goods, money, or land possessed by the agent on behalf of the principal. However, if a third party is entitled to the property in question, the agent may set up the title of such third party against the principal. An example is where the principal has wrongfully distrained X's goods and given them to an auctioneer. The latter can set up X's title as against the principal: *Biddle v Bond* (1865) 6 B & S 225.

However, if an agent receives money from his or her principal which belongs at law or in equity to a third party, the agent is not accountable to that third party unless he or she has been guilty of some wrongful act in relation to that money. Acting wrongfully involves: (a) knowingly participating in a breach of trust by the principal; (b) intermeddling with trust property otherwise than merely as an agent; (c) receiving or dealing with the money knowing that the principal has no right to pay it over or to instruct him or her to deal with it; (d) some dishonest act in relation to the money: *Carl-Zeiss Stiftung v Herbert Smith and Co (No 2)* [1969] 2 All ER 367, 384 per Edmund Davies LJ.

(6) The agent must act in the principal's interest. "No man can in this Court, acting as an agent, be allowed to put himself into a position in which his interest and his duty will be in conflict": *Parker v McKenna* (1874) LR 10 Ch App 96, 118 per Lord Cairns LC. The agent must, therefore, disclose to the principal any personal interest which may affect the performance of his or her duty to the principal. In the absence of proper disclosure, the principal may set aside the transaction and claim from the agent any profits which the latter has made from the transaction. Thus the sale of a house was set aside where the agent appointed to sell it had in fact secretly bought it himself: *McPherson v Watt* (1877) 3 App Cas 254. It is immaterial in such a case that the contract of sale is a fair one. The important point is that the principal was ignorant of what was happening: *Christie v Harcourt* [1973] NZLR 139.

An agent similarly cannot act for two principals. In *Farrington v Rowe McBride & Partners* [1985] 1 NZLR 83 (CA) the plaintiff's solicitors advised the plaintiff to invest money in a land development company, but failed to tell him that the group of companies of which the company in question was a member was the largest client of the solicitors and that some partners and their families had personal interests in the group. The company subsequently collapsed and the plaintiff sued the solicitors to recover his loss. The Court of Appeal held that the solicitors' involvement with the development group had created a conflict in their duty to the plaintiff as their client and to the group of companies as their client. The defendants should have disclosed all material facts concerning the double employment and advised the plaintiff to consider taking independent advice. They were, therefore, in breach of duty to their client and liable accordingly. See also *Day v Mead* [1987] 2 NZLR 443 (CA); *Elia v Commercial & Mortgage Nominees Ltd* (1988) 2 NZBLC 103, 296.

(7) The agent must account to his or her principal for all money received on behalf of the principal. In order for this duty to account to be properly performed, the agent should be in a position to know what he or she must pay the principal and the principal should be able to see whether the agent has fulfilled his or her duty. Therefore the agent should keep proper accounts and normally should keep the principal's property and money separate from his or her own and from that of others. There is a statutory obligation to keep separate accounts in certain cases: see, for example, Real Estate Agents Act 1976, ss 55-60; Law Practitioners Act 1982, s 89.

In *Westpac Banking Corporation v Savin* [1985] 2 NZLR 41 (CA) Richardson J observed that the general rule may be displaced and that it depends on the terms of the agency whether the agent is bound to keep the principal's money separate or is entitled to mix it with the agent's own. An agent appointed to sell two boats paid the proceeds of sale into its (overdrawn) trading account with the defendant bank. The agent went into liquidation and the principals sued the bank. It was held (i) that by paying the money into its own account the agent had acted in breach of fiduciary duty, for there was nothing to indicate the general rule should not apply, and (ii) that the bank having constructive notice of the breach it had to account to the plaintiffs for their property.

(8) The agent must not, without the principal's consent, make use for his or her own personal benefit of information acquired in the course of his or her employment as an agent. For instance, an employee should not be able to make use of confidential lists of his or her employer's clients,

after the agent has left the latter's employ and begun his or her own business in competition with the former employer's business: *SSC and B Lintas NZ Ltd v Murphy* [1986] 2 NZLR 436. However, if the agent obtained the information otherwise than while acting as an agent, he or she should be free to use it, although there are authorities to the effect that an agent will still be accountable to the principal for profits obtained from the use of information gained while acting as agent, even though the principal would not have wished or been able personally to use the information. These cases most frequently occur in the case of directors of companies: *Regal (Hastings) Ltd v Gulliver* (1967) 2 AC 134; cf *Peso Silver Mines Ltd v Cropper* (1966) 58 DLR (2d) 1. The rationale for the adoption of this harsh standpoint seems to be to encourage agents not to divide their loyalties.

(9) An agent may not make a secret profit from the performance of his or her duties as agent. The agent must account for all such profit. Failure to do so will disentitle the agent to his or her commission: *Boston Deep Sea Fishing and Ice Co v Ansell* (1888) 39 ChD 339.

The expression "secret profit" includes bribes (see *Mahesan v Malaysia Government Officers Co operative Housing Society Ltd* [1978] 2 All ER 405, 408), but extends to any secret financial advantage gained by the agent from the exercise of his or her authority. There need be no fraud on the agent's part: *Boardman v Phipps* [1967] 2 AC 46. He or she must still disgorge the secret profit.

Where an agent has accepted a bribe, the principal has alternative remedies available. He or she can either claim the bribe from the agent (as to taking accounts of profits, see High Court Rules R 384 et seq) or sue for damages for fraud in respect of his or her actual loss through entering into the transaction in respect of which the bribe was given (*Maheson, supra*).

An agent who makes a secret profit may also, in addition to civil remedies, be liable to conviction under one or more of the offences set out in the Secret Commissions Act 1910.

28.6 DUTIES OF THE PRINCIPAL

(1) The principal must remunerate the agent for services rendered, in terms of the express or implied contract between the parties. The intention of the parties with regard to remuneration depends in each case upon the terms of the contract. Where nothing is said as to remuneration, the circumstances may indicate that remuneration is to be paid. In such a case, the appropriate payment will be what is reasonable in the circumstances, or what is customary in the trade, profession, or business in which the agent is employed.

Whether a real estate agent is entitled to commission depends on whether, on the proper interpretation of the contract between the principal and the agent, the event has happened upon which commission is to be paid. In *Latter v Parsons* (1907) 26 NZLR 645 an owner agreed to pay commission to an agent if the agent could "sell" his property. The Court of Appeal held the commission was payable on the agent procuring a person approved by the vendor to enter into a binding contract of purchase, notwithstanding that the vendor released the purchaser from the contract in consideration of forfeiture by the purchaser of the deposit.

The decision may be compared with *Luxor (Eastbourne) Ltd v Cooper* [1941] AC 108. L engaged C to negotiate the sale of property. £ 10,000 commission was to be paid to C "on completion of the purchases". Offers were secured for the properties, but the agreement made with the purchasers was expressed to be "subject to contract". A binding agreement between L and the purchasers was not completed because L decided not to sell. C sued for commission but was unsuccessful. No sale had been made and there was no implied term in the contract between L and C that L should not act so as to prevent C from earning his commission.

It is possible for a land agent by clear and unequivocal language in the agreement by which he or she is appointed to become entitled to commission on securing an offer for a house or property to be sold. However, the decisions show that the Courts are reluctant to permit this to occur and construe land agents' agreements very strictly against them. After all, an offer may not mature into a binding contract and, unless it does, the vendor has not received the service which or she expected on appointing the agent. Examples of words construed to mean that a sale should actually be achieved are where the agent has agreed to introduce a person "willing and able to purchase": *Graham and Scott (Southlade) Ltd v Oxlade* [1950] 2 KB 257, "ready, able and willing to purchase": *Dennis Reed v Goody* [1950] 2 KB 277, and "prepared to enter into a contract to purchase": *Ackroyd & Sons v Hasan* [1960] 2 QB 144. In *Jaques v Lloyd D George & Partners Ltd* [1968] 1 WLR 625 commission was payable on the agent being "instrumental in introducing a person willing to sign a document capable of becoming a contract to purchase at a price which at any stage of the negotiations has been agreed by [the principal]". The agents' claim failed because (i) the meaning of the clause was so uncertain as to be unenforceable, and (ii) the agents had misrepresented the effect of the clause, having assured the principal orally that commission would be payable if they found a suitable purchaser and the deal went through. It will be remembered that a real estate agent cannot recover commission unless appointed in writing: Real Estate Agents Act 1976, s 62, supra, para 28.2.7.

The duty to remunerate the agent only arises where the agent has earned the remuneration. That is, the agent must show that he or she has caused the remunerating event to take place.

The principal's liability to pay the agent arises even though the principal has derived no benefit from the agent's act, as long as the agent has performed what he or she was employed to do: *Fisher v Drewett* (1879) 48 LJQB 32; *Mackay v Reeves* (1909) 28 NZLR 1114; *Latter v Parsons* (1907) 26 NZLR 645. If the agent has not done that, he or she is entitled to no remuneration, even if the principal prevented the agent from achieving his or her purpose, as long as what the principal did was legitimate under the contract, eg by rejecting the offer of a loan made by a lender introduced by the agent, in accordance with his or her task of finding a lender, on the grounds that the terms of the loan were unacceptable: *Fawcus v Bond St Brokers Ltd* (1967) 111 Sol Jo 495; *Hornbrook v Atkinson* (1912) 31 NZLR 86; *Salmons v Adams* (1908) 27 NZLR 610. In other words, there must be a default, ie wilful refusal or deceit by the principal before the agent can succeed. This aspect of a principal's duty to pay remuneration has arisen in respect of payment to estate agents who have not actually completed a sale (see cases cited above). The cases in this area show that everything turns on the terms of the agreement between principal and agent. If the contract expressly or impliedly reveals a term that the principal will not interfere, eg by himself or herself finding a purchaser, then the principal will be liable to the agent for breach of contract, to the extent of the commission involved (see *Alpha Trading Ltd v Dunnshaw-Patten Ltd* [1981] QB 290). If there is no such term in the contract, then the principal can negotiate and sell personally and will not be liable for commission *(Bentall, Horsley and Baldry v Vicary* [1931]1 KB 253).

There may be no liability to pay the agreed remuneration, even if the agent has done what was stipulated for, if the transaction on which the agent was employed was illegal. This is of course subject to the power which a Court has under the Illegal Contracts Act 1970 to validate what are otherwise illegal contracts: supra, para 5.4.

Similarly, the agent cannot receive remuneration if he or she has acted in breach of his or her duties under the contract of agency, or is otherwise guilty of misconduct. Thus a real estate agent who is required to obtain a deposit on the sale but who fails to do so is in breach of duty, and unless the principal has waived the breach he or she cannot recover any commission: see *Pemberton v Action Realty Ltd* [1986] 1 NZLR 286.

The principal must indemnify the agent against losses, liabilities and expenses, incurred in the performance of the undertaking. The extent of this indemnity depends on the agreement between the parties and the kind of business in which the agent is employed. More particularly, it will depend upon the nature of the authority granted to the agent, unless there is an express agreement excluding or cutting down the indemnity. To be entitled to the indemnity, the agent must have acted within his or her authority. There is no duty to indemnify an agent who has acted unlawfully, or in breach of duty or negligently: see *New Zealand Farmers' Co-operative Distributing Co Ltd v National Mortgage and Agency Co of New Zealand* [1961] NZLR 969; cf *Fraser v Equitorial Shipping Co Ltd* [1979] 1 Lloyd's Rep 103.

The agent has a right of lien over the principal's property if the principal has not satisfied his or her liabilities to the agent.

28.7 CONTRACTS BY AGENTS

In examining the effect of contracts made by agents, it is necessary to distinguish between different types of principal. First the name of the principal may have been revealed by the agent to the third party. Secondly, the third party may be aware that the agent is contracting as an agent, but is unaware of the principal's name. In both of these cases, then, the third party is aware that he or she is not contracting with the agent personally.

In the third sort of case, neither the existence nor the identity of the principal is made known to the third party. That party believes that the contract is with the agent personally.

These distinctions are relevant both as to the personal liability of the agent, and the question of whether the principal is bound by the agent's actions, and to what extent.

28.7.1 Where the principal is disclosed

In the first two of the above categories, the principal can be sued by and can sue the third party on the contract made by the agent. The agent must, however, have been acting within his or her authority (express, implied, usual or apparent) for the principal to be bound, or the principal must have ratified his or her actions. If the third party has actual or constructive notice of the agent's lack of authority, the principal will not be bound to any contract made by the agent, even if the agent appears to have authority.

As a general rule the agent for a disclosed principal incurs no personal liability on the contract, and the rights and liabilities of the principal and the third party are determined irrespective of any rights or liabilities of the agent. The agent may still, however, come into the picture where either principal or third party attempts to discharge his or her debt to the other by payment to the agent. If the third party leads the principal to believe that the agent has discharged the principal's liability to the third party, whereupon the principal pays the agent (ie changes his or her position vis a vis the agent), the third party cannot make the principal liable to pay again, even if the principal's liability to the third party has not, in fact, been discharged by the agent: *Heald v Kenworthy* (1855) 10 Exch 739, 746 per Parke B. In this way the principal may be discharged from further liability to the third party by payment to the agent. The third party may, equally, be absolved from liability to the principal upon settlement of the account with the agent, if either the agent had authority to receive payment on the principal's behalf, or if the agent has received payment, though unauthorised to do so, and has paid over to the principal, or if the principal has led the other party to believe that the agent is contracting as principal. Payment to the agent does not normally discharge the third party in any other case.

In certain circumstances an agent will be personally liable in respect of a contract which he or she has negotiated for and on behalf of a principal. These cases are as follows:

(a) The normal rule is always subject to the parties' contrary intention. Thus the agent may undertake or demonstrate an intention that he or she is personally liable to the third party: see eg *The Swan* [1968] 1 Lloyd's Rep 5. Again, the evidence may show a custom or usage of the agent's trade or business to this effect. The custom or usage, however, must not be repugnant to the terms of the written contract: *Hutchinson v Tatham* (1873) 8 CP 482, 487 per Brett J.

(b) The agent may be liable in tort in certain cases. Thus a land agent was liable to a purchaser for deceitful representations made prior to the contract between the principal and the purchaser: *Clemance v Hollis* [1987] 2 NZLR 471. Again, an agent who made a mistake in placing an order for fabric with its overseas principal on behalf of a New Zealand supplier was liable to that supplier for business loss suffered as a result of his negligence: *Milburn Tanner Ltd v Wales & Mckinlay Ltd* (1986) 1 NZBLC 102, 475.

(c) An agent who has no authority to contract as agent will be personally liable to the third party for breach of his or her implied warranty of authority. In *Collen v Wright* (1857) 8 E & B 647 Willes J explained the basis for the warranty as follows:

The fact that the professed agent honestly thinks that he has authority affects the moral character of his act; but his moral innocence, so far as the person whom he has induced to contract is concerned, in no way aids such person or alleviates the inconvenience and damage which he sustains. The obligation arising in such a case is well expressed by saying that a person, professing to contract as agent for another, impliedly, if not expressly, undertakes to or promises the person who enters into such contract, upon the faith of the professed agent being duly authorised, that the authority which he professes to have does in point of fact exist. The fact of entering into the transaction with the professed agent, as such, is good consideration for the promise.

It is apparent, then, that liability is founded upon a collateral contract between agent and third party. The agent represents that authority exists and the third party enters a contract in reliance on that representation.

(d) The agent may have contracted on behalf of a non-existent principal. At common law, whether a person contracting on behalf of a company to be formed is personally liable depends upon the contractual intention of the parties. While it is inherently likely that the parties would have intended the agent to be liable, any presumption to this effect is not irresistible: see *Elders Pastoral Ltd v Gibbs* [1988] 1 NZLR 596, where the overseas and New Zealand authorities are discussed. It may be, moreover, that this regime has been overtaken by statute. By s 42A(4) of the Companies Act 1955, unless a contrary intention is expressed in the contract the "agent" is personally liable on an implied warranty that the company would be incorporated and would ratify the contract. By s 42A(5) the damages recoverable for breach of warranty are the same as would be recoverable in an action for breach by the company of the unperformed obligations under the contract as if it had been ratified and cancelled. In the *Elders* case McGechan J inclined to the view that these provisions superseded the earlier law but in the end left the point open. Clause 158 of the Companies Bill 1990 continues the scheme in s 42A(4) and (5).

(e) An agent who signs a bill of exchange in his or her own name will be personally liable in the absence of words sufficiently indicating that he or she signs on behalf of a principal or in a representative capacity: Bills of Exchange Act 1908 s 26.

(f) At common law an agent who made a contract by deed became personally liable under it and able to enforce it. The principal could only sue or be sued on the deed if named as a party to it, and if it was signed in his or her name. Now, however, s 134 of the Property Law Act 1952 permits the donee of a power of attorney to sign in his or her own name and the instrument is as effectual as if it had been signed by the principal. An attorney signing his or her own name will not, therefore, incur personal liability under a deed.

28.7.2 Where the principal is undisclosed

In this third category of case, the agent is, so far as the third party is concerned, dealing on his or her own behalf and in his or her own name. In these circumstances the agent normally can sue and be sued on the contract in the ordinary way. However the third party may later find that in fact he or she is dealing with an undisclosed principal. If this is the case, then subject to the qualifications set out below, the undisclosed principal also may sue and be sued in his or her own name on any contract duly made on his or her behalf, so long as the agent was acting within the principal's authority. It might seem anomalous as being contrary to ordinary rules of privity (as to which see supra, para 6.3.5) that an unknown person should be able to enforce or be liable on a contract that he or she has not made. Considerations of commercial convenience, it seems, prompted development of the rule.

The qualifications to the general rule are as follows.

(a) If the agent is described in the contract as a principal, parol evidence may not be admissible to show that he or she has contracted as agent for someone else. The undisclosed principal cannot sue on the contract in such a case: *Humble v Hunter* (1848) 12 QB 310. However, such parol evidence is probably inadmissible only if the contract clearly shows that the party signing is the party who is the principal. If the contract is at all ambiguous in this respect, then parol evidence may be admissible to explain the contract: see eg *Murphy v Rae* [1967] NZLR 103; *Finzel, Berry and Co v Eastcheap Dried Fruit Co* [1962] 1 Lloyd's Rep 370, 375 per McNair J.

(b) The undisclosed principal cannot obtain rights on the contract where the contract expressly or by implication is intended to be confined in its operation to the parties themselves, so the possibility of agency is negatived: *Dillicar v West* [1921] NZLR 617, 629. In particular, if the agent's identity is material to the making of the contract – if, say, the third party is relying on the personal skill or solvency of the agent – then failure to disclose the existence of a principal will deprive the principal of his or her right to sue on the contract: see eg *Said v Butt* [1920] 3 KB 497.

(c) If the third party settles with the agent before discovering the existence of an undisclosed principal, this discharges the third party from further liability to the principal *(Coates v Lewes* (1808)1 Camp 444).

(d) The principal can be met with any defence which was available to the third party against the agent before the third party discovered the existence of the principal. Therefore, when an agent sells goods in his or her own name, but on behalf of an undisclosed principal, and the principal sues the purchaser for the price, the latter is entitled to show that he or she believed the agent to be the principal in the transaction; he or she would then have a right of set-off against the true principal for any sum owing to him or her by the agent before he or she became aware that such agent was not the principal. Set-off will not be allowed if the third party was aware that the agent was acting as agent, although the identity of the principal was not disclosed. Nor will set-off be available if, by the exercise of ordinary care or the making of usual inquiries, the third party would have become aware of agency. In *Montagu v Forwood* [1893] 2 QB 350 M employed B and Co as his agents to collect a debt from X. To do this B and Co properly employed F, who collected the debt. B and Co, owed F money, and F, not knowing at the time he was employed that B and Co were agents, claimed to set off the debt against the money owed him by B and Co. It was held that he was entitled to do so.

If the third party did not believe the agent to be the principal, that party cannot set off any claim he or she has against the agent against the principal. In *Cooke v Eshelby* (1887) 12 App Cas 271 C knew that L, when he contracted in his own name, did so sometimes on his own account and sometimes as agent. L, as agent for E, sold goods to C without disclosing his agency. It was held that C could not set off as against E a debt owed to C by L because C did not believe that L was contracting as principal.

(e) Once the agency has been disclosed the third party has the option of suing either the principal or the agent. If that party elects to sue the agent, he or she cannot subsequently make the principal liable. The election must, however, be final and unequivocal in order to bind the third party (*Clarkson, Booker Ltd v Andjel* [1964] 3 All ER 260).

(f) If the principal settles his or her account with the agent before the third party discovers the existence of the principal, then the third party cannot later sue the principal when the latter's existence is made known (*Armstrong v Stokes* (1872) LR 7 QB 598).

(g) The agent will be relieved from liability if the third party elects to sue the principal. If the principal himself or herself sues the third party, or has otherwise intervened, by way of prohibiting the agent from suing, or settling with the third party, the agent cannot sue on the contract: *Atkinson v Cotesworth* (1825) 3 B & C 647. However, the agent may still sue if he or she has a lien (or other interest) over the goods which are the subject-matter of the contract: *Robinson v Rutter* (1855) 4 E & B 954. If the agent sues on the contract, the third party can set up against him or her any defence which would have been available against the undisclosed principal: *Garnac Grain Co Inc v Faure and Fairclough Ltd* [1968] AC 1130.

28.8 DISPOSITIONS OF PROPERTY BY AGENTS

In this part we examine the extent to which dealings by an agent with money or property entrusted to him or to her by the principal or by a third party can affect the principal's legal position.

28.8.1 Rights of the principal as regards property in possession of the agent

The agent, if holding property as agent, cannot deny his or her principal's title. If employed to purchase property for his or her principal, the agent obtains title thereto, he or she holds it on trust for the principal: *Austin v Chambers* (1837-8) 6 Cl & Fin 1. The agent must account for, and pay over to the principal all moneys received by him or her as agent from third parties, even though the third parties claim entitlement to the money (*Bloustein v Maltz, Mitchell and Co* [1937] 2 KB 142). The agent will, however, be liable to repay money to a third party if he or she had received it through duress, fraud, mistake of fact, or there has been a failure of consideration: see Goff & Jones, *Law of Restitution*, (3rd ed, 1986), pp 707-711.

In respect of the above rights, the principal will have actions for account, breach of contract, or an action in quasi-contract for money had and received. If the agent has used the principal's money (or proceeds of sale of goods) to purchase other property, the principal may be able to recover such property (*Taylor v Plumer* (1815) 3 M & S 562), unless the property has been turned into money and mixed with a mass of other money, in which case tracing at common law is not available. However, the principal will probably be able to trace in equity.

28.8.2 Rights of principal as against third parties in possession of principal's property as a result of agent's unauthorised acts

The principal has as against the third party, an action in conversion, or a proprietary action to recover money, or an action for money had and received. As under the previous heading, if the money or property has become intermingled with the third party's own money, no common law tracing remedy exists. However, the equitable tracing remedy may still be available: *Re Hallett's Estate* (1880) 13 ChD 696; *Banque Belge Pour L'Etranger v Hambrouck* [1921] 1 KB 321.

The principal's right to recover from the third party may be denied in the following cases:

1   If the agent has acted without authority, the principal will still be bound by dispositions to third parties who took in good faith: *Lloyds and Scottish Finance Co Ltd v Williamson* [1965] 1 All ER 641. However, this exception is limited to cases where the agent has authority of some kind to deal with property, but goes beyond the bounds of that authority.

2   If the principal has held out the agent as having authority to act in respect of the title to the property, thereby misleading a third party, and the agent deals with the property as though he or she were actually authorised to do so, the agent will bind the principal. The third party will gain a good title to the property, and the principal is estopped from denying it: Sale of Goods Act 1908, s 23(1), supra, para 16.2.1. The test is whether the principal has armed the agent with the power to go into the world as the absolute owner of property: *Abigail v Lapin* [1934] AC 491, 499; *Eastern Distributors Ltd v Goldring* [1957] 2 QB 600; *RE Tingey and Co v John Chambers and Co* [1967] NZLR 785.

3   The Mercantile Law Act 1908 provides for circumstances in which mercantile agents, without any express authority, may be impliedly authorised to dispose of title to goods belonging to their principals: supra, para 16.3.

28.8.3 Rights of third party against agent or principal

The third party will have the right of suing the agent in respect of property which the principal has given to the agent, or allowed to remain in the agent's possession, if the agent is under some obligation to pay the money over to the third party. For instance, property of the principal's that is in the agent's hands may be assigned or charged by the principal in the third party's favour, in which case the agent is bound to pay over the moneys held by him or her upon receipt of notice of the charge or assignment: *Webb v Smith* (1885) 30 ChD 192. Again, if the agent agrees with the third party that he or she will pay him or her money held by the agent to the use of the principal, the third party may sue the agent: *Griffith v Weatherby* (1868) LR 3 QB 753.

The principal is not liable to the third party if he or she has directed the agent to pay the third party and the agent has not paid (*Williams v Everett* (1811)14 East 582). However, he or she will be liable for money or property of the third party which is received by the agent either while acting actually or apparently within the scope of his or her authority and misapplied by the agent, or while acting wrongfully or in an unauthorised way, as long as the money has been applied for the benefit of the principal: *Marsh v Keating* (1834) 1 Bing NC 198.

28.9 TERMINATION OF AGENCY

Agency may be determined in one of the following ways:

(a) Mutual agreement
(b) Notice of revocation by the principal
(c) Notice of renunciation by the agent.

These three situations are best considered together. In general the parties to a contract of agency, as with any contract, may agree to bring their relationship to an end or may terminate in accordance with the terms of the contract. If the contract is for a defined period, a purported termination before the expiration of that period may be actionable as a breach of contract: see, for example, *Re Premier Products Ltd* [1965] NZLR 50. Damages may include commission which would have been earned during the unexpired portion of the period: *Turner v Goldsmith* [1891] 1 QB 544. If the contract is silent on the matter it is a question of construction as to whether or how it is terminable. In such a case the Court may well conclude that it is terminable on reasonable notice: see, for example, *Martin-Baker Aircraft Co v Canadian Flight Equipment* [1955] 2 QB 556.

Revocation is not allowed without the agent's consent where the agent has been granted authority to act on the principal's behalf for the purpose of protecting some interest of the agent. In *Smart v Sanders* (1848) 5 CB 895 a factor was sent goods to sell on behalf of the principal. He later made advances to the principal on the security of the goods. The principal then countermanded his instructions to sell the goods but the factor nonetheless proceeded to sell them. It was held that the factor's authority was not irrevocable because it arose prior to and independently of the factor's interest in the proceeds of sale. The decision would have been different had the factor been put into possession with authority to sell and to repay himself out of the proceeds.

The Property Law Act 1952 deals with revocation of powers of attorney. Section 135(2) provides that every act or thing done by a donee of a power within the scope of that power after revocation of it shall be as effectual as if the revocation had not been made, as long as the donee had no notice of the revocation at the time (see also ss 136 and 137).

If the agent has completed what he or she was appointed to do, the principal cannot then purport to revoke his or her authority. Revocation will not affect any existing claims which the agent and principal have against each other. For instance, the principal can still sue the agent for breach of contract, and the agent can sue the principal for indemnity: see *Read v Anderson* (1884) 13 BD 779.

(d) If one or other party wrongfully repudiates the contract, ordinary principles apply and the contract is determined only on acceptance of the repudiation by the other: *Gunton v Richmond-upon-Thames LBC* [1981] Ch 448. However, this perhaps is a case where the innocent party in practice is obliged to accept the repudiation: supra, para 7.3.3.

(e) When the transaction undertaken has been performed the relationship of principal and agent is terminated, in the absence of contrary agreement. The same applies where the period fixed for the duration of the agency has expired.

(f) If the property which is the subject matter of the agency is destroyed, or ceases to exist, the relationship is terminated.

(g) The death of either principal or agent determines the agency.

(h) Mental incapacity of one of the parties also determines the relationship. However an incapable principal may remain liable for what the agent has done in his or her capacity as agent, for having been held out as having authority the agent can continue to exercise it until the third party becomes aware of the principal's incapacity. In *Drew v Nunn* (1879) 4 QBD 661, D, a tradesman, had given credit to N's wife with N's approval. N subsequently became insane, unknown to D, who continued to give the wife credit. N was held liable to pay for the goods himself.

The decision in *Yonge v Toynbee* [1910] 1 KB 215 muddies the waters. One T instructed his solicitors to defend him in a threatened action, and subsequently became insane. The solicitors, ignorant of their principal's insanity, proceeded with the defence, and took all necessary steps on their client's behalf. When Y discovered the insanity of T, he sought to have all proceedings struck out and to make the solicitors personally liable for all costs incurred, on the ground that their authority had been terminated by the insanity of T. It was held that the solicitors were liable, as they had warranted an authority which they had ceased to possess. If, however, the agent is still empowered to create a contractual relationship between the principal and the other party, as *Drew* holds, seemingly the principal should be exclusively liable.

(i) The bankruptcy of the principal terminates the agency as from the time of the first act of bankruptcy within the three months preceding the presentation of the bankruptcy petition: *Pearson v Graham* (1837) 6 Ad & El 899; Insolvency Act 1967, s 42.

Under s 47 of the Insolvency Act 1967, if the agent deals with a third party for valuable consideration, the third party acting in good faith and without notice of any act of bankruptcy committed by the principal, then the transaction will be valid;

(j) The contract between principal and agent can be terminated by frustration, for example, if it becomes illegal, impossible, or useless to continue the relationship.

Chapter 29

PARTNERSHIP

SUMMARY

29.1 DEFINITION OF PARTNERSHIP

Partnership is defined in s 4 of the Partnership Act as "the relation which subsists between persons carrying on a business in common with a view to profit".

29.1.1 Business

Section 2 of the Act defines "business" as including "every trade, occupation, or profession". However, it is clear that "business" must for this purpose be limited to what is recognised among businesspersons as commercial or professional business. The mere fact of co-ownership of an asset does not of itself create a partnership as to the thing co-owned. There must be a business carried on with respect to the asset: s 5(a). A "business" can exist even for a single undertaking of short duration: *Re Abenheim, Ex parte Abenheim* (1913)109 LT 219, 220 per Phillimore J.

29.1.2 Profit

The business must be carried on with a view to profit. By profit here is meant net profit: *Lyon v Knowles* (1863) 2 B & S 556; s 5(b). Even if a partnership is formed for the purpose of tax avoidance, it will still be a partnership if profit is intended to be made: *Newstead v Frost* [1978] 1 WLR 441.

29.1.3 Business carried on by, or on behalf of partners

The requirement that the business be carried on by, or on behalf of the alleged partners means that the mere carrying on of a business jointly with a view to profit does not constitute a partnership. The parties may, for example, be operating in the relationship of master and servant. Whether or not the relationship of partnership exists must depend on the real intention and contract of the parties. The mere participation in profit is not, by itself, a conclusive indicator of a partnership: see *Cox v Hickman* (1860) 8 HL Cas 268; *Davis v Davis* [1894] 1 Ch 393, 399 per North J.

The question of the ascertainment of whether or not a partnership exist, is also dealt with in s 5 of the Act. Section 5 provides as follows:

5. **Rules for determining existence of partnership** – In determining whether a partnership does or does not exist regard shall be had to the following rules:
(a) Joint tenancy, tenancy in common, joint property, or part ownership does not of itself create a partnership as to anything so held or owned, whether the tenants or owners do or do not share any profits made by the use thereof.
(b) The sharing of gross returns does not of itself create a partnership, whether the persons sharing such returns have or have not a joint or common right or interest in any property from which or from the use of which the returns are derived.
(c) The receipt by a person of a share of the profits of a business is prima facie evidence that he or she is a partner in the business, but the receipt of such a share of a payment contingent on or varying with the profits of a business does not of itself make him or her a partner in the business and, in particular, –
   (i)   The receipt by a person of a debt or other liquidated amount, by instalments or otherwise, out of the accruing profits of a business does not of itself make him or her a partner in the business or liable as such:
   (ii) A contract for the remuneration of a servant or agent of a person engaged in a business by a share of the profits of the business does not of itself make the servant or agent a partner in the business or liable as such:
   (iii) A person being the widow or child of a deceased partner, and receiving by way of annuity a portion of the profits made in the business in which the deceased person was a partner, is not by reason only of such receipt a partner in the business or liable as such:
   (iv) The advance of money by way of loan to a person engaged or about to engage in any business on a contract with that person that the lender shall receive a rate of interest varying with the profits, or shall receive a share of the profits arising from carrying on the business, does not of itself make the lender a partner with the person or persons carrying on the business, or liable as such:
        Provided that the contract is in writing, and signed by or on behalf of all the parties thereto:

(v) A person receiving by way of annuity or otherwise a portion of the
profits of a business in consideration of the sale by him or her of the
goodwill of the business is not, by reason only of such receipt, a
partner in the business or liable as such.

The rule stated in s 5(c), appearing as it does to contain a contradiction,
requires some explanation. In *Davis v Davis* supra, North J explained
s 5(c) as follows:

... the receipt by a person of a share of the profits of a business is prima facie
evidence that he or she is a partner in it, and, if the matter stops there, it is
evidence upon which the Court must act. But, if there are other circumstances
to be considered, they ought to be considered fairly together: not holding that
a partnership is proved by the receipt of a share of the profits, unless it is
rebutted by something else; but taking all the circumstances together, not
attaching undue weight to any of them, but drawing an inference from the
whole (399).

29.1.4 Co-ownership

Section 5(a) provides:

Joint tenancy, tenancy in common, joint property, or part ownership does
not of itself create a partnership as to anything so held or owned, whether the
tenants or owners do or do not share any profits made by the use thereof.

Merely because two or more persons are co-owners of property they are
not partners. There are many differences between partnership and co-
ownership, the most significant of which are:

(i)   partnership results from an agreement; co-ownership does not
necessarily rest on agreement. Persons may be co-owners under a
will or by operation of law.
(ii)   partnerships are created for the purpose of gain; persons owning
land as co-owners need not have this object.
(iii) a partner cannot transfer his or her share in a partnership without
the consent of the other parties; a co-owner is not subject to this
restriction;
(iv)   a partner is the agent of the firm; a co-owner is not the agent of his
or her co-owners unless he or she is specially given this authority.
(v)   a partner is not entitled to call for partition; a co-owner may seek
partition under the Property Law Act 1952, ss 140-143.

In *Davis v Davis* [1894] 1 Ch 393, it was held that two sons owned land
and buildings devised to them by their father as co-owners and not as
partners, even though they were partners in the business carried on on
the land.

29.1.5 Sharing gross returns

Section 5(b) provides:

The sharing of gross returns does not itself create a partnership, whether the
persons sharing such returns have or have not a joint or common right or

interest in any property from which or from the use of which the returns are derived.

The sharing of gross returns, unlike the sharing of net profits (see below), does not of itself create a partnership. In *Sutton and Co v Grey* [1894] 1 QB 285, an agreement was made between S and G under which G was entitled to half of the commissions earned by S in respect of transactions entered into by persons introduced by him. G was liable to meet half of the losses incurred. S and G were not partners because the commissions to be divided were gross returns, not net profits.

In *Cox v Coulson* [1916] 2 KB 177, Coulson, the lessee of a theatre, made an agreement with M, the manager of a theatrical company, under which Coulson agreed to provide the theatre and pay certain other expenses in return for sixty per cent of the receipts. M received the balance and agreed to provide the company and scenery. There was no partnership; the parties were sharing gross returns.

29.1.6 Sharing profits

Section 5(c) provides:

> The receipt by a person of a share of the profits of a business is prima facie evidence that he or she is a partner in the business, but the receipt of such a share or of a payment contingent on or varying with the profits of a business does not of itself make him or her a partner in the business, and, in particular –
>
> (i) The receipt by a person of a debt or other liquidated amount, by instalments or otherwise, out of the accruing profits of a business does not of itself make him or her a partner in the business or liable as such:
>
> (ii) A contract for the remuneration of a servant or agent of a person engaged in a business by a share of the profits of the business does not of itself make the servant or agent a partner in the business or liable as such:
>
> (iii) A person being the widow or child of a deceased partner, and receiving by way of annuity a portion of the profits made in the business in which the deceased person was a partner, is not by reason only of such receipt a partner in the business or liable as such:
>
> (iv) The advance of money by way of loan to a person engaged or about to engage in any business on a contract with that person that the lender shall receive a rate of interest varying with the profits, or shall receive a share of the profits arising from carrying on the business, does not of itself make the lender a partner with the person or persons carrying on the business, or liable as such:
>
> Provided that the contract is in writing, and signed by or on behalf of all the parties thereto:

For example, a man who lends money to another for use in his or her business, pursuant to a written contract that the borrower shall pay 1 % interest for every $100 net profit made, does not on that account become a partner in the business of the borrower.

> (v) A person receiving by way of annuity or otherwise a portion of the profits of a business in consideration of the sale by him or her of the goodwill of the business is not, by reason only of such receipt, a partner in the business or liable as such.

The purchaser of the goodwill of a business might agree to pay to the vendor 50% of the net profits for the next six years instead of an amount equal to the sum of the net profits for the past three years. The vendor under such an agreement does not thereby become a partner with the purchaser.

The first part of this subsection contains the only affirmative rule as to the existence of partnership. All of the other rules are negative. It will be noted that the sharing of profits is only prima facie evidence of partnership; that evidence can be rebutted by proof of a contrary intention.

A good illustration of this point is *Walker v Hirsch* (1884) ChD 450. The plaintiff and the defendant firm had agreed that for the part taken in the business by the plaintiff and a loan of £ 1,500 to the firm, he should receive a fixed annual salary of £ 180, and in addition should receive one-eighth share of the net profits, and bear one-eighth share of the losses. The agreement was to be determined by four months' notice on either side. The plaintiff had previously been a clerk to the defendants and continued to perform similar duties after the execution of the agreement. He was not introduced to customers as a member of the firm and his name was not included on letterheads, etc. The defendants became dissatisfied with the plaintiff and gave him notice to terminate the agreement. The plaintiff brought an action for winding up the partnership. The Court of Appeal held that on the true construction of the agreement the plaintiff was rather in the position of a servant than a partner and that no partnership existed. The fact that two or more persons share in profits from a business is only one of the circumstances to be considered. All of the circumstances must be taken into account. If the parties have agreed to share profits and losses it is probable, however, that the Courts will conclude that a partnership exists. In *Cox v Hickman* (1861) 8 HL Cas 268, a debtor assigned his business to trustees for the benefit of his creditors. The trustees carried on the business and paid the creditors from the profits. The creditors were held not to be partners in the business. Executors who carry on the testator's business in terms of his will are not partners: *Re Fisher and Sons* [1912] 2 KB 491.

In *Stekel v Ellice* [1973] 1 WLR 191 Megarry J considered the problem of so-called "salaried partners". The learned Judge said:

> The term "salaried partner" is not a term of art, and to some extent it may be said to be a contradiction in terms. However, it is a convenient expression which is widely used to denote a person who is held out to the world as being a partner, with his or her name appearing as partner on the notepaper of the firm, and so on. At the same time, he or she receives a salary as remuneration, rather than a share of the profits, though he or she may, in addition to his or her salary, receive some bonus or other sum of money dependent on the profits. Quoad the outside world it often will matter little whether a man is a full partner or a salaried partner; for a salaried partner is held out as being a partner, and the partners will be liable for his or her acts accordingly. But within the partnership it may be important to know whether a salaried partner is truly to be classified as a mere employee or as a partner (198).

He then continued:

> It seems to me impossible to say that as a matter of law a salaried partner is or is not necessarily a partner in the true sense. He or she may or may not be a partner, depending on the facts. What must be done, I think, is to look at the substance of the relationship between the parties; and there is ample authority for saying that the question whether or not there is a partnership depends on

what the true relationship is and not on any mere label attached to that relationship. A relationship that is plainly not a partnership is no more made into a partnership by calling it one than a relationship which is plainly a partnership is prevented from being one by a clause negativing partnership. ... If, there is a plain contract of master and servant, and the only qualification of that relationship is that the servant is being held out as being a partner, the name "salaried partner" seems perfectly apt for him; and yet he or she will be no partner in relation to the members of the firm. At the other extreme, there may be a full partnership deed under which all the partners save one take a share of the profits, with that one being paid a fixed salary not dependent on profits. Again, "salaried partner" seems to me an apt description of that one: yet I do not see why he or she should not be a true partner, at all events if he or she is entitled to share in the profits on a winding up, thereby satisfying the point made by Lindley on s 39. However, I do not think it could be said it would be impossible to exclude or vary s 39 by the terms of the partnership agreement, or even by subsequent variation (see s 19), and so I think that there could well be cases in which a salaried partner will be a true partner even though he or she would not benefit from s 39. It may be that most salaried partners are persons whose only title to partnership is that they are held out as being partners; but even if "salaried partners" who are true partners, though at a salary, are in a minority, that does not mean that they are non-existent.

29.2 CREATION OF A PARTNERSHIP

A partnership agreement need not be in writing. A partnership may result from an oral agreement. In *Gallagher v Schulz* (1988) 2 NZBLC 103,196 it was found that a partnership existed between G and S despite the facts that a written partnership agreement (which was never finally executed) named G and S's wife as the partners, and that the profit was not to be shared between G and S but between G and Mrs S. In practice, however, particularly where large businesses or complicated arrangements are involved, partnership agreements are generally reduced to writing in the form of a deed. This course of action is preferable because of the evidentiary problems which may arise when there is a dispute concerning the terms of the partnership agreement. The terms of a written agreement are more easily established.

The requirements of the Contracts Enforcement Act 1956, s 2, present certain problems where land is concerned. In *Griffiths v Graham* (1920) 15 MCR 41, the parties were engaged in land speculation as partners under an oral agreement. A property was purchased in the name of the defendant's wife, and on resale the defendant collected the whole of the profit and refused to account to the plaintiff for his share. The defendant set up the Statute of Frauds as a defence to a claim by the plaintiff. It was held that the action was not to recover land or any interest in land, but was a claim by one partner against the other to recover his or her share of partnership profits in a partnership undertaking; the statutory requirement that the contract be evidenced by writing did not apply.

On the other hand, where there is an oral agreement to become partners for the joint purchase and resale of a specific parcel of land with a view to subdivision and resale, it appears that this is an agreement for the disposition of an interest in land and, in the absence of part performance, the agreement to be enforceable must be evidenced by writing: *Imrie v Nisbet* (1908) 27 NZLR 783; *Cody v Roth* (1909) 28 NZLR 565.

If, on the other hand, there is more than a mere agreement to become partners, the matter may be different. If the parties have acted as partners, even though the partnership is to deal with land, then the partnership agreement may be proved by parol evidence: *Johnson v Murray* (1951) 2 WWR (NS) 447.

29.3 CAPACITY

Capacity to enter into a partnership is governed by the general law of contract: see supra. The following cases merit special attention.

29.3.1 Minors

At common law a minor may become a partner in a firm. The common law rules as to the capacity of minors and the capacity of a minor to enter into a partnership agreement have been modified and restated by the Minors' Contracts Act 1969: see 5.1.1 supra. A minor who is or has been married has full contractual capacity by s 4(1) of that Act, and may therefore become a partner and will be treated as an adult member of the firm.

A minor who has never been married, but who has attained the age of 18, is also treated as having full contractual capacity subject to certain provisions of a protective nature, discussed in 5.1.1 supra.

Minors who have never been married and are below the age of 18 are covered by s 6 of the Act, which provides that every contract entered into by such a minor other than one pursuant to s 75 of the Life Insurance Act 1908 or a contract of service, shall be unenforceable against the minor but otherwise shall have effect as if the minor were of full age.

Certain protective safeguards are again provided by s 6(2), as amended by the Minors' Contracts Amendment Act 1971, whereby the Court may, in the course of any proceedings or an application made for the purpose, inquire into the fairness and reasonableness of any contract to which s 6(1) applies at the time the contract was entered into. The wide powers conferred on the Court in this regard are discussed at 5.1.1, supra. It can be seen that, although minors may enter into partnership agreements, there are certain hazards involved for adults contracting with them. Until there are decisions on ss 5, 6 and 7 of the Minors' Contracts Act the scope of those provisions remains uncertain. Difficulties and uncertainties concerning those provisions can, of course, be avoided by the use of s 9(1) of the Minors' Contracts Act. Under this section every contract entered into by an unmarried minor shall have effect as if the minor were of full age if, before the contract is entered into by the minor, it is approved by a District Court. Resort to this procedure will provide a measure of security in the agreement for all the proposed partners, because the minor would then be bound by its terms as if he or she were an adult.

It is assumed that, in considering applications for approval under this section, Judges will have due regard to the ability of minors of tender years to give their consent to the terms of partnership agreements: see *Moore v Commissioner of Inland Revenue* [1959] NZLR 1046, 1050.

29.3.2 Aliens

Aliens, other than enemy aliens, are not generally subject to incapacity in New Zealand. An enemy alien may not enter into a partnership with a person resident in the territories of the Crown: *R v Kupfer* [1915] 2 KB 321.

29.3.3 Insanity

A partnership agreement made by a person not known to the other parties to be insane is binding, but if the other parties knew him or her to be insane the agreement may be repudiated by him: *Imperial Loan Co Ltd v Stone* [1892] 1 QB 599. Insanity is a ground for dissolution of the partnership by the Court; see infra.

A person subject to a property order made pursuant to Part III of the Protection of Personal and Property Rights Act 1988 (see supra 5.1.2) is incapable of exercising personally any of the powers vested in the manager in respect of any property to which the manager's powers extend. In making a property order the Court must determine which of the rights and powers specified in cl 1 of the First Schedule to the Act the manager is to have in respect of the property: s 29(3). Those powers include the power to carry on any trade or business of the person subject to a property order or carry on the business of any partnership in which the person is a partner: cl 1(f), First Schedule. However it appears that the Act does not restrict the capacity of a person subject to a property order to enter into a partnership.

29.4 ILLEGAL PARTNERSHIP

A partnership is unlawful if:

(a) it is forbidden by statute. The Companies Act 1955 provides that, except as provided in s 456 (1)(a) and (2), no partnership consisting of more than 25 persons shall be formed for the purpose of carrying on business for the purpose of gain. Other associations in excess of 25 members must be registered as a company. The Dental Act 1963 and the Law Practitioners Act 1982 prevent the formation of partnerships by persons unqualified in those professions. See also Human Rights Commission Act 1977, s 19; and

(b) it is formed for an illegal purpose or even an object contrary to international comity, eg the export of alcoholic beverages into the United States during the period when prohibition was in force: *Foster v Driscoll* [1929] 1 KB 470.

An unlawful partnership may be sued, but it cannot bring an action in the Courts. As to illegal contracts generally, see supra.

29.5 DURATION OF PARTNERSHIP

The term of the partnership is usually settled by the agreement. It may provide that the partnership shall continue during the joint lives of the partners or it may be for a specified term. It may provide that it shall be terminable on notice. A partnership at will is created where no express term is fixed; any partner may determine a partnership at will by giving notice of his or her intention to the other parties: s 29. The notice must be in writing if the partnership agreement is a deed: s 29(1).

Where the partnership was for a fixed term and is continued after that period without any new agreement, the rights and duties of the partners remain the same as they were at the expiration of the term so far as those are consistent with a partnership at will: s 30. A majority of the partners cannot expel any partner unless this power is expressly conferred by the partnership agreement: s 28.

29.6 RELATIONS BETWEEN THE FIRM AND THIRD PERSONS

The main rules with regard to the relations between partners and third persons are set out in ss 8 and 11 of the Act, as follows:

8. Power of partner to bind the firm: Every partner is an agent of the firm and his or her other partners for the purpose of the business of the partnership, and the acts of every partner who does any act for carrying on in the usual way business of the kind carried on by the firm, of which he or she is a member bind the firm and his or her partners, unless the partner so acting has in fact no authority to act for the firm in the particular matter, and the person with whom he or she is dealing either knows that he or she has no authority or does not know or believe him or her to be a partner.

11. Effect of notice that firm will not be bound by acts of partner: If it has been agreed between the partners that any restriction shall be placed on the power of any one or more of them to bind the firm, no act done in contravention of the agreement is binding on the firm with respect to persons having notice of the agreement.

These provisions can only be properly understood if one has some knowledge of the rules of agency. A partner may possess different types of authority to bind the firm. These are:

(a) Express. In these cases the partner will be contracting in accordance with the terms of the partnership agreement or with the consent of the other partners;

(b) Implied. The partner will not have express authority to contract but his or her authority is to be gathered from the surrounding circumstances;

(c) Apparent or ostensible authority. This is to be distinguished from implied authority which refers to powers actually (but impliedly) conferred on the partner. A partner has apparent or ostensible authority to bind the partnership, in those cases when it can be said that the partner has been clothed with authority to make the contract in question. The partner's authority may arise from prior transactions which the firm has accepted as binding or the contract may be so related to the firm's business that the partner would be understood to possess the authority to make it. Section 8 gives a statutory basis for much of what would otherwise fall within apparent or ostensible authority.

The position, therefore, in the light of the above provisions, is that if a partner exceeds his or her actual express or implied authority, then the firm will not be bound by transactions which he or she enters into with persons who know that he or she has exceeded his or her actual authority. If the third party has no such knowledge then the firm will be bound by acts which are within the partner's usual or apparent authority.

However, the requirements of s 8 should be borne in mind here. That is, in order to bind the firm the act must be done in relation to the partnership business. If the act bears no relation to the business then the firm could only be bound by ratification or estoppel. This requirement in s 8 is repeated in another form in ss 9 and 10 of the Act, which provide:

9. Partners bound by acts on behalf of firm: An act or instrument relating to the business of the firm, and done or executed in the firm name, or in any other manner showing an intention to bind the firm, by any person thereto authorised, whether a partner or not, is binding on the firm and all the partners:

Provided that this section shall not affect any general rule of law relating to the execution of deeds or negotiable instruments.

10. Partner using credit of firm for private purposes: Where one partner pledges the credit of the firm for a purpose apparently not connected with the firm's ordinary course of business, the firm is not bound unless he or she is in fact specially authorised by the other partners; but this section does not affect any personal liability incurred by an individual partner.

As to s 10, see *Kennedy v Malcolm Bros* (1909) 28 NZLR 457. It will be noted that in the case of s 10, unlike in s 8, it is enough if the purpose is apparently connected with the firm's ordinary course of business. Further, in relation to s 8, the act must be an act for carrying on business in the usual way.

In the case of commercial partnerships, and in the absence of any express prohibition, partners have implied authority to:

(i) sell any goods of the firm;
(ii) purchase on behalf of the firm any goods of a kind necessary for or usually employed in the business carried on by the firm;
(iii) receive payment of debts due to the firm, and give receipts or releases for them;
(iv) engage servants for the purpose of the partnership business;
(v) make, accept, indorse and issue bills of exchange and other negotiable instruments; under the Bills of Exchange Act 1908, s 23(b), the signature of the name of the firm is equivalent to the signature of all partners in the firm;
(vi) borrow money on the firm's credit and pledge the goods of the firm for that purpose;
(vii) instruct a solicitor in an action against the firm in respect of a trade debt.

See *Bank of Australasia v Breillat* (1847) 6 Moo PCC 152, 193: *Mercantile Credit Ltd v Garrod* [1962] 3 All ER 1103; *Mann v D'Arcy* [1968] 2 All ER 172.

In the case of non-commercial, eg professional, partnerships, partners have no authority to borrow or charge the partnership property: see eg *O'Connor v Waldegrave* [1928] NZLR 480.

Whether the business be a commercial or a non-commercial one, a partner has no authority under s 8 to do any of the following acts:

   (i)   to execute a deed, for an agent cannot bind his or her principal by deed unless the authority to do so is expressly conferred by deed;

   (ii) to give a guarantee in the firm's name;

   (iii) to submit matters to arbitration;

   (iv) to accept property in lieu of money in liquidation of a debt due to the partnership;

   (v) to authorise a third party to make use of the firm's name in legal or other proceedings.

Thirdly, in relation to s 8, the act must be done by a partner in his or her capacity as partner, and not in a private capacity: see s 9, supra.

The act of a partner done without actual authority for carrying on the partnership business in the usual way, will not bind the firm and other partners if the person with whom he or she is dealing knows either that he or she has no authority or does not know or believe him or her to be a partner.

This part of s 8 is similar to the agency rule but with one important difference. In the law of agency, an undisclosed principal is bound by the acts of his or her agent which are within the authority usually conferred on such an agent. However, in the law of partnership, s 8 operates to exonerate a "dormant" or undisclosed partner from liability where an "active" partner exceeds his or her actual authority when the above conditions are satisfied, namely, that the person dealing with the contracting partner either knows of the want of authority or does not know or believe him or her to be a partner. But dormant or undisclosed partners will still be liable if there has in fact been no excess of authority.

The case of *Watteau v Fenwick* [1893] 1 QB 346, is often referred to in connection with the liability of dormant partners, but this was not a case on partnership at all, but one on the liability of an undisclosed principal and usual authority in the law of agency. However, because Wills J felt compelled to remark on the position of a dormant partner, it may be useful to examine the case here.

The defendants were a firm of brewers who were the owners of a beerhouse. The licensee was the manager of the business, whose name also appeared over the door. Under the terms of the agreement made between the defendants and their manager, the latter was forbidden to buy any goods for the business except bottled ales and mineral waters; all other goods required were to be supplied by the defendants themselves. The manager bought other goods from a third party who gave him credit, being unaware of the existence of the brewers as principals. The action was brought to recover from the defendants the price of the goods delivered. It was held that the plaintiff was entitled to recover; the defendants were principals and therefore liable for all acts of their agent which were within the authority usually conferred upon an agent of his kind, although he had never been held out by the defendants as their agent, and although the authority actually given to him by them had been exceeded.

In the course of the judgment, probably by way of example rather than anything else, Wills J stated (349):

... But in the case of a dormant partner it is clear law that no limitation of authority as between the dormant and active partner will avail the dormant partner, as to things within the ordinary authority of a partner. The law of partnership is, on such a question, nothing but a branch of the general law of principal and agent, and it appears to me to be undisputed and conclusive on the point now under discussion.

It is submitted that to accept this dictum as a true statement of the liability of dormant or undisclosed partners is to overlook the closing words of s 8 of the Partnership Act 1908. Unlike an ordinary undisclosed principal, a dormant or undisclosed partner is clearly exonerated by s 8 from liability where there is excess of real authority by an active partner and the person dealing with the latter either knows of the want of authority or does not know him or her to be a partner.

29.7 LIABILITY FOR TORTS

The law as to the liability of a firm for the torts of its partners is set out in ss 13 and 14 of the Act, as follows:

> **13. Liability of the firm for wrongs:** Where by the wrongful act or omission of any partner acting in the ordinary course of the business of the firm, or with the authority of his co-partners, loss or injury is caused to any person not being a partner in the firm, or any penalty is incurred, the firm is liable therefore to the same extent as the partner so acting or omitting to act.

> **14. Misapplication of money received for firm, etc.** In the following cases, namely:
> (a) Where one partner acting within the scope of his apparent authority receives the money or property of a third person and misapplies it; and
> (b) Where a firm in the course of its business receives money or property of a third person, and the money or property so received is misapplied by one or more of the partners while it is in the custody of the firm, – the firm is liable to make good the loss.

> **15. Joint and several liability:** Every partner is liable jointly with his co-partners and also severally for everything for which the firm, while he is a partner therein, becomes liable under either of the two last preceding sections.

The provision in s 15 has the effect that the injured party may sue any or all of the partners, and judgment against one is not a bar to proceedings against another.

Under s 13, a firm of solicitors, for example, will be liable for the negligence of one of its partners: *Blyth v Fladgate* [1891] 1 Ch 337.

However, a firm will not be liable for a tort committed by a partner which is outside the scope of his or her authority: *Re Bell's Indenture* [1980] 2 All ER 425, 437 per Vinelott J.

In respect of fraudulent misrepresentations, the effect of s 6 of the Statute of Frauds Amendment Act 1829 (UK), which is still in force in New Zealand, is that a firm will not be liable for a fraudulent misrepresentation made by one of the partners even if the others knew and approved it and the only person who can be charged is the partner, signing the misrepresentation. Section 6 provides as follows:

No action shall be brought whereby to charge any person upon or by reason of any representation or assurance made or given concerning or relating to the character, conduct, credit, ability, or trade, or dealings with any other person, to the intent or purpose that such other person may obtain credit, money, or goods (upon), unless such representation or assurance be made in writing, signed by the party to be charged therewith: see *R T Turnbull and Co Ltd v Mackay and McDonald* [1932] NZLR 1300.

The signature of the firm is insufficient to satisfy s 6 even though all of the partners are privy to the misrepresentation: *Swift v Jewsbury* (1874) LR 9 QB 301.

Section 16 of the Act was included ex abundanti cautela, in order to make it clear that a firm is not liable for the act of a partner who is a trustee, and who, without the knowledge of his or her co-partners, brings the trust funds into the business as part of his or her capital. Section 16 provides:

> **16. Improper employment of trust property for partnership purposes:** If a partner, being a trustee, improperly employs trust property in the business or on the account of the partnership, no other partner is liable for the trust property to the persons beneficially interested therein: Provided that –
> (a) This section shall not affect any liability incurred by any partner by reason of his or her having notice of a breach of trust; and
> (b) Nothing in this section shall prevent trust money from being followed and recovered from the firm if still in its possession or under its control.

29.8 NATURE OF LIABILITY OF PARTNERS

Reference has already been made to s 15 of the Act, which describes the nature of partners' tortious liability. As regards contractual liability, s 12 provides:

> **12. Liability of partners:** Every partner in a firm is liable jointly with the other partners for all debts and obligations of the firm incurred while he is a partner; and after his death his estate is also severally liable in a due course of administration for such debts and obligations as far as they remain unsatisfied, but subject to the prior payment of his or her separate debts.

The result of s 12 was, at common law, that, with regard to debts and contractual obligations, a plaintiff could bring only one action, and not several actions, against the members of the firm.

However, under R 79 of the High Court Rules (or R 61 of the District Coult Rules 1948), an action can be brought in the firm name.

Section 94 of the Judicature Act 1908 provides that a judgment against one or more persons jointly liable shall not operate as a bar or defence to an action or other proceeding against any of such persons against whom judgment has not been recovered, except to the extent to which the judgment has been satisfied, any rule of law notwithstanding.

29.9 DURATION OF PARTNERS' LIABILITY

A partner is, generally speaking, liable for acts committed whilst he or she is a partner. A partner's liability ceases when he or she retires from the firm, or, in the event of a dissolution of the partnership, when the liquidation is fully complete: s 41. These rules are reflected in s 20 of the Act, which provides:

20. Liabilities of incoming and outgoing partners: (1) A person who is admitted as a partner into an existing firm does not thereby become liable to the creditors of the firm for anything done before he or she becomes a partner.

(2) A partner who retires from a firm does not thereby cease to be liable for partnership debts or obligations incurred before his retirement.

(3) A retiring partner may be discharged from any existing liabilities by an agreement to that effect between himself and the members of the firm as newly constituted and the creditors, and this agreement may be either express or inferred as a fact from the course of dealing between the creditors and the firm as newly constituted.

The same principle as in s 20(3) applies in the case of the death of a partner. It will be noted that the rules in s 20 may be varied by means of a novation.

Novation, in this context, is an agreement between the creditors, new or retiring partners, and continuing partners, under which the reconstituted firm assumes liability for past debts and obligations of the firm. Novation will effectively release a retiring partner from debts and obligations and place the obligations on the reconstituted firm. Such an agreement may be expressed or implied from the course of dealings between the creditors and the firm as newly constituted: s 20(3). See *Cycle Motor Supplies Ltd v Sinclair and Brown* (1909) 12 GLR 223.

Section 39 deals with the giving of notice to creditors of any change in the constitution of a firm, as follows:

39. Rights of persons dealing with firm against apparent members: (1) Where a person deals with a firm after a change in its constitution, he is entitled to treat all apparent members of the old firm as still being members of the firm until he has notice of the change.

(2) An advertisement in the *Gazette* shall be notice as to persons who had no dealings with the firm before the date of the dissolution or change so advertised.

(3) The estate of a partner who dies or who becomes bankrupt, or of a partner who, not having been known to the person dealing with the firm to be a partner, retires from the firm, is not liable for partnership debts contracted after the date of the death, bankruptcy, or retirement respectively.

29.10 HOLDING OUT AS PARTNERS

Section 17 of the Act provides:

17. Persons liable by "holding out": (1) Every one who, by words spoken or written, or by conduct, represents himself, or who knowingly suffers himself to be represented, as a partner in a particular firm is liable as a partner to any one who has, on the faith of any such representation, given credit to the firm, whether the representation has or has not been made or communicated to the person so giving credit by or with the knowledge of the apparent partner making the representation or suffering it to be made.

(2) Provided that where after a partner's death the partnership business is continued in the old firm name, the continued use of that name or of the deceased partner's name as part thereof shall not of itself make his or her executors or administrators estate or effects liable for any partnership debts or contracted after his or her death.

The doctrine of "holding out" is based on the law of estoppel. See *Tower Cabinet Co Ltd v Ingram* [1949] 2 KB 397.

A retired partner is not liable for debts and liabilities incurred after his or her retirement unless he or she is held out as a continuing partner. In order to prevent himself or herself being rendered liable, a retiring partner must notify personally all persons who have had dealings with the firm of his or her retirement and advertise his or her retirement by notice in the *Gazette*: s 39. Notice in the *Gazette* is sufficient to negative "holding out" so far as persons who have not previously dealt with the firm are concerned. The estate of a partner who dies or who becomes bankrupt, or of a partner who, not having been known to the person dealing with the firm to be a partner, retires from the firm, is not liable for partnership debts or contracts after the date of the death, bankruptcy, or retirement respectively: s 39(3).

29.11 THE RELATION OF PARTNERS TO ONE ANOTHER

In some cases the rights, duties and interests of the parties will be settled by the written partnership agreement. The agreement may define rights to profits, the sharing of losses, the provision of capital, the amount to be drawn by way of salary by each partner, the respective duties of partners and so on. But these rights and duties may be varied by the consent of all partners and such consent may be express or inferred from a course of dealing: s 22. The partnership articles, whether settled by deed or written agreement, may be varied by an oral agreement or by conduct.

29.11.1 Utmost good faith

It is an implied term of every partnership agreement that each partner must observe the utmost good faith and fairness towards his or her fellow partners. For instance, a power to expel a partner from the firm must not be exercised otherwise than in good faith. A partner cannot be expelled merely to enable the other partners to purchase his or her share on reasonable terms: *Green v Howell* [1910] 1 Ch 495, 504.

Another example is provided in the situation where one partner is selling his or her share to another. In such a case, both parties must disclose all relevant information which may bear on the value of the share that is being sold: *Law v Law* [1905]1 Ch 140. A sale in breach of this obligation is voidable and may be set aside.

Sections 31 to 33 of the Act contain rules which all flow from the general duty of good faith:

31. Duty to render accounts, etc:
   Partners are bound to render true accounts and full information of all things affecting the partnership to any partner or his legal representative.

32. Partners to account for private profits:
   (1) Every partner must account to the firm for any benefit derived by him without the consent of the other partners from any transaction concerning the partnership, or from any use by him of the partnership property, name, or business connection.

(2) This section applies also to transactions undertaken after a partnership has been dissolved by the death of a partner, and before the affairs thereof have been completely wound up, either by any surviving partner or by the representatives of the deceased partner.

33. Partner not to compete with firm:

If a partner, without the consent of the other partners, carries on any business of the same nature as and competing with that of the firm, he must account for and pay over to the firm all profits made by him in that business.

As to s 32(1), see *Bentley v Craven* (1853)18 Beav 75. C was a partner in a sugar refining firm, and was also the firm's buyer of its sugar. He also ran a separate business himself as a sugar dealer with the consent of his partners. In this latter capacity he became expert in the variation of prices of the sugar market, making a considerable profit of £853 in one year. Although he had charged his partners in the refining firm the market price for their sugar in that year it was held that he must account to them for any profit made at their expense.

As to s 33(1), this principle is illustrated by *Gibson v Tyree* (1901) 20 NZLR 278. T was the managing partner in the firm of Gavin, Gibson and Co, wholesale leather merchants. Toomer Bros were boot manufacturers who, being in debt to a number of creditors including the firm of Gavin, Gibson and Co, had assigned their assets for the benefit of their creditors. T was a trustee under the deed of assignment, which also authorised him to become the purchaser of the assigned estate. T, secretly and through an agent, then bought the whole estate and resold it in part to one P, a boot retailer, at a considerable profit. The goods so resold, together with the ordinary stock of the firm of Gibson and Co, could have been sold by that firm as a normal part of their business, so that other partners sought to make T account to them for the profit made. It was held that he was liable to account to his partners. Stout CJ rested his finding on the ground that the resale was in competition with the firm's business, and Williams J relied on s 32. Connolly J dissented on the ground that he did not consider that on the facts the resale was competitive.

29.11.2 Partnership property and duties of partners

Section 27 provides:

(a) All the partners are entitled to share equally in the capital and profits of the business, and must contribute equally towards the losses, whether of capital or otherwise, sustained by the firm.
(b) The firm must indemnify every partner in respect of payments made and personal liabilities incurred by him:
  (i) in the ordinary and proper conduct of the business of the firm; or
  (ii) in or about anything necessarily done for the preservation of the business or property of the firm.
(c) A partner making for the purpose of the partnership, any payment or advance beyond the amount of capital which he has agreed to subscribe is entitled to interest at the rate of five per centum per annum from the date of the payment or advance.
(d) A partner is not entitled, before the ascertainment of profits, to interest on the capital subscribed by him.
(e) Every partner may take part in the management of the partnership business.

(f) No partner shall be entitled to remuneration for acting in the partnership business. He is, of course, entitled to a share in the profits and to such remuneration as is fixed by the articles of partnership.

(g) No person may be introduced as a partner without the consent of all existing partners.

(h) Any difference arising as to ordinary matters connected with the partnership business may be decided by a majority of the partners, but no change may be made in the nature of the partnership business without the consent of all existing partners.

(i) The partnership books are to be kept at the place of business of the partnership (or the principal place if there is more than one), and every partner may when he thinks fit have access to and inspect and copy any of them.

All property and rights and interests in property originally brought into the partnership stock, or acquired (whether by purchase or otherwise) on account of the firm or for the purpose and in the course of the partnership business, are called "partnership property", and must be held and applied by the partners exclusively for the purposes of the partnership and in accordance with the partnership agreement: s 23(1).

Unless the contrary intention appears, property bought with money belonging to the firm is deemed to have been bought on account of the firm: s 24.

Unless the contrary intention appears, land held as partnership property is to be treated as between the parties (including the representatives of a deceased partner), and also between the heirs of a deceased partner and his or her executors or administrators, as personal and not real estate: s 25. This rule means simply that, in the absence of agreement to the contrary, partnership land is deemed as between the partners to have been converted into personal estate and will devolve as such on dissolution of the partnership.

The operation of s 25 is illustrated by *Moleta v Moleta* (1977) 3 NZ Recent Law 18, where Ongley J held that on dissolution, partnership land, being deemed to be personalty, could not be partitioned in terms of the Property Law Act 1952, s 140 which applies only to land.

The High Court or a Judge thereof may, on the application by summons of any judgment creditor of a partner, make an order charging that partner's interest in the partnership property and profits with payment of the amount of the judgment debt and interest thereon; and may by the same or a subsequent order appoint a receiver of that partner's share of profits (whether already declared or accruing), and of any other money coming to him or her in respect of the partnership, and direct all accounts and inquiries and give all other orders and directions which might have been directed or given if the charge had been made in favour of the judgment creditor by the partner, or which the circumstances of the case require: s 26(2). This is a ground for dissolution of the partnership: see infra.

The other partner or partners shall be at liberty at any time to redeem the interest charged or, in the case of a sale being directed, to purchase that partner's interest: s 26(3).

The question as to whether property is that of the firm, or of individual partners is of importance, since an increase in the value of partnership property belongs to the firm, whereas if the property is that of an individual partner, the increase belongs to him or her solely. The point is also of importance as between the creditors of the firm and those of the individual partners.

Whether property is or is not partnership property depends in the first instance on the express or implied agreement between the partners. There must be evidence of some intention to treat the property as part of the capital of the business: see *Waterer v Waterer* (1873) LR 15 Eq 402, cf *Davis v Davis* [1894] 1 Ch 393.

A writ of execution will not issue against any partnership property except on a judgment against the firm: s 26(1).

The decision of the High Court of Australia in *Harvey v Harvey* (1970) 120 CLR 529; 44 ALJR 159, concerns the use by the partnership of property, owned by one of the partners, for the purposes of carrying on the business of the partnership. A partnership was formed by oral agreement in 1946 between the appellant, who owned a pastoral property, and another firm, the members of which were his brother and his brother's adult sons, all successful graziers. The owner had fallen into ill health and had considered selling the property but was dissuaded from this course by his brother, who suggested that it should be run by the owner and the firm so as to give the brother's sons some experience in pastoral management and so that it would be available for the owner's youngest son, then aged six, if he should want it. As a result of this suggestion the partnership was formed.

It was agreed that the owner and the firm would carry on the pastoral business on the land; that the owner was to contribute certain stock and implements; that the firm was to contribute labour and skill but no other capital; that the owner was not to be active in the working of the business: and that expenses, including the cost of improvements, were to be borne and profits divided between the owner and the firm equally. There was no agreement that the land itself would be a partnership asset and it was not treated as such in the books of the partnership. Nor was there any agreement as to how the improvements to the land, regarded as necessary to all concerned, were to be dealt with in the accounts or on dissolution.

In 1958 an agreement was signed between the owner and his brother, purporting to bind the rest of his firm in the regulation of compensation payments by the owner to that firm for improvements made on the land, and also providing for the termination of the partnership in December 1958. However, because there was no evidence before the Court that the brother had been authorised by the firm to make the agreement, it need not concern us further. The pastoral partnership was finally determined on June 30, 1967, the land having been vastly improved by the clearing and cultivation of substantial areas, and the construction of fences, dams and bores.

The principal question raised was whether the appellant's land became a partnership asset. The majority of the High Court, Walsh and Menzies JJ, disagreeing with Barwick CJ and overruling Barbury CJ, in the Tasmanian Supreme Court on this point, held that where there was no agreement between the parties for the passing of the appellant's property to the partnership, it was not, in the absence of strong evidence to the contrary, to be deemed partnership property. The basis of the whole understanding was that the owner should retain the land, and at the end of the partnership it would be available for his or her youngest son. To treat the land as a partnership asset would have meant that, in the absence of some new agreement, it would have to be sold on the termination of the partnership and the proceeds made available for distribution. The fact that, while the appellant had expressly contributed certain stock implements to the business, no such mention was made of the land, and the fact that the accounts did not treat the land as a partnership asset also weighed with the Court.

A further question for the Court was whether the additional value of the property brought about by the improvements made to it in the course of the partnership business should be taken into account in the final accounts of the partnership. The majority view here was that the improvements were inseparable from the property and could not be owned separately from it. In the view of Menzies J it was anticipated that the profits would eventually take care of the cost of the improvements in any case. He agreed with Walsh J that there is no general principle that, in the absence of agreement, a partner whose property has been increased in value by the expenditure of partnership money is bound to allow the other partners to share in the increased value.

Finally, it was held by the whole Court that the final accounts should be adjusted to the extent that the owner had not been charged in the partnership accounts with the costs of making the improvements, and the owner's account should be debited with half the expenses but that in the making of the adjustments no allowance should be made for the labour contributed by the firm in effecting the improvements, for that was part of their agreed contribution to the partnership. As with the enhanced value of the land through improvements, it was ordered that the present market value of the stock and implements initially contributed by the appellant should be treated as part of his capital stake in the venture.

29.11.3 Capital profits and losses

Section 27(a), which applies unless modified by agreement of the partner, provides that all the partners are entitled to share equally in the capital and profits of the business, and must contribute equally towards the losses, whether of capital or otherwise, sustained by the firm. This rule, which takes no account of the proportions in which assets have been provided, can be excluded only by an agreement providing some other basis for sharing profits and contributing towards losses. An agreement that these shall be shared unequally may be inferred from the course of conduct of the parties and from the partnership accounts.

There is no necessary connection between the proportion in which the capital is contributed and the sharing of profits and losses, but there is an inference that the losses are to be borne in the same proportion as profits are shared. For example, A B and C entered into a partnership on the terms of A finding $1,000 capital, B $500, and C contributing skill and knowledge; profits and losses were to be shared equally. On dissolution, after payment of debts, loans, etc, the surplus assets amounted to $600 only. This means a loss of $900 which must be borne equally. The Act suggests that each partner would then pay in $300 so that A and B could be paid their respective capital balances of $1,000 and $500. But in practice each partner would be debited with his share of the loss and only those partners with resulting debit balances would have to make a contribution. Thus, in the example taken, C will pay in $300, which, together with the "surplus assets" of $600, will meet the final balances of $700 and $200 in the accounts of A and B. If, however, C through being insolvent is unable to pay the $300, this debit will be shared by A and B in the proportion of their original capital, ie A will lose $200 and B will lose $100 through C's default: *Garner v Murray* [1904] 1 Ch 57. A will then receive $500 and B $100 from the "surplus assets".

29.11.4 Alienation of shares

(a) NEW PARTNERS
No person may be introduced as a partner without the consent of all existing partners: s 27(g). If the partnership deed provides that one or more of the partners shall have the right to introduce a partner, a partner can compel the other partners to accept his or her nominee: *Byrne v Reid* [1902] 2 Ch 735. Whether the nominee can himself or herself enforce his or her acceptance by the firm depends upon the ordinary rules governing the scope of a contract: see ch 6 supra.

(b) EXPULSION
A majority of the partners cannot expel any partner unless a power to do so has been conferred by express agreement between the partners: s 28.

(c) ASSIGNMENT
A partner may assign his or her share in the assets or profits of the partnership. An assignment by any partner of his or her share in the partnership, either absolute or by way of mortgage, does not, as against the other partners, entitle the assignee, during the continuance of the partnership to interfere in the management or administration of the partnership business or affairs, or to require any account of the partnership transactions, or to inspect the partnership books. The assignee is entitled to receive only the share of the profits to which the assigning partner would otherwise be entitled, and the assignee must accept the account of profits agreed to by the partners: s 34(1). On dissolution, the assignee is entitled to receive the share of the partnership assets to which the assigning partner is entitled as between himself or herself and the other partners, and, for the purpose of ascertaining that share, to an account as from the date of the dissolution: s 34(2).

(d) CHARGING ORDER
An order charging the interest of a partner may be issued under s 26(2).

29.12 DISSOLUTION OF THE PARTNERSHIP

A partnership may be dissolved either by the Court or without recourse to Court proceedings.

29.12.1 Dissolution by the Court

On application by a partner the Court may declare a dissolution of the partnership in any of the following cases:

(a) Where a partner is shown to the satisfaction of the Court to be of permanently unsound mind; the application may be made either by any of the other partners or on behalf of the insane partner by his or her committee or next friend or person having title to intervene;

(b) Where a partner, other than the partner suing, becomes in any other way permanently incapable of performing his or her part of the partnership contract;

(c) Where a partner, other than the partner suing, has been guilty of such conduct as in the opinion of the Court, regard being had to the nature of the business, is calculated to affect prejudicially the carrying-on of the business;

(d) Where a partner, other than the partner suing, wilfully or persistently commits a breach of the partnership agreement, or otherwise so conducts himself or herself in matters relating to the partnership business that it is not reasonably practicable for the other partner or partners to carry on the business in partnership with him;

(e) Where the business of the partnership can be carried on only at a loss;

(f) Where circumstances have arisen which, in the opinion of the Court, render it just and equitable that the partnership be dissolved: s 38.

29.12.2 Dissolution otherwise than by the Court

Subject to any agreement between the partners, a partnership is dissolved:

(a) If entered into for a fixed term, by the expiration of that term: s 35(1)(a);

(b) If entered into for a single adventure or undertaking, by the termination of that adventure or undertaking: s 35(1)(b);

(c) If entered into for an undefined time, by any partner giving notice to the other or others of his or her intention to dissolve the partnership; s 35(1)(c). The partnership is dissolved as from the date mentioned in the notice as the date of dissolution, or, if no date is so mentioned, as from the date of the communication of the notice: s 35(2). Oral notice is sufficient except in the case of a partnership constituted by deed: s 29(2).

(d) By the death or bankruptcy of any partner: s 36(1);

(e) A partnership may, at the option of the other partners, be dissolved if any partner suffers his or her share of the partnership property to be charged for his or her separate debts: s 36(2).

Occasionally the question of the effect of a notice of dissolution may arise, particularly where two or more partners give notice to dissolve the partnership simultaneously or almost so. The question will usually be resolved on a construction of the partnership agreement: *Peyton v Midham* [1972] 1 WLR 8; [1971] 3 All ER 1215.

A partnership is in every case dissolved by the happening of any event which makes it unlawful for the business of the firm to be carried on or for the members of the firm to carry it on in partnership: s 37. See *Hugdell Yeates & Co v Watson* [1978] QB 451; [1978] 2 All ER 363, where a breach of the Solicitors Act 1957 (UK) dissolved the contract. The New Zealand Illegal Contracts Act 1970 might produce a different result: see 5.4 supra.

The retirement of a partner, or the admission of a new partner, constitutes in law the dissolution of the old partnership and the formation of a new one. It is not possible to avoid these consequences by agreement. The partners may agree in advance that all except any retiring member will continue in partnership, but the "continuing" partnership is in reality a new one: *Hadlee v Commissioner of Inland Revenue* [1989] 2 NZLR 447, 455.

A partnership may also be terminated by mutual agreement; see 8.2 supra, as to discharge of a contract by agreement.

29.12.3 Cancellation of partnership agreement for fraud or misrepresentation

Where a partnership contract is cancelled on the ground of the fraud or misrepresentation of one of the parties thereto, the party entitled to cancel is, without prejudice to any other right, entitled:

(a) To a lien on or right of retention of the surplus of the partnership assets, after satisfying the partnership liabilities, for any sum of money paid by him or her for the purchase of a share in the partnership and for any capital contributed by him or her; and

(b) To stand in the place of the creditors of the firm for any payments made by him or her in respect of the partnership liabilities; and

(c) To be indemnified, by the person guilty of the fraud or making the representation, against all the debts and liabilities of the firm: s 44.

An action for damages for fraud is also available: *Derry v Peek* (1889) 14 App Cas 337.

As the result of the Contractual Remedies Act 1979, if it were held to apply (see s 15(h)), the innocent party or parties would have the additional rights conferred by ss 4-10. See s 6 as to damages for fraudulent misrepresentation, discussed supra.

29.12.4 Consequences of dissolution

(a) PREMIUMS

Where one partner has paid a premium to another on entering into a partnership for a fixed term, and the partnership is dissolved before the expiration of that term otherwise than by the death of a partner, the Court may order the repayment of the premium or of such part thereof as it thinks just, having regard to the terms of the partnership contract and to the length of time during which the partnership has continued, unless:

(i) the dissolution is, in the judgment of the Court, wholly or chiefly due to the misconduct of the partner who paid the premium or

(ii) the partnership has been dissolved by an agreement containing no provision for a return of any part of the premium: s 43.

(b) PERSONS DEALING WITH FIRM

A third party who deals with a firm of partners may not realise that the partnership has altered with the retirement of one or more partners. If a retiring member still appears to be a partner after the change in the constitution of the firm (because, for example, the firm's letterhead listing the partners is not revised) a third party who deals with the firm may treat the retiring member (the "apparent partner") as a partner until the third party has notice of the change: s 39(1). Accordingly the apparent member may be held liable for the debts of the partnership incurred after the change in the partnership. But this does not apply where the apparent partner was not known by the third party to be a partner at all. In *Elders Pastoral Ltd v Rutherfurd* (1990) 3 NZBLC 101,899 (CA) E supplied goods to a partnership of which R was a partner, and continued to supply after R's retirement from the firm. E was not aware at the time that R was a party, and a fortiori did not know that she had retired. E subsequently learned of R's involvement and sought to make recovery from her post-partnership debts. Section 39(1) was held not to apply.

(c) NOTICE OF DISSOLUTION

On the dissolution of a partnership or retirement of a partner any partner may publicly notify the same, and may require the other partner or partners to concur for that purpose in all necessary or proper acts, if any, which cannot be done without his or her or their concurrence: s 40.

(d) CONTINUING AUTHORITY OF PARTNERS

After the dissolution of a partnership the authority of each partner to bind the firm, and the other rights and obligations of the partners, continue (notwithstanding the dissolution) so far as may be necessary to wind up the affairs of the partnership and to complete transactions begun, but unfinished, at the time of the dissolution, but not otherwise: s 41.

If the dissolution is caused by the death or bankruptcy of a partner, this authority devolves on the surviving or solvent partners alone, to the exclusion of the bankrupt partner or the personal representatives or the assignee of the deceased or bankrupt partner. The surviving partner may mortgage the partnership property to secure a debt of the firm, and persons dealing with a surviving partner are, in the absence of evidence to the contrary, entitled to assume that the mortgage is given in the proper course of winding up the partnership: *Re Bourne* [1906] 2 Ch 427.

(e) GOODWILL

On dissolution any partner may require that the property, including the goodwill, be sold. He or she may restrain any other partner from doing anything which tends directly to decrease the value of the goodwill, eg using the firm's name when an attempt is being made to sell the goodwill. When one partner dies, the right to the goodwill does not vest in the survivors entirely, and consequently it may be sold for the benefit of the deceased's estate.

In *Trego v Hunt* [1896] AC 7, 24, Lord Macnaghten described goodwill as "the whole advantage, whatever it may be of the reputation and connection of the firm, which may have been built up by years of honest work or gained by the lavish expenditure of money". As to the limitations placed on members of a firm that has sold its goodwill, Lord Herschell stated, pp 20-21:

> I think it must be treated as settled that whenever the goodwill of a business is sold the vendor does not, by reason only of that sale, come under a restriction not to carry on a competing business. . . . It does not seem to me to follow that because a man may, by his acts, invite all men to deal with him, and so, amongst the rest of mankind, invite the former customers of the firm, he may use the knowledge which he has acquired of what persons were customers of

the old firm in order, by an appeal to them, to seek to weaken their habit of dealing where they have dealt before, or whatever else binds them to the old business, and so to secure their custom for himself. This seems to me to be a direct and intentional dealing with the goodwill and an endeavour to destroy it if a person who has previously been a partner in a firm sets up in business on his own account and appeals generally for custom, he only does that which any member of the public may do, and which those carrying on the same trade are already doing. It is true that those who were former customers of the firm to which he belonged may of their own accord transfer their custom to him: but this incidental advantage is unavoidable and does not result from any act of his. He only conducts his business in precisely the same way as he would if he had never been a member of the firm to which he previously belonged. But when he specifically and directly appealed to those who were customers of the previous firm he seeks to take advantage of the connection previously formed by his old firm, and of the knowledge of that connection which he has previously acquired, to take that which constitutes the goodwill away from the persons to whom it has been sold and to restore it to himself. It is said, indeed, that he may not represent himself as a successor of the old firm, or as carrying on a continuation of their business, but this in many cases appears to me of little importance, and of small practical advantage, if canvassing the customers of the old firm were allowed without restraint. . . . I have so far dealt with the case as if the goodwill had been sold, but I think the rights and obligations must be precisely the same for present purposes when, on the creation of a partnership, it has been agreed that the goodwill shall belong exclusively to one of the partners.

A member of a firm that has sold its goodwill cannot canvass the customers of the firm, but he or she may invite the public generally to deal with him or her and in this way secure business from former customers.

(f) PROFITS

Where any member of a firm dies or otherwise ceases to be a partner, and the surviving or continuing partners carry on the business of the firm with its capital or assets without any final settlement of accounts as between the firm and the outgoing partner or his or her estate, then, in the absence of any agreement to the contrary, the outgoing partner or his or her estate is entitled, at the option of the outgoing partner or his or her representative, to such share of the profits made since the dissolution as the Court may find to be attributable to the use of his or her share of the partnership assets, or to interest at the rate of five % on the amount of his or her share of the partnership assets: s 45(1).

Where by the partnership contract an option is given to surviving or continuing partners to purchase the interest of a deceased or outgoing partner, and that option is duly exercised, the estate of the deceased partner or the outgoing partner, or his or her estate, as the case may be, is not entitled to any further or other share of profits; but if any partner assuming to act in exercise of the option does not in all material respects comply with the terms thereof he or she is liable to account in accordance with s 45(1), supra: s 45(2).

(g) DISTRIBUTION OF ASSETS

On the dissolution of a partnership every partner is entitled to have the property of the partnership applied in payment of the debts and liabilities of the firm, and to have the surplus assets after such payment applied in payment of what may be due to the partners respectively after deducting what may due due from them as partners of the firm: s 42, see *Re Ward (a bankrupt)* [1985] 2 NZLR 352 (CA).

In settling accounts between the partners after a dissolution of partnership the following rules shall, subject to any agreement, be observed:

(1) Losses including losses and deficiencies of capital, shall be paid first out of profits, next out of capital, and lastly, if necessary, by the partners individually in the proportion in which they were entitled to share profits.

(2) The assets of the firm, including the sums (if any) contributed by the partners to make up losses or deficiencies of capital, shall be applied in the following manner and order:

    (i) in paying the debts and liabilities of the firm to persons who are not partners therein;

    (ii) in paying to each partner rateably what is due from the firm to him or her for advances as distinguished from capital;

    (iii) in paying to each partner rateably what is due from the firm to him or her in respect of capital;

    (iv) the ultimate residue, if any, shall be divided among the partners in the proportion in which profits are divisible: s 47.

29.13 SPECIAL PARTNERSHIPS

The Act provides for the creation of special partnerships which permit persons to become special partners in a partnership without any responsibility for any debt of the partnership beyond the amount contributed in money as capital.

All persons forming a special partnership must, before commencing business, sign a certificate containing:

(a) The style of the firm. Such style of firm must contain the names of general partners only, with the addition of the words "and Company", which must be added as part of the firm-name, and, the general partners only may transact the partnership business;

(b) The names and places of residence of all partners, distinguishing the general from the special partners;

(c) The amount of capital contributed by each special partner, and also the amount contributed by the general partners to the common stock;

(d) The general nature of the business to be transacted;

(e) The principal place where the business is to be transacted;

(f) The time when the partnership is to commence and when it is to terminate.

A special partnership is not deemed to be formed until such certificate is acknowledged by each partner before a Justice of the Peace and registered in the High Court in a book to be kept open for public inspection.

A copy of the certificate must be published at least once in the *Gazette* and twice in a newspaper published at the intended place of business; failing such publication, the partnership is deemed general.

A special partner must not permit his or her name to be used in any contract, otherwise he or she will be deemed to be a general partner. No part of the certified capital may be withdrawn.

Any action respecting the business of any special partnership must be taken against the general partners only.

Special partnerships must not be entered into for banking or insurance nor for a period of more than seven years; any such partnership may be rendered at the end of that period or at the termination of any shorter period for which it was formed.

Chapter 30

THE NATURE OF INSURANCE

SUMMARY

30.1 DEFINITION AND CHARACTERISTICS OF INSURANCE

A contract of insurance is a contract whereby one person, the insurer, agrees in return for a money or other consideration called the premium, to pay a sum of money or its equivalent to another person, the insured, upon the occurrence of a specific contingency.

30.1.1 Contract

First, there must always be a binding contract and, as with any other transaction, the determination of this question is by reference to the general principles of contract law. Cognisance must, of course, be taken of a number of particular rules and statutory modifications to the common law that have special application to contracts of insurance. For example the contract of insurance is a contract of utmost good faith and this attracts to it special obligations pertaining to the duty of the contracting parties or their agents to disclose material information; and, certain doctrines, such as that of subrogation, have attained their fullest development and significance in the field of insurance law. Furthermore, various statutory incursions into the insurance arena have effected significant changes to the law governing the formation and performance of contracts of insurance; for example, the Insurance Law Reform Acts 1977 and 1985.

In some cases it may be difficult to classify a particular contract as one of insurance or non-insurance. A manufacturer undertakes that it will replace any of its products which are damaged or destroyed within a year of purchase; is this a contract of insurance, or merely some form of

451

warranty? See Hellner "The Scope of Insurance Regulation: What is the Insurance for the Purposes of Regulation?" (1963) 12 Am J Comp L 494. The Courts have relied upon several tests for determining whether a contract is one of insurance. For example, it may be asked whether the liability of the "insurer" is dependent upon a contingent event beyond its control?: see para 30.1.5 infra. Where a single contract has provisions of both an insurance and non-insurance kind, the test is whether the insurance provision is a major component of the contract as a whole or merely ancillary. Cf *The Motorcycle Specialists Ltd v Attorney-General* (1988) 5 ANZ Ins Cas 60-882.

30.1.2 Promise of money or money's worth

Secondly, the insurer must in return for the consideration called the premium agree to pay a sum of money or its equivalent on the happening of the specified contingency. As Channell J observed in the leading case of *Prudential Insurance Co v Inland Revenue Commissioners* [1904] 2 KB 658, 663:

> A contract of insurance then must be a contract for the payment of a sum of money, or for some corresponding benefit such as the rebuilding of a house or the repairing of a ship . . .

In *Department of Trade and Industry v St Christopher Motorists Association Ltd* [1974] 1 WLR 99 a contractual arrangement whereby the defendant association in return for a small annual sum undertook to provide its members with chauffeur services should they through injury or disqualification be prevented from driving, fell to be considered. The Department of Trade and Industry contended that by undertaking to provide these benefits the defendant association was carrying on an unauthorised "insurance business". Templeman J accepted this argument in that the learned Judge could see no logical difference between the association paying the chauffeur, and the association paying the member a sum of money representing the cost to him or her of engaging a chauffeur personally; paying the chauffeur for the member's benefit clearly fell within the meaning of the phrase "some corresponding benefit". In *Medical Defence Union Ltd v Dept of Trade* [1979] 2 WLR 686 Sir Robert Megarry VC cautioned against construing the ratio of the *St Christopher* case too widely. He pointed out that if the definition of the contract of insurance is extended beyond contracts where the obligation is to provide money or money's worth, the net may be too widely cast; if a contract of insurance is taken to embrace contracts promising the conferment of any benefit on the happening of some uncertain event, many professional and other bodies giving their members the right to advice and assistance would, to their astonishment, learn that in the eyes of the law they were carrying on the business of insurance. Megarry VC did concede that it would be possible to define the obligation of the insurer in terms of money or money's worth, *or the provision of services to be paid for by the insurer*, without endangering those contractual obligations that cannot fairly be regarded as constituting insurance contracts. This extension, would very neatly encapsulate the *St Christopher* type of case without affecting other organisations and bodies which confer the right to advice and assistance upon members where such provision in no way adds to the expenses of the body concerned. In the *Medical Defence Union* case the facts were as follows. The plaintiff was a company with some 80,000 members who were either medical practitioners or dentists. These members paid an annual fee and the Medical Defence Union were charged with the fulfilment of three main functions; namely, to conduct legal proceedings on behalf of members; to indemnify them against claims for damages and costs; and, to provide advice on medical, employment, and other matters. However, in terms of the memorandum and articles, a member had no right to require the Union to conduct proceedings on his or her behalf, and no right to indemnity against claims for damages. Members merely had the right to request that they be given assistance or an indemnity. Counsel for the Department of Trade contended that although this was not a right to money or money's worth, it was of value, and so was a benefit promised on the occurrence of some event. Megarry VC held that the plaintiffs were not carrying on the business of insurance. The Vice-Chancellor rejected the argument that the right to have an application for assistance or indemnity properly considered sufficed for a contract of insurance; a right to be considered for a benefit which is truly only discretionary is not sufficient. See also *C V G Siderurgica Del Orinoco S A v London Mutual Steamship Owners' Association Ltd* [1979] 1 Lloyd's Rep 557; Roberts (1980) 43 MLR 85.

The judgments in the *St Christopher* and *Medical Defence Union* cases were extensively quoted by Davison CJ in *The Motorcycle Specialists Ltd v Attorney-General* (1988) 5 ANZ Ins Cas 60-882. The question was whether the plaintiff, a licensed motor dealer, was obliged to make a payment pursuant to the Insurance Companies Deposit Act. That statute requires that a deposit be paid by any person carrying on insurance business within New Zealand. The plaintiff sought a declaration that it was not carrying on insurance business by virtue of offering to customers a hire purchase agreement in terms of which the payment of monthly instalments could be suspended for any period (up to a maximum of six months) during which the purchaser was disabled or unemployed. It was held that this was not an insurance provision. It did not provide for payment by the plaintiff of money or money's worth; rather the plaintiff simply forwent its contractual right to receive payments.

30.1.3 An uncertain event

Thirdly, there must be uncertainty as to whether the specified event will occur or not, or, as is the case with life insurance, uncertainty as to when the event will occur. In *Marac Life Assurance Ltd v Commissioner of Inland Revenue* [1986] 1 NZLR 694 (CA) the appellant Marac marketed "life bonds" which had the following features. The purchaser paid a single premium at the outset and depending upon the term of the bond (maturity dates of one, two, three, four, five or ten years were offered) was entitled to receive upon maturity a benefit calculated by adding an annual percentage increment to the amount of the premium. The Commissioner of Inland Revenue argued that the difference between the premium paid and the benefit received was interest and accordingly assessable income. Marac sought a declaration, inter alia, that the bonds were contracts of life insurance. The Court of Appeal without difficulty concluded that they were. The full benefit was payable upon either the maturity of the bond or the earlier death of the bondholder. Marac bore the risk from the inception of any bond that the bondholder would not survive the full term and that premature repayment would be required. This was a sufficient contingency to support the classification of the bond as a contract of life insurance.

In *Prudential Insurance Co v Inland Revenue Commissioners* [1904] 2 KB 658, 664, Channell J stated that the specified event must also be of a character more or less adverse to the insured in the sense that if it happened it must result in loss to the insured. However in *Gould v Curtis (Surveyor of Taxes)* [1913] 3 KB 84, the English Court of Appeal criticised this aspect of Channell J's judgment and it cannot be accepted that the event upon which payment is to be made must in some way be adverse to the interests of the insured. While adversity commonly will be present in fire and marine insurance, for example, the same cannot be said in respect of certain life insurance contracts. As Megarry VC observed in *Medical Defence Union Ltd v Dept of Trade* [1979] 2 WLR 686, 694:

> ... if a sum is made payable to a man on attaining a given age, or on living for a stated period of years, his or her feat of survival, can hardly be called an event that is adverse to his or her interests.

Therefore, while the specified event must have some uncertainty about it, there is no requirement that the event upon which payment is to be made must be adverse to the interests of the insured.

30.1.4 Insurable interest

In England in the mid-eighteenth century a gambling mania afflicted a great number of persons and it was commonplace for "insurance" to be effected on almost anyone or anything, regardless of whether the person effecting the insurance had any pre-existing interest in the subject matter of insurance. Abhorrence of this wagering within the insurance market led to the promulgation of the Marine Insurance Act 1745 and the Life Assurance Act 1774 which required that a person taking out a policy of marine or life assurance, respectively, must have an insurable interest in the subject matter of the insurance; that is, the person effecting the insurance had to stand in some legally recognised relationship to the subject matter of the insurance and the practice of "punters" wagering on the lives of prominent people, for example, was outlawed. The Life Assurance Act 1774 became part of New Zealand law on settlement (see *NZ Insurance Co Ltd v Tyneside Pty Ltd* [1917] NZLR 569; English Laws Act 1908, s 2) and the Marine Insurance Act 1908 (NZ) embodies the insurable interest requirement of its early English forerunner. While no specific legislation required that persons effecting insurance other than life or marine insurance should have an insurable interest in the subject matter of the insurance, an insurance contract entered into in respect of buildings, goods and against legal liabilities where the insured lacked an insurable interest would infringe the Gaming and Lotteries Act 1977, s 128, and, in addition, would fail to satisfy one of the basic requirements of such insurances, namely, that the agreement promises to provide the insured with an indemnity. The primary purpose of such insurances is to protect the insured from the economic consequences of fortuitous events, and it follows from this that the insured must have an interest in the subject matter of insurance, for without such an interest, the insured can suffer no loss and hence can obtain no indemnity.

(a) LIFE INSURANCE

Section 6 of the Insurance Law Reform Act 1985 abolishes the statutory requirement of an insurable interest in respect of life insurance. That provision provides:

> A contract of assurance on the life of a person is not void or illegal by means only of the fact that the insured under the contract does not have, or did not have when the contract was entered into, any interest in the life of that person.

However there are still restrictions on who may insure the life of a minor. This is because a minor is thought to be particularly vulnerable and may be even more at risk if a person has taken out insurance for large amounts on the life of the minor. Section 67(2) of the Life Insurance Act 1908 now provides that no person may effect a policy on the life of a minor who is under the age of 16 years. There are certain exceptions; for example, a parent or guardian of a minor may take out insurance on the minor's life.

(b) NON-LIFE INSURANCE

As far as contracts of general insurance are concerned s 7 of the Insurance Law Reform Act 1985 provides:

> (1) Except as provided in the Marine Insurance Act 1908, no person for whose use or benefit or on whose account a policy of insurance is made is required to have any interest in any event for the purposes of —
>
> (a) Any contract of indemnity against loss; or
>
> (b) Any contract of assurance on the life of a person.
>
> (2) Notwithstanding anything in Part IX of the Gaming and Lotteries Act 1977, but subject to subsection (1) of this section, no insurance shall be made by any person—
>
> (a) On any event whatsoever wherein the person for whose use or benefit or on whose account the policy is made has no interest; or
>
> (b) By way of gaming or wagering.
>
> (3) Every insurance made contrary to subsection (2) of this section is void.
>
> (4) Nothing in this section limits the provisions of the Marine Insurance Act 1908.

A number of points may be made in respect of this provision. First, the insurable interest provisions contained in ss 5 to 16 of the Marine Insurance Act 1908 remain intact and untouched by this section. Consequently a contract of marine insurance is deemed to be a gaming and wagering contract where the insured has no insurable interest or where the policy is made on ppi terms, that is, policy proof of interest clauses: Marine Insurance Act 1908, s 5.

Secondly, while there is no requirement that an interest be shown for purposes of any contract of insurance on the life of a person, s 7(2)(b) declares any such contract that is made by way of gaming and wagering to be void. Thirdly, there is no requirement that an insured demonstrate an interest for purposes of any contract of indemnity against loss. As Sir Robert Megarry VC explained in *Medical Defence Union Ltd v Department of Trade* [1979] 2 WLR 686, 690:

Indemnity insurance provides an indemnity against loss.... Within the limits of the policy the measure of the loss is the measure of the payment.

Therefore, in respect of indemnity insurance the insurer is under an obligation to reimburse the insured for his or her *actual* loss from the accepted risk; that is, the insured must be restored, subject to the terms and conditions of the policy to the financial position that he or she enjoyed immediately before the realisation of the peril insured against. The measure of indemnity is *the loss suffered by the insured* and not necessarily the value of the subject matter of insurance which is destroyed or damaged: *Falcon Investments Corp (NZ) Ltd v State Insurance General Manager* [1975] 1 NZLR 520, 522. Consequently, the insured under an indemnity policy must have an interest in the subject matter of the insurance, for without such an interest, he or she will be unable to prove a loss and will be disentitled from recovery under the policy. Therefore, notwithstanding that by virtue of s 7(1)(a) the validity of an indemnity policy is not dependent upon the existence of an insurable interest, the very nature of an indemnity policy dictates that an interest in the subject matter of insurance must be present before any compensation is payable.

However, the way is now clear to move away from the narrow confines of cases such as *Macaura v Northern Assurance Co* [1925] AC 619 towards a more liberal benefit/detriment test; that is, satisfaction of the indemnity principle simply demands that the insured show that he or she has suffered a loss through the occurrence of a defined event, and he or she does not have to go further and satisfy a strict proprietary test of insurable interest. The contractual requirement of an insurable interest is conceptually quite separate and distinct from the statutory requirement of insurable interest and, subject only to the terms of the policy in question, the insured should be permitted to recover in respect of events causing him or her economic loss notwithstanding the absence of a legal or equitable interest in the property that is destroyed or damaged. See now *Wijeyaratne v Medical Assurance Society NZ Ltd* [1991] 2 NZLR 332. However, it appears that the insured is not necessarily *limited* to recovering the amount of his or her loss. Where the policy was intended to cover the interest of some other person as well, and the insured has only a limited interest, the insured may nonetheless recover the full amount of the insurance, of course accounting to the third party for the amount representing the third party's interest. A common example is insurance taken out in the name of a bailee on property belonging to the bailor. In the absence of negligence the bailee is not to be liable to the bailor for the loss of the property and therefore cannot be said to suffer a loss, but has been permitted to recover the full amount: *A Tomlinson (Hauliers) Ltd v Hepburn* [1966] 1 AC 451. This rule depended upon finding that the bailee had an insurable interest, and survives in New Zealand notwithstanding that an insurable interest need not be demonstrated: see *Guardian Royal Exchange Assurance of New Zealand Ltd v Roberts* [1991] 2 NZLR 106.

Fourthly, there are those forms of insurance which are neither life insurance, marine insurance or indemnity insurance; eg personal accident policies and consumer credit insurance. These contracts may be described as contracts of contingency insurance as the amount recoverable under such policies is not limited, nor gauged, by reference to the actual loss of the insured; instead the contract secures the payment of a sum of money on the happening of a specified event, such as the insured's partial or total disablement, and the amount recoverable is not measured by the extent of the insured's pecuniary loss.

Of course, there will be exceptions; for example, where a personal accident policy provides for the reimbursement of *actual* medical expenses as opposed to a fixed payment per day, or where the benefits payable under a consumer credit policy are related directly to debts owing or the loss of income by the insured. Save in such cases of indemnity insurance, the requirement of an insurable interest remains. Thus, where a capital sum is payable in the event of specified injuries under the terms of a personal accident policy, the insured must have an insurable interest in the person who is the subject of the insurance. The retention of this requirement of insurable interest for non-indemnity general insurance contracts does introduce unnecessary distinctions within the class of general insurance and may give rise to drafting difficulties; moreover, given the general prohibition against, and invalidity of gaming and wagering transactions, the retention of this requirement seems unnecessary. It is probable that the separate treatment of non-indemnity insurance other than life insurance was not intended but is the consequence of poor drafting.

30.1.5 Event outside control of insurer

Finally, the event insured against must be outside the control of the insurer. This point was raised in both the *St Christopher* case [1974] 1 WLR 99, 106, and the *Medical Defence Union* case [1979] 2 WLR 686, 691, but in neither case was the resolution of this point necessary for the decision. Numerous transactions, such as contracts of service or repair, or manufacturers' guarantees or warranties, evidence the principal characteristics of contracts of insurance, namely the transfer and distribution of risk. In the absence of a requirement that the event insured must be outside the control of the insurer, it is no easy task to avoid categorising such transactions as contracts of insurance. For example, a typical manufacturer's guarantee will promise that goods are of a certain quality and that if they are not, the manufacturer will take certain steps to remedy any defect, replace the goods or refund any money paid. Assuming the terms of such a guarantee are embodied in a contract between the manufacturer and the purchaser of the product concerned, is this contract a contract of insurance? The manufacturer has undertaken to provide money or money's worth in the uncertain event of some defect manifesting itself in the product. If the defect is attributable to the poor quality of the product, the contingent event is not outside the manufacturer's control but could have been avoided. The contract is therefore not one of insurance. But should the guarantee extend to loss of the product through some purely fortuitous event, such as an accidental fire, the manufacturer has undertaken to indemnify on the occurrence of an event beyond its control, and the contract is accordingly one of insurance.

30.2 TYPES OF INSURANCE

30.2.1 Life insurance

Life insurance, or life assurance, takes several guises and it is useful at this stage to identify some of the main types of policies in use in New Zealand. A *Whole of Life* policy provides for the payment of the sum insured, plus any bonuses, on the death of the life insured. The allotment of a share in the profits of an insurance company to the contracted sum insured is called a bonus, and a policy giving this right to share in the profits is called a participating policy. In *Term* or *Temporary* insurance the life is held covered by a specified time and the sum insured is only payable if the person whose life is insured dies within this period. *Endowment* insurance provides for the payment of the sum insured, plus any bonuses, when the life insured reaches a certain age, or when a specific time has expired, or on the earlier death of the life insured. *Pure endowment*, however, describes a policy where the amount of the policy, plus any bonuses, is payable only if the life insured survives to a predetermined age or date. If death occurs before then provision usually is made for the return of the premiums paid with interest thereon. *Annuity is* a contract under which the insurer agrees to pay a fixed sum at regular intervals from an agreed upon date for a specified period of time or for the rest of the annuitant's lifetime. A *Superannuation* policy provides benefits for employees and their dependants in the form of a pension, or a lump sum upon retirement, death or disablement during employment. Usually the employer and employee each pay a share, the employee's share being based on his or her salary and wage, and deducted from it. An *Unbundled* policy combines the features of an endowment policy with a high savings return — the death cover aspect and investment/saving aspect of such a policy is separated into two clearly identifiable components.

30.2.2 Fire insurance

A contract of fire insurance, as defined in the Earthquake and War Damage Act 1944, s 2(1), means "a contract whereby any property is insured against loss or damage by fire, whether the contract includes other risks or not." This definition recognises that while the basic intention of the fire policy is to provide compensation to the insured in the event of there being damage or destruction to property by fire, the *basic fire* policy usually covers certain other specified risks such as damage to, or destruction of property by lightning and explosion. Furthermore the policy may be extended to cover such perils as storm, tempest and flood, riot and civil commotion, malicious damage, damage by aircraft, impact by motor vehicles, and so on. The common *houseowner's* and/or *householder's* policy will cover the above mentioned risks as well as perils such as burglary, breakage of glass plate and bursting of water pipes.

30.2.3 Property insurance – against loss, theft or damage

In motor vehicle insurance a substantial reduction in premium is given in the form of a "no claim bonus". This term means what it says and does not mean a "no blame bonus". Motorists find this strict interpretation irritating, particularly when their parked cars are damaged in their absence. But if the insurer is able to recover the cost of repairs from the negligent third party, the bonus may be reinstated.

The type of risk covered, loss arising from a comprehensive range of events and theft is far more extensive than in a fire policy. But an insured should read the "exceptions" in the policy carefully, ie the risks which are not covered. For example, a landlord might have a "comprehensive policy" but might include amongst its exceptions "malicious damage" and thus find that wanton damage done to his or her furniture and premises by a tenant was not covered.

30.2.4 Marine insurance

A contract of marine insurance is defined in the Marine Insurance Act 1908, s 3(1) as "a contract whereby the insurer undertakes to indemnify the assured, in manner and to the extent thereby agreed, against marine losses – that is to say, the losses incident to marine adventure." Therefore, for the contract to be one of marine insurance it is essential that the loss which is insured against is one incident to marine adventure, and the Act states that, in particular, there is a marine adventure when the subject matter of the insurance, such as the ship, the goods or the freight derivable from the employment of the ship, is exposed to or endangered by a maritime peril: s 4(2). Maritime perils mean "the perils consequent on or incidental to the navigation of the sea – that is to say, perils of the seas, fire, war perils, pirates, rovers, thieves, captures, seizures, restraints, and detainments of princes and peoples, jettisons, barratry, and any other perils, either of the like kind or designated by the policy": s 4(3); see *Shell International Petroleum Co Ltd v Gibbs; The Salem* [1983] 1 All ER 745 (HL).

The principal types of marine policy are:

(a) VOYAGE POLICY

The contract is to insure at and from, or from, one place to another: cf *Lobb v Phoenix Assurance Co Ltd* [1988] 1 NZLR 285 (CA). In this policy the insurer is discharged from liability if the ship does not sail from the port specified in the policy (s 44) or sails to a different destination from that specified (s 45), or where there is a voluntary change of the course of the voyage (s 46), or there is deviation without lawful excuse: s 47. However, deviation may be excused to save the ship or human life or through circumstances beyond the control of the master or the master's employer: s 50; likewise the insurer will remain liable if the goods have to be transhipped owing to the occurrence of a peril insured against: s 59.

(b) TIME POLICY

This is a contract to provide insurance for a particular period. It contains no restrictions as to place.

(c) MIXED POLICY

This policy makes the insurer liable only if the loss occurs during the specified period and in the course of the specified voyage.

(d) THE FLOATING POLICY

In this policy, the insured takes out cover for, say $200,000 for a period of 12 months and as each consignment of goods is shipped, the shipper makes a declaration as to the value of the shipment and the amounts declared is deducted from the total amount of insurance cover already paid for. All consignments of goods must be declared to the insurer. Failure in this respect is a ground for avoiding the policy.

(e) THE OPEN COVER

This is merely a contract of insurance with contractual obligations arising from the slip signed by the underwriter. Here there is an agreement to give cover on all goods shipped and the premium is fixed in accordance with the values shown on the declaration which the shipper is obliged to send to the underwriter concerned. There is generally a limit on the total amount of compensation payable by the underwriter concerned.

(f) THE VALUED POLICY

In this case, the value of the subject matter is specified and is conclusive except in the case of a constructive total loss. The value fixed by the policy is not conclusive for the purpose of determining whether there has been a constructive total loss: s 28(3).

(g) THE UNVALUED POLICY

The subject matter is described but the value is left to be determined later.

30.2.5 Liability insurance

Under a liability insurance policy, the insurer contracts to indemnify the insured against claims made against the insured by third parties for loss suffered by them as a result of their relationship with the insured or their using property belonging to the insured. The necessity for insurance against liability for personal injury or death disappeared with the enactment of accident compensation legislation. The current statute is the Accident Compensation Act 1982 which extinguishes any right to bring an action to recover damages arising out of personal injury by accident.

Professional negligence policies, sometimes with extensions covering dishonesty of employees and partners, are often taken out by doctors, solicitors and other professional people. A group scheme may be arranged for the particular profession.

A person may, despite the passing of the Accident Compensation legislation, choose to take out "Public Risk" insurance to cover himself or herself against liability arising through the death or accident of any member of the public, or accidental damage to property caused, for example, by the negligence of persons for whom the insured is responsible or by defects in his or her plant or the dangerous nature of his or her premises.

30.2.6 Loss of profits insurance – insurance against consequential loss

The ordinary fire policy does not cover losses from the diminution of trade consequent on a fire. But if profits have already been earned, eg where goods still in the possession of the insured have already been sold at an increased price, these profits may be covered by the indemnity provided by an insurance policy. Formerly an insurable interest was a basic requirement for a contract of indemnity. Now, however, it is not required except in respect of marine insurance: Insurance Law Reform Act 1985, s 7(1)(a) and (4). An owner of premises damaged by fire may be indemnified in respect of loss of net profits during the agreed period of indemnity, as well as standing charges such as salaries, rent, interest and additional costs incurred through renting new premises and equipment. Generally, the amount paid by the insurer is determined by a public accountant appointed in terms of the policy.

30.2.7 Guarantee insurance

These are contracts whereby the insurer undertakes to indemnify the insured against some default by a third person; for example, a creditor may insure against the non-payment of a debt. As the insurer indemnifies the insured against loss, the insurer is, after payment, subrogated (this term is discussed infra) to all the creditors' rights against the debtor: *Meacock v Bryant and Co* (1924) 59 TLR 51.

A fidelity policy is another form of guarantee insurance. This policy may protect an employer against misappropriation by an employee; eg it may provide insurance against theft of jewels, precious metals, etc handled by an employee in the course of his or her trade. The type of default for which the insurer will be responsible must be clearly defined. Thus, a policy indemnifying an employer against loss for "any act, neglect, etc" of the employee will provide protection only against claims from outsiders. It does not cover moral default of the employee causing direct loss to his employer: *Goddard and Smith v Frew* (1939) 109 LJKB 69.

30.2.8 Aviation insurance

This is a relatively new branch of insurance, but, like other forms of insurance, it has been influenced by marine insurance. Essentially, the same principles apply, modified however by international agreements: for example, the Warsaw and Supplementary Conventions which are given the force of law by the Carriage by Air Act 1967, s 7. That Act which binds the Crown also applies to the Cook Islands and the Tokelau Islands.

The Act contains limitations of liability and enjoins the Court to determine claims in a "just and equitable manner": ss 10 and 35. There is a two-year limit within which to bring actions. The legislation covers both domestic and international carriage by air, and covers not only persons and property but also animals (a term which is widely defined, eg to include insects).

Air carriers must insure: s 29. Contracting out of liability is forbidden: s 30. Because of the specialised nature of aviation insurance, and the enormous sums often involved, most brokers and underwriters are located in London.

30.2.9 Miscellaneous

Policies are available for long or short periods, eg death and accident cover for a single aircraft journey, and for a wide range of risks, eg a *pluvius* (rain) policy. This insurance cover may be taken out by a sporting body to provide for payment of a fixed sum as the estimated loss suffered by reason of poor attendance if an agreed number of millimetres of rain fall in a particular place during specified hours on the day of a sports gathering. Other risks that are commonly insured include insurance of money (loss of cash in transit or on the premises), baggage and travel insurance of all kinds, and insurance of dogs and livestock.

Chapter 31

NEGOTIATION AND FORMATION OF THE INSURANCE CONTRACT

SUMMARY

31.1   NON-DISCLOSURE
31.2   MISSTATEMENTS
31.3   AGENCY
31.4   FORMATION OF THE CONTRACT

31.1 NON-DISCLOSURE

31.1.1 Introduction

An insurance contract is a contract of the utmost good faith (uberrima fides) and although the duty of good faith is owed by both insured and insurer alike: see *Banque Keyser Ullman SA v Skandia (UK) Ins Co Ltd* [1987] 2 WLR 1300, appeal *Banque Financière de la Cité SA v Westgate Ins Co Ltd* [1989] 3 WLR 25 (CA), [1990] 3 WLR 363 (HL), in practice the duty imposes more onerous obligations upon the insured. One such obligation is the necessity for disclosure by the insured of all material facts relating to the insurance before the contract is entered into. Non-disclosure renders the contract voidable at the instance of the insurer.

The duty of disclosure is not based upon an implied term of the contract, but is a common law duty arising outside the contract: *Banque Financière* [1989] 3 WLR 25 (CA), 86-87; contra *McLeod v SIMU Mutual Assurance Association* (1987) 4 ANZ Ins Cas 60-784, 74,793. Non-disclosure does not fall within the scope of the Insurance Law Reform Act 1977 and continues to be governed by the common law: *Preece v State Insurance General Manager* (1982) 2 ANZ Ins Cas 77,804.

31.1.2 What must be disclosed?

The duty is to disclose all material facts. A fact is material, and should accordingly be disclosed to the insurer, if it is one which would influence the judgment of a prudent insurer in deciding whether to accept the risk and on what terms: *Avon House Ltd v Cornhill Insurance Ltd* (1980) 1 ANZ Ins Cas 60-429. As appears below (see 31.2.3), the same test is used to judge the materiality of a misstatement made by an insured in negotiating the contract.

It is well established that the absence of specific questions in a proposal form relating to a particular aspect of the insurance does not relieve the insured of the necessity to disclose all matters which are material to that aspect: *Misirlakis v New Zealand Insurance Co Ltd* (1985) 3 ANZ Ins Cas 60-633 (CA), 78,893). In *Schoolman v Hall* [1951] 1 Lloyd's Rep 139 the insured suffered a burglary loss which the insurer conceded was genuine; the insurer nonetheless sought to avoid liability on the basis that the insured had failed to disclose a criminal record. One argument raised by the insured was that since he had been asked 15 questions and had been required to guarantee the truth and accuracy of his responses, the information given in answer to the inquiries represented all the information that the insurer wished to have; that is, the insurer must be taken to have waived all other information. The argument was rejected by the English Court of Appeal which affirmed the generality of the duty of disclosure even where a proposal form is used.

Equally, however, it is clear that specific questions may have the effect of limiting disclosure if the insurer is to have waived disclosure of information falling outside those questions, and on balance recent cases suggest that the Courts will take a robust approach in favour of the insured in construing proposal forms in this regard: see *State Insurance General Manager v Hanham* (1990) 6 ANZ Ins Cas 60-990; *State Insurance General Manager v Peake* (1990) 3 NZBLC 99-194; *Nairn v Royal Insurance Fire and General (NZ) Ltd* (1990) 6 ANZ Ins Cas 61-010. It is possible that in some circumstances insurers may not rely upon non-disclosure of a particular fact as a ground for avoiding liability unless that fact is covered by a specific question. In *Peake* Chilwell J referred to the possible practice of insurers of refraining from including a specific question as to the insured's general criminal convictions and then seeking to rely upon non-disclosure of that precise aspect of the insured's past. Chilwell J accepted that this may amount to a breach of the duty of the utmost good faith on the part of the insurer (at 101, 839).

31.1.3 The scope of the duty of disclosure

It is frequently stated that the insured is under a duty to disclose all material facts which the insured in fact knows. This view was put most forcibly by Fletcher Moulton LJ in the leading case of *Joel v Law Union and Crown Insurance Co* [1908] 2 KB 863, 884:

> The disclosure must be of all you ought to have realised to be material, not of that only which you did in fact realise to be so. But in my opinion there is a point here which often is not sufficiently kept in mind. The duty is a duty to disclose, and you cannot disclose what you do not know. The obligation to disclose, therefore, necessarily depends on the knowledge you possess . . . [The] question always is, was the knowledge you possessed such that you ought to have disclosed it?

Nevertheless it is settled law that as far as marine insurance is concerned, the insured is *also* under a duty to disclose material facts which he or she *ought* to know: Marine Insurance Act 1908, s 18(1). This is clearly the case where, although the fact in question was never within his or her actual knowledge, the insured's ignorance was due to an intentional failure to make such inquiries as he or she might reasonably have been expected to be made in the circumstances. Similarly where the insured's failure to make inquiries is unintentional a marine policy is equally to be avoided where the insured should have made the inquiries in the ordinary course of business. Therefore it is clear that as far as marine policies are concerned the duty to disclose extends to all facts actually known and to all facts which the insured ought in the ordinary course of business to have known. The position as far as non-marine policies are concerned is less clearcut. However, it is submitted that on balance the position in New Zealand is the same for marine and non-marine insurances that is, the proponent or insured is under an obligation to disclose those matters of which he or she is in fact aware, and must disclose those matters of which he or she ought to have knowledge: *Blackley v National Mutual Life Association of Australasia Ltd* [1970] NZLR 919, 931; *Avon House Ltd v Cornhill Insurance Co Ltd* (1980) 1 ANZ Ins Cas 60-429, 77, 228.

The question of materiality is a question of fact to be decided in each individual case, but certain broad categories of material circumstances are generally accepted. First, all facts that suggest that the subject matter of insurance is exposed to more than ordinary danger from the perils insured against; that is, facts affecting the physical hazard. For example, the nature, construction and use of an insured building, or whether it is particularly exposed to danger, would be material facts affecting the physical hazard in property insurance. A proponent for life insurance must disclose facts relating to his or her health and any occupation, leisure time pursuits, or intemperate habits that may affect the duration of his or her life.

Secondly, those facts referable to the integrity of the insured such as character, qualities and reputation, that is, facts affecting the moral hazard. Under this head an insured is under an obligation to disclose, inter alia, previous convictions, previous losses and claims, and whether insurance has ever before been declined or cancelled. Whether criminal convictions are material to a particular risk depends upon the circumstances prevailing at the time the insurance proposal was completed, viz the nature of the offence, the penalty, the age and circumstances of the person concerned at the time, and the length of time which has elapsed since the offence: *Misirlakis v New Zealand Insurance Co Ltd* (1985) 3 ANZ Ins Cas 60-633 (CA); see further Clarke "The Disclosure of Criminal Information to Insurers" [1984] LMCLQ 100.

Thirdly, matters affecting the subrogation rights of an insurer may be material because if the insured has deprived himself or herself of the right to recover against third parties, the ultimate risk borne by the insurer is increased.

Fourthly, the insured must disclose gross over-insurance, but is not as a general rule bound to disclose that he or she is insured elsewhere unless such information is solicited in the proposal or elsewhere.

Conversely, the insured need not disclose facts which diminish the risk, nor facts within the knowledge of insurers, nor facts which it is superfluous to disclose by reason of any express or implied warranty; nor facts as to which the insurer waives information. Generally, see the Marine Insurance Act 1908, s 18(3).

The duty of disclosure exists up to the date of the conclusion of the agreement and whether the duty is broken or not depends upon the circumstances existing at the time the contract is made. With most types of insurance there is a new contract each year, as opposed to a continuing one (as with life insurance) and this reimposes a duty to disclose. The insured must with each renewal correct earlier representations that have become incorrect and disclose fresh material facts.

The onus of establishing that there has been a breach of the duty of disclosure rests upon the insurer. The insurer must prove, on a balance of probabilities, that the insured knew or ought reasonably in the ordinary course of business to have known, of the fact in question, but that the insured failed to disclose it and that it would have been material to a prudent insurer if disclosed. Expert evidence of persons engaged in the insurance business may be led but such evidence must be directed to the general practice of insurers as a class. Frequently, however, the materiality of an uncommunicated fact may be so obvious that it is unnecessary to call any expert evidence to establish this point.

Finally the effect of waiver is important. If the insured has, by non-disclosure, incorrect statement or failure to comply with express conditions, made it legally possible for the insurer to rescind the contract, the insurer may, nevertheless, either expressly or impliedly waive the default of the insured. Waiver would be implied, for example, where, after the insurer has discovered the breach of condition, the insurer continues to accept premiums. Any other acts leading the insured reasonably to believe that the insurer will not rescind the contract may subsequently prevent the insurer from underlying liability.

31.2 MISSTATEMENTS

31.2.1 General

An insurer usually requires the insured to complete a proposal form which elicits information about the risk to be insured. Invariably the insured signs a declaration warranting the truth and accuracy of the statements made in the proposal form. Where such warranty has become part of the contract by incorporation (usually by reference), the common law position is that the insurer may avoid the contract for any misstatement contained in the proposal form. This is so whether the incorrect statement is inaccurate in only a minor or even trivial respect, whether it is immaterial, or whether it has no connection with the cause of the loss when it occurs.

In respect of contracts generally a false or misleading statement may render the maker of that statement liable in damages and/or entitle the innocent party to cancel the contract entered into in reliance upon the misstatement: Contractual Remedies Act 1979, ss 6-10; see supra ch 7. However, the remedies as outlined in ss 6 to 10 of the Contractual Remedies Act apply only insofar as the contract fails to make express provision for misrepresentation or any of the other matters to which ss 6 to 10 relate: s 5 Contractual Remedies Act; cf *Turner v Metropolitan Life Assurance Co of NZ Ltd* (1988) 5 ANZ Ins Cas 60-861. On the assumption that most policies of insurance do make express provision for cancellation for misstatements by the insured, it is only in infrequent cases that the Contractual Remedies Act applies. One example might be a verbal contract of insurance where no mention is made of any remedy for misrepresentation.

Misstatements in the context of insurance are governed by the Insurance Law Reform Act 1977.

31.2.2 The Insurance Law Reform Act 1977

The Insurance Law Reform Act 1977 is the virtual enactment of a bill drafted by the now defunct Contracts and Commercial Law Reform Committee. In its first Report (*Aspects of Insurance Law*, 1975) the Committee took the view that in respect of each of the five matters considered, insurers "commonly draw insurance contracts in a manner that is so potentially unfair to the insured that legislative interference is necessary". One of these matters was the entitlement of an insurer to avoid liability for an immaterial or trivial misstatement.

(a) LIFE INSURANCE
First, a life policy cannot be avoided at all by reason only of a misstatement of the age of the life insured: s 7(1). Rather the insurer is entitled to adjust the sum insured or the premium, depending upon whether the age as misstated is greater or less than the true age of the life insured.

Secondly, in respect of all other misstatements, the insurer may not avoid the policy unless the misstatement was:

(a) substantially incorrect;
(b) material; and
(c) made either fraudulently, or within the period of three years immediately preceding the date on which the policy is sought to be avoided or the death of the life insured, whichever is the earlier: s 4(1).

A statement is substantially incorrect only if the difference between what is stated and what is actually correct would have been considered material by a prudent insurer: Insurance Law Reform Act 1977, s 6(1). The term "prudent insurer" is not defined in the Act but corresponds closely to the hypothetical "reasonable insurer": *Associated Oil Carriers Ltd v Union Insurance Society of Canton Ltd* [1917] 2 KB 184.

A statement is material only if that statement would have influenced the judgment of a prudent insurer in fixing the premium or in determining whether he or she would have taken or continued the risk upon substantially the same terms: Insurance Law Reform Act 1977, s 6(2).

(b) OTHER CONTRACTS OF INSURANCE
Contracts of insurance other than life insurance are governed by s 5 of the Insurance Law Reform Act 1977. Section 5 provides that the insurer may not avoid the contract

... by reason only of any statement made in any proposal or other document on the faith of which the contract was entered into, reinstated, or renewed by the insurer unless the statement –
(a) Was substantially incorrect; and
(b) Was material.

31.2.3 The test of materiality

Section 6(2) of the Insurance Law Reform Act 1977 provides that a statement is material only if it

> . . . would have influenced the judgment of a prudent insurer in fixing the premium or in determining whether he would have taken or continued the risk upon substantially the same terms.

This test, which is almost identical to that found in the Marine Insurance Act 1908, s 20(2) and reflects the common law test of materiality of non-disclosure, has created a sharp divide between the authorities as to its meaning. In particular, the words "influence the judgment of a prudent insurer" are ambiguous.

The first issue is whether the test is purely objective. In *Berger & Light Diffusers Ltd v Pollock* [1973] 2 Lloyd's Rep 442 Kerr J proposed a "mixed" test, inquiring whether, by applying the standard of the judgment of a prudent insurer, the insurer in question would have been influenced. Were this not the case, there might arise the situation where an insurer would be entitled to avoid a contract for non-disclosure of a fact which objectively a prudent insurer would have considered material, even though the particular insurer would not.

The weight of New Zealand authority is clearly in favour of a purely objective test. In *Avon House Ltd v Cornhill Insurance Ltd* (1980) 1 ANZ Ins Cas 60-429, a case of non-disclosure, Somers J refused to follow the mixed test proposed by Kerr J, who subsequently sitting in the English Court of Appeal stated that he had reconsidered the approach taken in *Berger* and thought it mistaken: *CTI International Inc and Reliance Group Inc v Oceanus Mutual Underwriting Association (Bermuda) Ltd* [1984] 1 Lloyd's Rep 476 (CA), 495. In *McLeod v SIMU Mutual Assurance Association* (1987) 4 ANZ Ins Cas 60-784 Williamson J considered that the statutory test was drafted in purely objective terms, and that this was supported by *Avon House*, which predated the application of the Act. But Williamson J noted, as had Kerr J in *Berger*, that the objective test favours the negligent insurer who would not have regarded a particular fact as material. The only New Zealand case against the trend is the decision in *Goldstar Insurance Co Ltd v Tegas* (unreported, High Court, Wellington, M 7/86, 21 August 1986, Heron J).

An unsatisfactory feature of the objective test is that in certain circumstances it cannot be applied without reference to the actual insurer. A misstatement in a proposal form is not material if the true position has been disclosed to the insurer's agent. In *Edwards v AA Mutual Insurance Co Ltd* (1985) 3 ANZ Ins Cas 60-668 the insured signed a proposal for insurance on his house, in which it was stated that the main living-rooms were constructed of gib board, a fire resistant material. What the insured in fact said to the insurer's agent who completed the form was that he thought the sitting-room walls *could* be gib board but that he was not sure. As it happened the sitting room walls were constructed of a non-fire resistant material. On the house being destroyed by fire the insurer repudiated liability on a number of grounds. One of these was the misstatement contained in the proposal.

Tompkins J held that the statement was substantially incorrect in terms of s 6(1) of the Insurance Law Reform Act, but that it was not material because, in the particular circumstances of the case, it would not have influenced the judgment of the prudent insurer since the knowledge of its incorrectness would be imputed to it by s 10(2): see infra 31.3.2.

The second ambiguity in the test of materiality concerns the meaning of the italicised words in the phrase *"influence the judgment* of a prudent insurer". The issue here is whether the test of materiality requires that the prudent insurer would have been influenced in the sense of making a different response, for example, by refusing the proposal or by requiring a higher premium or by imposing more stringent terms. Or is it sufficient merely that the prudent insurer would have chosen to know of the true position, although such knowledge would not have led him or her to insure on any other terms?

The same issue arises in assessing the materiality of a fact which has not been disclosed. In *Avon House* Somers J, after stating that the fact in question should have been disclosed, continued at 77, 228:

> That is not to say that upon disclosure [the insurer] would have increased the premium or refused the risk or accepted it on other terms. I think it probable that it would simply have continued to insure on the same terms ... But it was a matter for consideration and [the insurer] never had that opportunity to consider it.

The same approach was taken by the English Court of Appeal in the *Oceanus* case. For a fact to be material, it is necessary only that the undisclosed fact would have been one which the prudent insurer would have taken into account, whether or not the prudent insurer would then have adjusted the response to the proposal in any way. See too *Highlands Insurance Co v Continental Insurance Co* [1987] 1 Lloyd's Rep 109.

There is some support for the difference of response test in New Zealand cases: see *Edwards v AA Mutual Insurance Co* (1985) 3 ANZ Ins Cas 60-668; contra *Avon House Ltd v Cornhill Insurance Ltd* (1980) 1 ANZ Ins Cas 60-429; *Gibbs v NZ Insurance Co Ltd* (unreported, High Court, Auckland, A 172/80, 6 December 1983, Chilwell J). The strongest authority in favour is the decision of the New South Wales Court of Appeal in *Barclay Holdings (Aust) Pty Ltd v British National Insurance Co Ltd* (1987) 8 NSWLR 514.

In *Barclay* Glass JA, with whom Priestley JA concurred, said that a fact is material only if it would actually have influenced a prudent insurer to respond differently, because the relevance of the undisclosed fact is judged at the moment when the insurer is deciding whether or not to accept the risk and not at the moment when the insurer undertakes the investigation of the risk: 523. In other words, the point in time when the insurer determines whether to accept the insurance is the moment when the actual decision is made. The process of determination does not extend to the larger task of investigating all possibilities, some of which are then disregarded.

In a judgment which emphasised policy considerations, Kirby P said that the effect on the mind of the insurer should be something more than the effect produced by information which the insurer would generally be interested to have. It is strictly limited to those considerations which will ultimately determine whether or not the insurer will accept the insurance and, if so, at what premiums and on what conditions: 517.

31.2.4 Marine Insurance Act 1908

Section 20(1) of the Marine Insurance Act 1908 provides that:

> Every material representation made by the assured or his agent to the insurer
> during the negotiations for the contract, and before the contract is concluded,
> must be true. If it is untrue, the insurer may avoid the contract.

The question as to whether a representation is material or not is resolved
in much the same way as under the Insurance Law Reform Act 1977,
namely, a "a representation is material which would influence the
judgment of a prudent insurer in fixing the premium or determining
whether he will take the risk": s 20(2). A matter of fact is accepted as true
if it is substantially correct in the sense that the difference between what
is actually correct and what is represented would not be considered
material by a prudent insurer: s 20(4). While s 14 of the Insurance Law
Reform Act 1977 declares that the provisions of this Act must prevail in
the event of any conflict with the provisions of the Marine Insurance Act
1908, the two statutes are in perfect harmony as regards misstatements.
However, it should be borne in mind that s 20 of the Marine Insurance Act
1908 does not confine its attentions to written statements.

31.3 AGENCY

31.3.1 Transferred agency

Section 10(1) Insurance Law Reform Act 1977 was enacted to meet the
problem of "transferred agency" exemplified in *Newsholme Bros v Road
Transport & General Insurance Co* [1929] 2 KB 356 (CA). In that case an
agent of the insurer, who completed the proposal form, was held to be the
agent of the *insured* for that limited purpose only, with the result that the
insured was responsible for misstatements made by the agent. This
possibility is now excluded by s 10(1) which provides:

> A representative of the insurer who acts for the insurer during the negotiation
> of any contract of insurance, and so acts within the scope of his actual or
> apparent authority, shall be deemed, as between the insured and the insurer
> and at all times during the negotiations until the contract comes into being, to
> be the agent of the insurer.

The term "representative of the insurer" is widely defined. It includes
any servant or employee of the insurer and extends to any person entitled
to receive from the insurer commission or other valuable consideration
in return for negotiating or procuring the contract: s 10(3).

31.3.2 Disclosure to insurer's representative

Under s 10(2) the knowledge of a representative of an insurer acquired
before the insurer's acceptance of the proposal is imputed to the insurer.
The representative must have been concerned in the negotiation of the
contract; consequently information which is acquired by a representative of the insurer who is totally unconnected with the relevant transac-

tion is not imputed to the insurer. However, there is no requirement in s 10(2) that the representative act for the insurer. This distinguishes the subsection from s 10(1) which refers to an agent who acts within the scope of his or her actual or apparent authority. At common law an insurance broker is the agent of and acts for the insured, and accordingly s 10(1) will not usually apply to a broker. But s 10(2) does apply to a broker who, although the agent of the insured, may nonetheless qualify as the representative of the insurer by reason of receiving a commission: *Helicopter Equipment Ltd v Marine Insurance Co Ltd* [1986] 1 NZLR 448, 454; cf *Hing v Security and General Insurance Co (NZ) Ltd* (1986) 4 ANZ Ins Cas 60-696. Disclosure to the insurer's representative may be effective to bind the insurer even where no contract in fact results. In *Gaunt v Gold Star Insurance Co Ltd* [1991] 2 NZLR 341 Gallen J said:

> The wording of [s 10(2)] which (sic) could be construed as applying only where the contract of insurance has actually ensued but not necessarily so. The wording is apt to justify the view that the emphasis is on the negotiation rather than the completion.

31.4 FORMATION OF THE CONTRACT

31.4.1 The proposal

When a person desires insurance cover, the insurer requires a proposal form to be completed by the insured. This contains a number of questions dealing with the subject matter of the insurance and facts relevant to the risk involved. The proposal is what the term suggests – a proposition that the insurer should enter into a contract to grant insurance cover to the proponent. Although the proposal form generally provides that the proponent agrees to accept the policy subject to the conditions therein stated and that the truth of the answers in the proposal is the basis of the insurance contract, the payment of a premium by the proponent at the time the proposal form is handed in is merely a deposit pending the conclusion of a contract between the parties; payment alone does not create a contract between the proponent and the insurer.

The question of the time of making the contract of insurance is important. The ordinary principles of contracts apply to insurance. The contract is made when there is an unqualified acceptance by the insurer of the offer embodied in the proposal tendered by the proponent. If the premium has been fixed and the proposal form completed, communication of the assent of the insurance company to the proposal is an acceptance by the company and the insured can, if the contract so provides, claim compensation if the agreed risk takes place before the insured pays the premium or before the policy is issued: *Adie and Sons v The Insurance Corporation Ltd* (1898) 14 TLR 544.

But if the insurer increases the amount of the premium suggested at the time of the proposal or if the policy issued differs from the terms agreed to by the proponent when tendering the proposal, this amounts to a counter-offer by the insurer and no contract is completed until the insured accepts the modified terms: see, for example, *Capital Plumbing Service Pty Ltd v FML Assurance Ltd* (1986) 4 ANZ Ins Cas 60-687.

In *Phoenix Assurance Company of New Zealand Ltd v Campbell* (unreported, High Court, Auckland, M 314/75, 3 February 1976, Wilson J) an insurer got a proponent to sign a proposal form for insuring his motorcycle for $1,725. The premium was paid on this amount and there was no reference to the proponent having to meet any part of a claim he might make. The proposal did however stipulate that the proponent would accept the policy subject to the terms, conditions and exceptions contained therein. The proponent claimed for the total loss of his motorcycle and was told that the policy was subject to a deduction of $300 excess and that he would receive only $1,425. The policy was issued subsequently and showed an "excess" deduction of $300. Wilson J held that a provision in a proposal that a proponent agreed to accept a policy subject to the terms therein did not entitle the insurer to insert a term contrary to the terms of the proposal itself.

If the insurer accepts the proposal and then for the first time notifies the proponent of the amount of the premium, this is also a counter-offer and no contract arises until the proponent accepts the offer by agreeing to pay the premium indicated. Likewise if the insurer stipulates that no insurance will take effect until the premium is paid, there is no accepted offer giving rise to a contract of insurance until the insurer has accepted the premium – mere tender by the proponent is insufficient. In *Canning v Farquhar* (1886) 16 QBD 727 the insurer, after receipt of the proposal wrote fixing the premium and accepting the proposal but stated that "no assurance can take place until the first premium is paid." Three weeks later the proponent, Canning, fell over a cliff and four days later the premium was tendered on his behalf and the insurer was informed of the accident. The insurer refused the premium. Canning died shortly after. The Court of Appeal held that there was no life insurance contract.

The insured is entitled to assume, after receiving an acceptance of the proposal, that the policy issued will be substantially in the terms of the proposal, and if it is not the company may be bound by the terms originally agreed upon. For example, in *Braund v Mutual Life and Citizens Assurance Co Ltd* [1926] NZLR 529 an insured took out life and accident cover under a proposal in which accident was defined in general terms. The policy, when it was subsequently issued contained a condition in small print and difficult to read which provided that the insured was exempt from liability for certain specified accidents including hernia. The insured had an accident which caused hernia and the company declined to pay. It was held, that as the insured had not accepted this modification of the terms agreed upon, he was entitled to have the policy rectified in conformity with the proposal and was, therefore, entitled to compensation.

If the terms in the proposal form and the policy differ, the policy is the dominant document; however, if it can be proved that the policy differs from the terms of the contract made between the parties, the insured may bring action for the rectification of the policy and the enforcement of the original rights under the contract.

31.4.2 The cover note and the slip

The current business practice is to give the proponent immediate temporary protection by the issue of a cover note. If the receipt and cover note are combined, the receipt is usually termed a deposit receipt. In either case, the insurer is entering into an interim contract of insurance with the proponent terminable either at the end of a fixed period, on delivery of the policy, or on notification that the proposal for insurance has been declined. Generally, see *Smith v National Mutual Fire Insurance Ltd* [1974] 1 NZLR 278.

As the cover note is a contract of insurance the proponent is under a duty to disclose all material facts to the insurer prior to its conclusion, or the insurer may exercise its right to avoid liability: *Mayne Nickless Ltd v Pegler* [1974] 1 NSWLR 228; *Marene Knitting Mills Pty Ltd v Greater Pacific General Insurance Ltd* (1976) 11 ALR 167, 171.

Where insurance is placed with Lloyd's of London the following procedure is adopted. The prospective insured approaches a Lloyd's broker for cover; the broker then prepares a document known as a slip with details of the risk to be insured. This slip is then circulated among the various underwriters, ie insurers, operating at Lloyd's, and those who are prepared to undertake the insurance initial the slip for the proportion of the risk each is willing to assume. The act by the underwriter of initialling the broker's slip constitutes acceptance of insured's offer and creates an immediately binding contract between the parties, ie between each underwriter and the insured: *General Reinsurance Corporation v Forsakringsaktiebogalet Fennia Patria* [1982] QB 1022.

Sections 22 and 23 of the Marine Insurance Act 1908 as amended by the Amendment Act 1975 allow an action to be brought before the policy is issued but make it an offence for an insurer, who has been paid the premium, not to execute the said policy of insurance within 30 days of receiving payment

If a loss occurs before the issue of the policy, there will be no retrospective protection for the insured unless the policy so specifies, eg "lost or not lost" in marine insurance, or where a slip or cover note has been issued or, finally, where there was a contract by the insurer to issue a policy. If, without the knowledge of the insurer or insured, the loss had occurred before the issue of the policy, the policy will be void on the ground of common mistake as to subject matter or the underlying assumption of the contract. Obviously, if the insured was aware of the loss, and the insurer was not, a failure to disclose by the insured would make the policy voidable.

31.4.3 The policy

A contract of marine insurance needs to be evidenced by a policy: Marine Insurance Act 1908, s 26. No particular form of policy is required in the other types of insurance. Although an oral promise to insure given in consideration of a premium paid by the promisee would probably be enforceable, it is unlikely that any insurance company would adopt this practice. It is usual to set out in the policy the names of the insurer and the insured, the location and subject matter of the insurance, the period and amount of cover, the due date and amount of the premium and the conditions under which the liability of the insurer will arise.

Insurance contracts commonly contain a number of warranties, and in this insurance context, a warranty is a term of the contract of insurance which, if breached, entitles the insurer to repudiate the contract. Warranties take numerous and diverse forms and may embrace an infinite variety of circumstances, but the following categories may be isolated. First, certain warranties are implied into contracts of marine insurance; for example, there are implied warranties of seaworthiness and neutrality: Marine Insurance Act 1908, ss 37, 40. There is no counterpart to these implied warranties in other areas of insurance but it is common for express provision to be made in non-marine insurance to cover analogous situations; for example, an insured may be required pursuant to a motor vehicle policy to warrant that he or she will take all reasonable steps to safeguard the insured vehicle and its accessories and maintain it in an efficient condition: *AA Mutual Insurance Co v Stevens* [1982] 1 NZLR 349.

Secondly, the insured may be required to warrant the accuracy of all statements and promises made by the insured as to past or existing facts. It is common for a proposal to contain a declaration that the answers to various questions posed in the proposal are in every respect true, that the proposal and declaration shall be the *basis of the contract* and that the insured agrees to accept the insurer's policy; the policy itself usually contains such a recital incorporating the proposal and declaration. Such a "basis of the contract" clause elevates the statements and promises to which it refers to the status of warranties. The effect is that if an incorrect answer is given to any question, whether it is material or not, the insurer may repudiate liability, but this must now be read in the light of the Insurance Law Reform Act 1977, ss 4, 5.

Thirdly, an insured may give an undertaking as to the future that amounts to a promissory or continuing warranty. A warranty of this nature arises where the insured promises that facts will or will not exist during the continuation of the risk and not merely at its inception, and that any breach will entitle the insurer to terminate the risk and avoid the policy; for example, a commercial fire insurance policy may incorporate a warranty requiring that the insured maintain fire alarms, automatic sprinkler systems and other fire fighting equipment in good order.

Finally, the insured may be required to warrant that facts are or will be true to the best of his or her knowledge or belief; for example, an insured may declare that he or she is "not aware of any disorder tending to shorten life", and insofar as warranties of opinion or belief are concerned the insured is under an obligation to exercise reasonable care and there will only be a breach of warranty if he or she recklessly or dishonestly supplies an incorrect answer.

It is common for insurance policies to list a number of terms under the general heading of "conditions". These terms may cover matters such as misrepresentation, non-disclosure, misdescription, alteration of the risk, double insurance, payment of the premium, notice of the event insured against, and the claims procedure. Such terms may amount to warranties in the sense outlined above, and the words "warranty" and "condition" may be used interchangeably in the insurance context to describe a term in the contract of insurance the breach of which may entitle the insurer to repudiate its liability under the contract. However, it is a question of construction in each case whether a term expressed to be a condition possesses all the characteristics of a warranty having regard to the subject matter dealt with by the term and any related clauses setting out the effect of the breach.

Typically, a contract of insurance will make provision in respect of breaches; for example, the contract may provide that "the due observance and fulfilment of the terms, provisions, conditions and endorsements of this policy by the insured insofar as they relate to anything to be done or complied with by him and the truth of the statements and answers in the said proposal shall be conditions precedent to any liability of the company to make any payment under this policy": *South British Insurance Co Ltd v Irwin* [1954] NZLR 562. Therefore, in respect of breach of any warranty, condition, or indeed, any other term of a contract of insurance, the consequences attendant upon such a breach may be outlined in the policy itself. Where express provision is made for cancellation and/or damages, this provision will displace the operation of ss 6 to 10 of the Contractual Remedies Act 1979: see s 5 of that Act. However, s 15(h) of the Contractual Remedies Act 1979 does not affect "(a) any other enactment so far as it prescribes or governs terms of contracts or remedies available in respect of contracts, or governs the enforcement of contracts". Consequently any reliance upon an express term in a contract of insurance is subject, for example, to the provisions in the Insurance Law Reform Act 1977 and the Marine Insurance Act 1908. The Insurance Law Reform Act 1977 restricts the circumstances in which a policy may be avoided for misstatement (ss 4, 5, 7), provides that arbitration clauses are not binding on the insured (s 8), regulates the consequences to flow from a failure by an insured to comply with a clause requiring notice of claims (s 9), and curtails the efficacy of noncausative or temporal exclusion clauses (s 11). The Marine Insurance Act 1908, too, contains a number of provisions governing terms of contracts of marine insurance and prescribes the remedies available in respect of any breach; for example, s 34 provides that any failure to comply with a warranty as defined in the Act discharges the insurer from liability as from the date of the breach of the warranty – this is stated to be subject to any express provision in the policy, but it is plain that in the absence of any such provision in the policy the consequences as outlined in the Marine Insurance Act 1908 apply.

Therefore the consequences to be visited upon any breach demands that a careful appraisal and identification of the relevant term be undertaken – is it a warranty, "condition", a clause descriptive of the risk, or an innominate term? But, more importantly, the contract must be studied to ascertain whether any express provision for a remedy is made in relation to the relevant term. Where express provision is made then prima facie that is the remedy that will apply or consequence that will ensue, subject, of course, to any statutory provision to the contrary. Where the contract is silent as regards remedies then the provisions of the Contractual Remedies Act 1979 apply – again, this is subject to the provisions of any other statute.

The cover provided under a policy is commonly described in general terms, and it is the practice of insurers with a view to qualifying their undertaking to introduce exemptions which expressly exclude their liability where the loss is caused or the peril brought into operation by certain specified causes. The nature of these exceptions will vary according to the type of insurance concerned; for example in the case of a motor vehicle policy it is common to find an exclusion clause to the following, or like effect:

> The Company shall not be liable in respect of any accident injury loss damage
> or liability caused sustained or incurred whilst any vehicle . . . is . . . being
> driven in an unsafe condition. . . .

In many life insurance policies it is common to find an exemption clause
relieving the insurer of liability to make payment if the life insured dies:
"whilst (a) taking part in aviation in any capacity whatsoever except as
a fare paying passenger on a recognised airline, or (b) driving or riding
in any motor propelled vehicle engaged in any organised or unorganised
race or speed trial . . .".

Exclusion or exemption clauses often define the circumstances in
which cover is inapplicable in terms that are temporal, rather than
causative. The two examples given above are couched in temporal terms
and the effect of such clauses is that no causal link need exist between the
excepted circumstances and the actual loss. For example, in *State Insurance General Manager v Harray* [1973] 1 NZLR 276 the respondent insured's car was damaged in an accident. The appellant insurer refused to
indemnify the insured on the ground that the car was being driven
"whilst . . . in an unsafe condition" in breach of an exception in the policy.
Three tyres on the vehicle had less tread depth than required under the
relevant traffic regulation, but there had been no causal connection
between the worn tyres and the accident. However Roper J stressed that
the authorities are clear that when invoking temporal exception clauses
of this kind, there was no need for an insurer to prove such a connection.
As the Contracts and Commercial Law Reform Committee remarked in
their first report on *Aspects of Insurance Law* (April 1975), para 29:

> This seems to us wrong. Insurers are of course entitled to define the risks in
> respect of which they will indemnify by excluding circumstances that increase
> the risk. It is understandable that they should seek to define exclusions in
> temporal rather than causative terms for it is easier to prove (for example) that
> a vehicle was in an unsafe condition at the relevant time than that the unsafe
> condition caused the accident. But it is unreasonable for insurers to avoid
> liability on the grounds that the risk is increased where the loss results from
> some cause other than the circumstances relied on as increasing the risk.

Consequently the Committee recommended (para 30) that provision be
made to control non-causative exemptions, and this recommendation
has found statutory expression in s 11 of the Insurance Law Reform Act
1977:

11. Certain exclusions forbidden – Where —
   (a) By the provisions of a contract of insurance the circumstances in which the
       insurer is bound to indemnify the insured against loss are so defined as
       to exclude or limit the liability of the insurer to indemnify the insured on
       the happening of certain events or on the existence of certain circumstances;
       and
   (b) In the view of the Court or arbitrator determining the claim of the insured
       the liability of the insurer has been so defined because the happening of
       such events or the existence of such circumstances was in the view of the
       insurer likely to increase the risk of such loss occurring, —
   the insured shall not be disentitled to be indemnified by the insurer by reason
   only of such provisions of the contract of insurance if the insured proves on the
   balance of probability that the loss in respect of which the insured seeks to be
   indemnified was not caused or contributed to by the happening of such events
   or the existence of such circumstances.

There is a presumption in favour of a causal link and the onus of proof is upon the insured to demonstrate on a balance of probability that no such link exists.

Section 11 was successfully relied upon by the insured in *Norwich Winterthur Insurance (NZ) Ltd v Hammond* (1985) 3 ANZ Ins Cas 60-637. The vehicle driven by the insured skidded off the road, which was flooded, on to a river bank where it hit a tree. At the time of the accident the rear tyres of the vehicle were severely worn. The policy excluded the liability of the insurer if the vehicle was being driven in an unsafe condition. On the evidence Heron J found that the insured had discharged the onus of showing that the condition of the rear tyres had not contributed to the accident. In *New Zealand Insurance Co Ltd v Harris* (1990) 6 ANZ Ins Cas 60-952 (CA) a tractor was destroyed by arson while let out on hire. Under the policy the insured warranted that the vehicle would not be let out on hire. Applying s 11 the Court of Appeal held that the insured had discharged the onus of proving that the loss of the tractor was not caused or contributed to by non-compliance with the warranty. Cf *Lotus Manufacturing Co Ltd v Sun Alliance Insurance Ltd* (1987) 4 ANZ Ins Cas 60-782.

An early decision construing s 11 held that it was applicable to a dishonest misstatement at claim stage where the provision of true and accurate information concerning the event insured against was a condition precedent to the liability of the insurer: *Sampson v Gold Star Insurance Co Ltd* [1980] 2 NZLR 742, (although the insurer was held entitled to avoid liability for breach of the insured's common law duty of good faith). Barker J held that the requirement of s 11(b) was satisfied because the provision of false information was, in the view of the insurer, likely to increase the risk. However the false information was given after the loss in question had occurred and so could not have increased the risk of that loss occurring. It is now recognised that the decision *Sampson* is incorrect insofar as it holds that s 11 applies in such a case: see *Vermeulen v SIMU Mutual Assurance Association* (1987) 4 ANZ Ins Cas 60-812.

In the case of liability insurance, however, the conduct of the insured after the primary event giving rise to liability may fall within s 11. In *Nupin Distribution Ltd v Harlick* (1988) 5 ANZ Ins Cas 60-874 the insured Harlick was involved in an accident in which the plaintiff Nupin's trailer and load were damaged. At the time of the accident Harlick admitted liability both to the driver of the Nupin vehicle and a police officer. Almost three years later Harlick submitted a claim form to his insurer in respect of his liability to Nupin. The claim form contained a misstatement (that the Nupin driver had admitted liability) which Harlick knew to be untrue. The insurer repudiated liability on the ground, inter alia, that Harlick had breached the following policy conditions: (1) that notice of any accident be given as soon as possible; (2) that the benefit of the policy is forfeited if the claim is fraudulent or contained a false statement; and (3) that no admission of liability be made without the consent of the insurer. It was held that all three conditions fell within the scope of s 11: the loss was the extent of the insured's liability to a third party, which liability could be influenced by each of the three factors in point. However, Harlick failed to prove that the loss was not caused by or contributed to by the delay in giving notice or by his admission of liability. While his false statement did not contribute to the loss, the position would have been otherwise if the insurer had been lulled into a false sense of security. In the end the insurer was entitled to avoid liability.

An exception or exclusion clause in a policy will be construed strictly (*contra proferentem*) against the insurer as the wording of the exception is that of the insurer: *Skeggs Foods Ltd v General Accident Fire and Life Assurance Corporation Ltd* [1973] 2 NZLR 439; *New Zealand Municipalities Co-operative Insurance Co Ltd v Mount Albert City Council* [1983] NZLR 200, 205.

31.4.4 The premium

The premium is the consideration given by the insured in return for the insurer's undertaking to cover the risks specified in the policy. Usually the premium is in the form of a money payment, but there is no necessity for the consideration to take this form; for example, it could be the liability which a member of a mutual insurance society assumes to contribute towards the funds of the mutual society: *Lion Mutual Marine Insurance Association Ltd v Tucker* (1883) 12 QBD 176, 187. There is no general principle that a contract of insurance does not come into existence until the premium is paid: *Tapa v Attorney-General* [1977] 2 NZLR 435. However, it is common for insurers to stipulate that liability is confined to loss sustained "after payment of premium" or that "no insurance is in force until the premium is paid". The presence of such a provision is the determining factor where a loss occurs before the payment of a premium unless the requirement of pre-payment of the premium is waived by the insurer, or an estoppel can be raised which prevents an insurer from asserting that payment was not made.

An insured may be able to recover the premium payment in certain cases. The premium is generally money paid in consideration of the insurer accepting a certain risk and if the risk has attached even for a short period, there is no right to the repayment of the premium. If there is a total failure of consideration, the premium generally is recoverable by the insured. Where the policy is avoided ab initio by the insurer, the insured may be able to recover the premiums paid. A premium paid by the insured at the time he or she submits the proposal is recoverable if the insurer makes a material alteration in terms already agreed upon when the policy is issued; any qualified acceptance by the insurer is merely a counter offer and does not complete the insurance contract. It should always be borne in mind that where a policy is terminated according to its terms, either by the insurer or the insured, recoverability of the premium will depend upon the provisions of the policy; in the absence of any policy provision covering the consequences attendant upon any breach or termination then recourse must be had to the Contractual Remedies Act 1979. However, most policies do in fact make provision for the refund/forfeiture, in whole or in part, of the premium depending on the circumstances. Where a policy is illegal the rights and obligations of the parties are determined by reference to the Illegal Contracts Act 1970.

31.4.5 Renewal and risk

The insurer is liable only for loss which occurs during the period of the contract of insurance. Life insurance contracts are for a period of years or for a whole life. Despite the alteration in risk through the increasing age or illness of the insured, an insurer cannot decline to renew a life policy. But there is no reason why an insurer should provide any insurance cover if the premium is unpaid. In New Zealand the policy will not lapse so long as the arrears of premium and interest do not exceed the accumulated surrender value, which is applied in payment of the over-due premium: Life Insurance Act 1908, s 64: see infra. If an assured has a life policy with an overseas company, it is unlikely that the contract would be subject to the law of New Zealand and the insured estate might well lose the benefits of the policy if the insured died at a time when the premium was overdue.

Liability insurance and any policy of indemnity, such as fire or marine insurance, are generally contracts for the term of one year which are reviewed, at the option of the insurer, at the end of each successive period. Time of payment of the premium for renewal of insurance is of the essence of the contract and the insurer is not at risk if the premium is unpaid, unless a renewal receipt providing cover during the period the premium is unpaid is used by the insurer. Some insurers allow days of grace for the payment of the premium but if there is no undertaking to provide insurance cover during the days of grace, this concession may amount to nothing more than a promise to renew the insurance for a further period if the premium is paid during the days of grace, no protection being given until the premium is tendered and accepted: *Simpson v Accidental Death* (1857) 2 CB (NS) 257. The days of grace may even be nothing more than an invitation to make an offer of renewal by forwarding the premium. However, whether the tender of the premium is merely an offer by the insured or is the acceptance of an offer of renewal by the insurer, the insured must disclose any change of risk or loss suffered between the due date of payment of the premium and its acceptance by the insurer, otherwise the insurer will have the right of avoidance. If there is such an alteration in circumstances that the insurer is covering a different risk from that originally undertaken, the company is entitled to notification of the alteration before the policy is renewed for a further period. In either a life or an indemnity policy, if there is any alteration in the risk between the time of submitting the proposal and the conclusion of the contract, the insurer must be notified: *Dalgety and Co Ltd v AMP Society* [1908] VLR 481.

The insurer is liable only for damage to the subject matter insured. The insurer is not, unless such is expressly provided for, liable for any consequential loss such as loss of profits. The loss must be due to a fortuitous event and not be such as normally would occur. Even in an "all risks" policy there is no liability for fair wear and tear, inherent vice, the insured's own act, acts done with insured's concurrence or risks which it is not lawful to cover: *British and Foreign Marine Insurance Co Ltd v Gaunt* [1921] 2 AC 41, 57. With the exception of certain provisions of the Accident Compensation Act 1982 as to injuries sustained in the course of commission of an offence or crime, wilfully self-inflicted personal injuries, and suicide, an insured or anyone deriving title through him or her cannot claim compensation or loss due to his or her own wilful misconduct or crime; likewise, an insurer is freed from liability arising through a crime committed by a person entitled to benefit under the policy: *Gray v Barr* [1971] 2 QB 554; *Gardner v Moore* [1984] 1 All ER 1100 (HL). In

Cleaver v Mutual Reserve Fund Life Association [1892]1 QB 147 neither the wife, who had murdered her husband by poisoning, nor her estate was entitled to insurance moneys payable on his or her death. But the insured can recover if the loss is due to the act of some stranger without his or her knowledge or consent: *Midland Insurance Co v Smith* (1881) 6 QBD 561. The insured can also recover where the fortuitous event causing the loss arises through his or her own negligence or through the negligence or crime of a stranger: *Samuel v Dumas* [1924] AC 431. Thus, in *Harris v Poland* [1941] 1 KB 462; [1941] 1 All ER 204, the plaintiff, to prevent her jewels and bank notes being stolen, had hidden them under coal in the grate and later lit a fire and damaged them. It was held that she could recover for the damage done by fire.

Chapter 32

THE CLAIM AND ITS CONSEQUENCES

SUMMARY

32.1   THE CLAIM
32.2   SUBROGATION
32.3   DOUBLE INSURANCE AND CONTRIBUTION

32.1 THE CLAIM

32.1.1 Onus of proof

The onus is upon the insured to prove that he or she has sustained a loss within the terms of the policy; that is, the insured must show, on a balance of probabilities, that the event covered by the policy has occurred, that loss has been suffered by him or her as a result, and that the event is the dominant, effective or operative cause of the loss. Where the insurer has expressed its undertaking in general terms and has qualified a part of the undertaking by means of exception clauses, it is sufficient for the insured to bring himself or herself prima facie within the terms of the policy, leaving it to the insurers to prove that the case in fact falls within an exception. However, where the language used is such that the whole undertaking is qualified, the insured must bring himself or herself within the terms of the qualified undertaking. See, for example, *Munro Brice and Co v War Risks Association* [1918] 2 KB 78, 88; *Long v Colonial Mutual Life Assurance Society Ltd* [1931] NZLR 528.

32.1.2 Causation – *causa proxima non remota spectatur*

The Latin maxim above literally translated means "it is the immediate cause, not the remote one, which is considered". Among the many factors which may finally bring about the loss, the direct, dominant and efficient cause is the one which will decide whether the insurer is liable or not. In deciding the immediate cause of the loss, the standard of judgment is that of the ordinary, reasonable and prudent person, not that of an expert or

481

specialist; in other words, the standard is that of "the prudent insurer". An overly technical approach to the question of proximate cause must be avoided: *Techni-Chemicals Products Co Ltd v South British Insurance Co Ltd* [1977] 1 NZLR 311.

Lord Shaw stressed in *Leyland Shipping Co Ltd v Norwich Union Fire Insurance Society Ltd* [1916] AC 350, 369, that in the law of insurance the overriding principle is the need to examine the contract as a whole to ascertain what the parties really meant, ie, what they must have had in their minds when they spoke of cause in the contract. He said, "the chain of causation is a handy expression . . . causation is not a chain, but a net . . . the cause which is truly proximate is that which is proximate in efficiency." In the *Leyland* case a ship was torpedoed at sea, brought to harbour, and then sank at her moorings, becoming á total wreck. It was held by the House of Lords that the proximate cause of the sinking was the torpedoing, and that liability for this had been excepted by the terms of the policy. The proximate cause rule may, however, be excluded by the use of expressions such as "directly or indirectly caused by": *Coxe v Employers Liability Assurance Co Ltd* [1916] 2 KB 629. In this case the liability of the insurer, who had insured a cargo of coffee against seizure and the consequences of hostilities, depended on whether the wreck of the ship and the destruction of the cargo was due to a lighthouse being put out of action as a result of hostilities or whether it was due to "a peril of the sea". It was held that the proximate cause of the loss was the vessel being off course and striking rocks – a peril of the sea.

In *Samuel v Dumas* [1924] AC 431, a master and the crew deliberately scuttled a ship by opening the sea-cocks and boring holes in the sides. It was held that, although the ship foundered through the flooding of the vessel by the sea and this was the final link in the chain of causation, the dominant and operative event, the proximate cause in the chain of events leading to the loss, was the scuttling of the vessel and not "a peril of the sea".

In *Everett v London Assurance* (1865) 19 CB (NS) 126, a building insured against "such loss or damage as should or might be occasioned by fire" was damaged by concussion from a powder magazine half a mile away, which had caught fire. It was held that the concussion and not fire was the proximate cause of the damage.

However, obiter dicta, various cases and custom in fire insurance business have made it standard practice for fire insurance policies to cover consequential damage arising through bona fide and justifiable efforts to minimise loss by fire. Thus, loss through damage by water or chemical fire extinguishers, resultant damage, or even theft where furniture has been thrown out of windows, and the demolition of neighbouring buildings to prevent the fire spreading, are covered by a fire policy.

Injurious consequences following an accident will be considered to be proximately caused thereby unless some other event breaks the chain of causation. In *Travellers' Insurance Co v Robbins* 27 US App 547 (1894), where the insured suffered an injury from which he developed tetanus, and as a consequence of the tetanus became insane and then took his own life, the injury was held to be the proximate cause of the insured's death. It appears that if death is the final result of a series of events consequential on the insured risk taking place without the intervention of some independent cause, such insured risk will be held to be the proximate cause of death. Where an insured, dazed as a result of an accident, fell into water and died, death was held to have been caused by the accident: *Smith v Cornhill Insurance* (1938) 54 TLR 869.

The principle of proximate cause does not mean that there can be no step between the cause and the consequence. For example, in *Boiler Inspection and Insurance Co of Canada v Sherwin Williams Company of Canada Ltd* [1951] AC 319, certain equipment, including a steam jacketed bleacher tank, was insured against loss if directly damaged by an accident while the equipment was on the property of the insured. Loss by fire as an indirect result of an accident was expressly excluded. While the bleacher tank was being used to bleach turpentine, very heavy pressure developed and the door of the tank was blown off; a large body of gas escaped and on being mixed with the air ignited, exploded and shattered the building. It was held that the bursting of the tank was the dominant and proximate cause of the damage and that it was irrelevant that the fumes had to be mixed with air to become explosive or that some source of ignition was required.

32.1.3 Notice of loss

Insurance policies almost invariably require notice of any loss sustained by the insured to be given to the insured within a specified time and in a prescribed manner. Moreover it is common to find a clause requiring an insured to commence any legal action in respect of a claim within a prescribed period on pain of forfeiture of any possible benefit under the policy. At common law a failure to comply strictly with such clauses could be fatal to a claim: *Hollister v Accident Association of New Zealand* (1887) 5 NZLR 49. However, as a result of s 9 of the Insurance Law Reform Act 1977, time limits on claims under contracts of insurance do not bind the insured as tightly as previously; in the case of life policies no time limits bind the insured's representatives where the claim relates to the death of the insured, and, in respect of other insurance contracts, the insurer is only relieved of liability to the extent that he or she has been prejudiced by the non-compliance by the insured with the relevant provision: cf *Nupin Distribution Ltd v Harlick* (1988) 5 ANZ Ins Cas 60-874. *Bland v South British Insurance Co Ltd* (1990) 6 ANZ Ins Cas 60-998.

32.1.4 Settlement of claims

At one time it was common practice for insurers to provide in their policies that any dispute between the parties was not justifiable by the Courts unless the issue had first been submitted to arbitration. However, it is provided in s 8 of the Insurance Law Reform Act 1977 that arbitration clauses contained in a policy are not binding on an insured and that the insured may initiate Court proceedings immediately upon the insurers' rejection of any claim. Such a clause is only binding on an insured where it is contained in an agreement which is entered into *after* a difference or dispute has arisen between the insurer and the insured; an agreement to arbitrate entered into after a dispute has arisen is more likely to be freely entered into and to be the product of an informed choice based on factors such as relative costs and length of delays.

Actions on or in relation to contracts of insurance must be tried before a Judge without a jury: Insurance Law Reform Act 1977, s 12(1).

32.1.5 Fraudulent claims

In discharge of the duty of good faith the insured, in making a claim under the policy, must not knowingly make any false statement or withhold material information. At common law there must be an intention to deceive before a claim can be characterised as fraudulent. It is not necessary that the intention be to deceive the insurer. In *Sampson v Gold Star Insurance Co Ltd* [1980] 2 NZLR 742 the insured's intention in falsely describing the cause of an accident was to assist the insurer in pursuing a claim against a third party. The essential obligation is one of honesty: *Vermeulen v SIMU Mutual Assurance Association* (1987) 4 ANZ Ins Cas 60-812, 74,987. An innocent error cannot constitute a breach of the duty of utmost good faith: *Kinred v State Insurance General Manager* (1989) 5 ANZ Ins Cas 60-923.

Invariably insurers are not content to rely upon the insured's duty of good faith in making a claim and make express provision for the forfeiture of any benefit under the policy where the facts relating to a claim are not fully or accurately disclosed. A number of cases import a requirement of dishonesty or moral obliquity into the wording of the forfeiture clause: see *National Insurance Co Ltd v Van Gameren* [1986] 2 NZLR 374; *Lotus Manufacturing Co Ltd v Sun Alliance Insurance Ltd* (1987) 4 ANZ Ins Cas 60-782. The most influential has been *FAME Insurance Co Ltd v McFadyen* [1961] NZLR 1070 where a motor policy provided that the policy became void if "in any statement of declaration made in support of any claim there is any untruth or suppression by or on behalf of the Insured". Following a motor accident the insured submitted a Notice of Accident form which required the names and addresses of any witnesses to the accident. The insured failed to name two passengers in the vehicle as witnesses. Barrowclough J said that had the parties contracted on the basis of any inaccuracy or incorrectness in a statement made in support of the claim then the insurer would have been entitled to avoid the policy. But the expressions "untruth or suppression" and "inaccuracy or incorrectness" were not synonymous. The former expression generally connoted moral obliquity, and in the present case the insurer had not discharged the burden of proving this element.

The simple wording of the policy may entitle the insurer to avoid, whether the insured was acting in good faith or not. In *Purcell v State Insurance Office* (1982) 2 ANZ Ins Cas 60-812 one Saunders, the father-in-law of the insured, crashed the insured's vehicle and falsely stated in answer to a question in the claim form required to be completed by the driver that he had not consumed intoxicating liquor within six hours of the accident. The insured in signing the claim form was unaware of Saunders' falsehood. The insurer sought to avoid liability by invoking a condition of the policy which provided for forfeiture of all benefit under the policy should "any false declaration or statement" be made or used in support of a claim. An action by the insured on the policy failed both in the District Court and on appeal to Prichard J in the High Court. Although the trial Judge found "moral obliquity" to have been present in so far as the insured pressed his claim even after the falsehood came to his knowledge, Prichard J preferred to base his decision simply on the operation of the forfeiture clause. Undeniably a false statement was made and was used in support of the claim, therefore the forfeiture clause applied to exclude liability on the part of the insurer.

Similarly in *Vermeulen v SIMU Mutual Assurance Assocation* (1987) 4 ANZ Ins Cas 60-812 the insured under a motor policy denied having drunk any intoxicating liquor within six hours before the accident in question. This was incorrect; he had drunk two beers only fifteen minutes earlier. However, the Court accepted that he was not acting dishonestly: at the time of completing the claim form he was confused and disorientated as a result of concussion. The policy provided:

> When proposing insurance or making a claim, all statements are to be truthful. If any material statement is substantially incorrect this Policy will not operate.

Following *McFadyen* the insured's denial of consuming alcohol was not "untruthful", since he was not acting dishonestly. But the statement was material and substantially incorrect, and therefore the insurer was entitled to avoid.

An insurer is entitled to avoid liability for a claim where the insured has breached the duty of good faith by making a false statement in support of the claim, even though the insured may in fact have suffered a genuine loss. However in the Australian case of *GRE Insurance Ltd v Ormsby* (1982) 2 ANZ Ins Cas 60-472 a distinction was drawn between a valid claim supported by false evidence and a fraudulent claim. There the insured was, for the purposes of the appeal to the Supreme Court of South Australia, assumed to have adduced false evidence in order to bolster a claim conceded by the insurer otherwise to be entirely valid. It was held that the false evidence did not taint the claim. It is unlikely that this decision will be followed in New Zealand. In *New Zealand Insurance Co Ltd v Forbes* (1988) 5 ANZ Ins Cas 60-871 the Court of Appeal described it as "an exceptional case decided on its own facts and on a concession" and did not regard it as a statement of principle.

32.1.6 Quantum recoverable—indemnity

Contracts of indemnity insurance may be distinguished from contracts of contingency insurance. As Megarry VC explained in *Medical Defence Union Ltd v Dept of Trade* [1979] 2 WLR 686, 690:

> Indemnity insurance provides an indemnity against loss, as in a fire policy or a marine policy on a vessel. Within the limits of the policy the measure of the loss is the measure of the payment. Contingency insurance provides no indemnity but instead payment upon a contingent event, as in a life policy or a personal injury policy. The contractual sum is paid if the life ends or the limb is lost, irrespective of the value of the life or the limb.

Life insurance, accident insurance and most types of medical insurance can be classified as contingency insurances as the amount recoverable under such policies is not limited, nor gauged, by reference to the actual loss of the insured; the contract simply secures the payment of a sum of money on the happening of a specified event.

Conversely, with contracts of indemnity the insurer is under an obligation to make good the *actual* loss that the insured has sustained from the accepted risk: *Falcon Investment Corporation (NZ) Ltd v State Insurance General Manager* [1975] 1 NZLR 520, 522. A contract of indemnity provides such compensation as will restore the other party, as far as money can do so, to his or her original position, but it should not improve it. The amount of compensation will never exceed the amount for which the property is insured, but it may be less than that amount: *Aubrey Film Productions Ltd v Graham* [1960] 2 Lloyd's Rep 101. The reason for this is that the amount of insurance specified in an indemnity policy does not necessarily represent the measure of indemnity but merely indicates the maximum amount for which the insurer will be liable, the insured must still prove the extent of his or her loss. In each case the proper measure of indemnity is a matter of fact and degree. In the case of fire insurance over household effects the measure of indemnity will prima facie be the market value of the property lost or destroyed at the time and place of the loss: *Dawson v Monarch Insurance Co of New Zealand Ltd* [1977] 1 NZLR 372, 377. In some instances it may be difficult to identify the relevant market. In *Legal & General Insurance Australia Ltd v Eather* (1986) 6 NSWLR 390 jewellery insured under a multi-risks policy was stolen from a motor car. The jewellery had a specified value under the policy of some $27,000 being the valuation obtained from a valuer for the purpose of the insurance. This is the amount which would have been required to replace the jewellery from a dealer. Kirby P, dissenting on this point, held that the indemnity to which the insured was entitled was the amount which a dealer would have paid for the jewellery. By virtue of a dealer's mark-up of 100 per cent the amount was approximately half the replacement value. However the majority of the New South Wales Court of Appeal disagreed, stating that the relevant market was not what a dealer would have paid but what an ordinary person would have bought or sold the jewellery for, viz the full replacement value. Cf *Young v Commercial Union General Insurance Co Ltd* (1988) 5 ANZ Ins Cas 60-875.

In the case of stock in trade, the market value of the insured goods at the place and time of loss is the cost to the insured of purchasing replacement goods. If there is no ready market, then market value is assessed at the price of replacement at the place of manufacture plus the cost of carriage to the insured plus, if the insured is neither the manufacturer nor the importer, the profit those persons would have charged: *Haighi's Persian Trading Co Ltd v General Accident Insurance Co New Zealand Ltd* (1990) 6 ANZ Ins Cas 61-003.

As regards buildings the measure of indemnity may be calculated by reference to the market value of the destroyed premises, but commonly policies give the insured the option of reinstatement. The insured is not entitled to recover the cost of reinstatement, which invariably exceeds the market value of the building, unless rebuilding actually takes place: *Kerr v State Insurance General Manager* (1987) 4 ANZ Ins Cas 60-781; cf *Cannell v Commercial Union General Insurance Co Ltd* (1985) 3 ANZ Ins Cas 60-666.

Where the basis of assessment is the cost of reinstatement an allowance for betterment may be made, that is, in the absence of a policy condition to the contrary, some adjustment must be made to account for the fact that any building or article restored to its original state will almost inevitably be an improvement on the building or article as it existed at the time of the occurrence of the insured peril, as new materials will have been used to replace old.

A valued policy may be effected which provides for the payment of a fixed sum in the event of the total destruction or loss of the subject matter of insurance, irrespective of whether there has been any fluctuation in value, either up or down. The fact that the policy specified the value of an item of property does not necessarily mean that the policy is a valued policy: see *Young v Commercial Union General Insurance Co Ltd* (1988) 5 ANZ Ins Cas 60-875. The value stated is conclusive in the absence of fraud: *Burnand v Rodocanachi, Sons and Co* (1882) 7 App Cas 333, 335. Where a partial loss occurs, it was decided in *Elcock v Thomson* [1949] 2 KB 755 that the agreed value should also be applied, the insurer being liable for that proportion of the agreed value as is represented by the depreciation in the actual value of the subject matter; that is, the fraction of the actual loss to the actual value is applied as a fraction of the agreed valuation.

The quantum payable in respect of any loss is, of course, always subject to the terms and conditions of the policy. The policy may contain an excess clause under which the insured must accept liability for a specified amount of the loss; for example, the first $50 of each and every claim. Moreover, if a policy contains an *average* clause, then subject to ss 15 and 16 of the Insurance Law Reform Act 1985, the insured will only be entitled to recover the full amount of the loss if the property is insured for its full value at the time of the loss. If the loss is partial and he or she has not insured for the full value, the insured is deemed under a policy "subject to average" to be his or her own insurer for the difference in value and must bear a saleable proportion of the loss accordingly. Finally policies on goods frequently are transacted on a "new for old" basis; that is, the insurer undertakes in the event of the loss or destruction of the goods to pay the replacement, rather than the market value, and the insured may replace the lost or destroyed goods by equivalent new goods. Generally see AA Tarr, "The Measure of Indemnity under Property Insurance Policies" (1983) 2 *Canterbury Law Review* 107.

32.2 SUBROGATION

Subrogation is a doctrine derived from Roman Law, by means of which one person can "step into the legal shoes of another". It is the substitution of one person for another under such circumstances that the person substituted acquires the rights of that other in respect of a particular subject matter. The doctrine applies outside of the law of insurance, for example, to guarantors. The doctrine of subrogation allows an insurer who has paid for a total loss, either of the whole or, in the case of goods, of any apportionable part of the subject-matter insured, to take over the interests of the insured in whatever may remain of the subject matter so paid for. As a consequence, the insurer is thereby subrogated to all the rights and remedies of the insured in respect of that subject matter as from the time of the happening causing the loss.

Lord Blackburn, in *Burnand v Rodocanachi* (1882) 7 App Cas 333, 339:

> The general rule of law (it is obvious justice) is that where there is a contract of indemnity (it matters not whether it is a marine policy or a policy against

fire on land, or any other contract of indemnity), and a loss happens, anything which reduces or diminishes that loss reduces or diminishes the amount which the indemnifier is bound to pay; and if the indemnifier has already paid it then, if anything which diminishes the loss comes into the hands of the person to whom he or she has paid it, it becomes an equity that the person who has already paid the full indemnity is entitled to be recouped by having that amount back.

Suppose that A insured his or her home with the X Insurance Company. If the local electric supply authority, in pursuance of its powers, negligently connects up A's house and the house is destroyed by fire as the result of such negligence, A would be entitled to claim against the insurance company or against the electric supply authority. If, in fact, he or she claims; under the policy and the X Company pays the indemnity due by it, then the X company is entitled to bring an action in A's name against the supply authority. The chief rules applicable to this doctrine may be set out as follows:

(a) The principles applicable to subrogation are practically the same in fire and marine insurance; both of these are contracts of indemnity, but there is no right of subrogation in life assurance, which is not a contract of indemnity.

(b) Unless an insurer stipulates in the policy that it is entitled to exercise its rights of subrogation before making payment the full indemnity payable under the policy will have to be paid before the insurer commences proceedings against the third party. Payment made after the issue of the writ, but before the hearing, is insufficient to make the doctrine applicable: *Page v Scottish Insurance Corporation* (1929) 98 LJKB 308. A person suffering damage is entitled to full indemnity against this loss and any costs involved in asserting his or her claim: *National Fire v McLaren* (1886)12 Ont R 682. The right of the insured to full compensation from the third party responsible is not prejudiced by the doctrine of subrogation. A claim for full compensation may be made in the name of the insured and the insurer is entitled to be repaid only the money it has already paid out; the insured is entitled to any additional amount that is recovered: *Yorkshire Insurance Co Ltd v Nisbet Shipping Co Ltd* [1962] 2 QB 330; *Lucas v Exports Credits Guarantee Department* [1974] 1 WLR 909. But if the insurer takes an assignment of the insured's rights or if the insured has served notice of abandonment on the insurer, the latter is entitled to retain all that it receives through subsequent proceedings or dealings with the property insured: *Compania Colombiana de Seguros v Pacific Steam Navigation Co* [1965] 1 QB 101.

(c) If the insured recovers compensation from some third party and later obtains compensation for the sum lost under the policy of insurance, the amount received from the third party must be taken into account in adjusting the rights of the insurer and the insured. The latter may have to refund to the insurer the whole amount he or she has received from the insurer.

(d) If the insured receives the amount under the policy and subsequently recovers compensation for the loss from a third party, the insured must repay the insurer the amount so received out of the compensation moneys: *Castellain v Preston* (1883) 11 QBD 380. The insured will also have to reimburse the insurer if a third party is legally bound to make the damage good, as where a tenant has to repair premises occupied by him or her: *Darrell v Tibbitts* (1880) 5 QBD 560.

(e) The insured is, in any event, entitled to full compensation for the loss, and the insurer's right to reimbursement of moneys paid to the insured is subordinate to this right of full indemnity. An insured who has received compensation from his or her insurer must not do anything to prejudice any claim against the person responsible for the loss, but is still entitled to control proceedings for the establishment of this claim if he or she has not been fully indemnified by the insurer: *Commercial Union Assurance Co v Lister* (1874) LR 9 Ch 483; *Arthur Barnett Ltd v National Insurance Co of NZ Ltd* [1965] NZLR 874, 882. Once the insured has received full indemnity from the insurer, the insurer is in control of proceedings against the third party. However, this control does not extend to stopping the insured from bringing action against the person responsible, if the insurer decides not to sue. As the insurer's liability is limited to the extent of the indemnity payable he or she is entitled to require ex gratia payments or any goods returned where they have been stolen or, possibly, seized by an enemy, to be taken into account when assessing the amount of compensation to be paid.

(f) An insurer is bound by any contract affecting the property or risk made by the insured with any third party. If such contract was not disclosed to the insurer at the time of taking out the insurance, it might well be a ground for avoiding the contract for non-disclosure of a material fact: *Guthrie House Ltd v Cornhill Insurance Co Ltd* (1982) 2 ANZ Ins Cas 60-466. An insurer is likewise bound by any admission of liability or any settlement, compromise or waiver of rights made or granted by the insured in favour of the person responsible for the loss or any other person: *Phoenix Assurance Co v Spooner* [1905] 2 KB 753, 756. If a settlement or waiver takes place before payment by the insurer it will be freed from liability to the insured: *Fidelity Co v Gas Co* (1892) 150 Pa 8; if it takes place after payment by the insurer to the insured, the insurer can claim damages against the insured for the consequent loss: *Boag v Standard Marine* [1937] 2 KB 113, 128. Accordingly, an insured who has brought an action against a third party for compensation should obtain the consent of the insurer before he or she settles the action. Where the insured unilaterally compromises a claim against the third party to the prejudice of the insurer, the third party cannot rely upon the release given by the insured if the third party has notice, actual or constructive, of the insurer's interest: *Morganite Ceramic Fibre Pty Ltd v Sola Basic Australia Ltd* (1987) 11 NSWLR 189.

(g) The doctrine of subrogation may bring totally unanticipated financial disaster upon an employee. For example, an employee who has been held to be negligent in the performance of work for which he or she was employed, may find that he or she has to repay the employer's insurer the amount paid out by it to meet the employer's liability for the act of the employee: *Lister v Romford Ice and Cold Storage Co Ltd* [1957] AC 555; cf: *Morris v Ford Motor Co* [1973] QB 492. In England it was recognised that the exercise of subrogation rights in these circumstances could lead to industrial disharmony, and the insurance companies entered into a gentlemen's agreement not to take advantage of the decision in *Listers* case and to desist from bringing actions of this type against employees.

(h) It is not uncommon for insurers to agree not to exercise rights of subrogation in certain circumstances. In New Zealand the majority of motor vehicle insurers subscribe to a knock-for-knock agreement. This means that in the event of motor accident involving two motorists insured with different insurers, each insurer agrees to indemnify its own insured irrespective of who is at fault.

(i) Express subrogation clauses are common in policies of insurance. Such clauses may exclude or modify some of the conditions surrounding the exercise of subrogation rights at common law. For example, subrogation rights may be vested in the insurer before indemnification and the right to control proceedings or compromise proceedings may be at the insurer's discretion. Generally, see J Birds, "Contractual Subrogation in Insurance", [1979] JBL 124.

32.3 DOUBLE INSURANCE AND CONTRIBUTION

Double insurance exists where, at the time of the loss, two legally enforceable policies cover the same interest in the subject matter against the same risk: *North British and Mercantile Insurance Co Ltd v Public Mutual Insurance Co of the New Zealand* [1935] NZLR 678, 683; *Boys v State Insurance General Manager* [1980] 1 NZLR 87, 91-92.

Where the aggregate amount of the policies exceeds the amount necessary to indemnify the insured for his or her loss, the insurer is, in the absence of a condition to the contrary, entitled to call upon any of his or her insurers to pay the insured in full and the fact that the others are also liable will afford that insurer no defence. But the insurer who has paid out can call upon any others to contribute their share of the loss and pay their proportion of the amount already paid under the first policy. The principle of contribution applies to all types of indemnity insurance and the co-insurers must apportion the liability between themselves. In computing the contribution payable the Courts will be guided by what is equitable in the circumstances of the case, for as Kitto J put the matter in *Albion Insurance Co Ltd v Government Insurance Office of New South Wales* (1969) 121 CLR 342, 351, ". . . contribution must be based upon reason, justice and fairness". The methods of assessing contribution are discussed by AA Tarr, "Double Insurance", [1982] NZLJ 136.

Insurers have sought to exclude, limit or qualify their liability where double insurance has been effected. For example, a clause may absolve an insurer from liability should other insurance covering the same risk be in existence or be effected during the period of cover, unless the insurer is notified in writing of that other insurance. Alternatively, a policy may endeavour to restrict the insurer's liability to the loss in excess of that covered by the other insurance: *State Fire Insurance General Manager v Liverpool and London and Globe Insurance Co Ltd* [1952] NZLR 5, 29. A third permutation would be a clause which restricts the insurer's liability to a rateable proportion of any sum payable in the event of any loss; the introduction of such a clause into the insurer's policy prevents the insured from recovering full satisfaction from any one insurer and the insured is entitled only to a pro rata payment from each: *Commercial Union Assurance Co Ltd v Hayden* [1977] QB 804, 819.

Chapter 33

ASSIGNMENT OF POLICIES

33.1 LIFE POLICIES

An assignment of a life insurance policy is an assignment of the right to collect moneys falling due under the policy on the assignor's reaching a certain age or dying. At common law the assignor must have had an insurable interest when he or she took out the policy but the assignee did not require an insurable interest to support his or her claim; such insurable interest by the assignor is no longer required: Insurance Law Reform Act 1985, s 6.

A life policy is a chose in action and may be assigned by transfer indorsed upon the policy in the form set out in the Eighth Schedule to the Life Insurance Act 1908. The transfer must be signed by both the assignor and assignee and upon being registered by the company the policy is absolutely vested in the assignee who may sue on it in his or her own name. The assignment (unless it is made to the company) is not valid until it is registered: Life Insurance Act 1908, s 43.

If the assignment is upon trust, the trust must be effected by way of declaration in some separate instrument.

Where there is an equitable assignment of the policy, the assignment is registered by leaving the policy and assignment with the company which indorses the policy to that effect. The giving of notice of the assignment to the insurer is essential and is a condition precedent to the right to sue. An equitable assignment may also be created by the deposit of the policy with the assignee. If notice is not given, any payment by the insurer in good faith will be good against the assignee.

By the Life Insurance Amendment Act 1920, s 2, it is provided that where the policyholder has assigned a policy on his or her own life to his or her wife, or vice versa, and the assignee has died in the lifetime of the policyholder without having disposed of such policy by will and the sum assured exclusive of bonuses, or the premiums actually paid on the policy do not, at the date of the death of the assignee, exceed $9,000, such policy reverts to and vests in the surviving husband or wife as the case may be.

The Life Insurance Amendment Act 1920 also provides that the company in such a case may, without requiring probate of the will, where the policyholder has made a will, make a written declaration signed by the secretary that the executor of such will or the person entitled under the will to the policy is the holder of the policy. The company, however, may require probate of the will to be taken out.

As life policies do not require an insurable interest at inception or at the time of making the claim and are not policies of indemnity, there is no personal relationship between the assignee and the insurer. Consequently the insurer cannot validly object to any legally effective assignment.

33.2 MARINE INSURANCE

The Marine Insurance Act 1908, s 16, provides that where an insured assigns his or her interest in the subject matter, the insured does not transfer his or her rights under the policy unless it is so agreed. A marine policy may be assigned by indorsement or in any other customary manner before or after loss: s 51. No question of consent arises as the reputation of the assignee is of no importance to the insurer. A marine policy is a transferable interest. But the interest must be transferred before or at the time the original owner disposes of the subject matter of the insurance. An insured who has no insurable interest in the subject matter cannot assign the policy: s 52.

33.3 FIRE INSURANCE

The basic rule is that a contract of fire insurance is a personal contract between insurer and insured whereby the insurer undertakes to indemnify the insured in respect of *his or her* loss in the event of a fire and, as such, the contract is not one which runs with the land so as to pass the benefit on it to an assignee of the original owner, or which is so connected up with the subject matter of the insurance as to be transferred by the mere transfer of the subject matter: *Budhia v Wellington City Corporation* [1976]1 NZLR 766, 768. Therefore, for there to be a valid assignment of a fire policy the consent of the insurer must be obtained, or there must be a transfer of it by operation of law.

First, consider assignment with the consent of the insurer. Here it is doubtful whether "assignment" is the appropriate label to affix to the transaction at all. The "assignment" with the assent of the insurer may result in the creation of a new contract between insurer and the so-called "assignee"; that is, while the new contract may contain all the terms and conditions of the original contract it may constitute novation as distinct from an assignment. The advantage of novation lies in the fact that the insurer cannot rely on the acts of the original insured to claim that the policy is vitiated and hence that there is no liability to recompense the assignee. Under an assignment the assignee takes subject to the equities and the insurer is entitled to raise as against the assignee any defence which he or she would have available against the assignor. However, it must not be thought that every assignment with the consent of the insurer is, in reality, a novation. In *Mercantile Finance Corporation Ltd v New Zealand Insurance Co Ltd* [1932] NZLR 1107 the point was made that the *mere fact* that an insurer consents to the assignment of a policy or to the substitution of another insured for the original party does not constitute a new contract and does not prevent the insurer from afterwards asserting that the policy had already been avoided at the date of the assignment. The giving of consent does not stop the insurer from claiming subsequently that the policy was void ab initio or when assigned. Therefore the benefit of a fire policy may be transferred with the consent of the insurer; the legal classification of this transaction may be an assignment or a novation. If the transaction amounts to an assignment the assignee takes subject to any rights that the insurer has against the assignor and the assignor remains liable to perform his or her obligations under the contract of insurance. If the transaction amounts to a novation a new contract comes into being whereby the insurer releases the original insured who, in turn, undertakes the liability of the party released. As is plain from the *Mercantile Finance Corporation* case something more than the mere substitution of one person for another is required; namely, there must be the concurrence of this substitution with an intention or animus novandi that the original contract be discharged by a new one. The presence, or absence, of this mental element is determined by reference to the facts of the particular case.

Second, transfer of a contract of fire insurance by operation of law falls to be considered. This issue arises in connection with the sale and purchase of land and the relationship between vendor and purchaser during the period between the making of the contract of sale and the purchaser taking possession. In the absence of any express agreement to the contrary, both equitable ownership and risk pass to the purchaser on the formation of the contract of sale, and the purchaser must take a conveyance of the property and must pay the full contract price for it even if the property has been damaged or destroyed after the contract has been entered into: *Carly v Farrelly* [1975] 1 NZLR 356. Ordinarily the vendor's insurer would not be bound by an agreement between vendor and purchaser that an existing policy of insurance continue for the benefit of the purchaser, unless the consent of the insurer was first obtained. However, s 13(1) of the Insurance Law Reform Act 1985 now confers upon the purchaser a statutory right to the benefit of any insurance on the property taken out by the vendor. Section 13(1) provides as follows:

> During the period between –
> (a) The making of the contract for the sale of land and all or any fixtures thereon, and
> (b) The purchaser taking possession of the land and fixtures, or final settlement, whichever is the sooner—
> any policy of insurance maintained by the vendor in respect of any damage to or destruction of any part of the land or fixtures shall, in respect of the land and fixtures agreed to be sold and to the extent that the purchaser is not entitled to be indemnified under any other policy of insurance, enure for the benefit of the purchaser as well as for the vendor, and the purchaser shall be entitled to

be indemnified by the insurer under the policy in the same manner and to the same extent as the vendor would have been if there had been no contract of sale:

Provided that nothing in this subsection shall oblige an insurer to pay more in total under a policy of insurance than it would have had to pay if there had been no contract of sale.

The insurer is not obliged to pay more in total under the policy than it would have had to pay if there had been no contract of sale, and the purchaser must first look to any contract of insurance he or she may have effected in respect of the land and fixtures. The vendor's insurer is the "backstop" in the event of the purchaser being uninsured during this period, and obviously if the vendor is uninsured then the purchaser does not have this protection. The Act does not overlook complications that may arise through double insurance; for example, where the purchaser takes out his or her own insurance, the purchaser's policy may include a term avoiding the cover if the purchaser is otherwise entitled to an indemnity. It would be paradoxical if the statutory extension of a vendor's insurance cover were to vitiate insurance cover specifically arranged by the purchaser. Consequently, the Insurance Law Reform Act 1985, s 14, provides that a purchaser will be covered by any policy arranged by the purchaser notwithstanding that the policy includes a term purporting to avoid it for other insurance.

Other subsections to s 13 tie up some loose ends. For example, it is no defence for a vendor's insurer to reject a purchaser's claim because the vendor has suffered no loss in that he or she has been paid the purchase price: s 13(2)(a). Where, pursuant to a vendor's insurance policy, insurance monies for loss or damage to the land or fixtures are payable to a third person such as the vendor's mortgagee, then the purchase price payable under the contract of sale shall be reduced by the amount so payable to that person: s 13(3). It is possible to contract out of the obligations imposed by s 13, as subs (5) of that section provides that it shall not apply to the extent that the purchaser and vendor under a contract of sale expressly agree at any time.

Section 13 affords much needed protection to purchasers who are not aware of the common law rules as to passing of risk. The palliative of an action against the solicitor who failed to advise the client-purchaser of the need for insurance is both uncertain and subject to the delays of litigation: see *Fox v Everingham and Howard* (1984) 3 ANZ Ins Cases 60-547. Of course, in affording the benefit of a vendor's insurance to a purchaser, the insurer is forced, for a short time, to insure a risk that it is unable to assess; that is, because it must take the purchaser as he or she is even though it might otherwise choose to refuse to issue a policy to that person. However, the need to mitigate the common law outweighs this consideration and, in any event, the insurer's difficulties should be minimal as it is unlikely that the purchaser will damage the property in the short time for which the insurer would be liable to cover him.

Section 13 deals with the situation where the risk has already passed to the purchaser. Where a loss occurs before the risk passes, for example, before the contract of purchase and sale is concluded, the vendor may assign to the purchaser the right of indemnity which lies against the insurer, but not the right to reinstatement which is personal to the insured, ie the vendor: *Bryant v Primary Industries Insurance Co Ltd* [1990] 2 NZLR 142 (CA).

Chapter 34

REINSURANCE

SUMMARY

34.1   DEFINITION
34.2   DIFFERENCES

34.1 DEFINITION

Reinsurance may be defined as the insurance of contractual liabilities, incurred under the contracts of direct insurance or reinsurance. The notion behind reinsurance is the desire of an insurer to lay off part of the risk it has undertaken and reinsurance is in effect a means whereby the original insurer, who has underwritten direct business, distributes its potential liability by giving off part of its risks to another insurer (the reinsurer) with the object of reducing the amount of its possible loss. Some direct insurers reinsure other insurers, whilst other reinsurers contract nothing but reinsurance business.

As in any other contract of insurance one party, the insurer, promises that on the occurrence of a certain specified event it will either indemnify the other party, the insured, for any financial losses it may sustain, or pay to it a certain sum, and in return the insured agrees to pay the insurer an ascertainable amount known as a premium.

The direct or original insurer is sometimes known as the ceding company (passing to another insurer part of a risk or liability) and the other party being known as the reinsurer. The reinsurer may in turn reinsure the contract then being known as a retrocession with the ceding company being the retrocedent and the second reinsurer being the retrocessionaire.

34.2 DIFFERENCES

Reinsurance contracts differ from other classes of insurance contracts in three main ways:

495

1   An insurer contracts with a member of the public whereas a reinsurance contract is between two insurers.
2   The subject matter of insurance is some property or personal benefit exposed to loss or damage or some potential legal liability. A reinsurer only becomes indirectly interested in such primary losses insofar as it has undertaken to compensate the reinsured for the payments made.
3   All reinsurance contracts are contracts of indemnity whereas this is not necessarily the case for other insurance contracts, for example, life and accident policies.

The reinsurance market, sometimes in contrast to the insurance market, is truly international. Reinsurance enables domestic insurers to spread losses internationally. Clearly the most common reason why insurance companies fail is because of an unprovided increase in claims. This may occur for many reasons including the random occurrence of one or more very large individual losses or fluctuation of annual aggregate claims experienced around the mean. Reinsurance offers protection against such problems and enables insurers to deal much more flexibly in the market place. In short it spreads losses. Reinsurance is able to protect insurers from underwriting losses which may imperil their solvency and to stabilise underwriting results. It can enable that insurer to increase the flexibility and the size and types of risk and the volume of risks he can underwrite and can assist in the financing of insurance operations to the benefit of insureds.

Reinsurance is a contract of the utmost good faith and thus the reinsured is in the same position vis-a-vis its reinsurer as the original insured was to it when the original contract of insurance was made. However in reinsurance each party is an expert and consequently the duty of disclosure will be somewhat less onerous, for the reinsured is entitled to expect that the reinsurer will have an informed approach to the situation: *Southern Cross Assurance Company Ltd v Australian Provincial Assurance Association* (1935) 53 CLR 618, 628.

Sometimes representations made by an original insured are relevant to the validity of a reinsurance contract. It depends on the terms of the reinsurance contract. If an original insured before the conclusion of his or her insurance makes incorrect statements which are warranted true in the original policy and in turn are clearly stated to form the basis of the reinsurance contract, the reinsurer on discovering the truth is entitled to repudiate liability: *Australian Widows' Fund Life v National Mutual Life Association of Australia Ltd* [1914] AC 634. Alternatively the recital of an original declaration may be interpreted as simply informing the reinsurers of the declaration which formed the basis of the original policy.

For the relationship between identical terms in each of the insurance and reinsurance contracts, each term having a different effect by virtue of the law of the place at which the respective contracts were made, see *Forsikringsaktieselskapet Vesta v Butcher (No 1)* [1989] 1 All ER 402 (HL).

The original insurer, not the reinsurer, has the right to fix the terms of settlement under the original policy. The reinsurer is bound by any reasonable compromise made bona fide between the original insurer and the insured: *Western Assurance Company of Toronto v Poole* [1903] 1 KB 376. But it is not bound if the original insurer varies the terms of the policy with the insured or if it makes an ex gratia payment without the assent of the reinsurer: *MacKenzie v Whitworth* (1875) 1 Ex D 36.

The reinsurer's liability arises, in the absence of express agreement to the contrary, when the amount of the loss has been determined in the terms, of the original policy.

Chapter 35

TYPES OF INSURANCE CONTRACT

SUMMARY

35.1   LIFE INSURANCE
35.2   FIRE INSURANCE
35.3   MARINE INSURANCE
35.4   EARTHQUAKE AND WAR DAMAGE INSURANCE

35.1 LIFE INSURANCE

35.1.1 General

Life insurance is isolated for particular consideration because it is extremely important and is subject to a number of special rules. Life insurance is governed by the Life Insurance Act 1908 and its amendments. As discussed earlier (see para 30.2.1, supra), the modern forms of life policies are numerous and diverse ranging from the traditional whole life policy and term insurance through to endowment policies and investment linked life insurance.

35.1.2 Non-payment of premiums

No policy becomes void through non-payment of premium so long as the premiums and interest do not exceed the surrender value: s 64. The surrender value is the amount which the insurer is prepared to pay to the insured if he or she should terminate the policy. It is to be noted that additional surrender value, which can be applied in payment of premiums, will accrue during the years the policy is kept in force by the use of surrender value already accumulated. For example where the assured has taken out an endowment policy for $20,000 and bonuses at the age of 30, to mature at the age of 65, and cannot pay the premium at the beginning of the sixth year, approximately $1,040 would be available from surrender value and the present worth of bonuses. This amount would almost pay the premium during the next two years during which time additional surrender value and bonuses would accumulate. Generally, see *Spooner-Kenyon v Yorkshire General Life Assurance Co Ltd* (1982) 2 ANZ Ins Cas 60-476.

35.1.3 Insurance on the lives of minors

Insurance on the lives of minors is governed by ss 66A-D, 67A-E of the Life Insurance Act 1908. Section 66A states that a minor who is under the age of ten years may effect a policy on his or her own life if the contract is approved by a District Court pursuant to s 9 of the Minors' Contracts Act 1969. Sections 66A and 66B give a minor of or over the age of ten years power to effect a policy on his or her own life, but this may be subjected to judicial scrutiny under the provisions of the Minors' Contracts Act 1969; namely, if the minor is under the age of 16 years this power is subject to s 6 of the Minors' Contracts Act 1969, and, if 16 years or over, then this is subject to s 5(2) of the Minors' Contracts Act 1969. Moreover, while the minor is given extensive powers to deal with a policy owned by him, these powers are again subject to the protective mechanisms enshrined in the Minors' Contracts Act 1969; for example, while a minor of or over the age of 16 years may give discharges for the money payable under the policy, a Court may intervene pursuant to s 5(2) of the Minors' Contracts Act 1969 and grant relief where the life policy imposes a harsh or unconscionable obligation upon the minor or where the consideration for the minor's promise or act was so inadequate as to be unconscionable: s 66C(4)(a) Life Insurance Act 1908. Section 66D contains two presumptions as to age; that is, that so far as concerns the company issuing any policy, and so far as concerns any person claiming under any disposition of a policy made bona fide and for valuable consideration, it shall be conclusively presumed that the person *effecting* the policy was, at the time when that person effected the policy, of or over the age of ten years; and that the person who disposed of the policy was, at the time when that person disposed of the policy, of or over the age of 16 years. These presumptions facilitate the enforcement of policies and their provisions and throw the onus of rebuttal upon any challenger. Moreover, these presumptions do not apply where the issuing company or the third party recipient for value, had actual notice to the contrary, and the presumptions do not apply to any policy effected in accordance with a contract approved under s 9 of the Minors' Contracts Act 1969.

Sections 67, 67A, 67B and 67C of the Life Insurance Act 1908, address the questions of who may insure the lives of minors and how much may be recovered in the event that such a minor dies. The category of persons who may take out a policy on the life of a minor under the age of 16 years is severely restricted; namely, s 67(1) states that the parents or guardians, or one of them, or a person who has obtained the consent of the District Court may effect a valid policy on the life of such a minor. Moreover a joint insurance by a guardian or parent and the spouse of such guardian or parent is permissible. Section 67A re-enacts the substance of s 8(1)(b) of the Life Insurance Amendment Act 1921-22 by providing that it shall be lawful for any company to issue an endowment policy on the life of any minor of any age. Section 67B(1) provides that on the death of minor under the age of ten years the maximum amount recoverable by any proponent for all insurers will be limited to a return of premiums together with interest thereon *and* $2,000 (representing a rough approximation of the cost today of a funeral) or such larger sum as may from time to time be specified by Order in Council. Section 67C provides that no company shall pay, on the death of a minor who is under the age of 16 years, any sum under any policy issued after the commencement of the Insurance Law Reform Act to any person other than a person specified in s 67(1), or such person's executor or administrator, or a person to whom payment may be made under s 65(2) of the Administration Act 1969, or an approved assignee. Section 67D(1) provides that no company shall issue a policy on the life of a minor who is under the age of 16 years *unless* a statement explaining the effect of ss 67B and 67C is set out in the proposal for the policy and the person effecting the policy has signed a separate acknowledgement that that person is aware of the limitations imposed by those sections. Non-compliance with this requirement does not make the policy illegal, unenforceable or of no effect, but is an offence rendering the insurer liable on summary conviction to a fine not exceeding $1,000. Similarly s 67E declares it to be an offence for a company to contravene s 67B or s 67D, or for a person claiming on the death of a minor under the age of 16 years to produce a false death certificate or one that was fraudulently obtained, or for such person in any way to attempt to defeat the provisions of the Act with respect to payments upon the death of minors.

35.1.4 Form and registration of mortgages

In so far as a life policy provides for the payment of a determinable sum on the occurrence of a certain event, it is a form of security readily acceptable by lending institutions. Apart from the value of the policy at maturity date, it also has a surrender value after it has been in existence for some years. The Life Insurance Act 1908, ss 44, 45, 46, 47, 50 and 51, provide for the form and registration of mortgages.

Every mortgage made must be in the prescribed form signed by the mortgagor. The mortgage must be registered by leaving it, duly executed, with the policy and a certified copy of the mortgage, at the office of the insurance company. The secretary indorses on the policy and on the mortgage a memorandum evidencing the mortgage. The company retains the certified copy and returns the mortgage and policy duly indorsed, to the person who has left them at the office. No mortgage is valid unless registered, except when the mortgage is given in favour of the company issuing it, or if it is a mortgage of a policy issued by a company which has not established itself in New Zealand or which has no place of business in New Zealand. The company may require an indorsement on the mortgage acknowledging loans made by it prior to registration.

A mortgagee may sell the policy under the implied power of sale and may execute an assignment of the policy. Mortgages are discharged in the manner prescribed by the Act.

35.1.5 Payment of policy moneys without probate

In any case in which the insurance moneys due under the policy, including profits, do not exceed the sum of $9,000 the insurer liable under such policy may pay such sum to:

(a) the widow, widower, or children of the deceased;
(b) any person related by blood or marriage to the deceased, who undertakes to maintain his or her children; or
(c) any person who has control of any of the deceased's children who are minors, or any person who is entitled under the will or on the intestacy of the deceased or any person entitled to obtain administration of the estate of the deceased;

without either probate or letters of administration being taken out: Administration Act 1969, s 65(5) as amended.

35.2 FIRE INSURANCE

35.2.1 General

As has already been mentioned, fire insurance is a contract of indemnity. The indemnity is payable even if fire is caused by the negligence of the insured, or the wrong-doing of some third party. For the insurer to be liable, there has to be an actual fire and the loss must be caused by fire. Damage to goods caused by explosion or excessive heat where there is no actual fire, is not recoverable. If a fire results from an explosion and the subject matter is destroyed, this is treated as a loss by fire. For damage by smoke, see *Harris v Poland* [1941] 1 KB 462; [1941] 1 All ER 204. On the other hand, loss arising from the efforts made to extinguish or prevent a fire spreading are deemed to be natural and consequential damage by fire and the insurer is liable. An insurer is liable for damage caused by a fire following lightning, but not for the damage caused by the lightning itself, if no fire follows. At present there is no statute in New Zealand which deals specifically with fire insurance and no particular form is required for the policy. It is unusual to issue valued fire policies, the normal form being a contract to indemnify the insured for his or her loss up to a certain stated amount.

35.2.2 Cover notes and renewal receipts

The cover note is a separate contract containing an undertaking by the insurer to indemnify the proponent until it has been decided whether or not to accept the proposal. The issue of a cover note raises no presumption that the company will ultimately accept the proposal.

Normally, a contract of fire insurance is for one year only and is not automatically renewed, but it is the custom of many insurers to issue "renewal receipts". The conduct of the insurer and the insured as well as the terms of the renewal receipt and the policy determine whether the insurer remains liable irrespective of the payment of the premium.

35.2.3 Reinstatement

(a) PURSUANT TO CONTRACT
Most fire policies give the insurer an option to reinstate. This option to reinstate was introduced to enable insurers to ease the burden of a monetary payment to achieve indemnity, by arranging repairs which, in

some cases, might be carried out at much less expense. Furthermore such a clause may serve to protect an insurer against fraudulent claims and excessive claims.

The insurer is free to decide what it will do, and unless a time is fixed in the policy, the insurer has a reasonable time within which to come to a decision whether to pay the loss, or to repair: *Lake v Hartford Fire Insurance Co Ltd* [1966] WAR 161, 166. The insurer must make clear its election between the two alternatives by unequivocal words or conduct. The insurer may expressly notify the insured that it intends to exercise the option and reinstate the property insured, in which case no difficulty arises. However, an express election is not necessary as there may be a binding election by conduct, where the insurer has so conducted itself that the necessary implication is that an election has been made. It would be unreasonable to expect an insurer to elect to reinstate before it had adequate information to determine which of the two courses of action before it was the more advantageous. Therefore no act by the insurer for the purpose of ascertaining the extent of loss of damage, or the cost of reinstatement, can fairly be considered an election under which it is bound to reinstate. However, it would be prudent for an insurer to insert a term in the policy, that it not be called upon to elect, until it has obtained all the necessary estimates, plans and evaluations that are deemed necessary for a competent election to be carried out.

It is difficult to lay down any general principles as to what conduct constitutes an election, since in each case it would appear to be a question of fact. Jackson J in *Lake v Hartford Fire Insurance Co Ltd* [1966] WAR 161 stated that election is a unilateral act of the insurer which does not depend on agreement between the parties and it may be made expressly or it may be implied from an insurer's conduct. In this case a Holden motor car was extensively damaged in a collision. The car was insured for £500 subject to an excess of £10. The car was so badly damaged it was irreparable. The insurer offered to pay the pre-accident market value of the car less the £10 excess, that is, £390. The insured claimed he was entitled to the full £490. Because of the insured's default under a hire purchase contract on the car, the financier repossessed the car. Meanwhile the insurer, unaware of the seizure, had authorised the repair of the car at a cost of £305. The insured sued the insurer for £490 claiming that there was an election on the part of the insurer to pay the total loss, therefore it could not change his mind and repair. Wolff CJ, in a dissenting judgment, said that there must be some unequivocal act by the insurer which committed it to its choice under the policy. The Chief Justice mentioned several such acts by way of illustration: disposal of the property by salvage, or submission of the claim to arbitration. His Honour considered that in *Lake's* case all the insurer had done was to indicate a willingness to settle on the basis of total loss if the insured agreed and therefore there was no election. However, the majority of the Court considered that if an insurer negotiates with the insured on the basis that a money payment will be made in respect of the loss, it cannot later elect to reinstate the loss. On the other hand, if the negotiations really only relate to the *amount of the damage* suffered, there may be no election to reinstate. The fact that the insurers sent a letter to the insured conveying the information that the vehicle was a total loss is evidence enough of an election. The fact that the insured did not accept the amount then offered (£390) does not affect the position. This is because the election of the insurer is a unilateral act on its part and does *not* need the assent of the insured to give it force and effect. Therefore the majority found that there was a binding election not to reinstate.

In *Scottish Amicable Heritable Securities Association Ltd v Northern Assurance Co* (1883) 11 R (Ct of Sess) 287 prolonged negotiations between insurer and insured ensued following a claim in respect of a fire loss. The insured claimed money or reinstatement, but the insurer totally ignored the question of reinstatement and instead disputed the amount of loss and prepared to go to arbitration over it. Only when the insured commenced proceedings some 18 months after the fire did the insurers for the first time offer to reinstate. It was held that the offer was too late since it was clear that the insurers had elected to settle in money and the only point in dispute was the sum to be paid. On the other hand, where negotiations (including a cash offer) really only related to the amount of damage suffered, it was held in *Sutherland v Sun Fire Office* (1852) 14D (Ct of Sess) 775 that there had been no election not to reinstate. A stationer's stock and furniture was damaged by fire and before any formal claim was made, the insurer sent an expert to report on the damage. After a formal claim was made an offer of cash payment was made and declined by the insured. Subsequently, an offer to refer the valuation of damage to arbitration was also refused by the insured. The insurer then stated it would exercise its right to reinstate but the insured claimed that the insurer had elected to pay a sum of money. It was held that it was still open to the insurer to elect to reinstate. The only Judge to express any doubt was Lord Ivory who thought that the offer of a cash payment might have been an election to pay, but he found that the refusal to go to arbitration threw the whole question open again.

If the insurer elects to reinstate, the contract becomes a building or repair contract. However, the election does not constitute a fresh contract between insurer and insured, but the policy is read as if it had originally simply been one for reinstatement. Thus, in *Robson v New Zealand Insurance Co Ltd* [1931] NZLR 35 a motor vehicle policy gave the insurer the option of repairing the car if and when damaged, or of allowing the insured to do so and paying the cost thereof to the insured. A clause in the policy prohibited the insured from repairing the vehicle without the prior permission of the insurer having been obtained. The car was damaged in an accident and the insurer elected to repair the vehicle. However, these repairs were not carried out satisfactorily and the insured took the vehicle to his own garage to have the faulty repairs rectified. The insurer refused to pay for this work, relying on the clause requiring the prior consent of the insurer to any repairs effected by the insured. However, it was held that the insurer was liable, in that the clause as to the consent of the insurer was applicable only to the other option of the insurer, that is, of allowing the insured to do his own repairs and paying for them. On the election to reinstate, the policy had to read as simply one for reinstatement and as this contract had not been properly performed, the insured could recover damages assessed as the sum expended in rectifying the faulty repairs.

Once the insurer elects to reinstate it is bound by this decision and it cannot change its mind on discovering that its decision was unwise: *Lake v Hartford Fire Insurance Co Ltd* [1966] WAR 161, 167. The insurer must carry out the reinstatement to the reasonable satisfaction of the insured, and the reinstatement must be completed within a reasonable period of time. Once the insurer has exercised its election to reinstate, its liability is not limited either by the amount insured or by the amount of damage: *Swift v New Zealand Insurance Co Ltd* [1927] VLR 249.

Where reinstatement is impossible at the time when the insurer has to make an election, the insurer is left with the obligation to make a money payment. As Bowen LJ observed in *Anderson v Commercial Union Assurance Co* (1885) 55 LJQB 146, 150:

> It is clear law that if one of two things which had been contracted for subsequently becomes impossible, it becomes a question of construction whether, according to the true intention of the parties, the obligor is bound to perform the alternative or is discharged altogether.

Total discharge is unlikely to be the intention of the parties in any policy, and so where reinstatement is impossible the insurer's obligation is to make a money payment. However, Lord Esher MR cautioned against an approach that would construe impossibility of reinstatement where such reinstatement could be effected a reasonable distance away or in a reasonably-proximate form: *Anderson's* case, p 148. In such cases there is no impossibility such as to preclude the insurer from exercising its option to reinstate.

Finally, if it is impossible to reinstate because of some circumstance intervening after an election is made, there is authority that the insurer is nonetheless bound by the election and liable in damages for not reinstating despite the impossibility. In *Brown v Royal Insurance Co* (1859)1 E & E 853 the insurer elected to reinstate a house but, after this task had commenced, the house was condemned by the Commissioners of Sewers, who ordered that the house be demolished. The insured claimed damages for breach of the contract to reinstate, and it was held that the insurer had become bound by its election and that, even in the fact of this impossibility, the insurer must either perform the contract or pay damages for not performing it. However, this case was decided before the Courts developed the doctrine of frustration, and in any event in *Bank of New South Wales v Royal Insurance Co* (1880) 2 NZLR (SC) 337 Richardson J observed that if, through the want of title in the insured or from some other cause beyond the control of the insurer, it is impossible for the latter to enter on the premises and reinstate, the insurer is not bound by the election.

(b) STATUTORY REINSTATEMENT

In addition to the situation where an insurer may elect unilaterally to reinstate pursuant to a term of the contract, it may be compelled, or authorised, to so act by virtue of statute. Section 83 of the Fires Prevention (Metropolis) Act 1774 requires an insurer of houses and other buildings against fire to apply the policy monies, so far as they will go, towards rebuilding or reinstating an insured building damaged or destroyed by fire at the request of any person or persons interested in the building; and it authorises an insurer so to act if it suspects that the owner, occupier or other person who has insured the building was guilty of fraud or arson. The second limb of this provision adds little to the usual contractual right to reinstate, but the first limb may be used to compel an insurer to reinstate where a person interested in premises which have been damaged or destroyed by fire requires the insurer to expend the policy monies in this way. The policy and object of the section is to remove incentives to arson by an insured person with a limited interest in premises; while the contract of indemnity under the insurance policy may be completely enforced, all possibility of any profit accruing to the insured is taken away and so the inducement to commit arson is removed. This statute is in force in New Zealand: see *Cleland v South British Insurance Co Ltd* (1891) 9 NZLR 177; English Laws Act 1908.

The obligation of an insurer under s 83 arises only upon a definite request to reinstate by a "person interested" in the building. For example in *Cleland v South British Insurance Co* supra, the owner and mortgagees of certain land and buildings in Wellington sought to have the defendant insurance company expend money payable under a policy taken out by the lessee on the rebuilding and reinstating of the insured premises. The insurer was ordered, in accordance with s 83, to adopt this course of action. Consequently, the insurer is not entitled to refuse a request to reinstate by a person having some legal or equitable interest in the insured property, and the right to reinstatement is enforceable by mandamus or mandatory order: *Mylius v Royal Insurance Co Ltd* (1926) 38 CLR 477, 496.

The insurer does not have to expend the maximum sum payable under the policy, but only the amount which under the contract it was obliged to pay; that is, the insurer is only obliged to spend such sum on reinstatement as is commensurate with what the insured would be entitled to receive in a money payment: *Auckland City Corporation v Mercantile and General Insurance Co Ltd* [1930] NZLR 809. Statutory reinstatement diverges from contractual reinstatement in this regard, for as we have seen above, where the insurer elects to exercise its contractual right to reinstate its liability is not limited by either the amount insured or damage sustained. However, it is also plain that the insurer will only exercise its contractual right to reinstate where it believes this will be financially more advantageous to itself than would be the case where a money payment is made. Where the insurer has no option, as with statutory reinstatement, it would be most inequitable if its liability was not restricted to an amount not exceeding what the insured would have been entitled to receive in cash. The object of s 83 is to deter arson, and not to benefit persons interested in property.

The statutory right of reinstatement does not subsist unless monies are properly payable by the insurer under the policy. When for any reason the policy is avoided and nothing is payable thereunder, proceedings to enforce the statutory right by whomsoever they are taken must fail. Moreover, s 83 is subject to the proviso that if the person claiming the insurance money gives sufficient security to the insurer within 60 days after adjustment of the claim that the money will be expended on reinstatement, or the insurance money is disposed of among contending parties within this time period to the satisfaction of the insurer, the insurer ceases to be under any obligation to, or to be able to insist on its right to reinstate.

35.3 MARINE INSURANCE

35.3.1 General

The United Kingdom Marine Insurance Act 1906, on which the New Zealand 1908 Act is based, sets out the form of the marine policy in the First Schedule. This form was settled in 1779 in Edward Lloyd's Coffee House, where shipowners, captains and underwriters used to meet, and it followed the form of marine policy used in Italy in the sixteenth century. Modifications to this form have been made by the London Institute of Underwriters and these qualifying and additional clauses are known as Institute Clauses. Although this form of policy is not included in the New Zealand Act, the rules for the construction of terms used in this policy form are found in the Schedule to the Act. Space does not permit a full discussion of the various clauses commonly included in the policy, such as the *Inchmaree Clause, Running Down Clause (RDC)* and the *Suing and Labouring Clause* but it is necessary to draw attention to the *Warehouse to Warehouse Clause* which covers sea and land risks and also removes any doubt as to whether the goods are covered during the loading. The principal types of marine insurance policy are canvassed above (see 30.2.4, infra).

35.3.2 Maritime perils

Marine insurance is designed to cover loss arising out of lawful marine adventure. The insurer undertakes to indemnify the insured against the loss of a ship or goods, freight, passage money or other pecuniary benefits accruing from a voyage or the insured's liability to third parties arising out of maritime perils. Defeasible, partial and contingent interests are insurable.

There is a marine adventure where a ship, goods, or other movables are exposed to maritime perils. Section 4 defines maritime perils as:

> ... perils consequent on or incidental to the navigation of the sea – that is to say, perils of the seas, fire, war-perils, pirates, rovers, thieves, captures, seizures, restraints, and detainments of princes and peoples, jettisons, barratry, and any other perils, either of the like kind or designed by the policy.

Maritime perils are confined to perils of the sea, not perils on the sea. The term does not cover everything that happens at sea, but is confined to dangers of the sea and unexpected accidents arising in the course of navigating the seas. It does not include damage arising from the ordinary action of the wind and waves, nor such loss as arises through wear and tear, leakage, inherent vice of the cargo (s 55) or disaster arising from the negligence, lack of skill or the wrong-doing of the master or the crew. A maritime peril for the general purposes of marine cover relates to unexpected casualty, not to inevitable consequences. It covers accidents which may happen, not events which are certain to happen.

Section 34 declares that warranties in marine insurance are promissory warranties – undertakings that some particular thing shall or shall not be done or that some condition shall be fulfilled or that a particular state of facts does or does not exist. Compliance by the insured with the warranty is mandatory otherwise the insurer is discharged from liability from the date of the breach of warranty. An insurer in time of war might stipulate for an express warranty of the neutrality of both the ship and cargo, although normally there is no implied warranty of nationality of the ship.

In a voyage policy there is an implied warranty that the ship shall be seaworthy from the time of the commencement of risk to the port of destination: s 40. A ship is seaworthy when it is in such condition as to encounter with safety whatever perils a ship of that kind, loaded in the way it is, may fairly be expected to encounter in making the specified voyage at the time of the year in which it is undertaken.

A buyer of a ship has no insurable interest until the property in it passes to him: *Piper v Royal Exchange Assurance* (1932) 44 Ll L Rep 103. But a mortgagee having an equitable interest has an insurable interest in a ship.

In determining the measure of damages arising through a loss due to a maritime peril, it was decided in *Saunders and Co Ltd v Phoenix Assurance Co Ltd* [1953] NZLR 598 that where goods subject to Price Control are lost "the value of the property" for the purposes of insurance is the landed cost plus profit as limited by price orders and not the replacement cost. See too *Haighi's Persian Trading Co Ltd v General Accident Insurance Co New Zealand Ltd* (1990) 6 ANZ Ins Cas 61, 002.

Section 79 gives the insurer a statutory right of subrogation on payment for a total loss of the whole of the subject matter of the insurance or, in the case of goods, of any apportionable part.

35.3.3 Lost or not lost

This clause was first introduced into English policies at the beginning of the seventeenth century, when insurances were sometimes effected when there was no way of knowing whether the vessel had sailed or, if she had sailed, whether she had been wrecked. Insurance is frequently granted where there is no information as to the safety of the ship or cargo. The wards "lost or not lost" make the insurer liable whether the property is lost or the insured had previously lost his or her insurable interest.

The principle of good faith applies with equal force to both insurer and insured. If the insurer knows the ship or goods have arrived at their destination and there is no risk, or if the insured knows the ship or goods have been lost and the insurer does not, no legal obligation arises in the case of either party. It has been said that both parties must be in equal knowledge or in equal ignorance.

Section 7 provides that if the subject matter is insured "lost or not lost", the insured may recover although he or she may not have acquired his or her interest until after the loss, unless at the time of effecting the insurance, the insured was aware of the loss and the insurer was not.

35.3.4 Loss and abandonment

Loss may be either total or partial. Where there is partial loss, the insurer will pay only such proportion of the loss as corresponds with the ratio of the amount of the insurance to the total value of the subject matter.

(1) Total loss: May be actual or constructive: s 56. There is an actual total loss when the subject matter insured is destroyed or so damaged as to cease to be a thing of the kind insured or where the insured is irretrievably deprived of it. Where there is actual total loss no notice of abandonment need be given: s 57. For example, hides were insured from Valparaiso to Bordeaux. In consequence of sea damage, they arrived at Rio de Janeiro in a state of incipient putridity, and were sold there. Their state was such that they would have been wholly putrid if carried on to Bordeaux. This was an actual total loss: *Roux v Salvador* (1836) 3 Bing NC 266.

(2) A constructive total loss: Occurs where the subject matter insured is reasonably abandoned on account of its actual total loss appearing to be unavoidable or because its preservation would involve expenditure exceeding its value when recovered: s 60.

On a constructive total loss the insured may treat the loss as a partial loss or abandon the subject matter to the insurer. *Notice of abandonment* may be either written or oral and must show a clear election to abandon the subject matter to the insurer. It must be given with reasonable diligence after the receipt of reliable information and if it is not given, the loss is treated as partial: s 62 (1), (3); see generally Lord Chelmsford in *Currie & Co v Bombay Native Insurance Co* (1869) LR 3 PC 72, 79.

The insured must take some positive step, although he or she is allowed reasonable time to verify the facts. Once notice of abandonment is accepted by the insurer, it is irrevocable. "Abandoned" means "left", not "handed over to the insurer". Valid abandonment entitles the insurer to take over the interest of the insured in whatever remains of the subject matter and all proprietary rights incidental thereto: s 63.

35.3.5 Average

Section 81 of the Marine Insurance Act 1908 provides that where an insured is insured for an amount less than the insurable value, or, in the case of a valued policy, for an amount less than the policy valuation, the insured is deemed to be his or her own insurer in respect of the uninsured balance. Thus, if furniture worth $10,000 were insured for $6,000 and this furniture were forwarded by ship and half of it were destroyed, the insured would receive only 6000/10000 of the $5000 loss and thus be his or her own insurer to the extent of 40% of the value.

In marine insurance, the term *general average* refers to a partial loss deliberately and reasonably incurred in time of peril for the general benefit of all those interested in the marine adventure. Contribution to this loss must be made by all the owners whose property is saved, ie, by those interested in the ship, the freight and the cargo.

General average developed from a custom coming down from the very earliest time of sea-borne traffic and it is stated in the ancient Law of Rhodes in these terms:

> The Rhodian Law provides that if, in order to lighten a ship, merchandise is thrown overboard, that which has been given for all shall be replaced by contribution of all.

The liability to contribute to general average is based on the principles of common law; all those interested must make contribution whether they are insured or not. The Marine Insurance Act 1908, s 66, defines a *general average loss* as a loss caused by or directly consequent on a general average act.

There is a *general average act* where any extraordinary sacrifice or expenditure is voluntarily and reasonably made or incurred in time of peril for the purpose of preserving the property imperilled in the common adventure.

Where there is a general average loss, the party on whom it falls can call for a rateable contribution from the other parties interested, the contribution is called a *general average contribution*. For example, if a ship sprang a leak in the forward hold it might be necessary to jettison some of the cargo in that hold so as to raise the bow of the ship. The loss of the cargo so jettisoned is a general average loss, incurred for the safety of all parties, who must contribute even though their own goods are not damaged.

Subject to any express provision in the policy, where the insured has incurred a general average expenditure, he or she may recover from the insurer in respect of the proportion of the loss which falls upon him; and in the case of a general average sacrifice, the insured may recover from the insurer in respect of the whole loss without having enforced his or her right of contribution from the other parties liable to contribute. Of course the insurer having paid compensation is subrogated to this right of contribution.

If there has been a general average loss, the master of the ship usually gives notice to all those concerned that "a general average contribution is required" and will refuse to part with any part of the cargo until the contribution has been made or a bond has been entered into for due payment when the general average adjustment has been made. This is made either according to the principles of the port of destination or according to the York Antwerp Rules 1950 and the Rules of Practice of the Association of Average Adjusters. These rules are international in their application and provide for all the usual contingencies such as jettison of cargo for common safety, voluntary stranding, burning ship's material for fuel and cutting away wreckage.

Particular average: Is a partial loss due to purely accidental causes, such as stranding causing substantial interruption of the voyage, collision, or failure of refrigeration plant and is borne by the owner without any right of contribution from others interested in the same marine adventure. The loss is not in the nature of sacrifice of property and has conferred no benefit on the others interested in the adventure. Where the subject matter is warranted "free from particular average" (referred to as the FPA clause), either wholly or under a certain percentage, the insurer is not responsible for particular average losses except for certain specific events such as the stranding, sinking or burning of the vessel. Thus, the death of a racehorse through seasickness would be a particular average loss and, if the FPA clause applied, the owner would have to bear the whole loss himself or herself without any right of indemnity against the insurer.

35.4 EARTHQUAKE AND WAR DAMAGE INSURANCE

The preamble to the Earthquake and War Damage Act 1944 recites that the Act is designed "to make provision with respect to the insurance of property against earthquake damage and war damage". The Act provides that all property insured against fire is deemed to be insured to the extent of the indemnity value against earthquake and war damage: s 14(1). An Earthquake and War Damage Commission is established and this body is charged with the responsibility of making good by repayment, reinstatement or repair earthquake, war damage and extraordinary disaster damage: s 16. Under the Earthquake and War Damage Regulations 1984 protection also is afforded to the insured against damage caused by volcanic eruption, hydrothermal activity, and landslip, and the Earthquake and War Damage (Land Cover) Regulations 1984 provide that the Commission is liable to make good earthquake or landslip or disaster damage to land where the property is insured against fire.

An Earthquake and War Damage Fund is established and its chief source of revenue are premiums at the rate of 5 cents for each 100 dollars of insurance cover which are collected on behalf of the Commission by the various insurance companies and paid into this fund. The Act provides that this premium must be computed on the indemnity value; this value may be derived from the policy where it expressed the indemnity value, or may be certified by a registered architect, valuer, engineer, or surveyor: s 14(2A); see *Farmers Mutual Insurance Co Ltd v Bay Milk Products Ltd* [1989] 3 NZLR 647 (CA).

The insurance of any property under the Act and the regulations is subject to the same conditions as are set out in the contract of fire insurance, so far as they are applicable and are not inconsistent with the provisions of the Act and of the regulations: Earthquake and War Damage Regulations 1984, reg 6(2). The Earthquake and War Damage Commission is arrogated a wide power to pay or allow at any time the amount of any claim or claims lodged by any insured. Gresson J in *Low v Earthquake and War Damage Commission* [1960] NZLR 189, 190, described the situation as being one where ". . . Parliament has made the Commission itself the final Judge in what is, in a sense, its own cause". However the decision of the Commission in determining whether compensation is payable for a particular form of disaster may be quashed by the High Court, if in making it, the Commission contravened principles of natural justice. The Commission has an unrestricted discretion under Condition 4 in the schedule to the Earthquake and War Damage Regulations 1984 to cancel cover at any time, and the duty to refund part of the premium is not a condition precedent to the exercise of this discretion: *Earthquake and War Damage Commission v Graves and Walker* [1983] NZ *Recent Law* 342. However, the Commission on cancelling or reducing insurance on property must register a certificate against the land title and (on request) give reasons for such cancellation or reduction: reg 5A.

Part V

SECURED TRANSACTIONS AND HIRE PURCHASE

Chapter 36

CHATTEL SECURITIES

36.1 INTRODUCTION

The Chattels Transfer Act 1924 (as amended), deals with loans on the security of chattels other than motor vehicles within the meaning of the Motor Vehicle Securities Act 1989 and certain other exceptions. The reference to chattels hereafter is used in this limited sense. The purchase of chattels on hire purchase is governed by the Hire Purchase Act 1971 as well as the Chattels Transfer Act and its amendments. Hire purchase agreements will be discussed in the next chapter. The Chattels Transfer Act applies only to instruments in writing, not to oral transactions: *New Zealand Serpentine Ltd v Hoon Hay Quarries Ltd* [1925] NZLR 73. This does not mean that an oral agreement giving a security over a chattel is not valid. It simply means that anyone basing a claim on an oral agreement must rely on the general principles of contract and appropriate statutes such as the Sale of Goods Act 1908; on the other hand, he or she will not be penalised because of non-compliance with the Chattels Transfer Act as to registration. Both Acts relate only to chattels; mortgages and transfers of land are governed by the Land Transfer Act 1952 and the Property Law Act 1952.

515

The principal instruments which are affected by the Chattels Transfer Act (which will be referred to as "the Act" in this chapter) are:

(a) instruments by way of security; and
(b) hire purchase agreements; and
(c) bailments.

Instruments by way of security are commonly referred to as chattel securities, chattel mortgages and bills of sale, or, in the cases of sheep and cattle, as stock mortgages. Although the term "bill of sale" is frequently used by the business community to describe a chattel security, the use of the term is not strictly correct in a legal sense as under a bill of sale ownership of the goods may pass absolutely to the transferee.

36.2 THE PURPOSE AND SCOPE OF THE ACT

There are numerous situations where a person in possession of goods does not own them. Such a person may pass himself or herself off as owner and, the goods to an innocent third party, or borrow on the security of those goods. When this happens the complications associated with the *nemo dat quod non habet* rule arise; two innocent parties become embroiled in a dispute as to ownership and, of necessity, one must forfeit his or her interest in the goods.

The Act endeavours to prevent this sort of problem from arising and is specifically designed to protect the interests of persons who have proprietary interests in, but not the possession of goods. Generally speaking, the Act applies to all transactions which result in possession of goods being in someone other than the owner. To achieve its object of protecting creditors of an apparent owner and to counter the deceptions that may stem from a separation of ownership and possession, the Act establishes a system of registration providing for the registration of certain documents in accordance with the statutory provisions, the supposition being that the publicity attached to registration will counter deception by enabling the general public to ascertain whether or not a person has unencumbered ownership of goods in his or her possession. The underlying assumption of the Act is that anyone dealing with goods will check the register, because registration is notice to everyone of the instrument registered and its contents.

The types of transaction to which the Act applies may be illustrated by these examples.

First, let us assume that B has a piano worth $800 and, being financially embarrassed, raises a loan of $400 from L on the security of the piano. L, the lender (referred to in the Act as "the grantee"), will require B, the borrower (referred to as "the grantor"), to execute a chattel security over the piano. The chattel security will provide that the grantor "doth hereby assign transfer and set over the said piano by way of mortgage" to the grantee. Under the covenants implied in the chattel security by the Fourth Schedule of the Act, the grantee on default by the grantor is entitled "without giving to the grantor any notice, or waiting any time, and notwithstanding any subsequent acceptance of any payment . . . to enter upon any lands or premises whereon the chattels for the time being subject to this security may be, and take possession thereof and sell and dispose of the same".

Secondly, let us assume that L sells a piano worth $800 to B and B pays $400 on account. L may take a chattel security over the piano to secure the payment of the balance of the purchase price with interest. The chattel security will be substantially the same as in the first case. However, if L is a retail seller, then such a sale and "mortgage back" will be deemed to be a hire purchase transaction and subject to terms and provisions of the Hire Purchase Act 1971 (Hire Purchase Amendment Act 1974, s 2). See infra.

Thirdly, we may assume that L, who in this case is called the grantor, on selling the piano on terms to B (called the grantee), decides to give B no permanent proprietary rights in the piano until he or she pays the last instalment, and wishes to deny him or her the power to sell it to anyone else. L will then require B to sign a particular form of bailment called a hire purchase agreement. This agreement will give B the possession and the use of the piano, but will provide that the deposit is paid on account of rental or merely to secure an option to purchase the piano at the agreed price. Instalments of the purchase price are deemed to be payments of rental for the use of the piano. The agreement will further provide that if B (the grantee) parts with the possession of the piano, executes a security over it, breaks the agreement, becomes bankrupt, assigns his or her estate, allows a judgment against him or her to remain unsatisfied, or distress to be levied against him or her, his or her rights under the agreement are terminated and he or she is contractually bound to return the piano to the grantor. If the grantee fails to return the piano, a provision of the agreement will empower the grantor to enter the grantee's premises and repossess it. Alternatively the hire purchase agreement may take the form of a conditional agreement to sell.

Fourthly, L may enter into a lease or "renting agreement" where he or she simply bails the piano to B for a term at a set hiring charge. Office equipment, word processors, computers, industrial plant and electronic plant are now frequently acquired by users on lease. Lease or lease purchase agreements often fix the amount of the residual value at the end of the term. This may be the amount the conditional purchaser-lessee has to pay to complete the purchase at the end of the lease or it may determine how much a lessee not exercising any right to purchase has to pay or is entitled to receive. The lessee is entitled to the amount by which the market value of the leased goods exceeds this figure if he or she returns them in better than average condition at the end of the lease. But if he or she returns them in bad or damaged condition he or she will have to pay the lessor the difference between the market value and the residual value so agreed upon. Obviously the lessee's position will be governed by rises and falls in the market price.

In all four cases mentioned, L has the property in the piano but it is in B's possession. Possession of a chattel raises a presumption of ownership and most people will believe that B owns the piano and is free to sell or mortgage it as he or she pleases. From a practical point of view, the borrower or conditional purchaser must have the possession of and the responsibility for the care of chattels, subject to a chattel security or a hire purchase agreement. No lender, eg, a bank, would appreciate having possession of 150 cows given as security for an increase in a farmer's overdraft. The position of L above must be distinguished from that of a legal lien holder. Such liens are possessory in nature and therefore require L to *retain possession.* For example, the common law lien of an unpaid vendor, a car mechanic's lien or a solicitor's lien over his or her client's books, are all examples of possessory liens. Equitable liens do not depend on possession.

As mentioned earlier the purpose of the Act is to counteract the dangers arising from B being in possession of goods while the property in the goods has passed to, or remains with L. Such possession makes it possible for credit to be obtained through apparent ownership of goods, or for goods to be sold by persons who have no title to them. The Act therefore, has established a system of registration which protects a lender under a chattel security or a private vendor under a hire purchase agreement from seizure of his or her security or property by the Official Assignee, an assignee acting on behalf of creditors, an execution creditor or a bona fide purchaser or mortgagee for value. The Act does not require transactions relating to chattels to be put into writing, but it does require transactions, reduced to writing and subject to the Act, to be registered, if the legal rights of both parties are to be fully protected.

Registration is notice to everyone of the instrument registered and its contents, but not to the grantee of any prior registered instrument relating to the same chattels or any of them: s 4(1) and (3). The system of registration also provides protection for creditors and prospective purchasers of second-hand chattels, who are entitled to search the Chattels Register at the High Court Office without charge; by a search it can be ascertained whether there is a registered instrument over chattels in which they are interested. There is no central registry for the whole of New Zealand. A register of instruments affecting chattels has been established in towns where there is a High Court Office. The protection is accordingly limited to transactions which have taken place in the district where the search is made. This is clearly a major weakness in the present system. With the obvious transportability of chattels and the increased mobility of persons since this system of registration was first instituted in 1924, it is now quite likely that chattels, the subject of an instrument, could be taken and sold in Greymouth while the instrument, unknown to any potential purchaser, remains registered only in Auckland. The result is that the registers kept under the Act may not in fact give the "full story". Such a criticism, of course, goes to the very heart of the registration system. Either the register is efficient and shows *all* of the interest and charges, or it is of little assistance and value and should be discarded. A national register is therefore advocated. In this age of computer technology a national register is possible as is demonstrated by the setting up of the Motor Vehicle Security Register. Many of the provinces of Canada already operate computerised registers. If there is an unregistered instrument affecting the chattels, purchasers thereof and creditors are unaffected by it unless they have express notice of the instrument. Generally see Cain, "The Chattels Transfer Act: Oddities and Oddments" [1959] NZLJ 167, 168.

As the result of pressure by the trading community, a very wide range of chattels can be bought under customary hire purchase agreements which are exempt from registration. A purchaser of *second-hand* customary chattels should require evidence that the vendor has paid for goods he or she purports to sell. The vendor, himself, may be buying them under a customary hire purchase agreement, which does not require registration. See ch 37.

The Chattels Transfer Act 1924 (hereinafter referred to as "the Act") sets out the definitions in s 2. The Act commences by giving the relevant definitions, the most important of which are the definitions of chattels and instruments. Provision is made for the form and execution of instruments, the procedure for and the effect of registration as well as the consequences of failing to register. Sections 24-41 deal with instruments over various kinds of securities such as after-acquired chattels, stock, book debts, crops and wool. The discharge of chattel securities by the entry of a memorandum of satisfaction by the grantee, or in his or her absence by the Public Trustee, or on the order of a Judge is set out in ss 42-45. Sales of the mortgaged chattels by the Registrar of the High Court and by a sheriff or bailiff are covered by ss 46 and 47. Transfers of instruments, their effect and registration are dealt with in ss 55 and 56. Section 57 (as amended by s 3 of the Chattels Transfer Amendment Act 1970) sets out the provisions relating to customary hire purchase agreements; this section must be read in conjunction with the Hire Purchase Act 1971. The powers, covenants and provisions to be implied in instruments subject to the Act are set out in the Third and Fourth Schedules to the Act.

36.3 DEFINITIONS

36.3.1 General

The definition of "instrument" is of special importance because registration is necessary only if the document is an "instrument". The basic test to be applied to the document is, does it transfer or purport to transfer "the property in or right to the possession of chattels"?

The definition prevents receipts, declarations of trust and authorities to take possession from being effective to transfer ownership of chattels, in the possession of other people, to the holders of such documents, unless the documents are registered.

If the document is not an "instrument", eg, a customary hire-purchase agreement, it need not be registered in order to protect the seller's interest against claims of the Official Assignee or creditor of the person in possession of the goods. The following are the key definitions in the Act; for the remainder, reference should be made to s 2.

(1) Chattels means any personal property that can be completely transferred by delivery, and includes machinery, stock and the natural increase of stock, crops, wool and book debts but does not include:

- (a) chattels interests in real estate, title-deeds, choses in action (not being book debts), negotiable instruments; or
- (b) shares and interests in the stock, funds, or securities of any Government or local authority; or
- (c) shares and interests in the capital or property of any company or other corporate body; or
- (d) debentures and interest coupons issued by any Government, or local authority, or company, or other corporate body; or
- (e) motor vehicles within the meaning of the Motor Vehicle Securities Act 1989.

(2) Grantee means the party to an instrument to whom chattels therein referred to, or any interest therein, are thereby granted or assigned, or agreed so to be, and includes his or her executors, administrators, and assigns; and in the case of a company or corporation includes the successors and assigns of such company or corporation.

(3) Grantor means the party to an instrument who thereby grants or assigns, or agrees to grant to assign, chattels therein referred to, or any interest therein, and includes his or her executors, administrators, and assigns; and in the case of a company or corporation includes the successors and assigns of such company or corporation.

From the definition it may be seen that the grantee in an instrument by way of security is the lender and the grantor is the borrower; the verb "to grant", referring to the granting of the *interest* in the property. In a hire purchase agreement the grantor is the vendor and the grantee is the conditional purchaser or hirer. Similarly in a bailment, the lessor or bailor is the grantor, as he or she is granting an interest in his or her goods to the lessee (grantee).

(4) Instrument means and includes any bill of sale, mortgage, lien, or any other document that transfers or purports to transfer the property in or right to the possession of chattels, whether permanently or temporarily, whether absolutely or conditionally, and whether by way of sale, security, pledge, gift, settlement, bailment, or lease, and also the following:

(a) inventories of chattels with receipt thereto attached (see *Manchester Sheffield and Lincolnshire Railway Co v North Central Wagon Co* (1888) 13 App Cas 554 (HL);
(b) receipts for purchase money of chattels and other assurances of chattels (a receipt, being nothing more than an acknowledgement of payment, is not an instrument but, if it purports to confer a title, it is);
(c) declarations of trust without transfer (see *Re Allester Ltd* [1922] 2 Ch 211);
(d) powers of attorney, authorities or licences to take possession of chattels as security for any debt (see *Williams and Kettle Ltd v Official Assignee of Harding* (1908) 27 NZLR 871; 11 GLR 1);
(e) any agreement whether intended to be followed by the execution of any other instrument or not, by which a right in equity to any chattels or to any charge or security thereon or thereover is conferred. For an agreement to be an instrument under subpara (f) the agreement must confer the right in equity to the chattels. This is of particular importance. If the documentation only *evidences* an equitable right granted, for example, by oral contract, then the document will not be an instrument, and accordingly, will not be subject to the provisions of the Act (see *Shears and Sons Ltd v Jones* [1922] 2 Ch 802).

The copy of an inventory of chattels handed over by a trustee to a life tenant or other person with a limited interest under a will and signed by such life tenant or other person and the trustee shall be deemed to be an instrument under the Chattels Transfer Act 1924; Trustee Act 1956, s 39A (1) and (3).

Instrument does *not* include the following:

   (a) securities over, or bailments or leases of, fixtures (except "trade machinery" as defined by the Act), when mortgaged or leased in any mortgage or lease of any freehold or leasehold interest in any land or building to which they are affixed, and whether or not such fixtures are separately mortgaged or leased by mention thereof in separate words, and whether or not power is given by such mortgage or lease to sever such fixtures from the land or building to which they are affixed without otherwise taking possession of or dealing with such land or building;

   (b) assignments for the benefit of the creditors of the person making the same;

   (c) transfers of or agreements to transfer instruments by way of security (although it is not mandatory to register, a registered transfer or agreement would take priority over an unregistered one);

   (d) transfers or assignments of any ship or vessel or any share thereof if executed before the first day of October 1940, or if at the time of execution the ship or vessel is registered or required to be registered under the provisions of Part XII of the Shipping and Seamen Act 1952;

   (e) transfers of chattels in the ordinary course of business of any trade or calling;

   (f) debentures and interest coupons issued by any Government or local authority;

   (g) bills of sale of chattels in any foreign parts, or at sea;

   (h) bills of lading, warehouse-keepers' certificates, warrants, or orders for the delivery of chattels, entries in auctioneer's books or any other document used in the ordinary course of business as proof of the possession or control of chattels, or authorising or purporting to authorise, either by indorsement or delivery, the possessor of such document to transfer or receive the chattels thereby represented;

   (i) debentures and interest coupons issued by any company or other corporate body and secured upon the capital stock or chattels of such company or other corporate body;

   (j) mortgages or charges granted or created by a company incorporated or registered under the Companies Act 1955. The effect of this exemption is that chattel securities, or "interests" granted by companies are not subject to the provisions of the Act. However their security will be lost as against the liquidator or any creditor of the company if the charge or mortgage is not registered under the provisions of Part IV of the Companies Act 1955;

   (k) customary hire purchase agreements as defined in the Act;

   (l) mortgages or charges granted or created by a society registered under the Industrial and Provident Societies Act 1908.

(5) *Instrument by way of security* means an instrument given to secure the payment of money or the performance of some obligation.

(6) *Registration* means the filing of an instrument with schedule or inventories, or a true copy thereof, with the certificate of due execution.

(7) Stock includes any sheep, cattle, horses, pigs, poultry, ostriches, and any other living animals.

(8) Trade machinery means the machinery used in or attached to any factory or workshop, but does not include:

  (a) the fixed motive powers, such as water-wheels, and steam and other engines, and the steam boilers, donkey-engines and other fixed appurtenances of the said motive powers; or
  (b) the fixed-power machinery (such as the shafts, wheels, drums, and their fixed appurtenances) for transmitting the action of the motive powers to the other machinery, fixed and loose; or
  (c) the pipes for steam, gas, and water.

For example, in a country timber mill the boiler, steam engine, flywheel, shafting and pulleys would be treated as fixtures, whereas planing machines, saws and sanders would be treated as trade machinery, ie, chattels, and title to them would in certain instances depend on the provisions of the Chattels Transfer Act 1924. It is submitted, although there is no authority on the point, that electric motors, being customary chattels included in the Seventh Schedule, would also be treated as chattels although they comprise part of the "fixed motive powers".

The Court will examine the terms of a document very carefully to determine its effect and the real intention of the parties and whether through its basic operative provisions it falls into the category of "instrument" and requires registration for the benefit of the public. If such a document is not registered and nevertheless gives effective legal control of chattels to someone other than the person who has possession, the Court will deprive the person having title and control of his or her rights against others who have had bona fide dealings with the chattels or creditors or representatives of creditors of the person having possession.

Where chattels are seized under a power of distress in an agreement, given as a form of security for a present, future or contingent debt and in which the rental is arranged as a means of paying interest on such debt, the agreement will be treated as an instrument (and thus requires registration to protect the lender) as regards the chattels so seized: s 3. Thus in *Re Bowes* (1880) 14 ChD 725 (CA), a clause in a mortgage securing £ 7,090 purported to create a tenancy determinable by one week's notice at a rental of £ 8,000 per year of premises worth a rental of £ 140 a year. Distress levied by the mortgagee landlord on the chattels of the mortgagor tenant was set aside on the bankruptcy of the tenant. Had the rental been genuine and not a mere device to get additional security through distress, the document would not have been treated as a registrable instrument.

36.3.2 Instruments by way of security, and fixtures

Securities over, or bailments or leases of fixtures, are not instruments and accordingly are not subject to the provisions of the Act unless the security document enables the grantee to deal with the fixtures independently of the land or buildings including a separate power of sale. The question "what is a fixture?" can be difficult to answer. It will depend to a large extent on the facts of each particular situation. In general, fixtures are chattels which have become part of the land by reason of the object and purpose of affixation to the land. Depending on the circumstances they may become the property of the landlord, the mortgagee of the property, or remain the property of the tenant.

Fixtures are of interest for two reasons. First, if a chattel is a fixture, then any document which may otherwise have been "an instrument" will not be so and will not require registration. Naturally, the converse is true, that is if the chattel is *not* a fixture, then such document *will* require registration. The second reason for our inquiry into fixtures, although not of direct relevance at this point, relates to ownership of the chattel in question. If the chattel is a fixture, then it may belong to the mortgagee, the landlord, the hire purchase vendor or the tenant, depending upon the circumstances. If the chattel is *not* a fixture, then it will belong to the tenant in whose possession and control it is unless there is an agreement to the contrary. If that agreement is in writing, then it is an instrument and will require registration.

As stated, to determine whether a chattel is a fixture or not, one has to analyse the purpose of annexation. If it was the permanent and substantial improvement of the land or buildings, the item is a fixture. But if it was for a temporary purpose or for more complete enjoyment and use of it as a chattel, then it remains a chattel. The degree of annexation and the damage which would be caused to the land and building by the removal of the item may assist in determining the object or purpose of annexation. Pillars of brick and mortar built on a dairy floor to hold milk pans have been held to be chattels: *Leach v Thomas* (1835) 7 C & P 327. The walls and roof of a shed erected on a concrete base by being bolted thereto have been held to be chattels: *Webb v Bevis Ltd* [1940] All ER 247. In *Neylon v Dickens* [1979] 2 NZLR 714, Jeffries J held that a prefabricated three-bedroom dwelling erected on permanent foundations and connected to drainage, sewerage and power, was a chattel. Although the degree of annexation was high, there was no doubt from the evidence that on the erection of the structure there had been no intention of permanently erecting the structure on the land. See also *Trust Bank Central Ltd v Southdown Properties Ltd* (High Court, Auckland, CP 59/90, 13 February 1990, Robertson J) (joinery wrongly removed from mortgaged properties made subject of mandatory injunction to deliver up); criticised by S Dukeson in "Commercial Securities" in *Essays in Commercial Law* (Borrowdale and Rowe eds) 93,98-9.

Goods the subject of a *customary* hire purchase agreement shall always remain chattels regardless of their degree of affixation, and the vendor or bailor of the chattels, upon the giving of one month's notice, may remove the chattel if and when he or she becomes entitled to possession under the customary hire purchase agreement: Chattels Transfer Act 1924, s 57(7).

36.3.3 Bailments and leases

Bailments and leases are included in the category of instruments. Office equipment, machinery for manufacturing, heavy trucks, and equipment for loading goods, are often leased by finance corporations to business people (eg the lessee chooses the equipment and the financier pays for it and then leases it to the person who requires it for his or her business). This avoids heavy capital expenditure by the lessee and has certain income tax advantages. There appears to be no necessity to register such leases or bailments. Although such transactions, if written, are included in the definition of "instrument", it is submitted that there is no serious consequence or invalidity in not registering them. As will be seen in this chapter, failure to register has two consequences. First, to the extent that the chattels are in the possession or apparent possession of the grantor (the bailor or lessor), the agreement is void as against the Official Assignee and creditors: s 18. However, as s 18 applies only to the insolvency of the grantor, it is not applicable on the insolvency of the bailee, or lessee. The second disadvantage arising from failing to register an investment relates to the rights of ownership of the chattels which may be acquired by a bona fide purchaser from the lessee. However, it is submitted that the true owner, the bailor or lessor, can never be deprived of his or her rights of ownership by transactions subsequently entered into by a bailee (lessee) with third parties unless there is some form of agency agreement between the lessor and the lessee, or unless s 19 is regarded as an exception to the nemo dat rule. However, as the Act is not concerned with transactions as such but with documents affecting title to goods, it is submitted that s 19 does not have this effect.

36.4 REGISTRATION

36.4.1 Form

The definition in s 2 of "instrument" does not specify any formalities for a document to qualify as an instrument. However, the Act does make express provision for instruments by way of security. Section 33(1) provides that an instrument by way of security may be in the form specified in the First Schedule or be "to the like effect, with such variations or modifications thereof and additions thereto as are expressed in the instrument. "

36.4.2 Attestation

Section 20 of the Act expressly denies that sealing is essential to the validity of any instrument, but then provides that every instrument shall be attested by at least one witness, who shall add to his or her signature his or her residence and occupation. See *Te Aro Loan Co v Cameron* (1895) 14 NZLR 411. The effect of non-compliance was authoritatively stated by the Privy Council in *National and Grindlays Bank Ltd v Dharamshi Vallabhji* [1967] 1 AC 207, where the grantee of an instrument was sued in trespass for taking possession of securities over which there was an unattested instrument by way of security. It was held that a breach of s 20 did not affect the validity of the instrument *inter partes* but non-compliance meant that the instrument was incapable of registration; or, if registered, could not afford the grantee the benefits of registration. The action for trespass was dismissed.

36.4.3 Mechanics of registration

Section 5(1) of the Act (as substituted by the Chattels Transfer Amendment Act 1973, s 2) states that registration of an instrument is effected by filing the instrument and schedules, or true copies, in the High Court

Office of any Registrar in the provincial district in which the particular chattels were situated when the instrument was made or given. These documents are to be accompanied by a certificate as specified in the First Schedule, or one to like effect. This certificate is signed by a witness who certifies that he or she was present and saw the instrument annexed to his or her certificate (or a true copy of which is attached to his or her certificate) signed by the grantor and any other signatories to it and that he or she is aware that he or she commits an offence if he or she acts negligently in giving the certificate or knows it to be false. In *Philips Electrical Industries of New Zealand Ltd v Official Assignee* [1981] 2 NZLR 104 an instrument by way of security was filed in Court, but no certificate was attached. That fact was later notified to the solicitor acting who was also the witness. The solicitor-witness then executed such a certificate and attended the Court to have it annexed to the instrument, which could not, however, be located by the Court clerk. Thereupon the witness left the certificate with the clerk to attach to the instrument, but the certificate was never attached and was instead lost. Whether it would have been sufficient for the Court clerk to have annexed it to the instrument when it was found was left open. It was held that registration of the instrument was not effected because of the absence of the witness' certificate. See also *ANZ Banking Group (NZ) Ltd v John F Jones Ltd* [1984] 2 NZLR 29.

Registration must be effected in the High Court office of the district in which the chattels are situated at the time of the making of the instrument. Accordingly, if the security comprised road-making machinery situated in the Dargaville district, the copy of the original instrument would be filed in the High Court office at Whangarei. An abstract of the instrument would be sent to the main High Court office of the province being the Auckland Registry, where the Chattels Register is kept. The index to the Chattels Register is in a filing cabinet with drawers having the grantors' names arranged alphabetically.

Although there is no central register for the whole of New Zealand the principal cities keep a register not only of the instruments filed in their own registry but also of the smaller registries adjoining them. Auckland, for example, has a register of all the instruments registered in its own High Court office and also details sufficient to enable a person to find out whether any instrument has been registered in the Whangarei or Hamilton registries. Each registry retains the instruments filed in its own office. Consequently the only information available in Auckland about an instrument over road-making machinery situated at Dargaville would be the names of the grantor and the grantee, the name of the district in which he or she lived, the registration number in the Whangarei Registry, the type of instrument – instrument by way of security, bailment, lease, hire purchase agreement or conditional purchase agreement, the date of the instrument and whether registration had been renewed after five years. For details of the chattel itself and the terms binding the grantor and grantee it would be necessary to search the registered copy in the Whangarei Office.

Usually a search is undertaken to see if the person having possession of the chattels owns them. Consequently, to ascertain whether a security has been given by the person in possession, the search must be commenced by reference to the name of the grantor; but to determine whether goods are held under hire purchase (not customary) or bailment, reference must be made to a transaction under the name of the grantee. Searchers must be on the alert for cards out of alphabetical order. The Registrar cannot be held responsible if this occurs.

36.4.4 Time for registration

An instrument must be registered on the day of execution or within the following twenty-one days. If the Registrar's office is closed on the twenty-first day, registration may be made on the first following day of business. The instrument is protected against the consequence of non-registration during this period. An instrument affecting chattels in the Chatham Islands or islands not included in any particular provincial district, must be registered in the High Court office at Wellington. The time allowed for the registration of instruments executed out of New Zealand or in the outlying islands referred to above is ninety days from the execution thereof.

If there is more than one grantor, the date of execution is deemed to be the date of execution by the grantor who first executes the instrument: s 8. If the instrument is some form of bailment or lease, which is complete only when signed by all parties, the time for filing runs from the date on which the last signatory executed the document.

If an instrument is made in execution of any process of the Court, the name, residence and occupation of the person against whom such process is issued must be stated in the certificate which is filed on registration: s 6.

Registration must be renewed within five years of the previous registration. This is done by filing an affidavit of renewal, the form of which is set out in the First Schedule to the Act. The initial registration and any renewal of the registration is effective to protect the interests of the parties for five years from the date on which registration takes place:

36.4.5 Extension of time for registration

Under s 13, the time for registration may be extended and mistakes in the register may be corrected on the order of a Judge of the High Court, provided that he or she is satisfied that the omission or mistake was accidental or due to inadvertence. Likewise, if an instrument has been filed in the wrong High Court office, a Judge may order it to be transferred to the correct office and registered there.

The form of order and the considerations affecting the Court were settled in *Re Byers* (1905) 24 NZLR 903; 7 GLR 464, and in *Re Chattels Transfer Act 1908* (1914) 33 NLZR 1536. In *Byers'* case Edwards J said, at 904.

> ... the legislature must, I think, be taken to have assumed that the time would not be extended without fully protecting the rights and interests of all persons who might directly or indirectly be affected by the extension of the time for registration.

Under this order, the grantee undertakes that the interests of third parties will not be affected and counsel for the grantee undertakes that he or she will raise no objection if the order is set aside at the instigation of third parties or the Official Assignee. There is also power to grant an extension of time for the registration of an affidavit of renewal.

36.4.6 Miscellaneous provisions as to registration

A chattel security given by a company must be registered with the Registrar of Companies. If it is so registered, the grantee will have the same protection as he or she would have had under the Chattels Transfer Act. All persons shall be deemed to have notice of it and it cannot be avoided by the liquidator and the creditors of the company except in terms of the Companies Act 1955, s 102 (12).

But it must be remembered that s 102 of the Companies Act 1955 authorises only the registration of charges. True hire purchase agreements or conditional purchase agreements do not create charges within the meaning of s 102 and therefore will not be accepted for registration by the Companies Office. These agreements are registrable in the Chattels Transfer Registry.

Speight J in *Re Manurewa Transport Ltd* [1971] NZLR 909 (infra) deals with the respective priorities given by the registration of a floating charge under the Companies Act and an instrument by way of security under the Chattels Transfer Act.

SECURITIES FOR PAST ADVANCES
Registration will not protect a grantee where his or her security under the Act has been given in the period commencing 12 months before the filing of a creditor's petition and continuing up to adjudication or in the 12 months preceding a debtor's petition in bankruptcy (if there is no creditor's petition): Insolvency Act 1967, s 57(1). Such securities are voidable against the Official Assignee except as to:

(a) money actually advanced or paid; or
(b) the actual price or value of the goods sold or supplied by the grantee to the grantor contemporaneously with or at any time after the execution of the instrument.

Any unpaid purchase money for any property is deemed to be money actually advanced at the time of execution, if the instrument is executed within 21 days of the sale: Insolvency Act 1967, s 57 (2).

Securities given in pursuance of an agreement made prior to the 12 months period and securities in substitution for securities given before the commencement of the said period are not voidable at the option of the Assignee. Section 57 of the Insolvency Act, referring to voidable securities, is discussed more fully infra. However consider the case of *Farm Products Ltd v Bellkirk Poultry Farm Ltd* [1965] NZLR 1012.

In December 1964 E owed approximately £2,000 to the plaintiff. As the amount had been owing for some time and was unsecured, E executed an instrument by way of security over his flock of poultry and all produce from such poultry. In January 1965 E entered into an agreement to sell the poultry to the defendant, the agreement being conditional on the defendant being able to obtain a lease of the property on which the poultry were situated. The defendant did not secure an enforceable lease until May 1965. On 24 March 1965 E was adjudicated bankrupt on his own petition. Although there was a covenant in the instrument by way of security forbidding the grantor to sell without the consent of the grantee, it was clear that the grantee wanted the grantor to sell subject to his receiving the purchase money on account of the secured debt. The price was to be determined by valuation, and possession of the poultry was to be given three days after the date of the valuation. The valuation took place on 6 March 1965. McGregor J found that it was a sale of specific goods in respect of which both delivery and payment were postponed but that the deciding factor was that the sale was subject to an unfulfilled condition on 24 March 1965 (the date of adjudication) and that accordingly no property had passed to the defendant. To the extent that the instrument by way of security secured a past advance (the amount of approximately £2,000 owing in December 1964) it was void, as adjudication had taken place only three months after the execution of the instrument; the instrument was, however, valid to the extent that the plaintiff could prove it had made advances to E subsequent to the execution of the instrument.

36.5 EFFECTS OF REGISTRATION

36.5.1 Notice

Section 4(1) is the central point around which the Act is constructed; it states that, from the moment of registration, all persons are deemed to have notice of the existence and contents of the registered instrument. So where there is a registered instrument a third party cannot claim, for example, to come under the bona fide purchaser without notice exception to the nemo dat rule: *Guardian Trust and Executors Co Ltd v Equitable Loan and Finance Co Ltd* [1929] NZLR 702. Notice is only in respect of the instrument and not of any other interconnected transactions: *Re Lyford; Official Assignee v General Finance Ltd* (1990) 3 NZBLC 101, 727.

By virtue of s 4(3), registration is not in itself notice of the existence or contents of that instrument to the grantee of any prior registered instrument over the same chattels or some of them. A grantee of such prior registered instrument who makes further advances before receiving notice of the second registered instrument will have priority over the second grantee. This appears to make it imperative for the grantee of the second registered instrument to give notice to the grantee of the prior registered instrument. Once the first grantee receives notice, he or she has no priority over the second grantee for further advances unless the latter has consented to the further advance being made.

Except as provided in s 4(3), all persons are deemed to have notice of a security over chattels given by a company and of the contents of such security (so far as it relates to chattels) immediately upon registration of such security in the manner provided by the Companies Act 1955: Chattels Transfer Act 1924, s 4(2).

36.5.2 Priorities

Where more instruments than one are executed comprising in whole or in part the same chattels, priority is accorded in order of the time of their *registration*, not execution: s 22. A proviso to s 22 stipulates that a grantee claiming priority by virtue of an earlier registration must prove that when he or she executed the instrument he or she had no notice of the existence of any unregistered instrument: see *Powell v Harcourt* (1884) NZLR 2 (CA) 303, 306.

The relative priorities of a floating charge over company assets registered with the Registrar of Companies before the registration of a chattel security over one of the assets comprised in the floating charge was examined by Speight J in *Re Manurewa Transport Ltd* [1971] NZLR 909. A debenture creating a floating charge over the assets of a company was registered under s 102 of the Companies Act 1955 with the Registrar of Companies in July 1968. An instrument by way of security for repairs to a truck amounting to some $3,600 was given to a motor engineering firm and registered in September 1969. This truck was one of the assets of the company at the time it gave a floating charge over its undertaking. The contest was as to priority, in particular whether the later chattel security over a specific item took priority over the earlier floating charge. It appears that the motor engineering firm relinquished its workman's lien for the value of the repairs and let the company have its truck back on being given the instrument by way of security. The debenture contained a condition whereby the money secured should become immediately due and payable and the charge thereby created should attach and be affixed inter alia, if the company mortgaged, charged or encumbered any of its assets contrary to the provisions of the debenture without the prior written consent of the debenture holder. The debenture being a floating charge contained a condition permitting the company to deal with its property in the ordinary course of business but the company was not to create a mortgage or other charge upon any part of its assets in priority to the charge created by the debenture except with the written consent of the debenture holder.

His Honour held that pursuant to s 102 (2) of the Companies Act 1955, the grantee of the instrument by way of security had constructive notice of the contents of the debenture in accordance with s 4 (2) of the Chattels Transfer Act 1924. The debenture provided that the moneys due thereunder should become payable and the charge would attach and become affixed if the company mortgaged, charged or attempted to mortgage or charge any of its assets without the written consent of the debenture holder. This the company did and the floating charge automatically crystallised when the instrument by way of security was executed. It therefore had priority.

The Rural Intermediate Credit Act 1927, s 73, provides that any instrument by way of security under that Act shall have priority over any prior registered security if the grantee in the prior security joins in the latter security and agrees therein that it shall have priority.

If a grantor, who has given a security over his or her plant and stock wishes to lease his or her land, plant and stock to a third person, it appears that the grantee under the original security should give a bailment over the plant and stock to the third person and then register the bailment in the usual manner.

Registration effected more than five years previously ceases to have any effect: s 14.

36.6 EFFECTS OF NON-REGISTRATION

36.6.1 General

Failure to register an instrument within the required period in no way affects the validity of the instrument between the parties themselves: *Re*

Proudfoot [1961] NZLR 268, 276. However, as against certain third parties, the unregistered instrument is void in the circumstances set out in ss 18 and 19 of the Act. Furthermore, the title of the grantee of an unregistered instrument is liable to be displaced by that of a person claiming under a registered instrument: s 22.

36.6.2 Section 18

This section provides that where the time, or extended time, for registration has passed without due registration the instrument is deemed to be "fraudulent and void" as against:

(a) the assignee in bankruptcy of the person whose chattels are comprised in the instrument;

(b) the assignee or trustee acting under any assignment for the benefit of creditors of such a person;

(c) any sheriff, bailiff or other person seizing such chattels in due execution of the process of any Court;

provided the chattels comprised in the instrument are in the possession or apparent possession of the grantor or the person against whom the process is issued.

So the effect of s 18 is that because the instrument is deemed invalid the specified three classes of persons can ignore it and acquire rights over the chattels comprised in the instrument if they are still in the possession or apparent possession of the grantor at the relevant time. As the avoidance only applies to the extent that the chattels are in the possession or apparent possession of the grantor at or after the time of bankruptcy, or at the time of the execution by the grantor of an assignment for the benefit of creditors or of the execution of the process of any Court (as the case may be), it is important to examine the expression "apparent possession". No definition is given in the Act but the expression has been examined in a number of cases over the years.

In *Official Assignee of Casey v Bartosh* [1955] NZLR 287 a solicitor for a grantee whose instrument had not been registered purported to take possession of the chattels charged but was held on the facts to have done so ineffectively with the result that the Official Assignee succeeded in having the goods restored to general creditors. The solicitor had entered the business premises of the debtor, marked off the chattels covered by the instrument, and removed the keys to the premises. The premises remained closed and bankruptcy intervened before the grantee had shifted the chattels from these premises. Barrowclough CJ after conceding that the chattels were in the possession of the grantee's solicitor from the date on which the latter took the keys, stated, at 290:

> After that date, they were in Mr Ongley's (the solicitor for the grantee) possession; but they would remain in the apparent possession of the bankrupt because they were "in or upon the premises of the person making or giving the bill of sale" and they would so remain until something was done, which in the eyes of everybody who sees the goods, or who is concerned in the matter, plainly takes them out of the apparent possession of the grantor. What then was done, and was it enough to put an end to the apparent possession?
>
> All that was done was this: Mr Ongley and Mr Casey entered the shop by going through an alley-way to the back door. It was not proved that anyone

saw them enter or saw them in the shop. Mr Ongley then took possession and retained the keys. The shop, which had been closed down before, remained closed down. So far as the evidence went, there was no obvious change that could have been apparent to anyone but these two.

Therefore, a grantee cannot protect himself or herself against the consequences of non-registration by merely withdrawing his or her consent to the goods remaining in the grantor's possession; formal or symbolic taking of possession is not enough to put an end to the apparent possession of the grantor.

Bartosh's case may be contrasted with the earlier case of *Official Assignee v Colonial Bank of New Zealand* (1887) NZLR 5 SC 456. A bailiff purported to take possession of a debtor's stock in trade by taking an inventory and locking up the debtor's Lumsden store and had also taken money from the customers as the debtor stood beside him telling him the prices. The bailiff also counted cattle belonging to the debtor while they were grazing in a paddock but did nothing else to show that he had taken possession of them. It was held that the actions of the bailiff in seizing the stock in trade were sufficient and notorious in such a small country town so that the debtor was not in apparent possession of these goods. However, the debtor was in apparent possession of the cattle.

Where the grantor has parted with possession of goods to some third party such as a bailee, the question may arise as to whether those goods remain in the grantor's apparent possession. In *South Pacific Loan and Investment Co v Official Assignee of Wright* (1898) 17 NZLR 492, Prendergast CJ stated, at 496:

> Generally the possession of a simple bailee – for instance a bailee to take care of a thing – from the grantor of a bill of sale would be constructively the possession of the grantor – . . . but the possession of a pledgee from the grantor would not be the possession of the grantor.

Therefore, where chattels have been bailed by the grantor to some third party, whether or not they will be regarded as still being in the apparent possession of the grantor will depend on the nature of the bailment. In *Philips Electrical Industries of New Zealand Ltd v Official Assignee* [1981] 2 NZLR 104, over 50 television sets (being the subject of an invalidly registered instrument by way of security) were in the physical possession of persons who had hired them from the grantor of the instrument. It was held that these television sets were not in the apparent possession of the grantor as they were not reclaimable at the will of the grantor but subject to the rights of possession of the hirers. See also *Re Scott ex parte Vincent* (1906) 26 NZLR 116; 8 GLR 578.

A grantee with an unregistered security who seeks to protect himself or herself by seizing the chattels comprising the security must have brought them effectively into his or her possession before the commencement of the period of relation back if the grantor is adjudicated bankrupt. Apparent possession of the grantor may be terminated even though such termination is an illegal act on the part of the grantee: *Johns v Mullinder* [1916] NZLR 422; [1916] GLR 264. Notwithstanding the emphasis throughout the Act on the importance of registration, the grantee with an unregistered security may nevertheless be in a stronger position than other creditors in bankruptcy.

The operation of s 18 of the Act has been severely criticised. Mr G Cain, "Chattels Transfer Act: Seizure of Chattels by Grantee" [1960] NZLJ 391 observes:

> The chief purpose of the Act is surely to protect the s 18 group against the unregistered instrument, and, to go one further step back, to prevent the debtor from raising credit on the strength of his possession of goods which he does not own, or which are subject to secret charges. It is suggested that if the grantee under an unregistered instrument can effectively seize the chattels at the first breath of trouble this basic purpose of the Act is endangered. The test should not be the possession of the debtor at the time the rights of the s 18 group arise (the damage is likely to have been done at this stage) but at the time when the credit is obtained in the first place.

36.6.3 Section 19

Where an instrument has not been registered, s 19 states that such instrument shall not, without express notice, be valid and effectual as against any bona fide purchaser or mortgagee for valuable consideration, or as against any person bona fide selling or dealing with the relevant chattels as auctioneer, dealer, or agent in the ordinary course of business. By virtue of this section the grantee of an instrument who fails to register it is in danger of having his or her interest defeated by a subsequent purchaser, or ranked second in priority after the interest of a second mortgagee. It appears that a second mortgage will take priority over an earlier unregistered instrument even though the instrument creating the second mortgage is also unregistered. As Cain, "The Chattels Transfer Act: Oddities and Oddments" [1959] NZLJ 87, 88 points out "this is contrary to normal principles; if equities are equal, the first in time prevails". Section 19 also protects any auctioneer, dealer or agent who, by assisting the grantor to dispose of goods that are the subject of an unregistered security interest, has unwittingly laid himself open to legal action by the grantee. The categories of person identified in s 19 must act bona fide and without notice of the unregistered instrument to derive the protection of the section.

36.7 AVOIDANCE FOR DEFECTS OTHER THAN NON-REGISTRATION

36.7.1 General

Other circumstances besides non-registration are provided for in the Act which will avoid or invalidate an instrument as against the categories of persons, identified in ss 18 and 19. Before turning to a consideration of these circumstances it must be pointed out that whenever an instrument is invalidated as against the s 18 group of persons the apparent possession requirement is applicable; that is, where an instrument is invalid for some reason other than non-registration as against the s 18 group it is only invalid to the extent provided in s 18. This means that a grantee could protect himself or herself by seizing the chattels comprised in an invalid instrument and by taking them out of the possession or apparent possession of the grantor thereby preserving his or her security: *Re Franks* [1934] NZLR 886.

36.7.2 Inventory

It is usual to describe the chattels subject to an instrument in a schedule. However, if an instrument affects only one chattel, this is not necessary. In many cases the list of chattels given as security is so extensive that if schedules are not used the whole sense and continuity of the instrument is destroyed. If the chattels are insufficiently described, the instrument is valid to the extent and as against the persons mentioned in ss 18 and 19.

In terms of s 23, every instrument must contain an inventory or schedule of the chattels comprised therein, the instrument gives a good title only to the chattels described in such inventory or schedule. What constitutes an adequate description depends on the occupation of the parties and the surrounding circumstances. "A bay gelding" would probably be insufficient if the grantor was a racehorse breeder. Every effort should be made to describe the chattels in such a way that the chattels can be identified from the schedule or inventory.

  (a) Household furniture and effects: *Roberts v Roberts* (1884) 13 QBD 794; and
  (b) 400,000 envelopes as part of the description of the contents of the stationer's shop: *Sommers v Eiby* (1890) 8 NZLR 626.

In *Hylton Parker and Co Ltd v Medical Securities Ltd* (High Court, Auckland, CP 1315/89, 28 June 1989) Thorp J held that description of a motor vehicle by make, year and registration number was sufficient compliance under s 23. (Motor vehicles are now outside the scope of the Chattels Transfer Act.)

Generally, see *Eyre* v *McCullough* [1925] NZLR 395; *ANZ Banking Group (NZ) Ltd v John F Jones Ltd* [1984] 2 NZLR 29.

The question of the validity of a security over stock-in-trade is discussed, infra. As to the description of book debts, see below.

36.7.3 After-acquired chattels

After-acquired chattels are chattels to which the grantor of an instrument becomes entitled after the execution of the instrument.

Section 24 provides that an instrument over chattels which the grantor acquires or becomes entitled to after the execution of the instrument is void *to the extent* and as against the persons mentioned in ss 18 and 19. The instrument is, nevertheless, good between the parties thereto, and if the grantee seizes the chattels before the commencement of bankruptcy or before the assignment to an assignee for the benefit of creditors or seizure by an execution creditor, he or she will be entitled to the chattels. Likewise, a grantee who has taken an assignment of future book debts which become due to the grantor after the execution of the instrument is protected if he or she can secure payment before the above events: *Tailby v Official Receiver* (1888) 13 App Cas 523.

A proviso to s 24 excludes from its ambit those instruments which cover loans to buy the chattels specified in the instrument; although the chattels acquired with the loan money are strictly speaking after-acquired, the proviso deems them to have been acquired contemporaneously with the execution of the instrument. This proviso was considered in *Broadlands Finance Ltd v Shand Miller Musical Supplies Ltd* [1976] 2 NZLR 124. Shand Miller, the respondent in this appeal from a decision of the Magistrate's Court, dealt in musical instruments. H arranged to buy certain musical instruments from Shand Miller on hire purchase and got Shand Miller to give him a list on its own business paper setting out details of the instruments he was going to buy. H took the list to Broadlands which agreed to take a chattel security over the instruments H was going to buy and to lend him $850 on the instruments. The chattel security stated "whenever the grantor (H) is not at the time of giving this security the owner of the said chattels, then the loan is to be extended in whole or in part in the purchase of the said chattels".

The appellant contended that the clause above in the chattel security and the proviso to s 24 of the Act gave it a security over the musical instruments as H had undertaken to apply the loan of $850 in the purchase of the instruments and that as he had done so he must be deemed to have acquired the chattels contemporaneously with the execution of the chattel security.

But H had used the $850 merely to pay a deposit on the instruments and had entered into a hire purchase (conditional sale) agreement with Shand Miller under which he made default and never acquired title. It was not a customary hire purchase agreement and had not been registered. He also defaulted in meeting his payments under the instrument by way of security.

Quilliam J found that the conditional sale agreement, although not registered, was good between the parties and that Broadlands must fail in its action to get the musical instruments subject to the security back from Shand Miller, which had repossessed them. He said that as title to the instruments was to remain with the seller, H could not give what he had not got and that the proviso to s 24 should read "the grantor (H) shall be deemed to have acquired the said chattels, *if he acquired them at all*, contemporaneously with the execution of the instrument".

Until all instalments of the hire purchase agreement had been paid H never acquired title and there was no title he could pass to Broadlands. Furthermore Broadlands, having no title, was not a bona fide mortgagee and could not get any protection under s 19 of the Chattels Transfer Act.

See D McLauchlan, "Chattel Transfer— The Security That Never Was" [1977] NZLJ 118. See too *Re Lyford; Official Assignee v General Finance Ltd* (1990) 3 NZBLC 101, 727 which followed the *Broadlands* case.

Another area of difficulty with s 24 relates to s 50 which provides that the covenants of the Fourth Schedule to the Act are to be implied into every instrument by way of security. One of the covenants is that the grantor will replace any chattels that are destroyed or cease to exist and will, if required to do so by the grantee, execute any instrument that may be necessary to give the grantee security over these replacement chattels. It is clear that these replacement chattels are chattels acquired after the execution of the instrument. The position of such replacement chattels was considered by Stanton J in *New Zealand Creditmen's Association Ltd v Garvey* [1957] NZLR 1104. It was held in that case that the covenant implied by s 50 created an equitable security over such chattels as are replacing chattels. The execution and registration of a further instrument in respect of such replacement chattels is necessary to protect the grantee as against the ss 18 and 19 groups.

36.7.4 Defeasance

The defeasance clause, s 25, requires that the full agreement of the parties be put on record. If there is some unregistered document substantially modifying the provisions of the registered document, the whole object of registration is defeated. The registered instrument does not give adequate or accurate notice of the legal position to the interested parties.

For the purposes of s 25, a defeasance is a provision, declaration of trust or agreement which defeats the operation of an instrument, but is contained in some document other than the one which is registered. Even an oral condition may operate as a defeasance: *Christchurch Finance Co v Durant and Son* (1889) 7 NZLR 619.

Section 25(2) provides that if a document secures the payment of money, it shall not be necessary to write such document on the same paper so long as the date, the names of the parties thereto and the nature of the security are set forth in the instrument or some schedule thereto.

Non-compliance with s 25 means that the instrument is void to the extent and as against the persons referred to in s 18 as regards the property in or rights to the possession of any chattels comprised in or affected by such instrument.

Whether there is a defeasance or not, the instrument is good as between the parties. It is avoided only against the Official Assignee, the assignee for creditors and the execution creditor. The section refers to an instrument "given subject to any defeasance". This means that the defeasance must have been made either contemporaneously with, or prior to the execution of the instrument defeated. Any agreement made subsequently cannot operate as a defeasance. In *Guardian Trust and Executors Co Ltd v Equitable Loan and Finance Co Ltd* [1929] NZLR 702; [1929] GLR 485; a grantor had given a duly registered chattel mortgage over certain chattels in May 1927. In August 1927 the grantor signed a second instrument (in the form of a receipt) in favour of the grantee varying the terms of the original registered instrument. In February 1928 the grantor's wife, under an assumed name, purported to sell the chattels subject to the security to an auctioneer. It was held that:

(a) the second document was not a rescission of the original mortgage as no memorandum of satisfaction was in existence;

(b) it was not a defeasance as it had not been made before or at the time the original instrument by way of security was executed;

(c) as the original registered instrument had not been invalidated by the subsequent execution of the unregistered instrument, no title to the chattels passed to the auctioneer.

There is no logical reason why an agreement reached subsequently should be treated or regarded any differently; the principle that the register should truly reflect the position between the parties is breached as much by a subsequent secret agreement as by a contemporary one Cain: "The Chattels Transfer Act: Oddities and Oddments" [1959] NZLJ 87, 89.

36.7.5 Successive securities

A chattel security executed after a prior unregistered instrument over the same chattels (or any of them) as security for the same debt is avoided against the persons mentioned in s 18 (the Official Assignee, the assignee for creditors and an execution creditor) unless it was given bona fide for the purpose of correcting some material error in the first instrument and not for the purpose of evading the Act: s 34.

Some doubt as to correct procedure may arise where the chattel security is executed after there has been an agreement between the parties to end on the same security or if a chattel security is executed more than 21 days before the advance is made. Mr G Cain in [1959] NZLJ 104,105 suggests that as the agreement in the first instance does not *create* any mortgage or lien and does not *transfer* or purport to transfer the property in or the right to the possession of any chattels, but more evidences the earlier oral agreement, then the subsequent written document does not need registration. In the second situation, viz the execution of a chattel security more than 21 days before the advance is made, Mr Cain suggests that this written agreement is a nullity because as no money has passed, it secures nothing. However, it is submitted that if money is subsequently advanced, pursuant to the agreement previously entered into then *at the time of acquisition* of any chattels with the sums advanced, the lender will obtain an equitable mortgage or charge over those chattels: *Re Connolly Bros* [1912] 2 Ch 25. In this situation s 2(f) of the definition of "instrument" would render the original written agreement an agreement by which a right in equity to any chattels, or to any charge or security thereon or thereover is conferred. The applicability of this subparagraph depends upon whether or not the right in equity was *conferred by the agreement,* to be distinguished from, *as a result of* the agreement. In *Roberts v IAC (Finance) Pty Ltd* [1967] VR 321 the Supreme Court of Victoria held in a similar situation that such a charge could be regarded as created in the latter manner, ie *as a result* of the agreement, and therefore was not registrable. However, it is submitted that in that case the agreement was not in writing and neither the New Zealand nor Victorian sections would have applied. It is submitted that the better view is that subpara (f) will apply to any written agreement which is not merely evidential of an earlier oral agreement, if the mortgagee or charge-holder has to refer to the written agreement to establish that he or she is entitled to a mortgage. As regards after-acquired chattels or future goods and *Roberts'* case, see infra.

Section 34 is designed to prevent the evasion of the Act by persons seeking to avoid registration and giving notice to other parties of the transaction. The fact that the parties purport to discharge the already existing instrument and to give a fresh security will not exclude the operation of s 34: *In re Jensen* [1918] NZLR 121; [1918] GLR 50.

36.8 SAVING

It is sometimes desired to give security over stock, replacement stock, crops which have yet to be sown, or future clips of wool. If the provisions as to inventory and after-acquired chattels applied to such securities it would not be possible to give a valid security over such chattels. Replacement machinery and farming equipment are subject to a similar exemption.

Accordingly, it has been provided that s 23 (inventory), s 24 (after-acquired chattels) and s 25 (defeasance) shall not render an instrument void as to:

(a) stock, wool and crops; or
(b) fixtures, plant or trade machinery substituted for similar equipment described in the instrument; or
(c) tractors, engines, machines, vehicles and farming equipment described in the instrument and used upon the land described in the instrument;
(d) any chattels which the grantor under an instrument by way of security is required by the instrument to hold, until sold or while not leased or hired, on the property specified in the instrument if
   (i) the chattels are by their nature or description reasonably capable of identification and
   (ii) the grantor sells, hires out or disposes by hire purchase chattels of that nature: s 26, as amended by the Chattels Transfer Amendment Act 1974, s 3(1).

Where any chattels are subject to an instrument by way of security which but for the provisions of para (d) above, would have been void against the persons mentioned in ss 18 and 19 of the Act through inadequacy of description (s 23) or as not complying with the provisions of s 24 relating to after-acquired chattels, the proceeds of any sale, bailment or exchange of those chattels received by the grantor shall form part of the grantee's security, only to the extent that:

(a) the instrument expressly states that the proceeds form part of the grantee's security; and
(b) for so long as any such proceeds being money are kept by or on behalf of the grantor in a separate and identifiable fund: Chattels Transfer Amendment Act 1974, s 3(2).

Prior to the enactment of this amendment a trader could not give a satisfactory security over his or her stock in trade, because owing to its changing nature, it could not be adequately described. This amendment is designed to clarify the position of a dealer raising money to enable him or her to buy stock in trade required for his or her business. As a corollary to this new latitude afforded to traders, protection was given to customers of such traders. It would be inequitable and commercially disastrous to expect customers to inspect a chattels register before purchasing from a shop. Therefore the Chattels Transfer Amendment Act 1974, s 2, adds a new s 18A to the principal Act. The new section is headed "Protection to retail customers". In the first place the section gives protection to a person who has hired chattels in good faith and for valuable consideration from a person whose business it is to hire out chattels of that kind. If this person has given some form of security or an instrument entitling a third person to seize and sell the chattels so hired, such person cannot seize the chattels but must observe the hirer's rights under the bailment. Such person is bound by its terms but he or she is entitled to moneys payable under the bailment and to all other rights of the original bailor.

The bailee's rights are the same whether the bailment is registered or not. There is however no protection under this section for a bailee who is entitled or obliged to purchase the chattels.

In the second place a person who buys chattels in good faith and for valuable consideration from a retailer, who has given a security over the chattels to a lender, takes such chattels free from the security interest (whether registered or not) so given by the retailer. A security interest in chattels is one which secures the payment of money or the performance of an obligation as, for example, conditional contracts for the sale of chattels, hire purchase agreements or bailments securing the payment of money. Generally see D McLauchlan, *Legislation Note* (1976) 8 NZULR 83.

36.9 INSTRUMENTS OVER PARTICULAR TYPES OF SECURITY

36.9.1 Book debts

The provisions relating to book debts are set out in the Statutes Amendment Act 1939 (s 6) which is to be read with the Chattels Transfer Act 1924.

Book debts means debts owing to any person in the course of his or her trade or business, but do not include any debt secured or charged on land, or any debt owing to any person for or in respect of any milk, cream, or butterfat supplied by him or her to any butter factory, cheese factory, condensed-milk factory, or milk-powder factory: s 6(4).

Each book debt is treated as a separate chattel and shall be described by setting forth the amount of the debt and the name of the debtor or firm of debtors so far as is reasonably necessary to show by whom the debt is owing: s 6(3).

It would not matter if the debtors resided in some other part of New Zealand because the debt is deemed to be a chattel situated in the place where the creditor, that is the grantor of the instrument comprising such chattels, longest resided or carried on business during the six months preceding the execution of the instrument: s 6(2).

36.9.2 Crops

No security can be given over any crop (other than flax) which cannot be harvested within one year from the date of execution of the instrument: s 36. A security may be given over crops to be sown on the lands mentioned in the instrument or to be sown thereon or after they have been harvested, no matter where they are stacked or stored: s 35. The phrase "lands mentioned in the instrument" means lands mentioned in such a manner that persons reading the instrument may at any time be able to identify them: *Pyne, Gould, Guiness Ltd v Meredith and Co and John Mill and Co Ltd* [1926] NZLR 241; [1926] GLR 136.

The rights of a landlord or mortgagee of the land on which the crops are growing are not prejudicially affected by the instrument unless he or she has consented to it in writing: s 37. A registered instrument over crops is not extinguished by the subsequent sale, lease or mortgage of the land:

s 37. But the existence of such a registered instrument over a crop gives the grantee thereunder no right to block the sale of the land. A mortgagee selling the land under his or her power of sale would have first priority over the proceeds for the settlement of his or her claim and the grantee would be restricted to getting paid out of the balance of the proceeds.

The defeasance, after-acquired chattels and inventory clauses do not apply to this form of security: s 26.

The following power in an instrument by way of security over crops is implied by the Fourth Schedule to the Act. Upon default, the crops shall be harvested either by the grantor or the grantee at the grantee's option, but at the grantor's expense and delivered to the grantee who may sell the same in New Zealand or out of New Zealand and shall not be responsible for any efficiency on such sale. From the proceeds, the grantee shall pay the grantor the balance after deducting a sufficient amount to cover principal and interest, all charges and rent due.

Any contractor who has threshed a crop subject to a bill of sale and gives written notice of his or her claim to the grantee within ten days of the sale by the grantee shall be entitled to be paid out of the proceeds: Wages Protection and Contractor's Liens Act 1939, s 47.

36.9.3 Stock

Stock is personal property completely transferable by delivery and is therefore classified as chattels for the purposes of the Act. Under s 28 the stock must be described by some brand, earmark or other mark or by their sex, age, name, colour or other mode of description. The Act refers to the "name" of stock, but in the larger dairy herds the cows usually have numbers branded on them (except in the case of sheep) and this number, with the registered brand and earmark, is used for identification purposes. The description must be sufficient to render the stock reasonably capable of identification. In *Sowell v National Australia Finance Ltd* (1990) 3 NZBLC 101, 718 Doogue J held that the obligation was to provide a description which one would normally expect for the particular nature of the stock. Failure to comply under s 28 did not make the instrument unregistrable but meant that there was inadequate notice to the world of the security.

The requirement that the description of stock will make them "reasonable capable of identification" (s 25) depends largely on the stock in question; a description of a farmer's dairy herd by sex and age makes such stock reasonably capable of identification; a covenant "to ear mark" will be taken to have the same meaning "mutatis mutandis" as the covenant "will brand" in the Sixth Schedule and creates a duty to brand present and future stock and imposes a perpetual duty to brand while the security remains valid: *Official Assignee of Bailey v Union Bank of Australia* [1916] NZLR 9; [1916] GLR 78.

In the same case, on appeal, it was held that if the earmarks on the cattle are not the same as that specified in the instrument, the description is insufficient for the purposes of s 25 and invalid against the Official Assignee, but that the grantee can nevertheless rely on the provisions in s 26 that an instrument comprising stock shall be deemed to include all the stock he or she has covenanted to brand which are depasturing on the land described in the instrument: *Union Bank of Australia v Official*

Assignee of Bailey [1916] NZLR 873; [1916] GLR 449, CA. The fact that a brand is unregistered is irrelevant: *Honore v Farmers Co-operative Auctioneering Co Ltd and Official Assignee* [1923] NZLR 56. The land where the stock are depastured must also be described.

If the description is inadequate the instrument will be void to the extent and as against the persons mentioned in s 18 as regards such of the stock as cannot be reasonably identified. If the land on which the stock are depastured is not described, the instrument is not invalidated as between the parties, but even if the instrument is accepted for registration the grantee loses the benefit of registration: *Lee v Official Assignee* (1904) 22 NZLR 747; 5 GLR 269.

If, however, the grantee properly gains possession of the stock before the commencement of the grantor's bankruptcy or seizure by an assignee for creditors or an execution creditor, he or she can exercise his or her rights over them. The grantee must remove them from "the apparent possession" of the grantor.

Unless the contrary is expressed, an instrument over stock shall be deemed to include:

(a) the stock described therein;

(b) the natural increase of such stock; and

(c) all stock of the classes described being the property of the grantor and branded or marked as specified in the instrument or covenanted to be so branded or marked which are depasturing upon the land described therein: s 29.

Natural increase, after-acquired, and replacement stock, which fall within s 29, are included in the security. The provisions of s 29 as to natural increase apply to poultry but s 28, providing for branding and marking, does not.

The provisions as to defeasance, after-acquired chattels and inventory (s 23) do not apply to instruments over stock.

The following powers, covenants and provisions are implied by the Fourth Schedule in instruments by way of security over stock:

(a) That the grantee may enter and view the stock and that the grantor will, on receiving seven days' previous notice in writing, assist the grantee to view the stock. This provision is particularly necessary on a large sheep station;

(b) That all the stock described are grazing on the said lands and that the grantor will not further encumber the stock, reduce the specified number, change the general character or description of the stock, remove them from the land or sell the same except in the ordinary course of business. It appears that a farmer is entitled to sell stock in the ordinary course of business, but the grantee can secure the proceeds on demand from the grantor: *Bowden v King* [1921] NZLR 249; [1921] GLR 33; compare *Elders Pastoral Ltd v BNZ* [1989] 2 NZLR 180 where the Court of Appeal found a constructive trust in the circumstances.

(c) That the grantor will brand and earmark the stock only in the way specified in the instrument.

(d) That the grantor will maintain the stock in clean and healthy condition and will make an annual written return of the same when required by the grantee;

(e) That the grantee taking possession of stock branded or covenanted to be branded in the same way as the stock assigned shall have the same rights over these as over the assigned stock. Further, the grantor shall do everything to complete the assignment of any stock which subsequently becomes subject to the instrument;

(f) That the grantor will pay all charges on the stock assigned and, on his or her default, the grantee may pay the same, such amount and interest being a charge on the stock;

(g) That the grantee may enter and remain on the land where stock is depastured and use all implements and equipment on the land until the sale of the said stock to any purchaser thereof. Expenses of the same and interest are a charge on the stock. This provision is necessary to enable the grantee, who is exercising his or her power of sale, to graze and water the stock on the grantor's land until the next sale day.

36.9.4 Wool

A grantee may take security over the next ensuing clip from the sheep described in the instrument. The wool from the natural increase of sheep depasturing on the land mentioned in the instrument is also included in the security. The grantee is entitled to the wool, not only while it is growing, but afterwards when it is shorn wherever it may be: s 38. No subsequent sale or mortgage of the sheep affects the grantee's security: s 39.

The grantor of an instrument by way of security over sheep may, with the written consent of the grantee, give a valid security to a third person over the next ensuing wool clip of such sheep: s 40.

If the grantee is entitled to have the grantor execute a security over each clip of wool or is entitled to the delivery of the wool clips during the continuance of the instrument, then such grantee shall be deemed to have a lien or security over each clip without the execution of any special instrument.

In all instruments over sheep as security, there is an implied covenant that the grantor will deliver the wool clip to the grantee each year during the continuance of the security: s 41. The provisions as to defeasance, after-acquired chattels and inventory do not apply to securities over wool: s 26.

There is an implied power in an instrument by way of security under the Fourth Schedule to the Act that the grantee, on default by the grantor, may order him or her or some other person to shear the sheep and the increase thereof and to bale and deliver such wool for sale by the grantee. From the proceeds the grantee shall pay the grantor the balance after he or she has deducted sufficient for principal, interest charges and any rent due.

36.10 THE IMPLIED PROVISIONS OF THE ACT

36.10.1 General

For convenience and brevity, certain covenants, provisions and powers are implied in all instruments unless they are expressly negatived or varied. These implied provisions have the same binding force as they would have had if they had been expressly included in the instrument itself. As to negativing and varying, see *Elders Pastoral Ltd v BNZ* [1989] 2 NZLR 180 (CA).

In addition to certain provisions, certain phrases are very fully defined in the Fifth Schedule. By using these provisions, a very short document will adequately protect the parties. The expressions so defined are "upon demand", "further advances", "will, upon demand, pay the balance due upon the account current between them", "will insure" and "will brand, earmark and mark".

The powers, covenants and provisions implied in instruments over stock, crops and wool have already been summarised under their respective headings. The following covenants, however, have general application to all instruments by way of security and the covenants as to title also apply to hire purchase agreements.

(a) COVENANTS FOR TITLE IMPLIED IN ALL INSTRUMENTS

(a) The grantor has a good right and full power to assign the chattels free from encumbrances; and
(b) The grantor will do everything to complete the assignment of the chattels.

(b) COVENANTS IMPLIED IN INSTRUMENTS BY WAY OF SECURITY

The grantor covenants:
(a) to pay interest and principal;
(b) to pay interest on any further advances;
(c) not to prejudice the security and to pay rent for the land or premises where the chattels are situated, and
(d) to keep the chattels in good order and to repair or replace any which are damaged or destroyed and to execute a security over any chattels so replaced.

(c) PROVISOS AND AGREEMENTS IMPLIED IN INSTRUMENTS BY WAY OF SECURITY

(a) The grantor may have the possession and use of the chattels until default or the commencement of bankruptcy or until a judgment has remained unsatisfied for ten days;
(b) Bills of exchange or promissory notes shall not be considered as payment until they have been honoured;
(c) The grantee, upon default, the commencement of bankruptcy or failure to satisfy a judgment for ten days by the grantor, may seize and sell the security, repaying to himself the amount secured and the expenses of the sale and paying the balance to the grantor.

36.11 DISCHARGE OF AN INSTRUMENT BY WAY OF SECURITY

36.11.1 Entry of satisfaction

The form of memorandum of satisfaction is given in the First Schedule to the Act. Where the amount secured by the instrument has been paid off, the memorandum of satisfaction signed by the grantee and duly witnessed may be registered. Proof of destruction or loss of the original instrument may be tendered to the Registrar where necessary: s 42(3). A certificate of due execution is unnecessary where the witness is a Registrar, Notary Public, Justice of the Peace, Postmaster or solicitor, or if the grantee is the Housing Corporation, or the Rural Banking and Finance Corporation of New Zealand or the memorandum of satisfaction is made by a corporation under its official seal: Chattels Transfer Act 1924, s 24. From the time of filing such memorandum, the whole or the part of the debt and the grantee's interest in the chattels subject to the security is discharged: s 43. The interest of the grantee in the chattels so discharged shall vest in the person entitled to the equity of redemption (s 43), who will normally be the grantor unless his or her interest in the chattels has been sold, as, for example, under s 47.

If the grantee is absent from New Zealand, the Public Trustee may receive payment and sign the memorandum of satisfaction. A Judge, who is satisfied that the debt or obligation has been discharged, may, on application, order a memorandum of satisfaction to be filed: ss 44 and 45.

36.11.2 Sale by the Registrar of the High Court

Where both land and chattels have been mortgaged as security for a loan, the Registrar may, on default being made by the borrower, sell the chattels either together with, or separately from, the land in accordance with the provisions of the Property Law Act 1952.

36.11.3 Sale of the grantor's revisionary interest

Where the grantor is a judgment debtor and the judgment creditor issues execution against the chattels subject to an instrument by way of security, the grantor's interest may be sold. On receiving notice of sale, the grantee may take possession of the chattels so sold and will then hold the chattels in trust for the purchaser subject to payment of all moneys due under the instrument.

If the grantee elects to sell the chattels under his or her implied power of sale, he or she must deduct from the proceeds any amount due to him or her and hand the balance over to the purchaser from the execution creditor: s 47.

36.12 SALE BY THE GRANTOR

It is a punishable offence for the grantor of a chattel security to sell the chattels without the consent of the grantee or to impair the security by any other means: s 58.

36.13 TRANSFERS OF INSTRUMENTS

A considerable part of business today is done on extended credit terms. In fact, there has been such a phenomenal consumer demand created by the time payment system that the legislature both in England and New Zealand has taken steps to curb this type of trading by making a substantial portion of the purchase price payable by way of deposit and by curtailing the time allowed for repayment of the balance: Hire Purchase and Credit Sales Stabilisation Regulations 1957; revoked by the Revocation of Hire Purchase and Credit Sales Stabilisation Regulations 1983. The time payment system is normally carried out either by means of customary hire purchase agreements or by taking a chattel security for the unpaid balance. This system commonly leads to firms providing credit facilities for their customers beyond their financial resources.

In consequence, standing arrangements are frequently made with finance corporations whereby the customary hire purchase agreement or chattel security taken from the customer is sold outright at a discount or assigned by way of mortgage to the finance corporation with the dealer possibly undertaking a guarantee of the amount involved in each transaction. Again, the dealer may act as an agent on behalf of the finance corporation so that he or she receives payment from it, and technically the customary hire purchase agreement or chattel security is made by the customer with the corporation. Another method commonly used is that technically the dealer sells the article outright to the finance corporation for cash. The finance corporation then sells the article on hire purchase to the purchaser, although the latter in all probability is not aware of the exact nature of the transaction and believes that he or she is being allowed credit by the dealer. With regard to the effect of representations made by the dealer, see the Hire Purchase Act 1971, s 17.

The form of transfer of an instrument is set out in the Sixth Schedule to the Act. The transferee, his or her executors, administrators and assigns have exactly the same rights and obligations as the transferor: s 55. See also the Hire Purchase Act 1971, ss 18, 20, 21. On registration of a transfer the position is:

(a) a registered transfer has priority over an unregistered one;
(b) as between registered transfers, priority is given in the order of their time of registration: s 56.

The reversionary interest in chattels, being a chose in action, may be assigned by the grantor without registration: *Re Thynne* [1911] 1 Ch 282. Assignments of customary hire purchase agreements (which are excluded from the definition of instruments by s 2) are valid and effectual without registration.

Assignments of hire purchase agreements over motor vehicles are valid without registration under the Chattels Transfer Act 1924.

36.14 REFORM

The question of reform of chattels security has been discussed in ch 1. See 1.6.3 and the materials cited there. See also ch 40, post.

Chapter 37

HIRE PURCHASE AGREEMENTS

37.1 INTRODUCTION

The law of hire purchase in New Zealand is problematic. It is problematic because hire purchase, in terms of its form, is a transaction of sale but in terms of its substance and function, it is a security device. In addition, hire purchase is a species of credit transaction. As a credit transaction, hire purchase requires regulation in order to offer adequate protection to consumers. That protection requires a balance to be struck between consumer interests and the rights of creditors.

Dissatisfaction with New Zealand's existing credit and security laws has led to pressure for reform. Limited reform has been effected with regard to the security aspect of hire purchase at least in so far as motor vehicles are concerned. Under the Motor Vehicle Securities Act 1989, "security interest" has been defined to include hire purchase agreements. The term subsumes both "true" hire purchase agreements and conditional sale agreements. As "security interests" such agreements become registrable under the system established by that Act. In making hire purchase agreements registrable, Parliament has recognised the realities of the situation and treated hire purchase agreements as security devices. This reform only concerns security interests in motor vehicles. The Law Commission, on the other hand, has proposed comprehensive reform of the registration system for security interests in chattels and it too, under its draft Personal Property Securities Act, has defined "security interest" to include hire purchase agreements.

The schemes under the Motor Vehicle Securities Act and as proposed by the Law Commission address the personal property security aspect of hire purchase. The credit aspect has yet to be dealt with. In this regard the Hire Purchase Act 1971, the Chattels Transfer Act 1924 and the Credit Contracts Act 1981 all need to come under scrutiny. In the Australian states, reform, where it has been effected, has taken the path of modification of the concept of hire purchase itself.

Jacob Ziegel has described hire purchase as "the dark horse in the chattel security stable": Professor J S Ziegel, "Hire Purchase: the Dark Horse in the Chattel Security Stable" (1968) 3 Recent Law 228. It is a "dark horse" which needs to be thoroughly understood with regard to both the security and credit aspects.

37.2 HISTORY

37.2.1 Concept

In everyday parlance the term "hire purchase" is used interchangeably with such terms as "time payment", "instalment plan" and others, none of which have, in themselves, any legal significance and all of which describe methods of purchasing goods by way of instalments. The basic concept of a hire purchase agreement is encapsulated in the term itself: the purchaser who has possession of the goods hires them during the period of credit; the vendor retains title to them until the full purchase price is paid.

The term "hire purchase" is used to describe two types of agreement which are themselves conceptually distinct, the one from the other. The first is a bailment with an option to purchase. This is the transaction from which we derive the term "hire purchase" and such agreements are known as "true" hire purchase agreements. Conceptually it is not a contract of sale, although this is the function it performs. Legally, it takes the form of an agreement to lease or hire the goods, so that the purchaser (hirer) has possession of them, with the hirer paying a rental and having an option to purchase the goods outright. The rental is usually, though not necessarily, treated as instalments of the purchase price and the "instalments" are calculated so as to amount over a specified period to the full amount of the purchase price together with interest and other charges. The agreement may either provide that on payment of all instalments the hirer may exercise the option to purchase on payment of a further nominal sum or, more usually, it will treat payment of the final instalment as being the exercise of the option to purchase. Under this type of agreement, the purchaser can terminate the arrangement at any time and return the goods.

The second type of agreement is the conditional purchase agreement. This is a contract of sale under which the purchaser is given immediate possession of the goods but it is agreed that the property in the goods will remain in the vendor until all instalments of the purchase price have been paid. Under this type of agreement the purchaser has no right to terminate, although the vendor can, at any time on default by the purchaser, repossess the goods. Whichever form the agreement takes, the substance of the transaction remains the same. It is security for the sale of goods with the purchaser obtaining immediate possession and ultimately acquiring ownership on payment of specified instalments.

True hire purchase agreements and conditional purchase agreements must be distinguished from credit sales. A credit sale is an ordinary sale of goods where both possession and ownership pass immediately to the purchaser and the purchaser is allowed time in which to pay for the goods. Although it may be agreed that the price will be paid by a fixed number of instalments, such an arrangement does not amount to a hire purchase agreement. Once the property in the goods has passed and possession has been given to the purchaser, the vendor ceases to have any rights in respect of the goods. If the purchaser defaults in payment, the vendor's only remedy is a personal action on the debt.

True hire purchase agreements and conditional purchase agreements must also be distinguished from the chattel mortgage. Here, on sale, property and possession pass to the purchaser, who retains possession but assigns the property by way of mortgage to the vendor or other lender. In this chapter the terms "vendor" and "purchaser" will be used to refer to the parties to both conditional purchase and true hire purchase agreements.

37.2.2 Origins

The origins of hire purchase have been documented in the Crowther Committee's Report on Consumer Credit (the "Report of the Committee on Consumer Credit under the chairmanship of Lord Crowther", London, Her Majesty's Stationery Office, 1971, Cmnd 4596) from which the following account is taken.

The earliest evidence of hire purchase, or something like it, comes from France and the United States of America with the sale of furniture to the well-to-do. The furniture was leased at a rent for a stated period with an option to purchase for an agreed final payment at the end of the period. Very likely, in France, this arrangement grew out of the simple leasing of furniture by country-based noblemen for use in their town houses during their visits to the capital.

It seems that this system was in use, or came to be used, in England in the early nineteenth century and was soon applied to the supply of goods to the middle and working classes. In the late 1840s there was a boom in the sale of pianos to the middle classes on these terms. In the early 1860s the Singer Sewing Machine Company began selling its machines on hire, with an option to purchase and this extended the scope of "hire purchase" to skilled workers. Until the late 1870s the system was referred to as "the two year system" (sewing machines), "the three year system" (pianos) and the "hire system" (furniture). The term "hire purchase" (or "hire and purchase") was, to begin with, purely a colloquialism, and many so-called hire purchase agreements were in law conditional sale agreements because the "hirer" had no right to terminate the agreement and was under an obligation to carry it through to completion by paying the full price. This distinction became legally significant with the English Factors Act 1889 by which a conditional buyer could in certain circumstances pass title to an innocent purchaser.

In Victorian times hire purchase, using the term loosely, seems to have been largely confined to furniture, pianos and sewing machines among consumer goods. Other goods sold on instalment terms seem to have been bought mostly on credit sale: see paragraph 37.2.1. From the 1920s onwards the finance houses became an important element in instalment selling of the dearer kinds of goods-radios, household appliances and above all, cars, which required considerable finance for periods of perhaps two or three years. The need for finance companies arose because unless dealers extending credit to purchasing customers had vast resources they would rapidly reach the limit of credit they could grant on their own. As standards of living rose the demand for goods rose and the demand for credit to finance the purchases of those goods rose.

Hire purchase took on its modern form with the House of Lords decision in *Helby v Matthews* [1895] AC 471. This is the leading case on true hire purchase agreements (bailments with an option to purchase) and such agreements are commonly referred to as *Helby v Matthews* agreements. In this case the efficacy of the device was tested. In *Helby v Matthews*, B agreed to hire from the appellant a piano under an agreement which gave him an option to purchase the piano upon payment of the requisite number of instalments stipulated in the agreement. During the continuance of the agreement, B pledged the piano with a third party, the respondent, as security for an advance. In an action by the appellant against the respondent for conversion of the piano, the respondent argued that B had "agreed to buy the piano" and so could pass a good title under the English equivalent of New Zealand's present s 27(2) Sale of Goods Act 1908. This argument was upheld by the Court of Appeal but that decision was reversed by the House of Lords. The House of Lords took the view that there was no "contract by the seller to sell", but merely an offer to do so and there was no contract by the purchaser to buy.

The importance of the option to purchase lies in the fact that the hirer is unable to pass a good title to a third party under s 27(2) Sale of Goods Act 1908, for the purchaser is not "a person, having bought or agreed to buy goods". Since the property in the goods remains in the owner who lets them on loan, the retention of the ownership of the goods and the inability of the hirer to pass a good title, provide the owner with some measure of security in case of default on the part of the hirer. The hirer, on the other hand, obtains the benefit of the credit transaction in that he or she receives the possession and the use of the goods in advance of payment of the price and is then able to purchase the goods once the price has been paid.

It would, however, be wrong to regard a true hire purchase agreement as simply a bailment with an option to purchase added. The concept of hire purchase has become sui generis and one to which special rules of law apply. It is a "hybrid transaction", "autonomous" unto itself, to use Professor Guest's terms: Professor A G Guest *The Law of Hire Purchase*, London, Sweet and Maxwell (1966) p 12. This is clearly indicated in *Karflex v Poole* [1933] 2 KB 251, 264-26 where Goddard J said:

> Now it does not seem to me by any means to follow that the doctrines which were applied to ordinary simple bailments in bygone days apply to this modern class of bailment which has in it, not only the element of bailment, but also the element of sale . . . I do not think that hire purchase is an ordinary contract of bailment. The bailor who lets out the goods is not an ordinary

bailor, nor is the customer, who agrees to pay these instalments with the hope and intention of becoming the full owner, an ordinary bailee, and there are special contracts and special representations in such an agreement. . . .

Assessment of damages for breach indicates the "autonomous" nature of the concept. The measure of damages applicable is based on the assumption that the hirer will not elect to terminate the agreement during its currency and will proceed ultimately to purchase the goods. This reflects the true nature of the relationship between the vendor and purchaser rather than the strict legal relationship where the purchaser has an "option" to exercise.

D F Dugdale *New Zealand Hire Purchase Law* (3rd edn, 1978) Wellington, Butterworths, describes the position as follows:

> The hire purchase agreement is thus the offspring of an artificial union between the contracts of hiring and sale and this mixed parentage has resulted in many problems and complexities for until the legislature intervened the Courts were frequently faced with the need to determine whether in a particular set of circumstances the rights and liabilities of the parties were to be governed by the rules governing bailment, or by the rules governing sales of goods or by some hybrid mixture of both.

The leading case on conditional sale agreements is *Lee v Butler* [1893] 2 QB 138 and such agreements are commonly referred to as *Lee v Butler* agreements. In this case, an agreement, described as a "hire and purchase" agreement, was entered into between the plaintiff's assignor and a Mrs Lloyd, in which Mrs Lloyd agreed to hire certain furniture and to pay for it in the sum of £1 on the day following the execution of the agreement and £96 three months later. The agreement provided that the property in the furniture should remain in the plaintiff's assignor but that on payment of the sums mentioned above the furniture should "thenceforth be and become the sole and absolute property of the . . . hirer". During the term of the agreement and before the sums of money had been paid, Mrs Lloyd wrongfully sold and delivered the furniture to the defendant who received it in good faith. In an action by the plaintiff (the party to whom the person letting the goods had assigned his interest under the agreement) against the defendant for the return of the goods, the Court of Appeal held that the situation fell clearly within what in New Zealand is s 27(2) of the Sale of Goods Act 1908 and that the defendant had acquired good title to the goods. This decision was approved by the House of Lords in *Helby v Matthews* but was distinguished by it on the grounds that Mrs Lloyd was *bound* to purchase the goods. Conceptually, the two types of agreement are distinct each from the other but in New Zealand the Hire Purchase Act 1971, in s 2(1) defines "hire purchase" in such a way as to include both types and does not distinguish between them in any way for the purposes of the application of its provisions. A number of writers in other jurisdictions insist on dealing with the two concepts quite separately but it appears that in New Zealand "hire purchase" is sui generis and that the two types are species of the one genus. In these circumstances both kinds of agreement will be referred to in this chapter as "hire purchase agreements" unless it is necessary to make a distinction between them, in which case they will be described by their traditional names.

37.2.3 Legislative intervention

Parliament first intervened in hire purchase in New Zealand in 1939 with the Hire Purchase Agreements Act in that year. During the Depression years of 1931-36 many people defaulted under hire purchase agreements and many purchasers, despite having paid a major part of the purchase price, had goods "repossessed" or "snatched back": see the Crowther Report, supra, without any allowance for what they had paid. The Act enabled such people to obtain a partial refund of their payments. It also allowed purchasers a period following repossession in which they could pay arrears and repossession costs and then continue with the contract.

At one time purchasing goods on hire purchase carried with it a social stigma: see D F Dugdale *New Zealand Hire Purchase Law* (1978) p 4, note a. After the Second World War attitudes changed and the growth of the consumer society caused the volume of hire purchase trading to increase markedly. By the 1960s it was apparent that comprehensive reform was required to regulate this type of dealing, especially with regard to the protection of consumer interests. In 1971 a new statute was enacted.

D F Dugdale at pp 4 and 5, has summarised the reasons why the Hire Purchase Act 1971 was brought into being. First, it was enacted to make provision for requirements as to form; secondly, to regulate the terms to be implied in hire purchase agreements and to make them binding not only on a vendor but also on any assignee financier; thirdly, to limit a vendor's right to repossess; and fourthly, to strengthen the provisions of the 1939 Act regulating the rights and liabilities of the parties following repossession. The Act is, in short, a consumer protection measure.

From 1957 to 1983 hire purchase transactions in New Zealand were subject to economic regulation in the form of the Hire Purchase and Credit Sales Stabilisation Regulations made under the Economic Stabilisation Act 1948, s 3. The general purpose of the Act and the regulations made under it was to safeguard the economic stability of New Zealand. The general effect of the regulations was to require defined minimum deposits and maximum periods of credit where certain classes of goods were disposed of on terms requiring payment in instalments. These regulations, which were varied from time to time to give effect to government policy, were always very restrictive in the field of new motor vehicle purchases, requiring substantial deposits and very short periods in which to pay off the balance (50 per cent deposit and 12 months to pay the balance was common). Regulations under the Act prescribed strict formal requirements as well. The intention of the regulations was to restrict credit and the amount of currency in circulation in an endeavour to combat inflation. The regulations were revoked by the Revocation of Hire Purchase and Credit Sales Stabilisation Regulations and Economic (Motorcar Hiring) Regulations in 1983.

37.2.4 Mechanism

Hire purchase transactions involve a triangular mechanism. The seller, instead of disposing of goods direct to the customer, sells the goods to a finance company which lets them to the customer on hire purchase. It is from this three-cornered pattern that the legal problems of hire purchase arise. Where a dealer in goods wishes to meet the demands of customers for instalment credit facilities but lacks the capital to cope with such credit extension, the dealer can enter into either "direct collection" arrangements with a finance house, or undertake "block discounting". With direct collection the dealer sells the goods to a finance house and arranges for the finance house to supply the goods to the customer on hire purchase terms. This method is known as "direct" or "direct collection" business because the finance company is placed in direct contractual relationship with the customer and collects the instalments directly from the customer. Discounting involves the dealer itself in entering into the hire purchase contract with the customer and then selling the contract to the finance house. In this situation the finance house is not a party to the hire purchase contract but is a purchaser of the outstanding accounts resulting from it. With this method it is common for the dealer to continue collecting the instalments itself but, of course, as agent for the finance house. Agreements are commonly sold to the finance house at a discount in batches and the transaction is accordingly termed "block discounting".

The legal relationships in direct collection may be illustrated as follows:

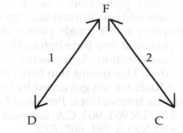

In the above diagram it can be seen that there is a sale by the dealer to the finance house and then hire purchase arrangements are entered into between the finance house and the customer. It can be seen that in this form of transaction, unlike block discounting illustrated below, the customer has no contractual relationship with the dealer at all. The dealer supplies the goods but the customer's contract is with the finance house.

With block discounting, the legal relationships may be illustrated as follows:

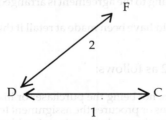

It can be seen above that the dealer enters into a conditional sale or hire purchase agreement with a customer and then assigns to the finance house the dealer's rights under that agreement which, depending upon the arrangement between the dealer and the finance house, may or may not include the dealer's underlying title to the goods. What the finance house is paying for is the money to be paid pursuant to the hire purchase terms and not the title to the goods themselves. Such outstanding sums of money are known as "receivables". As can be seen by comparison with the diagram for the legal relationships involving direct collection, there is no contractual relationship between the finance house and the customer of the dealer. The customer's contract is with the dealer alone. The finance house is the purchaser of the rights vested in the dealer under the conditional sale or hire purchase agreement. Relations between finance house and dealer can be on a *recourse* or *non-recourse* basis. Where the dealer is required to give recourse, the dealer must guarantee the buyer's performance under the agreement which has been assigned or the dealer must undertake to repurchase the goods if the buyer defaults.

37.3 THE HIRE PURCHASE ACT 1971

37.3.1 Transactions subject to the Hire Purchase Act 1971

"Hire purchase agreement" is defined in s 2 of the Act. Subsections (2)-(7) of s 2 represent extensions of the definition enacted in an attempt to effect comprehensive consumer protection. The definition in s 2(1) includes both true hire purchase and conditional sale agreements. Agreements under which the property in the goods passes absolutely at the time of the agreement or upon or at any time before the delivery of the goods, are excluded from the definition. Agreements "made otherwise than at retail" are also excluded. This means that hire purchase transactions between private individuals are not governed by the Act. The term "retail" also excludes wholesale transactions: *Provident Life Assurance Co Ltd v Official Assignee* [1963] NZLR 961, 965, CA; *Bateman Television Ltd v Coleridge Finance Co Ltd* [1969] NZLR 794, 807, 822.

In cases where the dealer arranges the sale, then assigns the goods to a finance company which contracts directly with the purchaser, s 2(2) makes the following provision:

> (2) For the avoidance of doubt, and without limiting the circumstances in which a hire purchase agreement may be made at retail, it is hereby declared that for the purposes of this Act a hire purchase agreement shall be deemed to be made at retail if –
> (a) The transaction leading to the agreement is arranged by a dealer or on his behalf; and
> (b) The agreement would have been made at retail if the dealer had been the vendor.

"Dealer" is defined in s 2 as follows:

> "Dealer" means a person, not being the purchaser or his agent or the vendor or his servant, who assigns or procures the assignment to the vendor of goods for the purpose of enabling the vendor to enter into a hire purchase agreement in respect of those goods or goods of that kind with the purchaser.

Section 2(3) provides that transactions which "in substance or effect" constitute hire purchase agreements are to be treated for the purpose of the Act as amounting to hire purchase agreements. This provision is clearly designed to prevent parties from evading the regime of the statute by fictitious means.

When the Hire Purchase Act was introduced in 1971, the chattel mortgage enjoyed some popularity as an avoidance device, as an outright sale followed by a mortgage back to the dealer did not fall within the scope of the Act and the consumer protection provisions in the Act were thereby circumvented. In consequence, the Act was amended in 1974 to deal with this problem. Subsections (5), (6), and (7) of s 2 of the Act were added by the Hire Purchase Amendment Act 1974. Subsection (5) provides that where it is a condition of any agreement to sell goods at retail that the buyer grants security over the goods for the whole or part of the purchase price and the property in the goods passes to the buyer subject to that condition, the transaction shall be deemed to be a hire purchase transaction. Subsection (6) provides that where the whole or any part of the purchase price of goods bought at retail is to be paid from a loan on the security of the goods sold, made by the seller or arranged by the seller with a lender of money, the sale and the loan shall together be deemed to be a hire purchase agreement made at the time of making the loan: see *Sudfelt v UDC Finance Limited* (unreported, Court of Appeal 174/86, 14 December 1987), and *Broadbank Corporation v Moffat* (unreported, Plt 5198/86, 14 October 1988, Guest DCJ). A lender of money making such a loan will for the purpose of the Act, be deemed to be the vendor and the seller shall be deemed to be the dealer, except that s 18 of the Act referring to the liability of the vendor's assignees shall apply as if the seller were the vendor and the lender of money was the assignee: s 2(7).

The effect of the s 2 definition of "hire purchase agreement" and the provisions of subs (2)-(7) is to ensure that a vast array of transactions is made subject to the provisions of the Act, so that the protection of the Act is extended to purchasers who have entered into transactions which are not in form "true" hire purchase agreements or conditional sales but are akin to them in substance. In these circumstances it is submitted that hire purchase is sui generis in New Zealand.

37.3.2 Subject-matter

The Hire Purchase Act 1971 is concerned with goods. Section 2 of the Act defines goods as follows:

"Goods" includes all chattels personal other than money or things in action.

"Chattels" are defined under s 2 of the Chattels Transfer Act 1924 as:

any personal property that can be completely transferred by delivery.

The area of potential problems with the subject-matter of hire purchase agreements relates to the concept of accession. Accession occurs where additional chattels (accessories) are attached to a principal chattel. Difficulties arise when the principal chattel is the subject of a hire purchase agreement. The one reported decision on this matter in New Zealand involves a very full judgment. The case is *Thomas v Robinson* [1977] 1 NZLR 385. The judgment of Speight J refers to an article by Professor

A G Guest in which Professor Guest proposes a number of tests to determine when accessories can be said to have merged with the principal chattel: "Accession and Confusion in the Law of Hire Purchase" (1964) 27 MLR 505.

Pursuant to the decision in *Thomas v Robinson* it would appear that accession disputes turn on whether the purchaser under the hire purchase agreement owns the accessories or whether they are owned by a third party. If the accessories are owned by a third party, the accessories will remain the property of that party unless they cannot be separately identified or, if they can be so identified, they cannot be detached from the original goods. If, however, the accessories are owned by the purchaser under the hire purchase agreement then the terms of the agreement must be looked to. Where the agreement provides that accessories will become the property of the vendor, that will be the case: see Professor A G Guest op cit. Where there is no provision made in the agreement then the law is uncertain. In *Regina Chevrolet Sales Ltd v Riddell* [1942] 3 DLR 159, referred to by Professor Guest, it was held that the correct test is whether the accessories are an integral part of the chattels to which they are affixed and necessary for its working. In cases such as this, ownership of the accessory passes to the vendor of the original goods under the hire purchase agreement. The Law Commission has made specific provision for security interests in accessions in its draft Personal Property Securities Act (Law Commission Report No 8): s 31.

37.3.3 Consumer protection

(a) FORMALITIES
Sections 4, 5, 6 and 7 of the Act set out the formal requirements for agreements governed by the Act.

Section 5 provides that every hire purchase agreement shall be in writing.

Section 5 makes the following provisions for execution of the agreement by the purchaser:

(a) Where the purchaser is an individual, by him personally or on his behalf by any person acting under authority conferred by a power of attorney:
(b) Where the purchasers are carrying on a business in partnership, by any person who has authority to execute it on behalf of the firm:
(c) Where the purchaser is a corporation, under the seal of the corporation or on its behalf by a person acting under its authority, express or implied.

Section 6(1) makes stipulations as to the contents of agreements governed by the Act:

(a) The agreement shall contain a description of the goods to which the agreement relates; and
(b) The agreement shall specify –
 (i) The number or the minimum number of instalments; and
 (ii) The amount or the minimum amount of each of those instalments; and
 (iii) The person to whom and the place at which the payments of instalments are to be made; and
 (iv) The date, or the mode of determining the date, on which each such instalment is payable; and

    (v) The full name and address of the vendor; and
    (vi) Where credit is extended through a variable credit account, the
        method by which periodic balances are calculated and by which
        interest is calculated on those balances; and
  (c) The agreement shall set out on its first page the financial details of the
     transaction in a form which is substantially the same as the form set out
     in Part I of the First Schedule to this Act; and
  (d) The agreement shall have endorsed on it a statement in the form set out
     in Part II of the First Schedule to this Act.

The statement referred to in s 6(1)(d) informs the purchaser that the purchaser is entitled to a copy of the agreement free of charge; that with the written consent of the vendor, which cannot be unreasonably withheld, the purchaser may assign the purchaser's rights under the hire purchase agreement; and that the purchaser has a right to complete the agreement at any time and in doing so is entitled to a rebate of some of the finance charges payable under the agreement.

Section 6(2) provides for the Minister of Justice to prescribe alternative requirements instead of those set out in s 6(1)(b) and (c). The Hire Purchase Agreements Notice 1972 was made pursuant to s 6(2) of the Act and this Notice allows a "fair estimate" of insurance premiums to be adopted temporarily for the purposes of s 6 and Part I of the First Schedule to the Act. Section 6(3) provides that the terms of an earlier hire purchase agreement may be incorporated by reference in a subsequent agreement between the same parties. Where there is such incorporation by reference, the vendor is liable to have to supply copies of both agreements if the purchaser so requests.

Section 7 of the Act makes provision for copies of hire purchase agreements to be supplied to purchasers.

Section 7(1)(a) provides that a copy of the agreement shall be given to the purchaser before the end of the period of 10 days beginning with the day after the date of the execution of the agreement by the purchaser. If the copy of the agreement is not given to the purchaser immediately after it is executed by the purchaser, the purchaser shall then be given a sales docket which sets out clearly the information specified in the Second Schedule to the Act, referred to above. Where the agreement is executed by the purchaser on a day later than the day on which it is executed by all the other parties, a copy of the agreement, marked in conspicuous letters with the words "PURCHASER TO KEEP THIS COPY" shall be given to the purchaser when the original is given to the purchaser for execution.

The intention of the Hire Purchase Act, then, is to ensure that purchasers receive full information about any transactions which they enter into which are governed by the Act. Section 4 of the Act deals with enforcement of the requirements under ss 5, 6 and 7.

Section 4(1) states that where the requirements of s 5 are not complied with then, unless the Court orders otherwise, the agreement, any contract of guarantee relating to the agreement and any security given by the purchaser or the guarantor in respect of money payable under the agreement, shall not be enforceable by the vendor.

Where a vendor fails to comply with the requirements of ss 6 and 7 of the Act then s 4(2) states:

(a) The liability of the purchaser for the cost of credit shall be extinguished; and
(b) The vendor shall repay any money already paid to him by any person on account of or in satisfaction of the cost of credit.

Section 4(3) goes on to provide that the enforcement provisions for ss 6 and 7 contained in s 4(2) shall not apply if the vendor shows:

(a) That the non-compliance was not of such a nature as to mislead or deceive the purchaser to his prejudice: or
(b) In any other case that the vendor has promptly remedied the non-compliance (in so far as it is capable of being remedied) on its being discovered or brought to his notice and has, where appropriate, compensated or offered to compensate the purchaser for the prejudice caused to him.

Section 4 has been considered by the Court of Appeal in *Industrial Steel and Plant Ltd v Smith* [1980] 1 NZLR 545. See also *Marac Finance Ltd v Ellis* (unreported, High Court, Rotorua, A35/79, 10 November 1983, Prichard J).

(b) VARIATION

Section 10 of the Act provides that parties to any hire purchase agreement may agree from time to time to vary that agreement. Where an agreement is varied, the variation shall not be enforceable by the vendor without the leave of the Court, and subject to any conditions imposed by the Court, unless a note or memorandum in writing of the variation is executed by the purchaser in accordance with s 5 of the Act and a copy if given to the purchaser immediately after the purchaser has executed it.

A note or memorandum must contain all the terms of the variation and as provided in s 10(4) must, in particular, show:

(a) The date on which the variation is made; and
(b) The amount of money then owing under the hire purchase agreement whether or not it is increased or reduced by the variation; and
(c) If the date of payment of any instalment is changed or if the amount of any of the instalments is increased or reduced by the variation, the particulars concerning the instalments mentioned in subparagraphs (i) to (iv) paragraph (b) of subsection (l) of s 6 of this Act.

These provisions are subject to subs (2) and (3) of s 10. Under subs (2) the vendor may give notice in writing changing the person to whom or the place to which payments of instalments are to be made.

Under subs (3) where the purchaser has made default in the payment of any money owing under a hire purchase agreement, the vendor need not comply with s 10(1) in respect of any variation in which the vendor agrees to forbear from exercising all or any of its remedies in respect of the default for a specified period or until a demand is made for payment or so long as the purchaser continues to make specified payments and the purchaser agrees to observe the conditions of the hire purchase agreement as varied. For subs (3) to apply, neither the amount of money owing nor the amount of any of the instalments must be increased except in accordance with any provision in the agreement for the payment of penalty interest. Any such variation shall be enforceable by the vendor without the leave of the Court.

(c) IMPLIED TERMS AND REPRESENTATIONS

Exemption clauses are proscribed by the Hire Purchase Act. Section 51 of the Act states that the provisions of the Act shall have effect notwithstanding any provision to the contrary in the agreement between the parties and it is further provided that s 56 of the Sale of Goods Act 1908, which could otherwise allow contracting out in conditional sale agreements, does not apply. Nevertheless provision is made for a limited degree of contracting out by the parties relative to second-hand goods: s 12(1)(d), and where there is a voluntary return of goods: s 24(6).

For statements that have induced a purchaser to enter into an agreement, we must turn to the Contractual Remedies Act 1979 to determine the scope of the protection offered. A purchaser may allege that the hire purchase sale was made on the basis of a representation or was subject to a condition precedent such as the reconditioning of an engine in a motorboat by the vendor before delivery to the purchasers. To avoid liability under any such representation or to defeat the effect of the condition precedent, vendors often include a clause in the following terms:

> The conditional purchaser admits that he has examined or caused to be examined the said chattels before making this agreement and that he has satisfied himself as to their condition and that he enters into this agreement solely and exclusively in reliance on such examination and upon his own judgment. The conditional purchaser further agrees that this agreement evidences the whole agreement between him and the vendor and that all conditions (precedent, subsequent or otherwise relevant) and warranties except those applying by virtue of the Hire Purchase Act 1971 are excluded and that no representation, warranty, promise or undertaking is or has been made or given by the vendor and no condition or term whatsoever has been imposed or stipulated for by or on behalf of the conditional purchaser prior to the execution of this agreement unless it is expressly incorporated herein.

The Contractual Remedies Act enables the Courts to go behind such clauses to ascertain the true state of affairs, "unless the Court considers that it is fair and reasonable that the provisions should be conclusive between the parties": s 4(1). In deciding whether a clause is conclusive or not the Court shall have regard to all the circumstances of the case, including the subject-matter and value of the transaction, the respective bargaining strengths of the parties, and the question whether any party was represented or advised by a solicitor at the time of the negotiations or at any other relevant time: s 4(1)(c).

In addition, there is the protection afforded by the Credit Contracts Act 1981. Under ss 10 and 11 of that Act the Court may reopen a contract where it considers the contract is oppressive or a party to a credit contract is exercising his or her rights and powers in an oppressive manner, or a party was induced to enter into the contract by oppressive means. Section 9 defines "oppressive" to mean oppressive, harsh, unjustly burdensome, unconscionable or in contravention of reasonable standards of commercial practice. Proceedings to reopen must be instituted in Court within six months after the date the last obligation to be performed under the contract is performed: s 12, Credit Contracts Act 1981.

(1) Liability for representations: The "triangular" nature of the relationship found under hire purchase transactions has already been discussed. This relationship may give rise to difficulties with regard to representations made to the purchaser. For example, with the direct collection method of financing, we have seen that the goods are sold by the retail dealer to a finance company which lets them on hire purchase to the consumer. It may be the case that the purchaser discussed the goods with the retailer and the retailer made all sorts of claims about the goods. The difficulty is that the consumer's hire purchase contract for the goods is with the finance company and on the face of it there is no contractual relationship between the retailer who actually supplies the goods and the customer who takes delivery. In these circumstances ss 17 and 18 have been enacted under the Hire Purchase Act to deal with this situation.

Sections 17 and 18 are intended to afford protection with regard to both the "direct collection" and "block discounting" methods of financing. The terms "vendor" and "dealer" are defined in s 2 of the Act. The definition of "dealer" has been set out in paragraph 37.3.1 above. For the purposes of "direct collection" financing the retailer is defined as a "dealer" for the purposes of the Act. A "dealer" is an intermediary between the vendor and the customer.

Vendor is defined as follows:

> "Vendor" means the person disposing of goods under a hire purchase agreement, and, if the rights of that person are transferred by assignment or by operation of law, includes the person for the time being entitled to those rights.

In the "block discounting" method of financing they are both classified as vendors for the purposes of the Act – the finance company has taken an assignment of the hire purchase agreement from the retailer who first disposed of the goods.

Section 17(1)(a) and (b) provides:

> (1) Every representation, warranty or statement made to the purchaser . . . , whether orally or in writing, by the dealer or any person acting on behalf of the vendor or dealer . . . in the course of negotiations leading up to . . . a hire purchase agreement shall confer on the purchaser –
>
> (a) As against the vendor, subject to section 18 of this Act, the same rights as the purchaser would have had if the representation, warranty, or statement had been made by the vendor personally;
>
> (b) As against the person who made the representation, warranty, or statement and any person on whose behalf such person was acting in making it, the same rights against them or any of them personally as the purchaser would have had if the purchaser had entered into the hire purchase agreement with the person who made the representation, warranty, or statement or the person on whose behalf that person was acting (as the case may be) as a result of the negotiations.

The wording of s 17(1) indicates that the assignee of a vendor is liable for representations or warranties made by the original vendor's agent but not for representations or warranties made by the original vendor personally. D F Dugdale in *New Zealand Hire Purchase Law* (1978) p 19, suggests that this is the result of an accidental omission when the legislation was drafted.

Section 17(2) makes provision for relief from vicarious liability for the innocent vendor who did not expressly or impliedly authorise the making of such a representation, warranty or statement. Innocent vendors have a right of indemnity from the person responsible or the person on whose behalf it was made in terms of that provision. If the vendor can prove that any such representation, warranty or statement was made without his or her knowledge or express or implied authority, then no action for damages in deceit shall lie against the vendor. Any claim made by a purchaser against the vendor's assignee under s 17 may not exceed the amount owing by the purchaser under the agreement at the date of the assignment and the assignee has rights of indemnity and subrogation: s 18(3), (4).

(2) Implied terms: A consideration of the implied terms under the Hire Purchase Act well illustrates the problems which can occur when transactions referred to as hire purchase are in fact of two kinds: a bailment with an option to purchase and a conditional sale. Prior to the enactment of the Hire Purchase Act 1971, where hire purchase took the form of a conditional sale the statutory conditions and warranties under the Sale of Goods Act were implied into such agreements except to the extent that they were expressly modified or excluded. In the case of true hire purchase agreements, there were no terms implied by statute as these agreements were not "agreements to sell" in terms of the Sale of Goods Act 1908. The Hire Purchase Act provides that the implied terms of the Sale of Goods Act shall not apply to either kind of agreement: s 16, Hire Purchase Act 1971. Instead, the Hire Purchase Act implies terms into both types of hire purchase agreement and, except to the limited extent provided in s 12(1)(d), the Act does not allow the parties to contract out of these obligations: s 51. Thus the 1971 Act overcame this problem.

With the passing of the Contractual Remedies Act 1979, the distinction between conditions and warranties was removed from our law of contract. Accordingly, the Hire Purchase Act was amended and the words "condition" and "warranty" were omitted from ss 11, 12, 13 and 14 of the Act: s 14(3) Contractual Remedies Act 1979.

If a purchaser under a hire purchase agreement wishes to cancel the contract for breach of an implied term, that party must show that the breach was sufficiently serious to satisfy the tests set out in s 7(4) of the Contractual Remedies Act. Section 7(4)(b) provides that the innocent party may cancel the contract if:

The effect of the misrepresentation or breach is, or, in the case of an anticipatory breach, will be –
(i)   Substantially to reduce the benefit of the contract to the cancelling party; or
(ii) Substantially to increase the burden of the cancelling party under the contract; or
(iii) In relation to the cancelling party, to make the benefit or burden of the contract substantially different from that represented or contracted for.

The implied terms under the Hire Purchase Act are set out in ss 11–14 and relate to title, merchantable quality, fitness for the purpose, sale by description and sale by sample.

For sales of motor vehicles, Part VII of the Motor Vehicle Dealers Act 1975 contains provisions which impose a variety of obligations on licensed motor vehicle dealers. Section 89 is dealt with in Chapter 38; s 90 requires that certain particulars be displayed in respect of second-hand motor vehicles; s 92 establishes the categories A to D for second-hand motor vehicles; s 93 creates obligations for the dealer in respect of the sale of second-hand motor vehicles; s 94 enables dealers to sell "C" category vehicles without a warranty; and s 95 deals with notices of defects. The Motor Vehicle Dealers Act governs all sales of motor vehicles by dealers, not just sales on hire purchase.

Unfortunately, when the Motor Vehicle Dealers Act was first enacted, it was worded in such a way that the substantive provisions of Part VII did not appear to apply to true hire purchase agreements, only to the conditional sale variety. Quite literally, Part VII was concerned only with "sales". This anomaly was dealt with by legislative amendment and in 1979 the Motor Vehicle Dealers Amendment Act was enacted so that both types of hire purchase agreement were made subject to the statutory regime.

(a) The implied term as to title – Section 11 of the Hire Purchase Act provides that:

In every hire purchase agreement there shall be implied –
  (a) A term . . . that the vendor will have the right to sell the goods at the time when the property is to pass:
  (b) A term . . . that the goods will be free from any charge or encumbrance in favour of any third party (other than a charge or encumbrance disclosed to the purchaser in writing by the vendor or the dealer before or at the time the agreement is entered into or a charge or encumbrance created by or with the express consent of the purchaser) at the time when the property is to pass:
  (c) A term . . . that the purchaser shall enjoy quiet possession of the goods except so far as it may be disturbed by the owner of any charge or encumbrance so disclosed or known or by the vendor where the purchaser is in default under the agreement.

(b) The implied term as to merchantable quality – This implied term, under s 12(1), provides that to be of merchantable quality, goods sold under a hire purchase agreement must at the time of delivery be reasonably fit for the purpose for which goods of that kind are commonly bought. This requirement is clarified by s 12(2) in as much as it is stated that the goods must be fit for their original purpose to the extent that may be reasonably expected having regard to their price or any description applied to them, for example, "sale" goods. The term is not implied under s 12(1):

  (a) As regards defects which are specified in the agreement if the vendor proves that the defects were specifically drawn to the purchaser's attention and accepted by him before the agreement was entered into; or
  (b) If the purchaser examined the goods or a sample of them before the agreement was entered into, as regards defects which the examination ought to have revealed; or
  (c) If the cash price of the goods exceeds $5,000 or such larger sum as may from time to time be specified by the Governor-General by Order in Council and the agreement expressly negatives such a term; or
  (d) If the goods are secondhand goods and –
    (i) The agreement contains a conspicuous statement signed by the purchaser in the following terms: "I understand that the goods to

which this agreement relates are secondhand goods and that *[Insert name of vendor]* does not promise that they are fit for use or for any particular purpose"; and

(ii) That statement is separately signed by the purchaser.

The original amount of $5,000 specified in s 12(1)(c) was subsequently increased to $15,000 by the The Hire Purchase (Specified Sums) Order 1980/270.

"Conspicuous statement" in terms of s 12(1)(d) of the Hire Purchase Act has been defined by the Courts. In *Terminus Car Court Limited v Lewis* [1975] 1 NZLR 260 it was held to mean "clearly visible, obvious or striking to the eye" of somebody who merely scans the agreement. The test is not whether it would be read by someone who reads the document in detail. Again in *Marac Finance Limited v Ellis* (unreported, High Court Rotorua, A35/79, 10 November 1983, Prichard J) it was held that a conspicuous statement was one that stood out as something apart from the general layout of the document. In this case no real significance was attached to the fact that the statement was one which had been signed by the purchaser, as the purchaser had also signed a statement to the effect that he acknowledged he had received a copy of the agreement when it was executed, and that was not the case: see also, *Clyde Engineering Ltd v Russell Walker Ltd* [1984] 2 NZLR 343 (CA). Where the procedures outlined in s 12(1)(d) are adopted, the vendor will escape liability for breach of the implied term as to fitness for purpose. In *Facer v Automobile Centre (Auckland) Limited* (unreported, M 287/75, February 1976, Henry J) a very old Daimler car was sold on hire purchase. The purchaser signed a "conspicuous statement" that the car was not fit for use for any particular purpose and this was held by the Court to be conclusive as excluding liability for the numerous defects that were later discovered. This decision must be compared with that in *Broadbank Corporation Ltd v Martin* [1988] 1 NZLR 446 where the Court held that the statement under s 12(1)(d) was not effective to protect Broadbank Corporation Ltd against their failure to comply with a specific condition in the agreement as to quality. The condition was found to be an essential term which went to the heart of the contract.

(c) The implied term as to fitness for purpose – Where the purchaser, expressly or by implication, makes known to the vendor or to the dealer the particular purpose for which the goods are required there is an implied term under s 13 that the goods will be reasonably fit for that purpose, whether or not that is a purpose for which such goods are commonly bought. Section 13(1) provides that the goods must at the time of delivery be reasonably fit for their purpose except where:

(a) The goods are secondhand goods and paragraph (d) of subsection (1) of section 12 of this Act is complied with; or

(b) The circumstances otherwise show that the purchaser does not rely, or that it is unreasonable for him to rely, on the vendor's skill or judgment.

Communication of the particular purpose to an employee or agent of the vendor or dealer puts the latter under a duty to comply with this term. A vendor is entitled to be indemnified by the dealer against any damage suffered by him or her through breach of the above term if the purchaser expressly or impliedly made known to the dealer, his or her agent or any servant of the dealer, the particular purpose for which the goods were required. Naturally the dealer would not be liable if the vendor had authorised the dealer to say that the goods were reasonably fit for the purchaser's purpose: s 13(2).

The implied terms of merchantable quality and fitness give a purchaser the right to reject or claim damages. If the defect results in injury to the property of a third party and damages are awarded to the third party against the purchaser, the purchaser is entitled to be indemnified by the vendor in respect of such liability: *Mowbray v Merryweather* [1895] 2 QB 640, (CA).

(d) The implied term as to description – There is an implied term that goods will correspond with the description under which they are sold: s 14(2).

(e) The implied term concerning goods disposed of by sample – Section 14 provides:

(1) (a) ... that the bulk will correspond with the sample in quality; and
     (b) ... that the purchaser will have a reasonable opportunity of comparing the bulk with the sample.
(2) ... if the goods are disposed of by reference to a sample as well as by description it shall not be sufficient that the bulk of the goods correspond with the sample if the goods do not correspond with the description.

(f) Assessment of damages – The damages that a purchaser may recover for breach of a term implied in a hire purchase agreement by the Act shall be assessed, in the absence of evidence to the contrary, on the basis that the purchaser will complete the purchase of the goods or would have completed that purchase if the goods had complied with that term: s 15. This provision was included to prevent vendors arguing that a purchaser under a true hire purchase agreement might elect not to exercise the option to purchase.

(d) REBATES FOR EARLY PAYMENT IN FULL
The situation concerning rebates for early payment in full is unsatisfactory. Prior to the Hire Purchase Act 1971, consumers were not entitled to a rebate where they elected to repay the amount outstanding before due date. Section 22 of the Act provides that the purchaser may at any time complete the purchase by tendering to the vendor the net balance due under the agreement. The net balance due is calculated by taking into account the rebates allowed by the agreement for early completion or the statutory rebates, whichever are the greater. Section 9(1) provides that, subject to exceptions set out in s 23, every hire purchase agreement shall contain one of the following statements:

"Early completion of this agreement will entitle the purchaser to rebates greater than the statutory rebates as follows: [*There shall follow a statement of the particulars.*]"
"Early completion of this agreement will entitle the purchaser to statutory rebates in accordance with s 23 of the Hire Purchase Act 1971."

Where any hire purchase agreement does not meet these requirements, the vendor under the agreement commits an offence: s 9(2).

Section 23(1) sets out the statutory rebates. They are:

(a) A rebate of the terms charges (the terms charges being the total cost of credit less any items included in that total for insurance or for maintenance or repairs):

(b) A rebate for insurance if the purchaser requires any contract for insurance in respect of which he has been debited with the premiums under the agreement to be terminated:

(c) A rebate for maintenance or repairs if the purchaser requires any contract for maintenance or repairs in respect of which he has been charged under the agreement to be terminated.

Subsections (2) (3) and (4) of s 23 set out the particulars for the rebates of terms charges, insurance and maintenance respectively. The exclusions are set out in subs (5) which provides as follows:

(5) The purchaser shall not be entitled to statutory rebates if –
(a) The aggregate amount of those rebates would be less than $1; or
(b) The cash price of the goods comprised in the agreement exceeds $5,000 or such larger sum as may from time to time be specified by the Governor-General, by Order in Council, for the purposes of this paragraph; or
(c) The purchaser is not bound to pay anything for terms charges, insurance, maintenance, or repairs; or
(d) Credit for the balance payable under the agreement is extended to the purchaser through a variable credit account and the purchaser is not bound to pay anything for insurance, maintenance, or repairs.

The original amount of $5,000 referred to in s 23(5)(b) has subsequently been increased to $15,000 by the Governor-General under the Hire Purchase (Specified Sums) Order 1980/270. The statutory method of calculating the rebate provided by ss 22 and 23 is known as the "Rule of 78".

In short, the Act provides in s 23 for a rebate if 90 per cent of the total cost of credit less any cost of insurance, maintenance or repairs, plus a refund of the unused proportion of the insurance premium and a percentage of maintenance or repair charges. The "Rule of 78" has this name because the sum of the digits from the number of months in a year adds up to 78. The use of this method of calculation has been strongly criticised by the Ministry of Consumer Affairs in its discussion paper, "Consumers and Credit", (1988), pp 66-71. The discussion paper gives the following explanation:

78 is a variable figure depending on the total term of the contract. In a 12 month contract it operates by allocating 12/78 of the cost of credit to the first instalment, 11/78 to the second instalment and so on down to 1/78 for the twelfth and final instalment. If the borrower decides to repay the balance still owing after having paid two instalments, (12/78 + 11/78 = 23/78) of the cost of credit, a rebate calculated at 90% of the remaining 55/78 of the full cost of credit shown in the contract will be payable to the debtor.

The formula is:

$$90\% \quad \times \quad \frac{\text{Cost of Credit}}{1} \quad \times \quad \frac{\text{Sum of the digits of the whole months to go}}{78}$$

For example, a car costing $10,000 is purchased on 12 months hire purchase terms. The finance rate is 36%. The cost of credit is therefore $3600.00 If early repayment is made after 6 months the calculation will be:

$$\frac{9}{10} \times \frac{3600}{1} \times \frac{21}{78} \quad - \quad \text{allowing a rebate of } \$872.31$$

The discussion paper records that during the transition of the Hire Purchase Act 1971 through Parliament the question of whether or not the rebate should be 80 per cent, 90 per cent or 100 per cent was debated. The figure of 90 per cent was eventually settled upon.

Parliament could have adopted, as an alternative, the *actuarial method*. Under this method the rebate for early repayment is calculated on the basis of the amount of interest accrued up to repayment date and the amount remaining unearned. The actuarial method provides a more accurate calculation. Whichever method of calculation is used there is the further question of whether or not the rebate should be for 100 per cent of the interest and charges outstanding or some lesser percentage, as is the case at present where only 90 per cent is allowed for. The view expressed by the Ministry of Consumer Affairs in its Discussion Paper is that the actuarial method should be adopted by Parliament for use in New Zealand and that the statutory rebate should be 100 per cent.

(e) VOLUNTARY RETURN OF THE GOODS BEFORE DUE DATE
Section 24 of the Act makes provision for voluntary return of goods by purchasers before completion of their contracts. The section provides that a hire purchase agreement may be terminated by a voluntary return of goods in three cases:

(1) The vendor may, before accepting a return of the goods, require the purchaser to enter into a written agreement which expressly excludes all the rights to which the purchaser would have been entitled under s 24 or upon repossession (ss 26 to 35 of the Act). There is, however, some measure of protection for the purchaser in that he or she must have had competent and independent advice as to the legal implications of the waiver before he or she enters into it: s 24(6).
(2) The hire purchase agreement itself may permit the purchaser to return the goods and terminate the agreement as in a true hire purchase agreement.
(3) Where no such right is included in the agreement, then the purchaser cannot voluntarily return the goods and terminate his or her obligations unless the vendor agrees to this taking place. Such a situation could hardly arise except in the conditional sale form of agreement and vendors are not likely to agree to it. Subsection (3) of s 24 provides that if the agreement fixes the amount to be paid by the purchaser in the case of voluntary termination then that shall be the maximum amount payable by the purchaser.

The first edition of this text, and the seventh of *Leys and Northey's Commercial Law in New Zealand*, contains the following paragraph:

> Where there is a voluntary return . . . the vendor must, unless he elects to regard the goods as having a value of not less than 80% of the cash price, act in the same way as if he had repossessed the goods, that is, the goods must not be sold until at least 21 days after a notice setting out the purchaser's rights has been served on the latter.

This statement is not, however, supported by authority.

This question has now been specifically considered in *W R Phillips Ltd v Carter* [1991] DCR 228. The point at issue involved the relationship of s 24 with s 28 of the Act. Section 28 contains the duties of a vendor after repossession of goods which are subject to a hire purchase agreement, including the giving of notice to the purchaser concerning the purchaser's rights. Judge Abbott in the District Court held that s 28 applied where a voluntary return of goods on hire purchase resulted in termination of the hire purchase agreement in terms of s 24(1) of the Act.

As in repossession, the purchaser can compel the vendor to sell if the vendor has not sold the goods within three months of the date of receiving them, and after the sale the purchaser is entitled to statements of account and possibly a right of refund. Subsection (5) emphasises that in the event of the voluntary return of the goods, the purchaser's rights are confined to the statutory refund.

If the vendor elects to regard the goods as having a value of not less than 80 percent of the cash price he or she must within fourteen days after the termination of the agreement serve on the purchaser a notice setting out the value which he or she attributes to the goods, the amount the purchaser would have to pay to settle the agreement and the balance owing by the vendor to the purchaser or by the purchaser to the vendor, as the case may be: s 24(4).

Where the goods have been voluntarily returned under (2) or (3) above, the amount payable to the vendor or to be refunded to the purchaser must be determined. The vendor must within ten days after the sale give a statement of account to the purchaser showing how much is to be paid by the vendor to the purchaser or by the purchaser to the vendor, as the case may be: ss 24(5), 32.

No action to recover the amount due to the purchaser shall be brought more than six months after service on the purchaser of this statement of account: s 33(2).

The voluntary return of goods leads to the question of minimum payment clauses also known as minimum hiring clauses. Where a voluntary return of goods is made, a determination must be made of what amount is due by the purchaser to the vendor to complete payments. Provision may be made in the hire purchase agreement that all the cash purchase price will become payable or that a certain percentage of the unpaid balance of the remaining instalments will become payable. Vendors using "true" hire purchase agreements have used such minimum payment clauses to minimise disadvantages arising from the purchaser's right to terminate the agreement at any time. Where a vendor terminates the agreement because of the default of the purchaser, the vendor is bound by the statutory provisions as to repossession and these provisions are not affected by minimum payment clauses. Section 24(3) states as follows:

> (3) Where any agreement fixes or makes provision for the fixing of the amount (if any) to be paid by the purchaser in the case of the voluntary

termination of the agreement by the purchaser, the amount (if any) that the vendor shall be entitled to recover from the purchaser shall not exceed that amount.

This provision is intended to ensure that the purchaser is not prejudiced by a voluntary return of goods

Under s 24(2) the rights and liabilities of the purchaser and vendor are determined as if the goods had been repossessed by the vendor on the day they were returned by the purchaser. There is an exception to this where the amount payable under a minimum payment clause is less than that recoverable under the repossession sections. The intention is that minimum payment clauses should operate to favour the purchaser.

37.3.4 Creditors' remedies: repossession

(a) THE RIGHT OF THE VENDOR TO REPOSSESS
The Ministry of Consumer Affairs' Discussion Paper "Consumers and Credit", (1988) states at p 72:

> Where goods are provided as security for performance of a contract and the debtor fails to abide by that contract a credit provider may repossess, ie take the goods to meet the debtor's obligation.

Sections 26 to 35 of the Act make provision for repossession and the rights and obligations of vendors and purchasers where repossession occurs. Section 26(1) makes provision that the vendor is entitled to repossess goods if:

(a) The purchaser is in default under the agreement; and
(b) The vendor has served on the purchaser a notice in writing in the form set out in the Third Schedule to this Act specifying the default complained of and, if the default is capable of remedy, requiring the purchaser to remedy the default within a period to be specified in the notice (being a period of not less than 10 days after the service of the notice on the purchaser); and
(c) The purchaser has failed within the period specified in the notice to remedy the default in so far as it is capable of being remedied.

It is an offence for a vendor to contravene these provisions and it is an offence for anyone wilfully and forcibly to obstruct a vendor or any agent lawfully exercising the vendor's right of possession: s 26(4), (5).

It is usual for a hire purchase agreement to contain a provision entitling the vendor on default of the purchaser to enter the premises where the purchaser is supposed to reside or carry on business or where the hire purchase goods are situated. If the vendor exercises this right in a manner or at a time which is unreasonable then the vendor commits an offence but no prosecution can be brought except with the leave of the Attorney-General: s 27. The provisions in the Act governing repossession have come in for much criticism. One of the problem areas concerns s 27: see Ministry of Consumer Affairs' Discussion Paper, "Consumers and Credit", (1988) p 73. The Act does not define "reasonableness" in this context. The Discussion Paper states that consumers' organisations are aware of instances where debtors have been disturbed late at night by repossession agents. Concern is expressed in the Discussion Paper over the forcible entry of premises and the suggestion is made that when such entry is desired it would be preferable if a Court order had to be obtained permitting the entry to be made.

After the service of the notice pursuant to s 26(1), or on possession of the goods, the purchaser can apply to the District Court for relief which can be granted if the request is reasonable, although it may involve a variation of the terms of the agreement: s 26(2). This right is in addition to the right of a purchaser to ask the Court to reopen a transaction and take accounts on the ground that the transaction is harsh and unconscionable.

If the Court decides that the application is vexatious it shall order the purchaser to pay the vendor the vendor's full costs, including reasonable costs incurred between solicitor and client, fees and other reasonable expenses incurred in connection with the application. In these circumstances the Court shall order that the purchaser shall have no right to introduce a buyer to take over the repossessed goods and the vendor will no longer be prevented from selling the goods before the expiration of 21 days from the service on the purchaser of the Fourth Schedule notice referred to, infra: s 26(3). The vendor is not required to serve a Third Schedule notice specifying default and the intention to repossess if the vendor has reasonable grounds to believe that the goods comprised in the hire purchase agreement have been or will be destroyed, damaged, endangered, disassembled, removed or concealed contrary to the provisions of the agreement. The onus of proving the existence of those grounds lies upon the vendor: s 26(4).

In the Discussion Paper of the Ministry of Consumer Affairs, "Consumers and Credit", (1988) p 75, forms of notice under the Act are criticised as difficult to understand. The suggestion is made that they should be rewritten in plain English.

Section 25 of the Act deals with successive agreements and agreements financed through variable credit accounts. This section offers protection to purchasers who agree to buy additional goods on hire purchase from vendors to whom they already have obligations under a hire purchase agreement relating to an earlier purchase. Similar protection is given to purchasers who enter into further hire purchase agreements (replacement agreements) affecting all or some of the goods included in an earlier agreement. The provision is intended to control the situation in which a vendor attempts to take an advantage by providing in a subsequent agreement that all goods subject to time payment might be repossessed although default affects only part of the goods or only those in the later agreement. Where there have been successive agreements the vendor shall not, without the leave of the Court, repossess goods comprising either the original or any successive agreement: *Development Finance Corporation v Industrial Steel and Plant Ltd* (unreported, High Court, Auckland, A 1603/79, 23 February 1982, Barker J). Where application is made for leave, the Court may make such order as it thinks fit, including an order for the specific delivery of some of the goods to the vendor and for the transfer to the purchaser of the vendor's title to the remainder of the goods. Any order may be made subject to the fulfilment by the purchaser or a guarantor of such conditions as the Court thinks just: s 25(3). The Court may postpone the operation of any such order on condition that the purchaser or any guarantor pays the unpaid balance of the total amount payable at such times and in such amounts as the Court, having regard to the means of the purchaser and of any guarantor, thinks just: s 25(4). Variable credit accounts are dealt with in s 25(2) which states:

> (2) Where goods are disposed of under a hire purchase agreement and credit is extended through a variable credit account then, unless that account relates for the time being only to that agreement, the vendor shall not, without the leave of the Court, exercise any power of taking possession of the goods comprised in the agreement.

(b) DUTIES OF A VENDOR AND RIGHTS OF A PURCHASER FOLLOWING REPOSSESSION

The vendor must within 21 days of repossessing the goods serve a Fourth Schedule notice on the purchaser and every guarantor of the purchaser: see *BNZ Finance Ltd v Castles* (unreported, High Court, Auckland, CP 2307/89, 6 April 1990, Master Towle). The notice states the vendor's estimate of the value of the goods and shows the amount to be paid within 21 days of service if the purchaser is to have his or her agreement reinstated. Alternatively it sets out details showing the amount required to pay off or settle the agreement. Finally there is the vendor's estimate of the value of the goods repossessed. This is important because the purchaser can introduce another buyer to take over at that figure. The Fourth Schedule "Summary of Your Rights" sets out in simple form the purchaser's rights under the repossession provisions of the Act. The notice also sets out in simple terms the events which may follow repossession. It invites the purchaser before the goods are sold to get them back either by reinstating the agreement by making good the default and paying the additional costs consequent on the repossession and redelivery of the goods or by settling the agreement, which means that the purchaser will have to pay the rebated "net balance due" under the agreement: s 22(3), plus the costs arising through the repossession and redelivery to the purchaser as well as any cost reasonably incurred by the vendor in making good the purchaser's default under the agreement. Then follows a warning that if the purchaser does not reinstate the agreement or pay it off the vendor is required to sell the goods after the lapse of 21 days following the service of the notice above but not more than three months after he or she took possession of the goods. Attention is drawn to the protection given to the purchaser by the Act. Thus the vendor must state without delay the estimate of the value of the goods repossessed made by the vendor. Linked with this is the purchaser's right to give the vendor notice in writing introducing a cash buyer who will buy the goods at not less than this estimated value: s 29(1)(b). This provision deters the vendor from valuing the repossessed goods at too low a figure. However, it must be appreciated that this estimate of value does not directly influence the actual open market value of the repossessed goods and in no case, except where there is a voluntary return pursuant to s 24(4), is the vendor required to give credit to the purchaser for an estimated value.

In para 5 of the "Summary of Your Rights" the purchaser is told that the purchaser can compel the sale of the goods if the vendor has not sold them within three months of repossession. Paragraph 6 informs the purchaser that the vendor must within 10 days after the sale give the purchaser a statement of account regarding a refund. Section 32 requires a written statement showing:

(a) The amount of the gross proceeds of the sale:
(b) The amount of the costs and expenses of and incidental to the sale:
(c) The amount required to settle the agreement . . . as at the date of the sale:
(d) The balance owing by the vendor to the purchaser or by the purchaser to the vendor, as the case may be.

The vendor must furnish this statement whether the vendor sells the repossessed goods of his or her own accord or through compulsion exercised by the purchaser as above: s 32.

To determine the maximum amount recoverable from the purchaser after the repossessed goods are sold by the vendor the net amount realised through the sale is deducted from the total amount required to settle the agreement as stated in the Fourth Schedule notice: s 34. For a discussion of this provision, see *Russell v Lancaster Motors Ltd and Anor* [1985] BCL para 1354 and *Marac Finance Ltd v McKee* (1988) 2 NZBLC 102, 867. In the latter case rebates had been allowed in the repossession notice, the s 32 notice and in the demand for payment. When proceedings were commenced, no allowance was made for a rebate in the amount claimed by the plaintiff. There was no warning that the rebate would not be allowed if proceedings were commenced. The point at issue was whether in these circumstances, allowance should have been made for a rebate in the amount claimed. The Court held that while there was no legal obligation to make the rebates, it was harsh and contrary to reasonable standards of commercial practice to have taken proceedings without a warning that failure to pay promptly would mean that the rebates would not be deducted. Finally, there is a warning that the purchaser must not delay in exercising his or her rights. Thus if the purchaser has not received a refund to which he or she is entitled or if the purchaser wishes to have a harsh and unconscionable agreement reopened he or she must bring proceedings in the appropriate Court within six months after receipt of the statement of account referred to above.

In *BNZ Finance Ltd v Haile and Anor* (unreported, High Court, Christchurch, CP 104/89, 1 June 1989, Master Hansen) H successfully resisted summary judgment proceedings on the grounds that the repossession notices sent lacked the second page containing a summary of rights available to a purchaser under the Fourth Schedule to the Act. The Court took the view that a failure to serve a purchaser with a proper notice would give rise to a defence.

(c) VENDOR'S DEFAULT IN CARRYING OUT STATUTORY DUTIES
A vendor failing to serve the Fourth Schedule notice within the 21 days following repossession is deprived of the right to recover from the purchaser the costs of repossessing the goods and the purchaser is not limited to the period of 21 days following repossession for reinstating the agreement or introducing a buyer of his or her choice to buy the goods. The purchaser can take either of these steps at any time before the goods are sold by the vendor: s 28(1), (2).

The vendor may sell the repossessed goods not less than 21 days from the service on the purchaser of the Fourth Schedule notice or after the expiration of the time specified in a notice served on the vendor by the purchaser stating that a buyer introduced by the purchaser is going to buy the repossessed goods, whichever is the later, or alternatively after a purchaser who has declared his or her intention to tender the money required to settle the agreement fails to make the payment: ss 28(5), 30.

However, the vendor would be entitled to sell the repossessed goods earlier if either the purchaser consented to this in writing (s 28(3)) or in the event of a District Court order made as a result of a vexatious claim for relief: s 26(3).

Under s 28(4):

(4) If the vendor acts in contravention of subsection (3) of this section –
(a) The liability of the purchaser for anything other than the amount financed under the agreement shall be extinguished; and
(b) The vendor shall repay any money already paid to him by any person on account of or in satisfaction of any amount in respect of which liability is extinguished by paragraph (a) of this subsection.

The vendor shall take all commercially reasonable steps to obtain the best price for the goods, which may be sold privately or by auction, or by public tender: s 28(6). See *Broadlands Finance Ltd v Hautapu Motors Ltd* (unreported, High Court, Wanganui, A 5/81, 10 November 1983, O'Regan J); *Marac Finance Ltd v McKee* (1988) 2 NZBLC 102, 867, and *AGC NZ Ltd v Phillips* (unreported, High Court, Auckland, CP 1268/88, 6 March 1990, Thomas J). Unless the goods are perishable or threaten to decline speedily in value the vendor shall give the purchaser reasonable notice of the time, place and manner of sale, including the reserve price. Both vendor and purchaser are entitled to bid or tender for the goods. In case of dispute the burden of proving that the sale was in accordance with these provisions rests on the vendor: s 28(9).

It may happen that a vendor does not wish to sell or delays unduly in selling the repossessed goods. If the vendor fails to sell the goods within the three months following repossession the purchaser may:

(1) Apply to the Court for an appropriate order compelling the sale of the goods; the Court has a discretion as to the order it makes; or
(2) Serve written notice signed by the purchaser requiring the vendor to offer the goods for sale by public auction without reserve within two months of the service of the notice.

The vendor and purchaser are both entitled to bid at this auction: s 31.

Section 35 is designed to meet the case of the vendor who has repossessed hire purchase goods only after attempts to compel payment through the Courts have failed, i e, where judgment has been obtained or a Court order but it has not been possible to enforce the judgment. Following repossession the Court may discharge or vary any prior judgment or order of the Court against the purchaser for the recovery of money so as to accord with the amount to be paid by the purchaser to the vendor or the amount to be repaid to the purchaser by the vendor as determined by ss 33 and 34 of the Act referred to above.

(d) PURCHASER'S RIGHT TO REINSTATEMENT OF THE AGREE-MENT
At any time in the 21 days following the service on the purchaser of the Fourth Schedule notice, during which the vendor is not entitled to sell the repossessed goods, the purchaser is entitled to pay or tender to the vendor the total amount shown in the said notice as a prerequisite to the reinstatement of the agreement. Likewise, the purchaser must remedy

any breaches of the agreement set out in the notice. Thereupon the vendor is bound to return the goods to the purchaser, who will hold them pursuant to the terms of the original hire purchase agreement and as though no breach had occurred: s 29(2).

If, although the vendor has returned the goods to the purchaser, some breach has not been remedied, the vendor is not entitled to repossess the goods a second time for the same breach unless at the time he or she returned the goods he or she served notice in writing on the purchaser specifying the breach and requesting the purchaser to remedy it. The vendor can, however, repossess the goods if the purchaser fails to remedy this breach within 14 days after service of this notice: s 29(3).

The Fourth Schedule notice, as well as setting out the details of the amount required to reinstate the agreement, provides an alternative solution for the purchaser's difficulties by supplying details of the net balance, after allowing a deduction of the statutory rebates, required to be paid by the purchaser if he or she elects to pay off the agreement. As with reinstatement, in the computation of the amounts to be paid the costs of repossession, storage, repairs and maintenance as well as the costs of remedying the purchaser's breaches of the agreement are taken into account, so that the vendor will not be "out of pocket": s 30.

In "Consumers and Credit", the Discussion Paper of the Ministry of Consumer Affairs, pp 75 and 77, the suggestion is made that where the consumer has repaid a specified percentage of the hire purchase loan then the credit provider should have to obtain a Court order before repossessing the goods. The rationale for this proposition is that the rate of depreciation in goods increases the longer the period of time the hire purchase agreement has been in existence. The result of this is that when goods are resold they often have a limited resale value. It is suggested in the Discussion Paper that in these cases it might be appropriate to encourage the credit provider to renegotiate repayment terms with the debtor. New Zealand legislation does not limit the right of the credit provider to repossess goods where a certain percentage of the total cost of the goods has been paid. In some jurisdictions a Court order is required before repossession can occur when a specified proportion of the total amount has been paid by the debtor.

37.3.5 Assignment

(a) ASSIGNMENT BY THE VENDOR
This matter has been dealt with in paragraphs no 37.2.4 and 37.3.3.

(b) ASSIGNMENT BY THE PURCHASER
Under s 20, the purchaser under a hire purchase agreement is entitled to assign his or her right, title and interest under the agreement. The right, title and interest of the party may pass by operation of law to his or her personal representatives but if it is the right, title and interest of a purchaser which is so passing by operation of law or the purchaser is a body corporate and its rights are passing to a liquidator, neither the personal representatives nor the liquidator shall be relieved from compliance with the provisions of the agreement in the event of the purchaser's bankruptcy: s 20(7).

Under s 20(6) no assignment authorised by s 20 shall constitute a breach of the terms of the hire purchase agreement nor shall it entitle the vendor to take possession of the goods.

A purchaser's right, title and interest may be assigned absolutely with the vendor's consent or, if that consent is unreasonably withheld, with the leave of the Court. A vendor shall not require payment or any other consideration for giving consent to an assignment but the vendor can make it a condition of granting consent that the purchaser shall make good all defaults under the hire purchase agreement. Consent shall be deemed to be unreasonably withheld if it is withheld by reason only of the colour, race or ethnic or national origins of any person: s 20(1)-(5).

Prior to the passing of the 1971 Act, vendors frequently inserted a clause in hire purchase agreements providing for the automatic termination of the agreement if the purchaser purported to assign his or her interest under it. This effectively prevented an assignee from obtaining any rights through an assignment by a purchaser. Under the present Act the parties cannot effectively do this and consequently such a clause is ineffective to stop the purchaser from assigning his or her rights under the agreement. The vendor can require the purchaser or the assignee to pay a reasonable sum to reimburse the vendor for legal or other expenses incurred by him or her in connection with the assignment: s 20(4).

The vendor may stipulate as a condition of granting consent that all defaults under the agreement be made good: see paragraph 37.3.6. This may prove to be a real problem where the purchaser wants to assign his or her interest because of financial difficulties and where the purchaser is in arrears with the instalments.

The method and effect of assignments by the purchaser are provided for in s 21. Every assignment by a purchaser must be in writing and must fully describe the assignee. A copy of the assignment must be served on the vendor within seven days after the date of its execution by the assignor. The assignee from a hire purchase buyer becomes personally liable to pay the instalments and to observe all the other terms of the hire purchase agreement and to indemnify the buyer in respect of such liabilities. A buyer and any guarantor, is not, unless it is otherwise agreed to in writing with the vendor, released from personal liability under the hire purchase agreement or the guarantee, as the case may be. This means that where there is an assignment and the instalments fall into arrears, the vendor has recourse against the assignee, the original purchaser and any guarantor that may have been a party to the hire purchase agreement.

37.3.6 Miscellaneous Matters

(a) INSURANCE

Section 40 of the Act makes provision for the insurance of goods which are subject to hire purchase agreements. The vendor may require the hire purchase goods to be insured at the purchaser's expense with an independent insurer nominated by the vendor during the period of the agreement in the name of the vendor and the purchaser and on such terms as the vendor would insist on if the arrangement of insurance had been left to him or her: s 40(1), (2), (4). If the purchaser wishes to change the insurer he or she can give written notice to the vendor of his or her intention and place the insurance with any reputable insurer carrying on business in New Zealand. The effects of subs (3) and (7) of s 40 are that the vendor cannot compel the purchaser to insure with an insurer which is controlled by the vendor or which is a subsidiary or the holding company or a subsidiary of the holding company of the vendor or dealer. See the comments of the Ministry of Consumer Affairs in its discussion paper "Consumers and Credit" (1988) on the question of insurance in consumer credit contracts.

Any no-claim bonus or rebate of a similar nature allowed by an insurer on hire purchase goods is to be credited to the purchaser and any person paying or allowing it to the vendor commits an offence: s 40(5). This provision is designed to overcome the problem of a secret commission or rebate paid by an insurer to the vendor arranging the insurance transaction.

The question whether the amount payable for insurance is to be included as forming part of the cost of credit and the procedure where there has to be an estimate of the cost of insurance is dealt with in chapter 24.

(b) REPAIRS

Where the agreement specifies that goods may be required or maintained only by the vendor or his or her nominee, s 42(1) provides that repair or maintenance by some other person shall not be a breach of the agreement if:

   (a) It is not practicable in the circumstances to have the repairs or maintenance carried out by the person specified or approved by or pursuant to the agreement; or

   (b) The repairs or maintenance are carried out in a proper and workmanlike manner.

Unless the agreement otherwise provides, work done by such other person absolves the vendor from any obligation to repair or maintain the goods at no cost to the purchaser: s 42(2).

(c) WORKERS' LIENS

Where a worker does work upon hire purchase goods in such circumstances that if the goods were the property of the purchaser the worker would be entitled to a lien thereon for the value of the work, then even if the agreement forbids the creation of a lien by the purchaser, the worker can still claim a valid lien unless he or she has notice of such provision at the time he or she commenced the work: s 43.

(d) NOTICES

Notices required to be served by the Act must be written, not oral. If they are sent by registered post they will be deemed to be delivered four days after posting: s 46(1). Although there is no reference to AR (acknowledgement registration) post in the Act, this is the most satisfactory way of ensuring delivery of the notice and having proof of its delivery. The Court will hold that there has been sufficient service if the notice is delivered or posted to the recipient at his or her usual or last known place of abode or business or at an address specified for that purpose in the hire purchase agreement. Most hire purchase agreements have a clause to the effect that the purchaser specifies the address set out in his or her description in the agreement as the address at which any relevant notices are to be served. The Act also makes provision for service on the agent of a person absent from New Zealand, and on the personal representatives of deceased persons. If service cannot be effected, the Court may give directions: s 46(5).

(e) ILLEGAL CONTRACTS

The Hire Purchase Act 1971 states that contravention of its provisions does not make the agreement illegal and that except as expressly provided by the Act, such contravention does not make the contract unenforceable and of no effect. The imposition of a fine (maximum $500) is the sanction employed by the Courts to prevent contravention of the Act. The intention is to keep the hire purchase agreement enforceable so that if there is a remedy for an aggrieved party it is still available: ss 48, 52. Both ss 6 and 7 of the Illegal Contracts Act 1970 are expressly stated to be "subject to any other enactment".

(f) GUARANTORS

Section 2 of the Act includes the definition of "contract of guarantee". For the purposes of the Act the term covers both a guarantee and an indemnity. We have already seen that a guarantor undertakes no more than contingent liability arising only where the primary debtor makes default, as contrasted with an indemnifier who undertakes primary liability for payment himself. But "guarantor" (as restrictively defined) does not include:

(a) a vendor — as, for example, where a trader disposes of goods and then assigns the hire purchase agreement to an assignee "with recourse" against the assignor, ie, the trader undertakes that he or she will make good any default by the purchaser in making payments to the assignee. See para 37.2.4.

(b) a person who enters into a contract of guarantee in the course of business carried on by him or her. This could arise perhaps where some additional party for a consideration has undertaken to guarantee payments due from a purchaser to a financier to whom the hire purchase agreement has been assigned. Alternatively, it may be the "dealer" who introduced the business (whereby the hire purchase agreement was to be made directly between the financier and the customer) but was required to be a guarantor or to find some other party to do so for reward. In some cases the dealer will enter into the hire purchase agreement in the capacity of the financing party's agent, yet in such case the dealer might be required to accept personal liability as guarantor.

Any variation of the contract between the vendor and the purchaser without the agreement of the guarantor shall discharge the guarantor from liability as well as persons described in (a) and (b) as undertaking obligations arising out of a hire purchase transaction.

Likewise, the same persons referred to in (a) and (b) above, along with guarantors and indemnifiers as defined in s 2 of the Act are not released from their obligations under their guarantees by reason of the operation of the Act or because the vendor, pursuant to the provisions of a hire purchase agreement, has taken possession of the goods contained therein: s 36(1), (2), (5).

The vendor must terminate the hire purchase agreement before calling on the guarantor to pay: *Reliance Car Facilities Ltd v Roding Motors* [1952] 2 QB 844; [1952]1 All ER 1355.

A guarantor's liability is, however, limited to the extent of the purchaser's obligations guaranteed. The guarantor may, however, have undertaken additional obligations (such as offering a security in support of the guarantee), in which case he or she will remain bound to that extent, irrespective of the termination of the purchaser's obligations.

Where the vendor has repossessed hire purchase goods any guarantor (reverting now to the restrictive definition of that term in the Act) who has paid money to the vendor under the guarantee shall have the like right in like manner to recover the money so paid as he or she would have had if the guarantor were the purchaser. In calculating the amount received by the vendor, all money paid and the value of any consideration provided by the purchaser shall be deemed to have been paid by the guarantor. This accords with the principle that a guarantor is a favoured debtor and ensures that the guarantor will be repaid in full before the purchaser gets any refund: s 36 (4).

Naturally, the guarantor will not receive anything more than he or she paid under the guarantee: s 36 (4).

A guarantor or indemnifier who has had to pay the vendor on the purchaser's default is entitled to be subrogated to the rights of the vendor over the purchaser to the extent of moneys so paid.

The terms of the guarantee or indemnity undertaken by the "business" guarantors referred to in paras (a) and (b) above will determine whether guarantors of this type will be entitled to the benefits of subrogation and perhaps to have the hire purchase agreement re-opened under the provisions of the Credit Contracts Act 1981.

(g) RIGHTS OF THE EXECUTION CREDITOR OF A PURCHASER
Section 47 of the Chattels Transfer Act makes it plain that execution can be levied against the grantor's interest in goods comprised in a chattel mortgage. There is no equivalent provision under the Hire Purchase Act. It is customary to include under the terms of a hire purchase agreement a clause to the effect that it is a breach of the agreement for the purchaser to allow a judgment or Court order against him or her to remain unsatisfied or for distress to be levied on his or her goods. Section 20 of the Hire Purchase Act states:

(1) The right, title, and interest of a purchaser under a hire purchase agreement may be assigned absolutely with the consent of the vendor or, if this consent is unreasonably withheld, with the leave of the Court.

. . .

(3) As a condition of granting his consent, the vendor may stipulate that all defaults under the hire purchase agreement shall be made good.

The question arises as to when the assignable interest of the purchaser may be taken in execution by the creditor. It is arguable that a bailiff or sheriff could take over and sell the purchaser's interest in the goods provided the execution was completed before the vendor had served a Third Schedule notice on the purchaser. If the bailiff or sheriff purported to sell the absolute property in the goods he or she would be liable in an action for conversion of the vendor's reversionary interest: *Lancashire Waggon Co v Fitzhugh* (1861) 6 H & N 502. The position is not clear. The vendor's consent is necessary as provided in s 20(1) Hire Purchase Act and the vendor could make his or her consent conditional on the purchaser making good the default. Obviously this would be a demand by the vendor that the purchaser should satisfy the judgment in respect of which distress was levied. It is important to bear in mind that the purchaser's right to assign under s 20 seems to involve a chose in action, that is to say, the purchaser's contractual right and does not refer to the goods themselves.

37.4 THE RELATIONSHIP OF THE HIRE PURCHASE ACT WITH THE CHATTELS TRANSFER ACT 1924

37.4.1 Registration of hire purchase agreements under the Chattels Transfer Act 1924

The Hire Purchase Act makes no provision for the registration of hire purchase agreements. However, such agreements clearly come within the definition of "instrument" or "customary hire purchase agreement" in the Chattels Transfer Act 1924, ss 2 and 57(1) respectively. They are therefore subject to the provisions of the Chattels Transfer Act scheme of registration discussed in Chapter 36. Hire purchase agreements of both types are "instruments" within the meaning of the Chattels Transfer Act. Both "transfer the right to the possession of chattels", the one by way of bailment and the other by way of sale. Both can therefore be registered, and, subject to the comments below, the protection of the Act can be obtained.

37.4.2 Customary hire purchase agreements

As can be seen above, with hire purchase agreements, possession of goods is placed in the hands of one party while ownership remains vested in another. This is clearly a situation that may lead to problems. Before the enactment of the Chattels Transfer Act in 1924 a vendor always had to register an agreement to avoid the possibility of goods passing to the Official Assignee in the event of the purchaser becoming bankrupt and also to prevent a conditional purchaser from passing good title to a bona fide purchaser or mortgagee. The difficulty with bankruptcy was the doctrine of "reputed ownership". Under s 61(c) Bankruptcy Act 1908, provision was made whereby there should pass to the Official Assignee not only the bankrupt's own goods but also goods –

> . . . at the commencement of the bankruptcy, in the possession, order, or disposition of the bankrupt by the consent and permission of the true owner, under such circumstances that the bankrupt is the reputed owner thereof:

In other words, property which did not belong to the bankrupt could vest in the Official Assignee, if the goods were held by the bankrupt in circumstances in which it was reasonable to infer that they were owned by him or her.

As the popularity of hire purchase trading increased many retailers were, it seems, prepared to take the risk of not registering, particularly when dealing with low priced articles. It was always possible for the vendor under an unregistered agreement to rebut the presumption of a bankrupt purchaser's reputed ownership, and prevent the goods from passing to the Official Assignee, by proving a notorious custom that such goods in such locality were commonly sold on hire purchase: see "Chattels Securities", the First Report of the Contracts and Commercial Law Reform Committee, presented to the Minister of Justice, September 1973 at p 9. By the 1920s it was clear that certain classes of goods were regularly sold on hire purchase and that possession of such goods did not of itself suggest ownership. The need to protect creditors and others dealing with the person in possession of such goods, by requiring registration of agreements accordingly ceased to exist. This gave rise to the customary hire purchase agreement, which is specifically excluded from the definition of "instrument" in the Chattels Transfer Act and does not therefore need to be registered for protection to be obtained.

Section 57 establishes "a list of chattels in which a custom rebutting reputed ownership was deemed to exist – hence the term": "Chattels Securities", the First Report of the Contracts and Commercial Law Reform Committee, at p 9. Section 57 of the Chattels Transfer Act 1924 defines a customary hire purchase agreement as follows:

(1) A customary hire purchase agreement is a deed or agreement in writing made between the owner of or a dealer in certain chattels and a conditional purchaser of those chattels where –
(a) The owner of or dealer in the chattels is either the manufacturer thereof or a person who is engaged in the trade or business of disposing of the goods or chattels of such nature or description;
(b) The deed or agreement provides either expressly or impliedly for delivery of possession to the conditional purchaser but that the property in the chattels shall not pass to the conditional purchaser, or shall only conditionally so pass until the completion of the payments to be made by him;
(c) The chattels the subject of the deed or agreement are described in the Seventh Schedule to this Act at the time when the agreement is made.

Section 57 provides that a customary hire purchase agreement may be either a "true" hire purchase agreement or a conditional purchase agreement. It is valid for all purposes without registration and the chattels will not pass to the Official Assignee on the bankruptcy of the purchaser. This applies to assignments, absolute or by way of mortgage, as well. The seller of chattels accordingly enjoys a safeguard against the operation of ss 18 and 19 of the Chattels Transfer Act. The purchaser has no right to dispose of the chattels: s 57(5), and the vendor's title is not affected by any purported disposition, whether by way of sale, mortgage or otherwise. Under s 20, Hire Purchase Act 1971, the bailee is empowered to transfer his or her interest in the hire purchase agreement and may do so absolutely: see paragraph 37.3.5. A bailee in this situation has to obtain the vendor's consent but if it is unreasonably withheld the Court can give consent. Here we are speaking of the assignment by the bailee of his or her interest in the agreement, not of an assignment of the chattels themselves.

In order to qualify as a customary hire purchase agreement, first, the transaction must be with the manufacturer or other person engaged in the business of disposing of chattels of such description or a finance corporation, and secondly, the chattels must be listed in the Seventh Schedule. The Schedule mainly deals with furniture, household appliances of all kinds, and farm equipment. The list has been added to over the years by Order in Council, yet boats and carpet are not listed nor are common products of our electronic "High-Tech" world. Hire purchase agreements for the sale of such products, at least where a conditional purchase agreement is used (this is in order to avoid the effects of s 27(2) Sale of Goods Act 1908), should be registered by the vendor in order to secure protection. Motor Vehicles have been removed from the list as from 1 April 1990 under the Motor Vehicle Securities Act 1989, which provides a separate system for motor vehicle securities: see Chapter 38.

If retailers purchase their stock for sale pursuant to hire purchase agreements then those agreements are excluded from the definition of customary hire purchase. An agreement covering the purchase by a retailer of chattels on the customary list entered into with a manufacturer of such chattels, a wholesale dealer in such chattels or a finance corporation under which the retailer takes possession of the chattels is not deemed to be a customary hire purchase agreement, pursuant to s 2(5), Chattels Transfer Amendment Act 1931. The effect of this provision is to safeguard the interests of bona fide purchasers buying from retailers. This amendment puts retailers in the position of mercantile agents enabling purchasers from them to enjoy the protection of s 3 Mercantile Law Act 1908. A vendor to a mercantile agent can enjoy protection only by registering the hire purchase agreement. Registration is available and necessary for the protection of the vendor's title as the agreement is not a customary hire purchase agreement.

Section 23 of the Chattels Transfer Act provides that every instrument shall contain a schedule of the chattels comprised in the instrument and gives good title only to the chattels described in the schedule. Instruments are void as against the persons mentioned in ss 18 and 19 in respect of any chattels not described in the schedule. This provision applies to customary hire purchase agreements: Statutes Amendment Act 1936, s 16. A defective description will not invalidate the agreement between the parties to the instrument if adequate evidence of identification can be given.

Customary chattels included in hire purchase agreements do not become fixtures if they are attached to the land. The sellers or bailors may remove them if they give one month's notice to the occupier of the land: s 57(7).

The question must arise as to whether or not s 57 should be retained. Perhaps it is the case that all hire purchase agreements should be registered. This question was considered in 1973 by the Contracts and Commercial Law Reform Committee in "Chattels Securities," at pp 10-11. The Committee states at page 10:

> . . . it is difficult to see any justification for the preservation of the distinction between customary hire purchase agreements and other types of hire purchase agreements. Plainly in our submission it should be abolished. . . .

The committee then goes on to recommend that the law should be such that unless an agreement is registered, a bona fide purchaser acquires good title. No move has been made to implement this recommendation.

37.4.3 Registration of non-customary hire purchase agreements

There has always been uncertainty over whether non-customary hire purchase agreements should be registered and it is surprising that, in the long history of the Chattels Transfer Act, Parliament has not moved to clarify the position. The uncertainty reflects the difficulty of accommodating the concept of bailment within the Chattels Transfer Act. The first point to determine is whether non-customary hire purchase agreements fall within the definition of instrument in s 2 of the Chattels Transfer Act. "Instrument" is defined in s 2 of the Act to include any document which purports to transfer the right to the possession of chattels, whether permanently or temporarily, whether absolutely or conditionally, and whether by way of bailment or lease.

In *Motor Mart Limited v Webb* [1958] NZLR 773 Turner J referred to the two types of hire purchase agreement in the following terms at p 786:

> In the *Helby v Matthews* type of agreement, the owner is always bound throughout – the hirer has an option to purchase. While the state of uncertainty as to the ultimate outcome subsists, and it is still uncertain as to whether the parties will ever be vendor and purchaser, their relationship is that of bailor and bailee. *Helby v Matthews* [1895] AC 471; *Karflex Limited v Poole* [1933] 2 KB 251, and in New Zealand, *Woods v Latham* (1907) 27 NZLR 50; 9 GLR 650. In the *Lee v Butler* [1893] 2 QB 318 type of agreement, the purchaser is always bound; the vendor, however, is not bound to transfer the property except in the event of the last payment being duly made. While the state of uncertainty as to the ultimate outcome subsists, and it is still uncertain whether the parties will ever be vendor and purchaser, their relationship I think is that of bailor and bailee.

Plainly there is an element of bailment in both types of agreement and they therefore fall within the definition of "instrument" in s 2. Both types of hire purchase agreement are effective and binding between the parties to them, whether the agreement is registered or not, but beyond this proposition it is necessary to examine each of the types of agreement separately.

(a) TRUE HIRE PURCHASE AGREEMENT
(1) Section 18 Chattels Transfer Act provides that where chattels secured by an unregistered agreement are in the possession or apparent possession of the grantor, the agreement is void as against the Official Assignee and the creditors. A true hire purchase agreement is in fact a bailment with an option to purchase. Under a bailment the grantor is the bailor. The purchaser, who would normally have possession, is the grantee. Section 18 concerns only the grantor's insolvency and it will have no bearing on the grantee's (purchaser's) insolvency: see *Booth MacDonald & Co Ltd v The OA of Hallmond* (1913) 33 NZLR 110.

(2) Section 19 of the Chattels Transfer Act provides that an unregistered instrument is not to affect the title acquired by a bona fide purchaser for value. Difficulties over this provision arise because of comments

made by Sir Michael Myers CJ in *General Motors Acceptance Corporation v Traders' Finance Corporation Limited* [1932] NZLR 1 where he took the view that failure to register a hire purchase agreement divests the owner of his or her interest as against the persons mentioned in s 19, that is to say, a bona fide purchaser or mortgagee. Myers CJ's remarks are probably obiter and appear to go beyond the scope of the section which is simply expressed to invalidate unregistered instruments. The owner's title is not created by or dependent on the instrument and therefore avoidance of the instrument will have no effect so long as the owner can establish his or her right to the goods which will not be in his or her possession.

The correct view, it is submitted, is that the bailor (lessor) of goods cannot be deprived of his or her rights of ownership by transactions subsequently entered into by the bailee (lessee) with third parties. Until there is a valid exercise of the option, the vendor's title to the chattels is unaffected and he or she does not have to rely on the agreement to prove ownership of them: *Bowmakers v Barnet Instruments* [1945] KB 655 and *Galyer v Massey-Harris Co (Ltd)* (1914) 33 NZLR 1392.

(b) CONDITIONAL PURCHASE AGREEMENT

Different considerations apply to the conditional purchase *(Lee v Butler)* agreement. As a conditional sale it is governed by the provisions of the Sale of Goods Act 1908. Section 27(2) of that Act enables the conditional purchaser to confer a good title on a purchaser in good faith and without notice. Where the agreement has been registered though, the proviso to s 27(2) applies and the sub-purchaser has constructive notice of the contents of the instrument. As with s 57(5) of the Chattels Transfer Act concerning customary hire purchase agreements, no title can then be conferred on the sub-purchaser. Section 27(2) may explain the *General Motors* case. The hire purchase agreement in that case was a conditional sale agreement and was therefore within the scope of the Sale of Goods Act. The grantee was a person who had "agreed to buy" within the meaning of s 27(2) and that provision had the effect of divesting the grantor of title when the grantee disposed of the goods to a bona fide purchaser: see discussion in the *Law of Commerce* by D Roebuck, P C Duncan and A Szakats, Wellington, Sweet & Maxwell (1968) pp 231-232.

From this discussion of the question of registration of non-customary hire purchase agreements the following principles appear:

(i)   both types of agreement can be registered;
(ii) with a true hire purchase agreement, there is no disadvantage to the owner of goods if he or she does not register the agreement;
(iii) the conditional purchase type of agreement must be registered to avoid the effects of s 27(2) of the Sale of Goods Act 1908.

The Legal Research Foundation has stated, "the very uncertainty of the point is highly undesirable" and in 1973 proposed that ss 18 and 19 be amended and all hire purchase agreements of both kinds be dealt with on the same footing: Appendix 1 of the First Report of the Contracts and Commercial Law Reform Committee, "Chattels Securities", p 33. See pp 33-34 for proposed amendments to ss 18 and 19.

37.5 DISPOSAL BY THE PURCHASER OF CHATTELS SUBJECT TO A HIRE PURCHASE AGREEMENT

37.5.1 Fraudulent disposition of goods by a purchaser

Section 44 of the Hire Purchase Act provides that every person who with intent to defraud the vendor parts with possession or purports to sell the hire purchase goods or removes or attempts to remove those goods or does any other act in relation to the goods, commits an offence and is liable to imprisonment and/or a fine.

37.5.2 Registered agreements

Registration of the hire purchase agreement is notice to all the world of the agreement and its contents. Registration protects a vendor from any unauthorised disposition by the purchaser, which otherwise would be valid under s 3 of the Mercantile Law Act 1908 and s 27(2) of the Sale of Goods Act 1908, as the vendor's title in both cases is defeated only by a disposition to a person who takes without notice of the vendor's interest. The position concerning a manufacturer or dealer who sells customary chattels on hire purchase to a retailer is set out above: see para 37.4.2.

37.5.3 Unregistered agreements

It is submitted that the buyer cannot dispose of goods which are subject to a true hire purchase agreement as he or she has no title to them: *Carmine v Howell* (1924) 19 MCR 103. It seems that a failure to register this type of agreement will not deprive a vendor of title as the vendor does not derive title through the agreement.

If a purchaser has entered into an unregistered conditional purchase agreement, other than a customary hire purchase agreement, he or she is a person who has "agreed to buy goods" and therefore s 27(2) of the Sale of Goods Act 1908 will apply. Section 27(2) provides that a sale, pledge or other disposition of goods subject to such an agreement or of the documents of title to them to a person acting in good faith and without notice of the vendor's interest will be valid: *Lee v Butler* [1893] 2 QB 138.

Section 57(5) of the Chattels Transfer Act 1924 prohibits any dealings by the purchaser with goods subject to a customary hire purchase agreement.

If it can be shown that the purchaser has acquired title, then any disposition by him or her of the chattel is binding on the vendor. For example, the vendor may pass title by requiring the purchaser to sign an order form before entering into a hire purchase agreement. If such a form can be construed as an unconditional contract of sale it will transfer title to the purchaser and the hire purchase agreement will not restore title to the vendor: *Dennant v Skinner and Collom* [1948] 2 KB 164; but see also *Paintin and Nottingham Ltd v Miller Gale and Winter* [1971] NZLR 164.

It is clear that the practice where the vendor requires the hirer under a hire purchase agreement to give a series of promissory notes which cover the hire payments as they become due does not vest the property in the goods in the hirer: *Campbell v OA of Buckman* (1909) 28 NZLR 875.

Even the discounting of the promissory notes given as security for payment in a hire purchase agreement will not convert a true hire purchase agreement into a contract of sale: *Modern Light Cars Ltd v Seals* [1934] 1 KB 32. A record of the promissory notes should be contained in the agreement to avoid their amounting to a defeasance, if the hire purchase agreement is an "instrument", and requires registration under the Chattels Transfer Act.

37.6. INSOLVENCY

37.6.1 The purchaser's bankruptcy

Under s 2(1) "purchaser" is defined to include someone to whom the purchaser's interest may be assigned by operation of law. This means that the Official Assignee succeeds to the rights of the bankrupt purchaser. The rights of the vendor of goods on hire purchase and the rights of the Official Assignee on the adjudication of the purchaser as bankrupt are set out in s 91 of the Insolvency Act 1967 as amended by s 54 of the Hire Purchase Act. If the vendor has repossessed the goods within the 21 days preceding the adjudication of bankruptcy and has not disposed of them, or if the vendor repossesses the goods after adjudication, the vendor must serve on the Official Assignee the notice under s 28(1) of the Hire Purchase Act: s 91(2). The Official Assignee then has one month to settle the agreement or to introduce a buyer: s 91(3). If the Official Assignee fails to do this the vendor may prove in the bankruptcy for damages in accordance with the formula in s 34 and must lodge with the proof of debt the s 28(1) notice and the s 32 statement. The Assignee will have the rights conferred on the purchaser by ss 28, 35 and 37. If the vendor has repossessed the goods but not disposed of them or if the vendor has not repossessed them, there is provision in s 91(5) for the vendor to assign the goods to the Official Assignee and prove in the bankruptcy for the net balance due to him or her. This appears to be the equivalent of the situation whereby a secured creditor abandons the security and proves in the bankruptcy as an unsecured creditor for the full debt. Where they are not inconsistent with s 91, the general provisions under s 76 of the Insolvency Act 1967 would seem to apply so that the Official Assignee is entitled to elect to continue or determine a contract.

Section 20(6) of the Hire Purchase Act 1971 has been dealt with above: see para 37.3.5. It would seem that it does not make ineffective a provision in a hire purchase agreement entitling a vendor to repossess the goods in the event of the purchaser's bankruptcy: see D F Dugdale *New Zealand Hire Purchase Law* (1978) p 44.

37.6.2 The purchaser's liquidation

Section 20(7) of the Hire Purchase Act provides that where the purchaser is a body corporate its liquidator may exercise the purchaser's rights subject to compliance with the provisions of the agreement. Section 20(6) does not appear to make ineffective a provision in a hire purchase agreement entitling a vendor to repossess the goods in the event that a liquidator for the purchaser is appointed. Section 307 of the Companies

Act 1955 provides that certain rules applicable to bankruptcies apply to the winding up of insolvent companies.

37.7 REFORM OF HIRE PURCHASE

The law of hire purchase in New Zealand is in need of reform. In Australia it has been significantly reformed. Reform in Australia has come with regard to consumer credit, with South Australia leading the way. In 1972, South Australia abandoned the concept of hire purchase in favour of a "consumer mortgage", which was exempted from the bills of sale legislation: Bills of Sale Act 1886-1972, s 28(2), and the Hire Purchase Agreements Act was repealed: Consumer Transactions Act 1972, s 4. The new Act provides that the property and any goods that constitute a hire purchase agreement, shall pass to the consumer on delivery of the goods to him or her, any provisions of any such contract by virtue of which the supplier is to take possession or dispose of the goods to which the contract relates shall be void and the rights of the supplier under any such contract shall be secured by a mortgage in terms prescribed by regulation. New South Wales repealed its Hire Purchase Act in 1981 as part of its credit control legislation and Victoria has also reformed its hire purchase laws. The Australian Capital Territory in the Credit Ordinance 1985, s 265, has repealed its hire purchase legislation and Western Australia has enacted reforms.

All these reforms relate to the credit aspect of hire purchase. The Molomby Committee: see the Molomby Report, printed by order of the Legislative Assembly of Victoria [C No 5] - 777/72, has considered the security aspect and recommended the adoption of a system based on Article 9 of the United States Uniform Commercial Code. This recommendation has not led to legislative amendment.

In New Zealand it is the security aspect of hire purchase which has been addressed in terms of reform, rather than the credit aspect. In New Zealand the report to the Law Commission by Professor Farrar and Mr O'Regan, "Reform of Personal Property Security Law", Law Commission Preliminary Paper No 6, (1988) also advocates the adoption of an Article 9 type system, and the Law Commission has responded to the report by preparing a draft Personal Property Securities Act, modelled on Article 9 principles. To date, however, the only reform to come about has been limited to security interests in motor vehicles under the Motor Vehicle Securities Act 1989. The Ministry of Consumer Affairs has considered the difficulties with the credit aspect of hire purchase in its discussion paper "Consumers and Credit" (1988).

The Law Commission has also considered the whole question of "unfair" contracts and proposed a scheme to deal with them: Preliminary Paper No 11, "'Unfair' Contracts", a discussion paper, Wellington 1990. In response to the Law Commission's proposals the Ministry of Consumer Affairs has acknowledged the need for legislation dealing with unfair contracts generally but has gone on to suggest that there is a need for legislation which is specific to consumer transactions: The Ministry of Consumer Affairs' Submission on Unfair Contracts, January 1991. The Ministry proposes that legislation about unfairness which is specific to consumer transactions be enacted by way of amendment to the Fair Trading Act 1986, the Credit Contracts Act 1981, the Hire Purchase

Act 1971, the Motor Vehicle Dealers Act 1975 and all other consumer legislation including proposed legislation covering consumer sales of goods and services and consumer credit contracts. The Ministry takes the view that consumer legislation should prescribe a duty of good faith and fair dealing, in respect of every transaction and a prohibition against unfair conduct in respect of the negotiation, settlement and carrying out of every transaction. As yet neither the Law Commission's nor the Ministry of Consumer Affairs' proposals have led to legislation. Comprehensive reform of both the security and the credit aspects of the law of hire purchase are needed but to date Parliament has not moved to give effect to such reform.

Chapter 38

MOTOR VEHICLE SECURITIES

SUMMARY

38.1	INTRODUCTION
38.2	THE PROBLEM
38.3	MOTOR VEHICLE SECURITIES ACT 1989
38.4	THE EFFECTS OF THE MOTOR VEHICLE SECURITIES ACT
38.5	REFORM OF PERSONAL PROPERTY SECURITY LAW

38.1 INTRODUCTION

In 1988, the Motor Vehicle Securities Bill was introduced into Parliament. The explanatory notes to the Bill stated that the principal objects of the proposed scheme were (a) to protect purchasers of motor vehicles that may be subject to security interests, and (b) to protect holders of security interests in motor vehicles in the event of debtors disposing of the vehicles. The Bill received the Royal Assent on 17 April 1989 and came into full force and effect on 1 April 1990.

The Act represents discrete legislation for security interests in motor vehicles. It establishes a registration system for such security interests which stands beside the existing registration systems under the Chattels Transfer Act 1924 and the Companies Act 1955. The existing systems have been the subject of criticism for many years: see Law Commission Preliminary Paper No 6, "Reform of Personal Property Security Law", a Report to the Law Commission by Professor J H Farrar and Mr M A O'Regan, yet reform has been restricted to security interests in only one specific class of chattel. Clearly the problems of security interests in motor vehicles are significant although they merely serve to illustrate the difficulties with the New Zealand registration systems for chattel securities relative to all forms of chattel.

38.2 THE PROBLEM

The origins of the Motor Vehicle Securities Act can be traced to a press statement of the then Minister of Justice on 7 October 1986. The Minister stated:

As the law stands it is very difficult for the purchaser of a used car to discover whether the vehicle is free of a prior interest, such as a hire purchase agreement or a chattel mortgage.

The Minister noted that there are between 20 and 25 cases of unauthorised sales each week, about ten of which result in the consumer losing title and paying the outstanding hire purchase debt of another, without compensation. The Minister went on to state that an impetus to change in the law had been brought about by the recent establishment of a centralised, computerised motor vehicle registration system and the implementation of a successful system in Victoria.

The problem is essentially that of the separation of ownership and possession. It arises when a person without title or authority to pass title to a motor vehicle, purports to do so in favour of a bona fide purchaser for value. For example, where title in a motor vehicle is held by a finance company under a hire purchase agreement, yet possession of both the vehicle and the registration certificate remains with the person whose name appears on the registration certificate, apparently the owner, who then attempts to sell the motor vehicle to a third party. Although most chattels are portable or mobile, the problem tends to have made its greatest impact with regard to the sales of motor vehicles.

The basis of this problem in New Zealand has always been twofold. First, a misapprehension on the part of consumers of the significance of registration under the Transport (Vehicle and Driver Registration and Licensing) Act 1986. Secondly, the lack of a single, comprehensive system of registration of security interests in motor vehicles. Writing of the first in "Security Interests in Motor Vehicles" [1974] NZLJ 498, Jeremy Pope stated that there is a common but mistaken belief that provided the person from whom the buyer is purchasing the vehicle is the registered owner and produces the registration certificate, that person in fact owns the vehicle and no further inquiries are called for. This is quite wrong. There is no system of title registration for motor vehicles in New Zealand. Registration under the Transport (Vehicle and Driver Registration and Licensing) Act 1986 is not evidence of ownership, nor does it create ownership. *Owner* is defined in s 2 of the Act as the person lawfully entitled to possession of the motor vehicle. Sections 20 - 26 make provision for the procedure for registering *change of ownership* with the Registrar of Motor Vehicles. The relevant sections use the term *owner*, but it is *owner* as defined in the Act and this is a reference to possession, not ownership as understood at common law.

The second limb of the problem has now been overcome by the introduction of the Motor Vehicle Securities Act which establishes a Register of Motor Vehicle Securities. This statute is concerned with security interests and accordingly the registration requirements under the Transport (Vehicle and Driver Registration and Licensing) Act 1986 continue to exist and must be complied with. The two statutes fulfil separate functions.

Recognising the problem of security interests in motor vehicles, the Post Office (now New Zealand Post Ltd) introduced in 1962 a system to ameliorate the difficulties. Since 1962 the Post Office has included on both "Application for Registration" and the "Notice of Change of Ownership" forms provision for the registered owner to assign possession of the Certificate of Registration to a third party. In these circumstances, a creditor can gain a considerable measure of protection by arranging for the registered owner of a vehicle bought on credit, such as hire purchase, to complete the assignment in the company's favour. Where this procedure has been followed, the certificate is held by the company until the hire purchase agreement is discharged. An application by the registered owner for a duplicate certificate of registration is not acted on until the person or firm to whom the original certificate was delivered confirms its destruction or loss and indicates to whom the duplicate should be delivered. Thus it is that a degree of protection is available to the legal owner and through that owner to the prospective buyers of vehicles in respect of which encumbrances exist. This system still operates.

The Chattels Transfer Act 1924 has been considered in Chapter 36. It was not able to give effective protection to purchasers of motor vehicles because there has never been a national register of chattel securities and, in any event, motor vehicles, prior to the Motor Vehicle Securities Act, were on the list of customary chattels for the purposes of hire purchase: see para 37.4.2.

The extent of the problem for both consumers and financiers was made clear in submissions to the Commerce and Marketing Select Committee when it was considering the Motor Vehicle Securities Bill. The Select Committee heard evidence from the NZ Financial Services Association that the problem of *out of trust* selling of motor vehicles, as it was referred to, was increasing significantly. An estimate was given that there had been a fourfold increase in this type of illegal selling in the twelve-month period from October 1987 to October 1988. The reason for the increase was attributed to an increased awareness of the deficiencies of the motor vehicle registration system and that there were no accurate means by which a finance company could check for fraud. This was a matter of serious concern to the association whose members' loans for motor vehicles approached $1 billion.

The amount of fraud was estimated to be between $2 million and $5 million with about 8,000 to 10,000 people involved. It was not limited to people with a known record for such dealings, with fraud occurring across all social, economic and age groups. In the Parliamentary debates on the second and third readings of the Bill specific reference was made by members to the impact of unemployment on the level of dishonesty in this area of motor car sales. The NZ Financial Services Association, in its submissions, stated that the level of fraud had a significant effect on the association's members' ability to reduce finance rates with as much as 0.5 per cent involved.

The Automobile Association also commented on the increase in fraudulent activity. The Automobile Association submitted that as many as 50 per cent of motor car sales and purchases were between individuals and not between licensed motor vehicle dealers and that this gave urgency to the whole question of reform: see para 38.5.

The Ministry of Transport stated to the Select Committee that the present motor vehicle registration system had serious flaws because a vehicle's identifying characteristics, engine and chassis numbers, were physically matched with the information on the register only in the event of an incident such as an accident or theft. An estimated 15,000 cars disappeared each year while the increase in unlicensed motor vehicles on the road was estimated to be between 10 per cent and 15 per cent. 32,436 motor vehicles were reported as stolen in 1986.

The need for increased consumer protection is obvious from the figures given above. The need for increased protection for creditors is obvious from submissions made by the New Zealand Bankers' Association. The Association was asked if it could advise the total amount of lending by its members on motor vehicles and the percentage of motor vehicles which might be subject to charges under debenture securities held by banks. The Association informed the Select Committee that it could not give the precise details sought as banking operations do not allow for the identification of such figures. However the Association did obtain from its members estimates which would appear to be indicative of the position. The Association submitted that total lending by its members would be about $17/20 billion of which about $140/150 million would be by way of 10,000/11,000 hire purchase agreements covering motor vehicles.

Besides hire purchase lending, direct lending to farmers would total something in excess of $1 billion. Security in many farming cases includes instruments registered under the Chattels Transfer Act 1924 covering farm stock, plant and *farm vehicles.* In terms of corporate customers, the Association estimated that members held in excess of 100,000 debenture securities which included a fixed charge over vehicles. The Association noted that most debenture securities would, in effect, include a security over a motor vehicle. On the basis of the above figures the Association estimated that conservatively there would be potentially 150,000/200,000 motor vehicles at least over which members would need to obtain specific details and then re-register pursuant to the motor vehicle securities legislation should it proceed to become law.

In making submissions, the Motor Vehicle Dealers' Institute stated that the 1987 Motor Industry Yearbook indicated, as at 30 June 1986, a total number of vehicles on the Register of Motor Vehicles of 2,477,132. In the estimation of the Institute, an accurate figure of potential entries on the Register of Motor Vehicle Securities would be 1,964,331. It was the view of the Institute that at any given time it would be unlikely that more than 50 percent of that total would be subject to a lien or subject to an encumbrance and therefore eligible for potential entry on the Register of Motor Vehicle Securities.

In adopting a system for the registration of security interests in motor vehicles New Zealand has been influenced by developments in Australia, where equivalent systems have been established throughout the 1980s. This is appropriate in view of the policy of Closer Economic Relations (CER) between the two countries. There is a Memorandum of Understanding on the Harmonisation of Business Law which Australia and New Zealand have entered into in support of CER. Harmonisation is problematic. Each Australian state has its own distinct system for registration of security interests in motor vehicles and the New Zealand system is different again. The New Zealand Law Commission has commented on the harmonisation of business law: see Report No 8, "A Personal Property Securities Act for New Zealand" and Report No 9, "Company Law Reform and Restatement". It has expressed the view that harmonisation might come through Australia following developments in the law in this country. To date, however, the various jurisdictions have continued to operate independently in the matter of reform and the system created by the Motor Vehicle Securities Act 1989, although influenced by Australian models, is unique to New Zealand.

38.3 MOTOR VEHICLE SECURITIES ACT 1989

38.3.1 Overview

The Motor Vehicle Securities Act became law on 17 April 1989 and came into full force and effect on 1 April 1990. The Act provides for the establishment of a register of security interests in motor vehicles under the control of a Registrar of Motor Vehicle Securities. "Security interest" is given a comprehensive definition in the Act and procedures are established for the registration of such interests. Any person may then apply to the Registrar for a certificate indicating whether or not a security interest is registered in respect of the vehicle. If the vehicle is stolen, this information can be put on the register. "Motor vehicle" is given a sweeping definition in the Act.

There are provisions in the Act governing dispositions of motor vehicles subject to security interests and a distinction is drawn between dispositions by licensed motor vehicle dealers to consumers, as defined, and other transactions. Broadly, the Act creates a system for the extinguishment of such security interests on the disposition of a vehicle. By way of example, if a purchase is made by a consumer from a licensed motor vehicle dealer, subject to exceptions, the security interest is extinguished and the dealer can be called on to compensate the holder of the security interest. If the purchase is from someone other than a dealer, extinguishment depends on notice as defined. Extinguishment does not occur where a vehicle is purchased from a thief. There are also provisions in the Act for priority of security interests.

The Act gives rise to consequential amendments to various other statutes including the Sale of Goods Act 1908, the Mercantile Law Act 1908, the Chattels Transfer Act 1924 and the Companies Act 1955.

38.3.2 The purpose of the Act

The Act has a two-fold purpose, as its Long Title tells us. It is:

> An Act to provide for the registration of security interests in, and other information relating to, motor vehicles, and to amend, in certain respects, the law relating to the disposition of and the creation of interests in motor vehicles subject to security interests.

38.3.3 Time frame

Although the Motor Vehicle Securities Bill received the Royal Assent on 17 April 1989, Parts I and V of the Act, subject to certain exceptions, did not come into force until 1 October 1989 and those exceptions together with Parts II to IV came into force on 1 April 1990.

Part I of the Act provides for the establishment of a Register of Motor Vehicle Securities and Part V sets out transitional provisions. In effect, the time delay enabled the machinery of the register to be set up between 1 October 1989 and 1 April 1990, with registration and searching operating from 1 April 1990. The concept of extinguishment, the priority rules and all other provisions came into operation from 1 April 1990.

38.3.4 Scheme of the Act

The scheme of the Act involves the key concept of extinguishment which is new to New Zealand law. The other fundamental provisions involve the mechanics of the registration system itself, the definition of security interests, non-extinguishment where a purchase is made from a thief, reimbursement by dealers where the holders of security interests suffer loss, and priority of security interests.

38.3.5 Definition of "motor vehicle"

"Motor vehicle" is defined in s 2 of the Act. The definition is as follows:

"Motor vehicle" or "vehicle" -
(a) Means a vehicle, including a trailer, that -
   (i) Is equipped with wheels, tracks, or revolving runners upon which it moves or is moved; and
   (ii) Is drawn or propelled by mechanical power; and
   (iii) Has a registration number or a chassis number, or both of those numbers:
(b) Includes any other vehicle that is declared in regulations made under this Act to be a motor vehicle for the purposes of this Act; but
(c) Does not include -
   (i) A vehicle running on rails; or
   (ii) An aircraft; or
   (iii) A trailer (not being a trailer designed solely for the carriage of goods) that is designed and used exclusively as part of the armament of any of Her Majesty's Forces; or
   (iv) A trailer running on 1 wheel and designed exclusively as a speed measuring device or for testing the wear of vehicle tyres; or
   (v) A vehicle designed for amusement purposes and used exclusively within a place of recreation, amusement, or entertainment to which the public does not have access with motor vehicles; or
   (vi) A pedestrian-controlled machine designed to perform some mechanical operation and not designed for the carriage of persons or goods; or
   (vii) A pedestrian-controlled forklift.

The definition of motor vehicle under the Act is wide and may be widened yet further as para (b) states that the definition includes any other vehicle as declared in regulations made under the Act to be a motor vehicle.

The s 2 definition includes trailers, caravans and "off-road" vehicles. "Trailer" is separately defined:

"Trailer" means a vehicle without motive power that is drawn or propelled, or is capable of being drawn or propelled, by a motor vehicle from which it is readily detachable.

"Caravan" is not expressly referred to in the definition of "motor vehicle" under the Motor Vehicle Securities Act but the definition expressly includes trailers and caravans clearly fall within the definition of "trailer".

38.3.6 Security interests

"Security interest" is defined in s 2 of the Act in very wide terms. It expressly encompasses the creditor's interest in the transactions of lease, "true" and conditional sale and purchase forms of hire purchase and the chattel mortgage. It also includes reservation of title, fixed charges created by companies and, for the purposes of Part II of the Act, discussed below, floating charges which have become fixed. It does not include the possessory lien or the pledge.

"Security interest" means an interest in or a power over a motor vehicle, whether arising by or pursuant to a document or transaction, which secures the payment of a debt or other pecuniary obligation or the performance of any other obligation. The definition includes the interests specified above, and expressly excludes the possessory lien and the pledge. The definition is more specific than that found in the Chattel Securities Act in Victoria. It is very wide and the intention is to cover as many situations as possible in which one person is in possession of a motor vehicle while another person has a financial interest in that vehicle.

There is no exclusion under the Act for very short-term transactions. The question is one of whether a debtor in a short-term transaction is less likely to sell the vehicle than a debtor in a long-term arrangement. The Act does not oblige secured parties to register their interests and they may decide to take the risk of having a vehicle sold if the burden of registration is disproportionate to the chance of the vehicle being sold. Similarly, there is no minimum term under which a lease need not be registered. Again, lessors need not register if they are willing to bear the risk of a vehicle being sold.

"Secured party" is defined as a holder of a security interest in a motor vehicle and, specifically, the definition includes lessors, owners under hire purchase agreements and mortgagees. Hire purchase agreements are defined to cover both the *Lee v Butler* [1893] 2 QB 318 (CA) and *Helby v Matthews* [1895] AC 471 types of agreement.

Immediately, then, it is clear that the Act favours *substance* rather than *form*. Transactions are classified in accordance with their substance and function instead of the form in which they are cast. Where the function is security, the definition of "security interest" applies.

Submissions to the Parliamentary Select Committee considering the Bill argued that the Bill should be extended to enable the registration of caveats. It was thought that these would be useful if a plaintiff was granted a Mareva injunction freezing the defendant's assets or if the Registrar was not satisfied that the security interest was properly registrable. It was also suggested that secured parties should be allowed to put notices on the register of an intention to register a security interest. Such a notice would last ten days and prevent any other prior registration in priority to the notice. These submissions were not adopted as they would not serve the Act's principal purpose of assisting potential purchasers by giving them information on the title of the vehicles they contemplate purchasing. Such notices do not exist in the Australian jurisdictions.

38.3.7 The registration system

The Act provides for the appointment of a Registrar of Motor Vehicle Securities: s 4, who is directed to establish and maintain a register of security interests in motor vehicles: s 5. This register has been given the name "Autocheck". The office of the Registrar is located in Manukau. The register is, however, a national register in that it contains records of security interests for the whole country. The register of security interests is the central concept around which the other provisions under the Act revolve. It is a *goods indexed* system requiring *notice* filing. Remarkably, there is no provision requiring the registration of the name of the debtor, only the secured party. In keeping the name of the debtor off the register the Act follows the approach taken in New South Wales. Privacy is the underlying rationale of the provision. Any information a purchaser or subsequent creditor needs to know about the debtor can be provided by the secured party.

Section 6 provides that a holder of a security interest in a motor vehicle may apply to the Registrar for the registration of that security interest. Section 6(2) states:

Every application for registration shall specify:
(a) The registration number and chassis number of the motor vehicle unless either of those numbers does not exist;
(b) The name and address of the secured party;
(c) The type and term of the security interest;
(d) The amount of the debt or details of the other obligation secured and;
(e) Such other matters as may be required by the Registrar.

It would seem that s 6(2)(e) could be used by the Registrar to require the name of the debtor to be registered.

Registration of the security interest involves the Registrar in entering in the register the date and time the application for registration was presented and the security interest registered, together with such other matters as the Registrar considers appropriate: s 7. Every security interest is to be entered in the register before 9 am on the next registering day and is deemed to be registered at 9 am on that day: s 8(1).

"Registration Day" is defined, for the purposes of s 8, as the first day on which the registry opens for the registration of security interests after the day on which the application is presented: s 8(2).

Applications to register security interests can be filed at any District Court office throughout the country unless application is made in Auckland, Wellington or Christchurch in which case application should be filed in the offices of the High Court.

The Registrar may make entries in the register noting that a motor vehicle has been reported stolen or otherwise unlawfully obtained: s 9. In doing this the Registrar acts on information which has been received from the Commissioner of Police: s 9(1). Such entries do not create security interests in the motor vehicles to which they relate: s 9(2).

The Department of Justice has prepared an "Information Kit" concerning the registration system under the Motor Vehicle Securities Act. This kit is issued to all secured parties registered under the Act. The kit explains the system and is divided into three parts: Introduction to the Electronic Data Interchange Service of the Motor Vehicle Securities

Register, Introduction to the Motor Vehicle Securities Register and Guide to the Motor Vehicle Securities Register for Secured Parties.

38.3.8 Searching

Searching the register is provided for in ss 10 to 13. Any person may enquire of the Registrar whether or not any security interest is registered in respect of any specified motor vehicle: s 10(1). To make the inquiry, the searcher needs to specify the registration number and chassis number of the vehicle, unless they do not exist: s 10(2). No alternative means of identification is specified in the Act if they do not exist. Identification of motor vehicles is a vexed question. The provisions in the original Bill, cl 7, together with the definition of motor vehicle, cl 2, have changed dramatically in terms of the final Act. It is clear that Parliament wanted certainty as far as identification of motor vehicles is concerned. Car registration plate numbers, engine numbers and chassis numbers have not proved to be an insuperable barrier to car thieves in the past. The Ministry of Transport is currently proposing the introduction of a system of "vehicle identification numbers" (VINS), registration and standards compliance at point of manufacture/entry and confirmation of owner and vehicle identity combined with annual vehicle inspection. If this scheme lives up to its promise, it could well overcome the problems of the past. At such time as this system is introduced the administration of the Motor Vehicle Securities Act should be adjusted to accommodate it. At that time presumably the VINS number would become the principal means of identification of a vehicle and as such used for searching by purchasers.

If an inquiry is made, the Registrar is directed by the Act to state whether or not a security interest is registered in respect of the vehicle by reference to the registration and chassis numbers: s 10(3). Again, there is no reference to what the Registrar is to do when these do not exist. Presumably identification is, in these circumstances, performed by way of reference to "such other matters as may be required by the Registrar" on registration: s 6(2)(e)

Where the Registrar has made an entry under s 9 that a vehicle has been reported as stolen or otherwise unlawfully taken and an inquiry is made in respect of that vehicle, the Registrar shall, "if the entry is made by reference to the numbers specified", state that such an entry has been made: s 10(4). This appears to import a requirement that entries under s 9 be by way of registration and chassis numbers, if the searching procedure with regard to stolen vehicles is going to be effective.

Search inquiries may be made by telephone.

Having made an inquiry of the Registrar, the searcher may then request of him or her a certificate in respect of a specified motor vehicle, to be identified by the registration number and chassis number unless these numbers do not exist: s 11(1) and (2).

On receipt of an application for a certificate, the Registrar shall issue a certificate stating:

(a) whether or not a security interest is registered in respect of a vehicle by reference to the numbers specified;

(b) if a security interest is so registered, the registered particulars of that security interest;

(c)　the date and time of issue;
(d)　the date and time at which the certificate will expire;
(e)　that the certificate will not offer any protection after it has expired: s11(3).

Where application is made for a certificate for the purposes of s 36(a) of the Act, which is discussed below and concerns reimbursement, s 11(4A), added by the Motor Vehicle Securities Amendment Act 1989, applies. There used to be a similar procedure for the issue of certificates in Victoria under the Chattels Transfer Act 1981 but it was abandoned under the 1987 Chattels Transfer Act. It may be that such a system will prove to be too cumbersome in New Zealand relative to the large number of requests that are bound to occur although such a procedure does still exist in New South Wales.

In submissions to the Select Committee the question was raised as to whether or not a guaranteed search note system should be introduced under the Act similar to that operating with regard to land under the Land Transfer Act 1952. The guaranteed title system relative to land transfer was introduced to overcome the problem of delay between the lodging of documents and their registration. For various reasons some time can elapse between lodgement and registration. The guaranteed search note system does not prevent the registration of adverse interests but, rather, it provides compensation if loss occurs because of the process of removing an adverse interest from the title or because of the adverse interest stopping a transaction altogether.

It seems that the lower value of motor vehicles justified a simpler approach. Three possible avenues were recommended:

(1)　Provide for a certificate valid at the date of issue and enable potential purchasers to make a telephone inquiry just before purchase to see if any further interests have been registered;
(2)　Provide for a certificate valid for a period of time, during which no interests may be entered on the register; and
(3)　Provide for a certificate valid for a period of time during which interests may be registered but specify that those interests do not prevail against the person holding the certificate.

The essential choice is between the person holding a certificate which does not freeze the register, as far as the certificate holder is concerned, as in choice (1) and a certificate which does freeze it as in (2) and (3). A meeting of potential users of the Motor Vehicle Securities Register convened by the Justice Department concluded that the fairest approach was to issue a certificate which freezes the register until the start of the next working day. Purchasers who obtain certificates would be able to rely on them for the remainder of the day. Any security interests received by the registry on that day would not be entered on the register. They would be held and entered, probably overnight, before the start of the next working day. The certificates would indicate in an appropriate manner the period of validity.

This approach amounts to a reasonable compromise between the rights of persons checking the register and those entering security interests. Persons checking the register can obtain a certificate valid for a period of hours. If the vehicle is not purchased within that period they may make a free telephone call to check the state of the register immediately before completing a purchase. Parties entering security interests would know that their securities would appear on the register at the start of the next working day.

If anyone applies for a certificate concerning a vehicle which the Registrar has been informed has been reported as stolen or otherwise unlawfully taken, the Registrar shall issue a certificate containing particulars of that entry if the entry has been made by reference to the vehicle's registration and chassis numbers: s 11 (4).

Every certificate issued by the Registrar in response to an inquiry expires at 9 am, on the day after the date of issue. The situation of the register in Manukau has the potential to pose a problem for the collection of certificates in view of the time-frame for their expiry. The Registrar will, however, make certificates available by way of fax: LawTalk 330. Certificates can be obtained by way of fax at the offices of the District Court throughout the country with the exception of Auckland, Wellington and Christchurch where certificates can be obtained by way of fax at the offices of the High Court. No certificate so issued shall state the amount of the debt or the details of the other obligation secured by any registered security interest: s 13.

The Registrar is directed not to disclose to any person the amount of the debt or the details of any other obligations secured by any registered security interest: s 13(2). Any holder of the security interest in a motor vehicle may request the Registrar to disclose the information entered in the register relating to the amount of the debt or the details of any other obligations secured by any other security interest registered in respect of the same vehicle. If the Registrar is satisfied that this information is needed to determine the priorities of any two or more security interests in respect of the vehicle, then he or she shall supply the information requested: s 50(5) and (6).

Where any registered security interest is discharged, the person entered in the register as the secured party shall within ten working days of the day on which the security interest is discharged apply to the Registrar for the cancellation of the registration. Where any registered security interest is extinguished under ss 24 or 25 which deal with dispositions by dealers to consumers, the person entered in the register as the secured party shall, within ten working days of the date on which that person becomes aware that the security interest has been extinguished, apply to the Registrar for cancellation of the registration: s 14(1) and (2). In any event, any secured party may at any time apply to the Registrar for the cancellation of the registration of his or her security interest: s 14(3). The Registrar, if satisfied that an application for cancellation is in order, shall cancel the registration of the security interest: s 14(4). Failure to cancel registration by a secured party attracts both civil and criminal liability as in Victoria. Every person commits an offence and is liable on summary conviction to a fine not exceeding $1,000 who fails, without reasonable excuse, to comply with the cancellation provisions set out above: s 15(1).

Any person who suffers loss or damage by reason of the failure of any other person to comply with the cancellation provisions may apply to a Disputes Tribunal for an order requiring such person to pay such compensation as the Tribunal considers just.

38.3.9 Discharge and cancellation

Where any registered security interest is discharged and the person entered in the register as the secured party fails to apply for the cancellation of the registration within ten working days of the date on which the security interest is discharged, the person who is the debtor may apply to the Registrar for the cancellation of the registration: s 16(1).

Where any registered security interest is extinguished pursuant to those provisions of the Act concerning dispositions by dealers to consumers, and the person entered in the register as the secured party fails to apply for the cancellation of the registration within ten working days of the date on which that person became aware that the security interest had been extinguished, the purchaser or the hirer or the lessee of the motor vehicle may apply to the Registrar for the cancellation of the registration: s 16(2).

On receipt of an application for cancellation in these circumstances, that is to say, by the debtor or the purchaser, the Registrar shall give to the person entered in the register as the secured party, a notice requiring that person to show cause, within ten working days of the date on which the notice was given, why the registration should not be cancelled: s 16(3). If any person fails within those ten working days to show cause to the Registrar's satisfaction why the registration should not be cancelled, the Registrar may cancel the registration of the security interest: s 16(4).

The Registrar may of his or her own motion cancel registration of a security interest. Where it appears to the Registrar that a person entered in the register as the holder of the security interest was not, when the application for registration was made, the holder of that interest or a registered security interest may have been discharged or extinguished and the person entered in the register as the secured party may have failed to apply for the cancellation of that registration, the Registrar may, by notice to that person, require that person to show cause, within ten working days from the date on which notice was given, why the registration should not be cancelled. If such person fails within those ten working days to show cause to the Registrar's satisfaction, the Registrar may, in his or her own discretion, cancel the registration of the security interest: s 17(2). Cancellations of security interests are deemed to take effect at 9 am, on the registering day following the day on which application for the cancellation is presented: s 19.

There is provision under the Act for amendment of registration particulars of a security interest and amendment takes effect on the same basis as cancellation: s 18.

All applications under Part I are to be in an approved form and fees are payable: ss 20 and 21.

38.3.10 False or misleading information

If any person makes a statement or supplies false or misleading information to the Registrar for the purpose of obtaining or retaining the registration of any security interest under the Act, that person becomes liable to a fine not exceeding $2,000: s 22(1). Any person who suffers loss or damage by reason of any other person committing such offence may apply to the Disputes Tribunal for an order seeking such compensation as the Tribunal considers just from that other person: s 22(2).

In submissions to the Select Committee it was suggested that a provision should be included in the Act stating that a registration would not be invalidated because of a fault by the secured party in supplying information, unless that fault misled another person. It is clear that faults in the information supplied to the Registrar do not invalidate the registration except that if the faulty information means that the security is registered against the wrong vehicle that could lead to the secured party losing its security.

38.3.11 Extinguishment

If registration is the cornerstone of the Act, extinguishment is the concept which stands next to it in importance. Again, the influence of Victoria is obvious as that jurisdiction has a regime of registration and extinguishment of security interests relative to motor vehicles.

The wording of the Act concerning extinguishment is dramatically different from the wording in the Bill as originally introduced into Parliament. The influence of submissions made by interested parties to the Select Committee considering the Bill is obvious in this regard.

The relevant provisions of the Act are as follows:

24. Extinguishment of security interest in case of consumer purchase from dealer – Where a consumer purchases a motor vehicle that is subject to a security interest from a dealer, –
(a) The security interest in that motor vehicle shall be extinguished; and
(b) The consumer shall acquire the vehicle free from the security interest; and
(c) Where title to the vehicle was vested in the holder of that security interest, title shall pass to the consumer.

25. Extinguishment of security interest in case of consumer hire purchase or lease from dealer – Where a consumer acquires from a dealer, under a hire purchase agreement or a lease, a motor vehicle that is subject to a security interest –
(a) The security interest in that motor vehicle shall be extinguished; and
(b) Where title to the vehicle was vested in the holder of that security interest, title shall pass to the dealer.

26. Relevance of notice of security interest - sections 24 and 25 of this Act shall apply whether or not the dealer or the consumer has notice of the security interest, and whether or not the dealer is the debtor, except where –
(a) The security interest is disclosed to the consumer in writing before the contract of sale becomes binding on the consumer, or, as the case may be, before the hire purchase agreement or lease is entered into; or
(b) The security interest is created by or with the express consent of the consumer.

27. Extinguishment of security interest in case of other purchases –
(1) Where a motor vehicle that is subject to a security interest is purchased otherwise than by a consumer from a dealer, and the purchaser does not have notice of the security interest at the time when the purchase price is paid or the exchange is made –
(a) The security interest in the motor vehicle shall be extinguished; and
(b) The purchaser shall acquire the vehicle free from the security interest; and

(c) Where title to the vehicle was vested in the holder of that security interest, title shall pass to the purchaser.

(2) This section is subject to the provisions of sections 30 and 31 of this Act.

28. Extinguishment of security interest in case of other hire purchases or leases -

(1) Where -

(a) Any person acquires, under a hire purchase agreement or a lease, an interest in a motor vehicle that is subject to a security interest; and

(b) That person does not have notice of the security interest at the time when the first payment is made under the hire purchase agreement or lease, as the case may be –

any secured party shall, notwithstanding any provision of the agreement between the secured party and the debtor, be bound by the terms of the hire purchase agreement or lease.

(2) Nothing in this section applies where the motor vehicle is acquired on hire purchase or is leased from a dealer by a consumer.

(3) This section is subject to the provisions of sections 30 and 31 of this Act.

Both the terms "consumer" and "dealer" are defined in s 2.
"Consumer" means any person other than:

(a) A manufacturer;

(b) A wholesaler;

(c) A dealer;

(d) A finance company.

"Dealer" means a holder of a motor vehicle dealer's licence issued under s 15 of the Motor Vehicle Dealers Act 1975. The definitions are thus clear.

The interesting matter here is how the Bill so strikingly changed its form as it passed through the stages from introduction to Parliament to becoming law. The vital question was that of affording protection to consumers while balancing that interest against that of secured parties. The role of motor vehicle dealers, when it stood between the two, was obviously seen as crucial.

Concern was expressed by interested parties to the Select Committee in submissions that the Bill as originally drafted would cause problems for parties supplying vehicles to motor vehicle dealers pursuant to Romalpa clauses. Submissions were made that the Bill would oblige such suppliers to register each motor vehicle and the security interest in it prior to dispatch to dealers. Such suppliers dispatch motor vehicles to a dealer on the basis that the supplier retains title until paid in full. On a retail sale the motor vehicle dealer registers the motor vehicle. The supplier is then divested of title but retains a charge on the proceeds of sale. Under the Bill as originally drafted, such suppliers ran the risk of financially distressed dealers registering and selling vehicles to other dealers or creditors. Such transactions would not be sales at retail and under cl 26 of the original Bill any security interest would be extinguished. Clearly there is a problem here.

In another submission it was argued that the protection given by cl 26 to purchasers should not extend to purchasers who are finance companies acting as financiers, licensed motor vehicle dealers, manufacturers as defined in the Motor Vehicle Dealers Act and wholesalers as defined in the Motor Vehicle Dealers Act. The argument ran that people buying motor vehicles who belong to these categories have sufficient knowledge of the motor vehicle industry either actually to know that the motor vehicle is being sold subject to security interests or to know that they should check the securities register. In the circumstances it was argued that it is unfair that they should have the protection of a clause designed to protect ordinary members of the public buying from dealers.

Another submission accepted that ordinary members of the public should have greater protection when buying from dealers than when buying privately and in another the view was taken that a registered security interest should always prevail.

These submissions were heeded as the amendments to the Bill were substantial. In the Act a clear distinction has been drawn between consumers on the one hand, and, on the other hand, purchasers who are motor vehicle manufacturers, wholesalers, dealers or financiers. This distinction is central to the extinguishment provisions under the Act.

38.3.12 Dispositions by dealers to consumers

(1) Disposition, notice and extinguishment: The Act provides that where a consumer purchases a motor vehicle that is subject to a security interest, from a dealer, the security interest shall be extinguished and the consumer shall acquire the vehicle free from the security interest. Where title to the vehicle is vested in the holder of that security interest, title then passes to the consumer: s 24.

So, too, where a consumer acquires a motor vehicle from a dealer under a hire purchase agreement or lease and the motor vehicle is subject to a security interest, the security interest is extinguished and, where title is vested in the holder of the security interest, title passes to the dealer: s 25.

Subject to certain exceptions, the security interest is extinguished regardless of whether or not it has been registered under Part I of the Act. The relevant concept is that of notice, rather than that of registration per se.

Extinguishment occurs whether or not the dealer or consumer has notice of the security interest, except where, first, the security interest is disclosed to the consumer in writing before the contract of sale becomes binding on the consumer, or, as the case may be, before the hire purchase agreement or lease is entered into, or, secondly, where the security interest is created by or with the express consent of the consumer: s 26.

The Act sets out rules for determining whether a person has notice of a security interest. A person has such notice if the security interest is registered or the person has actual knowledge of the security interest: s 29. Actual knowledge includes actual notice that a floating charge registered under the Companies Act 1955 has become fixed.

The provisions in the Act are subject to the situation whereby a security interest is registered with regard to a motor vehicle and the engine is later transferred to a second motor vehicle: s 33. In these circumstances, no person involved in the purchase or other acquisition, or the sale or other disposition of the second motor vehicle shall have notice of the security interest by reason only of the fact that it was registered in respect of the first vehicle: s 33.

Before the Select Committee it was argued that the question of the purchaser's right to the vehicle should not be determined by whether the purchaser had notice of the security interest. Rather, it was argued that it should be determined solely by whether the security interest was registered.

Registration as the sole test of the validity of a security interest against a purchaser has the attraction of simplicity. That is the system in the United States of America and parts of Canada. Its benefit is that it leads to absolute certainty.

On the other hand, it means that purchasers who actually know about unregistered security interests, are able to acquire title despite their knowledge. For this reason in New Zealand actual knowledge prevents a purchaser, a purchaser under hire purchase or a lessee from acquiring title.

(2) Reimbursement: This is a concept in its own right under the Act. The position is the same as that in Victoria. That is to say, a consumer can deal with confidence with a licensed motor vehicle dealer knowing that she or he will obtain a motor vehicle which is not encumbered by some prior security interest. The secured party can ultimately look to the Motor Vehicle Dealers Fidelity Guarantee Fund in order to have his or her loss made good.

(3) Purchase from a dealer: Where a motor vehicle already subject to a security interest is purchased from a dealer by a consumer and the security interest is extinguished under the Act, the dealer must pay to the secured party the amount outstanding under the debt or other obligations secured by the security interest: s 34. For this provision to apply, the dealer is required to have notice of the security interest at the time the purchase price is paid or an exchange is made: s 34(c). Payment must be made by the dealer to the secured party within seven working days from the date on which the secured party serves a claim for payment on the dealer. In the original Bill the period was twenty-eight days but in submissions to the Select Committee the Motor Vehicle Dealers Institute suggested the reduction to seven days which was ultimately adopted in the Act: s 34(d).

The definition of "notice" is set out above: see discussion of s 29. Where the dealer does not have notice, no claim for reimbursement arises. This is a very real incentive to register a security interest. Under s 36(b) a claimant for reimbursement on extinguishment of a security interest must submit a statement, where the security interest is unregistered, setting out the grounds on which it is believed that the dealer had notice of the security interest.

If the dealer fails to comply with the above requirements for reimbursement, the secured party may make a claim under Part III of the Motor Vehicle Dealers Act 1975 for payment by the Motor Vehicle Dealers Fidelity Guarantee Fund of the amount the dealer is required to pay to the secured party. This right of recourse to the Fidelity Guarantee Fund applies only where the vehicle disposed of by the dealer is a motor vehicle as defined in s 2 of the Motor Vehicle Dealers Act 1975. The effect of this is that there is no right of recourse to the Fidelity Guarantee Fund where the vehicle is either a caravan or a trailer.

The Act states in s 35, that the Fund is not liable to pay any amount to the secured party where that amount is recoverable from the purchaser of the motor vehicle because he or she still has a balance of the purchase price to pay, or would have been recoverable if the secured party had not unreasonably delayed in exercising its rights: s 35(2). The secured party is subrogated to the extent of the amount outstanding, to the person from whom the vehicle is purchased: s 43(1). Before exercising the rights of subrogation contained in s 43, the secured party must give notice in writing to the purchaser and if practicable, the person from whom the vehicle was purchased, first explaining that the purchaser is obliged to pay or deliver to the secured party any money or other property owing to the seller in reduction of the purchase price and secondly, summarising any other rights that the secured party intends to exercise.

The procedure for making claims for reimbursement by a secured party is set out in s 36. Where payment is made to the secured party either by the dealer or the Fund, the dealer or the Fund is subrogated to the extent of that payment to all rights and remedies the secured party would have had against the debtor and his or her personal representatives: s 37(1).

Where payment is made by the Fund, the Fund is subrogated to the extent of the payment to all rights and remedies the secured party would have had against the dealer and his or her personal representatives: s 37(2).

Company officers, employees or agents of the debtor or dealer may be held to be personally responsible for payment to the dealer or Fund of any amounts paid by them: s 37(3).

Notwithstanding anything in the Companies Act 1955 or any other Act or any rule of law, any amount that the Fund is entitled to recover from the dealer company, shall, in the event of the winding up of the company, be paid in priority to all other debts in accordance with s 308(1)(d) of the Companies Act 1955 and the provisions of that section and of s 101 of the Companies Act shall apply to it accordingly: s 37(4).

In submissions to the Select Committee it was argued that what was to become s 45(2) should be deleted. The effect of this would have been that the secured party would not be obliged to exercise its right to subrogation under s 43 before claiming from the Fund. Another submission considered that third parties who were finance companies, dealers, manufacturers or wholesalers should not be able to claim on the Fund at all. These submissions were not adopted. The logic of the system demands that the Fund be available as a "back-stop" to all secured parties. All secured parties must be able to resort to the Fund if the dealer cannot provide the money.

(4) Dealer granting a lease or making a hire purchase agreement: Where a motor vehicle, subject to a security interest, is purchased on hire purchase from a dealer or leased from a dealer and the security interest is extinguished under the Act, the dealer must pay to the secured party the amount outstanding under the debt or other obligation secured by the security interest. Again, reimbursement depends on notice: the dealer must have notice of the security interest at the time when the first payment under the hire purchase agreement or lease is made. Payment must be made within seven working days after the date on which the secured party serves a claim for payment on the dealer: s 38(1).

If the dealer fails to comply with these provisions, the secured party may make a claim for payment by the Motor Vehicle Dealers Fidelity Guarantee Fund: s 38(2). Again, this right of recourse applies only where the vehicle disposed of by the dealer is a motor vehicle as defined in s 2 of the Motor Vehicle Dealers Act 1975.

The Fund is not liable to pay to the secured party any amount otherwise recoverable from the hirer or lessee of the motor vehicle under the Act or would have been so recoverable if the secured party had not unreasonably delayed in exercising its rights: s 38(3).

There is a procedure laid down under the Act for making claims for reimbursement: s 36 as amended by s 2 of the Motor Vehicle Securities Amendment Act 1989, s 38(4), and rights of subrogation apply as discussed above under s 37 with such modifications as may be necessary.

The secured party can itself receive the balance of payments due under the hire purchase agreement or lease where its original security interest has been extinguished: ss 38(3) and 32. The secured party is entitled to demand and give receipts for money payable under the hire purchase agreement or lease and to exercise all other rights and powers of the person who disposed of the vehicle under the hire purchase agreement or lease, as if that person's rights under the hire purchase agreement or lease had been assigned to the secured party. The secured party must give notice in writing to the hirer or lessee before exercising these rights: s 32(2).

38.3.13 The Motor Vehicle Dealers Act 1975

Licensed motor vehicle dealers have been subject to exacting obligations with regard to title when selling motor vehicles since the enactment of the Motor Vehicle Dealers Act 1975. The Act is essentially a consumer protection measure. It was drawn in such a way as to ensure members of the public dealing with licensed motor vehicle dealers that they could do so with the complete confidence of obtaining clear title to the vehicle they wished to purchase.

Section 89 was enacted to deal with this matter. In its original form, subs (1) did two things: (1) Section 89(1)(a) implied the condition into contracts that the seller of a new or secondhand vehicle was the "true owner"; and (2) Section 89(1)(b) provided that the vehicle would be free from any charge or encumbrance in favour of a third party unless it had been disclosed to the purchaser in writing before the sale.

Under s 89(2), anyone who suffered loss because of a breach of subs (1), was, subject to certain exceptions (s 40(3), (4) and (4A)) entitled to make a claim against the Motor Vehicle Dealers Fidelity Guarantee Fund.

With the passing of the Motor Vehicle Securities Act 1989, s 89(1)(b) has been consequentially repealed as from 1 April 1990. Plainly it is no longer needed as the Motor Vehicle Securities Act sets up a new regime governing dispositions by licensed motor vehicle dealers to consumers of motor vehicles subject to security interests.

Again, it is a cornerstone of the Motor Vehicle Securities Act that consumers can enter into transactions with dealers with complete confidence. Section 89(1)(a), supported by s 89(2), and the Motor Vehicle Securities Act, complement each other and the consumer can rest assured that he or she will receive good title free of security interests.

Section 89(1)(a) cannot be excluded from transactions by the agreement of the parties. Section 107(1) of the Motor Vehicle Dealers Act provides that the provisions of Part VII of the Act shall have effect notwithstanding any provision to the contrary in any contract of sale or other agreement. Section 89 falls within Part VII: see the note by the

Executive Director of the Motor Vehicle Dealers Institute Inc, "Motor Vehicle Dealers Fidelity Guarantee Fund" [1990] NZLJ 339.

38.3.14 Dispositions other than by dealers to consumers

As with transactions between consumers and dealers, extinguishment occurs both in the case of sales and hire purchase and leases but where the disposition is not made by a dealer to a consumer, registration under the Act prevents extinguishment.

(1) Purchases: Where a motor vehicle which is subject to a security interest is purchased otherwise than by a consumer from a dealer and the purchaser does not have notice of the security interest when the purchase price is paid or the exchange made where there is a trade-in, the security interest is extinguished and the purchaser acquires the motor vehicle free from the security interest. Where title to the vehicle is vested in the holder of the security interest, title passes to the purchaser. Title will, of course, commonly be vested in the holder of the security interest: s 27. "Notice" means actual notice or registration under the Act. Registration therefore protects the interest of the secured party.

The term "otherwise by a consumer from a dealer" requires consideration. "Consumer", as we have seen, is defined to mean any person other than the following: a manufacturer, a wholesaler, a dealer, a finance company. Clearly then, under s 27, any of these persons purchasing from a dealer, from each other or from a consumer will come within the ambit of the provision. The dealer who buys from a consumer is at risk and will need to search the register to secure protection. So, too, the dealer who buys from a manufacturer, a wholesaler or another dealer, as is commonly done. A finance company which enters into hire purchase arrangements with a consumer and buys the motor vehicle from the consumer in order to sell it back to the consumer on hire purchase will be at risk.

The above provision is subject to s 30. Extinguishment will not occur unless the motor vehicle is purchased or acquired from the debtor or a person who is lawfully in possession of the vehicle or has assumed ownership of it where the debtor has lost the right to possession of it or is estopped from asserting an interest in the vehicle against the purchaser. There is, then, no extinguishment where there is a purchase from a thief.

Section 27 is also subject to s 31. This section applies only where a person who is not a consumer purchases or acquires a motor vehicle from someone who is also not a consumer. For example where a dealer purchases from a manufacturer or wholesaler or another dealer, even from a finance company where repossession has occurred. If the person purchasing or acquiring the vehicle knows that the sale or other disposition (hire purchase agreements and leases would come within this term) is not in the ordinary course of business of the other person, unregistered security interests with regard to the vehicle will not be extinguished. Under the Act it is presumed that a person does not know that a sale or other disposition is not in the ordinary course of business unless the contrary is proved: s 31(3). This provision seems to be designed to catch unusual transactions. Only those within the ordinary course of business cause unregistered security interests to be extinguished.

(2) Hire purchase or leases: Where any person acquires, under a hire purchase agreement or a lease, an interest in a motor vehicle that is subject to a security interest and that person does not have notice of the security interest at the time when the first payment is made under the hire purchase agreement or lease, the prior security interest shall be extinguished or, to use the language of the statute, the secured party shall "be bound by the terms of the hire purchase agreement or lease": s 28. The provision does not use the term "extinguishment" although it appears in the shoulder note. Section 38(1) (d) refers to a security interest "extinguished" under s 28. Again, "notice" means either actual notice or registration under the Act. Registration protects the interest of the secured party. This provision is subject to ss 30 and 31 discussed above involving acquisition of a motor vehicle from a thief and transactions which are not in the ordinary course of business. Section 32 sets out the rights of a secured party in the event of a subsequent hire purchase agreement or lease and these have been discussed above.

38.3.15 Miscellaneous provisions under Part II of the Act

(1) Registration under the Companies Act: A security interest in a motor vehicle may be extinguished notwithstanding that the charge which creates or evidences the security interest, or the charge under which the security interest otherwise arises, is registered under the Companies Act 1955: s 39. Registration of the company charge under the Motor Vehicle Securities Act would prevent extinguishment except in the case of a purchase by a consumer from a dealer, as we have seen. Fixed charges with regard to motor vehicles may be registered under the Act, but not floating charges: see the definition of "security interest" in s 2, discussed above.

(2) Charge over proceeds of sale: The extinguishment of any security interest in a motor vehicle shall not affect any security interest that may exist in respect of the proceeds of sale of the vehicle. This provision clearly caters for rights of tracing under Romalpa clauses: s 40.

(3) Revival of security interest on cancellation of contract for purchase of motor vehicle: Where a purchaser contracts to purchase a motor vehicle which is subject to a security interest and that security interest is extinguished pursuant to the Act and the contract for the purchase of the motor vehicle is then repudiated or rescinded, the security interest revives and continues in full force and effect as if it had not been extinguished. Where a security interest revives in this manner the title to the vehicle revests in the person in whom it was vested immediately before the security interest was extinguished. The security interest can then be re-registered by the Registrar. These provisions, contained in s 41 of the Act, apply both to purchases by consumers from dealers and to "other" purchases.

(4) Revival of security interest on cancellation of hire purchase agreement or lease entered into with dealer: Where a consumer enters into a hire purchase

agreement or lease with a dealer in respect of a motor vehicle that is subject to a security interest and the security interest in the motor vehicle is extinguished under the Act and the hire purchase agreement or the lease is itself rescinded or cancelled then the security interest revives and continues in full force and effect as if it had not been extinguished: s 42(1). Where a security interest revives in this way the title to the vehicle revests in the person in whom it was vested immediately before the security interest was extinguished: s 42(2). The security interest can then be re-registered by the Registrar: s 42(3). This provision relates only to extinguishment where a transaction is entered into with a dealer.

Section 25 of the Act deals with extinguishment of a security interest in the case of a consumer taking a hire purchase agreement or a lease from a dealer and s 28 deals with security interests in "other" cases of hire purchase or lease. Under s 25 extinguishment occurs and the secured party may look to the dealer, supported by the Motor Vehicle Dealers Fidelity Guarantee Fund for reimbursement of the loss suffered. Under s 28 the secured party whose interest is extinguished may in turn receive the payments owing under the hire purchase agreement or lease pursuant to s 32. The different consequences under ss 25 and 28 account for the fact that s 42 deals only with extinguishment under s 25 where the transaction is conducted with a dealer.

(5) Secured party subrogated to rights of seller against purchaser: Section 43 has been dealt with above. Two questions arise with regard to it. The first is whether the wording is wide enough to enable the secured party to require the handing over of a trade-in vehicle as part payment of the purchase price. The second relates to the priority of the subrogation rights against either an assignee of a hire purchase agreement or the holder of a debenture over the assets of the dealer which includes a charge over the book debts of the dealer. With regard to the first question, as "the purchase price" is defined to include "any valuable consideration" under s 2, it seems a purchaser would be obliged to hand over a trade-in vehicle to a secured party who stepped into the shoes of the party from whom the vehicle was purchased. As regards the second question, it seems that s 43 would have the effect of giving priority to the finance company to which the hire purchase agreement was assigned. The section provides for the secured party to be subrogated to the rights "of a person from whom a vehicle was purchased". If that person has assigned his or her rights, there are no rights for the secured party to be subrogated to. However, the secured party continues to have rights against the dealer or the Fund where extinguishment takes place pursuant to s 24. Where the purchase is not by a consumer from a dealer loss could occur and this must be seen as an inducement to the secured party to register the secured interest under the Act. The position with regard to the debenture holder is less satisfactory. The secured party has the same rights to enforce payment as the dealer but the provision in the Act does not say that the payments recovered are subject to the debenture holder's interest. The rights of a debenture holder in this position are not clear.

(6) Liability of agent: Under s 44 a person acting as an agent of a debtor is not liable for conversion, or any other tort in respect of interests in chattels, by selling or otherwise disposing of a motor vehicle subject to a

security interest, if the person did not have notice of the security interest at the time when the person sold or disposed of the vehicle.

(7) Repossession: In submissions to the Select Committee the point was raised that means should be included in the Act to inform secured parties when their security interests are extinguished because of a sale by a dealer. This submission was concerned about the effect on a secured party which tried to repossess a vehicle from a person who had acquired good title through purchasing from a dealer. It seems that this problem will not arise in those cases where the secured party has recourse against the dealer, who originally sold the vehicle, on the default of the debtor. This is a common arrangement. In the remaining cases the problem will occur only if secured parties repossess vehicles without making contact with the persons who appear currently to be in possession of them. Repossession agents who do not give advance notice of repossession must always run the risk that they will repossess an item to which they are not entitled.

38.3.16 Priorities

Part III of the Act deals with priority of security interests. The scheme of priorities follows the Victorian model up to a point but there are significant differences. As in Victoria, the Act does not have any bearing on the priority of company charges: s 45. Also as in Victoria, a registered security interest takes priority over an unregistered security interest with regard to the same vehicle: s 46. The time of registration determines priority between competing security interests, again as in Victoria: s 47. We can thus have a situation where a security interest is created but not registered before a subsequently created security interest is registered. The subsequently created but first registered charge takes priority.

These priority rules apply notwithstanding that when an application for registration of a security interest is presented for registration, the holder of the security interest has "express, implied or constructive notice" of an earlier security interest or that the motor vehicle is in the possession of another secured party: s 48. This is quite different from the position in Victoria. The first situation is not expressly covered under the Victorian Act. The second is dealt with by granting priority to the party with possession.

The question was raised before the Select Committee whether the statutory priority would prevail over the voidable preference rules. The Act is directed to ensuring that time of registration is the rule for determining priority with regard to competing securities. It seems that there is no intention of altering the law of voidable preference or voidable securities in ss 56 and 57 of the Insolvency Act 1967. The Act provides that nothing in Part III, which contains the provisions dealing with priorities, shall limit these sections of the Insolvency Act. Sections 309 and 311 of the Companies Act which concern voidable preferences and voidable securities are not affected either but that is of no consequence here as the priority rules do not apply to company charges.

Priority of unregistered security interests follows the traditional concept that the first in time prevails. Thus any two or more unregistered security interests in respect of the same vehicle shall have priority in relation to each other according to the time at which each security was created or otherwise arose. In Victoria, unregistered security interests are governed by general principles of law.

There are priority provisions for further advances: s 50, and there are provisions expressly permitting postponement of priority: s 51, thereby overcoming with regard to motor vehicles a problem experienced relative to chattels generally under the Chattels Transfer Act 1924. The priority rules are subject to the extinguishment provisions under ss 25 and 28 concerning subsequent hire purchase agreements and leases. In other words, the provisions for extinguishment are not affected by the priority rules. This is necessary because ss 25 and 28 themselves deal with competing securities: s 52.

Part III of the Act attempts to establish a comprehensive scheme of priorities under the Act and appears to achieve its aim except for the uneasy relationship it has with company charges. Clearly registration is the priority point.

38.3.17 Compensation

The Act makes provision, as is the case in the Australian States, for compensation for loss or damage arising from acts or omissions of the Registrar: ss 54, 55, 56 and 57.

38.3.18 General provisions

(a) The Act creates an offence where a person with intent to defraud a secured party purports to sell or otherwise dispose of any motor vehicle that is subject to a security interest. The maximum fine is $2,000.00: s 58.

(b) Contracting out of the Act is prohibited, subject to some limitations. First, where neither party is a consumer, contracting out is permitted, s 59(2)(a), and secondly, terms other than those dealing with extinguishment may be modified, restricted or excluded: s 59(2)(b). Hence, for example, parties may establish their own priority provisions. Attempts otherwise to exclude the Act are punishable by a fine of $1,000 on summary conviction: s 59(3). Section 56 of the Sale of Goods Act 1908, the contracting out provision of that Act, is to be read subject to s 59 of the Motor Vehicle Securities Act: s 59(4).

(c) Sections 46 to 48 of the Chattels Transfer Act 1924 concerning sales by the Registrar and sale of the grantor's interest in chattels in execution are stated to apply to motor vehicles under the Motor Vehicle Securities Act: s 60.

(d) Section 61 of the Act deals with constructive notice of registration under the Companies Act 1955. It provides that for the purposes of any Act other than the Motor Vehicle Securities Act, all persons shall be deemed to have notice of a security interest given wholly or partly in respect of motor vehicles by a company registered under the Companies Act 1955 and of the contents of that security interest, in so far as it relates to motor vehicles, immediately upon the registration of the security interest in the manner provided by the Companies Act 1955. It should be noted that this provision relates to the purposes of Acts other than the Motor Vehicle Securities Act and that it amounts to notice both of the security interest and of the *contents* of that security interest. This provision apparently tries to make it clear that the registration system under the Companies Act is effective notwithstanding the existence of the Motor Vehicle Securities Act and its own registration provisions. The relationship of the two Acts is discussed below: see para 38.4.3 (1).

(e) Savings. Section 62 provides that except to the extent that the Motor Vehicle Securities Act expressly provides otherwise, nothing in the Act shall prevent any purchaser of a motor vehicle acquiring title to the vehicle by virtue of any provision of the Sale of Goods Act 1908 or by virtue of any other enactment or rule of law, or modify, restrict or exclude any other right or remedy that a person would have had if the Motor Vehicle Securities Act had not been enacted.

(f) Section 65 provides that where an offence against the Motor Vehicle Securities Act has been committed by a company and it is proved to have been committed with the consent or connivance of a person who is a director, manager, or secretary or other officer of the company, that person shall be guilty of the same offence and shall be liable to the same penalty as the company.

(g) There are also miscellaneous provisions concerning delegation, service and regulations. Enactments affected by the new statute are discussed below. Regulations have been promulgated. The Motor Vehicle Securities (Fees) Regulations 1990 set out fees for various matters including registration of a security interest and applications for certificates under s 11.

38.3.19 Transitional provisions

An Act effecting such major change as this one does, creates a difficult period of transition. What of the existing securities over motor vehicles under the old system? Do they need to be reregistered, and if so, what priority do they enjoy? Part V of the Act attempts to answer such questions. The "transitional period" is defined as 1 October 1989 to 31 March 1990: s 68. During this period the provisions concerning application for registration: s 6, registration: s 7, stolen motor vehicles: s 9, the provisions for cancellation and amendment: ss 14 to 18, and those concerning forms, fees, false/misleading statements and exemption from liability: ss 20-23, are to apply with such modifications as may be necessary: s 69. The Act provides that every person who as at 1 October 1989 is the holder of a security interest in respect of a motor vehicle may, before the end of the transitional period, apply to the Registrar for the registration of that security interest under the new Act: s 70(1); see s 70A for fees.

If a person becomes the holder of a security interest during the transitional period, that person may, before the end of that period, apply to the Registrar for registration of that security interest: s 70(2); see s 70A for fees. Every security interest in respect of which an application for registration is presented during the transitional period shall, if the application is in order for registration, be deemed to be registered at 9 am on 1 April 1990. Nothing in this provision shall apply if the registration of the security interest has been cancelled before that time: s 71.

As has been discussed above, s 47 accords priority to registered security interests in accordance with their time of registration. In terms of application for registration in the transitional period, s 47 notwith-standing, priority depends on the time at which the security interest was created "or otherwise arose": s 72. This is subject to two further provisions. First, where two security interests are registered over the same motor vehicle under the Chattels Transfer Act and those interests are then registered during the transitional period under the Motor Vehicle Securities Act, they will continue to enjoy the order of priority they had under the Chattels Transfer Act: s 73. Secondly, where instruments over motor vehicles were not registered within the time limits imposed by the Chattels Transfer and Companies Acts, they may be registered under the Motor Vehicle Securities Act, if they amount to security interests within the meaning of the Motor Vehicle Securities Act: s 74(1) and (2). In such cases, the security interest is registered as if it had only been created or otherwise arisen on the date on which the application for registration was received by the Registrar: s 74(3). Under s 75 registration of any instrument under the Chattels Transfer Act 1924, so far as it comprises or affects any motor vehicle, shall, as from the end of the transitional period, cease to be of any effect.

38.3.20 Consequential amendments

(1) Mercantile Law Act 1908: Section 3 of the Mercantile Law Act has been discussed above (see para 16.3) concerning the rule nemo dat quod non habet and its exceptions. It will be recalled that under s 23(2)(a) of the Sale of Goods Act 1908, s 3 of the Mercantile Law Act becomes one of the exceptions to the nemo dat rule enabling good title to pass where a disposition of goods is made by a mercantile agent in the terms provided under the Act. If the Motor Vehicle Securities Act is to be effective, clearly an amendment to these provisions is required. A "mercantile agent" is wide enough in definition to cover licensed motor vehicle dealers, whose business it is to sell cars and who are therefore at the centre of the scheme of the Motor Vehicle Securities Act. Accordingly, a new subs (1A) is inserted in s 3 of the Mercantile Law Act as follows:

> Where the goods are a motor vehicle and a security interest in respect of that vehicle has been registered under the Motor Vehicle Securities Act 1989, the person taking under any disposition of the vehicle shall be deemed to have notice that the person making the disposition has no authority to make it, unless it is proved that such authority did exist.

Where registration under the Motor Vehicle Securities Act is performed then, a mercantile agent cannot confer good title on a purchaser unless he or she has actual authority to do so. The Act is silent on who bears the burden of proof. This exception to the nemo dat rule is accordingly abrogated where registration is performed, but not otherwise.

(2) Sale of Goods Act 1908, s 23(2): Section 23(1) of the Sale of Goods Act restates the rule nemo dat quod non habet, and goes on to create the exception to the rule involving estoppel. Section 23(2) provides that nothing in the Sale of Goods Act shall affect:

> (a) The provisions of the Mercantile Law Act 1908, or any other enactment enabling the apparent owner of goods to dispose of them as if he were the true owner thereof;

(b) The validity of any contract of sale under any special common law or statutory power of sale or under the order of a court of competent jurisdiction.

The mercantile agency exception to the nemo dat rule has been discussed above, as have special powers of sale see paras 16.3, 16.7.

It is clear that if the Motor Vehicle Securities Act is going to be effective, it has to be stated that the provisions of the Sale of Goods Act are subject to the Motor Vehicle Securities Act. If this were not so, the relationship of the two Acts would be uncertain as far as motor vehicles are concerned, as it would not be clear if the nemo dat rule and its exceptions operated in the face of the regime established under the new Act. Accordingly, there is added to s 23(2) a further provision, s 23(2)(c) as follows:

... nothing in this Act shall affect – ...
(c) The provisions of the Motor Vehicle Securities Act 1989 enabling a purchaser of a motor vehicle to acquire good title to the vehicle.

Sale of Goods Act 1908, s 27(2): This provision has also been discussed above: see paras 16.6 and 37.5.3. It deals with the buyer in possession of goods transferring the title to another and is a further exception to the nemo dat rule. The proviso to the section deals with the question of notice by way of registration under the Chattels Transfer Act 1924. The Motor Vehicle Securities Act creates an additional proviso, dealing with registration under the new Act. It states:

Provided further that, in the case of a motor vehicle, if the lien or other right of the original seller is created or evidenced by, or arises under, a security interest registered under the Motor Vehicle Securities Act 1989, then the person receiving the motor vehicle shall be deemed to have notice of the existence of that security interest and the registered particulars in respect of it.

As we have seen, s 25 of the Motor Vehicle Securities Act provides that registration under the Chattels Transfer Act shall cease to be of any effect as from the end of the transitional period, 31 March 1990, with regard to motor vehicles. In the circumstances the existing proviso to s 27(2) also ceases to have effect with regard to motor vehicles as it refers only to registration under the Chattels Transfer Act. Accordingly there is a need for a new proviso to take its place with regard to motor vehicles.

(3) Chattels Transfer Act 1924: With the transfer of security interests over motor vehicles from the Chattels Transfer Act to the Motor Vehicle Securities Act, motor vehicles have been added to the list of exclusions from the definition of chattels under s 2 of the Chattels Transfer Act: Para (e) of the s 2 definition of "chattels" under that Act. Also, the words, "motor vehicles of all descriptions" have been removed from the list of customary chattels in the Seventh Schedule of the Act. Under the Motor Vehicle Securities Act, then, motor vehicles cease to be subject to s 57 of the Chattels Transfer Act: they are no longer customary chattels. Motor vehicles, that is to say, motor cars, and caravans are, then, in this respect, placed on an equal footing. This amendment has given rise to the need for further legislation and this has taken the form of the Chattels Transfer Amendment Act 1990 and the Companies Amendment Act 1990. These

Acts were introduced into Parliament as the Motor Vehicle Securities (Assignments) Bill.

Motor vehicle dealers commonly sell motor vehicles to customers under hire purchase agreements and assign the benefits of those agreements either absolutely or by way of mortgage to a financier. Traditionally these assignments have not had to be registered in order to enjoy protection because motor vehicles have been defined as "customary chattels" in terms of the Chattels Transfer Act 1924. With the removal of motor vehicles from the customary list under the Motor Vehicle Securities Act, registration would have been necessary in the absence of further statutory amendment.

The Bill was introduced to preserve the exemption from compliance with the registration requirements of the Companies Act 1955 and the Chattels Transfer Act 1924 in respect of assignments of hire purchase agreements over motor vehicles. It was intended from the outset that the Bill should be divided into two separate Acts which would take effect from 1 April 1990, when the Motor Vehicle Securities Act would also take full force and effect.

Assignments by way of mortgage of customary hire purchase agreements have been exempted from registration under the Companies Act 1955 since 1931, in consequence of s 2(8) of the Chattels Transfer Amendment Act of that year. The purpose of the Companies Amendment Act 1990 is to continue that exemption and it does so by adding subs (13) to s 102 of the Companies Act.

The Chattels Transfer Amendment Act 1990 creates s 19B of the Chattels Transfer Act 1924. It provides that both absolute assignments and assignments by way of hire purchase agreements over motor vehicles are valid and effectual without registration under the Chattels Transfer Act 1924. This was the position pursuant to s 57(3) of the Chattels Transfer Act 1924 prior to the advent of the Motor Vehicle Securities Act.

(4) The Companies Act 1955: Under the Motor Vehicle Securities Act, s 102(2) of the Companies Act is amended by the addition of para (cc) which provides that a charge on any motor vehicle of the company shall be registered with the Registrar of Companies pursuant to the established procedure under s 102. The relationship of the Motor Vehicle Securities Act with the Companies Act is discussed below.

(5) The Motor Vehicle Dealers Act 1975: There are various amendments to this Act to accommodate the provisions of the Motor Vehicle Securities Act with regard to claims on the Fidelity Guarantee Fund where purchases are made by consumers from dealers. Sections 30, 31, 39 and 40 are all amended. Most significantly and following logically from the introduction of the new scheme for consumer purchases from dealers, s 89(1)(b) is repealed. Section 89(1)(b), it will be recalled, is that provision which requires licensed motor vehicle dealers to give clear title to motor vehicles sold by them to their customers: see "Motor Vehicle Dealers Fidelity Guarantee Fund" [1990] NZLJ 339

(6) The Disputes Tribunals Act 1988: Motor Vehicle Securities Act disputes are brought within the jurisdiction of the Disputes Tribunal.

38.4 THE EFFECTS OF THE MOTOR VEHICLE
SECURITIES ACT

38.4.1 Method of reform

Reform of the law of chattels security can be dealt with in three ways. The first method involves the introduction of an improved registration system for security interests. The second, the introduction of a title registration system and the third, the amendment of the rule nemo dat quod non habet and its exceptions: see D F Dugdale [1987] NZLJ 101.

Under the Motor Vehicle Securities Act the first method has been adopted and a new system of registration of security interests for motor vehicles has been introduced. This new system creates further exceptions to the nemo dat rule. The rule nemo dat quod non habet is fully preserved as regards purchases from a thief. Under s 30, extinguishment does not occur in such circumstances. The exceptions arise because extinguishment of interests enables dispositions of otherwise defective titles to be made, with the claims of holders of security interests defeated where the disposition is made by licensed motor vehicle dealers to consumers or, in "other" transactions, where the notice provisions are not satisfied. The new system also modifies already existing exceptions. Section 3(1A) of the Mercantile Law Act 1908 has been discussed above as has the new provision under s 23(2) of the Sale of Goods Act 1908 which subjects the whole Sale of Goods Act to the Motor Vehicle Securities Act. The changes involve both the nemo dat rule and its exceptions and the proviso to s 27(2).

The amendments to the rule and its exceptions do not turn on questions of principle but on the accommodation of a new scheme of registration. The considerations are essentially practical. It is clear that the Motor Vehicle Securities Act is not intended as a revision of the rules in the Sale of Goods Act. All that has been undertaken is an amendment of that Act to accommodate the establishment of the new scheme under the Motor Vehicle Securities Act.

In these circumstances there will continue to be cases where there is nothing in the Motor Vehicle Securities Act to help the innocent third party purchaser, as is illustrated in this example given by Professor D W McLauchlan in "Motor Vehicle Securities: The Quagmire Deepens" [1989] NZLJ 211, 213. O sells her car to B, a rogue, who gives a cheque for the price which is drawn on insufficient funds. O contacts the police, thereby effecting a rescission of the contract which revests title in O. B then sells to T who takes in good faith.

As Professor McLauchlan states, although there is some authority for the view that T obtains good title under the nemo dat exception in s 27(2) of the Sale of Goods Act 1908, there is a strong argument that s 27 (2) does not apply. If s 27 (2) does not apply, O's ownership interest arising from the rescission does not fall within the definition of "security interest" under the Motor Vehicle Securities Act. Neither T nor any subsequent purchaser will acquire good title and the situation is no different if the purchase is made from a licensed motor vehicle dealer. The Motor Vehicle Securities Act is concerned only with transactions involving security interests, not the general reform of the nemo dat rule and its exceptions.

38.4.2 Problems involving security over motor vehicles

Traditionally, the fundamental problem with security interests in motor vehicles in New Zealand has been the inadequacy of the system of registration for such interests. This inadequacy has facilitated dishonest dealings with motor vehicles and has produced unsatisfactory results with competing interests. A new system of registration of security interests now exists. The matter to be considered is whether it is adequate to overcome the problems of the past. Let us examine four hypothetical situations.

(1) Theft with sale to an innocent third party: In this case the motor vehicle subject to a security interest is stolen from a consumer, or the secured party, and is purchased by an innocent third party either from the thief or from someone who has acquired it from the thief. Where the purchase is from the thief, s 30 applies and whether the security interest is registered or not, extinguishment does not occur. The same is so where the purchase is from someone who has acquired the motor vehicle from the thief unless that person is a licensed motor vehicle dealer in which case the loss will be the dealer's when she or he sells the vehicle. Title will pass to the purchaser and the dealer will have to meet the secured party's loss under the security interest: s 24 – s 25 applies where a consumer acquires a motor vehicle from a dealer under a hire purchase agreement or a lease. Section 30 applies to "other" dispositions only, not those involving a purchase by a consumer from a dealer. In any event, registration does not matter where the purchase is *from* a licensed motor vehicle dealer provided that it is a consumer as defined under the Act who is making the purchase as the security interest will be extinguished unless one of the exceptions applies as discussed above.

(2) Sale to an innocent third party: In this case a private individual (consumer) sells his or her motor vehicle, which is subject to a security interest, to an innocent third party without disclosing the secured party's interest and without obtaining the secured party's consent to the sale. If the security interest is registered, that amounts to notice: s 29, and the security interest is not extinguished: s 27 – consider also s 28, leaving the rights of the secured party intact. If it is not registered, the case will turn on whether the innocent third party has actual notice. If the third party does not have such notice, the security interest will be extinguished.

(3) Competing interests of creditors: The situation here is one where a consumer purports to transfer to a creditor a security interest in a motor vehicle where a security interest already exists and the consumer does so without disclosing the existence of the first security interest and without obtaining the secured party's consent to the subsequent transaction. Registration is the determining factor here. If the first creditor has registered its security interest and thereby become a secured party, that security interest is protected. If it has not been registered, the second creditor, by registering, can take priority over the first creditor's security interest: s 47. It does not matter in this case that the second creditor had express, implied or constructive notice of the earlier security interest nor that the vehicle was in the possession of the other creditor: s 48. If both

creditors' security interests are unregistered, the first in time of creation prevails. Extinguishment does not arise here because there is no sale, either outright or on hire purchase terms.

(4) Consumer sale of motor vehicle to an innocent third party who then creates a security interest in the motor vehicle: This is the situation where a consumer has a motor vehicle which is subject to a security interest, and sells the motor vehicle to an innocent third party without disclosing the security interest and without seeking the secured party's consent. The new purchaser then purports to create a security interest in the motor vehicle in favour of another creditor. Notice is the determining factor. If the original security interest is registered or the purchaser has actual notice of it, that security interest will not be extinguished and the creditor of the seller is protected. If it is not registered and the purchaser does not have actual notice of it, it will be extinguished and the security interest of the purchaser's creditor will prevail: s 27.

In view of these examples, can it be said that the Motor Vehicle Securities Act strikes a fair balance? In all cases where there is a purchase either outright or on hire purchase terms from a dealer, the responsibility is the dealer's to clear prior encumbrances, not the consumer's. If the dealer is free of notice, as defined, of a security interest, when he or she acquires a vehicle for sale, he or she can conduct business without fear. Consumers can always deal with licensed motor vehicle dealers with the confidence that they will receive an unencumbered vehicle. The position of licensed motor vehicle dealers purchasing their stock is considered below.

Theft, from the example given, might be thought to work hardship on the innocent purchaser, but under s 9, details of the stolen motor vehicle can be entered on the register. Hardship would seem to apply then only when the owner of the vehicle fails to report the theft to the police. The Commissioner of Police will, presumably, as a matter of course, notify the Registrar of all thefts reported to the police.

The second situation considered above, sale to an innocent third party, appears to strike a fair balance. The emphasis is on registration. If creditors register and purchasers search the register, all interests are fairly served. If creditors do not register, they put themselves at risk and if purchasers do not conduct searches, they stand at risk.

The question of priorities is a difficult one. New Zealand has tackled the problem in a manner different from that in Victoria. In Victoria, registration is the linchpin of priority, regardless of notice otherwise. This creates a logically consistent system but not one which is necessarily fair. A creditor may be beaten to registration without any dilatoriness on his or her part at all and thereby lose priority.

The fourth situation of a consumer sale of a motor vehicle to an innocent third party who then creates a security interest in the motor vehicle, depends on notice and, again, a fair balance seems to be struck. The rules act as an incentive to creditors to ensure the existence of notice by means of registration.

The system, then, is not perfect but in terms of the examples given, it is only the priority question which appears troublesome. There are other situations, though, which will be considered below which illustrate problems created by the Act.

38.4.3 Problems under the new scheme

The scheme of the Motor Vehicle Securities Act is a vast improvement on the former system for registration of security interests in motor vehicles under the Chattels Transfer Act. The new scheme creates a centralised, national register, it classifies security interests in accordance with their substance and function instead of their form so that hire purchase agreements, financial lease arrangements and Romalpa provisions become registrable, and it removes motor vehicles from the list of customary chattels in the Seventh Schedule to the Chattels Transfer Act. In addition, it realigns the balance of interests with regard to execution creditors and assignees in bankruptcy. The Act is intended to have the effect that security interests in motor vehicles are valid against them without registration and this produces a result which is the opposite of s 18 of the Chattels Transfer Act. There are, however, problem areas under the Motor Vehicle Securities Act.

(1) Relationship with the Companies Act 1955: Traditionally in New Zealand there has been a dual system of registration for chattel securities with separate schemes operating under the Chattels Transfer Act 1924 and the Companies Act 1955. Under this system, any charge which would be registrable as a chattels security when created by an individual and which is created by a company, must be registered with the Registrar of Companies: s 102(2)(c), Companies Act 1955, and not under the Chattels Transfer Act. This has created two systems of registration, one for individuals and one for corporate bodies. Indeed, the matter is even more complex than this. The question of which rules apply to company securities, whether they must be registered and where they must be registered, is fraught with difficulty. Aside from registration under the Motor Vehicle Securities Act, some company securities have to be registered under the Companies Act, some under the Chattels Transfer Act and some do not have to be registered at all. For a full discussion of this topic see Professor D W McLauchlan, "Corporate Personal Property Secured Transactions – Chattels Transfer Act, Companies Act or Neither?" [1978] NZLJ 137.

The intention of the Motor Vehicle Securities Act is for the scheme of the Companies Act with regard to charges to remain in full force and effect independent of the Motor Vehicle Securities Act. New Zealand's dual system of registration of securities over personal property under the Chattels Transfer Act 1924 and the Companies Act 1955, therefore becomes a triple system with the advent of the Motor Vehicle Securities Act. This is unfortunate and would not have occurred if the entire law of personal property security had been overhauled and amended. The difficulties of piecemeal reform are highlighted by what must be seen as the uneasy relationship of the Motor Vehicle Securities Act with the Companies Act. These comments apply equally to the relationship of the Motor Vehicle Securities Act with the Industrial and Provident Societies Act 1908.

The s 2 definition of "security interest" under the Motor Vehicle Securities Act tells us that company charges over motor vehicles come within the definition if they are fixed charges, or, for the purposes of Part II of the Act, if they are floating charges which have become fixed. Under the consequential amendments, s 102 of the Companies Act is extended to cover charges over a company's motor vehicles. In these circumstances it seems that all charges are registrable under the Companies Act, fixed charges are registrable under both Acts and floating charges which become fixed over motor vehicles then become "security interests" under the Motor Vehicle Securities Act for the defined purposes of notice and extinguishment. This is cumbersome and may prove problematic as far as floating charges becoming fixed is concerned.

The Motor Vehicle Securities Act deals with the floating charge in terms of s 29 of the Act. Section 29(1)(b) states that for the purposes of the Act, a person has notice of a security interest if the person has actual knowledge of that security interest, including, in the case of a floating charge that is registered under the Companies Act 1955, actual notice that it has become fixed. Actual notice, then, becomes the key factor under the Motor Vehicle Securities Act: actual notice that the floating charge has become fixed.

What of the floating charge which has become fixed? Does it give rise to a registrable security interest under the Motor Vehicle Securities Act? In s 2, "security interest" is defined to include *for the purposes of Part II of the Act,* any floating charge created by a company registered under the Companies Act 1955 that has become fixed in relation to a motor vehicle. Part II is concerned with dispositions, notice and extinguishment. It is Part I which governs registration. Floating charges which have become fixed do not therefore appear to be security interests for the purposes of registration. The s 2 definition appears to relate directly to s 29, which sets out the rules for determining whether a person has notice of a security interest under the Act. Section 29(1)(b) is discussed above and concerns floating charges registered under the Companies Act 1955 becoming fixed. Floating charges which become fixed over motor vehicles do appear, then to be security interests only for the limited purposes defined in Part II of the Act.

The question which now arises is that of the impact the system of dual registration under the Companies and Motor Vehicle Securities Acts will have on priority disputes. Should a dispute over priority arise, s 45 of the Motor Vehicle Securities Act tells us that priority of company charges is determined purely in terms of the law as it existed before the enactment of the Motor Vehicle Securities Act. Registration, it seems, will not necessarily be the priority point where company charges are concerned.

The priority of competing mortgages and charges will be governed by the ordinary rules of common law and equity. In general, the first in time of creation prevails except that an equitable interest is liable to be defeated by a later legal interest taken for value and without notice.

There are four situations which need to be considered regarding priority:

1   where registration is performed under both Acts;
2   where registration is performed only under the Motor Vehicle Securities Act;
3   where registration is performed only under the Companies Act; and
4   where registration is not performed under either Act.

1   Plainly, registration of fixed charges should be carried out under both Acts.

2   If registration is performed only under the Motor Vehicle Securities Act, s 103 of the Companies Act has to be considered. Section 103 provides that charges which have not been registered under s 102 shall be void against the liquidator and any creditor of the company. The section also provides that charges registrable under any other Act are not avoided. As fixed charges over motor vehicles are registrable under the Motor Vehicle Securities Act, this exception to avoidance under s 103 appears to apply and such charges will not be avoided for non-registration under the Companies Act. Floating charges will continue to be void under s 103 for non-registration.

3   If registration is performed only under the Companies Act, the non-registration under the Motor Vehicle Securities Act will not, it seems, affect the validity of the security interest because registration under the Motor Vehicle Securities Act is not mandatory and non-registration does not invalidate the security interest on the insolvency of the grantor. Registration of a further charge under both Acts will not disturb the priority position because under s 45 the priority of charges created by a company registered under the Companies Act shall be determined as if Part III of the Motor Vehicle Securities Act had not been enacted.

4   If registration is not performed under either Act further consideration has to be given to s 103 of the Companies Act. This refers to charges registrable under any other Act. The provision uses the term "registrable" not "registered". Accordingly, such a charge would not be void as against a liquidator and creditors if not registered under that other Act. Actual registration is not required for validity to be preserved: see *Re Mountain View Property Holdings Ltd* [1972] NZLR 1 and *Re Universal Management Ltd* [1983] NZLR 462. Although valid, such a charge seems to be liable to be defeated in priority by a subsequently created legal interest taken for value and without notice.

Registration under the Companies Act may have a very real bearing on the outcome of a priority dispute because of the terms of s 61 of the Motor Vehicle Securities Act. Section 61 provides that, except for the purposes of the Motor Vehicle Securities Act, registration under the Companies Act of a security interest given wholly or partly in respect of motor vehicles will constitute constructive notice of the security and of its contents so far as it relates to motor vehicles. This means that registration of a floating charge under the Companies Act will continue to give notice, at least in so far as the charge affects chattels, of a clause which prohibits the creation of subsequent charges ranking in priority to or pari passu with the floating charge: s 61 preserves the law as held in *Re Manurewa Transport Ltd* [1971] NZLR 909.

Section 39 states that the provisions of Part II which deal with dispositions of motor vehicles subject to security interests, shall apply and a security interest in a motor vehicle may be extinguished, notwithstanding that the charge which creates or evidences the security interest, or the charge under which the security interest otherwise arises, is registered under the Companies Act 1955. We have yet to see how the Courts deal with the relationship of the two Acts.

(2) Licensed Motor Vehicle Dealers: The Motor Vehicle Securities Act deals with dispositions by licensed motor vehicle dealers to consumers on a different footing from "other" dispositions. Is the Act unduly harsh in its treatment of such dealers? The fact that the licensed motor vehicle dealer must convey clear title to a consumer, unless agreed otherwise, means that such dealers must be punctilious in their observance of the search procedures under the Act when they acquire motor vehicles themselves for sale. If they are not, they may be confronted with a claim for payment by the secured party under s 34. Notice, as defined, is the determining factor and if the dealer has such notice, the dealer is liable. If the dealer fails to meet the claim for payment, the consumer is protected by way of recourse to the Motor Vehicle Dealers Fidelity Guarantee Fund though not where caravans and trailers are concerned: see 38.3.12. This does not relieve dealers of liability because they all contribute to the Fund by way of annual levy. Default could lead to the refusal of the Motor Vehicle Dealers Licensing Board to renew the dealer's licence.

It can be said, of course, that the fact that the public can buy with absolute confidence when purchasing from a dealer is a positive fact working in favour of increased sales. Far from being detrimental to dealers then, the Act may be seen as a benefit to them. Certainly it is an inducement to them to adopt proficient procedures when buying and selling vehicles.

(3) "Other" transactions: Sections 27 and 28 of the Motor Vehicle Securities Act turn on notice as defined. They are relevant to dealers in the area of acquisition of stock. A dealer who acquires stock from a manufacturer, wholesaler, member of the public or another dealer will not be bound by a security interest unless he or she has notice of it and it will be extinguished. This applies to "trade-ins" but not to transactions which are not in the ordinary course of business: s 31. "The ordinary course of business" is a difficult term to define. The provision appears to be designed to catch unusual transactions and certainly those which are suspect in some way. Reservation of property clauses are defined as security interests under the Act: s 2 definition of "security interest". They are registrable and are therefore, for the purposes of the Act, in the ordinary course of business. Suppliers must be alert to register such provisions to retain their protection. Again, dealers must be vigilant with their searching. It is important that they take title to their stock within the period of duration of the certificate of entry in the register: ss 11 and 12, especially with trade-ins and purchases from the public, otherwise they will be at risk. For wholesalers and manufacturers, it is important that they register their security interests for their own protection. The provisions of the Act relative to the acquisition of stock would seem to do no more than ensure that licensed motor vehicle dealers act prudently when stocking their showrooms and yards.

38.5 REFORM OF PERSONAL PROPERTY SECURITY LAW

The Motor Vehicle Securities Act brings about effective reform of the law of security interests in motor vehicles. The call for reform in this jurisdiction, is, however, a wider one. In response to the report of Professor J H Farrar and Mr M A O'Regan contained in the Law Commission's Preliminary Paper No 6, the Law Commission, only days after the Motor Vehicle Securities Act received the Royal Assent, published its Report No 8, "A Personal Property Securities Act for New Zealand". Report No 8 contains a draft Personal Property Securities Act, based on North American models, which comprehensively reforms the entire law of chattel securities in this country. To date the publication of the draft Act has not led to the introduction of a Bill into Parliament. Appendix "C" of the report sets out provisions, based on Part II of the Motor Vehicle Securities Act, for a separate regime for security interests in motor vehicles, to be incorporated in either the draft Personal Property Securities Act or the Motor Vehicle Dealers Act 1975, should a separate regime for such security interests be thought to be necessary. Comprehensive reform such as is contemplated by the draft Personal Property Securities Act renders the need for a separate regime for security interests in motor vehicles entirely unnecessary.

Chapter 39

THE FLOATING CHARGE

SUMMARY

39.1   FIXED AND FLOATING CHARGES
39.2   THE NATURE OF A FLOATING CHARGE
39.3   REGISTRATION
39.4   CRYSTALLISATION
39.5   EFFECT OF CRYSTALLISATION
39.6   FLOATING CHARGES AND RESERVATION OF PROPERTY CLAUSES

39.1 FIXED AND FLOATING CHARGES

A company is an artificial person and as such can not only create the types of fixed security which a natural person can create but it can also create a floating charge. Before we consider the nature of a floating charge it will be useful to recapitulate on the nature of a fixed charge. The most common asset charged is land and the most common mortgage over land is a security interest by way of a registered legal mortgage under the Land Transfer Act 1952. The charge specifically attaches to the land and the company cannot dispose of the land without the consent of the holder of the charge. The charge has to be registered under the Act. An unregistered mortgage takes effect as an equitable mortgage. A fixed charge over chattels in the case of an individual, as we have seen, must be effected under the Chattels Transfer Act 1924 which requires registration of a schedule of the assets secured. Such a charge in the case of a company can only be registered with the Registrar of Companies. Equitable mortgages and charges can also be created over chattels. Intangible property, such as an insurance policy or shares in another company, can be the subject of a fixed legal or equitable charge. The former requires transfer into the name of the chargee, whereas the latter does not. Book debts, also a species of intangible property, are now governed by the Chattels Transfer Act 1924 as amended. Motor vehicles are subject to the Motor Vehicle Securities Act. A floating charge is not a fixed charge. It is a species of equitable charge whose character was first recognised by the English Court of Appeal in Chancery in *Re Panama, New Zealand and Australian Royal Mail* (1870) 5 Ch App 318. Its juridical nature, however, was not worked out until the 1900s.

39.2 THE NATURE OF A FLOATING CHARGE

39.2.1 A shifting equitable charge on assets of a going concern

A floating charge is a present equitable charge which is not specific but shifting until crystallisation when it settles and becomes a fixed equitable charge. In *Government Stock Investment Co v Manila Railway Co* [1897] AC 81, 86 Lord Macnaghten described a floating charge as follows:

> A floating security is an equitable charge on the assets for the time being of a going concern. It attaches to the subject charged in the varying condition in which it happens to be from time to time. It is the essence of such a charge that it remains dormant until the undertaking charged ceases to be a going concern, or until the person in whose favour the charge is created intervenes.

Seven years later he said in *Illingworth v Houldsworth* [1904] AC 355,

> I should have thought there was not much difficulty in defining what a floating charge is in contrast to what is called a specific charge. A specific charge, I think, is one that without more fastens on ascertained and definite property or property capable of being ascertained and defined; a floating charge, on the other hand, is ambulatory and shifting in its nature, hovering over and so to speak floating with the property which it is intended to affect until some event occurs or some act is done which causes it to settle and fasten on the subject of the charge within its reach and grasp. . . .

The three common characteristics of a floating charge are now recognised to be that: (1) it is a charge on a class of assets of a company, present and future; (2) that class is one which in the ordinary course of business changes from time to time; (3) by the charge it is contemplated that until some future step is taken by or on behalf of the chargee the company may carry on its business in the ordinary way: Romer LJ in *Re Yorkshire Woolcombers Association Ltd* [1903] 2 Ch 284, 295. In fact, the members of the class change rather than the class itself. Although a floating charge does not create a fixed charge until crystallisation it has nevertheless been held that it creates a floating equitable interest before crystallisation: *Landall Holdings Ltd v Caratti* [1979] WAR 97. Whether this amounts to an equitable interest in the full sense is controversial. It nevertheless creates a security interest. See further Farrar and Russell *Company Law and Securities Regulation in New Zealand*, 166; W J Gough, *Company Charges* and D W McLauchlan (1979) 4 Otago LR 396. The significance of such an interest is that it is only defeasible by a transaction in the ordinary course of business. A transaction not in the ordinary course of business takes subject to the security interest created by the charge even though crystallisation may not have taken place: *Hamilton v Hunter* (1983) 7 ACLR 295. If the transaction is substantial it may, in any event, give rise to crystallisation on the basis that the company has ceased to carry on business: *Re Woodroffes (Musical Instruments) Ltd* [1985] 2 All ER 908.

39.2.2 The company's power to carry on business

The company has power to carry on business in the ordinary course. In other words it has a limited, not an absolute, right to dispose of its assets free of the charge before crystallisation. However, the Courts have given a wide interpretation to transactions in the ordinary course of business. Thus sales, leases, mortgages, charges, liens, payment of debts and other transactions effected with a view to carrying on as a going concern have all been held to be within the scope of the power: see, generally, the decision of the New South Wales Court of Appeal in *Reynolds Bros (Motors) Pty Ltd v Esanda Ltd* (1984) 8 ACLR 422. This will normally predicate a transfer of equivalent value in the sense of quid pro quo.

39.2.3 Restrictive clauses

Because of the latitude shown by the Courts to companies which have created floating charges, it has become the general practice to insert a cause forbidding the creation of any mortgage or charge ranking in priority to, or pari passu with the floating charge. Such a clause seems to have been first introduced in *Palmers Company Precedents* in 1877. The principal significance of such a clause is its effect on priorities. In English law unless there is knowledge of such a clause the holder of a subsequent charge is not postponed: *Wilson v Kelland* [1920] 2 Ch 306. In New Zealand, however, the position is as follows:

(1) in so far as the charge is part of a fixed and floating charge which covers land, this may amount to an equitable mortgage which can be the subject of a caveat under the Land Transfer Act 1952. (This will be so if there is a covenant for further assurance which constitutes an agreement to enter into a legal mortgage.)

(2) in so far as the charge covers chattels and book debts by virtue of s 4(2) of the Chattels Transfer Act 1924 (as amended) there is notice of the contents including a restrictive clause;

(3) in so far as the charge covers other property, ie choses in action which are not book debts, there is no notice of the contents but there is the possibility of actual or inferred knowledge based on the fact that such clauses are common and a copy of the charge can be inspected on a search.

39.3 REGISTRATION

A floating charge is subject to two separate systems of registration under the Companies Act 1955. First, it must be registered in the Company's own Register of Charges: s 111(1). Copies of the charge must be kept with the Register: s 110(1). In addition and more importantly, a copy of the floating charge or particulars thereof must be registered with the Registrar of Companies under s 102 of the Companies Act 1955. Failure to register the charge within 30 days of creation makes it void as against the liquidator and any creditor: s 103(1). However, under s 108 it is possible to apply to the High Court for registration out of time and rectification of the Register.

39.4 CRYSTALLISATION

39.4.1 Clear cases

It is settled law that crystallisation occurs on the winding up of the company, even where the winding up is a member's voluntary winding up for the purpose of reconstruction of the company: *Re Crompton and Co Ltd* [1914] 1 Ch 954. It is also settled law that crystallisation occurs where a receiver is appointed: *Re Florence Public Works Co* (1878) 10 ChD 530.

39.4.2 Unclear cases

In a number of the earlier English cases there is a suggestion that a floating charge crystallises on the company ceasing to be a going concern. Occasionally, this is described in terms of ceasing to carry on business. In *Hamilton v Hunter* (1983) 7 ACLR 295, it was accepted that this could be a ground for crystallisation in Australia. See further Farrar and Russell *Company Law and Securities Regulation in New Zealand*, 168-9. In *Re Woodroffes (Musical Instruments) Ltd* [1985] 2 All ER 908 Nourse J recognised that the cessation of a company's business gave rise to crystallisation.

Further, a more troublesome question is whether crystallisation occurs when an event happens which is expressly mentioned in the charge as an automatic crystallisation event. In New Zealand such clauses are common and are frequently linked with restrictive clauses. In *Re Manurewa Transport Ltd* [1971] NZLR 909, Speight J expressly upheld such a clause. In that case a company operated a carrying business and had created a floating charge which contained the usual form of restrictive clause forbidding the creation of further mortgages without consent. There was also an express clause which provided that the charge should "attach and become affixed" on the happening of a number of events one of which was the breach of the restrictive clause. After the company had delayed paying its garage bills the garage seized a truck and refused to release it until they were given a chattel security. This was duly registered but the consent of the debenture holder was never obtained. The matter fell for decision on the company's insolvency. Speight J decided in favour of the debenture holder. *Re Manurewa Transport Ltd* has been followed in the Australian cases of *Deputy Federal Commissioner of Taxes v Horsburgh* (1984) 83 ATC 4, 823 and *Re Obie Pty (No 2)* (1984) 2 ACLC 67 and the English case of *Re Brightlife Ltd* [1987] Ch 200. On the other hand a different view was taken in the Canadian case of the *Queen v Consolidated Churchill Copper Corporation Ltd* (1978) 5 WWR 652. In that case the clause in question was not an explicit automatic crystallisation clause and therefore the dicta about automatic crystallisation are arguably obiter. However, Berger J said that automatic crystallisation was not justified on the authorities, nor justifiable in terms of policy. The balance of authority rests with *Re Manurewa Transport Ltd*.

39.5 EFFECT OF CRYSTALLISATION

On crystallisation the floating charge becomes a fixed equitable charge. The effect of this in the case of book debts is that they are equitably assigned to the debenture holder, subject to subsisting equities at the time of crystallisation. This means that they are subject to rights of set-off existing at that time but crystallisation breaks the mutuality required for set-off so that it is not possible to set-off pre-receivership and post-receivership debts: *NW Robbie and Co Ltd v Whitney Warehouse Co Ltd* [1963] 3 All ER 613. See also *Rendell v Doors and Doors Ltd* [1975] 2 NZLR 191. The full legal effects of crystallisation depend on whether the crystallisation has been due to the appointment of a receiver or liquidation. For a detailed discussion see Farrar and Russell, *Company Law and Securities Regulation in New Zealand*, chs 34 and 35.

39.6 FLOATING CHARGES AND RESERVATION OF PROPERTY CLAUSES

Because secured and preferential creditors scoop the pool of assets when a debtor becomes insolvent trade creditors can lose out. Although they may have what in the USA is known as "street knowledge" of the debtor's affairs through operation in the same locality this may not be enough to protect them. On the European continent it is common for suppliers to reserve property or title in the goods supplied until the debt is paid. This is a standard form of commercial security. As we have seen it is in fact allowed by the Sale of Goods Act 1908, ss 19 and 21 but until recently it has not been common except in the shape of the conditional sale form of hire purchase and in export sales.

However in *Aluminium Industrie Vaassen v Romalpa Aluminium Ltd* [1976] 2 All ER 552 the English Court of Appeal was faced with a simple and complex reservation of property clause. A simple reservation of property clause reserves property in the goods supplied until the price is paid. A complex clause purports to attach either to proceeds of subsales of the goods or to new goods produced using the original goods as ingredients or components. In the *Romalpa* case the clause in question was a literal English translation of a Dutch standard form and contained the words "fiduciary owner" which was standard Dutch security language. The English Court, however, applying English law held that in the circumstances the simple clause could be combined with an equitable right to trace the goods or their proceeds. This latter right was an equitable right which was not registrable as a charge under the Companies Act. The Court did not consider the operation of the complex clause. For discussion of this and subsequent cases see B Collier *Romalpa Clauses: Reservation of Title in Sale of Goods Transactions*.

In *Re Interview Ltd* [1975] IR 382, an Irish case, it was said that where goods are subject to a reservation of property clause this may be defeated by a sale by the buyer in possession to a bona fide subpurchaser under the equivalent of our Sale of Goods Act 1908, s 27(2). A similar view was taken in the earlier New Zealand Magistrates' Court decision in *Dayton Monyweight Scale Co v Mather* (1923) 18 MCD 86. See too *Four Point Garage Ltd v Carter* [1985] 3 All ER 12.

A simple reservation of property clause is probably not a registrable instrument under s 2 of the Chattels Transfer Act 1924, because it is part of a transfer of chattels in the ordinary course of business of a trade or calling. It also does not give rise to a registrable charge under the Companies Act 1955. Where there is a complex clause which purports to attach to the proceeds of sale this may be construed as a charge on book debts and registrable under the Chattels Transfer Act as amended by the Statutes Amendment Act 1939, s 6, or the Companies Act 1955, s 102(2)(f): see *Pfeiffer Weinkellerei-Weinenkauf GmbH & Co v Arbuthnot Factors Ltd* [1988] 1 WLR 150; *Tatung (UK) Ltd v Galex Telesure Ltd* (1989) 5 BCC 325.

A clause which enables the seller to enter on land and remove goods supplied even if they have been incorporated into a building was held not to give rise to an interest capable of protection by caveat under the Land Transfer Act: *Carter Holt Harvey Merchandising Group Ltd v Southern Cross Building Society* (unreported, High Court, Auckland, M 2061/90, 18 April 1991, Master Gambrill). For a discussion of whether such goods become fixtures to the land, see *Trust Bank Central Ltd v Southdown Properties Ltd* (unreported, High Court, Auckland, CP 59/90, 1 May 1991, Robertson J).

A complex clause which purports to attach to mixed goods may be held to a fixed equitable charge or a floating charge. In *Re Bond Worth Ltd* [1980] Ch 228 a complex clause which allowed the buyer to sell the mixed goods was held to a floating charge. This would need to be registered under s 102(2)(d). If there is no such power the interest reserved may still be construed as a chattel security and registrable under s 102(2)(c): *Borden (UK) Ltd v Scottish Timber Products Ltd* [1981] Ch 25.

On the other hand the decision of the English Court of Appeal in *Clough Mill Ltd v Martin* [1984] 3 All ER 982 recognised that simple reservation clauses are effective and not registrable in England and that complex clauses are not necessarily invalid because the buyer retains certain powers over the goods. As a result of *Hendy Lennox (Industrial Engines) Ltd v Graham Puttick Ltd* [1984] 2 All ER 152 and *Re Andrabell Ltd* [1984] 3 All ER 407 it appears that whether there is any recourse to the proceeds of subsale depends on whether the relationship between buyer and seller happens in the circumstances to be of a fiduciary nature. Each case and contract must be looked at individually. There is probably no presumption of a fiduciary relationship even if a bailment existed *(Re Andrabell Ltd* but cf *Hendy Lennox).* See JH Farrar and Chiah Kim Chai [1985] JBL 160 for a discussion of factors to be considered when determining whether a fiduciary relationship exits. See also N Palmer [1984] All ER Annual Review 31.

The English cases were applied by Barker J in *Len Vidgen Ski and Leisure Ltd v Timaru Marine Supplies (1982) Ltd, Goodchild and Johnstone* [1986] 1 NZLR 349. The case involved the supply of goods to a company on credit subject to a clause which provided:

4 OWNERSHIP

Risk in any goods supplied by the company to a customer shall pass when such goods are delivered to the customer or into custody on the customer's behalf but ownership in such goods is retained by the company until payment is made for the goods and for all other goods supplied by the company to the customer. If such goods are sold by the customer prior to payment therefore and if they shall become constituents of other goods then the proceeds of sale thereof shall be the property of the company.

The period of credit had expired and the company went into receivership. Some of the goods were sold by the receivers after the receivership. Barker J held that the goods unsold remained identifiable and the plaintiff was entitled to reclaim them. If they were sold, the plaintiff was entitled to the proceeds of sale by way of damages for conversion. As regards goods sold before the receivership, the clause here, unlike that in *Romalpa* and *Andrabell*, referred expressly to the proceeds of sale and provided that they should be the property of the plaintiff. In other words, there was an indication that the company would be accountable to the plaintiff, and this justified the implication of a duty to keep the proceeds separate from its own moneys. On the other hand, the existence of credit tended to negate the idea of a fiduciary relationship. Nevertheless, the term of credit had expired and on balance, his Honour concluded there was a duty to account. The plaintiff was, therefore, entitled to the entire proceeds of the sub-sales unless there was a surplus over the original debt. It is arguable that this goes too far. In *Re Country Stores Pty Ltd* [1987] QdR 318, on the other hand, Williams J was not willing to imply an obligation to account in a standard supply agreement in respect of groceries. The buyers carried on the business of retail grocers and purchased 80 per cent of their stock from the seller. There was a bailment but no agency relationship. In the recent case of *NZ Forest Products Ltd v Pongakawa Sawmill Ltd (in rec)* (unreported, High Court, Auckland, CP 1672/89, 7 March 1991) Henry J held that sawn timber was identifiable as being a product made from logs supplied under a reservation of property clause and was subject to a reservation of property clause. These cases highlight the need for careful drafting of such clauses to reduce the risk of erratic judicial construction.

Chapter 40

THE PROPOSED PERSONAL PROPERTY SECURITIES ACT

SUMMARY

40.1 INTRODUCTION
40.2 OVERVIEW
40.3 PRACTICAL IMPACT
40.4 HARMONISATION OF LAWS
40.5 FUTURE PROGRESS

40.1 INTRODUCTION

As we have seen in Part V, New Zealand has a complicated system of personal property security law. Prior to the introduction of the Motor Vehicle Securities Bill the Law Commission, as part of the review of the Companies Act 1955, sent Professor J H Farrar and Mark O'Regan to Canada and USA in 1988 to look at Article 9 of the Uniform Commercial Code and the Canadian Personal Properties Securities legislation. After widespread consultation in North America, Professor Farrar and Mr O'Regan produced a report published as Law Commission Preliminary Paper No 6 *Reform of Personal Property Security Law* in May 1988. The report considered that the optimal reform was to adopt the US system of Motor Vehicle Title for motor vehicles as well as Article 9 but recognised that this was beyond the resources of a small country like New Zealand. It, therefore, favoured legislation substantially based on the latest Canadian models. A committee of experts was set up to prepare a Bill which was contained in Report No 8 *A Personal Properties Securities Act for New Zealand*. The committee comprised a law commissioner, leading commercial law practitioners, three academic lawyers and an accountant. The report contained a draft Bill which followed the British Columbia model reasonably closely. There were, however, some significant differences. The Bill was reviewed to attempt a plain English style of drafting wherever possible. This was achieved only partially due in large part to the innate complexity of the subject matter. A number of provisions were not included since they were thought undesirable in principle or inappropriate for New Zealand conditions. The main difference in the New Zealand draft is the omission of remedies which is perhaps an unfortunate omission likely to undermine the whole reform since the old forms would not have been decently buried and, through their remedial regimes, will be capable of ruling from their graves. There was a division of opinion on the committee of experts on this question which was ultimately resolved by the pragmatic consideration that this would inevitably bog the Bill down in the glacially slow review of consumer protection currently being undertaken by the Ministry of Consumer Affairs. For that reason also, consumer protection measures were generally excluded from the Bill. The Law Commission's report on *Company Law Reform and Restatement* contained receivership provisions which are to be inserted in the Property Law Act and applicable to all property and all debtors, corporate and non-corporate.

40.2 OVERVIEW

The draft Bill follows the North American models of Article 9 of the Uniform Commercial Code and the Canadian Personal Property Securities legislation. In doing so it has the following general features:

(1) *Uniform rules:* The Bill sets out a regime of uniform rules for all types of security interests regardless of the distinctions of form under the present law. Thus chattel mortgages, leases, conditional sale agreements, Romalpa clauses, fixed and floating charges, floorplan agreements and so on are subsumed under the common concept of "security interest".

(2) *Perfection:* The Bill enables a creditor with a security interest in personal property to perfect that security interest. Once a security interest has "attached" to personal property, which occurs when a debtor grants a security interest in property to a creditor and the creditor gives value, the creditor can perfect the security interest either by registration of the financing statement at the Personal Property Security Registry or by taking possession of the property.

(3) *Registration:* Most secured transactions will involve registration of the financing statement which will give details of the security interest. This will be the subject of a computerised national register on which the details of all security interests will be entered. The current practice of registering copies of security agreements will disappear but the register will give enough information to inform people of the basics of the security arrangement. The Bill also gives rights to certain parties to obtain copies of the securities agreement from creditors in appropriate circumstances.

(4) *Priorities:* The Bill attempts a comprehensive set of priority rules for competing security interests. In most cases the priority will be determined by the first to file rule but the Bill entitles purchase money creditors to obtain a super-priority over earlier registered floating security interests.

(5) *Transaction costs:* The introduction of a national comprehensive computerised registry with the facility for online filing and searching should greatly reduce transaction costs of lending. Whether the advantages of this will be passed on to the borrower remains to be seen.

40.3 PRACTICAL IMPACT

The existence of a common regime for corporate and non-corporate borrowers will remove the necessity for small businesses to incorporate so as to create a floating charge. Under the new regime floating charges as such will no longer be relevant since there will be the possibility of creating a fixed charge over circulating assets. One consequence of the adoption of the North American system will be that it will give the original bank lender a monopoly over security arrangements of a debtor since the bank is likely to take broad generic security. In principle this seems undesirable and seems to happen more in Canada than the United States. It is tempered somewhat by the super-priority given to purchase money security interests. Another major consequence of the introduction of a PPSA will be that the law will be regulated by reference to substance rather than form. At the moment, particularly in the area of Romalpa clauses, haphazard results depend on the formal logic of the documentation. This tends to be produce the possibility of real injustice.

40.4 HARMONISATION OF LAWS

Since the PPSA is based on the North American models there will be a measure of harmonisation of New Zealand Personal Property Security Law with those of the Canadian provinces and the United States. In adopting a PPSA New Zealand will, however, depart from the predominantly English model which is currently in force in the Australian states. For this reason the project was referred to the Australian authorities for consideration under the Closer Economic Relations agreement with Australia. The matter was in turn referred to the Australian Law Reform Commission, the New South Wales Law Reform Commission and the Victoria Law Review Commission. Some of the New Zealand personnel involved in the Law Commission project were made consultants to those Commissions. Initially the Australian Commissions produced a draft report which favoured the concept and then proceeded to engage in a number of alterations of points of detail which seem to be at odds with fundamental concepts of the North American model. This was strongly criticised by a number of commentators in North America and New Zealand and, following a meeting between the Australian Law Reform Commission and the New Zealand Law Reform Commission, a decision was taken by the Federal Attorney-General to prefer the New Zealand version.

40.5 FUTURE PROGRESS

In the light of the above it is likely that a Personal Property Securities Bill will be introduced early in 1992. Because of the delay the Companies Bill will be enacted retaining the existing charges provisions. It is still not clear what the precise interface with the Motor Vehicle Securities Act 1989 will be. Presumably that Act together with the Chattels Transfer Act and the company charges provisions of the Companies Act 1955 will be repealed.

PART VI

COMPETITION LAW

Chapter 41

ASPECTS OF THE COMMERCE ACT 1986

SUMMARY

41.1	INTRODUCTION
41.2	FUNDAMENTAL CONCEPTS
41.3	THE GENERAL PROHIBITION SECTION – s 27
41.4	EXCLUSIONARY PROVISIONS
41.5	PRICE FIXING
41.6	USE OF A DOMINANT POSITION
41.7	RESALE PRICE MAINTENANCE

41.1. INTRODUCTION

41.1.1 Scheme of the Act

(a) STATUTORY OBJECT

The object of the Commerce Act 1986, the role of some of its key provisions, and the influence of overseas antitrust legislation on the New Zealand law are nicely encapsulated in the following passage from the High Court's judgment in *Union Shipping NZ Ltd v Port Nelson Ltd* [1990] 2 NZLR 662 at pp 699-700:

> The object of the Commerce Act is evident in its long title: "An Act to [promote] competition in markets within New Zealand . . .". The emphasis is upon [promoting] "competition". In the words of Richardson J delivering the decision of the Court of Appeal in *Tru Tone Ltd & Ors v Festival Records Retail Marketing Ltd* (1988) 2 NZBLC 103,286 at p 103, 291 [1988] 2 NZLR 352 at p 358. "It is based on the premise that society's resources are best allocated in a competitive market where rivalry between firms ensures maximum efficiency in the use of resources." It is the [promotion] of competition which the Court is directed to foster. Parliament as a matter of policy has decided benefits will flow from that course. Whether such is a correct economic or social analysis is not a matter for the Court. Within that objective, the particular objectives of ss 27 and 36 are clear. Section 27 prohibits contracts, arrangements or understandings, which substantially lessen competition. Section 36, following in the footsteps of a tradition at least as old as the Sherman Act (USC 15 ss 1-7) recognises that even in competitive markets dominant positions do

arise which in the end can generate anticompetitive activity. Accordingly it is intended to prohibit the use of such dominant position within a market for serious anticompetitive purposes. Such provisions are directed at the protection of the concept of competition as such. They are not directed at the protection of individual competitors, except insofar as the latter may promote the former. In the trade practices area, the 1986 Act clearly follows in a general way a number of approaches adopted in Australia under the Trade Practices Act 1974, which in turn in some areas pick up principles developed under United States antitrust legislation. Developments and approaches in those jurisdictions can be kept in mind accordingly. The legislation to no small extent breaks new ground, reflecting the increasing complexity and maturity of the commercial environment in this country in recent decades and the demands which that has imposed. It is legislation of a type where the Courts should not hesitate to adopt necessary purposive approaches in line with *Northland Milk Vendors Association Inc v Northern Milk Ltd* [1988] 1 NZLR 530 paying due respect to legislative policy.

One may draw several points from the above passage. First, the Commerce Act has mixed legal/economic content. Second, the Act focuses on the promotion of competition, not on the protection of individual competitors. Third, this is an area of the law where the Australian developments are of considerable relevance as to a lesser extent are the American. Finally, the Courts should not hesitate to apply purposive interpretations to the legislation. Throughout this Chapter, the writer will invoke these points to help analyse and clarify the law.

(b) THE SUBSTANTIVE PARTS OF THE ACT
Like most antitrust statutes, the Commerce Act is concerned with two types of phenomena which give rise to or buttress market power, viz (a) restrictive trade practices, and (b) market forms and behaviour which, collectively, one may describe as the market dominance problem.

In addressing the above types of phenomena, the Commerce Act employs a number of prohibitions which are classified into categories designated by Parts.

Part II of the Act deals with "Restrictive Trade Practices". Normally one associates such practices with concerted conduct that is anti-competitive in nature. While Part II embraces such conduct, it does not limit itself to concerted activity. Part II singles out the more blatant types of anti-competitive conduct – exclusionary arrangements (s 29), horizontal price fixing (s 30) and resale price maintenance (ss 37 and 38) – for special condemnation, ie, the conduct is illegal per se without any need for the plaintiff to show that it has the purpose or effect of substantially lessening competition. Many other manifestations of concerted behaviour may have a detrimental effect on competition in a particular fact situation. To ensure such behaviour is subject to scrutiny under the Act, Part II contains a general prohibition section (s 27) which employs a rule of reason approach ie the Court or Commission examining a challenged practice will condemn it only if the party attacking it establishes that the practice has the purpose or effect of substantially lessening competition in the market as a whole. As noted above, Part II is not limited to concerted behaviour. It also regulates the use of a dominant market position for certain anti-competitive or exclusionary purposes (s 36). Unlike the other substantive parts of the Act, Part II is of fundamental importance to all those engaged in commercial activity. For this reason, the Chapter will limit itself to a discussion of the practices falling within its ambit.

Part III of the Act, regulating "Business Acquisitions" (referred to prior to the Commerce Amendment Act 1990 as "mergers and takeovers") reflects a concern for the structural dimension of market dominance. The key provision in Part III, s 47 prohibits any person from acquiring assets of a business or shares if, as a result of the acquisition that person or another person would be, or would be likely to be, in a dominant position in a market, or that person's or another person's dominant position in a market would be, or would be likely to be, strengthened. If the acquirer is to avoid the consequences of contravening the section, it will need to apply to the Commerce Commission for an authorisation. For a useful discussion of the business acquisition provisions, see Y van Roy, *Guidebook to New Zealand Competition Laws* (2nd edn, 1991) ch 9. Berry & Riley (1991) 21 VUWLR 91 provide a more technical analysis. M N Berry canvasses the important recent case law and policy changes in "The Application of Competition Laws to Business Acquisitions in New Zealand" in *Institutional Investors and the New Takeover Regime* (J Farrar ed, forthcoming June 1992).

Part IV of the Act, providing for the imposition of price control in circumstances of restricted competition allows the Commerce Commission to scrutinise the performance of dominant firms.

Finally, Part V of the Act provides for most of the practices caught by the Act, and business acquisitions, to be authorised, in effect allowed to continue, by reference to prescribed public benefit tests.

(c) EXCEPTIONS

(1) Matters specifically authorised by any enactment: Section 43(1) provides:

> (1) Nothing in this Part of this Act applies in respect of any act, matter, or thing that is, or is of a kind, specifically authorised by any enactment or Order in Council made under any Act.

Section 43(2) seeks to clarify the scope of the exception by providing that an enactment or Order in Council does not provide specific authority if it provides in general terms for an act, matter or thing notwithstanding that it requires or is subject to approval or authorisation by a Minister of the Crown, statutory body or a person holding any particular office.

The Privy Council in *Apple Fields Ltd v New Zealand Apple and Pear Marketing Board* [1991] 1 NZLR 257 (PC) took a narrow view of the exception. At issue was whether a second-tier capital levy imposed by the Board on new growers and growers wishing to expand production was "specifically authorised" by the Apple and Pear Marketing Board Act 1971. Section 31(1) of that Act empowers the Board, with the approval of the Fruitgrowers' Federation, to "impose on growers levies of such nature and incidence as the Board thinks fit" and these might be imposed on "all growers, or on any class or classes of growers": s 31 (2). The Court of Appeal unanimously held that the levies were specifically authorised and hence fell within the protection of the s 43 statutory exception. In overturning the Court of Appeal, the Privy Council rejected the emphasis the Court of Appeal judgments had put on the role of producer boards. It saw the matter simply as a question of construction. Was s 31

particular enough to constitute a "specific authorisation" under s 43? The
Privy Council set out its views on s 43 at p 265.

> Section 43(2) makes it abundantly clear that a statutory authorisation embracing
> a class of acts which may or may not amount to restrictive practices is not a
> specific authorisation which will satisfy s 43(1). This is so even if, as here, the
> particular act in question is not only authorised generally by the statute, but
> also requires under the statute, and has obtained, the specific authority of the
> Minister. This seems to their Lordships to indicate that nothing less will do
> than either a statutory authorisation of the very act in question or, if it is one
> of a class or kinds of authorised acts, that the whole authorised class would if
> not so authorised, fall foul of the prohibition in Part II of the Act of 1986.

While not insisting that every act of the kind authorised must be anti-
competitive, the Privy Council took the view that the statute must
authorise acts of a kind "of which the preponderant majority will
continually operate in an anti-competitive way".

(2) Specific exceptions – s 44: Section 44 excludes from the operation of Part
II the following:

— partnership agreements between individuals insofar as the agreement relates to the terms of the partnership, the conduct of the
partnership business and competition between the parties:
s 44(1)(a);

— contracts, arrangements or understanding, or covenants where
the only parties thereto are or would be interconnected bodies
corporate: s 44(1)(b);

— contracts containing provisions restricting the work individuals
may engage in during, or after the termination of, the contract:
s 44(1)(c);

— contracts for or covenants for the sale of a business or of shares in
the capital of a body corporate carrying on a business that is solely
for the protection of the purchaser in respect of the goodwill of the
business: s 44(1)(d);

— contracts, arrangements or understandings whereby a person is
obliged to comply with the standards of dimension, design, quality or performance proposed or approved by the Standards Association of New Zealand or by any prescribed association or body:
s 44(1)(e);

— contracts, arrangements or understandings containing provisions
relating to remuneration and conditions of work: s 44(1)(f);

— contracts, arrangements and understandings relating exclusively
to the export of goods or services provided that particulars are
submitted to the Commerce Commission within 15 days of making the arrangement: s 44(1)(g);

— actions undertaken in concert by users of goods or services otherwise than in trade against the suppliers of those goods or services:
s 44(1)(h);

— contracts, arrangements or understandings containing provisions
relating exclusively to international shipping to or from New
Zealand: s 44(2). This exemption does not apply to the carriage of
goods to or from a ship or the loading or unloading of a ship:
s 44(3).

(3) Statutory intellectual property rights: Section 45 exempts provisions authorising any act that would otherwise be prohibited by reason of the existence of a statutory intellectual property right. The exemption does not cover provisions which contravene ss 36, 36A, 37 and 38.

Sections 36(2) and 36A(2) exempt from the prohibitions contained in those sections actions taken solely to enforce an intellectual property right.

The law relating to restraint of trade and breaches of confidence are not affected by the Commerce Act: s 7(1) and (2).

(d) PENALTIES AND REMEDIES

Under s 80, the Commission may institute proceedings in the High Court for recovery of pecuniary penalties from persons who have contravened any of the provisions of Part II of the Act. Such proceedings must be brought within three years of the contravention: s 80(5). As a result of the Commerce Amendment Act 1990, the maximum penalty in respect of a body corporate is $5,000,000, and for other persons $500,000.

Note that s 80 extends to those who attempt to contravene a provision of Part II or induce, or attempt to induce, any other person, whether by threats or promises or otherwise, to contravene such a provision. The section also catches the activities of those who aid, abet, counsel, procure, conspire with others or are in any way, directly or indirectly knowingly concerned in or a party to the contravention.

The contraventions of Part II may also be the subject of injunction proceedings before the High Court. The Commission or any other person may apply for injunctions: s 81.

Persons who suffer loss or damage by a contravention of Part II are entitled to institute civil proceedings for the recovery of the actual amount of the loss or damage incurred: s 82. A private plaintiff can also seek an injunction or obtain a declaration. As to the latter, see *Commerce Commission v Fletcher Challenge Ltd* (1989) 2 NZBLC 103,463 at p 103, 513.

41.1.2 Administration of the Act

(a) THE COMMERCE COMMISSION

(1) Membership, terms of appointment, meetings, staff: The Commerce Commission was originally established by the Trade Practices (Commerce Commission and Pyramid Selling) Act 1974. It operated under the Commerce Act 1975 but was wound up under s 116 of the Commerce Act 1986. However, Parliament re-established it under Part I of the 1986 Act with the membership being unchanged.

The Commission is a body corporate with perpetual succession and a common seal: s 8(2). It may acquire, hold or otherwise dispose of real and personal property, and may sue or be sued in its corporate name: s 8(3).

The Commission consists of not less than three nor more than five members (of whom at least one shall be a barrister and solicitor, of not less than five years standing) appointed by the Governor-General on the recommendation of the Minister of Commerce. The Minister is obliged to consult with the Attorney-General in the case of any person who is a barrister and solicitor. One member is appointed as Chairman of the Commission and another as Deputy Chairman. The Minister is not to recommend any person unless, in the opinion of the Minister that person is qualified by virtue of his or her knowledge of or experience in industry, commerce, economics, law, accountancy, public administration, or consumer affairs: s 9(1)-(4).

Members hold office for terms not exceeding five years but are eligible for reappointment: s 10(1). The Act provides for the appointment of associate members in relation to a specified matter or class of matters: s 11. The Governor-General may terminate the appointment of a member for disability, bankruptcy, neglect of duty, misconduct or failure to comply with the financial disclosure provisions of the Act: s 13(1)-(2).

Section 14 requires the disclosure of financial interests where the member has an interest in a business or body corporate that would in accordance with the rules of natural justice disqualify the member from taking part in the consideration or determination of any matter. Disclosure is to the Chairman, or in the case of a financial interest held by the Chairman, to the Minister.

The Chairman convenes meetings of the Commission at such times as he or she determines. The quorum at such meetings is three with the Chairman having a deliberative vote and, in the event of an equality of votes, he or she also has a casting vote. The Chairman may give directions regarding procedures. s 15(1)-(7).

The Chairman may direct the Commission to sit in separate Divisions, with each Division having its own Chairman: s 16.

The Commission may appoint such employees as it thinks fit for the efficient performance and exercise of its powers and functions: s 17.

(2) Functions of the Commission: The Commission's principal functions are threefold. It has an enforcement role, a decision-making role and an investigative role.

In its enforcement role, the Commission may institute proceedings in the High Court for the recovery of pecuniary penalties under s 80 for breaches of Part II of the Act (restrictive trade practices). It may also apply to the High Court for injunctions: s 81. In respect of business acquisitions (mergers and takeovers) it may seek pecuniary penalties (s 83), injunctions (s 84) and divestiture of assets (s 85). As far as controlled goods and services are concerned, the Commission may prosecute in the District Court for offences seeking the imposition of fines (s 86) and apply to the High Court for injunctions (s 87).

The Commission's decision-making role relates primarily to authorising certain restrictive trade practices (anti-competitive arrangements, exclusionary provisions and resale price maintenance) which would otherwise be prohibited (s 58(1)-(6)); granting clearances to business acquisitions which do not result in a person acquiring or strengthening a dominant market position (ss 66(3) and 67(3)); authorising business acquisitions on the ground that they have sufficient public benefit to outweigh the detriment constituted by the acquisition or strengthening of a dominant market position (s 61(3)); and authorising maximum, actual or minimum prices for controlled goods and services (s 70).

The Commission's investigative role relates to matters that constitute or may constitute, a contravention of the Act, or are relevant to the making of an authorisation or clearance decision by the Commission. The officers and employees of the Commission undertake this task.

The three roles of the Commission were the subject of judicial comment in *Fisher & Paykel Ltd v Commerce Commission* (1990) NZBLC 101,655 at p 101, 660:

> It should be noted that the Commission has cast upon it by the statute three quite different roles. In some circumstances, it can be an investigator and prosecutor. Yet it must act judicially when determining applications such as that made to it by F & P. As Mr Fogarty's thoughtful submissions pointed out this statutory schizophrenia has some similarities with the functions of the United States Federal Trade Commission and the Australian Trade Practices Commission. Under earlier legislation in New Zealand, the investigative and adjudicative process were undertaken by separate entities. But the legislature saw fit in 1986 to combine both functions in the one body.

Section 25 requires the Commission to make available information on its functions and powers, and the purposes and provisions of the Commerce Act.

The Commission is independent of both the political and executive branches of Government. Section 26, however, requires the Commission in exercising its powers under the Act, to have regard to the economic policies of the Government as transmitted in writing to the Commission by the Minister. The Minister is obliged to publish any such statement of economic policy in the *Gazette* and table it in Parliament as soon as practicable after its transmission. The High Court examined the nature of s 26 in *New Zealand Co-operative Dairy Co Ltd v Commerce Commission* (1991) 3 NZBLC 102, 059. See also *Re New Zealand Kiwifruit Exporters Association (Inc) – New Zealand Kiwifruit Coolstores Association (Inc)* (1989) 2 NZBLC (Com) 104,485.

(3) Powers of the Commission: Section 98 empowers the Commission to require, by written notice, a person to furnish information, produce documents or give evidence which it considers necessary or desirable for the purpose of carrying out its functions and exercising it powers under the Act.

Gallen J considered the scope of s 98 in *Telecom Corp of New Zealand v Commerce Commission* (1991) 3 NZBLC 101, 962. His Honour ruled that the Commission has power to seek information only where it is relevant to the investigation, which must itself be one authorised by the Act. It is for the Commission to decide if the material sought is relevant; this does not mean, however, that the Commission has an unrestricted right to seek whatever information it chooses. But the onus on the Commission to show a degree of relevance would be a very easy one to discharge.

The Commission may authorise an employee to obtain a search warrant to enable the employee to enter premises, search for and receive relevant documents or articles and things, inspect documents and take copies or extracts therefrom in order to ascertain whether any person has or is contravening the Act: ss 98A and 98B.

Section 99 empowers the Commission to receive in evidence any statement, document, information or matter that it considers will assist it to deal effectively with the matter before it, whether or not that evidence would be otherwise admissible in a Court of law. The Commission may require the evidence to be given on oath.

Non-compliance with the provisions of s 98 or obstructing an employee of the Commission acting pursuant to a warrant issued under s 98A is an offence, carrying a fine not exceeding $10,000 in the case of an individual or $30,000 in the case of a body corporate.

(4) The role of the Commission in appeals: It is now well established that the extent of the Commission's role in appeals from its own determinations will depend upon whether the other parties will fully canvass the issues in the appeal before the Court. The Court of Appeal formulated guiding principles in *Goodman Fielder Ltd v Commerce Commission* [1987] 2 NZLR 10 at p 20:

> In both Courts Mr McGrath has raised the question of the role of the Commission in appeals from it under the Commerce Act. He mentioned observations, said to have an inhibiting effect, in *New Zealand Engineering etc Industrial Union of Workers v Court of Arbitration* [1976] 2 NZLR 283, 284-284, about the well-established principle that judicial bodies should strive not to enter the fray in a way which might appear to favour the interests of one of the parties. Those observations do not apply in their terms or spirit to a case where considerations of public interest and the effective administration of an Act arise, especially if there is no other party to put those considerations adequately before the appellate Court. In such a case it is right that the Commission should help the appellate Court to whatever extent the Commission and that Court find consistent with the Commission's public responsibility.

In accordance with these principles, the Commission has played an active part in appeals where no other party presented argument in support of the Commission. See, for example, *New Zealand Co-operative Dairy Company* (supra); *Hoyts Corp Holdings Operations (NZ) Ltd v Commerce Commission* (High Court, Auckland, CL 44/91, 17 December 1991, Henry J and R G Blunt Esq). In contrast, in *Telecom Corp of New Zealand Ltd v Commerce Commission* (High Court, Wellington, AP 279/90, 10 December 1991, Greig J, W J Shaw Esq and Professor M Brunt), where two other parties actively opposed Telecom's appeal, the Commission did not contest the merits of the appeal and did not actively oppose the appellant or support its own decision. It did however, make submissions on what it considered were two questions of principle and on one going to the effective administration of the Commerce Act.

(b) THE HIGH COURT
The High Court plays a pivotal role as a decision-making body under the Commerce Act 1986. The Court has jurisdiction under s 75(1) to hear and determine a wide variety of proceedings. In the case of contraventions of Part II of the Act (restrictive trade practices), the Court is required to deal with the recovery of pecuniary penalties under s 80, applications for injunctions under s 81 and actions for damages under s 82. Contraventions of Part III of the Act (business acquisitions) may involve the recovery of pecuniary penalties under s 83, applications for injunctions under s 84 and proceedings to divest shares or assets under s 85. In the case of contraventions of Part IV of the Act (control of prices), the Court is required to determine applications for injunctions under s 87 and for orders under s 89.

Section 79 provides for the relaxation of the rules of evidence in that it allows the Court to receive in evidence any statement, document, or information that would not be otherwise admissible if the Court considers it to be of assistance. Note that s 79 does not apply to criminal proceedings, the pecuniary penalty provisions (ss 80 and 83) or in proceedings for a declaration: see *Auckland Regional Authority v Mutual Rental Cars (Auckland Airport) Ltd* [1987] 2 NZLR 647 at p 654.

The standard of proof for all types of civil proceedings under the Act is the ordinary civil standard. In *Tru Tone Ltd v Festival Records Retail Marketing Ltd* [1988] 2 NZLR 352 at p 358 the Court of Appeal said that it could see no support "either in principle or specifically under this legislation for requiring 'a high degree of probability'" – the phrase used by Barker J in the High Court [1987] 2 NZLR 647 at p 660.

The Act provides for the appointment of lay members who must be qualified by virtue of their knowledge or experience in industry, commerce, economics, law or accountancy: s 77(2). For the purposes of its appellate jurisdiction in respect of Commission determinations, s 77(9) mandates the High Court to be comprised of a Judge and at least one lay member. In respect of proceedings which relate to any of ss 27 to 29, 36, 36A, or 47 of the Act, a Judge of the High Court may elect to sit with one or more lay members: s 78(1).

A dissatisfied party to any appeal before the High Court from any determination of the Commission, may, with the leave of the High Court or the Court of Appeal appeal to the Court of Appeal: s 97(1). The decision of the Court of Appeal on such appeals is final: s 97(4).

In the case of other appeals from the High Court the normal rules relating to appeals apply. Ultimately, a dissatisfied litigant may appeal to the Judicial Committee of the Privy Council. One such appeal has already occurred, viz *Apple Fields Ltd v New Zealand Apple and Pear Marketing Board* [1991] 1 NZLR 257 (PC).

41.2 FUNDAMENTAL CONCEPTS

There are a number of fundamental legal and economic concepts which are basic to an understanding of the Commerce Act 1986.

41.2.1 Contracts, arrangements and understandings

Apart from the unilateral behaviour of dominant firms and the coercive practices of individual suppliers engaged in resale price maintenance, the focus of the Commerce Act is on collusive action arising from an agreement. This emphasis on agreement is soundly based as cooperation increases the risk of anti-competitive action, expands market power, creates an anti-competitive restraint not otherwise possible and surrenders important decisionmaking autonomy on a matter of competitive significance: P Areeda, 6 *Antitrust Law* (1986) at para 1402(b). The Commerce Act encapsulates the notion of agreement in terms of a broad formula, viz "contract arrangement or understanding". This is similar to the "contract, combination or conspiracy" language of s 1 of the Sherman Act 1890 although the tendency in the United States is to interpret the s 1 language as embodying a single concept rather than a trinity.

(a) "CONTRACT"
Section 2(6) of the Commerce Act gives the word "contract" an extended meaning which includes leases or licences of any land or building. As used in the Commerce Act, "contract" probably refers to any contract,

whether express or implied, formal or informal, which is enforceable (or would be enforceable apart from the Commerce Act provision) by legal proceedings and also probably encompasses those contracts which, though still on foot, are rendered unenforceable or voidable because of some imperfection or vitiating factor: G Taperell, R Vermeesch & D Harland, *Trade Practices and Consumer Protection* (3rd edn, 1983) at p 199.

(b) "ARRANGEMENT"

Unlike "contract", the term "arrangement" almost defies definition. Indeed, the Judges have expressly forsworn any attempt to define it. Nevertheless, the concept has been the subject of analysis by United Kingdom, Australian and New Zealand Courts, and, as a result, it is possible to identify the essential elements of an arrangement. The word arrangement is not a term of art. Accordingly, one should construe it in its ordinary or popular sense. It embraces the situation where each of two or more parties intentionally arouses in the other an expectation that he or she will act in a particular way. Such obligations may be purely moral, binding in honour only.

(1) The Basic Slag *case:* The leading United Kingdom case is *Re British Basic Slag Ltd's Application* (1962) LR 3 RP 178, *affirmed* (1963) LR 4 RP 116 (CA). Several steel companies formed British Basic Slag Ltd (Basic) to purchase their slag and sell it as fertiliser. The steel companies, each of which nominated one director to Basic's board, owned all its capital. Each steel company signed an agreement with Basic giving Basic the exclusive right to purchase the company's slag. Each of the agreements was in similar terms. Uncontradicted evidence tendered on behalf of the companies was that there had been no prior communication between the individual steel companies as to the terms of the agreement and that each company had acted according to its individual judgment. Also, the execution by one company of its agreement was not conditional on the execution of similar agreements by the other companies. Nevertheless, Mr Justice Cross, at first instance, held that there was an arrangement between the steel companies to enter into common form agreements. In so finding, Cross J had regard to the history of the trading relationship of the parties, to the fact that each steel company had its nominee director on the board of Basic, thus allowing each director to keep his steel company informed of the discussions preceding the signing of the contracts, and that a memorandum endorsed on each contract named the other companies which in fact entered into similar contracts. As to the elements of an arrangement, Cross J said at p 196:

> [A]ll that is required to constitute an arrangement not enforceable in law is that the parties to it shall have communicated with one another in some way, and that as a result of the communication each has intentionally aroused in the other an expectation that he will act in a certain way.

Cross J then dealt with an objection that the steel companies could not have entered into an arrangement because there were no "mutual rights or obligations" within the principle that Upjohn J had established in the earlier case of *Re Austin Motor Co Ltd's Agreements* (1957) LR 1 RP 6. Cross J rejected that argument, saying at p 197:

But what Upjohn J was concerned to point out there was that you could not have an arrangement within the meaning of s 6 [of the United Kingdom Restrictive Trade Practices Act 1956] unless the parties to it both accepted obligations. He was not directing his mind to the question as to how stringent the obligations had to be, and I see nothing in that case which is inconsistent with the view which I have formed in the present case.

The steel companies appealed and the definition of "arrangement" given by Upjohn J in the *Austin* case and by Cross J were both approved. Wilmer L J considered at p 146 that there was no inconsistency between the two definitions:

> For when each of two or more parties intentionally arouses in the others an expectation that he will act in a certain way, it seems to be that he incurs at least a moral obligation to do so. An arrangement as so defined is therefore something "whereby the parties to it accept mutual rights and obligations".

Lord Justice Diplock also embraced this line of reasoning. His Lordship stated at p 154:

> "Arrangement" is not a term of art; and in section 6(3) of the Act of 1956 I agree with my Lords that it bears the meaning that an ordinary educated man would ascribe to it. It involves a meeting of minds because under section 6(1) it has to be an arrangement "between two or more persons", and since it must be an arrangement under which restrictions are accepted by two or more parties it involves mutuality in that each party, assuming he is a reasonable and conscientious man would regard himself as being in some degree under a duty, whether moral or legal, to conduct himself in a particular way or not to conduct himself in a particular way as the case may be, at any rate so long as the other party or parties conducted themselves in the way contemplated by the arrangement.

Diplock L J then referred to the requirements of an arrangement as Cross J had stated them and added at p 155:

> I think that I am only expressing the same concept in slightly different terms if I say without attempting an exhaustive definition, for there are many ways in which arrangements may be made, that it is sufficient to constitute an arrangement between A and B, if (1) A makes a representation as to his future conduct with the expectation and intention that such conduct on his part will operate as an inducement to B to act in a particular way, (2) such representation is communicated to B, who has knowledge that A so expected and intended, and (3) such representation or A's conduct in fulfilment of it operates as an inducement, whether among inducements or not, to B to act in that particular way.

On its surface, this alternative definition of Lord Diplock's does not require either mutual intercommunication or mutuality of obligation; for these reasons it has attracted criticism: see, for example, J G Collinge, *Restrictive Trade Practices and Monopolies, Mergers & Take-overs in New Zealand* (2nd edn, 1982) at pp 152-54. Because of this, it is useful to distinguish the alternative definition from his Lordship's generally accepted definition quoted earlier, which stresses mutuality of obligation.

When considering the meaning of arrangement in the context of the Commerce Act 1986 and the Trade Practices Act 1974, the New Zealand

and Australian judiciary have followed the United Kingdom Court of Appeal's approach in *Basic Slag*: see, for example, *Top Performance Motors v Ira Berk Ltd* (1975) ATPR para 40-004 per Smithers J; *Auckland Regional Authority v Mutual Rental Cars (Auckland Airport) Ltd* [1987] 2 NZLR 647. One must note, however, that unlike the situation prevailing under the United Kingdom Restrictive Trade Practices Act, the Australasian legislation does not require any need to prove a restriction as such, or to prove that two or more parties accept restrictions.

(2) The Mileage Conference *case: Basic Slag* emphasised that the parties to an arrangement must have communicated with each other. However, the United Kingdom Restrictive Practices Court qualified this requirement of mutual intercommunication in *Re Mileage Conference Group* (1966) LR 6 RP 49 where the Court held that in certain circumstances *observed conduct* may substitute for intercommunication.

Because of the importance of the observed conduct principle one must examine the factual situation in *Mileage Conference*. Prior to the 1956 United Kingdom Act coming into force, eight tyre manufacturers, members of a trade association, had an agreement not to tender to supply tyres to fleet operators at a rate lower than the lowest rate that any member insisted upon at a meeting held in accordance with a specified procedure, without first notifying the other members. The object was to ensure that each manufacturer when putting in his quotation knew the lowest rate which any of his competitors was mindful to quote. The parties registered the agreement under the 1956 Act, but they did not seek to defend it before the Restrictive Practices Court and gave the Court an undertaking in the usual form, ie not to enforce the agreement and not to make any other agreement to the like effect.

Before giving the undertaking the parties had terminated the agreement and had entered into a new "rate notification scheme". There was a compulsory part of the scheme requiring members to notify the secretary of the rates they *had actually quoted* the operators. There was also a permissive part under which the members could also notify the secretary of rates which they *proposed to quote*, and any changes in them, and the secretary would then notify these to other members. As the parties operated it, the permissive part of the scheme meant that no member would quote a rate lower than the lowest rate notified, without first notifying the secretary of that lowest rate. Each company in fact operated under the permissive part of the scheme and the result was that the rates eventually quoted were identical or very close.

The Registrar of Restrictive Practices alleged that the parties were in breach of their undertaking. In rebuttal, the parties relied on the fact that before they adopted the scheme the secretary informed members that they must neither agree with each other that they would all operate the permissive part of the scheme nor discuss with each other any proposed rates. The Restrictive Practices Court accepted that each party had decided quite separately and independently to operate the permissive part of the scheme and there was no verbal intimation to each other of their respective decisions and intentions.

The Court accepted that at the outset there may have been no arrangement. But when it became obvious that all the parties had decided to operate the permissive part of the scheme, a scheme which would operate only if the others did so too, there then arose in the Court's view mutual obligations to continue to operate the scheme in return for the benefits received from it. In rejecting the argument that an arrangement cannot arise out of observed conduct, the Court said at p 102:

> The law is not so subtle or unrealistic as to involve the conclusion that, while an arrangement can come into being as a result of information as to one another's intentions supplied in words or writing or by a nod or a wink, it cannot come into being as a result of information as to one another's intentions derived from their actual and continuing conduct towards one another.

The significance of *Mileage Conference* is that it shows that mutual intercommunication is not essential to the creation of an arrangement – in certain circumstances observed conduct may make up for the lack of intercommunication. Nevertheless, one must place some limit on the observed conduct principle otherwise it would embrace "conscious parallelism", ie the common practice among firms in a concentrated industry of conducting their similar businesses in a uniform manner, aware that their counterparts are pursuing the same course of action. To avoid this result, an English commentator, James Cunningham, in *The Fair Trading Act 1973* (1974) at p 211 has suggested that the observed conduct principle will apply only where the conduct in question includes the acceptance of benefits, acceptance in such circumstances as to give rise to a corresponding obligation.

(c) "UNDERSTANDING"
The Australasian case law and commentary has tended to equate "arrangement" with "understanding", although the Courts have recognised that the term "understanding" may catch collusion achieved by even less formality than an arrangement.
 The Courts accept that, as in the case of an arrangement, there must be a meeting of minds before an understanding can be found. Smithers J spelt out this requirement in the *Top Performance* case (supra) at p 17,116:

> It seems to me . . . that an understanding must involve the meeting of two or more minds. Where the minds of the parties are at one that a proposed transaction between them proceeds on the basis of the maintenance of a particular state of affairs or the adoption of a particular course of conduct, it would seem that there would be an understanding within the meaning of the Act.

Smithers J also discussed the meaning of understanding in *L Grollo & Co Pty Ltd v Nu-Staff Decorating Pty Ltd* (1978) ATPR para 40-086 at p 17,842:

> I have to remember that the concept of an understanding is broad and flexible. It may arise merely where the minds of the parties are at one that a proposed transaction proceeds on the basis of the maintenance of a particular state of affairs or the adoption of a particular course of conduct.

Franki J in *Trade Practices Commission v TNT Management Pty Ltd* (1985) ATPR para 40-512, while citing with approval Smithers J's remarks in *Grollo*, questioned whether an understanding was a broader concept. His Honour said at p 46,098:

[I] would not necessarily reject a proposition that the requirements for entering into an understanding may be somewhat different and more easily satisfied than the requirements for making an arrangement.

In *Trade Practices Commission v David Jones (Australia) Pty Ltd* (1986) 64 ALR 67, Fisher J cited with approval the above remarks of both Smithers J and Franki J. His Honour also referred to the decision of the High Court of Australia in *Federal Commissioner of Taxation v Lutovi Investments Pty Ltd* (1978) 140 CLR 434, where Gibbs and Mason J J at p 444 made the following observations regarding the requirements of an arrangement in the context of the Australian Income Tax Assessment Act 1936:

> It is, however, necessary that an arrangement should be consensual, and that there should be some adoption of it. But in our view it is not essential that the parties are committed to it or are bound to support it. An arrangement may be informal as well as unenforceable and the parties may be free to withdraw from it or to act inconsistently with it, notwithstanding their adoption of it.

Fisher J interpreted this statement of the elements of an arrangement as applying equally to an understanding. Applying it to the facts before him, his Honour had no difficulty in inferring an understanding notwithstanding that the conduct would be contrary to company policy or that employees could only implement it with the approval of a superior.

In *Auckland Regional Authority v Mutual Rental Cars (Auckland Airport) Ltd* [1987] 2 NZLR 647, the first New Zealand case under the Commerce Act 1986 to examine the expression "contract, arrangement or understanding", Barker J briefly canvassed the Australian authorities and expressed agreement with the view that there must be a meeting of minds before the Courts could infer an understanding or arrangement. His Honour also noted at p 662 that "it is hard to see how the meeting of minds necessary to constitute an understanding can be reached without some communication between the parties similar to that required to constitute an arrangement".

(d) IS MUTUALITY OF OBLIGATION REQUIRED?

An issue which has been the subject of discussion in the Australian cases is whether it is enough that the arrangement restrains or benefits only one party or whether there must be a reciprocity of restraint. As noted above, the United Kingdom cases have stressed mutual rights and obligations but the explicit United Kingdom statutory requirement that the legislation applies only where two or more parties accept a restriction explains this insistence on reciprocity in the case law. The absence of such a requirement from the Australasian legislation gives room for argument as to whether mutuality is a necessary prerequisite for an arrangement or understanding.

The matter arose in *Trade Practices Commission v Nicholas Enterprises Pty Ltd* (1979) ATPR para 40-126. Fisher J, after reviewing the United Kingdom and Australian authorities on the meaning of "arrangement or understanding", said at p 18,342:

> A significant feature of each of [these authorities] is the emphasis placed upon the necessity for each of the parties to have communicated with the other, for each to have raised an expectation in the mind of the other, and for each to have

accepted an obligation qua the other. These are in my opinion the essential elements of the requisite meeting of minds.

On appeal, the Full Federal Court of Australia in *Morphett Arms Hotel Pty Ltd v Trade Practices Commission* (1980) ATPR para 40-157 upheld the decision of Fisher J, but Bowen C J, who delivered the opinion of the Full Court, made an important obiter statement at p 42,234 on the mutuality issue:

> As at present advised, it seems to me that one could have an understanding between two or more persons restricted to the conduct which one of them will pursue without any element of mutual obligation insofar as the other party or parties to the understanding are concerned.

The Trade Practices Commission strongly relied on Bowen C J's statement in the subsequent case of *Trade Practices Commission v Email Ltd* (1980) ATPR para 40-172. As Lockhart J in that case found that neither of the two defendant companies had any sense of obligation qua the other, his Honour did not explore fully the question of mutuality. Nevertheless, his Honour did make the observation at p 42,377 that one could normally expect reciprocity of commitment:

> For my part I find it difficult to envisage circumstances where there would be an understanding involving a commitment by one party as to the way he should behave without some commitment by the other party. Unless there is reciprocity of commitment, I do not readily see why the parties would come to an arrangement or understanding.

But having made this point, Lockhart J, no doubt with Bowen C J's remarks in *Morphett Arms* in mind, said (ibid):

> [I] incline to the view that there is no necessity for an element of mutual commitment between the parties to an arrangement or understanding such that each accepts an obligation qua the other; although in practice such cases would be rare.

The *David Jones* case (supra) suggests that such cases do in fact exist. Following a price war, Zellen, a distributor of Sheridan bed linen, promoted a meeting in March 1984 with Adelaide retailers to discuss their retail prices. At the beginning of April 1984, the price structure of the retailers exhibited significant uniformity. There was evidence that Zellen had given the parties at the meeting a list of stipulated prices for the relevant products. The Trade Practices Commission alleged that Zellen and the retailers had made an arrangement or understanding which had the effect or likely effect of fixing prices for Sheridan bed linen products in the Adelaide metropolitan area. Fisher J found for the Trade Practices Commission. His Honour relied on the circumstantial evidence to infer that the parties had arrived at the alleged understanding. This evidence revealed both an incentive and an opportunity to arrive at such an understanding as well as subsequent concurrent acts of, and the lack of sworn evidence from the respondents.

In considering the position of Zellen, Fisher J observed that as a wholesaler, Zellen was only indirectly, if at all, a party to the price fixing provision and not subject to any obligation in respect thereof. The retailers did not require Zellen to implement this provision of the

understanding; his task was to advise discounting retailers of its existence. Referring to Lockhart's statement in *Email*, Fisher J considered that
Zellen's position may be one of the rare cases Lockhart J had in mind. His
Honour ruled that a person may be a party to an understanding provided
he or she is aware of, although not necessarily committed to each
provision of the understanding.

While the issue has not yet arisen in the New Zealand context, one
perhaps may ascribe some significance to the fact that Barker J in
Auckland Regional Authority (supra) cited with apparent approval Lord
Diplock's alternative definition of arrangement which on its surface does
not require either mutual intercommunication or mutuality of obligation. Barker J, while acknowledging the need for communication between the parties, did not refer to any need for mutuality of obligation.

In summary, the element of mutuality of obligation required under
the wording of the United Kingdom Act is not a prerequisite under either
the Australian or New Zealand legislation so it is possible to envisage an
arrangement or understanding which one of the parties will pursue
without there being any corresponding obligation on the other. Normally, however, business people will not enter into an arrangement or
arrive at an understanding unless there is some *quid pro quo* or some sort
of commitment on either side.

41.2.2 Proof of the contract, arrangement or understanding

Plaintiffs may sometimes prove a contract, arrangement or understanding by direct evidence. This is often possible where the concerted action
is the result of an express agreement. However, in most situations direct
evidence of the contract, arrangement or understanding is not present
and Courts must infer the necessary concerted action from circumstantial evidence.

(a) MINIMAL EVIDENCE NEEDED
Two leading United States Supreme Court cases illustrate the minimal
evidence necessary for inferring an understanding from circumstantial
evidence.

(1) Interstate Circuit: In *Interstate Circuit Inc v United States* 306 US 208
(1939), the United States Government alleged that eight major film
distributors had conspired with two large first-run exhibitors to impose
restrictions on independent second-run cinemas. There was no direct
evidence of agreement or communication among the distributors, and
the distributors never met the defendant exhibitors. However, one of the
latter had written a letter to each of the eight distributors naming them
all as addressees, which set out two demands relating to the distribution
of second-run releases, viz (1) that distributors set a minimum admission
price for second-run releases; and (2) that they should require the
exhibitors not to show the films as part of a double programme. The aim
was to increase the profitability of films for the first-run exhibitors by
making it impossible to see them cheaply on a second-run. Soon after the
receipt of the letter, all eight distributors complied with the demands and
made the necessary modifications to their contracts.

The Supreme Court held there was sufficient evidence of an agreement. The Court relied on four factors:

(1) Each distributor knew that the exhibitor had approached all the other distributors with the same proposals.
(2) Each distributor made substantially identical alterations to their contract and the modifications were complex.
(3) The imposition of the restrictions was feasible and profitable only if all the distributors adhered to them.
(4) The failure of the distributors to call their local managers as witnesses to deny the existence of an agreement suggested that the testimony of the latter would have proved unfavourable.

While one can readily agree with the Court's view that the circumstantial evidence supported the finding of concerted action, the Court in a very broad dictum at p 226 seemed to suggest that unlawful concerted activity could be the basis for liability:

> While the District Court's finding of an agreement of the distributors among themselves is supported by the evidence, we think that in the circumstances of this case such agreement . . . was not a prerequisite. It was enough that, knowing that concerted action was contemplated and invited, the distributors gave their adherence to the scheme and participated in it.

Subsequent lower Court decisions relied on *Interstate Circuit* to infer conspiracies from uniform refusals to deal or other parallel business activity: see, for example, *Milgram v Loew's Inc* 192 F 2d 579 (3rd Cir 1951) *cert denied* 343 US 929 (1953).

(2) Theatre Enterprises: In *Theatre Enterprises Inc v Paramount Film Distributors Corp* 346 US 537 (1954), the Supreme Court made it clear that while parallel business behaviour is admissible circumstantial evidence of conspiracy it does not "conclusively" demonstrate an illegal agreement. The plaintiff owned a modern suburban theatre in Baltimore. The defendants, the major film distributing companies, each refused to lease first-run films to the plaintiff. The plaintiff alleged there was an agreement between the defendants not to deal with him but he adduced no evidence of agreement except the fact that all the defendants had refused to give him first-run releases. Moreover, the defendants gave evidence of legitimate business reasons for not treating the plaintiff's theatre as a suitable place for a first release. There was also no evidence that all defendants knew that the others had received or turned down an offer by the plaintiff to guarantee distributors against any loss of revenue. In contrast to their behaviour in *Interstate Circuit*, the distributors' responsible officers specifically denied any collaboration. In rejecting the plaintiff's claim, the Supreme Court specifically addressed the "conscious parallelism" issue, at pp 540-41:

> The crucial question is whether respondents' conduct toward petitioner stemmed from independent decision or from an agreement, tacit or express. To be sure, business behaviour is admissible circumstantial evidence from which the fact finder may infer agreement. But this Court has never held that proof of parallel business behaviour conclusively establishes agreement or, phrased differently, that such behaviour itself constitutes a Sherman Act offense. Circumstantial evidence of consciously parallel behaviour may have made heavy inroads into the traditional judicial attitude toward conspiracy; but "conscious parallelism" has not yet read conspiracy out of the Sherman Act entirely.

(b) THE "PLUS FACTORS" APPROACH

Since *Theatre Enterprises* United States Courts have typically required circumstantial proof in addition to conscious parallelism before inferring the existence of an agreement. Courts sometimes refer to the necessary additional proofs as "plus factors". Plus factors which the Courts most frequently cite are: (1) conduct contrary to the self-interest of each firm acting independently; (2) the existence of a motive for concerted action; (3) that the defendant was unable or unwilling to rebut or explain uniform behaviour; (4) evidence that the parties had opportunities to discuss pricing or evidence of actual communication; and (5) the use of facilitating practices such as delivered pricing and artificial product standardisation. Even if a single plus factor standing alone is not sufficient, the Courts may be willing to infer an agreement from a number of factors taken together: see, for example, *C-O-Two Fire Equipment Co v United States* 197 F 2d 489 (9th Cir) *cert denied* 344 US 892 (1952).

The United States Courts, however, have taken cognisance of the fact that prices in an oligopolistic industry tend to move in a parallel, or oligopolistically interdependent fashion. In *Pevely Dairy Co v United States* 178 F 2d 363 (8th Cir 1949), *cert denied* 339 US 942 (1950), the structure of the St Louis milk market obviously influenced the decision. The Eight Circuit Court of Appeals noted that: (1) Pevely Dairy and St Louis Dairy, the two corporate defendants, processed 63 per cent of the fluid milk sold in St Louis; (2) there was little difference between the products of the two companies; (3) the costs of labour and materials were identical for both; (4) the two alleged conspirators had not communicated with one another; (5) government regulations on the price of milk had limited their freedom to compete; and (6) sound business judgment could support each pricing decision. In reversing the Trial Court's finding of a price fixing conspiracy, the Eighth Circuit said at p 368:

> [W]hen there are only two or a few sellers, their fortunes are not independent. There can be no actual or tacit, agreement - that is all. Each is forced by the situation itself to take into account the policy of his rival in determining his own, and this cannot be construed as a "tacit agreement" between the two.

The Court concluded that "every price change was made not as the result of any understanding or agreement but because of economic factors": ibid.

(c) TIGHTENING OF THE STANDARDS

As a result of its recent decisions in *Monsanto Co v Spray-Rite Service Corp* 465 US 752 (1984) and *Matsushita Electric Industrial Co v Zenith Radio Co* 106 S Ct 1348 (1986) it is apparent that the United States Supreme Court is tightening the standards of circumstantial proof in conspiracy cases.

(1) Monsanto: Reflecting its more tolerant attitude toward nonprice vertical restraints as expressed in *Continental TV Inc v GTE Sylvania Inc* 433 US 36 (1977), the Court in *Monsanto* made it clear that evidence of frequent contact and communications between a supplier and complaining distributors is insufficient to support the inference of a vertical conspiracy. The Court rejected the argument that one could infer a conspiracy to fix resale prices solely from the supplier's termination of a price-cutting distributor following on in response to prior complaints

from competing distributors. In order to establish a conspiracy in dealer termination cases, the Court held at p 764 that a plaintiff must satisfy the following standard:

> [T]here must be evidence that tends to exclude the possibility of independent action by the manufacturer and distributor. That is, there must be direct or circumstantial evidence that reasonably tends to prove that the manufacturer and others had a conscious commitment to a common scheme designed to achieve an unlawful objective.

(2) Matsushita: The Supreme Court carried over its scepticism about the probative value of circumstantial evidence into the horizontal context in *Matsushita*. In that case, the plaintiffs tendered evidence of the defendants' parallel conduct and concerted action and alleged that the defendants were parties to a predatory pricing conspiracy. Relying on Chicago School economic theory that predatory pricing is irrational business behaviour, the Court viewed the allegation of a predatory pricing conspiracy in the circumstances of the case as highly implausible. Having found that the defendants lacked any plausible motive to engage in an economically irrational conspiracy, the Court held at p 1361 that:

> [l]ack of motive bears on the range of permissible conclusions that might be drawn from ambiguous evidence: if [the defendants] had no rational economic motive to conspire, and if their conduct is consistent with other, equally plausible explanations, the conduct does not give rise to an inference of conspiracy.

Moreover, the Court stated, "if the factual context renders [the plaintiffs] claim implausible – if the claim is one that simply makes no economic sense – [the plaintiffs] must come forward with more persuasive evidence to support their claim than would otherwise be necessary": at p 1356. In making out a claim of conspiracy, the Court, quoting *Monsanto*, ruled that "a plaintiff ... must present evidence `that tends to exclude the possibility that the alleged conspirators acted independently'": ibid, and "conduct as consistent with permissible competition as with illegal conspiracy does not, standing along, support an inference of antitrust conspiracy": ibid.

Matsushita appears to establish that even if the plaintiff proves that the defendants had a strong motive for concerted action and had engaged in consciously parallel behaviour, this will be insufficient to infer conspiracy. This is because motive to conspire does not sufficiently preclude the possibility that the defendants' behaviour was the product of independent decisionmaking and not illegal agreement.

(d) THE AUSTRALIAN EXPERIENCE

While the Australian Courts have referred to the leading American cases on inferring agreement from circumstantial evidence, the judicial application of the economic principles on which the American cases are based has sometimes left a lot to be desired. This is particularly true of the decision of Mr Justice Lockhart in *Trade Practices Commission* v *Email* (1980) ATPR para 40-172.

(1) The Email *case: Email* involved a duopoly. Email and Warburton Franki were the only Australian manufacturers of kilowatt hour meters,

selling about 98 per cent of them to electricity supply authorities. Email, the larger of the two, had between 60-70 per cent of the market between 1968 and 1978. There was no import competition. In addition to exchanging price lists prior to implementing identical price increases and submitting identical tenders, the two respondent companies engaged in a variety of collaborative activity.

Lockhart J found that the exchange of price lists was done for "sound commercial reasons". These reasons were: (1) that Email's action of sending price lists to its competitor was "in furtherance of its price leadership and was in no way intended as some form of signal to Warburton Franki": at p 42,374; (2) that Email believed that price competition would force Warburton Franki to leave the market exposing Email to possible liability under s 46 of the Trade Practices Act 1974 (corresponding to s 36 of the Commerce Act 1986); and (3) that Email wished to preserve harmonious relationships with the supply authorities which wanted to preserve dual sourcing. His Honour explained the respondents' behaviour as follows (at p 42,371):

> By sending its price lists to Warburton Franki, Email helped Warburton Franki follow the Email prices if it chose to do so; but there was no obligation to do so; and this ensured price stability. By Warburton Franki receiving the Email prices quickly, the price leadership situation could operate quickly. Email was confident that Warburton Franki would follow its prices based on previous experience. The receipt by Email of Warburton Franki's price list was of little significance to Email.

His Honour concluded by saying that it was not the exchange of price information that led to the identical prices. Rather, "[t]his was produced by market forces, competition and the necessity for Warburton Franki to follow Email": at p 42,380. Lockhart J was willing to accept that parallel conduct may constitute evidence from which one might infer an arrangement or understanding but he noted that "when a credible explanation is given by the defendant it may be sufficient to negate the inference of an arrangement or understanding": at p 42,370. His Honour found the evidence of the company officials reliable and that neither company was under any obligation qua the other. In his Honour's view, this meant that no price fixing arrangement or understanding existed.

Granted that the special nature of the oligopolistic market involved undoubtedly played an important part in the *Email* determination, nevertheless the decision is disturbing in that it fails to recognise that the respondents' behaviour may have been due to "collusive price leadership" rather than the non-collusive "barometric price leadership" explanation which the Court accepted. For a discussion of the various types of price leadership and their relevance to competition law, see Miller & Round (1982) 10 ABLR 251.

(2) The Allied Mills *case:* A more satisfactory treatment of parallel conduct in an oligopolistic market is seen in *Trade Practices Commission v Allied Mills Industries Pty Ltd* (1980) ATPR para 40-178. The case involved allegations of price fixing against five manufacturers of liquid glucose. Competition in the industry was non-existent until the aggressive entry in late 1975 of a new entrant. A vigorous price war ensued. During the price war two of the established sellers tried independently on separate occasions to lead the price back up. Both attempts were unsuccessful.

However, in August 1976 all five producers met in their capacity as exporters of gluten. In September, almost simultaneously, all five producers raised glucose prices back up to their pre-price war levels. They also refused to cut prices to gain new customers, contrary to their earlier behaviour. The respondents initially defended the case on the basis of non-collusive price leadership and conscious parallelism. In rejecting this line of argument, Shepherd J invoked Lockhart J's comment in *Email* (supra) at p 42,370 that "parallel conduct may constitute circumstantial evidence from which an arrangement or understanding may depend. It depends on the facts of each case". His Honour noted at p 42,458 that *Email* was not authority for the proposition –

> ... that in no circumstances will evidence of parallel pricing provide evidence of an arrangement or understanding. There are cases in which it may do so. In a case where that was the only allegation one would certainly hesitate a long time before striking out a statement of claim.

In addition to the parallel conduct, his Honour also relied on the meetings between the parties and their refusal to cut prices to gain new customers. His Honour concluded that there was a real question to be tried. The approach adopted by his Honour is akin to the "plus factors" approach which the American Courts have embraced.

41.2.3 Attempts to reach an agreement

Unlike s 1 of the Sherman Act, the Commerce Act 1986 extends to attempts to reach an agreement. Section 80(1)(b) of the Act provides for the imposition of pecuniary penalties where the Court is satisfied on the application of the Commerce Commission that a person has attempted to contravene any of the provisions of Part II of the Act. Paragraph (d) of s 80(1) provides for similar liability where a person has induced or attempted to induce any other person whether by threats or promises or otherwise, to contravene any of the Part II provisions. In addition to the pecuniary penalties under s 80(1), persons involved in making an attempt may be the subject of a restraining injunction under s 81 on the application of either the Commission or any other person. An attempt to contravene Part II, however, cannot be the subject of a damages claim.

(1) The Tubemakers *case:* In *Trade Practices Commission v Tubemakers of Australia Ltd* (1983) ATPR para 40-358, Toohey J considered the elements necessary to constitute an attempt to enter into an arrangement or arrive at an understanding. The respondents, Tubemakers Ltd and its subsidiary, Steel Supplies Ltd, were members of a trade association of Western Australian steel distributors, ISSCA. The respondents had discussed between themselves the declining profitability of the group's operations in Western Australia. At a specially convened meeting of ISSCA, the manager of Steel Supplies, after a general discussion on the lack of profitability in the steel business in Western Australia stated that henceforth his companies would limit discounts to 12 per cent. Before this announcement, the regional manager of Tubemakers had informed those present that it was a matter of urgency that greater profits be made and that he would support whatever initiative was undertaken to improve profitability. He thereupon left the meeting.

The Trade Practices Commission alleged that, by reason of the actions of the regional manager of Tubemakers and the manager of Steel Supplies, both of these companies had attempted to contravene ss 45(2)(a)(ii) and 45A of the Trade Practices Act (corresponding to ss 27 and 30 of the Commerce Act) and had attempted to induce others to do the same. The decision of the Federal Court of Australia turned on the mental elements necessary to prove the alleged contraventions. Toohey J held on the basis of the established criminal law principles that it was necessary to establish the relevant intention, that is that the respondents acted with the intention of bringing about an arrangement or understanding with other steel merchants controlling the discounts allowed by merchants to customers. The respondents conceded that the intended arrangement or understanding would, if completed, contravene ss 45(2)(a)(ii) and 45A of the Act. However, the respondents contended that it was necessary to show that the officials made the statements at the meeting in the expectation that an arrangement or understanding would result from them. Toohey J was prepared to accept that the statements must carry within their terms the potential for an arrangement or understanding but considered that it would introduce an unnecessary and unwarranted element into the notion of attempt to suggest that there must be such an expectation in addition to the intention to bring about the arrangement or understanding.

(2) The Parkfield *case:* The Full Court of the Federal Court of Australia in *Trade Practices Commission v Parkfield Operations Pty Ltd* (1985) ATPR para 40-639 provided further guidance on what constitutes an attempt to make an arrangement or arrive at an understanding.

Parkfield owned and operated petrol stations in the Newcastle and Maitland areas. Parkfield's manager, C, suggested to S, the manager of XL Petroleum Ltd, that XL raise its outlets' petrol prices to 44.8 cents per litre if the other petrol retailers in the area raised their prices to 45.3 cents per litre. Later C informed S that he had got the other retailers to agree to raise their prices to 45.3 cents per litre. S refused to agree to the suggested price increase. The Trade Practices Commission alleged that Parkfield and C had thereby attempted to make an arrangement with XL and other petrol retailers in the area in contravention of the Australian equivalents of ss 27 and 30 of the Commerce Act.

Fox J, at first instance ((1985) ATPR para 40-526), held that the Trade Practices Commission had not established its cases against the respondents and dismissed the application. His Honour thought that the proposal C suggested to S was too nebulous to constitute an arrangement or understanding or a proposal for such. His Honour expressed the view that for conduct to constitute an attempt, the conduct must reach a reasonably advanced stage of carrying out that which is being attempted and that on the evidence before him there still remained much to be done to achieve the arrangement.

The Full Court (Bowen C J, Smithers and Morling J J) overturned Fox J's decision. Following *Tubemakers,* the Full Court held that the Trade Practices Commission only needed to prove that Parkfield intended to make an arrangement between itself, XL and such other petrol retailers as might be persuaded to be parties to it, and that, as the first step in making that arrangement, it attempted to make an arrangement between itself and XL. The Court held that an attempt must involve the taking of a step toward commission of the illegal act and that it is not sufficient that it be merely remotely connected or preparatory to the commission of it. Applying this principle to the facts, the Court held that C's conversations with S were steps toward the making of an agreement with XL and other retailers to raise prices and these conversations were immediately, and not merely remotely, connected with the making of that agreement, or the attempt to make it. One could not reasonably regard the conversations as having any purpose other than progressing the making of an agreement to which C hoped that XL and other retailers would be parties. The Court further held that there was no warrant for holding that the conduct in question must have reached an advanced stage before it can constitute an attempt within the meaning of the Act.

(3) Enforcement policy: In some cases, the enforcement authorities have failed to establish the existence of a price fixing arrangement in circumstances where an attempt charge may well have succeeded. See *Trade Practices Commission v Leslievale Pty Ltd* (1986) ATPR para 40-687; *Trade Practices Commission v J J & Y K Russell Pty Ltd* (1991) ATPR para 41-132; *Commerce Commission v The Wellington Branch of the NZ Institute of Driving Instructors* (1990) 3 NZBLC 101,913. This point will not have been lost on the authorities; in the future we are likely to see greater reliance on the attempt provisions.

41.2.4 The concept of competition

The concept of competition is of fundamental importance to the operation of the Commerce Act 1986. The object of the Act as expressed in the Long Title is "to promote competition in markets within New Zealand".

Section 3(1) defines "competition" as meaning "workable or effective competition". The phrase "effective competition" previously appeared in the objects clause of the Commerce Act 1975, s 2A, which referred, *inter alia*, "to the need" to secure "effective competition" in industry and commerce in New Zealand.

A definition of "workable competition" which has found favour with the New Zealand Courts: see *Auckland Regional Authority* (supra) at p 671; *Fisher & Paykel Ltd v Commerce Commission* (1990) 3 NZBLC 101,655 at p 101,678, is that given by J D Heydon in 1 *Trade Practices Law* (2nd ed 1989) at p 1,548:

> Workable competition means a market framework in which the pressures of other participants (or the existence of potential new entrants) is sufficient to ensure that each participant is constrained to act efficiently and in its planning to take account of those other participants or likely entrants as unknown quantities. To that end there must be an opportunity for each participant or new entrant to achieve an equal footing with the efficient participants in the market by having equivalent access to the means of entry, sources of supply, outlets for product, information, expertise and finance. This is not to say that particular instances of the items on that list must be available to all. That would be impossible. For example, a particular customer is not at any one time freely available to all suppliers. Workable competition exists when there is an opportunity for sufficient influences to exist in any one market which must be taken into account by each participant and which constrains its behaviour.

(1) The Visionhire/Sanyo *discussion of "effective competition":* In a leading merger case under the Commerce Act 1975, *Visionhire/Sanyo* (1984) 4 NZAR 288, the Commerce Commission made the following observations concerning the concept of "effective competition" at p 290:

> It is not necessary in this case to examine in detail the term "effective competition", but broadly it envisages a market structure in which there is an absence of power in any relevant market to raise price and/or decrease services or to exclude entry by others to such market. Some guidance as to factors relevant to determining whether such a market structure exists was given by the Australian Trade Practices Tribunal in the *Queensland Co-operative Milling Association case* (1976) 1 TPC 109 as follows:
>
> "Competition is a process rather than a situation. Nevertheless, whether firms compete is very much a matter of the structure of the markets in which they operate. The elements of market structure which we would stress as needing to be scanned in any case are these: (1) the number and size distribution of independent sellers, especially the degree of market concentration; (2) the height of barriers to entry, that is, the ease with which new firms may enter and secure a viable market; (3) the extent to which the products of the industry are characterised by extreme product differentiation and sales promotion; (4) the character of "vertical relationships' with customers and with suppliers and the extent of vertical integration; and (5) the nature of any formal stable and fundamental arrangements between firms which restrict their ability to function as independent entities."

The Chairman of the Commerce Commission, Mr John Collinge, elaborated on the *Visionhire* statement in an address in September 1984 in which he emphasised that behavioural factors can play an important role in competition analysis:

> [B]ehaviour in the market and the conduct of the participants may influence the determination of the Commission as to whether effective competition exists in any given market. Conduct may therefore be relevant to determining whether the market structure is satisfactory. In adopting this test, the Commission brought New Zealand very much into line with tests adopted in Australia, a result which may not be insignificant with the increasing impact of Closer Economic Relations.

In several subsequent decisions, the Commerce Commission, under both the 1975 and 1986 Acts, has reaffirmed the *Visionhire* formulation of effective competition, although without extending the analysis of the concept in any significant manner.

(2) The Trade Practices Tribunal's discussion of competition in QCMA: One must read the *Visionhire* statement in the context of the Trade Practices Tribunal's decision in *Queensland Co-operative Milling Ass'n (QCMA)* (1976) ATPR para 40-012, which is now universally regarded as the starting point in any discussion of effective competition in the Australasian context.

By stating that "[c]ompetition is a process rather than a situation", the Tribunal is drawing attention to the dynamic aspects of competition resulting from the continual evolvement of new marketing and economic conditions and technological developments with which participants in the market have to contend. For a discussion of the dynamic aspects of competition, see, for example, F Fisher, J McGowan &

J Greenwood, *Folded, Spindled and Mutilated: Economic Analysis and US v IBM* (1983) ch 2; R Brenner, *Competition: the Leapfrogging Game* (1987). This approach is in marked contrast to the static structural situation of the theoretical concept of perfect or pure competition which assumes markets composed of numerous sellers, homogeneous products, free entry and complete information. There are few, if any, markets such as this in the real world; hence the unsuitability of the pure competition model as a workable policy standard.

The Tribunal explained the role of competition and its dynamic features as follows at p 17,245:

> [I]n identifying the existence of competition in particular industries or markets, we must focus upon its economic role as a device for controlling the disposition of society's resources. Thus we think of competition as a mechanism for discovery of market information and for enforcement of business decisions in the light of this information . . . .
>
> This does not mean that we view competition as a series of passive, mechanical responses to "impersonal market forces". There is of course a creative role for firms in devising the new product, the new technology, the more effective service or improved cost efficiency. And there are opportunities and rewards as well as punishments. Competition is a dynamic process; but that process is generated by market pressure from alternative sources of supply and the desire to keep ahead.

Unlike the Commerce Act 1986, the Australian Trade Practices Act 1974 does not define "competition". Nevertheless, the Tribunal in *QCMA* endorsed the concept of workable or effective competition as an appropriate standard for decisionmaking under the Australian Act. The Tribunal commented at pp 17,245-46:

> As was said by the US Attorney-General's National Committee to Study the Antitrust Laws in its Report of 1955 (at p 320): "The basic characteristic of effective competition in the economic sense is that no one seller, and no group of sellers acting in concert has the power to choose its level of profits by giving less and charging more. Where there is workable competition, rival sellers, whether existing competitors or new potential entrants into the field, would keep this power in check by offering or threatening to offer effective inducement . . .".
>
> Or again, as is often said in US antitrust cases, the antithesis of competition is undue market power, in the sense of the power to raise price and exclude entry. That power may or may not be exercised. Rather, where there is significant market power the firm (or group of firms acting in concert) is sufficiently free from market pressures to "administer" its own production and selling policies at its discretion. Firms may be public spirited in their motivation; but if their business conduct is not subject to severe market constraints this is not competition. In such a case there is substituted the values, incentives and penalties of management for the values, incentives and penalties of the market place.

The Tribunal, reflecting contemporary economic and marketing realities, recognised the importance of rivalry in terms of both price and nonprice factors. It stated at p 17, 246:

> Competition expresses itself as rivalrous market behaviour. In the course of these proceedings two rather different emphases were placed upon the most useful form such rivalry can take. On the one hand it was put to us that price

competition is the most valuable and desirable form of competition. On the
other hand it was said that if there was rivalry in other dimensions of business
conduct – in service, in technology, in quality and consistency of product – an
absence of price competition need not be of great concern.

In our view effective competition requires both that prices should be
flexible reflecting the forces of demand and supply and that there should be
independent rivalry in all dimensions of the price - product - service packages
offered to consumers and customers.

Having outlined its views on the appropriate concept of competition to
be employed, the Tribunal then identified the five elements of market
structure which it considered decisionmakers should scan in any particular case. By "market structure" is meant all those competitive characteristics of a market that condition (or constrain) a firm's production and
selling policies: M Brunt, "Economic Overview" in *Monash Trade Practices Lectures* (1975). The five elements the Tribunal listed (which are set
out above in the extract from *Visionhire*) represent the leading elements
of market structure that industrial organisation economists commonly
employ in analyzing the state of competition in a market. See generally
F M Scherer, *Industrial Market Structure and Economic Performance* (2nd
edn, 1980). After listing the criteria, the Tribunal identified barriers to
entry as the most important element of market structure on the ground
that "it is the ease with which firms may enter which establishes the
possibilities of market concentration over time; and it is the threat of the
entry of a new firm or a new plant into a market which operates as the
ultimate regulator of competitive conduct". For recent commentary on
barriers to entry, see P Geroski, R Gilbert & A Jacquemin, *Barriers to Entry
and Strategic Competition* (1990); Schmalensee (1987) 56 Antitrust L J 41;
Salop (1986) 31 Antitrust Bull 551; Ordover & Wall (1988) 2 Antitrust (No
2) 12.

(3) Judicial discussion of competition: The judicial reaction to the *QCMA*
analysis has been very favourable. In the *Ansett/Avis* merger case (1978)
ATPR para 40-017, Northrop J drew upon the *QCMA* criteria and the
decision of the European Court of Justice in *United Brands v Commission*
[1978] ECR 207 in analysing whether a proposed merger between Ansett
Transport Industries Ltd (Ansett) and Avis Rent-a-Car-Systems Pty Ltd
(Avis) would result in Avis being in a position to control or dominate the
Australian car rental market in breach of s 50 of the Trade Practices Act.
Northrop J at p 17,720 identified the following factors as being relevant
to the assessment of dominance:

   (1) The firms operating in the market and the degree of market concentration,
       ie market share.
   (2) The capacity of Avis to determine prices for its services without being
       consistently inhibited in its determinations by other firms.
   (3) The height of barriers to entry.
   (4) The extent to which the products of the industry were characterized by
       extreme product differentiation.
   (5) The character of corporate relationships and the extent of corporate
       integration.

Four of the five factors for assessing dominance outlined by Northrop J
are structural criteria which are for all practical purposes identical with

the structural competition criteria the Tribunal laid down in *QCMA*. The Court estimated Avis' share of the car rental market as between 43-46 per cent with Kay-Hertz and Budget following with 17 and 16 per cent respectively. The Court found that Avis did not have power to determine its prices independently because the smaller operators were offering active competition, including price competition. There were no substantial barriers to entry, and a number of local operators were currently moving onto the national scene. Notwithstanding its advantage in advertising, Northrop J found substitutability between Avis' service and those of the competitors. Having considered these factors, the Court concluded that Avis would not be in a position to dominate the car rental market.

While the *Ansett* decision gave the judicial seal of approval to the approach developed by the Tribunal in *QCMA*, Northrop J extended the analysis by the formulation of a significant conduct criterion, viz the extent to which Avis was "consistently inhibited" by its competitors. This development may account for the Chairman of the Commerce Commission's remarks in September 1984, referred to above, that conduct as well as structure is a relevant factor in determining whether effective competition exists in any given market.

Like their Australian counterparts, the New Zealand Courts have looked to *QCMA* for guidance. The High Court's comments in *Fisher & Paykel* (supra) underscore the importance of the *QCMA* analysis of competition, at p 101,680:

> The relationship between workable competition and market power can be gleaned from a study of the often cited dicta in *QCMA*. We make no apology for not reproducing the familiar expose of competition, not because we disagree with it – on the contrary, we agree wholeheartedly with it, but we think it so well known as to make its quotation unnecessary.

A perceptive understanding of competition as a process was displayed by the High Court in *Tru Tone Ltd v Festival Records Retail Marketing Ltd* (1988) 2 NZBLC 103,081. *Tru Tone* concerned the legality of maximum resale price maintenance on records under ss 27 and 36 of the Commerce Act; retailers challenging the practice argued that records that made it into the "charts" constituted a separate market for the purposes of s 36 of the Act. The Court justifiably rejected this argument holding that even an outstanding popular album's "charting records are too short-lived to qualify as any form of dominance". The Court said at p 103,089:

> We accept the evidence called for the plaintiffs that when an album is charting well a sizeable percentage of popular album purchasers will want that product and will not be prepared to substitute it for some other. But in view of the short average time that such an album remains popular we see the albums which displace it in the chart ratings as clear substitutes. And it is clear from the evidence that at any one time when an album is enjoying popularity, promotion of another is gathering momentum. In our view the places at the top of the charts are a constant battle ground in which rivalrous conduct abounds.

The Court of Appeal affirmed this approach ([1988] 2 NZLR 352). Richardson J elaborated on the dynamic aspects of the industry as follows, at p 360:

Viewed in relation to product and time the single album definition of market ignores commercial realities. It focuses on short run phenomena. It presents a snapshot rather than a moving picture of continuing commercial activity. Supply to distributors is not acquired on an album by album basis but by licensors giving rights to any album produced by the artist or label. In arranging supply the distribution achieves economies of scope in what is a continuing activity. And retailers and consumers along with distributors are dependent on a flow of new albums to join and, in part, to displace existing albums – a process recognised and encouraged in the promotional and pricing arrangements. Promotion is undertaken in accordance with normal competitive practice for the purpose of differentiating one album from a whole range of possible substitutes and the evidence of promotion of particular albums by retailers emphasising price concessions belies the argument that purchasers of albums are not price sensitive. The emphasis on product differentiation arises precisely because there is a range of products competing for the consumer's attention. And the movement of albums in and out of the charts and their constantly shifting positions are clear evidence of the manner in which, and the extent to which substitution takes place.

(4) Relevance of the structure-conduct-performance paradigm: The developments in the case law underscore the basic usefulness of the structure-conduct-performance paradigm in competition analysis. For a discussion of the paradigm in the antitrust context, see Carstensen (1983) 16 UC Davis L Rev 487; Weiss (1979) 127 U Pa L Rev 1104. According to the paradigm, the interplay of various factors – the basic conditions of the market, market structure and the conduct of buyers and sellers – determine performance in a particular industry. The Trade Practices Tribunal incorporated the paradigm in *QCMA* but, arguably, in listing the main elements of market structure as it did, the Tribunal placed too great an emphasis on structure to the neglect of conduct and performance factors. Later cases, particularly the *Ansett/Avis* and *Tru Tone* decisions, have helped remind us that competition is the outcome of a complex interaction of factors involving the whole market environment.

41.2.5 The concept of market

The Commerce Act 1986 makes liability under most of its substantive provisions (ss 27, 28, 36 and 47) depend in one way or another on the identification of a market or markets in which the impugned conduct has injured competition. Even the per se offences of horizontal price fixing (s 30) and exclusionary arrangements (s 29) require a limited market analysis in that those sections require that two or more parties be "in competition with each other". Market definition is also relevant in assessing detriment and public benefit under the various authorisation tests.

Professor Geoffrey Walker attributes the explicit recognition of the market concept in the Australasian legislation to the importance which other jurisdictions, particularly the United States, have accorded the concepts of market definition and market power in recent years: Walker (1980) 11 Fed L Rev 386 at p 387. Since the enactment of the Trade Practices Act in 1974, these concepts have undergone further development in the United States, as witnessed by the promulgation of the US Merger Guidelines in 1982 and 1984 and the increasing tendency for United States Courts to employ market power tests when assessing competitive effect. For a critical review of the contemporary United States developments, see Pitofsky (1990) 90 Colum L Rev 1805.

While the Australasian Courts have drawn on the traditional United States case law on market definition, in the main, they have initially looked to the decisions of the Australian Trade Practices Tribunal for guidance. Reflecting its economist membership, that body adopts an economics-based approach to questions of market definition and market control.

(a) THE TRADE PRACTICES TRIBUNAL'S DEFINITION OF MARKET

As with the related concept of competition, the Trade Practices Tribunal's decision in *QCMA* is the starting point on any discussion of market. The Tribunal in that case made the following fundamental statement (at p 17,247):

> A market is the area of close competition between firms or, putting it a little differently, the field of rivalry between them. . . . Within the bounds of a market there is substitution – substitution between one product and another, and between one source of supply and another, in response to changing prices. So a market is the field of actual and potential transactions between buyers and sellers amongst whom there can be strong substitution, at least in the long run, if given a sufficient price incentive. . . . Whether such substitution is feasible or likely depends ultimately on customer attitudes, technology, distance, and cost and price incentives.
>
> It is the possibilities of such substitution which set the limits upon a firm's ability "to give less and charge more". Accordingly, in determining the outer boundaries of the market we ask a quite simple but fundamental question: If the firm were to "give less and charge more" would there be, to put the matter colloquially, much of a reaction?

The Tribunal expressed the concept more formally in *In re Tooth & Co Ltd; In re Tooheys Ltd* (the *Brewery Ties* case) (1979) ATPR para 40-013 at p 18,196:

> [C]ompetition may proceed not just through the substitution of one product for another in use (substitution in demand) but also through the substitution of one source of supply for another in production or distribution (substitution in supply). The market should comprehend the maximum range of business activities and the widest geographic area within which, if given a sufficient economic incentive, buyers can switch to a substantial extent from one source of supply to another and sellers can switch to a substantial extent from one production plan to another. In an economist's language, both cross-elasticity of demand and cross-elasticity of supply are relevant.

(b) THE STATUTORY DEFINITION OF MARKET

In *Edmonds Food Industries Ltd/W F Tucker Co Ltd* (Commerce Commission Decision 84, 21 June 1984), a merger decision under the Commerce Act 1975, the Commerce Commission laid down some general principles relating to market definition which the Commission has referred to and applied in a number of its subsequent decisions:

> A market has been defined as a field of actual or potential transactions between buyers and sellers amongst whom there can be strong substitution, at least in the long run, if given a sufficient price incentive. In delineating the relevant market in any particular case there is a value judgement which must be made which involves, for example, an assessment of pertinent market

realities such as technology, distance, cost and price incentives; an assessment of the degree of substitutability of products; an appreciation of the fact that a market is dynamic and that potential competition is relevant; and an evaluation of industry viewpoints and public tastes and attitudes. Particularly important in this process is industry recognition (both by supplier and purchaser) and recognition by the consumer. Ultimately the judgment as to the appropriate market – and its delineation by function, product and area – is a question of fact which must be made on the basis of commercial common sense in the circumstances of each case – see, for example, the United Kingdom case of *Wire Ropes* (1964) LR 5 RP 146,204.

The pragmatic nature of the *Edmonds/Tucker* definition appears to have impressed the framers of the Commerce Act for they incorporated the "fact" and "commercial commonsense" components in the statutory definition of market contained in s 3(1) of the 1986 Act as originally enacted. That provision read: "'Market' means a market for goods and services within New Zealand that may be distinguished as a matter of fact and commercial common sense".

In contrast, the Australian statutory definition of market is expressed in more conventional economic terms. Section 4E of the Trade Practices Act, as inserted by the 1977 Amendment, provides:

> For the purposes of this Act, "market" means a market in Australia and, when used in relation to any goods or services, includes a market for those goods or services and other goods or services that are substitutable for, or otherwise competitive with, the first-mentioned goods or services.

In the *Auckland Regional Authority* case (supra), counsel sought to distinguish the two statutory definitions, arguing that the reference to "fact and commercial common sense" in the New Zealand definition meant that a New Zealand Court should give more weight to the views of businesspeople in the market place when defining the relevant boundaries of the market. Barker J had no difficulty in rejecting this proposition, at p 669:

> In my view, that submission is simplistic; the reference in the Act to commercial common sense (as distinct from any other kind of common sense) as the yardstick by which to determine a market is another and more straightforward way of articulating the Australian standard. The matters in the Australian definition must enter the Court's assessment of "fact and common sense". The assessment must be made from a consideration of the composition of and the forces in the market. The perceptions of the participants can only be part of the necessary information available.

His Honour stressed the advantages of New Zealand Courts drawing on the Australian experience, at p 670:

> I should have been sorry to have reached an opposite conclusion and to have held the cases on the Australian definition inappropriate; the impetus for the legislative change in New Zealand in the trade practices area came from the Australia/New Zealand Closer Economic Relations trade agreement (the CER agreement) which substituted for the enforcement machinery of earlier New Zealand trade practices legislation, the Australian Court-centred legislation. In these early days of the operation of the Act in this country, it will be helpful to be able to draw on the Australian experience which, in turn takes into account decisions of the United States Courts on the anti-competition

laws of that country (notably the Sherman Act); those laws provided much of the foundation for the Australian legislation.

A somewhat different approach is evident in the Court of Appeal's judgment in *Tru Tone* (supra). In delivering the judgment for the Court, Richardson J, after citing the definition of market formulated by the Commerce Commission in *Edmonds/Tucker*, commented at p 359:

> In focusing in the definition in s 3(1) on distinguishability as a matter of fact and commercial commonsense the legalisation has carefully avoided giving prominence to any particular criterion. In particular, the test is not substitutability as such, although that will ordinarily be an important consideration; and, as is recognised in the passages cited, "market" is ordinarily regarded as a multi-dimensional concept with dimensions of product, functional level, space and time.

The above passage apparently influenced Holland J's approach to the interpretation of s 3(1) in *Apple Fields Ltd v New Zealand Apple and Pear Marketing Board* (1989) 2 NZBLC 103,564 for, after citing Richardson J's comments in *Tru Tone*, his Honour observed at p 103,577:

> The definition of "market" is not the same as that in the Trade Practices Act in Australia and this renders some of the observations in Australian cases to be of little assistance.

Tipping J in *New Zealand Magic Millions Ltd v Wrightson Bloodstock Ltd* [1990] 1 NZLR 731 also noted the differences between the Australian and New Zealand definitions and cautioned against giving too much weight to substitutability, at p 746:

> While I acknowledge that questions of substitutability are certainly relevant in delineating a market in New Zealand, they are by no means the be all and end all of the exercise and care must be taken not to give too much weight to that or any other aspect. It is a matter of weighing all the relevant considerations and then, against our statutory definition, distinguishing the relevant market as a matter of fact and commercial common sense. Matters pertaining to economics and economic theory are relevant but must be kept in perspective in the light of the direction to the Courts inherent in the definition.

Concern that the New Zealand Courts could interpret the s 3(1) definition as displacing the economic approach in s 4E of the Trade Practices Act undoubtedly explains the legislative decision in the Commerce Amendment Act 1990 to repeal the s 3(1) definition and replace it with a new definition that more closely resembles the Australian one. The new definition contained in s 3(1A) defines "market" as "a reference to a market in New Zealand for goods or services as well as other goods or services that, as a matter of fact and commercial commonsense, are substitutable".

The new definition was the subject of judicial comment in *Telecom Corp of New Zealand Ltd v Commerce Commission* (High Court, Wellington, AP 279/90, 10 December 1991). There, the High Court (Greig J, Mr W J Shaw and Professor M Brunt) did not see s 3(1A) as giving rise to any new change in focus. The Court said, at pp 23-24:

This is the first occasion on which the Court has been required to assess the implications of the amendment.... The practical effect of the revised wording appears to be no more than to make the relevance of economic substitutability explicit. It thus resolves some doubts that had been previously expressed, and confirms the relevance of the main line of New Zealand decisions (such as *Auckland Regional Authority* and *Tru Tone* at first instance and on appeal) and of Australian authorities (such as *QCMA, Tooth and Tooheys, Queensland Wire*). The retention of reference to "commercial commonsense", a term that first appeared in *Edmonds Food Industries Ltd/W F Tucker & Co Ltd* (Commerce Commission, Decision No 84), affirms the traditional New Zealand emphasis upon the need for a commercially realistic factual base. We see no source of conflict or tension in the juxtaposition of the two elements, substitutability and commercial commonsense, in this formulation. Compare Barker J in *Auckland Regional Authority* at 669-670.

The Court then noted that in both Australia and New Zealand, the Courts had said, in effect, that a mechanical reliance upon substitution criteria in a contextual vacuum was not sufficient. In endorsing the view that "market" is an instrumental concept, the Court commented, at p 33:

Hence the boundaries should be drawn by reference to the conduct at issue, the terms of the relevant section or sections, and the policy of the statute. Some judgment is required, bearing in mind that "market" is an instrumental concept designed to clarify the sources and potential effects of market power that may be possessed by an enterprise. In the words of Mason C J and Wilson J in *Queensland Wire* at p 187: "Defining the market and evaluating the degree of power in that market, are part of the same process....". As to the degree of substitutability that is pertinent in a particular case, the Full Court of the Australian Federal Court offers a test for cases regarding monopolisation and merger: one should not use a definition so wide (eg the "hot beverage market" for tea and coffee) that "it would thwart the objectives of provisions such as ss 46 and 50 of the Act". (*Arnotts* case at 576.)

(c) DIMENSIONS OF THE MARKET
Although Courts often confine their analysis of the market to the product and geographic dimensions, a two-dimensional focus may ignore important questions. For as Professor Maureen Brunt explains in *Competition Law and Policy in New Zealand* (R Ahdar ed 1991) ch 9 at p 130:

A market has product, space, function and time dimensions. Between what set of *products* can customers and suppliers switch? Within what geographic *space*? Is the focus to be on the selling *function*, and how many levels or stages of production and distribution is it appropriate to distinguish in order to assess the scope for substitution through trade? Finally, how much *time* is needed for customers and suppliers to make their adjustments in response to economic incentives?

The four dimensions Professor Brunt identifies merit separate attention.

(1) *Product market:* Like their overseas counterparts, the Australasian Courts and tribunals recognise substitutability as a central criterion for determining which products are to be included in the relevant market. The enactment of s 3(1A) has resolved any doubts concerning the appropriateness of this approach in the New Zealand context.

(a) Demand substitution – The classic case concerning substitutability is *United States v E I du Pont de Nemours & Co* (the *Cellophane* case) 351 US 377 (1956) where the United States Supreme Court adopted "cross-elasticity of demand" and "reasonable interchangeability" of use as product market tests. At issue in the case was the question of whether the relevant product market was cellophane (in which 75 per cent of the sales were from du Pont's production) or flexible packaging materials (in which cellophane constituted less than 20 per cent of the sales). The Court, in a majority opinion, held that cellophane's distinct physical characteristics were not sufficient to constitute a product market, so long as buyers might readily use other market alternatives for their purposes. The Court reasoned at pp 394-95, 400:

> Because most products have possible substitutes we cannot . . . give "that infinite range" to the definition of substitutes. Nor is it a proper interpretation of the Sherman Act to require that products be fungible to be considered in the relevant market.
>
> . . . .
>
> . . . In considering what is the relevant market for determining the control of price and competition, no more definite rule can be declared than that commodities reasonably interchangeable by consumers for the same purpose make up this "part of the trade or commerce", monopolisation of which may be illegal.
>
> . . . .
>
> An element for consideration as to cross-elasticity of demand between products is the responsiveness of the sales of one product to price changes of the other. If a slight decrease in the price of cellophane causes a considerable number of customers of other flexible wrappings to switch to cellophane, it would be an indication that a high cross-elasticity of demand exists between them; that the products compete in the same market.

The Court formulated the following test at p 404: a "market is composed of products that have reasonable interchangeability for the purposes for which they are produced - price, use and qualities considered".

Applying these tests, the Court found that a "very considerable degree of functional interchangeability" existed between cellophane and other flexible wrappings. On this point, the Court emphasised that sales of cellophane for several different uses were price sensitive, ie in response to price and quality changes, many customers switched from cellophane to other materials. The Court concluded that the market in question was not the market for cellophane only but for all flexible wrapping materials.

Chief Justice Warren, writing for the minority, argued that the relevant market was cellophane. He pointed to the different physical components of the products and, more importantly, to the higher price of cellophane. Warren CJ commented at p 418: "We cannot believe that buyers, practical businessmen, would have bought cellophane in increasing amounts over a quarter of a century if close substitutes were available at from one-seventh to one-half cellophane's price". The Chief Justice also challenged the conclusion of the majority that there was great price sensitivity to sales of cellophane; his Honour levelled criticism at the majority for not taking into account the conduct of sellers. The Chief

Justice noted at p 417 that "[p]roducers of glassine and waxed paper . . . displayed apparent indifference to du Pont's repeated and substantial price cuts" and that internal reports of du Pont indicated that du Pont considered that the sole competition for cellophane "will come from competitive cellophane and from non-cellophane films made by us or others": at p 418.

While economists have confirmed the minority's view that du Pont had monopoly power, the *Cellophane* market definition test (reasonable interchangeability based on cross-elasticity of demand) remains the basic test for market delineation purposes. However, in applying that test, the majority made a logical error which has become known as "the *Cellophane* trap". Professors Posner and Easterbrook (now Judges) explain the error in their casebook, *Antitrust : Cases, Economic Notes and Other Materials* (2nd edn, 1981) at p 362:

> To include products that were good substitutes for cellophane *at the price at which cellophane was being sold by its sole producer* begged the question whether the producer had a monopoly. If he had a monopoly and was charging a monopoly price, that would make substitutes attractive which at a competitive price would be considered grossly inferior alternatives. In fact it seems almost certain that the cross-elasticity of demand between cellophane and other flexible packaging materials for many important uses would have been very low had cellophane been sold at a price substantially nearer its cost.

To avoid the *Cellophane* trap, decisionmakers should ideally examine substitution by reference to competitive prices rather than prevailing price, although this may not always be administratively practical. Awareness of the trap, however, should alert decisionmakers to an analytic snare that they might otherwise overlook.

Australian commentators argue that the application of the test of cross-elasticity or substitutability should be in terms of *close* substitutes, in preference to the wider "reasonable interchangeability" test articulated in *Cellophane*: see, for example, Walker (supra) at p 399. The Trade Practices Tribunal has explicitly and consistently defined the product market in terms of close substitutes. *See Re Tooth & Co Ltd; Re Tooheys Ltd* (supra) at p 18,196; *Re Howard Smith Industries* (1977) ATPR para 40-023 at p 17,336; *QCMA* (supra) at p 17,247. The New Zealand Courts are likely to follow the same approach. For example, the High Court in *Hoyts Corporation v Commerce Commission* (High Court, Auckland, CL 44/91, 17 December 1991, Henry J and R G Blunt Esq) recently said at p 14:

> The term "close substitute" was used by the Commission and by both counsel in their submissions, and although that qualification is not expressed in the statutory formulation it would seem to capture its intent.

Although the data necessary to prepare precise cross-elasticity estimates is usually not available, this is not fatal as it is possible to use the notions of response elasticities without undertaking quantitative measurement. Trade witnesses' descriptions of past trends, and questions designed to elicit the likely consumer and rival producer "reaction" in the event of a price rise are likely to suffice for purposes of market definition.

(b) Supply substitution – Courts and antitrust authorities in a number of jurisdictions are increasingly acknowledging the role of supply substitution in the market definition process. Professor F M Scherer (supra) at p 60 explains the basic rationale:

> Groups of firms making completely nonsubstitutable products may nevertheless be meaningful competitors if they employ essentially similar skills and equipment and if they can quickly move into each other's product lines should the profit lure beckon.

The Trade Practices Tribunal has repeatedly acknowledged the relevance of elasticity of supply. In *Re Howard Smith* (supra) the Tribunal said at p 17,336:

> [A]n important consideration in identifying a market is the ease of substitution by suppliers as well as by buyers. In other words, can suppliers readily substitute one type or quality of product or service for another or can they vary the quantities supplied at different locations if there are differences in the prices which they can obtain at those locations?

Similarly, in the *Brewery Ties* case (supra), the Tribunal noted at p 18,198 that because "producers have a significant degree of flexibility in shifting their output as between the bulk and packaged forms" this warranted including both forms of beer in the same product market.

The High Court of Australia in *Queensland Wire Industries Pty Ltd v Broken Hill Pty Co Ltd* (1989) 167 CLR 177 endorsed the relevance of substitution in supply. Toohey J, after referring to s 4E and the test of interchangeability of products on the demand side, said at p 210:

> [I]n delineating the scope of the product market demand substitutability has often been emphasised at the expense of supply substitutability.
> But this does not mean that supply substitutability is irrelevant to the task of market definition: see *Europemballage Corp and Continental Can Co Inc v E C Commission* [1973] 1 ECR 215, [1973] 12 CMLR 199. Rather, the definition of the relevant market requires a consideration of substitutability both on the demand and on the supply side.

His Honour then noted the previous Australian decisions where the concept had been recognised and referred to some of the American and EEC literature.

Dawson J also made reference to the concept at p 199:

> In setting the limits of a market the emphasis has historically been placed upon what is referred to as the "demand side", but more recently the "supply side" has also come to be regarded as significant. The basic test involves the ascertainment of both supply and demand, that is to say, the extent to which the supply of or the demand for a particular product responds to change in the price of another product. Cross-elasticities of supply and demand reveal the degree to which one product may be substituted for another, an important consideration in any definition of a market.

The *Telecom* decision (supra) reaffirmed the relevance of supply side substitution in the New Zealand context.

Supply substitution is closely related to the ease of entry. Both involve a switchover of production facilities. One can distinguish them by the time and difficulty necessary to achieve such a switchover. Professor Scherer (supra) at pp 60-61 addresses the problem as follows:

How quickly must firms be able to shift over between products to be classified in the same industry? Given a long enough period and sufficient investment, shifts in production activity more accurately described as "new entry" than as "substitution" can take place. A distinction between substitutability in production and ease of entry (ie where barriers to entry are minimal) must be drawn. At the risk of being somewhat arbitrary we should probably draw the line to include as substitutes on the production side only existing capacity that can be shifted in the short run, ie without significant new investment in plant, equipment, and worker training.

The issue discussed by Scherer arose in *Telecom* (supra). The case involved an unsuccessful appeal against the determination of the Commerce Commission, Decision No 254 (17 October 1990), which declined the authorisation of the acquisition by the appellant, Telecom, of management rights for the radio frequency spectrum AMPS-A. AMPS is an abbreviation of Advanced Mobile Phone System. The Commission found that Telecom's ownership and control of the Public Switched Telephone Network (PSTN) gave it a dominant position in both the voice telephony (fixed) market and the voice telephony (mobile) market. It considered that the acquisition of AMPS-A by Telecom would strengthen its dominance in the voice telephony (mobile) market. It declined to grant authorisation as, in its view, the detriments outweighed any public benefit. On appeal, counsel for Telecom submitted, *inter alia*, that the Commission failed to take a long-run approach leading it to focus only on mobile telephone technology actually operating in the New Zealand commercial market at the time of the decision, rather than including the numerous alternative technologies which were either currently available or are on a development path. Counsel submitted that if the purpose of the exercise was to assess the market power of an incumbent, one should extend the market on the supply side to include both substitution in production and entirely new entry in order that all relevant market constraints be considered. The High Court rejected the validity of this approach at pp 38-39:

> [I]n accordance with standard procedure in litigation of this type, the timeframe for market definition is not identical with the timeframe for assessing market constraints when account is taken of the potential for new entry. The phrase in common use "to enter a market" contemplates that market boundaries are placed about buyers and sellers already in existence. We include within the market those sources of supply that come about from deploying existing production and distribution capacity but stop short of including supplies arising from entirely new entry. Thus "the long run" in market definition does not refer to any particular length of calendar time but to the operational time required for organising and implementing a redeployment of existing capacity in response to profit incentives.

However, the Court did accept that the Commerce Commission in its general orientation and its approach to market definition adopted too short a time perspective. While endorsing the Commission's treatment of the mobile telephone service as a product market distinct from the fixed telephone service, (the high price of the cellular service was decisive in making this distinction), the Court was critical of the Commission for not canvassing explicitly the new wireless-based products and services for inclusion in the relevant markets.

(2) Geographic market: The geographic dimension of the market is concerned with the appropriate area within which decision-makers should measure market power. Professor Herbert Hovenkamp in *Economics and Federal Antitrust Law* (1985) at p 70 defines the concept as follows:

> The relevant geographic market for antitrust purposes is some "section of the country" in which a firm can increase its price without (1) large numbers of its customers immediately turning to alternative supply sources outside the area; or (2) producers outside the area quickly flooding the area with substitute products. If either of these things happens when the firm attempts to charge a supracompetitive price then the estimated geographic market has been drawn too narrowly and a larger market must be drawn to include these outside suppliers.

The scope of a geographic market may be as small as a city (or even a part thereof), a region or nationwide. Increasingly, commentators and overseas enforcement authorities are recognising that markets may extend beyond national markets. Section 3(1A) of the Commerce Act refers to a market as being one within New Zealand; however, s 3(3) specifically provides that in determining the effect of competition in such a market decisionmakers are to take account of "all factors that affect competition in that market including competition from goods or services supplied or likely to be supplied by persons not resident or not carrying on business in New Zealand". These requirements appear to allow appropriate account to be taken of foreign competition while restraining the jurisdiction of the Commerce Act to New Zealand markets. Such a view, however, may need to be qualified by virtue of the interpretation given to s 3(3) by Tipping J in *New Zealand Magic Millions Ltd v Wrightson Bloodstock Ltd* [1990] 1 NZLR 731 at p 759. According to his Honour, s 3(3) requires the potential goods or services to be supplied *in New Zealand*; it is not sufficient, for example, if the goods or services are currently being supplied in Australia by persons not resident or carrying on business in New Zealand.

Geographic market definition is not an abstract exercise, but depends upon the nature of the product and the competitive conditions facing the particular firm or group of firms: B Klein in *27th Annual Advanced Antitrust Seminar : Mergers, Markets and Joint Ventures* (1987) at p 255. Economists consider firms to be in the same geographic market if they are so located that they are able to exert a restraining influence on each other's exercise of market power. The type of evidence used to define geographic markets includes: the location of buyers; the sales patterns of the relevant firms; the excess capacity of firms outside the immediate geographic area that are capable of shifting production; and market barriers that might limit the ability to sell in particular areas (including transportation and distribution costs, customer convenience, and customer preferences for the products of particular customers). As with the relevant product market, elasticities of demand and supply are important in determining the relevant geographic market.

For an important Australian case exploring acceptable approaches to determining the relevant geographic market, see *Trade Practices Commission v Australian Meat Holdings* (1988) ATPR para 40-876, and on appeal (1989) ATPR para 40-932.

(3) Functional dimensions: The functional dimensions of the market (such as manufacturing or importing, wholesaling or retailing) may play an important role in overall market analysis. *Telecom* (supra) is an example of a case where functional dimensions were important. There, the High Court outlined the following principles governing functional identification and their application to the case before it at pp 37-38:

> If we ask what functional divisions are appropriate in any market definition exercise the answer, plainly enough, must be whatever will best expose the play of market forces, actual and potential, upon buyers and sellers. Whenever successive stages of production and distribution can be co-ordinated by market transactions, there is no difficulty : there will be a series of markets linking actual and potential buyers and sellers at each stage. And again, when pronounced efficiencies of vertical integration dictate that successive stages of production and distribution must be co-ordinated by internal managerial processes, there can be no market. But a feature of this application is the presence of the integrated PSTN [Public Switched Telephone Network] linking all members of the community in innumerable two-party and multi-party communications; and there is also the possibility of some market transactions along the way, ie in interconnections with duplicate or by-pass networks and in leased circuits as permitted by the incidence of economics of scale and scope.
>
> In this case (and with no artificial regulatory requirements limiting the freedom of entry to particular segments of the network, as in the United States) we think it best to regard the functional delineation of the standard telephone services as the whole PSTN, comprising the largely fixed facilities for the supply of local, national and international service to households, firms and interconnected suppliers (such as Clear). The PSTN comprises both the trunking network and the local loop.

For the mobile telephone service, however, the Court distinguished three functional levels. First, network operation and service supply such as that conducted by Telecom Cellular Ltd, providing service, including air time, on a wholesale basis for Telecom Approved Service Providers (TASPs). Second, distribution of connections, continuing access and usage, such as that provided by the four "service providers", the TASPs. Finally, the retailing of mobile service contracts and hand sets such as that conducted by the over 150 Telecom dealers.

The Court found the Commission's market definition inadequate in its treatment of the functional dimension of the market. In particular, it was critical of the Commission for its failure to identify the PSTN as the fundamental ingredient of the standard telephone service and, also, for making no reference to the various functional levels in the provision of the mobile service. The Court indicated that its own findings led it to give the PSTN greater prominence in its decision than did the Commerce Commission. It also indicated that wholesale distribution and retailing were of some relevance in its assessment of dominance in the mobile telephone market.

(4) Temporal dimension: Every market definition presents a question of time: over what period should one assess the degree of substitutability in defining a market? In the *Brewery Ties* case (supra), the Tribunal explained at p 18,196 that it was concerned with substitution possibilities in the longer run:

It is plain that the longer the period allowed for likely customer and supplier adjustments to economic incentives, the wider the market delineated. In our judgment, given the policy objectives of the legislation, it serves no useful purpose to focus attention upon a short-run, transitory situation. We consider we should be basically concerned with substitution possibilities, in the longer run. This does not mean we seek to prophesy the shape of the future – to speculate upon how community tastes or institutions or technology might change. Rather, we ask of the evidence what is likely to happen to patterns of consumption and production were existing suppliers to raise price or, more generally, offer a poorer deal. For the market is the field of actual or potential rivalry between firms.

As we have seen, the High Court in *Telecom* was concerned with the time element. The Court, after having rejected Telecom's argument that supply substitution and new entry should both be taken into account for market definition purposes, addressed the question of whether its approach took sufficient account of the dynamics of the telecommunications industry (at p 39):

> The question arises as to whether the exclusion of entry possibilities from market definition gives adequate recognition to the dynamic forces playing about this unique industry. We think it does. Market definition is but a first step, albeit an important step, in the analysis of dominance, detriment and public benefit. We would not wish to deny that technological change can transform market boundaries, that the implementation of technological change by business conduct can undermine market structures. But if market boundaries are subject to change, it does not mean that they are non-existent. What is essential is that market boundaries should be described in terms that do not unwittingly preclude consideration of prospects for new entry, as would, for example, a description of a market as the cellular telephone services market, rather than the mobile telephone services market; and further that the consideration of constraints upon market incumbents, as is required by s 3(8), should pay adequate and appropriate regard to dynamic forces.
>
> Supply substitutability and new entry can be closely related. (Indeed, we are conscious that in the extreme case of "perfect contestability", in the language of economics, with "hit and run entry" associated with "zero sunk costs" supply substitutability and "zero entry" are indistinguishable.) Just as it is a matter of judgment and of analytical convenience as to precisely where to draw the market boundary about substitutes in demand, so it can also be a matter of judgment and of analytical convenience as to precisely where to draw the market boundary, about existing supply "capacity". In the case before us . . . we think it appropriate to view the core "capacity" possessed by an incumbent in the mobile telephone business as usage of relevant spectrum, network facilities and wireless technology in New Zealand.

41.3 THE GENERAL PROHIBITION SECTION - s 27

41.3.1 Introduction

(a) BACKGROUND

Section 27 of the Commerce Act is the catch-all provision: the section applies to all types of anti-competitive arrangements whether they be horizontal or vertical. Unlike ss 29 and 30, it does not matter that none of the parties are in competition with each other; there must, however, be duality of action in the form of a contract, arrangement or understanding. In the absence of this element, the section has no application.

The section has much in common with s 1 of the Sherman Act which prohibits "[e]very contract, combination ... or conspiracy, in restraint of trade or commerce ...". One significant difference between the New Zealand and American provisions is that s 27 does not limit itself to provisions which are restrictive in nature; the prohibition applies to both restrictive and non-restrictive conduct. The key question under s 27 is whether the provision has the purpose or effect of substantially lessening competition in a market.

The section is based on s 45 of the Australian Trade Practices Act 1974. In its original form, s 45 was worded in a manner similar to s 1 of the Sherman Act in that it prohibited contracts, arrangements or understandings "in restraint of trade or commerce". Those responsible for the drafting of the original version of s 45 no doubt intended "restraint of trade" to have a meaning similar to its counterpart in s 1 of the Sherman Act and not the narrower meaning that the words "covenant in restraint of trade" have at common law. The High Court of Australia, however, in *Quadramain Pty Ltd v Sevastapel Investments Pty Ltd* (1976) 133 CLR 390 opted for the common law meaning, thus importing into s 45 all the technical limitations of the doctrine of restraint of trade at common law. The *Quadramain* decision led to a major redrafting of s 45. In the new version of s 45, enacted in 1977, the draftsperson made no reference to "restraint of trade" or related concepts (cf the recommendation of the Swanson Committee Report (August 1986) at para 4,11.8)). Instead, s 45 incorporated a test of anti-competitiveness which applies to every provision whatever the nature of the agreement or provision may be. To ensure that provisions in relation to covenants annexed to or running with an estate or interest in land would be subject to the Act, the draftsperson added new provisions to s 45 replicating to a large degree the prohibitions and exemptions applying to provisions in contracts, arrangements and understandings.

The New Zealand legislation follows the Australian approach but the draftsperson has simplified the drafting and has separated out the various prohibitions in the form of separate sections. Section 27 contains the general prohibition applying to contracts, arrangements and understandings while s 28 applies a similar prohibition to covenants. The analysis of the s 27 test of anti-competitiveness is equally applicable to s 28.

(b) THE STATUTORY PROVISIONS
Section 27 of the Commerce Act provides:

(1) No person shall enter into a contract or arrangement, or arrive at an understanding, containing a provision that has the purpose, or has or is likely to have the effect, of substantially lessening competition in a market.
(2) No person shall give effect to a provision of a contract, arrangement, or understanding that has the purpose, or has or is likely to have the effect, of substantially lessening competition in a market.
(3) Subsection (2) of this section applies in respect of a contract or arrangement entered into, or an understanding arrived at, whether before or after the commencement of this Act.
(4) No provision of a contract, whether made before or after the commencement of this Act, that has the purpose, or has or is likely to have the effect, of substantially lessening competition in a market is enforceable.

41.3.2 Analysis of s 27

(a) SOME PRELIMINARY DEFINITIONS

(1) Person: Section 27 is addressed to "persons". Section 2(1) defines "person" as involving "a local authority and any association of persons whether incorporated or not". Trade and professional bodies are obviously an "association of persons" and hence a person for s 27 purposes. The conduct of such bodies as well as their constitutions, rules and codes of ethics may be open to attack under s 27. Members of such bodies may easily become parties to anti-competitive arrangements resulting from recommendations and decisions of general meetings and ruling bodies relating to such matters as price dissemination schemes, terms and conditions of trading or methods of marketing, credit reporting schemes, product certification programmes, and rules governing membership qualifications and expulsions. Note the special deeming provisions in s 2(8)(a) and (b) which overcome any technical difficulties that might otherwise arise in imposing liability on members. See also *Re Wellington Fencing Materials Association* [1960] NZLR 1121 which suggests that the concepts of arrangement and understanding will encompass a wide range of association activity.

The decision of the Commerce Commission in *Re Speedway Control Board of New Zealand (Inc)* (1990) 2 NZBLC (Com) 104,521 has revealed that non-profit organisations such as sporting bodies may face problems under s 27 if anti-competitive conduct is involved.

It is well-established under company law that a company's articles of association constitute a contract between the company and each of its shareholders and between the shareholders themselves. For a recent case where the Federal Court of Australia held that a provision in a company's articles of association was anti-competitive in terms of the Australian equivalent of s 27, see *Eastern Express Pty Ltd v General Newspapers Pty Ltd* (1991) ATPR para 41-128.

(2) "Enter into" and "arrive at": The Act does not define the term "enter into". It can be contrasted with the Australian equivalent term "make". Prior to the 1977 amendment of s 45(2), the Australian legislation employed the words "entered into". The 1977 amendment deleted "entered into" and substituted "arrived at". In addition, the amendment gave an expansive definition of "arrived at", viz "arrive at" in relation to an understanding, includes reach or enter into": s 4(1). A similar definition appears in s 2(1) of the Commerce Act. The terms in the definition were the subject of judicial comment in *Trade Practices Commission v Nicholas Enterprises Pty Ltd* (1979) ATPR para 40-126 where Fisher J said at p 18,347:

> It may well be that the notion of "entering into an understanding" postulates the concept of this occurring at a particular moment of time between two persons in each others presence whereas an understanding may be arrived at over a subsequent period when, for example, by a series of acts the proposal is adopted by the other party.

(3) "Give effect to": By s 27(2) and (3), the parties are prohibited from giving effect to the provision of a contract, arrangement or understand-

ing, whether entered into or arrived at before or after the commencement of the Act. Section 2(1) defines "give effect to" as follows:

> "Give effect to", in relation to a provision of a contract, arrangement, or understanding, includes –
>> (a) Do an act or thing in pursuance of or in accordance with that provision;
>> (b) Enforce or purport to enforce that provision.

In *Tradestock Pty Ltd v TNT (Management) Pty Ltd* (1978) ATPR para 40-056, Smithers J made the following comment at p 17,571 on the equivalent Australian definition:

> It is to be observed that an act done by way of implementation of a contract, arrangement or understanding would necessarily be done in "pursuance thereof". If the only acts struck at by the Act are those done by way of implementation of the contract, arrangement or understanding then there is no work left to be done by the words "or in accordance with". And there is good reason for thinking that those words are intended to cover the situation where what is done is or may be done for reasons other than to implement the understanding.

(4) Why is s 27(4) limited to contracts?: The reader will note that s 27(4) only makes contracts, and not arrangements or understandings unenforceable. Of the three types of agreement, only a contract is a legally enforceable agreement. Thus, it was unnecessary for the draftsperson to include arrangements or understandings in the subsection as these would not be enforceable in a Court of law anyway.

(b) NEED FOR A CONTRACT, ARRANGEMENT OR UNDERSTANDING
As previously mentioned, for s 27 to apply there must be a contract, arrangement or understanding. See "Fundamental Concepts", 41.2, for a discussion of these terms.

(c) PURPOSE OR EFFECT
The prohibition will apply if a provision of an arrangement has the prohibited *purpose* or *effect* or is *likely to have* the prohibited effect. A plaintiff needs to satisfy only one of these limbs. If a provision has the prohibited purpose, it does not matter that the purpose is not achieved, or was unachievable. Alternatively, if the provision has or is likely to have the prohibited effect, that suffices, irrespective of whether it has the prohibited purpose or not.

(1) Purpose: As we shall see, the meaning and nature of "purpose" is a recurrent theme in the analysis of most of the restrictive trade practices provisions in Part II of the Act.

(a) The meaning of purpose – To date, the most detailed discussion of the meaning of purpose under the Commerce Act is that of the High Court (McGechan J and Mr G Blunt) in *Union Shipping NZ Ltd v Port Nelson* [1990] 2 NZLR 662 at p 707.

> The concept of anticompetitive "purpose" arises under both ss 27 and 36. Under the statutory definition in s 2(5) "purpose" is not confined to "sole

purpose". Engaging in multi-purpose conduct which includes that anticompetitive purpose, will suffice as long as that anticompetitive purpose is "substantial". "Substantial" means "real or of substance". Like so many mental concepts, the reference to "purpose" has its difficulties. The word is not merely "intention". Intention to do an act, which is known will have anticompetitive consequences, in itself is not enough. "Purpose" implies object or aim. The requirement is that "the conduct producing the consequences was motivated or inspired by a wish for the occurrence of the consequences": Donald and Heydon *Trade Practices Law* (1989) para 5-400 at p 2,621.

(b) Nature of the purpose test – The High Court also drew attention to the difference of judicial opinion as to whether "purpose" was to be ascertained objectively or subjectively. The reader is referred to the "Exclusionary Provisions", 41.4, and "Use of a Dominant Position", 41.6, parts of this Chapter for a full discussion of this question.

This part of the commentary will focus on the New Zealand judicial discussion of the objective versus subjective approach under s 27. The matter arose in *Auckland Regional Authority v Mutual Rental Cars (Auckland) Airport Ltd* [1987] 2 NZLR 647 where Barker J said at p 664:

> Section 2(5)(a) provides that a provision is deemed to have had or to have a particular purpose if it was included in the understanding or arrangement for the purpose or purposes that included that purpose and that purpose was a substantial purpose. The subsection provides for an objective test, see *Dandy Power Equipment Pty Ltd v Mercury Marine Pty Ltd* (1982) ATPR para 40-315; (1982) 44 ALR 173, at p 267.

Smithers J in that case referred to the equivalent provision in the Australian Act as needing to be interpreted objectively. He relied on tax cases in which the subjective purpose, motive or intention of a taxpayer was held irrelevant in interpreting tax evasion legislation which was concerned with the character of acts done and of transactions.

His Honour made these remarks in the context of s 29 but later in his judgment he affirmed that they also applied to s 27:

> "Purpose" under s 27 must be interpreted objectively as for s 29 . . . . I note Smithers J at p 207 noted – that a plaintiff will be able to prove anticompetitive purpose "if it proves that the overt acts done in the course of engaging in the conduct were intrinsically of such a character that it is proper to infer therefrom that the purpose of the engaging in those acts was substantially to lessen competition in a relevant market".

One can find support for Barker J's view of purpose in the High Court's decision in *Tru Tone Ltd v Festival Records Ltd* (1988) 2 NZBLC 103,081 at p 103,092, although the Court in that case was satisfied on both subjective and objective tests that the defendant's purpose was not anti-competitive.

The Commerce Commission's majority determination in *Re Fisher & Paykel Ltd (No 2)* (1989) 2 NZBLC (Com) 104,377 discussed the nature of the purpose test in s 27 and opted for the objective approach. On appeal, the High Court (Barker J and Mr G Blunt) considered that the majority was right in holding such a view: *Fisher & Paykel Ltd v Commerce Commission* (1990) 3 NZBLC 101,655 at p 101,663.

There is still much doubt, however, whether the objective approach is the correct one. Holland J in the High Court in *Apple Fields Ltd v NZ Apple and Pear Marketing Board* (1989) 2 NZBLC 103,564, after noting the conflicting New Zealand and Australian authorities, made the following observations on purpose in the context of s 27 at p 103,578:

> The use of both the words "purpose" and "effect" in the one sentence tends to support the view that "purpose" means what was intended to result whereas "effect" means what is likely to result but it must always be borne in mind that the statute is speaking of the purpose or likely effect of the provision contained in the arrangement rather than the arrangement itself or the parties to the arrangement.

The High Court in *Union Shipping* (supra) canvassed the authorities in some detail, but focused its attention primarily on the purpose test in s 36. The Court did, however, draw attention at p 708 to the fact that Smithers J qualified his remarks in *Dandy Power* but that his Honour's qualifications were not included in the passage cited by Barker J in *Auckland Regional Authority*.

As well as the doubts raised in the New Zealand case law, the great bulk of the Australian authority favours a subjective approach to purpose in the context of the Australian equivalents of ss 27 and 29. The "Exclusionary Provisions", 41.4, commentary canvasses the Australian case law.

Even if the Courts opt for a subjective interpretation of purpose, this will not prevent them drawing the necessary inferences from conduct and other circumstances, as well as relying on direct evidence from the parties themselves.

(c) Difference between s 27 anti-competitive purpose and s 36 exclusionary purpose – Plaintiffs will sometimes allege that conduct has both an anti-competitive purpose in terms of s 27 as well as one or more of the exclusionary purposes listed in s 36(1)(a)-(c).

The Courts have indicated that a finding of purpose under s 36 does not necessarily mean that the purpose limb of s 27 is also satisfied. This is seen in *Union Shipping* (supra). That case involved a claim by a shipping company and an associated stevedoring company (USSL) that the actions of a port company, Port Nelson Ltd (PNL), in seeking to impose a contract on USSL requiring the latter to use PNL forklifts and drivers, or to pay a wharf user levy, contravened ss 27 and 36 of the Commerce Act. The Court found that PNL was in a dominant position and that one of its purposes in seeking to impose the terms was to prevent or deter USSL from engaging in competitive conduct in a market in which stevedores operate in Nelson. This constituted a breach of s 36(1)(b). The Court said that the finding of purpose meant that the likely effect on USSL would be to prevent or deter it from engaging in competitive conduct. But the Court distinguished injury to USSL from injury to competition as a whole. Although USSL held some 90 per cent of the Nelson stevedoring market, there were other potentially significant operators, past and present. Barriers to entry were low and labour was readily available. While USSL adduced some evidence of likely detrimental effects upon itself, the Court found the evidence to be limited and general in nature and did not extend beyond USSL. The Court concluded that USSL had not fulfilled the onus on it of establishing a sufficient likelihood that PNL's actions, if successful, would substantially lessen competition in the market as a whole. The Court, therefore, found that PNL had not breached s 27.

The same issue arose in *ASX Operations Pty Ltd v Pont Data Australia Pty Ltd* (1991) ATPR para 41-069. There, the Full Federal Court of Australia (Lockhart, Gummow and von Doussa JJ) considered an appeal in respect of the Trial Judge's finding that the Australian Stock Exchange (ASX) and its subsidiary, ASX Operations Ltd (ASXO), in imposing particular contractual terms in their agreements with Pont Data, had breached s 46(1)(b) and (c) of the Trade Practices Act (corresponding to s 36(1)(a) and (b) of the Commerce Act). Having made these findings in respect of s 46, the Trial Judge said that the agreements in question contravened the anti-competitive purpose limbs of s 45(2). The Full Court disagreed with the Trial Judge that one could make such an inference. In commenting on the relationship between purpose as used in s 45(2) and s 46, the Full Court said at p 52,068:

> Subsection 45(2) is more narrowly drawn than para 46(1)(b) in the sense that when read with subsec 45(3), one is concerned to ask whether the purpose was one of substantially lessening competition in any market in which ASX or ASXO supplies or acquires goods or services or would, but for the provisions in question, supply or acquire them, or be likely to do so. As his Honour pointed out, the reference in subsec 45(2) to the lessening of competition is to be read as including a reference to preventing or hindering it. Nevertheless, the purpose must be one of *substantially* lessening competition, in the sense we have given that term earlier in these reasons.

The Full Court found that as the contravention of s 46(1)(b) was not supported on the evidence, on the facts of the case it followed that there could be no purpose of substantially lessening competition in terms of s 45(2). The Full Court did uphold the Trial Judge's finding in respect of s 46(1)(c), but was not prepared to infer from this that the agreements had the purpose of substantially lessening competition in the broader sense of s 45. The Court did, however, find that the agreements had a substantial anti-competitive effect under s 45(2).

(2) Likely effect: It is important to note that the effect limb of s 27 has two components: *actual effect* and *likely effect*. A plaintiff may invoke either or both. Whether an arrangement has the relevant effect or likely effect is a question of fact in each case: *Re Weddel Crown Corp Ltd* (1987) 1 NZBLC (Com) 104,200 at p 104,212. Actual results are relevant when one is considering the "effect" of an arrangement whereas "likely effect" involves considering results that may happen. The degree of likelihood of the results occurring is thus of primary importance.

A leading New Zealand case on "likely" in the context of competition law is *Air New Zealand v Commerce Commission* [1985] 2 NZLR 338. There, Davison C J discussed the meaning of "likely" in s 76 of the Commerce Act 1975 ("is or is likely to be contrary to public interest") and in s 80 ("the occurrence or likely occurrence of one or more of the effects described in section 21 . . ."). The Chief Justice equated "likely" with "probable" and cited by way of support the following dicta of the Australian Trade Practices Tribunal in *Queensland Co-operative Milling Association case* (1976) ATPR para 40-012 at p 17,243:

We are to be concerned with probable effects rather than with possible or speculative effects. Yet we accept the view that the probabilities with which we are concerned are commercial or economic likelihoods which need not be susceptible of formal proof. We are required to look into the future but we can be concerned only with the foreseeable future as it appears on the basis of evidence and argument relating to the particular application.

The Chief Justice in the *Air New Zealand* case, after noting that it was difficult to differentiate clearly between "likely" and "probably" in any sensible degree, proffered the following approach, at p 342:

> On a graduated scale one might place expressions of likelihood in the following order of certainty – possible; distinct or significant possibility; reasonably probable; probable; highly probable.
>
> However, when one eliminates from the expression "likely", possible or speculative effects as did the Australian Trade Practices Tribunal, then the additional certainty required to eliminate those effects takes one into the realm of probability or, expressed differently, to a state of mind where one has some degree of assurance that the contemplated result will eventuate.

The most extensive discussion of the phrase "likely to have the effect" under s 27 is in *Mobil Oil Corporation v The Queen in Right of New Zealand* (International Centre for Settlement of Investment Disputes, Washington DC, Case ARB/87/2, 2 May 1989, International Arbitral Tribunal: Hon Sir Graham Speight, Professor Maureen Brunt and Stephen Charles QC). After citing the relevant passage from *Air New Zealand*, the panel made the following observations on Davison CJ's approach to "likely" at para 8.2.29:

> As the Chief Judge of the Australian Federal Court said in *Tillmann's Butcheries* [(1979) ATPR para 40-138 at p 18,495 per Bowen C J], "The word 'likely' is one which has various shades of meaning". Upon a close reading of the *Air New Zealand* passage we are now not convinced that the shade of meaning expressed by Davison C J is captured by the phrase "more probable than not". All that is required is to eliminate from the graduated scale of expressions "possible or speculative effects" so that one is left with all the others or, expressed differently, a "state of mind where one has some degree of assurance that the contemplated result will eventuate". Nor are we convinced that the Australian Tribunal in *QCMA* is to be read as requiring effects that are more probable than not. The emphasis in the quoted passage, as Davison CJ says, is upon the elimination of "possible or speculative effects" to give "commercial or economic likelihoods which may not be susceptible of formal proof".

After canvassing the case law on "likely" and noting that not all the interpretations coincided with a test of "more probably than not", the panel stated at para 8.2.33:

> It is commonly accepted that the legal context is of significance. We ourselves are also troubled by an approach that would isolate the word "likely" too sharply from the immediately surrounding words of s 27. It may be that a lower degree of probability or possibility could apply if the envisaged consequences for competition in the market were "very" substantial. We notice that the Australian Trade Practices Tribunal in recent years (ie since the time of *QCMA* and *Howard Smith*) has not found it necessary to isolate this element when applying its statutory authorization test.

At para 8.3.25, the panel drew a distinction between the civil standard of proof (the balance of probabilities) and the standard of likelihood. The panel interpreted the former requirement "as governing the degree of conviction with which we might hold our conclusion regarding likelihood".

The panel concluded its discussion with the following observation at para 8.2.36:

> While the hearing proceeded on the basis that "likely to have the effect" referred to the future, we do not read the application of this phrase as necessarily restricted to the future. The more compendious reference could well be to the likelihood of effect – past, present and future. The causal connection between trade practice and effect need not be 100% but merely "likely", it is not only the future for which causality is less than 100% certain.

The points made by the panel in *Mobil Oil* at paras 8.2.29, 8.2.33 and 8.2.35 were adopted by Greig J in *Broadcast Communications Ltd v Commerce Commission* (High Court, Wellington, CP 1132/90, 10 December 1991). The plaintiff, Broadcast Communications, sought judicial review of the Commerce Commission's finding in Decision No 256 (30 November 1990) that if Telecom did not acquire the AMPS-A radio frequency band but did acquire the TACS-B band that would not result in Telecom strengthening its already dominant position in the fixed and mobile voice telephony markets. Broadcast Communications submitted that the Commission had applied the wrong test to the question of whether the acquisition was likely to strengthen Telecom's dominance. As to this claim Greig J commented at p 20:

> I think that the real issue in this case is not the meaning of the word "strengthening" but the application of that in the way in which the statute requires, namely, that it "would be likely". The real point in this case is the meaning of "would be likely". It is important to note that the phrase is "would be likely". That is doubly conditional. It is that phrase, in the context of the Act and its purpose, that has to be applied by the Commission in satisfying itself whether or not there is a strengthening.

After canvassing relevant New Zealand and Australian authorities, including *Air New Zealand v Commerce Commission* and *Mobil Oil*, his Honour said at p 25:

> The whole of the phrase must be construed in its context. The purpose of the Act is to prevent competition. The acquisition of dominance is proscribed unless there are benefits which outweigh the detriments. Increase to or strengthening of that dominance is also proscribed and in terms in which the Commission deciding the question had to be satisfied only that that increase "would be likely". I do not think that that does mean "probable" or "more than a 50% chance". It means more than a possibility or a speculation but it "would be likely" if it could well happen if it is even less than an even chance less than probable but is more than a possibility.
>
> In this case I think that the wrong test was applied by the Commission. It is plain that they thought that there was more than a mere possibility and were left in some doubt, lingering though it may be, as to the likely effects of the acquisition. It was not satisfied that dominance would not be strengthened. I think that in the end the Commission found, and indeed there was no other finding possible, that an increase in strengthening of dominance would be likely.

Having found that the Commission erred in law in applying the wrong test, his Honour made an order setting aside the Commission's decision.

(d) "SUBSTANTIAL"

Before there can be a breach of s 27 the lessening of competition involved must be "substantial". The meaning of the term is thus of considerable importance. As Wilcox J observed in *Eastern Express Pty Ltd v General Newspapers Pty Ltd* (1991) ATPR para 41-128 at p 52,906:

> The word enables, and requires, the courts to determine what degree of restriction is compatible with a competitive environment.

No definition of "substantial" appears in the Australian legislation. In contrast, the Commerce Act defines "substantial" as meaning "real or of substance". This definition has general application apart from s 47(3) and (4) (concerning business acquisitions).

It is generally thought that in framing this definition, the legislature had in mind Dean J's comments in *Tillmanns Butcheries Pty Ltd v The Australasian Meat Industry Employees' Union* (1979) ATPR para 40-138 at p 18,500:

> In the context of sec 45 D(1) of the Act, the word "substantial" is used in a relative sense in that, regardless of whether it means large or weighty on the one hand or real or of substance as distinct from ephemeral or nominal on the other, it would be necessary to know something of the nature and scope of the relevant business before one could say that particular actual or potential loss or damage was substantial. As at present advised, I incline to the view that the phrase, substantial loss or damage in sec 45 D(1) includes loss or damage that is, in the circumstances, real or of substance and not insubstantial or nominal.

Although given in the context of s 45D (the Australian secondary boycott provision), Keely J applied Deane J's view to the s 47(10) competitive effect and purpose test in *Cool & Sons Pty Ltd v O'Brien Glass Industries Ltd* (1981) ATPR para 40-220. His Honour said at p 43,003 that the substantial lessening of competition required by s 47(10) "must be capable of being fairly described as a lessening of competition that is real or [of] substance as distinct from a lessening that is insubstantial, insignificant or mini-mal". On appeal ((1983) ATPR para 40-376), Fox J (with whom Sheppard J agreed) said at p 44,455 that Keely J's understanding of "substantially" was not wrong.

The Commerce Commission in *Re Weddel Crown Corp Ltd* (1987) 1 NZBLC (Com) 104,200 assumed that the comments of Deane J and Keely J had influenced the New Zealand legislature. The Commission said at p 104,212:

> Accordingly, it seems reasonable to assume that "real or of substance" in New Zealand was intended to mean not insignificant, not ephemeral, not nominal or minimal. Of course, as Deane J says, such a test conceals a lack of precision. In this respect, the evaluation of the question of degree, based on the criterion of "not insignificant, ephemeral, nominal or minimal" must be a matter of judgment for the appropriate adjudicating body.

The Commission majority determination in *Re Fisher & Paykel Ltd (No 2)* (supra) endorsed this approach as did the High Court on appeal (supra) which also cited the following passage from the *Mobil Oil* arbitration case (paras 8.2.19-8.2.20):

> Thus we take the term to mean not nominal or ephemeral but not large or weighty either. In accordance with universal competition law practice (New Zealand as well as Australian) we regard the term as importing relativity, here assessed by reference to the impact of the practice upon the functioning of the relevant market. Compare, for instance, Lockhart J in the Australian case *Radio 2UE Sydney v Stereo FM* (1982) ATPR 43-912 at p 43,918: "In the context of sec 45 the word 'substantial' is used in a relative sense. The very notion of competition imports relativity. One needs to know something of the businesses carried on in the relevant market and the nature and extent of the market before one can say that any particular lessening of competition is substantial."
>
> Further, we accept the Crown's submission on this point, that substantially is "to be judged in competition terms, and therefore, some matters have more importance than others. The height of barriers to entry is the most important element of market structure".
>
> Plainly in the end, it is a matter of judgment as to whether the hindering of competition is of sufficient importance in the context of the policy of the legislation for remedial action to be taken.

(e) LESSENING OF COMPETITION

(1) Evaluation of whether competition has been substantially lessened: Smithers J's remarks in *Dandy Power Equipment Pty Ltd v Mercury Marine Pty Ltd* (supra) at pp 43,887-8 affords assistance as to the way Courts should apply the test of substantially lessening competition:

> To apply the concept of substantially lessening competition in a market, it is necessary to assess the nature and extent of the market, the probable nature and extent of competition which would exist therein but for the conduct in question, the way the market operates and the nature and extent of the contemplated lessening. To my mind one must look at the relevant significant portion of the market, ask oneself how and to what extent there would have been competition therein but for the conduct, assess what is left and determine whether what has been lost in relation to what would have been, is seen to be a substantial lessening of competition. I prefer not to substitute other adverbs for "substantially". "Substantially" is a word the meaning of which in the circumstances in which it is applied must, to some extent, be of uncertain incidence and a matter of judgment. There is no precise scale by which to measure what is substantial. I think . . . the word is used in a sense imparting a greater rather than a lesser degree of lessening. Accordingly in my opinion competition in a market is substantially lessened if the extent of competition in the market which has been lost, is seen by those competent to judge to be a substantial lessening of competition. Has competitive trading in the market been substantially interfered with? It is then that the public will suffer. . . .
>
> Although the words "substantially lessened in a market" refer generally to a market, it is the degree to which competition has been lessened which is critical, not the proportion of that lessening to the whole of the competition which exists in the total market. Thus a lessening in a significant section of the market, if a substantial lessening of otherwise active competition may, according to circumstances, be a substantial lessening of competition.

The importance of Smithers J's formulation in *Dandy Power* is underlined by the New Zealand Courts having invoked it in most of the cases involving a competition assessment under s 27. After citing the above passage from *Dandy Power*, the arbitration panel in *Mobil Oil* (supra) made the following observations on the formulation (at para 8.2.22):

> We draw three points in particular from the passage: the first is the desirability of interpreting the phrase "substantial lessening of competition" as a whole; the second is the manner in which relativity is to be approached; and the third, and most important for this arbitration, is the manner in which causality is to be assessed. As to this last, we are required to assess the competitive functioning of a relevant market, with and without the disputed practice . . .

Also helpful in evaluating whether competition is substantially lessened, is the list of questions the Commerce Commission formulated in *Re Weddel Crown* (supra) at p 104,212. The Commission thought the list would assist in determining a practice's impact on competition, although it added that the questions were not necessarily exhaustive or conclusive:

- What is the extent to which competition is foreclosed by the agreement, etc, and what alternatives do others in the market have?
- Does the agreement have the effect of threatening independent initiatives of operators in the market?
- Does the agreement have the effect of causing operators in the market to compete less vigorously?
- Does the agreement enable the parties thereto to exercise power over others, eg, over persons contracting with the parties or their competitors?
- Does the agreement affect the ability or desire of potential entrants to enter the market in question?

The majority determination in *Re Fisher & Paykel Ltd (No 2)* (supra) formulated guidelines specifically designed to assess the competitive effects of vertical restraints. The Commission described the guidelines as a useful adjunct to the *Weddel Crown* tests. The High Court, however, did not favour such an approach, cautioning against any "guidelines" which have no foundation in the statute.

(2) Net approach – pro and anti-competitive effects: Section 27 is concerned with the "net" effect on competition. The majority determination in *Re Fisher & Paykel* (supra) dealt with this issue as follows at p 104,395:

> It was . . . submitted by the applicant that, in determining whether a practice substantially lessened competition in any market, both pro-competitive effects and anti-competitive effects had to be taken into account. Counsel opposing the application did not take issue with this submission. In the view of the Commission, should the circumstances make it appropriate, it is necessary to take into account all effects of the restrictive clause which is the subject of the inquiry in ascertaining whether the test in sec 27 is met. To take into account some effects on competition only would not be realistic. Further, sec 3(3) of the Act provides that "all factors that affect competition in that market" must be taken into account, and it appears to embrace those factors which enhance competition as well as those which lessen it. If, for example, it could be shown that the net effect of the clause was to promote competition, then there can be no "substantial lessening of competition" in terms of sec 27.

The High Court endorsed this approach as well as the majority's view that efficiencies as well as inefficiencies had to be evaluated when applying the s 27 test. The Court also noted that non-competition public benefits were more appropriately dealt with at the authorisation stage.

(f) MARKET
The "Fundamental Concepts", 41.2, part of this chapter discusses the concept of "market" and the role of substitutability in delineating the relevant market in some detail. The reader is referred to that discussion.

(1) Statutory provisions relating to competition and market: In "Fundamental Concepts" the writer canvassed the statutory definitions of "competition" and "market". Certain other statutory provisions are also relevant when applying the s 27 test.

Section 3(2) provides that a reference to a lessening of competition includes a reference to a preventing or hindering of competition. There are some types of anti-competitive conduct where a plaintiff may have little difficulty in establishing by inference a hindering of competition but where he or she may have trouble in establishing an actual lessening of competition in any quantitative sense. Trade association price agreements are an example. See *Re New Zealand Master Grocers' Federation* [1961] NZLR 177 at p 191.

Section 3(4)(a) provides that in assessing the anti-competitive purpose or effect of a provision, a reference to a market includes the market in which a party to the arrangement (or interconnected body corporation thereof) supplies or acquires or is likely to supply or acquire goods or services or would, but for the relevant provision, be likely to do so. This part of the subsection is similar to s 45(3) of the Australian Act; however, s 3(4)(b) goes beyond the Australian position by referring to "[a]ny other market in which those goods may be supplied or acquired". G Q Taperell, R B Vermeesch & D J Harland in *Trade Practices and Consumer Protection* (3rd edn, 1983) at p 215, illustrate the effect of the Australian provision with the following example:

> Thus, for instance, an arrangement between manufacturers may have an effect on the prices at which their suppliers or customers buy and sell, but, assuming the manufacturers do not and are not likely to enter the market in which the suppliers and customers operate, the effect on those markets is not to be considered.

By virtue of s 3(4)(b), in New Zealand, one could consider the effect of the arrangement in the markets in which the suppliers and customers operate.

Section 3(4) provides for the aggregation of provisions to help assess overall anti-competitive effect. The subsection provides that a provision is to be examined along with the provisions of any other arrangement to which the person, or any interconnected body corporate thereof, is a party. If the cumulative effect of all the provisions has the requisite anti-competitive effect in the same market, then s 3(5) deems the provision in issue also to have that effect. Note one should only aggregate the provisions of other arrangements when applying s 27 to the person who is a party to all of them: Taperell, Vermeesch & Harland (supra) at p 218. Through a probable drafting oversight this point is not made explicit in s 3(5), but such a construction is necessary if the subsection is to operate as intended: BM Hill & MR Jones, *Competitive Trading in New Zealand* (1986) at p33, para 3.2.

In similar fashion s 3(7) provides for the aggregation of conduct, if the conduct engaged in and the same or similar conduct, when taken together, have the requisite anti-competitive effect.

(g) *HECAR* AS A CASE STUDY

The case of *Hecar Investments No 6 Pty Ltd v Outboard Marine Australia* (1982) ATPR para 40-298 highlights the importance of the interrelated concepts of "competition" and "market" when evaluating whether competition is substantially lessened. *Hecar* illustrates that judicial failure to come to terms with these economic concepts may well result in a Court arriving at the wrong decision.

At issue was whether the refusal of a supplier (OMA) to supply Evinrude outboard motors to a dealer (Hecar) because the latter had acquired or would not agree not to acquire a competing brand, Suzuki, had the purpose or effect of substantially lessening competition in a market under s 47(10) of the Trade Practices Act (the Australian exclusive dealing section).

A leading economist, Dr Neville Norman, gave evidence as to the economic meaning of competition. Surprisingly, Franki J treated the evidence as being irrelevant for the purposes of the Trade Practices Act, at p 43,704:

> Dr Norman, an economist, gave evidence. He has outstanding academic and professional qualifications as an economist. He expressed the view that there was frequently a difference between the meaning and the use of the word "competition" in business and economics. He said that in economics competition refers, inter alia, to the capacity and ability of the market (once defined) to adopt new techniques of production and distribution, to respond to variations in the needs and requirements of the buyers, to avoid excessive profits or selling costs, and to distribute goods and services efficiently.
>
> If, as Dr Norman said, the meaning of "competition" in a business setting differs from its meaning in an economic setting, then, since the Act is directed to business situations, the word should be given the ordinary meaning it bears in such business. For this reason I do not find Dr Norman's evidence of assistance.

His Honour preferred the view of a business witness, a Mr Nettleship, whom his Honour described as "a well qualified and experienced businessman". Mr Nettleship stated that "competition is the supplying of alternatives to satisfy a market".

Applying this definition of competition, Franki J ruled at p 43,705 that as the refusal to supply was likely to lessen or hinder the opportunity of a purchaser to view two competing brands side by side this constituted an effect on competition "at least in a situation where there are no Suzuki outboard motors on display in close proximity to the premises of Hecar". His Honour considered that Hecar had established that the refusal to supply was likely to have the effect of substantially lessening or substantially hindering competition under s 47(10).

Franki J's rejection of the economic meaning of competition is difficult to comprehend. Section 4E of the Australian legislation makes it clear that Courts must consider competition in the context of a market made up of rival suppliers of goods and services. His Honour's approach treats competition in absolute terms and would result in every retailer being permitted to sell all brands of a product irrespective of whether the store next door is doing exactly the same. Failure to analyse the structure of the market led Franki J into the classic error of equating injury to a competitor with injury to competition. His concern about the shopping convenience of consumers is also misplaced; a competitive market will ensure the ready availability of competing brands, albeit not always on a side by side basis.

By coincidence, a strikingly similar factual situation to *Hecar* came up for decision contemporaneously in *Dandy Power Equipment Pty Ltd v Mercury Marine Pty Ltd* (1982) ATPR para 40-315. In that case, Smithers J made the following observation at p 43,887 concerning competition:

> To my mind, competition in a market is the sum of activity engaged in by persons in promoting the sale to potential buyers of the goods with which the market is concerned.

His Honour considered both the retail and wholesale markets in the selling of outboard motors to be highly competitive. In contrast to Franki J, he rejected the argument that the displaying of competing brands of outboard motor side by side would intensify price competition in the industry. Taking into account the competitive state of the retail and wholesale markets and the fact that the termination of the plaintiff's franchise involved only a small number of outboard motors, and also the fact that the plaintiff still had indirect access to the defendant's brand as well as other brands, Smithers J concluded that the refusal to supply did not have the purpose or effect of substantially lessening competition in any relevant market.

The *Hecar* case meanwhile was appealed to the Full Federal Court of Australia: (1982) ATPR para 40-327. In a joint judgment, Bowen C J and Fisher J referred with approval to the *QCMA* case and the decision of Smithers J in *Dandy Power*, observing at p 43,983:

> It would seem that "competition" for the purposes of s 47(10) must be read as referring to a process or state of affairs in a market. In considering the state of competition a detailed evaluation of the market structure seems to be required. In the *Dandy case* Smithers J regarded as necessary an assessment of the nature and extent of the market, the probable nature and extent of competition which could exist therein but for the conduct in question, the operation of the market and the extent of the contemplated lessening.

Their Honours had little difficulty in rejecting Hecar's argument that there is a significant connection between the convenience of prospective customers in comparing brands "side by side on the same floor" and competition in the market. They found that there was "no evidence that OMA's refusal to supply Hecar had or would be likely to have the result of altering the market structure so as to produce an anti-competitive effect, for example there is no evidence that barriers to entry have been raised, nor that price competition has been reduced": p 43,984.

Fitzgerald J, in a separate opinion, agreed that the Full Court should allow the appeal and made the following important statement at pp 43,988-89:

> It would, I think, be an unusual and exceptional case in which it could be shown that competition in a generally competitive market was or was likely to be substantially lessened by a refusal to supply one or a number of competitive retailers in the market with a product otherwise freely available and competitively marketed. Further, where there is a market which is generally competitive, it plainly does not follow that conduct which affects the balance of competition by advantaging or disadvantaging a particular dealer

or dealers or a particular product or product necessarily lessens the competition in the market.

In addition to the above statement of general principle, his Honour formulated a number of tests which he considered Hecar had to satisfy if it was to sustain a charge of substantial lessening of competition. His Honour pointed out that Hecar had failed to establish that OMA's refusal to supply was or was likely to have:

(1) any effect on the capacity of consumers in the market to influence the market;
(2) any effect on the capacity of the dealers or products in the market to continue, or on fresh entry into the market;
(3) any effect on a capacity or willingness of dealers in the market to meet the present or future requirements of consumers in the market or to respond to variations in these requirements;
(4) any effect on the cost or profit structures in the market or its efficiency otherwise;
(5) any effect upon the product range, including brands, sizes, finishes, colours, etc available in the market;
(6) any effect upon prices, terms, standards, service, etc in the market;
(7) any effect on the number or identify of the retailers in the market, or the number, location, or convenience and accessibility of retail outlets, or on any other aspect of the efficient retail sale and distribution of outboard motors in the market. . . .

The significance of the Fitzgerald tests is that they place relatively little emphasis on the narrow structural criteria of concentration or market shares. Read with the Northrop approach in *Ansett/Avis*, one can see the Fitzgerald tests as a continuing refinement of a workable standard of effective competition extending beyond purely structural criteria.

41.3.3 Authorisation

The Commerce Commission has power to grant authorisation for s 27 conduct. Section 58(1)-(4) provides that the Commission may grant an authorisation on the application of any person who wishes to enter into or give effect to a contract, arrangement, or understanding, or covenant, to which ss 27 or 28 would or might apply.

The test for authorisation of ss 27 or 28 conduct is found in s 61(6) which provides that the Commission shall not grant an authorisation unless it is satisfied that the practice "will in all the circumstances result, or be likely to result, in a benefit to the public which would outweigh the lessening in competition that would result, or would be likely to result or is deemed to result therefrom".

The Commission in *Re Weddel Crown* (supra) at p 104,214 outlined its methodology for assessing whether or not to grant an authorisation:

(i) What is the relevant market (or markets) in which the effect of the practice upon competition is to be evaluated?
(ii) Is the practice for which approval is applied for, one to which sec 27 . . . of the Act applies? (See sec 58(1).) . . .
(iii) To what extent does the contract or arrangement in question result in a "lessening of competition" in the market or markets affected by the practice. (See s 61(6).)

(iv) What are the effects caused by the lessening of competition referred to above?

(v) Does the contract or arrangement result or will it be likely to result in a benefit to the public. (See sec 61(6).)

(vi) Does the net public benefit which is found to exist from the practice outweigh any net competitive detriment from the lessening of competition in the relevant market?

The majority of the Commission in *Weddel Crown* decided that the mere making of an application for authorisation was not enough to give it jurisdiction. The Commission took the view that s 58(1), as it then stood, required it to form the view that the practice to which the authorisation related contravened s 27. The then Department of Trade and Industry in its discussion paper, *Review of the Commerce Act* (August 1988) at pp 54-58, expressed concern as to the Commission's approach. This concern led to s 19 of the Commerce Amendment Act 1990 adding the words "or might apply" into ss 58(1)-(8) of the principal Act. While the purpose of the amendment was clear, the Commission in *Re The Insurance Council of New Zealand* (1990) 2 NZBLC (Com) 104,564 expressed the view at p 104,568 that it did not change the jurisdictional requirement:

> [W]hile the amendment clarifies the applicant's position, it does not appear to necessitate an alteration in the Commission's methodology for considering such applications. The Commission is still required to consider public benefits, and weigh them against competitive detriments. There would be no point in going through this process, if the practice did not substantially lessen competition ie did not give rise to competitive detriments. In effect, therefore, the Commission will begin by considering the threshold issue of whether or not there is an arrangement which substantially lessens competition.

For a detailed analysis of the authorisation process, see Ahdar in *Competition Law and Policy in New Zealand* (R Ahdar ed, 1991) ch 12. The High Court recently reviewed the concept of "public benefit" in *Telecom Corp of New Zealand v Commerce Commission* (supra).

41.4 EXCLUSIONARY PROVISIONS

41.4.1 Section 29 and its coverage of boycott conduct

Section 29 of the Commerce Act is intended to prohibit what is commonly referred to in antitrust law as a concerted refusal to deal or group boycott. The Act employs the terminology of an "exclusionary provision" to encompass this type of activity. Section 29(1) defines the term as follows:

(1) For the purposes of this Act, a provision of a contract or arrangement or understanding is an exclusionary provision if –

(a) It is a provision of a contract or arrangement entered into, or understanding arrived at, between persons of whom any 2 or more are in competition with each other, and

(b) It has the purpose of preventing, restricting, or limiting the supply of goods or services to, or the acquisition of goods or services from, any particular person or class of persons, either generally or in particular circumstances or on particular conditions, by all or any of the parties to the contract, arrangement or understanding, or if a party is a body corporate, by a body corporate that is interconnected with that party; and

   (c) The particular person or the class of persons to which the provision relates
        is in competition with one or more of the parties to the contract, arrangement
        or understanding in relation to the supply or acquisition of those goods
        or services.

The Act prohibits any person from entering into a contract or arrangement or arriving at an understanding that contains an exclusionary
provision: s 29(3). The prohibition also applies to giving effect to an
exclusionary provision: s 29(4). The prohibition applies whether the
contract etc was made before or after the commencement of the Act:
s 29(5). No exclusionary provision of a contract, whether made before or
after the commencement of the Act, is enforceable: s 29(6).

There is an absolute prohibition attaching to conduct falling within
s 29, ie the practice is illegal per se subject only to the possibility of the
Commerce Commission granting an authorisation.

The Commerce Amendment Act 1990 made an important change to
s 29 by adding para (c) to s 29(1). The effect of the new paragraph is to
require that the particular person or class of persons to whom supply or
acquisition is restricted be a competitor of one or more of the parties to
the boycotting arrangement.

To understand the scope of s 29, both before and after the enactment
of the Commerce Amendment Act, one must have some acquaintance
with the various types of boycott.

One useful classification of boycotts is that by Hadden (1985) BUL Rev
164 at pp 169-72:

> Boycotts can be classified according to the relationship between the target and
> the conspirators. Thus, in a direct boycott in which the target is either a
> supplier or a customer, the target stands in a vertical relationship with the
> boycotting parties; that is, the target either sells to or buys from the members
> of the conspiracy. The boycott mechanism operates when the conspiracy
> members refuse to deal, or threaten to refuse to deal with the target. The result
> of these tactics is either a discontinuance of economic relations between target
> and conspirators, or a favourable change of terms on which the conspirators
> deal with the target. . . . Joint action permits the members of the conspiracy to
> gain an advantage over the target which would not be available to each acting
> alone.
>
>   In another classic form, the indirect boycott against competitors, the target
> is a competitor of the conspirators. In order to coerce or injure the target, the
> conspirators enlist the assistance of the target's suppliers or customers by
> threatening them with a direct boycott. The target is then threatened with
> deprivation of access to goods from suppliers it shares with the conspirators,
> or of access to customers which it shares with the conspirators. If the target
> refuses to accede to the conspirator's wishes, the target is excluded from the
> market or injured in its ability to compete effectively on an equal basis.
>
>   A third type of boycott is the direct boycott against competitors where
> competitors take action directly against other competitors. Such a boycott
> requires an existing economic relationship between the competitors and the
> target the interruption of which can cause injury to the target. For example, the
> competitors as a group may control a facility that is necessary for effective
> competition. Control over this facility gives the group the power to enforce
> terms of commercial conduct; the group may deny a target access to the
> facility, and thereby exclude it from the market or seriously impair its ability
> to compete.

There is United States Supreme Court authority for condemning all three types of boycott as illegal per se, although the current application of the per se rule to boycott activity must now be read in the light of the Supreme Court's decision in *Northwest Wholesale Stationers v Pacific Stationery and Printing Co*, 472 US 284 (1985).

Prior to its amendment in 1990, s 29 of the Commerce Act had the potential to embrace all the above types of boycott. The insertion of para (c) into the body of s 29(1), however, has dramatically curtailed the ambit of s 29 effectively limiting its operation to the third type of boycott. As far as the second type of boycott is concerned, s 29 would only apply if the target's suppliers or customers succumb to the pressure exerted on them by the parties to the boycott and join the conspirators in the boycott. The Australian legislature has not seen fit to amend s 4D of the Trade Practices Act, the Australian equivalent of s 29, along the lines of the New Zealand provision. This means that there is a considerable difference between the New Zealand and Australian trade practices law as far as the scope of the exclusionary provisions sections are concerned.

The reasons why the New Zealand legislature decided to limit the scope of s 29, and the merits of the change, will be discussed later in this commentary.

41.4.2 The justification for treating boycotts as per se illegal

As we have seen, a group boycott can either drive a competitor completely from the market or make it significantly more difficult for the firm to compete. One can argue that since the primary concern of antitrust law is to protect *competition* and not *competitors*, the per se rule should not be invoked in the absence of detrimental market effect. See generally Bauer (1979) 79 Colum L Rev 685. Such an argument overlooks business and public expectations that the antitrust laws ought to protect individual firms from forms of "unfair practices" which will drive them from the market. While some commentators dismiss such "populist" notions as being divorced from the real goals of antitrust law, viz the promotion of efficiency and competition, a study of comparative antitrust jurisprudence reveals a recurrent concern with unfair exclusionary practices, particularly where joint market power or a dominant firm is involved. For illustrations of United Kingdom and EEC judicial hostility to group boycotts, see *Daily Mirror Newspapers Ltd v Gardiner* [1968] 2 QB 762; *Brekkes v Cattel* (1970) LR 7 RP 150; *Belgian Wallpaper Manufacturers' Agreement* [1974] 2 CMLR D 102 (Comm), [1975] ECR 1491 (ECJ). To ignore this strand of thinking, is to deny the importance of social and political values inherent in any system of antitrust law. See generally Hovenkamp (1982) 51 Geo Wash L Rev 1; Schwartz (1979) 127 U Pa L Rev 1051; Sullivan (1975) 75 Colum L Rev 1214.

The relationship between "fair" competition and "free" competition is perhaps more complementary than many commentators are prepared to concede. Taking a long-run dynamic view of the market, an economy is likely to be healthier if the number of competitors is not privately determined and there is freedom of exit and entry. As Professor Bauer (supra) observes at pp 698-89:

Even if the boycotted party is not eliminated or diminished as a market force, the concerted refusal to deal may deprive the firm of entrepreneurial freedom and force it to conform to conduct – such as pricing, selection of goods sold, choice of suppliers or customers – which is arbitrarily determined by another. Absent the boycott, a company might bring new products on the market, sell through new distributive channels or to different customers, offer new services to consumers or package the product differently. The concerted refusal to deal deprives the businessman of this flexibility, and may therefore rob society of lower prices, better quality products and services, and ultimately of goods themselves.

Group boycotts are also condemned because of societal distrust of the private power in the hands of the combination. Professor Milton Handler in (1959) 59 Colum L Rev 834 at p 866 stated:

> [A] boycott smacks of a licensing system . . . imposed by private groups for private reasons. The boycotting parties determine who shall remain in, and who be excluded from a field of economic activity.

The coercion of third parties by private groups, carrying with it as it does connotations of self-help, private licensing and mob rule explains much of the judicial and legislative hostility toward boycott activity.

While the case for the per se treatment of group boycotts is a strong one, there are always likely to be some cases where legitimate efficiencies or other societal benefits may justify exclusionary conduct. Given the wording and concepts embodied in s 29 of the Commerce Act, it may be that the judiciary will adopt a rule of reason approach to the section and sift out what are obviously pro-competitive or neutral self-regulatory arrangements from those which are clearly in violation of both the letter and intent of the legislation. It is also open to the parties to any arrangement containing an exclusionary provision that appears to come within the ambit of s 29 to apply to the Commerce Commission for an authorisation.

41.4.3 Constituent elements of s 29

(a) NEED FOR A CONTRACT, ARRANGEMENT OR UNDERSTANDING

For s 29 to apply, there must be a contract, arrangement or understanding. See "Fundamental Concepts", 41.2, for a discussion of these terms.

The importance of showing concerted action between at least two competitors is seen in *Auckland Regional Authority v Mutual Rental Cars (Auckland Airport) Ltd* [1987] 2 NZLR 647. There, Budget failed to establish that there was an understanding between the ARA, Avis and Hertz to exclude it from Auckland airport. At most there were two lots of two-way arrangements between the ARA and Avis and the ARA and Hertz. The s 29 claim therefore failed.

(b) TWO OR MORE OF THE PARTIES MUST BE "IN COMPETITION WITH EACH OTHER"

A provision of a contract, arrangement or understanding is an exclusionary provision only where at least two of the parties to the contract, arrangement or understanding are "in competition with each other": s 29(1)(a).

It is not necessary that all the parties to the arrangement be in competition with each other; it is sufficient if at least two of the parties are competitors. Note that the party alleged to have restricted supply or acquisition need not necessarily be competitive with any other party to the arrangement.

Subsection (2) of s 29 broadens the normal understanding of a competitive relationship. The subsection reads:

> For the purposes of subsection (1)(a) of this section, a person is in competition with another person if that person or any interconnected body corporate is, or is likely to be, or, but for the relevant provision, would be or would be likely to be, in competition with the other person, or with an interconnected body corporate, in relation to the supply or acquisition of all or any of the goods or services to which that relevant provision relates.

Where a body corporate is a party to the arrangement it is sufficient if an interconnected body corporate of such party is in competition with another party or a body corporate interconnected with another party. For example, if A is a manufacturer and B is a retailer, s 29(2) will deem them to be in competition with each other if A's retail subsidiary, C, is competitive with B. Likewise, if A is a manufacturer and B is a wholesaler and both have retail subsidiaries which are competitive with each other, the subsection will deem A and B to be in competition with each other. This deeming rule poses problems for dual distribution systems. A corporate manufacturer with a retail subsidiary may supply other retail distributors on terms limiting the persons to whom those distributors may resupply the goods. Government accounts, for example, may be reserved for the manufacturer's retail subsidiary. Such an arrangement would appear to satisfy all the elements of s 29. The same problems would arise even in the absence of a parent/subsidiary relationship provided the manufacturer was also engaged in retailing.

Section 29(2) makes it clear that the parties in competition with each other must be competitive in relation to the goods or services to which the boycott relates. This point arose in *ASX Operations Pty Ltd v Pont Data Australia Pty Ltd* (1991) ATPR para 41-109. At issue was a provision in the "Foreign Agreement" between ASXO and Pont Data prohibiting the latter from wholesaling the supply of "Signal C" information to non-Australian users. The Full Court of the Federal Court of Australia (Lockhart, Gummow, von Doussa JJ), invoking the Australian equivalent of s 29(2), held that the provision was not an exclusionary provision because Pont Data had not shown that the parties were competitive or likely to be competitive in relation to the supply of Signal C information to non-Australian users.

In its primary decision, *ASX Operations Pty Ltd v Pont Data Australia Ltd* (1991) ATPR para 41-069, concerning, inter alia, the "Dynamic Agreement", the Full Court found that Pont Data and ASXO (through its subsidiary JECNET) were competitors in relation to the sale of the information contained in Signal C and that the provisions in the agreement obligating Pont Data not to supply the information to any person other than a licensee who was a party to the agreement breached s 4D of the Australian Act.

The question of whether real estate agents compete with each other for the acquisition of real estate advertising services arose in *Eastern Express*

Pty Ltd v General Newspapers Pty Ltd (1991) ATPR para 41-128. The applicant company whose shareholders were mainly real estate agents began publishing a newspaper, the *Eastern Express*, in February 1990 to compete with the longstanding local Sydney eastern suburbs newspaper, the *Wentworth Courier*, published by the respondent companies trading in partnership as Eastern Suburbs Newspapers (ESN). A major source of revenue for both newspapers was display real estate advertisements. From February 1990 the *Wentworth Courier* revised its advertising rates with substantial reduction in price and began a comparative advertising campaign to publicise this. The paper also made reference to real estate agents owning shares in a newspaper, suggesting that this might not be in the best interests of vendors.

The applicant unsuccessfully claimed that the respondents were engaging in predatory pricing in order to damage or eliminate it as a competitor in contravention of s 46 of the Trade Practices Act (corresponding to s 36 of the Commerce Act). The respondents cross-claimed against the applicant company and some of its real estate agent shareholders alleging that a provision in the company's articles of association requiring "A" class shareholders to place a quota of advertising in the *Eastern Express* was an exclusionary provision under s 4D of the Australian Act. The quota was related directly to the amount of advertising which each real estate agent shareholder had customarily placed with the *Wentworth Courier*.

To succeed in its s 4D cross-claim, the respondents had to show: (1) that the real estate agent shareholders were competitive with each other; and (2) that they were competitive in respect of the services to which the quota provisions related. Wilcox J held that the respondents had not established either requirement. His Honour outlined the respective arguments and his views thereon as follows at p 52,905:

> [ESN's] counsel accept that it is not enough that the contract was made, amongst other persons, between shareholders who are real estate agents in competition with each other for the listing and sale of properties. By force of s 4D(2), the relevant competition must relate to the supply or acquisition of goods or services to which the contract relates. However, they say that the agents compete with each other for the acquisition of real estate advertising services. In that connection, they point to evidence that some advertisers prefer certain parts of the newspaper for the placement of their clients' advertisements. Some preferred pages, such as the back of the newspaper and right hand pages, carry an extra loading.
>
> Counsel for the cross-respondents dispute that the agents are in competition with each other, in the relevant sense. They say that the supply of advertising space in local newspapers is, in effect, infinite; any competition for preferred pages in a particular newspaper is *de minimis* and, in any event, that competition is not affected by the quota provisions.
>
> I think that these submissions are correct. But, as the argument *de minimis* involves a matter of degree upon which opinions may vary, I prefer to rest my rejection of ESN's case under s 4D(1)(a) on the latter point.
>
> Subsection (2) requires that the relevant competition be "in relation to the supply or acquisition of all or any of the goods or services to which the relevant provision of the contract ... relates". In the present case, ESN argues that there is competition in respect of the acquisition of services. If the word "services" is defined broadly, so as merely to refer to real estate advertising services, it may justly be said that these are services to which the quota provisions relate. But ESN's difficulty is that the agents are not in competition with each other in relation to services generally. Even on the ESN argument, the agents engage

in a limited competition for some preferred pages of the newspaper. If the word "services" is defined narrowly, to accommodate the limited nature of the competition (as, for example, by defining the relevant "services" as advertising on certain preferred pages of either newspaper) these are not services to which the quota provisions relate. The dilemma for ESN is that on no reading of the word "services", does the area of competition coincide with the area of contractual regulation.

It is not clear whether the parties must be in competition with each other at the time when they entered into the arrangement or whether, it is sufficient to satisfy the section if they become competitive at some later time.

There is Australian authority in support of the view that the parties must be in competition at the time they entered into the arrangement. In *Australian Broadcasting Commission v Parrish* (1980) 27 ALR 573, St John J, at the interlocutory stage, noted that in s 4D there is an exclusionary provision only "if the parties to the contract *are* competitive with one another". In his Honour's view, the present tense meant that the parties must be competitive at the time they entered into the agreement. Franki J expressed a similar view in *Trade Practices Commission v TNT Management Pty Ltd* (the *Tradestock* case) (1985) ATPR para 40-512. His Honour observed at p 43,135:

> I consider that the time when the question of competition is to be determined is the time when the arrangement was made or the understanding arrived at.

No New Zealand Court has yet examined the issue; however, the Commerce Commission in *Re South Pacific Tyres Ltd* Decision No 247 (3 May 1990) preferred the broader view, viz, s 29 can catch an arrangement having an exclusionary provision if at any time the parties become competitive. The Commission invoked s 29(2) in support of its view, at para 37:

> For the purposes of s 29(1)(a) it is not necessary that the parties actually be in competition with each other. It is sufficient, in terms of 29(2) that they "are or are likely to be" or "but for the relevant provision would be or would be likely to be". Thus s 29 is not avoided, for example, by entering into an otherwise "exclusionary arrangement" prior to one party entering the relevant market.

An example where the exclusionary provisions section failed to catch a classic boycott because the parties were not in competition with each other is seen in *Jewel Food Stores Pty Ltd v Hall* (1990) ATPR para 40,931. A licensing system in New South Wales allocated defined areas to particular vendors of pasteurised milk. A retailer could only obtain New South Wales milk from the vendor responsible for the area in which the retailer was located. The New South Wales vendors' sales regions did not overlap. The plaintiff, Jewel, conducted a chain of supermarkets in New South Wales which offered pasteurised milk for sale to customers. From time to time, Jewel obtained additional milk supplies from Victorian suppliers at a cheaper price than was available from New South Wales vendors. However, Jewel also needed New South Wales milk to sell in its stores. The Amalgamated Milk Vendors Association Inc at a meeting expressed the view that the supply of New South Wales milk to Jewel stores should cease while the stores sold interstate milk. Following the meeting, supply of New South Wales milk to all but two Jewel stores stopped. There was little doubt that the Milk Vendors Association and the milk vendors had acted in concert to withhold supplies of milk from Jewel in order to force it to stop acquiring and selling Victorian milk. Although the case exhibited all the characteristics of a classic primary boycott, the case did not proceed under s 4D of the Australian Act. There were two reasons for this. First, under the licensing system the milk vendors were not in competition with each other; second, neither were they corporations as required under s 4D(1). For these reasons, Jewel sought to rely on s 45D(1) (the secondary boycott provision) as this provision applies to natural persons as well as to corporations. Jewel failed in the Federal Court: (1989) ATPR para 40-931, but the Full Court (by majority) allowed its appeal: (1990) ATPR para 40-997. However, the High Court of Australia by a majority of 3 to 2 held that s 45D(1) did not apply: *Devenish v Jewel Food Stores Pty Ltd* (1991) ATPR para 41-098.

It is instructive to examine how the *Jewel* case would have proceeded assuming the factual situation arose under s 29 of the Commerce Act. The fact that the milk vendors were not corporations would have been irrelevant under s 29. But as in the case of s 4D(1), the non-competitive status of the milk vendors would have prevented s 29 from applying. But even if the milk vendors were or were likely to be in competition with each other, Jewel may still not have succeeded under s 29 because of the requirement in s 29(1)(c) that the person or class of persons to whom supply or acquisition is restricted be a competitor of one or more of the parties to the boycotting arrangement. Jewel, being a supermarket, could only have satisfied this requirement if the milk vendors also sold at the retail level. If this was not the case, Jewel would have been forced to rely on s 27 and would have had to prove that the parties to the arrangement had either the purpose or effect of substantially lessening competition in a market. This would have been difficult to establish.

(c) PURPOSE OF PREVENTING, RESTRICTING OR LIMITING

Assuming that the plaintiff has proven the existence of an arrangement between at least two or more competitors, the next step is for the plaintiff to demonstrate that a provision of such arrangement has the "purpose" of preventing, restricting or limiting supply in any of the ways described in para (b) of s 29(1). It is important to note that it is the provision – not the contract, arrangement or understanding – which must have the requisite purpose. It should also be noted that unlike ss 27 or 30, s 29 does not refer to the effect or likely effect of a provision; the purpose of the provision is the operative test. It is irrelevant whether the purpose is achieved or could be achieved.

(1) The time at which purpose is to be ascertained: As with the "in competition" element, it is not clear from s 29 when the purpose of a provision is to be judged. The change in tense from "entered into" and "arrived at" in para (a) to "has the purpose" in para (b) suggests that an arrangement not having the requisite purpose when entered into could become unlawful if the requisite purpose manifested itself at any later time. Assuming this view to be correct, is there a notional new arrangement for the purposes of s 29(3) (entering into an arrangement) or is the plaintiff limited to invoking s 29(4) (giving effect to an arrangement)? The

contrary view is that s 29 would not apply unless the exclusionary purpose existed at the time the parties entered into the arrangement. Australian commentators have suggested the wording of s 4F(a) of the Australian Act lends some support to this view in that sub-paragraph (i) of s 4F(a) refers to the purpose for which a provision *was* included in the arrangement. The equivalent New Zealand provision, s 2(5)(a)(i), however, uses the words *was* or *is* included.

(2) The relevance of the Australian s 45D authorities on purpose: Some Australian commentators have suggested that plaintiffs will have little difficulty in satisfying the purpose test of s 4D of the Trade Practices Act. Relying on decisions given in the context of s 45D of the Australian Act, commentators have noted that it is the immediate purpose rather than the long-term or ultimate purpose that is relevant. In the words of Dr Steven Corones, "[i]f the immediate purpose is to prevent, restrict or limit the supply or acquisition of goods or services, s 4D applies even though the ultimate purpose may be pro-competitive": S G Corones, *Competition Law and Policy in Australia* (1990) at p 224. See also Pengilley (1988) 3 Canta L Rev 351.

One should be cautious about applying the above views to s 29. As mentioned, the Australian commentators' views are based, largely, on a body of case law on s 45D of the Trade Practices Act. No equivalent provision appears in the New Zealand legislation. The Australian Commonwealth Parliament inserted s 45D into the main body of the Trade Practices Act in 1977 following a recommendation by the Swanson Committee. The conduct of concern to the Committee was secondary boycotts where employees of one employer place a boycott upon the dealings of that employer with another person. As finally enacted, s 45D was not confined to employee conduct, but most litigation has involved unions and unionists. The section has been a very controversial one; on 12 September 1984, the Australian Labour Government introduced the Trade Practices Amendment Bill which proposed the repeal of ss 45D and 45E. The Bill was defeated in the Australian Senate.

There are several differences between ss 4D(1) and 45D(1) of the Trade Practices Act. Mason CJ canvassed these in his dissenting judgment in the *Jewel* case (supra). Regarding the purpose component of the two sections, the Chief Justice made the following observations at p 52,561:

> A further lack of symmetry between the sections is evidenced by the fact that the "likely effect" of any exclusionary provision is not taken into account in considering a breach of s 45(2)(a)(i) or (b)(i) [corresponding to s 29(3) and (4) of the Commerce Act], the purpose for making the exclusionary provision being the key concept. Section 45D(1), on the other hand, is not only concerned with the purpose of any concerted conduct but, as an essential element of liability, also requires that the likely effect of such conduct be the cause of substantial loss or damage to the business of the corporation. Further, the purpose referred to in s 4D(1) is required by s 4F(a)(ii) to be "a substantial purpose". In the case of s 45(d)(1), there is no requirement that the purpose for engaging in the proscribed conduct be "a substantial purpose", it being sufficient if it was one of several purposes: s 45D(2).

The High Court in *Jewel* was not required to address the issue of purpose; however, the Full Court in *Jewel Food Stores Pty Ltd v Amalgamated Milk*

Vendors Association Inc (1990) ATPR para 40-997 did deal with the matter in some detail. The majority (Sheppard and Wilcox JJ) cited with approval the Full Court's first decision on s 45D in *Tillmanns Butcheries Pty Ltd v The Australasian Meat Industry Employees' Union* (1979) 27 ALR 367. There, Bowen CJ, with whom Evatt J agreed, dealt with duality of purpose as follows at p 374:

> Nevertheless, the fact that a union and its members acting together have a union purpose does not necessarily exclude the possibility that they had, also, the purpose of causing substantial loss or damage to the business of the corporation. The statement of Evatt J in *McKernan v Fraser* (1931) 46 CLR 343 is apposite. His Honour in that case (at p 403) said: "Sir Godfrey Lushington said, in special reference to combined action against employers or non-unionists on the part of unionists, that to ask the question whether they acted to defend their own trade interests or to injure their economic adversary for the time being is equivalent to asking of a soldier, who shoots to kill in battle, whether he does so for the purpose of injuring his enemy or defending his country. The analogy is sound because combined strike action is usually undertaken for the purpose of causing harm to the employers and for the improvement or maintenance of the standard of unionists".

After citing several other cases which have adopted the approach laid down in *Tillmanns Butcheries*, Sheppard and Wilcox JJ observed at p 50,992:

> Ordinarily, the purpose of inflicting damage upon the business of a person is to cause that person to modify its behaviour in some way for the advantage of the person occasioning the damage of its members. In other words, the damage is a means to an end. Consequently, although a primary purpose of the milk vendors was to protect their own businesses, another purpose which they had was to damage or injure the applicant's business. That was the means by which they intended to achieve their primary purpose.

The dissenting Judge in the Full Court in *Jewel*, Spender J, took a somewhat different approach to purpose. His Honour said at p 51,000:

> If as is usually the case, the result of concerted action is the causing of damage to the target, it does not at all follow that at least one of the purposes for which the conduct was engaged in was the causing of damage. This approach which attributes as a purpose that which frequently is not a purpose but a means, is to be contrasted with the true position as indicated by Viscount Simon LC in *Crofter Hand Woven Harris Tweed Company Limited v Veitch* (1942) AC 435.

In the passage Spender J quoted from Viscount Simon's judgment, the Lord Chancellor said:

> The test is not what is the natural result to the plaintiffs of such combined action, or what is the resulting damage which the defendants realize or should realize will follow, but what is in truth the object in the minds of the combiners when they acted as they did.

Spender J suggests (at p 51,001) that before it might properly be said that one of the purposes was to cause substantial loss or damage, something in the nature of "independent malevolence" should be required.

An editorial comment in the CCH report of the Full Court's decision in *Jewel* (1990) ATPR para 40-997 at p 50,985) is sympathetic to Spender

J's general approach to purpose, but suggests that the test of "independent malevolence", redolent of the law of common law conspiracy, prescribes too high a standard of proof. In the commentator's view:

> The better course might be to require a showing of alternative means of achieving the ultimate purpose, a task which will be relatively simple in typical secondary boycott cases but which will at least give some weight to the fact that purpose is an independent element of the contravention, and will serve to distinguish those cases where a breach of s 45D should not be found.

In addition to Spender J's comments, some earlier decisions: see, for example, *Nauru Local Government Council v Australian Shipping Officers Association* (1978) ATPR para 40-087, support the view that it is open to defendants to argue that the purpose of the secondary boycott was not to cause substantial loss or damage, but rather to preserve some business interest or to further some union objective. Since *Tillmanns Butcheries*, however, such an approach has not found favour with the Courts. Sheppard and Wilcox JJ in *Jewel* (supra) acknowledged at p 50-991 that the bulk of authority prevents any argument for invoking an ultimate purpose:

> As we see the case, there can be no doubt that the respondents possessed such a purpose. It is true that this purpose was an immediate purpose rather than an ultimate purpose; but it is too late in the day to contend, at least in this Court that the only type of purpose which may satisfy a description in sec 45 D(1)(b) is an ultimate purpose.

For the purposes of interpreting s 29 of the Commerce Act, it is the writer's view that the New Zealand Courts should not place too great a reliance on the interpretation of purpose given in the context of s 45D of the Trade Practices Act. First, as Mason CJ pointed out in the *Jewel* case, there are considerable differences between ss 4D(1) and 45D(1). Secondly, the s 45D cases have not played a significant role in any of the decided s 4D cases. Thirdly, the approach of the Australian judiciary to s 45D is arguably explained by the nature of the section and the circumstances which led to its introduction. No such circumstances attach to s 29. Finally, the High Court of Australia has yet to address the issue of purpose either in the s 4D or s 45D context.

(3) The New Zealand approach to purpose: To date, the most detailed discussion of purpose under the Commerce Act is that of the High Court (McGechan J and Mr G Blunt) in *Union Shipping NZ Ltd v Port Nelson Ltd* [1990] 2 NZLR 662. In drawing a distinction between "purpose" and "intention", the Court said at p 707:

> Like so many mental concepts, the reference to "purpose" has its difficulties. The word used is not merely "intention". Intention to do an act, which it is known will have anticompetitive consequences, in itself is not enough. "Purpose" implies object or aim. The requirement is that "the conduct producing the consequences was motivated or inspired by a wish for the occurrence of the consequences": Donald and Heydon *Trade Practices Law* (1989) para 5,400 at p 2,621.

The Court gave the following example to illustrate its point that a party who intentionally carries out an action which it knows will have anti-competitive results need not necessarily have an anti-competitive purpose, at p 707-708:

> Refusal to supply may be designed to eliminate, but it may be due to poor performance or credit rating. The activity covered will not be prohibited, despite foreseen anticompetitive effects, if it arises for unrelated legitimate business reasons, without purposive pursuit of those anticompetitive outcomes in themselves.

In similar vein, Wilcox J in *Eastern Express* (supra) drew a distinction between the purpose to be inferred from certain conduct and the natural result of that conduct. His Honour said in the context of rejecting a s 46 predatory pricing allegation at p 52,896:

> The mere admission by Messrs Hannan of a recognition that the aggressive activity which they thought necessary for the successful defence of *Wentworth Courier* would damage *Eastern Express* is not an admission by them that damage was a purpose of their activity. The statement is equally consistent with a recognition that it would be a result.

The High Court's distinction of purpose and intention in *Union Shipping* has much in common with Spender J's discussion of these terms in the *Jewel* case (supra). After discussing the rejection in Australian criminal law of the proposition that a person intends the natural consequence of his or her acts, his Honour said at p 50,996:

> More importantly in the present case, "intention" is not "purpose", and it is wrong to treat the concepts as interchangeable. The section does not require simply that the conduct be engaged in with the intention of causing substantial loss or damage; and it is wrong to equate a finding of the existence of that intention to a finding that the conduct was engaged in for the purpose of causing substantial loss or damage.
>
> It is true that the effect of sec 45 D(2) and para 4F(b) is that a person is deemed to be engaged in conduct for a particular purpose if the person engaged or engages in the conduct for purposes that included or include that purpose and that purpose was or is a substantial purpose. Those provisions recognise that persons can engage in conduct for a number of purposes. If logically a distinction is properly to be maintained between means and ends, it is, I believe, wrong to characterise the means by which a purpose is sought to be achieved as a co-existing purpose.

Unlike their Australian counterparts, the New Zealand Courts have not painted themselves into a corner over purpose. There is sufficient flexibility in the concept of purpose as defined in *Union Shipping* to ensure that pro-competitive conduct will not be struck down under s 29.

(4) Is purpose used objectively or subjectively?: It is unclear whether "purpose" in the context of s 29 denotes an objective or subjective test.

Some commentators and Judges have argued that an objective test is called for in those sections of the Act which refer to the "purpose" of the provision of a contract, arrangement or understanding. Franki J in *Trade Practices Commission v TNT Management Pty Ltd* (1985) ATPR para 40-592 adopted this view in relation to s 4D(1)(b) of the Trade Practices Act. His Honour said at p 46,136:

It is always difficult to decide whether the word purpose is used subjectively or objectively. In my opinion, in general, where one is concerned with the purpose of a provision in an arrangement or understanding, it is the objective purpose which is relevant. Where one is concerned with the purpose of a person in the doing of an act, it is usually the subjective purpose which is relevant. However, the meaning of the word must depend on its context.

From a policy perspective, it would be unwise for a Court to ignore subjective intent in the context of the exclusionary provisions section. This is because of the inherent problems in distinguishing legitimate collective refusals to deal from unlawful ones – subjective intent has a useful role in helping the Court make a distinction.

One can find support for the subjective approach in *Hughes v Western Australian Cricket Association Inc* (1986) ALR 662. In that case, Toohey J, after reviewing the Australian authorities on "purpose" said at pp 688-89:

> I accept the view that it is the subjective purpose of those engaging in the relevant conduct with which the Court is concerned. All other considerations aside, the use in subsec 45(2) of "purpose" and "effect" tends to suggest that a subjective approach is intended by the former expression. The application of a subjective test does not exclude a consideration of the circumstances surrounding the reaching of the understanding.

More recently, the Full Federal Court of Australia in *ASX Operations Pty Ltd v Pont Data Australia Pty Ltd* (1991) ATPR para 41-069 affirmed the subjective test in relation to s 4D. In reaching this view, the Full Court placed considerable reliance on s 4F of the Australian Act (corresponding to s 2(5) of the Commerce Act):

> In its operation upon provisions stated to have a particular purpose, sec 4F uses the words "the provision was included in the contract ... for that purpose or for purposes that included or include that purpose". This indicates that sec 4F, in this operation, requires one to look to the purposes of the individuals by which the provision was included in the contract, arrangement or understanding in question. It therefore directs attention to the "subjective" purposes of those individuals.
>
> . . . .
>
> Section 4F has application also to subsec 45(2) in so far as it is directed to "exclusionary provisions", as spelled out in s 4D. In our view, there should be applied to the expression in subsec 4 D(1), "the provision has the purpose . . .", the same "subjective" construction we favour in reading the references in subsec 45(2) itself to the purpose of provisions of a contract, arrangement or understanding.

Although the bulk of Australian authority favours a subjective approach to s 4D, it is possible that the New Zealand Courts will opt for an objective test for both ss 27 and 29: see *Auckland Regional Authority* (supra) and *Fisher & Paykel Ltd v Commerce Commission* (1990) 3 NZBLC 101,655.

In practice, the issue whether "purpose" is used objectively or subjectively may not prove to be of any great significance, given the legislative aids to proving purpose and the fact that the prohibition is not a criminal provision. Even if the Courts ultimately adopt a subjective test they will rely on inferences drawn from conduct, from the wording of the provision and the terms of the arrangement concerned, as well as on direct evidence from the parties themselves: G Tapperell, R Vermeesch & D Harland, *Trade Practices and Consumer Protection* (3rd edn, 1983) at p 168.

(5) The relationship between purpose as used in s 29 and s 36: There are indications that the Courts may interpret the purpose tests in ss 29 and 36 in a uniform manner even though the wording and focus of the purpose provisions in the two sections differ. On policy grounds this move is to be welcomed. For as Professor Barry Kellman has observed in *Private Antitrust Litigation* (1985) at p 42:

> Culpable exclusion has two manifestations: as the product of concerted agreement to foreclose a victim from a market and the product of unilateral exercise of monopoly power.

A recent example of a Court's willingness to accept that a finding of purpose under the misuse provisions also satisfies the purpose test of the exclusionary provisions section is found in *ASX Operations Pty Ltd v Pont Data Australia Pty Ltd* (1991) ATPR para 41-069. There, the Full Federal Court of Australia confirmed the Trial Judge's finding that ASX and ASXO, in imposing particular contractual terms in their agreements with Point Data, did so with the purpose of preventing Pont Data competing with ASXO in the wholesale information market and deterring it from competing with JECNET in the retail market. Such conduct breached s 46(1)(c) of the Trade Practices Act (corresponding to s 36(1)(b) of the Commerce Act). Having confirmed the Trial Judge's finding, the Full Court proceeded on the assumption that the upholding as to "purpose" in the setting of s 46(1)(c) also provided a sufficient footing for a holding of purpose for s 4D.

A similar approach is also discernible in Cooke P's judgment in *New Zealand Apple and Pear Marketing Board v Apple Fields Ltd* [1989] 3 NZLR 158. While the interpretation of "purpose" was not directly in issue in the Court of Appeal, Cooke P did express disagreement with the Trial Judge's findings on purpose. The President stated that the Board in imposing a second-tier levy on new growers and existing growers expanding production, had set out to reduce the attraction to enter the industry or make new plantings. By achieving some degree of fairness the levy, at the same time, inevitably carried out a policy or purpose of restricting production. The President concluded at p 162:

> On the evidence and the Judge's analysis of the facts, I cannot avoid the conclusion that the arrangement for the levy between the Board and the Federation, however well motivated, has had a substantial purpose of deterring entry into the apple-growing industry or increases of production.
>
> That view means that there also have been breaches of s 29 and s 36 unless the statutory exception about to be considered applies.

The significance of the judicial willingness to inter-link ss 29 and 36 is that it demonstrates that the Courts are unlikely to take a narrow view of the purpose test in s 29 and will be prepared to consider both objective and subjective factors.

(6) Must all the parties to the agreement share the required purpose?: There is judicial support for the view that all the parties to the arrangement must

share the required purpose. *Carlton and United Breweries (NSW) Pty Ltd v Bond Brewing New South Wales Ltd* (1987) ATPR para 40-820 involved a struggle between the then two largest brewery concerns in Australia, United and Carlton (Carlton) and Bond Brewing (Bond) for supremacy in the New South Wales beer market. Two major breweries and hotel owners, Tooheys Ltd and Tooth & Co Ltd, had traditionally dominated this market. In 1983, Carlton purchased the New South Wales brewery business of Tooth but not its 266 hotels. A term of the 1983 agreement was that Tooth would not sell the hotels for five years, and that when it did it would give the right of first refusal to Carlton. In the meantime, Bond had acquired Tooheys, the other major New South Wales brewery. This brought Bond/Tooheys into direct competition with Carlton in the New South Wales beer market. In May 1985, Tooth agreed to give to Bond/Tooheys head leases over most of its 266 hotels. This would enable Bond/Tooheys to increase its sale of beer at the expense of Carlton. Carlton sought an interlocutory injunction restraining the implementation of the agreement alleging, inter alia, that it contained an exclusionary provision and consequently was in breach of s 45(2)(a)(i) of the Trade Practices Act (corresponding to s 29(3) of the Commerce Act).

Wilcox J found that the agreement did not fall within s 4D(1)(b) as it did not have the required purpose. His Honour had no doubt that Bond/Tooheys in entering into the agreement had the purpose of reducing the supply of Carlton's beer to Tooth's hotels but that there was no evidence to indicate that Tooth shared this purpose. His Honour accepted that Tooth was aware that Tooheys wished to acquire the leases in order to improve its market share; "but to say that a party is aware of the purpose of another party is a very different thing from saying that the former shared the latter's purpose": p 48,880. According to his Honour, there was no reason to suppose that Tooth was actuated by any purpose other than that of obtaining the best bargain which was commercially attainable.

Wilcox J's ruling has significant implications, particularly if the New Zealand Courts do not confine themselves to the parties' immediate purpose but also take account of their ultimate aim or object. Potential problems may arise in indirect boycotts where the conspirators first exert pressure on the target's suppliers or customers. Assuming that the conspirators are successful in coercing the target's suppliers or customers to join the boycott and withhold supply or orders from the target, it is difficult to argue that all the parties to the boycott have the same common purpose. The purpose of the parties who are competitors of the target is to drive the target from the market; the purpose of the parties who are the target's suppliers or customers is to maintain their dealings with the target's rivals. Nevertheless, it is possible to argue that all share the same immediate purpose, viz to restrict supply or acquisition to or from the target. As it is likely that the Courts will construe such a purpose as a substantial one, then in terms of s 2(5)(a) of the Act it may not matter that not all the parties share the same ultimate object or aim.

One should not overlook that Wilcox J gave his ruling in the context of interlocutory proceedings. While the ruling appears appropriate in the case before his Honour, its rigid application to the more conventional types of boycott situations would seriously undermine the effectiveness of the section.

(7) Preventing, restricting or limiting: The exclusionary provision must have the purpose of preventing, restricting or limiting supply to, or acquisition from, any particular person or class of persons or to, or from, these persons in particular conditions: s 29(1)(b).

The words "preventing, limiting or restricting" are quantitative in nature. Total prohibition (you cannot have any) is covered by the use of "preventing" and partial prohibition (you may not have more than X quantity) by the use of "limiting". Howard Schreiber in *The New Deal in Trade Practices* (1977) at p 62 gives the following example of the role of "restricting":

> If A and B agree that they will each supply only on a C.O.D. basis that would be an agreement to supply any amount ordered but containing, nonetheless, an exclusionary provision – that the supply is subject to a restriction on credit.

The words "in particular circumstances" or "on particular conditions" are already encompassed by the word "restriction"; the draftsperson probably inserted them out of an abundance of caution: Schreiber (supra).

On its surface, s 29 appears to be tripartite in structure. Mason CJ in *Jewel* (supra) at pp 52,559-60, however, doubted whether the section was so limited. The Chief Justice said that a tripartite interpretation requires one to read into s 4D(1)(b) the word "directly" as governing "preventing, restricting or limiting". His Honour did not favour reading the section in this way and said that s 4D could cover the following example: A and B could prevent, restrict or limit the acquisition of goods or services from C by impeding a fourth party D from acquiring goods or services from C or alternatively, by inducing D not to acquire goods or services from C.

(d) "ANY PARTICULAR PERSON OR CLASS OF PERSONS"

In terms of s 29(1)(b) the exclusionary provisions must be aimed at a "particular person or class of persons".

As originally enacted, s 4D of the Trade Practices Act was limited to exclusionary provisions aimed at "particular" persons. Section 4D was the subject of judicial interpretation in *Trade Practices Commission v TNT Management Pty Ltd* (1985) ATPR para 40-512 where the Australian Trade Practices Commission alleged a collective boycott by freight forwarding companies of Tradestock Pty Ltd. Tradestock wished to enter the business of transport brokering, an activity which was opposed by the National Freight Forwarders Association (NFFA). The NFFA held various meetings to discuss Transport Brokerage Agencies. It recorded minutes to the effect that such Agencies were not in the industry's best interests. Whilst the minutes of the NFFA meetings were worded in generality, Tradestock was specifically referred to in the minutes of two of the meetings. It should also be noted that Tradestock was the only transport broker in existence at the time. At the hearing on the merits, the Trade Practices Commission established that a contract, arrangement or understanding had been entered into and that as a result a concerted refusal to deal had taken place. However, the defendants successfully argued that the arrangements in question were not exclusionary provisions within the meaning of s 4D. Franki J, in dealing with the "particular persons" issue, contrasted the words "particular persons" in s 4D with the wording of s 47 of the Australian Act which draws a distinction between "particular persons" and "classes of persons". His Honour concluded at p 46,136:

> I accept the submissions of the defendants in this regard that an arrangement or understanding not to deal with a class or category of persons does not satisfy the requirement of an arrangement or understanding not to deal with "particular persons". However, the word "persons" will also include the singular. That conclusion is sufficient of itself to answer the claim made of giving effect to an exclusionary provision.

A somewhat different approach to the particularity requirement is evident in *Bullock v The Federated Furnishing Trades Society of Australasia (FFTSA)* (1985) ATPR para 40-509, a case decided shortly before the *Tradestock* decision. There, a union had allegedly used its industrial power to force carpet suppliers to sign agreements to the general effect that they would not give any work to independent contractors but instead would employ their own labour. A number of self-employed carpet layers who were commonly employed as independent contractors sought interlocutory injunctions against the FFTSA, alleging, inter alia, a breach of the exclusionary provisions section. In relation to this claim, Gray J found insufficient particularity for the purposes of s 4D. His Honour said at p 46,040:

> In my view, none of the agreements relevant to this proceeding would fall within the definition of "exclusionary provision" in sec 4D. The reason for this is that in each case the agreement intends to exclude all carpet buyers and not particular persons from operating otherwise than in accordance with its terms. In my view, sec 4D is plainly designed to apply to provisions which exclude particular persons in the sense of persons whose identity is known or can be ascertained. It is not directed towards the exclusion of the entirety of the available body of persons who could conceivably be called upon to perform or supply the relevant services.

On appeal ((1985) ATPR para 40-577), the Full Federal Court disagreed with Gray J's view on the particularity issue. Woodward J (with whom Sweeney J agreed) said at p 46,696:

> [I]n my view, it is clearly arguable that "self-employed carpet layers" or at least "the self-employed carpet layers who have in the past been employed by the carpet suppliers who have been forced to sign the FFTSA agreement" are particular persons within the meaning of the Act. It is arguable that particular persons may be identified by general description, or as members of a designated class without being individually named.

Having regard to the provisions of s 4F, Smithers J took the view that it was necessary to inquire not so much what were the words of the relevant provision in the agreements but whether, whatever the nature of the provision, it was included in the agreement for the purpose of preventing the acquisition of services from particular persons in particular circumstances or on particular conditions. His Honour expressly rejected the argument that since the provision excluded all carpet layers it could not be regarded, in any sense, as excluding particular carpet layers. Because the provisions had the purpose of preventing the corporate respondents

705

from acquiring carpet laying services from the persons from whom they customarily acquired such services, Smithers J felt that the provisions had sufficient particularity to satisfy the requirements of s 4D.

In *Hughes v Western Australian Cricket Association (Inc)* (1986) ATPR para 40-736, Toohey J said at p 48-046 "the existence or otherwise of "particular persons' is to be determined as a matter of substance and not of form". A rule of the Cricket Council of the Western Australian Cricket Association (WACA) precluded a player from taking part in a cricket match, other than a match recognised by the Australian Cricket Board or WACA, without the consent of the Cricket Council. At a meeting on 4 November 1985, the WACA and its associated clubs amended the rule to provide that any player found in breach thereof was automatically disqualified until reinstated by the Cricket Council. Although the amended rule did not refer to individual cricketers and was of general application, Toohey J had no doubt that it was aimed at the applicant, cricketer Kim Hughes, as well as others who had participated in rebel tours of South Africa. His Honour was of the opinion that the decision to amend the rule at the meeting on 4 November constituted an under-standing between the clubs and the WACA, which understanding con-tained an exclusionary provision.

In order to overcome the perceived difficulties arising from Franki J's narrow interpretation of "particular persons" in the *Tradestock* case, the Trade Practices Revision Act 1986 amended s 4D by inserting the words "or classes of persons" after "particular person". The particularity re-quirement is now the same in both the New Zealand and Australian exclusionary provisions sections.

The broadening effect of the 1986 Australian amendment is seen in *ASX Operations Pty Ltd v Pont Data* (1991) ATPR para 41-069. Pont Data contended that the provisions in the Dynamic Agreement obligating it not to sell or supply the information contained in Signal C to any person other than a licensee who was a party to the agreement in question constituted an exclusionary provision. The appellants argued that there was no exclusionary provision as the particularity requirement of s 4D could not be satisfied. The Full Court at p 52,070 responded to the appellants' argument as follows:

> It was said that the persons or classes of persons excluded must still be identified if sec 4D is to apply. That may be conceded, but they are identified, in the present case, by the characteristic that they may not be supplied with the information in question unless they accept and become bound by the restraints imposed by the Dynamic Agreement. Such persons come within a category or description defined by a collective formula: cf *Pearks v Mosley* (1880) 5 App Cas 714 at 723. They ordinarily would be treated as constituting a particular class, even though at any one time the identity of all the members of the class might not readily be ascertainable. What distinguishes the class and makes it particular is that its members are objects of an anticompetitive purpose, with which sec 4D is concerned.

The New Zealand Courts have not yet considered the particularity requirement. The Commerce Commission's decision in *Re The Insurance Council of NZ (Inc) (Nuclear Risks Exclusion Agreement)* Decision No 244 (6 March 1990) illustrates the point that the particularity requirement will not be satisfied if the arrangement is aimed generally. The agreement in issue excluded the supply of nuclear risks insurance to *all* persons and so did not satisfy the criterion of due particularity set out in s 29(1)(b).

(e) BOYCOTT "VICTIM" MUST BE IN COMPETITION WITH ONE OR MORE OF THE BOYCOTTING PARTIES

(1) The genesis of s 29(1)(c): The Commerce Amendment Act 1990 introduced an additional requirement into the definition of an exclusionary provision in the form of para (c) of s 29(1). The new provision requires that the particular person or the class of persons to whom the provision relates must, in relation to the supply or acquisition of the restricted goods or services, be in competition with one or more of the parties to the contract, arrangement or understanding.

The genesis of the reform stems from the then Department of Trade and Industry's discussion paper, *Review of the Commerce Act 1986* (August 1988). The Department in advocating reform of s 29 drew heavily on a paper by Dr Warren Pengilley for support for its views as to the perceived deficiencies of s 29. Dr Pengilley's paper has since been published in (1988) 3 Canta L Rev 357.

In its *Review*, the Department placed considerable importance on the fact that an exclusionary provision need not have a purpose of lessening competition. In the Department's view, this could lead to conduct being condemned as per se illegal notwithstanding that the conduct had no anti-competitive results. The Department cited an example of a professional golfing association excluding a professional golfer from a tournament because of that person's poor tournament record. According to the Department, the exclusion would breach s 29 because it has the "purpose of preventing, restricting or limiting the supply of goods or services" from any particular person, by the parties to the contract. The Department also cited an example from Pengilley's paper of an arrangement for the television coverage of a sports event with "black outs" in the area where the event was taking place in order to encourage local people to attend the actual event. According to Pengilley, "there is no doubt that the immediate purpose is to deny services to certain identifiable persons or institutions"; however, invoking United States decisions, Pengilley argues that the provision's purpose is not anti-competitive but pro-competitive. Again drawing from Pengilley, the Department suggested that the phrase "class of persons" extended the scope of s 29 such that trade associations implementing a policy of refusal to deal with non-members would now fall within the prohibition.

Having canvassed the perceived deficiencies of s 29, the Department considered that there was merit in introducing a competition test into s 29. The test would require that an exclusionary provision had the purpose of substantially lessening competition between the parties to the arrangement and the persons at whom the boycott was aimed. The Department also suggested that consideration should be given to requiring the boycotted party to be in competition with those taking the action. The Department noted that such an approach would be more in line with the current United States position.

As it eventuated, the Department's first recommendation was not acted on; its second recommendation, and presumably its less preferred one, was given legislative endorsement.

In the writer's view, the Department acted precipitately in advocating reform of s 29. It was too quick to assume that the hypothetical situations discussed by Dr Pengilley would be decided in the manner he suggested. As discussed earlier in this commentary, several Australian commentators have assumed that the Courts will treat "purpose" in the same way as they have approached it in s 45D. Such an assumption may be valid in the Australian context, but, for the reasons indicated earlier, the New Zealand Courts may be most reluctant to adopt the s 45D line of cases on purpose. Second, the Department fails to mention the potential role of the Long Title to the Commerce Act viz "An Act to promote competition in markets within New Zealand and to repeal the Commerce Act 1975". The Long Title is likely to play an important role in the interpretation of s 29. The Courts could use it to confine the scope of s 29 to matters having a bearing on competition. The Trade Practices Act lacks a competition-oriented Long Title; furthermore, observers have commented on the greater willingness of the New Zealand Courts to adopt a purposive approach to the interpretation of commercial legislation compared to their Australian counterparts. Finally, the Department overlooks the ways in which the Courts have dealt with characterisation problems in the price fixing area. As we shall see, there is a growing realisation that literal price fixing is not necessarily price fixing in the antitrust sense. Similarly, not every concerted refusal to deal need be exclusionary in nature. There is a role for the rule of reason in the interpretation of s 29.

(2) The relevance of the American law: If interpreted along the lines suggested by Dr Pengilley and the Department of Trade and Industry, one must concede that s 29 in its original form would have resulted in an "overkill" situation. The insertion of paragraph (a) in s 29(1), however, has resulted in the section now having a serious "underkill".

The rationale for adding s 29(1)(c) is the belief that the new element would harmonise the section with the United States law on collective boycotts. This assumes, first, that the American boycott law is well-settled and, second, that the per se rule is limited to those boycotts where the victim is a competitor of the boycotting parties. Neither assumption, however, is well-founded.

(a) The unsettled status of the American law – As far as the first assumption is concerned, the comments of Justice Brennan delivering the opinion of the United States Supreme Court in *Northwest Wholesale Stationers v Pacific Stationery and Printing Co* 472 US 284 (1985) are apposite, at p 294:

> "Group boycotts" are often listed among the classes of economic activity that merit per se invalidation under s 1 of the Sherman Act. Exactly what types of activity fall within the forbidden category is, however, far from certain "[T]here is more confusion about the scope and operation of the per se rule against group boycotts than in reference to any other aspect of the per se doctrine." L. Sullivan, *Law of Antitrust* 229-230 (1977). Some care is therefore necessary in defining the category of concerted refusals to deal that mandate per se condemnation.

Justice Brennan then noted the circumstances under which the Court had applied the per se rule to past boycott cases (ibid):

Cases to which this Court has applied the per se approach have generally involved joint efforts by a firm or firms to disadvantage competitors by either "directly denying or persuading or coercing suppliers or customers to deny relationships the competitors need in the competitive struggle." ... In these cases, the boycott often cut off access to a supply, facility, or market necessary to enable the boycotted firm to compete, ... and frequently the boycotting firms possessed a dominant position in the relevant market.... In addition, the practices were generally not justified by plausible arguments that they were intended to enhance overall efficiency and make markets more competitive. Under such circumstances the likelihood of anticompetitive effects is clear and the possibility of countervailing procompetitive effects is remote.

Justice Brennan, however, made it clear that "a concerted refusal to deal need not necessarily possess all of these traits to merit per se treatment": p 295. His Honour concluded with a brief review of the status of the per se concept and the group boycott prohibition, at p 298.

A plaintiff seeking application of the per se rule must present a threshold case that the challenged activity falls into a category likely to have predominantly anticompetitive effects. The mere allegation of a concerted refusal to deal does not suffice because not all concerted refusals to deal are predominantly anticompetitive. When the plaintiff challenges expulsion from a joint buying cooperative, some showing must be made that the cooperative possesses market power or unique access to a business element necessary for effective competition.

Even though the Supreme Court's opinion in *Northwest* exhibits a marked degree of caution in applying the per se rule to group boycotts, the Court failed to develop a general test for identifying those collective refusals to deal which do warrant per se treatment. Rather, it developed a specific test for an individual type of collective refusal to deal, viz an expulsion from a joint buying arrangement that appeared to have efficiency-enhancing characteristics. In line with its recent price fixing cases, the Court sanctioned the need for a collective refusal to deal to undergo a characterisation process to determine whether it is almost certain to prove anticompetitive.

Northwest left many questions unanswered concerning the precise scope of the per se rule as applied to group boycotts. However, two subsequent Supreme Court decisions, *Federal Trade Commission v Indiana Federation of Dentists* 476 US 447 (1986) and *Federal Trade Commission v Superior Court Trial Lawyers* 493 US 411 (1990) indicate that the Court will have little hesitation in condemning group boycotts under either a per se rule or a "truncated" rule of reason if they involve a naked restraint of trade.

While the most recent Supreme Court boycott decisions suggest appropriate lines of inquiry when considering the interpretation of s 29, perhaps of greater relevance for our purposes are the lower Federal Courts' decisions prior to *Northwest* that developed their own analysis for determining whether or not a collective refusal to deal should receive per se treatment. Unlike the Supreme Court decisions, these cases dealt with refusals which lacked an obvious anti-competitive character. The problem confronting the lower Courts was that the decisions of the Supreme Court in *Klor's Inc v Broadway-Hale Stores Inc* 359 US 207 (1959) and *United States v General Motors Corp* 384 US 127 (1966) appeared to have foreclosed any considerations of purpose and motive when determining the validity of concerted refusals to deal.

The most prominent of the lower Courts' decisions was *E A McQuade Tours Inc v Consolidated Air Tour Manual Committee* (CATM) 467 F 2d 178 (5th Cir 1972) *cert denied* 409 US 1009 (1973). McQuade, who was in the business of offering tour packages, sued CATM, an organisation of air carriers which published a tour manual for travel agents. In the case of one particular hotel, CATM refused to list McQuade as an available option despite the fact its tour package had been included for the hotel in the previous year. CATM's refusal was based on McQuade's failure to provide CATM with the written authorisation from the hotel. McQuade, relying on Supreme Court authority, contended that its exclusion from the manual was a per se violation of s 1 of the Sherman Act. The Fifth Circuit Court of Appeals held that CATM's refusal was not a per se boycott. Referring to the Supreme Court cases, the Court said at pp 186-87:

> In all of these cases, the touchstone of per se illegality has been the purpose and effect of the arrangement in question. Where exclusionary or coercive conduct has been present, the arrangements have been viewed as "naked restraints of trade", and have fallen victim to the per se rule. . . . We conclude that resort to the per se rule is justified only when the presence of exclusionary or coercive conduct warrants the view that the arrangements are a "naked restraint of trade". Absent these factors the rule of reason must be followed in determining the legality of the arrangements.

The Court's opinion makes it clear that coercion or exclusion were significant, not as results, but only as objectives. The Court concluded that all major Supreme Court decisions finding group boycotts per se illegal fell into three categories: (1) horizontal combinations among traders at one level of distribution whose purpose was to exclude direct competitors from the market; (2) vertical combinations at different marketing levels designed to exclude a direct competitor of a member of the combination; or (3) combinations that are designed to influence coercively the trade practices of boycott victims rather than to eliminate competition. Only if an agreement fell within one of these categories should a Court invoke the per se rule.

In the case before it, the Court found there had been no coercive conduct or exclusionary intent on the part of the defendants nor had there been any conspiracy between CATM and the plaintiff's competitors. Accordingly, the Court concluded that the rule of per se illegality was not appropriate and that the conduct should be judged under the rule of reason.

The purpose-based characterisation process formulated by the Fifth Circuit in *McQuade* proved influential with a number of federal circuits either relying expressly upon it or developing a similar analysis of their own to distinguish those collective refusals to deal deserving per se treatment from those requiring the complete rule of reason examination. See, for example, *Worthen Bank & Trust Co v National Bankamericard Inc* 485 F 2d 119 (8th Cir 1973) *cert denied* 415 US 918 (1974); *De Filippo v Ford Motor Co* 516 F 2d 1313 (3rd Cir 1975).

It is interesting to speculate whether those responsible for the drafting of s 4D of the Australian Act were influenced by the *McQuade* line of cases.

The Fifth Circuit modified its *McQuade* approach in *United States v Realty Multi-List Inc* 629 F 2d 1351 (5th Cir 1980). The Department of Justice alleged that members of a real estate multiple listing service (RML) had formed a group boycott in violation of s 1 of the Sherman Act. The Court considered the question as to whether the membership criteria for the service operated as a group boycott of those real estate agents who did not qualify. While reiterating the purpose-based standard of *McQuade*, the Court, influenced by the Supreme Court's price fixing characterisation approach in *Broadcast Music Inc v Columbia Broadcasting Systems Inc* 441 US 1 (1979), added an efficiency-creating component to the analysis. The Court said at p 1367:

> The presence of purposefully exclusionary or coercive conduct is a strong indication that the boycott is a naked restraint of trade; indeed, if no other purposes are present, this purpose will warrant outright condemnation of the practice. In light of our discussion of the per se rule, however, . . . it is also necessary to inquire further to determine whether the practice is at least potentially reasonable ancillary to joint efficiency-creating economic activity.

The Court, while recognising that RML's challenged practices – refusing to deal with non members and restricting membership – might potentially be reasonably ancillary to RML's existence, was not convinced that they were reasonable in this case. The Court observed at p 1371:

> [W]here a broker is excluded from a multiple listing service with the requisite market power without an adequate justification in the competitive needs of the service both the broker and the public are clearly harmed.

The Court remanded the case for consideration of the anti-competitive effect of the membership rules.

(b) Need there be a competitive relationship between the victim and the boycotting parties under American law? – Those who argue that the American law requires the victim to be in competition with the boycotting parties commonly cite as authority *Smith v Pro Football Inc* 593 F 2d 1173 (DC Cir 1978). There, the Court stated at p 1178 the group boycott concept only applied to "a concerted attempt by a group of competitors at one level to protect themselves from competition from non-group members who seek to compete at that level". The Court found support for its view in Professor Lawrence Sullivan's *Handbook on the Law of Antitrust* (1977) ch 3 paras 89-90. Sullivan argued that the per se rule should be limited to "classic boycotts" which he defined as "an effort by a group of traders to exclude or inhibit a competitor trying to enter or compete in their market either by themselves not dealing with the competitor or by coercing or inducing one or more suppliers or customers not to deal with him": p 255, n 5.

As Sullivan acknowledged, the Supreme Court's two motion picture cases involving concerted refusals to deal presented a problem. In *Paramount Famous Lasky Corp v United States* 282 US 30 (1930) film distributors concertedly agreed not to deal with exhibitors who failed to comply with the arbitration clause in a standard form contract used by all the distributors. The Court described the arrangement as "necessarily and directly" tending to destroy competition. In *United States v First*

National Pictures Inc 282 US 44 (1930), the same distributors agreed not to deal with new theatre owners unless they either assumed the obligations of prior owners or deposited cash security with the distributors' credit committee. Referring to *Paramount* and two earlier boycott cases, the Supreme Court condemned the agreement.

While Sullivan concedes that "the casebooks and commentators tend to group *Famous Lasky* and *First National Pictures* with boycott cases", he points out that the Supreme Court did not use the term boycott in either case. In order to keep the per se rule respecting boycotts coherent, Sullivan favoured labelling arrangements concertedly setting trade terms as "loose-knit concerted action" which would be subject to rule of reason analysis.

Shortly after the publication of Sullivan's treatise, the Supreme Court addressed the meaning of "boycott" in *St Paul Fire & Marine Insurance Co v Barry* 438 US 531 (1978). St Paul, one of only four sellers of medical malpractice insurance in Rhode Island, convinced the other three sellers to refuse to sell to St Paul's insured physicians until those physicians accepted new terms from St Paul. The plaintiff physicians, unable to obtain the insurance necessary for practice, challenged the conduct as an illegal boycott. The principal issue on appeal was whether the alleged conspiracy was immunised from Sherman Act coverage by the McCarran-Ferguson Act, which permits the States to regulate the "business of insurance" but provides for Sherman Act coverage of "any agreement to boycott, coerce or intimidate". The defendants admitted that the conduct may have been anti-competitive but denied it was a boycott because St Paul was not a competitor of the physicians and did not intend or attempt to exclude those competitors. The defendants cited Sullivan as authority for the proposition that the boycotters and the ultimate target must be in a competitive relationship. Rejecting this view, the Court said at p 543:

> As the labor-boycott cases illustrate, the boycotters and the ultimate target need not be in a competitive relationship with each other. This Court has held unlawful concerted refusal to deal in cases where the target is a customer of some or all of the conspirators who is being denied access to a deserved good or service because of a refusal to accede to particular terms set by some or all of the parties. See, eg *Paramount Famous Lasky Corp v United States* 282 US 30 (1930).

The problem with Sullivan's requirement is that it leads to an overly-formalistic approach to boycott law. Professor Robert Heidt in (1986) Vanderbilt L Rev 1507 in discussing Sullivan's view comments at p 1510, n 16:

> Granted, being the plaintiff's horizontal rivals may increase the defendants' incentive to use self-regulation in order to put the plaintiff at a competitive disadvantage. Too much, however, is made of this factor. The result is a distressing, formalistic tendency to decide these cases by diagramming the defendants' and the plaintiffs' relative positions in the chain of distribution and then jumping to conclusions based on that diagram.

The problem is compounded in the New Zealand setting because it is the "victim" of the boycott, ie the particular person to whom supply or acquisition is restricted, who must be in competition with one or more of the boycotting parties. In the United States, the focus is on the ultimate target of the boycott, thus allowing the Courts to apply the per se rule to indirect boycotts against competitors, even though the immediate victim is a supplier or customer. The classic indirect boycott case is *Fashion Originators Guild of America Inc v Federal Trade Commission* 312 US 457 (1941). Members of a Guild who designed and manufactured women's dresses sought to prevent "style piracy" through an agreement to refuse to deal with retailers who had purchased from the target manufacturers that sold copies. Through collective action, the Guild "persuaded" over 12,000 retailers to "cooperate" with the Guild's boycott. Those retailers who did sell a copyist's work were subject to an elaborate system of private trial and appellate tribunals. The Supreme Court had no difficulty in condemning the boycott at p 468:

> The purpose and object of this combination, its potential power, its tendency to monopoly, the coercion it could and did practice upon a rival method of competition, all brought it within the policy of the prohibition.

We can conclude our discussion of the American law with the observations that cases like *Famous Lasky, First National, St Paul* and *Fashion Originators*, all of which involved blatant anti-competitive conduct, would not be subject to the s 29 prohibition as the victims were not in competition with the boycotting parties. All of the above cases, however, would arguably contravene the Australian boycott law.

(3) *Reliance on s 27 as an alternative to s 29:* An observer, conceding that s 29 has been severely limited by subs 29(1)(c), might well argue that if the conduct is so egregious a plaintiff should have no difficulty in succeeding under s 27. But this overlooks the differences between the two sections and the rationale for having an exclusionary provisions section. Assuming that the plaintiff is unable to satisfy s 29(1)(c), and the exclusion of the plaintiff from the market does not have the requisite purpose or effect of substantially lessening competition in a market, the boycott will escape condemnation under both ss 27 and 29 even though it may involve a naked restraint of trade. Professor Kellman (supra) at p 65 aptly sums up the rationale for condemning exclusionary conduct under a test of the type contained in s 29:

> [I]n all contexts of concerted efforts to exclude competitors, a court analyzing defendant's actions must focus solely on the nature of the defendant's conduct. The courts should not limit inquiry to what effects flow from the activity alleged to be antitrust culpable. Action which is exclusionary in nature violates the law if it unreasonably hinders plaintiff's attempts to compete in a marketplace of unfettered competition where skill and integrity are rewarded. Concerted exclusionary conduct may manifest itself either as a refusal to associate, a conventional boycott or an unreasonable refusal to deal. Each of these paradigms of anti-competitive activity illustrate a constant principle; it is illegal for independent actors to join together for the purpose of inhibiting the normal competitive forces, processes, or outcomes of the marketplace. Conduct designed to achieve such an end is antitrust culpable even without demonstrable proof of adverse effects on consumer welfare.

While it is acknowledged that there are important exceptions to the per se ban on group boycotts under American law, one must not overlook that the United States Courts have considerable flexibility in applying the rule of reason. This is well illustrated by *Federal Trade Commission v Indiana Federation of Dentists* 476 US 447 (1986). There, the Supreme Court invalidated under the rule of reason an agreement by a group of dentists to withhold patient x-rays from insurance companies. The x-rays were used to serve as a peer-review check on the appropriateness of the dentists' charges and as a cost containment mechanism. The Court declined to invoke the per se doctrine because the classic characteristics of a group boycott were lacking. The Court was also reluctant to condemn the rules of a professional association where the economic impact of the practices was not immediately obvious. Applying the rule of reason, the Court concluded that the Commission's finding of illegality was amply supported both factually and legally. The agreement had clear anti-competitive characteristics – it limited consumer choice and increased the cost for insurers and patients of obtaining needed information. The Court rejected the argument that either definition of a market or proof of market power was required; rather "the [FTC's] finding of actual sustained adverse effects on competition . . . is legally sufficient to support a finding that the challenged restraint was unreasonable even in the absence of elaborate market analysis": at p 461.

The Court's "truncated" rule of reason analysis was appropriate in the circumstances; the dentists' agreement was a naked restraint of trade. Such an approach, however, is not possible under s 27 of the Commerce Act. That section mandates a full market inquiry. It is interesting to note that the Seventh Circuit Court of Appeals which had earlier considered the case conducted a full market analysis and found the dentists lacked market power: 745 F 2d 1124 (7th Cir 1984). The Supreme Court reversed the Seventh Circuit's decision. In the New Zealand context, *Dentists* would not have been examined under s 29 because the insurance companies were not in competition with the dentists.

When considering the respective roles of ss 27 and 29, one cannot ignore the cost question. Section 29 cases will often involve David and Goliath situations. In most cases, the per se nature of s 29 will mean that litigation is likely to be more expeditious and less expensive than that generated under s 27. The *Tradestock* case demonstrates that a small firm may be wiped out financially if it challenges powerful firms alleged to have engaged in exclusionary behaviour. That case involved both full rule of reason analysis as well as consideration of the then new s 4 D. A small firm may well forgo litigation under s 27 if the s 29 route is closed to it.

(4) Section 29(1)(c) and potential competitors: As we have seen, s 29(2) deems a person to be in competition with another person if that person is or is likely to be, or but for the relevant provision, would be or likely to be, in competition with the other person. The subsection, however, expressly states the deeming rule applies "[f]or the purposes of subsection (1)(a) of this section. . . ." As no reference is made to s 29(1)(c), on the surface it appears that a potential competitor who is the subject of the exclusionary provisions will not be able to rely on s 29(2).

It would be a gross violation of the policy underlying s 29(1)(c) if this interpretation was adopted. For as Professor Sullivan (supra) has said:

> A classic boycott is an effort by a group of traders to exclude *or inhibit a competitor trying to enter or compete in their market* either by themselves not

dealing with the competitor or by coercing or inducing one or more suppliers or customers not to deal with him (emphasis added).

The Courts are likely to overcome this probable drafting oversight by applying a purposive interpretation to s 29 in accordance with the principles expounded by the Court of Appeal in *Northland Milk Vendors Assn Inc v Northern Milk Ltd* [1988] 1 NZLR 530. Cooke P in that case said at pp 537-38:

> This is one of a growing number of recent cases partly in a category of their own. They are cases where, in the preparation of new legislation making sweeping changes in a particular field, a very real problem has certainly not been expressly provided for and possibly not even foreseen. The responsibility falling on the Courts as a result is to work out a practical interpretation appearing to accord best with the general intention of Parliament as embodied in the Act – that is to say, the spirit of the Act. . . . Obviously therefore a great deal turns on the need for the Courts to appreciate and give weight to the underlying ideas and schemes of the Act.
> It can be helpful, even crucial, to have statements of general principle or purpose in the Act itself. . . . Whether or not the legislature has provided those aids, the Courts must try to make the Act work while taking care not themselves to usurp the policy making function, which rightly belongs to Parliament. The Courts can in a sense fill gaps in an Act but only in order to make the Act work as Parliament must have intended. See *Goodman Fielder Ltd v Commerce Commission* [1987] 2 NZLR 10 as to the Commerce Act 1986, a case which illustrates both aspects of that proposition.

The underlying ideas and scheme of the Commerce Act are readily ascertainable from the Act's Long Title and its substantive provisions. Both ss 29 and 30 are per se provisions; both have a requirement that the parties to the arrangement be "in competition with each other". Subsection 2 of ss 29 and 30 allows potential competitors to satisfy the competitive relationship requirement. The legislative intention prior to the Commerce Amendment Act 1990 regarding these two sections was clear – potential competitors were to be dealt with on the same basis as actual competitors. Although s 29(2) does not expressly apply to s 29(1)(c), one can regard this as an oversight. It is likely that the Courts will decide that s 29(2) impliedly relates to s 29(1)(c), since to allow a boycotting group to exclude a potential competitor, but not an actual competitor, would be contrary to the scheme and purpose of the Act.

41.4.4 Authorisation of exclusionary provisions

Section 58(5) and (6) provide that the Commerce Commission may grant an authorisation on the application of any person who wishes to enter into or give effect to a contract, arrangement or understanding to which s 29 would or might apply.

The test for authorisation of exclusionary conduct is found in s 61(7) which provides that the Commission shall not grant an authorisation unless it is satisfied that the entering into, or giving effect to, the exclusionary provision would likely result in "such benefit to the public" that it should be permitted. The subsection does not specifically require a weighing of public benefit against competitive or public detriment. Nonetheless, the Commerce Commission in *Re New Zealand Stock Ex-*

change Decision No 232 (10 May 1989) at para 62 followed the Australian practise and interpreted "such benefit to the public" as "a net or overall benefit after any detriment to the public has been taken into account".

Applicants normally have a difficult task in satisfying the authorisation test. This is because in many cases their conduct, though not necessarily anti-competitive, gives rise to no public benefit: see *Re South Pacific Tyres Ltd* Commerce Commission Decision No 247 (3 May 1990). However, in *Re New Zealand Stock Exchange* (supra) the Commission granted authorisation to an exclusionary agreement citing as public benefit the efficient operation and confidence in the capital and securities market which is essential to the market's existence. The Commission noted that the Exchange's objective admission criteria helped to ensure competence of members and thus increased public confidence. The Commission is likely to decline authorisation where is no causal connection between the claimed benefits and the restrictive arrangements: see *Re Speedway Control Board of New Zealand (Inc)* (1990) 2 NZBLC (Com) 104,536. The chances of success will be greater where the arrangement is likely to result in economic efficiencies. Section 3A, introduced by the Commerce Amendment Act 1990, requires the Commission, when considering public benefits, to have regard to any efficiencies which will result, or be likely to result, from the practice. Thus, the Commission is likely to authorise an exclusionary provision where it is an integral part of a joint productive efficiency-enhancing venture and is no more restrictive than necessary.

41.5 PRICE FIXING

41.5.1 Overview

The Commerce Act 1986 renders collusive price fixing arrangements illegal per se. Parties to such arrangements are subject both to penalty action by the Commerce Commission and to private action. To obtain immunity from such action, it is necessary for the parties to a price fixing arrangement to apply to the Commerce Commission for an authorisation. The possibility of the Commission granting authorisation for a price fixing arrangement is not great.

Analysis of the statutory ban starts with s 27. That section prohibits provisions in contracts, arrangements or understandings that have the purpose or have or are likely to have the effect, of substantially lessening competition in a market. It is s 30, however, which effectively prohibits price fixing by deeming such conduct for the purposes of s 27 to have a substantially anti-competitive purpose or effect.

A similar situation applies to price fixing covenants with ss 28 and 34 performing a similar role to ss 27 and 30. The analysis of s 30 is equally applicable to s 34.

One must read the deeming provision of s 30 along with ss 31 to 33, for these sections exempt from the deemed illegality certain types of pricing arrangement: viz joint venture pricing; recommended prices issued by associations with 50 or more members; and joint buying and promotion arrangements. The exempted arrangements are still, however, subject to the substantial lessening of competition test contained in s 27.

41.5.2 Analysis of s 30

(a) NEED FOR A CONTRACT, ARRANGEMENT OR UNDERSTANDING

For s 30 to apply, there must be a contract, arrangement or understanding. The concept of a contract, arrangement or understanding and the methods of proof thereof have been discussed above.

(b) NEED FOR PROVISION OF CONTRACT ETC TO HAVE THE PURPOSE, EFFECT OR LIKELY EFFECT OF FIXING, CONTROLLING OR MAINTAINING THE PRICE FOR GOODS OR SERVICES, OR ANY DISCOUNT, ALLOWANCE, REBATE OR CREDIT IN RELATION TO THOSE GOODS OR SERVICES

(1) Meaning of "price fixing": Competitors may *fix* prices by agreeing on the actual amount of a price, or agreeing on a formula or some other method of calculation. If price is expressly or tacitly agreed to, the Courts will construe the agreement as price fixing. The fact that there is no "penalty" for parties not adhering to prices fixed or agreed is immaterial: *Federal Trade Commission v Pacific States Paper Trade Association* 273 US 52 (1927).

It is important to note that s 30 applies not only to arrangements which actually fix prices, but also to those which *provide* for the fixing, controlling or maintaining of prices. An arrangement may create a basis or system which "provides" the means for the price to be fixed etc either currently, or at some time in the future, or only in certain circumstances. Arrangements by competitors to employ specific devices that facilitate collective pricing would be caught. One must distinguish the collusive situation, however, from that where members of an oligopoly "tacitly" employ such devices but their conduct falls short of a contract, arrangement or understanding. For discussion of this topic, see Hay (1982) 67 Cornell L Rev 439; Clark 1983 Wis L Rev 887; Carstensen 1983 Wis L Rev 953.

Although the dictionary meaning of "fix" suggests an element of permanency, this is not an essential element of price fixing. This was made clear by Lockhart J in *Radio 2UE Sydney Pty Ltd v Stereo FM Pty Ltd* (1982) 62 FLR 437. His Honour, after referring to dictionary meanings, stated (at p 449):

> In my view the fixing of a price for the purpose of s 45A [the Australian equivalent of s 30 of the Commerce Act] does not connote an element of permanency, but generally suggests the settling or determining of a price that is not instantaneous or merely ephemeral. A person may fix a price for his goods knowing that he may wish to vary it at some future time, but generally not so soon as would to business people be regarded as merely momentary or transitional.

In a subsequent Australian case, *Trade Practices Commission v Parkfield Operations Pty Ltd* (1985) 5 FCR 140, Fox J said (at p 143):

> [P]rices can be "fixed" even if all that is proposed is an increase to a certain figure, without any provision as to when or by what machinery, or what amount, a further change may take place. Assurance of permanency, or long duration or constant relativity is not necessary.

On appeal the Full Federal Court of Australia confirmed this view, stating that there was no requirement that the provision should have the purpose of fixing, controlling or maintaining a price for any length of time: (1985) 7 FCR 534.

(2) The characterisation question: In *Radio 2UE*, supra, Lockhart J considered the vexed question of whether he should characterise conduct which in the literal sense fixes prices as price fixing for the purposes of the Act, even though the conduct allegedly improves competition. The case concerned the propriety of two radio stations offering to purchasers of radio time a combined rate card, which aggregated the two stations' separate charges. There was no evidence that the radio stations consulted each other before determining their own rates. On the facts, Lockhart J concluded that the setting of the combined rate did not involve any understanding that each station would maintain its rates for a continuous period. His Honour took the view that the agreement for the combined card rate did not substantially lessen, but rather improved, competition in the Australian market for radio advertising. Lockhart J expressed the following views on the characterisation question at p 448:

> The Court's task is to characterise the conduct before it in a given case. Care must be taken in performing that task because, by its very nature, the violation of s 45A is deemed, for the purpose of s 45, to substantially lessen competition per se. Such a finding may have far reaching consequences to the competitors concerned.
>
> It is important to distinguish between arrangements . . . which restrain price competition and arrangements which merely incidentally affect it or have some connection with it. Not every arrangement between competitors which has some possible impact on price is per se unlawful under the section. Nor in my view was s 45A introduced by Parliament to make arrangements unlawful which affect price by improving competition. It is fundamental to both ss 45A and 45 [corresponding to ss 30 and 27 of the Commerce Act] that the relevant conduct, in purpose or effect, substantially lessens competition or would be likely to do so. If competition is improved by an arrangement I cannot perceive how it could be characterised as a price fixing arrangement within the ambit of these sections. This case is an example in my view of such an arrangement.

In view of Lockhart J's finding that the radio stations had not entered into any price fixing arrangement, his Honour's observations on the interpretation of s 45A of the Australian Act must be regarded as obiter. On appeal the Full Federal Court of Australia confirmed Lockhart J's ruling that the combined card did not involve a price fixing arrangement, and suggested, without reaching a concluded opinion on the point, that the arrangement would also not have breached ss 45(2) and 45A had the parties not been free to vary their individual rates at any time: (1983) 68 FLR 70. However, the Full Federal Court declined to express any view as to whether Lockhart J was correct in suggesting that a price fixing arrangement which is shown to have in fact a net advantageous effect on competition cannot constitute a breach of the price fixing provisions.

Commentators in the main reacted sharply to Lockhart J's interpretation of s 45A. See, for example, Blakeney & Freilich (1986) 60 ALJ 668. Most writers viewed the section as a statutory embodiment of the American per se rule not admitting of any competition analysis once the plaintiff has established the requisite degree of price fixation. These commentators argued that the genesis of s 45A was the United States Supreme Court's landmark decision in *United States v Socony-Vacuum Oil Co* 310 US 150 (1940), which established beyond doubt that horizontal price fixing was illegal per se. Furthermore, any flexibility in the application of the rule possible under the American antitrust law had been foreclosed in the Australasian context by the statutory deeming provision which was conclusive of Parliament's intention. Professor Robert Baxt, however, took a different view. Writing in (1983) 57 ALJ 423, Baxt applauded Lockhart J's analysis, describing it as imparting "the correct antitrust principles from the United States". Baxt also saw the decision as allaying concern that commentators had expressed in Australia "that where per se offences were introduced in the legislation the Courts would be likely to read these provisions too rigidly, and not adopt what has been described in the American jurisprudence as a *rule of reason* approach".

It is unfortunate that neither Lockhart J, nor any of the commentators mentioned above, referred to the contemporary developments in United States price fixing law. Although the rule of per se illegality for horizontal price fixing remains in force in that country: see *Federal Trade Commission v Superior Court Trial Lawyers Association* 493 US 411 (1990), the way in which Courts view the rule was considerably altered by the Supreme Court's decision in *Broadcast Music Inc v Columbia Broadcasting Systems Inc* 441 US 1 (1979). In that case, the Supreme Court recognised that "[n]ot all arrangements among actual or potential competitors that have an impact on price are per se violations of the Sherman Act or even unreasonable restraints": at p 23. The case involved a price fixing challenge to Broadcast Music's practice of pooling copyrights on musical works owned by individual composers and then licensing use of the works only on a pooled basis. The Court held the per se rule inapplicable, although it found that the defendant's activity was "price fixing in the literal sense: the composers and publishing houses joined together into an organization that sets its price for the blanket licenses it [sold]": at p 8. The Court stated that "price fixing' is a shorthand way of describing certain categories of business behaviour" that are per se unlawful but cautioned that characterising conduct as price fixing "is not a question simply of determining whether two or more potential competitors have literally "fixed' a price": at p 8. The Court observed that rather than being a "naked restraint of trade", the blanket licence accompanied a useful integration of competitors, and that "[j]oint ventures and other cooperative arrangements are also not usually unlawful, at least not as price-fixing schemes, where the agreement on price is necessary to market the product at all": at p 23.

The importance of *Broadcast Music* is that it shows that the United States Supreme Court was willing to entertain the argument that business persons could engage in literal price fixing for pro-competitive purposes. In such circumstances the conduct would not amount to "price fixing" within the meaning of the per se rule. The difficulty with the decision is that the Court did not give a doctrinal basis for its ruling, although it did use language and illustrations that would enable subsequent Courts to accommodate the decision within the ancillary restraints doctrine.

Judge, later Chief Justice, Taft formulated the ancillary restraints doctrine in *United States v Addyston Pipe and Steel Co* 85 F 271 (6th Cir 1898) *modified* 175 US 211 (1899). The doctrine makes a distinction between "naked" and "ancillary" restraints. A "naked" restraint of trade is an agreement in which the parties have no significant dealing other than the elimination of competition; such agreements have no redeeming virtues and are deserving of condemnation. In contrast, an "ancillary" restraint of trade is an agreement which is subordinate and collateral to a separate, lawful business purpose. The restraint is needed to make a desirable business transaction or integration either efficient or possible. To escape condemnation, an ancillary restraint must be essential, not merely helpful or useful, to the implementation of the underlying transaction. Moreover, the restraint cannot be more restrictive or extensive than necessary to meet the parties' needs. The ancillary restraints doctrine provides a useful test by which potentially pro-competitive agreements are elevated from the illegal per se category to a rule of reason analysis.

The application of the ancillary restraints doctrine is seen in *National Collegiate Athletic Association (NCAA) v Board of Regents* 468 US 85 (1984), another landmark case in contemporary United States price fixing law. In *NCAA*, the Supreme Court confirmed that in factually complex situations it is legitimate for the fact finder to conduct an initial screening to determine whether the challenged activity is likely to have predominantly anti-competitive effect. The case concerned a Sherman Act, s 1 challenge to an NCAA arrangement with major television networks that, in relevant part, effectively fixed the prices paid for telecasts of college football games. The Court held that it would judge under the rule of reason standard horizontal restraints on the price or kind of television rights that member schools could offer to broadcasters because the case involved "an industry in which horizontal restraints on competition are essential if the product is to be available at all": at p 101. Although employing the rule of reason, the Court stated at p 104, n 26 that –

> ... there is often no bright line separating per se from Rule of Reason analysis. Per se rules may require considerable inquiry into market conditions before the evidence justifies a presumption of anti-competitive conduct.

The Court held that the existing NCAA television contract violated the Sherman Act under the rule of reason since it reduced member output, restrained member prices, and frustrated the ability of member institutions to respond to consumer preferences. Describing the television plan as a "naked restraint on price or output", the Court rejected NCAA's proffered justifications for employing the restrictions: at p 110.

While some commentators have criticised the Supreme Court for departing from the per se rule in a case where there was a naked restriction on price and output: see for example, Liebler (1986) 33 UCLA L Rev 1019, the Court's analysis is in line with its *Broadcast Music* standard. One can readily accommodate both cases within the *Addyston Pipe* naked/ancillary restraints methodology. Counsel in *Radio 2UE* appear to have overlooked the *Broadcast Music* decision. This is unfortunate as the issues in the two cases were very similar. The application of *Broadcast Music's* ancillary restraints principles would have enabled Lockhart J to have formulated a more principled basis for his interpretation of s 45A. Note, however, that the application of the doctrine would cast doubt on the correctness of the Full Federal Court's broad dictum that there would have been no breach of ss 45(2) and 45A even had the parties not been free to vary their individual rates at any time. The dictum is at odds with the doctrine's principle that an ancillary restraint cannot be more restrictive or extensive than necessary to meet the parties' needs. In *Broadcast Music*, the Supreme Court considered it significant that copyright owners were free to negotiate individually with potential users of the musical works.

To date, decision makers in Australia and New Zealand have not explicitly invoked the doctrine of ancillary restraints. However, two Australian Trade Practice Commission decisions explicable in terms of the doctrine are *Electric Lamp Manufacturers (Australia) Pty Ltd* (1982) ATPR (Com) para 50-033 and *Interflora Australian Unit Ltd* (1976) 3 TPCD [421]. In *Electric Lamps*, the Commission, after initially viewing certain restraints as anti-competitive, changed its mind in its final determination and regarded the restraints as an indispensable part of the joint venture operating agreement contributing indirectly to the aims of the venture itself, the latter being adjudged to be in the public benefit. *Interflora* was a single commissioner's decision. The Commissioner, Dr Warren Pengilly, thought that it was impossible to see how the Interflora scheme could operate without the recommended price provisions. In both cases, the ancillary restraints were needed to make the integration both efficient and possible.

In New Zealand, the characterisation issue was discussed by the Commerce Commission in *Re Insurance Council of New Zealand* (1989) 2 NZBLC (Com) 104,477, where the Commission ruled that an agreement among signatory members to remove a cost element in the costing of motor vehicle insurance did not amount to "price fixing". While recognising that, in a technical sense, any agreement by competitors in a market which has an influence on or interferes with the setting of a price amounts to price fixing, the Commission, following Lockhart J's approach in *Radio 2UE*, stated at p 104,482 –

> . . . for that interference to have any significance in a competition sense the price that is so fixed must not be "instantaneous or merely ephemeral", "momentary or transitory", or be the result of arrangements which "merely incidentally affect it".

The parties had agreed to remove the cost element in order to reduce or eliminate administrative and litigation costs, a saving which was likely to be passed on to consumers. The cost element agreement did not have a net effect of substantially lessening competition, as once the cost element had been removed the price for motor vehicle insurance then moved in accordance with "normal competitive pressure". Furthermore, the competitive conditions under which the industry operated made it unlikely that a cartel could successfully operate.

While Lockhart J's distinction between "arrangements which directly or indirectly restrain price competition" and those which "merely incidentally affect it" is a useful starting point on the characterisation issue, decision makers have to be careful not to lose sight of the statutory test. Arrangements which "merely incidentally affect" price may not satisfy the effect limb of s 30; however, they may still be caught if they have the *purpose* of price fixing. See Jackson (1983) 11 ABLR 310 at pp 316-18. The difficulty with the *Insurance Council* decision is not the Commission's factual finding – this can be supported on a purpose and effect analysis. Rather, the difficulty lies in the Commission's failure to articulate an operational methodology that legal advisers could usefully employ to determine when arrangements that have an indirect impact on price fall outside the ambit of s 30. Having embarked on the task of examining the characterisation question, the Commission could have explored the issue in more detail, taking cognizance of the contemporary American case law as well as the critical commentary on *Radio 2UE*.

At this stage, it is too early to predict how the New Zealand Courts are likely to approach the characterisation issue, and, in particular, whether they will be prepared to acknowledge the need for a competitive impact threshold analysis in ambiguous cases. Unlike the situation in the United States, the New Zealand legislation, through its authorisation provisions, allows for the canvassing of efficiency arguments which a rigid application of the per se rule might otherwise stifle. Commentators are divided on the question of whether the flexibility exhibited in the recent American cases can be accommodated within the confines of the Australasian statutory ban against price fixing. Compare S C Corones *Competition Law and Policy in Australia* (1990) at pp 229-31 with Stevens & Dean in *Competition Law and Policy in New Zealand* (R Ahdar ed, 1991) ch 10.

(3) Arrangements "controlling" or "maintaining" price: By employing the words "control or maintain", those responsible for the legislation have indicated that the per se ban on price fixing should extend to arrangements which, while not prescribing any agreed price or uniform method for computing it, nevertheless affect the mechanism of price formation.

The United States Supreme Court's opinion in *Socony-Vacuum*, supra, has obviously influenced the framers of the legislation. Speaking for the majority, Justice Douglas encapsulated the Court's view in a passage at p 223, which has become the definitive pronouncement on the scope of the price fixing rule:

> Under the Sherman Act a combination formed for the purpose and with the effect of raising, depressing, fixing, pegging, or stabilizing the price of a commodity . . . is illegal per se.

On policy grounds, it is desirable that the New Zealand Courts construe the phrase "fix, control or maintain price" broadly, along the lines suggested by the Supreme Court in *Socony-Vacuum*, supra. There is a danger, however, that the Courts may focus narrowly on the constituent words of the phrase. There is some evidence of this in *Radio 2UE* (1982) 62 FLR 437 where Lockhart J began his analysis of the phrase under discussion by referring to dictionary meanings of the words "fix" and "maintain". His Honour said, at p 449 that "[g]enerally, to maintain a price assumes that it has been fixed beforehand". On appeal, the Full Federal Court expressed the view, at p 72, that "the word 'fixing' in s 45A takes its colour from its general context and the words used with it . . .": (1983) 68 FLR 70. But the Full Court went on to say that there must be "an intention or likelihood to affect competition before price 'fixing' can be established". If the members of the Full Court were suggesting a need to prove intention in every case, their comment ignores the plain words of the section which clearly indicate that "purpose" and "effect" are disjunctive.

Maximum price arrangements are likely to run foul of s 30 if they have the effect of controlling or maintaining price. Courts have condemned such arrangements in the United States because "such agreements, no less than those to fix minimum prices, cripple the freedom of traders to sell in accordance with their judgment": *Kiefer-Stewart Co v Joseph E Seagrams & Sons* 340 US 211, 213 (1951). See also *Arizona v Maricopa County Medical Society* 457 US 332 (1982). Advocates of the "consumer welfare" approach to antitrust law believe that such judicial concern is misplaced and argue that harm to competition should be the sole concern of antitrust law. See, for example, Blair & Fesmire (1986) 37 Syracuse L Rev 43; Easterbrook (1981) 48 U Chi L Rev 886. Section 30 of the New Zealand Act, however, with its focus on competition between the parties to the agreement, rather than in the market as a whole, would appear to accommodate the United States decisions outlawing maximum horizontal price fixing agreements. See Ahdar (1989) 13 NZULR 271. On strict competition grounds, the condemning of maximum price arrangements is justified, since prices proclaimed as maxima are often in practice followed as minima. Also, a cartel may use maximum prices as a profit-pooling device. The authorisation provisions are available to accommodate those arrangements which do have positive public benefits. See *Re New Zealand Kiwifruit Exporting Association (Inc) – New Zealand Kiwifruit Coolstores Association (Inc)* (1989) 2 NZBLC (Com) 104,485.

Quota agreements for production or supply will usually have the direct effect of controlling or maintaining prices. A scheme of this kind was in issue in *United States v Socony-Vacuum Oil Co*, supra. To prevent "distress gasoline" from small refiners depressing market prices, the major oil companies entered into an informal agreement to purchase from the smaller refiners all their distress gasoline. They did not make any agreement regarding price, except that they were to make purchases at the "fair going market price". Because they had the storage capacity and developed distribution systems, both of which the smaller refiners lacked, the major oil companies were successful in removing much of the distress gasoline from the market. The Supreme Court had no difficulty in discerning from the evidence a purpose to raise and to stabilise prices. Although not substantively necessary in light of the clear evidence of purpose, the Court also found that the arrangement had an elevating and stabilising effect on prices.

Market division either on a product, geographic or customer basis may also serve as a substitute for price fixing. See *Palmer v BRG of Georgia Inc* 111 St Ct 49 (1990). In many cases it may be easier to divide the market and share it, rather than try to agree on the prices to be changed. Market division also has the advantage of avoiding non-price competition which in the traditional price fixing arrangement tends to dissipate cartel profits. If the arrangement operates so as to "control or maintain" the price of the goods concerned, it will be subject to the s 30 deeming rule.

Agreements controlling the flow of goods or services to the market, collusive tendering and bidding arrangements, and market sharing schemes stand out as obvious candidates for challenge under s 30. Apart from these likely targets, a wide range of commercial practices could be potentially at risk under s 30. Where any doubt exists, parties to commercial arrangements would be well advised to consider modifying their arrangements or availing themselves of the authorisation provisions.

(4) Meaning of "price", "discount", "allowance", "rebate" and "credit": Section 2(1) broadly defines "price" as including:

> valuable consideration in any form, whether direct and indirect, and includes any consideration that in effect relates to the acquisition or disposition of any interest in land, although ostensibly relating to any other matter or thing.

Resort to the statutory definition may assist in determining whether an agreement relates to price. It does not follow, however, that because a matter falls within the statutory definition of price any agreement relating thereto is itself illegal. Section 30 will prohibit the agreement only if it has the purpose or has or is likely to have effect of fixing, controlling or maintaining price, not because the matter directly agreed upon is "price".

To prevent simple avoidance, an ideal price fixing law should extend beyond price to cover methods for making adjustments to price: J D Heydon, 1 *Trade Practices Law* (1989) p 2227. This is the reason why the New Zealand legislature has extended s 30 beyond price to strike at agreements which have the purpose or effect of fixing, maintaining or controlling "any discount, allowance, rebate or credit in relation to goods or services . . .".

A wide range of adjustment benefits and concessions fall within the rubric of "discount, allowance, rebate or credit". Often it will be difficult to classify a benefit under one or other of the four terms. The principal reason for this is that there is considerable overlap between discounts, allowances, rebates and credits.

Agreements between competitors fixing the discount for payment in cash, or within 30 days, or fixing common quantity discounts would be examples of discount agreements. Trade discounts are another example although these need not necessarily involve a reference price.

"Allowance" is probably the widest of the four terms, covering deductions from price generally. It would catch agreed restrictions as to "trade-in" allowances on the purchase of new goods and also agreements on common freight allowances. The question of indirect price fixing involving the fixing of an allowance arose in *Trade Practices Commission v Nicholas Enterprises Pty Ltd* (1979) 40 FLR 74. Fisher J held that an arrangement between hotel proprietors to fix the allowance given on sales of beer at 14 bottles to the dozen fell within the Australian equivalent of s 30.

The commercial community normally understands the term "rebate" as a return of a sum of money after the purchaser has paid the full price. Price and rebate are often inseparable. Any type of horizontal fixing of rebates may run foul of s 30. Aggregated rebate cartels, ie agreements by which customers' rebates depend on their total purchases from all participating suppliers, have been a favourite target of antitrust enforcement agencies.

Australian commentators have questioned whether "credit" refers to credit terms, for example, thirty days. The Australian section uses the words *"a* credit". The indefinite article does not appear in s 30 of the Commerce Act which suggests that the draftsperson may have intended that the word should extend to credit terms. The fact that the word appears in the singular also lends weight to the argument that the term encompasses credit facilities.

Irrespective of whether credit terms are covered by "credit" or the broader concepts of "allowance" or "discount", any agreement relating to such terms will be subject to s 30. The United States Supreme Court reviewed the relationship between credit terms and price fixing in *Catalano Inc v Target Sales Inc* 446 US 643 (1980). In that case, beer wholesalers in California agreed to withdraw 30- to 40-day interest-free credit previously offered to retailers, and required that all future sales be in cash in advance or upon delivery. The Supreme Court held that the agreement was a form of price fixing and condemned it as per se illegal.

(c) SIGNIFICANCE OF "SUPPLIED", "ACQUIRED" AND "RESUPPLIED"

The words "supplied or acquired" in s 30(1)(a) make it clear that the Act's prohibition against agreements to fix prices is not exclusively directed to seller competitors. The Act also prohibits agreements between purchasers that affect prices. See *Re New Zealand Grape Growers Council (Inc)* (1991) 2 NZBLC (Com) 104,573.

This reflects the situation prevailing under the Sherman Act. American examples of illegal buyer price fixing agreements include *Mandeville Island Farmers Inc v American Crystal Sugar Co* 334 US 219 (1948) (sugar refiners agreeing to pay uniform price for sugar beet) and *United States v Champion International Corp* 557 F 2d 1270 (9th Cir 1977) *cert denied* 434 US 938 (1978) (bid-rigging by buyers of government timber).

By virtue of s 30(1)(b), the prohibition will also catch provisions in arrangements that fix, control or maintain *resupply* prices of goods. Thus, if competitors are parties to an arrangement designed to affect the prices charged by others in the *resupply* of their goods, s 30(1) will deem the arrangement to be substantially anti-competitive and thus prohibited by s 27.

No doubt the draftsperson directed this provision at collective resale price maintenance. It may well have application in oligopolistic industries where producers can tacitly coordinate their own selling prices without the need for an arrangement or understanding. However, in order to stabilise industry prices the producers may collectively agree on the resale prices that they will recommend to retailers.

The definition of "resupply" in s 2(4)(e) of the Act extends to situations where the goods are in an altered form or condition from that in which they were originally supplied. Further, the definition includes supply to another person of other goods incorporating the originally supplied goods. The statutory definition of "resupply" has the effect of extending the scope of s 30 to encompass collective resale price maintenance in a number of franchising and licensing contexts.

(d) TWO OR MORE OF THE PARTIES MUST BE "IN COMPETITION WITH EACH OTHER"

To succeed under s 30 a plaintiff does not have to demonstrate anti-competitive effect; however, a plaintiff does have to prove that the defendant parties are "in competition with each other". Thus, the legislature has aimed the section at horizontal arrangements. A purely vertical price fixing arrangement escapes condemnation under s 30 but would be subject to the per se ban on resale price maintenance contained in s 37 of the Act.

In most cases, it is unlikely that the requirement that the parties be "in competition with each other" will prove to be an obstacle to plaintiffs. The reasons for this are as follows. First, s 30(1)(a) uses the word "competition" alone and does not limit it to competition in a market. Secondly, s 30(2) provides that the reference in s 30(1)(a) to supply or acquisition by persons "in competition with each other" includes a reference to persons who *but for* the price fixing provision *would be* or would be *likely to be* "in competition with each other" in relation to the supply or acquisition of the goods or services. Section 30(2) thus clearly embraces potential competitors. Finally, the only firms likely to enter into a price fixing arrangement will normally be actual or potential competitors. Otherwise, why should two firms enter into an agreement to restrain the forces of rivalry if one of them is not in a position actually or potentially to constrain, or to be constrained by, the other's independently formulated strategies? See Round (1984) 12 ABLR 86.

However, in the Australasian context the fact that the requirement is expressed in statutory form may lead, at least initially, to prolonged debate as to whether the parties to an alleged price fixing arrangement are in fact competitors. This was the case in *Trade Practices Commission v Nicholas Enterprises Pty Ltd*, supra, where Fisher J was confronted with the question of whether two hotels who had been found to be parties to a price fixing arrangement in relation to the sale of bottled beer were in competition with each other. His Honour, relying on the opinion evidence of a chainstore executive and census work travel statistics, answered the question in the affirmative. The somewhat pragmatic view of competition adopted in the case suggests that once a plaintiff has established a horizontal price fixing arrangement, a Court is unlikely to receive with much sympathy the defence that the parties were not in competition with each other.

In a two-party situation it is clear that each must compete with the other if the deeming provision in s 30(1) is to apply. But if there are more than two parties, must all the parties to the agreement be "in competition with each other"? For a detailed discussion of this point, see Jackson (1983) 11 ABLR 310. An affirmative answer to this question is possible if one treats the words "or by any of them", appearing in paras (a) and (b) of s 30(1), as relating only to the goods or services supplied and having no limiting effect on the phrase "in competition with each other". This is a strained interpretation and would give rise to easy avoidance of the section. The more likely interpretation is that s 309 catches *all* parties to a price fixing arrangement regardless of their competitive status provided at least two of the parties acquiring or selling the goods or services in question are in competition with each other. On this construction, the words "each other" qualify "by any of them", so that "each" simply refers to any of the parties who have supplied goods or services. This interpretation finds support in the remarks of Fisher J in *Trade Practices Commission v David Jones (Australia) Pty Ltd* (1985-86) 64 ALR 67 (at p 93):

> The words "or by any of them ... in competition with each other" may indicate that it is not necessary for all of the parties to the understanding to be engaged in the supply of goods and thus in competition with each other in that market

for the deeming provision to be available. Alternatively it could mean that it is not necessary for them all to be in competition although it would appear essential for at least two to be engaged in the supply of goods to the market otherwise there would be no competition. The crucial words "or by any of them" indicate the necessity for at least two parties to the understanding to be in competition with each other. Either construction of the section supports the view that it is not essential for all parties to the understanding to be in competition with each other.

The *David Jones* case was concerned, inter alia, with the question of whether a wholesaler could be found to have contravened the Australian equivalents of ss 27 and 30 of the Commerce Act by being a party to a price fixing understanding with retailers, even though the wholesaler was not in direct competition with the retailers. Fisher J held that a person who participates in discussions leading to an understanding may be a party to that understanding provided he is aware of, although not necessarily committed to, each provision of the understanding. Furthermore, his Honour thought that it is not necessary for the parties to the understanding to be limited to those who are in competition in the same market. Applying these principles to the facts before him, his Honour found that the wholesaler was a party to an illegal price fixing arrangement. His Honour also made the observation that he would have held the wholesaler to have aided and abetted the respondent retailers to contravene the price fixing sections but for the fact that the wholesaler had not been so charged.

41.5.3 The statutory exemptions from s 30

(a) JOINT VENTURE PRICING

(1) Introduction: In ordinary circumstances, the terms of a joint venture arrangement will either touch directly upon the price of the goods or services that the joint venture will make available, or delegate price fixing to an executive board or officer. Because s 30 may have deemed any pricing aspects of a joint venture between competitors or potential competitors to be unlawful regardless of competitive impact, the legislature, in s 30(2), has exempted joint venture pricing of the type described from the deeming effect of s 30. In the absence of such an exemption, joint ventures would have found it difficult to engage in joint marketing without infringing the ban on price fixing.

(2) Statutory definition of joint venture: Section 31(1)(a) provides a definition of "joint venture". Two types of joint venture are covered by the definition, viz. (1) an unincorporated joint venture carried on by two or more persons whether or not in partnership; and (2) one carried on by a body corporate the joint venturers have formed for the purpose of carrying on a joint activity. Note that in the case of the latter, the body corporate performs the joint activity; the joint venturers themselves are only involved in activity jointly in the sense of their joint control of, or ownership, in the joint venture corporation.

(3) Analysis of s 31(2)(a)-(c): Section 31(2)(a)-(c) removes from the ambit of s 30 certain types of joint venture activity.

Section 31(2)(a) permits the parties to an unincorporated joint venture to fix the price at which jointly produced goods are to be jointly marketed or, alternatively, to fix the price at which each joint venturer may separately market his or her share of the joint product. In the latter case, the joint venturers may take advantage of the exception only if each takes and markets a share of the product proportionate to his or her interest in the joint venture. For goods to be "jointly produced" it appears that each party will need to play a genuine role in the physical process of production. It will not be sufficient that the goods (the subject of the productive process) are jointly owned.

Section 31(2)(b) permits fixation of the price of services where either the joint venture supplies the services or the parties themselves supply the services in proportion to their respective interests in the joint venture.

Section 31(2)(c) relates to a joint venture carried on through the mechanism of a body corporate.

Section 31(2)(c)(i) permits fixation of the price at which the corporation supplies the goods it produces. There is nothing in subpara (i) to permit producers to agree upon the price at which they will sell their respective products by the device of selling to a joint venture marketing vehicle resupplying at a price fixed by the parties. The corporate vehicle must both produce and market.

Section 31(2)(c)(ii) permits fixation of the price at which the joint venture corporation supplies services. The joint venturers may control the prices at which the corporation supplies the services irrespective of whether the corporation itself or others do the actual supplying. However, this rule does not apply where a shareholder, or any body corporate interconnected with a shareholder, supplies the services on behalf of the corporation. To have allowed joint venturers themselves to supply services in the name of a joint venture corporation would have provided an obvious means of avoiding the effect of s 30 in relation to price fixing of services.

(4) *The competitive impact of joint ventures:* The legislature has exempted joint venture activity of the type set out above from liability under s 30 presumably because it considers such ventures may be a good way of attaining commercial efficiency and development. However, the Courts can still strike down under s 27 all joint ventures, including those exempted from the operation of the deeming effect of s 30, if they have the purpose or effect of substantially lessening competition. In assessing the competitive impact of joint ventures, one must bear in mind that there will be other restrictions, apart from price controls, which may have a detrimental effect on competition. One will need to consider all the provisions of the joint venture arrangement, and of all other arrangements to which the joint venturers are party: s 3(5). It may be that the Courts will treat all reasonable restrictions necessary for the formation and efficient operation of the joint venture as not being caught by s 27. This is the position in the EEC. See *Commission Notice Regarding Restrictions Ancillary to Concentrations* OJ 1990 C 203/5.

(5) *The scope for authorisation:* Joint venturers wishing to avoid the consequences of ss 27 and 30 may avail themselves of the authorisation procedures contained in the Commerce Act. Section 61(6) of the Act

requires that the Commission be satisfied that the joint venture arrangement will result in a benefit to the public which will outweigh the lessening in competition that would result from the arrangement. In many cases, the ground for concluding that a benefit to the public will result is that the joint venturers will add a new endeavour to the economy. Further, applicants will no doubt argue that the new endeavour is not anti-competitive because it is beyond the capacity of any of the parties acting independently and does not therefore displace competition. It may be the only way of effecting economies of scale, or of enabling the parties to engage in costly research and development, or of ensuring that technologically sophisticated high volume production is commercially feasible. However, while such arrangements may well justify joint venturing to the point of production, competition policy questions arise when the joint venturers agree not only on joint production but also on the joint marketing of that product. In its authorisation decisions, the Australian Trade Practices Commission has made it plain that it will need to be convinced that in the circumstances of a particular project there is no realistic alternative to joint venture marketing, or at least the joint pricing element of it. In some recent determinations, the Australian Commission has granted authorisation for a joint venture pricing agreement for only a limited period of time. From a commercial perspective, however, such limited term authorisation may endanger the validity of long term sales contracts which in turn may endanger the fate of the joint venture structure itself. For an excellent analysis of the Australian experience of joint ventures and joint marketing, see Williamson [1989] AMPLA Yearbook 39.

(b) RECOMMENDED PRICES BY GROUPS OF 50 OR MORE PERSONS

(1) Background: Trade association recommended price agreements have been the main type of collective pricing arrangements in New Zealand. In the light of the experience under the Trade Practices Act 1958 and the Commerce Act 1975: see Hampton (1981) 1 Canta L R 198, one might have expected that the legislature would have made trade association price agreements illegal per se, subject only to the possibility of the parties applying for an authorisation of individual schemes. Instead, the legislature in enacting s 32 has chosen to follow the post-1977 Australian approach of exempting from the deeming effect of s 30 price recommendations made by groups with 50 or more members.

The 50-member criterion was the subject of comment by the Commerce Commission in *Re Chemists Guild of New Zealand (Inc)* (1987) 1 NZBLC (Com) 104,058, at p 104,062:

> The rationale of the exemption for contracts, arrangements and understandings between 50 members is not clear from the Act but where there are 50 members, or more, then a competitive environment may be more likely to exist than when there is a lesser number of members. Further, it may be that where there are more than 50 members there is likely to be a genuine trade association set up by the industry to deal with matters of general common interest to members, with the result that it is less likely to be a group of people combining with the objectives of fixing or controlling prices or some other aspect of the business conduct of its members. Whatever the precise rationale of the section, a similar provision applies in Australia and we note, incidentally, that there

has been no attempt in New Zealand to adjust the number of 50 participants downwards in recognition of the smaller economy. The privilege is given under the Act only to major trade associations representing a larger number of members.

Unlike the Australian legislation, the New Zealand Act contains a deeming provision, s 2(8)(b), providing that any recommendation issued by an association or body of persons to its members, or any class thereof, shall be deemed to be an arrangement between those members and between the association and those members. It is irrelevant that the rules of the association do not bind members to comply with the recommendations. The existence of the deeming provision overcomes any problems of proof that might otherwise arise for plaintiffs when alleging that members acting on a recommendation were acting pursuant to an arrangement.

The effect of the deeming provisions contained in s 2(8)(a) and (b) is to render all the members of an association liable for pecuniary penalties, damages and injunctions available under Part IV of the Act for the association's conduct, irrespective of particular members' involvement. Section 2(9)(a) mitigates this situation somewhat as it provides that liability will not arise where members expressly notify the association in writing that they dissociate themselves from the contract, arrangement or understanding and do so dissociate themselves. Members will also avoid liability where they can establish that they had no knowledge and could not reasonably have been expected to have had knowledge of the offending contract, arrangement or understanding: s 2(9)(b). A similar "lack of knowledge" defence exists under United States law. See *Kline v Coldwell Banker & Co* 508 F 2d 226 (9th Cir 1974) *cert denied* 421 US 963 (1975).

(2) Recommended prices must be genuine: The essential feature of a recommendation is that while it may identify a particular course of action, the adoption of it by any person is genuinely discretionary: B M Hill & M R Jones, *Competitive Trading in New Zealand* (1986) p 70. In *Chemists' Guild*, supra, the Commission stated at p 104,062: "it is quite clear from the Act that [recommended price lists] must have the purpose or effect of an aid to enable members individually to decide the price at which they sell". The Commission went on to list a number of actions which would be strong evidence that the prices in the list were not genuine recommended prices:

(1) the pressing of members not to discount from the recommended price or the pressing of members to use the margins recommended;
(2) the offering of inducements or special privileges to members to achieve the foregoing;
(3) the pressuring of suppliers not to supply, or to supply upon relatively unfavourable terms, to members who discount;
(4) announcements by the association to members that the price in question will rise or the making of similar statements to the effect that the recommended prices have some form of status or validity;
(5) agreements by individual members with each other to keep to the recommended price.

Any attempted or actual enforcement of the prices would destroy any notion of the prices being genuine recommended prices. If prices are not of this nature then the protection afforded by s 32 is lost.

(3) Legal status of price recommendation schemes: Assuming the existence of genuine recommended prices, what is the legal status of a price recommendation scheme under the Commerce Act 1986? There is the possibility that the recommendation may fall outside the Act altogether. This will be so where the recommendation does not have either the purpose or effect of fixing, controlling or maintaining price or any significant anti-competitive impact. However, because the inherent nature of recommended price schemes tends to create uniformity of prices, the number of schemes falling outside both ss 27 and 30 is not likely to be high.

This being the case, it is important to determine whether the association has 50 or more members. An association satisfying this requirement can claim the benefit of the s 32 exemption and can make a price recommendation to its members which will be exempt from the deeming effect of s 30. However, the Courts could still strike down under s 27 recommended price schemes involving 50 or more members if the arrangement substantially lessens competition in a market.

Where an association with fewer than 50 members issues a price recommendation, it will be automatically subject to the prohibition in s 27 if it has the purpose or effect of fixing, controlling or maintaining price in terms of s 30. Most schemes will have the effect of "maintaining" price. Even if the recommendation falls outside s 30, it may still be subject to the prohibition in s 27 if a plaintiff can show that the scheme has the requisite anti-competitive purpose or effect.

(4) The competitive impact of price recommendation schemes: The Commission in *Chemists' Guild*, supra, at pp 104,062-73 identified the following criteria which it thought would assist in determining whether or not a recommended price scheme would give rise to a substantial lessening of competition:

   (1)   the amount of business done by association members as compared with the market as a whole;
   (2)   the number of association members compared with others in the market;
   (3)   the degree to which members accept and adopt price recommendations;
   (4)   the degree to which a list and an association's involvement in the recommendations inhibit members in engaging in competition with each other;
   (5)   the ease of entry to the industry by a non-association member.

The Courts may not require the party challenging the recommended price agreement, which will normally be the Commerce Commission, to establish an actual substantial lessening of competition if the plaintiff can demonstrate that there is *potentiality* for competition in the absence of the agreement. The Trade Practices Appeal Authority adopted such an approach in *Re New Zealand Master Grocers' Federation* [1961] NZLR 177, where Judge Dalglish ruled that a detailed investigation of prices to demonstrate that an anti-competitive effect was actually realised in practice was not required. His Honour stated at p 191:

> The public is entitled to whatever benefits would flow from reductions in price brought about by competition. No estimate can be made as to the extent to which prices might be reduced, but ... price reductions have from time to time occurred and have caused some concern to the Federation.

The fact that s 3(2) of the Commerce Act 1986 allows "lessening of competition" to be read as including a reference to a preventing or hindering of competition assists the interpretation canvassed above.

No doubt defendants will invoke the decision of Davison CJ in *Hotel Association of New Zealand (HANZ)* (unreported, High Court, Wellington, M 326/78, 4 March 1980, addendum issued 2 April 1981) to counter this reasoning. In *HANZ*, the Chief Justice found that a recommended price scheme was not contrary to the public interest test contained in s 21 of the Commerce Act 1975 even thought the evidence showed uniform adherence to price lists, policing of deviations, mark-up pricing practices based on traditional percentages rather than a realistic assessment of costs and the existence of a 35 percent market share in a licensed industry. However, one can distinguish the *HANZ* decision on the ground that the Chief Justice was primarily concerned with the effect of the practice on prices, rather than on competition as such. For a detailed analysis of the *HANZ* case, see Hampton, supra.

On a conservative view, most association recommended price schemes would seem to be at risk of being struck down under s 27. One must temper this conclusion, however, by ascribing some weight to the fact that the legislature has seen fit to accord privileged treatment to recommended price schemes with 50 or more members. Such schemes may, therefore, be treated with some sympathy by the Courts and are unlikely to figure highly on the Commerce Commission's list of enforcement priorities.

(5) The scope for authorisation: Recommended price schemes may be the subject of an authorisation application; this is so regardless of the number of members involved. From experience gained under the 1958 and 1975 trade practices legislation, and also from the Australian experience: as to which see Wallace (1976) 4 ABLR 175, one can only predict that the chances of authorisation for a recommended price scheme will be small.

One area where there may be scope for a successful application is where a scheme provides costing assistance to small businesses and is not considered anti-competitive. The chances of authorisation are likely to be good where a small business trade association whose members are competing with other larger firms can demonstrate that a recommended price scheme can assist the efficiency of its members by saving them valuable time and cost by providing them with information that helps their competitiveness and viability. See *Re Retail Confectionery and Mixed Business Association (Victoria)* (1978) 4 TPCD [565] and *Applications of Various "Small Business" Trade Associations* (1978) 4 TPCD [561].

Rather than encourage reliance on recommended price schemes, the Australian Trade Practices Commission has suggested that small business trade associations offer forms of assistance to their members that provide them with information to set their own prices and assist them with their own costing. In pursuance of this policy, the Commission has raised no objection to the circulation of time manuals detailing times taken to carry out various repair tasks in relation to motor vehicles. See *Victorian Automobile Chamber of Commerce* (1976) 1 TPCD [348]. The Commission has also approved of calculation tables and formulas for calculating charge out rates but allowing for individual members to insert their own profit margins. See *Master Painters, Decorators and Signwriters Association of South Australia* (A 6003 9 April 1979). The Commission has also indicated its tolerance of small business trade associations distributing lists of selling prices based on various gross percentage mark-up figures allowing individual members to select the mark-ups appropriate to their own business thus saving them the time and money of calculating their own price lists. See *Pharmacy Guild of Australia* (A59 24 November 1977). Authorisation of schemes involving any of the above methods is not likely to be granted where the scheme is simply a recommended price arrangement in another form. See generally W Pengilly, *Trade Associations, Fairness and Competition* (1981) at pp 117-121.

(6) Professional fee schedules: Professional associations are one of the groups likely to claim the benefit of the s 32 exemption, particularly now that mandatory fee schedules are subject to control under the Act.

The Commerce Act 1986 dropped the special exemption for professional fees introduced by the Trade Practices Amendment Act 1971 and carried forward into the Commerce Act 1975. Under the 1986 Act a mandatory fee scale would clearly have the purpose and effect of fixing, controlling or maintaining price in terms of s 30 and thus the deeming rule providing for per se illegality would apply.

Although s 32 provides an incentive for professional associations to convert a mandatory fee scale into a purely recommended one, the section by no means eliminates antitrust concerns. This is because of the tendency for recommended fee scales to lead to price uniformity. If this situation occurs, the likelihood of a Court striking down a recommended fee scale under s 27 is high. There is also the possibility that price recommendations will be made by groups of local practitioners whose membership may fall short of 50 persons. Assuming that the recommended price arrangement has the purpose or effect of maintaining prices, then by virtue of s 2(8)(b) all members of the group will be liable to penalty action for breaching the per se ban on price fixing unless they can bring themselves within the protection of the s 2(9)(a) or (b) defences.

A professional association would be wise to seek authorisation for any proposed recommended pricing activity. It is highly unlikely that the Commerce Commission would grant authorisation in respect of minimum fee schedules preventing members from engaging in price competition. The Commission's attitude is likely to be similar to that adopted by the Australian Trade Practices Tribunal in *Re Association of Consulting Engineers of Australia (ACEA)* (1981) ATPR para 40-202. This was an application for authorisation of the code of ethics of the ACEA which banned fee competition among professional consulting engineers. The Tribunal regarded the ban on fee competition as sufficiently serious to outweigh any public benefit flowing from the arrangement. While condemning ACEA's price fixing activities, the Tribunal did allow that body to promulgate a recommended reference scale. The Tribunal directed that the scale should be introduced by words along the following lines:

> The fees provided for in this scale, which is a reference scale only, are fees which provide, for the average firm of consulting engineers, a reasonable level of profitability. However, consultants and prospective clients are free to negotiate fees on any basis whatsoever, including bases which are not at all related to the scale.

The Tribunal took account of the fact that the ACEA had available to it surveys of practice performance prepared at the University of New England which would enable the ACEA to factually support the statement in the introductory words that the fees provided for the average firm of consulting engineers a reasonable level of profitability. While not restricting ACEA to the sources of information from the University of New England surveys, the Tribunal made it clear that the statement in the introductory words ought not to be made except on a basis of fact or reliable opinion.

(c) JOINT BUYING AND PROMOTION ARRANGEMENTS

Section 33 provides that s 30 does not apply to the price of goods or services "collectively acquired, whether directly or indirectly by parties to the contract, arrangement or understanding": s 33(a), or "for the joint advertising of the price for the resupply of goods so acquired": s 33(b).

(1) Analysis of the statutory exemption: The exemption applies only to goods or services "collectively acquired". The term "collectively" is not defined, though it would seem from the use of the phrase "collectively acquired" in s 33(a) and the phrase "joint advertising" in s 33(b) that the acquisition need not be a joint acquisition in order to be treated as collective. The words "directly or indirectly" suggest that the legislature intended a wide variety of purchasing schemes to have the protection of the exemption. An arrangement whereby scheme members appoint the one agent to buy their total requirement or one involving the formation of a jointly owned buying group would seem to qualify as collective acquisitions. This would not be the case where members join together for promotional purposes but acquire their goods independently. The exemption requires collective action both at the point of acquisition and the point of advertising for resupply.

The exemption does not apply to the joint advertising of services, nor the joint advertising of goods not collectively acquired. While parties to arrangements involving the joint advertising of collectively acquired goods may agree on the *advertised* resupply price, the exemption stops short of allowing the parties to agree to sell at that price. Accordingly, any arrangement for joint advertising must not oblige participants to resell at the advertised price.

(2) The competitive impact of joint buying and promotion schemes: The justification for exempting joint buying and advertising schemes from the per se ban is because such schemes often do not detrimentally affect competition. Through collective action, a group of small traders can achieve economies of scale not otherwise open to them as individual

entities. By gaining access to facilities and expertise which are commonly available only to larger competitors, group members may be able to compete more effectively against their larger rivals. This may increase, not decrease, competition.

Early in the operation of the Australian legislation, the Trade Practices Commission expressed a willingness to approve schemes involving small retailers combining and jointly promoting their goods. In *Pharma-Buy* (1974-5) ATPR (Com) para 8,645, the Commission granted clearance to a buying and promotion group of 40 pharmacists in Melbourne. The Commission considered that any restraint of trade that resulted from the arrangement did not have and was not likely to have a significant effect on competition. In reaching this view, the Commission enumerated the following matters as being of relevance:

(1) The small number of participants in the scheme as a proportion of retail pharmacies as a whole.
(2) The relatively small turnover of each pharmacy.
(3) The few products involved in the promotion.
(4) The fact that products involved are marketed through a number of other large outlets.
(5) The widely scattered location of participants.
(6) The inability of participants significantly to influence price in the market as a whole.
(7) The fact that the promotion allows small outlets access to expertise and group buying, which facilities are commonly available to larger competitive outlets.
(8) The fact that the promotion in no way affects the freedom of each individual retailer to carry competitive lines.

The Trade Practices Commission has applied the *Pharma-Buy* logic in subsequent decisions and the Commerce Commission is likely to follow it in New Zealand. The Australian enforcement authority, however, has not been oblivious to the anti-competitive potential of joint buying and advertising schemes. In its guideline on the subject: see Information Circular No 15, *Joint Advertising, Marketing and Promotion Arrangements*, 12 May 1976, the Trade Practices Commission stresses that traders should not use joint arrangements of the type under discussion as a cloak for restrictive arrangements; traders should not use them where a substantial number of competitors in the industry as a whole or in any particular geographic location are involved and neither should they use them –

> . . . if the promotion consists of both large and small industry members. The effect of such an arrangement is likely to be that of restraining trade or commerce rather than giving to the smaller organisations the advantages enjoyed only by the large.

The Commission's Circular also emphasises that the promotion scheme must be voluntary, that there should be no disciplining of members for not taking part in any promotion, that there be no suggestion that members should not deal with any particular manufacturers or supplier, and that members should have the freedom to price as they think fit.

Given the scale of buying groups which have been emerging in New Zealand over the past few years, the Commerce Commission should adopt a cautious attitude to *large-scale* buying group activities. While s 33 exempts certain joint buying and advertising schemes from the per se ban on price fixing, all joint buying and advertising arrangements, including those exempted by s 30, fall for analysis under the general competition test of s 27. The factors identified by the Trade Practices Commission in its decisions and Information Circular will be relevant in determining whether buying groups will pass this test or not. It should be noted, however, that the pre-1977 Australian decisions and Circular were concerned with the question of whether or not the arrangement was likely to have a significant effect on competition in terms of the clearance test in operation at the time under the Australian legislation. The clearance test was abolished as from 1 July 1977. Nevertheless the pre-1977 Australian experience is still valuable when assessing competitive impact under s 27.

(3) The scope for authorisation: To avoid any legal uncertainty, parties to proposed joint buying and promotion schemes may seek authorisation of their proposed arrangements. Under the Commerce Act 1975, the Commerce Commission approved several such schemes on the grounds that "overall, they are competitive tools (against other distributors of like products) and in fact enhance competition at the retail level". See *Chemists' Guild* (supra) at p 104,063.

The earlier New Zealand experience, and the post-1977 Australian authorisation decisions, indicate that joint buying groups comprised of small traders should have little difficulty in satisfying the authorisation test. See *Re Application of Pharmacy Guild of Australia (Queensland Branch)* (1983) ATPR (Com) para 50-053.

41.5.4 Price information exchanges

(a) THE NATURE AND ECONOMIC EFFECTS OF PRICE INFORMATION EXCHANGES

Experience has shown that when legislation has made explicit price fixing agreements illegal, business groups have often replaced them by arrangements to exchange price information designed to serve the same purpose as the former agreements but in a more informal and hence less easily detectable manner. Competitors, either by explicit agreement or practice, may contact one another directly for price information or they may send such information to a coordinating body such as a trade association for compilation and distribution to the membership.

Regardless of the method employed, prices are likely to become more uniform and stable. The proponents of information exchanges contend that the resulting price uniformity is a manifestation of the increased transparency of the market. This improves the allocative mechanism of the price system and intensifies competition. Antitrust authorities, however, view price information exchanges with considerable suspicion. Their concern is that, irrespective of purpose, the effect of improved information about business rivals will lead to a greater likelihood of interdependence. This is particularly the case in oligopolistic markets. Greater interdependence may facilitate collusion or coordinated pricing and it may inhibit downward price movement. The British experience has been that whenever a price information agreement has been abolished competition has intensified, and as a rule prices have fallen. See D Swan, D O'Brien, W Maunder & W Howe, *Competition in British Industry* (1974) at pp 158-63.

(b) LEGAL ANALYSIS OF PRICE INFORMATION EXCHANGES
The legal analysis of a price information exchange starts with the question: Is there an agreement? An agreement, whether it be a contract, arrangement or understanding is required for the purposes of ss 27 and 30 of the Act. Membership of a trade association, formal or informal, which encourages the exchange of data, will satisfy the agreement requirement: see s 2(8)(b) and *Re Wellington Fencing Materials Association* [1960] NZLR 1121, 1134-35. A practice by competitors of exchanging price information may or may not develop into an arrangement or understanding. Compare *Mileage Conference* (1966) LR 6 RP 49 with *Trade Practices Commission v Email Ltd* (1980) 43 FLR 383. Agreement on compliance with particular prices is not necessary. In this regard s 30 is similar to the American law prevailing under s 1 of the Sherman Act. But American law requires that the necessary effect of a price information exchange must be to limit price competition substantially. By contrast, s 30 requires only that the arrangement (ie the arrangement to exchange information) has the *purpose* or has the *effect* or is *likely to have the effect* of fixing, controlling or maintaining the prices at which the parties, or any of them, supply or acquire goods or services. Proof of maintenance or control of prices *in the market* is not necessary.

Another difference between the American and New Zealand law, is that in New Zealand there is no need to isolate any restraint of trade. A New Zealand plaintiff thus has an easier task than his or her American counterpart in establishing the necessary causal nexus between the exchange and the stabilisation of prices. But, as in the United States, the onus will still be on the plaintiff to adduce sufficient evidence of prices following a pattern such as to warrant an inference of control or maintenance. See *Rosefielde v Falcon Jet Corp* 701 F Supp 1053 (DNJ 1988). As Heydon points out, "[t]he mere reduction of fluctuations in price may not be sufficient to establish maintenance": J D Heydon, 1 *Trade Practices Law* (1989) at p 2273. Establishing the fixing, controlling or maintaining element of s 30 may prove to be the Achilles heel for plaintiffs in a section otherwise weighted in their favour. A price stabilising effect short of maintenance, however, may still trigger liability under s 27.

(c) SCOPE FOR LAWFUL INFORMATION EXCHANGES
The United States case law and practice, particularly the decision of the Supreme Court in *Maple Flooring Manufacturers' Association v United States* 268 US 365 (1925), has influenced the views of the Australian Trade Practices Commission on what is and what is not acceptable in an information exchange. The Australian Commission set out general principles in Information Cjrcular No 14, *Market Information Agreements*, 28 April 1976. Note, however, that the Information Circular was concerned with the clearance test in force at the time, viz whether market information agreements would be likely to have a *significant* effect on competition.

The New Zealand Commerce Commission adopted the Australian principles in *Re NZ Medical Association* (1988) 7 NZAR 407 but noted that "[t]hese are general principles only and do not apply if there is found, in fact, to be a substantial lessening of competition". The principles may be summarised as follows:

(1) The agreement should be a genuine information exchange directed towards information generally.
(2) The information should be collected independently and anonymously.
(3) The agreement should assume the anonymity of members, and the information should be of such a nature as to be generalised naming no particular consumer or producer.
(4) The industry structure should be such that particular members, producers or consumers cannot be identified from the figures obtained.
(5) The scheme should be voluntary.
(6) The results should be available to any persons (including non-industry persons) on request.
(7) The figures collected from the survey should not be used as a vehicle for recommending or policing pricing or other policies.
(8) The information should be limited to past historical fact. Pre-notification of prices or trading terms should not occur.
(9) The frequency with which information is provided by the parties and how closely up to date it is, will be of relevance in assessing the likely competitive effects of the arrangement.

An information exchange complying with the above criteria is likely to withstand any legal challenge. If complete protection is desired, the parties should apply for an authorisation. This is likely to be granted; alternatively, the Commission may rule that the provisions do not fall within s 27. See *Medical Association*, supra, and *Application by the Insurance Council of New Zealand Inc* Decision No 240 (13 October 1989).

41.5.5 Authorisation of price fixing:

Unlike the Australian position, authorisation is possible for all types of price fixing arrangements whether for goods or services.

(a) INTERPRETATIONAL ISSUES
The Commerce Act provides for the authorisation of horizontal price fixing in an oblique way. Section 58(1)-(4) provides that the Commerce Commission may grant an authorisation on the application of any person who wishes to enter into or give effect to a contract, arrangement or understanding, or covenant, to which ss 27 or 28 would or might apply. No specific reference to s 30 appears within s 58. However, because s 30 is only a deeming provision and the actual prohibition against price fixing stems from s 27 specific reference to s 30 is not essential. An indirect reference to s 30 is contained in s 61(6) which provides that the Commission shall not grant an authorisation under s 58(1)(a) to (d) unless it is satisfied that the conduct "will in all the circumstances result or be likely to result, in a benefit to the public which would outweigh the lessening of competition that would result, or would be likely to result or is deemed to result therefrom". One can only logically interpret the reference to

deemed anti-competitive effect as pertaining to the deeming provisions of ss 30 and 34.

The question arises as to what competition analysis, if any, the legislation requires when the Commission weighs proven public benefit against a deemed lessening of competition. On a literal interpretation of s 61(6), one can argue that the Commission must take as read the deemed lessening of competition found to exist, and that no further competition analysis is necessary. The difficulty with this view is that it undermines the rationality of the balancing test contained in s 61(6), which logically would seem to require the Commission to weigh actual benefits against actual competitive detriment. One can explain the reference to "deeming" in s 61(6) as simply pertaining to the question of whether or not the practice falls within s 27 by virtue of the deeming provision of s 30. On this view, a deemed lessening of competition in the context of s 61(6) does not prevent the Commission from investigating the competitive impact of the practice. Indeed, the legislation seems to mandate such an inquiry.

The Commerce Commission had to decide between these two divergent views in *Re New Zealand Vegetable Growers Federation (Inc)* Decision No 206 (9 July 1987), the first authorisation application concerned with s 30. It came down firmly in favour of investigating actual competitive detriment. This view was not questioned on appeal.

However, the High Court did comment on the nature of the inquiry the Commission is obliged to undertake. See *New Zealand Vegetable Growers Federation (Inc) v Commerce Commission No 3* (1986-88) 2 TCLR 582 at p 588. Counsel for the appellants argued that the Commission, in assessing competitive detriment, had failed to consider the impact of the practice on all aspects of competition, both beneficial and detrimental, in the market as a whole. Instead, it had focused on the lessening of competition associated with that element of the market that was the subject of the practice. Counsel for the Commission argued that the deeming provision was controlling and that the Commission had carried out the weighing exercise by first making a *factual* assessment of *the degree* of the substantial lessening of competition which was *deemed* to exist. In commenting on this argument, the High Court said at p 588: "We do not find it necessary to make a final decision on [the] argument". Instead, the Court found that there was ample evidence that the Commission had taken account of all factors affecting the degree of lessening of competition in its decision. Although the Commission did not use the words "in the market as a whole", the Court was "not persuaded the Commission thereby failed to lift their eyes off one corner of the mosaic to look at the whole picture": at p 589.

(b) AUTHORISATION DETERMINATIONS
Of the Commission's three authorisation applications involving price fixing, three deserve special comment.

(1) Vegetable Growers: The *Vegetable Growers* application was lodged by various trade associations of fruit and vegetable growers ("the growers"). The application concerned a practice whereby growers collectively imposed uniform charges on new and secondhand returnable and non-returnable fruit and vegetable containers used for distributing fruit and vegetables from production units to retail stores through the central

marketing system. An accountant calculated the charges, basing them on a weighted average of the cost of purchasing each container from the manufacturers. The grower and the retailer shared these charges equally. The merchants who operated the auction markets administered the system.

The practice had existed for more than 50 years. The Trade Practices and Prices Tribunal had granted approval to the practice in 1974, subject to a number of conditions: Decision No 35, 29 August 1974. With the advent of the Commerce Act 1986, the approval ceased to have effect. The growers lodged an application for authorisation under the new Act and also sought provisional authorisation for the practice. The Commission granted the latter: Decision No 118, but eventually declined the authorisation application: Decision No 206. The growers were successful in obtaining in the High Court an order under s 95 of the Act staying the final determination of the Commission pending an appeal thereof: *New Zealand Vegetable Growers Federation (Inc) v Commerce Commission (No 2)* (1986-88) 2 TCLR 576. The Administrative Division of the High Court dismissed the growers' appeal in *New Zealand Vegetable Growers Federation (Inc) v Commerce Commission (No 3)*, supra.

The Commission, in its final determination: Decision No 206, had no difficulty in categorising the practice as price fixing within the meaning of s 30. The Commission also considered that the arrangement substantially lessened competition in terms of s 27. In reaching this view, the Commission took into account the following factors: approximately 95 per cent of all growers who send produce through the marketing system imposed the charge; it affected all purchasers of produce through that system; and the price of a container was a very real part of the cost of buying the produce contained therein. The Commission ruled that the relevant market was the sale of fruit and vegetables in containers when sold by merchants through the central marketing system.

Having satisfied itself that the practice came within both ss 27 and 30, the Commission then considered the actual degree of lessening of competition and its effects. The Commission rejected the growers' contention that pricing produce and containers separately made the true cost of the produce more transparent. The Commission also had little sympathy with the growers' claim that the collective container charge helped redress an imbalance in the respective market power between growers and retailers. Further, the Commission believed that there were competitive alternatives to the present system and observed that the restrictive practice may have impeded the development of these alternatives.

When it came to examining the effects of lessening the competition, the Commission emphasised that the practice kept prices higher than they would be otherwise. Further, the Commission observed that the system of average cost pricing for the containers reduced the incentive for the grower to increase the standard of packaging or to be innovative in relation thereto. The practice also denied retailers a range of choice based on price and standard of container. The Commission acknowledged that it was difficult to qualify the detrimental effect, but noted that those who gave evidence against the practice saw them as being very real.

The growers advanced the following public benefit claims: (1) the practice minimised administrative costs and simplified the auction market with resultant benefit to the public; (2) irrespective of the system employed, the consumer will always pay the cost of the container; (3) uniform container charges encouraged the use of quality packaging and led to standardisation with resultant benefits of efficiency and reduced costs; (4) by being able to ignore the container charge buyers could concentrate upon their bid for the produce thereby leading to a better and truer price for the produce; and (5) since both grower and retailer obtained the benefit of using the containers, it was only fair that both should bear an equal charge.

The Commission rejected all these claims. As the growers had not established any public benefit, the Commission, in terms of s 61(6), declined to authorise the practice. No balancing or weighing process was thus necessary. Nonetheless, the Commission concluded that detriment resulted from the degree of lessening of competition arising from the practice.

The High Court showed a marked reluctance to interfere with the discretionary judgment of the Commission. The Court noted that the Commission is an expert body and the procedures set out in the Commerce Act are specifically designed to ensure quality in the decision making process. In the Court's view, there were no grounds for interfering with the decision of the Commission. It had not reached the wrong conclusion in its finding that the practice substantially lessened competition and had not erred in its finding that the practice had no public benefit.

(2) Kiwifruit Exporters: *Re New Zealand Kiwifruit Exporting Association (Inc) – New Zealand Kiwifruit Coolstores Association (Inc)* (1989) 2 NZBLC (Com) 104,485 involved the Kiwifruit Exporters Association and the Coolstores Association ("the applicants") seeking authorisation to enter into and give effect to a national collective pricing agreement (NCPA) which was part of a wider agreement providing for the conditions and standards of primary coolstorage of kiwifruit. The Kiwifruit Exporters Association acted as agents for and on behalf of kiwifruit growers. The price fixing provisions related to a scale of maximum load-out charges for kiwifruit held in coolstore and charged by coolstore operators.

A primary argument of the applicants was that the NCPA held prices down. The Commission accepted the validity of this argument stating that the agreement was likely to have a restraining influence on the price for coolstorage generally. However, the Commission believed that the price established under the agreement was likely to be the norm, rather than a maximum price under which rebating occurs. The Commission also thought that the NCPA provided a disincentive to upgrade facilities and services and failed to take into account regional variations. Both these factors meant that some coolstorage charges from a significant number of coolstores were higher than they should be. The Commission concluded that the NCPA caused a significant lessening of competition.

The applicants advanced several public benefit claims but the Commission found that the majority of these either did not necessarily accrue directly from the NCPA or that there was insufficient evidence to support them. However, the Commission did acknowledge the validity of the claim that the NCPA assisted the efficient flow of fruit so as to aid the cooperative marketing of fruit overseas. The Commission believed that significant weight should be given to this benefit.

When it came to balancing, the Commission thought the scales were evenly balanced between the benefits and detriments. The Commission noted that there were several unusual features of the case which should be taken into account, viz: (1) the agreements allowed growers to combine and redress the lack of bargaining power which they have as against coolstores; (2) there were relatively few domestic implications in the agreement as it related entirely to the cost of coolstorage of kiwifruit for export; (3) kiwifruit is one of the most important horticultural crops; (4) all in the industry were agreed upon the desirability of the agreement; and (5) those whom the Act sought to protect from the deemed detriment of the NCPA (the growers), indicated that they saw their interests as being best served by the agreement.

Taking these factors into account, the Commission decided that on balance the public benefit outweighed the lessening in competition. In order to ameliorate the perceived detriments arising from the NCPA, the Commission invoked its powers under s 61(2) and imposed various conditions to its authorisation. The conditions related to equal representation of growers, coolstores and exporters in the negotiation of the NCPA, and the provision of differential payments for regional variations and to reflect differences in the quality of service.

(3) Grape Growers: In *Re The New Zealand Grape Growers Council (Inc)* (1991) 2 NZBLC (Com) 104,591, the Grape Growers Council ("the Council") sought authorisation for the collective registration and fixing of grape prices amongst growers themselves, and between growers and processors.

The price fixing arrangement was formalised in certain contracts entered into by grape growers and processor companies. Both parties to the contract appointed equal numbers of representatives to a joint committee whose major purpose was to determine grape pricing for the coming vintage. Other terms and conditions were also determined by agreement. The outcome applied to all growers contracted to the processor company.

The Council and individual growers supported the practice; it was opposed by several wine companies and the Wine Institute of New Zealand.

The Commission, invoking *Re British Basic Slag* (1962) LR 3 RP 178 (Ch D); (1963) LR 4 RP 116 (CA), ruled that though the individual contracts were vertical in nature, the joint committee pricing clauses resulted in horizontal price fixing arrangements. Section 30 thus applied to these provisions which were deemed to substantially lessen competition in terms of s 27.

The Commission was also of the view that other common terms of the contracts when taken together, in terms of s 3(5), also substantially lessened competition. The term of the Penfolds contract (99 years) and the Montana contract (10 years) had the effect of making new entry less likely. The limits on changes in volume and variety of grape restricted competition between individual growers and lessened incentives for individual buyers, to which the Commission gave a high detriment weighting. The joint funding by all Penfold growers of vine removal reduced the effect of market forces on the production and sale of grapes.

The Commission thought that the practice had the effect of increasing the price of grapes, and by dulling price signals, reduced efficiency and innovation. This in turn imposed a cost on the wine industry which lessened its ability to sell on the international market, and to compete against imports on the domestic market. The Commission noted that any lessening in the competitiveness of the wine industry could ultimately impact on the future viability of the grape growing industry.

The Commission considered that the public benefits from the practice were minor. While accepting that there were likely to be some cost savings from the reduced cost of negotiating prices collectively, rather than individually, the Commission thought that such savings fell within the "slight to small" category. As regards the alleged benefit of price stability, the Commission thought that while price stability could reduce uncertainty and risk, the effects could be beneficial only if the more stable prices provided an accurate reflection of market signals. This was not the situation in the case before it. While conceding that grape growers were currently in a relatively weak bargaining position, the Commission thought that this, in part, arose from the present oversupply of grapes. The Commission stated that as a general rule, it would accept the desirability of equalising bargaining power if the buyer was in a position of such strength as to be able to exercise monopoly power. However, the Commission found that Montana, the largest wine producer and purchaser of grapes in New Zealand, was not in such a position. Given this finding, the Commission was not prepared to accept equality of bargaining power as a public benefit. The Commission did accept the argument that the growers' committee, which negotiated prices, could be expected to be more informed as to market conditions than most individual growers. Consequently, in respect of some issues, they could achieve a more efficient outcome from the negotiations than individual negotiators. However, the Commission concluded that the extent of the disadvantage faced by individual growers was not substantial and not such as to provide more than a marginal amount of public benefit. The final public benefit argument related to the stability of rural communities. The Commission was dubious of this argument but recognised that some benefits derived from collective bargaining could have some minor beneficial impact on rural communities. The Commission concluded that the public benefits from the practice amounted to no more than a moderate amount and was not such as to outweigh the detriments from the lessening in competition. Accordingly, it declined to authorise the practice.

Various sectors of the rural industry have criticised the *Grape Growers* decision. It is unfortunate that the Commerce Commission did not discuss the decision of the Australian Trade Practices Commission in *Ardmona Fruit Products Co-op Ltd* (1987) ATPR (Com) para 50-065. That decision involved a successful application by the Processed Apple and Pear Committee for authorisation of an arrangement relating to the setting of annual minimum prices for apples and pears agreed upon in joint discussion between growers and processors. The Committee consisted of one producer and one processor representative from each of the States elected by the respective grower bodies or processing groups. In its decision, the Australian Commission reiterated its acknowledgment of the special position of primary producers and accepted the view that price stability in a primary industry can represent a benefit to the public. While stressing that the freedom of prices to respond to a market situation was a key element in the process of competition, the Commission believed that there were two factors in the instant case that ameliorated the adverse effects of the arrangement on price flexibility. The first related to the opportunity for growers to be involved collectively in the negotiating process, enhancing their bargaining position and thus providing them with countervailing power. The second factor was that the Committee set a *recommended* minimum price with processors and growers being free to negotiate independently of the recommended price. The Commission viewed this freedom as significant because it identified the arrangement as a true recommended price scheme as distinct from a price fixing scheme.

One can make several comments on the *Ardmona* decision. First, it illustrates that the Australian Commission views the rural industry as deserving of special consideration vis-a-vis the Trade Practices Act 1974. See generally, Trade Practices Commission, *Rural Guideline* (August 1989). Secondly, it shows that the Australian Commission is prepared to accept the notion that collective action by growers can ameliorate anti-competitive effect not only where the growers confront a monopoly buyer, but also in industries where buyers may be several in number. Finally, the decision illustrates the important role that government departments can play. In addition to submissions by producers, processors and industry groups, relevant state and federal government departments made submissions in support of the application. Although the Commerce Commission in *Kiwifruit Exporters* made a statement of general principle welcoming input from government departments and organisations, no such bodies made submissions in *Grape Growers*.

One can make the observation that had the Australian experience been explored in detail in *Grape Growers* and had the arrangement in issue been structured to take account of the observations made in *Ardmona* and *Kiwifruit Exporters*, the Commerce Commission would most likely have taken a more sympathetic view of the practice.

(c) OBSERVATIONS ON THE AUTHORISATION OF PRICE FIXING
In general terms, one must welcome the authorisation determinations of the Commission which clearly demonstrate that applicants seeking authorisation of a horizontal price fixing arrangement will have a difficult task establishing public benefit claims. Even if they establish such claims, applicants will still have an uphill task in satisfying the Commission that the established benefits outweigh the anti-competitive detriment, which in the great majority of price fixing arrangements is likely to be substantial.

While this conclusion may lead some observers to query the wisdom of the New Zealand legislature in providing for the authorisation of price fixing in the first place, the New Zealand legislative scheme does have the virtue of allowing parties to allegedly output-enhancing arrangements to argue efficiency claims without being confined by the boundaries of the per se standard. The existence of the authorisation provisions may well prevent the erosion of the per se rule in judicial proceedings, something which the American case law demonstrates is a very real danger. Authorisation may be the safety valve needed to allow the statutory per se standard to remain intact.

41.6 USE OF A DOMINANT POSITION

41.6.1 Introduction

Section 36 of the Commerce Act 1986 performs the role of regulating the conduct of market dominant firms in New Zealand. The section is entitled "Use of a dominant position in a market" and reads:

> (1) No person who has a dominant position in a market shall use that position for the purpose of -
> (a) Restricting the entry of any person into that or any other market; or
> (b) Preventing or deterring any person from engaging in competitive conduct in that or in any other market; or
> (c) Eliminating any person from that or any other market.
> (2) For the purposes of this section, a person does not use a dominant position in a market for any of the purposes specified in paragraphs (a) to (c) of subsection (1) of this section by reason only that that person seeks to enforce any statutory intellectual property right within the meaning of section 45(2) of this Act in New Zealand.
> (3) Nothing in this section applies to any practice or conduct to which this Part of this Act applies which has been authorised pursuant to Part V of this Act.

The provisions of the section are directed not to the creation and continued existence of dominant firms, but to a dominant firm's use of its economic power for certain proscribed anti-competitive purposes. Section 36 is modelled largely on article 86 of the Treaty of Rome and s 46 of the Trade Practices Act 1974; the section also has parallels with s 2 of the Sherman Act 1890 insofar as that section applies to conduct.

While s 36 of the Commerce Act 1986 closely parallels s 46 of the Trade Practices Act, there are a number of significant differences between the two sections. The most obvious is the difference in the threshold tests. Most commentators are of the view that the New Zealand test of "a dominant position in a market" represents a higher threshold of market power than the Australian test of "a substantial degree of power in a market". The New Zealand provision, however, does not contain the words "take advantage of that power"; instead, s 36 employs the more neutral expression "use that [dominant] position". Section 36 has no equivalent to s 46(7) of the Australian Act which expressly permits a Court to infer a proscribed purpose from circumstantial evidence. However, this subsection appears to confer no power that is not already available to a Court under common law. In contrast to the Australian law, the New Zealand provision specifically deals with the enforcement of intellectual property rights.

The Australian section is headed "misuse of market power" while the New Zealand provision is entitled "use of a dominant position in a market". In this commentary both sections will be referred to as the misuse provision.

41.6.2 Constituent elements of s 36(1)

Section 36 has three fundamental elements which are contained in subs (1). It prohibits:

1   a person who is in a dominant position in a market;
2   from using that position;
3   for the purpose of restricting entry in a market, deterring competi-
    tive conduct in a market or eliminating a person from a market.

Each of these elements will be examined in turn.

(a) DOMINANT POSITION IN A MARKET
"Dominant position" is defined in s 3(8) as follows:

> (8) For the purposes of sections 36 and 36A of this Act, a dominant position in
> a market is one in which a person as supplier or an acquirer of goods or
> services, either alone or together with any interconnected body corporate, is
> in a position to exercise a dominant influence over the production, acquisition,
> supply, or price of goods or services in that market, and for the purpose of
> determining whether a person is in a position to exercise a dominant influence
> over the production, acquisition, supply, or price of goods or services in a
> market regard shall be had to –
> (a) The share of the market, the technical knowledge, the access to materials
>   or capital of that person or that person together with any interconnected
>   body corporate:
> (b) The extent to which that person is constrained by the conduct of competitors
>   or actual competitors in that market:
> (c) The extent to which that person is constrained by the conduct of suppliers
>   or acquirers of goods or services in that market.

Key elements of the s 3(8) definition are "person", "in a position",
"dominant influence" and "market".

(1) Person: Section 36 is addressed to "persons". Section 2(1) defines
"person" as including a local authority, and "any association of persons
whether incorporated or not". This means that a person is not necessarily
a separate legal entity. If a separate legal entity could only occupy a
dominant position, commercial groups could easily evade s 36. The
phrase "any association of persons" appears to encompass an association
of persons operating as a single business unit or commercial entity. For
example, an unincorporated joint venture would fall within the definition.

Trade associations are obviously an "association of persons" and
hence a person for s 36 purposes. However, the express reference in s 3(8)
to a person as "a supplier or an acquirer of goods or services" limits the
application of s 36 to those situations where the trade association is itself
a supplier or an acquirer of goods or services and is in a position to
exercise a dominant influence over the production, acquisition, supply,
or price of those goods or services. By virtue of the s 3(8) reference to
suppliers and acquirers, s 36 encompasses the activities of the monopsonist
as well as those of the monopolist, ie both market suppliers and enterprises which acquire goods or services are subject to the prohibition.

Section 3(8) provides that a person may occupy a dominant position
"either alone or together with any interconnected body corporate".
Under s 2(7), two firms are "interconnected bodies corporate" if they are
in a holding or subsidiary relationship or if they are both subsidiaries of
the same company or are subsidiaries of companies which are themselves interconnected. Thus the Act regards all members of a group of

companies as one "person" in deciding whether a dominant position exists.

In the absence of any interconnected body corporate link, there is little scope for aggregating the power of two or more firms. The concept of "an association of persons" probably does not extend to "shared monopoly", that is, where two or more unrelated firms, each of whom is individually not in a position to dominate a market but who together control a dominant portion of the market, act to protect that position by restraining competition. Even if the two firms are loosely associated by an anti-competitive arrangement, they would not as a unit be a supplier or acquirer of goods or services and thus not be a person for s 36 purposes. While the section does not cover joint dominance, circumstances could arise in a tightly oligopolistic market in which more than one firm could arguably be said to be in a position to exercise a dominant influence over the market. If this was the case, then each of these firms occupying such a position could run foul of s 36, if they engaged in the proscribed conduct with the requisite purpose. Australian authority supports this view. In *Tytel Pty Ltd v Australian Telecommunications Commission* (1986) 67 ALR 433, Jackson J said at p 437: "The terms of s 46(1) do not seem necessarily to require that only one corporation satisfy the test at any one time." His Honour made these remarks in respect of the pre-1986 Australian thresh-old test, viz being in a position to substantially control the market – a test not dissimilar to the New Zealand dominance test. Note, however, that the Commerce Commission currently holds the view that only one firm can be dominant at any given time within a particular market.

(2) In a position: A firm must already be in a position to exercise a dominant influence over a market before s 36 can operate. However, it is unnecessary that the firm *actually* be exercising the dominant influence. The firm, however, must have the power and capacity to exercise such influence without undue delay. Australian case law suggests that the section may apply even if the firm has not entered a market; apparently it is sufficient if the firm is in a position to enter with the capacity to exercise a dominant influence over that market at short notice. See *Victorian Egg Marketing Board v Parkwood Eggs Pty Ltd* (1978) 33 FLR 294; *Tytel,* supra, at p 437.

(3) Dominant influence: The first part of s 3(8) defines a dominant position in terms of the ability to exercise a dominant influence over production, acquisition, supply or price. This approach essentially corresponds with the economic definition of market power. Many commentators, how-ever, define market power more narrowly in terms of the ability of a firm to increase its profits by reducing output and charging more than a competitive price for its product: see, for example, H Hovenkamp, *Economics and Federal Antitrust Law* (1985) at p 55. But as Professor William Shepherd points out in *Market Power & Economic Welfare* (1970) at p 34:

> . . . net income [of a firm enjoying market power] may be enlarged either by adjusting prices or quantities sold, or by pushing down prices of inputs (as well as revising the quantity of inputs per output), which is usually referred to as technical change. For each such move, there are often many alternative strategies which the firm may use and combine.

In encompassing an expansive perspective of market power, s 3(8) better captures the essence of dominance than the conventional short-hand formulation of market power expressed in terms of increased price and reduced output.

The existence of a dominant position implies more than a predominant market share linked with the power to influence one or more of the market variables mentioned in s 3(8): the firm must have a major influence over one or more of the variables: see A Jacquemin & H de Jong, *European Industrial Organisation* (1977) at p 229.

The EC Commission highlighted this attribute of dominance in *Re Continental Can Co* [1972] CMLR D 11, the first decision under art 86 of the Treaty of Rome to analyse the concept of a dominant position in some detail at D 17:

> Undertakings are in a dominant position when they have the power to behave independently, which puts them in a position to act without taking into account their competitors, purchasers or suppliers. That is the position when, because of their share of the market, or because of their share of the market combined with the availability of technical knowledge, raw materials or capital they have the power to determine prices or to control production or distribution for a significant part of the products in question. This power does not necessarily have to result from an absolute domination enabling the undertakings which hold it to eliminate all will on the part of their economic partners but it is enough that they be strong enough as a whole to ensure those undertakings an overall independence of behaviour, even if there are differences in intensity in their influence on the different partial markets.

This definition, which the European Court of Justice implicitly accepted on appeal ([1973] ECR 215), has been particularly influential in Australian and New Zealand thinking on the meaning of dominance.

As stated earlier, the mere ability to influence or affect price is not sufficient to satisfy the dominance test. Transitory aggressive pricing of a supplier in a very competitive market may have a devastating influence on the price of a commodity in the market, notwithstanding that the firm has no capacity to sustain the price reduction for a significant period of time having regard to the effect which a sustained price reduction would have on its profitability. In no sense could such a firm satisfy the s 3(8) definition of dominance. The ability of a firm to exercise a dominant influence over prices, production etc depends on it possessing a substantial degree of market power. Further, its ability to exert such influence must be sustainable over time. A firm which is forced to follow does not "determine" or "influence", but a firm which has the ability to lead independently and sustain that lead over time does have the requisite degree of power needed to satisfy the dominance test: J G Collinge, *Restrictive Trade Practices and Monopolies, Mergers & Takeovers in New Zealand* (2nd edn, 1982) at p 398.

The wording of s 3(8) makes it clear that it is not only discretion in setting prices that is important; discretion in making other market decisions is also relevant. Existing firms have discretion over their market decisions only when they enjoy some advantage over others who may be considering whether to enter the market or expand their output. Such market discretion presupposes the absence of close substitutes and the existence of barriers to entry or expansion, preventing new competition from arising even when supply is profitable: Korah (1978) 53 Notre Dame L Rev 768 at p 770.

Paragraphs (a)-(c) of s 3(8) provide a non-exhaustive list of factors which the Court must take into account in determining whether a person is in a dominant influence. The para (a) factors (market share, technical knowledge and access to materials or capital) encompass a number of important structural determinants of market power; one can trace the genesis of the list to the EC Commission's definition of dominance in *Continental Can*. The EC influence in also seen in paras (b) and (c) which concern the question of whether the alleged dominant firm faces constraints by the conduct of actual and potential competitors, suppliers and acquirers. See *United Brands Co v Commission* [1978] 1 ECR 207 ground 65; *Hoffman-La Roche v Commission* [1979] ECR 461 ground 38. See also Korah (1980) 17 CMLR 395. The inclusion of paras (b) and (c) in s 3(8) recognises that a dominant firm enjoys market power due to the absence of competitive pressures upon it. The reference to behavioural constraints is significant, since such constraints may be used to negate an inference of market dominance based on structural factors, for example, a large market share.

Two indicators of market power not mentioned in s 3(8) but worthy of consideration are: (1) patterns of conduct; and (2) persistent profitability.

Evidence of patterns of conduct may assist in establishing market power. The European Court of Justice in *United Brands,* supra, stated at ground 68 that in determining whether a dominant position exists "it may be advisable to take account if need be of the facts put forward as acts amounting to abuses without necessarily having to acknowledge that they are abuses". In other words, conduct can be evidence of dominance. But an important qualification must be made: the conduct must be of a type that could be practised only by a dominant firm: Hay & Vickers in *The Economics of Market Dominance* (D Hay & J Vickers eds, 1987) at p 38.

Courts have been remarkably reluctant to infer the existence of market power from a firm's profitability. In *Trade Practices Commission v Ansett Transport Industries (Operations) Pty Ltd* (1978) ATPR para 40-071, Northrop J expressed the view at p 17,720 that "the profitability of a firm is not of real assistance in determining dominance". His Honour pointed out that there will often be no yardstick by which one may measure profitability. In adopting this approach, Northrop J was reflecting the view of the European Court of Justice in *United Brands,* supra. In that case, the Court stated at p 491:

> An undertaking's financial strength is not measured by its profitability; a reduced profit margin, or even losses for a time, are not incompatible with a dominant position, just as large profits may be compatible with a situation where there is effective competition.

While there is general agreement among jurists and economists that profitability is an unrealistic measure of short-run market power, nevertheless, a number of economists believe that *persistent* excess profits provide a good indication of long-run power: see, for example, Schmalensee (1982) 95 Harv L Rev 1789 at p 1806.

To date, there has not been any landmark case on the meaning of dominance in the context of s 36. It is significant that in several of the decided s 36 cases the High Court has mentioned the relevance of the EC law, pointing out that s 3(8) is derived from case law on art 86 of the Treaty of Rome: see, for example, *Auckland Regional Authority v Mutual Rental Cars (Auckland Airport) Ltd* [1987] 2 NZLR 647 at p 679; *Tru Tone Ltd*

v Festival Records Retail Marketing Ltd, (1988) 2 NZBLC 682 103,081 at
p 103,088 (HC). The Commerce Commission's interpretation of dominance in the merger context has not played any significant role in any of
the s 36 cases decided to date, although Tipping J in *New Zealand Magic
Millions Ltd v Wrightson Bloodstock Ltd* [1990] 1 NZLR 731 did cite with
approval *Lion Corporation Ltd v Commerce Commission* [1988] 2 NZLR 682.
In the latter case Davison CJ endorsed the Commission's approach to
s 3(8) which it had adopted in two of its merger decisions, viz *News Ltd/
Independent Newspapers Ltd* (1987) 1 NZBLC (Com) para 99-500 and
Magnum Corp Ltd/Dominion Breweries Ltd (1987) 1 NZBLC (Com) para 99-
504.

In its original form, s 3(8) applied to both the misuse and merger
provisions. However, as a result of the Commerce Amendment Act 1990,
the s 3(8) definition is now limited to ss 36 and 36A. A new s 3(9) applies
to mergers, referred to in the Act as "business acquisitions". Apart from
the s 3(9) definition applying to two or more persons that are "associated" together, the two statutory definitions of dominant position are the
same. Nevertheless, the recasting of the statutory definition of "a dominant position" may mean that the Courts in s 36 cases will feel less
inclined to be influenced by merger decisions. It should not be overlooked that the dominance test performs a different role in the misuse
and merger provisions: in the s 36 context, the concept of a dominant
position is used merely as a jurisdictional threshold, whereas in the
merger provisions the acquisition or strengthening of a dominant position is the substantive test for determining whether a particular business
acquisition contravenes the Act.

(4) Market: The conduct of a person cannot contravene s 36 unless that
person has a dominant position in *a market.* The delineation of the
relevant market is important because it is only by reference to the supply
or acquisition of some description of goods or services that a Court can
assess the respondent's market power. The concept of the relevant
market has been discussed above.

One aspect of market definition, that does warrant some additional
discussion in the s 36 context is the extent to which the Courts are free to
tailor the market concept to the conduct at issue. It must always be borne
in mind that the relevant market is a tool for resolving legal questions. For
as Areeda and Turner explain in 2 *Antitrust Law* (1978) at p 348:

> One cannot determine the degree of market power that merits concern, or,
> consequently, the "proper" market definition, without reference to the legal
> context in which the issue arises. One must consider what is under attack, the
> substantive rules of liability that govern the particular case and the relief that
> is in issue.

For an excellent discussion of this aspect of market definition in the
Australasian context, see Brunt in *Competition Law and Policy in New
Zealand* (R Ahdar, ed, 1991) ch 9.

There are indications that the Australasian Courts will approach the
market definition exercise in the manner advocated by Areeda and
Turner. Two of the judgments in *Queensland Wire Industries Pty Ltd v
Broken Hill Pty Co Ltd* (1989) 167 CLR 177, the leading Australian case on
s 46, touch on the issue under discussion. In their joint judgment,

Mason CJ and Wilson J emphasised the inter-relatedness of the concepts of market and market power, at p 187:

> The analysis of a s 46 claim necessarily begins with a description of the market in which the defendant is thought to have a substantial degree of power. In identifying the relevant market it must be borne in mind that the object is to discover the degree of the defendant's market power. Defining the market and evaluating the degree of power in that market are part of the same process, and it is for the sake of simplicity of analysis that the two are separated.

More specifically, Deane J spoke of the need to keep in mind the actual conduct alleged when defining the market at p 195:

> In the case of an alleged contravention of the provisions of s 46(1) there will ordinarily be little point in attempting to define relevant markets without first identifying precisely what it is that is said to have been done in contravention of the section.

Any problem arising from the New Zealand Act's employment of a common definition of dominant position for both the misuse and merger provisions assumes less importance once it is recognised that there can be some degree of relativity in a Court's conception of market to the conduct at issue. Compare the judicial approach to the delineation of the car-rental market in *Auckland Regional Authority*, supra, (a s 36 case) with that adopted in *Ansett*, supra, (a merger case).

(b) "USE THAT POSITION"

(1) Meaning of "use": To breach s 36 a firm must have used its dominant position for one or more of the proscribed purposes. By using the neutral word "use", Parliament indicated that it did not intend that the words "use that position" should serve as the test for distinguishing a legitimate use of a dominant position from a misuse of such a position. In the s 36 context the purpose requirement performs this role. This is in marked contrast to art 86 of the Treaty of Rome where the notion of misuse of power is largely embodied in the objective concept of "abuse": see *Hoffman-La Roche v Commission* [1979] ECR 461 at p 541. Consequently, the role of intent assumes much less significance in that jurisdiction.

The High Court of Australia's decision in *Queensland Wire*, supra, has confirmed the above interpretation of "use". As mentioned earlier, s 46 of the Australian Act uses the expression "take advantage of". The High Court equated "take advantage of" with "use", unanimously rejecting the view of the Trial Court Judge, Pincus J, that the words should be given a pejorative interpretation. Pincus J had suggested that the phrase required that the defendant be doing something reprehensible; in his Honour's view some element of unfairness or predatoriness had to be present. Mason CJ and Wilson J in their joint judgment thought that words such as "predatory", "unfair" or "reprehensible" were ill-defined and were rendered superfluous by the purpose requirement. Their Honours said at p 191:

> It is unclear precisely what the phrases are supposed to mean, but they suggest some notion of hostile intent. For our part, we have difficulty in seeing why an additional, unexpressed and ill-defined standard should be implanted in

the section. The phrase "take advantage of" in s 46(1) does not require a hostile intent inquiry – nowhere is such a standard specified. And it is significant that s 46(1) already contains an anti-competitive purpose element. It stipulates that an infringement may be found only where the market power is taken advantage of for a purpose proscribed in para (a), (b) or (c). It is these purpose provisions which define what uses of market power constitute misuse.

Other members of the High Court expressed similar views.

Queensland Wire has become the leading authority on the misuse provision in both Australia and New Zealand. Recently, the New Zealand Court of Appeal in *Electricity Corp Ltd v Geotherm Energy Ltd* (unreported, 4 October 1991, CA 169/91) endorsed the approach of the Australian High Court at p 15:

> The interpretation of s 46 adopted by the High Court of Australia indicates a similar approach to that dictated by the New Zealand s 36. The distinction between vigorous legitimate competition by a corporation with substantial market power and conduct that contravenes the section is in the purpose of the conduct. Market power can be exercised legitimately or illegitimately.

(2) The "causation" issue: Now it is firmly established that the "use" or "take advantage of" element does not imply any notion of misuse, attention is likely to focus on the "causation" requirement inherent in the words "use that position". These words imply that there must be a connection between the impugned behaviour and the dominant position. The precise nature of this connection, however, is open to argument.

Logically, in the absence of any connection between the dominant position and the impugned conduct there can be no violation of s 36, even though the dominance and purpose elements are satisfied. The Australian case of *Williams v Papersave Pty Ltd* (1987) ATPR para 40-781 illustrates this. A director of the respondent firm discovered that the applicant planned to lease premises and operate in competition with the respondent. He approached the agent of the lessor with a view to the respondent obtaining the premises. The applicant sought an injunction to prevent the respondent from obtaining the lease on the grounds that such action would contravene s 46 of the Australian Act. Shepherd J found that although the respondent had a substantial degree of power in the relevant market and had acted with the requisite purpose there was no violation of the section. This was because the respondent had not taken advantage of its market power – its conduct "could as easily have been committed by a company having little market power": at p 48,525. The fact that the terms of the lease offered to the respondent were the same as those offered to the applicant influenced Shepherd J. His Honour noted that "this is not a case where a corporation has endeavoured to induce a lessor to give it a lease by offering terms and conditions more advantageous to the lessor than those proposed by the other party" (ibid).

The Full Federal Court upheld Shepherd J's decision on appeal: (1987) ATPR para 40-818. All three members of the Full Court agreed with Shepherd J's view that the respondent in offering to take the lease was not taking advantage of its market power. Fox J made the following pertinent comment at p 48,866:

[A] corporation which has market power does not take advantage of it whenever it is placed in juxtaposition with a competitor, and acts adversely to it. While a company having substantial power in a market is perhaps not free to do therein, or in relation thereto, all that another person or corporation without that power may be free to do, the forbidden area must be related to the market and the market power, so that it can be seen that the market power is taken advantage of for one of the stated purposes.

Counsel raised the "causality" issue in *Queensland Wire*, supra, but the Justices confined their discussion of it to the particular conduct before them. Certain of the Justices' statements, however, support the view that to take advantage of one's market power is to do something which can only be done because of one's market power: see Mason CJ and Wilson J   at p 192; Dawson J at p 202; and Toohey J at pp 215-16.

The basic thrust of the Justices' reasoning seeks to confine the role of the misuse provision to conduct which has its source, either wholly or partially, in market power. Applying this reasoning to s 36, to fall within the section a firm must both possess market power (a dominant position) and use that power for any one or more of the three specified purposes. The way s 36 is constructed appears to restrict the range of conduct the section catches to that which could not be achieved, either in performance or effect, without reliance upon market power. For further elaboration of this view, see Hampton in *Competition Law and Policy in New Zealand* (R Ahdar ed, 1991) at pp 194-204. See also Y van Roy, *Guidebook to New Zealand Competition Laws* (2nd edn, 1991) at pp 150-53; Hanks & Williams (1990) 17 MULR 437.

In contrast to the approach adopted in *Papersave* and *Queensland Wire*, Tipping J in *Magic Millions*, supra, appears to have afforded little significance to the use element. His Honour said at p 761:

> As a first observation I would have thought that if a person having a dominant position acts in a particular way with a prohibited purpose in mind it is almost axiomatic that such person has used his dominant position for a prohibited purpose. . . .
> It seems to me that the key question is not so much whether a dominant party has used its dominant position but rather whether or not its conduct is proved to have been for one of the proscribed purposes. . . .
>
> . . . .
>
> I would venture the following proposition. It is not a breach of s 36 if a person, albeit with a dominant position, simply acts in a competitive manner. It would be an irony if such conduct could be attacked because it is competition which the Act is designed to promote. However if someone with a dominant position takes some action for a purpose proscribed by s 36 then clearly they are using their dominant position in a manner which s 36 prohibits.

A somewhat different view of the significance of the use element is discernible in the judgment of the High Court (McGechan J and Mr G Blunt) in *Union Shipping NZ Ltd v Port Nelson Ltd* [1990] 2 NZLR 662. That case involved a claim by a shipping company and an associated stevedoring company that the actions of a port company, Port Nelson Ltd (PNL), in seeking, directly or through imposition of a levy, to require the shipping company and stevedore to use port company forklifts and port company employee drivers on the Nelson waterfront, contravened ss 27 and 36 of the Commerce Act. The Court made the following observations on the "use" element at p 706:

> Section 36 provides that no person, who has a dominant position in a market shall use that position for proscribed purposes. There must be "use" of dominant position for infringement. The section does not say that no person who has a dominant position in a market shall "act" for proscribed purposes. The evidence of Dr Williams and the submissions for PNL took the stance that there is no "use" of dominant position where a person simply is doing something which would be done in a competitive situation in any event. Put so baldly, and as a theoretical proposition few would disagree. If a person simply acts in a normal competitive fashion, as he would whether dominant or not, that person hardly can be said to be "using dominance". PNL in its submission seeks to build on this proposition, through Dr Williams' theory of expansion through economies of scope, to a position where it is said PNL demands for use of its own forklifts or additional payments are steps PNL would take in a normal competitive situation, irrespective of dominance. Ultimately this is a question of fact.

After discussing the competitive pressures that PNL would be subject to if the situation were truly competitive, with another port nearby, the Court concluded at p 101,646:

> We do not accept that in imposing a requirement for plant hire, or additional payment, PNL is acting as it would in a competitive situation, and is not using its dominant position. Its present demands are possible only because of its dominant position. Its demands, at times stark, are a use of that dominance.

Whatever reservations there may have been regarding the significance of the use element, the role of that element has now been clarified by the Court of Appeal's decision in *Electricity Corp Ltd v Geotherm Energy Ltd* (unreported, 4 October 1991, CA 169/91). In its judgment delivered by Gault J, the Court (Cooke P, Gault and McGechan JJ) made several important observations concerning the meaning and ramifications of the phrase "use that position".

First, the Court confirmed that the use and purpose elements are analytically separate and that a plaintiff has to establish both elements to prove a contravention of s 36, at p 9:

> The conduct prohibited by the section is the use of the dominant market position for the proscribed purposes. There will be circumstances in which the use of the market position and the purpose are not easily separated but the two requirements must be kept in mind.

Secondly, while recognising the desirability of harmony in the trade practices law of New Zealand and Australia, the Court of Appeal drew attention to possible differences between s 46 of the Australian Act and its New Zealand counterpart, at pp 15-16:

> [W]e are not satisfied that use of a market position necessarily is the same as use of market power. It is arguable that "use of a dominant position" is to be construed as use of the market power flowing from that position. But equally a position in which unconstrained discretionary conduct is open may be "used" without engaging in that conduct – as by threatening to do so.

Thirdly, the Court made it clear that the conduct subject to the prohibition need not be confined to market activity in the production, acquisition, supply or pricing of goods or services, at p 16:

> Clearly it extends to conduct capable of "influencing" those market elements. There must, however, be a clear and direct link between the influence and the dominant position.

Fourthly, the Court emphasised that the conduct in question must be considered in its commercial context. Referring to the refusal to supply conduct in *Queensland Wire*, the Court observed at pp 16-17:

> It was not the conduct itself that amounted to a use of market power for a prohibited purpose but the conduct in the market context for the particular anti-competitive purpose. This illustrates the difficulty in separating use of market dominance and purpose.

Finally, the Court expressed the view (which it described as a tentative one) that it was not convinced that the position under the Australian provision and that under s 36 will necessarily be the same in all cases. In conjunction with this statement the Court cited at p 17 the following passage from Hampton in *Competition Law and Policy in New Zealand* (R Ahdar ed, 1991) at p 204:

> Although s 3(8)(a)-(c) contains a non-exhaustive list of factors that aid in market power analysis, one must bear in mind that the concept of market power employed in s 3(8) extends beyond the narrow economic notion, viz the ability of a firm to profitably raise price above marginal cost. The s 3(8) test is whether a firm "is in a position to exercise a dominant influence over the production, acquisition, supply or price of goods or services" in a market. This expansive notion of market power would embrace rights, powers or advantages that enable the firm to exercise a major influence over one or more of the market variables mentioned. Assuming such rights et cetera contribute to the firm's dominance, the taking advantage of such rights will involve the "use" of the firm's dominant position . . . .

(3) The market power/non-market power distinction: A number of Australian cases have drawn a distinction between the exercise of market power and the exercise of some other power or right. According to the Judges deciding these cases, only the former falls within the ambit of s 46. See *Top Performance Motors Pty Ltd v Ira Berk (Queensland) Pty Ltd* (1975) 24 FLR 286 at p 290; *Ah Toy J Pty Ltd v Thiess Toyota Pty Ltd* (1980) 30 ALR 271 at p 275; *Warman-International Ltd v Envirotech Australia Pty Ltd* (1986) 11 FCR 478 at p 502; *Williams v Papersave* (1987) 73 ALR 475 at p 491.

The distinction between the taking advantage of legal rights and the use of market power, however, overlooks the fact that the possession and exercise of such rights may be intertwined with the dominant firm's market power. For this reason, Australian commentators have criticised the above decisions: see, for example, Walker (1976) 50 ALJ 89 at p 92.

Carried to its logical conclusion the distinction between the exercise of market power and the exercise of some other power or right would effectively eviscerate the misuse provision of any real meaning: in most cases, it would not be too difficult for counsel to characterise a respondent's conduct as involving the taking advantage of a legal right or other power, as distinct from the taking advantage of market power.

No doubt recognising this, Pincus J in *Queensland Wire* (1987) 16 FCR 50 at p 65 implicitly rejected the validity of the distinction:

> [T]he expression "take advantage of", although loose, was probably not intended to require that what has been done was *purely* an exercise of power in the market place, as opposed to an exercise of the power of an owner qua owner or a contracting party qua contracting party. Powers of these kind are components of market power.

Dawson J in the High Court ((1989) 167 CLR 177 at p 202) made it plain that he regarded the distinction as unhelpful:

> Nor is it helpful to categorize conduct, as has been done, by determining whether it is the exercise of some contractual or other right. . . . The fact that action is taken pursuant to the terms of a contract has no necessary bearing upon whether it is the exercise of market power in contravention of s 46.

Further, in *Australasian Performing Right Association Ltd v Ceridale Pty Ltd* (1991) ATPR para 41,074 the Full Court of the Federal Court of Australia said, at p 12,129, of the *Top Performance* line of cases:

> These cases have now to be read in the light of the meaning attributed by the High Court to the words "take advantage of" in *Queensland Wire Industries Proprietary Limited v The Broken Hill Proprietary Company Limited and Anor* (1989) 167 CLR 177; see especially per Dawson J at p 202.

Such comments would appear to signal the judicial abandonment of the distinction in Australia. Unlike their Australian counterparts, the New Zealand Courts have never shown any enthusiasm for the argument. See *Bond & Bond Ltd v Fisher & Paykel Ltd* (1987) 1 NZBLC 102,622; *Auckland Regional Authority*, supra. More recently, the Court of Appeal in *Electricity Corp*, supra, after noting the comments of Dawson J in *Queensland Wire* and the Full Court in *Australasian Performing Right Association*, commented at p 22:

> If those views are considered to be open on the Australian s 46 it can be argued with some strength that the exercise of statutory rights will not necessarily be beyond the scope of New Zealand s 36. As s 3(8) indicates, technical knowledge and access to materials and capital are factors in the capacity to influence production and supply and going to market dominance. If in a particular case they are an element of a dominant position and are used in the course of the exercise of statutory rights for a proscribed purpose s 36 might be breached.

(c) THE PURPOSE REQUIREMENT

(1) The need to show purposive conduct: The words "for the purpose of" make it clear that only intentional or purposive conduct by a dominant firm comes within the ambit of s 36. Liability arises under the section only when a dominant firm uses its market power for the purpose of achieving one or more of the results listed in s 36(1)(a)-(c). However, it is not necessary that the result be actually achieved. Conversely, the fact that certain acts or practices engaged in by dominant firms achieve or attain the consequences set forth in s 36(1)(a)-(c) is not of itself sufficient to make the section applicable to those acts or practices. Before liability can arise,

a plaintiff must prove that the impugned acts or practices constitute the use of a dominant position for one or more of the proscribed purposes.

(2) Meaning of "purpose": It is necessary to draw a distinction between "purpose" and "intention". One can have an intention to do an act, knowing that it will have anti-competitive consequences, yet not have the requisite purpose required by the section. For liability to arise, there must be a purposive pursuit of the anti-competitive outcome. Heydon suggests: "What may be required is proof that the conduct producing the consequences was motivated or inspired by a wish for the occurrence of the consequences": JD Heydon, 1 *Trade Practices Law* (1989) at p 2621. The High Court in *Union Shipping NZ Ltd v Port Nelson Ltd* (supra) at p 707 endorsed this view; the Court also cited Toohey J's statement in *Queensland Wire* (1989) 167 CLR 177 at p 214 that "[t]he reference to "for the purpose of' carries with it the notion of an intent to achieve the result spoken of in each of the paragraphs in s 46(1)". Following *Queensland Wire*, the Court emphasised that once anti-competitive purpose is established, any inquiry into the motives of the person using the dominant position becomes irrelevant.

(3) Does "purpose" denote an objective or subjective test?: It is unclear whether "purpose" denotes an objective or subjective test. Barker J in *Auckland Regional Authority*, relying on Smithers J's observations in *Dandy Power Equipment Pty Ltd v Mercury Marine Pty Ltd* (1982) 64 FLR 239, favoured an objective approach to "purpose".

In contrast to Smithers J's approach in *Dandy Power*, Toohey J in *Hughes v Western Australian Cricket Association Inc* (1986) 69 ALR 660, after reviewing the Australian authorities on purpose, opted for the subjective test. Note, however, that neither *Dandy Power* nor *Hughes* concerned the misuse provision.

In *Apple Fields Ltd v New Zealand Apple and Pear Marketing Board* (1989) 2 NZBLC 103,564 (HC), Holland J, after noting the different views of Barker J and Toohey J, expressed the view that purpose in the context of s 36 denotes a subjective test, at p 103,581:

> It is significant that it is the use of the position for the purpose which must be considered. The context satisfies me that at least in this provision the appropriate test of "purpose" is a subjective one.

Apple Fields demonstrates that the judicial preference regarding the appropriate test can make a difference to the outcome of a case. The applicants in that case had applied to the High Court, inter alia, for a declaration that a second tier levy imposed by the Apple and Pear Marketing Board on new growers and existing growers expanding production was in breach of ss 27, 29 and 36 of the Commerce Act. In relation to the s 36 claim, Holland J said at p 103,581:

> I am not persuaded that the Board, in adopting this proposal . . ., ever did so for the *purpose* of restricting entry into the market or preventing or deterring any person from engaging in competitive conduct in the market. Its purpose was to recover from those entering the market or increasing production a fair proportion of the capital costs created by such entry or increase.

The applicants, however, were successful in their s 27 claim because His Honour thought that while the purpose of the levy was not to lessen competition, the likely effect was to do so. That transgressed the section.

The Apple and Pear Marketing Board successfully appealed Holland J's decision: [1989] 3 NZLR 158. The Court of Appeal, however, determined the case on the basis that the levy was "specifically authorised" by the Apple and Pear Marketing Act 1971 and hence fell within the scope of the statutory exception contained in s 43 of the Commerce Act. The Privy Council subsequently overturned the Court of Appeal's decision on the s 43 issue ((1991) 3 NZBLC 101,946). While the interpretation of "purpose" was not directly in issue before the Court of Appeal, Cooke P did express disagreement with Holland J's findings on purpose. The President stated that the Board, in imposing the levy, had set out to reduce the attraction to enter the industry or make new plantings. By achieving some degree of fairness the levy, at the same time, inevitably carried out a policy or purpose of restricting production. In Cooke P's view, the levy, "however well motivated, has had a substantial purpose of deterring entry": at p 162. It is unfortunate that Cooke P did not discuss the authorities on "purpose" or express a point of view on whether "purpose" denotes a subjective or objective test. Cooke P's approach, however, seems consistent with the objective test.

Subsequent to the Court of Appeal's decision in *Apple Fields*, Tipping J in *Magic Millions*, supra, came out firmly in favour of a subjective approach to purpose, although His Honour did not cite any authorities for his view, at p 762:

> When one is talking of purpose one is really talking about what a party has in mind. It is clearly a subjective matter. Unless that party gives evidence . . . as to its purpose then the Court is left to infer with what purpose a person acts from all the available and relevant materials.

Union Shipping, supra, the most recent decision to discuss the question, contains a detailed survey of the authorities on "purpose". After canvassing the relevant case law, the Court commented at p 709:

> We must say we are reluctant to adopt an entirely subjective approach. As the development of the law of contract rather demonstrates, the commercial field is one in which objective ascertainment of states of mind has much to commend it. We would be sorry to see the objectives of s 36 inhibited by any undue subjectivity as to purpose, perhaps more natural to the criminal law. However, in the light of Tipping J's firmly expressed view, we will leave the question of principle open.

The Australian Courts have not addressed the subjective/objective issue in any detail. What judicial discussion there has been, however, lends support to the subjective approach: see *Taprobane Tours WA Pty Ltd v Singapore Airlines Ltd* (1990) ATPR para 41-054 at p 51,706; *ASX Operations Pty Ltd v Pont Data Australia Pty Ltd* (1991) ATPR para 41-069 at p 52,059 (Full Federal Court of Australia).

(4) Proof of purpose: Even if the Courts opt for a subjective interpretation of purpose, this will not prevent them drawing the necessary inferences from conduct and other circumstances, as well as relying on direct evidence from the parties themselves.

Section 2(5)(b) of the Commerce Act 1986 has resolved the problem of multiple purposes which caused so much difficulty at common law. Under that provision it is sufficient if a requisite purpose (that is one directed to s 36(1)(a), (b) or (c)) is one among other purposes, so long as the requisite purpose was a substantial one.

The utility of s 2(5)(b) is seen in the Australian case of *Mark Lyons Pty Ltd v Bursill Sportsgear Pty Ltd* (1987) 75 ALR 581. The respondent supplier argued that its purpose in withholding in-line ski boots to the applicant was to prevent conduct which could bring the product into disrepute. Wilcox J, however, held that the applicant had established that one of the purposes actuating the respondent was to deter or prevent the applicant from engaging in competitive conduct. This was sufficient to trigger s 46(1)(c).

Any difficulty in proving the mental state of a corporation has been overcome by s 90(1), which provides that where it is necessary to establish the state of mind of a body corporate, it is sufficient to show that a director, servant or agent of the body corporate, acting within the scope of his or her actual or apparent authority, had that state of mind.

(5) The proscribed purposes: The use of a dominant position will be unlawful if it has the purpose of producing one or more of the consequences specified in paras (a), (b) and (c) of s 36(1) either in the market where the dominant firm has power or in another market.

Paragraph (a) (restricting entry) embraces any kind of exclusionary activity directed at potential competitors.

Paragraph (b) (preventing or deterring competitive conduct) overlaps with both paragraphs (a) and (c): it is likely that "deterring . . . competitive conduct" would encompass both "restricting" entry into a market and "eliminating" a person from a market. Paragraph (b), however, would cover certain cases not falling within (a) or (c). A target firm may already be in the market, and although it may not be eliminated or substantially damaged by a dominant firm's behaviour, yet it may be constrained by that behaviour, that is, prevented from acting with full competitive vigour. The paragraph would also have application to a person who seeks to engage in competitive behaviour in a market but who does not contemplate entry on a permanent basis, for example, a manufacturer wishing to dispose of excess stock by selling direct to the public. If a dominant wholesaler or retailer threatened the manufacturer with reprisals such conduct could be caught by para (b): G Q Taperell, R B Vermeesch & D J Harland, *Trade Practices and Consumer Protection* (3d edn, 1983) at p 231.

The s 36(1) paragraphs refer to the restricting, deterring or eliminating of "any person". The words "any person" suggest that the prohibition will apply even though the dominant firm need not necessarily intend to damage a *particular* person. Much exclusionary conduct engaged in by dominant firms is directed at the general threat of future competition.

The references to "that or any other market" in paras (a) - (c) make it clear that the exercise of market power need not necessarily take place in the market in which the respondent enjoys a dominant position. Section 36 imposes no limitation on where or how the exercise of market power must take place: *S A Brewing Holdings Ltd v Baxt* (1989) ATPR para 40-942 at p 50,278. It may be availed of in the market in which the respondent is dominant or in some other market. That other market may differ in terms of product, area or function.

Likewise, the section does not require that the dominant firm must compete in the same market as the party alleged to have been harmed by the dominant firm's conduct. An attempt by a dominant firm to extend or leverage market power from one market to another would be caught under s 36.

A literal reading of the paras (a) - (c) suggests that a dominant firm will breach the section when it uses its position with the intention of harming some "person": the section does not appear to require proof of an intention to harm competition.

Nevertheless, there are indications in *Queensland Wire* that in the absence of harm to competition, the Courts will be reluctant to find a breach of the misuse law. The joint judgment of Mason CJ and Wilson J is the most explicit on this point. In the course of rejecting the argument that "take advantage" incorporates an intent element, their Honours stress that the object of s 46 is the protection of the interests of consumers through the promotion of competition. In commenting on the role of provisions like s 36 of the Commerce Act, the High Court in dicta in *Union Shipping*, supra, said at p 700:

> Such provisions are directed at protection of the concept of competition as such. They are not directed at the protection of individual competitors, except in so far as the latter may promote the former.

In view of these judicial observations, the Courts are unlikely to find a violation where the impugned conduct does not threaten or undermine competition.

41.6.3 Types of conduct caught by s 36

The misuse provision is "open-ended" in that, once the other elements of the offence are established, s 36 catches *any* behaviour which constitutes a use of a dominant position for one or more of the proscribed purposes.

The following commentary will examine four kinds of conduct that might well run foul of the section but the discussion of the categories of conduct examined is not exhaustive.

(a) PREDATORY PRICING

(1) Nature: In general terms, predatory pricing is where a predating firm adopts a pricing policy involving a reduction of price in the short-run so as to drive competing firms out of the market or to discourage new entry. The rationale of such a policy is to gain higher profits in the long-run than the predator would have earned had there been no short-run price reduction. Joskow & Klevorick: (1979) 89 Yale L J 213 at p 219-20.

For predation to be successful, the predator must not only be able to drive out rivals, but also keep them from re-entering the industry once the predator has raised price. The dominant firm can make the threat to predate more credible by making irrecoverable investments, for example, in plant capacity that enable low cost future expansion. Sunk cost investments may increase the viability of predating by lowering a predator's costs of expanding output and by alerting rivals contemplating re-entry that future predatory pricing episodes are a distinct possibility.

(2) Is predatory pricing a rational strategy?: Chicago School scholars argue that predatory pricing is not a rational strategy: see McGee (1958) 1 J L & Econ 137; R Bork, *The Antitrust Paradox* (1978); Easterbrook (1981) 48 U Chi L Rev 263. These scholars contend, assuming that the predator has a larger market share, predation is more costly to the predator than the victim, and that as the duration of the campaign and market share increases, so do the costs. The victim may also act to prevent the predator from reaping future monopoly profits, for example, the victim might enter into long-term contracts with customers (who would not want to see a competing supplier disappear), find financing to ride out the price cutting or shut down and wait for prices to rise. Even if the predator does succeed in eliminating the victim, recoupment of losses will be doubtful as post-predation supracompetitive prices will attract new entrants into the industry. McGee argues that instead of engaging in costly predatory pricing campaigns, a dominant firm is more likely to merge with its smaller competitors: (1980) 23 J L & Econ 289.

While the McGee/Bork/Easterbrook argument that predatory pricing is an irrational strategy and should not occur in the real world has been influential, recent scholarship demonstrates that the argument is incorrect and that at least as a matter of economic theory, it may be rational strategy for a dominant firm to engage in predatory pricing: see Hay (1990) 58 Antitrust L J 913; Rap (1991) 59 Antitrust L J 595.

Departing from the world of single-market firms with complete information, economists have recently developed reputation and signalling models involving multi-market firms where the potential victim cannot determine whether an established firm's price cutting policy is either predatory or the result of normal competition. Further, these models assume that the victim is likewise ignorant or uncertain of exactly what strategy the established firm will follow in the future. Lacking information about the established firm's costs, entrants will base their expectations about future predation on past conduct, giving the established firm an incentive to build a reputation as a predator. Signalling models are a more recent development hypothesising that an established firm may find it worthwhile to induce an entrant to exit a market by falsely signalling a cost advantage. The very signalling that induces the entrant to leave the market also persuades others not to enter. For reviews of the recent literature see, Ordover & Saloner in 2 *Handbook of Industrial Organization* (R Schmalensee & R Willig eds, 1989) 537; Ordover & Wall (Summer 1987) 1 Antitrust 5; Baker (1989) 58 Antitrust L J 649.

Under the new theories of predation, immediate exit of the entrant because of predation is not essential. Predation may still be rational even though the conduct may merely delay entry or induce an entrant to curtail its production: Pitman (1989) 34 Antitrust Bull 231.

(3) Standards for assessing predatory pricing: A recurrent problem with predatory pricing is how are Courts to distinguish the occasional case of predation from very low, very aggressive, but lawful pricing.

In 1975, Professors Areeda and Turner proposed that Courts should determine predatory pricing suits using an objective cost-based standard: (1975) 88 Harv L Rev 697. Specifically, a price above short-run marginal cost is not predatory; one below is. Since marginal costs are frequently unmeasurable, Areeda and Turner suggest using average variable cost in practice as a proxy for short-run marginal cost. According to Areeda and Turner, the cost-based test obviates any necessity to inquire into the alleged predator's intent.

The Areeda-Turner article generated an avalanche of commentary – much of it highly critical of both the reliance on cost-based tests generally and the use of average variable costs in particular. See, for example, Scherer (1976) 89 Harv L Rev 869; Williamson, (1977) Yale L J 284; Baumol (1979) 89 Yale L J; Joskow & Klevorick (1979) 89 Yale L J 213; Koller (1979) 24 Antitrust Bull 283. Despite this academic criticism, United States Courts, particularly in the period immediately following the Areeda-Turner article's publication, enthusiastically embraced the test, although most Courts treated the variable costs threshold as establishing a presumption of guilt or innocence rather than as an absolute rule. Further, all Courts, even those repudiating variable cost as an appropriate threshold, accepted the principle that they could appropriately presume intent from price-cost relations. For surveys of the American case law see, Hurwtitz & Kovaic (1982) Vanderbilt L Rev 63; Liebeler (1986) 61 Notre Dame L Rev 1052; Austin (1990) 58 Antitrust L J 913.

Some scholars have proposed alternative cost-based standards. Professor Douglas Greer advocates a two-part standard keyed to average total cost: (1979) 24 Antitrust Bull 233. According to Greer, pricing below average total cost, plus substantial evidence of predatory intent suggests predatory conduct. Professor (now Judge) Richard Posner favours a long-run marginal cost test combined with intent to exclude an equally efficient competitor: R Posner, *Antitrust Law: An Economic Perspective* (1976) at pp 184-95. Because marginal costs are difficult to determine, Posner would substitute average costs from the firm's balance sheet, resulting in a test which would look to full average cost based on the company's books.

Rejecting static bright-line tests between a price that is predatory and a price that is not, Professor Oliver Williamson, supra, has devised a "dynamic" rule to cope with predatory pricing in the context of entry. He proposes an "output restriction rule" which would prevent a dominant firm from expanding output in the face of new entry for a twelve- to eighteen-month period. Tackling the same problem, but with a different solution, Professor William Baumol suggests that a dominant firm be free to reduce prices in the face of entry, but restricted from revising them for a period of years if the entrant leaves the market.

Professor F M Scherer, supra, argues that the Areeda-Turner test is deficient in that it does not have as its goal long-run welfare maximisation; long-term economic welfare is sometimes maximised when a monopolist's price exceeds its marginal costs and in other cases when its price drops below marginal costs. Scherer proposes a rule of reason approach to determine the welfare maximising price.

Perhaps the most promising of all the tests proposed to date, is Joskow and Klevorick's, supra, "two-tier" approach. The first stage involves a Court examining the market's structural characteristics, such as barriers to entry and concentration levels, to determine whether long-term monopoly power is a serious possibility thus making the market conducive to predatory pricing. If the structural analysis reveals an absence of market power, the inquiry proceeds no further. If the analysis shows that the market is conducive to monopolisation, the Court proceeds to the second stage which involves a detailed inquiry into the alleged predator's pricing behaviour. The second tier stage incorporates a number of cost-based tests, takes account of predatory pricing in the context of entry and accords some relevance to intent.

(4) Relevance of the American standards to New Zealand competition law:
While at first glance the various standards discussed above seem disparate, one can discern considerable common ground among a number of the proposals.

Virtually all the proposals, either implicitly or explicitly, assume that the predator has some real measure of market power. Without market power a predator will not be able to recoup its losses as it will lack the ability to engage in supracompetitive pricing in the post-predation phase: see *AA Poultry Farms Inc v Rose Acre Farms Inc* 881 F2d 1396 (7th Cir 1989).

In the s 36 context, the market power requirement translates into a finding of dominance. A dominant position implies a competitive advantage enabling the dominant firm to remain powerful over time. Such an advantage may stem, inter alia, from market share, access to capital, economies of scale, excess capacity, first mover advantages or product differentiation. In addition to these factors, actual conduct may sometimes be useful evidence of dominance, for example, an ability to practise a persistent policy of price discrimination.

The jurisdictional threshold of dominance required under s 36 of the Commerce Act 1986 is analogous to the first tier of the Joskow-Klevorick test, although the inquiry under s 36 would need to explicitly consider the structural and behavioural factors mentioned in s 3(8)(a)-(c), as well as other relevant factors.

Assuming the dominance element is satisfied, attention will shift to the "use" and "purpose" elements. In a predatory pricing case, the purpose inquiry will assume primary importance. As noted earlier,   s 36(1) does not require evidence of actual competitive injury; however, the plaintiff must show that the dominant firm engaged in the pricing conduct for the purpose of achieving one or more of the effects listed in s 36(1)(a)-(c).

When conducting the purpose inquiry, a Court will be free to examine all relevant factors. A Court is likely to prefer a broad-based rule of reason approach, such as Scherer advocates, over a narrow cost-based standard. Cost-based standards, however, are still likely to be at the heart of any inquiry: see *Eastern Express Pty Ltd v General Newspapers Pty Ltd* (1991) ATPR para 41-128. But Australasian Courts are likely to be wary of embracing any one particular cost test. Indeed, the Explanatory Memorandum accompanying the Australian Trade Practices Revision Bill specifically cautions against such an approach at para 54:

> In regard to predatory pricing in *Victorian Egg Marketing Board v Parkwood Eggs Pty Ltd* Bowen C J left open the question whether in the ordinary course a monopolist can engage in predatory price cutting only if the price is below some particular cost, and not where the price set, although it may deter competitors, is one which merely does not maximise the monopolist's profit.

It is not the intention of s 46 that pricing, in order to be predatory, must fall below some particular cost. The prohibition in the section may be satisfied "notwithstanding that it is not below marginal or average variable cost and does not result in a loss being incurred". Certainly, though, where a corporation with the requisite market power is, in the absence of countervailing evidence that its pricing was not aimed at destroying actual or potential competition, selling at below average variable cost there may be grounds for inferring that it is taking advantage of its power for a proscribed purpose.

The flexibility inherent in the above statement has much to commend it. Sales below average variable cost may often occur for commercially justifiable reasons, for example, establishing a presence in a competitive market, liquidating excess inventory or obsolete merchandise, severe excess capacity in the industry etc. In the absence of any exclusionary purpose, such activity will not breach s 36. Conversely, a dominant firm deliberately pursuing a predatory pricing strategy will not be able to escape liability simply by relying on the fact that its prices are above average variable cost: see *AKZO Chemie BV v Commission* (Case 62/86, judgment of the European Court of Justice of 3 July 1991. Not yet reported).

(b) NONPRICE PREDATION

(1) Nature: Predatory conduct is not limited to pricing conduct. Recently, commentators have paid considerable attention to nonprice predation, which may be defined as strategic behaviour designed to raise rivals' costs or impair their ability to generate demand for their products. Sullivan & Harrison, in *Understanding Antitrust and its Economic Implications* (1988) at p 239, describe nonprice predation (also known as raising rival's costs (RRC)) as follows:

> The theory is that a firm may cause the costs, and ultimately the prices, of a competitor to increase. The effect is to create an umbrella under which the firm then has the freedom to raise its own prices above competitive levels. Raising the cost of a rival could either increase the market power of the firm or simply enable it to maintain existing power. Moreover, possession of market power is not necessarily required in order to cause the cost of a rival to increase. Thus, the activity could fulfil the conduct component of either a charge of monopolization or of attempt to monopolize.

For an excellent analysis of the theories, literature and case law on nonprice predation, see ABA Antitrust Section: Monograph No 18, *Nonprice Predation under Section 2 of the Sherman Act* (1991).

Nonprice strategies have several qualities which make them attractive to a predatory firm. First, they are much less expensive to the predator to implement than predatory pricing. If a predator can successfully impose cost increases on its rivals, they will be forced to quickly reduce output, allowing the predator to immediately raise price or market share. Thus it is unnecessary for the predator to sacrifice profits in the short run for "speculative and indeterminate" profits in the long run. No deep pocket is required. Nor is it necessary for the predator to force rivals to exit. Further, in some situations it may be relatively inexpensive for a predator to raise rivals' costs substantially. For example, a mandatory product standard may exclude rivals while being virtually costless to the predator.

A second advantage of nonprice predation is that it creates fewer legal risks. It may be difficult for an enforcement agency or a private plaintiff to detect and prove that a predator deliberately undertook a course of conduct with a view to raising rivals' costs. However, a predator's anti-competitive intent will usually be transparent where it persuades some government agency to impose constraints on its rivals but not on itself. In the United States the *Noerr-Pennington* doctrine will often protect this type of conduct; the doctrine exempts challenged acts that constitute the petitioning of government for a policy that may competitively favour the petitioner. The doctrine does not, however, protect the intent to harm one's competitors by the litigation or government process itself. Thus, the Seventh Circuit Court of Appeals in *Grip-Pak Inc v Illinois Tool Works* 694 F 2d 466 (7th Cir 1982) *cert denied* 461 US 958 (1983) observed at p 472:

> The line is crossed when [the] purpose is not to win a favourable judgment against a competitor but to harass him, and deter others, by the process itself – regardless of outcome – of litigating.

For allegations of this type in the New Zealand context and a tentative discussion of whether this type of conduct will constitute a breach of s 36, see *Electricity Corp Ltd v Geotherm Energy Ltd*, supra. See also *Cadbury Schweppes Pty Ltd v Kenman Developments Pty Ltd* (1991) ATPR para 41-116.

A third advantage of nonprice predation is that predators can use it in numerous circumstances. Since nonprice predation is cheaper than price predation, it can be effective in a larger number of markets. Unlike the theories of reputation-based predatory pricing, nonprice predation does not presuppose that the predator be a multi-market or multi-product firm; nor does it presuppose the existence of asymmetric information. All firms, even local ones, would benefit if their rivals' costs go up dispropor-tionately to their own: OECD, *Predatory Pricing* (1989) at p 13.

Examples of conduct which may raise rivals' costs or the costs of new entry include: predatory product innovation; redesigning systems so as to render the components incompatible with those of rivals; raising switching costs making it difficult for consumers to switch in the future to a new entrant's product; and buying up industry supplies of scarce resources in an effort to prevent rivals from using them. Mention has already been made of action taken before regulatory agencies and the creation of product standards. The proponents of RRC have also applied the theory to exclusionary practices which have long given rise to antitrust concern such as group boycotts, vertical price squeezes, denial of access to "essential facilities" and exclusive dealing.

(2) Application to exclusive dealing: It is worthwhile to examine the contri-bution that RRC has made to our understanding of exclusive dealing. Historically, Courts and commentators have perceived foreclosure as the anti-competitive harm flowing from exclusive dealing. The earlier treat-ment of foreclosure, however, has not been satisfactory because it has failed to explain how supply contracts enable firms to raise prices to supracompetitive levels and/or maintain prices at such levels. The theory of RRC addresses this problem.

Krattenmaker and Salop have developed a model which focuses the impact of exclusive dealing on the costs of competitors: see (1986) 96 Yale

LJ 209. From the viewpoint of the manufacturer who wishes to distribute a product, dealerships are an input. In the terminology of Krattenmaker and Salop, the manufacturer purchases an exclusionary right when it enters into an exclusive arrangement with an input supplier.

Krattenmaker and Salop identify four ways in which exclusive arrangements can raise rival manufacturers' costs. First, the buying manufacturer may purchase exclusionary rights from some or all of the lowest-cost and/or best-located input suppliers with the result that rivals are forced to shift to higher cost and/or poorly-located substitutes. Second, the buying manufacturer may limit supply by obtaining exclusionary rights from a large percentage of existing input suppliers. Faced with insufficient non-foreclosed suppliers, and assuming barriers to entry and expansion in the input market, rivals are likely to face higher inputs as demand drives up the price of inputs. The RRC literature describes this strategy as "real foreclosure" because the buying manufacturer gains control of the input with the ability to restrict supply and raise the price. Third, the buying manufacturer may induce input suppliers not to deal with rivals or to charge high prices. Fourth, costs to rivals may rise if the non-foreclosed input suppliers are few enough so as to be able to collude over price.

The above methods have the effect of raising rivals' costs thereby inducing them to restrict their production or exit which causes the market price of the product to rise. The theory thus explains how exclusive dealing may endow the purchaser of the exclusionary rights with the power to raise or maintain prices above the competitive level.

It is useful to view the *Fisher & Paykel* case through the lens of the RRC theory: see *Re Fisher & Paykel Ltd (No 2)* (1989) 2 NZBLC (Com) 104,377; *Fisher & Paykel Ltd v Commerce Commission* (1990) 3 NZBLC 101,655. Opponents of the exclusive dealing practice engaged in by Fisher & Paykel would, no doubt, invoke the first two methods identified by Kattenmaker and Salop to explain the anti-competitive nature of the practice. Those who view Fisher & Paykel's practice more benignly, however, would undoubtedly argue that the assumptions underlying these methods were not met in the circumstances of the case. While the RRC theory is unlikely to reduce the controversy surrounding the case, it does at least provide a more intellectually rigorous methodology for examining the effects of the practice than does the traditional foreclosure theory. For a useful commentary on the RRC model as applied to exclusive dealing, see MacCrommin & Sadanand (1989) 27 Osgoode Hall L J 709.

(c) INDUCING PRICE DISCRIMINATION

Unlike the Trade Practices Act 1974, the Commerce Act contains no specific provisions prohibiting price discrimination. Section 36, however, has considerable potential as an anti-discrimination measure particularly as a means of controlling what competition law authorities commonly see as the most harmful form of price discrimination, viz the practice of powerful buyers with monopsony power inducing suppliers of important goods and services into granting discriminatory discounts.

To succeed in a s 36 case involving the inducing of price discrimination, a plaintiff needs to show that the buyer was in a dominant position, that the buyer used that position to induce the discrimination and that the buyer engaged in the conduct for one or more of the proscribed purposes.

An ability to bargain for discriminatory discounts may evidence a buyer's dominance. This may indicate the existence of monopsony power and a relationship of dependence of the seller upon the buyer. One may also infer dominance from the structure of the market in which the buyer operates, including the availability of alternative distribution outlets to the seller. In the retail area it may be difficult for the plaintiff to establish dominance, as on the surface there appears to be considerable ease of entry and exit in the retail industry, thus making the existence of monopsony power unlikely. In reality, many sections of the New Zealand and Australian retail industries are highly concentrated with buyers enjoying considerable market power. This was one of the reasons which led the Australian legislature in 1986 to change the threshold test in s 46 from one of "substantial control" to one of "a substantial degree of power in a market". This allows plaintiffs to invoke the Australian misuse provision in oligopolistic structured industries.

Assuming the Court finds the buyer to be in a dominant position, there arises the question of what behaviour represents the use of this position. One must remember that the right of a buyer to bargain for discounts and to go elsewhere if those discounts are not forthcoming is an essential feature of the free-market system and should not be unduly hampered. So is the buyer using a dominant position by threatening to switch suppliers or produce the product internally, or otherwise refusing to buy from a supplier unless discounts are obtained? Recalling earlier discussion of the "use" element, such threats could represent a "use of a dominant position" as their effectiveness depends on the buyer being in a dominant position.

The most difficult task confronting a plaintiff will be to prove that the buyer engaged in the inducing conduct for one or more of the proscribed purposes. It will not be enough for the plaintiff to show that the buyer has used its monopsony power to obtain a discriminatory benefit, although the nature of the inducing conduct may be probative in establishing the buyer's purpose. Unless the plaintiff can establish the buyer's awareness of the discriminatory nature of the benefit, its magnitude, and the sensitivity of the price discrimination in the particular market, a Court is not likely to infer an exclusionary purpose. These factors have proved decisive in showing culpable knowledge under s 2(f) of the Robinson-Patman Act 1936 (the American price discrimination statute) prohibiting buyers from knowingly inducing or receiving illegal price discrimination. The burden on the plaintiff may not be too imposing where the buyer has demanded a substantial discount be made available exclusively to it as this could indicate a desire to harm other competitors: see *Fred Meyer Inc v Federal Trade Commission* 359 F 2d 351 (9th Cir 1966) *reversed on other grounds* 390 US 341 (1968). The recurrence of the inducing conduct would also count against the buyer. An express cost justification defence is not available to the buyer under s 36; however, cost justification evidence may help to refute an allegation of exclusionary intent.

In sum, plaintiffs have the potential to use s 36 to control the inducement of price discrimination by powerful buyers where the practice results in competitive injury. The chief weakness of s 36 as an effective form of legal control in this area stems from the use of dominance as the threshold test. Adopting the Australian threshold test of a substantial degree of power in a market would do much to strengthen s 36's potency as an effective weapon against the misuse of monopsony power.

(d) REFUSALS TO DEAL

Refusals to deal by dominant firms have always figured prominently in overseas antitrust litigation. This is also likely to be the case under the Commerce Act 1986. Indeed, the small-scale nature of most markets in New Zealand means that often customers will be dependent on a dominant supplier. A refusal to deal on the part of a dominant supplier may leave a trader without any alternative sources of supply; hence, there will be an incentive for that person to challenge the refusal under s 36.

While the language of s 36 and s 2 of the Sherman Act differ, one may find useful guidance in the United States case law as to the circumstances under which a refusal to deal may give rise to antitrust liability.

(1) United States cases: A unilateral refusal to deal is lawful under the Sherman Act unless, as the Supreme Court noted 70 years ago in *United States v Colgate & Co* 250 US 300 (1919), the firm refusing to deal has a "purpose to create or maintain a monopoly": at p 307. In the absence of such a purpose, a firm acting on its own can refuse to deal for any reason or for no reason at all. Not surprisingly, plaintiffs have seized on the monopoly exception to the *Colgate* doctrine and have argued that the refusal to deal at issue has been done with intent to preserve a monopoly.

The United States cases directly addressing the issue of intent are of particular relevance to the New Zealand scene because they have effectively required a finding of specific intent – a notion not dissimilar to the concept of "purpose" as employed in the Commerce Act. Because there is rarely direct evidence of intent, United States Courts have been prepared to evaluate the monopolist's conduct to determine whether under the circumstances of the case, the conduct at issue demonstrates an illegal intent to destroy competition. If the conduct gives rise to an inference of anti-competitive intent, then the monopolist is subject to liability under s 2.

An early United States case emphasising the role of a monopolist's intent is *Eastman Kodak Co v Southern Photo Materials Co* 273 US 359 (1927). Kodak had a monopoly position as a manufacturer of photographic suppliers; it also competed with independent distributors. In order to integrate vertically and control retail distribution, Kodak began buying distributorships. By 1910, Kodak had acquired control of all distributorships in Atlanta with the exception of Southern Photo who declined to sell to Kodak. Kodak then refused to sell photographic supplies to Southern Photo except at retail prices. The Supreme Court had no difficulty in inferring from the circumstances a purpose to monopolise.

A similar situation arose in *Poster Exchange Inc v National Screen Service Corp* 431 F2d 334 (5th Cir 1970) *cert denied* 401 US 912 (1971). There, a vertically integrated producer/distributor of motion picture advertising accessories refused to supply a local distributor. The Fifth Circuit Court of Appeals held that the defendant "intentionally used the monopoly power it had at the manufacturing level to eliminate [the plaintiff] as a competitor at the distributor-jobber level": p 339. Applying *Eastman Kodak*, the Fifth Circuit ruled that "the use of monopoly power at one level to drive out competition at another" constituted a violation of s 2: ibid.

The above two cases illustrate that a monopolist's extension of power from one stage of the market into another provides a strong indication of anti-competitive intent and this justifies the imposition of liability under s 2.

United States Courts have also inferred intent where a company with monopoly power on one level of the market refuses to deal in order to maintain or expand its monopoly on that same level of the market. The leading case is *Lorain Journal Co v United States* 342 US 143 (1951). A newspaper possessing a monopoly in the advertising market in a particular locality refused to sell advertising space to local businesses that also placed advertisements with a competing radio station. The Supreme Court enjoined the newspaper from continuing the practice. The Court declared that the newspaper was refusing to deal with the local businesses for the sole purpose of eliminating threatening competition. The newspaper's diversion from its established course of conduct gave rise to the inference of anti-competitive intent. The sudden refusal, coupled with the identity of the refused customers, clearly revealed an anti-competitive intent.

While some lower Courts follow *Lorain* and search for an illicit motive, such as a monopolist's desire to increase its competitive advantage, other Courts have increasingly begun emphasising the overall impact of a monopolist's refusal to deal. See, for example, *Byars v Bluff City News Co* 609 F 2d 843 (6th Cir 1979). The latter approach prohibits only unreasonable refusals to deal – the Court weighs the anti-competitive impact of the refusal to deal against the business or efficiency justification for the monopolist's practices.

Arguably, the Supreme Court in its most recent refusal to deal decision, *Aspen Skiing Co v Aspen Highlands Skiing Corp*, 472 US 585 (1985), has reconciled these two divergent approaches. In *Aspen*, the Court held that a dominant firm violated s 2 of the Sherman Act by refusing to continue to co-operate with its smaller competitor in a joint venture which had operated successfully for a number of years. The joint venture involved the marketing of a joint pass (the all-Aspen pass) to the four downhill ski facilities at Aspen, Colorado. Aspen Skiing Company (Ski Co) owns three of the facilities and Aspen Highlands Skiing Corporation (Highlands) owns the fourth. As well as withdrawing from the venture, Ski Co refused to sell any of its own ski tickets to Highlands when that firm tried to market its own version of an all-Aspen ticket. The effect of Ski Co's action was to deny consumers their preference for a four-area pass; Highlands suffered severe financial losses; and Ski Co turned away potential customers.

In the District Court, a jury found that Ski Co had monopolised the Aspen downhill skiing market in violation of s 2 of the Sherman Act. The Tenth Circuit affirmed. Because Ski Co had not contested the jury's finding of monopoly power, the Supreme Court focused exclusively on the issue of exclusionary conduct. The Court, in a unanimous judgment, observed that although monopolists are under no general duty to co-operate with competitors, they do not enjoy an unqualified right to reject joint ventures with competitors. The Court declared that the right not to deal exists only "[i]n the absence of any purpose to create or maintain a monopoly": p 600. Because such a purpose is present when there are no valid business or efficiency reasons for the refusal to deal, the Court considered whether such reasons were present in the instant case. While Ski Co argued that a concern about the quality of Highland's facilities explained its conduct, the Court concluded that there was no substance to this argument.

In evaluating Ski Co's conduct, the Court suggested a three-prong test to determine whether a lawful monopolist intentionally maintained its power through exclusionary means or with exclusionary purposes: first, whether the monopolist's conduct adversely affected consumers; second, whether the monopolist's conduct hampered rivals' ability to compete; and third, whether valid business considerations justified the monopolist's conduct. On this test Ski Co's conduct was clearly exclusionary: it harmed consumers, it caused its rival severe financial hardship and valid business or efficiency reasons could not justify it.

The significance of the *Aspen* three-prong test is that it re-establishes intent as a relevant criterion in a s 2 inquiry. At the same time the test confirms the lower Courts' approach that proof of a valid business purpose negates the inference of monopolistic intent. Where *Aspen* differs from the decisions of the lower Courts is the prominence it gives to evidence of specific intent as helping a Court distinguish between predation and legitimately competitive exclusions. This approach is similar to that of the High Court of Australia's in *Queensland Wire*. *Aspen* is, therefore, likely to be highly influential in the development of the Australasian law on refusals to deal.

(2) Australian cases: The leading Australian case on refusal to deal is *Queensland Wire*. The case concerned a refusal by The Broken Hill Proprietary Company (BHP), producing 97 percent of the steel produced in Australia and supplying 85 percent of the country's steel and steel products, to supply Queensland Wire Industries Ltd (QWI) with "Y-bar" feed stock for the production of star picket fence posts. BHP was the only producer of Y-bar in Australia and maintained a policy of selling Y-bar only to Australian Wire Industries Ltd, AWI, a wholly-owned subsidiary of BHP and a competitor of QWI in the rural fencing materials market. QWI wanted supply of the Y-bar in order to manufacture its own star picket posts, and thereby be in a position to supply the large pastoral houses with assembled fencing. Only BHP was in a position to supply these houses with the full range of rural fencing products. Eventually BHP did offer to supply QWI with Y-bar but only at unrealistically high prices.

Pincus J, at first instance ((1987) 16 FCR 50) found that BHP had both the substantial degree of market power required under the section and the prohibited purpose. Nevertheless, his Honour found no breach of s 46 because, in his view, BHP, by refusing to sell to QWI, did not take advantage of its market power. As we have seen Pincus J thought that "take advantage of" should be interpreted in a pejorative sense and not in a neutral way. Applying this interpretation to the facts of the case, Pincus J ruled that while the effect of BHP's monopoly may be to keep prices up, BHP had done nothing commercially reprehensible by refusing to supply QWI with Y-bar. According to his Honour, turning all of one's product into a finished product rather than selling it is not predatory or unfair.

The Full Court of the Federal Court of Australia dismissed QWI's appeal ((1988 17 FCR 211) because in its view, as BHP had never supplied

Y-bar to anyone, there was no market involved and hence "the taking advantage of" element was not satisfied.

The High Court of Australia allowed QWI's further appeal ((1989) 167 CLR 177), unanimously rejecting Pincus J's view that the words "take advantage of" should be given a pejorative meaning. The High Court also unanimously rejected the approach of the Full Court that "trade or traffic" had to be involved before a market could exist. Thus Deane J said at p 196: "[A] market can exist if there be the potential for close competition even though none in fact exists".

In finding for QWI, the High Court appears to have been influenced by BHP's leveraging conduct. Thus, in discussing Pincus J's finding that BHP refused to supply fell at least within para (b) of s 46(1) in that it was aimed at excluding QWI from the star picket post market, Mason CJ and Wilson J said (at p 193) that this market was "not the most informative one on which to focus". Their Honours commented (ibid):

> The evidence regarding the importance to BHP of being the only supplier of the full range of rural fencing products indicates that it is in the market for rural fencing products where those advantages lie and where BHP's market power is being extended. Pincus J's finding of an impermissible purpose remains applicable, however, because star picket posts are a constituent element of a product which competes in the rural fencing market. So, although it is sufficient to describe the infringement in terms of s 46(1)(b), preventing the entry of a rival into a market, it would be more apt to describe that purpose in terms of s 46(1)(c) "deterring or preventing a person from engaging, in competitive conduct" in a market.

The High Court was also influenced by the lack of a legitimate commercial reason for the refusal to supply. BHP offered other products of its rolling mills, all of which faced a degree of competition, for sale; Y-bar was the only product not offered for sale. Thus, adverse conclusions could be drawn from the fact that the refusal to supply was not in accordance with BHP's normal policy.

The Justices assumed that had BHP been operating in a competitive environment it would not have refused to supply QWI. Its conduct was possible only because of the absence of competitive constraint.

Having found that BHP was in contravention of s 46(1), the High Court remitted the case to the Federal Court for further hearing and determination of the question of relief. No hearing was necessary as the parties settled the matter.

Injunctive relief in cases of refusal to supply raise a number of complex issues: for example, should a Court order supply and, if so, at what price and how is that price to be supervised in the future? For a discussion of these issues, see Wright (1991) 19 ABLR 65.

Another significant Australian refusal to supply case is *Trade Practices Commission v CSR Ltd* (1991) ATPR para 41-076. The Trade Practices Commission alleged that CSR, one of Australia's largest companies engaged, inter alia, in the manufacturing of plasterboard and related products, misused its substantial market power for ceiling materials in Western Australia. As at March 1988, CSR supplied about 55 per cent of plasterboard in the States of Australia, other than Western Australia. Since 1970 CSR has been the sole manufacturer of plasterboard in Western Australia. Its largest wholesale customer in the State was North

Perth Plaster Works Ltd (North Perth). Until January 1987, North Perth acquired all of its supplies of plasterboard from CSR. Early in 1987 North Perth starting sourcing some of its requirements from Boral Australian Gypsum Ltd (Boral) which supplied the 45 per cent of plasterboard outside of Western Australia that was not supplied by CSR. After several discussions between CSR and North Perth concerning the latter's arrangements with Boral, CSR wrote to North Perth indicating that it would be discontinuing plasterboard supplies to the latter as it was not prepared to supply products to a wholesaler where such supplies were either to supplement the Boral range, or "top up" short falls in supply from Boral. North Perth complained to the Trade Practices Commission who brought proceedings against CSR for pecuniary penalties and injunctive relief for breaches of ss 46 and 47 (the exclusive dealing section of the Australian Act). CSR subsequently admitted that its conduct breached both sections.

In assessing the appropriate penalty, French J gave a useful discussion of the general principles governing enforcement and the recovery of pecuniary penalties. His Honour reiterated previously expressed judicial concern that the present day value of the maximum penalty no longer reflected the seriousness with which Parliament in 1974 intended contravention of the restrictive trade practices part of the Act to be treated.

As far as the case before him was concerned, his Honour said that the fact that there was no clear evidence of loss or damage to Boral, North Perth or the consuming public, was of considerably less significance than the fact that CSR's conduct was directed at Boral at a time when Boral was seeking to enter the market through its association with North Perth at a time when North Perth was vulnerable to any discontinuity in supply from Boral. CSR's size and the size of its market share were elements in its market power which was enhanced by the geographical isolation of the market and the associated barriers to new entry. Its conduct was deliberate. Purpose was admitted and the involvement of senior management, not just in Western Australia, was clear. Further, there was little convincing evidence of a corporate culture seriously committed to the need to comply with the requirements of the Act. His Honour assessed the penalty at $A220,000.

(3) The essential facilities doctrine: An alternative to the intent-focused approach to unilateral refusals to deal is the "bottleneck monopoly theory" or the "essential facility doctrine" as it is more commonly called. As William Tye explains, "[t]he gist of the "essential facilities' concept as applied in the antitrust law is that one competitor has control of the facility and is able to foreclose effective competition in one or more other relevant markets by denying a competitor's access to the facility". Tye (1987) 8 Energy L J 337.

The most frequently cited formulation of the essential facilities doctrine is the Seventh Circuit Court of Appeal's in *MCI Communications Corp v American Telephone & Telegraph (MCI v AT&T)* 708 F2d 1081 (7th Cir) *cert denied* 464 US 891 (1983). AT&T at the time was a vertically integrated telephone company controlling most local telephone facilities. AT&T refused to interconnect MCI's long distance service with local switching and distribution facilities, limiting the kinds of service MCI could offer customers. The Seventh Circuit held that local telephone exchanges are "essential facilities" and that AT&T had a duty to allow MCI access to those local exchange facilities. The Court defined the test for essentiality as follows at p 1132-33:

> The case law sets forth four elements necessary to establish liability under the essential facilities doctrine: (1) control of the essential facility by a monopolist; (2) a competitor's inability practicably or reasonably to duplicate the essential facility; (3) the denial of the use of the facility to a competitor; and (4) the feasibility of providing the doctrine.

In its analysis of "feasibility" the Court found that AT&T could advance "no legitimate business or technical reason" for its refusal.

As well as laying down a four part test, the Court provided a rationale for applying the doctrine (at p 1132):

> [A] refusal may be unlawful because a monopolist's control of an essential facility (sometimes called a "bottleneck") can extend monopoly power from one stage of production to another, and from one market into another. Thus, the antitrust laws have imposed on firms controlling an essential facility the obligation to make the facility available on non-discriminatory terms.

The above statement identifies monopoly leveraging as a central concern motivating the essential facilities doctrine – the concern is that an entity with monopoly power on one level of a market will use that power to gain control on another level of the market.

The essential facilities doctrine has evolved through three related lines of cases — traditional group boycott cases: see, for example, *Northwest Wholesale Stationers Inc v Pacific Stationery and Printing Co*, 472 U S 284 (1985); joint venture essential facility cases: see, for example, *United States v Terminal Railroad Association* 224 US 383 (1912); and single firm bottle-neck cases: see, for example, *Otter Tail Power Co v United States* 410 US 366 (1973). William Blumenthal notes that "[o]ver the last decade, the three lines have largely converged, although the convergence may not yet be complete. The resulting legal standards hold many ambiguities": Blumenthal in *The Cutting Edge of Antitrust: Exclusionary Practices* (ABA Antitrust Section 1989) at p 12. In recent years scholars have explored the nature and scope of the doctrine and have developed a number of proposals for alternative legal rules regarding the application of the doctrine: see, for example, Boudin (1986) 75 Geo L J 395; Cirace (1986) W Va L Rev 677; Ratner (1988) 21 U Cal Davis L Rev 327; Werden (1987) 32 St Louis U L J 433; Note (1983) Colum L Rev 441; Note (1988) 74 Va L Rev 1069. While the doctrine appears to be firmly embedded in United States antitrust law, some commentators are in favour of according a very narrow role to the doctrine, particularly in the context of single firm activity: see, for example, P Areeda & H Hovenkamp, *Antitrust Law* paras 736.1, 736.2 (Supplement 1990).

An issue concerning the application of the doctrine that is of particular interest in New Zealand and Australia is the role of intent. Some recent cases distinguish the "intent" theory from the essential facilities doctrine on the basis that the former focuses primarily upon the subjective intent of the monopolist's state of mind while the latter emphasises the effect of the denial of access on competition. See, for example, *Aspen Highlands Skiing Corp v Aspen Skiing Co*, 738 F2d 1509 at pp 1520-21 (10th Cir 1984).

Nevertheless, these Courts have recognized that there are "overlapping considerations".

The majority of Courts, however, impose a duty on the controller(s) of a vertically integrated or jointly owned essential facility in situations where the Court presumes that the likely intent of the controller(s) in denying access is anti-competitive. Issues of anti-competitive intent are linked with the consideration of the legitimacy of asserted business justifications for the denial of access. Thus even though a plaintiff user may satisfy a Court that a facility is essential, the defendant controller(s) may escape liability by demonstrating a valid business reason for refusing to deal. See, for example, *Town of Massena v Niagara Mohawk Power Corp*, 1980-2 Trade Cas (CCH) para 63,526 (NDNY 1980), (refusal to "wheel" power justified because of engineering deficiencies in plaintiff's subtransmission plan). According to this view, the valid business reason outweighs the presumption that the facility controller(s) intended to restrict competition.

A useful judicial discussion emphasising the overriding importance of intent in essential facility cases is Chief Judge Tjoflat's dissenting Eleventh Circuit opinion in *Consolidated Gas Co of Florida v City Gas Co of Florida* 912 F2d 1262 (1990). In the course of his opinion, his Honour made the following observations at p 1295:

> The essential facilities doctrine . . . is nothing more than a mechanism that aids courts in evaluating circumstantial evidence to determine whether the evidence supports an inference of anti-competitive intent. Given a certain type of fact pattern the doctrine's four part test [as identified in *MCI v AT&T*] will generally give rise to such an inference. Absent that type of fact pattern, however, even if the facts of the case could be found to satisfy the test they would not support an inference of anti-competitive intent. Such an inference depends on more than the four elements of the test; it arises from the larger factual context – the circumstantial evidence – of the case as a whole. The four elements of the doctrine therefore may indicate, but by no means define, the kind of refusal-to-deal cases in which an inference of anti-competitive intent is justified.

As regards the required fact pattern, his Honour identified three necessary features. First, the defendant must already be engaged in the business of providing access to the essential facility. Second, the defendant must be vertically integrated: it must operate on another level of the market, and the facility must be essential to its operation on that level as well. Third, the defendant, in control of an essential facility at one level of its operations must compete on the second level of operation with other entities that also require access to the essential facility in order to operate at the second level. Given these three factual features his Honour contended that any attempt by the defendant to restrain competitors' access to the essential facility becomes significant for antitrust purposes: under the circumstances, the conduct gives rise to an inference of anti-competitive intent.

While not all commentators would necessarily agree with Tjoflat CJ's characterisation of the doctrine, most analysts would agree with his Honour's view that the mechanical application of the doctrine's four part test is by itself insufficient to impose liability. In the New Zealand context, a mechanical application of the doctrine is no substitute for the need for a plaintiff user to demonstrate that it has satisfied all the constituent elements of s 36. One of those elements is proving the requisite anti-competitive purpose. As Tjoflat CJ observed, the doctrine can aid the Court in evaluating circumstantial evidence to determine whether the evidence supports an inference of anti-competitive intent. The doctrine is thus compatible with s 36 – in certain circumstances it can perform a useful evidentiary role.

To date, the New Zealand Courts and policymakers have given a mixed reception to the doctrine. In *Auckland Regional Authority*, Barker J invoked the essential facilities doctrine in reaching the view that Auckland Airport constituted a separate and identifiable geographic market for rental-car services. His Honour held that the Auckland Regional Authority, the controller of the airport, in entering into two exclusive contracts with Avis and Hertz had used its dominant purpose for a proscribed exclusionary purpose. Some observers have argued that the case did not lend itself to the application of the doctrine: no monopoly leveraging was involved and the ARA did not compete on the second level of operation (the airport car rental market). As we have seen, the latter requirement is not essential under s 36 but as Areeda and Hovenkamp,supra, have observed (at para 736.2e), if a monopolist does not compete in the affected market, efficiency concerns are likely to motivate its actions.

The High Court in *Union Shipping*, supra, addressed the doctrine in some detail. After reviewing the American authorities and commentary and the New Zealand and Australian Courts' treatment of the doctrine, the Court commented at p 705:

> We are reluctant unreservedly to import a doctrine, both controversial and as yet untested before the United States Supreme Court, into development of New Zealand competition law at this early formative stage. A wrong turning at this point may prove painfully difficult to correct.

Both the Commission and the Ministry of Commerce have issued discussion papers on the doctrine: see K M Vautier, *The Essential Facilities Doctrine*, Occasional Paper No 4, Commerce Commission, March 1990; Ministry of Commerce *Guarantee of Access to Essential Facilities*, Discussion Paper, December 1989.

Despite some of the reservations expressed in the above cases and commentary, one should not be too quick to write off the essential facilities doctrine. The doctrine has potential application in the so-called natural monopoly industries and may have possible scope in some of the sectors undergoing radical re-structuring, for example, the health care industry.

(4) Use of a dominant position in trans-Tasman markets: The Commerce Amendment Act 1990 inserted s 36A into the main body of the Commerce Act 1986. Section 36A is in similar terms to s 36 prohibiting any person who has a dominant position in a market in New Zealand, Australia or a combined New Zealand and Australian market from using that position for the purpose of restricting entry to a market, or preventing or deterring any person from engaging in competitive conduct in a market, or eliminating any person from a market. The anti-competitive activity, however, must relate to a market other than a market for services.

The enactment of s 36A must be seen as part of harmonisation of trans-Tasman business laws under the Australia and New Zealand Closer Economic Relations Trade Agreement (ANCERTA). The Australian and New Zealand governments reviewed ANCERTA in 1988 and agreed to accelerate free trade in goods. In accordance with that agreement, the legislatures in both countries recently repealed the antidumping laws involving trans-Tasman trade and enacted legislation extending the misuse provisions in each country's trade practices legislation to cover the use of market power within trans-Tasman markets. Section 36A is the resulting New Zealand provision while s 46A of the Trade Practices Act is the Australian equivalent.

In the absence of antidumping laws, officials expect that greater reliance will be made of the misuse provisions to control trans-Tasman predatory pricing. As mentioned earlier, the Australasian misuse provisions have different threshold tests. It would be unfair if Australian firms engaging in predatory pricing in New Zealand escaped condemnation because they did not satisfy the New Zealand threshold test, while New Zealand firms engaging in the same practice in Australia were caught because of that country's lower threshold. For this reason, an alignment of the two tests is a distinct possibility.

While predatory pricing will be an obvious candidate for attack under the trans-Tasman misuse provisions, it must not be overlooked that the sections are general in nature. In the first action under s 46A of the Australian Act, *Berlaz Pty Ltd v Fine Leather Care Products Ltd* (1991) ATPR para 41-118, the conduct alleged to be in breach of s 46A involved the termination of a distributorship agreement. Pincus J denied the Australian distributor injunctive relief because it was not possible to conclude that the purpose of the New Zealand supplier in terminating the agreement was the suppression of competition or the deterring of competitive conduct. A distinction had to be drawn between purpose and consequence. The supplier's purpose in acting as it did was not to eliminate or damage the applicant as a competitor, although no doubt the supplier knew that by terminating the distribution agreement it would be likely to have one or both of those results.

For informative commentary on the trans-Tasman misuse and ancillary provisions, see Waincymer (1990) 18 ABLR 267; Vautier in *CER and Business Competition* (K Vautier, J Farmer & R Baxt, eds, 1990) at pp 73-114; Y van Roy, *Guidebook to New Zealand Competition Laws* (2nd edn, 1991) at pp 166-173.

41.7 RESALE PRICE MAINTENANCE

41.7.1 Overview

In very general terms, resale price maintenance ("RPM") can be defined as a practice whereby a supplier of a certain commodity prescribes a minimum price which resellers have to observe on resale.

Section 37(1) of the Commerce Act 1986 prohibits completely the practice of RPM involving goods, ie it is illegal per se. As a result of the Commerce Amendment Act 1990, however, the practice may now be authorised. By s 37(2) a person, referred to in the section as a supplier, is taken to have engaged in the practice of RPM if that person does any of the five acts referred to in s 37(3).

It is only suppliers of goods who may fall within one or more of the s 37(3) categories of RPM. The s 37 provisions do not regulate the conduct of persons who receive goods, though such conduct may be regulated by the provisions of the Act involving concerted action as well as by the ancillary liability provisions.

While s 37 is limited to supplier conduct, s 38 extends the coverage of the legislation by prohibiting RPM by third parties.

Maximum RPM involving the fixing of a price ceiling falls outside the scope of the RPM provisions, but other provisions of the Act, particularly ss 27 and 36, may apply to maximum RPM if it is being used for an anti-competitive purpose or effect. For a recent case where distribution contracts involving maximum RPM were held not to contravene either ss 27 or 36, see *Tru Tone Ltd v Festival Records Retail Marketing Ltd* (1988) 2 NZBLC 103,081 (HC); [1988] 2 NZLR 352 (CA).

Finally, a supplier who enjoys a dominant market position and who engages in RPM type conduct has to contend with possible liability under s 36 of the Act. This will be so even though the particular conduct may fall outside the scope of s 37.

41.7.2 Key concepts

Before discussing the various categories of prohibited conduct, it is necessary to examine certain key concepts which are of general application.

(a) SPECIFIED PRICE
The RPM provisions are aimed at suppliers imposing minimum resale prices upon subsequent sellers of their goods. To achieve the legislative aim, the Act employs the concept of selling goods at a price "less than a price specified" in all the prohibited categories of RPM. Whether a supplier has specified a price is thus of primary importance in deciding whether the supplier has breached the RPM provisions.

(1) The s 37(4) deeming provisions: Section 37(4), which applies to all of the prohibited categories of RPM, contains a number of deeming provisions which particularise various ways in which a supplier might specify a price. The subsection, however, is not an exhaustive definition of the methods of specifying a price: *The Heating Centre Pty Ltd v Trade Practices Commission* (1986) 65 ALR 429 at p 432 per Lockhart and Wilcox JJ.

The provisions, inter alia, embrace the situations where a supplier relies on a price specified by others or arrived at by calculations.

If the specification is by another person, the supplier will be deemed to have specified that price only if it makes it known that it adopts that price as the price below which its goods are not to be sold: s 37(4)(a).

The qualification does not apply when a person acting on behalf of, or by arrangement with, the supplier specifies a price or does any other constituent act of RPM. There the Act deems the supplier to have specified the price or engaged in the other act: s 37(4)(e). The Australian Courts have held that the phrase "on behalf of" extends further than the law of agency. Thus a servant or agent engaging in RPM will bind the supplier even though such person may not have had the authority to bind the supplier under the general law of agency. See, for example, *Trade Practices Commission v Bata Shoe Co of Australia Pty Ltd (No 2)* (1980) 44 FLR

149 at p 159. In addition to s 37(4)(e), the general provisions of s 90(2) and (4) provide that any conduct engaged in on behalf of a supplier will be deemed to be engaged in also by the supplier, provided the person acting on behalf of the supplier acts within the scope of his or her actual or apparent authority. No doubt suppliers will seize on the s 90 requirement of actual or apparent authority to argue that the same requirement should be read into s 37(4)(e). Even if the Courts accept this argument, the Australian case law shows that Courts are likely to hold that pricing conduct is normally within the scope of the servant's or agent's apparent authority even though such person may not have been authorised by the supplier to engage in RPM. See *Bata Shoe* (supra); *Commissioner of Trade Practices v Caltex Oil (Australia) Pty Ltd* (1974) 23 FLR 457.

The specification of a formula may be sufficient to attract liability. Section 37(4)(b) deems the supplier to have specified a price "where a set form, method, or formula is specified by or on behalf of the supplier and a price may be ascertained from, or by reference to, that set form, method or formula". Where another person specifies the formula, the supplier will be deemed to have specified the price only if it makes it known that it adopts that price as the price below which its goods are not to be sold: s 37(4)(c). *Caltex Oil* (supra) provides an example of a supplier invoking a formula specified by another person. Smithers J said, at p 474:

> [T]he notification by Caltex to Heath's that the price which it desired Heath's to adopt was three cents less than the Victorian Automobile Chamber of Commerce recommended price or three cents less than the ordinary retail price constituted a specification by Caltex of a formula by reference to which the price might be ascertained.

The scope of the RPM practices is considerably broadened by the deeming provision in s 37(4)(d) which reads:

> Where the supplier makes a statement to another person of a price that is likely to be understood by that person as the price below which the goods are not to be sold, the price shall be deemed to have been specified by the supplier as the price below which the goods are not to be sold.

By virtue of its inclusion in s 37(4), the provision applies to all of the prohibited categories of RPM. This is not the case under the Australian RPM legislation where a similar provision to s 37(4)(d) appears as a separate category of prohibited conduct, viz s 96(3)(f) of the Trade Practices Act 1974. For Australian case law on s 96(3)(f), see *Commissioner of Trade Practices v Dalgety Australia* (1973) 22 FLR 62; *Trade Practices Commission v Bata Shoe Company of Australia Pty Ltd (No 2)* (1980) 44 FLR 149; *Trade Practices Commission v BP Australia Ltd* (1985) 7 FCR 499 *affirmed* by the Full Federal Court (1986) ATPR para 40-701; *The Heating Centre Pty Ltd v Trade Practices Commission* (1986) 65 ALR 429.

Section 37(4)(d) is extremely wide and will capture behaviour which might not otherwise be caught. The words "makes a statement to another person", which do not appear in s 96(3)(f) of the Australian Act, indicate the need for actual communication of the statement. There is no limitation, however, on the means by which the supplier may communicate the statement.

The test of whether a statement of a price "is likely to be understood" as the price below which the goods are not to be sold is an objective one. The Full Federal Court of Australia in *Trade Practices Commission v BP Australia Ltd* (1986) ATPR para 40-701 per Lockhart J made the following observations on the equivalent Australian provision, at p 47,655:

> Paragraph (f) is a provision of wide application. The phrase "likely to be understood" requires an objective test. The test does not look to the intention of the supplier in making the statement but is measured by its likely effect on "the second person". Where the supplier communicates his intention to the second person the statements made are relevant, not as indicating the supplier's intention but as evidence of the contents of the statement made which will bear upon the second person's understanding of the statement. In determining whether the statement of a price is likely to be understood in the sense stipulated in the paragraph the text of the statement and all the relevant circumstances surrounding the making of it are to be considered.

(2) Price need not be specified exactly: It is not necessary that a supplier specify an *exact* price. An approximate specification will suffice. In *Bata Shoe* (supra), the wholesale agent of a shoe supplier pressured Woolworths Ltd to sell footwear "somewhere near the selling price of Gowings Ltd in Sydney". Holding that this was a sufficient specification of price, Lockhart J said, at pp 159-160:

> The fact that a price is stated to be within a range of a particular figure or that otherwise an element of approximation is introduced, does not detract from the true character of the price as being a specified price.

In *Trade Practices Commission v Mobil Oil Australia Ltd* (1984) 55 ALR 527, Toohey J suggested that a supplier may specify a price by reference to some standard well known to the parties from which they may ascertain a price.

The price, however, must be able to be defined. In *Peter Williamson Pty Ltd v Capitol Motors Ltd* (1982) 61 FLR 257, Franki J accepted that the price could be defined as a so-called "go" price or as a price within some range but said that there must be some method of fixing and ascertaining the relevant price or the relevant price range.

(3) Specification of recommended price: In some circumstances, a supplier issuing a list of "recommended" prices may be held to have "specified" a price as the minimum price "below which the goods are not to be sold". This was the case in *Mikasa (NSW) Pty Ltd v Festival Stores* (1971) 18 FLR 260 *affirmed* (1972) 127 CLR 617. Mikasa, a supplier of dinnerware, had a long-standing policy of refusing to supply discount stores of which Festival Stores was one. Mikasa had always made this clear, not once but on a number of occasions. The Australian Commonwealth Industrial Court found as a fact that the only reason Mikasa declined to supply goods was because Festival Stores was likely to sell those goods at less than the price in Mikasa's catalogue, and that price, although a recommended price, was in the circumstances of the case, "a price specified ... as the price below which the goods are not to be sold": at p 268. The High Court of Australia confirmed the decision of the Industrial Court.

The *Mikasa* decision should be contrasted with that of Franki J in *Peter Williamson* (supra). Peter Williamson alleged that its BMW dealership

had been improperly terminated by Capitol Motors and that the termination was in breach of the Australian equivalent of s 37(3)(d)(ii) of the
Commerce Act. Under the terms of the dealership agreement, Capitol
Motors had issued a suggested price list which Franki J accepted as
constituting genuine "recommended prices". Dealers allowed significant discounts and his Honour accepted that Capitol Motors did not
enforce the recommended price list in any way. His Honour found that
the termination of the dealership was for legitimate commercial reasons.
Franki J rejected the proposition that *Mikasa* stood for the proposition
that in all cases a refusal to supply after recommendation of a price
converted that price into a price specified by the supplier as the price
below which the goods are not to be sold. His Honour held that in the case
before him, even though there was a recommended price, there was no
"specified" price below which Williamson was not to sell. The failure to
establish this key element proved fatal to Williamson's case.

(4) Reference to a previously distributed document: In *The Heating Centre* case
(supra) the Full Federal Court of Australia considered the question of the
extent to which the requirement for the supplier to specify a minimum
resale price could be satisfied by reference to a document that had been
distributed previously. According to Lockhart and Wilcox JJ, but not
Pincus J, this requirement could be satisfied by reference to such a
document, provided the supplier makes it clear that references to pricing
matters are to be understood as references to the prices listed in the
document. Thus, a statement there should be "no discounting" can be
regarded as a statement as to a "price specified" when it is clear that the
speaker is saying that the reseller must not sell below the prices listed on
an existing price list. In *Trade Practices Commission v Sony (Australia) Pty
Ltd* (1990) ATPR para 41-031, Pincus J accepted the majority view but
indicated that the statement and the earlier document must be sufficiently closely connected in time and other circumstances before one
could make the inference of inter-relatedness.

(b) "SUPPLY" TO "ANOTHER PERSON"
All the types of prohibited RPM conduct involve "supply" of goods to
"another person". The meaning of these words is important for the
purpose of determining whether agency transactions are subject to the
RPM legislation. As regards the indicia of agency, see *International
Harvester Co v Corrigans Hazeldine Pastoral Co* (1958) 100 CLR 644; J D
Heydon, 1 *Trade Practices Law* (1989) at pp 3553-54.
    The term "supply" as related to goods is defined in s 2(1) as including
(and thus not limited to) "supply (or resupply) by way of gift, sale,
exchange, lease, hire or hire purchase".
    It is possible that a delivery of possession of goods under a bailment
may constitute a supply: see, for example, *Commonwealth v Sterling
Nicholas Duty Free Pty Ltd* (1971) 126 CLR 297 at p 309 per Menzies J. If this
is the case, then the delivery of goods to an agent on consignment would
amount to a supply of goods.
    Against this, one can argue that on an *ejusdem generis* interpretation of
the words mentioned in the definition of "supply", a passing of ownership or other title is required, thus excluding agency arrangements:
Pengilley, in *Competition Law and Policy in New Zealand* (R Ahdar ed, 1991)
at p 260.

Irrespective of the precise scope of "supply", agency transactions may fall outside the ambit of the RPM legislation for other reasons. First, the term "another person" implies a person who possesses a legal personality separate from that of the supplier. As Heydon (supra) observes at p 3552, an agency relationship between the supplier and the second person would seem to deny this separate personality, as normally the act of an agent is deemed to be the act of its principal.

Secondly, even if an agent is "another person", it is difficult to see how one can regard such a person as "selling" the goods. In the absence of any definition in the Act of the word "sell" or "sale", the normal elements involved in a sale of goods will need to be satisfied. A key element is the transferring of property in the goods. An agent does not have legal capacity to transfer property since it has never been vested in him or her; he or she "sells" as agent only and receives and accounts for the price to the supplier. One cannot properly regard an agent, therefore, as "selling" the goods. This means that the agent's principal can stipulate the price at which the goods are to be sold without infringing the RPM legislation: cf *United States v General Electric Co* 272 US 476 (1926); *Mesirow v Pepperidge Farm Inc* 703 F 2d 339 (9th Cir 1983); *Illinois Corporate Travel Inc v American Airlines* 806 F 2d 722 (7th Cir 1986). This suggests an avenue for avoiding the provisions of the Act.

In the United States and Canada, suppliers have been tempted to circumvent the bans upon RPM by instituting the practice of consignment selling involving large scale conversion to agency transactions. In *Simpson v Union Oil Co* 377 US 13 (1964), the United States Supreme Court struck down an oil company's widespread use of a sham consignment system as a violation of s 1 of the Sherman Act. However, the Court recognised that price maintenance in a bona fide consignment to a distributor could still be lawful. In the 1976 amendments to the Combines Investigation Act, since re-enacted as the Competition Act 1985, the Canadian Federal Parliament saw fit to permit the Restrictive Trade Practices Commission to forbid a supplier from introducing consignment selling for the purpose of controlling resale prices: Competition Act 1985, s 76. Such a provision could usefully be incorporated in the New Zealand legislation.

In the absence of such a provision, the New Zealand Courts can be expected to scrutinise carefully large-scale agency arrangements, particularly where their antecedents are agreements for sale and resale, to ensure that they are not sham arrangements for allowing suppliers to impose RPM on independent resellers. It is to be hoped that the New Zealand Courts will look at the functional relationship of the parties rather than merely invoking the formal passing of title test. Intervention is warranted where the resellers are functionally independent of the supplier. See, for example, *Trade Practices Commission v Pye Industries Sales Pty Ltd* (1978) ATPR, para 40-088 (relationship was one of buyer and seller rather than principal and agent). However, where the agents are functionally more like sales employees than independent dealers, there is likely to be a legitimate use of consignment selling and little basis for antitrust concern with a supplier's efforts to control the resale prices of his agents. See generally Rahl (1966) 61 Nw U L Rev 1.

(c) "SELLING"

The various categories of prohibited RPM conduct refer to *sale* by another person at a price less than a price specified by the supplier.

A supplier will sometimes stipulate that a reseller advertise the goods at a specified minimum price, even though no control over actual selling prices may be provided for. Under the original 1971 Australian RPM legislation, suppliers argued (see, for example, *Caltex Oil* (supra)) that such action did not constitute an attempt to induce the reseller from *selling* at a price below a specified price, but was merely an attempt to induce the reseller from *advertising* the prices at which it was likely to sell the goods. Because the practice did not restrict a reseller from selling at any price it may decide upon, suppliers argued that it was not conduct in the nature of RPM.

The 1971 Australian RPM legislation was carried forward into the Trade Practices Act 1974; however, to forestall any further argument of the type discussed above the draftsperson inserted a new provision in the RPM legislation expanding the reference to selling to include references to advertising, displaying, or offering goods for resale. A similar provision appears in s 37(5) of the Commerce Act.

The RPM legislation in both Australia and New Zealand, therefore, covers the practice by which a supplier stipulates minimum prices at which a reseller may advertise goods, as distinct from selling goods. It must be remembered, however, that before a contravention of the RPM legislation can occur, the supplier must specify a price as the price below which the goods are not to be advertised for sale. Merely inducing or attempting to induce a reseller not to advertise at a particular price is not sufficient. This point is made clear by Smithers J in *Trade Practices Commission v Stihl Chain Saws (Aust) Pty Ltd* (1978) ATPR para 40-091, at p 17,892:

> If the substance of what the defendant had intimated to MBS was merely that they were not to advertise at a particular price that would not offend s 48 of the Act [corresponding to s 37(1) of the Commerce Act] unless as between the parties it was understood that that price was unacceptable because it was less than some other price which was specified in the sense of being chosen by the defendant and communicated to MBS as the price below which MBS were not to advertise the goods.

The *Stihl* case also demonstrates the real possibility that resellers may construe suppliers' recommended prices as specified minimum advertised prices. Smithers J said, at p 17,892:

> The question is whether when the defendant intimated that it desired MBS not to advertise its discount prices, the recommended retail price played a role as the benchmark, a level designated by the defendant as the level of price below which MBS were not to advertise the goods for sale.

His Honour had no difficulty in finding that Stihl had used the recommended price as a benchmark:

> When the defendant intimated its desire or requirement that MBS not advertise discount prices, it was saying that its desire or requirement was that MBS should not advertise at a price less than the recommended retail price. In that context the recommended retail price was the price specified by the defendant as the price below which MBS should not advertise the goods for sale.

41.7.3 The s 37(3) categories of prohibited conduct

(a) MAKING IT KNOWN THAT SUPPLY IS SUBJECT TO AN RPM CONDITION

In terms of s 37(3)(a), the supplier engages in RPM by "making it known to another person that the supplier will not supply goods to the other person unless the other person agrees not to sell those goods at a price less than a price specified by the supplier".

It is the supplier's action, or of someone acting on its behalf or by arrangement with it, in making it known to the other person that any supply to that person is subject to the condition that it shall not sell below a specified minimum price that constitutes the prohibited conduct. Whether the other person accepts the supplier's condition or whether the supplier actually withholds the supply of goods is irrelevant. See, for example, *Bata Shoe* (supra); *Trade Practices Commission v ICI Australia Petrochemicals Ltd* (1983) ATPR para 40-364.

The phrase "making it known" suggests not only that the other person must know of the supplier's intention but also that the supplier intended that person to have such knowledge: Heydon (supra) at p 3611. As Pincus J observed at p 47,434 in *The Heating Centre* case (supra), "the information specified must be conveyed by one means or another, but not necessarily in the precise terms set out in the statute". A supplier may adopt a variety of means, whether oral, written or by conduct, to make its intention known. One obvious way is direct communication with the other person. But less direct means would suffice. Thus, an announcement in the press or in a trade journal may suffice, provided the other person reads the announcement with the requisite understanding.

The word "agrees" lends itself to the argument that the supplier will not be engaging in s 37(3)(a) conduct unless it requires of the other person a binding agreement. To insist on a formal agreement, however, would be to frustrate the obvious intent of the provision. It is unlikely that the Courts will adopt such a narrow view of the section.

However, in *The Heating Centre* case (supra), all members of the Full Federal Court agreed that there was a difference for the purposes of the Australian equivalent of s 37(3)(a) between a supplier threatening not to supply a reseller who sells below a specified price and a supplier threatening not to supply a dealer unless the latter *agrees* not to sell below that price. Although the effect of the threat may be the same in both cases and although the parties may not draw the distinction themselves, it is important legally because, as a matter of statutory interpretation, only the latter conduct is within s 37(3)(a). In the context of the RPM provisions as a whole, however, the distinction drawn by the Full Court is only of technical importance for the threat of non-supply unaccompanied by any reference about agreeing not to discount is likely to be caught under s 37(3)(b) or (d).

In the *Sony* case (supra), Pincus J ruled that the person who is refused supply must be the same person to whom the RPM condition was made known. In his Honour's view, the two references to "other person", referred to in the Australian legislation as "second person", in s 37(3)(a) clearly identify the same person. In the case before him, his Honour held that para (a) did not apply because the supplier communicated its intention to a retail dealer but actually supplied the goods to an associated warehouse company.

(b) INDUCING SALE AT OR ABOVE A SPECIFIED MINIMUM PRICE AND THE EXCEPTION FOR RECOMMENDED PRICES

Section 37(3)(b) conduct involves "[t]he supplier inducing, or attempting to induce another person not to sell, at a price less than a price specified by the supplier, goods supplied to the other person by the supplier or by a third person who, directly or indirectly, has obtained the goods from the supplier".

The type of behaviour prohibited by s 37(3)(b) covers both unsuccessful and successful efforts by the supplier. "An attempt" to induce need not be successful whereas "to induce" suggests success.

Where an attempt to induce is alleged it is necessary to prove intention, but where inducement is alleged, intention is not required to be proven. It is only necessary to prove the conduct proscribed. See *Trade Practices Commission v Mobil Oil Australia Pty Ltd* (1984) 55 ALR 527.

"Induce" in the context of s 37(3)(b) involves the exercise of persuasion or influence upon a person with a view to having that person act in a particular way. The Australian Courts have given a wide meaning to inducement. Pincus J in *The Heating Centre* case (supra) proffered the following view of the term at p 47,434:

Counsel argued that there must be an "inducement" as that word is commonly used in the law. It is true that the word ordinarily refers to some proffered advantage or disadvantage, promised or threatened, to follow from following or failing to follow a stipulated course of action. There is no reason, however, to read into para (b) a necessity to find that anything is offered in exchange, so to speak, for not discounting; mere persuasion with no promise or threat, may well be an attempt to induce. Apart from that, here it appears that there was an inducement in the sense referred to by counsel, namely a threat to discontinue supply.

Depending upon the circumstances, what some suppliers may regard as mere "exhortations" may also be held to be inducements. For example, in the *Stihl* case (supra) the defendant company through its employees urged one of its retail stockists who had been supplying a former Stihl dealer with Stihl products at a discount of 20 per cent of the recommended retail price to discontinue the practice, but that if supply did continue then it should be at a discount no higher than 10 per cent. Smithers J found that the conduct came within the Australian equivalent of s 37(3)(b) even though it appears that no threats, disadvantages or promises of benefit were involved.

Threatening to cease the subsidising of advertising costs will amount to inducing conduct. In *Trade Practices Commission v Sharp Corporation of Australia Pty Ltd* (1975) 8 ALR 255 the Court found that the defendant company had engaged in conduct which amounted to an attempt to induce, by writing a letter to a retailer which read:

Would you please note that all future advertisements for Sharp Electronic calculators should show our uniform retail prices.

You will realize the difficulties that variations in prices advertised per calculator could cause both this company and yourselves, and would like to stress one point ie the Sharp Corporation will be unable to subsidize any advertising for electronic calculators that does not comply with the above request.

I thank you for your assistance in the above.

The Trade Practices Commission has successfully invoked the Australian equivalent of s 37(3)(b) in several cases. See, for example, *Trade Practices Commission v Pye Industries Sales Pty Ltd* (1978) ATPR para 40-088; *Trade Practices Commission v Madad Pty Ltd* (1979) 40 FLR 453; *Trade Practices Commission v Kensington Hiring Co Pty Ltd* (1981) ATPR para 40-256. In the recent case of *Trade Practices Commission v Penfolds Wines Pty Ltd* (1991) ATPR para 41-071, however, the Commission failed to establish a breach of the provision. Lee J said at p 52,087:

It is obvious that Penfolds attempted to induce Foodland to increase its prices, but I remain unpersuaded by the evidence that it attempted to induce Foodland not to sell, or advertise for sale, Penfold's products at a price *less* than a price specified by Penfolds, namely the price set by Penfolds for those products in its "direct deal" price lists.

The Commission has appealed Lee J's decision.

The legislature has seen fit to allow suppliers to engage in the practice of *recommending* resale prices. For criticism of such a policy, see Anderson (1979) 54 Wash L Rev 763; Pickering (1978) 2 Journal of Consumer Policy 97.

To give effect to this policy, the draftsperson has inserted a declaratory provision in the form of s 39. The section provides that for the purposes of s 37(3)(b) a supplier will not be taken as inducing, or attempting to induce, "merely because" of (a) a statement of price being applied to the goods or on the covering, label, reel or thing in which the goods are supplied, provided the statement is preceded by the words "recommended price"; or (b) the supplier notifies in writing to the other person a recommended price which includes, whether expressly or by implication, "a statement to the effect that the price is a recommended price only and that there is no obligation to comply with the recommendation".

Paragraph (a) of s 39 recognises that it is usually impractical to use a statement of the type referred to in para (b) on the goods themselves or on the covering, label, reel or thing in or with which goods are supplied. In such circumstances the words "recommended price" are sufficient.

However, in order to obtain the protection afforded by the section in circumstances other than those mentioned in para (a), any writing that refers to the actual notification of recommended prices must contain a qualifying statement of the type indicated in s 39(b).

While s 39 provides a presumption in favour of a supplier who complies with the requirements of the section, non-compliance need not necessarily result in an infringement of s 37(3)(b). No doubt there will be many cases where a failure to comply with s 39 will occur, but where, nevertheless, a supplier will not be regarded in all the circumstances as having engaged in inducing conduct. This will be so where a price was not understood, or not likely to be understood as anything other than a genuine recommendation carrying no sanction.

Conversely, compliance with s 39 will not prevent an infringement of s 37(3)(b) if the supplier has gone beyond strict compliance and has engaged in inducing conduct. Thus, in the *Mikasa* case (supra), there were catalogue price lists stating that prices were recommended only and there was no obligation to comply therewith. Nevertheless, in examining the course of Mikasa's conduct with its customers, the Industrial Court had no difficulty in finding that the supplier had indicated that failure to

comply with the recommended prices would produce adverse consequences. One of the Industrial Court judges, Joske J, concluded that, in
the light of all the facts, the notification in the catalogue price lists was "no
more than a subterfuge". The High Court of Australia endorsed the
finding of the Industrial Court.

(c) AGREEMENT NOT TO RESELL BELOW A SPECIFIED PRICE
Section 37(3)(b) prohibits the supplier entering or offering to enter into an
agreement for the supply of goods to another person, one of the terms of
which is, or would be, that the other person will not sell the goods at a
price less than that specified, or would be specified, by the supplier.

By using the word "agreement" the subsection may encompass only
legally enforceable agreements. At general law "agreement" normally
means a legally enforceable one and not merely an arrangement or
understanding: see *Wain v Warlters* (1804) 5 East 10 at pp 16-17.

Under the Commerce Act 1975, the expression "agreement or arrangement" was used in the provisions requiring concerted action. Section
23(11) of the 1975 Act made it clear that it was irrelevant whether the
parties intended their actions to be legally enforceable or not – "gentlemen's agreements" were thus included in the scope of the statutory
provisions. The framers of the Commerce Act 1986 chose to replace
"agreement or arrangement" with the broad formula of "contract, arrangement or understanding". No definition of "agreement" appears in
the 1986 Act. One can argue that had Parliament intended unenforceable
agreements to be caught under s 37(3)(c) it would have employed the
contract, arrangement or understanding wording or at least have carried
forward the s 23(11) definition into the 1986 Act. The failure of Parliament
to do either of these things means that the Courts may interpret "agreement" narrowly in the sense that it has at general law. A Court, however,
may reject such an argument as too formalistic. From a policy point of
view it is desirable that "agreement" should encompass arrangements
which are not legally binding.

The mere offer to enter into an agreement is sufficient to attract liability
under the subsection. Section 2(2)(d) of the Act defines the word "offer"
in broad terms:

> A reference to a person offering to do an act, or to do an act on a particular
> condition, includes a reference to the person making it known that the person
> will accept applications, offers, or proposals for the person to do that act or to
> do that act on that condition, as the case may be.

The definition overcomes the technical common law distinction between
an offer and an invitation to treat. Section 37(3)(c), therefore, potentially
applies to a wide range of pre-contractual negotiations.

Section 37(3)(c) has not given rise to much case law. This is not
surprising given that there are far more subtle ways of imposing RPM
than through an agreement. Nevertheless, legal advisers often have to
excise RPM conditions when perusing draft commercial agreements
which suggests that businesspersons are not sufficiently aware of the
serious legal consequences attaching to RPM. For an example of a blatant
contravention of the subsection, see *Trade Practices Commission v Baxmix
Australia Pty Ltd* (1985) ATPR para 40-534. As noted above, pre-contractual negotiations are fraught with potential danger for the unsuspecting
businessperson inclined to view RPM benignly.

(d) WITHHOLDING SUPPLY FOR REASONS INVOLVING SPECIFIED MINIMUM PRICES

Paragraphs (d) and (e) of s 37(3) involve the withholding of supply from another person (the reseller) for RPM reasons.

Section 37(3)(d) catches withholding where the reseller:

(i) has not agreed to the condition mentioned in section 37(3)(a); or
(ii) has sold or is likely to sell goods supplied at a price less than that specified by the supplier. The goods in question may be supplied indirectly through a third person, e.g. a wholesaler, jobber or distributor.

Section 37(3)(e) is similar to s 37(3)(d), except that the roles of the reseller and third persons are the reverse of those in s 37(3)(d)(ii), ie the supplier withholds supplies from the reseller because a third person further down the chain who has obtained goods, whether directly or indirectly from the reseller, has not or is not likely to abide by minimum specified prices.

Where the reseller has been selling or advertising the supplier's goods at reduced prices at the time of, or shortly before, the withholding, there will be little difficulty in establishing that the reseller is "likely to sell" at less than a price specified. This will also be the situation where, as in the *Mikasa* case, a prospective customer who has not before dealt in the supplier's goods, has a known policy of refusing to be bound to sell at resale prices specified by manufacturers, or wholesalers, or advertises widely that the goods which it offers for sale are sold at the greatest possible discount: G Q Tapperell, R B Vermeesch & D J Harland, *Trade Practices and Consumer Protection* (3rd edn, 1983) at p 406. In the latter situation, there need be no evidence that the supplier has told the prospective customer what the specified price is: *Mikasa* (1972) 127 CLR 617 at p 645 per Menzies J. For as Pincus J said in the *Sony* case (supra) at p 51,489, the supplier "might not do so if he did not intend to supply anyway".

(1) The meaning of withholding supply: Section 40 deems a number of factual situations to constitute withholding supply for the purposes of s 37(3)(d) and (e). The list of circumstances is not exhaustive but it is unlikely that there would be a withholding of supply which does not fall within the section. The various circumstances will be examined in turn.

(a) Refuses or fails to supply (s 40(a)) – If a supplier *refuses* or *fails* to supply goods to, or as *requested by*, another person, the supplier is deemed to withhold the supply of goods from that person.

The OECD report, *Refusal to Deal* (1969), notes that a "refusal" presupposes firstly that a buyer has approached the supplier and has made a written or oral request for the supply of certain goods; secondly that the supplier has not granted the request. Such analysis accords with Taylor J's dictum in the Australian case of *Attorney General v Dalgety Trading Co Ltd* [1966] ALR 194 that there cannot be a refusal without an "intimation" of the supplier's decision to refuse supply as requested.

Non-response on the part of a supplier may amount to a failure to supply goods as requested. But something more than a mere omission to respond is probably required: the Courts will probably look for some element of deliberateness.

787

The phrase "as requested by" gives the section wide meaning. The commercial status of the person making the request is irrelevant. This is seen from Smithers J's decision in the *Stihl* case (supra). The defendant company there terminated a distributorship of one of its retail dealers (MBS). MBS sought reinstatement as a dealer but was refused. Smithers J considered the reinstatement on the basis that MBS had no outstanding contractual rights to supplies and was, in effect, a mere member of the public who requested supplies on dealership terms. Nevertheless, his Honour ruled that the refusal on the part of the defendant was a withholding of supplies within the meaning of the Australian equivalent of s 40(a). However, his Honour made it clear that the refusal of itself did not constitute a contravention of the RPM legislation; before that could occur the plaintiff would have to show that the withholding of supply was committed for a reason specified in s 37(d) or (e) of the Act.

(b) Supply on disadvantageous terms (s 40(b)) – Paragraph (b) of s 40 deals with discriminatory treatment in the actual or suggested terms of the agreement to supply. The word "disadvantageous" is used without providing any point of comparison. In order to determine whether terms are "disadvantageous" it will be necessary to compare them to terms applied in previous dealings, or, in the case of a first supply, with terms applicable to others carrying on business in similar circumstances to the person alleging disadvantageous treatment. In some cases, a Court will have little difficulty in finding the terms are disadvantageous. An example of blatant disadvantageous treatment is seen in *Attorney General v Dalgety Trading Co Pty Ltd* (supra). The normal terms of trade were 30 days for payment. When the complainant began price-cutting he immediately became subject to COD plus a surcharge of 25 percent. A similar situation arose in *Direct Holdings Ltd v Feltex Furnishing of New Zealand Ltd* (1986) 1 NZBLC 102,616.

(c) Less favourable treatment (s 40(c)) – Paragraph (c) of s 40 deals with the situation where a supplier supplies goods to another person but in doing so "treats that person less favourably, whether in respect of time, method, or place of delivery, or otherwise, than the supplier treats other persons to whom the supplier supplies the same or similar goods".

Heydon (supra) observes at p 3646 that the provision concentrates on conduct in the course of supplying, whereas para (b) deals with the making of the contractual terms. Unlike para (b), this provision is limited to cases where comparison with other persons supplied is possible. Where there is no possibility of comparison, the case can only come within para (b).

Heydon also advances the argument that as the specific items of treatment listed all relate to delivery, then, on *ejusdem generis* principles, any other matters can only be delivery matters. Even if that argument were rejected, Heydon is of the opinion that the less favourable treatment must be in respect of circumstances connected with the implementation of supply, for example, delivery, credit, allowances, packing of goods, etc.

(d) Causing or procuring another to withhold supply (s 40(d)) – If the supplier causes or procures another person to act as stated in paras (a), (b) or (c), the supplier is itself regarded as withholding the goods.

An example of this provision is seen in *Trade Practices Commission v Pye Industries Sales Ltd* (1979) 2 ATPR para 40-088 where Pye Sales, a wholesale supplier of television sets procured a related company, Pye Finance, to withhold supplies of television sets to a retailer who continued to advertise them at a price less than that charged by other retailers in the area.

(2) The reason for withholding: Unlike the Commerce Act 1975, the 1986 legislation has no general provision regulating "unjustifiable" unilateral refusals to supply. Leaving aside possible liability under s 36, a supplier can lawfully withhold supplies from another person for reasons unconnected with RPM. It is only where the supplier is motivated by an RPM reason that the conduct becomes unlawful.

The question arises of what is the position where there are two or more reasons for withholding supplies, one of which is RPM. In such circumstances, is the withholding "for the reason" of RPM so as to fall within paras (d) or (e) of s 37(3)? In *Mikasa* (1972) 127 CLR 617 the High Court of Australia unanimously held that the words "for the reason that" in the 1971 Australian equivalent of s 37(3)(d) did not mean "for the sole reason". In an oft-cited statement, Barwick CJ said at p 634:

> In my opinion it is not correct to so emphasise the participle in the phrase *for the reason that* as requiring the withholding of the supply to be for one reason only. In my opinion, if the likelihood that the would-be purchaser would sell at less than the specified price is an operative reason for withholding that supply, the supplier engages in the practice of RPM, however many reasons the supplier may in effect have for not supplying the goods to the would-be purchaser. The likelihood of price cutting is not required, in my opinion, to be the predominant reason; it is enough for this to be an operative reason, that is to say, a substantial reason in the totality of reasons for the withholding of supply.

The view of the High Court obviously influenced the drafting of s 4F(b) of the Trade Practices Act 1974, inserted into the main body of the Act by the Trade Practices Amendment Act 1977. Section 2(5)(b) of the Commerce Act 1986 is in similar terms to s 4F(b). The subsection provides that a person is deemed to have engaged, or to engage in conduct for a particular reason if the person engaged or engages in conduct for reasons that included that reason and that reason was or is a substantial reason.

As to the meaning of "substantial", s 2(1A) defines the term to mean real or of substance. Franki J gave a somewhat more helpful definition in *Peter Williamson* (supra) at p 265:

> In my opinion it is not possible to place precise limits on the meaning of the word "substantial" in s 4 F. I consider that the proscribed reason in s 96(3)(d) [corresponding to s 37(3)(d) of the Commerce Act 1986] must be one of real significance in the decision to withhold supply of goods, or to adopt the words of Barwick CJ an "operative" reason.

The ramifications of s 2(5)(b) are seen in *Ron Hodgson (Holdings) Pty Ltd v Westco Motors (Distributors) Pty Ltd* (1980) 29 ALR 307. In 1975 Westco granted a franchise to Hodgson in respect of Mazda cars. In February 1979, Westco gave Hodgson notice of termination of the franchise. Hodgson, alleging a breach of the Australian equivalent of s 37(3)(d)(ii), sought an injunction in the Federal Court of Australia restraining Westco from terminating the franchise.

Franki J found that Westco had good commercial reasons for terminating the franchise. However, he also found on the evidence that Westco had a policy of discouraging discount advertising and that it had communicated this policy to Hodgson. Invoking the assistance of the Australian equivalent of s 2(5)(b), his Honour said at p 320:

> [T]he franchise was terminated for a reason which included, as a substantial and operative reason, that the applicant has sold or was likely to sell, or had advertised or was likely to advertise, Mazda vehicles at a price less than that specified by the first respondent.

Having found that Westco had engaged in RPM, his Honour ruled that this was a proper case for injunctive relief.

Pengilley, ((supra) at p 264) has expressed the opinion that the *Ron Hodgson* decision "gives rise to innumerable commercial difficulties": Dr Pengilley makes the point at p 266 that a supplier has –

> . . . far greater freedom, either in terminating a reseller or in refusing to deal with an applicant for supplies, if there are no retail price lists in existence, recommended or otherwise. This is because there can be no "specified" price and a "specified" price is a prerequisite in triggering the operation of s 37.

Counsel for the appellants in *The Heating Centre* case (1986) 65 ALR 429 made a valiant attempt to circumvent the hazards posed to suppliers by s 2(5)(b) by advancing the argument that the subsection is a deeming provision which applies only to language in the Act referring expressly to "engaging in conduct". Counsel submitted that since the Australian equivalent of s 37(1) uses the words "shall not engage in the practice of resale price maintenance" the section could not have its interpretation assisted by s 2(5)(b). Pincus J, with whom Lockhart and Wilcox JJ agreed on this point, rejected this argument at p 442 on the grounds that s 2(5)(b) "is not expressed to apply only when one finds a reference to particular words and is apt to catch provisions which, however expressed may be said to deal with the question of engaging in conduct". The Full Court concluded that s 2(5)(b) did apply to s 37(3)(d)(ii) and that as a substantial reason for The Heating Centre's refusal to deal with a particular reseller was apprehension that the latter would sell at a discount, its conduct in so refusing was RPM. This was so, even though it was accepted that at least a substantial reason for The Heating Centre's conduct was its desire to have a limited number of dealers.

(3) *Proof of reason for withholding:* It is frequently difficult for a person taking proceedings against a supplier to prove that the supplier withheld goods for the reason of RPM. To overcome this problem, s 42 provides that in certain circumstances a Court may presume that goods have been withheld for an unlawful reason unless the supplier can prove that they were withheld for some other reason.

To call this presumption into play the plaintiff must prove:

(a) that supplies of goods were withheld within the meaning of s 40;
(b) that immediately before the supplier so acted, it had been supply-

ing goods of the kind withheld to either the person in respect of whom the contravention is alleged or another person carrying on a similar business; and

(c) that within the previous six months the supplier become aware of a matter referred to in s 37(d) or (e).

If these conditions are fulfilled it shall be presumed, in the absence of evidence to the contrary, that the reason for the withholding of supply of goods was one of those proscribed in s 37(d) or (e).

There are certain limitations on the use of the provision. First, the withholding must be of a kind contemplated by s 40 otherwise the presumption will not apply. Secondly, the words "had been supplying" in s 42(1)(b) indicate that "some continuity of supply ... is contemplated by the section": *Festival Industries Pty Ltd v Mikasa (New South Wales) Pty Ltd* (1971) 18 FLR 260 at p 284 per Spicer CJ and Smithers J. Thirdly, the requirement in s 42(1)(c) necessitates the plaintiff proving a particular awareness by the supplier. Finally, s 42(2) excludes the use of the presumption where proof of disadvantageous or unfavourable treatment consists "only" of a discriminatory method as to time or method of payment or the giving of security. The non-application of the presumption in these latter circumstances is understandable as it is desirable that businesses should have flexibility in credit matters. Where the presumption does not apply, other proof will be required.

In the great majority of cases none of the above limitations should present a problem to the plaintiff.

41.7.4 Resale price maintenance by third parties

(a) THE GENESIS OF THE PROVISIONS

The origin of s 38, which prohibits RPM by third parties, lies in Australian legislative proposals to deal with RPM problems in the Australian petroleum industry: see V Venturini, *The Administration of the Murphy Trade Practices Act* (1980) at pp 309-15. In February 1976, the Australian Trade Practices Commission alleged that the Transport Workers' Union was co-operating with the oil companies to maintain the retail price of petrol in Sydney. Apparently, the Union policy was to withhold delivery of petrol from service stations displaying "discount boards". Such a policy was pursued because of a belief that discounting affects the employment and earnings of tanker drivers. The problem confronting the Trade Practices Commission was that the Union, not being a supplier, could only be proceeded against if it could be shown to have aided and abetted an oil company. This was difficult to show as the Union's acts directly maintained the price rather than aiding and abetting an oil company to maintain it.

Legislative changes to the Australian RPM legislation to deal with the above problem have been mooted on a number of occasions. In its Green Paper, *Trade Practices Act: Proposals for Change* (February 1984), the Australian Labour Government discussed, inter alia, the case for repealing the secondary boycott provisions of the Trade Practices Act 1974, introduced into the main Act in 1977, and extending the RPM provisions to cover price maintenance activities by non-suppliers but subject only to the remedy of injunction. On 12 September 1984, the Government introduced the Trade Practices Amendment Bill which proposed the repeal of the secondary boycott provisions. The Bill was defeated in the Senate. On 9 October 1985, the Government introduced the Trade Practices Amendment Bill 1985, providing for a large number of changes to the 1974 Act. Although based in large part on its February 1984 proposals, the 1985 Bill, since enacted as the Trade Practices Revision Act 1986, did not propose any change in the existing law relating to secondary boycotts or RPM.

The decision of the New Zealand Labour Government not to include secondary boycott provisions in the Commerce Act 1986 undoubtedly smoothed the way for the New Zealand RPM legislation to be extended to cover third parties.

(b) DEFINITION OF "THIRD PARTY"

The s 38(1) proscription is directed against "persons", referred to in the section as "third parties". A third party can be any type of "person" within the statutory or ordinary meaning of that term. The definition of "person" in s 2(1) includes "a local authority and any association of persons, whether incorporated or not". The inclusive definition of "person" encompasses virtually all types of legal and natural persons, including public and local authorities, companies, trade associations, trade unions, and employees, officials and members of such bodies. In the context of the RPM provisions, however, it is clear that "third parties" are not suppliers of the goods which are the subject of the alleged price maintaining activity.

(c) THE CATEGORIES OF RPM BY THIRD PARTIES

(1) Making it known that the third party proposes to engage in hindering conduct: s 38(1)(a): In terms of s 38(1)(a) it is an offence for a third party to make it known that it proposes to engage in conduct, whether alone or in concert with any other person, that will hinder or prevent the supply of goods to, or the acquisition of goods from, another person unless that person agrees not to sell those goods at a price less than a price specified by the third party.

The meaning of the phrase "make it known" has already been discussed in the context of s 37(3)(a).

By s 2(2)(a) of the Act, a reference to engaging in conduct shall be read as a reference to doing or refusing to do any act. Section 2(2)(c) elaborates on this by providing that a reference to refusing to do any act includes a reference to refraining from doing it (otherwise than inadvertently) or making it known that the act will not be done. Thus, where a third party either withholds goods or delivery or threatens to do so, ie makes it known that it will not do an act, it engages in conduct within the meaning of s 38(1).

The third party may act alone or in concert with any other person. The term "in concert" is very general. The ordinary meaning of the term refers to the agreement of two or more persons in a design, plan or enterprise. The term has been the subject of judicial interpretation in the context of s 45D of the Australian Trade Practices Act 1974 (the secondary boycott provision). Bowen CJ in *Tillmanns Butcheries Pty Ltd v AMIEU* (1979) ATPR para 40-138 said at p 18,493 that –

... [a]cting in concert involves knowing conduct, the result of communication between the parties and not simply simultaneous actions occurring spontaneously.

In *AMIEU v Mudginberri Station Pty Ltd* (1985) ATPR para 40-624, Keely and Pincus JJ stated at p 47,073 that –

... [t]he notion of acting in concert involves contemporaneity.

Moreover, mere mental support without any current overt participation does not amount to acting in concert. It does not matter that the acts performed by one participant are different from those of the others provided they form part of the plan of action or give effect to the understanding or "concert" between the participants.

Supply or acquisition can be hindered or prevented by direct action such as refusal to supply or deliver or by less direct means such as threats, warnings or persuasion. The conduct engaged in must be causally connected to the hindrance or prevention.

It is arguable that because of the use of the word "agrees", the third party will not be practising RPM unless he/she requires of the other person a binding agreement. Such a view, however, is overly formalistic and is unlikely to be adopted by the Courts.

Section 38(1)(a) would apply to the type of conduct that was alleged to have occurred in the Australian petroleum industry. The subsection would also apply where a reseller, observing a certain percentage mark-up or a supplier's recommended prices, threatens a discounting reseller that it will take steps to ensure that supply to the latter will be hindered or prevented unless it falls into line with the former's pricing policies.

(2) Engaging in conduct for the purpose of inducing RPM: s 38(1)(b): Section 38(1)(b) makes it an offence for a third party to engage in conduct, whether alone or in concert with any other person, that will hinder or prevent the supply of goods to, or the acquisition of goods from, another person for the purpose of inducing that person not to sell those goods at a price less than a price specified by the third party.

Unlike s 38(1)(a), where the third party can incur liability by merely threatening to engage in hindering conduct, s 38(1)(b) requires the third party to have actually engaged in hindering conduct before liability can be incurred.

The meaning of "engage in conduct", "in concert" and "hinder or prevent" have already been discussed in the context of s 38(1)(a).

The third party must have engaged in the hindering conduct for the *purpose* of *inducing* another person not to sell the goods at a price less than a price specified by the third party. Many actions under s 38(1)(b), no doubt, will be defended on the basis that the conduct engaged in was motivated by a primary purpose not directly related to RPM, for example, a desire to protect jobs. However, in terms of s 2(5)(b) of the Act liability will be incurred if the hindering conduct was motivated in part by an RPM purpose and that purpose was or is a substantial purpose for engaging in the conduct.

Because of the purpose requirement it is necessary to prove an intention to induce. However, success in the effort to induce is not necessary; hence the subsection may be relied upon by sellers of goods who are resisting direct or indirect pressures from third parties not to sell their goods below a specified price.

Section 38(1)(b) embraces the situation where one or more competitors of a discounter threaten to quit buying from a supplier unless the latter takes action to persuade the discounter to adhere to stipulated prices. The prices, however, must be specified by the third party. For example, the complaining reseller may demand that the supplier convey to the discounter that unless the latter raises its prices to the level of those of the complaining reseller, supply will be withheld. The supplier need not necessarily have a policy of specifying minimum prices or even a policy of recommending resale prices. In contrast to s 37, the specification must be made by the third party. As with s 37, failure to demonstrate the necessary specification will prove fatal to a plaintiff's case. Section 38(3) and (4) contain similar deeming provisions to those contained in s 37(4) and (5) of the Act.

(d) POSSIBLE LIABILITY UNDER OTHER PROVISIONS

Section 38 recognises that RPM is often dealer-induced. But unlike the position in the United States, as to which see *Monsanto Co v Spray-rite Service Corp* 465 US 752 (1984) and *Business Electronics Corp v Sharp Electronics Corp* 485 US 717 (1988), there is no need to prove an agreement between the third party and the supplier either to terminate the discounter's distributorship or to fix resale prices.

If there is evidence of an agreement, then in addition to liability under s 38 a possible contravention of s 27 may be involved. Where two or more competitors act in concert with the supplier, their conduct may amount to a breach of the exclusionary provisions contained in s 29 of the Act. The parties to such an arrangement may also contravene the s 30 horizontal price fixing provisions. Both collective boycotts and price fixing are per se illegal. In addition to possible liability under these provisions, the supplier's conduct in inducing, or attempting to induce, RPM will constitute a contravention of one or more of the categories of s 37(3). The competitors may also be a party to a s 37 contravention by virtue of the aiding and abetting provisions contained in ss 80(1)(b), 81(c) and 82(1)(b) of the Act. A dominant supplier terminating or threatening to terminate a discounter also runs the risk of incurring liability under s 36; this will be the case even though no specified minimum price may be involved: *Mark Lyons Pty Ltd v Bursill Sportsgear Pty Ltd* (1987) 75 ALR 581. Finally, a supplier attempting to induce its competitors' dealers to engage in RPM will run foul of ss 80(1)(b) and 81(b) for attempting to contravene ss 27 and 30: see *Commerce Commission v BP Oil New Zealand Ltd* (1991) 3 NZBLC 102,092 where the Court imposed a penalty of $40,000 on the supplier and $8,000 on its employee for attempt conduct.

(e) PREVALENCE OF DEALER-INDUCED RPM

It is interesting to note that pressure from competing resellers appears to have been responsible for the supplier's RPM conduct in the two reported cases to date under the New Zealand RPM legislation. In the first such case, *Direct Holdings Ltd v Feltex Furnishing of NZ Ltd* (supra), the plaintiff was a furniture retailer offering goods at a substantial discount. One of its suppliers changed the terms of trade as between itself and the plaintiff, requiring that payment be made on a cash basis and adding a surcharge to its normal wholesale price. Previously it had supplied the retailer on credit and granted discount from the wholesale price. The plaintiff alleged that the change in terms of trade had been introduced as a result of threats by a competitor to remove its custom from the supplier. The plaintiff advanced several heads of liability. First, it alleged that the supplier was in breach of s 37(3)(b) by attempting to induce it not to sell at discounted prices. Secondly, the plaintiff contended that the supplier's decision to change the terms of trade was the result of an arrangement or understanding in breach of s 27 of the Act. Thirdly, as against the competitor, the plaintiff alleged a breach of s 29 based on concerted activity undertaken by the competitor in conjunction with other trade competitors with the purpose of limiting the supply of goods to the plaintiff. Finally, the plaintiff argued that the competitor, by persuading the supplier to increase the price of its goods to the plaintiff, was attempting to lessen competition in terms of s 27. Holland J granted interim injunctions against both the supplier and the competitor to restore supply on the same terms as other retailers, and to prevent action being taken in relation to the supplier's other customers.

In the second case, *Commerce Commission v Herberts Bakery Ltd* (1991) 3 NZBLC 101,996, the defendant bakery company entered into an arrangement for the supply of bread to a restaurant. After an initial supply, the distribution manager of the bakery telephoned the restaurant and requested that it lift its prices to the full recommended retail price per loaf as pressure was being put on the distribution manager by a rival of the restaurant. The restaurant declined and received no further bread. When the Commerce Commission investigated the matter, the distribution manager confirmed the telephone conversation but the general manager of the bakery denied that it was acting under pressure, stating that the restaurant was not meeting the minimum daily requirement of 24 loaves. The defendant company, however, later conceded liability under the Commerce Act. In an oral judgment, Fisher J imposed a penalty of $5,000 on the company. While focusing on the clear breach of s 37(3)(b), his Honour observed at p 101,997, "[t]here are various other provisions in Pt II of the Act which appear to have been contravened in the present case . . .".

What the preceding discussion illustrates is that RPM conduct is fraught with potential liability under a whole raft of provisions, not only for suppliers but also for all those involved in the practice.

Given the time lapse since the enactment of the Commerce Act 1986 and the considerable number of successful RPM prosecutions, albeit most of them Australian, the commercial community has been well and truly put on notice that engaging in RPM is likely to be met with heavy penalties.

41.7.5 Authorisation of RPM

(a) POLICY CHANGES

As originally enacted, the Commerce Act 1986 did not provide for the authorisation of RPM, also known as vertical price fixing. Several commentators observed that it was anomalous that the Act denied the possibility for authorisation of vertical price fixing while allowing it in respect of horizontal price fixing. Of the two practices, virtually all commentators agree that horizontal price fixing is likely to be the more pernicious because it almost always has anti-competitive effects and almost never has pro-competitive ones, and thus is unlikely to be of net economic benefit.

While commentators once held the same attitudes in respect of RPM, contemporary scholarship has revealed a range of efficiency explanations for the practice and has demonstrated that under some circumstances RPM may be welfare-enhancing. The "new learning" in respect of RPM has led to calls to relax the per se rule that governs the practice in most countries.

New Zealand officials have acknowledged the insights of the "new learning". In its review of the Commerce Act 1986, the then Department of Trade and Industry tentatively suggested that the absolute ban on RPM be modified: *Review of the Commerce Act 1986: A Discussion Paper* (1988) at p 39. This suggestion firmed into a policy change with the enactment of the Commerce Amendment Act 1990, s 19 of which added RPM to the list of authorisable practices. The Australian legislature has made no similar change in respect of the Australian RPM legislation.

(b) EFFICIENCY EXPLANATIONS FOR RPM

(1) Telser's special services theory: The efficiency explanation for RPM that has gained the most recognition hypothesises that manufacturers impose price restraints upon their resellers to insure the provision of special services. Professor Lester Telser advanced this "special services" theory in his 1960 article "Why Should Manufacturers Want Fair Trade?" (1960) Journal of Law & Economics 86. Telser persuasively argued that, in certain circumstances, it could be in the manufacturer's best interests to limit price competition among its dealers. Telser explained that the manufacturer could benefit when it wanted a dealer to furnish a potential customer with services associated with the product.

By "services", Telser meant not only delivery, credit, and repair, but also point-of-purchase sales promotions or information about the particular product. Services include any dealer activities that may increase demand. Having dealers supply these costly services benefits the manufacturer whenever the resulting stimulative effect on demand exceeds the depressing effect of the higher price charged to consumers.

In addition to showing how demand could be stimulated by higher prices, Telser explained why price floors were needed. He pointed out that resellers who provide special services to consumers, and who incur the costs associated with the provision of such services could be taken advantage of by other resellers who provide no services, incur fewer costs, and are therefore able to offer the product for sale at a lower cost. Consumers, after utilising the pre-sales services of the higher priced resellers, will be induced to buy from lower priced sellers who take a "free ride" on the services offered by their higher priced competitors. These free-riding activities discourage the sellers who are being taken advantage of from continuing to provide services, thus harming the manufacturer and consumers. To deal with this problem, the manufacturer can establish minimum retail prices so that resellers are forced to compete by providing special services with the product and not by reducing the resale price.

For a study assessing the relative importance of special services as an explanation of RPM, see P M Ippolito, *Resale Price Maintenance: Economic Evidence from Litigation* (1988). See also Hanks & Williams (1987) 15 ABLR 147.

(2) The welfare effects of the special services theory: Scholars of the Chicago School of antitrust analysis, building on Telser's work, have postulated that vertical restraints, including RPM, are generally welfare-enhancing because they usually increase output. The following comments of Professor (now Judge) Richard Posner are illustrative of the Chicago view: see (1981) 48 Chi L Rev 6 at p 21.

> If [the firm's] output expanded, the [vertical] restriction must have made the firm's product more attractive to consumers on balance, thereby enabling the firm to take business from its competitors. This is an increase in interbrand competition and hence in consumer welfare, which is the desired result of competition. The increase must exceed any net reduction in intrabrand competition considered in both its price and service.

The Chicago School view that RPM is generally welfare-enhancing is based on the premise that greater output is normally associated with improved consumer welfare. This assumption, however, has been attacked by economists such as Professor William Comanor, who has demonstrated that even though RPM may increase output, the practice can result in a reduction in consumer welfare: see Comanor (1985) 98 Harv L Rev 983.

The crucial point in Comanor's analysis is that a profit-seeking firm pays attention only to the preferences of marginal consumers (those who lack knowledge about the product) in deciding whether to increase the level of services and promotion for its product. If marginal consumers value the extra services more than their cost, and increase their purchases of the product as a result, the manufacturer will find it profitable to impose vertical restraints such as RPM. The RPM-generated additional services or promotion, however, may have value only to customers at the margin and have little or no value for infra-marginal customers, ie well-informed consumers who value the product highly and do not cease purchasing it when its price rises. Comanor and Kirkwood explain how despite increased output, RPM could still harm consumers as a whole: see 3 Contemporary Policy Issues 9 at p 13 (Spring 1985).

> Although marginal consumers would gain from the extra services, infra-marginal consumers might be hurt. If the latter prefer to purchase the manufacturer's product at a lower price (without additional services), RPM would reduce their welfare. Moreover, the welfare losses to these consumers may outweigh the gains to marginal consumers. When this possibility is recognized, the link between the interests of producers and consumers – presumed by many to hold in a purely vertical context – is effectively broken.

While conceding that evidence about the prevalence of the anti-competitive instances of RPM is not yet available, Comanor and Kirkwood believe that such instances may be quite frequent if one makes the plausible assumption that substantial quantities of products are bought by knowledgeable infra-marginal consumers who place little value on information services provided by dealers. Until more extensive evidence is available, Comanor and Kirkwood believe that policymakers should be cautious about proposals to weaken the current per se rule against RPM. An exception could, however, be made in the case of new entrants. This is because few prospective purchasers of a new entrant's product are likely to be knowledgeable; most purchasers are likely to be ignorant and in need of advice. Consequently purely vertical RPM is more likely to increase efficiency in the case of a new entrant than it would in the case of an established firm.

(3) Quality signalling theories: The limitation of Telser's theory to explain the adoption of vertical RPM in situations where products require little, if any, presales services, has led some economists to formulate generalised free rider theories that emphasise the importance of establishing and maintaining product reputation and/or sales outlets. See Marvel & McCafferty (1984) 15 Rand Journal of Economics 346; Goldberg (1984) 79 Nw U L Rev 736.

These theories assume that if certain products are to be established and promoted effectively, retailers with a high quality image must carry the product. By using the services of such retailers, the manufacturer conveys a quality signal to customers assumed to be unable to judge a product's quality prior to purchase. It should be noted that the retailer's premises and its general methods of doing business convey the quality signal, rather than the price of the product per se. To the extent that cultivating a high-quality image requires resources, retailers with images of higher quality require higher mark-ups over the manufacturer's price relative to retailers with lower quality images. The manufacturer may rely on RPM under these circumstances because having products available in the type of retail outlets which present consumers with a correct signal of the product's quality and relative value may be an efficient way of stimulating demand for the products. Without RPM, a free rider problem might emerge in that consumers, observing that high-quality stores carry certain products, might purchase those products in discount stores. This could result in the high-quality stores refusing to stock the manufacturer's products with a consequent reduction in consumer demand and/or a debasement in their quality.

Although the quality certification theories add considerably to our understanding of RPM the welfare effects of such theories are still ambiguous at this stage. The theories, however, lend weight to the argument that a new entrant's product may need the protection of RPM in the early stages of its life cycle if it is to gain brand recognition and consumer acceptance.

For United States and Australian case studies where quality and style certification theories may explain the RPM conduct involved, see Goldberg (1980) Am Bus L J 225; Goldberg (1982) 23 Wm & Mary L Rev 439; Lindgren & Entrekin (1973), ABLR 130; Hampton (1989) 4 Canta L Rev 75.

Another efficiency explanation for RPM is the outlets hypothesis. This theory postulates that, under certain circumstances, manufacturers may have incentives to impose RPM when the total demand for their product is positively related to the density of retail distribution. See Reagan (1986) 9 Research in Law & Economics 1.

Unlike the free rider theories discussed above, the outlets hypothesis does not explain RPM in terms of encouraging dealers to compete through the provision of services. Rather, an astute manufacturer will impose RPM when on balance the gains from obtaining additional outlets through RPM-induced subsidisation of relatively high cost retailers more than offset any demand-reducing of higher prices associated with the protected resale margins. According to the theory, the increase in demand in response to additional outlets might allow the manufacturer to realise cost savings associated with economies of scale. This may lead to final consumer prices being lower under RPM than under competitive conditions. Even in instances where the manufacturer possesses significant market power and the effect of RPM is to raise final consumer prices, the net effect of the RPM will be to increase the quantity sold.

Even though traditional retailers are likely to benefit from this type of RPM, low-cost retailers will be prevented from capturing the gains that would be available to them in the absence of fixed prices and passing their lower distribution costs on to consumers. This factor is likely to weigh heavily against any application for dispensation from the per se ban: see *Re Chocolate and Sugar Confectionery* (1967) LR 6 RP 338. In the absence of special public interest circumstances, as to which see *Re Net Book Agreement* (1962) LR 3 RP 198 and *Re Medicaments Reference (No 2)* (1970) LR 7 RP 267, it seems unlikely that the outlets hypothesis would find favour with a competition authority.

(c) ANTI-COMPETITIVE EXPLANATIONS FOR RPM

(1) Retailer collusion: The most popular, and historically the most important, explanatory hypothesis for RPM relates to the existence of retailer collusion. Traditional retailers, wanting to protect themselves against discounters and wanting a way to prevent destabilising cheating from within their own group, combine to coerce manufacturers into the establishment of an RPM programme. The retailers use the manufacturer as a central body to enforce compliance with cartel prices. It is assumed that the retailers have sufficient market (monopsony) power to impose their will upon the manufacturer.

The result of such action is identical to that achieved by a horizontal price fixing agreement except that a vertical form masks the scheme. Using RPM in this form may be more effective than if the retailers relied solely on agreements among themselves. Reliance on horizontal agreements allows new retailers to enter and undercut the cartel members. Because of the advantage of using vertical price fixing, it has been "theorized . . . that the motivation for resale price fixing often – perhaps usually or even almost always – comes from retailers": L Sullivan, *Handbook of the Law of Antitrust* (1977) at p 383.

Given the existence of the Commerce Act 1986 and the more competitive commercial environment of the last decade, formal RPM cartels involving retailer groups entering into agreements with manufacturers to impose price restraints or exacting such restraints from manufacturers, are not likely to be very common. However, retailer-induced RPM can effectively occur in a number of ways that do not involve an agreement in the legal sense of that term. Pressure from a single prestigious dealer may cause a manufacturer to initiate RPM, even though, in the absence of such pressure, the firm would prefer to distribute its products without a price restraint. The manufacturer may also succumb to pressures exerted independently by several independent dealers. Again, there is no agreement or cartel in legal terms. Even if there are no dealer complaints, the manufacturer may be fearful that the existence of price competition might cause some incumbent full-price retailers to refrain from handling its product. As noted above, retailer-induced RPM is commonplace. As yet, no theory adequately explains how countervailing efficiency considerations, if any, outweigh the anti-competitive effects.

(2) Manufacturer collusion: Manufacturers may impose RPM to facilitate collusion. If members of a manufacturers' cartel merely set uniform selling rates to buyers at the next level of distribution, there is always the temptation on the part of one or more cartel members (usually the more efficient) to offer secret discounts to resellers. Assuming that the price reductions pass through to consumers, this could affect market sales and shares of the cartel members. To prevent cheating of this sort, manufacturers can fix resale prices. Any deviation from the fixed resale prices would alert the cartel members to the possibility that one or more of their members was price shading or that the agreed resale prices were not being effectively enforced. Thus, it would be easy to detect possible cheating.

To avoid detection, it would be possible for a manufacturer to shade selling prices but to insist that its retailers maintain resale prices. It would be rational for a manufacturer to engage in such behaviour if it resulted in retailers increasing their purchases of the manufacturer's brand at the expense of other members' brands. However, the more retailers that the manufacturer has to negotiate with, the more likely that its discounting activities would become known to the trade generally. To prevent such discounting, the cartel may insist on a policy of exclusive dealing between individual manufacturers and their retailers. Under these conditions, a manufacturer would have little incentive to cut prices, unless higher retail margins, made possible by the secret price cuts, led retailers to push more aggressively the manufacturer's product, thus generating higher sales.

While economists have long recognised the manufacturer cartel theory of RPM, see, for example, Telser (supra) at pp 96-105, some recent commentators suggest that collusive RPM by manufacturers is so unlikely as to be of no real policy concern: see, for example, Ornstein (1985) 54 Antitrust Bull 401. However, the New Zealand experience under the Trade Practices Act 1958 shows that the practice is not unknown in New Zealand: see *His Master's Voice (NZ) Ltd v Simmons* [1960] NZLR 25; *Re the Pricing and Marketing of Hormone Weedkiller Preparations* Decision No. 19 of the Trade Practices and Prices Commission (1 February 1965), *affirmed* by the Trade Practices Appeal Authority (2 October 1965). Over many years, sections of the farming community have made complaints against the agricultural chemical industry alleging collective pricing behaviour and collective refusal to supply farmer co-operatives. The Commerce Commission is currently carrying out an investigation of the pricing practices within the industry: *Fair's Fair* (Issue No 12, November 1991 at p 1).

(3) Other uses of RPM by manufacturers: In addition to the use of RPM as
a means of policing a horizontal price agreement among manufacturers,
RPM can be used to co-ordinate oligopolistic behaviour. Price competition in retailing can be an independent source of instability in the
individual market shares of a group of oligopolistic suppliers. Retail
price competition can destabilise prices at the supplier level, causing
competition at that level to be more frequent and intense than otherwise.
Thus, it is in the interests of suppliers, proceeding collusively or
oligopolistically, to suppress price competition at the retail level. The
frequent instances of oil refining companies engaging in RPM are arguably explained on this basis. If this is the case, any relaxation of the per
se rule would only make it more difficult for independently-owned retail
outlets to engage in price competition.

RPM may also feature in more complex marketing arrangements
designed to induce dealer loyalty and minimise the threat of new entry.

The introduction of RPM is merely one way in which some tangible
benefit may be conferred upon distributors. Often RPM will be accompanied by exclusive dealing and a policy of selective distribution. In a small
economy like New Zealand's, the use of RPM and other types of vertical
restrictions in the manner described is likely to be more harmful than in
a large open economy.

(d) DOES THE "NEW LEARNING" JUSTIFY ALLOWING AUTHORI-
SATION OF RPM?

The economic analysis of RPM reveals a range of anti-competitive and
pro-competitive explanations for the practice. While scholars recognise
the possibility that RPM can have one or more of a number of functions,
they dispute the relative probability of the practice being either efficiency-enhancing or anti-competitive, either in individual cases or on
balance.

Nevertheless, even those scholars who oppose any relaxation of the
per se ban on RPM concede that some exception is warranted in the case
of a new firm or product.

The recent legislative amendment allowing for authorisation of RPM
enables the Commerce Commission to take account of the "new learning", particularly as it applies to new entrants.

Before the Commission can make a determination granting an authorisation in respect of RPM it must be satisfied that the engaging in the
practice of RPM, or the act or conduct to which the application relates,
will in all the circumstances result, or be likely to result in such a benefit
to the public that the practice or act should be permitted: s 61(8).

The public benefit that applicants are most likely to invoke is efficiency. The nature of the product provides important clues about the
likelihood of efficiencies being generated by RPM. The special services
argument for RPM presumes a complex product with important presales
services provided by the dealer. Where the product is homogeneous and
there are few or no presale services provided by the dealer, the Commission is unlikely to be receptive towards an efficiency argument: Larner,
in *Economics & Antitrust Policy* (R Larner & J Meehan eds. 1989) at p 136.

Where the dealer's role is important either in the form of tangible
services, certification of the quality of the product, or location, RPM can
foster efficient distribution: Larner (ibid). In these circumstances the
Commission may be prepared to recognise an efficiency-enhancing role

for RPM, particularly if the applicant is a new entrant or the product is new.

The Commission is only likely to be sympathetic to an RPM authorisation application where there is vigorous inter-brand competition. This is unlikely to be present in a highly concentrated industry or one dominated by a powerful firm. A new entrant attempting to break into such an industry may, however, be viewed more favourably.

Even if an applicant demonstrates that RPM is efficiency-enhancing this does not necessarily mean the Commission will equate the claimed efficiencies with public benefit. What may be privately beneficial need not necessarily be beneficial from a welfare point of view: see Rey & Tirole (1986) 76 Am Econ Rev 92.

Apart from efficiency, public benefit arguments acceptable to the Commission are likely to be few. In *Re Net Book Agreement* (1962) LR 3 RP 198 and *Re Associated Booksellers* [1962] NZLR 1057, the United Kingdom Restrictive Practices Court and the New Zealand Trade Practices Appeal Authority respectively accepted the validity of the public benefit argument that RPM resulted in the greater availability of, and lower price for books of a technical, educational and cultural nature because of the cross-subsidisation involved between these books and the more popular fast-moving titles. However, it is doubtful whether these decisions would be decided the same way today; rather the contrary approach adopted by the Australian Trade Practices Tribunal in *Re Books* (1972) 20 FLR 256, denying RPM on books, is more likely to accord with the pro-competitive thrust of the Commerce Act 1986. The deregulation of the pharmacy industry and the acceptability of discounting within the industry generally would also undermine many of the arguments that led the United Kingdom Restrictive Practices Court to uphold RPM in *Re Medicaments Reference (No 2)* (1970) LR 7 RP 267.

On the detriment side of the ledger, the imposition of RPM is likely to lead to an increase in price, at least in the short-run, and the elimination of intra-brand price competition. Strong public benefit evidence will be needed before the Commission is likely to authorise a practice the effect of which is to increase price and eliminate competition in the market-place.

Part VII

INSOLVENCY

Chapter 42

INSOLVENCY AND BANKRUPTCY

SUMMARY

42.1 INTRODUCTION

42.1.1 Definitions

Insolvency is the inability to pay one's debts: *Re Muggeridge's Settlement* (1859) 29 LJCh (NS)288, 289. Commercial insolvency is the inability to pay one's debts as they fall due: cf s 2(3) of the Sale of Goods Act 1908. What might be described as ultimate insolvency is the inability to pay one's debts after realising all one's assets: see *Nicholson v Permakraft (NZ) Ltd (in liq)* [1985] 1 NZLR 242, 249. Insolvency is not necessarily the same as bankruptcy, although the two concepts overlap. A person who is insolvent is not necessarily bankrupt in the technical sense. Bankruptcy is the name given to the form of proceedings whereby a debtor who has committed certain acts and defaults is divested of his or her property which is vested in an officer of the Court, the Official Assignee, to be equitably distributed among his or her creditors according to the statutory priorities. The bankrupt debtor is then, unlike the insolvent person, discharged from liability for payment of all debts provable in the bankruptcy. Whereas insolvency is a matter of fact, bankruptcy denotes the status of a person and is a question of law: Spratt and MacKenzie's *Law of Insolvency*, (2 ed), 5.

Receivership is a secured creditor's remedy over the property of a debtor. Although it can be used against an individual debtor it is usually used in the case of partnerships and companies. In its oldest form the receiver simply collected the rents and profits of the property. In its modern form, combining the office of receiver with that of manager, the receiver carries on the business with a view to its sale as a going concern.

Winding up or liquidation – the two terms are synonymous – are the corporate equivalent of bankruptcy in the case of an insolvent company. Bankruptcy as such only applies to natural persons, not to companies. Winding up can also take place in respect of a solvent company as a prelude to the distribution of its surplus assets to members and its ultimate dissolution. In this book we shall only deal in detail with bankruptcy and alternatives thereto but before we do so we shall briefly review the history of the whole area of law.

42.1.2 History

(a) BANKRUPTCY
There was no bankruptcy at common law. The first general legislation was in the reign of Henry VIII. The legislation only applied to traders until 1861 in England and the Debtors and Creditors Act 1862 in New Zealand. Until legislation in 1705-6 there was no possibility of discharge from Bankruptcy – once a bankrupt always a bankrupt. However once discharge was possible traders were placed in a more favourable position than nontraders who could never escape the incubus of their debts in the period before 1861-2.

Originally the administration of bankruptcy was in the hands of Commissioners of Bankruptcy. The modern system of Official Assignees was introduced in the nineteenth century as a result of corruption and delay in the administration of bankrupt estates.

The history of the law represents an attempt by the law to reconcile three separate interests – the creditor, debtor and public interests. The early law was very much weighted in favour of creditors. The person as well as the property of the bankrupt could be taken into their control. The law gradually recognised the interests of debtors, originally only trade debtors. By the nineteenth century there was increasing awareness of the public interest in favour of honest and efficient processing of insolvencies and the rehabilitation of honest debtors.

(b) RECEIVERSHIPS
Receivership was an ancient equitable remedy whose scope was enlarged in the nineteenth century with the growth of joint stock companies and the development of the floating charge.

In order to protect the receiver and the secured creditor from the strict liability imposed on a mortgagee in possession of a debtor's assets it became common to provide for the receiver to be appointed agent of the company. This practice was later legitimated by statute although it represents an awkward fiction since the company has little control over him.

Reforms in 1980 have helped to clarify the receiver's powers and his or her relationship with the liquidator of an insolvent company. A proposal to introduce creditors' management on the lines of official management in Australia was dropped although a similar procedure is in force in the United Kingdom.

Receiverships are dealt with in Farrar and Russell, *Company Law and Securities Regulation in New Zealand,* ch 34.

(c) WINDING UP

Originally companies were not subject to Bankruptcy. The affairs of a chartered or statutory company could be the subject of ad hoc investigation by the Board of Trade. In 1844 it was possible for them to be subjected to Bankruptcy proceedings but there was an ill-defined relationship between the jurisdiction of the Court of Chancery and the Bankruptcy Court which was finally resolved in England in 1856 when the basis of the modern system of Winding Up was introduced. This was generically separate from personal Bankruptcy although certain Bankruptcy rules were applied to the winding up of insolvent companies.

Winding up could be either compulsory – under an order of the Court – or voluntary. Provision was made for voluntary winding up under the supervision of the Court and this became redundant in 1933 when creditors voluntary winding up was introduced. Voluntary winding up subject to supervision was abolished in 1980.

Winding up is dealt with in Farrar and Russell, op cit, ch 35.

(d) ALTERNATIVES

It has always been possible for a debtor to enter into some kind of composition or arrangement with his or her creditors as an alternative to Bankruptcy. Legislation in the nineteenth century was enacted to facilitate this by providing for procedures for application to the Court and registration of the deed. These were supplemented by the provisions for proposals and summary instalment orders in Parts XV and XVI of the Insolvency Act 1967.

In the case of companies the main procedure is s 205 of the Companies Act 1955 which provides for a scheme of arrangement. It is possible to provide for a moratorium under s 205. Section 205 is dealt with in Farrar and Russell, op cit, 374.

42.1.3 Present administration

Bankruptcy and compulsory winding up are now dealt with by the Commercial Affairs Division of the Justice Department. The Insolvency Amendment Act 1976, s 2 provides for the appointment of an Official Assignee for the whole of New Zealand. In this text we shall use the term "Assignee" to refer to that official and his or her Deputies.

42.2 BANKRUPTCY

42.2.1 The Court

Bankruptcy procedure is governed by the provisions of the Insolvency Act 1967, the Insolvency Rules 1970 and the Insolvency Regulations 1970. For convenience of reference, in this Part the Insolvency Act 1967 will be hereafter referred to as "the Act", a section of an Act will be referred to as "s", a rule as "R", and a regulation as "reg". The Court having jurisdiction in bankruptcy is the High Court: s 5.

Appeals from the decisions of the High Court may be made to the Court of Appeal in the manner and within the time prescribed by R 65. There is no right of appeal to the Privy Council from the Court of Appeal: *Nunns v Licensing Control Commission* [1968] NZLR 57 (CA).

42.2.2 An overview of bankruptcy procedure

Bankruptcy proceedings are commenced by a petition to the High Court. This petition may be filed by the debtor, in which case he or she is adjudicated bankrupt at the date of the filing of the petition. No Court hearing is necessary. A creditor may file a petition provided that the debtor owes to him or her (or if two or more creditors file the petition there is owing to them), a liquidated sum of not less than $200 and the debtor has committed an act of bankruptcy within the three months preceding the filing of the petition: s 3.

Let us consider a typical proceeding in bankruptcy. Let us assume that a meeting of the debtor's creditors has been called by him or her for the purpose of discussing his or her financial difficulties. Section 19(4) provides that where a meeting is called and a majority in number and value of the creditors present at that meeting pass a resolution requiring him or her to file a debtor's petition or the debtor consents to file a petition and fails to do so, he or she has committed an act of bankruptcy. The debtor should file his or her own petition as requested, and he or she will be adjudicated bankrupt at the date of filing: s 28. If he or she fails to file his or her own petition, then any creditor to whom a liquidated sum of not less than $200 is owing may file a creditor's petition within three months from the time the debtor called the meeting: s 23. Such creditor will allege the calling of the meeting of creditors and the adoption of the creditors' resolution, or the debtor's failing to file his or her own petition after consenting to do so, as the act of bankruptcy on which the petition is founded.

At the hearing, the petitioning creditor must appear unless he or she is excused by the Court. If the Court is satisfied as to the facts alleged in the petition and that the debtor has been duly served, the debtor may be adjudged bankrupt: s 26. Adjudication by the Court is not necessary if the debtor has filed his or her own petition. On adjudication, all the debtor's property is vested in the Assignee who is required forthwith to give notice of the debtor's adjudication by advertisement in the local newspapers: s 31. No assignment to the Assignee of personal property is necessary. The Assignee is also entitled to the bankrupt's land, but it is only after registration of a transmission that he or she appears on the title as the registered proprietor.

Immediately upon adjudication, the bankrupt may select with the concurrence of the Assignee, and retain for his or her own use tools of trade to the value of $100, furniture and personal effects not exceeding $300 in value: s 52. With this exception, the Assignee becomes entitled to all property, both real and personal, vested in the bankrupt at the commencement of bankruptcy or acquired by him or her before discharge: s 42. In our example, commencement of bankruptcy is the time at which the debtor called the meeting of creditors. It is at this time that he or she committed the act of bankruptcy on which he or she was subsequently adjudged bankrupt.

The Assignee is given wide powers of investigation. For example, Forms 3 and 4 of the Regulations prescribe 43 questions to be answered by the bankrupt businessperson. The Assignee also brings into the bankrupt's estate certain property disposed of by the bankrupt or money which he or she has paid in the period preceding adjudication. For example, under s 54 any gift of property made in the five years preceding adjudication is voidable against the Assignee unless the donee can prove that the bankrupt, at some time between the date of settlement and adjudication, was able to pay his or her debts without using the property settled. Under s 55, if the debtor, whether solvent or not, has bought land for another person or erected buildings on, or otherwise improved, land belonging to such person in the two years preceding adjudication, that person may be compelled to refund the amount paid or the value of the improvements to the Assignee, failing which the Court may direct the sale of the land.

The Assignee in exercise of his or her powers under the doctrine of relation back, which entitles him or her to all property belonging to the bankrupt at the commencement of bankruptcy, can upset transactions with the bankrupt in the period between commencement of bankruptcy and the date of adjudication. The period of relation back may extend for several months before adjudication. This period goes back to the first available act of bankruptcy.

On adjudication, the debtor is prohibited from obtaining credit for $100 or more without disclosing that he or she is an undischarged bankrupt: s 128(g). He or she cannot, if still an undischarged bankrupt, leave New Zealand within three years following adjudication without the consent of the Assignee: s 128(f), regs 40, 41. If he or she holds a public office he or she may find that he or she is automatically disqualified from remaining in his or her position. Thus he or she is disqualified to act as a Member of Parliament, a municipal officer such as a mayor or council-lor, a company director, auctioneer or land agent. Sections 33 and 60 require the bankrupt to give the Assignee a detailed statement of his or her assets, debts and liabilities, to provide a list of his or her creditors, to surrender his or her books and papers and also to assist in getting in and realising his or her property.

The bankrupt may be imprisoned if he or she has failed to keep proper books of account for the three years prior to his or her adjudication: s 127.

The bankrupt receives statutory protection against legal proceedings to recover debts. Practically all proceedings already commenced are after advertisement of adjudication, stayed: s 32.

The Assignee must summon the first meeting of creditors: s 34. The time and place of such meeting must be advertised. The creditors mentioned in the bankrupt's list are notified by post. Creditors, before being entitled to vote at the meeting, must have duly proved for the debts owing to them: s 40(1)(b). Subsequent meetings may be called by the Assignee or by the Assignee on the requisition of one-fourth in value of creditors who have proved their debts: s 36. The Assignee is required to bring all the bankrupt's property, including any possessions he or she may have overseas, under his or her control. If he or she finds certain property cannot readily be sold, he or she may disclaim it by filing a written notice of disclaimer in the High Court. Any person who is affected by this disclaimer may prove in the bankruptcy for the amount of damage he or she has suffered: s 75.

During the period of bankruptcy the Assignee, with the consent of the creditors expressed by resolution, may make such allowance as he or she thinks just for the support of the bankrupt and his or her family: s 53(1).

The bankrupt's property is usually sold by public auction or public tender: s 72(1). From the proceeds of the sale of the debtor's property the Assignee meets claims in the following order:

(a) costs and expenses of the bankruptcy including costs and expenses in procuring adjudication;

(b) commission payable to the Official Assignee;

(c) claims for wages or salaries and any holiday pay due to any employees of the bankrupt to a maximum of $1500 per employee. The first week's wages payable by an employer to an injured employee under the Accident Compensation Act 1982. Fees for legal and accounting services are protected by s 73(2);

(d) tax deductions made by the bankrupt from employees' wages;

(e) debts admitted in the bankruptcy excluding those in (f) below;

(f) unpaid wages to bankrupt's spouse if employed in the bankrupt's business and certain other deferred debts; and

(g) interest on debts admitted in the bankruptcy: s 104(1)(a)-(h).

If there is any surplus, interest may be allowed on proved debts and then the balance is paid to the bankrupt: s 104(1)(i) and (j).

The payments to the preferential creditors are first made, then a dividend is paid to creditors having debts admitted from bankruptcy. A final dividend distributing the balance of the estate is made later: s 105. Distributions of dividend are advertised.

At any time after adjudication the bankrupt may apply for his or her discharge: s 108. Notice of his or her intention to apply must be advertised and the Assignee and all creditors must be given notice not less than two weeks before the date of the hearing. Failing objection by the Assignee or a creditor, the bankrupt is automatically discharged after the expiration of three years from adjudication: s 107(1). The Assignee must file a full report on the estate and conduct of the bankrupt prior to the hearing: s 109(2). A copy of the report must be sent to the bankrupt: R 76. The Assignee shall in January of each year send a certificate of discharge to each bankrupt discharged the previous year: reg 48. The Assignee or any creditor may oppose the application and examine the bankrupt on any matters relating to the bankruptcy. This power is rarely used. If the Court is satisfied with the Assignee's report on the conduct of the bankrupt and no valid objection to the bankrupt's application has been raised the order of discharge will be granted. If the Court is not satisfied, the order may be refused or granted subject to certain conditions: s 110. The fact that the Court has refused or suspended the discharge of a bankrupt may be published: s 118(1). If the Assignee or a creditor objects to the discharge of the bankrupt, either at the time of application for discharge by the bankrupt or at the end of three years after adjudication, a public examination of the bankrupt may be held: s 109(1).

If discharge is refused the bankrupt may repeat his or her application for discharge at a later date: s 108. Provision is made for publication annually in the *Gazette* of a list of undischarged bankrupts: s 118.

Discharge releases the bankrupt from all provable debts not tainted with fraud or not subject to Court order or statutory provision to the contrary, whether such debts were in fact proved or not: ss 114, 45.

If, in the course of the two years following the making of the order of discharge, facts come to light which would have justified the Court in refusing to make the order at the time when application was made the Court has power to reverse the order of discharge. The debtor once again resumes his or her status as a bankrupt: s 112.

Finally, the Court has power under ss 119 and 120 to annul an order of adjudication if the Court is satisfied that the order should not have been made, that the financial position of the bankrupt has changed substantially or that the Court has approved a composition under Part XII of the Act. The effect of annulment is that legally the debtor is regarded as not having been adjudicated bankrupt and such part of his or her property as has not yet been sold by the Official Assignee revests in him or her automatically. Annulment must be advertised forthwith by the Assignee: R 82.

As soon as practicable after the advertisement of the distribution of the final dividend, the Assignee shall submit to the Audit Office a statement of accounts and balance sheets showing in detail his or her receipts and payments. The report of the Audit Office together with the statement of accounts and balance and balance sheet so submitted is open to inspection by the bankrupt, and creditor or other person interested. The Assignee, after advertising the filing of the accounts and report, applies to the Court for an order releasing him or her from administration of the estate. Any surplus money or unclaimed dividend from the estate is paid to the Public Trust Office. After twelve months from the declaration of the final dividend such money is carried to the Bankruptcy Surplus Account which fund is to meet any claims made on it by order of the Court: ss 132-134. Any creditor who has not received his or her dividend may make application for payment to the Assignee, who will in a proper case claim the money from any surplus funds or unclaimed dividend lodged in the Bankruptcy Surplus Account with the Public Trustee and make payment to the creditor.

42.2.3 Persons subject to bankruptcy law

(a) GENERAL RULE
The general rule is that every person who has contractual capacity and is subject to the law of New Zealand is subject to the Bankruptcy Law of this country.

(b) MINORS
Terms such as "infant" and "minor" for general purposes are determined by the Age of Majority Act 1970, s 4, which states that a person attains full age when he or she attains the age of twenty years. This provision, however, does not affect the provisions of the Minors' Contracts Act 1969, which determines the enforceability of debts incurred by young people.

Minors may be made bankrupt when they have failed to pay a legally enforceable debt.

For many years it was believed that minors not only enjoyed a favoured position under the law of contract, but that they also had complete protection from bankruptcy proceedings. This protection of minors from bankruptcy proceedings may have arisen through the early emphasis on the criminal aspect of bankruptcy. The first Bankruptcy Act 1542, specifically referred to the bankrupt as an "offender". Thus it appears that the Court would annul adjudication if a minor presented his or her own petition and would dismiss a creditor's petition against a minor even if the minor had fraudulently misrepresented himself or herself as being an adult.

Today the Minors' Contracts Act 1969 determines the legal liability of young people for debts incurred by them. The topic is discussed fully in para 5.1.1 supra, to which reference should be made. The principle that jurisdiction in bankruptcy should be determined by the legal enforceability of the debt and not on the status of infancy was established in *In a Debtor (Ex p Commissioners of Customs and Excise v The Debtor)* [1950] Ch 282; [1950] 1 All ER 308 (CA). In that case the English Commissioners of Customs and Excise recovered judgment for unpaid purchase tax against a mother and her daughter, aged 20, who were wholesale traders in cosmetics. The Court of Appeal rejected the arguments that infants should not be adjudicated bankrupt owing to their special status, public policy, and absence of precedent, and held that where an infant has incurred a legally enforceable debt, she may be adjudicated bankrupt.

The Minors' Contracts Act 1969 makes the following contracts enforceable against persons under the age of 21:

(a) a contract entered into by a person of 18 or more except where the Court declares such contract to be unenforceable: s 5.
(b) contracts made by married persons under the age of 18: s 4(1).
(c) contracts of service or life insurance: s 5(1).
(d) contracts made by persons under the age of 18 where the Court on application is satisfied the contract is fair and reasonable and makes an order enforcing it against the minor: s 6.
(e) contracts approved by the Court at the time they were made: s 9.

(c) ADJUDICATION OF ALIENS; PROPERTY OUTSIDE NEW ZEALAND

An alien who becomes liable in New Zealand for non-payment of a debt due on a judgment enforceable in New Zealand and who has committed an available act of bankruptcy in New Zealand may be made bankrupt.

An alien living abroad cannot be made bankrupt merely because he or she contracts a debt in the course of running a business in New Zealand: *Ex parte Blain, Re Sawers* (1879) 12 ChD 522.

The method of service on persons overseas is set out in R 21. A bankrupt shall execute such powers of attorney, transfers and other instruments and do all things in relation to his or her property outside New Zealand as required by the Assignee or by any direction of the Court: s 60(d).

(d) AMBASSADORS OR DIPLOMATS ACCREDITED BY A FOREIGN GOVERNMENT

Ambassadors or other diplomats appointed to New Zealand by another country and bona fide members of their staff, whether New Zealand citizens or not, cannot be made bankrupt. Where, however, a member of the staff, being a New Zealand citizen, can be shown to have obtained his or her appointment in order to defeat his or her creditors he or she cannot claim immunity; *Re Cloete* (1891) 9 Morr 195. Diplomatic status is usually proved by a certificate from the Minister of External Relations and Trade. The privileges, immunities and capacities of the Commonwealth Secretariat and persons connected therewith are set out in the Diplomatic Privileges and Immunities Act 1971.

(e) MEMBERS OF PARLIAMENT

Members of Parliament are entitled under certain conditions to an adjournment of any civil proceedings which would otherwise have been heard, in the period extending from ten days before the holding of any session of the General Assembly to 30 days after the termination of the session: Legislature Act 1908, s 265.

(f) CONVICTS

Since the enactment of the Penal Institutions Act 1954, a prisoner can be adjudged bankrupt on his or her own or a creditor's petition.

(g) MENTALLY DISORDERED PERSONS

A mentally disordered person within the meaning of the Mental Health Act 1969 is legally incapable of committing an available act of bankruptcy where the intention of the debtor is a necessary part of the act of bankruptcy, eg the giving of a fraudulent preference. But the Court will not stay proceedings where the debtor has become insane after the commencement of bankruptcy: *Ex parte Layton* (1801) 6 Ves 434. It does not appear to have been decided whether a debtor's petition can be filed by a person mentally disordered or by anyone purporting to act on his or her behalf.

The Court has general jurisdiction and control over the estates of mentally disordered persons and over guardians of such persons: Judicature Act 1908, s 17.

The Third Schedule of the Mental Health Act empowers the Public Trustee to institute appropriate proceedings to protect the estate of a mentally disordered person who is a protected patient within s 82 of Mental Health Act or to consent to any judgment or order against him. Although there is express power to take appropriate steps to apply for a summary instalment order or to get an order of adjudication against someone owing money to the mentally disordered person, there are no specific provisions for the institution of or collaboration in bankruptcy proceedings in relation to the estate of the mentally disordered person. It appears that the Public Trustee's powers in this respect arise by implication from the provisions of para 2(a)(i) of the Third Schedule of the Mental Health Act which gives him or her power to institute or consent to proceedings concerning the property of the patient.

The maintenance and care of the mental defective is the primary concern of the Court in its lunacy jurisdiction and consequently creditors may be prevented from applying the assets in the estate for the satisfaction of their debts: *Re P (a Mental Patient)* [1928] GLR 334.

If there are assets available after provision has been made for the maintenance of the mentally disordered person, such assets should be applied in satisfaction of creditors' claims: *Re Farnham (No 2)* [1896] 1 Ch 836, 841.

(h) PARTNERSHIPS

Rules 23 and 47 set out the procedure for filing a petition against a partnership or for the adjudication of one partner without including the others. Provision is made for the disclosure of the names of the partners other than the one against whom proceedings are being taken.

(i) SECOND BANKRUPTCY

When an undischarged bankrupt becomes bankrupt a second time the Assignee in the second bankruptcy is entitled to all property acquired by the bankrupt in the period between his or her first adjudication and his or her discharge in the second bankruptcy. When the Assignee in the first bankruptcy receives notice of a petition for a second adjudication against the bankrupt he or she shall hold any property then in his or her possession which has been acquired by or devolved on the bankrupt since adjudication. If the debtor is adjudicated a second time he or she shall transfer all such property (less his or her costs and expenses) to the Assignee in the later bankruptcy. In most cases it will be the same Assignee in both bankruptcies, so it will be merely a matter of transferring these assets to a different account.

The Assignee in the first bankruptcy is entitled to any assets in the second bankruptcy which were acquired independently of the creditors of the latter bankruptcy. Likewise, if property has devolved on the bankrupt the Court may order that all or any of such property shall be credited to the creditors in the first bankruptcy.

Any surplus after administration in the second bankruptcy is completed shall be paid to the Assignee of the first bankruptcy to be treated as an asset in the first bankruptcy: s 59. But no commission on this surplus is payable to the Assignee of the later bankruptcy: reg 46.

No dispositions or payments by the Assignee in the former bankruptcy shall be upset on the debtor being adjudicated a second time.

42.3 ACTS OF BANKRUPTCY

42.3.1 General

The acts of bankruptcy do not fall into any general pattern. They may be evidence of insolvency or they may be acts prejudicial to the general body of creditors, but an act of bankruptcy must be a personal act or default of the debtor. Again some of the acts may be committed out of New Zealand although they must be intended to take effect in New Zealand. They may be voluntary acts on the part of the debtor or acts done against the debtor's will to compel payment by him. The third clause of the petition sets out the act of bankruptcy on which the creditor relies; this must have taken place within the three months preceding the filing of the petition: s 23(b).

The acts of bankruptcy are set out in s 19 of the Act. Owing to the significance of these acts to the future status of the insolvent a strict construction should be given to them in the Courts: *Ex parte Chinery* (1884) 12 QBD 343, 346. A number of decisions of the Courts assist in interpreting the statutory provisions.

42.3.2 The acts of bankruptcy

A debtor commits an act of bankruptcy if:

(a) In New Zealand or elsewhere, he or she makes a disposition of all or substantially all of his or her property to a trustee for the benefit of all or any of his or her creditors.

(b) In New Zealand or elsewhere he or she fraudulently or with intent to prefer a creditor makes a payment, incurs an obligation, disposes of or creates a charge over any of his or her property.

(c) With intent to delay or defeat his or her creditors he or she departs or attempts to depart from New Zealand, remains out of New Zealand, or departs from his or her dwellinghouse, otherwise absents himself or herself or keeps to any premises to avoid his or her creditors.

(d) Being a judgment debtor, he or she fails within 14 days after the day of service to comply with a bankruptcy notice or secure or compound for the judgment debt therein and cannot set up a counterclaim of equal or greater amount than the judgment debt, such counterclaim being one that he or she could not set up in the action in which the judgment was obtained.

(e) He or she gives notice of suspension of payment to any of his or her creditors.

(f) At a meeting of creditors he or she admits that he or she is insolvent and a majority in number and value of those present pass a resolution that he or she should file a debtor's petition or if he or she consents to file a debtor's petition and fails within the following 48 hours to do so.

(g) Possession has been taken under execution issued against him or her or his or her property, and the judgment is not satisfied within seven days of possession being taken.

(h) A writ of sale against his or her land or any interest therein has been delivered to a Sheriff and such land or interest has been advertised for sale, provided that if the judgment on which the writ of sale is issued is satisfied within seven days of the said delivery and advertisement, no act of bankruptcy shall have been committed.

(i) A return of nulla bona has been made to any execution issued against him or her or his or her property.

(j) With intent to prejudice his or her creditors or to prefer one creditor above another, he or she removes or attempts to remove any of his or her property from one place, or conceals or attempts to conceal any of his or her property.

(k) He or she, being a person required by law to keep a trust account, fails for seven days to satisfy a judgment for the non-payment of trust moneys.

Each of these acts of bankruptcy will be examined in turn.

(a) ASSIGNMENT TO A TRUSTEE FOR THE BENEFIT OF ALL OR ANY CREDITORS
Section 19(1)(a) provides that a debtor commits an act of bankruptcy if:

> In New Zealand or elsewhere, he makes a disposition of all or substantially all of his property to a trustee for the benefit of all or any of his creditors.

The essential feature of this act of bankruptcy is that the assignment must put practically the whole of the debtor's property out of his or her control although it need not be for the benefit of all creditors. This type of arrangement must be distinguished from the statutory composition in Part XII of the Act, which is available only in cases where the debtor has already been adjudicated bankrupt. Furthermore, it is quite distinct from the proposal in Part XV, wherein the insolvent submits a scheme to satisfy his or her creditors which, if it is accepted by the creditors, is sent on to the Court for its approval.

An assignment for the benefit of creditors must be in the usual form and, wherever executed, it must be intended to operate in accordance with the law of New Zealand. Normally, creditors who have signed it, acted under its provisions, or who, although they have not signed it, have been aware of it without registering their dissent, cannot use it or the circular convening the meeting of creditors to fix the terms of the assignment as an available act of bankruptcy. They can, however, use an independent act of bankruptcy such as non-compliance with a bankruptcy notice as a foundation of their petition unless the terms of the assignment preclude them from taking individual proceedings.

Although this is an act of bankruptcy, an assignment is really a private arrangement between a debtor and his or her creditors and rarely results in adjudication. A debtor may find himself or herself unable to meet the demands of his or her creditors and, after asking an accountant to investigate his or her affairs, a meeting of creditors is called. At that meeting it may be decided that the debtor should assign the major part of his or her property to the account or some nominee of the creditors who will act as a trustee on their behalf. The assignment takes the form of a deed made between the debtor, and trustee and the creditors. It is generally worded to include any creditors who, although they may not sign the deed, signify their acceptance in writing when the trustee has subsequently communicated with them.

A mere declaration of trust or an agreement to assign is not sufficient. The assignment must be a formal instrument in the usual form adopted by conveyancers for such purposes and it must transfer substantially the whole of the debtor's property to the trustee for distribution amongst the creditors: *Re Spackman, Ex parte Foley* (1890) 24 QBD 728. Where an assignment leaves a debtor in a position of obvious insolvency, it is an assignment of substantially the whole of his or her property: *Re Hooper, Ex parte Official Assignee* [1951] NZLR 704; [1951] GLR 361.

The transfer of substantially the whole of a debtor's assets to effect a composition is an act of bankruptcy; but creditors who receive payments under such a composition in good faith and without notice of any other available act of bankruptcy are protected by s 47(1)(d), (e) if the debtor is subsequently adjudicated bankrupt. Where the debtor fraudulently conceals the existence of other creditors at the time of making the composition, the creditors who have received payment prior to the filing of the debtor's petition in bankruptcy are not prejudiced: *Re Cochrane* [1925] NZLR 15.

The fact that payments made under an assignment or composition are protected against the doctrine of relation back does not prevent their being treated as acts of bankruptcy: *DOA v Bank of New Zealand* (1915) 17 GLR 717.

If the assignment is made to a person who gives value as a purchaser it is not an act of bankruptcy even if the money is applied in payment of creditors. The real test is whether the debtor has transferred to his or her creditors or any of them the major part of his or her property in satisfaction of his or her debts.

A petitioning creditor who has been privy to a deed of assignment whether he or she signed it or not, or who has acted in such a way as to show his or her approval of the deed, cannot use it as an act of bankruptcy. *Re Aburn* (1908) 27 NZLR 442; 10 GLR 306; and *Victor Weston Ltd v Morgensterns* [1937] 3 All ER 769. Assent, recognition or approval of the deed or even passive acquiescence may prevent a creditor alleging it as an act of bankruptcy: *Re a Debtor* [1936] 1 Ch 165.

(b) FRAUDULENT DEALING OR FRAUDULENT PREFERENCE

Section 19(1)(b) of the Act states that a debtor commits an act of bankruptcy:

> If, in New Zealand or elsewhere, he fraudulently, or with intent to give any creditor a preference over other creditors,
> (i)   makes any disposition of his property or any part thereof; or
> (ii) creates any charge thereon or gives any security thereover, or
> (iii) makes any payment; or
> (iv) incurs any obligation.

Disposition is defined in wide terms by s 2. It refers to transfers, settlements, leases, mortgages, trusts created, the surrender of rights, the exercise of powers of appointment and all the usual means by which one person may diminish the value of his or her own property and "increase the value of the estate of any other person".

This act, which results in an increase in the value of one person's estate at the expense of the insolvent's estate, is envisaged as either unjustly enriching a particular creditor or someone other than a creditor. It is, in fact, a transaction defrauding the general body of creditors and having the effect of preventing or being designed to prevent an equitable distribution of the assets to which the creditors are entitled.

A debtor, realising he or she is insolvent, may sell his or her car worth $15,000, to a friend for less than its value, say $12,000. He or she may also give a creditor who has treated him or her favourably, a chattel security over his or her piano to secure a debt incurred two years earlier. In such a case the sale of the car will fraudulently transfer $3,000 worth of assets to the friend at the expense of creditors who, if the debtor proves to be insolvent, may not be paid in full. The chattel security will also have been given with the obvious intention of preferring that creditor. If it was signed within the twelve months preceding the filing of a petition in bankruptcy it will be voidable: s 57.

The fraudulent disposition of property or surrender of property rights by a debtor in the shadow of impending bankruptcy is of vital importance. Payments for inadequate or no consideration may be made or property may be transferred or mortgaged in order to favour a particular creditor; the debtor may so deal with his or her assets that all his or her creditors are deprived of their proper judicial remedies against his or her property. Again, he or she may deal with his or her property in such a way that future creditors will not have the rights to which they would normally be entitled, as, for example, where he or she executes a power of appointment to take effect on the happening of some future event. Finally, he or she may voluntarily incur an obligation to the detriment of his or her creditors, even to the extent of allowing a judgment to be taken against him or her either collusively or by failing to set up a valid available defence.

Voidable dispositions, securities and preference are fully discussed in ch 45 infra.

(c) DEPARTING OR AVOIDING CREDITORS WITH INTENT TO DEFEAT OR DELAY THEM

Under s 19(1)(c) a debtor commits this available act of bankruptcy if:

> With intent to defeat or delay his creditors, he departs, or attempts to depart, or is about to depart, out of New Zealand, or (being out of New Zealand) remains out of New Zealand, or departs from his dwellinghouse, or otherwise absents himself, or keeps to any premises or to part thereof to avoid his creditors.

The essence of this act of bankruptcy is the debtor's denial of himself or herself to his or her creditors coupled with an intention to defeat or delay them.

Intention to defeat or delay must be alleged in the petition: *In re Skelton, Ex parte Coates* (1877) 5 ChD 979. It is the intention of the debtor that is material and not the actual effect on the creditors. If the debtor can show a valid reason for his or her departure, he or she will not have committed an act of bankruptcy although creditors are in fact delayed: *Re Stephany, Ex parte Meyer* (1871) 7 Ch App 188. A person is held to intend the necessary consequences of his or her acts, and intent will be presumed where it is obvious that departure will cause delay to the creditors. Thus, where a debt is unenforceable out of New Zealand, and the debtor is in financial difficulties, whether he or she has his or her permanent domicile in New Zealand or not, his or her departure from New Zealand gives rise to a strong presumption of intention to defeat or delay creditors: *Re Cohen, Ex parte the Bankrupt v Inland Revenue Comrs* [1950] 2 All ER 36. See also *Bryan v LMVD Finance (NZ) Ltd* (unreported, High Court, Christchurch, B110/83, 4 November 1983, Hardie Boys J); [1983] BCL 1090.

Again, when a debtor, on being pressed by his or her creditors, leaves New Zealand, there is strong evidence of an intention to defeat or delay them. Generally, it is not an act of bankruptcy if a foreigner comes to New Zealand for a temporary purpose and then returns to his or her own country: *Ex parte Crispin* (1873) LR 8 Ch App 374. A New Zealand debtor, having his or her permanent residence abroad, does not commit an act of bankruptcy by returning there: *Re Trench, Ex parte Brandon* (1884) 25 ChD 500.

The circumstances in which a debtor departs from his or her dwellinghouse or keeps to any premises must show an intention to defeat or delay creditors. Section 19(1)(c) will apply if a debtor denies himself or herself to his or her creditors, either by keeping away from his or her usual place of business or house or by staying in any premises and refusing to see anyone. Intentional denial of himself or herself to his or her creditors by a debtor has been established in cases where a debtor has kept away from a particular creditor, adopted an assumed name, left his or her usual place of business and given no address, given orders to his or her employees that he or she will see no one, gone out from his or her own house only at night and even where he or she failed to keep appointments. A debtor can, however, refuse to see anyone at unreasonable hours without committing this act of bankruptcy. If the act of bankruptcy alleged is departure from his or her dwellinghouse, it is necessary to prove that he or she is alive and elsewhere: *Re Stranger, Ex parte Geisel* (1882) 22 ChD 436.

Absenting oneself is a continuing act of bankruptcy, and accordingly the petition can be filed at any time not later than three months after the absence has ceased; on the other hand, the title of the Official Assignee will relate back only to a time three months before the date of the filing of the petition and not to the time when the absence commenced: *Re Burrows* [1944] Ch 49.

(d) NON-COMPLIANCE WITH A BANKRUPTCY NOTICE
Under s 19(1)(d) a debtor commits this act of bankruptcy if:

A creditor has obtained a final judgment or final order against the debtor for any amount, and, execution thereon not having been stayed, the debtor has served on him in New Zealand, or, by leave of the Court, elsewhere, a bankruptcy notice under this Act, and he does not, within 14 days after the service of the notice in a case where the service is effected in New Zealand, and in a case where the service is effected elsewhere then within the time limited in that behalf by the order giving leave to effect the service, either comply with the requirements of the notice or satisfy the Court that he has a counterclaim, setoff, or cross demand which equals or exceeds the amount of the judgment debt or sum ordered to be paid, and which he could not set up in the action in which the judgment was obtained, or the proceedings in which the order was obtained.

In practice this is the most common act of bankruptcy relied on. Almost all involuntary bankruptcies are based on this ground. A creditor adopting this procedure files in the High Court a request for the issue of a bankruptcy notice. This notice may be issued in respect of a debt of any amount and requires the debtor to pay within the 14 days following the day of service. If he or she fails to pay or secure the debt or set up a counterclaim of equal or greater amount than the debt claimed, he or she will have committed an act of bankruptcy available for any creditor.

Section 19(1)(d) empowers a creditor who has obtained a final judgment for "any amount" (not necessarily $200 or more), and in respect of which execution has not been stayed, to serve a bankruptcy notice on the judgment debtor requiring him or her within 14 days following the day of service to pay the amount of the judgment debt, either to the creditor issuing the notice or to an agent acting on his or her behalf. Section 19(1)(d) of the Act and Form 15 of the Rules permit a bankruptcy notice to be issued for the outstanding balance of a judgment debt. Any person who is for the time being entitled to enforce a final judgment or final order shall be deemed to be a creditor who has obtained a final judgment or final order. If the debtor does not pay the debt, he or she must satisfy the creditor or the Court by giving a security or making an arrangement or a composition in respect of the said sum with the creditor.

A bankruptcy notice may be set aside on proof that the debt has been satisfied. Proof of a dispute is not enough for this purpose: *Re Wells, ex parte Sewell* (unreported, High Court, Christchurch, B 80/88, 3 May 1988, Tipping J).

A bankruptcy notice may be set aside on application by a debtor who files an affidavit with the Registrar giving evidence of a genuine counterclaim equal to or exceeding the amount of the judgment debt and being one which could not have been set up in the action for judgment on the debt on which the notice was founded. The debtor may supplement the bare outline of facts in the affidavit filed with the Registrar with such evidence as is necessary to support his or her application at the hearing: *Re A Debtor, ex parte The Debtor v H Tossoun* [1963] 1 WLR 51; [1963] 1 All ER 85 (CA). The filing of the affidavit operates as an application to set aside the bankruptcy notice. No act of bankruptcy shall be deemed to have been committed until the application has been determined: R 41(4). As to the meaning of counterclaim and the necessity for a fair, large and liberal interpretation, see *Potemkin v Protector Safety Ltd* (unreported, High Court, Auckland, B1106/86, 10 September 1986, Doogue J).

A debtor, as an alternative to setting up a counterclaim, may move to set aside a bankruptcy notice on the ground that it does not follow the judgment on which it is based, that it is irregular in form, that there was not due service of the notice or that repayment has been made. Two or more judgments cannot be included in the same bankruptcy notice: *Re Low* [1891] 1 QB 147.

The lodging of an appeal does not amount to a stay of execution. If the creditor accepts a cheque or a promissory note from the debtor within the 14 day period, this will be a conditional payment and the creditor cannot take any further steps under the notice until it is known whether or not the cheque will be met: *Bolt and Nut (Tipton) Ltd v Rowlands, Nicholls and Co Ltd* [1964] 2 QB 10; [1964] 1 All ER 137 (CA).

A bankruptcy notice may be issued for any amount, and if the debtor fails to comply with it, any creditor may allege it in a bankruptcy petition provided he or she is owed $200 at least. Where the amount stated in the bankruptcy notice is $200 or more, payment into Court of a sum sufficient to reduce the debt below $200 will not affect the creditor's right to petition: *Re Morris* (1909) 29 NZLR 152.

A foreign judgment may constitute the judgment debt stated in the bankruptcy notice, provided such judgment is enforceable under the Reciprocal Enforcement of Judgments Act 1934. Where there is a judgment against two or more jointly, a bankruptcy notice may be served on one without including the others: *Re Low, ex parte Gisbon* [1895] 1 QB 734.

If the debtor can prove that but for the act or omission of the creditor the judgment debt in respect of which the bankruptcy notice was issued would have been paid, the notice will be set aside: *Bracia Czeczowiszka v Otto Markus* [1936] 1 All ER 944.

The Act also provides that the consequences of non-compliance shall be stated in the notice, viz the commission of an act of bankruptcy. It further provides that the notice is not invalidated by an over statement of the amount due unless the debtor gives notice, within the 14 days allowed to him, that he or she disputes the notice on the ground of such mis-statement: s 20(b). The costs of an unsuccessful execution cannot be added to a judgment debt to make up the amount stated in the notice: *Re Eva, Ex parte Robertson Bros Ltd* [1927] NZLR 652; [1927] GLR 440. On the other hand, the debtor is deemed to have complied with the bankruptcy notice, if, within the time allowed, he or she takes such steps as would have complied with the notice if the amount had been correctly stated: s 20(b).

A bankruptcy notice may be issued against a minor if the debt is legally enforceable against him: *In re a Debtor, ex parte Commissioners of Customs and Excise v The Debtor* (supra).

This act of bankruptcy may be used by any other creditor if the creditor who served the notice has been paid after the lapse of the 14 days specified: *In re Powell, Ex parte Powell* [1891] 2 QB 324.

If the Court sets aside a bankruptcy notice, it may, at the same time, declare that no act of bankruptcy has been committed: R 43.

(e) NOTICE TO ANY CREDITOR OF SUSPENSION OF PAYMENT
Section 19(1)(e) provides that a debtor commits an act of bankruptcy if:

He gives notice to any of his creditors that he has suspended or is about to suspend payment of his debts.

To constitute this act of bankruptcy there must be an unqualified unconditional notice deliberately given by a debtor to a creditor (not merely a person making a claim for damages) or to his or her representative, from which an ordinary man of business would understand that, if he or she did not accept less than was due to him, debtor would have to suspend payment of his or her debts: *In re Crook, ex parte Crook* (1890) 24 QBD 320. This notice often takes the form of a circular sent out to creditors by a debtor inviting them to attend a meeting to discuss his or her position which, taken in relation to all the circumstances, shows that the debtor is unable to meet his or her liabilities in full and that the debtor intends to refuse to pay his or her debts in full for the time being. Generally, it is a reasonable inference that it would be dishonest for the debtor to pay any of his or her creditors between the date of the notice and the date of the meeting: *Re Dagnall, Ex parte Soan and Morley* [1896] 2 QB 407. Notice of a temporary suspension of payments is sufficient to constitute this act of bankruptcy. Generally, an offer is made in the circular or at the meeting of creditors and it can be reasonably inferred that, if the offer is rejected, payments will be suspended.

Whether a notice to creditors can be held to be a notice of suspension of payment depends on the wording of the notice in relation to the circumstances known to the creditors. If a notice is sent out by a debtor's representative who is known to be well acquainted with the debtor's financial position and the notice shows that the debtor's financial position is too bad to allow of any payments to be made in the meantime, that the creditors are to be given a statement of the debtor's financial position, and that there is an intention to deal with the creditors collectively the notice will be regarded as a notice of suspension of payments although there is no direct statement to that effect: *Official Assignee of Simon v Arnold and Wright Limited* [1967] NZLR 552. The notice may be oral: *In re Walker, Ex parte Nickoll* (1884) 13 QBD 469. If in the prevailing circumstances it appears that the debtor is giving notice that he or she will suspend payments if the creditors will not accept the proposition he or she has made with regard to his or her debts, the notice he or she has given may be treated as an act of bankruptcy: *Crook v Morley* [1890] 24 QBD 320 (CA); [1891] AC 315.

In *Re Paterson, Ex parte Boyack and Oats* [1936] NZLR suppl 65, the solicitors of the debtor in a circular letter calling a meeting of creditors stated, "It is Mr Paterson's intention to pay everyone if given time" and at the meeting of creditors the debtor stated that he or she was unable to pay his debts. The Court held that each of these events constituted an act of bankruptcy.

Notice may be given to only one creditor, but this will not be accepted as an act of bankruptcy as readily as a notice to creditors generally: *Hill's Trustee v Rowlands* [1896] 2 QB 124. The statutory provision refers to "debts", which leads to the inference that a refusal to pay one particular debt as opposed to a general denial of a creditor's claims, will not as a rule be held to be an act of bankruptcy.

The notice of suspension must not be subject to a condition. The statement "If you do not supply me with bricks, I shall not be able to carry out my contracts and shall have to stop payments", was held not to constitute an act of bankruptcy in *Re Phillips, Ex parte Thomas and Co* (1897) 76 LT 531. In *Clough v Samuel* [1905] AC 442 it was held that a mere admission of insolvency is not sufficient. A stockbroker admitted that he was insolvent and would have difficulty in meeting his commitments on due date and accordingly requested his customers to close their accounts with him. This was held not to be an act of bankruptcy. But a statement by a debtor that he or she can pay nothing may be an act of bankruptcy as in *Re Miller* [1901] 1 KB 51, where a debtor in conversation with one of his creditors said, after a severe drop in the value of securities on the Stock Exchange, that he was "utterly penniless" and that "he could not pay anybody".

Where a letter is written genuinely with a view to effecting a settlement of a dispute, it may be marked *without prejudice* and cannot be produced in Court as evidence. But a notice of suspension of payments so marked may be produced in Court to establish an act of bankruptcy. It is not regarded as an attempt to settle a dispute, but rather as a conditional threat if an offer is refused: *Re Daintrey, Ex parte Holt* [1893] 2 QB 116.

If a creditor is estopped by conduct from treating a deed of assignment as an act of bankruptcy, he or she will not be allowed to rely on the circular convening the meeting to discuss the deed as a notice of suspension of payment and use it as an act of bankruptcy on which to base a petition: *Re Hawley, Ex parte Ridgway* (1897) 4 Mans 41.

The mere calling of a meeting of creditors is not by itself an act of bankruptcy. Where, however, the debtor cancels the notice calling the meeting and states that he or she is going to file a debtor's petition on a particular date, this is a notice of suspension of payment and an act of bankruptcy, whether he or she does file his or her petition or not: *In re Taylor, Ex parte Carter Merchants Ltd* [1962] NZLR 507.

(f) A DEBTOR AT A MEETING OF CREDITORS HAVING ADMITTED INSOLVENCY IS REQUIRED TO FILE A DEBTOR'S PETITION OR CONSENTS TO DO SO
Section 19(1)(f) provides that a debtor commits an act of bankruptcy if:

If at any meeting of his creditors he admits that he is in insolvent circumstances, and if either –
(i) A majority in number and value of the creditors present at the meeting by resolution at the meeting require him to file a debtor's petition; or
(ii) He consents to file a debtor's petition and he does not within 48-hours (excluding any holiday) from the time of his consent file the petition.

The meeting may be called by either the debtor or his or her creditors. The wording of the Act appears to call for an admission of insolvency by the debtor at the meeting as a prerequisite to either of the other events constituting the act of bankruptcy. The presentation of a set of accounts by an accountant clearly showing the state of insolvency is insufficient unless it is accompanied by such an admission made by the debtor or someone acting on his or her behalf.

There seems to be no obligation that creditors should attend the meeting personally. A creditor may be represented by an agent who can vote on his or her behalf unless the creditor is one who has some special qualifications or is entitled to be present only by virtue of some contract by which attendance at meetings in a representative character is regulated, eg as a director of a company: *In re Wood (A Bankrupt)* [1959] NZLR 742.

(g) SEIZURE OF GOODS UNDER A WRIT OF EXECUTION

Section 19(1)(g) provides that a debtor commits an act of bankruptcy if:

> Possession has been taken under execution issued against him or his property on any legal process and the judgment or order in respect of which the execution is issued is not satisfied within seven days after possession has been taken: Provided that, where an interpleader summons has been taken out in regard to the property seized, the time elapsing between the taking out of the summons and the time when the proceedings on the summons are finally disposed of, settled, or abandoned shall not be taken into account in calculating the said period of seven days.

An interpleader summons is an application by a third party claiming as his or her own, goods which have been seized in execution. For example, where furniture or a car has been seized, the debtor's spouse will sometimes claim that the goods seized belong to the spouse and not the debtor. The ownership is determined at a hearing before a District Court Judge, but in the meantime the bailiff cannot sell the goods so seized.

No act of bankruptcy has been committed until the seven days have elapsed.

In every action where judgment has been given or payment of any sum of money has been ordered and the terms of the judgment have not been carried out or payment has not been made, a District Court Judge, at the request of the party seeking to enforce such judgment or order, may, whether the time allowed for giving notice of appeal has expired or not, grant a distress warrant directed to the bailiff of the Court.

The bailiff takes possession of the goods of the debtor (except tools of trade to the value of $100 and household furniture and effects and clothing to the value of $300) and sells them by auction after a lapse of not less than seven clear days from the time of taking possession.

The judgment creditor who has sold his or her debtor's property under an execution may allege this act of bankruptcy in a subsequent petition for the bankruptcy of the debtor: *Re Smith* (1867) 16 LT 643.

This act of bankruptcy is available for any creditor whether he or she was the one on whose judgment the distress warrant was issued or not.

(h) ADVERTISEMENT OF A WRIT OF SALE

Section 19(1)(h) provides that a debtor commits an act of bankruptcy if:

> A writ of sale directed against any land of the debtor or any interest therein has been delivered to a sheriff, and that land or interest has been advertised for sale, in at least one newspaper published or circulating in the town or district

in which the land is situated, under that process: provided that, if the judgment or order in pursuance of which the writ of sale issued is satisfied within seven days after the said writ of sale has been both delivered to the sheriff and advertised, no act of bankruptcy shall have been committed.

If the creditor wishes to sell the debtor's land, he or she must apply to the High Court which may issue a writ of sale. A creditor who, having registered a charging order against the debtor's land, decides to have it sold, may adopt the same procedure. Under a writ of sale the sheriff may:

(a) Seize any moneys, bills of exchange, or securities for money of the debtor and deliver the moneys to the party suing out the writ;

(b) Seize the chattels of the debtor (with the exception of the $400 worth of personal goods noted above) and sell them seven clear days after the sale is advertised. The chattels are sold before any land of the debtor is sold;

(c) Advertise the sale of and sell the land of the debtor. No seizure of the land is necessary before the sale.

No act of bankruptcy comes into existence until the writ of sale has been advertised and default in satisfying the judgment has continued for seven days after such advertisement. This act of bankruptcy is available to any creditor.

A bailiff or a sheriff who seizes and sells property of the debtor, in pursuance of a writ of execution issued to satisfy a judgment exceeding $100, must hold the proceeds of the sale, less his or her costs, for 14 days after the sale. If he or she receives notice of the presentation of a bankruptcy petition in that period he or she must, in the case of a debtor's petition, hand over the balance of the proceeds or any moneys paid to him or her to avoid execution to the Assignee. If he or she has notice of the filing of a creditor's petition he or she must await the disposal of the petition, and if adjudication follows the petition he or she must hand over the said balance or the moneys so paid to the Assignee. The Court has, however, a discretionary power to set aside the Assignee's rights in favour of the execution creditor: s 50.

When a sale under a writ of sale or distress warrant is advertised, prompt action should be taken by other creditors. It may be advisable to file a creditor's petition, founded on possession being taken or advertisement of the sale of land, to prevent the execution creditor gaining an advantage over the others.

The sheriff may be authorised to sell a debtor's land by virtue of an order made by a District Court Judge under the Wages Protection and Contractors' Liens Act 1939, but this is not an execution under a writ of sale: *Re Davies* (1907) 26 NZLR 254.

(i) RETURN OF NULLA BONA

Section 19(1)(i) provides that the return of nulla bona (no goods on which distress can be levied) to a distress warrant levied to execute an unsatisfied judgment constitutes an act of bankruptcy.

(j) REMOVAL OR CONCEALMENT OF PROPERTY WITH INTENT TO PREJUDICE CREDITORS OR TO PREFER A CREDITOR

Section 19(1)(j) provides that a debtor commits an act of bankruptcy if:

With intent to prejudice his creditors or to prefer one creditor above another, he removes or attempts to remove any of his property from any place or conceals or attempts to conceal any of his property.

The inclusion of the words "with intent" may make proof of this act of bankruptcy difficult, particularly where it is sought to prove a desire to prefer a creditor. A presumption of intent to prejudice creditors may be a logical implication if creditors are deprived of assets to which they were entitled owing to the removal or concealment by a debtor of his or her property.

(k) FAILURE TO SATISFY A JUDGMENT FOR THE NON-PAYMENT OF TRUST MONEY BY A PERSON REQUIRED BY LAW TO KEEP A TRUST ACCOUNT

Section 19(1)(k) provides that a person entrusted with trust funds commits an act of bankruptcy if:

He is required by law to keep a trust account and any Court has given judgment against him for non-payment of trust money and the judgment is unsatisfied for seven days.

Certain professional men and others, who handle large sums of money belonging to members of the public, are required by law to keep trust accounts under the supervision of independent auditors. For example, solicitors to whom purchase, mortgage and estate moneys are paid and land agents receiving deposits on property transactions, must keep up-to-date trust account records. It is not the failure to keep the records, however, but the failure to satisfy the judgment which is the act of bankruptcy .

Chapter 43

PROCEDURE UP TO AND AFTER ADJUDICATION

SUMMARY

43.1 THE PETITION

43.1.1 The filing of the petition

All bankruptcy proceedings are commenced by the filing in the proper Court of a petition either by the debtor or a creditor. A petition cannot be withdrawn after filing without the leave of the Court: s 26(10). However the Court rarely raises any objection to the withdrawal of a petition by consent. Where a petitioning creditor had been paid by a third party and asked for leave to withdraw his or her petition it was held that the Court has no power to make an order of adjudication unless another creditor has been substituted as petitioner: *Re Mann* [1958] 3 All ER 660.

Section 26(9) empowers the Court to substitute another petitioning creditor if the original petitioner is not proceeding with due diligence or if at the hearing he or she offers no evidence. The petitioner so substituted must file a fresh petition but can rely on the act of bankruptcy in the original petition. In *Ronaldson v Dominion Freeholds Ltd* [1981] 2 NZLR 132 the Court of Appeal held that a substituted creditor could only rely on an act of bankruptcy so long as it was available to the petitioning creditor when the original petition was issued.

Application to be substituted as petitioner in lieu of a petitioning creditor who has failed to proceed with due diligence must be made before the period of three months after the act of bankruptcy alleged in the petition has expired. A petitioning creditor has the right to refuse to accept payment of his or her debt once the petition has been lodged, and it is almost his or her duty to refuse to do so: *Re Ell* (1886) NZLR 4 (CA) 114. In the Australian case *Re Snowden, Ex parte Deputy Commissioner of*

Taxation [1970] ALR 229, it was suggested that a creditor might take part payment of a debt on the condition that it was accepted only if the balance was paid and the petition in bankruptcy dismissed. No creditor's petition can be filed if the act of bankruptcy alleged therein has occurred more than three months before the filing; the extension of the period of relation back could well be disadvantageous to those who had dealings with the bankrupt prior to adjudication: *Re J (A Debtor)* [1967] NZLR 763. If a debtor against whom a bankruptcy petition is filed dies, the proceedings in the matter shall, unless the Court otherwise orders, be continued as if he or she were alive and if the debtor's death occurs before service of the summons and petition, the Court may order service to be effected on his or her administrator or such other persons as it thinks fit: R 54.

If the Court is satisfied that prompt personal service cannot be effected because the debtor is avoiding service of the bankruptcy summons and petition, it may order substituted service: R 27(1).

43.1.2 Place for filing petition

A bankruptcy petition must be filed:

(a) Where the debtor resides in New Zealand, in the office of the High Court nearest by the most practical route to the place in which he or she has resided or carried on business for the longest period during the six months immediately preceding the time when the petition is filed;

(b) Where the debtor is in custody, in the office of the High Court nearest by the most practicable route to the place in which he or she is in custody.

(c) Where the debtor is absent from New Zealand or the petitioning creditor cannot ascertain the place of his or her residence, in the office of the High Court nearest by the most practicable route to the place in which the petitioning creditor resides or carries on business.

(d) Where the debtor has never been resident in New Zealand, in the office of the High Court nearest by the most practicable route to the place in which the petitioning creditor resides or carries on business.

(e) Where the act of bankruptcy alleged is attempting to depart from New Zealand or keeping to or keeping away from the bankruptcy's premises, in any office of the Court.

Proceedings are not invalid if taken in the wrong Court, but the Rules provide that they may, on application by the creditor or the debtor, be transferred to the proper Court: s 13(2)(a).

An application for annulment by a debtor who had deliberately filed his or her petition in the "wrong Court" was refused. It was held that the Court had jurisdiction in respect of the petition: *Re Patterson* (1907) 27 NZLR 171; 10 GLR 84.

43.1.3 Appointment of Assignee as receiver

If after the filing of a petition it appears that the assets of the debtor are in jeopardy, a creditor may ensure that they are safeguarded. At any time after the filing of a creditor's petition but before adjudication a creditor may apply to the Court for the appointment of the Assignee as receiver and manager of the whole or any part of the debtor's property.

The creditor must deposit with the Assignee such sum as the Court directs to meet the consequent expenses of the Assignee, but this sum may be refunded if the debtor is subsequently adjudicated bankrupt: R 10(1), (4).

On such appointment being made (in addition to any further order that may be made at the request of the Assignee or any creditor) the Court may authorise the Assignee to:

(a) Sell perishable property or any property which is rapidly depreciating in value.
(b) Take possession of or control the debtor's property.
(c) Exercise such control over the debtor's business as the Court considers necessary for the conservation of his or her property.

After notice of such appointment has been advertised no execution against the debtor or his or her property shall be issued or proceeded with except with the consent of the Court and under such conditions as the Court thinks fit.

43.1.4 The debtor's petition

Form 16 of the Rules sets out the details of a debtor's petition. On the filing of the petition, the debtor immediately becomes bankrupt and is in the same legal position as if an order adjudging him or her a bankrupt had been made: s 21. Filing is complete on delivery of the petition by an authorised person to the proper officer (usually the Registrar) with the intention that it should be filed: *Ramsford v Maule* (1873) LR 8 CP 672. As the filing of a debtor's petition is equivalent to an order of adjudication, it appears that a debtor's petition cannot be withdrawn even with the leave of the Court; the only step that can be taken is to move for annulment of adjudication under s 119(a) where it is provided that adjudication may be annulled . . .

. . . where the Court is of the opinion that an order of adjudication should not have been made.

Adjudication on a debtor's petition may be annulled where such a petition is an abuse of the process of the Court: *In re Aekins, Ex parte Aekins* (1911) NZLR 1021; 13 GLR 688.

Unfortunately, the Courts are reluctant to annul adjudication even though it arises from a debtor's petition apparently filed with the sole object of defeating a judgment creditor: *Re Painter* [1895] 1 QB 85; and *Re Dunn* [1949] Ch 640; [1949] 2 All ER 388.

If a bankrupt's financial position has improved since he or she filed his or her own petition or if his or her conduct has been unsatisfactory, creditors or the Assignee may before the bankrupt's discharge apply for an order under s 45 compelling the bankrupt to pay a lump sum or to make periodic payments to the Assignee. Discharge does not release the bankrupt from complying with this order: s 114(c).

43.1.5 The creditor's petition

The conditions under which a creditor is entitled to file a bankruptcy petition against a debtor are set out in s 23 of the Act, which provides that he or she shall not be so entitled unless:

(a) The debt owing from the debtor to the petitioning creditor, or, if two or more creditors join in the petition, the aggregate amount of debts owing to the several petitioning creditors, amounts to a sum not less than $200; and

(b) The debtor, whether before or after incurring such debt, has committed an act of bankruptcy within three months before the filing of the petition; and

(c) The debt is a liquidated sum payable either immediately or at some certain future time.

Two points arise for consideration, first that the debt need not be owing at the time the act of bankruptcy is committed, although it must be owing at the date of the presentation of the petition. Secondly, the debt may be a liquidated sum payable at some certain future time.

The commission of the available act of bankruptcy within the three months preceding the filing of the petition is the foundation of bankruptcy proceedings. Once a liquidated debt of $200 has been incurred, even though payment is not due to the petitioning creditor for some time a petition in bankruptcy may be filed, apparently on the theory that the commission of the act of bankruptcy indicates that payment of the debt is at least in doubt. Although payment of the future debt cannot be demanded forthwith, the date of payment must be certain and not dependent on a contingency. Thus a petition could be filed on a debt of $200 or more for goods supplied, if the seller had allowed the debtor credit by taking as payment a bill of exchange due at some later date: *Re Raatz, Ex parte Raatz* [1897] 2 QB 80.

When considering the significance of a creditor being able to cite a debt payable in the future in the bankruptcy petition it must be borne in mind that the power of the Court to make an order of adjudication under s 26 is discretionary and a creditor would not file a petition and pay the necessary costs if there was little likelihood of the order being made.

The debt cannot be a mere claim for damages, it must be certain in amount, due for payment on a specified date, and legally enforceable; it cannot be statute barred: *Ex parte Tynte* (1880) 15 ChD 125; nor can it be a sum claimed in respect of an illegal transaction.

A creditor need not be beneficially entitled to receive the debt; he or she can file a petition against a debtor in a representative character. Thus the Official Assignee in the bankruptcy of a creditor or an assignee under a statutory assignment under the Property Law Act 1952, s 130, can file a petition. Where there has been merely an equitable assignment of a legal chose in action then both the creditor and the assignee should be joined as co-petitioners: *Thompson v Bruce L Mills* (unreported, High Court, Wellington, CB 110/86, 2 December 1986, McGechan J). The executors of a deceased creditor can petition, provided they take out probate before the hearing of the petition. A minor can petition; this is usually done through his or her next friend. A trustee to whom a debt is owed must include the beneficiary in the petition unless the beneficiary is not sui juris by reason of infancy or other incapacity. All joint creditors must join in a petition based on a joint debt: *Brickland v Newsome* (1808) 1 Camp 474. But if one joint creditor has died, the survivor or survivors may petition. Where two or more bankruptcy petitions are filed against the same debtor or against joint debtors, the Court may consolidate the proceedings: R 56.

Where a petition is presented by a mortgagee or other secured creditor, the Court shall not make an order of adjudication, unless the creditor satisfies the Court that the amount of the debt exceeds the value of the security by at least $200: s 25.

A creditor who is privy to a deed of assignment, whether he or she executed it or not, cannot allege the deed as an act of bankruptcy: *In re Aburn* (1908) 27 NZLR 442; 10 GLR 306. See also s 26 (3).

Where the petitioning creditor is an incorporated company, the petition must be executed in the name of the company under its seal. It must not be in the name of an officer of the company. If the petition is presented in the name of an officer of the company purporting to act with the authority of the company, the Court has no power to give leave to amend the petition. The affidavit verifying the petition is, however, made by an officer of the company. Rules 45 and 46 provide for the attestation and verification of documents.

Where a creditor alleges non-compliance with a bankruptcy notice as the available act of bankruptcy, he or she must, if he or she is not the creditor responsible for the issue of the bankruptcy notice, obtain and file an affidavit from the creditor concerned verifying the default which constitutes the act of bankruptcy.

A tender of part or the whole of the debt even with costs after presentation of the petition need not be accepted by the petitioning creditor, *Re Ell, Ex Parte Austin and Haskins* (1886) NZLR 4 CA 114, and *Re Gentry* [1910] 1 KB 825.

As s 26 (9), (10) prevents a petition being withdrawn without the consent of the Court, and further provides for the substitution of a petitioner in place of a petitioner who wishes to discontinue, a petitioning creditor cannot undertake, on accepting payment of his or her debt and costs, that proceedings will not continue. If a creditor accepts payment without costs and the petition is withdrawn with the leave of the Court there appears to be no valid claim available to the creditor for recovery of the costs to the proceedings which he or she has abandoned: *Re Peacock, ex Parte Provincial Discounts Ltd* [1956] NZLR 365. Section 26(9) provides for substitution of a creditor, not substitution of a debt: *Re Mailo, ex Parte General Finance Ltd* (High Court, Auckland, B533/85, 15 April 1986 Henry J).

43.2 THE COURT'S POWERS

43.2.1 Disposal of the petition

If the insolvent files his or her own petition, he or she is automatically adjudicated bankrupt without any Court hearing taking place: s 21. It appears that the insolvent cannot withdraw his or her own petition, nor has the Court power to grant him or her leave to withdraw it: s 30. The

Court can, however, annul his or her adjudication: s 119. If a creditor's petition is filed:

(a) The debtor may be adjudged bankrupt;
(b) The petition may be dismissed;
(c) Proceedings may be stayed; or
(d) The Assignee may be appointed as a receiver and manager of the debtor's property.

The hearing of a petition shall not be adjourned for more than one month unless the Court is satisfied that the adjournment will not be prejudicial to the general body of creditors: R 58.

If a creditor neglects to appear on his or her petition, no subsequent petition against the same debtor or debtors, or any of them, either alone or jointly with any other person, shall be presented by the same creditor in respect of the same act of bankruptcy without the leave of the Court: R 59.

The Court may make an order of adjudication against a debtor who does not appear: R 60. Where a debtor has absconded, the Court may hear a creditor's petition at an earlier date than the date given in the summons for adjudication: R 57.

If a petitioner does not proceed with due diligence or offers no evidence at the hearing, the Court may substitute another creditor to whom at least $200 is owing by the debtor. Such a creditor must file a fresh petition, but he or she can rely on the act of bankruptcy alleged in the original petition: s 26(9).

43.2.2 Adjudication

A Court hearing follows the filing of a creditor's petition. The allegations in the creditor's petition are:

(a) that a debt of not less than $200 is owing from the debtor to the petitioning creditor, or if there is more than one petitioning creditor that the debts owing to them collectively amounts to not less than $200:
(b) that the debt is a liquidated sum;
(c) that the debtor has committed an available act of bankruptcy within the three months before the filing of the petition; and
(d) that either the petitioning creditor has no security for his or her debt or if he or she has a security the amount of the debt exceeds the value of the security by not less than $200.

Usually formal evidence is given by the petitioner confirming the allegations in the petition, and if the debtor does not oppose the petition an order of adjudication will be made in the course of a few minutes. It is clear that the Court is under no compulsion to make an order of adjudication, as the Act has added the words "in its discretion" to the words "may adjudge the debtor bankrupt" which appeared in the repealed Bankruptcy Act 1908. Section 26(1) of the Act states:

> The Court, on being satisfied that the allegations stated in a creditor's petition are true may, in its discretion, adjudge the debtor bankrupt.

A creditor whose debt is insufficient to support a bankruptcy petition may buy another debt to make up the necessary $200, but a petition by a creditor who has bought a debt and filed a petition, not to recover the debt but for some ulterior purpose such as to stifle or delay a suit then pending by the debtor against the creditor, may be dismissed: *In re Cooper ex parte Coleman and Clarke* (1882) 1 NZLR 301 (CA).

43.2.3 Dismissal of petition

The Court may dismiss a creditor's petition if:

(a) It is not satisfied with the proof of the allegations in the petition;
(b) The creditor neglects to appear at the hearing of the petition (see R 59);
(c) It is satisfied that the debtor is able to pay his or her debts;
(d) The debtor has made a disposition of all or substantially all of his or her property to a trustee for the benefit of his or her creditors generally;
(e) He or she has made a proposal for the payment of his or her creditors under s 140 of the Act or has applied for a Summary Instalment Order under s 146. In such a case the Court may either dismiss or stay the petition. If an order for costs is made in favour of the petitioner they may be ordered to be paid out of the insolvent's estate;
(f) It is just and equitable not to make an order of adjudication or for other sufficient cause no order should be made: s 26(2), (3).

Where the creditor's petition relates to more than one debtor, the Court may dismiss the petition as to one or more of them: s 26(8).

If the debtor intends to oppose a petition he or she must file a notice with the Registrar specifying the statements which he or she intends to dispute and serve on the petitioning creditor or his or her solicitor a copy of the notice before the time of the hearing: R 55 and Form 20.

Section 26(2) gives the Court ample power to refuse adjudication where the object of the petition is not the equitable distribution of the debtor's assets, eg the petition may be the culmination of pressure by a particular creditor. Thus, where a petitioning creditor had brought continuous pressure upon an insolvent in order to make him act fraudulently in relation to his other creditors, and give the petitioning creditor an unfair advantage, the petition was dismissed: *Re Eggers* (1912) 31 NZLR 1123; 14 GLR 573. For a discussion of a bank's conduct which was held not to amount to abuse of process but which nevertheless influenced the Court to dismiss a petition see *Meates v Bank of New Zealand* (unreported, High Court, Greymouth, B5/83, 2 September 1983, Hardie Boys J; [1983] BCL 919). For dismissal of a precipitate petition by the Inland Revenue see *Re Le Lievre, ex parte District Commissioner of Inland Revenue* (unreported, High Court, Christchurch, B160/86, 11 February 1987). See also *Uittenbogaard v Commissioner of Inland Revenue* (High Court, Rotorua, B355, 356/86, 19 January 1988, Master Gambrill). Attempted extortion by the petitioning creditor is a ground for dismissing a petition: *Re Otway, Ex parte Otway* [1895] 1 QB 812. A collateral motive on the part of the petitioning creditor is not sufficient to justify the Court in refusing an order unless it amounts to fraud: *Re Ewing, Ex parte Morgan* (1905) 24 NZLR 808; 8 GLR 213. An ulterior private motive such as the expulsion of a member from a partnership is not necessarily a fraud on the Court (*King v Henderson* [1898] AC 720) and although an action will lie for maliciously obtaining an order of adjudication, the petitioning creditor can successfully defend himself or herself by proving there was a legally enforceable debt sufficient to support a petition and an available act of bankruptcy at the time of filing the petition: *Bayne v Blake* (1909) 9 CLR 347.

The Court may refuse adjudication:

(a) Where there are no assets: *In re Betts, Ex parte Betts* [1897] 1 QB 5C. It is submitted that this could constitute "for other sufficient cause". The additional fact in this case that the debtor was already an undischarged bankrupt would have no relevance in view of s 59 of the Act, which sets out the position where an undischarged bankrupt is adjudicated a second time.

(b) Where the creditor has refused payment of part of a debt so that he or she could keep the sum owing up to the $200 necessary to support a petition in bankruptcy: *In re a debtor, Ex parte Lawrence* [1928] 1 Ch 665. A creditor may refuse to accept payment once he or she has filed a petition in bankruptcy.

(c) Where there is only one creditor: *In re Hecquard, Ex parte Hecquard* (1889) 24 QBD 71.

(d) Where the only asset of the debtor is an interest determinable on bankruptcy, eg a life interest determinable on the adjudication of the debtor: *Re Otway, Ex parte Otway* (supra).

43.2.4 Stay of proceedings

The Court may stay proceedings:

(a) Where the act of bankruptcy alleged in the petition is failure to comply with a bankruptcy notice or to pay trust moneys and an appeal is pending from the judgment or order. The Court also has power to dismiss the petition on this ground although it is unlikely to be used until the result of the appeal is known.

(b) As an alternative to dismissing the petition where a debtor denies his or her liability for the debt alleged and gives such security for the debt and costs as the Court requires.

(c) At its own discretion on such terms and subject to such conditions as it thinks fit.

Where proceedings have been stayed in order to test the validity of a petitioning creditor's debt, R 63 makes provision for resumption of proceedings if the debt is found to be valid and for the dismissal of a petition with costs where the decision has been against the validity of the debt.

A stay of proceedings, but not dismissal of the petition, has been allowed where the debtor showed that he had himself brought an action which if successful would enable him to pay his debts in full: *Re Keir* [1916] GLR 264 and *In re Twidle* [1916] NZLR 748; [1916] GLR 533.

43.2.5 Appointment of Assignee as receiver

Under s 27 the Court, on the application of a creditor, has a discretion to appoint the Official Assignee as receiver and manager of the whole or part of the debtor's property at any time after the filing of a creditor's petition and before adjudication. Any order may authorise the taking of possession of any property, the sale of perishable or depreciating property and the exercise of such control as the Court directs. No order shall be made to control the debtor's business except to the extent necessary to conserve the debtor's property.

43.3 PROCEDURE AFTER ADJUDICATION

43.3.1 Duties of the bankrupt

Section 30 provides that the order of adjudication is final and conclusive with respect to its validity and shall not be impeached at law or in equity. This does not, however, preclude an application for annulment under s 119.

Immediately adjudication takes place, the Registrar notifies the Assignee, who forthwith advertises it in the local newspapers and in the *Gazette*: s 31, regs 15, 16. On being notified by the Registrar of the debtor's adjudication, the Assignee sends out a notice to the bankrupt stating that he or she has been adjudicated bankrupt and that he or she is required to complete certain forms enclosed relating to his or her assets and liabilities and to answer a long list of questions relating to his or her affairs. He or she is also given a time at which to attend at the Assignee's office for examination about his or her bankruptcy and is called on to attend a meeting of creditors, the time and place of which will be given to him or her later. The form of this notice is set out in Forms 1-4 of the First Schedule of the Regulations and it also sets out the statutory duties of the bankrupt and in particular warns him or her that if he or she does not comply with these duties he or she will be liable to a penalty: s 38, reg 18.

The forms relating to the bankrupt's assets and liabilities call for details of his or her secured and unsecured creditors, hire purchase commitments, his or her real estate, and a list of book debts and other assets not already listed. If the bankrupt has been in business in the three years preceding adjudication he or she must give details about his or her business, his or her drawings, whether all moneys received were banked and his or her reason for the loss he or she has shown.

The bankrupt shall to the utmost of his or her power aid in the realisation of his or her property and the distribution of the proceeds amongst his or her creditors. In particular he or she shall:

(a) Immediately upon adjudication give up his or her books and papers in his or her own possession and give details of those in the possession of anyone else; also all information necessary for the preparation of a balance sheet of his or her estate must be given to the Assignee: s 61(1).

(b) Within a reasonable time prepare and deliver to the Assignee full, true and detailed balance sheets and accounts of his or her trading and stocktaking for any period not being earlier than three years before the commencement of bankruptcy. The bankrupt for this purpose may have full access to all his or her books and papers in the possession of the Assignee and may with the Assignee's concurrence, have the assistance of an accountant at the expense of the estate: s 61(2).

(c) Give a complete and accurate list of his or her property and of his or her creditors and debtors and such other information as to his or her property as the Assignee requires; and attend before the Assignee whenever called upon to do so.

(d) Disclose to the Assignee any property acquired by him or her before his or her discharge and divisible amongst his or her creditors.

(e) Supply to the Assignee information regarding his or her expenditure and sources of income after adjudication.

(f) Execute such powers of attorney, transfers, deed, and instruments, and generally do all such acts and things in relation to his or her property (whether within or outside New Zealand) and the distribution of the proceeds amongst his or her creditors, as are required by the Assignee or prescribed by rules made under the Act or directed by the Court.

(g) Deliver to the Assignee on demand any of his or her property that is divisible amongst his or her creditors and is in his or her possession or control.

(h) Deliver on demand to the Assignee or anyone authorised by him or her any property that is acquired by him or her before his or her discharge.

(i) Notify the Assignee immediately in writing of any change of his or her address, and any change of his or her employment and of any change of his or her name.

An undischarged bankrupt shall not without the consent of the Assignee or the Court:

(a) Enter into or carry on any business alone or in partnership, or
(b) Be a director or take any part in the management of a company; or
(c) Manage or control any business carried on by or on behalf of or be in the employ of the bankrupt's wife or husband, a lineal ancestor or descendant of the bankrupt, the wife or husband of such an ancestor or descendant, a brother of the bankrupt, the wife of such a brother, a sister of the bankrupt, and the husband of such a sister: s 62.

An undischarged bankrupt is not allowed to take part in the real business of a company and it is irrelevant whether any action taken by him or her is subject to the approval of someone else: *Re Newth* [1974] 2 NZLR 760.

Section 188 of the Companies Act 1955 makes it an offence for an undischarged bankrupt to act as a director or to be concerned directly or indirectly with the management of any company.

43.3.2 Meeting of creditors

The procedure to be followed by the Assignee at this stage is set out in Part II of the Rules and in regs 3-22. His or her duty is to obtain full information about the bankrupt's assets and liabilities and to protect and get in the property of the bankrupt in order to realise it and distribute it amongst the creditors. To obtain this information, the Assignee insists on the bankrupt complying with the duties detailed above and also holds meetings of creditors and has the power to compel the debtors of the bankrupt to submit to various examinations.

Section 34 provides that unless the Assignee considers special circumstances justify delay, the first meeting of creditors shall be called not later than 14 days after the bankrupt has filed with the Assignee the statement relating to his or her assets, liabilities and creditors as well as the answers to the questions referred to above. Even when the bankrupt fails to file this statement within the 14 days following adjudication, the meeting shall not be delayed for more than 28 days after adjudication. Notice of the meeting is given by post and it is also advertised: s 34(2). Unless the Court otherwise orders, proceedings at meetings are not invalidated through some creditors not having received notice of the meeting: s 40(6). The Assignee shall, unless such information has not been supplied by the bankrupt, send to each creditor with the notice of the meeting details of the bankrupt's assets, liabilities and creditors and a summary of the bankrupt's explanation of his or her insolvency: s 35. Proof of debts shall be submitted to the Assignee as soon as may be, and he or she will endorse on the proof of debt form his or her admission or rejection of the proof: regs 23, 24.

Section 37 (2) provides that the bankrupt must submit to an examination in respect of his or her property and creditors and that he or she must sign a written statement of his or her evidence if so required by the Assignee. This examination is normally combined with the first meeting of creditors and is of particular importance.

Where it is obvious that the bankrupt estate will yield only a small dividend and it is difficult to get creditors to attend, one creditor and the Assignee may constitute a quorum: s 38. Provision is made for the representation of creditors by s 39.

If the bankrupt has no available assets, the Assignee shall not be required to incur any expense in relation to his or her estate without a guarantee from the creditors: reg 63.

At the meeting of creditors, where the examination of the bankrupt is also held, the Assignee, who is the chairman, usually reads the written statement forwarded by the bankrupt explaining the circumstances leading to the bankruptcy. The bankrupt is then sworn in as a witness and the Assignee reads the statement of the debtor's assets and liabilities and has the debtor swear to the truth of that statement.

The Assignee then conducts a searching examination with regard to goods purchased and moneys received by the bankrupt in the period preceding adjudication and how such moneys have been disposed of. Detailed questions on such matters as to whether all moneys were paid into the debtor's bank account and whether receipts were given for all moneys received and a demand for the production of receipts for all moneys paid by the bankrupt as well as the bankrupt's answers to the prescribed questions are usually effective in putting a fairly complete picture before the creditors. The creditors also ask questions and give information as to the bankrupt's transactions. All the questions and answers are taken down by the associate of the Assignee and this record is typed out and signed by the bankrupt shortly after the examination.

In the course of the examination it may be apparent that penal offences under the Act have been committed by the bankrupt, but no immediate action will be taken by the Assignee until independent proof can be obtained. At the end of the meeting the Assignee usually comments on the facts which have been brought out and indicates whether in his or her opinion the bankrupt has been merely unfortunate or whether his or her insolvency has been brought about by incompetence and recklessness or other cause. If dissatisfied with the position he or she may advise the bankrupt not to apply for his or her discharge for at least 12 months.

Minutes of the proceedings kept and signed by the Official Assignee are prima facie evidence of what passed at the meetings.

An ordinary resolution shall be carried by a majority of creditors or their representatives present and voting thereon unless a creditor of his or her representative demands that it shall be decided by a majority in value.

A creditor is not entitled to vote if:

(a) He or she has not proved his or her debt; but the Assignee is empowered to admit proof at the meeting so as to enable the creditor to vote, but proof in this summary fashion does not entitle the creditor to claim that he or she has proved his or her debt for other purposes in the bankruptcy;

(b) He or she is a secured creditor and has not valued, surrendered or realised his or her security;

(c) His or her debt is secured by a bill of exchange, unless he or she is willing to treat the liability of everyone antecedently liable as a security for the debt, and to value such security and deduct it from the amount of his or her proof. A creditor seeking to prove in respect of a bill of exchange may be required to produce the bill before proving: s 40 (1), (2), (3).

No person shall vote in favour of any resolution which would directly or indirectly place him, or his or her partner or employer or employee, or the creditor whom he or she represents, or the creditor's partner or employer or employee, in a position to receive any remuneration out of the estate of the debtor otherwise than as a creditor rateably with the other creditors of the debtors: s 40(4).

Subsequent meetings may be summoned by the Assignee and must be summoned by him or her when required by one-fourth in the value of the creditors who have proved: s 36. The bankrupt shall, if required by the Assignee, attend all meetings of creditors: s 37(2). The Assignee is an officer of the Court, and the bankrupt's failure to attend such a meeting is contempt of Court: s 15(3).

A creditor who, not being on oath, makes a defamatory statement about the bankrupt at a meeting of creditors is not absolutely privileged. He or she is probably protected if he or she is being examined on oath: *Searl v Lyons* (1908) 27 NZLR 524.

43.3.3 Appointment of committee or expert to assist Assignee

Creditors may by resolution appoint an expert or a committee to assist the Assignee in the administration of the estate: s 41.

43.3.4 Examinations of the bankrupt

There are various examinations to which the bankrupt must submit. In the course of examinations made under the authority of the Act the bankrupt and others who are examined are bound to answer all questions relating to the business or property of the bankrupt, the causes of bankruptcy and the disposition of the bankrupt's property.

The bankrupt or any other person who is examined about matters relating to a bankruptcy by the Court, the Assignee or a District Court Judge shall not be excused from answering any question on the ground that his or her answer might lay him or her open to a criminal charge. But any such answer shall not be admissible as evidence in any criminal proceeding against the person concerned, except on a charge of perjury arising out of his or her statement or answer; s 70. Again, a bankrupt or other person who makes a statement which is false in any material particular or who wilfully misleads the Assignee or who refuses without lawful justification to answer any question put to him or her is not entitled to this privilege and is liable to summary conviction and may be imprisoned: ss 128 (1) (c), 164.

(a) EXAMINATION OF THE BANKRUPT BY THE ASSIGNEE AND HIS OR HER CREDITORS

This usually takes place at the first meeting of creditors, as we have seen, and its main purpose is to find out what property and money the bankrupt has had during the years immediately preceding adjudication and what has happened to it.

(b) PRIVATE EXAMINATION

A private examination under s 68 may take place either before or after the debtor's discharge. The following persons may be summoned to appear for examination before the Assignee, some other Assignee or a District Court Judge, and may also be required to produce and surrender to the Assignee books or papers relating to the property and dealings by the bankrupt:

(a) The bankrupt himself or herself;
(b) The spouse of the bankrupt;
(c) Any person suspected of being indebted to the bankrupt or of having in his or her possession any property, books or papers of the bankrupt or having information about the bankrupt's property, trade, dealings, income or expenditure.

Any person required to attend this examination must have tendered to him or her reasonable expenses of his or her attendance thereat. Should a person whose evidence is necessary for the bankruptcy proceedings and who has no reasonable excuse for not attending have to be arrested, he or she may be ordered to pay the expenses of his or her arrest and examination. If the bankrupt, or such other person, fails to appear on summons he or she may be arrested and brought before the Court. The examination must be committed to writing and the examinee must sign the written report, if so required.

The examination by the Assignee is a judicial proceeding and the person being examined is a witness giving evidence on oath. The typewritten transcript of the evidence given by a bankrupt should be signed by him or her as provided by s 68(3), otherwise its accuracy may be challenged. The bankrupt or other person may be represented by a solicitor and his or her answers to his or her solicitor will form part of his or her examination.

The examination is private; only those taking part in it are entitled to be present.

The District Court Judge or the Assignee may in his or her discretion permit the bankrupt to be present throughout. No report of this examination will be published save with the consent of the Court on the application of the Assignee.

The private examination provides suitable machinery for dealing with a bankrupt whose conduct is unsatisfactory or who is suspected of concealing his or her property. It may also be used when there is an application for the reversal of the order of discharge under s 112.

(c) PUBLIC EXAMINATION

The primary object of a public examination under s 69 is the protection of the public and it should take place only where the fullest investigation of the bankrupt's transactions should be made and publicised. As such examinations have sometimes served a scandalous rather than the public interest, it is not usual to hold them. A further reason for not holding the public examination is that the substantial expense of a High Court hearing increases the costs of administration which must be paid in priority to creditors' claims.

On the application of the Assignee or the creditors pursuant to an ordinary resolution passed at a meeting of the creditors at any time after adjudication and before an absolute order of discharge, the bankrupt may be required to submit to a public examination. At least seven days' notice of intention to hold such an examination must be advertised and given to the bankrupt and his creditors. The provisions relating to the payment of expenses to people attending from a distance, their liability to pay expenses if they fail to appear, and the power to compel attendance at examination by the arrest of the people concerned, if they fail to appear, apply to both public and private examinations. At the beginning of the examination the Judge presiding usually asks the bankrupt whether he or she is satisfied that due notice has been given and the other formalities have been complied with.

Prior to the examination, the Assignee must file a report on the bankrupt's conduct and his or her estate.

The Assignee or any creditor who has proved may examine the bankrupt. The bankrupt is examined on oath and must answer all questions allowed by the Court. The purpose of the public examination is to protect the public as well as to obtain for the creditors full disclosure of the conduct of the bankrupt, his or her assets and liabilities.

Again here the bankrupt cannot refuse to answer incriminating questions. His or her duty to answer is unaffected by the fact that he or she may be awaiting trial for a criminal offence relating to his property. The Court may decide to adjourn the public examination until the trial has taken place but this course is not obligatory: Re Atherton [1912] 2 KB 251. Notes of the examination are put into writing and after being read over by the bankrupt are signed by him or her. Such evidence may be used against the bankrupt in subsequent proceedings against him or her. The written notes of the examination are available for inspection by any creditor.

An order of the Court that a bankrupt's examination is finished should not be made until his or her affairs have been sufficiently investigated.

Non-committal answers or discursive explanatory statements, not being direct answers to the questions put, are unacceptable. An order that the examination is finished should not be given by consent of the parties: *In re Wallace, Gunson, Neale and Co* [1960] NZLR 769.

Public examinations usually take place immediately before the hearing of an application for discharge, but where the interest of the public is involved or the Assignee considers that the debtor is not co-operative or making full disclosure the public examination may be held before the assets of the bankrupt have been realised and dividends paid to the creditors.

If the Assignee considers that the bankrupt has committed an offence under the Act, he or she must lay the facts before the Crown Solicitor; s 129. If the latter certifies that there are reasonable grounds for prosecution, the Assignee lays an information against the bankrupt.

Chapter 44

POWERS OF THE OFFICIAL ASSIGNEE

SUMMARY

44.1 GENERAL

The principal powers of the Assignee are concerned with getting control of the debtor's property, selling it to the best advantage, and distributing the proceeds, but he or she has special additional powers such as disclaiming unsaleable property (ss 75, 78), terminating contracts (s 76), as well as facultative powers such as the right to transfer company shares and Government and local body stock (s 74).

On adjudication, the Assignee becomes entitled to exercise the legal rights of the bankrupt over any property to which the bankrupt may become entitled from the time of the commencement of bankruptcy until his or her discharge. He or she may also acquire rights to seize property which has been transferred by the bankrupt to others in the period preceding adjudication. The bulk of the property passing to the Assignee is, however, that which was vested in the bankrupt at the commencement of bankruptcy or was acquired by him or her during bankruptcy but before discharge.

If the bankrupt has any property outside New Zealand which he or she may validly dispose of by law, he or she must at the request of the Assignee execute all documents necessary to vest such property in the Assignee: s 60(d).

Where, as mentioned above, the Assignee is exercising any rights of transfer enjoyed by the bankrupt over stock, shares or other property transferable in the books of a company and standing in the bankrupt's name, the various persons whose acts or consents are necessary must, whether there is a provision to the contrary in the articles or not, at the request of the Assignee do all things necessary to enable such transfer to be completed: s 74(1), (2).

The Assignee is entitled to all the rights the bankrupt had to recover his or her property and he or she can intervene and claim any real or personal property to which the bankrupt was entitled at the time of the commencement of bankruptcy or to which he or she becomes entitled between the commencement of bankruptcy and discharge: s 42(2)(a), (b).

No person can withhold possession of books or papers against the Assignee whether he or she is claiming a lien for professional service or otherwise. But a person (other than the spouse of the bankrupt) claiming for professional service in regard to the bankrupt's books, deeds or instruments and who otherwise would have had a lien over such books deeds or instruments, may be treated as a preferential creditor for an amount not exceeding $100: s 73.

To establish his or her right to real or personal property devolving upon the bankrupt or to which he or she becomes entitled between adjudication and discharge, the Assignee must take steps to intervene and claim it: s 49(1)(a). Bankers who have complied with the provisions of the Act in s 49(5) dealing with money, securities or negotiable instruments on behalf of the bankrupt are deemed to have dealt with the bankrupt for value and there are special provisions relating to execution creditors (see infra). Neither a bankrupt nor anyone claiming through him or her has any power to recover any of the bankrupt's property or to release anyone from any obligations relating to such property: s 44(a). The Court may also order any debtor, who owes money to the bankrupt, to pay the debt to the Assignee. The bankrupt must not execute any power of appointment which will defeat any interest to which he or she might have been beneficially entitled before discharge in default of appointment: s 44(b). For example, a debtor may have been left a farm by his or her father subject to a power of appointment to his eldest son, either during his or her lifetime or by will on his or her death. If the debtor has leased the farm and is receiving the rental, he or she cannot on adjudication exercise the power of appointment in favour of his or her son so as to deprive his or her estate of the rental he or she was receiving.

44.2 ENFORCING SURRENDER OF PROPERTY

The Assignee or any creditor may take steps to prevent the debtor absconding, removing or concealing his or her property or destroying his or her books. After adjudication the Assignee may get a search warrant in order to seize the debtor's property, wherever it is situated, as well as get an order for possession of his or her premises. Rules 28-31 set out the procedure relating to search warrants, warrants to arrest and warrants of seizure. The bankrupt is not allowed to enter into any business or control or manage a business run by any close relatives: s 62; *Re Newth* [1974] 2 NZLR 760. See supra 43.3.1.

44.3 GENERAL ADMINISTRATIVE POWERS OF THE ASSIGNEE

The general administrative powers of the Assignee are to be found in s 71 of the Act, to which reference should be made. These powers are set out in considerable detail and are expressed to be in furtherance and not in limitation of all other powers vested in the Assignee. The Assignee can exercise these powers (except the power to sell property) without the concurrence of the creditors. Details of the procedure to be followed by the Assignee are to be found in regs 3-25.

The powers specified are designed to confer on the Assignee all the rights and authority the bankrupt had over any property as well as any rights the bankrupt had or could have had to bring, defend and compromise any claims, refer disputes to arbitration, and give valid receipts for money received.

The Assignee is also given power to mortgage the bankrupt's property but the money raised must be used for a purpose to which money realised by the sale of the bankrupt's property could be applied. Money may be expended in repairs or renovation of the bankrupt's property, whether the work is necessary for salvage or for routine maintenance.

The Assignee is further authorised to employ and remunerate any person to transact any business arising in the course of administration of the bankrupt's estate and to appoint agents or attorneys in or out of New Zealand.

Any power conferred on a trustee by the Trustee Act 1956 may be exercised by the Assignee over the bankrupt's property.

The Assignee may, for the benefit of the bankrupt's estate and with the approval of the Controller and Auditor-General, invest money not required for immediate disbursement. Other moneys should be banked: s 81, reg 47.

The Assignee may surrender building society shares to any society: s 72(3). This course might be advisable if the shares are not readily saleable privately.

Section 71(o) gives the Assignee a discretion in the management and distribution of the estate. Although the Act gives no express power to grant a lease of the bankrupt's property, it appears that the giving of a lease would be a matter within the discretion of the Assignee. This would not extend to granting a lease for a long term, but would apply to the granting of, say, a monthly tenancy till the Assignee was able to sell the property: *Re Calcinai* [1937] NZLR 701; [1937] GLR 446.

The Assignee is not liable for anything done by him or her in the course of administration by reason only that the order of adjudication is discharged or annulled: s 138. Nor is the Assignee liable for costs when proceedings are brought against him or her in regard to matters affecting a bankrupt estate: R 11.

44.4 THE POWER OF SALE

The Assignee may sell the whole or any part of the bankrupt's property by public auction or public tender with power to buy in at any such auction. The property of the bankrupt must not be sold until after the date of the first meeting of creditors except in the case of:

(a) Perishable property; and
(b) Property the sale of which would be prejudiced by delay or in respect of which extra expenses would be incurred by delay, provided that the creditors are first consulted: s 72(4).

He or she may sell privately:

(a) Any perishable property;
(b) Any unsold property previously offered for sale by public auction or public tender;
(c) Any property which, by reason of its nature, situation, value or other special circumstances, he or she considers it unnecessary or inadvisable to sell by public auction or public tender;
(d) Any property for which authority has been given by a resolution of creditors to sell by private contract;
(e) Company, Government, or local body securities, provided they are sold through a registered stock exchange.

If the bankrupt was a member of a dissolved partnership, the Assignee may not sell the book debts and goodwill of the joint business: *Re Motion, Maule v Davis* (1873) LR 9 Ch 192.

Where there is an assignment of the bankrupt's business and goodwill, the bankrupt cannot be compelled to enter into any covenant preventing him or her from re-entering the same type of business, or from soliciting his or her old customers. Whether a debtor files his or her own petition in bankruptcy or whether he or she enters into a deed of assignment for the benefit of his or her creditors, he or she does not thereby constitute the relationship of vendor and purchaser between himself and the ultimate purchaser of the property: *Green and Sons Ltd v Morris* [1914] 1 Ch 562. The bankrupt cannot, of course, represent himself or herself as carrying on the original business which has been sold, but it seems clear that, apart from the financial failure of the business beforehand, the fact that the buyer has no protection from subsequent competition from the bankrupt makes the goodwill practically valueless.

A chose in action may be sold by the Assignee: *Taylor v Knapman* (1883) NZLR 2 SC 265.

A mortgagee may buy in the security if it is sold either by his or her directions or on demand by the Assignee. But see s 90(5)(b).

The title acquired by anyone under the exercise of the Assignee's power of sale can be invalidated only on the ground of fraud, but not on the ground that no case has arisen to authorise a sale or that the power of sale had been improperly or irregularly exercised: s 72(6).

44.5 POWER TO CARRY ON THE BUSINESS OF THE BANKRUPT

The Assignee is entitled to carry on the business of the bankrupt so far as this is necessary or expedient for the beneficial disposal of the same: s 71(g), but not with the sole intention of benefiting the bankrupt: *Clark v Smith* [1940] 1 KB 126; [1939] 4 All ER 59 (CA). If the majority of creditors resolve that the Assignee is to carry on the business for any purpose other than for disposing of it for the benefit of the estate, eg the making of a profit, the resolution will not bind the dissentient minority and the Court will declare the resolution invalid: *In re Batey, Ex parte Emmanuel* (1881) 17 ChD 35.

The bankrupt may apply to the Assignee for leave to carry on his or her business. The Assignee may, if he or she is satisfied with the reasons for the application and after having regard to the interests of the bankrupt, the creditors and the community, grant such leave: regs 33, 34.

The Assignee may appoint the bankrupt or some other person to carry on the business on behalf of the creditors: s 71(g).

44.6 POWER OF OFFICIAL ASSIGNEE TO PAY FOR SERVICES RENDERED PRIOR TO ADJUDICATION

The Assignee may pay for services rendered which are beneficial to creditors. If he or she is in doubt he or she should ask the Court for directions: s 85, R 9; *In re Green, Ex parte Park* [1917] 1 KB 183.

Reference has already been made to the right of persons who have rendered services to the bankrupt in respect of accounting and legal matters to claim up to $100 by way of fees as preferential creditors. Where a solicitor for the debtor has opposed bankruptcy proceedings and has been paid by the debtor before adjudication, such costs are irrecoverable by the Assignee: *In re Sinclair, Ex parte Payne* (1885)15 QBD 616. Again where a solicitor rendered services to a debtor prior to his or her committing an act of bankruptcy and also between the commencement of bankruptcy and adjudication. It was decided that he or she was entitled to retain out of moneys held by him or her on behalf of the debtor the amount of costs incurred before the commencement of bankruptcy, but not for subsequent services: *In re Hardy* (1901) 19 NZLR 845; 3 GLR 193. On the other hand payments made to an accountant for services rendered in connection with an assignment for creditors which has not become operative are recoverable by the Assignee: *Re White* (1898) 5 Mans 17.

In *Re Stephens* [1929] NZLR 254, creditors called on a debtor to assign his or her estate to trustees for the benefit of creditors. The trustees got in the estate and were in the process of realising it when the debtor was adjudicated bankrupt. One creditor objected to the trustees being given preferential payment for their services. It was held that the Official Assignee had no discretion to deviate from the order of payments prescribed by the Act (now s 104), but that the Assignee having accepted the work done by the trustees in the realisation of the estate, they were his agents and entitled to fair remuneration, and that this remuneration should come under s 104(1)(a) as costs, allowances and expenses properly payable by the Assignee in the exercise of his office.

In administering the estate of the bankrupt, the Assignee must have regard to the resolutions of creditors in general meeting, but if the Assignee or any dissenting creditor thinks that the resolution is unjust, an application should be made to the Court for directions. Apart from this provision, the Assignee can use his or her own discretion in the management and distribution of the estate: s 84.

The Court will not interfere with the exercise of the Assignee's discretion unless it is proved that he or she is acting in a totally unreasonable fashion: *Re Peters, Ex parte Lloyd* (1882) 47 LT 64. Again, if the

Assignee is in doubt about any question concerning the management of the estate, he or she may apply to the Court for directions and when acting on such directions, he or she is free from personal responsibility in the discharge of his or her duty in that particular matter: s 84. The bankrupt, any creditor or any other person aggrieved by any act or decision of the Assignee may, within 21 days of such act or decision, appeal to the Court: s 86.

44.7 THE RULE IN *EX PARTE JAMES*

The so-called rule in *Ex parte James (Re Condon, ex p James)* (1874) LR 9 Ch App 609, [1874-80] All ER Rep 388) is a leading principle of bankruptcy administration. In essence it provides that an Official Assignee as an officer of the Court, may be restrained from enforcing a claim or remaining money if it is:

> not honourable — if it were not high minded — if it would be contrary to natural justice — if it would be shabby — if it would be a dirty trick for him to retain it.

(per Scrutton LJ, summarising earlier formulations of the principle in *Re Wigzell, ex parte Hart* [1921] 2 KB 835 at 858) In *Re Tyler* [1907] 1 KB 865, 873; [1904-7] All ER Rep 181, 185 c-d Buckley LJ expressed it in a more temperate way:

> Assuming that he (the officer of the Court) has a right enforceable in a Court of Justice, the Court of Bankruptcy or the Court for the administration of estates in Chancery will not take advantage of that right if to do so would be inconsistent with natural justice and that which an honest man would do.

The true basis of the principle is that the Courts have two functions — one to decide the rights between the parties and the other to administer estates. In administering estates the Court by its officer may find itself in the position of a quasi litigant. As Farwell LJ said in *Re Tyler* (p 871), in such circumstances "It would be insufferable for this Court to have it said of it that it has been guilty by its officer of a dirty trick". The problem with the principle is that it represents a matter which is almost exclusively one of ethics rather than law. As Salter J said in the Divisional Court in *Re Wigzell* [1921] 2 KB at 845 (approved in the Court of Appeal, pp 852 and 859):

> Legal rights can be determined with precision by authority, but questions of ethical propriety have always been, and will always be, the subject of honest difference among honest men.

However, it can be argued that the discretion must be acted on on judicial principles (per Vaughan Williams LJ in *Re Tyler* [1907] 1 KB 865, 870) and what the Courts are concerned with is not plumbing the depths of ethical propriety, but recognising particular cases of ethical impropriety when they see them. This is analogous to the point that whereas it is difficult exhaustively to define good faith it is possible to identify particular instances of bad faith. Indeed there is a close link between the rule in *Ex parte James* and bad faith.

Thus where money recovered by an execution creditor was paid to the trustee in bankruptcy under a mistake of law, it was held that the trustee, being an officer of the Court, could not take advantage of the ordinary rule of law that money paid under a mistake of law was irrecoverable and that he or she must refund the money so paid: *Re Condon, Ex parte James* (1874) 9 Ch App 609. On the other hand in *Re Byers, Ex parte Davies* [1965] NZLR 774 Davies offered by tender to the Official Assignee to purchase a section of land in a bankrupt estate valued at £250 for £700. He made this inflated offer through his failure to identify the section correctly, which was not due to carelessness but to an error in sign-posting the road and in no way due to any action by the Official Assignee, who had described the land correctly. In such circumstances, when the mistake is unilateral, the Court had no power to rectify or avoid the contract prior to the Contractual Mistakes Act 1977.

Perry J adopted the view that, while the Official Assignee had a duty to safeguard the rights of creditors, it is not his duty to enrich them, and on motion for directions his Honour adopted the rule in *Ex parte James* to the effect that the Court will order the Official Assignee, being an officer of the Court, to act in an honourable and high-minded way in refraining from enforcing an unjust though legally enforceable claim.

The application of the principle expressed in the rule in *Ex parte James* is in the discretion of the Court, but generally the rule will be applied where the Assignee has known the facts and has taken no steps to correct the position, or where the transaction in question has been carried out by the Assignee. The principle should not be applied indiscriminately and it should not be invoked unless the estate of the bankrupt for disposition amongst his or her creditors have been unjustly enriched at the expense of the claimant: *Government of India v Taylor* [1955] AC 491, 513; [1955] 1 All ER 292, 300.

The general principle applies to cases of money paid under a mistake of law as well as fact. In *Re Tyler, Ex parte Official Receiver* [1907]1 KB 865 a debtor had requested his wife to pay the premiums on a life assurance policy. The trustee in bankruptcy knew the wife had been paying the premiums for six years in the erroneous belief that she was going to benefit under the policy. The Court decided that the trustee could not take the policy moneys without refunding the premiums so paid.

The Judicature Act 1908, ss 94A and 94B, states that if relief could be granted if the mistake was wholly one of fact, then that relief shall not be denied by reason that the mistake was one of law, whether or not it was in any degree also one of fact. Recovery of money paid under mistake, whether of law or of fact, may be denied wholly or partly if the person from whom relief is sought received the payment in good faith and has so altered his or her position in reliance on the validity of the payment that it is inequitable to grant relief.

A further factor in deciding to what extent the principle is applicable is the duty of the Assignee to administer the bankrupt's estate for the benefit of creditors. This duty imposes limitations on the scope of the principle. Accordingly, what might be a dishonourable thing on the part of the bankrupt may not necessarily be dishonourable when done by the Assignee in order to protect the assets for the creditors: *Scranton's Trustee v Peace* [1922] 2 Ch 877.

Chapter 45

PROPERTY PASSING TO THE OFFICIAL ASSIGNEE

SUMMARY

45.1 GENERAL

The Assignee's title to the bankrupt's property is based primarily on s 42(2) of the Act, which, subject to the qualifications referred to in this chapter, provides that:

> . . . the property and powers of the bankrupt to vest in the Assignee and be divisible amongst his creditors shall comprise the following:
> (a) All property whatsoever and wheresoever situated belonging to or vested in the bankrupt at the commencement of the bankruptcy, or acquired by or devolving upon him before his discharge;
> (b) The capacity to exercise and to take proceedings for exercising all such powers in or over or in respect of any property whatsoever and wheresoever situated as might have been exercised by the bankrupt for his own benefit at the commencement of the bankruptcy or before his discharge.

But the following property does not pass to the Assignee:

> (a) The interest of a bankrupt spouse in a joint family home under the Joint Family Homes Act 1964 and his or her protected interest in the matrimonial home, the family chattels, and other matrimonial property interests under ss 8,11, and 20 of the Matrimonial Property Act 1976;

851

(b) Any property held in trust by the bankrupt for any other person (s 42(3)) other than for a spouse of a bankrupt: s 43;

(c) Tools of trade estimated by the Assignee not to exceed $100 in value: s 52;

(d) Household furniture and effects, including clothes of himself or herself and his or her family, estimated by the Assignee not to exceed $300 in value: s 52.

The creditors may resolve to give a more liberal allowance. Goods being acquired on hire purchase are not included – they do not belong to the bankrupt and the owner's interest in those goods is not prejudiced.

As has already been stated, the property and rights belonging to the bankrupt at the commencement of bankruptcy or acquired by him or her in the period between the commencement of bankruptcy and adjudication pass to the Assignee under the doctrine of relation back: see 42.2.2 supra and 46.2 post. The property and rights acquired by the bankrupt in the period between adjudication and discharge are discussed in ch 46 infra.

Section 42, vesting the bankrupt's property in the Assignee, may be regarded as an absolute statutory assignment but the Assignee is not obliged to give notice to the persons affected, which is necessary in the case of an assignee under an assignment within the Property Law Act 1952, s 130. The Assignee takes the property "subject to equities".

The indefeasibility of title provisions (ss 62 and 63) of the Land Transfer Act 1952 do not restrict the power of the Assignee in getting control of land sold or mortgaged during the period of relation back, acquired or improved by the bankrupt on behalf of another as provided in s 55, or disposed of as provided in s 58. The Assignee can stop any dealing with the legal interest in any land subject to ss 42, 43, 54, 56, 57 and 162 of the Insolvency Act and s 60 of the Property Law Act 1952 before he or she appears on the title as registered proprietor following registration of a transmission to him or her: ss 42(5), 55(4) and 58(7). Relief for a person unjustly deprived of his or her title to land is provided for in ss 47 and 58 (6).

45.2 INTERESTS DETERMINABLE ON BANKRUPTCY

An owner of property cannot defeat his or her creditors by entering into a contract providing for the disposal of it if he or she should go bankrupt: *Mackintosh v Pogose* [1895] Ch 505, 511; or by providing for a gift over in the event of his or her bankruptcy: Ex *parte Jay re Harrison* (1880) 14 ChD 19. Apart from common law the provisions of the Act (s 54, voidable gifts; s 56, voidable preferences; s 57, voidable securities) give the Assignee adequate powers to avoid transactions of this type. But a donor of property is entitled to determine who is to enjoy his or her bounty and provided he or she has not passed an absolute interest to the donee, he or she may settle his or her property upon a person with a gift over on the happening of a certain event, such as the bankruptcy of the donee. If, however, the certain event refers only indirectly to bankruptcy, as for example, where he or she has specified that the donee's interest shall pass to someone else on the donee's assigning, alienating, or encumbering his or her property, it is then necessary to decide whether such assigning or alienating is a voluntary or an involuntary act. Prima facie, a debtor's petition in bankruptcy is a voluntary act, whereas adjudication on a creditor's petition is an assignment of the debtor's property under compulsion. For example, in *Re Harvey ex parte Pixley* (1889) 60 LT 710, there was a proviso in the will for the determination of a life interest on the life tenant "alienating, charging, encumbering or disposing of the income". The tenant was adjudicated bankrupt on a creditor's petition. It was held that the gift over did not operate to deprive him of his interest, as the assignment under bankruptcy was an involuntary act.

Quite apart from the determinable interest which any donor may create in his or her property at common law, it is also lawful either in a will or in a settlement on marriage to provide that any interest given in such will or settlement to a beneficiary shall not pass to the Assignee in bankruptcy or be seized in execution. This restriction on forfeiture or alienation of property applies only where the beneficiary is a child or grandchild of the testator or a husband or wife in a marriage settlement: Property Law Act 1952, s 33.

Where a debtor has entered into a covenant giving the lessor the right to re-enter if he or she should assign a lease, his or her subsequent adjudication, whether on a debtor's petition or not, is regarded as an act done under compulsion. It has been held that only a voluntary assignment gives the lessor the right to re-enter: *In re Riggs, ex parte Lovell* [1901] 2 KB 16. Consequently, the Assignee is entitled to the lessee's interest in the lease which he or she is entitled to disclaim, if he or she thinks fit. If a lease provides that it shall be automatically determined on the bankruptcy of a lessee, the lessee's interest terminates on bankruptcy and the Assignee is bound thereby but subject now to relief against forfeiture under the Property Law Act 1952, s 118, as amended.

If the lease gives a right exercisable at the option of the lessor to cancel a lease on the bankruptcy of the lessee and the lessor exercises this right the Assignee may be entitled to recover some compensation from the lessor, eg an allowance for improvements as provided in the lease.

45.3 AFTER-ACQUIRED PROPERTY

45.3.1 General

Section 42(2)(a) provides that all property belonging to or acquired by or devolving on the bankrupt between the commencement of bankruptcy and discharge passes to the Assignee. A distinction must be made, however, between property which is acquired by the bankrupt during the period of relation back and property acquired in the period between adjudication and discharge. A legal fiction is created under which all property to which the debtor was entitled between the commencement of bankruptcy and his or her adjudication belongs to the Assignee; subject to certain exceptions, the Assignee is entitled to recover any of this property that the debtor disposes of during the period of relation back. The Assignee is also entitled to any real or personal property which the bankrupt acquires between adjudication and discharge, but, if he or she does not interfere and claim it, the bankrupt can give a good title to this property to any one who deals with him or her in good faith and for value: s 49(1)(a). The Assignee can, by application to the Court, recover the proceeds from such dealing by the bankrupt after a reasonable allowance has been made for the maintenance of the bankrupt and his or her family: s 45.

The same section gives the Assignee the right to a Court order requiring the bankrupt to make periodic payments in reduction of his or her debts from money payable to the bankrupt in the future, and an order of this type is not necessarily cancelled on his or her discharge: s 45(2), (3).

45.3.2 Property acquired between adjudication and discharge

Where, after adjudication but before discharge, a person transfers property, or pays money to a bankrupt in respect of an obligation incurred before adjudication, such transferor may be called upon by the Assignee to account to him or her directly for such property or money whether he or she knew of the bankruptcy or not. Of course, if the property or money is still recoverable from the bankrupt himself or herself, the Assignee will not take action against the person making the transfer or payment.

Section 42(2) makes it clear that the Assignee is entitled to any property acquired by the bankrupt between adjudication and discharge. But it is a defeasible right; if the Assignee has not intervened and claimed this property the bankrupt can sell or mortgage it, whether it be real or personal, provided the purchaser or mortgagee is acting in good faith and for value. In fact, s 49(1) refers to "transactions" which may include other dealings besides sales and mortgages and it may well be that such a transaction is in good faith and for value, although the value of the bankrupt's estate is not increased thereby.

There is, however, no validity in the suggestion that the bankrupt is entitled to after-acquired property until the Assignee intervenes and claims it. The bankrupt has a power of disposition which can defeat the Assignee's title, where the Assignee has failed to perfect it by intervention. If there has been no intervention by the Assignee, the bankrupt has power to sue for such property in his or her own name, to confer an unimpeachable title thereto and to create rights thereover in favour of third parties, whether they were aware of the bankruptcy or not. A third party may enter into a transaction with a bankrupt in good faith, despite the fact that he or she knows of the bankruptcy. But he or she must give value to enjoy the protection of s 49(1)(a). A person who does not give value and fails to make inquiry into the bankruptcy may be unable to show good faith: *Re Bennett* [1907] 1 KB 149. A person defending an action by a bankrupt for the recovery of after-acquired property must establish not only the bankruptcy, but also that the Assignee has intervened. The bankrupt also has the right to protect his or her property against wrongdoers.

Lord Greene MR in *Re Pascoe* [1944] Ch 219; [1944] 1 All ER 281, in considering the protection given to third parties dealing with the bankrupt, said at 225 [284]:

> That protection operated in two ways. First, third persons who acquired property in a transaction of the kind described had a good title to it which could not be impugned by the trustee in bankruptcy. Secondly, a party to such a transaction with an undischarged bankrupt could not set up as against the undischarged bankrupt the title of the trustee unless, of course, the trustee had

intervened.In other words, the bankrupt was entitled to deal with his after-acquired property by means of transactions with third persons of the kind specified, and as against him the person with whom he dealt could not dispute his title, but these cases clearly do not establish the proposition that, as between the bankrupt and the trustee, after-acquired property belongs to the bankrupt until the trustee claims it. I can find no support for that proposition.

In *Gough v Fraser* [1977] 1 NZLR 279 (CA) it was held that a bankrupt is competent to sue in respect of after-acquired property unless and until the Assignee intervenes and claims the property. This principle applies whether the bankrupt has received his or her discharge or not.

The bankrupt is required to disclose to the Assignee any property acquired by him or her before discharge: s 60(b). Default in making such disclosure is a summary offence: s 128(1)(a).

In the interests of creditors the Assignee is bound to be vigilant in claiming after-acquired property because if he or she fails to make his or her claim for some time he or she may be obliged to respect the rights of third persons. The right of the Assignee in relation to land subject to the Land Transfer Act acquired by the bankrupt after adjudication is clear. As soon as the Assignee registers a transmission, he or she can deal with it as the registered proprietor thereof. Until the Assignee has intervened and a transmission to him or her has been registered the bankrupt can transfer the property to a bona fide purchaser for value, and the transferee will have a valid title against the Assignee.

If, however, a bankrupt were to mortgage or sell property and dispose of the proceeds before the Assignee had a reasonable opportunity of intervention, this conduct would probably be reported in detail in the Assignee's report which is presented to the Court on the hearing of an application for discharge under s 109(2). The effect of such an unfavourable report might well be the dismissal of the application for discharge or suspension of discharge for a period to mark the disapproval by the Court of the conduct of the bankrupt.

All executions and attachments in good faith completed before intervention by the Assignee against property acquired by or devolving upon the bankrupt between adjudication and discharge for debts incurred by the bankrupt after adjudication are valid against the Assignee: s 49(1)(b).

Assets acquired by an undischarged bankrupt who has started to trade again and who subsequently becomes bankrupt a second time belong to the creditors of the second bankruptcy in preference to those of the first.

45.3.3 Transactions between the bankrupt and third persons

It is clear that persons acting bona fide and for value who enter into transactions (a comprehensive term) with the bankrupt in regard to real or personal property acquired after adjudication are protected provided the Assignee has not already intervened: s 49(1)(a). Also the transaction will be valid whether or not it was known that the bankrupt had been adjudicated bankrupt: *Cohen v Mitchell* (1890) 25 QBD 262. The bankrupt is accordingly entitled to sue on contracts made after adjudication of a contract for personal services entered into before adjudication: *Bailey v*

Thurston and Co Ltd [1903]1 KB 137. Failing prior intervention by the Assignee, he or she can bring an action to recover any property to which he or she becomes entitled after adjudication. He or she can also bring an action for damages for breach after adjudication or to enforce any rights relating to the property.

The Assignee may, through non-intervention after becoming aware of what is taking place, be estopped from his or her denying the right of the bankrupt to deal with property and to give a good title to a third party.

An action for specific performance may be brought by a bankrupt purchaser. If he or she has, from after-acquired funds, the money to pay and the Assignee has not intervened, the contract appears to fall into the category of transactions bona fide and for value relating to after-acquired property. See also *Dyster v Randall and Sons* [1926] Ch 932, 940; [1926] All ER Rep 151, 155.

45.3.4 Transactions between the bankrupt and his banker

The position of bankers who have dealings with undischarged bankrupts in the period between adjudication and discharge is set out in s 49(3), (5).

Consideration must be given to the rights and liabilities of a bank which has met a bankrupt's cheques, both before and after it has ascertained that its customer is a bankrupt, having no reason to believe he or she has been discharged from bankruptcy.

Advertisement of adjudication gives rise to a presumption that a bank is aware of its customer's bankruptcy. Immediately a bank is aware of the bankruptcy of a customer it must inform the Assignee of the existence of the account and make no payments from the account unless, after one month from when the information has been given to the Assignee, no instructions have been received from him or her. The bank is under no duty to give this information if it is satisfied that the account is held on behalf of another person: s 49(5).

Receipt of money or securities or negotiable instruments by a bank from, or by the direction of the bankrupt are deemed to be transactions for value and are accordingly protected. Likewise, any payment or delivery of a security or a negotiable instrument by a bank to, or by the direction of a bankrupt is similarly deemed to be for value and protected: s 49(3). This protection is qualified by the bank's duty to act in accordance with the Assignee's directions referred to in the preceding paragraph.

45.4 PERSONAL EARNINGS OF THE BANKRUPT

Section 42(2)(a) establishes the title of the Assignee to wages and salary whenever earned. Personal earnings are the proceeds of the personal labour of the bankrupt, although such earnings need not be on a daily or weekly basis. Thus commission earned personally by a bankrupt commission agent has been held to be personal earnings: *Affleck v Hammond* [1912] 3 KB 162. But profits from a business, or royalties from the publication of books, or a purely voluntary allowance paid to a bankrupt do not fall under this heading and the whole amount due from these sources passes to the Assignee. It is usual for the Assignee to rely on s 45(1), (2), to secure personal earnings in excess of the amount required to maintain the bankrupt and his or her family. This practice of the Assignee appears to follow from the Australian decision *Federal Commissioner of Taxation v Official Receiver* (1956) 95 CLR 300, which related to a refund of income tax to an employee in respect of an excess of deductions made by the employer and paid to the Commissioner of Taxation. However, the Australian Bankruptcy Act provides in s 101 as follows:

> Subject to this Act, where a bankrupt is in receipt of pay, pension, salary, emoluments, profits, wages, earnings, or income, the trustee shall receive for distribution amongst the creditors so much thereof as the Court, on the application of the trustee, directs.

There is no equivalent provision in the New Zealand legislation.

The position in New Zealand is that s 42 vests all earnings and income (whether arising from personal exertion or otherwise) in the Assignee. *Re Roberts* [1900]1 QB 122, which was followed in New Zealand in *Re Burney, ex parte Official Assignee* [1955] NZLR 1071, established that a bankrupt is entitled to so much of his or her earnings after adjudication as is necessary to maintain the bankrupt and his or her family.

The general practice, is to allow the insolvent to retain all his or her personal earnings. In this way the initiative of the bankrupt to improve his or her financial position is not stifled. The Assignee, if he or she is of the opinion that the bankrupt is receiving more income than is proper, and that a portion of the bankrupt's income ought be diverted toward settlement of the bankrupt's debts, can apply under s 45 to the Court for an order.

Section 45 provides that on an application before the date of a conditional or absolute order of discharge by any creditor or the Assignee, the Court, having regard to the circumstances of the bankruptcy, the bankrupt's conduct, earning power, responsibilities and prospects, and after making a reasonable allowance for the maintenance of the bankrupt and his or her spouse and family, may order the bankrupt to make to the Assignee:

(a) payment of a lump sum, and; or
(b) periodic payments for a period determined by the Court.

To give effect to this the Court may assign or charge not only moneys due to the bankrupt at the time but also moneys payable to him or her in the future: s 45(2). It is necessary to distinguish between a mere expectancy and money due for payment in the future. The former only becomes property of the debtor when it matures into a vested interest. Should an expectancy not vest until after discharge, then the discharged bankrupt takes the property free of the Assignee. The latter payments are property of the debtor which passes to the Assignee. This is a present right to receive money in the future and is an existing vested proprietary interest in that debt. It follows therefore that any expectancy which becomes vested prior to discharge will vest in the Assignee.

Such moneys shall be applied in payment of debts in accordance with the priorities stipulated in s 104.

Although the Court may vary, suspend or cancel any order or remit arrears thereunder, the order is not cancelled merely by reason of the discharge of the bankrupt: s 45(3), (4).

The following decisions clarify the position. In *Re Byrne, ex parte Henry* (1892) 9 Mor 213, it was decided that the Assignee is entitled to personal earnings which are owing to the bankrupt at the time of the commencement of bankruptcy, even though they are not actually paid until after the bankrupt's discharge.

If the earnings are no more than sufficient for the support of the bankrupt and his or her family, the Assignee will not be able to secure any portion of them: *Williams v Chambers* (1847) 10 QB 337. If the earnings are more than sufficient for this purpose the Assignee has a right to claim them: *Re Roberts* [1900]1 QB 122. This power is sparingly used as it is against the policy of bankruptcy law to dissuade a bankrupt from using his or her full earning capacity. Compare *Re Burney, ex parte Official Assignee* [1955] NZLR 1071, 1076; and *Re Te Rangi* [1961] NZLR 942.

Should a bankrupt who has been ordered by the Court to make payments out of his or her earnings in reduction of his or her debts, make default the onus will be on him or her to show the default was not wilful: s 46. The High Court has power to treat disobedience to a Court order as contempt of Court and punishable by fine or imprisonment.

If the Assignee has not already intervened, the bankrupt is entitled to bring an action for his or her personal earnings: *Affeck v Hammond*, supra. However, a bankrupt is not *entitled* to all his or her personal earnings (including refunds of taxation by the Inland Revenue Department which result from an excess of PAYE provisions of the Act).

In *Re Bertrand* [1980] 2 NZLR 72 a debtor was adjudicated bankrupt in October 1973. Between October 1973 and March 1974 he was employed on wages. Income tax was deducted at source and paid to the Inland Revenue Department in accordance with the PAYE provisions of the Income Tax Assessment Act 1957 then in force. Subsequently, and while the bankrupt remained undischarged, it was found that the income tax due by him in the year ended 31 March 1974 had been overpaid by $208.91. The Commissioner of Inland Revenue refused to pay this refund to the Assignee on the ground that s 28(2) of the Income Tax Assessment Act (now s 362(2) of the Income Tax Act 1976) required the Commissioner to make a refund of tax "to the employee". The Court of Appeal held that:

1   A refund of income tax payable to the taxpayer by the Commissioner came within the wide definition of "property" in s 2 of the Insolvency Act 1967 and was thereby subject to s 42(2) of that Act whereby "all property whatsoever and wheresoever situated belonging to or vested in the bankrupt at the commencement of the bankruptcy, or acquired by or devolving upon him or her before his or her discharge" is vested in the Assignee.

2   Section 42 of the Insolvency Act 1967 included earnings from personal exertion and thereby included refunds of income tax deducted at source from such earnings.

3   Section 29(2) of the Income Tax Assessment Act (now s 362(2) of the Income Tax Act was not intended to supersede the general law of bankruptcy. It had nothing to do with the operation of the Insolvency Act 1967.

The Court of Appeal discussed the decision of *Re Gunson* [1965] NZLR 769. This case involved the status of an income tax refund in respect of excess PAYE deductions made by an employer and paid to the Commissioner. Moller J held that the refund of tax had not lost its character as "earnings", and as the Assignee had taken no steps to claim any part of the bankrupt's earnings, the refund should be paid to the bankrupt, not to the Assignee. This decision was distinguished on the ground that the decision of the Judge was based upon concessions of counsel made at the trial.

The Assignee takes the property of the bankrupt "subject to equities". *King v Faraday (Michael) and Partners Ltd* [1939] 2 KB 753; [1939] 2 All ER 478 suggests that a charge given by a debtor before the commencement of bankruptcy over such amount of his or her personal earnings (wages or salary) as are in excess of the requirements of himself and his or her family, is valid against the Assignee. Where, however, a debtor assigned his or her future professional earnings under a deed of arrangement, it was held that his or her subsequent adjudication defeated the title of the trustee under the deed. The Court saw no justification for treating the future professional earnings of a debtor on a different basis from the profits of a business and accordingly held that the trustee in bankruptcy was entitled to them: *In re De Marney* [1943] Ch 126; [1943] 1 All ER 275.

45.5 PROPERTY BELONGING TO OTHERS PASSING TO THE OFFICIAL ASSIGNEE

The bulk of the property passing to the Assignee is the property owned by the bankrupt himself. However, certain property not owned by the bankrupt also passes to the Assignee. This is generally property which has passed from the bankrupt to volunteers (transferees who have given no consideration) or to transferees who have given inadequate consideration and thus received a voidable gift, or to favoured creditors and to those who have had dealings with the bankrupt which amount to fraud in regard to the other creditors. More precisely, the following classes of property belonging to others can pass to the Assignee:

(a) Dispositions of property made by the bankrupt during the period of relation back: s 42.

(b) Property which has passed to another, but which is claimed by the Assignee on the ground that the transaction was a fraudulent conveyance under the Property Law Act 1952, s 60.

(c) Property controlled by the bankrupt but transferred to another person through the exercise of a power of appointment by the bankrupt (s 44), *Re Taylor's Settlement Trusts, Public Trustee v Taylor* [1929] 1 Ch 435; [1929] All ER Rep 367.

(d) Voidable gifts (s 54) of property, mortgages or payments made by the bankrupt falling into the category of voidable preferences: s 56.

(e) Voidable securities: s 57.

(f) Property or the value of improvements thereon paid for by the bankrupt on behalf of another: s 55.

(g) Property of the debtor taken in execution, where the execution has not been completed before adjudication or before notice has been received by the execution creditor of either the filing of a petition in bankruptcy or of the commission of an act of bankruptcy by the debtor: s 50.

Likewise, unless the Court orders to the contrary, where the judgment on which execution was founded exceeds $100, and notice that a bankruptcy petition has been presented against the debtor is served on the sheriff's agent or bailiff in the 14 days following the sale of the debtor's property, the balance of the proceeds after deduction of costs will be paid to the Assignee: s 50(4).

(h) Chattels subject to an unregistered instrument by way of security and which are in the possession or apparent possession of the grantor of the instrument (ie, the person who originally owned the chattels): Chattels Transfer Act 1924, s 18.

(i) Any money or other property belonging to one spouse and lent or entrusted to the other spouse for the purpose of any trade or business will be regarded as part of the latter's estate in the event of bankruptcy: s 43(1), (2). A similar provision applies to inter-spouse loans of money for any purpose, ie whether for business or trade or otherwise.

Similarly, any security or charge given over the property of a bankrupt spouse as security for the money or property lent or advanced by the other spouse for the purpose above is voidable by the Assignee: s 43(3). But the money or property shall not be treated as being part of the bankrupt's estate nor shall the security, unless it has been given for past consideration, be regarded as voidable if the lending or entrusting of the property or the security or charge was given in good faith more than four years before adjudication. See *Re Hale* [1974] 2 NZLR 1.

(j) Property which has been disclaimed by a beneficiary about to become bankrupt.

Section 82 of the Administration Act 1969 provides that for the purposes of the Insolvency Act and the consequential protection of creditors, any beneficiary who disclaims property to which he or she would have been entitled either under a will or in the intestacy of a deceased person will be deemed to have accepted the disclaimed interest.

If the disclaimed interest has by reason of the disclaimer passed to other persons, such other persons will be deemed to have had the disclaimed interest transferred to them by the original beneficiary.

These provisions enable the Assignee in certain instances to recover property to which a bankrupt beneficiary would have been entitled but for the disclaimer.

The same section exempts the administrator from liability if he or she distributes the disclaimed interest to those entitled in consequence of the disclaimer of the beneficiary provided that the administrator had no reason to believe that the disclaiming successor was about to become bankrupt or was in fact bankrupt, or that the disclaimer was void or about to become voidable. Again no action lies against the administrator for having failed to inquire whether such successor was about to become bankrupt.

(k) Goods on hire purchase can be treated as if they belonged to the bankrupt purchaser in certain circumstances: s 91, as amended by the Hire Purchase Act 1971, s 54.

45.6 PROPERTY WHICH DOES NOT PASS TO THE ASSIGNEE

Certain property belonging to the bankrupt does not pass to the Assignee. In some cases, there is a provision in the Insolvency Act itself to this effect; in other cases the protection is derived from another statute or the common law.

45.6.1 The Insolvency Act 1967

By virtue of the Insolvency Act the following property does not pass to the Assignee:

(a) Property held by the bankrupt in trust for another person: s 42(3). Only property in which the bankrupt has a beneficial interest is available for his or her creditors. Where, however, a bankrupt holds property in trust and also has a beneficial interest therein, the legal estate vests in the Assignee subject to the trust: *St Thomas' Hospital v Richardson* [1910]1 KB 271.

Creation of a trust by a debtor in the shadow of impending bankruptcy may be calculated to defeat creditors and be avoided by the Assignee as a voidable gift: ss 54, 58.

(b) An execution creditor who has completed his or her execution or attachment before adjudication or before notice of the filing of a petition or of the commission of an act of bankruptcy can retain the proceeds against the Assignee: s 50(1), (2).

(c) Payments to creditors, transfers and assignments by the debtor for valuable consideration and contracts or other transactions for valuable consideration are not invalidated even if they took place between the time of commencement of bankruptcy and the date of adjudication, but the person dealing with the debtor must prove that he or she acted in good faith and that at the time of the transaction he or she had no notice of any act of bankruptcy committed by the debtor: s 47(1). Persons acquiring a property interest from people who have acquired such property from the bankrupt obtain even greater protection: s 47(1)(c).

(d) Property, real or personal, acquired by the bankrupt between adjudication and discharge and disposed of by the bankrupt before intervention by the Assignee to someone acting in good faith and for valuable consideration: s 49(1)(a).

(e) Property acquired by the bankrupt between adjudication and discharge whereon execution has been levied in good faith in respect of debts incurred by the bankrupt after adjudication and before intervention by the Assignee: s 49(1)(b).

(f) The bankrupt, on adjudication, has the right to retain tools of trade to the value of $100, and household furniture and personal effects to the value of $300: s 52(1).

(g) The Assignee, with the consent of creditors expressed by resolution, may make an allowance of money out of the bankrupt's property to the bankrupt or a member of his or her family for the support of the bankrupt and his or her family. Apart from this, the Assignee may allow him or her to retain at the time of adjudication up to $40 in his or her possession or in a bank account for the maintenance of himself or herself and his or her family: s 53.

(h) Property may be disclaimed and contracts may be terminated by the Assignee: ss 75, 76, 78, 79.

45.6.2 Other statutory provisions

The following statutory provisions are relevant:

(a) Certain policies of life insurance held by a person who died or was adjudicated bankrupt before 1st April 1986 cannot be seized by the Assignee. Life Insurance Act 1908, ss 65 and 66 repealed by Insurance Law Reform Act 1985, s 4 as from that date.

(b) The Matrimonial Property Act 1976 is designed to recognise the equal contribution of husband and wife to the marriage partnership and, to provide for a just division of the matrimonial property (s 8) including farm homesteads, between spouses on separation, dissolution of the marriage or in the event of one spouse being adjudicated bankrupt. Basically his or her Act provides for the equal sharing (s 11) of matrimonial property which comprises primarily the matrimonial home and family chattels (including the family car) (s 2).

If one spouse is adjudicated bankrupt creditors having a security over any of the matrimonial property are not prejudiced (s 46). The spouse of the bankrupt has a protected interest to the extent of $10,000 or one half of the equity (after deduction of any mortgage) in the matrimonial home, or the sum of $10,000), whichever is the lesser in value: s 20(2)(b).

The Joint Family Homes Act 1964 makes provision for dwelling houses, town houses or flats occupied by a husband or wife to be registered as joint family homes. If either spouse becomes bankrupt, no order for mortgage or sale will be made if the net value of the property is not in excess of $10,000 plus the amount of any mortgage, lien or other charge to which the property is subject: ss 16, 17, 20.

(c) The Estate and Gift Duties Amendment Act 1976 which has allowed automatic estate duty exemption for the matrimonial home and the protection given to the spouse of the bankrupt by the Matrimonial Property Act 1976 has made the Joint Family Homes Act 1964 of little consequence.

Registration of the property as a joint family home does not affect the interest of any person holding a mortgage, or a charge or a lien over it under the Wages Protection and Contractors' Liens Act 1939.

Only a Registrar of the Maori Land Court may make an order vesting in the Assignee the beneficial freehold interest of the bankrupt in Maori freehold land owned by him or her in severality or owned jointly with others. The Assignee has no power to disclaim any interest vested in him or her by such an order: Maori Affairs Act 1953, s 445   (1)(4).

(d) Social Welfare benefits, Government Superannuation, War Pensions and pensions under the National Provident Fund Act 1950 and its amendments.

The Assignee is not entitled to superannuation contributions repaid with accrued interest to the contributor: *Re Duckett, ex parte Minister of Education v McLeod* [1964] Ch 398; [1964] 1 All ER 19 CA.

(e) Friendly Society benefits; Friendly Societies Act 1909, s 99.

(f) Purely personal rights of action, eg an action for defamation, Defamation Act 1954.

(g) Compensation for injury and death caused by an accident.

Section 89 of the Accident Compensation Act 1982 states that any compensation moneys for accident or death held by the Accident Compensation Commission are not assignable and also that compensation for non-economic loss related to physical injury and lump sums payable on account of injury through accident are not assets in the estate of a bankrupt entitled thereto.

(h) Any tax deductions made by an employer shall be held in trust for the Crown and shall not pass to the Assignee as part of a bankrupt employer's estate: Income Tax Act 1976 s 365(1).

45.6.3 Under common law

(a) The Assignee takes the bankrupt's property "subject to equities." His or her title is no better or no worse than that of the bankrupt. Thus, if a bankrupt purchaser has taken delivery of goods on credit, the Assignee is not bound to return them, but if the sale and delivery arose through fraud of the bankrupt, then the vendor can rescind the contract and recover his or her goods: *Tilley v Bowman Ltd* [1910] 1 KB 745. The Assignee takes the bankrupt's property subject to all charges and liabilities which affect it when his or her title arises, whether he or she has notice of such charges and liabilities or not. The ordinary rule, where there is conflict between the claims of the various assignees and encumbrances, is that the one who first gives notice to the person liable obtains priority, unless he or she was aware of the earlier interest. But the Assignee cannot, merely by giving notice before the mortgagee or assignee, obtain priority over a good equitable mortgage or assignment of a chose in action given for valuable consideration before the commencement of bankruptcy: *In re Wallis, ex parte Jenks* [1902] 1 KB 719. Notice is not necessary to establish the Assignee's title to any property or rights belonging to the bankrupt at the time of the commencement of bankruptcy or which becomes his or hers between the commencement of bankruptcy and adjudication.

An equitable assignment of a debt, future personal earnings or profits of a business which accrue before the commencement of bankruptcy but are payable after that time is valid against the Assignee. If the debt or earnings are not due or the profits have not been determined before the commencement of bankruptcy, the assignment is not good against the Assignee: *Official Assignee of Bredow v Newton King Ltd* [1926] NZLR 198; [1925] GLR 172.

Claims by the bankrupt, statute-barred under the Limitation Act 1950, cannot be enforced by the Assignee.

(b) Property subject to the rule in *Ex parte James* does not pass to the Assignee. See the discussion of the rule at 44.7 ante.

(c) Interests determinable on bankruptcy do not pass to the Assignee, nor do mere possibilities or expectancies of property which are not realised before discharge; see supra. But any device by the debtor to defeat the laws of bankruptcy, such as providing for the alienation of some of his or her property to a third person, if he or she should be adjudicated bankrupt will be held to be void. In this connection we have already referred to s 44, which states that a bankrupt shall not exercise, either before or after his or her discharge, any power of appointment or any other power vested in him or her to defeat any contingent or other interest to which, in default of exercising this power, he or she would have been beneficially entitled at any time before his or her discharge: 42.2 supra.

(d) Legal aid granted to a debtor before adjudication to enable him or her to bring an action may be withdrawn when he or she is adjudicated: Legal Aid Act 1969, s 24(1)(c).

(e) Where a vendor has sold goods on credit but has not delivered them to the bankrupt, the Assignee cannot claim delivery without paying the full purchase price; similarly, where credit has been allowed on a contract for delivery by instalments, the vendor is not bound to continue delivery to the Assignee until the goods already delivered as well as the goods to be delivered in the future have been paid for in full: *Ex parte Chalmers, Re Edwards* (1873) LR 8 Ch 289.

45.7 DISCLAIMER OF ONEROUS PROPERTY

45.7.1 General

It has already been explained that the Assignee takes over the bankrupt's property subject to all its liabilities. Included in the property vested in the Assignee there may be shares with a liability for calls, unprofitable contracts, property unsaleable or not readily saleable because it binds the possessor to make certain payments, leases of land subject to onerous covenants, etc. The policy of bankruptcy law is to reduce the bankrupt's estate to a net balance and divide it among the creditors. The Assignee is liable personally, in so far as the bankrupt's estate is insufficient, to meet the liabilities in connection with the property vested in him. The intention of s 75, which permits disclaimer by the Assignee, is to relieve him or her from liability in respect of onerous obligations of the bankrupt and to do so with as little disturbance as possible to the rights of third persons.

The Assignee may abandon property of a bankrupt as worthless: *Re Butler-Harrison* [1959] NZLR 427. Disclaimer must not be confused with abandonment. Liabilities connected with the property are not released by abandonment, but the Assignee has no rights against the abandoned property thereafter. But with disclaimer the bankrupt and his or her estate are freed from any further liability in respect of the property on discharge. The only remedy for a person injured by disclaimer is to prove in the bankruptcy.

Section 75 sets out the procedure for selling unsaleable or not readily saleable property acquired before or after adjudication, with the exception of shares, and the effect of disclaimer in detail. Although the Assignee may have tried to sell or may have taken possession of or exercised rights of ownership in respect of the bankrupt's property, he or she may, within twelve months after adjudication or within the time as extended by the Court, disclaim in writing such onerous property. The power of disclaimer extends to property acquired by the bankrupt after adjudication: s 75(1). The disclaimer must be signed by the Assignee personally and filed in the Court: Reg 43, Form 10. If the Assignee is unaware of the property after the lapse of one month from adjudication, the twelve months will run from the time he or she becomes aware of it: s 75 (1). If the Assignee does not disclaim immediately he or she may be liable for voluntary waste committed by him: *Re Wharfe* [1981] 2 NZLR 700.

Any person interested in the property may apply to the Assignee in writing, requiring him or her to decide within 28 days of receiving such notice, whether he or she will disclaim the property or not. Failing disclaimer within the 28 days or within the extended time allowed by the Court, the Assignee loses his or her right to disclaim: s 75(3).

The Court may vest the property disclaimed in any person interested in it on application by such person or the Assignee, eg, in a sub-lessee where the lessee goes bankrupt. The Court may vest the property by way of compensation in some person who had some liability in respect of the disclaimed property which was not discharged by the disclaimer. The property may even be vested in the bankrupt and he or she can retain it against the Assignee. On such vesting order being made no transfer or assignment is necessary. But the rights of any under-lessee, sub-tenant or mortgagee are not prejudiced by such order; s 75(4), (5).

45.7.2 Effects of a disclaimer

(a) The personal liability of the bankrupt in the disclaimed property ceases as from the date of disclaimer. If shares are disclaimed, the Assignee ceases to be a member of the company as from the date the shares vested in him or her. As long as the Assignee is not placed on the register of shareholders, he or she incurs no liability and disclaimer is unnecessary: s 78.

(b) The liabilities of the bankrupt's estate are determined as from the date of the disclaimer.

(c) The personal liability of the Assignee in respect of the disclaimed property is discharged as from the time such property vested in him or her.

(d) Except as provided in (a), (b) and (c) above, the disclaimer shall not affect the rights and liabilities of lessors and other third parties: s 75 (2),

Any person suffering loss is entitled to prove for it in the same way as if it were an ordinary debt: s 75(9).

Consideration will now be given to the effect of disclaimer of leases.

45.7.3 Disclaimer of leases

(a) The Court has power to vest disclaimed property in any person whom the Court thinks fit: s 75(4). If a registered lessee has mortgaged his or her lease and is now bankrupt, the Registrar shall, if the Assignee disclaims the lease, vest the lease in the mortgagee upon written application by him: Land Transfer Act 1952, ss 125, 126. If, for example, no one is willing to take the property, the Court may vest it in the reversioner (the owner of the property subject to the lease). The reversioner is not entitled to be reimbursed out of the bankrupt estate for the costs of an order vesting the property in him or her. It is the practice of the Land Registry Office to register disclaimers which are treated as transmissions.

(b) It may be that the sub-lessee applies to the Court for the disclaimed land to be vested in him or her. If the Court grants the applicant it will vest the property in the applicant on the same terms and subject to the same liabilities and obligations as the bankrupt was subject to under the lease at the date of adjudication: s 75(7).

(c) Section 75(4) empowers the Court to vest the property in the bankrupt, who can hold the property despite any subsequent claim by the Assignee.

(d) At the same time as the Court makes a vesting order with regard to disclaimed leasehold property it may make such order as it considers just with regard to fixtures, tenant's improvements, etc (generally matters where the tenant was entitled to compensation on termination of a lease): s 75(6).

(e) Where, following disclaimer, land subject to a rent charge is vested in the Crown or some other person, neither the Crown nor such other person shall be held liable for any rent due up to the date on which possession was taken under the vesting order. The person taking possession under a vesting order is naturally liable for rent falling due after he or she has taken possession: s 79.

(f) On disclaimer of a lease, the lessor is entitled to prove for the present value of the difference between the future letting value of the premises and the rent to be paid under the lease: *Ex parte Inglis In re Paulin* (1886) NZLR 4 SC 338.

(g) On disclaimer, a surety for the rent is discharged: *Stacey v Hill* [1901] 1 QB 660.

(h) The lessor cannot prove for the cost of revesting the property in him or her, but apart from the special provisions of ss 75 and 77, his or her rights and powers shall not be prejudiced.

Sometimes, after the formal disclaimer of a lease, the Assignee may wish to keep the bankrupt's assets or to carry on the bankrupt's business temporarily in the premises held under the disclaimed lease. In these circumstances, it appears to have become customary to pay the original rental in full for this period, defining it as "use and occupation" rental. Some authority for this procedure may be implied in the power to carry on the bankrupt's business: s 71(g).

45.8 ASSIGNEE'S DUTIES WHERE LAND IS SUBJECT TO A MORTGAGE

Section 80 defines the duties and rights of the Assignee, the mortgagee and the bankrupt in relation to land subject to mortgage or a charge.

The Assignee shall either:

(a) disclaim the bankrupt's equity of redemption in the mortgaged land; or

(b) register a transmission of the land under the Land Transfer Act 1952. This will be the usual procedure, and the Assignee will then be the registered proprietor of the land subject to the mortgage or charge; or

(c) give notice to the mortgagee or chargee that he or she does not intend to register transmission or cannot register a transmission.

The Assignee may decide neither to disclaim nor to register a transmission but just let the bankrupt continue in possession. The bankrupt would then have to meet current outgoings from personal earnings or money devolving upon him or her after adjudication. But the bankrupt would know where he or she stood, particularly if he or she improved the land. Section 80(3) provides:

. . . if the bankrupt is in possession of the interest in the land at the time of the adjudication and remains in possession thereof until his discharge from the bankruptcy, then, as from his discharge, the Assignee shall not be entitled to claim the interest in the land unless he obtains the consent of the Court. The Court may give or refuse to give consent having regard to the good faith of the bankrupt, the length of time from the date of adjudication, the value of the improvements made by the bankrupt, and all other relevant matters.

It will be seen later that usually it is only where there is annulment of adjudication that any property remaining in the hands of the Assignee revests in the debtor, for the discharge of a bankrupt does not terminate the right of the Assignee to property in the bankrupt estate.

Where the Assignee does not register transmission, and whether or not notice is given as in (c) above that the Assignee is not registering a transmission and the mortgagee or chargee enters into possession or sells, he or she is liable to account to the Assignee as if he or she were the registered proprietor of the land.

Chapter 46

THE EFFECT OF BANKRUPTCY ON ANTECEDENT TRANSACTIONS

SUMMARY

46.1 INTRODUCTION
46.2 THE DOCTRINE OF RELATION BACK
46.3 VOIDABLE DISPOSITIONS AND PAYMENTS BY THE BANKRUPT

46.1 INTRODUCTION

46.1.1 Antecedent transactions in bankruptcy

In the shadow of his or her impending bankruptcy, a debtor may take steps to safeguard his or her financial interests at the expense of the creditors. Generally, he or she will be the first to be aware of his or her unsound financial position and, being forewarned, may attempt to conceal property or deal with it in such a way as to prevent his or her creditors receiving the benefit from it. Again, he or she may forget that a debtor must be just before he or she is generous and give property away or sell it to his or her friends for inadequate consideration. Sometimes, he or she may feel that, because certain creditors have treated him or her favourably, they should be paid in full although this preference results in the other creditors receiving proportionately less than they would otherwise have received.

On the other hand, some creditors may recognise the debtor's financial weakness before the others, and may seize the debtor's goods under a writ of execution or bring pressure upon the debtor to give him or her a security or to make payment in full under the implied threat that, if he or she does not do so, he or she will be forced into bankruptcy with all its detrimental publicity.

For these reasons adjudication in bankruptcy takes effect retrospectively. To begin with, when we refer to bankruptcy, we are not referring merely to the period between adjudication and discharge, but also to the period running from the commencement of bankruptcy. Furthermore, the status of bankruptcy has far-reaching effects, extending well before the commencement of bankruptcy. Those who have received gifts from the debtor several years before his or her adjudication may find that they have to return to the Assignee the property that they had taken in good faith.

These principal transactions caught by the claw back provisions are:

(a) those covered by the doctrine of relation back: s 42, as modified by ss 47, 48 and 51;
(b) voidable gifts: s 54;
(c) improvements made by the bankrupt to the property of another: s 55;
(d) voidable preferences: s 56;
(e) loans by wife to husband and by husband to wife: s 43;
(f) securities for past advances: ss 43(3), 57.

In addition, the following two topics must be considered under the heading of antecedent transactions in bankruptcy:

(a) the rights of execution creditors against the Assignee: ss 27(3), 50, particularly in the period of relation back;
(b) fraudulent conveyances under the Property Law Act 1952, s 60.

46.1.2 Transactions before and after adjudication

Three periods have to be considered. The first period is that preceding the commencement of bankruptcy. Voluntary transactions by the debtor during this time may be avoided by the operation of the Property Law Act 1952, ss 60-61. Any alienation of property with intent to defraud creditors is voidable. Accordingly, the alienation of property is good until it is actually avoided; hence, prior to avoidance, the person who has acquired title from the debtor can give a good title to a purchaser for value who has no notice of the fraud.

Voluntary settlements of property in the five years preceding adjudication, gifts and transfers of property for inadequate consideration, not made in consideration of marriage for the benefit of the settlor's spouse or children, are, subject to s 54, voidable at the Assignee's option. The value of improvements made and sums paid for the purchase of land or other property within the two years preceding adjudication by the bankrupt on behalf of someone else are recoverable by the Assignee: s 55.

The second period is the period of relation back. This period extends from the first available act of bankruptcy to the date of adjudication. The debtor has very limited powers to deal with his or her property other than the personal earnings to which he or she becomes entitled during this period.

The third period is that between adjudication and discharge. For valuable consideration the bankrupt can confer rights over or deal with real or personal property acquired during this period if the Assignee has not intervened and claimed it.

But the Court will prevent a creditor obtaining preference over other creditors by completing his or her execution after adjudication or where a deceased debtor's estate is insolvent: *George Lee and Sons Ltd v Olink* [1972] 1 WLR 214.

46.2 THE DOCTRINE OF RELATION BACK

46.2.1 General

The effect of the doctrine of relation back contained in s 42 is to make bankruptcy commence at a time earlier than adjudication. The doctrine entitles the Assignee to claim certain property formerly belonging to the bankrupt, but disposed of by him or her prior to adjudication. The doctrine is intended to protect creditors from loss resulting from the debtor having improperly dealt with his or her assets in the period immediately preceding adjudication. It also prevents a creditor who has forced the debtor to pay him or her in full during that period from retaining that advantage. It provides protection against an insolvent tradesman who, in order to defeat his or her creditors, has formed a company to take over his or her business and its assets. It is a recognition of the principle that the creditors are entitled to an equitable distribution of assets. It also gives the Assignee the power to make a thorough investigation of the debtor's transactions which took place before adjudication. The central feature of the doctrine of relation back is the predating of the Official Assignee's title to the debtor's estate to the commencement of bankruptcy.

46.2.2 The commencement of bankruptcy

Section 42(4) determines the time of the commencement of bankruptcy as follows:

(a) If a creditor's petition has been filed, bankruptcy relates back to and commences at the time of the act of bankruptcy on which the order of adjudication is made, or if the bankrupt is proved to have committed more acts of bankruptcy than one, the bankruptcy shall relate back to and commence at the time of the first of the acts of bankruptcy proved to have been committed in the three months immediately preceding the filing of such petition.

Bankruptcy shall not relate back to any act of bankruptcy prior to that alleged in the petition unless at the time of committing the prior act of bankruptcy the debtor owed some creditor or creditors not less than $200.

(b) If adjudication takes place on a debtor's petition and no creditor's petition has been filed, bankruptcy commences when the debtor's petition is filed, but if the debtor has committed an act or acts of bankruptcy, then bankruptcy commences at the time of the first act of bankruptcy committed by him or her in the three months preceding the filing of his or her own petition.

The period between the filing of the petition and the preceding available act of bankruptcy is known as the period of "relation back".

As one or two months usually elapses between the filing of the creditor's petition and adjudication, relation back may extend for some four or five months before adjudication: Re Quartley (1910) 30 NZLR 270; 13 GLR 331.

46.2.3 The effect of relation back

Under the doctrine of relation back, the Assignee's title to the debtor's estate arises not as from adjudication but from the commencement of bankruptcy. The effect of adjudication is retrospective; this gives rise to difficulties. If a debtor deals with his or her property after committing an act of bankruptcy, the validity of the transaction depends upon whether he or she is subsequently adjudicated bankrupt. Not only does adjudication divest the bankrupt of his or her title to property owned by him or her at the date of adjudication, but it also brings into effect the absolute statutory assignment of the bankrupt's property to the Assignee provided for in the relation back section of the Act (s 42) and allows the Assignee to treat any transactions with the bankrupt's property during this period as transactions with property to which he or she had no title. If, during this period, he or she transfers or mortgages his or her assets, he or she is theoretically transferring or mortgaging the Assignee's property. A mortgagee or transferee of land gets no protection from registration under the Land Transfer Act 1952, but the doctrine of relation back will not overrule the Joint Family Homes Act 1964 which prevents certain property from passing to the Assignee: s 42(5). Unless the transferee or mortgagee can bring himself or herself within the protection of s 47, the transaction will be void. The debtor cannot pay money he or she owes; in theory it is the Assignee's money he or she is paying. It has been said that a debtor who has committed an available act of bankruptcy is a "a financial leper" for the following three months; those who deal with him or her in that period may suffer if a petition in bankruptcy is presented against him or her.

In *Re Pollitt, Ex parte Minor* [1893] 1 QB 455, a debtor's solicitor refused to act for him unless he was paid £ 30 for future costs. The solicitor then prepared a deed of assignment in favour of creditors which was executed by the debtor. Lord Esher MR allowed the solicitor to retain £ 6 for work done prior to the execution of the assignment, but ordered the remaining £ 24 to be paid to the trustee in bankruptcy. In the course of his judgment, he said, at 457:

> . . . the deed of assignment which had been prepared by the solicitor was executed by the debtor; its execution was an act of bankruptcy, and the solicitor knew that it was. The title of the trustee in the subsequent bankruptcy related back to that act of bankruptcy. What does that mean? The result of the relation back is that all subsequent dealings with the debtor's property must be treated as if the bankruptcy had taken place at the moment when the act of bankruptcy was committed. The debtor must be considered as having become a bankrupt the moment the deed was executed. Then, he being a bankrupt, all the money which he then had, and all the money which was owing to him, passed to the trustee in the bankruptcy for the purpose of being distributed by him amongst the bankrupt's creditors.

An accountant or solicitor who has been requested to act for a debtor, who is known to have committed an act of bankruptcy, may be in some doubt as to whether he or she will receive payment in full, a fractional payment, or nothing at all for his or her services. It appears that the Court has a wide discretion in the matter, but generally professional costs incurred by the bankrupt during the period of relation back will not be allowed unless the Court considers that the professional services rendered were of substantial benefit to the creditors. No person can claim a lien and withhold the bankrupt's books of account and other documents relating to the business of the bankrupt. However, any person (other than the spouse of the bankrupt) to whom money is owing for services performed in connection with such books and documents and who otherwise would have had a lien on those books and documents is entitled to prove as a preferential creditor in the fourth priority for fees not exceeding $100: s 73. The right of retention of funds in a solicitor's hands and also his or her right of set off against such funds and the question of proving for costs incurred by the debtor in the period immediately preceding adjudication were considered in *Re British Folding Bed Co* [1948] Ch 635; [1948] 2 All ER 216.

46.2.4 Transactions protected against the doctrine

(a) LOCAL BODIES
Section 3(1) provides that nothing in the Act shall affect the right of any local authority to recover rates or to enforce any judgment for rates by selling or leasing the land on which the rates are payable.

(b) EXECUTION CREDITORS
The right of an execution creditor, who has completed his or her execution or attachment during the period of relation back, to retain the proceeds thereof is discussed at 43.2.6, infra.

(c) PURCHASERS FROM A BAILIFF OR SHERIFF
Seizure and sale under a writ of execution constitutes an act of bankruptcy of which the purchaser necessarily has notice. If, however, the purchaser is acting in good faith, he or she acquires a good title to the goods so sold: s 50(7).

(d) LANDLORD DISTRAINING FOR RENT
If a landlord has levied distress for unpaid rent prior to the advertisement of the tenant's adjudication he or she may proceed with the distress and recover the rent owing: s 50(5).

(e) STATUTORY PROTECTION AGAINST THE DOCTRINE
Section 42(5) states:

> Nothing in the Land Transfer Act 1952 shall restrict the operation of this section and nothing in this section shall affect the operation of any other enactment or rule of law which prevents any property from passing to the Assignee.

Thus the Joint Family Homes Act 1964 may prevent a house registered under this Act from passing to the Assignee. See infra.

On the other hand, the Hire Purchase Act 1971 facilitates the acquisition by the Assignee of goods in the possession of a bankrupt purchaser. See supra.

The Insolvency Act makes substantial qualifications to the Assignee's rights to upset transactions entered into during the period of relation back. These transactions are:

(i) Bona fide payments or dispositions by the bankrupt for valuable consideration: s 47, infra.
(ii) Bona fide payments or delivery of property to the bankrupt: s 48 infra;
(iii) Payments made by execution debtors and completed executions and attachments: s 50;
(iv) Voidable gifts and settlements: s 54;
(v) Improvements made by the bankrupt on the property of others more than two years before his or her adjudication: s 50;
(vi) Voidable securities: s 57;

(f) ASSIGNEES OF CERTAIN PAYMENTS FROM DAIRY FACTORIES AND MILK SUPPLY AUTHORITIES: s 51

46.2.5 Persons dealing with the bankrupt during the period of relation back

Section 47 protects any payment by the bankrupt to any of his or her creditors, any disposition by the bankrupt for valuable consideration, or any disposition of property for valuable consideration provided that person had:

(i) no notice of any available act of bankruptcy; and
(ii) otherwise acted in good faith; and,
(iii) the payment, disposition, contract, dealing or transaction took place before adjudication.

Section 47(1)(c) also states that the Assignee cannot invalidate:

(c) Any deposition of property made for valuable consideration by –
   (i) A person who became entitled to the property under a disposition made by the bankrupt, or
   (ii) A person who became entitled, whether before or after the adjudication of the bankrupt, to the property through a person to whom subparagraph (i) of this paragraph applies.

The object of these provisions is to provide protection for persons who have acquired property which originally belonged to the bankrupt. For example, let us assume that in the period of relation back B (who later was adjudged bankrupt) gave a boat (worth $500) to C, who was unaware that B had committed an act of bankruptcy and was insolvent. C then gives the boat to his or her brother D, who has never heard of B. D sells the boat to E for $500.

E gets a good title to the boat because he has acquired the boat for valuable consideration *through* a person to whom para 1(c) applies. Anyone subsequently acquiring the boat, whether by way of gift or otherwise, also gets a good title. If the boat had remained in the hands of C, the Assignee could have recovered it, as no valuable consideration had passed from him to B for the boat: ss 47(1), 58(2)(a), (b). If the boat had remained in the hands of D he could not have retained it against the Assignee, as although he had acquired it from "a person who became entitled to the property under a disposition made by the bankrupt" the disposition was not for valuable consideration.

In the circumstances above it appears that the Assignee could recover from D the amount paid by E to D. The gift of the boat from B to C was a voidable gift: s 54. Section 58(2)(a) empowers the Court to recover the value of property acquired by a person otherwise than for valuable consideration from a person who became entitled to the property through a voidable gift by the bankrupt.

The protection given to these transactions is subject to compliance with the following conditions:

(1) The person (other than the bankrupt) with whom the first transaction was entered into had not at that time notice of any available act of bankruptcy committed before that time. If a person claiming the protection of s 47 has been put "on inquiry" and wilfully abstains from finding out whether such an act has been committed, he or she is subject to all the consequences of the doctrine of relation back. He or she cannot plead that he or she did not make the logical inference from the facts any more than he or she could escape the consequences of formal notice of an act of bankruptcy by alleging that he or she had not read the notice: *Ex parte Snowball, Re Douglas* (1872) LR 7 Ch App 534. In a similar position are those who knew that the debtor had done a certain act but were unaware that it was an available act of bankruptcy. The law proceeds on the basis that ignorance of the law is no excuse. This condition does not apply to the sub-purchaser mentioned in s 47(1)(c)(ii) above, in so much as he or she may become entitled after adjudication and still be within the protection of s 47.

(2) Such person otherwise acts in good faith.

(3) The transaction took place before adjudication: s 47(1).

In *Re Richardson, Official Assignee v Totalizator Agency Board* [1959] NZLR 481, the Assignee brought an action to recover from the TAB $3,600 invested with it by the debtor and $3,000 paid to her by way of dividends during the period of relation back. It was conceded that the TAB was unaware that the debtor had committed an act of bankruptcy or that a petition had been filed for adjudication in bankruptcy.

The Court took the view that "the totalizator, though not actually banned, is certainly not blessed" and was "an instrument for betting and gambling", and held that ss 69 and 70 of the Gaming Act 1908 made the $3,600 paid for wagering irrecoverable. As the payments by way of dividend were made without knowledge of an act of bankruptcy in good faith, they were irrecoverable by virtue of s 82(b) (now s 47).

Apart from that, s 82A (now s 48) made the payments to the debtor irrecoverable as they were made before adjudication in the ordinary course of business by the TAB, which had no knowledge of the presentation of a petition in bankruptcy.

The question of payments and transfers of property made by and to the debtor is one of practical importance. A creditor acting in good faith who is unaware that the insolvent, making payment to him or her, has committed an act of bankruptcy is entitled to retain payment: s 47(1). It has already been pointed out that any transfer of property or dealing therewith for consideration by a bankrupt is valid if the other party to the transaction acts in good faith and is unaware of the commission of an act of bankruptcy by the bankrupt: s 47. However, property transferred or money paid to a person in the period of relation back who is aware of the commission of an act of bankruptcy may be recovered by the Assignee should adjudication take place subsequently.

Section 48 refers exclusively to payments or deliveries of property to or to the order of a person who has been or subsequently is adjudged bankrupt or to the order of the assignee of such a person. The receipt of such a person or his or her assignee is a sufficient discharge to the person so paying or delivering property, provided the payment or delivery was made before the advertisement of adjudication. This qualification gives rise to the possibility that the transaction may take place after adjudication and accords with the earlier part of the section which refers to a person 'who has been . . . adjudged bankrupt".

However, before such payment or delivery can be treated as a good discharge for the person making it, he or she must satisfy the Court:

(a) That he or she had no knowledge of the adjudication, whether it has been advertised or not, or the presentation of a petition; and

(b) That the payment or delivery was made either in the ordinary course of business or otherwise in good faith.

If a debtor should pay a secured creditor, the latter, if he or she is unaware that a petition for the bankruptcy of the debtor has been filed, may hand back the securities to the debtor. It appears that this is in order whether the secured creditor knew that the debtor had committed an act of bankruptcy or not: s 48.

A person owing money to the debtor may feel it incumbent on him or her to pay what he or she owes. If a person so paying knows that a petition in bankruptcy has been filed for the adjudication of the debtor, he or she cannot pay him or her without running the risk of having to pay a second time on demand by the Assignee in the exercise of his or her powers under relation back. Prima facie, the right to collect any moneys falling due in the period of relation back is vested in the Assignee. If the debtor demands payment or sues for payment of a debt to him, and the person who owes the money knows that a petition in bankruptcy has been filed, he or she should state that he or she will pay the money into Court. The Court will retain it until the person entitled to it is determined, and if the debtor persists in bringing an action, the person who has paid the money into Court will generally be allowed costs.

It seems clear that s 48 makes the refusal of direct payment to the debtor justifiable only if the person who owes the money knows that the debtor has had a petition in bankruptcy filed against him. The person who has property of the debtor or owes money to him or her could deliver the property or pay even if he or she is aware of the commission of an act of bankruptcy by the debtor: s 48. The debtor's receipt will be a valid discharge of the obligation.

An assignment to a trustee for the benefit of creditors is an act of bankruptcy. If no petition has been filed against the debtor, moneys due to him or her may be paid to the trustee of the assignment, but the trustee cannot safely pay out these moneys, or any other funds, for that matter, to creditors until three months have elapsed after the execution of the assignment.

It is submitted that ss 47 and 48 are mutually exclusive, as a payment or delivery to a bankrupt can be validly made by a person who has had notice of the commission of an act of bankruptcy by the bankrupt, provided the person so delivering or paying has taken reasonable steps to make sure that no petition in bankruptcy has been filed.

Section 48 clarifies the position of people who have made payments or delivered property to the bankrupt or in accordance with his or her directions. Section 47 restricts the powers of the Assignee to upset "dispositions" of property made by the bankrupt and contracts and other transactions entered into with him or her during the period of relation back. Three elements must all be present in the latter transaction – the provision of valuable consideration coupled with good faith on the part of the person dealing with the bankrupt and a lack of knowledge of the commission of an act of bankruptcy. Thus any creditor acting in good faith who has no notice of an available act of bankruptcy may retain any payment made to him or her by the bankrupt during the period of relation back, provided it cannot be set aside as a voidable preference: s 56.

A transaction which is in fact an act of bankruptcy may be protected by s 47, provided the person claiming protection has given value and acted innocently, ie he or she must neither have known nor have had reason to suspect that the transaction was an act of bankruptcy: *Shears v Goddard* [1896] 1 QB 406.

Likewise, creditors who, before adjudication, receive payment from a trustee under a composition are protected by s 47 if they are acting in good faith and are unaware that the payment under the composition is a fraud on the creditors who are not a party to it: *Re Cochrane* [1925] NZLR 15; [1924] GLR 554. A creditor who takes an assignment of substantially the whole of a debtor's estate, knowing that the debtor is insolvent and that there are other creditors, contravenes the policy of bankruptcy law. As he or she cannot show good faith, his or her act being a fraud on the other creditors, he or she will not receive any protection from the Act nor, in particular, from s 47: *Commercial Union Assurance Co Ltd v New Zealand Express Co Ltd* (1905) 8 GLR 166.

No protection is afforded by s 47 against the provisions relating to voidable gifts (s 54), improvements to or the purchase of property of any kind on behalf of another (s 55), execution creditors (s 50), and voidable preferences and voidable securities (ss 56, 57).

46.2.6 Rights of execution creditors and duties of Sheriff

One special but common situation is the clash which arises between the rights of the Official Assignee and competing creditors who have levied execution. This is governed by s 50 which also deals with the position of the Sheriff.

Under s 50(1) a creditor who has issued execution against the goods or land of a debtor or has attached any debt due to him or her is entitled to retain the benefit if he or she has completed the execution or attachment.

(a) before adjudication and
(b) before notice of the filing of a petition or the commission of an act of bankruptcy other than the immediate execution or attachment.

What constitutes completion differs according to whichever method of execution etc is employed. Section 50(2) provides that execution against goods is completed by seizure and sale, execution against land by sale or in the case of an equitable interest by appointment of a receiver and attachment of debts by receipt of the debt.

Section 50(4) deals with the position of the sheriff where he or she holds the net proceeds of an execution for a judgment for more than $100 or payment is made to avoid a sale. The sheriff must hold the money for 14 days. If he or she receives notice in that time of the filing of a bankruptcy petition he or she must pay the proceeds to the Assignee in the case of a debtor's petition but in the case of a creditor's petition he or she must hold them until the petition is disposed of and account to the Assignee only after adjudication. In any other case the execution creditor is entitled to be paid. Section 50(7) protects a bona fide purchaser from a sheriff. Section 50(8) gives the Court a discretion to set aside the rights of the Assignee under the section to such extent and subject to such terms as it thinks fit: see *Coulsons Ltd v Dyer* [1960] NZLR 281.

46.3 VOIDABLE DISPOSITIONS AND PAYMENTS BY THE BANKRUPT

46.3.1 General

We have referred above to s 60 of the Property Law Act 1952 and we shall examine it in more detail in a moment.

The Insolvency Act gives full recognition to the fact that a debtor may bring about his or her bankruptcy by reckless or irresponsible generosity or by inability to assess his or her financial situation; it also recognises that a debtor seems that bankruptcy is inevitable may, in a mood of defiance or antagonism towards his or her creditors, dispose of assets he or she knows that he or she cannot retain.

Section 19(1)(b) of the Act states that a debtor commits an act of bankruptcy if he or she fraudulently, or with intent to give any creditor a preference over other creditors:

(a) makes a disposition of his or her property or any part thereof; or
(b) makes any payment; or
(c) incurs any obligation.

This act of bankruptcy together with s 42 (relation back) would in some instances be sufficient for the Assignee to claim back any property made over fraudulently or with the intent to prefer any creditor. However, the limitation of the relation back provision is that s 42 can only relate back to acts of bankruptcy committed within the three months preceding the filing of the petition. Hence the Assignee will in cases outside this period have to rely on ss 54 (voidable gifts), 55 (recovery of moneys spent for the benefit of others), 56 (voidable preferences), 43(3) and 57 (voidable securities). Thus, apart from the rule that the Assignee is entitled to all the bankrupt's assets from the time of the commencement of bankruptcy, the Assignee can set aside settlements, gifts, partial gifts, repudiate promises to make gifts, and recover moneys spent for the benefit of others and property originally belonging to the bankrupt but disposed of by him or her or the value thereof. Registration under the Land Transfer Act 1952 will not protect the recipient of such property: s 58.

Section 54 avoids any gift made by the bankrupt within two years preceding adjudication, or within five years before adjudication unless the donee proves that the donor was at the time of making the gift (or at any time thereafter) able to pay his or her debts without the aid of the property comprised in the gift or settlement. Where the consideration for any disposition is inadequate and the Court is satisfied that it was the intention of the debtor to make a gift of the difference or inadequacy, then the Court can order the donee to pay to the Assignee the difference or any part thereof.

Section 54 (6) defines "gift" for the purposes of the section as any disposition made otherwise than in good faith and for valuable consideration. This definition stresses the lack of probity and the diminution of the bankrupt's estate. Valuable consideration has been defined as "consideration moving to the debtor which replaced the property extracted from his or her creditors": *Re a debtor, ex parte Official Receiver v Morrison* [1965]1 WLR 1498, 1505; [1965] 3 All ER 453, 457.

The definition of "gift" refers to "any disposition", which is defined in very wide terms: s 2. Two clauses of the definition of "disposition" are particularly significant in this context. They are:

(a) Any conveyance, transfer, assignment, settlement, delivery, payment or other alienation of property, whether at law or in equity.

(f) Any transaction entered into by any person with intent thereby to diminish, directly or indirectly, the value of his or her own estate and to increase the value of the estate of any other person.

Section 55 provides that where a bankrupt has improved land or property of another or has purchased land or property in the name of or on behalf of another, then if the bankrupt is adjudicated bankrupt within two years of so doing, or within five years and that other person cannot show that the bankrupt was able to pay his or her debts without the aid of the money or other property comprised in the disposition, then the Court may order that other person to pay to the Assignee the value of the improvements or the amount expended. The Court has a discretion under s 55(3) to reduce the amount payable to the Assignee in cases where that other person has acted in good faith, has altered his or her position in the belief that the actions of the bankrupt were valid, and the Court is of the opinion that it would be inequitable to order payment of all or any part of the amount otherwise payable.

Section 56 provides that where a debtor, unable to pay his or her debts from his or her own money, makes any transfer of property, gives a charge on property or suffers any execution against his or her property, then these actions may be voidable against the Assignee. If any of these arrangements is made with a view to giving any creditor a preference, then if made within two years of adjudication it is voidable as against the Assignee. If there was no intention to prefer, then they are voidable if made within one month of adjudication or where service of the petition on the debtor precedes adjudication by more than one month, then such actions are voidable if entered into in the period following service of the petition.

Section 43 provides that money lent by one spouse to the other spouse for any purpose, or other property of one spouse entrusted to the other spouse for the purpose of any trade or business carried on by that other spouse, upon bankruptcy of that other spouse, shall form part of the estate of that other spouse unless it can be shown that the lending or entrusting was in good faith and took place more than four years prior to adjudication.

Subsection (3) provides that any securities given to protect any moneys lent or property entrusted by one spouse to the other shall also be voidable as against the Assignee unless they too were entered into in good faith, more than four years before adjudication.

Section 57 renders voidable any charge or security given by a debtor over his or her property within the period commencing 12 months before the filing of a petition and ending on adjudication. This section will not affect securities given to secure money actually paid to the debtor or the price or value of property sold or supplied to the debtor at the time of or after execution of the securities.

46.3.2 Fraudulent dispositions under the Property Law Act 1952, s 60

This section provides:

(1) Save as provided by this section. every alienation of property with intent to defraud creditors shall be voidable at the instance of the person thereby prejudiced .

(2) This section does not affect the law of bankruptcy for the time being in force.

(3) This section does not extend to any estate or interest in property alienated, to a purchaser in good faith not having, at the time of the alienation, notice of the intention to defraud creditors.

A number of points should be noted about the section:

(1) It makes the disposition voidable not void.

(2) It applies irrespective of adjudication and there is no time zone.

(3) It only applies if there is an intent to defraud. This is a question of fact in each case. It may sometimes be inferred for instance when the debtor's remaining assets are insufficient to arrest his or her debts but it can be rebutted if the debtor can prove no actual intention to defraud: *Re Wise* (1886) 17 QBD 290.

(4) A purchaser in good faith and without notice is protected. Purchaser includes a lessee and mortgagee or other person for valuable consideration: Property Law Act 1952, s 2. It is necessary, therefore, to prove absence of valuable consideration or knowledge of the debtor's fraudulent intention: *OA of Harding v Harding* (1913) 16 GLR 448 (transfer pursuant to ante-nuptial agreement set aside because of complicity by wife in husband's fraud.)

(5) Every disposition voidable under s 60 is an act of bankruptcy under s 19(1)(b) of the Insolvency Act 1967.

46.3.3 Voidable gifts

The old law gave limited powers to the Assignee to recover property given away by the bankrupt in the period preceding adjudication. It was more remarkable for its inconsistency than its clarity. The present provisions simply pose the question: Are the creditors going to get less than the true value because this transaction took place? If the answer is affirmative, whether the creditor's funds are reduced by the whole value of the property transferred or by only part of the value of such property, it is a gift made by the bankrupt at the expense of his or her creditors. The Court may make such order as is appropriate for the recovery of the property, its value or the amount by which the creditors' funds are reduced. No question arises these days as to whether the gift has retained its identity or whether moneys received by the donee as a result of the gift are traceable.

Section 54(3) deals with the partial gift and makes it clear that the recipient of property from the debtor must not only give valuable consideration but it must be "adequate consideration in money or money's worth". Otherwise the Court on being satisfied that the intention of the debtor was to make a gift of the difference in value between the consideration and the gift and that the gift was voidable against the Assignee, may order the donee to pay to the Assignee an amount not exceeding the value of the difference.

However, a donee who has received a total or a partial gift from the debtor through failing to give any consideration or giving only partial consideration can prove that he or she had given consideration prior to the gift. The Court, contrary to the general principle that consideration must be present or future, may, if it thinks just and equitable, take into account past consideration and treat it as valuable consideration: s 54(7).

The Assignee may avoid the following transactions:

(a) any gifts where the donor is adjudged bankrupt within two years after making the gift;

(b) gifts not included in (a) above but being made in the five years preceding adjudication unless the donee can prove:

(i) that the donor could at the time of making the gift or at any time after that up till adjudication pay his or her debts without the aid of the property comprised in the gift, and

(ii) that if the gift was a settlement the settlor's interest in the property passed to the trustees of the settlement on the execution thereof: s 54(1), (2).

To be subject to s 54, the settlement must be one of property belonging to the settlor or property over which he or she has unqualified legal control at the time of settlement. In Re Schebsman [1944] Ch 83; [1943] 2 All ER 768 a company agreed to pay an employee leaving its service certain sums over a period of years and in the event of his death to make payment to his widow or daughter. The employee was adjudged bankrupt and died soon afterwards. The trustee in bankruptcy claimed the payments to be made to the widow as being a voidable voluntary settlement but it was held that the debtor was not entitled to any property under the agreement; the agreement merely provided for payments to be made to third parties. Accordingly, there was no settlement within the provisions of the section.

The burden of proving that a settlement was not made in good faith or was not made for adequate consideration will rest on the Assignee. The question whether the donor was, at the date of the gift, able to pay his or her debts without recourse to the property settled must be decided on an objective, not a subjective, basis. The responsibility for such proof rests on the recipient.

A covenant or contract made in consideration of his or her own marriage by the bankrupt, either for the future payment of money for the benefit of the bankrupt's spouse or children or for a future settlement on them of property in which at the time of marriage he or she had no interest, is voidable against the Assignee subject to the qualification below: s 54(4).

There is no general presumption of bad faith where a debtor settles property for the benefit of his or her spouse and children. The section is aimed at settlements purporting to deal with property which the settlor does not own at the time of his or her marriage. If the settlor is unable to transfer the property or make the payment before the commencement of bankruptcy but does make it after the commencement of bankruptcy it is in fact a dealing with the Assignee's property in the period of relation back, and, apart from that, there must inevitably be a strong suspicion that the debtor in the shadow of impending bankruptcy is taking steps to defraud his or her creditors. The covenant or contract (ie the obligation to pay or transfer property) may not be set aside if the bankrupt had made the payment or transferred the property before the commencement of bankruptcy. If the Assignee does set aside the covenant or contract the persons entitled may prove in the bankruptcy but will rank only ninth in the priority of payments.

Although the Act recognises to some extent the validity of the obligation if carried into effect by the bankrupt, it provides machinery for the recovery of the value of any property transferred or payments made to the spouse or children in fulfilment of the contract or covenant.

Section 54(5) provides that any payments (not being payments of premiums on a life assurance policy) and any transfers of property in pursuance of a post-nuptial contract or covenant referred to above, shall be voidable against the Assignee unless the recipient can prove that:

(a) The payment or transfer was made more than two years before adjudication; or

(b) That at the time of payment or transfer or at any time thereafter up to the adjudication the bankrupt could have paid all his or her debts without recourse to this money or property.

The solvency of the settlor must be established either immediately after the payment or transfer or at some time subsequent to the payment or transfer. The recipient is defeated if there is no period of solvency after the transfer or payment has been made.

(c) That the payment or transfer was made in pursuance of a covenant or contract to pay money or transfer property expected to come to the settlor from or on the death of a particular person named in the covenant or contract, eg a share in a deceased estate or an interest in property to which the bankrupt had become entitled from a particular person under a trust or a power of appointment. To come into this exclusion the payment or transfer by the bankrupt must have been made within the three months following the time when the money or property came into the possession or under the control of the bankrupt.

It is important to note that the transactions above are voidable, not void. The title or right of the recipient is not affected until adjudication takes place. The general principles of law relating to voidable titles will protect persons giving valuable consideration and acting in good faith without notice of any defect in the title, who have acquired property from a transferee from the bankrupt. Section 58(5), which does not extend to the doctrine of relation back, states that the person receiving the property or payment directly from the bankrupt is not protected even if he or she has acted in good faith and for "valuable" (as distinct from "adequate") consideration, but the Assignee has no right of recovery against a person who, acting in good faith and giving valuable consideration (eg a sub-purchaser), has received the property from someone to whom the disposition was originally made by the bankrupt.

People who have to return money or property through the operation of s 54(5) above are also entitled to claim dividends as deferred creditors ranking equally with the claims of spouses who have lent money or entrusted property to the bankrupt.

Consideration received from any source may prevent a property transaction being treated as a voidable gift.

The person providing consideration need not necessarily be the person who is to receive the benefit of the settlement. He or she is merely the person at whose request the settlement is made and who in good faith furnishes the consideration for compliance with his or her request. The consideration given by such a person may confer no benefit on the settlor; it may merely be a detriment suffered by the purchaser. On the other hand, the settlement may benefit a stranger to the consideration. In short, a person giving consideration need not purchase for himself or herself but may purchase for others.

In *Hance v Harding* (1888) 20 QBD 732 a doctor was spending the bulk of his earnings on drink, and on a woman with whom he was infatuated. His father, concerned for the welfare of his son's wife and children, persuaded the son to settle two life assurance policies on his wife and children; in consideration of this settlement the father settled leasehold property so that the income therefrom would pay the premiums on the life policies and the balance would be available for the wife and children. He also released a debt of £ 214 which the son owed to him. The son was adjudicated bankrupt within the next two years and died. The trustee in bankruptcy claimed the insurance policies. It was held that the father was a purchaser because he had given something to get a benefit for other persons, viz his son's family, and accordingly had given valuable consideration . The transaction was in good faith and not in fraud of creditors because the father was attempting to alleviate the difficulties and misfortune of his son's family and did not have in contemplation the possible insolvency or bankruptcy of his son. The settlement of the policies on the bankrupt's family was accordingly valid.

In *Re Humphries* (unreported, High Court, Auckland, B 15/84, 15 October 1986, Henry J) payments by trustees of a trust set up by a man who later became bankrupt to his de facto wife were held to be for valuable consideration and not to be voidable gifts. The de facto wife had a claim to a beneficial interest in the property sold and for maintenance for their son. As to the meaning of valuable consideration, see *Re Austin (a bankrupt)* [1982] 2 NZLR 524; *Barton v Official Receiver* (1986) 161 CLR 75 (High Court of Australia). See too 43.3.6 infra.

All the provisions above apply equally to a bankrupt wife, giving or settling property on her husband.

Registration of his or her interest under the Land Transfer Act 1952 will not protect the donee where he or she has received a voidable free gift of land; the Court, on the application of the Assignee, can either make an order that the donee transfer the land in question to the Assignee or that the donee shall pay to the Assignee a sum of money not exceeding the value of the land at the time when the disposition was set aside: s 58(2). It is to be noted that it is not the value of the land when the disposition was made. If the disposition had taken place some four or five years previously in a period of rapidly increasing land prices, this power might be extremely serious for the donee. It appears improbable that the Court would order the land to be transferred to the Assignee if the donee had built on it, but nevertheless the donee might be compelled to raise a second mortgage at a punitive rate of interest. Where there has been a partial gift of land, the Court cannot make an order for the land to be transferred to the Assignee but may, after having regard to all the circumstances, order a payment to be made to cover the deficiency in consideration. Although this might be justifiable in principle, there seems to be some inconsistency here: s 54(3) seems to indicate that the sum that may be fixed by the Court is to be determined at the time of the partial gift – "The difference between the value of the property disposed of and the value of the consideration". Where no consideration has been given, the time for the determination of the value of the property is the time when the gift was set aside: s 58 (2)(b). There could well be a very great difference in the value of the property at these two different times; these sums are admittedly only maximum figures and subject in each case to the Court's discretion.

Where there is a settlement of a joint family home by one spouse in favour of the other, the Joint Family Homes Act 1964 overrules the Insolvency Act 1967 and the gift cannot be set aside by the Assignee: s 3(2).

However the District Land Registrar must cancel the registration of a joint family home certificate on the application of the Assignee where there was no advertisement of the application and the settlor was adjudged bankrupt within two years of registration.

46.3.4 Purchase of property for another person or improvements made thereon by the bankrupt before adjudication: s 55

The same test may be applied to this transaction as to the voidable gift. Have the funds available to creditors for the payment of their debts been reduced through the bankrupt's action? If the bankrupt's estate has been diminished it is a form of gift by the bankrupt made at the expense of his or her creditors and consequently, if this transaction takes place in the two-year period or the five-year period preceding adjudication the Assignee can take the steps necessary to recover from the person benefiting the amount by which the bankrupt estate was diminished.

For the section to apply the improvements must have been made on the land of another and the bankrupt's estate must have been diminished because he or she made the improvements.

In *Official Assignee of Andrew v Johnston* [1974] 1 NZLR 79 a debtor, prior to his adjudication in bankruptcy, paid a deposit on a section but was allowed into possession of it before he paid the balance of the purchase price. As soon as he entered into possession he paid for clearing and drainage work on the section. However, he was unable to pay the balance due on the section and the vendor rescinded the agreement for sale and purchase and re-entered into possession of the land. Following the adjudication of the purchaser the Assignee sued the vendor for the value of the improvements but did not succeed. Henry J held that, prior to the rescission of the contract, the debtor was in sole possession of the land and was in equity the owner of the land subject to his meeting his obligations under the agreement. At the time the improvements were made it was not the land "of another person". Any decrease in the bankrupt's assets arose from the bankrupt's default under the agreement not through his carrying out the improvements.

As s 55 is chiefly aimed at purchases of land and improvements on land, the Court when dealing with an application by the Assignee must first ascertain the value of the improvements made or the price paid for the land or property and order the person benefiting to pay to the Assignee this amount, together with the consequent legal expenses, interest, rates, and other charges: s 55(2)(a).

It is only if the person benefiting does not comply with this order that the Court may order the land or part of the land purchased, or the land on which the improvements have been made, to be sold by the Assignee. If the land is sold, the Court can transfer the land to the purchaser and make any vesting order necessary: s 55(2)(b). Registration of his or her title to the land under the Land Transfer Act 1952 will not protect the person whose land is being sold: s 55(4). The Court may order the land or part of the land purchased, or the land on which the improvements have been made, to be sold by the Assignee. If the land is sold, the Court can transfer the land to the purchaser and make any vesting order necessary: s 55(2)(b). Registration of his or her title to the land under the Land Transfer Act 1952 will not protect the person whose land is being sold: s 55(4).

In order that any deficiency in the consideration received by the bankrupt or the value of any improvements made may be recovered for the benefit of the bankrupt estate, s 55(2)(c) directs the proceeds of the sale to be used in the following manner:

> The Assignee shall retain the whole or so much of the amount so ascertained as is necessary, along with all other assets in the estate, to pay the creditors in full (including the payment of interest under section 104 of this Act), and any balance of the amount shall be paid to the other person [the person benefiting]. Where any money has been retained by the Assignee under this paragraph and the creditors have been paid in full, any surplus of the proceeds of the bankrupt's estate shall be paid to the said other person to the extent of the amount so retained before any payment is made to the bankrupt.

Section 55(3) empowers the Court to refuse to make any order for payment or to make an order for payment of a sum less than the ascertained value or price above if:

(a) The person benefiting acted in good faith and has altered his or her position in the reasonably held belief that the bankrupt's action was valid and would not be set aside, and

(b) In the opinion of the Court it is inequitable to order payment of all or any part of the amount, as the case may be.

This power of restoration of the bankrupt's assets applies where the bankrupt, without receiving adequate consideration, had, prior to adjudication, conferred a benefit on another person by:

(a) Erecting buildings upon or improving the land or property of that other person; or

(b) Purchasing land or other property in that other person's name; or

(c) Providing money for such purpose (including payments for legal expenses, interest, rates, etc); or

(d) Paying instalments for the purchase of any land or property in the name of another;

and in consequence of such action has diminished his or her assets.

This power, however, is exercisable only if the bankrupt did any of these acts:

(a) Within the two years preceding his or her adjudication; or

(b) Within the five years preceding his or her adjudication, unless the person benefiting can prove that the bankrupt was at the time of the act referred to or at any time thereafter able to pay all his or her debts without the aid of the money or other property comprised in the disposition.

In *Official Assignee of Roberts v Roberts* [1955] NZLR 263, R, who was a builder, was adjudicated bankrupt on 12 October 1953 and a dividend of 14 cents in the dollar was paid. When R applied for his discharge, the Assignee sought an order under s 76 (now s 55) on the ground that R had made improvements on his wife's land. It was proved that R had with his own labour erected a house with materials and on land owned by his wife. It was also proved that during that time he received no payment for his work but that his wife supported the bankrupt and his family during that period. It was estimated that had R taken employment he would have received $30 per week (less tax) and that his wife had expended approximately that amount in maintaining the family. Thus, even if he had taken other employment, the creditors would not have benefited. No order was made; Turner J stated, at 266:

> The reality of the transaction is that the husband worked for the wife in improving her property, and she, instead of paying him in cash, assumed his liability for maintaining the family. It is clear that no creditor lost anything by this proceeding, for, if the bankrupt had worked for outside employers for wages, as it was contended he should have done, there could still have been no surplus from his funds out of which the creditors could have expected to receive any payment.

Any debt incurred by a bankrupt to purchase land for another is recoverable by the Assignee as money expended on that other person's behalf: *Re Boyland ex parte Official Assignee* [1932] NZLR 1256; [1933] GLR 70. Failing such repayment, the Judge may direct the Assignee to sell the land and to deduct from the proceeds so much of the money expended or the value of the improvements as with the other estate assets shall be sufficient to pay the creditors 100¢ in $1, with interest. The person whose land was sold will then, if sufficient funds are available, be reimbursed in full.

46.3.5 Voidable preferences

(a) GENERAL

Section 56 is designed to prevent the debtor robbing Peter to pay Paul. An insolvent debtor loses his or her right to decide who will be paid first and certainly is not entitled to decide who will be be paid in full and who will only be paid a portion of what is owed by him.

If the transaction favouring the particular creditor takes place in the *month* immediately preceding adjudication or in the period between the service of a creditor's petition on an insolvent and his or her adjudication, the motive of the debtor and any intention to prefer are irrelevant. The transaction may be avoided by the Assignee at any time after the service of the petition, and this period may extend for more than a month: s 56(3). The Assignee is entitled to avoid only such transactions as occur within this statutory period. Transactions entered into within the *two years* preceding adjudication by an insolvent debtor with a view to preferring a creditor, a trustee or a guarantor for that creditor may also be avoided by the Assignee as voidable preferences. In this case, the transactions must be entered into "with a view to giving that creditor or any surety or guarantor for the debt due to that creditor a preference over the other creditors". The transactions covered by both classes of case are:

(1) every conveyance or transfer of property; and
(2) every charge made thereon; and
(3) every obligation incurred and every execution under any judicial proceeding suffered; and
(4) every payment made (including any payment made in pursuance of a judgment or order of a Court) by a person unable to pay his or her debts as they fall due.

For cases falling in the first class the following elements must be established:

(a) an act of the kind specified;
(b) by a person unable to pay his or her debts as they become due from his or her own money;
(c) the act must be in favour of a creditor;
(d) it must have been done within one month of the adjudication.

For cases falling in the second class (a)-(c) must be established and the act must have been done with "a view to giving that creditor . . . a preference over other creditors" and within two years of the adjudication.

In the leading but curiously unreported decision of *Re Northridge Properties Ltd* (unreported, High Court, Auckland, M46-49/75,77/75, 13 December 1977) Richardson, J said about (a), (b) and (c):

As to [(b)], several points are clear. First the expression is concerned with the position of the debtor at the time the charge or payment is made or other specified act takes place. It is not relevant that in the past he has been unable to pay his debts as they fall due, or that it is likely that in the future he will be unable to pay his debts as they become due. The concern is with the present. But, in considering the present position, regard may properly be had to the recent past; whether he has, in recent weeks, been able to meet his debts as they become due. And in determining ability to meet debts as they become due, account must be taken of outstanding debts. They have to be paid or allowed for in answering the question. Second, "as they become due" means as they become legally due.

Third, the reference to payment, "from his own money" has not been interpreted strictly to require a debtor to keep sufficient on hand at all times for that purpose. It seems to me to follow, and as a prudent commercial consideration, that the possibility of converting a non-cash asset into a cash asset should not be taken into account for the purpose of assessing solvency unless realisation of the asset in that way was in contemplation by the debtor at the time. Fourth, if, as is well established, convertibility of non-cash assets on hand may be taken into account in determining solvency, so too must debts becoming due while that conversion takes place. Moreover, the words "as they become due" involve consideration of the debtor's position over a period not at an instant of time. It is a moving picture of his financial position rather than a still shot.

His Honour cited *Bank of Australasia v Hall* [1907] 4 CLR 1514 where Higgins J said, at 1554:

The critical words are "as they become due"; so that, on the one hand, a debtor in making a payment or giving a security to a creditor has to take into account, not only his debts immediately payable, but his debts which will become payable; and on the other hand, he is not obliged to keep money always in hand to meet debts not immediately due. It is sufficient if he sees to it that he will be in a position to get enough moneys of his own to pay each debt as and when it becomes due.

Griffith CJ said at 1527-1528:

. . . the debts referred to are not his or her debts "then" payable, but his debts "as they become due" – a phrase which looks to the future. No doubt, only the reasonably immediate future is to be looked to.

No doubt when debts are not due at the date the impugned security is given, it is necessary to tread very warily before taking them into account. But for example, where it is clear that non-cash assets would have to be realised by the debtor and that an on-demand debt is about to be called up and would be called up before that could be achieved, it would be flying in the face of commercial reality to disregard altogether that impending obligation to pay in determining ability to pay debts as they become due. Finally, the test of insolvency is an objective one. The belief or state of mind of the debtor is not relevant here, although it is of critical importance when considering the third requirement of the section that the act was done with a view to giving a preference.

(b) A VIEW TO GIVING A PREFERENCE

Richardson J in *Re Northridge Properties Ltd* (supra) made some interesting remarks about the view to giving a preference. He quoted the *Shorter Oxford English Dictionary* definition of "view" as:

4.   "An aim or intention: a design or plan; an object or purpose" and "with a view to" is:

(a)   with the aim or object of attaining, effecting or accomplishing something

and said:

It is not surprising then that, in describing this ingredient, the Courts have used such terms as "intent", "motive", "object", "purpose", and reason". I do not find it necessary for the purpose of this case to analyse the expression in detail. It is sufficient to say that, while "view" may be reasonably close in meaning to "intent", what is to be assessed is the ulterior intent rather than simply the immediate intent of the debtor in making the charge or payment: *Sharp v Jackson* [1899] AC 419; *Re Reimer* (1896)15 NZLR 198; *Official Assignee v Wairarapa Farmers' Cooperative Association Ltd* [1925] NZLR 1. A view to preferring a creditor requires a conscious decision which is an act of free will. So payment made in response to real pressure from the creditor may not be voluntary, in which case it is not within the section *(Re TW Cutts* [1956] 1 WLR 728). To come within s 56 there must be a dominant intention to prefer a particular creditor. It need not be the only intention.

He cited Salmond J in *Official Assignee v Wairarapa Farmers Cooperative Association* [1925] NZLR 1, 8 when the latter said:

There is no fraudulent preference unless his real, dominant, and substantial motive was a desire to prefer the particular creditor over his other creditors. It is not enough that he knew that the necessary result of the payment was to give that creditor an advantage over the others and to prevent the equal distribution of his assets among his creditors. It is necessary that this should have been the operative reason for which he made the payment. If his real reason was something else – some benefit, for example, to be obtained for himself – the transaction cannot be attacked as a fraudulent preference. This is so even though the act of the bankrupt may have been consciously dishonest as amounting to a use of his money for his own purposes instead of distributing it equally among his creditors. The only fraudulent preference recognised by the Bankruptcy Act is the act of an insolvent debtor in preferring one creditor to another, not the act of preferring himself to his creditors.

Richardson J then said that the onus is on the person seeking to impeach the transaction to establish the view to prefer. The onus may be discharged by direct evidence of the state of mind of the debtor or by necessary inference from all the circumstances. *Re Northridge Properties Ltd* was noted in [1983] NZLJ 44 and has been followed in subsequent decisions. See, for example, *Nangeela Properties Ltd v Westpac Banking Corporation* (1986-7) 3 NZCLC 99, 588 (CA); and *Re Radio Times Communications Ltd* (1984) 2 NZCLC 99, 671.

Historically, this was a jury matter and there are a number of factors which negate the view to prefer. That is to say they are not exceptions as such but practical factors which, a Judge would advise a jury, would tend to negate the view to prefer. There must be a free exercise of the debtor's will. The preference must be a voluntary act carried out in the desire to treat the creditor more favourably than the others: *Official Assignee v Wairarapa Farmers Co-operative Association Ltd* [1925] NZLR 1; [1924] GLR 449.

Essentially, the transaction must have been entered into by a debtor free from all pressure or fear of legal consequences or even of apprehension of curtailment of credit as in *Re Clay* (1896) 3 Mans 31, where an insolvent trader met his acceptances as they became due, as refusal of payment would have put an end to this credit.

Pressure exerted on the debtor is irrelevant in deciding whether a preference is voidable unless it is genuine and results in effective compulsion. A debtor in a completely hopeless financial position will not be likely to be influenced by threats to sue him or her: *Ex parte Hall, Re Cooper* (1882) 19 ChD 580.

There is no pressure where the legal and social penalties are inevitable despite the payment being made: *Re T W Cutts* [1956] 1 WLR 728; [1956] 2 All ER 537. In this case a defaulting solicitor had stolen sums from a number of clients and his defalcations had been detected. He decided to make reparation to his best client but this could not stave off his eventual punishment and disgrace, and it was held to be a voidable preference. Lord Evershed MR, discussing dominant intention and sense of moral obligation, observed, pp 541 and 542:

> ... it is notorious that human beings are by no means always single-minded, the intention to prefer which must be proved is the principal or dominant intention. There may also be a valid distinction for present purposes between an intention to prefer and the reason for forming and executing that intention ...
>
> For if a debtor deliberately selects for payment A in preference to all his other creditors, it cannot to my mind matter in the absence of other relevant circumstances, whether A is the debtor's oldest friend, closest relative or best client. On the other hand, where a debtor owing money in all directions has also robbed his employer's till, he may, knowing himself to be insolvent, elect to reimburse the till in order that, when the crash comes, the damaging fact of his robbing may not be discovered. Or a debtor may elect to make a particular payment under pressure of some threat or to obtain for himself some immediate and material benefit or to fulfil some particular obligation. In these cases the reason for the payment affects, essentially, the intention in making it. ...
>
> Though the question of pressure in some form or another has, in the reported cases, often been the crux of the matter, it is plain that an inference of intention to prefer may be displaced in many other ways than by showing that the debtor acted under pressure.

Good faith on the part of the creditor himself and ignorance that he or she was being preferred will not prevent the transaction being upset as a voidable preference, even though he or she can show valuable consideration which may also be adequate consideration: *Official Assignee v The King* [1922] NZLR 265; [1922] GLR 172.

Payment made in the ordinary course of business to a creditor, uninfluenced by any belief that the debtor was insolvent, would lead to a presumption that preference of the business creditor was not the debtor's dominant intention but rather that his or her trading connections should continue, thus making it possible for him or her to retrieve his or her financial position. But payment is not made in the ordinary course of business where the course of business is being ended and practically the only available assets are being taken by the creditor to protect himself from loss: *Re Dunneman ex parte The Trustee* (1935) 8 ABC 148, 154. A security given to secure a further advance to enable the debtor to carry on and not to strengthen the position of the creditor is not a voidable preference: *In re Fairbrother Official Assignee v Baddeley* (1906) 25 NZLR 546; 8 GLR 225.

Payments to State Departments (the Crown) can be treated as voidable preferences: *Re Butler* [1981] 2 NZLR 149.

In *Re Hooper, ex parte the Official Assignee* [1951] NZLR 704; [1951] GLR 361 in 1949 H arranged with F, a supplier, to provide him with materials and send him monthly accounts. H got most of his income from building contracts with the Land and Survey Department, which, on the certification of these monthly accounts, paid F the amount owing. H, although receiving further supplies, failed to forward further statements to the Department, and a debt of $1,710 became owing by H to F. The Department was holding $820 on account of H. F persuaded H to sign an assignment directing the Department to pay the $820 held by it to F. On the bankruptcy of H it was held that the assignment was in pursuance of an agreement made between H and F before the liability was incurred, and that it was not fraudulent and the Assignee had not proved that H's substantial and dominant motive was to prefer F.

The burden of proving both the insolvency of the debtor and his or her dominant intention rests on the Assignee. Once these are established the onus then shifts to the creditor to establish a negating factor or exemption: *Re Ciminiello* [1981] 2 NZLR 495.

All this difficulty in determining the essential element of voidable preference could be obviated if the legislature provided that the result or the fact that a preference had been made was all that had to be taken into consideration, or if the wording of the Australian Bankruptcy Acts, "having the effect of giving that creditor . . . a preference" were substituted for the words "with a view to giving that creditor . . . a preference" in our own s 56(1)(a): see KC Chiah [1986] 12 NZULR 1.

For a detailed discussion of the English section see JH Farrar [1983] JBL 390. For a dated but useful discussion of New Zealand Laws see Spratt and MacKenzie, *Law of Insolvency* (2 ed) by PD McKenzie, 153 et seq.

(c) PREFERENCE OF GUARANTORS

The Assignee is empowered by s 56(1) to avoid any transaction intended to prefer any creditor, trustee for such creditor, or guarantor of the sum due to the creditor. This enables the Assignee, subject to the right of the Court to adjust the respective liabilities of the guarantor and the person receiving a payment under the voidable preference, to recover from such person any amount paid, although it is the guarantor who is in fact preferred. The guarantor, even though he or she has not yet paid, being able to prove in the bankruptcy of the debtor, is "a creditor" within the words of the section. The practical result of this provision is that the original creditor having been compelled to return any moneys he or she has received under the voidable preference will demand payment from the guarantor .

It has been decided that the term "surety" or "guarantor" includes a person who has merely deposited securities, although he or she may not have personally undertaken to pay the creditor on default of the debtor: *Re Conley, ex parte The Trustee v Barclay's Bank Ltd* (1938) 54 TLR 641.

46.3.6 Voidable securities

Securities or charges over a debtor's land or other property are voidable against the Assignee, if they are given within the following periods:

(a) If there is a creditor's petition then in the period commencing 12 months before the filing of the petition and ending upon adjudication. (The period in this case will extend for more than 12 months.)

(b) If there is no creditor's petition but the debtor has filed a petition then in the 12 months preceding the filing of that petition: s 57(1).

The security is not voidable in so far as it relates to:

(a) Money actually advanced or paid, or the actual price or the value of the property sold or supplied, or any other valuable consideration given in good faith by the grantee of the security or charge to the grantor at the time of or at any time after the execution thereof.

(b) A security over any property of the grantor securing unpaid purchase money, such security being executed not later than 21 days after the purchase of the property. Thus a mortgage back executed by the purchaser over the property he or she has bought or a mortgage over other property of the purchaser is valid, if it is given within 21 days following the purchase: s 57(2).

"Valuable consideration" in s 57(2) means more than in the law of contract. Some real value was necessary although this might not represent equivalent value. Mere forbearance to sue was inadequate: *Re Williams (a bankrupt)* (High Court, Wellington, B 175/84, 2 October 1986, Greig J). See too *Barton v Official Receiver* (1986) 161 CLR 75 (High Court of Australia) (voidable settlement case).

In *Re Holm* [1974] 2 NZLR 455 a debtor was allowed an overdraft of $2,000 by a bank. The overdraft increased rapidly and two months later was in excess of $6,000. In June 1971 the debtor executed a mortgage in favour of the bank and in September 1971 he was adjudicated bankrupt. The Assignee after adjudication gave notice to the bank saying that in the terms of s 58 of the Act he was setting aside the mortgage. This notice was disputed by the bank and the Assignee then applied to the Court to confirm that this mortgage, given within the period of 12 months preceding the filing of the creditor's petition and ending with adjudication was voidable. It was conceded that the bank gave consideration by undertaking that it would not sue the debtor. It was then a question as to whether the bank was acting in good faith and it was contended by the bank that as the Assignee had instituted the proceedings the burden rested on him to prove the bank was not acting in good faith. The Court set the mortgage aside and found that the burden of proving good faith rested on the bank as the grantee of the security and that the bank did not act in good faith (s 57(2)) as it must have been aware that other creditors would not be paid if the mortgage was upheld. See also *Re Austin (a bankrupt)* [1982] 2 NZLR 524.

Section 57(3) relates to those cases where a security has been granted within the 12-month period securing indebtedness made up of advances prior to the granting of the security and advances made thereafter. Section 57(2) renders the latter advances safe from the Assignee. However, the earlier advances made prior to the granting of the security would be voidable as against the Assignee. If during the period prior to adjudication the insolvent made certain repayments, it would be advantageous for the creditor to appropriate these repayments to the earlier, and voidable, advances. However, s 57(3) provides that all payments received by the grantee from the grantor thereafter, shall be deemed to be repayments of money advanced or paid to the grantor by the grantee at the time or after the security was given or to be payments of the actual price or the value of the property sold or supplied by the grantee to the grantor or payments for other valuable consideration given in good faith to the grantor by the grantee on or after the execution of the security or charge: s 57(3).

These provisions do not apply to payments received by trading banks in good faith in the ordinary course of business and without negligence: s 57(3).

The Act refers to the "actual price or value" of property sold. It is submitted that if the actual price was much above the value the transaction could be avoided under other sections of the Act.

It would appear that this section includes mortgages of land as well as securities over chattels. The 21-day time limit provided in s 57(2)(b) could cause problems for the unpaid vendor of land taking a mortgage back to secure the balance of the unpaid purchase price. If the agreement for sale and purchase is entered into without reference to the mortgage then a settlement is usually longer than 21 days after the agreement and the mortgage given the vendor on settlement would not be saved by s 57(2)(b) upon the purchaser's later insolvency. However, this problem can be overcome by stating in the agreement for sale and purchase that the purchaser agrees to grant a mortgage to the vendor to secure the balance of the unpaid purchase price. It is submitted that this promise to grant a mortgage is, in fact, an equitable mortgage sufficient in its own right to support a caveat and, being a charge or mortgage granted within the 21 day period, is protected by s 57(2)(b) from avoidance by the Assignee under s 57(1) should the purchaser be adjudicated bankrupt within the next 12 months.

Securities or charges given pursuant to an agreement made before the commencement of the 12 month period above are not affected, nor are securities or charges given in substitution for existing securities or charges executed before the commencement of the said period.

46.3.7 Loans of money or property to bankrupt spouses

Where a husband or wife is adjudicated bankrupt, any money lent by the other spouse to the bankrupt for any purpose or any property lent or entrusted for business purposes within the *four* years preceding the adjudication of the borrower shall be treated as assets in the bankrupt borrower's estate: s 43(1), (2).

It is to be noted that land or other property is affected by this provision only if it is lent or entrusted for business purposes; no such limitation is placed on a loan of money.

Any security given to the lender by the bankrupt borrower is voidable against the Assignee unless it is proved by the person who so asserts that the security or charge was given in good faith and more than four years before the adjudication. The advance or transfer of assets must be given at the time of the giving of the charge or security. Securities given for past advances are in all circumstances voidable by the Assignee: s 43(3). In *Re*

Berry [1978] 2 NZLR 373 (CA) the bankrupt and his wife were joint owners of a house property. It was accepted that the wife by reason of her cash contributions was entitled to a 77 per cent interest in this property. The husband, who was a builder, got into serious financial difficulties and the wife and the husband raised a mortgage of $6,000 on this property so that the husband could meet his most pressing debts. The husband was adjudicated bankrupt and the Assignee sold the house and proposed that the equity of both the husband and the wife should be distributed after payment of the mortgage. The wife applied to the High Court claiming that the mortgage had been raised solely for the purpose of the husband's business and should be discharged only from his share of the proceeds of the sale. Casey J in the High Court considered that the equitable doctrine of exoneration applied. The doctrine provides that where the property of a married woman is mortgaged to raise money for the payment of her husband's debts, it is presumed in the absence of evidence showing an intention to the contrary, that she meant to charge her property merely by way of security and in such a case she is in the position of a surety and she is entitled to be indemnified by her husband and to throw the debt primarily on his estate to the exoneration of her own. The Court of Appeal held that the husband and wife had entered into the transaction jointly, as co-debtors. There was no suggestion that the husband should be the principal debtor. The transactions did not give rise to any obligations by the husband to the wife. Accordingly the Assignee was quite right to deal with the property as he proposed.

However, s 104 gives the lending spouse a slight concession, in so far as he or she can claim as a creditor in the bankrupt estate in the ninth priority, that is, after all ordinary creditors have been paid in full and interest has been paid on all debts proved. See 47.7.2 post.

The disabilities referred to in s 43 above are imposed on a spouse who has lent money or property in the same circumstances and within the four years preceding a Court order for the administration of a deceased insolvent estate under Part XVII of the Insolvency Act 1967.

A lending spouse can prove as an ordinary creditor or assert his or her rights under the security for the loan only if such lender can prove:

(a) that the lender acted in good faith; *and*
(b) that the loan was made or the security was given before the four year period referred to above: s 43(1), (2), (3).

46.3.8 The assignee's right to recover property or value

As a result of an antecedent transaction the bankrupt may have disposed of land, personal property or money, which should be available for the payment of his or her creditors. A voidable disposition of land by the bankrupt months or even years before his or her adjudication may put the transferee in an unenviable position. He or she may have built a house on the land financed by a mortgage for repayment of which, apart from the security over the land, he or she is personally responsible and the land itself may have doubled in value.

If the Assignee decides to avoid the transaction the Court may, on application by the Assignee, do one of three things:

(1) Order the transferee to transfer the land back to the Assignee: s 58(2)(a). It is most unlikely that the Court would make such an order in the circumstances above.

(2) Order the transferee to pay to the Assignee a sum not exceeding the value of the property *when the disposition was set aside:* s 58(2)(b).

This order could, owing to the rise in price of the land, coupled with the transferee's financial commitment under the mortgage, put him or her in an impossible position.

(3) Refuse to make any order for recovery or make an order providing for payment of only part of the present value of the land transferred.

Before deciding to refuse an order or make an order for only partial reimbursement of the bankrupt estate, the Court would need to be satisfied that:

(a) the transferee had received the property in good faith and had altered his or her position in the reasonably held belief that the transfer to him or her was validly made and would not be set aside; and

(b) it was inequitable to order recovery of the property, recovery of part of the value, or recovery in full, as the case may be: s 58(6).

An order for the transfer back of land or other property or an order for the reimbursement of the value of such land or other property may be directed against a transferee of such property, his or her personal representative (if the transferee had died) or any person claiming through him or her subject to the reservation below.

The order may be made in favour of the Assignee or an appointee under Part XVII of the Act if the insolvent transferor is dead: s 58(1).

To secure an order of the Court under s 58 the Assignee files a notice in the form prescribed and causes it to be served on the persons who have to be served in accordance with reg 42.

Section 58(2) is designed to resolve the difficulties created by *Re Gunsbourg* [1920] 2 KB 426, which recognised that a person dealing directly with a bankrupt might be protected from a claim by the Assignee provided that such person had given valuable consideration and had no notice of an act of bankruptcy committed by the bankrupt. Nevertheless, in the same case it was held that such protection did not extend to persons subsequently acquiring the property from the person dealing directly from the bankrupt. In short, the person acquiring personal property directly from the bankrupt was protected if he or she had no notice of an available act of bankruptcy and had given valuable consideration; but anyone who subsequently became entitled to the property was not protected. Section 47(1)(c) has been included in the Act to remedy this injustice.

Sections 47 and 58 should be read together, as there is no reason to assume that the two sections are mutually exclusive.

Section 58(1) makes no reference to s 42 (relation back) transactions. Nevertheless, s 58(4) clearly records that the remedies given to the Assignee by s 58 are additional to all other rights and remedies available to the Assignee. Furthermore, as we have seen above, s 58(6), somewhat inelegantly, confers a discretionary relief which is completely unrestricted in scope.

If the Court sets the disposition aside under s 58(2), the person dealing directly with the bankrupt is not protected merely by giving valuable consideration and acting in good faith. It is submitted that the consideration must be adequate consideration so that the bankrupt estate is not diminished. On the other hand, persons subsequently acquiring property comprised in the disposition, eg sub-purchasers, are protected if they act in good faith for valuable consideration, whether or not it was adequate. It appears that the Assignee cannot recover property or the value thereof from an agent who received it on behalf of a creditor whom the bankrupt intended to prefer: *Re Morant ex parte Trustees* [1924] 1 Ch 79.

Under the Bankruptcy Act 1908 it was doubtful whether the Assignee had any claim against a transferee or mortgagee of land once the interest of such transferee or mortgagee was registered on the title. The Insolvency Act, however, provides that nothing in the Land Transfer Act 1952 shall affect the operation of s 58. Registration will not protect any transferee or mortgagee, whether he or she has dealt with the bankrupt for valuable consideration or not.

Section 58, as we have seen, empowers the Assignee to recover property, real or personal, mortgaged to secure an advance for business purposes to the spouse of the bankrupt (s 43(3)), as well as property constituting voidable gifts (s 54), voidable preferences (s 56), and voidable securities (s 57). Similarly, the Assignee may recover any property or the value of any property which is a fraudulent conveyance under s 60 of the Property Law Act 1952 or which in accordance with s 162(e) is deemed to be a fraudulent, void or voidable transaction which took place during the lifetime of a deceased insolvent.

Section 58 omits any reference to s 42, which makes it clear that any land transferred by a bankrupt during the period of relation back is a transfer of the Assignee's land and further provides that nothing in the Land Transfer Act 1952 deprives the Assignee of his or her title to land so alienated: s 42(5). Nor does s 58 refer to s 55, dealing with improvement to or the purchase of property by the bankrupt for another person. Here it is clear that land is involved and the consequences of taking land from another person are generally much more serious than any acts in relation to personal property. The person against whom the Assignee claims is given as a first option the right to make a monetary payment before having the property sold. In any case the Court has the right to refuse an order for payment if the person concerned acted in good faith and has so altered his or her position in reliance on the validity of the bankrupt's action that it is inequitable to make an order: s 55(3). Nevertheless, it is further provided that nothing in the Land Transfer Act 1952 shall prevent the Court from directing the Assignee to sell the land and making any vesting order for that purpose: s 55(4).

We have already seen that, subject to the qualification above, the Assignee's powers to recover property disposed of by the bankrupt and to claim a compensatory payment are additional and not in any way restrictive of the rights and remedies of the Assignee: s 58(4).

Chapter 47

PROOF OF DEBTS AND DISTRIBUTION

SUMMARY

47.1   GENERAL
47.2   PROCEDURE FOR PROOF
47.3   PROVABLE DEBTS
47.4   PROOF BY SECURED CREDITORS
47.5   PROOF IN PARTICULAR CASES
47.6   CREDITORS WHOSE CLAIMS ARE NOT PROVABLE
47.7   DISTRIBUTION OF THE BANKRUPT'S ASSETS

47.1 GENERAL

On adjudication the majority of the creditors of the bankrupt are no longer entitled to enforce their claims. They must satisfy the Assignee that they are claiming the correct amount, which is done by submitting a "proof" of their debts in the form prescribed by the Regulations; reg 23. If their proof is admitted, the creditors must accept in full satisfaction of their claim such proportionate payment as the assets of the bankrupt allow by way of dividends. If bankruptcy is annulled, a creditor may again enforce his or her claim through the Courts.

This procedure, by which a creditor establishes his or her right to payment from the bankrupt's estate, must not be confused with the peremptory admission or rejection of proof allowed by s 40 at a creditors' meeting to determine solely the question of whether the creditor is entitled to vote or not.

The general rule is that discharge releases the bankrupt from all provable debts except those tainted with fraud, those for which judgment is entered on discharge, payments that the Court has ordered the bankrupt to make in reduction of his or her debts, and certain orders for maintenance of dependants or made in the course of matrimonial disputes: s 114.

Because most provable debts are released on the bankrupt being discharged from bankruptcy, creditors who have provable debts are virtually obliged to tender proof no matter how small the dividend may be. In fact he or she will be released from liability for provable debts whether any dividend has been paid or not.

47.2 PROCEDURE FOR PROOF

Form 7 in the Regulations sets out the form in which proof is tendered. The form must be signed by the creditor or someone having knowledge of the debt, and it must be delivered or sent by post to the Assignee as soon as may be: reg 23, s 88(2). The phrase "as soon as may be" does not prevent a creditor proving late. The procedure and powers of the Assignee in the admission and rejection of proofs is set out in s 89 of the Act. Trade discounts must be deducted and credit for any contra account given: s 92.

The creditor should post or submit his or her proof to the Assignee as soon as possible after adjudication. The cost of proof must be borne by the creditor, unless the Court otherwise orders: s 88(3). Proofs admitted or amended more than two months after adjudication are at some disadvantage for dividend purposes. A creditor who has proved may inspect the proofs of other creditors before the first meeting (s 88(4)), and he or she may apply to the Court to reverse the decision of the Assignee to admit another creditor's proof: *Re Taylor* [1934] NZLR 1117. The Court may, if it thinks that a proof has been improperly admitted, on the application of the Assignee or the bankrupt or any creditor, after notice to the creditor who made the proof, expunge the proof or reduce its amount. A creditor who has amended his or her proof by increasing the amount after a dividend has been paid, shall not disturb dividends already paid, but may be paid out of any moneys remaining in the Assignee's hands: s 105.

The Assignee must examine any proof submitted and shall endorse on the proof of debt form whether he or she admits or rejects the claim and whether the claim is preferential or not: reg 24. If he or she rejects the claim he or she shall give notice of the rejection and the reason therefor to the creditor: s 89(3), reg 25, Form 8. The Court will decide on the admissibility of the proof where the Assignee fails to decide within 14 days after notice to decide upon it has been given to him or her by the bankrupt or any creditor: s 89(6).

A creditor, whose proof has been rejected by the Assignee, must within 21 days of receiving notice of rejection apply to the Court to reverse the decision, otherwise the rejection shall be final: s 89(4). If the Assignee is uncertain of the validity of a proof, he or she may summon before him or her and examine on oath the person tendering the proof or any other person capable of giving evidence with regard to the debt: s 89(2). If either person fails to appear he or she can have such person arrested and brought up for examination: s 68(4).

Any creditor of the bankrupt may, on giving notice to the Court, be joined as a party to proceedings concerning proof by another creditor: s 89(7).

Where the sum claimed in a disputed proof does not exceed $12,000 proceedings are heard in the District Court, with a right of appeal to the High Court. The Court may direct costs to be paid by the bankrupt or any party other than the Assignee: s 89(10).

47.3 PROVABLE DEBTS

47.3.1 General rule

Under s 87 all debts and liabilities, present or future, certain or contingent, to which the bankrupt is subject at the time of adjudication, or to which he or she becomes subject before discharge, by reason of any obligation incurred before adjudication, are provable in bankruptcy, except:

> Any fine or penalty imposed or order for payment of money made pursuant to any conviction or under section 19 of the Criminal Justice Act 1985. . . .

Even debts contracted after the creditor has had notice of the commission of an act of bankruptcy are provable.

The provisions of any other Act as to the recovery of any such sum of money are not otherwise affected.

47.3.2 Contingent debts

If the Assignee assesses the value of a contingent debt, or if the Court, on appeal against the Assignee's decision to reject the proof on the ground that the value cannot be determined, does so estimate the value of the debt it is provable in bankruptcy: ss 98, 99.

Default assessments of income tax may require examination by the Assignee. Contingent claims such as the liability of a guarantor to pay the creditor, the contingent liability of the assignor of a lease to indemnify the lessor, and contingent claims for unliquidated damages are all provable debts to be estimated at the date of adjudication: *Ellis and Co's Trustee v Dixon Johnson* [1924] 1 Ch 342. Contingent claims for fraud or fraudulent breach of trust may be treated as a provable debt or the injured party may postpone his or her claim and rely on s 114(a), (b), which provides that such debts are not released by a discharge in bankruptcy. No proof is allowed where there is merely a possibility that costs will be awarded against the bankrupt.

47.3.3 Unliquidated claims

Whether these arise from tort or contract, an estimate of the amount may be made or contingent provision for payment may be made by the Assignee, and such amount will be treated as a provable debt. Although proof may be made for an unliquidated claim, such a claim cannot be used as a debt for the foundation of a bankruptcy petition: ss 87(1), 23(c).

47.3.4 Debts payable at a future time

The present value of the debt at the date of adjudication is estimated and proved, but no discount is deducted from a debt payable within three months of adjudication: s 95. Alimony, being a judicial assessment of the husband's obligation to maintain his wife, cannot be affected by the bankruptcy of the husband. It is an obligation which as a matter of public policy must survive such proceedings. As discharge does not release a bankrupt from future payments of maintenance and other sums ordered to be paid in matrimonial disputes, these are not to be treated as provable future debts: s 114(d). But arrears under a maintenance order at the date of adjudication and both arrears and payments due in the future under a separation agreement are provable debts.

For a detailed treatment of this topic see *Spratt and MacKenzie's Law of Insolvency* (2 ed, 1972), pp 218-220.

Proof may be made for arrears of rent, the present value of future loss of rental and breaches of covenant which have occurred prior to proof of the debt: *Metropolis Estates Company Ltd v Wilde* [1940] 2 KB 536. Rental for the future "use and occupation" of the premises after adjudication must be paid in full.

A life annuity may be capitalised and proof for the sum found may be made: *Re Rothermere* [1945] 1 Ch 72; [1944] 2 All ER 593.

47.3.5 Statute-barred debts

These debts are not provable. It appears that a debt which was not barred by the Limitation Act 1950 at the date of adjudication but which would subsequently have become barred during the bankruptcy, is provable. But the right of recovery in these circumstances is exercisable only in Bankruptcy, not in other proceedings: *Re Benzon* [1914] 2 Ch 68.

47.3.6 Proof for interest

Proof for interest may not be made unless:

(i) interest is authorised by statute or by rule of law; or
(ii) interest is allowed by the Court in entering judgment; or
(iii) the claim is based on an agreement providing for the payment of interest.

Interest may be claimed only up to the date of adjudication: s 94. The position of a creditor or mortgagee who does not prove in a bankruptcy is unaffected by the bankruptcy and in realising his or her security he or she is entitled to claim interest down to the date of payment of the principal sum: *Re Securitibank Ltd* [1980] 2 NZLR 714.

47.4 PROOF BY SECURED CREDITORS

A secured creditor is a person holding a mortgage, charge, lien or security on the property of the debtor, whether given directly or indirectly through another person, as a security for the debt due to him or her from the debtor: s 2. From the definition it appears that a creditor who has a security over the property of a third party is not a secured creditor, nor is a creditor who is entitled to exercise rights under a guarantee. Either creditor can elect to prove for his or her whole debt.

Insolvency may affect the rights of a security holder if:

(a) the giving of the security was an act of bankruptcy; or

(b) the security is voidable; or
(c) the security is void under the Chattels Transfer Act: s 18.

A secured creditor will usually retain his or her security and not prove in the bankruptcy, see eg *Re Cassidy (a bankrupt)* [1982] 2 NZLR 524. If there is likely to be a surplus after the creditor has realised his or her security and paid himself from the proceeds, the Assignee will arrange for the secured creditor to sell the security for cash, and so make the surplus available to the estate.

If the secured creditor realises his or her security, he or she may prove for the balance due to him or her after deducting the net amount realised: s 90(1). He or she can apply the proceeds from the realisation of his or her security on discharge of his or her non-preferential claim and prove for the preferential part of his or her claim: *Re William Hall (Contractors) Ltd (In Liq)* [1967] 1 WLR 948 [1967] 2 All ER 1150.

When, however, the secured creditor elects to prove in the bankruptcy, he or she must either surrender his or her security to the Assignee for the benefit of creditors and prove for the whole debt or else state particulars of his or her security and his or her assessment of its value in his or her proof and prove only for the remaining balance: s 90(4). If the value stated is made bona fide on a mistaken estimate or the security has dropped in value, he or she may amend his or her proof: s 90(6).

A secured creditor who has surrendered his or her security may change his or her mind. With the leave of the Court and probably the payment of costs he or she may at any time before the sale of his or her security either:

(i) Withdraw the surrender and rely on the security; or
(ii) Submit a fresh proof of debt: s 90(3).

If the Assignee is dissatisfied with the assessment of value made by the secured creditor, he or she may order that the security be sold, and, if the sale is by public auction, the secured creditor or the Assignee on behalf of the state may bid for the purchase of the property. Likewise, a secured creditor after having valued his or her security may decide to sell. In both cases the amount realised will be substituted for the secured creditor's valuation and his or her proof will be amended accordingly: s 90(8).

Where a security is so valued by the secured creditor, the Assignee may at any time redeem it on payment to the creditor of the amount at which he or she valued it: s 90(5)(a).

The substituted valuation may result in the secured creditor having to refund to the Assignee part of the dividend he or she has received; on the other hand he or she may be entitled to an additional payment, but there will have to be money available for the payment of dividends; he or she will not be entitled to disturb dividends already paid: s 90(7).

The secured creditor may at any time, by notice in writing, require the assignee to elect whether he or she will exercise his or her power to redeem or require it to be realised. If the Assignee does not, within six months after he or she receives the notice, signify in writing to the creditor his or her election to exercise the power, he or she shall not be entitled to exercise it, and the interest in the property comprised in the security which is vested in the Assignee shall vest in the creditor, and the amount of his or her debt shall be reduced by the amount at which the security has been valued: s 90(5). This subsection will not be used frequently, as secured creditors will prefer to rely on their securities.

Subject to s 90(5), the secured creditor shall not receive more than 100 cents in $1 and interest as allowed in s 94. Although the general rule is that provable debts are released by discharge, and most securities will be given for provable debts, nevertheless discharge will not affect the creditor's right to his or her security.

47.5 PROOF IN PARTICULAR CASES

The Act sets out rules governing proof by creditors in particular cases, some of which are discussed below.

47.5.1 Right of set-off

The existence of a right of set-off is determined as at the date of adjudication.

A creditor of the bankrupt is allowed to set off in full a debt owed by him or her to the bankrupt against a debt owed by the bankrupt to him. Such set-offs have the effect of paying the creditor 100 cents for each dollar claimed against the bankrupt estate.

There are two prerequisites to any such set-off (s 93):

(i) That the person claiming the benefit of any set-off had no notice of an available act of bankruptcy committed by the bankrupt. The creditor claiming the benefit of the set-off shall, in his or her proof, declare that he or she had at the time of giving credit no notice of such an act of bankruptcy.

(ii) That there must be mutuality of debts, credits or dealings. This "mutuality" exists if the debt, credit or dealing against which it is to be set off, is between the same parties. For example a joint debt cannot be set off against a separate debt; nor a debt due to three partners against a debt due from two of them. Mutuality must exist, and be ascertained as at the date of adjudication: *Re Milan Tramways Co, Ex parte Theys* (1884) 25 ChD 587.

Mutuality is essential before the right of set-off is allowed, and the creditor must have the beneficial interest and not merely a legal interest in the debt owed by the bankrupt. Thus, he or she cannot claim a right of set-off for a debt owed to him or her as trustee against money owed by him or her personally to the bankrupt: *Re Guthrie and Allied Companies* (1901) 4 GLR 155; *Shand v Atkinson Ltd* [1966] NZLR 551. Similarly, trust money held by a solicitor cannot be retained as a set-off on the bankruptcy of the client: *Official Assignee of Reeves and Williams v Dorrington* [1918] NZLR 702; [1918] GLR 568.

In *Rolls Razor Ltd v Cox* [1967] 1 QB 552 the Court of Appeal held that parties cannot contract out of the provisions of s 93 of the Insolvency Act 1967.

47.5.2 Hire purchase agreements

The vendor's right to payment of the unpaid balance where the Assignee of a bankrupt purchaser's estate decides to complete the purchase of hire purchase goods and the vendor's right of proof where he or she has not repossessed the goods or has repossessed the goods but not sold them has already been discussed, supra.

47.5.3 Double proof

The general rule is that there cannot be two proofs in respect of what is in substance one debt, but double proof may be made where:

(a) The bankrupt, at the date of adjudication, is a member of two or more different firms or is a sole contractor and also a member of a firm, and there have been distinct contracts with the same creditor. Proof may be made in respect of the contracts against each of the properties respectively liable on such contracts.

(b) Where there is liability for the same debt by the same person in two different legal capacities. Thus, if the firm A, B & C and A, B and C as individuals gave a joint and several promissory note to a creditor and the firm is adjudged bankrupt, proof can be made against the partnership assets for the whole amount and also against the private estates of the partners, A, B, and C, in their individual capacities: s 97.

Section 82, relating to the keeping of accounts and the application of the estates in a joint bankruptcy, is still paramount where purely partnership or private debts are concerned.

For a discussion of the general rule see *Barclays Bank Ltd v TOSG Trust Fund Ltd* [1984]1 All ER 628 (CA); 1060 (HL).

47.5.4 Wages

Employees may submit proofs as ordinary unsecured creditors for any amount due to them in excess of the preferential claim allowed under s 104.

47.5.5 Deferred creditors

Certain creditors have their claims postponed until all other creditors have been paid in full (though not all deferred debts rank equally as between themselves). It appears that they are not entitled to prove, even for the purpose of voting, until the other creditors have been paid in full. Some authority for this proposition in regard to claims deferred by the Partnership Act 1908, s 6, is found in *Ex parte Taylor, Re Grason* (1879) 12 ChD 366.

The following creditors' claims are postponed until other creditors' claims have been fully satisfied:

(a) Claims for moneys lent or property entrusted by a husband or wife to the other for use in his or her business or for moneys lent for any purpose at all. Such property or the moneys so lent are treated as assets in the bankrupt estate of the wife of husband, as the case may be. See s 43(1), (2), supra.

(b) Claims by a settlor's husband, wife or children under a covenant or contract made in consideration of marriage for future payment of money or for the settlement of property in which the settlor had no interest at the time of settlement: s 54(4).

(c) Where the creditor has lent money to another on the basis that he or she will receive a rate of interest varying with the profits or a share of the profit; Partnership Act 1908, s 6. The same Act provides that the claims of partners on dissolution are deferred until all other creditors have been paid.

(d) Where the vendor of the goodwill of a business has arranged to receive payment therefor by a share of the profits of the business; Partnership Act 1908, s 6.

47.6 CREDITORS WHOSE CLAIMS ARE NOT PROVABLE

Discharge from bankruptcy does not release the bankrupt from debts which are not provable, but such creditors cannot compel payment of their claims until after the debtor is discharged. If they get judgment during the debtor's bankruptcy, they cannot levy execution until after discharge. A creditor with a debt he or she cannot prove can wait until the debtor is in a stronger financial position and then compel payment in full instead of accepting a mere token payment in full satisfaction of his or her claims. The Court is not, however, prevented from enforcing payment of fines and penalties.

47.7 DISTRIBUTION OF THE BANKRUPT'S ASSETS

In general, each creditor receives the share of the bankrupt's assets in the proportion that his or her debt stands to the total indebtedness, but there are certain exceptions to this general rule.

47.7.1 Debtor's right to retain personal possessions

Section 52 provides that the bankrupt is entitled within seven days of adjudication or within such further time as the Assignee allows to select and retain:

(a) Necessary tools of trade to the value, in the opinion of the Assignee, of $100; and
(b) Necessary household furniture, effects and wearing apparel to the value of $300.

The qualification "necessary" means tools required by the bankrupt to earn his or her living, not equipment in a business such as a cash register: *Re Douglas* [1959] NZLR 1214, 1216; nor does the furniture to which the bankrupt is entitled include office furniture.

The allowance may exceed $100 and $300 respectively if the creditors so resolve. This provision does not affect the rights of any party to a chattels security or hire purchase agreement over the goods selected by the bankrupt.

If the tools of trade or the furniture and personal and household effects selected by the bankrupt are less than $100 and $300 in value, the bankrupt is not entitled to some other form of property to make up the difference: s 52(1)(a) and (b).

It is essential for the bankrupt to show good faith in the exercise of this right. A bankrupt who omits certain chattels from his or her statement of affairs or arbitrarily appropriates certain articles without coming to an agreement with the Assignee as to their value cannot defend his or her action by maintaining he or she was exercising his or her right of selection under s 52. The allowance made to the bankrupt for furniture and household effects may, in the event of his or her death, be exercised by a member of the family approved by the Assignee or the Court: s 52(3).

47.7.2 Preferential payments

When the Assignee is distributing the assets of the estate he or she must, subject to the provisions of any other enactment and in terms of s 104, pay the claims thereon in the following order:

First priority – Costs, charges, allowances and expenses incurred by or payable by the Assignee. These include allowances made to enable the bankrupt to comply with his or her duties under the Act.

Where, prior to adjudication, a trustee for the benefit of creditors takes steps to realise the estate and his or her work is accepted by the Assignee payment of reasonable costs for his or her services may rank equally with other costs already mentioned: *Re Stephens* [1929] NZLR 254.

Second priority – Costs and expenses incurred by the creditor or (in accordance with the scale prescribed) the costs of the debtor's solicitor in having the debtor adjudicated bankrupt.

Third priority – The Assignee's commission.

Fourth priority – (a) Arrears of wages or salaries due to a servant or worker for time or piecework or commission earned during the four months immediately preceding adjudication, but not exceeding $1500. Holiday pay falling due on the termination of employment, whether such termination preceded adjudication or not, is included in this priority but not so as to increase the amount of $1500 above. The definition of "holiday pay" and "wages" should be noted in s 104(3).

Any additional sum for salary or wages must be proved for in the ordinary way: s 104(1)(f). Whether a person is or is not a servant or worker will depend upon the actual terms of his or her employment. A managing director has been held not to be a clerk or servant; a secretary of a company was held to be a servant. Control or direction by an employer is necessary to establish the claimant's status as a servant (*Re Ashley and Smith Ltd, Ashley v The Company* [1918] 2 Ch 378), but a person performing piecework on commission has been held to be a servant.

Wage claims by the spouse of the bankrupt's business are relegated to the seventh priority: see below.

Any person who has, within the four-month period above, advanced money which has been used to meet the preferential claims for wages, salary and holiday pay shall have, to the extent his or her advance has not been recouped, the same rights of preferential payment from the bankrupt estate as the original claimant.

Trading banks making such advances or receiving repayments have a special dispensation: s 104(2).

Employers are required by the Accident Compensation Act 1982 to pay an injured employee his or her full wages for the first week of his or her disability. This compensation up to the amount of $1500 is included in the fourth priority if the employer has been adjudicated bankrupt. Accident Compensation Act 1982, s 58.

The Volunteer's Employment Protection Act 1973, ss 6, 15, provides that the Court may order an employer who has dismissed an employee who has volunteered to undertake service in Her Majesty's armed forces to pay 16 normal weeks pay not exceeding $200. This claim will also be in the fourth priority if the employer was adjudicated bankrupt and had dismissed the employee before a creditor had filed petition in bankruptcy against the employer or the employer had filed his or her own petition.

(b) All sums ordered by the Court to be paid out of the bankrupt's estate by way of partial refund of any fee or premium paid in respect of the apprenticeship which had terminated through adjudication.

(c) Solicitors' and accountants' fees in lieu of a lien over documents with a limit of $100 for each claimant: s 73(2).

All debts in the fourth priority abate rateably where there is insufficient money to pay them in full.

Unpaid GST ranks after the fourth priority category: s 42(2)(a), Goods and Services Tax Act 1985.

Fifth priority – First, tax payments deducted by the bankrupt from the wages or salaries of employees but not paid over to the Commissioner of Taxes; Income Tax Act 1976, s 365(2)(a).

Secondly, where a seller of "lay-by" goods cannot supply the goods he or she contracted to deliver to the purchaser on completion of payments by the latter the purchaser shall be a preferred creditor ranking between the fifth and sixth priorities to the extent of the payments he or she has made to the bankrupt seller: Layby Sales Act 1971, s 11.

Sixth priority – Debts admitted in the bankruptcy not already provided for but excluding those in the seventh priority. Proved debts include claims for income tax of self-employed persons. All sixth priority claims rank equally and abate pari passu if there is insufficient to pay them in full.

No payment can be made in respect of these debts unless the claims above have been paid 100¢ in $1.00. The Crown is entitled to no priority, as such.

Seventh priority – (a) Unpaid wages owing to the bankrupt's spouse if employed in the bankrupt's trade or business.

(b) Claims of a person who lends money to a business with interest varying with the amount of profit made or by the vendor of goodwill to whom "payment will be made by a share in the profits of a business, and to a person claiming the return of capital assets he or she has employed in a business". However the following deferred debts are excluded:

(i) Certain loans made or property entrusted by a spouse to the bankrupt. These are treated as part of the bankrupt's estate if made within the four years preceding adjudication. The claim for the return of such loan or payment of the value of the property is treated as a deferred debt and falls into the ninth priority: s 43.

(ii) Covenants or contracts made in consideration of marriage for a future payment of money or in respect of property in which the settlor had no present interest: s 54(4). This also falls into the ninth priority.

(Both (a) and (b) categories are payable rateably, ie if need be will abate proportionately.)

Eighth priority – Payment of interest from the date of adjudication on all debts admitted in the bankruptcy except those in ss 43 and 54(4) above. Eleven percent interest is allowed on High Court judgments.

Ninth priority – Payment of the debts referred to in ss 43 and 54(4) above, with interest thereon from the date of adjudication.

Tenth priority – The surplus to the bankrupt, except where s 55(2)(c) requires a refund to be made to any person who has paid to the bankrupt estate the ascertained value of property purchased by the bankrupt for him or her or the value of the improvements effected to the property of another by the bankrupt under s 55(2)(c).

47.7.3 Dividends

It is the duty of the Assignee to collect and realise the bankrupt's assets. The Act gives a direction that no dividend shall be paid out until two months after adjudication. Subject to the retention of sufficient funds to meet the costs of administration, the Assignee shall thereafter, with all convenient speed, declare and distribute dividends amongst the creditors who have proved, treating the creditors in the order of priority laid down in s 104.

Any of these creditors may, in case of undue delay after the two months aforesaid, apply to the Court for an order that the Assignee proceed with the distribution of dividends forthwith: s 105(3). Likewise, s 86 allows a creditor who is dissatisfied with the administration of the bankrupt's estate to appeal to the Court against the decision by the Assignee. The bankrupt has a similar right of appeal under the same section if he or she can show that there is or could be, with an alteration in the methods of administration, a surplus in the estate: *Re a Debtor* [1949] Ch 236.

Notice of the time and place of payment of the dividend should be sent to the creditors and advertised. Generally, there are two dividends paid – the first one distributing the major portion of the estate and the final dividend distributing any smaller amounts which may subsequently come into the hands of the Assignee when the estate is fully realised.

Except where the dividend has been declared more than four months after adjudication, the Assignee shall make provision for provable debts appearing from the bankrupt's statement to be owing to persons:

(a) So far distant that in the ordinary course of communications they have not had time to tender their proofs or establish them if disputed;
(b) Whose address is unknown to the Assignee;
(c) Whom the Assignee believes not to have had notice of the bankruptcy;
(d) Who have debts provable in respect of claims not yet determined.

The Court may order the Assignee to make such provisions although the dividend is being paid more than four months after adjudication: s 105(5), (6).

Where a creditor proves late, he or she is entitled to the same proportionate part of his or her debt as the other creditors had received previously – but there must be sufficient funds for this in the hands of the Assignee. A creditor proving late cannot disturb dividends declared before he or she proved his or her debt.

If a creditor on the due amendment of his or her proof increases his or her claim he or she shall be entitled to be paid an extra dividend in due proportion on such extra amount, again provided that there are sufficient funds in the hands of the Assignee – he or she, also, is not entitled to disturb dividends declared before land. If a creditor amends his or her proof so that this claim is reduced, he or she shall make a proportionate refund to the Assignee.

Creditors of joint debtors shall receive nothing from their respective separate estates until the separate creditors have been fully paid and vice versa.

The creditors of one bankrupt partner jointly indebted with other partners shall not receive any dividend out of his or her separate (private) estate until all his or her separate creditors have been paid in full; s 106.

Chapter 48

DISCHARGE AND ANNULMENT

48.1 DISCHARGE

48.1.1 Automatic discharge

Up till the passing of the Insolvency Act approximately 80 percent of the people who were adjudicated bankrupt failed to apply for a discharge. This has been remedied by s 107 of the Act, which provides for automatic discharge from bankruptcy after the expiration of three years from adjudication. No application to the Court is necessary. However, the bankrupt is not entitled to automatic discharge if:

(a) The Assignee or (with the leave of the Court) a creditor, who has proved, has entered an objection; or
(b) The bankrupt is still undischarged from an earlier bankruptcy; or
(c) He or she has to be publicly examined and has not undergone that examination; s 107(3), (6).

A certificate of discharge shall be sent by the Assignee in January to any bankrupt discharged in the previous year: reg 48.

There is nothing to prevent a bankrupt from applying to the Court with a view to getting an earlier discharge: s 108.

48.1.2 Discharge on application by the bankrupt

If an order of discharge is not granted on application by the bankrupt he or she can make further applications from time to time (s 108) unless the Court in refusing the discharge stipulates the earliest date on which he or she can apply again: s 110(d).

909

Where a bankrupt intends to apply to the Court for an order of discharge pursuant to s 108 of the Act, notice of the time and the place at which he or she proposes to make the application shall be advertised by him or her and sent to the Assignee and all creditors who have proved their claims at least twenty-one days before the day so proposed: R   75.

If the bankrupt applies for his or her discharge himself or herself, or if his or her automatic discharge after three years is opposed by the Assignee or any creditor, the Assignee must, not less than seven days prior to the date of hearing file in the Court a report on the bankrupt's affairs, the causes of his or her bankruptcy, the manner in which he or she has performed his or her duties and other matters of assistance to the Court in reaching its decision. A copy of the report must be sent to the bankrupt: s 109(2), R 76. Statements in the Assignee's report without an affidavit in support are accepted as evidence by the Court and such evidence shall be deemed to be sufficient of the matters reported unless there is evidence to the contrary: R 35, but see *Re Dutton*, infra. Any creditor opposing the discharge on grounds other than those mentioned in the Assignee's report shall give notice of his or her opposition, setting out the grounds thereof, to the Assignee and to the bankrupt, not less than three days before the hearing: s 109(4), R 77.

Section 69 makes provision for public examination of the bankrupt by the Court before the grant of an absolute order of discharge. The Assignee may file a statement in Court that a public examination is desirable or the creditors may pass an ordinary resolution certified by the Assignee to like effect. This is also filed in Court. The public examination is held as soon as practicable after the expiration of seven days after notice of the filing of such statement or resolution is given to the bankrupt. Notice of intention to hold the examination is advertised and sent to the creditors.

Again if a creditor or the Assignee objects to the automatic discharge of the bankrupt under s 107 above and has not withdrawn his or her objection, the bankrupt shall, as soon as practicable after the expiration of three years from the date of adjudication, be publicly examined concerning his or her discharge: s 109(1). If a creditor objects he or she must first obtain the leave of the Court to object and then file in the Court Form 24 of the Rules with a copy of the Court order granting leave to object. The creditor must serve a copy of the notice on the Assignee: R 73, s 107(3).

The public examination adds substantially to the costs of the administration of the estate and it should not be held unless it seems probable that the bankrupt has committed an offence or the creditors desire personally to investigate the bankrupt's affairs and the pattern of conduct in his dealings with others. The provisions relating to this examination have been discussed at 43.3.4, supra.

If the public examination is held, counsel for the bankrupt usually asks the Court for an order that the bankrupt's affairs have been sufficiently investigated and that his or her examination is finished: s 69(7).

If the bankrupt has been evasive in his or her answers or the conduct of his or her affairs has been scandalous or reckless of the interests of those who have had dealings with him or her and it appears that additional relevant information may be obtained through the publicity attendant on the examination, the Judge, at his or her discretion or on the application of a creditor, may declare that the bankrupt's affairs have not been sufficiently investigated and the examination is not finished. It is for the Court to decide whether the bankrupt's affairs have been sufficiently investigated; the mere consent of the parties taking part does not determine the question of whether the bankrupt's examination is finished: *In re Wallace Gunson, Neale and Co* [1960] NZLR 769. No public examination can be conducted, nor can any order of discharge be granted by the Registrar; such hearings must take place before a Judge in open Court: s 5.

Where the bankrupt applies to the Court for discharge or automatic discharge at the end of the three years following adjudication is opposed by the creditors, the Court will be strongly influenced, in dealing with the application for discharge, by the Assignee's report on the bankrupt's co-operation and conduct.

Creditors, in their own interest, should pay particular attention to any change in the financial circumstances of the bankrupt and the property coming into his or her control during the period between adjudication and discharge.

The dictum of Vaughan Williams LJ in *Re Gaskell* [1904] 2 KB 478, 482, is frequently quoted in support of an application for discharge. This dictum was referred to with approval by Ostler J in *Re Jones* [1926] NZLR 318; [1926] GLR 252, and there appears to be a tendency to treat it as a general principle for the guidance of the Court in granting an order of discharge. Vaughan Williams LJ stated:

> ... the overriding intention of the Legislature in all Bankruptcy Acts is that the debtor on giving up the whole of his property shall [in the absence of misconduct on his part] be a free man again, able to earn his livelihood, and having the ordinary inducements to industry.

The conditions attached by the learned Judge to the bankrupt becoming a free man again should be examined closely. The two conditions are: first, that a bankrupt should surrender his or her property and, secondly, absence of misconduct in the conduct of his or her business affairs. It is submitted that misconduct on the part of the bankrupt is not restricted to penal offences committed by the bankrupt, but includes irresponsible acceptance of credit and the use of the property of others, coupled with any subsequent disregard of the creditors' or property owners' interests.

The first condition requires that the bankrupt should give up the whole of his or her property. "Property" in bankruptcy includes not only property owned by the bankrupt at the time of the commencement of bankruptcy or even at the date of adjudication, but also "future" property: s 2. Furthermore, s 42(2)(a) specifically states that the property passing to the assignee and divisible amongst his or her creditors comprises:

> All property whatsoever and wheresoever situated belonging to or vested in the bankrupt at the commencement of the bankruptcy, or acquired by or devolving upon him or her before his or her discharge.

A surrender of all the bankrupt's property to the Assignee at the date of adjudication is insufficient. If there is a long period of time between adjudication and discharge, the onus is on the bankrupt to establish that his or her "property", as defined above, has in fact been made available to creditors, although it is submitted that the emphasis of the current legislation on rehabilitation of the bankrupt even before discharge (s 49) must be recognised where after-acquired property is concerned. Likewise, so long as the bankrupt has faithfully reported any acquisition of property subsequent to adjudication to the Assignee he or she will have complied with the spirit of the law. In *Re Dutton, ex parte Auckland Aero Club* (unreported, 1955) Stanton J disregarded the report of the Official Assignee which favoured discharge being granted to the bankrupt, and made discharge conditional on the bankrupt making payments out of his or her excess earnings, above the normal requirements for his support. The amount of dividend already paid was only a few pence in the pound and the debt was incurred through the destruction of an aircraft in complete disregard of Civil Aviation Regulations. It was proved that the bankrupt, who was single, had spent several hundred pounds in flying since adjudication, that he had made at least one substantial gift of money, had been in constant employment and was, at the time of making application for discharge, earning high wages as a topdressing pilot.

The Court of Appeal in England has issued a warning of the danger in citing as a general principle observations on a particular set of facts. In *Re Smith* [1947] 1 All ER 769, 771, Lord Greene MR, said in reference to the dictum of Vaughan Williams LJ in *Re Gaskell:*

> I myself always hesitate to extract from observations on the exercise of a discretion general principles which will operate to fetter that discretion in the future. We have been warned many times, especially in recent years, of the impropriety of attempting to lay down principles which would fetter a discretion in dealing with the facts of some individual case. . . . It may well be that [the principle] was a helpful angle with which to regard the facts of that case but, with all respect, it gives me no great assistance in dealing with the facts of this case. . . .

48.1.3 The order of the Court on an application for discharge

At the hearing of an application for discharge or at any examination where the automatic discharge of the bankrupt is opposed the Court may:

(a) Grant an immediate order of discharge;
(b) Grant an order of discharge subject to such conditions (including consenting to any judgment or order for the payment of any sum of money) as it thinks fit, or suspend an order for discharge for such time as it thinks fit;
(c) Grant an order of discharge with or without such conditions as it thinks fit to take effect at a specified future date;
(d) Refuse an order of discharge, in which case the Court may specify the earliest date on which the bankrupt may apply again to the Court for an order of discharge: s 110.

No restrictions are placed on the Court by the present Act in deciding whether to give the bankrupt his or her discharge or not. Thus the Court is not debarred from granting an unconditional discharge on the ground that the bankrupt had been guilty of an offence under the Act, or of misconduct or gross negligence in conducting his or her business. Nor is the bankrupt debarred from being given an immediate order of discharge on the ground that the preferential claim for wages had not been met in full.

An order of the Court made under s 110 above overrides the provision for automatic discharge in s 107.

Any judgment entered with the consent of the bankrupt under (b) above may be varied by the Court: s 110(3).

The Court may, on the application of a bankrupt, grant an absolute order of discharge where the bankrupt has failed to comply with a conditional order, provided the bankrupt cannot justly be held responsible for the failure to comply: s 113.

The fact that the order of discharge has been suspended or refused may be published: s 118(1). Suspension of discharge should be regarded as a mark of disapproval by the Court and a form of punishment of the bankrupt.

Where the Court is not satisfied with the bankrupt's conduct generally and considers that facilitating his or her entry into business again is contrary to public interest, discharge should be refused: *Re Martin, Ex parte James* [1952] NZLR 142; [1952] GLR 150. In granting an order of discharge, the Court will have regard, not only to the interest of the creditors, but also to the interests of the community. Thus discharge will not be granted subject to such harsh conditions that the bankrupt cannot hope to better his or her position: *Re Badcock* (1886) 3 Morr 138.

The Court cannot suspend the order of discharge for a certain period and at the same time make it subject to conditions. The powers under s 110(b), (c) and (d) cannot be exercised concurrently: *Re Atwill* [1958] NZLR 873.

Any agreement made by a creditor not to oppose the debtor's discharge in consideration of the payment of part of his or her debt is illegal. In *Re Hubber* [1954] NZLR 907, a conditional order of discharge was granted to a bankrupt subject to his or her consenting to judgment being entered for a total debt owing to one creditor. The bankrupt refused to consent to this condition, but later entered into an agreement with the creditor concerned to pay him or her a portion of this debt provided he or she would not oppose his discharge. The agreement was held to be illegal as tending to pervert the course of justice.

No agreement by creditors which virtually condones an offence by the bankrupt will affect the Court. Thus the Court will not grant a discharge to a bankrupt who has absconded from the jurisdiction, whether the creditors have agreed to the discharge or not: *Re McAlpine* (1913) 15 GLR 654.

48.1.4 Effect of discharge

An order of discharge releases the bankrupt from most provable debts, irrespective of whether they have been proved or not. But the following debts are not released:

(a) Debts incurred by fraud or fraudulent breach of trust to which he or she was a party;

(b) Debts whereof he or she has obtained forbearance by any fraud to which he or she was a party;

(c) Debts in respect of which he or she has consented to judgment being entered by the Assignee as a condition of discharge (s 110 (b));

(d) Any payments that the Court prior to absolute discharge has ordered the bankrupt to make in reduction of his or her debts (s 45(1), (3)); this type of obligation could never be classed as a provable debt;

(e) Any amount payable under a maintenance order under the Family Proceedings Act 1980, s 102. Neither the adjudication of one spouse nor his or her subsequent discharge from bankruptcy will affect the rights of the other spouse to claim payment from the Assignee of his or her "protected interest" of $10,000 or half of the proceeds from the sale of the matrimonial home (whichever is the lesser in value): Matrimonial Property Act 1976, ss 20, 8, 11, 12.

(f) Debts not provable in bankruptcy pursuant to s 87.

Contrary to general principles, the order of discharge does not release a surety for a debt due by the bankrupt, nor does it release partners, co-trustees or co-contractors of the bankrupt: s 116.

But where a creditor brings action in respect of a provable debt, the order of discharge is conclusive evidence of the bankruptcy (and the consequential release of the provable debt) against the creditor: s 115. The defence is available even if the creditor's name was omitted from the list of creditors: *Elmslie v Corrie* (1878) 4 QBD 295.

A debt is not treated as statute barred unless it was so barred at the date of adjudication. If it is statute barred at this date, then it is not a provable debt: s 87(1).

In order of discharge does not release a bankrupt from the following types of liability or obligation:

(a) Fines or penalties or orders for the payment of money made pursuant to any conviction or under s 19 of the Criminal Justice Act 1985.

(b) Negative covenants. A bankrupt is deemed to retain his or her power of refraining from doing things. Thus in *McCarthy v Mace* (1885) NZLR 3 SC 57, the defendant had sold his brewery business and covenanted not to sell ale in Wellington for 21 years. It was held that the bankruptcy of the defendant did not release him from his covenant.

(c) Future rental due on a lease which has not been disclaimed is not a provable debt and accordingly is not released on discharge: *Metropolis Estate Co Ltd v Wilde* [1940] 2 KB 536; [1940] 3 All ER 522.

(d) A debt subject to a mortgage owed to a debtor who did not prove: *Lamont v Bank of New Zealand* [1981] 2 NZLR 142.

Generally promises by a bankrupt to pay provable debts are not enforceable. If a debtor before discharge promises to pay a provable debt he or she will be bound if new consideration for this promise is given: *Wild v Tucker* [1914] 3 KB 36; likewise, a debtor who has been discharged from bankruptcy may be bound to pay a debt which has been released, provided new consideration for this promise is given: *Jakeman v Cook* (1878) 4 Ex D 26.

48.1.5 The position of the bankrupt after discharge

(a) RESTRICTION ON ENGAGING IN BUSINESS
The Court, before or when granting an order of discharge, may make an order prohibiting the bankrupt after discharge from doing the following things without the leave of the Court:

(a) Entering into or carrying on any business, either alone or in partnership;

(b) Being engaged in the management or control of any business carried on by or on behalf of, or being in the employ of, any of the following persons, namely, the bankrupt's wife or husband, a lineal ancestor or descendant of the bankrupt, the wife or husband of such an ancestor or descendant, a brother of the bankrupt, the wife of such a brother, a sister of the bankrupt, and the husband of such a sister;

(c) Acting as a director or participating in the management of any company.

An order of this type cannot be made after the bankrupt has received his or her discharge.

The period of restriction need not be limited in time but the Court may at any time cancel or vary the order: s 111.

(b) DUTIES OF THE DISCHARGED BANKRUPT
An application for discharge may be granted before the final dividend is paid, but the discharged bankrupt must continue to help in the realisation and distribution of the estate, if so required by the Assignee or the Court: s 117. For example, the bankrupt may be entitled to a share in a deceased estate subject to a life interest. The Assignee would notify the trustees of his or her claim, but the creditors might not receive the final dividend for many years.

Section 45 of the Act provides that the Court, at any time before the granting of an absolute order of discharge, may after considering the bankrupt's financial position, his or her conduct and after making a reasonable allowance for the maintenance of the bankrupt's spouse and family, order the bankrupt to pay a lump sum or make periodic payments in reduction of his or her debts. Such an order is not cancelled by an order of discharge.

Section 118 empowers the Secretary of Justice to publish a list of undischarged bankrupts from time to time.

48.1.6 Reversal of order of discharge

On application by the Assignee or any creditor made within two years of the absolute or conditional order taking effect, the Court may reverse the order of discharge. Facts must be established which, had they been known at the time of granting the order of discharge, would have justified the Court in refusing the order. The application will not be considered by the Court if these facts could have been discovered by the exercise of reasonable diligence at the time the order of discharge was made. The reversal shall not prejudicially affect those who have contracted with the debtor since his or her discharge, and any property acquired by the bankrupt since discharge shall vest in the Assignee subject to all equities and encumbrances and shall be applied by the Assignee, in the first instance, to satisfy debts incurred since the date of the order so reversed: s 112.

48.2 ANNULMENT OF ADJUDICATION

Annulment is a discretionary power of the Court and may not be desired by the debtor concerned, particularly if he or she has resorted to bankruptcy to escape his or her normal liabilities. It should not be granted if, in the circumstances, an application by the bankrupt for discharge would have been refused, nor is the Court in any way bound because all the creditors consent to an order of annulment being made.

An order of adjudication improperly made cannot be rescinded under the inherent discretionary power of the Court. It has immediate effect in respect of the bankrupt's property. The proper course is to annul the order: *Re Byron, Ex parte Commissioner of Inland Revenue* [1964] NZLR 508.

48.2.1 Circumstances in which an order of annulment may be made

Upon the application of the Assignee or any person interested, adjudication may be annulled under s 119.

(a) Where in the opinion of the Court an order of adjudication should not have been made.

Adjudication obtained for an ulterior motive, amounting to an abuse of the process of the Court, may be annulled. Of course it may turn out that the "bankrupt" is in fact solvent. Unanimous consent of all creditors to the application for annulment is no ground for making such an order: *Re Flateau* [1893] 2 QB 219 (CA). Misfortune suffered by the bankrupt not arising out of misconduct or recklessness may be accepted as justification for the submission that the order of adjudication should not have been made. The fact that the only debt was unenforceable is not a ground for annulment "if the debtor honestly believed on reasonable grounds that he was unable to pay his debts": *Re Harry Dutton* [1949] Ch 640; [1949] 2 All ER 388. Where a minor has been adjudicated bankrupt on a legally enforceable debt there now appears to be no ground for an application for annulment on the ground of infancy: *Re a Debtor, Ex parte Commissioners of Customs and Excise v The Debtor*, 42.2.3, 42.3.2, supra. The Court has a discretion to annul an order of adjudication based on an unenforceable debt due by a minor but the existence of other enforceable debts is a ground for refusing annulment: *Re Davenport, Ex parte The Bankrupt v Eric Street Properties*, 39.2.3 supra.

(b) Where the Court is of the opinion that the liability of the bankrupt to pay his or her debts should be revived because since the date of adjudication there has been a substantial change in the financial circumstances of the bankrupt. In *Clegg v Hanson* (unreported, High Court Palmerston North, B 75/86, 15 September 1987, Greig J) the bankrupt was not insolvent in a balance sheet sense but was unable to pay his debts as they fell due. He had borrowed to pay his debts. Although the Official Assignee did not oppose an annulment Greig J refused an order on the ground that there had been no substantial change of circumstances.

(c) Where the Court has approved a composition under Part XII of this Act.

In all cases under (a) and (b) above the Court exercises its discretion. Thus an order of annulment may be refused where the debtor's conduct does not merit annulment: *Re Taylor, Ex parte Taylor* [1901] 1 KB 744.

Paragraph (a), supra, is expressed in very wide terms; paragraph (b) is a reminder that creditors are entitled to claim through the Assignee property acquired by or devolving on the bankrupt after adjudication and before discharge. In the past there has been a tendency for creditors to accept the situation as it appeared at the first meeting of creditors, and Assignees may have felt that if creditors were not vigilant in their own interests there was little reason for them to assume the role of blood-hounds instead of watchdogs. Paragraph (a) gives the Court full powers to annul adjudication where the bankrupt is using adjudication as a means of evading legal liability, or in any case where bankruptcy is being used for some purpose other than an equitable distribution of assets amongst creditors and the relief of the debtor from liability which he or she has no reasonable expectation of being able to meet. This does not imply that a debtor cannot file a petition in order to protect himself or herself from legal process for debts he or she cannot pay. Thus, in *Re Devine, Ex parte Gyde* [1952] NZLR 646, Fair J said that, in his view, the Bankruptcy Act was not intended to enable persons to avoid payment of debts owing by them which by reasonable efforts they might discharge. However, he felt he was bound by the decision of the Court of Appeal in England in *Re Dunn* supra and with some reluctance, held that the filing by the bankrupt of a petition in order to avoid the enforcement of payment of a judgment obtained against him was not an abuse of the process of the Court. See also the note on *Re a Debtor, ex parte the Debtor v Allen* [1967] Ch 590, [1967]1 All ER 668.

The Court may annul adjudication after the debtor has obtained his or her discharge without proof that the debts have been paid in full: *Ex parte Firth* (1893) 11 NZLR 7.

If a bankrupt has paid in full debts admitted to proof, it is reasonable to infer that there has been "a substantial change in the financial circumstances of the bankrupt since the date of adjudication", and therefore an application for an order of annulment should be granted: *Re Hansen (A Bankrupt)* [1971] NZLR 927.

(d) Section 11 of the Act provides that proceedings under the Act shall not be set aside owing to inaccuracy or omission, provided no person is injuriously affected thereby. The Court has jurisdiction to direct that the irregularity be rectified and order that the proceedings continue. Where application is made to annul an order of adjudication on the ground of defective procedure the Court may, subject to any prior order made under s 11 above, annul the original order of adjudication, have the defect corrected and order the petition to be reheard as if no order of adjudication had taken place: s 119(4).

The order of annulment takes effect from the date on which it is made. But where the Court, as in (a) above, is of the opinion that the debtor should not have been adjudicated in the first place then it is effective, from and after, the date of adjudication: s 119(2), (3). Theoretically the debtor is regarded as never having been made bankrupt.

48.2.2 Effect of annulment

Upon annulment the balance of the property vested in the Assignee under bankruptcy revests in the bankrupt. Annulment does not affect the validity of any prior disposition of the bankrupt's property made by the Assignee. It appears that a creditor who has proved in the bankruptcy and whose proof has not been rejected by the Assignee, or a creditor who has not proved in the bankruptcy, are both entitled to claim payment of the debts from a debtor whose bankruptcy has been annulled: *More v More* [1962] Ch 424; [1962] 1 All ER 125. But a claim for a debt, proof of which was rejected by the Assignee, being something "duly done" by the Assignee (s 120(2), is not revived by an order of annulment: *Brandon v McHenry* [1891] 1 QB 538 (CA). The Assignee is not liable for any act done by him or her by reason only that an order of adjudication is either discharged or annulled: s 138.

Chapter 49

ALTERNATIVES TO BANKRUPTCY

SUMMARY

49.1 GENERAL

There are statutory and non-statutory alternatives to the Bankruptcy procedures discussed above. The non-statutory alternatives are either a private composition or arrangement with creditors to accept less than 100 cents for each dollar of indebtedness or assignment by the debtor of substantially all his or her assets to a trustee for the benefit of creditors. Both of these take place before an adjudication. There are two problems with either of these non-statutory alternatives. First, unless all the creditors agree to the composition or arrangement, and are in some way bound to it, any dissident creditor may subsequently seek to collect his or her whole debt. The second problem for any non-statutory alternative is that unless the creditor acknowledges in writing that he or she accepts a lesser sum in satisfaction of the original of the original debt, he or she will not be bound and could subsequently issue proceedings for the balance of the debt. The Court may prevent such a creditor bringing a bankruptcy petition (s 26(3)), but the Court does not appear to have any power to prevent the creditor levying execution against any of the goods or assets of the debtor at any time within the limitation period for bringing his or her action.

The statutory alternatives are designed specifically to overcome each of these problems. In essence the statutory alternatives provide that if all the necessary procedures are complied with then all the creditors are bound by the arrangement. The statutory alternatives are:

(1) Composition: Part XII of the Insolvency Act 1967. This alternative is open to debtors *after* they have been adjudicated bankrupt. Acceptance of the composition by the creditors and approval by the Court will annul the adjudication of Bankruptcy; s 123(2).

(2) Proposal: Part XV of the Insolvency Act 1967. This is a pre-adjudication alternative which has the advantage of preventing the debtor formally being adjudicated. The procedure is discussed below. The effect is to bind all creditors and release the debtor from all his or her debts.

(3) The Summary Instalment Order: Part XVI of the Insolvency Act 1967. This is another pre-adjudication procedure. Its application is restricted to insolvents whose total indebtedness is less than $4,000. This alternative is discussed further below. Essentially the summary instalment order procedure amounts to a Court supervised budget whereby the debtor repays his or her debts, or an agreed portion thereof, from his or her income or earnings over a period of time.

49.2 PRIVATE COMPOSITION

In its narrowest sense, an insolvent debtor making a private composition before adjudication keeps his or her assets and agrees to pay to his or her creditors a certain sum being less than 100 cents in the $1 in return for a release from his or her debts. Thus the operative part of a composition in this form would be expressed as follows:

> Now the creditors do hereby severally agree with the debtor that in consideration of the payment to each of them of a composition of 2 cents in the dollar on the amount of their respective debts within 2 days from the date of this agreement the creditors will severally accept the same in full satisfaction and discharge of the said debts due to them respectively and will on the receipt of the said composition give the debtor a release from the said debts.

It will be noticed that in this clause the creditors undertake to release the debtor on *payment* of a composition. If the deed makes *payment* the consideration for the discharge of the debtor, default by him or her generally entitles the creditors to sue for the whole of the balance of their unpaid debts. If, however, the creditors agree to accept the *promise* of the debtor in full satisfaction then, on default of the debtor, the claim is generally limited to the balance owing under the composition. In a composition the debtor usually agrees to make the necessary payments by instalments on set dates and further obtains a guarantee from one or two sureties who undertake to make good any default in payment by him.

A composition can be made by the debtor giving each creditor a bill of exchange for a sum smaller than his or her debt. Attention is drawn, however, to the provision of the Judicature Act 1908 where s 92 provides that an acknowledgment in writing by a creditor, or by any person authorised by him or her in writing in that behalf, of the receipt of a part of his or her debt in satisfaction of the whole debt shall operate as a discharge of the debt. Accordingly it is necessary to have the creditor acknowledge in writing the arrangement concluded.

49.3 ASSIGNMENT TO A TRUSTEE FOR THE BENEFIT OF CREDITORS

49.3.1 General

This is sometimes called a deed of arrangement or a private composition and, like the composition above, is made before the adjudication of the debtor. Also, like a composition, its primary object is to provide for an equitable distribution of the bankrupt's available resources and to benefit creditors generally. Sometimes an assignment will be accepted if it is in the creditors' interest that the debtor's business should be carried on for a period.

The trustee in such a case ought to make the contracts necessary for the conduct of the business in the debtor's name thus avoiding personal liability and refrain from taking the business in his or her own name.

An assignment may forestall an execution creditor intending to levy execution on the debtor's property and gain an advantage over the other creditors.

There are certain obvious advantages and disadvantages in the above arrangements. From the point of view of the debtor, there is the advantage that he or she avoids the publicity involved in bankruptcy. Both creditors and the debtor also avoid the delay and rigidity of bankruptcy proceedings.

There are certain disadvantages from the point of view of the trustee and also of the creditors in so far as a disposition of substantially the whole of the debtor's property is an act of bankruptcy, and may be used as the foundation of a creditor's petition. The position of the trustee is therefore uncertain for at least three months following the execution of the deed. Assignment for the benefit of creditors has been discussed as an act of bankruptcy at 42.3 supra. Reference should be made to these pages in connection with the powers available to assenting and non-assenting creditors to upset the deed of assignment and treat it as an act of bankruptcy.

Sometimes an insolvent debtor may, without prior consultation with his or her creditors, appoint a trustee and assign the major part of his or her property to him or her for realisation amongst the creditors. This is a risky method of procedure in that the trustee himself, or the terms of the trust, may not be acceptable to creditors, or the debtor may fail to obtain the consent of all the creditors to the arrangement.

The better procedure is to call a meeting of creditors who agree with the debtor on the choice of a trustee, the terms of the trust and the amount and nature of property to be transferred to the trustee. The creditors undertake, in consideration of the assignment of this property, not to take any legal steps to enforce their claims and to accept a part payment in full settlement. Such a deed of assignment is effective as soon as it has been delivered to the trustee or to the creditors, whether it has been delivered as an escrow or not. An assignment is revocable if the debtor assigns property to a trustee to pay all or some of his or her creditors and no creditor is named as a party to the deed or, if the creditors are named but are unaware of its existence and do not execute it: *Ellis and Co v Cross* [1915] 2 KB 254. Such a deed is nothing more than a power of attorney, revocable at the discretion of the debtor or his or her personal representatives. The trustee under such a deed cannot prevent an execution creditor seizing the property of the assignor.

If the disposition is for adequate consideration it may not be voidable under the Insolvency Act or any other statute, and certainly if it does not dispose of substantially the whole of the debtor's property it is not an available act of bankruptcy.

Assent of all the creditors to the assignment is important. It prevents any creditor from using it as an act of bankruptcy. However, the mere attendance at a meeting of creditors does not amount to assent and there is authority for saying that a creditor owes no duty to express dissent. Undue delay in expressing dissent may raise a presumption of assent.

A trustee under a deed of assignment who has performed services such as collecting and preserving assets cannot recover his or her costs, if creditors do not assent to the assignment: *Re Zakon* [1940] Ch 253.

It is not essential for all creditors to execute the assignment. Mere concurrence or acting on the deed will make it binding on them; *Ex parte Jerrard, Re Chambers* (1837) 3 Deac 1, 7. But a creditor's assent does not bind him or her if it has been induced by fraud or misrepresentation, or if there is any secret agreement between the debtor and another creditor: *Re Milner* (1885) 15 QBD 605. The property to be retained by the debtor should be specifically described and a trustee who allows other property to remain in his or her possession is personally liable to the creditors: *Re Pilling* (1873) LR 8 Ch 711.

Although the debtor is generally permitted to retain more than the $100 worth of tools of trade and $300 worth of personal possessions allowed to the bankrupt under s 52 of the Insolvency Act, the greater part of his or her property is assigned to the trustee. As the trustee is the legal owner of the property assigned and as he or she has no power of disclaimer, he or she should see that all onerous property is excluded from the assignment. Such property is left in the name of the debtor but he or she is required to make a declaration of trust in the deed that he or she will deal with such property as directed by the trustee.

49.3.2 The duties, rights and liabilities of the parties to an assignment

(a) THE TRUSTEE

(1) The trustee derives his or her powers from the general law relating to trustees and the Trustee Act 1956; he or she must rely on the deed for any special powers. In cases of doubt he or she should call a meeting of creditors.

(2) He or she is entitled only to such remuneration as is provided in the deed or is actually voted to him or her by the creditors.

(3) He or she holds the assigned property upon the following trusts:

    (i) To sell the property;
    (ii) To deduct costs from the proceeds;
    (iii) To make provision for the preferential claims in bankruptcy;
    (iv) To meet the claims of creditors upon the agreed terms;
    (v) To return any surplus to the debtor.

(4) He or she is empowered to require satisfactory proof by the creditors of debts.

(5) He or she must act impartially and prudently.

(6) He or she must keep proper accounts and, upon paying a dividend, he or she should send a statement to each creditor.

(7) If the deed becomes void through the debtor being adjudicated bankrupt, the trustee will have to account to the Assignee for all property he or she has received.

(8) In any case, he or she should not pay out until the deed has been executed and come to the knowledge of the creditors, as his or her authority in the meantime is revocable at the discretion of the debtor.

(9) He or she should not sell up the debtor's property or distribute dividends until three months have passed following the execution of the deed, as it may be upset on bankruptcy proceedings being taken by some creditors of whose existence he or she is unaware. In such a case he or she may not be entitled to his or her expenses and charges and will have to account fully for all property he or she has received. Further, a trustee may find himself treated as a trespasser by the Assignee or he or she may be held to be an agent accountable for all property received and profits made.

(10) If he or she does not dispose of any of the assigned property until at least three months after the execution of the Assignment and it proves to be void, he or she will not be bound to account to the Assignee for any transactions with or payments made out of the debtor's property in accordance with the terms of the trust, provided that he or she can show that he or she had no reason for suspecting the deed was void. Even if the deed proves to be void, the Assignee can elect to treat the trustee as his or her agent and refund to him or her any expenses incurred bona fide in the interest of creditors.

(11) If the Assignee does not elect to treat the trustee as his or her agent, the trustee may not be able to recover expenses and charges incurred during his or her trusteeship.

(12) It appears that a trustee is unwise to assent to any arrangement whereby the effects of the debtor are handed back to him or her, even though such a course is authorised by all the creditors who have executed the assignment. He or she certainly should not take the risk if there is any chance of a petition in bankruptcy being presented against the debtor within the three months following the execution of the deed. Another difficulty arises from the fact that the signatories to the deed may not include all the creditors, and other creditors may have the right to come in and participate during the continuance of the trust. A trustee would be liable for a breach of trust if he or she dealt with the estate in a manner contrary to the provisions of the deed.

(13) If a trustee under an assignment takes possession of the property of a debtor who is subsequently adjudicated bankrupt on a petition alleging the assignment as the act of bankruptcy, the Assignee has the option of treating him or her as his or her agent or as a trespasser. If he or she is treated as an agent, he or she is entitled to reimbursement as in (10) above, but if the Assignee deals with him or her as a trespasser he or she will have to hand over any property of the bankrupt remaining in his or her control and account for the value of any property he or she has disposed of: *Re Prigoshen* [1912] 2 KB 494.

(14) Sometimes a provision is inserted in the deed giving the trustee power to settle with a dissentient creditor, even to the extent of paying him or her 100c in the $1. From a strictly legal point of view, this clause is considered improper but it is sometimes expedient that such a dissentient creditor be paid in full rather than have the assignment upset by a subsequent bankruptcy proceedings.

(b) THE DEBTOR

(1) Usually he or she is entitled to freedom from judicial process for recovery of debts including bankruptcy proceedings, unless default is made under the assignment.

(2) He or she is entitled to a full discharge from the debts specified if the terms of the composition are carried out.

(3) He or she is normally entitled to any surplus of the assigned estate after payment of all costs and the fulfilment of the terms of the assignment. But sometimes the creditors are entitled to divide any surplus pro rata.

(4) He or she may, however, be adjudicated bankrupt if the composition fails to carry out the expressed intention of the creditors, or if any creditor who has not agreed to the composition files a bankruptcy petition.

(5) Creditors may be unwilling to provide in the deed of arrangement for the immediate release of the debtor and consequently it may be necessary to state that release will take effect upon compliance with all its terms. Thus, if a composition is made, the agreement might depend upon the fulfilment of other conditions, such as disclosure by the debtor of any after-acquired property and full co-operation by the debtor in the collection and realisation of his or her estate.

(c) THE CREDITORS

(1) A creditor, who has given his or her implied assent to the arrangement by conduct, is deemed to have elected to abide by its terms and is entitled to share in the assets assigned although he or she may not have executed the document.

(2) The Court will sometimes allow (or even order) a creditor who has failed to signify his or her assent within the time specified by the deed to be made a party to it and share in the benefits:

(3) A creditor is entitled to payments in accordance with the terms of the composition out of the proceeds of the sale of the assigned property after the deduction of costs and preferential payments in bankruptcy.

(4) His or her rights against third parties or sureties are generally not prejudiced by entering into a composition.

(5) Normally, the creditor cannot institute legal proceedings for the recovery of debts against the debtor or for making him or her bankrupt so long as the terms of the assignment are being carried out.

(6) Even if a creditor does file a petition in bankruptcy based on such a disposition, the Court may, if it appears desirable that the estate should be administered under that disposition, order that the making of the disposition shall not be an act of bankruptcy and, stay or dismiss the petition and include him or her in the assignment on the same terms as the other creditors: Insolvency Act 1967, s 26(3).

49.4 STATUTORY COMPOSITIONS UNDER PART XII

49.4.1 General

In essence Part XII provides for the making of a composition *after* adjudication whereby the creditors accept in full satisfaction of their debts some arrangement for payment of less than 100 cents in the dollar. The composition has to be approved by the Court under s 122 and embodied in a deed which is executed by the Official Assignee and the bankrupt. The deed is then confirmed by the Court which annuls the adjudication under s 123.

49.4.2 The procedure

Under s 121 after adjudication the creditors may by special resolution accept a composition in satisfaction of their debts. Notice of the meeting must state generally the terms of the proposal for composition and be accompanied by a report of the Assignee thereon. Section 121(4) contains a special provision for computing the requisite majority. If the proposal provides for the payment in full of creditors whose debts do not exceed a particular amount that class of creditors is not to be reckoned either in number or value.

When the confirming resolution has been passed either the bankrupt or the Assignee may apply to the Court to approve the composition and notice of the application must be given to every creditor: s 122(1). Before approving the composition the Court must hear a report of the Assignee as to the terms of the composition and the conduct of the bankrupt and hear any objection which may be made by a creditor: s 122.

The Court has a discretion under s 122(3). It may refuse to approve the composition if it is of the opinion:

(a) that the provisions of section 121 of this Act have not been complied with; or
(b) that the terms of the composition are not reasonable or not calculated to benefit the general body of creditors; or
(c) that the bankrupt has committed any such misconduct as would justify the Court in refusing, qualifying, or suspending his or her discharge; or
(d) that for any reason it is not expedient that the composition should be approved.

With regard to s 122(3)(b) it has been held that for a composition to "benefit the general body of creditors" it must give the creditors an advantage they would not obtain in the bankruptcy: *Re Aylmer, ex parte Bischoffsheim* (1887) 19 QBD 33 (CA). The burden of proof of the fairness and reasonableness of a composition rests on those who put it forward. The matter is ultimately one of discretion for the Court but in practice the Court will be unlikely to refuse a composition which has the unanimous support of all the creditors: *Re Rogers, ex parte Rogers* (1884) 13 QBD 438, 449; *Re Flew, ex parte Flew* [1905] 1 KB 278; [1904-7] All ER Rep 548 (CA).

No composition can be approved which does not provide for the payment in priority to other debts of all debts directed to be so paid in the distribution of the property of a bankrupt: s 122(4). In other words the bankruptcy priority rules set out in s 104 must be complied with. A composition which has been approved by the Court is binding on all the creditors so far as it relates to any debts due to them which were provable in the bankruptcy: s 122(5). Although the Court has power to correct accidental or formal errors or omissions in a composition which has been approved no alteration in the substance of a composition can be made: s 122(6). The approval of the Court is conclusive as to the validity of the composition: s 122(7).

As soon as the Court has approved the composition the bankrupt and Assignee must execute a deed of composition to carry it into effect. This must then be produced at the Court and confirmed by it: s 123(1). Once the Court has confirmed the deed it is entered and filed in the Court and the Court annuls the adjudication. The deed is thereupon binding in all respects upon all the creditors as if they had executed it. Subject to the provisions of the Land Transfer Act 1952, the bankrupt's property covered by the deed vests according to the provisions of the deed: s123(2). An endorsement of the entry of the deed in the records of the Court is made on the deed which is then returned to the Assignee: s 123(3).

Provision is made by s 124 for enforcement of the composition. Any person aggrieved may apply to the Court for an order that the particular default be remedied: s 124(1). Application is by motion made in the summary manner: s 124(2). Section 124(3) provides that notwithstanding the provisions of the composition and the annulment of the adjudication the Court continues to have exclusive jurisdiction over the enforcement of the deed of composition; matters arising in connection with the bankrupt's property or affairs; the claim of a person to be a creditor; and the taxation of costs or charges of professional persons employed under the deed.

If the confirming resolution is not passed within one month after the passing of the preliminary resolution or if the composition is not approved by the Court within one month after the passing of the confirming resolution or if the deed of the composition is not executed by the bankrupt within seven days after approval by the Court, the bankruptcy proceedings continue: s 125(1).

49.5 PROPOSALS

49.5.1 General

Proposals by a debtor to his or her creditors under Part XV which are based on Canadian legislation differ from statutory compositions, in that they deal with the debtor's financial situation *before* he or she is adjudicated bankrupt. Section 26(3) of the Act empowers the Court, on application of the trustee appointed or the debtor or any creditor, to declare that the making of the disposition or proposal shall not be deemed to be an act of bankruptcy, and to stay the filing of or dismiss any petition filed. Once the proposal has been approved by the Court it is binding on all creditors whose debts are provable, as well as the insolvent.

An insolvent person, ie, a person who is not bankrupt but is unable to meet the debts that would be provable in his or her bankruptcy as they become due (s 139), may make a proposal to his or her creditors for the satisfaction of his or her debts. The proposal may include all or any of the following:

(a) An offer to assign all or any of his or her property to a trustee for the benefit of his or her creditors;
(b) An offer to pay his or her debts by instalments;
(c) An offer to compromise his or her debts at less than one hundred cents in the dollar;
(d) An offer to pay his or her debts at some time in the future;
(e) Any other offer for an arrangement for the satisfaction of his or her debts: s 140(2).

The insolvent may offer a security at the same time or may induce someone to guarantee his or her undertakings.

The proposal, signed by the insolvent, shall nominate a provisional trustee who acknowledges in writing that he or she will act: s 140(5). It must be in Form 32 as prescribed by R 83 and shall be accompanied by a statement of affairs set out in Form 33, verified by affidavit showing particulars of the insolvent's assets, debts, and liabilities, the name, address, and occupation of every creditor of the insolvent, and the securities held by each creditor: s 140(4).

The proposal is filed in the High Court nearest to where the insolvent resides. Neither the proposal nor any security or guarantee tendered with it may be withdrawn without the consent of the Court pending the decision of the creditors and the Court: s 140(6). The time of filing determines the time at which creditor's claims are settled: s 140(7); and the time when the trustee named in the proposal becomes the provisional trustee: s 141(1).

The provisional trustee should forthwith call a meeting of creditors, advertise the time and place thereof, and post to every known creditor:

(a) A notice of the date, time, and place of the meeting;
(b) A condensed statement of the assets and liabilities of the insolvent;
(c) A copy of the proposal and particulars of any security or guarantee: R 83 and Forms 32, 33 and 34 of the Rules;
(d) A form of proof of debt;
(e) A voting letter in the form prescribed by reg 51, Form 14: s 141(2).

Only the creditors who have proved their debts may record their assent or their dissent to the proposal by letting the provisional trustee have their voting letter either at or before the meeting of creditors, and such letter will have the same effect as if the creditor had voted personally at the meeting: s 141(3).

The insolvent shall attend the meeting of creditors and may be examined as to his or her affairs: reg 54. It is an offence for an insolvent to make a false statement to, or to mislead, the trustee: s 164. Resolutions are passed by a majority in number and three-fourths in value of those who vote personally or through persons representing them (s 39), or by voting letter: s 111(3). This form of resolution is set out in Form 17 and does not fall into the pattern of either an ordinary or a special resolution. The creditors may confirm the appointment of the provisional trustee nominated by the insolvent or they may replace him. They may accept the proposal or alter it (s 142 (2)), and may, with the consent of the insolvent, include provisions for the supervision of the insolvent's affairs: s 142(4). They may reject the proposal, in which case the chairman of the meeting will return it to the Court endorsed over his or her signature, "Not accepted by creditors", whereupon the Registrar of the Court shall cancel the proposal: s 140(8).

49.5.2 Approval of proposal by Court

Upon acceptance of the proposal by creditors, the trustee shall prepare his or her report on the proposal. The report will state the date on which the insolvent lodged the proposal (a copy of which will be attached) in the Court as well as the date on which the creditors were notified of the calling of a meeting of creditors and the date when the meeting was held.

A true copy of the resolution accepting or amending the proposal and passed by the required majority of creditors is attached as an exhibit to the report.

The trustee sets out in the report details of the assets with an estimate of their fair realisable value and particulars of the liabilities of the debtor. Finally, he or she either recommends the proposal or disapproves of it, in either case setting out his or her reasons: R 85, Form 35.

The trustee shall forthwith apply to the Court for its approval and notify the insolvent and all known creditors of the date of hearing.

At the hearing the Court hears any objections by creditors but may not alter the substance of the proposal. It may refuse approval if it is of the opinion:

(a) That the provisions of Part XV of the Act have not been complied with; or
(b) That the terms of the proposal are not reasonable or are not calculated to benefit the general body of creditors; or
(c) That for any reason it is not expedient that the proposal should be approved.

No proposal shall be approved by the Court if it does not provide for the payment in priority to other claims of all claims directed to be so paid in the distribution of the property of a bankrupt and for the payment of all proper fees and expenses of the trustee of and incidental to the proceedings arising out of the proposal: s 143(3), (4).

It may be noted that misconduct of the debtor is not specifically stated as a ground for refusing approval of the proposal, although it is one of the grounds for refusing to approve a statutory composition: s 122(3)(d).

The approval of the Court is conclusive as to the validity of the proposal and makes it binding on all creditors who have provable debts and are affected by the terms of the proposal: s 143(5). The words "and are affected by the terms of the proposal" seem merely to recognise that the proposal terms may affect various debts differently; however, it is quite clear that once the proposal has Court approval, s 144(1) prevents all creditors with provable debts from instituting or continuing bankruptcy proceedings, or seeking to recover moneys by other legal means.

For a discussion of the legislation see Barker J in *Re Falconer* [1981] 1 NZLR 266. His Honour said, at 271, that the dominant purpose of the legislation is to provide the opportunity for a person in financial difficulties to make proposals to his or her creditors which, if they are accepted will give him or her a chance to trade his or her way out of financial difficulty without the stigma of bankruptcy. It is essential to the concept of a proposal under Part XV that all creditors must be bound by it.

49.5.3 Effect of approval by the Court and duty of trustee

The insolvent is bound to do all things necessary to give effect to the proposal when it has been approved by the Court: s 143(8).

After approval by the Court no creditor with a provable debt shall, except with the leave of the Court, given on such terms as the Court thinks fit:

(a) File a creditor's petition against the insolvent or proceed with a creditor's petition already filed; or

(b) Enforce any civil remedy against the property or person of the insolvent; or

(c) Commence any legal proceedings to recover his or her debt; s 144(1).

Once the proposal has been approved by the Court, the trustee must take control of the property subject to the proposal and must administer and distribute it in accordance with the terms of the proposal. He or she may sell the property in the manner directed by the proposal, or if there are no such directions he or she may exercise the same powers of sale as are available to the Assignee in s 72 of the Act: s 144(2). The form of the proposal determines whether the trustee holds the debtor's property as an assignee or an agent. It does not vest automatically in him or her.

The trustee has substantially the same rights as the Assignee in regard to the admission or rejection of proofs of debt: s 89(1), (3), (8), reg 58.

An abstract of receipts and payments for each preceding six months of his or her administration must be filed with the Registrar by the trustee. Also he or she must file a final abstract covering the period from the last abstract filed up to the date he or she ceased to act. In either case, such abstract must also include the figures for previous periods. A trustee who defaults in filing these returns may be fined: s 144(3), (4).

The Registrar of the Court may order the trustee's accounts to be audited by a chartered accountant. The Court may order the trustee to make good any loss arising through his or her misfeasance, negligence or default: reg 61.

When a trustee dies or becomes incapable of acting or desires to be relieved of his or her duties, the creditors may, by resolution at a meeting called for that purpose, appoint some other person willing to act to be the trustee.

The Court may, on the application of the insolvent or any creditor, remove a trustee and appoint another person as trustee in his or her place: reg 62.

49.5.4 Cancellation or variation of the proposal

Any creditor or the trustee may apply to the Court for a variation or cancellation of the proposal. An order to this effect may be made if the Court is satisfied:

(a) That the facts disclosed in the affidavit of the insolvent accompanying the proposal did not substantially set out the true position or that the insolvent gave wrong or misleading replies at his or her examination and that it was unlikely that the proposal would have been accepted had the true facts been disclosed; or

(b) That the insolvent has failed to carry out or comply with the terms of the proposal; or

(c) That the proposal cannot be proceeded with without injustice or undue delay to the creditors generally; or

(d) That for any other reason the proposal ought to be varied or terminated.

At the same time, upon the request of the applicant or any other creditor the Court may adjudge the insolvent bankrupt: s 145(1). The insolvent himself or herself may decide to file a debtor's petition (s 21), whereupon the proposal shall be deemed to be cancelled by the Court: s 145(4).

No contract, disposition of property or payment duly made by the trustee shall be made invalid by the cancellation of the proposal or the adjudication of the insolvent: s 145(3). But any of the insolvent's property still vested in the trustee and not disposed of by him or her at the time of the cancellation of the proposal shall, subject to s 42 of the Act, re-vest in the insolvent without the necessity of any transfer or assignment: s 145(2).

49.6 SUMMARY INSTALMENT ORDERS: PART XVI

49.6.1 General

The procedure to be followed and the forms to be used are set out in the Summary Instalment Orders (District Courts) Rules 1970. An explanatory note setting out the advantages to an insolvent and what he or she is required to do follows Form 6 of these Rules. The purpose of such an order is to facilitate payment by the debtor of his or her debts by instalments out of income rather than to sell up his or her possessions and distribute the proceeds amongst his or her creditors.

Where a judgment debtor cannot pay forthwith debts that would be provable in his or her bankruptcy, any creditor or the debtor may apply to a District Court for a summary instalment order. Note that it is the District Court, and not the High Court, which deals with these orders. This procedure is available on either the creditor or debtor alleging that the judgment debtor cannot pay and also that the judgment debtor's total unsecured debts do not exceed $4,000. But no summary instalment order shall be made if payment of the instalments made without default would extend over more than three years: s 146(1), (12). Once the order is made the debtor is protected from all proceedings to recover any debts included in the application: s 148, R 14.

An application by a debtor shall be in Forms 3 and 4, in which the debtor states a creditor has obtained judgment against him or her and that he or she owes his or her creditors, whom he or she has listed, unsecured debts provable in bankruptcy which would amount to not more than $4,000. He or she further states that he proposes to pay "X" cents in the dollar in either weekly, two weekly or monthly instalments: s 146(2). Added to this is a statement of his or her affairs setting out his or her age, his or her employer, his or her weekly earnings, his or her regular weekly outgoings, whether he or she is married, single or separated from his or her spouse, and his or her dependants. Other details to be included are particulars of his or her secured and unsecured creditors, with their respective debts and the reasons why he or she cannot meet these debts. When the Registrar of the Court receives the application he or she appoints a day for the hearing of the application and notifies the debtor and all creditors of the day so appointed: RR 7, 8.

If a creditor applies he or she shall file Form 5 in duplicate, and a copy of this application and a copy of Form 4, setting out details of the debtor's affairs, shall be served on the debtor, who must complete this and verify it with a statutory declaration before the expiration of 14 days from his or her being served with the notice of application: R 10.

The person serving the debtor with this notice shall tender to him or her any allowances or travelling expenses which are payable to him. If the debtor fails to file his or her statement of affairs a summons may be issued to compel his or her attendance, followed by a warrant for his or her arrest if necessary; R 11. The procedure at the hearing is set out in R 16.

The District Court Judge should, before making an order, hear any creditors or debtors who wish to be heard, and satisfy himself or herself that the debtor's total unsecured debts are not more than $4,000. The District Court Judge shall make such order as he or she thinks practicable in the circumstances. Although a summary instalment order is not invalidated by reason only that the debtor's debts exceed $4,000, this fact shall be brought to the notice of the Court, which may set aside the order; s 146(13). In addition to directing payments by instalments, the District Court Judge may make an order affecting the debtor's future income and the disposal of goods owned by him or her: s 146(4), (8).

A creditor who wishes to object to an order being made may give notice of his or her objection to the Registrar, the debtor and the applicant creditor (if applicable) not less than three clear days before the hearing. The notice may be in the form of a letter: R 15.

49.6.2 Supervisors

If an order is made a person is usually appointed by the Court to assist the debtor in the management of his or her financial affairs. While the order remains in force this person, who is called a "supervisor", is responsible for supervising the way in which the debtor manages his or her money matters. He or she advises the debtor and assists him or her in budgeting for the living expenses of himself or herself and his or her family and plans with him or her for the payment of his or her outstanding debts. The supervisor may, with the sanction of a Court order, require the debtor's employer to pay the debtor's wages to him or her for deposit in a separate bank account. The account will generally be held in the name of the debtor and the supervisor: RR 23, 27, Form 20. An amendment to the Rules SR 1971/285 R 3 empowers the Court to direct that the supervisor may account for money so paid to him or her in a different manner, provided that it is satisfied that the debtor is receiving adequate training in handling money and budgeting his or her income.

The supervisor may be required to provide a bond in favour of the Registrar to secure performance of his or her duties as supervisor: R 18. Such wages or salary are recoverable as a debt from the employer, and the supervisor's receipt shall be a discharge to the employer. The supervisor must see that the reasonable living expenses of the debtor and his or her family are paid out of the income or wages so received: s 146(9), (10).

Any payment that is wilfully made by an employer to any person in contravention of any such direction shall not discharge the liability of the employer to the supervisor in respect of the amount so paid, unless the payment is made with the consent of the supervisor or of the District Court or to some person other than the debtor who has a prior legal claim thereto: s 146(10).

The Court may make an order providing for the disposal of goods owned or possessed by the debtor: s 146(8)(b). The Court may decide not to make an appointment, in which case the relevant provisions of the Act shall apply as if the debtor were the supervisor, except that he or she shall have no authority to decide questions relating to the proof of debts or the right of any person to be included as a creditor in the administration of his or her estate. These decisions will be made by the Registrar of the District Court, if the debtor is acting as supervisor: ss 146(5), (7), 147(b), (c), (d).

Procedure for replacement of a supervisor is set out in R 25.

49.6.3 Proofs of debt

Where a summary instalment order has been made, the following provisions shall apply:

(a) Notice of the order shall be sent by the supervisor to every creditor of whom he or she has notice or whose name is shown on the application by the debtor or who has proved.
   This notice is sent out by the debtor himself or herself if no supervisor is appointed: s 146(7).

(b) Subject to the provisions of s 147 any creditor of the debtor, on proof of his or her debt before the supervisor, shall be entitled to be included as a creditor in the administration of the estate of the debtor under the order to the amount of his or her proof;

(c) Any creditor may, by application to the District Court which made the order, object to any proof accepted or rejected by the supervisor, and that Court may give such directions in the matters as it thinks proper as to the acceptance or rejection of the proof;

(d) Any person who, after the making of a summary instalment order, becomes a creditor of the debtor may, if he or she elects to do so on proof of his or her debt before the supervisor, be included as a creditor in the administration of the estate of the debtor, but shall not be entitled to any dividend under the order until the creditors included in the administration, having been creditors before the making of the order have been paid in accordance with the provisions of the order: s 147.

It appears that, failing an election under (d) above, a "subsequent" creditor could take independent proceedings to collect his or her debt, for what these might be worth.

Every creditor shall within 14 days after an order is made lodge a proof of his or her debt with the supervisor, who may admit or reject it (wholly or in part). Notice of rejection must be given to such a creditor. With the leave of the supervisor a creditor may amend his or her proof. If there is no supervisor, proof should be tendered to the Registrar: RR 20, 21. The rights of creditors proving late are set out in R 22.

49.6.4 Disbursement of money paid by debtor

Money paid under a summary instalment order shall be distributed by the supervisor in the following order:

(a) In satisfaction of the costs of administration in accordance with the prescribed scale;
(b) When applicable, in satisfaction of the taxed costs of the creditor making the application;
(c) In liquidation of the debts in accordance with the order;
(d) In payment to the debtor of any surplus.

When the amount received under a summary instalment order is sufficient to meet all amounts payable under paras (a), (b) and (c) above the debtor shall be discharged from the unsecured debts to which the order relates: s 149.

49.6.5 Supervisor or debtor to render accounts

Within one month or such longer period as the Registrar may allow after the expiration of six months from the making of an order and at the end of every subsequent period of six months until the order is set aside or rescinded or discharged or its administration completed, the supervisor (or, if no supervisor has been appointed the debtor), shall file in the Court accounts, supported by a bank statement or other statement of account showing his or her receipts and payments during the previous period of six months.

All accounts filed by a supervisor or debtor under this rule shall be inspected by the Registrar and may be audited at any time by any person whom the Registrar may appoint, and the supervisor or debtor shall for the purpose of the audit produce to the auditor all books of account, documents, and papers relating to the administration of the affairs of the debtor.

The costs of the audit shall be deemed part of the costs of administration payable by the debtor: R 26.

49.6.6 Duty of debtor

The debtor must give detailed information about his or her property, earnings, name and address of his or her employer, either in his or her own application to the Court or to the supervisor. If he or she defaults in paying any sum due under the summary instalment order, he or she shall, unless the contrary is proved be deemed to have had sufficient means to pay and to have refused or neglected to pay it. On default by the debtor all proceedings stayed may be resumed or commenced, and any order under the Imprisonment for Debt Limitation Act 1908 may be enforced: s 150.

It is an offence for a debtor during the currency of a summary instalment order made against him or her to obtain credit for himself or herself or incur liability on behalf of another for $100 or more from a person without informing that person of the order: s 51. An information may be laid within two years after the commission of the offence. Insolvency Amendment Act 1972: ss 2, 3.

The debtor, any creditor, the supervisor, or the Registrar, may apply for the discharge or variation of the order, and the Court may make such order as it thinks fit: s 146(14).

The procedure to be followed if the debtor does not comply with the order is set out in RR 30, 31.

Chapter 50

THE ADMINISTRATION OF THE ESTATES OF DECEASED INSOLVENTS

SUMMARY

50.1 GENERAL

Part XVII of the Act makes provision for the administration of estates where there are insufficient assets to pay the debts of a deceased. In such a case a creditor of the deceased may find that there is no person against whom he or she can take proceedings to recover payment or part payment of his or her debt, because the executor named in the deceased's will does not take out probate, as he or she is not prepared to undertake the problems inherent in the realisation and distribution of an insolvent estate. By adopting the procedure laid down in this Part of the Act a creditor can resolve his or her dilemma and ensure that someone is appointed to realise the assets of the deceased and distribute the proceeds fairly by applying the principles of Bankruptcy Law.

The appointee under this Part of the Act takes control and deals with that part (and it will usually be substantially the whole) of the deceased's estate which is available for distribution to meet administration charges, funeral, medical and hospital charges and other debts owed by the deceased: s 162(1)(b). Certain assets and rights of action which are not, in the terms of this Part of the Act, available to meet these claims may remain vested in and under the control of the deceased's executor or another administrator: s 153(3). Property of the deceased which would not have passed to the Assignee had the deceased been adjudicated bankrupt prior to his or her death does not pass to an appointee under

935

Part XVII. Thus superannuation, social welfare benefits and various types of pensions which were due but unpaid at the date of death do not pass to the appointee.

The deceased may have met his or her death through an accident and earnings related compensation or a lump sum by way of compensation may be payable to his or her dependants under the Accident Compensation Act 1982: ss 81-2. Again, he or she may have had a life assurance policy, which is protected against the claims of creditors for the benefit of the deceased's family to the extent of $4,000, and bonuses accrued due on that sum if he or she died before 1st April 1986: Insurance Law Reform Act 1985, s 4. The moneys payable to the estate of the deceased by way of compensation or reserved by statute for the protection and benefit of his or her family form no part of the estate available for administration by the appointee under Part XVII: ss 153(1), (3), 162(1)(b).

The appointee may be the administrator named in the will of the deceased or holding office under letters of administration, or alternatively the Assignee or the Public Trustee or some other person appointed by the Court, unless the Court otherwise directs. If the Court considers that the estate would be better administered by someone other than the present or prospective administrator it may order that any administrator already appointed shall cease to administer the estate and that the Assignee, the Public Trustee or some other person shall be appointed: s 158. Provisions relating to applications under this Part of the Act by the Public Trustee or the Maori Trustee administering the estate of insolvent deceased Maoris are set out in s 160. The whole of the available estate at the date on which the application for appointment is made to the Court vests in the appointee when the order is made: ss 153(1), 159(1).

50.2 APPLICATIONS UNDER PART XVII

An administrator or a person applying for administration, who ascertains that the money and assets which can be conveniently realised in the estate are insufficient to meet the claims against the estate, may file a notice of motion in the High Court to have the available estate administered under Part XVII. "Administrator" includes a trustee corporation in any case where it is deemed to be an executor or administrator by reason of having filed an election to administer: Administration Act 1969, s 2. The Public Trustee and the Maori Trustee are included in this term. The administrator must at the time of filing the application or at such later date as may be prescribed or allowed by the Court also file an account showing the assets, debts and liabilities of the deceased so far as they are known to him or her: s 154(1), (3); RR 87, 88, Forms 39, 42, 43. The account of assets, debts and liabilities must be filed in triplicate within 14 days of making the application. It must be verified by affidavit.

This application affecting the estate available for the payment of debts may be joined with an application for the grant of probate or letters of administration to enable the administrator to deal with other assets or interests of the deceased which are not subject to the provisions of Part XVII: s 154(2).

Any creditor of the estate whose debt would be sufficient to support a bankruptcy petition or any person beneficially interested in the estate may apply to the Court to have the estate administered under Part XVII if:

(a) The administrator has not made application under this Part of the Act and still fails to do so within 21 days after being requested in writing to do so, or

(b) No administrator has been appointed and no application under Part XVII has been made in the four months following the death of the debtor. But application can be made before the expiration of four months if:

  (i) The debtor committed an act of bankruptcy within the three months before his or her death;

  (ii) The estate which should have been available for creditors is diminishing: s 155, R 89, Forms 40 and 41.

In *Moulder v Fischer* [1979] 2 NZLR 662 the divorced spouse of a testator claimed to be a creditor and applied to have the estate administered under Part XVII. The whole of the estate was the proceeds of life policies which were protected against creditors by ss 65 and 66(3) of the Life Insurance Act 1908. The Court of Appeal held, at 665:

> Where the creditor proves his debt and establishes that there are insufficient assets to pay creditors in full it is for those resisting the making of an order to establish grounds why it should not be made. It is essentially the same approach as is the case on a bankruptcy petition.

Where an application is made by a creditor, or any person beneficially interested after a request has been made to an administrator and the administrator has failed within 21 days to make an application, the Court may direct the administrator to file the account of the deceased's assets and liabilities within such time as the Court directs. "A creditor of the estate of the deceased" apparently includes those who become creditors after the date of the decease.

Notice of the application must be given to any administrator already appointed or to such person as the Court directs: s 156, R 89.

50.3 JURISDICTION OF THE COURT

Registrars of the High Court are empowered to deal with applications under Part XVII which are joined with an application for a grant of probate or letters of administration: s 157(2).

The Court has the same jurisdiction as the Court in Bankruptcy where an application under Part XVII is pending or where an order for the administration of the estate under Part XVII has been made: s 161.

On the hearing of the application the Court may make an order for the estate to be administered under Part XVII or it may dismiss the application.

The Court will not make an order if it is reasonably probable that the available estate will be sufficient for the payment of the debts of the deceased *and* that the creditors will not be prejudiced by the estate being administered in the usual way. Any creditor making application must prove his or her debt: s 157(1).

An affirmative inference from the use of "and" in the provision above is that the Court may make an appointment even where application is made in respect of a solvent estate, if it is being administered in a manner prejudicial to the creditors.

Where someone other than the original administrator is appointed under this Part of the Act, the original administrator shall immediately deliver to the appointee an account of his or her dealings and administration of the deceased estate and other particulars required by the appointee: R 93. Likewise, any person who has intermeddled in the estate or taken on the administration of the estate without authority may be ordered by the Court to furnish an account of his or her administration: R 94.

The widow or widower is, however, entitled to select and retain as her or his own property necessary household furniture and effects (but not if the assets are encumbered or are assets of any other kind) to which she or he would have been entitled under the estate of the deceased to the value of $300. With the consent of the creditors, the appointee may allow the widow or widower to retain furniture and effects to a greater value than $300 and also make an allowance of money out of the estate for the support of the widow or widower or any member of the family: s 159(2) (3), (4). The value of the furniture and effects will be determined by the appointee, probably in relation to current auction prices for secondhand goods of this type.

An application for an order under this Part of the Act by a creditor or a person otherwise beneficially interested on the ground that the administrator has failed to make such an application shall not be granted (without the consent of the administrator) sooner than two months after the grant, unless:

(a) The deceased committed an act of bankruptcy in the three months preceding his or her death;or
(b) The administrator has preferred or is about to prefer any creditor; or
(c) The administrator in the opinion of the Court is not properly administering the estate: s 157.

Notice of application under this Part of the Act shall, if an order to administer is made thereon, be deemed equivalent to notice of an act of bankruptcy. Thereafter an administrator making any payment or disposing of the estate property shall not be discharged from liability therefor: s 162(1)(d). The appointee has the same powers as the Assignee, which include the power of examining persons about the property of the deceased: s 162(1)(a).

Section 159(1) provides that on an order to administer under this Part of the Act being made by the Court the whole of the deceased's estate as at the date of the presentation of the application is vested in the appointee, that is, the deceased's property subject to such charges, liens and rights subsisting in other persons as at that date: *Hasluck v Clark* [1899] 1 QB 699 (CA). But property devolving upon the administrator after that date is not vested in the appointee who succeeds him: *Re Jack Evelyn Sabine (deceased), Jessie Sabine Respondent* (1958) 18 ABC 188.

However, no payments made or acts done by an administrator in good faith before he or she received notice that an application was to be made under Part XVII are invalidated: s 163.

When an order has been made, the appointee shall proceed to realise, administer and distribute the estate in accordance with the law and practice of bankruptcy (s 159(1)) and shall have the same authority, powers and functions as the Assignee: s 162(1)(a).

The Public Trustee or the Maori Trustee administering an apparently insolvent estate may elect to administer an estate under Part XVII of the Act: s 160(1), (2). Alternatively, either of these officials could technically bypass Part XVII entirely, pursuant to s 160(3), so long as s 162(1)(b) priorities are observed.

For an application under Part XVII to overcome the effect of charging orders see *Re Piercy (dec'd) ex parte Baynes* (unreported, High Court, Invercargill, M52/87, 11 March 1988, Tipping J). The order was made. The charging orders had not been made absolute more than three months before the date of the order: s 162(1)(g).

50.4 CARRYING ON THE BUSINESS OF THE INSOLVENT DECEASED

If an appointee properly incurs debts in the administration of the estate, he or she is entitled to an indemnity from estate assets: *Hope v Public Trustee* [1943] NZLR 398.

An appointee should sell any business as a going concern within a reasonable time; if he or she cannot he or she should realise the business assets. He or she can carry the business on with the consent of the creditors and be entitled to an indemnity from them if he or she incurs liabilities in so doing. But if he or she carries on the business without their consent for more than a reasonable time to dispose of it as a going concern, he or she is not entitled to an indemnity and he or she may be liable to the creditors for losses incurred. Express authority in the will to carry on the business does not affect the appointee's liability or strengthen his or her position: *Re Millard, Ex parte Yates* (1895) 72 LT 823 (CA).

In *Re Brooks (deceased), Official Assignee v Brooks* [1942] NZLR 523; [1942] GLR 314 the defendant was the executrix of, and sole legatee under, her husband's will. Her husband died as a result of a motor accident in which three passengers were injured. As the estate proved to be insolvent, the Official Assignee was later appointed to administer the estate under Part IV of the Administration Act 1908 (now the Insolvency Act 1967, Part XVII). Acting under s 3 of the Law Reform Act 1936, the passengers had claimed compensation against the husband's estate. A claim was also made by the deceased's mother for moneys alleged to have been lent by the mother to the son many years before. After her husband's death the defendant continued to run her husband's business and took substantial personal drawings for herself. During her administration of the estate, the defendant paid the mother's claim in full, although her correspondence showed that she knew the estate was insolvent. It was held:

(1) That the carrying on of the business was a breach of trust against the creditors and that the defendant must repay the amount of her personal drawings and make good the loss arising from carrying on the business.

(2) That the Law Reform Act 1936 s 3 gave the passengers status as creditors after the death of the husband although their demands were in the nature of unliquidated damages.

(3) That the defendant had no right to prefer any creditors; the defendant must pay to the plaintiff such sum as would enable an equal dividend to be paid to the passengers as would have been payable to them had the defendant not preferred the other creditors.

(4) That the mother's claim was of such a nature that the defendant should not have paid it without a judgment of the Court and that the amount paid to her should be made available for the payment of the other creditors. Further, that the mother should not be entitled to be a creditor of the estate.

50.5 PRIORITIES OF CREDITORS

The relevant date for determining the amount of the debts for which proof is being made and for settling the priorities of payment is the date of death. The date of death is treated as if it were the date of adjudication in bankruptcy.

In accordance with s 162(1)(b) the appointee shall observe the following priorities in distributing the available estate of the deceased debtor:

First: Administration costs, whether incurred before or after the making of the order.

Second: Reasonable funeral expenses.

Third: Medical and (so far as they are lawfully recoverable) reasonable hospital and maintenance expenses in any institution incurred in the three months immediately before the death of the deceased.

Fourth: Claims and interest according to the priorities stipulated in s 104 of the Act.

Fifth: Any surplus after payment of the claims above shall be returned to any administrator handling the part of the estate not subject to the order under Part XVII, or if there is no such administrator it shall be distributed as directed by the Court.

No agreement by the deceased insolvent with any of the creditors can change the statutory order of priorities for the distribution of assets: *Re Rothermere* [1943] 1 All ER 307.

50.6 AVOIDANCE OF TRANSACTIONS PRIOR TO DEATH

Proceedings to set aside gifts, voluntary settlements and to recover moneys expended in improving purchasing or assisting to purchase property for other persons shall be taken only with the leave and subject to such terms as are imposed by the Court. Before leave is granted the Court will require the appointee to disclose the condition of the estate and whether it is likely that sufficient money will be realised thereout to pay creditors without recourse to the property given away or acquired for others. Leave will not be granted unless such property is necessary to pay debts (and interest thereon) in full: s 162(1)(f). Under s 162(3) the voidability of transactions is to be judged as if the deceased had been adjudicated at the time of his or her death. Voidable transactions have been dealt with in 46.3 supra.

Executions, unless they were completed more than three months before the making of an order under Part XVII, are voidable as against the appointee thereunder: s 162(1)(g).

50.7 DISPOSAL OF ANY SURPLUS AFTER CREDITORS HAVE BEEN PAID IN FULL

The appointee may pay any surplus, after the creditors have been paid in full, to the administrator of such part of the deceased's estate as was not vested in the appointee. But if there is no administrator, the appointee must make application to the Court for an order disposing of the surplus. He or she must make an affidavit to the effect that no grant of administration has been made to any person, that the creditors have been paid in full and that the surplus, amounting to $X, will be applied as set out in the affidavit: R 96, Form 46. The interests of person entitled under the will are determined as at the date when the surplus is available for distribution.

Part VIII

DISPUTE RESOLUTION

Chapter 51

THE RESOLUTION OF COMMERCIAL AND CONSUMER DISPUTES

SUMMARY

51.1   INTRODUCTION
51.2   NON LEGAL DISPUTE RESOLUTION
51.3   LITIGATION
51.4   ARBITRATION
51.5   MEDIATION AND CONCILIATION
51.6   SPECIAL CHARACTERISTICS OF CONSUMER DISPUTE RESOLU-
        TION AND CONSUMER PROTECTION LAW

51.1 INTRODUCTION

In commercial law a dispute may arise due to the refusal or failure of one party to perform his or her contractual obligations. For instance a supplier may supply defective products or the buyer may refuse to pay the price in whole or in part. Many such disputes never get near to a law Court. This does not necessarily mean that the law and lawyers are not used but simply that the parties use the law to arrive at a settlement without litigation. For many commercial contracts and especially consumer contracts, law and lawyers may not be used at all. Indeed some business people would argue that this ideally should always be the case. However, even here the law is in the background providing, as it were, a backcloth to the contract and potential disputes.

If a dispute arises the parties may settle it by ad hoc agreement. They may even plan a system to deal with it eg a complaints procedure. Failing this they may: (a) litigate; (b) arbitrate; (c) mediate; (d) conciliate their dispute.

Litigation involves the use of legal proceedings and ultimately the Court. Depending on the amount involved the parties may use:

(i)   the Disputes Tribunal;
(ii) the District Court; or
(iii) the High Court.

Within certain limits there is a right of appeal from the District Court and the High Court on points of law and within narrower limits on points of fact. The right of appeal from Disputes Tribunals is much more restricted. Litigation normally involves the adversarial system. It "is in many respects like a civilised war": R M Goode, *Commercial Law*, 943. It involves not only legal analysis and preparation of a case but also the assembling of evidence and the use of tactics, all with the object of presenting of one party's case to the best advantage. The contest takes place according to rules. Lawyers have certain professional duties to each other and the Court as well as their clients. Thus all relevant facts and documents have to be put before the Court. The Court sits as umpire not as participant. It does not call witnesses of its own motion, other than expert witnesses. It ultimately gives a reasoned decision. Most litigation in practice is settled and never gets to Court. This is for a variety of reasons but principally because of cost.

Litigation involves delay as well as cost. The Judge is not usually an expert in the field. Hearings are normally in public. For these reasons commercial people at dispute with each other prefer arbitration although this is not necessarily cheaper in the long run. One or more arbitrators are appointed by Court or by the parties under some mechanism agreed by them. The parties have more control over the proceedings and when hearings are held. The Court nevertheless has certain residual controls over arbitration proceedings.

As alternatives to litigation and arbitration the parties may prefer mediation or conciliation. Mediation involves a third party assisting the disputants to arrive at an agreed solution. Conciliation overlaps with mediation to some extent but perhaps presupposes a more active role for the intermediary. Both mediation and conciliation are developing at the municipal and international levels as means of settling disputes.

51.2 NON LEGAL DISPUTE RESOLUTION

51.2.1 General

Formal use of contract remedies to settle disputes tends to be unusual except possibly for collection of uncontested debts. In larger commercial contracts businesspeople sometimes plan for dispute resolution but the planning is often incomplete. Smaller items tend to be bought and sold on standard form conditions and sometimes where the contracting parties are both businesspeople there is a "battle of the forms" with uncertainty as to which set of standard conditions applies. Where, however, there is a larger contract especially for a building or civil engineering project it is likely to be negotiated on the basis of sophisti-cated standard forms by experienced people; similarly in the case of export trade contracts involving carriage by sea or air.

The law tends to see contracts in an atomistic way whereas the reality of many commercial contracts between businessmen is that they are part of an ongoing relationship between the parties. The parties wish to continue dealing with each other. Here too detailed a contract or, too legalistic an approach, may erode the goodwill necessary for that rela-tionship. Here too the loss of future business is itself an effective sanction. Time and effort goes into building these networks on which both parties may rely. The existence of such a relationship tends to cut down transaction costs of investigating alternative sources of supply and resolving disputes. Litigation and arbitration are expensive.

For useful discussion of non legal dispute resolution between businesspeople see Macauley, 28 *American Sociological Review* 55; Beale and Dugdale (1975) 2 BJLS 45 and Beale, "Remedies for Breach of Contract", 4-10 on which this is based.

51.2.2 Negotiation and settlement

Although there is obviously an overlap between this and 51.1.3, there are nevertheless certain legal characteristics of negotiation and settlement which are worth discussing in their own right.

Once litigation is commenced there are three ways in which a defendant can put forward a proposal to settle the plaintiff's claim:

(a) payment into Court;
(b) an open offer;
(c) a "without prejudice" offer.

A payment into Court will usually be less than the amount claimed but will be sufficient to make the plaintiff consider whether he or she should go on. If he or she accepts it he or she will recover his or her costs to date. If the plaintiff elects to proceed to Court and recovers less than the sum paid into Court he or she will be ordered to pay the defendant's costs from the date of the payment into Court.

An open offer is an offer which is not marked "without prejudice". In practice it is uncommon because the defendant will feel that if declined it will bias the Judge against him or her.

A "without prejudice" offer is one so marked and which thus cannot be disclosed to the Court unless it is accepted. It is without prejudice to one's legal rights and is very common in practice. See generally, RM Goode, *Commercial Law*, 961-2.

51.3 LITIGATION

51.3.1 Small claims

(a) DISPUTES TRIBUNALS
Small claims in New Zealand up to $3000 in respect of disputes in contract or quasi-contract or in tort for destruction, loss, damage or injury to property are handled by disputes tribunals set up in the major centres under the Disputes Tribunals Act 1988 and governed by the Disputes Tribunal Rules 1989/34. The jurisdiction can be extended up to $5000 by agreement of the parties.

The Tribunals are set up as special divisions of selected District Courts. Each tribunal is presided over by a referee, appointed from the persons selected by an assessment panel on the basis of their suitability. Legal qualifications are not necessary.

The primary function of the Tribunal is to endeavour to achieve a settlement between the parties to a dispute, that is conciliation is the primary objective with adjudication an essential but secondary aim. Where adjudication is necessary the tribunal is directed to:

> ... determine the dispute according to the substantial merits and justice of the case, and in doing so shall have regard to the law but shall not be bound to give effect to strict legal rights or obligations or to legal forms or technicalities (s 18(6) Disputes Tribunal Act 1988).

Furthermore, in s 18(7) of the Act the tribunal is empowered to disregard certain exemption clauses. Moreover, the Tribunal is allowed to receive and take account of such evidence as it thinks fit, whether or not such evidence would be admissible in a Court of law: s 40(4). The Tribunal is also empowered to seek out, on its own initiative, further information (s 40(2)), may appoint an investigator to make detailed inquiries on any matter (s 41), and may adopt such procedure as it best considers suited to the ends of justice (s 44). Therefore it is clear that the legislature has aimed at achieving the maximum level of informality commensurate with efficiency and the more active role attributed to the Tribunal, although at odds with the traditional adversary system approach, may counteract any deficiencies in presentation or informational deficiencies: Dr AA Tarr, PhD thesis.

There are very detailed provisions which cut down an insurer's right of subrogation and give limited rights of participation in the proceedings. These are contained in ss 29-35.

(b) PROCEDURE

The institution of proceedings before a Tribunal is simple and inexpensive. The claimant need only fill out a claim form giving the particulars of his or her claim and file it, with a small fee, with the Registrar of the District Court. The Registrar will give the claimant any assistance requested in filling out the form, and subsequently will advise both claimant and the respondent of the time and place of the hearing. In the event of the parties coming to a settlement after a claim has been lodged, the claimant simply advises the Registrar in writing that he or she wishes to withdraw. The hearing itself is very informal and in accordance with this informality and a desire to keep costs down, barristers and solicitors and other persons regularly engaged in advocacy work before other types of tribunals may not appear in a representative capacity before Disputes Tribunals: s 38(2), (7). This exclusion however does not extend to an appeal: per Judge Inglis QC in *Hewitt v King* (1983) 2 DCR 111. The Referee may allow representation by some other person in special circumstances, provided that person has personal knowledge of the case and authority to bind the claimant; for example, a representative may be appointed for a minor or handicapped person. Hearings are heard in private and the confidential nature of proceedings is thought to be less inhibiting to claimants and respondents.

Under s 19 the Tribunal may make seven types of order: the claim may be dismissed; payment of money required; work ordered to be performed; a declaration of non-liability made; specific chattels ordered to be delivered; harsh or unconscionable agreements varied or set aside; and agreements which have been induced by fraud, misrepresentation or mistake may be varied or set aside. Under s 43 the Tribunal is prevented from ordering that costs be awarded against a party unless that party's claim is frivolous or vexatious.

   The Act also makes provision for transfers, rehearings and appeals. Proceedings may be transferred from the Tribunal to the District Court on the application of either party or of the Tribunal's own motion in a proper case (s 36); for example, the Tribunal may decide that the matter would be better resolved before the District Court. Proceedings commenced in a District Court that has a Disputes Tribunal as a division of it must be transferred to the tribunal if the defendant so requests in his or her notice of intention to defend, and in every other case proceedings may be transferred on the application of either party or of a District Court Judge or Registrar's own motion: s 37.

   The Act allows for rehearings where a party has not complied with an order, where the Tribunal has decided a case in the absence of one of the parties, and whenever the initial proceedings do not culminate in a settlement. An appeal to the District Court is possible only on the grounds that the hearing or an investigator's inquiry called for by the Tribunal were carried out unfairly and prejudicially affected the outcome of the proceedings. There is no provision for an appeal for error in law, so subject to the Tribunal's power to rehear cases and its duty of observing the principles of natural justice, a Tribunal's orders are final.

(c) ASSESSMENT OF SYSTEM

The Disputes Tribunal system thus has considerable flexibility and novelty. Its power to disregard exemption clauses, the rules of evidence, and the adversarial approach together with the ban on legal representation all carry within themselves greater flexibility and potential for ad hoc justice. At the same time these very advantages lead to uncertainty and the resulting equity may very well vary with the length of the Referee's foot. Experience of disputes procedures in England and Wales in the County Courts even without these features tends this way.

   The Minister of Justice addressing the national seminar of Disputes Referees in 1985 gave the following statistics:

Year	Tribunals	Applications
1980	5	1081
1981	9	2211
1982	13	4104
1983	18	5413
1984	21	5569

He favoured a further increase in the jurisdiction and wider use of the Tribunals but had this to say about the operation of the system:

   The Tribunal system will succeed only if people are persuaded that their disputes will be *satisfactorily* resolved more cheaply and more quickly than if they used the Court system. Much turns on that word "satisfactory".
   Referees have a much freer hand in arriving at rulings on a case than a Judge would have. Decisions are very much more secure from appeal. Any mistakes made about the rights and wrongs of the law cannot be challenged.
   The decision cannot be scrutinised or rectified by anyone, unless the way proceedings were carried out was unfair and prejudiced the result. The words of the statute allow common sense and a broad notion of justice to be applied.
   Referees are entitled to regard a fair and evenhanded resolution of a

dispute as more important than legal doctrine and precedent. But because their decisions may only be altered in very limited circumstances, they have, it seems to me, a strong duty to be sure their decisions are correct in the first place. No-one expects them to be law professors. But the common law which shaped contract law was just that common. A distillation of shared experience.

Many people organise their affairs on the basis of legal rights and obligations generally known and understood. Or they take the trouble to ascertain from statutes what standards of behaviour and commercial probity are recognised in law, and what remedies are available for breach of these standards.

They have a right to expect that referees will "have regard to" these laws. Referees have an absolute obligation to do so.

Referees may feel that other factors in a particular case make a difference to the strict operation of the law. Then it is their task to weigh up just where, and to what extent, the decision should depart from the law.

All this may sound very theoretical and far removed from the practicalities of dealing with two angry people who are at loggerheads. But the notion is central to the service Disputes Tribunals provide.

The reputation and continued effectiveness of the Tribunals hinges on the referee's understanding of the competing claims of the disputants, and an ability to reach a decision which both parties can understand and accept. It must seem to be fair to people of varied social and cultural experience. Tribunals are a direct response to an evident community need.

Since 1985 the figures have substantially increased and are as follows:

Year	Tribunals	Applications
1985		7436
1986		9114
1987		10,934
1988		11,272
1989/90	56	15,630

51.3.2 The District Court

The general jurisdiction of the District Court in actions in contract is limited to claims not exceeding $50,000 after a set-off of any debt or demand claimed or recoverable by the plaintiff which has been admitted by the plaintiff in his or her claim or demand. Most actions commence with a request to the Court to issue a summons, together with a statement of claim. The summons is then served on the defendant. The summons may be in respect of either an ordinary action or a default action. The latter is generally only used to recover a liquidated claim, ie a claim for a certain sum where there is unlikely to be a dispute. The default action is used for debt collecting. Unliquidated claims eg a claim for unliquidated damages for breach of contract are the subject of an ordinary action.

After the summons has been served the defendant must file a notice of intention to defend, within seven days. In the case of a default action where no notice is filed, the plaintiff may obtain judgment for his or her claim, together with costs, without a Court hearing. Where a notice of intention to defend is filed, the procedure will be the same as in an ordinary action. Costs and execution of judgment are basically the same as in the High Court and are dealt with below. Appeals lie from the District Court to the High Court.

51.3.3 The High Court

The High Court, unlike the Disputes Tribunal and the District Court, has unlimited jurisdiction. Proceedings in the High Court are normally commenced by filing a statement of claim and notice of proceeding served on the defendant. The defendant, if he or she does not concede the claim, must file a statement of defence which may be accompanied by a counterclaim for damages against the plaintiff. In England it is common to have detailed pleadings in the large and more complex cases but this is less common in New Zealand. Before the case comes on for trial the parties may seek the following interlocutory relief:

(a) injunctions;
(b) discovery and interrogatories.

The plaintiff may apply for an interlocutory injunction to preserve the status quo pending trial. Frequently he or she will apply ex parte, ie without notice to the other side, and the Court may grant an injunction for a short time pending service on the defendant. When the summons is heard the Court may continue or discharge the injunction. In recent years the so-called Mareva injunction has developed out of the inherent jurisdiction of the Court to prevent a defendant from avoiding a potential judgment by transferring his or her assets abroad or dissipating them pending the trial. The test is:

(a) the plaintiff must show a good arguable case (as a minimum requirement);
(b) this must not be looked at in isolation but in the light of the whole of the evidence before the Court;
(c) then, whether refusal would involve a real risk that judgment in the plaintiff's favour would remain unsatisfied because of either:
  (i) removal of assets from the jurisdiction; or,
  (ii) dissipation of assets within the jurisdiction: *Ninemia Maritime Corp v Trave Schiffahrtsgesellschaft mbH & Co KG* [1984] 1 All ER 398 (CA).

It has been held that the New Zealand Courts have inherent power to grant a Mareva injunction: *Donselaar v Mosen* [1976] 2 NZLR 191; *Hunt v BP Exploration* [1980] 1 NZLR 104. See J K Maxton [1983] NZLJ 142, 198; C B Cato [1980] NZLJ 270; R J Calnan [1981] 9 NZULR 279.

Discovery and interrogatories are means whereby the parties may obtain information regarding their opponent's case. Discovery is of documents in the party's possession. Interrogatories are questions as to material matters raised in the pleadings. These must be answered by affidavit and may normally be used as evidence at the trial. A striking new order developed at the same time as the Mareva injunction is the so-called Anton Piller order named after the decision in the English Court of Appeal in *Anton Piller KG v Manufacturing Processes Ltd* [1976] Ch 55. This is an order obtained ex parte before service of a writ requiring the defendant to admit representatives of the plaintiff on to his or her premises to inspect and if necessary remove his or her documents and records. The purpose of the order was to combat piracy in sound and video reproduction by illegal operators of little financial substance. The Anton Piller order received a set back in *Rank Film Distributors Ltd v Video Information Centre* [1981] 2 All ER 76 when the House of Lords held that the defendant in proceedings for infringement of interlocutory rights enjoyed the usual privilege against self incrimination by discovery or answers to interrogatories. Where the defendant is liable to prosecution under the Crimes Act 1961 this could operate as a serious limitation. In England the matter has been dealt with by statute: Supreme Court Act 1981 (UK), s 72.

It has been held that the High Court in New Zealand has jurisdiction to make Anton Piller orders: *Busby v Thorn EMI Video Programmes Ltd* [1984] 1 NZLR 464 (CA). See JK Maxton [1985] NZLJ 307. The majority of the Court of Appeal regarded the question of privilege as a matter of judicial discretion. See the criticisms of Maxton op cit 316.

Summary judgment may be obtained by the plaintiff where he or she satisfies the Court that the defendant has no defence to a claim in the statement of claim or to a particular part of it: High Court Rules, R 136.

Costs are in the discretion of the trial Judge when the case comes on for trial. Before then the matter is sometimes the subject of practice rules. Normally costs follow the event, ie the loser has to pay not only his or her own but his or her opponent's costs.

Judgment which is unsatisfied may be enforced by such procedures as charging order, writ of sale or writ of possession in respect of assets of the defendant.

Appeals lie from the High Court to the Court of Appeal and thence in certain cases to the Judicial Committee of the Privy Council.

51.3.4 The need for a Commercial Court or List

On a number of occasions there have been proposals for the establishment of a Commercial Court or Commercial List. Thus the Contracts and Commercial Law Reform Committee argued the case for special provision for commercial causes in 1974 in its report "Commercial Causes". Such institutions have existed in London since 1895, New South Wales since 1903 and Victoria since 1978 and work well in practice. The main arguments in favour are:

(1) speed;
(2) specialist personnel;
(3) the ability to dispense with procedural and evidential formalities and work to fixed hearing dates, and
(4) the fact that many commercial disputes can be resolved by a ruling at an early stage on a preliminary point which will not necessarily be of law.

The main arguments against are:

(1) speed is not only desirable in commercial dispute resolution;
(2) similarly with specialisation and streamlining of procedures;
(3) New Zealand is a small country with a relatively small judiciary which may not be able or willing to provide such a specialised function; and

(4) expedition is not necessarily the rule in the English Commercial Court.

See generally the useful paper by Dr LS Sealy, "The Business Community: Is it being Served?" in 1984 New Zealand Law Conference Principal Papers, 21, 23-25 and the Draft Report of the Working Party considering a Scheme for the Introduction of a Commercial List at the High Court in Auckland. The Draft Report recommended a pilot scheme whereby commercial causes (which would include company and intellectual property disputes as well as the matters covered in this book) filed in the High Court in Auckland would on payment of a higher fee be placed on a separate "fast track" list to be called within say three weeks of service for issues to be identified and directions to be given and, if appropriate, a fixture to be made. There would be strict judicial supervision of pre-trial procedures. It has been contended that many of the arguments raised apply to all civil litigation and strict judicial supervision of this kind should be extended under the new High Court Rules: (1985) *The Capital Letter* No 33,1. The Commercial List was introduced in Auckland and has been a success. The experiment continues but so far such a list has not yet been introduced in the other main centres. There has not been felt to be a compelling need to do so.

51.4 ARBITRATION

51.4.1 General

Arbitration is a method of settling disputes by the decision of one or more persons called arbitrators, instead of seeking an order of the Court. The law governing the settlement of disputes by arbitration, apart from those involving industrial relations, is found in the Arbitration Act 1908 and the amending Acts of 1938 and 1952. In this chapter all references to "the Act" will be to the Arbitration Act 1908 and the section references will be to the same Act.

The Act and its amendments bind the Crown, but the Crown cannot compel a dispute, in which it is involved, to be decided by arbitration without the consent of the Attorney-General: s 24.

For there to be a submission to arbitration, there must be an intention to hold a judicial inquiry in a judicial manner to settle differences which have arisen or shall arise, as distinct from a mere valuation or appraisement for the purposes of preventing differences from arising: *Re Hammond and Waterton* (1890) 62 LT 808.

51.4.2 Types of reference

Reference to arbitration may be made in the following cases:

(a) By order of the Court under inherent jurisdiction;
(b) By order of the Court under the Arbitration Act ss 14 and 15;
(c) Under certain statutes;
(d) By consent of the parties out of Court.

The last type of reference, in which the arbitrator derives his or her authority directly from the agreement of the parties, is the one with which we are most concerned.

(a) REFERENCES BY ORDER OF THE COURT UNDER INHERENT JURISDICTION

In these references the authority of the arbitrator or "referee" is derived from the order of the Court directing the reference. The Court has inherent jurisdiction to make an order for reference to arbitration in any case where the parties decide the matter is to be determined by an arbitrator instead of the Court. When such an order is made, the Court action is stated while arbitration proceedings take place. The arbitrator appointed under such a reference is not an officer of the Court and he or she derives his or her powers from the consent of the parties as shown in the order of reference.

(b) REFERENCES BY ORDER OF THE COURT UNDER SECTIONS 14 AND 15

The Arbitration Act empowers the Court, subject to the right in appropriate cases to have the case tried by jury, to refer any question arising in any case (other than criminal proceedings by the Crown) to any official or special referee for inquiry or report: s 14. Sections 61 and 62 of the District Courts Act 1947 give District Court Judges similar powers.

Section 14 of the Arbitration Act gives power to refer "any question arising in any cause" for report. The report by this special referee is merely informative and is not binding on the Court: *Papps v Canterbury Furnishers* [1959] NZLR 1037. It may be adopted wholly or partially and if it is so adopted it may be enforced as a judgment or order.

Section 15 of the Act provides for the trial of the whole matter or any question of fact arising therein by an arbitrator and there is no suggestion that the arbitrator's decision can be disregarded by the Court. This section provides that in any case or matter (other than criminal proceedings by the Crown):

(1) if all the parties interested, who are not under disability, consent; or
(2) if the question in dispute consists wholly or in part of matters of account; or
(3) if the cause or matter requires any prolonged examination of documents or any scientific or local investigation which cannot in the opinion of the Court conveniently be made before a jury or conducted by the Court through its ordinary officers,

the Court may at any time order the whole cause or matter or any question or issue of fact arising therein to be tried before an arbitrator agreed on by the parties or before an officer of the Court.

In the cases falling under ss 14 and 15 the arbitrator is deemed to be an officer of the Court: s 16. His or her report or award, unless set aside by the Court, is equivalent to the verdict of a jury. The Court has the same powers of supervision over a reference under order of the Court as it has in the case of references by consent out of Court. Thus it may set the award aside, remit it for reconsideration, remove the arbitrator or compel the statement of a special case: s 17. The remuneration of the arbitrator is fixed by the Court: s 16. A strong case must be made out by the applicant before the Court will deprive the other party of his or her right to have his or her action tried by the ordinary tribunals. Where the parties cannot agree as to the appointment of an arbitrator then the only course, apart from an ordinary trial, is to refer the matter to an officer of the Court for his or her report: *Spencer v Rough and Hooper* [1927] NZLR 345; [1927] GLR 312.

(c) REFERENCES UNDER PARTICULAR STATUTES

Certain statutes provide for the reference of disputes to arbitration either by agreement of the parties or on a compulsory basis. In references under an Act of Parliament, the subject matter of the references prescribed by, and the authority of the arbitrator is derived from the particular statute in question. The provisions of the Act and amending Acts generally apply to these particular forms of arbitration unless they are inconsistent with the provisions of the statute under which the arbitration takes place. Certain provisions, such as the rules relating to costs and the powers of the Court on the removal of the arbitrator, etc, do not apply.

(d) REFERENCES BY CONSENT OUT OF COURT

(1) *The submission:* Every reference by consent of the parties out of Court originates in a submission, and a submission is defined in s 2 of the Act as:

> . . . a written agreement to submit present or future differences to arbitration, whether an arbitrator is named therein or not, or under which any question or matter is to be decided by one or more persons to be appointed by the contracting parties or by some person named in the agreement.

Where there is a reference by consent out of Court, the authority of the arbitrator is derived from and limited by the parties' submission to arbitration and by the provisions of the relevant statutes.

(2) *Form of the Submission:* A submission may be either oral, written or made by deed. No particular form is required and the parties can amend it at any time before the arbitrator has given his or her award, provided that such alteration is made in writing and signed by all the parties. Neither the arbitrators, nor the umpire, can alter the submission. Under common law there may be an oral submission to arbitration. But this is unsatisfactory as proof of the exact terms agreed upon may be difficult and either party even after proceedings have commenced, can revoke the arbitrator's authority and refuse to continue. The provisions of the Act and amending Acts do not apply and consequently all the terms of the submission must be agreed upon. The Court has no authority to enforce the award, even with the consent of the parties. It would be necessary for the successful party to bring an action and establish his or her right to an order to give effect to what had already been decided by arbitration.

It is provided by the Second Schedule of the Act and the amendments thereto that, unless a contrary intention is expressed, the following provisions are implied in written submissions:

(a) if no other mode of reference is provided, the reference shall be to a single arbitrator;

(b) if the reference is to two arbitrators, the two arbitrators shall appoint an umpire immediately after they are themselves appointed;

(c) if the arbitrators have delivered to any part to the submission or to the umpire a notice in writing stating that they cannot agree, the umpire may forthwith enter on the reference in lieu of the arbitrators;

(d) the parties must submit to examination on oath and must produce all books, papers or documents within their possession that are called for and do all other things required by the arbitrators or umpire;

(e) witnesses may be examined on oath;

(f) the award shall be final and binding on the parties and on those claiming through them;

(g) the costs of the reference and the award shall be at the discretion of the arbitrators or umpire;

Section 14 of the Arbitration Amendment Act 1938 provides that any provision in a submission to the effect that any party shall in any event pay any part of the costs will be void unless it is part of an agreement to submit to arbitration a dispute which arose before the making of such agreement. If the award does not provide for costs, any party to the reference may, within 14 days after the award has been published, apply to the arbitrator for an order directing by and to whom costs shall be paid and after hearing any party desiring to be heard, the arbitrator may amend his or her award by making directions as to the payment of costs;

(h) the arbitrators or umpire shall have the same power as the Court to order specific performance of any contract other than a contract relating to land or any interest in land;

(i) the arbitrators or umpire may make an interim award.

51.4.3 Arbitrators and umpires

(a) DIFFERENCE BETWEEN AN UMPIRE AND A THIRD ARBITRA-TOR

An umpire acts alone and his or her decision is necessary only when two arbitrators have disagreed or when the award has not been made within the time specified in the submission. He or she hears the evidence at the same time as the two arbitrators, but this is merely to save time and expense in case he or she should be called upon to give a decision. He or she should take no part in the proceedings until the two arbitrators disagree. An umpire must give a decision on the whole question and not only on the points on which the arbitrators differ unless, of course, the submission otherwise provides. The third arbitrator does not act alone but acts with the others, and when a third arbitrator has been appointed, the other two are not entitled to proceed on the reference until he or she joins them in the hearing.

(b) POWERS OF ARBITRATORS AND UMPIRES

The arbitrator is empowered to make an award on all the questions comprised in the submission and the parties in the submission may confer on him such other incidental powers as they think fit. If the umpire is called on to act in substitution for the arbitrators, he or she has the same powers as the arbitrators originally appointed.

Where the submission is a *written* one, and does not contain any contrary provision, the arbitrators or umpires have the following powers:

(a) to examine the parties and their witnesses on oath or affirmation: s 8;

(b) to give directions as to the payment of costs: Arbitration Amendment Act 1938, s 14;

(c) to state a special case for the opinion of the Court: Arbitration Amendment Act 1938, s 11;

(d) to correct any clerical mistake or error in the award arising from any accidental slip or omission: s 8;

(e) to make an interim award; Arbitration Act 1908, 2nd Schedule;

(f) to order specific performance of any contract not relating to land or an interest in land: Arbitration Act 1908, 2nd Schedule.

An arbitrator has no power to order the parties to give security for costs unless it is so provided in the submission.

An arbitrator or umpire may, however, enforce his or her remuneration by a lien on the submission and the award.

It has been said that an arbitrator may, for his or her own guidance, consult persons of expert knowledge or skill on questions arising in the course of the reference, but it is not advisable that he or she should do so except with the knowledge and consent of the parties. An arbitrator or umpire may, and frequently does, obtain legal assistance as to the general conduct of proceedings. An arbitrator is entitled to take the advice of counsel and base his or her award on such advice: *Proudfoot v Turnbull* (1883) 1 NZLR (CA) 247. An arbitrator or umpire should not confer with the party who has appointed him.

An arbitrator or umpire may *not* delegate to another the powers which the parties have, by their submission, given to him.

An arbitrator in a commercial dispute can rely on his or her own knowledge and experience as regards the quality of goods and can assess damages even without evidence being put before him or her as to the amount: *Mediterranean and Eastern Export Co v Fortress Fabrics Ltd* [1948] 2 All ER 186. However, he or she must not take the parties by surprise. He or she must disclose knowledge of facts not known to the parties and allow them to deal with them: *Thomas Borthwick (Glasgow) Ltd v Faure Fairclough Ltd* [1968] 1 Lloyd's Rep 16.

The arbitrator must apply the law, not principles of equity in the broad, non technical sense. In this respect, systems such as New Zealand based on the English tradition differ from some Continental European systems. The reason for the English approach is that it would make judicial review impossible: *Orion Compania Espanola de Seguras v Belfort Maatshoppij Voor Algemene Vazekgringeen* [1962] 2 Lloyd's Rep 257.

(c) LIABILITY OF ARBITRATORS AND UMPIRES

An arbitrator or umpire is not liable for want of skill or care. It is, however, probable that if the arbitrator or umpire is guilty of fraud, he or she would be liable in damages to the party who has suffered as a result of his or her fraudulent conduct.

51.4.4 The award

The arbitrator must confine himself to the matters submitted to him or her under the submission, but he or she must decide all of them. If he or she fails in either respect, the award is liable to be set aside.

An award should settle the allocation of costs. No exact form of award need be given, but although it appears from the amending Act that the award need not be in writing, it is normally delivered in this form. The requisites of a valid award are:

- (a) It must be certain. If it cannot be interpreted by the Court the award is bad;
- (b) It must be legal, possible and reasonable. Thus it cannot order a person to do something which is not within his or her power; nor can it contain a direction which the arbitrator has no jurisdiction to make;
- (c) It must be final in the sense that it cannot be conditional, unless an alternative is provided in case the condition cannot be fulfilled: see *Harrison v Bolton* [1985] 1 NZLR 457.
- (d) It must deal with all matters included in the reference.

But if a particular issue was not included in the terms of reference for an earlier arbitration between the parties, neither party can be barred from claiming relief by subsequent arbitration from damage arising from such excluded issue: *Purser and Co (Hillingdon) Ltd v Jackson* [1976] 3 All ER 641.

An arbitrator or umpire may make an interim award. Apart from this, an arbitrator's or umpire's authority is ended on the making of an award although s 8 gives him or her power to correct a clerical mistake arising from an accidental slip or omission.

51.4.5 The powers of the Court, in relation to arbitration proceedings

(a) GENERAL

The Courts provide effective machinery for the institution of arbitration proceedings, for the control of improper conduct during the course of proceedings and for the amendment, setting aside or the enforcement of awards made by arbitrators. In *Czarnikow v Roth Schmidt and CAO* [1922] 2 KB 478, Bankes, LJ, stated, at 484:

> That they [arbitration proceedings] will continue their present popularity I entertain no doubt, so long as the law retains sufficient hold over them to prevent and redress any injustice on the part of the arbitrator, and to secure that the law that is administered by an arbitrator is in substance the law of the land and not some home-made law of the particular arbitrator.

Many of the powers of the Court facilitating the institution and conduct of arbitration proceedings are provided by the Arbitration Amendment Act 1938, First Schedule. In addition to a power to subpoena witnesses, take evidence on oath and to remove an arbitrator or umpire who does not use reasonable despatch in proceeding with the reference, the Court may make orders for:

(a) Security for costs;
(b) Discovery of documents and interrogatories;
(c) The giving of evidence by affidavit;
(d) The examination of witnesses out of the jurisdiction;
(e) The preservation, interim custody or sale of any goods which are
      the subject-matter of the reference;
(f) Securing the amount in dispute;
(g) The detention, preservation or inspection of any property which
      is the subject of the reference;
(h) Interim injunctions or the appointment of a receiver.

Control over the conduct of arbitration proceedings can be exercised
by the Court through its power to revoke the submission and declare that
a reference to arbitration shall not be a condition precedent to the
institution of proceedings in Court. In *Re Frankenberg and Security Company* (1894) 10 TLR 393, where the company had appointed its own
manager as arbitrator, an order was made that another arbitrator must be
appointed within a week or the submission would be revoked.

The Court also has power to remove an arbitrator and to appoint a new
arbitrator or umpire where there is obvious bias or misconduct on the
part of the arbitrator or umpire appointed under the submission. Where
the appointment of an arbitrator or umpire is revoked by leave of the
Court or if, after having entered on the reference, either is removed by the
Court, the Court may, on the application of any party to the submission,
either: (a) appoint a person to act in place of the person removed; or (b)
order that the submission shall cease to have effect with respect to the
dispute referred: Arbitration Amendment Act 1938, s 5(2).

(b) POWER TO STAY
The Court has power to stay legal proceedings if:

(a) the proceedings concern a matter agreed to be referred;
(b) there is no sufficient reason why that matter should not be re-
      ferred;
(c) the applicant has not filed a defence or taken any other steps; and,
(d) the applicant remains ready and willing to do everything neces-
      sary to the proper conduct of the arbitration (s 5, 1908 Act, as
      amended by Amendment Act, 1952).

The onus of proof is on the party who wants to keep out of arbitration.
The Court has a discretion and may refuse a stay if questions of law are
involved and the dispute is thus best dealt with by the Court: *Roose
Industries v Ready Mix Concrete* [1974] 2 NZLR 246 (CA); *Royal Oak Mall
Ltd v Savory Holdings Ltd* (Court of Appeal, CA 106/89, 2 November
1989). Another consideration is whether the grant or refusal of a stay will
avoid duplication of proceedings with the attendant consequences of
delay, additional costs and the risk of conflicting decisions: *The Eschersheim*
[1976] 1 All ER 411 (CA). A stay may be refused if the defendant's
breaches of contract have impoverished the plaintiff so that he or she
cannot afford to arbitrate: *Fakes v Taylor Woodrow Construction Ltd* [1973]
QB 437 (CA).

Two modern cases illustrate the exercise of the Court's discretion. In
Codelfa-Cogefar (NZ) Ltd v AG [1981] 2 NZLR 153 White J granted a stay

of legal proceedings in an engineering dispute which involved a dispute over the methods used and the adequacy of the equipment supplied. In *Anthony Argyle Ltd v UEB Waihi Ltd*, (unreported, High Court, Invercargill, A19/93, 15 October 1983, Roper J); [1983] BCL 1096 the Judge refused a stay of legal proceedings in an action in bailment, negligence and breach of statutory duty for loss of wool sent for scouring which was destroyed in a fire. He did so largely on the ground that the likelihood was that the hearing would be protracted and involve difficult questions of law which would have made it inappropriate for hearing before arbitrators with no expertise in the law.

In granting a stay of legal proceedings, Hillyer J in *Wilsons (NZ) Portland Cement Ltd v Gatx-Fuller (Aust) Pty Ltd* (unreported, High Court, Auckland, M1530/82, 15 December 1983); *Cap Letter*, 1984, 4/5/B, upheld a Mareva injunction, saying that there was no reason in principle why it should not be available to a claimant who was seeking to commence an arbitration.

(c) SPECIAL CASE STATED
The Court may consider a special case stated by an arbitrator or umpire regarding a question of law or an award or part of an award and may direct a special case to be stated as to an interim award or on a question of law arising in the course of a reference even though proceedings on the reference are still pending: s 11, 1938 Act. In such proceedings the Court gives its opinion as consultant and there is no appeal.

(d) REMISSION AND SETTING ASIDE OF AWARDS
The Court has power under s 11 of the 1908 Act to remit any matter for reconsideration of the arbitrator or umpire. It has power under s 12 of the 1908 Act to set aside the award if it was improperly procured or where the arbitrator has misconducted himself or the proceedings. It may also set aside an award where: (a) the arbitrator has erred in law; (b) where the contract was illegal and void from its inception; or (c) where the arbitrator is not qualified in the manner contemplated by the submission. There is no time limit specified for filing an application to set aside but it has been held that it must be made within a reasonable time of publishing the award: *Kenneth Williams & Co Ltd v Martelli* [1980] 2 NZLR 596; *Castleton Securities Ltd v Metropolitan Life Assurance Co of NZ Ltd* (High Court, Christchurch, CP 58/89, 12 October 1989, Williamson J).

51.4.6 Enforcement

By virtue of s 13 of the 1908 Act and s 12 of the 1938 Act an award may, with leave of the Court, be enforced as a judgment. When an award has been made and no application has been made to the Court to set it aside, the Court will give leave to enforce it unless it is unclear or there is some real ground for doubting its validity: *Mackintosh v Castle Land Co* [1973] NZLR 194. An award will carry interest at the same rate as a judgment debt unless otherwise provided: s 13 of the 1938 Act.

51.4.7 Reform

The Law Commission produced a Report No 20 on Arbitration. This reviews the main overseas models and favours the UNCITRAL Model

Law on the basis that this strikes the right balance between arbitral autonomy and judicial supervision. The draft Act includes additional provisions to adapt the Model Law for the purposes of "domestic" arbitration. Parties to a domestic arbitration may contract out of these additional provisions and parties to an international arbitration may contract with them.

51.5 MEDIATION AND CONCILIATION

While the parties have more control over arbitration than litigation, they have even more control in mediation and conciliation. The foundations of arbitration, mediation and conciliation are the same – acceptance or the will of the parties. However, while acceptance and conciliation are inherent in arbitration some parties are reluctant even to trust an arbitrator to sit in judgment on them and indeed the nature of some disputes are such that even arbitration may be inappropriate. This is classically the case where there is an ongoing relationship between the parties or a need for greater informality. In the past China has declined to accept adjudication and arbitration but has favoured conciliation. The role of a conciliator is described in Article 7 of the 1980 UNCITRAL Conciliation Rules:

(1) The conciliator assists the parties in an independent and impartial manner in their attempt to reach an amicable settlement of their dispute;

(2) The conciliator will be guided by principles of objectivity, fairness and justice, giving consideration to, among other things, the rights and obligations of the parties, the usages of the trade concerned and the circumstances surrounding the dispute, including any previous business practices between the parties;

(3) The conciliator may conduct the conciliation proceedings in such a manner as he or she considers appropriate, taking into account the circumstances of the case, the wishes the parties may express, including any request by a party that the conciliator hear oral statements, and the need for a speedy settlement of the dispute;

(4) The conciliator may, at any stage of the conciliation proceedings, make proposals for a settlement of the dispute. Such proposals need not be in writing and need not be accompanied by a statement of the reasons therefor.

Thus while an arbitrator is not only a Judge but a conciliator in the broadest sense of friend of the parties, a conciliator in the technical sense is not a Judge at all. He or she does not deliver a judgment or award.

In New Zealand a Community Mediation Service was set up on a trial basis in Christchurch in 1984: see Jane Chart [1981] 1 Canta LR 271; [1983] NZLJ 39. This eventually came to an end on a formal basis. There are also signs that commercial interests, independently of this scheme but perhaps influenced by it, are beginning to experiment with mediation and conciliation as an alternative dispute resolution mechanism: see (1984) 7 *Capital Letter*, 33, 1. In 1989 the New Zealand Commercial Disputes Centre Limited was incorporated to facilitate and manage the resolution of domestic and international commercial disputes by means of conciliation, mediation, arbitration and similar techniques. It has languished due to an unwillingness of the Government to commit public money to the project.

In the USA commercial mediation usually commences with each party's case being presented by their respective lawyers accompanied by senior management to an independent chairman (often a retired Judge). The chairman then offers an educated opinion as to the likely cost, duration and result of pursuing the matter in the Courts. The teams then withdraw and consider a settlement. Many major disputes have been speedily resolved in this way: AH Hermann, *The Financial Times*, 23, 30 August, 1984. A variation on the theme in the USA is the so-called Mini-trial which is not a trial but the use of a neutral adviser to moderate, pose questions and identify the salient issues. The adviser performs a lower key role than a mediator or conciliator and only gives his or her opinion as to how a Court would decide the dispute, if asked. Such an opinion is not binding but can be used in further negotiations. These take place between senior management who, having heard the reviews by the legal experts, then go off and engage in problem solving. The resolution of the dispute lies with them. The term Mini-trial is, therefore, a complete misnomer. There is arguably a need for such procedures in New Zealand. Although litigation is much cheaper here than in the USA and UK it necessarily involves a lawyer's perception of the dispute.

51.6 SPECIAL CHARACTERISTICS OF CONSUMER DISPUTE RESOLUTION AND CONSUMER PROTECTION LAW

Consumer disputes may be dealt with by the Disputes Tribunals or the District Court. They rarely reach the High Court because of the amount involved. There is some basis in the law for representative or class actions in consumer disputes where there are a number of similar plaintiffs and a common defendant. Provision for representative actions exists in R 78 of the High Court Rules. This provides:

> Where two or more persons have the same interest in the subject-matter of a proceeding, one or more of them may, with the consent of the other or others, or by direction of the Court on the application of any party or intending party to the proceeding, sue or be sued in such proceeding on behalf of or for the benefit of all persons so interested.

In practice it is difficult to establish a sufficient common interest and the rules about costs make it impracticable. The consumer may lose and be responsible for the defendant's costs and unable to recover them against other members of the class. Representative and class actions are more developed in the USA than in New Zealand and other Commonwealth countries although reform has been considered in Canada and Australia.

A more important question is the availability of legal aid. In New Zealand the present financial conditions are such that only the comparatively poor are eligible and in practice over 90% of all civil legal aid applications are in respect of domestic proceedings in the District Court.

More important still than legal procedures and legal aid is the provision of adequate consumer information and advice. This is at the forefront of the policy of the Ministry of Consumer Affairs and is consistent with current thinking in the Department of Justice.

It is arguable that Consumer Protection has characteristics which transcend conventional law and legal procedures. Commercial Law has traditionally been the most dynamic area of the legal system. It is then not really surprising that part of it should show signs of breaking away and absorbing some of the characteristics of administrative law. Perhaps the next stage will be to have action on behalf of consumers as a class brought by a public servant or independent officer like the Director General of Fair Trading in the United Kingdom.

Appendix A

INTERESTS IN LAND

Because comparisons have been made in this book with interests in land and it is desirable that accountancy students should have a basic acquaintance with certain aspects of real property law which they are likely to meet in practice, a short note on the system of registration of titles and on certain dealings with land has been included.

THE LAND TRANSFER SYSTEM

This system has virtually replaced the earlier "deeds system" which was a registry of *deeds* (which occasionally still have to be searched).

The Land Transfer Act 1952 provides for a registry of *titles* in which the original certificate of title is held and for the issue to the registered proprietor of a duplicate freehold or leasehold certificate of title. The original certificates of title are held by the Land Registry Office of the district in which the land is situated. All instruments affecting land must be registered in the Land Registry Office for the district in which the land is situated. Dealings with land, eg, mortgages, transfers, leases and easements can be, and almost always are, entered in the register and recorded on the duplicate certificate of title. This system of registration of title enables a registered proprietor to show what interest he or she has in the land and permits a purchaser or mortgagee to deal with him or her on the basis of what is disclosed by the certificate of title. The register is open to search by the public.

Persons who deal in good faith with the registered proprietor and have provided some consideration and who themselves become the registered proprietor by registering against the title the instrument creating the interest dealt with, secure the protection of the Act: ss 62, 182 and 183.

Certain fundamental principles characterise the Land Transfer Act. First, it is by registration of the instrument under which he or she claims that a person acquires a *legal* interest in the land. Until registration, he or she has only an *equitable* interest: s 41; see *Catchpole v Burke* [1974] 1 NZLR 620 (CA). Priority as between persons claiming an interest in the land is determined by the time of registration of the instrument under which each claims. For example, the memorials (entries) on a certificate of title might record the following dealings:

965

(a) A mortgage by the registered proprietor to a lender "discharged" at 10.20 am, 1 June 1991;

(b) A transfer by the registered proprietor to a buyer registered at 10.21 am, 1 June 1991;

(c) A mortgage of the land by the buyer to a different lender registered at 10.22 am, 1 June 1991.

Secondly, the estate of the registered proprietor is generally paramount and is protected by the Act unless he or she has been a party to fraud (ss 62, 63). This is often described as the indefeasibility principle, applied by the Privy Council in *Frazer v Walker* [1967] NZLR 1069; [1967] AC 569. Fraud means actual dishonesty on the part of the person registered as proprietor and not merely constructive fraud. Provisions of the Insolvency Act 1967, already discussed, may affect the indefeasibility of the title of a person who has acquired an interest in the land of a registered proprietor who is subsequently adjudicated bankrupt.

Thirdly, registration is notice to all persons; they are affected with notice of what would have been discovered by a search of the original certificate of title held by the Land Registry Office. Because certain dealings, eg, liens, land and income tax charges and caveats, are registered only against the original certificate of title, it is essential that a search be made of that title and that a purchaser should not rely on the duplicate certificate held by the vendor. Rates become a legal charge on land when struck. A charge for rates does not appear on the title until much later. This explains the need to sign a receipt for payment of all rates when settling a land transaction.

Fourthly, bona fide purchasers or mortgagees who give valuable consideration and who deal with the registered proprietor on the faith of the register secure a good title on registration of the instrument under which they claim. For instance, in *Frazer v Walker*, supra, the mortgagees whose mortgage was forged and the purchasers at the mortgagees' sale both obtained good titles on registration, having acted in good faith and given consideration. However, to obtain protection the dealing must be with an *actual* registered proprietor, not a non-existent (fictitious) person, as in *Gibbs v Messer* [1891] AC 248, where the purchasers did not obtain an indefeasible title.

Fifthly, the registered proprietor holds the land subject only to other interests which have been registered on the title. He or she holds the land free from all unregistered interests: s 62. There are limited exceptions, the most important relating to easements (for example, rights of way) which have been executed, but omitted from the title. There is also an exception in the case of fraud, but the Act specifically provides that knowledge that unregistered interests exist "shall not itself be imputed as fraud": s 182. However, the Courts have interpreted this provision restrictively, and have been ready to find that fraud exists where a purchaser has acquired land with notice of unregistered interests, and intending to defeat them: *Efstratiou v Glantschnig* [1972] NZLR 594.

Sixthly, no notice of any trust may be made on a Land Transfer title. The purchaser or mortgagee can confidently deal with the registered proprietor; he or she need not inquire whether the registered proprietor is a trustee or whether he or she is acting in breach of trust. If, however, he or she is given notice that the transaction is in breach of trust, he or she should not complete the transaction with the registered proprietor. Registration of an instrument known to be in breach of trust would amount to fraud. The section forbidding the entry of trusts on the title and the other provisions mentioned facilitate dealings with land and do not require purchasers to inquire into the circumstances in which the registered proprietor acquired his or her estate.

CERTIFICATE OF TITLE

Every registered proprietor of an estate of freehold is entitled to a certificate of title describing his or her estate. Certificates can also be issued in respect of a leasehold interest in land. The certificate of title gives a legal description of the land with reference to a survey plan and states the interest of the registered proprietor in the land. A diagram is indorsed on the title showing the boundaries.

The Land Transfer (Compulsory Registration of Titles) Act 1924 provided for the bringing of all land under the Land Transfer Act. It also permitted the issue of "limited" titles where the Examiner of Titles was not satisfied with the evidence of entitlement to an interest in the land or where the boundaries were not adequately defined by survey. Registered proprietors with limited titles do not have the full protection of the Act.

A certificate of title, in addition to describing the land and naming the registered proprietor, will also have indorsed on it a number of memorials, ie, entries signed by the District Land Registrar or an Assistant Land Registrar. Among the memorials commonly found on certificates of title are fencing covenants, mortgages, easements, transfers and covenants restricting the use of land. A fencing covenant usually provides that the vendor of the land shall not be liable to contribute towards the cost of erection or maintenance of boundary fences. The title and the memorials set out on it show the nature of the interest of the registered proprietor and how he or she has dealt with it. The title reference is shown at the top right-hand corner, eg, volume 598, folio 77. This means that the original title will be found in the volume numbered 598, on page 77.

The Unit Titles Act 1972 has simplified the separate ownership of airspace to provide mortgageable and transferable leasehold tenures for tenants and owners of flat and office units in multi-storey buildings. A simple stratum title within the Land Transfer system results from the deposit of a unit plan. Existing schemes under the Companies Amendment Act 1961 may be converted to stratum estates.

TRANSFERS

A memorandum of transfer is the prescribed means of transferring an interest in land and of creating a right of way or other easement or a profit a prendre. If a registered proprietor wishes to execute a power of appointment or create a limited interest in land, the memorandum of transfer, suitably modified, is also the means by which this is done.

The transfer must refer to the folium of the register in which the original certificate of title is bound and contain a precise statement of the estate or interest to be transferred or created. This document, signed by the registered proprietor, is stamped (where necessary) and then lodged, together with the duplicate certificate of title, with the Land Registry Office for registration.

After registration, a memorial is entered on the original and duplicate certificates of title evidencing the registration of the dealing. The memorial signed by the District Land Registrar is conclusive evidence of the registration of the instrument.

EASEMENTS AND PROFIT A PRENDRE

If the registered proprietor wishes to create a right of way, a drainage easement, or a right to enter on the land and take part of its produce, eg, to take shingle, he or she can do this by a memorandum of transfer modified to meet the circumstances of the case. On registration of the instrument, a memorial showing the nature of the rights given is entered on the title.

COVENANTS RELATING TO LAND

Sometimes property owners, or purchasers of property, enter into "covenants" that they will use, or refrain from using, their land in a particular way for the benefit of adjoining property. For example, a property owner may covenant not to build other than a single-storey dwelling on his or her land so as to preserve the view of his or her neighbour. Such a covenant may be notified on the title to the property under s 126A of the Property Law Act 1952, although this "notification" is not true "registration" under the Land Transfer Act 1952, and gives the covenant no greater operation than it already had: s 126A(1)(b). However, a covenant binds all subsequent purchasers of the land as an equitable interest, and notification on the title ensures they have notice of it.

The law on this topic changed in 1987, for the first time allowing *positive* covenants to bind subsequent purchasers and to be notified on the title. Before that time only negative (or "restrictive") covenants had those consequences.

MORTGAGES

A mortgage (which is a species of contract) of Land Transfer land is a charge on, not an assignment of, the interest of the mortgagor. By signing a memorandum of mortgage over land, the mortgagor charges his or her land with payment of the moneys borrowed and enters into a number of covenants with the mortgagee the principal covenants being a personal undertaking to repay the principal sum in the manner specified in the memorandum, a covenant to pay interest at the rate specified on the dates agreed and a covenant to insure and to maintain the mortgaged property.

On registration of the memorandum of mortgage (in duplicate), the mortgagee secures a legal charge on the land. Until registration, he or she merely has an equitable charge on the land. The deposit of the certificate of title, even if accompanied by a memorandum stating the reasons for the deposit, does not in New Zealand create an equitable mortgage of the land. After the memorandum of mortgage is registered, a memorial is entered on the mortgagor's title; when the discharge or release of the mortgage is registered, a further memorial evidencing the discharge of the mortgage is stamped across the memorial referring to the mortgage. When the mortgagee's remedies against the mortgagor have become statute barred, the mortgagor is entitled to apply to the High Court to have the mortgage discharged. The Court may, in its discretion, make an order discharging the mortgage.

After he or she has mortgaged his or her land, the mortgagor still has an "equity of redemption", ie, he or she has the right to have the mortgage discharged on repayment of the principal and interest secured by the mortgage. His or her right to redeem continues even after the due date of repayment has passed; at any time prior to sale by the mortgagee, the mortgagor is entitled, on payment of principal and interest, to have the mortgage discharged. The law does not permit a mortgagor's equity of redemption to become "clogged" by provisions inconsistent with his or her right of repayment. In *Bannerman, Brydone, Folster and Co v Murray* [1972] NZLR 411 (CA), it was held that an option to purchase exercisable by the mortgagee was a clog on the equity of redemption because it prevented the mortgagor from regaining his or her property when he or she repaid the mortgage. The mortgagor is entitled to sell the mortgaged land, and if the mortgage is not repaid on sale, the purchaser then assumes responsibility for observing the covenants in the memorandum of mortgage.

A mortgagee secures certain rights by virtue of the mortgage. He or she is entitled to custody of the certificate of title and any insurance policy (if he or she is the first mortgagee); he or she can sue the mortgagor for arrears of principal and interest; he or she can enter and take possession of the mortgaged land and thereby acquire the right to payment of rent if the mortgaged premises are tenanted; he or she can sell the mortgaged property and sue the mortgagor if there is any deficiency after sale; he or she can grant a lease of the land after he or she has entered into possession.

The Property Law Act 1952 and the Land Transfer Act 1952 contain provisions concerning mortgages, the powers of the mortgagee and covenants as between the parties. Some of these provisions can be negatived or modified by agreement between the parties.

CAVEATS

These are in the nature of warnings to those searching a title of some dispute or contention affecting the land, or some unregistered interest in it. The most common form is the caveat against dealings. No transfer of or charge on the land can be registered while such a caveat is on the title. For example, a person who is purchasing land under a long-term agreement for sale and purchase will usually lodge a caveat to protect his or her interest and prevent the registration of a transfer to anyone else. Memorials of caveats are entered in red ink on the Registry copy of the title.

If a person who has lodged a caveat receives notice of an application to register a competing dealing, the caveat will lapse within 14 days unless the caveator applies to the High Court for an order continuing the caveat. Caveats are quite often litigated, sometimes as a result of applications of the kind just mentioned, sometimes as a result of someone challenging the right of the person concerned to caveat the title in the first place.

LEASES

The person granting a lease, which is a species of contract, is called the lessor; the person to whom the lease is granted is called the lessee. The lessee, unless the contrary is provided in the lease, may sub-let to a sublessee, or assign his or her interest to an assignee.

Many lease documents provide that there is to be no sub-lease or assignment without the lessor's consent, but in such a case the lessor's consent may not be unreasonably withheld.

A lease for three years or more must be registered under the Land Transfer Act 1952 otherwise it may be displaced by a later lease. A lease for less than three years may be registered. However, many leases are created by unregistered documents in the form of a deed, an agreement to lease, or a tenancy agreement. Such leases, although not protected by the provisions of the Land Transfer Act are perfectly valid and enforceable between lessor and lessee.

A lease may be granted for any term, but the term must be definite. A lease for a term to end on the marriage of the lessor's eldest son is for an indefinite or uncertain term and is void. Leases are sometimes granted for terms of 21 years, with a right of renewal (eg, Glasgow leases under which the tenant's improvements vest in the landlord) or for a term of 99 years. Some leases are granted for even longer terms, eg, 999 years. At the other end of the scale, some leases are for a very short term, and some are terminable by notice (often a month) on either side. Such arrangements are often called tenancies. If no term is agreed, the tenancy is deemed to be a monthly tenancy terminable on one month's notice by either party. A right of renewal in a lease gives the lessee the option of requiring the lessor to grant him or her a lease for a further term at the expiration of the current term provided the option is exercised in accordance with the lease. There is normally a provision for a revaluation and a consequent adjustment in the ground rent payable.

A lease or tenancy agreement usually contains a number of covenants, eg, an agreement or promise to pay rent, rates and insurance, a covenant to keep the premises in good repair and a covenant to grant a renewal. The covenants set out in the Property Law Act 1952 bind the parties to a lease unless the contrary is agreed.

If the lessee commits a breach of a covenant in the lease, the lessor may re-enter and forfeit the lease. There are provisions in the Property Law Act 1952 under which a lessee can apply to the Court for relief against forfeiture. There are special provisions for Crown tenants in the Land Act 1948.

A lease must be distinguished from a licence. A lease confers on the lessee exclusive possession (ie a right to exclude all other persons including the lessor); it confers a right of property in return for rent. A licence is merely the grant of a permission to someone to enter on the owner's land. Thus a lodger has only a licence: *Street v Mountford* [1985] AC 809, 817-818, as does a person with the right to sell confectionery in a theatre: *John Fuller & Sons Ltd v Brooks* [1950] NZLR 94, and a person with the right to depasture sheep on land which is also open to the public: *Mayor of Christchurch v Pyne, Gould, Guinness Ltd* [1928] NZLR 318. The mere fact that parties *call* their arrangement a lease or a licence is not all-important; it is the substance that matters: *Street v Mountford* supra. Deciding which it is, can sometimes be a matter of considerable difficulty. However, modern tenancy legislation often expressly applies to both sorts of arrangement; the Residential Tenancies Act 1986, for example, defines in great detail the sorts of arrangement to which it applies.

RESIDENTIAL TENANCY LEGISLATION

For many years the law has attempted to regulate leases and tenancies of dwellinghouses to ensure that there is fair treatment of tenants by landlords, and vice-versa. The current legislation in New Zealand is the Residential Tenancies Act 1986. It gives security of tenure to tenants by providing they cannot be put out with less than 90 days' notice (or 42 days' if the landlord requires the premises for certain purposes); however, if the tenants are behind with their rent or otherwise in breach of the tenancy agreement a Tenancy Tribunal may make an order for the tenancy to be terminated. There are also provisions limiting the amount of any bond the landlord may require, and regulating rent increases; a Tenancy Tribunal may, on application by a tenant, make an order reducing the rent to a market rent. There are also obligations on the landlord to maintain a reasonable state of repair, and on the tenant to keep the premises tidy and clean and not to damage the premises. Tenancy Tribunals are constituted by the Act, with jurisdiction to determine disputes between landlords and tenants. Except with the consent of a Tribunal, it is unlawful for a landlord to refuse to let premises to a person on the ground that the person has children, or is unemployed; it is also unlawful under the Human Rights Commission Act 1977 to discriminate against persons on the grounds of race, colour, sex, marital status, or religion.

Tenancy legislation of this kind is always politically controversial. It is a matter of considerable difficulty to maintain a fair balance between both sides. If the wrong balance is struck it can have a substantial effect on the housing market.

Appendix B

NEW ZEALAND COURTS

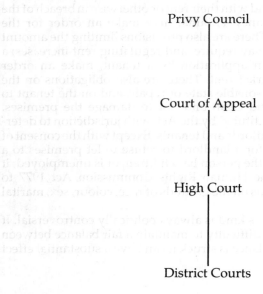

Privy Council

Court of Appeal

High Court

District Courts

Justices of the Peace may exercise part of the criminal jurisdiction of the District Court.

Disputes Tribunals have been established in the main centres. A limited appeal lies to the District Court.

Appendix C

THE PRESENT COURTS STRUCTURE IN ENGLAND AND WALES

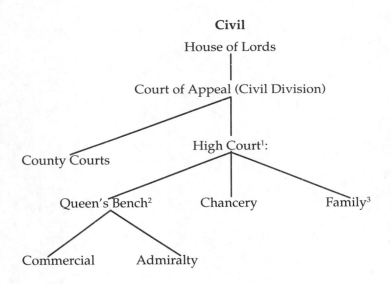

Civil

House of Lords

Court of Appeal (Civil Division)

High Court[1]:

County Courts

Queen's Bench[2]   Chancery   Family[3]

Commercial   Admiralty

Criminal

House of Lords

Court of Appeal (Criminal Division)

Crown Court

Magistrates Courts

973

1   Each Division of the High Court has a Divisional Court which
     exercises a species of appellate jurisdiction. Thus appeals from the
     matrimonial jurisdiction of the Magistrates' Courts go to the
     Divisional Court of the Family Division. There can also be appeals
     by a procedure known as case stated from the Magistrates' and
     Crown Courts to the Divisional Court of the Queen's Bench
     Division. This is irrational but historically explicable.
2   Under the Judicature Acts, there were also Common Pleas and
     Exchequer Divisions. These merged with the Queen's Bench Divi-
     sion in 1881.
3   Under the Judicature Acts, there was a Probate Divorce and
     Admiralty Division. This was changed by the Administration of
     Justice Act 1970, which created the Family Division and trans-
     ferred Admiralty to Queen's Bench and Contentious Probate to
     Chancery.

Appendix D

GLOSSARY OF LATIN TERMS

Ab initio: from the beginning.

A fortiori: all the more so, with stronger reason.

A priori: reasoning from first principle, deductively.

Assumpsit: literally, he or she has undertaken, but used commonly to describe an action on a simple contract.

Bona fide: in good faith.

Causa proxima et non remota spectatur: it is the immediate cause (of the loss) not the remote (indirect) one which is taken into consideration.

Consensus ad idem: agreement on the same thing, mutuality of wills.

Contra bonos mores: against good morals.

Contra proferentem: against the person responsible for putting it forward or giving evidence of the fact.

De facto: in fact though usually not in law.

Del credere agent: an agent usually for a higher commission who undertakes to indemnify his or her principal if the buyer fails to pay the principal.

Delegatus non potest delegare: an agent is not permitted to appoint another to act on his or her behalf.

Dictum, dicta: a saying, sayings. For *obiter dicta,* see below.

Ejusdem generis: of the same kind or nature.

Ex post facto: from something done afterwards.

Ex turpi causa, non oritur actio: a right of action does not arise from a disgraceful or immoral consideration.

Fructus industriales: crops produced by human labour.

Fructus naturales: crops produced naturally without human labour.

Ignorantia legis neminem excusat: ignorance of the law does not excuse anyone.

Infra: below.

In pari delicto: equally in the wrong.

In pari delicto potior est conditio defendentis: the parties being equally in the wrong, the defendant is in the more powerful position.

Inter alia: among other things.

Inter partes: between the parties.

In personam: usually an action against a person not involving title to property.

In rem: an action to determine claims to property or title or status.

In terrorem: as a warning.

In vacuo: in a vacuum, in the abstract.

Nisi: unless.

Non est factum: it is not my deed.

Nulla bona: no goods (exclusive of $400 worth of personal possessions and tools of trade).

Obiter, obiter dictum: a statement or comment, not binding upon future Courts, though it may be respected according to the reputation of the Judge, the eminence of the Court and the circumstances in which it came to be pronounced.

Pari passu: on an equal footing.

Per pro: for and on behalf of.

Per se: by or in itself.

Prima facie: on the first view (without taking other factors into consideration).

Profit à prendre: a right to enter on land and take part of its substance or produce.

Quaere: it is a question.

Quantum meruit: as much as he or she has earned (a payment proportionate to the amount earned).

Quid pro quo: that received in return.

Res extincta: things which do not exist.

Res sua: his or her own things or property.

Restitutio in integrum: total restoration.

Simpliciter: absolutely, universally.

Supra: above.

Uberrimae fidei: of the utmost good faith.

Ultra vires: beyond the powers of.

Appendix E

THE NEW ZEALAND STOCK & STATION AGENTS' ASSOCIATION CONDITIONS OF SALE

The Conditions of Sale set out below shall be binding upon all sellers and bidders in all transactions entered into at this place whether by auction, private contract or otherwise. In particular, these Conditions of Sale shall be binding upon all sales conducted by whatever means by members of the Constituent Stock & Station Agents Associations which are members of the New Zealand Stock & Station Agents' Association. They shall be so binding notwithstanding that they may not be read aloud at any stage and whether or not any announcement is made concerning them at any time during which business is transacted. The conduct of any person in employing the Auctioneer as his agent or in inspecting any Stock or in making any offer or bid for any Stock shall be deemed to be an acceptance of these Conditions of Sale.

1 INTERPRETATION

1.1 In these Conditions of Sale unless the context otherwise requires:

"Auctioneer" means the company, firm or person whose licence to sell by auction is held by the person conducting this sale as auctioneer, unless the context shows that it is intended to mean only the person conducting this sale as auctioneer;

"Embryo" means a fertilized egg from a donor animal;

"Flush" means the available Embryos to be flushed from the uterus of a donor animal following insemination by semen of a specified sire;

"Liquidated Damages" means damages which are calculated on the basis of interest on the full amount of the Purchase Price and any other moneys owing under these Conditions calculated in the manner described in clause 6.2 from the date of sale until payment in full. It shall also include all costs including without limitation legal costs incurred in the recovery of the Purchase Price or other moneys owing;

"Overdue Accounts" means those accounts which the Auctioneer or Stock & Station Agent has issued pursuant to payment arrangements entered into (being normally payment within 14 days) and which have not been paid within the terms of such arrangements;

"Purchase Price" means, unless otherwise announced by the Auctioneer, the price which is bid by the successful bidder plus the amount of goods and services tax on that price at the applicable rate;

"Semen" means sperm from an animal offered for sale measured in straws and certified in writing by an approved Artificial Insemination Technician as to fertility rating, identity, origin and quality of storage;

"Share" means the percentage interest in any live animal held by the seller;

"Stock" means and includes live and dead Stock, chattels, unfertilised ova, Stud Stock or Shares in any of the foregoing, and, where appropriate, includes any Embryo Flush and any Semen which has been offered for sale. All terms relating to live Stock shall apply (with the necessary changes being made) to all other forms of Stock described in this definition;

"Stock & Station Agent" means a person who is a member of a district Stock and Station Agents Association; and

"Stud Stock" means Stock which is registered in the Stud Book.

1.2   Words importing the singular shall include the plural and vice versa and one gender includes all others.

1.3   A reference to any legislation includes modification or re-enactment of, legislation re-enactment in substitution for or a regulation, order-in-council or other instrument from time to time issued or made under, that legislation.

2. GENERAL RULES OF AUCTION

2.1   The buyer sháll be the highest bidder at the fall of the hammer. If any dispute should arise the Stock shall by put up again and resold or the dispute otherwise settled at the Auctioneer's discretion. The decision of the Auctioneer shall be binding.

2.2   The Auctioneer reserves the right to refuse to accept any bid. No person shall advance in bidding less than an amount from time to time nominated or directed by the Auctioneer.

2.3   Every buyer is deemed, by virtue of his bid, to authorise either the Auctioneer or the clerk of the Auctioneer to sign the Sale Book of Memorandum of Agreement as buyer on his behalf. The signing of such a document by the clerk of the Auctioneer shall be as binding upon both the seller and the buyer as if the Auctioneer had signed it himself.

2.4   Every person who makes a bid is deemed to be bidding as a principal and the person to whom Stock is knocked down shall be and remain responsible for payment of the Purchase Price notwithstanding any subsequent disclosure of agency or any acceptance or acknowledgement of that agency by the Auctioneer.

2.5 The name, description, and address of the seller, as given by the seller, will in all cases be furnished to a bidder or buyer if required, and in case of any dispute the remedy of the buyer shall be against the seller only, and in no case or under any circumstances against the Auctioneer, who is to be regarded to all intents and purposes as agent for a disclosed principal.

2.6 There shall be no fictitious or fraudulent bidding.

2.7 The Auctioneer reserves the right to require all bidders to enter their name and address in a register prior to the commencement of any sale.

3 SELLER'S RIGHTS TO BID

3.1 The sale of any lot or lots is subject to the right of the seller or his agent to one bid only (the price of such bid to be the "reserve price").

3.2 If the seller or the seller's agent makes a bid and no further bid is made, the person who made the bid prior to the reserve price may purchase the lot or lots at the reserve price before the next pen is offered.

4 BUYER'S RISK – NO WARRANTIES

4.1 All lots are available for inspection prior to the sale and all bidders shall be deemed to have carefully inspected the Stock and have made their bids as a result of their own inspection and not on any other basis.

4.2 The Stock are sold with all faults which they may have at the time of sale whether or not such faults are discoverable by inspection.

4.3 The buyer acknowledges that no representations warranties guarantees or conditions were given to him in respect of the Stock and nor did he rely on any affirmations or statements made at the time of the sale or arising from any of the conditions of the sale. All representations conditions and warranties which might otherwise be implied by law are, to the extent permissible by law, excluded and negatived.

4.4 Clause 4.3 should not apply only if the buyer is able to produce a written statement before the commencement of the sale of the appropriate lot signed by the seller, or the Auctioneer on the seller's behalf, which expressly gives a representation warranty guarantee or condition. Failure to produce such a statement shall be conclusive proof that no representations warranties guarantees or conditions were given.

4.5 The Auctioneer gives no warranty as to the seller's title to the Stock nor to the validity of any description or particulars of any Stock offered for sale.

4.6   If any error or misdescription is made as to title, age, number, sex, condition, or any other particular of any Stock offered for sale, the same shall not annul the sale, but such compensation shall be allowed to the buyer by the seller as the auctioneer, acting as expert for both parties, shall determine at his complete discretion. If the buyer and seller are unwilling to accept the Auctioneer's determination, they must adjust the matter between themselves. In the event of any dispute between the buyer and the seller no lot is to be returned to the Auctioneer.

5 TERMS OF SALE

5.1   Each lot in all cases shall, immediately on the fall of the hammer, be at the risk of the buyer, who must remove the same within the time specified by the Auctioneer. Prior to the fall of the hammer the Stock will be at the sole risk of the relevant Seller and the Auctioneer shall not be in any way liable or responsible whether as bailee or otherwise for any loss of, damage to or the passing of disease or other condition to or from any Stock.

5.2   All Stock shall be paid for in cash immediately on the conclusion of the sale unless the Auctioneer shall prior to the putting up of any lot or lots otherwise specify or the buyer is able to make other arrangements satisfactory to the Auctioneer with one of the following:
(a) the Auctioneer acting in the capacity of the buyer's Stock & Station Agent; or
(b) another authorised person acting as the buyer's Stock & Station Agent.

5.3   The property in the Stock purchased shall not pass to the buyer until payment of the Purchase Price and all money owing under these Conditions including without limitation Liquidated Damages, if any, is made in full by or on behalf of the buyer to the Auctioneer.

5.4   If the Purchase Price is not paid in full and another arrangement made in accordance with clause 5.2:
(a) the Auctioneer may deliver the Stock to the buyer without receiving payment in full for such Stock and the buyer shall then hold such Stock on trust for the seller until the buyer himself (and not a Stock & Station Agent acting as agent for the buyer) has made payment in full; and
(b) the buyer shall be deemed to have requested and authorised the Stock & Station Agent acting for him to, on his account, pay the Purchase Price in full to the Auctioneer or credit the seller's account with the Auctioneer with that sum and to debit the buyer's account with the Purchase Price or such part of it as shall have not been paid by the buyer and, if the Auctioneer thinks fit, he shall do so and may deduct and retain his selling commission and charges when paying the balance of the Purchase Price to the seller.

5.5 Where the buyer's Stock & Station Agent credits the seller's account with the Purchase Price and debits the buyer's account with that amount, the seller agrees that all his rights relating to the Purchase Price and the Stock shall automatically be transferred or subrogated to the buyer's Stock & Station Agent. In the event that it should be necessary for a formal record of such transfer or subrogation to be made, the seller appoints the Auctioneer or the clerk of the Auctioneer to sign those documents as may be required on his behalf.

5.6 The seller and the Auctioneer agree that, unless the Auctioneer shall specify otherwise, all sales of Stock shall be subject to goods and services tax by virtue of the agreed application of the provisions of section 60(5) of the Goods and Services Tax Act 1985, irrespective of whether goods and services tax would otherwise by payable in respect of the sale of the Stock.

5.7 No buyer shall be entitled to withhold payment for pedigree Stock pending execution and delivery by the seller of transfer of the same registrable in the Stud Book and the remedy of the buyer on failure to receive such registrable transfer shall lie against the seller alone and not the Auctioneer.

5.8 Where Stock is to be sold by weight:
(a) the weight at which the Stock shall be sold is the weight recorded at the time specified by the Auctioneer on the certified scales used at any sale-yard venue and such weight shall bind both buyer and seller; and
(b) the seller shall advise the Auctioneer as to whether the Stock will be sold on an individual weight or other basis. If the Seller does not so advise the Auctioneer the method of disposal shall be at the discretion of the Auctioneer.

5.9 As a pre-condition to the Auctioneer selling Stock, the seller shall arrange for delivery to the Auctioneer of releases of all securities which have been granted over the Stock to be sold.

6 PAYMENT

6.1 Subject to any special arrangements that may be made in respect of any lot between the seller and the buyer, pursuant to clause 5 the buyer's Stock & Station Agent (including the Auctioneer if he acted as the buyer's Stock & Station Agent), in addition to all other rights and remedies of the Auctioneer express or implied, and notwithstanding the Sale Book or Memorandum of Agreement may have been signed by the Auctioneer or the clerk of the Auctioneer on behalf of or as agent for the buyer, shall be entitled to recover from the buyer as a debt due on demand by the buyer to the buyer's Stock & Station Agent, the full amount of the unpaid Purchase Price and all other money owing to him under these Conditions including without limitation Liquidated Damages and goods and services tax (if any) until payment is made by the buyer in full.

6.2 For the purpose of determining the amount of Liquidated Damages, interest shall be considered as accruing from day-to-day on all monies payable under these terms and conditions including, without limitation, goods and services tax at such rate for the time being charged by the buyer's Stock & Station Agent on Overdue Accounts and any such interest money remaining unpaid on the dates observed by the buyer's Stock & Station Agent for the capitalisation of interest shall itself carry interest in like manner as the unpaid Purchase Price and shall be deemed part of the unpaid Purchase Price. The current interest rate and the dates for capitalisation of interest (if any) shall be advised to the buyer on request.

6.3 The rights and remedies of the buyer's Stock & Station Agent or the Auctioneer under these conditions shall not be affected by reason of the selling commission and charges of the Auctioneer having been deducted in any payment made by the buyer's Stock & Station Agent to the seller, and as between the buyer and the buyer's Stock & Station Agent or the Auctioneer, as appropriate, the buyer waives all rights of set off, if any, the buyer as between the buyer and the seller may have against the seller.

7 REPOSSESSION AND RESALE

7.1 If the Stock is delivered to the buyer pursuant to clause 8 before the buyer has paid the Purchase Price in full, the buyer irrevocably gives the seller, the seller's employees and agents and the buyer's Stock & Station Agent leave and licence without notice to enter upon any premises occupied by the buyer as often as may be reasonably necessary and to search for, inspect and repossess the Stock without incurring any liability whatsoever for such actions notwithstanding that the buyer may have been declared bankrupt or, if a company, be in receivership or in liquidation.

7.2 Should the Stock be repossessed in accordance with this clause, the seller or the seller's agents or the buyer's Stock & Station Agent may resell the Stock by auction, private contract or otherwise without notice to the buyer. Such sale shall be at the buyer's risk and expense, any loss (including any goods and services tax imposed in respect of the sale and resale) on the resale shall be recoverable from the buyer as a debt due upon demand together with Liquidated Damages.

7.3 The buyer shall not be entitled to any surplus arising from the resale of the Stock.

7.4 The Auctioneer shall be under no liability for the loss, if any, incurred by the seller by reason of the failure on the part of the buyer to complete his purchase.

8 DELIVERY

8.1   In the event of either seller or buyer or both being absent at time of delivery into or out of the saleyards, the Auctioneer or any authorised employee of the local Stock & Station Agent shall be deemed to have been authorised to tally the Stock sold, and his figures are to be accepted as final.

8.2   Should Stock be removed by the buyer or his agent without authority of the Auctioneer, the buyer shall be liable for the numbers as entered in the Auctioneer's book.

8.3   The buyer agrees with the Auctioneer that any person to whom delivery of Stock may be given, nominated or appointed by the buyer, or by the Auctioneer purporting to act on behalf of the buyer, shall for all purposes be deemed to be the employee of the buyer, and the Auctioneer shall not in any way be liable or responsible for any act or omission of such person. The Auctioneer will not be responsible for any claims by any such person for compensation for loss as a result of accident.

8.4   The buyer agrees that notwithstanding any instructions or directions given by him to the Auctioneer or any servant of the Auctioneer as to the method or time of trucking, holding, feeding, watering or otherwise tending any Stock for any period, or as to the route to be followed by any driven or trucked Stock, or the numbers of drovers to be employed, the Stock shall remain at the buyer's risk, and no liability whatever shall attach to the Auctioneer or any servant of the Auctioneer for any loss or damage occasioned to such Stock.

8.5   The Auctioneer or any responsible employee of the Auctioneer shall be at liberty at his discretion, if in his opinion it is desirable or imperative in the interest of the buyer or for the benefit of any Stock, to disregard, vary or modify the directions or instructions of the buyer and adopt other procedure altogether or in part. In any such event the decision of the Auctioneer or any responsible employee of the Auctioneer shall be final and binding, and neither the Auctioneer nor any of its servants shall be liable to the buyer for any damage or loss incurred by the buyer consequent on the carrying out, disregard, variation or modification of his instructions or directions.

8.6   All expenses of whatsoever nature incurred by the Auctioneer on behalf of the buyer or seller for the care, maintenance and transit of Stock purchased or sold shall be at the expense in all respects of the seller prior to the fall of the hammer or the buyer after the fall of the hammer (as applicable) and may together with Liquidated Damages be recovered by the Auctioneer from the seller or buyer (as applicable) as a debt due upon demand. The buyer or seller, as applicable, shall also be liable for any goods and services tax payable in respect of payments due under this clause.

9 STOCK NOT SOLD

9.1 Any Stock not sold shall be at the risk of the seller and the Auctioneer shall not be responsible whether as bailee or otherwise to the seller for any loss of damage to or the passing of disease or other condition to or from such Stock.

9.2 The seller agrees with the Auctioneer that any person to whom return of Stock to the seller may be given, nominated or appointed by the seller or by the Auctioneer acting on behalf of the seller shall for all purposes be deemed to be the employee of the seller and the Auctioneer shall not be in any way liable or responsible for any act or omission of such person and the auctioneer will not be responsible for any claims by such person arising out of the return of such Stock. The provisions of clauses 8.4 and 8.5 shall apply in connection with Stock not sold substituting the word "seller" for the word "buyer" throughout those clauses.

9.3 Any Stock not sold at the auction may be sold privately before removal from the sale yards, and these Conditions shall apply to such sales. Notwithstanding that the auction sale may have been concluded, the Auctioneer shall continue to be agent for the seller in such sales, and the signing of the buyer's name in the Auction Sale Book on behalf of the buyer by the Auctioneer or the clerk of the Auctioneer shall constitute as binding an agreement for sale and purchase as between seller and buyer as if such Stock were sold at auction, and the Auctioneer shall be entitled to be paid in all respects as if such Stock had been actually sold at the auction, pursuant to these Conditions.

10 COMPLIANCE WITH STATUTES AND REGULATIONS

10.1 Every seller shall comply with all duties and obligations imposed on him by all relevant statutes, regulations, orders-in-council or any other regulatory instruments and he shall comply with any other obligation he may have as a result of his ownership of the Stock.

10.2 Prior to delivery of the Stock to the saleyards the seller shall disclose to the Auctioneer all information which directly or indirectly relates to the health of Stock or any other matter of whatsoever nature:

(a) which the Auctioneer is or may in turn be required to disclose to bidders; or

(b) which the seller is or may be under an obligation (whether legal or otherwise) to disclose to the buyer; or

(c) which relates or may relate to a duty or obligation (whether legal or otherwise) on the part of the seller in relation to the seller's Stock.

10.3 The seller shall indemnify the Auctioneer for any costs expenses and losses he may sustain as a result of the seller's failure to comply with this clause 10.

10.4 In relation to any breach of the seller's obligations as set out above the buyer's only remedy shall be an action against the seller.

11 MISCELLANEOUS

11.1 Every person attending the sale or entering the sale yards shall do so at his own risk, and the Auctioneer shall not be in any way liable or responsible for any accident whatsoever to any such person.

11.2 The Auctioneer shall issue any tax invoice, credit note, or debit note required under the Goods and Services Tax Act 1985, and the seller shall not issue any such tax invoice, credit note, or debit note. As a precondition to the Auctioneer selling the Stock, the seller shall provide the Auctioneer with the goods and services tax registration number of the seller together with such other information relating to the goods and services tax registration of the seller as the Auctioneer may require. The issue of a goods and services tax invoice by the Auctioneer shall not affect in any way the buyer's claim to title in the Stock.

11.3 The Auctioneer shall be entitled to charge buyers and sellers of Stock yard usage fees and other fees associated (plus goods and services tax) whether specified in these Conditions or elsewhere with the sale of Stock.

12 NON DEROGATION

Nothing in these Conditions shall in any way derogate from the right of the Auctioneer to charge and recover commission and any other fees and disbursements (and goods and services tax thereon) from the seller as may have been agreed between the Auctioneer and the seller at any time and in any manner.

Reproduced with the kind permission of the New Zealand Stock & Station Agents' Association.

Index

Index

Index

Index